THE
ANNUAL REGISTER
Vol. 250

THE
ANNUAL REGISTER

World Events 2008

Edited by
D.S. LEWIS

Deputy Editor
WENDY SLATER

FIRST EDITED IN 1758
BY EDMUND BURKE

Colophon from 1758 volume.

ProQuest®

Start here.

The 2009 Annual Register: WORLD EVENTS, 250th Ed.
Published by ProQuest
7200 Wisconsin Ave.
Bethesda, MD 20814
United States of America and
The Quorum
P.O. Box 1346
Barnwell Road
Cambridge UK, CB5 8SW

ISBN: 978-1-60030-828-4 / ISSN: 0266-6170

British Library Cataloguing in Publication Data
The Annual Register—2009
1. History—Periodicals
909.82'8'05 D410

Library of Congress Catalog Card Number: 4-17979

Set in Times Roman by
NEW AGE GRAPHICS, Silver Spring, MD, USA

Printed in the USA by
THE SHERIDAN BOOKS, Chelsea, MI, USA
Jacket Design: JOHN C. MOSS
Printed on permanent recycled paper, acid-free.

CONTENTS

CONTRIBUTORS

	James Bishop, Chairman of the advisory board
	Philip M.H. Bell, Senior Research Fellow, University of Liverpool
	D.S. Lewis, PhD, Editor of *The Annual Register*; former Editor *Keesing's Record of World Events*
	M.R.D. Foot, Professor of Modern History, University of Manchester, 1967-73; nominated to *The Annual Register* advisory board by The Royal Historical Society, 1972-2002
	Richard O'Brien, Partner, Outsights; nominated to *The Annual Register* advisory board by The Royal Economic Society since 1995

PART I

	Paul Rogers, PhD, Professor of Peace Studies at Bradford University and Global Security Consultant to Oxford Research Group

PART II

	Harriet Jones, MSc, PhD, Senior Research Fellow, Institute of Contemporary British History
	Michael Kandiah, MA, PhD, Lecturer in Contemporary British History and Director of the Oral History Programme, Centre for Contemporary British History, Institute of Historical Research, University of London
	Charlotte Lythe, MA, Honorary Research Fellow in Economic Studies, University of Dundee
	Gwyn Jenkins, MA, Director of Collection Services, The National Library of Wales, Aberystwyth
	Alan Greer, PhD, Reader in Politics & Public Policy, Associate Head, School of Politics, University of the West of England, Bristol
	Dan Hough, PhD, Lecturer in Politics, University of Sussex
	Martin Harrison, Professor of Politics, University of Keele
	Mark Donovan, PhD, Senior Lecturer in Politics, Cardiff University of Wales; Editor, *Modern Italy*
	Martin Harrison (see France)
	Mary Hilson, PhD, Lecturer in Contemporary Scandinavian History, University College, London
	Martin Harrison (see France)
	William Chislett, Former correspondent of *The Times*, Spain, and the *Financial Times*, Mexico; author on Spain for the Elcano Royal Institute

PORTUGAL	**Martin Eaton,** PhD, FRGS/IBG, Reader in Human Geography, University of Ulster at Coleraine
MALTA	**Dominic Fenech,** DPhil, Professor of History, University of Malta
GREECE	**Susannah Verney,** PhD, Lecturer in Department of Political Science and Public Administration, University of Athens; editor, *South European Society and Politics*
CYPRUS	**Robert McDonald,** Writer and broadcaster on Cyprus, Greece and Turkey
TURKEY	**A.J.A. Mango,** PhD, Orientalist and writer on current affairs in Turkey and the Near East

PART III

POLAND	**George Sanford,** MPhil, PhD, Professor Emeritus of East European Politics, University of Bristol
ESTONIA, LATVIA, LITHUANIA	**Richard Mole,** MPhil, PhD, Lecturer in the Politics of Central Europe, University College London
CZECH REPUBLIC, SLOVAKIA	**Sharon Fisher,** MA, PhD, Analyst specialising in East European political and economic affairs, Global Insight
HUNGARY	**Daniel Izsak,** Journalist; former European Affairs Specialist & Desk Editor, BBC World Service
ROMANIA	**Gabriel Partos,** MA, Balkan Affairs Analyst/Editor, Economist Intelligence Unit
FORMER YUGOSLAV REPUBLICS	**Marcus Tanner,** MA, Author; Editor *Balkan Insight*
BULGARIA, ALBANIA	**Genc Lamani,** MA, Journalist, BBC World Service News and Current Affairs
RUSSIA, WESTERN CIS	**Wendy Slater,** MA, PhD, Deputy Editor, *The Annual Register*; former Lecturer in Contemporary Russian History, University College London
CAUCASUS	**Elizabeth Fuller,** Caucasus Analyst, Radio Free Europe/Radio Liberty, Prague

PART IV

UNITED STATES OF AMERICA	**James D. Miller,** PhD, Associate Dean, Department of History, Carleton University, Ottawa
CANADA	**Will Stos,** MA, PhD candidate, Department of History, York University, Toronto
MEXICO, CENTRAL AMERICA, CARIBBEAN	**Peter Clegg,** MSc, PhD, Senior Lecturer in Politics, University of the West of England, Bristol
ARGENTINA, BRAZIL, SOUTH AMERICA	**Kurt Perry,** Freelance writer specialising in Latin America

PART V

ISRAEL, PALESTINE	**Darren Sagar,** MA, Freelance writer specialising in Middle Eastern and South-East Asian affairs
EGYPT, JORDAN, SYRIA, LEBANON	**David Butter,** MA, Chief Energy Analyst Economist Intelligence Unit; Editor *Business Middle East*; Editor ViewsWire Middle East
IRAQ	**Darren Sagar** (see Israel etc.)

| SAUDI ARABIA, YEMEN, ARAB GULF STATES | **James Gavin,** contributing editor, *Gulf States Newsletter* |

SUDAN   **Ahmed Al-Shahi,** MLitt, DPhil, Former lecturer in Social Anthropology, University of Newcastle Upon Tyne

LIBYA, TUNISIA   **Yahia Zoubir,** PhD, Professor of International Relations & International Management, Euromed, Marseille

ALGERIA, MOROCCO, WESTERN SAHARA   **Hakim Darbouche,** PhD, Deputy Editor, *Mediterranean Politics*

PART VI

HORN OF AFRICA   **Colin Darch,** PhD, Senior Information Specialist, African Studies Library, University of Cape Town

KENYA, TANZANIA, UGANDA   **William Tordoff,** MA, PhD, Emeritus Professor of Government, University of Manchester

NIGERIA, GHANA, SIERRA LEONE, THE GAMBIA, LIBERIA   **Guy Arnold,** Writer specialising in Africa and North-South affairs

FRANCOPHONE AFRICA   **Kaye Whiteman,** Former publisher, *West Africa*

GUINEA BISSAU, CAPE VERDE, SÃO TOMÉ AND PRÍNCIPE   **Christopher Saunders,** DPhil, Professor, Department of Historical Studies, University of Cape Town

PART VII

DEMOCRATIC REPUBLIC OF CONGO, BURUNDI & RWANDA, MOZAMBIQUE   **Colin Darch** (see Horn of Africa)

ANGOLA, ZAMBIA, MALAWI   **Christopher Saunders** (see Guinea Bissau etc.)

ZIMBABWE   **R.W. Baldock,** PhD, Managing Director, Yale University Press; writer on African affairs

BOTSWANA, LESOTHO, NAMIBIA, SWAZILAND, SOUTH AFRICA   **Elizabeth Sidiropoulos,** MA, Director of Studies, South African Institute of International Affairs (SAIIA), Johannesburg; and **Terence Corrigan,** Researcher, SAAIIA

PART VIII

IRAN   **Ali M. Ansari,** PhD, Professor of History, University of St Andrews

AFGHANISTAN   **D.S. Lewis,** PhD, Editor of *The Annual Register*

CENTRAL ASIAN REPUBLICS   **Shirin Akiner,** PhD, Lecturer in Central Asian Studies, School of Oriental and African Studies, University of London

INDIA, PAKISTAN, SRI LANKA, BANGLADESH, NEPAL, BHUTAN   **David Taylor,** PhD, Senior Lecturer in Politics with reference to South Asia, School of Oriental and African Studies, University of London

MAURITIUS, SEYCHELLES, COMOROS, MALDIVES, MADAGASCAR   **Malyn Newitt,** PhD, JP, Charles Boxer Professor of History, Department of Portuguese, King's College, London

PART IX

BURMA (MYANMAR), THAILAND, MALAYSIA, BRUNEI, SINGAPORE, VIETNAM, CAMBODIA, LAOS   **Stephen Levine,** PhD, Professor and Head of School of History, Philosophy, Political Science and International Relations, Victoria University of Wellington

INDONESIA, EAST TIMOR, PHILIPPINES	**Norman MacQueen,** MSc, DPhil, Head of Department of Politics, University of Dundee
CHINA, HONG KONG, TAIWAN	**Xiaoming Huang,** PhD, Senior Lecturer in East Asian politics, Department of Political Science and International Relations, Victoria University of Wellington
JAPAN	**Ian Nish,** PhD, Emeritus Professor of International History, London School of Economics and Political Science
NORTH AND SOUTH KOREA	**J.E. Hoare,** PhD, Consultant on East Asia; former chargé d'affaires in Pyongyang
MONGOLIA	**Manduhai Buyandelger,** PhD, Assistant Professor of Anthropology, MIT

PART X

AUSTRALIA	**James Jupp,** AM, MSc (Econ), PhD, FASSA, Director, Centre for Immigration and Multicultural Studies, Australian National University, Canberra
PAPUA NEW GUINEA	**Norman MacQueen** (see Indonesia etc.)
NEW ZEALAND, PACIFIC ISLAND STATES	**Stephen Levine** (see Burma etc.)

PART XI

UNITED NATIONS	**David Travers,** Lecturer in Politics and International Relations, Lancaster University; Specialist Advisor on UN to House of Commons' Foreign Affairs Committee
DEFENCE ORGANISATIONS	**Paul Cornish,** PhD, Carrington Chair in International Security and Head of International Security Programme, Chatham House, London
ECONOMIC ORGANISATIONS	**Paul Rayment,** MA, Former Director of the Economic Analysis Division of the UN Economic Commission for Europe, Geneva
COMMONWEALTH	**Derek Ingram,** Consultant Editor of *Gemini News Service*; author and writer on the Commonwealth
FRANCOPHONIE	**Kaye Whiteman,** (see Francophone Africa)
NON-ALIGNED MOVEMENT AND GROUP OF 77	**Peter Willetts,** PhD, Visiting Professor of Global Politics, Department of International Politics, City University, London
ORGANISATION OF THE ISLAMIC CONFERENCE	**Darren Sagar** (see Israel etc.)
EUROPEAN UNION; COUNCIL OF EUROPE	**Michael Berendt,** Expert on affairs of the European Union
ORGANISATION FOR SECURITY AND CO-OPERATION IN EUROPE; EUROPEAN BANK FOR RECONSTRUCTION AND DEVELOPMENT	**Michael Kaser,** MA, DLitt, DSocSc, Emeritus Fellow St Antony's College, Oxford, and Honorary Professor University of Birmingham
OTHER EUROPEAN ORGANISATIONS	**Martin Harrison** (see France etc.)
AMERICAN AND CARIBBEAN ORGANISATIONS	**Peter Clegg** (see Mexico etc.)
ARAB ORGANISATIONS	**Darren Sagar** (see Israel etc.)
AFRICAN ORGANISATIONS AND CONFERENCES	**Christopher Saunders** (see Cape Verde etc.)

EURASIAN ORGANISATIONS
ASIA-PACIFIC ORGANISATIONS

Shirin Akiner (see Central Asia)
Stephen Levine (see Burma etc.)

PART XII
ECONOMY

Paul Rayment (see Economic Organisations)

PART XIII
MEDICAL, SCIENTIFIC AND
    INDUSTRIAL RESEARCH

INFORMATION TECHNOLOGY
ENVIRONMENT

Neil Weir, FRCS, Consultant otolaryngologist and
Lorelly Wilson, Honorary Teaching Fellow,
University of Manchester
Kristian Saxton, CEO of software consultancy, Aethernet
Tim Curtis, Regional Editor, *Keesing's Record of World
Events*; writer on international affairs

PART XIV
INTERNATIONAL LAW

EUROPEAN COMMUNITY LAW

LAW IN THE UK

LAW IN THE USA

Christine Gray, MA, PhD, Fellow in Law, St John's
College, Cambridge
N. March Hunnings, LLM, PhD, Editor, *Encyclopedia
of European Union Law: Constitutional Texts*
Jonathan Morgan, MA, Fellow in Law, Christ's
College, Cambridge
Robert J. Spjut, ID, LLD, Member of the State Bars of
California and Florida

PART XV
RELIGION

Mark Chapman, PhD, Vice Principal, Ripon College
Cuddesdon, Oxford, Reader in Modern Theology at the
University of Oxford and Visiting Professor at Oxford
Brookes University; **Peter Oppenheimer**, MA, President,
Oxford Centre for Hebrew and Jewish Studies; **Shaunaka
Rishi Das**, Director, Oxford Centre for Hindu Studies,
Oxford; **Colin Shindler**, PhD, Reader in Israeli and
Modern Jewish Studies,School of Oriental and African
Studies, University of London; **Timothy Winter**, MA,
Sheikh Zayed Lecturer in Islamic Studies, University
of Cambridge

PART XVI
OPERA
MUSIC

BALLET & DANCE

THEATRE

CINEMA
TV & RADIO

George Hall, UK correspondent of *Opera News*
Francis Routh, Composer and author; founder director
of the Redcliffe Concerts
Jane Pritchard, Curator of Dance, the Victoria and
Albert Museum of Performing Arts, London
Matt Wolf, London theatre critic of *The International
Herald Tribune* and Bloomberg News and contributing
editor and chief critic for the new theatre.com website
Derek Malcolm, Cinema critic, *The Guardian*
Raymond Snoddy, Freelance journalist specialising in
media issues, writing for the *Independent*

VISUAL ARTS   **Anna Somers Cocks,** Group Editorial Director,
                               The Art Newspaper
ARCHITECTURE   **Jay Merrick,** Architecture correspondent, *The*
                               Independent; writer for *New Statesman*, *Blueprint*,
                               Monument, and *ArtReview*; and novelist
LITERATURE   **Alastair Niven,** OBE, Principal, Cumberland Lodge;
                               formerly Director of Literature, British Council

PART XVII
SPORT   **Paul Newman,** Chief Sports Feature Writer,
                               The Independent

PART XVIII
DOCUMENTS AND REFERENCE   **D.S. Lewis** and **Wendy Slater**

PART XIX
OBITUARY   **James Bishop,** Former Editor of *The Illustrated London*
                               News and Foreign News Editor of *The Times*

PART XX
CHRONICLE OF 2008   **D.S. Lewis** and **Wendy Slater**
THE ANNUAL REGISTER ARCHIVE: **Philip M.H. Bell** (see Extracts from Past Volumes)
  MAJOR WORLD EVENTS 1758-2008

MAPS   **J&L Composition Ltd**

ABBREVIATIONS AND ACRONYMS

AC	Arctic Council
ACP	African, Caribbean and Pacific states associated with EU
ACS	Association of Caribbean States
ADB	Asian Development Bank
AL	Arab League
ALADI	Latin American Integration Association
AMU	Arab Maghreb Union
ANZUS	Australia-New Zealand-US Security Treaty
APEC	Asia-Pacific Economic Co-operation
ASEAN	Association of South-East Asian Nations
AU	African Union
Benelux	Belgium-Netherlands-Luxembourg Economic Union
BSEC	Black Sea Economic Co-operation
Ancom/CA	Andean Community of Nations
Caricom	Caribbean Community and Common Market
CBSS	Council of the Baltic Sea States
CE	Council of Europe
CEEAC	Economic Community of Central African States
CEFTA	Central European Free Trade Agreement
CEI	Central European Initiative
CENSAD	Community of Sahel-Saharan States
CIS	Commonwealth of Independent States
COMESA	Common Market of Eastern and Southern Africa
CPLP	Community of Portuguese-Speaking Countries
CSTO	Collective Security Treaty Organisation
CWTH	The Commonwealth
DRC	Democratic Republic of Congo
DR-CAFTA	Dominican Republic-Central American Free Trade Agreement
EAC	East African Community
EBRD	European Bank for Reconstruction and Development
ECB	European Central Bank
ECO	Economic Co-operation Organisation
ECOWAS	Economic Community of West African States
EEA	European Economic Area
EEC	Eurasian Economic Community
EFTA	European Free Trade Association
EU	European Union
G-8	Group of Eight
G-7	Group of Seven
G-77	Group of 77
GCC	Gulf Co-operation Council
GDP	Gross domestic product
GNI	Gross national income
HIPC	Heavily Indebted Poor Countries
HIV/AIDS	Human Immunodeficiency Virus/Acquired Immune Deficiency Syndrome
IBRD	International Bank for Reconstruction and Development

IDA	International Development Association
IEA	International Energy Agency
IGAD	Inter-Governmental Authority on Development
IGO	Inter-governmental organisation
IMF	International Monetary Fund
IPCC	UN Intergovernmental Panel on Climate Change
IOC	Indian Ocean Commission
ISP	Internet service provider
MDG	Millennium Development Goals
Mercosur	Southern Common Market
NAFTA	North American Free Trade Agreement
NAM	Non-Aligned Movement
NASA	the US National Aeronautics and Space Administration
NATO	North Atlantic Treaty Organisation
NC	Nordic Council
NGO	Non-governmental organisation
OAPEC	Organisation of Arab Petroleum Exporting Countries
OAS	Organisation of American States
OECD	Organisation for Economic Co-operation and Development
OECS	Organisation of Eastern Caribbean States
OIC	Organisation of the Islamic Conference
OIF	International Organisation of Francophonie
OPEC	Organisation of the Petroleum Exporting Countries
OSCE	Organisation for Security and Co-operation in Europe
PACE	Parliamentary Assembly of the Council of Europe
PC	Pacific Community
PFP	Partnership for Peace
PIF	Pacific Islands Forum
PPP	Purchasing power parity
PRGF	Poverty Reduction and Growth Facility
SAARC	South Asian Association for Regional Co-operation
SADC	Southern African Development Community
SCO	Shanghai Co-operation Organisation
SELA	Latin American Economic System
UAE	United Arab Emirates
UEMOA	West African Economic and Monetary Union
UK	United Kingdom of Great Britain and Northern Ireland
UNESCO	United Nations Educational, Scientific and Cultural Organisation
USA	United States of America
WHO	World Health Organisation
WMO	UN World Meteorological Organisation
WTO	World Trade Organisation

ACKNOWLEDGEMENTS

THE editor gratefully acknowledges his debt to a number of individuals and institutions for their help with sources, references and documents. Acknowledgment is also due to the principal sources for the national and IGO data sections (showing the situation at end 2008 unless otherwise stated), namely *Keesing's Record of World Events* (Keesing's Worldwide), the World Bank Group website, the *Financial Times* (London), the FCO website (for UK Overseas Territories); National Statistics (for UK populations); National Statistics, Republic of China (for Taiwan). Whilst every effort is made to ensure accuracy, the Board and the bodies which nominate its members, the editors, and the publisher disclaim responsibility for any opinions expressed or the accuracy of facts recorded in this volume.

GNI per capita at PPP is a measure of gross national income that allows a standard comparison of real price levels between countries by using the PPP (purchasing power parity) rate. At the PPP rate, one international dollar has the same purchasing power over domestic GNI that the US dollar has over US GNI. PPP GNI per capita is PPP GNI divided by mid-year population.

FOREWORD TO 250TH ANNIVERSARY VOLUME
OF *THE ANNUAL REGISTER*

Neither Edmund Burke nor his publisher Robert Dodsley could possibly have imagined that their brainchild, described in its first edition as "a view of the history, politicks and literature of the year 1758," would still be flourishing, and developing, after two-and-a-half centuries.

My own first contact with *The Annual Register* came in the early 1950s, when as a fledgling journalist I found myself sitting on an aircraft next to a budding diplomat, an affable and confident young Englishman who was later to become British ambassador to a number of countries, including the USA. At that time he was about to take up a junior post in a country he had not been to before, and was busy studying some sheets of printed paper, which turned out to have been copied from the last ten years of *The Annual Register*. "Essential reading when you're going to a new country," he explained. "Many of us are regular subscribers," he added. "Or if we're not, we mug it all up in one of the libraries."

I followed his advice during my career as a foreign correspondent, and never travelled without having first scanned the *Register* for its history of recent events in the country I was flying to. It was following a tour in Africa that I wrote my first report for the book, on the "British Dependent Territories", which was published in its 200th edition.

The advance of technology since those days has recently brought the 250 years of *The Annual Register* online. I only wish this facility had been available in my younger days; how much easier life would have been. Even in an era marked by an explosion of electronic information, *The Annual Register* remains a key source for all those who need to keep abreast of world events, to check their facts, do some research into any period since 1758, or learn more about the world in which they live and work.

James Bishop
Chairman of the Advisory Board of *The Annual Register*.

ENDORSEMENTS OF *THE ANNUAL REGISTER*
BY ITS NOMINATING INSTITUTIONS

British Council

THE British Council was founded in 1934. Since then it has been playing its part in every corner of the world. There could hardly, therefore, be a publication with which to be more appropriately involved than *The Annual Register.* The stories which the *Register* tells each year are the same stories with which the Council interacts, whether they are political, educational or cultural. As a source of reference *The Annual Register* is invaluable whether we work online or accompanied by book shelves. It is comprehensive, accurate, detailed and perceptive. It has no axe to grind, though this is not to say that the individual contributors are without opinions; they simply hold them in a measured and responsible way. The British Council is proud to be a nominating organisation to the Advisory Board of *The Annual Register* and congratulates this superb and influential publication on achieving its 250th anniversary. It is unlikely that there is an older or more reliable record of information in the English-speaking world. Through *The Annual Register* facts about nations and cultures can be easily checked. The political and intellectual movements of the past can be traced from their origins, while today's world is laid out before the reader in manageable sections. This is an indispensable publication; a great link between the eighteenth century and the present day. In every decade it has reinterpreted its mission, so that it is kept constantly fresh and illuminating. The British Council is seventy-five years old, a youngster by comparison with *The Annual Register*, but it shares the same objective belief in the value of unbiased information and recording.

Martin Davidson, CMG
Chief Executive of the British Council.

British Science Association

THE British Science Association (formally known as the British Association for the Advancement of Science) is delighted to be associated with *The Annual Register* in its 250th year.

The Annual Register provides a unique record of the progress of science and many other topics over 250 years. The very great value of this record is its contemporary reporting by experts in the field, so that every breakthrough, invention and theory is seen in the light that prevailed at the time, rather than with hindsight. The birth in 1831 of the British Association for the Advancement of Science—"the most distinguished men of science from every part of the empire"—is recorded, as are very detailed reports of many of the subsequent meetings of an institution praised in *The Annual Register* for "the benefits to science from its efforts". Many great scientific advances are first reported at the meetings of the Association, the discovery of Neptune for example in the 1846 volume, while the 1871 *Annual Register* records how the publication of Darwin's *Descent of Man* resulted in sharp debate at the Oxford meeting. The Darwin family features even earlier, with Charles's grandfather Erasmus Darwin's publication of *Zoonomia* discussed in the 1794 edition.

Some of the very earliest scientific observations—Halley's Comet and the transit of Venus (AR 1758)—are there, all reported at first hand. There is a contemporary report of Marconi's first trans-Atlantic wireless communication (AR 1901). Because these are contemporary accounts, they make extremely interesting reading. It is amusing to read the discussion and debate, and indeed the delicate way in which *The Annual Register*'s science writer so many years ago reported findings which today we take for granted. As an example, he tiptoes carefully around the quantum theory of atomic structure, not yet sure whether it will be accepted: "Professor Planck's hypothesis that energy is emitted in definite units or quanta, a view so contrary to preconceived ideas that it is not surprising that the veterans in physics reserved judgment on its merits." (AR 1913).

The Annual Register and its online version are a goldmine for students of the history of science; there is a feast of facts, ideas and personalities within its pages. We applaud the editors, the contributors and the publishers, who have ensured that this exceptional historical record has been maintained every year. We hope that the publication will continue to thrive well into the future. Our congratulations on your 250th birthday!

Roland Jackson
Chief Executive of the British Science Association.

Royal Economic Society

THE 250-year span of *The Annual Register* takes us from the Enlightenment days of Adam Smith and *The Wealth of Nations* to the early 21st century crisis of markets on a global scale. Economic thinking has evolved steadily over this period and has often challenged conventional modes of thought. As the UK's learned society for economics, the Royal Economic Society has been delighted to be associated with *The Annual Register* as it has recorded the cycles in economic affairs and developments in economic thinking. Adam Smith judged Edmund Burke, the book's first editor, to be "the only man I ever knew who thinks on economic subjects exactly as I do, without any previous communications having passed between us". As a scholarly record of economic events and trends—from the smallest economies to the largest, and from micro to macro—*The Annual Register* helps to connect the complex strands of current economic activity.

In recent volumes, *The Annual Register* has drawn attention to one of today's major political economy issues, globalisation, a theme which links us directly with the political philosophy debates in which Burke engaged. With confidence in the current status quo under fire, analysts need to be able to learn through the contemporary observations on the turbulent events of the past. Today we can reflect on *The Annual Register* of 1929 where the most spectacular event was "the collapse of the great gambling movement of the New York Stock Exchange. As the 'boom' progressed it seemed likely to last until eternity. This gave birth to a new economic philosophy of a disastrous kind." And what of the years before the Crash? *The Annual Register* of 1928 provides fascinating reading, reporting on the long decade of difficulties in recovering from the Great War and observing "Abroad the chief events were the most amazing prosperity of the United States and the still more amazing speculation on the NYSE", and coining the wonderful phrase "Wall Street reflected some of its glory upon Throgmorton Street."

Pessimists may possibly sympathise with Burke's lament on the death of Marie Antoinette that "the age of chivalry is gone; that of sophisters, economists, and calculators has succeeded, and the glory of Europe is extinguished forever." The Royal Economic Society, however, looks forward to the next 250 years of *The Annual Register* with confidence.

Sir John Vickers
President, Royal Economic Society

Royal Historical Society

THE Royal Historical Society has been associated with *The Annual Register* for over 60 years, and we are delighted to congratulate the *Register* on its 250th volume in unbroken series. Fifty years ago Asa Briggs wrote that "For 200 years *The Annual Register* has provided a sustained and successful example of the writing of contemporary history", and this remains true to the present day. The content of the *Register* has changed enormously over its long life, from its 18th century concentration on British and European affairs to its present world-wide coverage; the vigorous opinions—not to say prejudices—of Edmund Burke's time have given way to a remarkable degree of balance, detachment and accuracy. *The Annual Register* is an important source for historical research, and indeed has become a part of history in itself, while remaining a treasure trove for the general reader. The Royal Historical Society extends its warmest congratulations to *The Annual Register* on the publication of its 250th volume, and wishes it every success in the future.

C.D.H. Jones
President, Royal Historical Society.

Royal Institute of International Affairs

I HAVE greatly appreciated the opportunity to serve as a contributor to *The Annual Register* since 1970 and as a member of the Advisory Board representing the

Royal Institute of International Affairs (Chatham House) since 1973. The formal connection between *The Annual Register* and Chatham House dates back to 1947 when Ivison S. Macadam, the director general of the Royal Institute of International Affairs, became the book's editor. One of Macadam's innovations was the introduction of the Advisory Board, which continues to support the editor of *The Annual Register* to this day and which has throughout its existence included a nominee of Chatham House. Both institutions are seen as integral to furthering an understanding of international relations. *The Annual Register* will undoubtedly continue to flourish, as it has done for two-and-a-half centuries, providing a unique reference source to scholarship and government worldwide, and I am delighted to offer my congratulations on this notable anniversary.

Michael Kaser
Royal Institute of International Affairs

Royal Society of Medicine

THE Royal Society of Medicine is proud to be associated with *The Annual Register* in its 250th year.

The Annual Register has recorded the major medical discoveries of the last 250 years and celebrated the lives of eminent medical men and women. In the early years papers were submitted to *The Annual Register* by the anatomist and surgeon John Hunter (AR 1780), by his pupil Edward Jenner (AR 1788), and by his brother-in-law, Sir Everard Home (AR 1805). Meetings of medical societies, both national and international, have been chronicled. The inaugural dinner to celebrate the formation of the Royal Society of Medicine in 1907 was reported in *The Annual Register*, as was the opening of the Society's new building at 1 Wimpole Street (AR 1912).

The Royal Society of Medicine—which is dedicated to the promotion of multidisciplinary education and professional matters relating to medicine, dentistry, veterinary medicine and their allied professions—greatly values the link with *The Annual Register*, which gives its membership an abundance of information, not only related to biological sciences and medicine but also to events occurring throughout the world, in the arts, the law, religion and sport. This contemporary writing by experts in their fields has the value of presenting the facts as they are perceived at that particular time. This provides, together with the online archive of the whole *Annual Register*, an invaluable asset for historians.

We congratulate the editors, contributors and publishers who have ensured the continued existence of this exceptional historical record.

Professor Robin Williamson
President, Royal Society of Medicine.

EXTRACTS FROM PAST VOLUMES

250 years ago

1758. *A World War.* A war between the maritime powers is felt in all parts of the world. Not content with inflaming Europe and America, the dissensions of the French and English pursued the tracks of their commerce, and the Ganges felt the fatal effects of a quarrel on the Ohio. But here the scene is changed greatly to the advantage of our nation; the bravery of Admiral Watson and Colonel Clive re-established the military honour of the English.

225 years ago

1783. *Treaty of Versailles with the United States of America.* From this point of view of our total inability to engage in another campaign, with any prospect of bringing it to a more favourable conclusion than the last, it was argued that peace on any terms ... was preferable to a continuation of the war. But it was asserted, in the second place, that the peace did not stand in need of such a defence, and that the terms obtained were fair and honourable ....

200 years ago

1808. *Insurrection against French rule in Spain.* Thus far we have seen Buonaparte carrying on his design by intrigue and fraud; by which means he considered it as accomplished. But the Spaniards, not only in the provinces of Spain, but in the colonies, started up simultaneously, as if moved by one indignant soul into an attitude of defence and defiance, and declared war against their perfidious and insolent oppressor ....

175 years ago

1833. *Antipathy of the President [Andrew Jackson] to the Bank of the United States.* ... on whichever side the right and law might be, the conduct of the President led to disastrous results in the mercantile world. The deposits being withdrawn, the bank necessarily diminished its issues, and lessened its discounts; all operations of buying and selling were thus discouraged and impeded; a stagnation of trade ensued; property was depreciated; and bankruptcies and failures were multiplied on all sides.

150 years ago

1858. *British India.* After the passing, in the month of August this year, of the Acts which abolished the East India Company, and transferred our Indian possessions to the direct government of the Crown, a Royal Proclamation was drawn up and transmitted to the Governor-General, who on the 1st of November, published it at Allahabad, where he was then staying.

125 years ago

1883. *Volcanic eruptions in the island of Java, by an eye-witness.* On the 26th [August] loud reports and detonations were heard from the direction of Krakatau, and towards evening the sea became unusually agitated, the water assuming a colour of inky blackness .... [Next morning] an immense wave, about 30 metres high, swept without warning over Anjer, completely ruining the place and penetrating inland to the distance of about two miles.

100 years ago

1908. *The Young Turks.* The year 1908 will be memorable in Turkish history as that of a revolution carried out with a moderation, wisdom and spirit of conciliation unprecedented in the revolutionary records of other countries. The 'Young Turkish' party ... did not strike its blow for a constitution until it was assured of the support of the army.

75 years ago

1933. *Germany: Hitler in power.* The complete Nazification of Germany was only carried out by a merciless persecution of all those of diverging views. For dealing with the masses of prisoners special concentration camps were opened. A conservative estimate puts the number of the inmates of these camps at 100,000 by the end of the year.

50 years ago

1958. *China: the Great Leap Forward.* One outstanding factor in this prodigious production drive was the organisation of People's Communes throughout the rural areas .... The working members of a commune were said to be awakened at 5 a.m. by a bugle call, given a short period of physical exercises, and then marched off to their labours, which extended, with an interval for meals until 6 p.m. They then had to undergo small arms drill, before being dismissed for a night's rest.

25 years ago

1983. *Poland: Visit by Pope John Paul II.* Crowds totalling an estimated 14 million pressed to see the Pope and hear him. The spirit of self-identity was repeatedly demonstrated through the persistent display of posters and slogans, chants and prayers, through periodic marches of Solidarity supporters, and through 'V for Victory' signs massively displayed at each gathering.

PREFACE

As James Bishop notes in this year's Foreword, it is unlikely that Edmund Burke, the founding editor of *The Annual Register*, or his publisher, Robert Dodsley, could have envisaged that their book would still be flourishing a quarter of a millennium after the appearance of its first volume. Nor could they have imagined that the publication's 250 year archive would be available to a global readership through the wizardry of the Internet.

In acknowledgement of *The Annual Register's* 250th anniversary, the current volume contains some novel features. We have included a personal essay by M.R.D. Foot, an eminent historian and a close associate of the *Register* over many decades, which chart's the book's evolution and its historical significance. We have also included a list of the single most significant world event for each year of the book's existence, complied by another respected historian, Philip M.H. Bell. Both of these features highlight the longevity of the *Register* and the scale of change which has occurred during its lifetime.

As Burke emphasised in his preface to the 1758 volume, *The Annual Register* aims to take the events of a year—these "broken and unconnected materials"— and, through a work of "more labour than may at first appear", unite them into "one connected narrative". In so doing it goes beyond the mere recording of reference information and attempts to fashion a work of history from events so recent that they remain white hot. Although in years to come more academic history will be written, benefiting from less molten source material which allows more time for scholarly reflection, the *Register* remains an invaluable repository of contemporaneous history. It is a record not just of what has happened in a particular year, but of the historical significance of these events *as seen at the time* by those experiencing them.

With this in mind, in this volume we have departed from tradition and included a piece by Richard O'Brien which imagines how the world might have changed by the year 2059, a date upon which *The Annual Register* will, we hope, celebrate its 300th anniversary. The piece aims not just to provoke debate about the direction in which the world is evolving, but also to provide a clear record about how the future is seen at this moment, a record which we hope will entertain readers in 50 years' time as well as those of today.

Each of the innovations within this year's volume is in keeping with Burke's stated aim of including "matters of a lighter nature; but pleasing even by their levity; by their variety; and their aptitude to enter into common conversation".

It is inevitable that the *Register's* 250th anniversary should emphasise its relationship with Edmund Burke, although in truth the publication has been fortunate to have benefited also from the talents of many of those editors who succeeded him over the years. It has also derived much of its authority and unique style from the quality of its contributors whose ability and loyalty have been a mainstay of the book's success. Many of these have graced the publication with their knowledge over several decades and there is no better occasion than this for the current editor and publisher to thank them for their invaluable contribution to the *Register's* continuing success.

Since the post-war period *The Annual Register* has had an advisory board to support and assist the editor. This was established in 1947 as "a recognition of the need for specialisation in these complicated times". As such, it was an indication of how much the world had changed since Burke's time. Members of the advisory board bring with them the support of the learned institutions which nominate them (see pp. xx-xxiii). The book has been fortunate that so many of its board members, like its contributors, have given generously not just of their expertise but also of their time and experience, with the result that the publication has benefited from a strong tide of continuity. This commitment is exemplified by the board's current chairman, James Bishop, whose association with the book extends unbroken for over 50 years.

It is fitting that the 250th volume of *The Annual Register* should deal with momentous events. As the book goes to press the world faces an economic crisis of a severity not seen since the 1930s. The depth and duration of the recession remain unknown, as does the efficacy of many of the weapons being deployed to combat it. Its long-term impact, particularly in terms of the level of debt being passed on to future generations, is also uncertain. The initial challenge which the crisis presented lay in devising ways of controlling a financial conflagration which, because of deregulation and globalisation, had spread with an unprecedented speed. On a more profound level the challenge lies in the creation of an economic system which can once again command public confidence and respect. In this sense it appears that, even after economic recovery has been effected, laissez faire capitalism will never be quite the same. It is not just that greater government regulation seems inevitable. Something more fundamental has been exposed. The result is that the morality which underpinned the supremacy of the market mechanism has been fatally compromised and will have to be recast in such a way as it no longer places at its core unfettered and reckless avarice.

The economic crisis was also instrumental in bringing about the other key development of 2008 in that it helped to decide the outcome of the US presidential election. This elevated Barack Obama, a young, charismatic, but relatively unknown senator, to the White House. Much was made of the fact that this was the first time that a non-white candidate had been chosen to lead the world's most powerful country and the degree to which this breakthrough provided a form of closure to the (comparatively recent) segregationist past of the USA. Historically, however, it may well be that the true significance of Obama's success lies not in his mixed race but in the degree to which race was not a significant issue in his election. The tenor of his campaign and the manner of his victory suggested the long overdue dawn of "post-racial" politics—an environment where, in the words of Haile Selassie—made famous by the singer Bob Marley—"the colour of a man's skin is of no more significance than the colour of his eyes".

Obama's victory over John McCain was determined not by his ethnicity but by his undoubted ability, for his election represented a triumph of the candidate of ideas over the man of action; the intellectual over the soldier; the future over the past. Not since the election of Franklin D. Roosevelt in 1932 had Americans chosen such an unapologetically intellectual candidate as their president—a man who dealt easily in the currency of sophisticated ideas and whose elitism translated itself as a willingness to engage in a higher form of political discourse. It was a break with the recent past which was applauded throughout the world.

That Obama should have been compared to Roosevelt was inevitable as he, like the earlier president, inherited a range of problems on a breathtaking scale. As Obama prepared to take office at the end of 2008 the colossal burden of expectations weighed heavily upon him: wars to be dealt with, the environment saved, intractable global disputes resolved, the USA's international reputation repaired, and a world economy to be stabilised and then remade. Not within living memory had so much been expected of an incoming US president. Time would be judge to his success.

D.S. Lewis
Editor, *The Annual Register*
Aquitaine, April 2009.

THE ANNUAL REGISTER

FOR THE YEAR 2008

THE ANNUAL REGISTER 250TH EDITION:
A PERSONAL HISTORY

The 250th anniversary of The Annual Register *is marked with a specially commissioned piece from M.R.D. Foot, b. 1919, army officer 1939-45, professor of modern history at Manchester University 1967-73, who served as the Royal Historical Society's represen-tative on the advisory board of* The Annual Register *from 1972 to 2002. The article examines the history of the AR, concentrating particularly upon the post-war years, and assesses the significance of this historic publication today.*

THIS is the 250th volume of *The Annual Register*. The Accademia dei Lincei in Italy has been publishing learned articles since the late Renaissance, and both the *London Gazette* and the *Proceedings of the Royal Society* are nearly a cen-tury older than *The Annual Register*; but even in this austere company the AR can hold up its head as a lasting contribution to humankind's understanding of the world in which it lives.

Edmund Burke, founder-editor of *The Annual Register*, wrote the original volume, covering 1758, which appeared in 1759. Every calendar year since has had its own volume. There were several rival versions of the AR in the late 18th century, one or two of them copying precise details of the original, down to the publisher's own title-page symbol; their existence forms a librarians' nightmare. But by the early 19th century there was one undisputed title, which has continued uninterrupted to the present day.

For the 200th edition, covering 1958 and duly appearing in 1959, Asa Briggs wrote a foreword in which he laid down the role of *The Annual Register* as an instance of contemporary history, safely renewed from year to year. It contin-ues to provide a first serious historian's look at each calendar year's events, with addenda to establish the particular flavour of each year. Its authorship is now multiple—84 was last year's total of contributors—a necessary proliferation since Burke's day, when the editor wrote virtually the entire volume himself.

In 1947 a new editor, Sir Ivison Macadam—who succeeded Mortimer Epstein, editor since 1920, who had just died—introduced an advisory board, the members of which were to be nominated by various learned societies. Macadam explained, in his preface to the 1947 volume, that this innovation was "a recognition of the need for specialisation in these complicated times". It was my own honour and privilege to succeed Professor W.N. Medlicott as the Royal Historical Society's member of this board, on which I had the delight of serving for over 30 years, thus acquiring some insights into the AR's editorial process. The board meets regularly with the editor and the publisher, to discuss all aspects of the title, including the recruiting of contributors and the distribution of subjects in the forthcoming issue. The editor is usually glad of the board's advice, but retains responsibility for the content, and uses his own initiative to fill in any gaps that accident may open up.

Over the years, the general body of contributors has built up some degree of collegiate feeling and has the opportunity to express this to the advisory board and the editor at an annual gathering over a dinner. Most of the AR's contributors are academics or journalists; all of them are experts in their field. They share a belief that the AR is of lasting benefit to scholars. The body of contributors is in constant slow flux as the editor seeks to maintain and improve its quality; yet the book is remarkable for the consistency of authorship. Several of the AR's current contributors have been associated with the title for more than a quarter of a century, and a handful for even longer.

Necessarily, the AR deals with the recent past, rather than with prospects for the future (although this anniversary edition does include a special forward-looking piece by Richard O'Brien, which follows this retrospective essay). *The Annual Register* reckons to provide an informed digest of what the world's news media have presented as the principal events of the relevant year, before even contemporary historians have themselves published much that bears on the subject; exactly as Lord Briggs (not then ennobled) pointed out. As a rule, the AR provides the earliest authoritative historical coverage for each year. Unlike much of the news media, it rarely seeks to prophesy—its contributors are mindful of Macaulay's remark that prophecy in politics is the most foolish occupation open to man—but it does record the forebodings of others. The environment chapter in 2003, for instance, gave prominence to a German report on the ghastly effects of the disappearance of the Gulf Stream, should that result from disproportionate carbon emissions, which upset the balance of nature. That humankind may now be teetering on the brink of an ecological catastrophe can have been inferred from the AR's pages for at least a decade.

Later, more fully informed historians, working on archives that may not be released for 30 or 50 years or longer, may be able to modify or even to contradict the views that the AR puts forward, but those views remain as a testimony at least to what each age thinks of itself: what seem, at the time, to be the most impressive changes in world history and in the ways in which life is lived. The growth and decay of political parties can be traced in the AR's pages; so can the careers of the most eminent public men and women. Part of the AR's unique value lies in its ability to set these figures in their context and record who was thought significant at the time.

Even the most ardent apostles of Fernand Braudel, who drew attention to the longue durée rather than the transient event as the dominant factor in history, should be prepared to admit that single events or single personalities do, now and again, shift the pace and direction of human development. The 20th century's history would have been entirely different had it not been for the presence of Lenin, Hitler, Einstein, Churchill, Roosevelt, and Mao. Similarly, social and industrial development sometimes stems from the work of single inventors and entrepreneurs, although the importance of these is not always apparent to contemporary observers.

Though the first earth satellite, the Soviet *Sputnik*, was duly recorded in the edition for 1957, not every major invention makes its mark in the AR immediately, because it is not always clear to the contemporary historian which innovations will endure. The Stockton to Darlington railway, now hailed as the opening of the powered railway age (there were railways, or at least rutways, in stone age Somerset), passed unnoticed in 1825, though the opening of the line from Liverpool to Manchester in 1830 attracted full comment. In fact, this was largely on account of the accidental death of the man who had secretly been running British spies into France in the Napoleonic wars, and is much better known for how he came to die: William Huskisson. Michael Faraday, on whose discoveries in electricity much of contemporary life is based, received a glowing obituary in 1867, but little other notice. Telephone, typewriter, bicycle, motor car, powered aircraft have made similar unheralded approaches to daily use. The Wright brothers' first powered flight in 1903 was unrecorded for that year, though Blériot's flight in an aircraft from Calais to Dover in 1909 was recorded (as had been a flight by balloon in the opposite direction, in 1785). I recall a meeting of the advisory board at which a new scientific adviser remarked that much of British industry was, by the time he was speaking, computer-regulated, but he had yet to see in the AR any mention of computers at all, a defect he remedied at once. The Internet was first discussed in the 1993 volume although, as the author of the information technology article noted, "the Internet was scarcely new", having evolved from a computer network established by the US defence department in 1969.

The ownership and copyright of *The Annual Register*, even before Burke's death, lay with its publishers, a consortium at first, settling down for over a century with the great house of Longman's. Longman's eventually became part of Pearson plc, a large publishing conglomerate, but the AR retained its Longman imprint. However, in 1995 the AR, along with the rest of the Longman current affairs list, was transferred to Cartermill, a division of Pearson, which was interested primarily in electronic publishing. After languishing for three years neglected by Cartermill, the AR was sold to Jonathan Hixon, a US publisher, as a minor part of a deal involving his purchase from Pearson of *Keesing's Record of World Events*.

Ructions followed. The chairman of the advisory board, the eminent H.V. Hodson, was unhappy that the AR had fallen into American ownership. Mr Hodson had succeeded Sir Ivison Macadam as the book's editor and chairman of the advisory board in 1973; in 1988, Mr Hodson had been succeeded as editor by

Alan Day but he retained, until his death in 1999, his position as chairman of the board, a post in which he was succeeded by Dr D.S. Lewis, the editor of *Keesing's Record of World Events*. Meanwhile, relations were deteriorating between the AR's new publisher, Mr Hixon, and its editor, Mr Day, with the result that the latter's contract was not renewed when it expired in 2000. Several contributors, including the invaluable Verena Hoffman, the assistant editor, resigned in sympathy with Mr Day. Most felt that the AR—as the Duke of Wellington once said of the King's government—must be carried on and held to their tasks. The AR survived this rocky period, with Dr Lewis stepping down from the chairmanship of the advisory board to take over as editor, the post he continues to hold, and James Bishop, the longest serving member of the advisory board, having joined in 1971, taking over as its chairman. The editorial capacities were broadened with the creation in 2002 of the post of deputy editor, which continues to be filled by Dr Wendy Slater.

Although he had not set out to acquire the AR, the new publisher took seriously his duties as custodian of such an historic title and was instrumental in making available its archive in electronic form. Indeed, Mr Hixon's interest in electronic publishing made the AR available to a wider readership than ever before. Under his stewardship, the entire 250-year archive was digitised and made available electronically to libraries and institutions throughout the world. In addition to holding an electronic archive, some libraries also continue to maintain their complete printed runs of the AR. The London Library, for example, shelves *The Annual Register* in print on either side of the fireplace of its main reading room in St James's Square, at hand for any scholar who needs to consult it.

At the end of 2005, Mr Hixon sold the AR to its current US publisher, ProQuest (formerly CSA). Whilst the company's headquarters are in Washington, DC, it has major branches in Oxford and Cambridge in the UK. Thus, Harry Hodson's dying wish—that the AR be brought back into British hands—has been nominally accomplished. The book's tone remains resolutely British, rather than American, although in recent years it has become more international in outlook. It has, for example, added to its longstanding listing of the British cabinet a list of the members of the cabinet of the president of the United States and, more recently still, a list of the members of the European Commission and the Nobel prizewinners for each year.

During the past half-century, there has been a major shift in world politics, seldom noticed by the news media: the number of the world's independent sovereign states has more than doubled. There were fewer than 80 in 1958; there are now more than 160. An after-effect of the 20th century's two world wars was that the governing elites of the world's great empires lost their will to govern. The Hohenzollern, Habsburg, Romanov, and Ottoman empires all dissolved in 1917-22; neither Hitler nor Mussolini could sustain their imperial attempts; the British and French empires had been broken up by the early 1960s, the Belgians gave up their Congo; and the Soviet empire that had succeeded the Tsars had collapsed by the end of 1991. Today's Russia keeps some degree of control over several successor states and the USA enjoys huge influence in many parts of the world; but the general effect of the dissolution of empires has been the multiplication of small states, each with its own ensign, head of state, postage stamps, national anthem, and other symbols of independence.

It is not the first time in world history that there has been such a shift: think of the kingdoms that succeeded to Alexander the Great's empire after his unexpected death in 323 BC, or the proliferation of bodies that resulted from the collapse of the Roman empire in the west in 476 AD, or the many republics in South America that succeeded Spanish and Portuguese rule in that continent. The shift in the 20th century has been described as the fall of colonialism. Today, colonialism has a bad world press, deriving from Lenin's powerful pamphlet, *Imperialism: the highest stage of capitalism*, of 1916, which rested in turn on J.A. Hobson's book, *Imperialism: a study*, published in 1902. Far too few people have read the challenge to them both contained in Lionel Robbins's *The Economic Causes of War*, because Jonathan Cape published it at the outbreak of another world war in 1939 and it got few reviews and too little notice. I just overlapped with Robbins on the AR's advisory board, and can testify to his extraordinary blend of common sense and historical insight.

The AR makes it a rule to cover every independent state in the world. (The current editor must surely be glad that he does not have to cope with each of the 300 or so statelets that, before Napoleon's day, composed what in 1871 became a single Germany.) The AR's coverage of the world economy has grown steadily for about a century; the Royal Economic Society nominates a member of the editorial board, who helps to ensure its quality. As editor, Mr Day, an economist by background, made an important innovation in placing at the head of every country article a summary giving each country's size, population, form of government, head of state, capital city, language, currency, membership in main international bodies, and estimated gross national income per capita. This has increased the AR's value for diplomats, economists, commentators, and students of international affairs. The summaries exemplify the AR's working principles: accurate information, providing the foundation for informed and stylish analysis.

For most of the 19th and early 20th centuries, the AR devoted its early chapters to a summary of the course of English politics, and from about 1890 to about 1950 a sizeable section on the British Empire followed, before a chapter or two on "foreign history". Sir Ivison Macadam, who long worked at Chatham House (the Royal Institute of International Affairs) and directed it in the 1950s, as well as Mr Hodson, a fellow of All Souls and a former editor of the *Sunday Times*, both had worldwide interests and shifted the AR to a less wholly English outlook. US ownership has accentuated this welcome trend towards a more balanced survey of world affairs. The AR's range of contributors gives it a multiplicity of perspectives, which means that its growing global readership has the benefit of a view of the world from beyond specific country borders.

Moreover, since the foundation of the League of Nations in 1919 the AR has devoted increasing space to international organisations, now numerous. The book also conveys the flavour of each year by noting major achievements and trends in literature, music, drama, opera, art, architecture, and sport, as well as science, religion, the law; and has added sections on film, radio, and television as they have developed. It takes care to shun the passion for celebrities that affects some of the news media, though great film stars such as Charlie Chaplin or Marlene Dietrich receive their entries in the longstanding obituary section. This now covers figures of genuine weight in the world; it used to be almost confined to royalty and members of Society. It now includes architects, judges, trade unionists, generals, actors, savants, authors, entrepreneurs, editors, singers: many sorts of personage of an adequate degree of distinction. Among these obituaries, one gem deserves lasting recall: the conservatoire at Milan once observed that the young Giuseppe Verdi, one of its unsuccessful students, had "no musical talent".

The latest four editors (Macadam, Hodson, Day, and Lewis) have transformed the AR from what it had been from Burke's day to Epstein's—an English-centred summary of each year, with excurses on the main events abroad—into a much more global analysis, by experts, of worldwide developments. The principal trends in international politics—such as the dissolution of the Soviet Union; the inability of the USA to impose itself as the single superpower; the emergence of China and India from the wings onto the superpower stage; the diminution of Great Britain from great power to moderate standing; the intermittent authority of the United Nations, established to replace the League of Nations in 1945—can all be observed in the AR's pages. So can the growth of terrorism, much enhanced in its danger by the rapidity of modern communications, as well as by the fanaticism of some of its practitioners. The arrival of the suicide bomber has upset a lot of security equations, which now need reformulating. A potential suicide bomber was once ready to attack Hitler, but was frustrated by one of the Fuhrer's abrupt changes of programme; the genre has developed a good deal since. Moreover, the international trade in drugs, which goes far back, even before Burke's time, has now proliferated so far that it has become entangled with other criminal enterprises and helps to supply them with money.

The 20th century's two world wars, which it was conceited enough to call the first and second—there had been plenty before—received, of course, the AR's full attention, as did the consequent revolutions in Russia, China, and elsewhere. (The 1917 volume had an engaging reference to "a certain M. Trotsky", described as "the incarnation of Bolshevism", who was to be heard of again.) The conclusion of the world war of 1939-45 was brought on by the first use of nuclear power in anger, at Hiroshima and Nagasaki in 1945. The last half-century has been the age of the hydrogen bomb, a weapon that makes the bombs used at Hiroshima and Nagasaki look puny; and the unspoken assumptions on which current international politics rest include the knowledge that these bombs exist, that several independent powers possess them, and that it is not inconceivable that they might one day be used. It is to this knowledge that an unusually long period of peace (at least nominal peace) between the world's great powers is due. No sensible statesman is going to expose his country to bombardment by H-bombs. Unhappily for the world, not all leading statesmen are always sensible.

However, the post-1945 peace led to wars by proxy, with client states engaging in non-nuclear conflict, encouraged, armed, and advised by larger powers. These campaigns have been fully covered by the AR. The book has also reported on the more elusive asymmetrical combats between sovereign states and guerrilla fighters, motivated by a range of ideologies, from right to left, encompassing criminals, fanatics, and those motivated by the desire for national liberation. The resources of conventional armaments are not always enough against the angry temper of an aroused nation, as England long ago found out in Ireland, and the United States learned again in the 1960s and 1970s in South East Asia.

One of the great shifts in the international economy since the last world war has been the emergence of the oil-owning states of the Middle East as dominant influences upon much of world trade and development, because of the world's industries' reliance upon oil as a source of power. This domination cannot last for ever: either the oil will run out, or alternative sources of power will be developed, or both, before long. For now this imbalance remains, further complicated by religion, geography, and the recrudescence of piracy off the Horn of Africa, close to a major oil shipping route. These are all issues whose significance the AR's writers must try to assess, even as they are evolving around them. Despite the inherent difficulties of this task, the AR's experts frequently succeed with distinction, as illustrated by Paul Rayment's article on the world economy in the volume covering 2007. Even before it was clear that the world was entering a recession that threatens to be as severe as that of the 1930s, Mr Rayment put his finger on injudicious lending by banks to "subprime" mortgage holders in the USA as the start of the current rot. Taxpayers the rich world over will have to bear the consequences of this recklessness for some years yet.

For half a century it has been the task of the advisory board's representative from the Royal Historical Society to produce brief extracts from earlier volumes of *The Annual Register*, to remind readers of the AR's continuous coverage of the past. Philip Bell, senior research fellow at the University of Liverpool, in the 2008 edition picked from the volume for 1857 the view that the eruptions in India that year were not "a merely military mutiny...but something more". This is an issue still debated among historians, but worthy of notice as an instance of the AR's capacity for insight. The same perspicacity was manifest in the AR's recognition of Nazi Germany's anti-Semitic legislation in the mid-1930s. The passage from legislation to annihilation was marked by several gloomy reports in 1942-44, at a time when there was little public knowledge of the Holocaust. When the extent of the Nazi crime received worldwide attention in 1945 with the liberation of German concentration camps, the AR estimated the death toll as at least 4 million.

The AR has also consistently recorded the lighter side of human affairs. The sports covered within its pages have varied with the taste of the times. The Oxford and Cambridge boat race, first rowed at Henley in 1829, had, by this writer's childhood, become a principal London festival. A report of the race has sometimes taken up several pages, but in the volume for 2007 rowing did not appear in the sports chapter at all. In the 1890s, when Lord Rosebery's horses twice won the Derby while he was prime minister, horse racing got plenty of attention, whereas in 2007 it got less than a page. When the Olympic games were revived in 1896, they received brief notice, with most attention centred on the long distance race, now known as the Marathon, which celebrated Pheidippides's original run from Marathon to Athens in 490BC. It was won by "a young peasant named Louis, from the village of Amarusi" in two hours and 58 minutes. In 1936 the games were only noticed as a great propaganda triumph for Germany, then already under Nazi domination.

More than 50 pages in the AR for 1851 went on listing the prize winners at the Great Exhibition in Joseph Paxton's Crystal Palace in Hyde Park. The same issue included over 30 pages of births and marriages, of those in or on the edge of Society, a practice long discarded by the book's modern editors. The Oxford and Cambridge class lists for the BA degree were then included as a matter of course. Much of the chronicle sections of mid-19th century *Annual Registers* were taken up by reports of natural disasters and by details of criminal trials: valuable material now for social historians and fascinating for the general reader. The Whitechapel murders of 1888, for instance, were noted briefly, but not attributed to Jack the Ripper, who claimed in letters to Scotland Yard to have delighted in them and whose exploits remain a lurid sensation to this day; how like the AR not to have used his sensationalist moniker.

In the past half-century it has become possible for the AR to include illustrations; most recently, illustrations in colour. This has been a welcome development. When colour illustrations, then much more expensive, were mooted in Longman's day, the publisher threatened to close the publication down if the advisory board persisted in requesting them. The book's current editor, backed by the publisher, has sought to use memorable photographs to highlight characteristic moments in each year, making the book more palatable to a visually more literate readership, less used than were our forefathers to handling long columns of dense print.

Everyone who writes for the AR is aware of its historical importance. Contributors to *The Annual Register* are writing for the record, and must strive to be as accurate as possible, even though they are routinely grappling with trends and developments, which are as yet unclear or incomplete. As A.E. Housman once reminded us all, "accuracy is a duty and not a virtue": a doctrine not often enough remembered by today's news media. Nevertheless, although authoritative in tone and content, in its modern format the AR is anything but dull or predictable. In addition to bringing expertise to bear upon their subjects, the writers frequently display a degree of wit and humour, which entertains as much as it informs. In this respect, and despite its great evolution over 250 years, the AR remains true to the founding principles of its first editor, Edmund Burke. Long may it flourish!

M.R.D. Foot

THE ANNUAL REGISTER 300TH EDITION: A PERSONAL FUTURE

To mark the 250th edition of The Annual Register, *we publish a piece of informed speculation about how the AR—and the world—might be 50 years hence, on the occasion of the book's 300th edition. The article by Richard O'Brien, Partner, Outsights, who has been the Royal Economic Society's representative on the AR advisory board since 1995, looks at the emerging trends of 2008 to suggest potential futures. The piece is written from the perspective of an AR reader in 2059.*

ONE of the great advantages of modern publishing is that we can instantly compile our own personalised version of *The Annual Register* on a theme of our choice, drawing on the erudite essays that are constantly fed into AROnline. This year, I have chosen as my theme "Spaces in the past 50 years". In true AR tradition, my personalised volume is based on the finest scholarship and is written in "plain English". It also always throws in enough anniversaries to remind me how long some things take to happen and how quickly the world can advance. My personal themed AR compilation supplements my regular AR from AROnline, which is also "personalised" but where the search engine decides what interests me: this at least keeps the information flow down to a manageable amount.

To develop my theme of "Spaces in the past 50 years", I have chosen to look at five spaces that extend my vision beyond a simple geographical review of the world. I have chosen to look at the new spaces that we now populate (on Earth, beyond the Earth, and in virtual reality); the spaces that we have had to abandon; and the developments in understanding what goes on inside our heads, in our "inner space". Hopefully, my personalised AR will give me some good ideas to discuss tomorrow evening with my great grandchildren, who somehow seem to be always one step ahead of me.

EMERGENT SPACES: THE POLES AND SIBERIA. Most of the coverage that the AR has given to the great emergent spaces of the 21st century—the North and South Poles and the Russian Far East—has been due to three interlinked reasons: governance, natural resources, and climate change. Fifty years ago there was intense focus on the melting Arctic ice, at the time the most visible manifestation of the impact of climate change as polar bears migrated and ice collapsed dramatically onto the last few tourist ships plying the region. We discovered our planet's climate history stored in the polar ice core readings. The melting of the polar ice, happening faster than expected, raised our sea levels and, most controversially, now does seem to be taking northern Europe closer to a new ice age, scientists always having been sharply divided on whether the North Atlantic "conveyor belt" of warm air would, indeed, shut down.

The Arctic governance question has been intense, ever since Russia dramatically planted its flag on the seabed 50 years ago (see AR 2008, p. 109). The Ilulissat Declaration of 2008 (see Documents) between the five coastal states of Canada, Denmark, Norway, the Russian Federation, and the USA, agreed that the issues would be worked out within current legal regimes (such as the Law of the Sea Convention, the International Maritime Organisation, and the Arctic Council), as opposed to under a new regime or "Arctic treaty". Whilst that has held up as a framing principle, the competition for Arctic resources has involved many more countries and allies—not least the EU, through Denmark, its sole representative amongst the "Arctic five"—because, unlike Antarctica, there has been little land emerging from the ice. Early estimates of the Arctic accounting for almost one-quarter of the world's undiscovered, technically recoverable energy resources have, as always, proven very wide of the mark, and competition has intensified as the world's resources have become closer to their much predicted "final depletion". Policing the fabled Northwest Passage that opened in 2007 (see AR 2008, pp. 461, 465), bringing Asia much closer to Europe, has also had to be assured in a world of increasing sea piracy and crowded shipping lanes.

Literally at the other end of the world the change has been dramatic. The priest of Trinity Church, regarded back in 2008 as the only permanent resident of Antarctica (the population of which at the time fluctuated seasonally between 1,000 and 5,000), would have a hard time ministering to today's population of 3 to 4 million, equivalent to around one-half to two-thirds of that of countries such as New Zealand, Ireland, or Denmark. For a human touch, I see that last year, in 2058, the first person to be born on the Antarctic landmass, (and, curiously, also the only person known to us to have been the first human born on any continent), returned from Argentina to celebrate his 80th birthday there. In four years time they are also planning to mark the 150th birthday of the first person to be born in the South Polar region itself. Indeed, as the AR celebrated its first quarter century in 1786, sealers on South Georgia were becoming the first semi-permanent residents of the region; and it was back in 1775 (when the AR was less than 20 years old) that Captain Cook was the first to see Antarctica. The continent has grown up with the AR (and, of course, "Antarctica" has been a separate editorial section in the AR for quite some time).

Inevitably, people, plus resources, and a landmass have raised the governance stakes. This year will mark the centenary of the signing of the first Antarctic Treaty (1 December 1959, see AR 1959, pp. 416-17), which has been the framework for intense debates in recent years. Antarctica remains a special place for the world's scientists. Better access has cut the cost of research, but scientists complain about the changing conditions: no longer is it the pristine place unsullied by human habitation. Like the Arctic, the melting of the region has been seen as a major cause of the rising sea levels, whilst researchers, such as those at Cape Roberts, are learning much about our climate history from their ice core investigations, still important in trying to understand how mankind can alleviate climate change and what still lies ahead.

When the Poles were less accessible, the risks of serious conflict were limited, even between the major powers who could "afford" to travel there. That has all changed. The major powers now struggle to police both regions, although, as a result, they have tended to reach settlements between themselves in order to focus on disruptive forces, to manage the influx of climate change refugees and resource speculators with easy access to technology, as well as to protect the wildlife diversity, itself changing, for climate change refugees are not only human.

The third great space to emerge from under the ice has been Siberia. Though it continues to be located entirely within one sovereign state, the Russian Federation, this has not diminished the governance or territorial controversies. As with other emergent spaces, control over the resources has been a key variable. At the advent of the 21st century, Siberia alone accounted for almost 90 per cent of Russia's natural gas production, 70 per cent of its oil and coal output, most of its reserves of non-ferrous and rare metals, and large amounts of explored chemicals. It had half of Russia's forests (many now consumed by fire), and more than half of its water and hydropower resources. Lake Baikal held 20 per cent of the world's freshwater reserves (whilst neighbouring China suffered from one of the world's worst water deficits). Retaining control over the region has been a challenge for Russia, not least as the Russians are now a minority in their own territory. If you visit today, you will notice that most of the population is Asian in origin, with the Chinese constituting the largest ethnic group. At first, much of the Chinese labour in the region was transient, but as numbers have increased more have stayed. The challenge of "dual integration" posed by President Vladimir Putin many years ago remains key: integration of this vast landmass and growing population into Russia, and of the area into the Asian region. In retrospect, that the integration has taken place without conflict has been a success.

The other success has been in tackling the great methane question. Fifty years ago, one of the enormous uncertainties was the impact of the methane—a gas with 20 times more impact as a greenhouse gas than CO_2—being released from the Arctic seabed and the melting tundra. As a resource, it was said to dwarf global coal reserves. Global co-operative investment in technology by the world's scientists, and in infrastructure by the energy industry and governments, has enabled much of the methane to be tapped and controlled in ways that were unforeseen in 2008.

Much of the region is physically changed from 50 years ago, as the tundra has melted and been replaced by the thermokarst landscape of rounded grass hillocks, the appearing and then disappearing lakes, the grass and scrubland, the landslips and exposed rocks. Access is still difficult, with the old infrastructure built on ice no longer usable and huge costs involved in connecting this space to the rest of the world, with the priorities lying in piping and transporting its resources.

DISAPPEARING SPACES. As the ice has melted, so coastal lands have "disappeared" below the sea. Low lying islands and the highly populated delta areas have been the first to be affected—Bangladesh, the Nile, the Chiang Jiang or Yangtze delta in China, the Godavari River delta in western India—areas where people have been traditionally vulnerable. But it took a long time for people living by the sea, everywhere, to understand that their seas would rise too. With more than half the US population living in coastal cities, the magnitude of the potential "invasion" was slowly realised. It was not necessary to be hit by Hurricane Katrina (see AR 2005, pp. 121-24), or be already below sea level, to be at risk; much of urban life has been affected. The communities that have coped the best have generally done two things: assessing realistically the size of the threat and developing a comprehensive plan. Strategies for dealing with the threat have ranged from raising barriers, which produced some alleviation, to planned relocation, which turned out not to be so hard for those countries such as the USA, which has either built or remodelled 80 per cent of today's buildings. The cost of rebuilding elsewhere, and better, clearly was not impossible, and it was sensible to build new capacity in safer areas for the additional millions in our cities. In the next 50 years the challenge will intensify in many ways, eroding coasts and the natural environment, not just our cities.

People are, however, seeking other ways of looking at the rise of sea levels, by starting to populate the sea itself. This idea has not really caught on yet, but as population and seas rise further then maybe 50 years from now we will have to think differently about the notion: we are still losing usable land to desertification, to falling water tables, and to mankind's continued destruction of the quality of land. While some of the more dire predictions made in 2008 of the impact of climate change could be ignored as they concerned a date long in the future—2100—we now find ourselves more than halfway there.

OUTER SPACE. It is now just over a century since mankind achieved what once would have been purely a journey for the imagination: travelling into Space (a capital "S" is still warranted). Very recently, we have had a spate of centenary anniversaries. The year 2057 marked the centenary of the launch of the first man-made Earth satellite, the Soviet *Sputnik* (see AR 1957, pp. 468-70); in 2058 we celebrated 100 years since the first attempt at a direct hit on the Moon, the 100th birthday of the USA's National Aeronautics and Space Administration (NASA), and the coining of the word "aerospace"; and this year, of course, marks 90 years since the first Moon landing (see AR 1969, pp. 376-81). Perhaps the initial leg of this journey was just over 150 years ago with the first powered flight in 1903. But since the flurry of the Soviet-US Space race, things seemed to slow down, budgets were cut, and Space became less important. With hindsight, we can see that this was a classic S-curve, where, after the first flurry of attention, and after the dramatic breakthrough and event, things settled down to consolidate, before the next advance was made.

Travel to Space has started to become routine, with civilians booking their tourism tickets and plans to develop space hotels. The famous nanotube Space elevator has been built. We have also seen 50 years of steadily pushing back the frontiers of our knowledge and achieving an even better familiarity with Space. Three dimensional mapping has helped people grasp the geography, while cheap microsatellites have slashed the cost of access to Space. We know so much more about the physical attributes of the planets. We are now mining the Moon. Perhaps our familiarity with Space was raised several notches during the 2029 and 2036 close encounters with Apophis, the asteroid that threatened twice to collide with Earth.

We have extended our political and economic governance of Space. This has not been without its tensions, given the competition to lay claim to the resources of Space and the need to govern the territory where the world's communications network is located and where, now that access is so much easier, rogue elements could be devastatingly disruptive. It is also now 100 years since the first proposals were made to the UN to avoid Outer Space becoming a battleground. These were put into legislation a decade later, in 1967, with the Outer Space Treaty (see AR 1967, p. 143), which was modelled on its predecessor, the 1959 Antarctic Treaty, the first of these so-called non-armament treaties (see AR 1959, pp. 416-17). Keeping Outer Space conflict free in the past 50 years has been hard and the risks are clearly rising alongside the opportunities. Perhaps most disappointing are the new risks we have created, the immense Space debris problem not only constantly disrupting communications but also a greater potential danger to us than any asteroid.

INNER SPACE. If travel to Space was once a journey to the imagination, so also was the journey to somewhere much closer: into our minds, physically close, but far from being properly understood. Scientific revolutions have been truly phenomenal in the past 50 years, even if the famous "singularity" (the explosion of intelligence caused by self-improving machines) has not come to pass. We have been able to create artificial life. Robots are part of our daily lives and have "rights and responsibilities". Nanoscience has revolutionised the ways in which we can manipulate our environment. But one science that has truly taken us into uncharted territory has been neuroscience. Just as medicine floundered for centuries before the body itself was properly understood, so before the 21st century neuroscience was quite primitive. The real revolution for mankind, however, has come from the consequences of this development. Our understanding of how the mind works takes us so close to what we have labelled values, beliefs, or the soul, and challenges our own sense of personal responsibility. The advances have been shaped in combination with other sciences, such as the neuroimaging advances in information technology, the advances in biology and genomics, and the linking with behavioural sciences.

For the world's religions this has been as revolutionary as the advances in geology in the 19th century, when fossils challenged the stories of Noah's Flood and the theory of evolution challenged the Biblical story of the Creation. Already 50 years ago, as neuroscience began to be able to predict more of what people would think or do, our Nobel laureates were asking, "Is there free will after all?" Now we seem to take for granted our new knowledge about what we know: 50 years ago it was pretty clear that we were on the edge of some "tipping point". Coming alongside the new ability to create "artificial life"—the physical side of ourselves—mankind has truly been transformed.

In practical terms, it means that we can now treat and often avert many of the so-called diseases of old age, such as Alzheimer's and Parkinson's. This has proved crucial now that (in richer countries at least) we expect to live to at least

90 years and want to enjoy a full life. Becoming a centenarian is no longer so special, even though holding down a full time job at 100 is still quite remarkable. We are expected to work until 90 years old before we qualify for any full pension, although many people "retire" earlier if they have saved enough to be able to make that choice. We can now repair our brains with replacement parts, which have become as commonplace as other body part substitutes. IBM's plan to create a "brain" by 2030, combining neuroscience with information technology, was completed well ahead of time. Again there has been a major practical advance: we can link our own brain signals directly to our computing equipment, now that we can identify the way in which particular brain signals work. It certainly seems to help those with brain injuries and the mentally impaired, where lost capabilities can be supplemented or "replaced".

Some of our discoveries have perhaps not been a big surprise, but merely confirmed what we used to call "common sense" and observed behaviour. In the same way, the limited genetic information we gained some 50 years ago was no more predictive than just knowing about our parents and grandparents. Combined with other advances in cognitive psychology, genomics, and biology we can now manage behaviours much better: for example, drug additions can be both understood and treated. Perhaps predictably, this has not reduced our use of drugs, the variety of which has increased greatly, but only made us more liberal in their use, knowing that there is a "cure".

Neuroscience has also taken communication to a new level: indeed, we now "talk to the animals" or, rather, we are better interpreting their sounds and influencing animals themselves. Animal rights groups have been strongly opposed to much of this work, especially that which has led to the greater use of animals in warfare. As ever, science has created new challenges for society simultaneously with the solutions that it has provided. Looking back, though, one great relief is that societies have at least not rejected science, something that has been a constant danger.

VIRTUAL SPACE: EVERYWHERE AND NOWHERE. The "net" is getting close to its centenary from its earliest creative days. Fifty years ago, it was well embedded in society, taken for granted in fact, and now we work in multiple worlds. In 2007, it was being said that "by 2050, the first child will be born that does not actually distinguish between the virtual world and the real world, because these virtual worlds will be that convincing." Why did they think it would take that long? Whilst the success of the pioneering online commercial site, "Second Life", was often dismissed with the counter-reaction of "get a life", online activity soon became as acceptable as personal interaction, just as, over time, the telephone became a perfectly acceptable way of dealing with people.

It took a few more breakthroughs to get us where we are today. Embedding chips in everybody has been essential. First, it was made near essential as a means of monitoring and administering health to our bodies and of carrying private information and literally all that people once had to remember: a great improvement on a losable plastic card, memory stick, or any of the various devices one can see in the online (virtual) museum. Secondly, data security has had to be well protected. It is still not perfect, but the legal world remains one step ahead of the illegal (yes, that distinction holds). Thirdly, socially we have had to accept that the virtual world is a truly alternative space in which to spend our lives. Fifty years ago "gaming" was one of the hot trends in information technology, creating new worlds in which people could play. In some senses, this was no different from the escapism enjoyed in films, art, and books for centuries; and, just as films and television were once believed to distort and influence people's visions of reality, gaming became more than escapism, as people began to find it harder to differentiate between their real and their virtual lives. Meanwhile, so-called "reality TV" was often quite the opposite, with its artificially created environments in which to watch selected people play out a so-called life reflecting modern mores, a laboratory experiment deliberately cordoned off from the rest of us.

Ultimately, the big achievements of virtual space have been threefold. First, in the extension of who and what participates in the virtual world, linking humans with other forms of biological life and with artificial life. Secondly, in overcoming the danger that we would be smothered by the avalanche of knowledge: we take it for granted now, but managing the volume of data and the complexity of the connections has been an immense task. Thirdly, the fact that we have been able to deliver on the great hopes for artificial intelligence.

Because we now live our lives on- and offline, to use the old distinction, we have, as with all other spaces, had to develop governance mechanisms. Although it was developed by the US military in conjunction with relatively closed research environments, the Internet had a culture of openness and freedom, regarding governance as a necessary evil to be minimised. It now has the full trappings of governance, based on the early efforts of ICANN (Internet Corporation for Assigned Names and Numbers) and multilateral intergovernmental arrangements. There really is no distinction between online and offline governance, any more than there is any sense of difference between virtual and real. As many have said, it's all in the mind, and one century and one decade after the publication of George Orwell's *1984*, we each still have one of those, don't we?

Richard O'Brien
1. 1. 2059

2008: THE YEAR IN REVIEW

THE year 2008 started with a broad international focus on two quite different issues—international security and the state of the global economy—and a more specific focus on the US presidential election campaign.

Concerning security, Pakistan's opposition leader Benazir Bhutto had been assassinated just four days before the start of the year and this resulted in a widespread concern over the potential for instability in that country. This was in the context of a winter of violence in Afghanistan, where the previous annual experience of a winter lull in the fighting had failed to materialise. Moreover, a steady increase in foreign troop deployments in Afghanistan had been accompanied by a greater recognition that the Federally Administered Tribal Areas (FATA) of western Pakistan were outside the control of the Pakistan government and had acquired the status of ungoverned space that was greatly useful to Taliban militias and their al-Qaida militant associates.

In Iraq, there was evidence at the start of the year that the "surge" in US troops was having some effect in limiting the violence, even if at least 1,000 civilians were still being killed each month, but a sudden increase in violence in the early weeks of 2008 suggested that optimism might be premature. Even so, there was still a widespread perception that the Iraq war might be diminishing, with the possible result being that the "war on terror" of the administration of US President George W. Bush was shifting its focus from Iraq to Afghanistan and western Pakistan. There was little pretence that the al-Qaida movement was in disarray, and concern that developments in Yemen, Somalia, and Afghanistan all suggested that this unusual trans-national entity had the capacity to evolve and adapt.

In relation to the world economy, the second half of 2007 had been a time of extraordinary upheaval, as the full impact of the "subprime" mortgage crisis in the USA became apparent and was having substantial effects across the world. The start of 2008 was therefore marked by considerable uncertainty and a palpable sense of unease. Optimistic assessments suggested that the crisis might be considerable but would be limited primarily to the financial sector, without having a great impact on the "real" economy of commodity markets, industry, and labour. Pessimistic assessments discounted this, predicting that 2008 would be the year in which an apparently internal financial crisis, limited primarily to the USA, was, in reality, the start of a global upheaval that was unpredictable in its impact, except that it would be long lasting and potentially as traumatic as that of the 1930s.

In the event, the more pessimistic assessments were closer to the actual experience of the year. Casualties in the USA included investment banks Bear Stearns, Merrill Lynch, and Lehman Brothers; the world's largest insurance company (AIG); and the two major federal mortgage institutions, Fannie Mae and Freddie Mac. Banks in Iceland collapsed, Russian oligarchs saw billions of dollars wiped off the value of their assets, and banks and building societies in the UK and several other western European countries were forced to seek massive government bailouts that amounted to partial nationalisation. The parlous state of the international financial system was illustrated by the collapse in December of an investment business built up by a pillar of the New York financial establishment, Bernard L. Madoff. Investors lost US$50 billion in a pyramid fraud, which had escaped the attention of the regulatory authorities for decades.

Perhaps most remarkable of all was the manner in which some of the financial giants of the USA were only saved by federal intervention that would have been declared akin to socialism just a few months earlier. The impact of the US financial crisis on global confidence was particularly marked because Wall Street had been seen as the living proof of the success of an untrammelled free market. That one of the world's leading financial centres could experience such manifest problems was an indication not just that confidence was misplaced but that there were deep seated problems with the entire global economy. This was supported by the rapid rise in unemployment in many countries towards the end of the year: in the United States alone, 2.6 million jobs were lost in 2008, the worst year since demobilisation in 1945. Multinational job losses were the real indicators that the world was moving into a period of recession that went far beyond a crisis in the financial sector.

The main focus for the financial crisis was upon its impact on the main economies, especially those of the North Atlantic community and East Asia. The primary response centred on the immediate effects of the crisis, with individual countries bringing in a range of measures to prevent collapse in their banking systems. Intergovernmental responses involved plans for improvements in international financial co-operation, including an effective early warning system and a more comprehensive framework for transnational responses. There were also plans drafted for an independent "college of supervisors" to provide systematic monitoring of the world's major companies and financial institutions. The emphasis throughout was on preventing a further deterioration in the status of the world's leading economies.

What these actions did not address was the more deep seated issue of rising global inequalities and the impact that the recession would have on the poorer communities that comprised the majority of the world's population. Most of the advanced economies, moreover, had well-developed welfare systems that provided some relief for the poorer sectors of their communities, whereas for most of the world such systems simply did not exist. The context for this issue was that the impressive economic growth of the world economy in recent decades did not bring socioeconomic justice; most of the fruits of economic progress were experienced by about one-fifth of the global population. This "elite" might be concentrated in the countries of the North Atlantic community, but it was transnational in the sense that it included probably close to 200 million people in China, over 100 million in India, and substantial minorities in Brazil, Russia and elsewhere. The most significant effect, if one rarely noted beyond specialist analysis, was that this division had been widening year-on-year and had reached remarkable proportions. A study from the UN University's world institute for development economics research in Helsinki reported that the richest 10 per cent of the world's people owned 85 per cent of household wealth and that the poorest 50 per cent owned barely 1 per cent.

This trend towards a global elite of many hundreds of millions of people was accompanied by another trend, which was welcome in very many ways but which interacted with these growing divisions. This was the remarkable improvement in education, literacy, and communications across much of the South, a product of intense effort over many decades. The penetration of primary education into most communities had been truly impressive and, over the last decade, had at last included a greater degree of gender equality, but one of its primary effects was to ensure that people in marginalised communities were far more aware of their own marginalisation. This, in turn, readily led to resentment and anger.

Two examples of this effect were evident during 2008, in China and India. For many years China had experienced impressive economic growth, often of the order of a 10 per cent increase in GDP per annum, but that growth was highly unequal and concentrated primarily in major coastal cities. As a result there was a marked increase in social unrest that caused the authorities deep concern, even if this was largely unreported outside China. One governmental response was to establish a new network of well-equipped public order units, 600-strong paramilitary forces located in 32 cities across China in order to maintain control in times of civil disturbance. As the world economic crisis deepened during 2008, the Chinese authorities became hugely concerned that they would be unable to maintain their previously impressive levels of economic growth, with a consequent negative impact on social cohesion. One response in early November was to announce a two-year economic stimulus package valued at US$586 billion. Much of this investment would be directed to rural areas, where the loss in remittances from migrant workers in cities was expected to have damaging social consequences.

The other major economy that was being watched with great concern was India, where the impressive economic growth had been even less evenly distributed than in China. A major effect of the wealth-poverty divide was a rise in the instances of civil unrest. These took the form both of revitalised secessionist movements, especially in north-east India, and a marked upsurge in activity by the neo-Maoist Naxalite movement. The Naxalites were originally active more than two decades previously and most analysts had assumed that they had declined to the point of obscurity. Their rebirth was remarkable: in 2008 they were active in 185 districts in 17 out of India's 26 states and were being described by Indian government sources as India's greatest internal security problem.

The world-wide socioeconomic divide, in combination with a more educated and knowledgeable population, also produced a strong reaction to the rapid increases in food prices in the early part of 2008. The last instance of a global food crisis was in 1973-74 but, unlike then, 2008 was marked by widespread food riots, especially in Africa and Central America.

By the end of the year, after many months of financial disarray, the actions of the major economies were focused almost entirely on their domestic situations, with little emphasis on international co-operation. Furthermore, what co-operation was developing scarcely related to the impact of the global recession on the world's poorer communities. The social and political consequences of this narrow outlook were unpredictable, but the evidence from China and India suggested that revolts from the margins were likely to grow.

In terms of the human consequences of warfare in 2008, the conflicts in the Darfur region of Sudan and the eastern area of the Democratic Republic of Congo were the worst anywhere in the world, with little immediate prospect of an end. In eastern Africa, the instability in Somalia became more widespread as Ethiopian troops failed to secure the greater Mogadishu region and African Union peacekeeping troops could only safeguard a small enclave within the capital. The government controlled very little territory and the Shahab Islamist faction continued to expand its areas of influence in the south and centre of the country. In the coastal areas of the north of Somalia there was no central control. Instead there was a marked rise in piracy as fishermen combined with paramilitary and criminal elements in the astonishingly successful evolution of their joint abilities to hijack large merchant vessels and hold them for ransom. Of around 10,000 commercial ships transiting the Gulf of Aden in the first six months of 2008, 71 were boarded, 12 were hijacked, and 11 fired upon. In total, 190 crew members were taken hostage and seven were killed. Some ships were held hostage for many months and by November, some US$30 million was believed to have been paid in ransom. Piracy reached new levels of audacity in November, when Somali pirates captured the supertanker *Sirius Star* 450 nautical miles off Kenya's coast.

In the early months of 2008 the security situation in Iraq showed signs of improved stability, although levels of violence were not lower than in 2003 and 2004, shortly after the termination of the Saddam Hussein regime. Much of the improvement was attributed to the effects of the US military "surge" in 2007-08, but US defence department officials were deeply reluctant to see troop levels further reduced beyond the ending of the surge, for fear that the gains would be reversed. In part, this was an acknowledgment that the surge was only one factor behind the decrease in violence. A ceasefire by Muqtada al-Sadr's Mahdi army, the rise of the "awakening movement" among Sunni communities opposed to Islamist militancy, and the much clearer geographical separation of confessional groups were other significant factors.

Nevertheless, one consequence of the security improvement was the development of a "narrative of victory" in Republican Party circles in the United States. A forceful argument was developed that the Bush administration's military posture in Iraq was, at last, working and that Democratic presidential candidate Barack Obama's proposal for an early withdrawal of troops would snatch defeat from the jaws of victory. This narrative had only limited effect on the presidential election campaign, however, and was unable to overturn a domestic weariness with the war. In the event, Obama's victory in November had relatively little to do with the situation in Iraq: his powerful rhetoric, an exceptionally well-organ-ised and financed campaign, and the impact of the economic crisis were all far more significant. The result did mean, though, that President-elect Obama would have considerable freedom to decide on the speed of troop withdrawal. While US forces would be likely to remain entrenched in Iraq in various capacities for many years to come, 2008 did appear to be the year in which the focus moved from Iraq towards Afghanistan.

The consequences of the Iraq intervention were not easy to predict but nearly six years of war had seen at least 100,000 civilians killed, 120,000 detained without trial—some for lengthy periods—and the reputation of the United States sullied by torture, rendition, and widespread prisoner abuse. While these costs were grievous for US standing across the Middle East and south-west Asia, the main impact might be quite different and singularly long-lasting. In 1980s Afghanistan, many thou-sands of resistance fighters gained combat experience fighting in a largely rural environment against well armed, but often poorly trained, conscript Soviet troops. The eventual withdrawal of those Soviet forces was interpreted as a huge victory for the Afghan resistance and the foreign paramilitaries that had joined the conflict. Indeed, it was subsequently seen by al-Qaida strategists as the veritable crippling of a superpower, which also provided a generation of combat-trained jihadists, some of whom formed the operational core of the al-Qaida movement.

In the Iraq of the mid-2000s, a new cohort of jihadist paramilitaries gained combat experience against very well equipped volunteer US troops and Marines in the largely urban environment of Iraq. While most were Iraqis, large numbers came from Saudi Arabia, Yemen, Egypt, Algeria, and other countries across the region. Many of them died in Iraq but most did not. Even were the Iraq war to scale down considerably in 2009-10, this new generation would be available for operations elsewhere, and 2008 saw clear evidence that weapons and tactics devel-oped in Iraq were being used in Afghanistan, western Pakistan, and even Somalia.

In Afghanistan, in particular, 2008 saw a steady increase in violent conflict and US military commanders argued for a major expansion in their operations, involv-ing the deployment of many thousands of additional troops. Other NATO states were deeply reluctant to make substantial additional commitments and even the UK, which planned to pull put all its troops from Iraq by mid-2009, was unlikely to increase its commitment in Afghanistan. As of mid-2008 there were over 60,000 foreign troops in the country, the majority of them from the USA. In Octo-ber an additional combat brigade of 4,000 troops was ordered to deploy from Jan-uary 2009 but there were indications that local US military commanders were urging the need for three more combat brigades. By the end of the year it was expected that at least 20,000 additional US troops and Marines would be deployed to the country during 2009. With some modest additions from other NATO states this would take the foreign forces close to 90,000. Significantly, this new empha-sis on Afghanistan was one aspect of US security policy where the incoming Obama administration was committed to a bipartisan approach.

The focus of international attention on Afghanistan and Pakistan came in a con-text of increased paramilitary activity within Pakistan and also in India. The destruction of the Marriott Hotel in Islamabad in September was one major incident but even more significant was a carefully executed attack by a paramilitary group on numerous targets in the Indian financial capital of Bombay (Mumbai) two months later. The targets of the attack included guests in two leading international hotels, who were held hostage for several days resulting in intensive worldwide media coverage.

Towards the end of the year, US forces stepped up their attacks on al-Qaida and Taliban groups in western Pakistan. Attempts to use US special forces in these operations were rebuffed by the Pakistani armed forces and one consequence was the increased use of armed drones. On several occasions this resulted in numerous civilian casualties, with a consequent antagonism to US policy within Pakistan. Nevertheless, there was every indication that 2009 would see an increase in US operations both in Afghanistan and Pakistan, with no guarantee that the activity of Taliban, al-Qaida, and other paramilitary groups would decrease. Within Afghanistan, the Taliban was financed by income from heroin and morphine exports which were increasingly refined within the country in order to increase their export value. There were also indications that many Taliban supporters saw their activities as part of a wider international jihad, rather than being merely a nationalist insurgency.

Beyond all of this loomed the idea of global jihad that underpinned the al-Qaida movement. This remained strong throughout 2008, even as the movement became more dispersed and fragmented. It received a substantial boost at the end of the year with the start of a new conflict in Gaza. Just as the Israeli siege of west Beirut in 1982 had fuelled a perception of anti-Islamic action, so the new conflict in Gaza could readily be portrayed in a similar manner, involving the unequivocal support of the "far enemy" (the USA) for the key "near enemy" of Israel. Perhaps least understood in the United States and Israel was al-Qaida's eschatological foundation. Although in many ways an unusual transnational revolutionary movement with defined political aims, it had its roots in a radical religious ideology that meant that it operated in a timescale stretching over many decades, with the leadership not expecting to achieve the movement's objectives in their own lifetimes. This demanded a sense of political perspective that was very difficult for conventional Western governance to embrace.

The middle months of 2008 saw a sudden crisis develop in South Ossetia, leading to tensions between the USA and Russia, and this was paralleled by entrenched Russian opposition to US plans for a forward-based missile defence system in Eastern Europe, as well as a crisis at the end of the year in the transport of Russian gas exports through Ukraine. While there was extensive talk of a new "cold war" and a continuing Russian sensitivity to its wider international status, the reality of the brief South Ossetia conflict was that it showed how decrepit were Russia's conventional armed forces. At the end of the year there were indications that the incoming Obama administration would show a more conciliatory US approach towards Russia, but that this would require a positive Russian response if it was to lead to a sustained improvement in relations. (Although the incoming

US administration showed little sign of major policy changes in relation to Israel, there was likely to be an attempt to improve relations with Iran, and Russian cooperation could be of some value in this regard.)

In other respects, the real changes expected from the Obama administration would relate to more sustained responses to the recession within the USA and a major shift in US attitudes to climate change. Throughout 2008 evidence grew that climate change would become one of the defining global issues of the mid-21st century. Four aspects of this issue became more significant. First, there was substantial evidence that the rate of change in the global climate was actually speeding up and was repeatedly exceeding the predictions made by the detailed climate modelling being conducted principally in the USA and the UK. A second aspect was that a number of positive feedback mechanisms were already at work. Among these was the decline in sea ice coverage in the polar regions, the result being that open water absorbed more solar radiation than sea ice, thus warming the sea and further increasing the rate of melting. Another feedback mechanism was that the melting of Arctic permafrost was beginning to release large quantities of methane from previously frozen decomposing vegetation, and methane was a far more potent climate change gas than carbon dioxide.

A third aspect of climate change was the increasing recognition that it would have a much greater impact on the tropical and sub-tropical regions that were home to most of the world's poorer people, who would be least able to cope. Finally, it was becoming steadily more apparent that combating climate change required far greater cuts in carbon emissions than any government was prepared to countenance. Cuts of 80 per cent in emissions were required within no more than two to three decades, and most were required by 2025.

If the probable impact of climate change was integrated with the widening global socioeconomic divide, the prospect was of a fractured and constrained global community that had the potential for social and political instability.

A number of military centres and security thinktanks in the USA and western Europe had come to embrace the idea of a volatile and uncertain global environment of insecurity, in which climate change and poverty were potential drivers of conflict. Amidst some innovative thinking, there remained a tendency to develop military responses that still depended primarily on ensuring the security of their own states or alliances. This was termed "liddism": keeping the lid on insecurity, rather than addressing the underlying causes.

Four trends that were apparent during 2008 were reminders that such a control paradigm might not be sustainable. In Iraq the expenditure of more than one thousand billion US dollars and the fielding of a substantial part of the world's most powerful army were only slowly gaining control of a five-and-a-half-year long insurgency, which rarely involved more than a few thousand paramilitaries. Moreover, arising from that insurgency were techniques of asymmetric warfare that were proliferating, not least to Afghanistan. Secondly, the extraordinarily potent attack on multiple targets in Bombay showed that a small but determined group of paramilitaries could require a powerful state to use most of its federal counterterrorism forces in responding to just one operation, taking several days to bring the situation under control. A third example was the spread of piracy off the east coast of Africa, eventually requiring the assembly of a substantial international fleet of warships in an attempt to bring it under control. Whatever was to happen in 2009, one consequence would be that many hundreds, and possibly thousands, of young men would have learnt the techniques of piracy and many would be available for hire to use them elsewhere.

Finally, and most potently, the forceful Israeli assault upon Gaza at the end of the year was predicated on a feeling of considerable vulnerability in the face of the crude rockets fired from Gaza into towns and cities in southern Israel. While a small proportion of the devices had been smuggled into Gaza, most were produced in back street workshops and were wildly inaccurate. Yet their crudeness did not in any way limit their psychological impact. Thus, devices manufactured by mechanics operating in an impoverished and blockaded environment were able to affect significantly a state that had some of the world's most sophisticated military equipment and weaponry and was strongly supported by the world's sole superpower.

Individually, each of these factors might have been of only moderate significance. Together they served as a forceful reminder that 2008 demanded a more thorough examination of approaches to international security than had yet been envisaged.

Paul Rogers

II WESTERN AND SOUTHERN EUROPE

UNITED KINGDOM—SCOTLAND—WALES—NORTHERN IRELAND

UNITED KINGDOM

CAPITAL: London   AREA: 243,610 sq km   POPULATION: 61,034,000 ('07)
OFFICIAL LANGUAGES: English; plus Welsh in Wales, Gaelic in Scotland, Irish and Ulster Scots in
    Northern Ireland   POLITICAL SYSTEM: multiparty monarchy
HEAD OF STATE: Queen Elizabeth II (since Feb '52)
RULING PARTY: Labour Party (since May '97)
HEAD OF GOVERNMENT: Prime Minister Gordon Brown (since June '07)
MAIN IGO MEMBERSHIPS (NON-UN): NATO, CWTH, EU, OSCE, CE, PC, OECD, G-8
CURRENCY: pound sterling (end-'08 US$1=£0.6955, €1=£0.9669)
GNI PER CAPITA: US$42,740, $34,370 at PPP ('07)

WHILE a tragedy for the economy, 2008 was a great year for fans of the Westminster political soap opera, which was dominated by the remarkable fall and rise of Prime Minister Gordon Brown. For most of the year the news was so bad for the government that by the end of the summer a Conservative landslide at the next election seemed assured. But as the financial crisis intensified sharply in September and October, it was Brown's proposal for recapitalising the banks that provided a model for global action. Statesmanlike and self-assured, Brown experienced a reversal of fortune, meaning that by the end of the year all bets were off as to the result of the next general election.

POLITICS. As the year began, Brown was rebuilding his team at the prime minister's office, making several heavyweight appointments of enormous significance. On 7 January it was announced that Stephen Carter, chief executive officer of the corporate communications company, Brunswick Group, had been appointed principal special adviser in charge of political strategy, communications, and research. On 23 January it was announced that Jeremy Heywood, talented former personal private secretary to Brown's predecessor, Tony Blair, would return to Downing Street in the new role of permanent secretary at No.10, to run the civil service aspect of the prime minister's office.

A change of luck was not immediately noticeable, however, as a series of controversies stole the political limelight during the first half of the year. In January it was disclosed that Peter Hain, who combined the posts of Welsh secretary with secretary at the department of work and pensions, had failed to declare over £100,000 in donations to his unsuccessful 2007 Labour Party deputy leadership bid. An enquiry launched by the Electoral Commission was extremely embarrassing for Hain and, under mounting pressure, he resigned on 24 January following the announcement that his campaign finances would be subject to a police investigation. It was announced on 5 December that no one would be prosecuted (see p. 42).

Hain's departure triggered a cabinet reshuffle, in which a number of young politicians were promoted. Culture Secretary James Purnell replaced Hain at work and pensions, and Andy Burnham filled the post left vacant at the department of culture, media and sport. Caroline Flint was promoted to become housing minister, a post which became vacant as Yvette Cooper was appointed chief secretary to the treasury. Paul Murphy became Welsh secretary. Shriti, Baroness Vadera, became parliamentary under-secretary of state for the department for business, enterprise and regulatory reform.

A furious backbench revolt at the end of April over the abolition of the 10p band of income tax forced the government to issue concessions to compensate the 5.3 million families affected. Local elections at the beginning of May were a disaster for Labour. The party's share of the national vote fell to 24 per cent, its lowest since the 1960s, and in London's mayoral contest incumbent Ken Livingstone was defeated by Conservative candidate Boris Johnson. The publication of several unflattering political memoirs was a further source of embarrassment, and hopes of a political recovery in 2009, based on an economic upturn, faded as Bank of England Governor Mervyn King warned that "the 'nice' decade is behind us" with the economy "travelling along a bumpy road". Public fears of a looming recession were confirmed when Caroline Flint inadvertently allowed her pessimistic cabinet briefing paper on housing to be photographed while walking into No. 10 on 13 May. By the end of the month, Labour's support was trailing in opinion polls by 14 points, the worst at any time since the height of Tory Prime Minister Margaret Thatcher's popularity. By this stage the government was understood to be so divided on political strategy that when Labour deputy leader Harriet Harman wore a stab proof vest to accompany police on patrol in south London at the beginning of April, the press joked that she needed to wear it for cabinet meetings.

By-elections reflected these problems. At Crewe and Nantwich, Conservative candidate Edward Timpson defeated Tamsin Dunwoody by a resounding 7,860 votes on a swing of 17.6 per cent in a key contest triggered by the death of her mother, veteran Labour MP Gwyneth Dunwoody, on 17 April (see Obituary). At Glasgow East on 24 July, a Labour majority of 13,507 was overturned by the Scottish National Party which won a narrow victory on an astounding swing of 22 per cent (see p. 40).

By July the knives were out for Brown within his own party. At the end of August, Chancellor of the Exchequer Alistair Darling told the press that economic conditions were the worst in 60 years, contradicting the prime minister's more confident position. With Foreign Secretary David Miliband waiting in the sidelines to seize the throne and Darling openly exasperated, critics charged that the government had become hopelessly dysfunctional at the moment when firm leadership was most needed. Calls for a leadership election came from a group of around 15 rebels, but with no clear successor, senior party figures were said to be convinced that Brown was still the best placed person to lead Labour through the economic storm that was gathering in ferocity.

Brown began to reassert control over the cabinet on 16 September, when he insisted to colleagues that speculation about leadership must be put aside during the economic crisis. The party rallied behind his leadership at its conference in the third week of September and further support came from *Harry Potter* author J.K. Rowling, when it was announced that she had made a £1 million donation to the cash-strapped party. Brown's speech to the party on 23 September, introduced by his popular wife Sarah, admitted to mistakes but stressed the need for "fairness" in government and was generally well received. In a surprise move, Transport Secretary Ruth Kelly—a critic of Brown—used her platform at the conference to announce her resignation, citing family reasons.

There were two big surprises in the post-conference reshuffle. Veteran minister Margaret Beckett returned as housing minister, replacing the less experienced Caroline Flint; and jaws dropped when it was announced that the outgoing EU commissioner for trade, Peter Mandelson, would return to cabinet as business secretary. Mandelson's stature, competence, and experience placed him in a de facto deputy prime ministerial role, transforming the power dynamics of the government. Mandelson and Brown had long ago fallen out over the leadership of former prime minister, Tony Blair, but the two were now apparently "joined at the hip". (For full UK cabinet list, see Documents.)

The tabloid press had sorely missed Mandelson and the inevitably salacious gossip and intrigue that seemed to follow in his wake, and they did not have long to wait for more. Conservative Shadow Chancellor George Osborne could not resist revealing that Mandelson had been "dripping poison" about Brown only weeks before, when the two had both holidayed at the Corfu villa of their mutual friend, financier Nathaniel Rothschild. Appalled at this "bad form", Rothschild wrote a furious letter to *The Times* alleging that at the same house party Osborne had taken the opportunity to attempt to solicit an illegal donation for the Conservatives from Russian aluminium billionaire Oleg Deripaska, whose yacht was moored close by. It soon transpired that Mandelson had stayed on the yacht with his pal Deripaska when the Rothschild villa grew crowded, in turn leading to speculation over the extent to which this friendship represented a conflict of interest for an EU commissioner. The press had enormous fun with all of this and the whole affair reflected awfully well on Brown, who had spent his holiday at the quiet English seaside town of Southwold with his wife and children, where no foreign billionaires were spotted.

It was Brown's leadership in co-ordinating the global response to the autumn financial crisis, however, that did more than anything else to improve his standing. His £50 billion rescue package for the banking system, announced on 8 October, was viewed as a model for the rest of the world and on 13 October Nobel prize winning economist Paul Krugman declared that Brown had possibly saved the international financial system; quite a feat, considering that he had for the past decade been in charge of the economic policies that led up to the disaster. Improbable as it seemed, the prime minister was soon being asked how it felt to be described as a super hero: "Flash Gordon" had arrived.

The impact of all this was already evident at the 6 November by-election at Glenrothes in Scotland, where Labour candidate Lindsay Roy defied pundits and held the seat with a comfortable majority (see p. 40). By the end of the year, polling data—

while inconsistent—suggested that support for Labour was growing, although the party was still trailing the Conservatives by around 5 per cent. There was also mounting speculation that Brown would opt for a spring general election in 2009. This was hugely frustrating for Conservative party leader David Cameron. He had started the year in a strong position and seemed to have captured the agenda in British politics with modernisation proposals for radical welfare reform based on what he called a "post-bureaucratic era". But Conservatives could not sound more plausible than Brown on the economy, and financial matters increasingly dominated the headlines.

Like Labour, the Conservatives had their share of scandal. On 30 January, Derek Conway, MP for Old Bexley and Sidcup, announced that he would step down at the next election, following his suspension from the parliamentary party and banishment from the House of Commons for 10 days after it was revealed that he had paid up to £77,000 to his sons for work that they did not actually undertake as "researchers". Yet the Conservatives took control of 12 councils in the local elections at the beginning of May, winning victories in the north of England as well as in their traditional electoral strongholds. When this victory was followed by the Conservative by-election triumph at Crewe and Nantwich, Cameron appeared to be building a convincing basis for a general election land-slide. In a sign of earnest preparation for government, Francis Maude was put in charge of an "implementation team" designed to address inexperience in the shadow cabinet by assigning experienced mentors to each member.

The most significant gain for the party was in London, where Boris Johnson, Conservative MP for Henley, was elected mayor. Johnson had become a house-hold name in recent years as a journalist and television personality. However, his previous management experience was limited to editing *The Spectator* magazine and there were doubts over his qualifications for the job of mayor. His first appointment, as deputy mayor for young people with responsibility for tackling the causes of youth crime, was east London youth worker Ray Lewis. On 4 July, Lewis would resign amid a string of allegations going back more than a decade and which he denied, including financial misconduct, sexual harassment, and deception. Other moves proved to be more successful, if no less dramatic. At the beginning of August, Johnson openly endorsed US presidential candidate, Barack Obama, in a snub to Republican contender, John McCain. On 2 October, Metropolitan Police Commissioner Sir Ian Blair was forced to resign under pressure from Johnson. Blair, perceived to be too close to New Labour, had been a controversial figure and the decision was widely applauded, as was Johnson's announcement of an investigation into racism in the Met.

Conservative Shadow Home Secretary David Davis resigned his seat following the Commons vote in June on 42-day detentions (see below) to campaign on the issue of civil liberties. Cameron quickly appointed Dominic Grieve as his permanent replacement. Davis's decision was an odd one, given that his party had also opposed the measure, but the resulting by-election at Haltemprice and Howden, at which Davis was re-elected, unopposed by Labour, succeeded in drawing attention to the issues raised by opponents of the bill.

The dramatic escalation of the financial crisis in September was more problematic for Cameron, who introduced a number of last minute changes to the party conference. Gone was the triumphalist mood of impending victory, as Cameron banned champagne and scrapped a video celebration of recent by-election victories. Policy announcements, such as George Osborne's commitment to a two-year freeze on council tax, were wiped from the headlines. Instead Cameron sought to look calm and authoritative, offering Brown bipartisan support. The prime minister's rising stature and the fragility of the market made it difficult for Cameron and Osborne to criticise the government. When on 14 November Osborne warned that government borrowing on a huge scale might lead to a run on the pound, for example, he was widely criticised for a lack of judgement.

The swinging polls explained commentators' interest in the Liberal Democrat party and its newly elected leader, Nick Clegg, who, it was felt, might prove to be the pivotal figure in the formation of the next government. Clegg's debut as party leader in the House of Commons on 9 January was respectable, but his authority was undermined when three members of his front bench team resigned at the beginning of March in defiance of a three line whip to abstain on the vote to hold a referendum over the EU Lisbon Treaty. They were joined by 10 backbench party members who also voted in favour. More generally, the party was divided philosophically between those who believed in the power of the state and therefore leaned towards collaboration with Labour, and those who favoured a more liberal, Conservative approach. At the party's conference in Bournemouth in the middle of September, Clegg put tax cuts at the heart of his election strategy as he sought to give voters a clear, progressive alternative to Labour. Shadow Treasury Spokesman Vincent Cable, however, made the deepest impression, gaining a standing ovation following his confident speech on the economy.

In other political news, House of Commons Speaker Michael Martin drew criticism because his controversial personal record was thought to conflict with his chairing of an inquiry into MPs' expenses. His competence came further into question in November, following the arrest by counter terrorism police officers of the Conservative shadow home office immigration minister, Damian Green, on suspicion that he had actively encouraged a home office official to leak documents over a two-year period. Green was held for nine hours at a central London police station in a move that was labelled "Stalinesque" by an outraged David Cameron. Without a warrant, police officers conducted simultaneous searches at four locations, including—in a serious breach of constitutional protocol—Green's office in the House of Commons. This was universally condemned in the press, although on 30 November Home Secretary Jacqui Smith defended the right of the police to conduct independent investigations where criminal activity was suspected. In a statement to the Commons on 3 December, Martin blamed a subordinate for authorising the search. His resignation would have prompted an unwelcome by-election in Glasgow and he retained the post of Speaker.

THE ROLE OF THE STATE, JUSTICE AND COUNTER-TERRORISM. The balance between the state and the individual had emerged as a defining political debate in Britain and was manifested in 2008 on a number of levels. An increase in the power of the state was justified by the prime minister when he unveiled the long-awaited national security strategy on 19 March, establishing an advisory National Security Forum. Other measures included the publication of the previously confidential "register of risks", which detailed current threats to the UK. Brown reported that around 2,000 individuals were being monitored for terrorism related activity. The monitoring organisation, Privacy International, warned that state surveillance in Britain was far more widespread than elsewhere in Europe and criticised the paucity of government powers of oversight on the many agencies with the authority to monitor private activities.

In January, the case against foreign office official Derek Pasquill collapsed spectacularly, when it was admitted that he had acted in the public interest by leaking a number of documents to the press that exposed weaknesses in government contact with Muslim groups and British collusion in the secret and illegal US rendition of terrorist suspects. The case, which had dragged on for two years since Pasquill's arrest at the beginning of 2006, questioned the use of the Official Secrets Act, which appeared to have been employed to protect the reputation of some ministers and officials. Foreign Secretary David Miliband acknowledged on 21 February that US planes on "extraordinary rendition" flights had twice stopped on British soil on the island of Diego Garcia, stating that the incidents had only recently been admitted to the government by US officials. The Official Secrets Act was also used to prosecute UK customs investigator Atif Amin, who was alleged to have leaked information concerning his officially suppressed investigation into the nuclear smuggling activities of Pakistani scientist Abdul Qadeer Khan in 2000 (see AR 2004, p. 301).

On 4 February Justice Minister Jack Straw announced an inquiry to establish why, in apparent violation of the Wilson doctrine that banned the tapping of MPs' telephones, Labour MP Sadiq Khan's conversations with one of his constituents, terrorism suspect Babar Ahmad, were recorded during two prison visits in 2005 and 2006. On 6 February Gordon Brown told the House of Commons that evidence obtained from telephone tapping should be made admissible in court, provided the security services agreed. The announcement followed the publication of a review of the use of intercept evidence chaired by former civil servant Sir John Chilcott. A cross party committee of privy councillors, led by Chilcott, would work with a government implementation team to draw up the new guidelines.

The counter-terrorism bill published on 24 January proposed to extend the limit on pre-charge detention for up to 42 days "if exceptional circumstances require it". The second reading of the bill was postponed in March by Home Secretary Jacqui Smith, as the scale of backbench opposition became clear, and cabinet ministers were reportedly divided on how to proceed. Critics feared that the measure would be viewed as an attack on the Muslim community, thereby reducing co-operation with police and intelligence agencies. Concessions presented to MPs at the beginning of June helped to reduce the scale of the rebellion, but the bill only passed through the Commons on 11 June with the last minute support of the Democrat Unionist Party. When the bill was overwhelmingly rejected in the House of Lords on 13 October the government reluctantly dropped the proposal.

Breaches of data security were reported at regular intervals during 2008. A laptop computer belonging to a Royal Navy recruitment officer was stolen from a car in Birmingham in January. It contained personal details of 600,000 people who had applied to or considered joining the Navy over the past 10 years. A senior civil servant was suspended in June, and charged under the Official Secrets Act in September, after highly classified intelligence documents were left on a commuter train. The discovery of a memory stick in a pub car park, containing user names and passwords, led to the emergency closure at the end of October of the government's Gateway website, through which people accessed tax, benefits, and other government services; and Work and Pensions Minister James Purnell apologised for accidentally leaving confidential correspondence on a train. (These incidents followed the loss in November 2007 of two computer disks containing details of all recipients of child benefit, some 25 million families.) Not only was all of this embarrassing for government, but it called into question plans for a national identity card scheme backed by a database containing personal details, including biometric identifiers, of everyone in the country. Government commitment to the scheme appeared to be slipping: a strategy paper leaked in January showed that its implementation schedule had been postponed.

Finally, 2008 saw the formal inquest into the killing by Metropolitan Police officers of Jean Charles de Menezes in 2005. After being directed by the coroner, Sir Michael Wright, not to reach a verdict of unlawful killing, the jury returned an open verdict on 12 December, rejecting the claim by Scotland Yard that the young Brazilian had been killed lawfully on 22 July 2005 as part of an anti-terrorism operation following the 7 July 2005 bombings (see AR 2005, p. 15; 2008, p. 19). The victim's family had lost confidence in the proceedings and dramatic protests at the inquest were not reported until after the verdict had been delivered, on the instructions of the coroner.

OTHER DOMESTIC NEWS. Immigration remained among the public's top concerns in 2008, and in particular the question of the extent to which new migrants were displacing British workers. Statistics suggested that two in three jobs created since 1997 had been filled by migrants. A report published in January by the left-of-centre think tank, the Institute of Public Policy Research, claimed that this was due to the aging British population and to emigration: the number of UK-born people of working age fell by 272,000 in 2006-07. It was acknowledged that the economy had benefited significantly from the arrival in recent years of skilled migrant workers from countries such as Poland. However, the new "points based" immigration system introduced in April for non-EU would-be immigrants was designed, in Brown's words, to "reserve British jobs for British workers".

Policy makers on all sides were frustrated by the apparent failure of the welfare system to move a significant number of the 5 million people in receipt of benefits back into the workplace to fill those vacant jobs. At the beginning of January, Gordon Brown marked the 10th anniversary of his welfare "new deal" by announcing a number of new reforms to address the needs of the long-term unemployed, those on incapacity benefits, and lone parents. Ministers at the department for work and pensions indicated that cash rewards for unemployed people who completed back-to-work training would be extended whilst benefits would be cut for those who refused jobs, as the focus of policy shifted from unemployment to employability. On 20 February James Purnell proposed that 250,000 long-term unemployed should have to work or train for a month in order to continue receiving unemployment benefit. The intention to proceed with legislation along these lines was announced in the Queen's speech at the beginning of December. The Conservative blueprint for welfare reform, published on 8 January, was more radical, and proposed that every welfare recipient who refused three "reasonable" job offers should have benefits withdrawn for up to three years.

Fifty-five teenagers were murdered in the UK in 2008, a figure that reinforced public fears over the perceived rise in knife crime and violent gang-related activity. Official statistics, however, showed that violent crime overall was continuing to fall. The police announced on 11 August that the number of people charged with knife possession in London had fallen by half in the past four years. With every incident renewing the debate, however, a "people's march" through central London on 20 September was held to raise awareness of the issue.

Government proposals to raise the school leaving age to 18 by 2015 were approved when the Education and Skills Act 2008 received royal assent in November. While critics feared that the measure was illiberal and might criminalise disaffected young people who refused to continue in education or work-related training, supporters argued that the new regulation would be the best way to improve the prospects of disadvantaged young people with few qualifications. On 29 February Children and Schools Minister Ed Balls announced the acceleration of the city academy programme in the next two years, following a favourable report on the impact of the new schools, which replaced failing secondary schools in disadvantaged communities.

Two shocking cases of child abuse raised concerns about the competence of child protection agencies. An urgent inquiry into the care of children in the London borough of Haringey was ordered on 12 November as details emerged over the death of 17-month old "Baby P" after months of abuse and neglect. The case suggested that his death was preventable, but had occurred because of poor management and judgement of the various agencies involved in investigating his situation. This included the news that ministers had failed to act on information provided by a social worker employed by the council, who had written letters of complaint in February 2007 regarding faults in the borough's children's services department. Concern escalated at the end of November when it was revealed that agencies in Lincolnshire and Sheffield had failed to investigate clear signs of a 20-year catalogue of abuse in a family whose father had repeatedly raped and impregnated his two daughters, now in their 30s.

A new generation of nuclear power stations was given the go-ahead in January as the government sought to meet its commitment to reduce carbon emissions. The decision was criticised for having failed to seek meaningful public or expert consultation. Critics warned that new nuclear power stations would take years to build and would not provide a magic solution to the country's future energy needs. On 26 June Gordon Brown presented a renewable energy plan that proposed incentives for the private sector to invest £100 billion in schemes that could create a large number of "green collar" jobs and meet the EU target of producing 15 per cent of the country's energy from renewable sources by 2020. On 16 October the new energy and climate change secretary, Ed Miliband, committed the UK to cutting greenhouse gas emissions by 80 per cent by 2050.

Meanwhile, the controversy over whether to build a third runway at Heathrow airport drew attention in November, amid indications that the government was inclined to endorse the proposal, first raised in a 2003 white paper. Brown met backbench MPs opposed to the plan on 11 November, and Transport Secretary Geoff Hoon stressed the importance of the aviation industry to Britain's economy. On 4 December Hoon announced that a decision on the issue would be delayed until 2009.

In February, it was announced that the government would have to bail out the agency, Transport for London, following the collapse of Metronet, the company at the heart of the private finance initiative negotiated in the late 1990s to repair London's aging underground tube train infrastructure. This was embarrassing for Gordon Brown, who as chancellor of the exchequer, had insisted upon the scheme. On 27 May, Metronet came into public ownership and Transport for London confirmed that it would invest a total of £1.4 billion in the company over the following 12 months. This was still feared to be insufficient to fill the funding gap, which was revealed in September to be much higher than earlier estimates.

Two thousand police were mobilised on 6 April as the Olympic torch relay was met in London by protestors against China's human rights record. Meanwhile, London's preparations to host the 2012 Olympics were given a glowing report by the international organising committee inspection team in May. Work was proceeding smoothly, with construction of the Olympic stadium beginning three months ahead of schedule. The 2008 Beijing Olympic and Paralympic Games were a triumph for UK athletes, or "Team GB", as they were embarrassingly dubbed by marketing people. A victory parade in London was held in August upon their return, to celebrate the country's most successful games for a century. The 300 athletes at the Olympics finished fourth in the world medal table, with a total of 19 gold, 13 silver, and 15 bronze medals. The 206-strong Paralympic team came second, after China, and won 42 gold medals.

On the first weekend of April the Queen called off an elaborate diamond wedding anniversary party at the Ritz—to be thrown for her and Prince Philip by friends—on the grounds that it seemed inappropriate, given the parlous state of the economy. Elaborate celebrations for the 60th birthday on 14 November of Prince Charles, the Prince of Wales, went ahead however, and included a dinner at Buckingham Palace, followed by a party at his country estate, Highgrove. The inquest into the death of Charles's first wife, Diana, Princess of Wales, found on 8 April that she and Dodi al Fayed had been unlawfully killed by the reckless driving of their chauffeur, Henri Paul, and paparazzi photographers in Paris in August 1997. Following the verdict, Dodi's father, Mohamed al Fayed, finally dropped his legal battle over the couple's deaths (see Documents; AR 1999, p. 28; AR 1997, pp. 4-7).

FOREIGN POLICY. Fighting for social justice and against poverty in the developing world lay at the heart of the prime minister's foreign policy, and throughout the year he pressed world leaders to honour their commitment to the UN's Millennium Development Goals (MDG) to halve the number of the world's poor and make basic education globally available by 2015 (see AR 2008, pp. 529-33). At the G-8 summit in Japan in July he prevented a dilution of the 2005 Gleneagles agreement to give US$25 billion in aid to Africa annually (see AR 2005, pp. 5-6). In an address to the Lambeth Conference of Anglican bishops on 24 July, he reiterated the MDG commitments and endorsed the march of more than 500 bishops through central London in support of them. At September's emergency UN summit to discuss the issue, he urged a redoubling of efforts to fund the global fight against hunger, malaria, infant mortality, and lack of education.

Britain's relations with the EU were dominated by legislation to ratify the Lisbon Treaty which replaced the failed European constitutional treaty in 2007. The ratification bill was controversial because all three main parties had promised a referendum on the constitution at the time of the last election, and the government rejected holding a referendum on the Treaty, even though it was similar to the earlier proposals. Attempts to force a referendum were defeated on 5 March, when MPs voted by a majority of 140 to approve the bill. On 13 June the government announced that it would still ratify the treaty in spite of the results of the Irish referendum that had rejected it (see p. 47). The bill received royal assent after being passed in the House of Lords on 18 June and the Treaty was ratified shortly thereafter.

A Downing Street summit on 29 January between EU leaders marked Gordon Brown's first major European initiative as prime minister. Aimed at fostering concerted action to mitigate the impact of the global financial crisis, Brown encouraged the establishment of more transparent mechanisms to detect potential risk and more rigorous regulation of the banks. France's President Nicolas Sarkozy made a 36-hour state visit to the UK on 26 March, arriving by horse-drawn carriage at Windsor Castle, where he stayed with his glamorous wife, Carla Bruni. The visit was brought to a close at a joint press conference, at which the two leaders spoke of an "entente formidable" following a meeting of ministers from both governments.

Britain's relations with Russia remained cool, exemplified by the latter's harassment of the staff of the British Council and BP offices in Russia. The embattled head of BP's Russian oil venture, TNK-BP, left the country on 24 July after what was described as an "orchestrated campaign". Talks between Russia's President Dmitry Medvedev and Brown at the G-8 summit the previous week were reportedly tense and relations deteriorated further when, days later, Russia unexpectedly used its UN Security Council veto to block UN sanctions against Zimbabwe's President Robert Mugabe, an initiative on which Brown had taken the lead. Gordon Brown warned on 31 August that the UK would not be held to ransom by Russia, after another tense conversation with Medvedev amid fears that the crisis in South Ossetia could escalate into an energy war.

Relations with the USA remained warm, in spite of open differences over military strategy. On 16 April Brown delivered a foreign policy speech in Boston which stressed the urgency of collaborative action between Europe and the USA and called for a restructuring of the major international organisations to reflect the changing needs of the new century. He met the three main presidential candidates on the following day. Following the 4 November presidential election, Brown described President-elect Obama as "a true friend of Britain", and David Cameron applauded the result as a "stunning victory and a beacon of hope, and opportunity and change".

Pakistan's Prime Minister Pervez Musharraf met Brown in London on 28 January amid tensions over his country's human rights record and British concerns that Pakistan provided a training ground for violent extremists, exemplified by the escape of British terrorism suspect, Rashid Rauf, while in the custody of the Pakistani intelligence services the previous month. A meeting on 16 September with Pakistan's new President Asif Ali Zardari in London discussed counter-terrorism and it was thought that the president had agreed to establish a unit to monitor more rigorously suspected extremists of Pakistani origin in the UK.

In his 21 July speech to the Israeli Knesset (legislature), Brown denounced Iran's nuclear weapons programme and signalled that the UK would be willing to support a military strike against Iran if all other diplomatic routes were to fail.

Brown's trip to India and China in January, accompanied by two dozen business leaders and university vice-chancellors, was intended to stress the importance of global markets to the future of the UK economy. In Beijing, an agreement was reached to expand trade between the two nations to US$60 billion by 2010; this included a memorandum of understanding signed to encourage UK firms to work on eco-friendly projects in China.

DEFENCE, IRAQ AND AFGHANISTAN.   At the start of 2008, the UK's overstretched armed forces faced a treasury proposal to cut £4.5 billion from the defence budget over the next three years, including reducing the number of submarines in service, cancelling an order for new destroyers, and cutting the number of Eurofighter Typhoon jets. On 3 July, however, the government announced that it would proceed with plans to build two new aircraft carriers, which would be the largest and most expensive in British naval history, helping to secure thousands of jobs in UK shipyards.

It was no secret as the year began that the government was anxious to with-draw the 4,000 troops stationed in Basra in southern Iraq, and under pressure from anti-war campaigners Brown promised in March that he would endorse a future inquiry into the decision to go to war, but not while UK troops were still on the ground. The operation, which in September 2007 had retreated outside Basra city to the relative safety of the airport (see AR 2008, pp. 23-24), served little purpose in 2008 other than to provide a multi-national fig leaf for US President George W. Bush, although the UK did continue to train Iraqi forces. Relations with Iraqi Prime Minister Nouri al-Maliki became tense in March, when he launched operation "Charge of the Knights" to drive the Shia militia out of Basra, and UK forces stayed largely aloof from the fighting. Eight hun-dred US troops had to be deployed from other parts of the country before order could be restored, and the further withdrawal of UK forces was postponed. In London on 1 May, Brown and Sir Jock Stirrup, chief of the defence staff, met the US commander in Iraq, General David Petraeus, to smooth things over. Brown visited both Baghdad and Basra in July, where he outlined a four-point plan on training, political progress, reconstruction, and preparing the airport facility, in order to strengthen Iraqi control before UK troops could withdraw. Al-Maliki told an interviewer dismissively on 13 October that British forces were "no longer required". With genuine improvements in security in Basra in 2008, UK defence sources signalled on 9 December that withdrawal would resume in the spring, with the objective of bringing the last troops home by June 2009.

It was a difficult year for the 7,700 UK forces deployed in Helmand province in southern Afghanistan, where 42 troops lost their lives in 2008. On 25 Janu-ary the government rejected claims by the Afghan president, Hamid Karzai that British and US forces were failing in Helmand province. Yet the deteriorating security situation there was manifested by suicide bombings that week which killed seven people, including the province's deputy governor. Tensions were already evident between US and British military commanders over differing approaches to countering the growing strength of the Taliban insurgency. British plans to support local militias and community defence initiatives were viewed sceptically by the USA. After the US "Drudge Report" website revealed on 28 February that Prince Harry had been secretly serving in Afghanistan since December as a forward air controller, he was recalled for security reasons. On a surprise visit to Afghanistan on 21 August, Brown com-pared soldiers to Olympic heroes. On 15 December, he confirmed that another 300 troops would be sent to Afghanistan, prior to the 2009 elections there. Figures released the same day showed that fighting was continuing to escalate, with deaths and serious injuries among British troops at the highest rate since the conflict began.

Harriet Jones

THE ECONOMY IN 2008.　On 1 January Prime Minister Gordon Brown stated that 2008 was "going to be a difficult year". This was to prove to be an understatement. In August the chancellor of the exchequer, Alistair Darling, said that he believed that the UK faced "arguably the worst" economic downturn in 60 years. He also indicated that this downturn would be "more profound and long lasting" than previously expected.

In his March budget, however, Darling suggested that the country was in a good position to "weather the economic storms" that were being created by the global economic instability, which had come about in consequence of the credit crunch that developed in 2007 (see AR 2008, pp. 436-40). Even so, he acknowledged that it had affected the country's growth rates, which had fallen short of predictions.

To help ameliorate the effects on households of deteriorating economic conditions, Chancellor Darling's March budget cut 2 pence off the basic rate of income tax, made more money available to alleviate child poverty, increased funding for those looking for work, and raised fuel payments to pensioners. To address concerns of the City (London's financial centre), the budget toned down proposals relating to taxation to be levied on non-domiciled aliens resident in the UK. (At same time higher taxes were imposed on alcohol, cigarettes, and on polluting cars.)

During the first months of the year the Bank of England, the UK's central bank, feared that inflation remained a major threat to the health of the economy. In January, in consequence of high food prices and a 15 per cent increase in household energy bills (largely the result of petroleum reaching US$100 per barrel), the Bank's monetary policy committee (MPC) maintained its interest rate at 5.5 per cent. By August petroleum prices had risen to US$140, which pushed domestic fuel prices upwards by 35 per cent over a six month period. The high cost of petroleum over the summer led to the bankruptcy of a number of UK airlines—Maxjet, Silverjet and XL—which had left thousands of British holidaymakers stranded abroad.

In February, as a record number of companies announced profits warnings, the Bank's MPC agreed to cut the base interest rate to 5.25 per cent. This was despite the fact that the consumer price index (the government's measure of inflation) was running at just over the target 2 per cent. In April the base interest rate was cut to 5 per cent, partly because the UK's stock market's performance had been uninspiring during the early months of 2008. Rather than put funds into stocks and shares, investors preferred to hold gold bullion, which had hit a record high of US$1,000 an ounce in March. In May, inflation hit 3 per cent, a percentage point above the government's target, and it rose again in June, to 3.3 per cent. Nevertheless, the governor of the Bank of England, Mervyn King, announced that an interest rate rise would probably push the economy into a dramatic downturn. His assessment was based on the news that the UK's gross domestic product (GDP) growth for the first quarter of 2008 had been revised down to just 0.3 per cent. Additionally, official data showed that families were dipping into their savings to cover ordinary expenses.

Conditions continued to decline in July, with retail sales staying flat as households reined in their spending. In August official statistics indicated that economic growth had ground to a halt in the second quarter of the year. The UK services sector, the backbone of the economy, had grown by just 0.2 per cent, while manufacturing output had fallen by 0.8 per cent. Exports also fell as demand dropped from Europe, the UK's main trading partner. Domestic household spending contracted that month by 0.1 per cent. However, over the summer inflation reached a 16-year high, hitting 5.2 per cent, making the Bank of England reluctant to cut interest rates to spur the economy.

With the nationalisation in February of Northern Rock, the UK's fifth largest mortgage lender, which had run into trouble in 2007 (see AR 2007, pp. 27-28) and for which no appropriate buyer had been found, the British banking sector's problems were believed to have been largely solved. However, in the middle of September 2008, following the collapse of Lehman Brothers in the USA and as the global banking system took a battering, British banks looked vulnerable and the UK money markets froze. Lloyds TSB announced that it was in merger talks with the Halifax Bank of Scotland (HBOS) group. The government had been encouraging these talks because it feared that otherwise HBOS might fail. As the merged institution would become a banking giant, the government had to set aside anti-monopoly legislation, but the details of the merger remained unresolved at the year's end. The government had to step in when Bradford & Bingley, the UK's ninth largest mortgage lender, found itself on the verge of collapse. By the end of September, with no suitable purchaser coming forward, the bank's £50 billion mortgage wing was nationalised, while the deposit and branch network was sold to the Spanish Santander group. Within a fortnight of this move, the government found that it had to inject a huge amount of taxpayers' money into the banking system, with £37 billion going to the Royal Bank of Scotland (RBS), HBOS, and Lloyds TSB. The government now owned 60 per cent of the former and 40 per cent of the latter two (on condition that they merge). Barclays, which had purchased Lehman Brothers' core assets, discovered that it too needed more liquidity, but it chose not to accept government money. Instead, it decided to raise around £7.3 billion from foreign, mainly Middle Eastern, investors. While bank shares initially rose as a result of this injection of liquidity, by December they were sharply lower and were declining. This was partly because of concerns about the stability of the international banking system and partly because it was feared that UK banks' bad debts would continue to rise. HBOS confirmed such fears, when it revealed that its bad debts on mortgages and unsecured lending had risen to £1.7 billion over the year.

To promote confidence in the banking system, the government announced in October that the first £50,000 of individuals' saving deposits in any one banking group would be guaranteed. However, for the approximately 230,000 savers in the failed Iceland-based Internet banks operating in the UK, recovering their deposits had proved considerably more complicated. As a result the government froze these Icelandic banks' UK assets, which resulted in a diplomatic incident between the two countries, and it set aside £800 million to compensate British savers. In addition to individuals, many British local authorities held substantial deposits in these Icelandic banks (see pp. 64-65).

After September, like most central banks around the world, the Bank of England aggressively lowered its interest rates. In early October it cut rates to 4.5 per cent, after having kept them at 5 per cent for over six months, and it further announced new measures to help stimulate interbank lending. However, official figures showed that the UK economy had continued to contract by 0.6 per cent in the third quarter. Consequently, the Bank further trimmed rates to 3 per cent in November and then to 2 per cent in December. These cuts brought Bank of England interest rates to their lowest levels since 1951.

However, despite calls from Prime Minister Brown to pass on these cuts to borrowers, many banks were reluctant to do so. HBOS, the UK's biggest mortgage lender, announced that it would cut standard variable rate (SVR) mortgages by just one-quarter of 1 per cent. Nationwide, the UK's biggest building society, cut only 0.69 of a percentage point. Only HSBC, Bristol & West, and Lloyds TSB reduced their SVR mortgages in line with the Bank of England cuts. Part of the reason for this was that the London Interbank Offered Rate (LIBOR, the average rate that banks charge each other for loans), while falling steadily as a result of the Bank of England cuts, did not fall as far or as fast.

Underpinning the poor performance of the UK banking sector was the collapse of the British housing market. Nationwide reported that house prices dropped by 15.9 per cent over the year, while Halifax said prices fell by 16.2 per cent. In November the cost of the average home fell to a two-year low to just over £196,000. The Royal Institution of Chartered Surveyors reported that in the final quarter of 2008 the housing market had been at its weakest for three decades. The difficulties in obtaining a mortgage meant that first-time buyers were virtually squeezed out of the market as lenders demanded higher deposits. The 100 per cent mortgage had all but vanished.

Mortgage debt contracted at the fastest rate since records began almost four decades previously. The Bank of England reported in December that equity withdrawal fell for a second successive quarter. The Bank said that people were paying off £5.7 billion of their home loans in the third quarter of 2008 after a £2 billion repayment in the second quarter. This situation had not occurred for more than a decade, with the trend in the third quarter the most marked since 1970. At the same time, the Financial Services Authority (FSA) reported that 13,161 homes were repossessed by lenders, a 92 per cent increase on the same period of 2007, as rising household bills and the squeeze on lending took their toll on struggling borrowers.

The number of those unemployed stood at 1.92 million between September and November, an increase of 131,000 unemployed on the previous three months and the highest level since September 1997. Further tens of thousands of jobs were cut in December, increasing the number of people claiming job-seeker's allowance by 77,900, to 1.16 million. The unemployment rate was 6.1 per cent for the three months to the end of November, compared with 5.2 per cent in the same period of 2007.

Retailers discounted early and heavily over the Christmas shopping period. Consequently, retail sales jumped 1.6 per cent, with the sale of household goods increasing by 4.5 per cent. Non-store sales, including from Internet retailers, saw a 6.4 per cent growth. However, as a result of the discounting, the value of sales dropped by 0.8 per cent compared with 2007, the worst performance since records began in 1986. Discount food retailers like Lidl and Aldi continued to report healthy sales but mid-market shops suffered, including Marks & Spencer, Britain's biggest retailer, which at the end of the year shed 1,200 jobs and announced the closure of nearly 30 food-only stores. A string of established chain stores collapsed, like Woolworths, Allied Carpets, and MFI, the UK's largest furniture retailer, leaving in their wake thousands of job losses.

The value of the pound sterling dropped precipitously. In the summer sterling was trading at around US$2 but slipped to US$1.40 in December, a rate not seen since 1985. The drop of sterling in relation to the euro was more significant, with the currencies nearly at parity towards the end of 2008, a fall of some 35 per cent in sterling over the year. However there were no currency benefits for the UK, as exports fell sharply in the final months of the year. Sales of goods abroad fell 5.8 per cent to a seasonally adjusted £19.8 billion over December. Imports of goods slipped by 1.8 per cent to £28.2 billion, signalling the weakening of domestic demand.

The manufacturing sector was in a deep recession, with output down 4.9 per cent from a year earlier after October's figures were released, the biggest drop since June 2002. Output fell for eight consecutive months to October, the longest run of contraction since 1980. Falling car production was one of the chief reasons for the slump in output. New car sales in November were 37 per cent down on the previous year.

The government's efforts to mitigate the decline included the announcement, in Chancellor Darling's November pre-budget report, of tax cuts of £20 billion and an expansion of public spending, principally by bringing forward large construction projects. These moves doubled the national debt to £1 trillion. One of the tax cuts that the chancellor announced was the temporary reduction of value added tax (VAT) from 17.5 per cent to 15 per cent, which took effect from 1 December.

The National Grid reported that the demand for electricity had fallen over Christmas. Thousands of Polish workers had returned home as the year ended. Unsurprisingly, the UK economy officially slipped into recession in the final quarter of the year, thus ending 15 years of continuous growth.

Michael Kandiah

SCOTLAND

CAPITAL: Edinburgh   AREA: 78,313 sq km   POPULATION: 5,144,200 (official estimate, mid '07)
OFFICIAL LANGUAGES: English and Gaelic   POLITICAL SYSTEM: devolved administration within UK
HEAD OF STATE: Queen Elizabeth II (since Feb '52)
RULING PARTY: Scottish National Party (since May '07)
HEAD OF GOVERNMENT: First Minister Alex Salmond (SNP) (since May '07)

THE major shock on the political scene in Scotland during the year was the outcome of a (Westminster) parliamentary by-election held in the Glasgow East constituency in July. The previous member, David Marshall, had resigned on health
grounds from what was one of the safest Labour seats in Scotland, in which he
had held a majority of 13,507 at the 2005 general election. The seat was captured
by John Mason of the Scottish National Party (SNP) by 361 votes. The decline at
UK level of the popularity of the Labour party had been compounded in Scotland
by the resignation in June of the Scottish Labour leader, Wendy Alexander, after
she was found to have failed to register donations to her leadership campaign. It
was felt that one of the reasons for Labour's disastrous showing was the failure of
the UK prime minister, Gordon Brown, to campaign in a Scottish election, despite
the very active role played by the Scottish first minister and SNP leader, Alex
Salmond. Lessons seemed to have been learned, because in the other (Westminster) by-election in Scotland, in November, the Glenrothes seat—which had
become vacant because of the death of the respected sitting member John Mac-
Dougall—was held for Labour by Lindsay Roy, albeit with a reduced majority.
The Labour campaign in Glenrothes was focused on the claimed failures of the
SNP in government in Scotland, and was actively supported by Brown, whose
own constituency neighboured Glenrothes. Both Scottish Labour and the Scottish
Liberal Democrats elected new leaders during the year. Iain Gray succeeded
Wendy Alexander, and Nicol Stephen, who resigned for personal reasons, was
replaced as Scottish Liberal Democrat leader by Tavish Scott.
    The other major shock to Scotland during the year was financial. Both the
Bank of Scotland and the Royal Bank of Scotland were sufficiently damaged by
the turmoil in financial markets that they had to submit to partial nationalisation
and, in the case of the Bank of Scotland, an unwanted merger. The Bank of Scotland had been founded in 1695 and in 2001, following its merger with the Halifax bank, renamed itself as HBOS, but much of its headquarters activity
remained in Edinburgh. Following unsuccessful attempts by HBOS to persuade
existing shareholders to take up a rights issue, the UK government's rescue plan
for the bank, announced in October and conditional on its merger with Lloyds
TSB, represented government ownership of about 44 per cent of its assets. In
December, HBOS was duly merged with Lloyds TSB: whilst the Bank of Scotland brand was to be kept, it was less certain how much activity other than retail
banking was to be kept in Scotland. The Edinburgh-based Royal Bank of Scotland had also absorbed various other businesses in its history since its foundation
in 1727, notably National Westminster Bank in 2000. It, too, failed to achieve
the desired outcome of a rights issue, and the October rescue arrangements saw
the UK government acquire about 60 per cent of the bank. For both banks, the

trouble stemmed from major losses on investments, particularly overseas, and a rise in bad debt. The Scottish financial sector had prided itself on its long traditions of prudence, so the losses incurred by the banks were a major blow to the reputation of a key part of the Scottish, particularly the Edinburgh, economy.

Various aspects of the public finances created controversies within and between the various levels of government in Scotland. The Scottish government had decided on political grounds that it would not pursue the private finance initiative method of obtaining private sector funding for infrastructure projects, but instead would use the Scottish Futures Trust (SFT). The SFT, launched in May, was to be a new not-for-profit company, in the public sector, pooling central and local government finance and expertise and drawing finance from a Scotland-wide municipal bond, with planned expenditure of up to £150 million per annum. In November, two pathfinder areas were announced, the first to be in south-east Scotland and the second in the north of Scotland, with total funding of £2.8 million.

It remained unclear, however, how the SFT would be able to attract private sector finance and the SFT was not considered as even part of the solution when questions arose about the funding of the new Forth Road Bridge. In February, the last road bridge tolls in Scotland, on the Tay and Forth bridges, were abolished. The Scottish government had committed itself to a new bridge, either to replace or to complement the existing Forth road bridge, which was suffering structural problems and was at times severely congested. The cost of the new bridge, to be completed by 2016, had been estimated at £4 billion, but it was not clear how the bridge would be financed. It would be inconsistent with other policies to levy tolls, so the cost would have to be met from public funds. Although the government announced in December that it would be possible, by retaining the existing bridge, to cut the cost of the new crossing to between £1.72 billion and £2.34 billion, the question of how the funding was to be raised remained open. The Scottish government proposed to the UK treasury that the new bridge be paid for over 20 years out of the capital budget Scotland would receive from UK taxes. At the end of the year, it was clear that the treasury would not countenance this proposal, in which case the bridge could be built only at the cost of delay to other important infrastructure projects.

Two men accused of involvement in the 2007 attempted terrorist attack on Glasgow airport (see AR 2008, p. 18) were tried in London. Bilal Abdullah had been arrested at the scene and was tried together with Mohammed Asha. Abdullah, who had worked as a doctor in Scotland, admitted some involvement and was in December sentenced to at least 32 years imprisonment. Asha, also a doctor, was found not guilty of all the charges he faced, and at the end of the year was resisting attempts to have him deported. Meanwhile, Abdel Baset al-Megrahi, the Libyan who had in 2001 been convicted of involvement in the 1988 Lockerbie bombing (see AR 2001, pp. 47-48), was granted a second appeal against his conviction, to be heard in 2009. In November it was also disclosed that he was terminally ill, but he was refused interim liberation.

Plans were being actively made during the year to promote Scottish tourism in 2009 under the banner of "year of homecoming", chosen to coincide with the 250th anniversary of the birth of Robert Burns and aimed principally at the descendants of emigrants. One significant step was the approval by the Scottish Parliament of the Scottish register of tartans, to protect, promote and preserve the traditional checked cloth patterns, which were estimated to contribute some £350 million per annum to the Scottish economy.

Charlotte Lythe

WALES

CAPITAL: Cardiff   AREA: 20,755 sq km   POPULATION: 2,965,900
OFFICIAL LANGUAGES: Welsh & English   POLITICAL SYSTEM: devolved administration within UK
HEAD OF STATE: Queen Elizabeth II (since Feb '52)
RULING PARTIES: Labour/Plaid Cymru coalition (since July '07)
HEAD OF GOVERNMENT: First Minister Rhodri Morgan (since Feb '00)

THERE were few indications in the early months of the year of the economic downturn which was to have a major impact on Wales in the autumn. The Welsh Assembly government coalition between Labour and Plaid Cymru seemed stable and it was the secretary of state for Wales, Peter Hain, who made the news in January. He left the UK cabinet to clear his name following allegations over his campaign fund for the Labour deputy leadership contest in 2007. Hain claimed that his failure to declare £103,000-worth of donations was an "innocent mistake" and later in the year the police dropped their investigation (see p. 24).

Hain was replaced as secretary of state for Wales by Paul Murphy, an experienced politician but not one considered to be an enthusiastic devolutionist, and there were concerns that this would have an impact on the relationship between the Assembly and the UK legislature in Westminster. Indeed during the year, concern was expressed at the National Assembly that the Legislative Competence Orders, the first stage in the convoluted method whereby the Assembly could legislate, were being held up by Westminster, leading to tensions between UK members of Parliament and Welsh Assembly members. This came to a head in the autumn over the "right to buy" housing legislation.

The general decline in the support for Labour was reflected in the results of the local authority elections held in May. Labour lost 122 seats and overall control in a number of authorities, such as Torfaen, Merthyr Tydfil, Flintshire, and Caerphilly, where it had previously been considered impregnable. Plaid Cymru made gains, but lost overall control of Gwynedd, following several defeats to candidates from a new group, Llais Gwynedd (Gwynedd's Voice), which campaigned mainly on the issue of the closure of small schools. The Conservatives gained ground, winning control of Monmouthshire and the Vale of Glamorgan, while the Liberal Democrats consolidated their grip on Cardiff, Swansea, and Wrexham. However the highest number of councillors in Wales had stood as independents with the result that local authorities tended to be run by an assortment of coalitions based on deals and compromises.

There was one casualty in the Welsh Assembly government cabinet when, following a series of public blunders, the minister for heritage, Rhodri Glyn Thomas, resigned in July to be replaced by the steadier hand of Alun Ffred Jones. In November, Kirsty Williams, the Assembly member for Brecon and Radnor, became the first female head of a political party in Wales, when she was elected leader of the Welsh Liberal Democrats.

The decision made by ITV in September to cut programmes in the regions and nations of Britain was considered a major blow to plurality in broadcasting in Wales. At the same time, Trinity Mirror, the biggest newspaper owner in Wales and the largest regional publisher in Britain, decided to close three local papers in north Wales. Earlier in the year the proposal to establish a Welsh-language daily newspaper foundered due to a lack of public funding.

The announcement in February that Airbus Broughton had won the second biggest defence contract ever in Britain, a massive US$40 billion order for 179 refuelling tankers for the US Air Force, was a major boost for the economy in north-east Wales. However the good news was soon reversed during the summer as the global economic crisis unfolded. The first signs came in July with job losses in the financial services sector and, in the second half of the year, thousands of jobs were lost in residential construction, as some of the biggest companies, such as Redrow, struggled to cope with falling demand as new mortgages became increasingly difficult to obtain. By November manufacturing industries were affected, with Bosch, a major employer, announcing that it was shedding 200 staff at its Miskin plant. The most significant blow to the south Wales economy came when Hoover announced that it was considering closing its factory at Merthyr Tudful, leaving more than 300 jobs under threat. The iconic Hoover factory, which had produced washing machines since 1948, was one of the first post-war examples of inward investment from overseas, and the then US-owned company had provided employment for generations of south Wales workers. Its potential closure was considered to be a symbolic indicator of difficult times.

In December it was reported that the unemployment figure for Wales had risen to 6.6 per cent, with a further 14,000 people out of work during the third quarter of the year. At the same time, that other sign of recession—falling house prices— saw Wales post its biggest annual decline in prices, with a reduction of 13.4 per cent during 2008, the largest percentage decrease in the UK.

The Welsh Assembly government's response to the recession was to organise three all-Wales economic summits attended by Assembly chiefs, business leaders, and others. A number of measures were proposed that were intended to support the economy by accelerating capital spending projects, improving skills, and helping local firms secure more work from the public sector. At the end of the year, First Minister Rhodri Morgan described the Welsh economy as a sick patient. He claimed, "The patient is sick but they're having blood transfusions, there's oxygen masks on, there's sort-of drips and all these different things and eventually the patient gets better. At this moment we don't know when that's going to be."

Despite the economic gloom, it was a momentous year for Welsh sportsmen and women. In soccer, Swansea City were promoted to the Championship, as First Division champions, and Cardiff City reached the FA Cup Final for the first time since 1927. Joe Calzaghe proved himself to be one of the outstanding boxers of his generation, with two stunning victories in the USA. Inspired by the diminutive but elusive winger, Shane Williams, the Welsh rugby team won the grand slam by winning all their matches in the Six Nations Championship. At the Beijing Olympics and Paralympics, Welsh sportsmen and women were particularly successful, with the Paralympian swimmer, David Roberts, capturing four gold medals. The cyclist, Nicole Cooke, not only won an Olympic gold medal in a thrilling race but soon afterwards became world champion, a remarkable achievement.

Gwyn Jenkins

NORTHERN IRELAND

CAPITAL: Belfast   AREA: 18,843 sq km   POPULATION: 1,759,148 (official est. mid '07)
OFFICIAL LANGUAGES: English, Irish & Ulster Scots   POLITICAL SYSTEM: devolved administration
    within UK
HEAD OF STATE: Queen Elizabeth II (since Feb '52)
RULING PARTIES: Democratic Unionist Party (DUP), Sinn Féin (SF), Ulster Unionist Party (UUP),
    & Social Democratic and Labour Party (SDLP)
HEAD OF GOVERNMENT: First Minister Peter Robinson (DUP) (since May '08)

THE year 2008 witnessed the end of an era with the retirement of Ian Paisley from frontline politics. In early March, he announced that he would resign as first minister and leader of the Democratic Unionist Party (DUP) in May, but would stay on as a Northern Ireland Assembly member (he also stepped down as leader of the Free Presbyterian Church in January). Following his unanimous election as DUP leader, Peter Robinson was confirmed as first minister of the Northern Ireland executive (devolved government) on 5 June, with Martin McGuinness of Sinn Féin remaining deputy first minister.

Paisley's son, Ian Paisley jr, also resigned in February as a junior minister because of pressure over his alleged links with the private developer of a proposed visitor centre at the Giants Causeway. Paisley jr was replaced by party colleague Jeffrey Donaldson, but resumed his position as one of the DUP members on the Northern Ireland Policing Board. In other developments, after months of talks the Ulster Unionist (UUP) and Conservative parties agreed to closer formal co-operation.

Although devolved government had resumed in May 2007, its operation was far from smooth and continuing tensions between the DUP and Sinn Féin at times threatened the very existence of the power sharing executive. In particular, controversy still surrounded the transfer from the UK Parliament at Westminster to the Assembly at Stormont of powers over policing and justice. Despite the urging of the British and Irish governments, the DUP reaffirmed its opposition to the devolution of policing while structures of the Irish Republican Army (IRA) remained in existence, demanding evidence that the IRA army council had been completely disbanded. For its part, Sinn Féin threatened to withdraw from the executive if a date for speedy devolution of powers was not agreed. Tensions again came to the surface prior to Robinson's nomination as first minister when Sinn Féin considered blocking his appointment until major disagreements had been resolved (mainly in relation to policing but also over education reform, a proposed Irish language act, and the future of the Maze Prison site). The situation was eased only after the intervention of the British and Irish governments, which brokered a solution that saw UK Prime Minister Gordon Brown convene a meeting with Robinson and McGuinness to discuss a mechanism for dealing with contentious issues.

Some progress was made in August when it was decided that there would be a single minister and department for policing and justice; moreover both the DUP and Sinn Féin agreed that they would not put forward a candidate for the portfolio, leaving the role open for one of the other parties in the Assembly. In an important report in early September the Independent Monitoring Commission (IMC) made clear its view that the IRA army council was "by deliberate choice...no longer operational or functional". In the light of this, talks resumed between the DUP and Sinn Féin, although the former still wanted republicans to make a public pledge that "the IRA was gone for good". Crucially there was still no consensus on the timing of the transfer of powers, despite a plea by Gordon Brown when he addressed the Assembly on 16 September. A meeting of the executive (which had not met since June) due on 18 September was cancelled, as Sinn Féin continued its boycott of formal proceedings in protest at the lack of political progress. However both Robinson and McGuinness did travel to Edinburgh for a meeting of the British-Irish Council, where they held talks with the Irish taoiseach (prime minister). Eventually the DUP and Sinn Féin found a formula for resolving the dispute over justice and policing, but although the deal included agreement on the appointment of an attorney general for Northern Ireland it did not set a specific deadline for the transfer of powers.

The executive resumed normal operation on 20 November, focusing much of its attention on how to cushion Northern Ireland from the effects of the global economic downturn. Despite the disagreements, "normal" political progress was made in crucial areas. In January the executive agreed a £18 billion budget, its programme for government, and an investment strategy for the three years to 2011, including a contribution of €60 million from the Irish government towards innovation funding. While the Assembly approved the programme, the Social Democratic and Labour Party (SDLP) voted against (as did the Alliance Party) despite the fact that its executive minister supported the plans.

Much effort was put into attracting inward investment. In April then First Minister Ian Paisley and Deputy First Minister Martin McGuinness travelled to New York for the announcement that the city was to help fund Northern Ireland's infrastructure development by investing US$150 million of its pension fund's income. In May a major international investment conference was held in Belfast, attended by senior US figures as well as by Prime Minister Gordon Brown and Taoiseach Brian Cowen. In July the Bombardier aerospace company announced major investment in its Shorts plant in Belfast, reinforced by loans and grants totalling £150 million provided by the British government, after heavy lobbying from the executive. At the end of the year the executive also announced a £200 million package to offset the effects of the economic slowdown.

Other important policy developments included the decision to reorganise local government by replacing the 26 councils created in 1972 with 11 new district "super councils" (although the two Ulster Unionist ministers voted against). In the light of this, Secretary of State Shaun Woodward agreed to a two-year postponement of the local elections due in 2009. Following negotiations with the UK government, water charges due to be implemented in 2009 were postponed. In September the executive announced that charges for medical prescriptions would be abolished from 2010 and free public transport within Northern Ireland for everyone aged 60 or above was also introduced. However controversy continued to surround proposals for the reform of the education system, with the DUP opposing Sinn Féin's plans to end the "11 plus" transfer system between primary and secondary schools, insisting that some form of academic selection on the basis of ability should be retained.

On the security front, several attacks on members of the police illustrated the continuing threat posed by dissident republican organisations, such as the Real IRA and the Continuity IRA. In May, for example, an off duty policeman was the target of a booby trap car bomb attack in Co. Tyrone and in June two officers were injured when a roadside landmine only partially exploded in Co. Fermanagh. In August three officers were the target of an attempted rocket attack in Co Fermanagh, in which Semtex explosive was used, and in Co. Armagh dissident republican elements were blamed for a series of attacks on the police involving gunshots and petrol bombs.

Alan Greer

REPUBLIC OF IRELAND—GERMANY—FRANCE—ITALY—BELGIUM—
THE NETHERLANDS—LUXEMBOURG

REPUBLIC OF IRELAND

CAPITAL: Dublin   AREA: 70,270 sq km   POPULATION: 4,366,000 ('07)
OFFICIAL LANGUAGES: Irish & English   POLITICAL SYSTEM: multiparty republic
HEAD OF STATE: President Mary McAleese (since Nov '97)
RULING PARTIES: coalition of Fianna Fáil (FF), Green Party, Progressive Democrats (PD),
    & independents
HEAD OF GOVERNMENT: Prime Minister/Taoiseach Brian Cowen (FF) (since May '08)
MAIN IGO MEMBERSHIPS (NON-UN): EU, OSCE, CE, OECD, PFP
CURRENCY: euro (end-'08 £1=€1.0344, US$1=€0.7194)
GNI PER CAPITA: US$48,140, $37,040 at PPP ('07)

THREE core issues dominated debate in 2008: the resignation of Taoiseach Bertie Ahern, the referendum on the EU Lisbon Treaty, and the fallout from the global financial crisis. The year began with Ahern still embroiled in controversy over his personal finances and tax affairs (see AR 2007, p. 36) and in February he appeared before the Mahon Tribunal for the third time. Despite eventually winning a legal challenge in the High Court (in May) to several aspects of its work, for example regarding demands for access to privileged information, he came under increasing political pressure. Opinion polls showed an increase in the percentage of respondents who did not believe his evidence and in late March two Fianna Fáil councillors called on the taoiseach to resign before local elections due in 2009. In early April, Ahern announced that he would resign on 6 May after 11 years in office, commenting that his decision was motivated solely by the best interests of the country, not by events at the Mahon Tribunal.

On 7 May the Dáil (legislature) approved Brian Cowen (unanimous choice as leader of Fianna Fáil) as taoiseach, by 88 votes to 76. In the ensuing government reshuffle major changes included the appointment of Mary Coughlan as tánaiste (deputy prime minister) and minister for enterprise, trade and employment; Mícheál Martin took over at foreign affairs, Brian Lenihan became minister for finance, and Dermot Ahern minister for justice. Fianna Fáil's coalition partners retained their portfolios but from November the position of Minister for Health Mary Harney of the Progressive Democrats (PDs) came under scrutiny following the decision of a special conference of the PDs in favour of dissolving the party (which in March had elected Senator Ciaran Cannon as leader).

Before his resignation there was concern in the political establishment that Ahern's personal travails were distracting attention from major issues, especially the referendum on the Lisbon Treaty. On assuming office, Brian Cowen identified winning the referendum as his most urgent task, a desire shared by all of the main parties. Sinn Féin was the main party voice on the "no" side, but also crucial in a diverse collection of opposed interests was the Libertas organisation, set up and partly funded by businessman Declan Ganley to campaign against the Treaty. At the beginning of the year polls showed a clear majority of committed voters in favour (around two to one), but by late April there was a narrowing of the lead held by the "yes" campaign, and the final weeks of the campaign saw a big increase in support for the "no" side.

In the referendum on 12 June, the Lisbon Treaty was rejected by 53.4 to 46.6 per cent, on a turnout of 53 per cent. Just ten of the 43 constituencies voted in favour, and "no" supporters were particularly concentrated among 25-34-year olds, in the working class socio-economic groups, among women, and in rural areas. The most important factor underpinning the "no" vote was lack of information about, or understanding of, the Treaty. While the government stated that it "accepted and respected the verdict" of the people, it was careful not to rule out the possibility of another vote. Indeed, at an EU summit in Brussels in December it agreed to hold a second referendum in 2009 in exchange for concessions relating to domestic policy (neutrality, abortion laws, and taxation) and the retention of a Commissioner for each member state, all important specific factors in the "no" vote.

The economy slowed dramatically, aggravated by the effects of the global financial crisis. In September, data showed that Ireland was officially in recession and figures at the end of the year indicated that the shortfall in the public finances for 2008, at more than €8 billion, was far larger than predicted. Unemployment reached 8.3 percent, its highest level since September 1996. With falling tax receipts, in early July the government announced a package of measures designed to save €440 million in public spending in 2008 and €1 billion in 2009.

With the worsening financial situation the budget was announced six weeks earlier than usual on 14 October. Described by Fine Gael leader Enda Kenny as "one of the most swingeing and savage" in years, it heralded a further round of tax increases and spending cuts. Several decisions fomented public controversy, not least proposals to increase school class sizes and to remove universal entitlement to the medical card for people over 70 years of age. Public opposition forced the government to propose several increases in the income eligibility thresholds, to remove the proposed means test, and to propose negotiations with the medical profession on a revision of the structure of the medical card scheme. In the political fall-out, a revolt within Fianna Fáil led to the resignation of Wicklow TD (Dáil member) Joe Behan, and independent TD Finian McGrath also withdrew his support for the government.

During the international banking crisis in mid-September, the financial regulator introduced a ban on the short selling of stocks, and on 20 September Minister for Finance Brian Lenihan announced an increase in the statutory deposit guarantee from €20,000 to €100,000. This was quickly followed by a decision to guarantee all deposits and borrowings for the six Irish-owned banks for the next two years (eligibility subsequently was extended to some non-Irish banks with a major presence in Ireland). In December the government announced a recapitalisation programme of up to €10 billion for three large financial institutions under which it would take preference shares (giving the state 75 per cent control of Anglo Irish Bank) in an effort to ensure the long term sustainability of the banking sector.

At the end of a difficult year, the popularity of Fianna Fáil and the government had suffered badly from the financial and budget crises. A poll taken in November indicated that just 18 per cent of respondents were satisfied with the performance of the governing coalition.

During 2008 the deaths occurred in April of former President Patrick Hillery (1976-90) and in December of Conor Cruise O'Brien, former cabinet minister, civil servant, UN official, writer, academic, and newspaper editor (see Obituary).

Alan Greer

GERMANY

CAPITAL: Berlin   AREA: 357,050 sq km   POPULATION: 82,268,000 ('07)
OFFICIAL LANGUAGE: German   POLITICAL SYSTEM: multiparty republic
HEAD OF STATE: President Horst Köhler (since July '04)
RULING PARTIES: "Grand Coalition" of Christian Democratic Union/Christian Social Union
   (CDU/CSU) and Social Democratic Party (SPD)
HEAD OF GOVERNMENT: Chancellor Angela Merkel (CDU) (since Oct '05)
MAIN IGO MEMBERSHIPS (NON-UN): NATO, EU, OSCE, CE, CBSS, AC, OECD, G-8
CURRENCY: euro (end-'08 £1=€1.0344, US$1=€0.7194)
GNI PER CAPITA: US$38,860, $33,820 at PPP ('07)

WITH 2009 promising to be a year of genuine political intrigue (no fewer than seven high profile elections in Germany were planned for that year), the year 2008 was always likely to be deprived of the drama and energy that elections inject into public life. The most noteworthy events of Germany's year were soon-to-be US President-elect Barack Obama's visit to Berlin to speak in front of hundreds of thousands of enthusiastic supporters in high summer and, as the year wore on, the impending doom that another US export—the credit crunch—was bringing to the German economy.

Obama's July speech in front of an estimated 200,000 people at the Victory Tower in the centre of Berlin was remarkable for a number of reasons. Obama appeared more rock star than politician and his calls for change and freedom were enthusiastically welcomed. Not since John F. Kennedy's famous 1963 speech condemning the building of the Berlin Wall had a foreign politician made such an impact on the German consciousness (see AR 1963, p. 260). That Obama chose Germany for his principle campaign speech away from American soil was also an indication that the somewhat strained relationship between the two countries, which had characterised the Bush era, was about to end.

Enthusiasm for Obama could not, however, disguise the malaise that was settling over other aspects of German public life. German troops stationed in northern Afghanistan were coming under sustained attack and an already controversial mission was beginning to lose support among the population. Selling the federal army's activities abroad to an intrinsically sceptical public was never easy, and the news filtering back from the Hindu Kush did nothing to help the government's cause. The government nonetheless continued to stress that the mission was largely a humanitarian one, despite the fact that the situation was becoming increasingly dangerous for the 3,500 German soldiers serving in Afghanistan. Yet support for the mission within Germany's political class remained broad and it appeared that an increased number of troops would be stationed in the country for at least one more year.

By the autumn of 2008 foreign policy questions had retreated into the background as the impending economic crisis took centre stage. This was particularly galling for Angela Merkel's Christian Democrat-led "Grand Coalition", which had presided over a clear improvement in economic fortunes during the first half of the year. Unemployment had fallen to a record post-unification low, whilst Germany continued to defend its unofficial title as "export world champion" (and that included China). The government was still talking about balancing the budget, and although demand within Germany remained weak, prospects for economic growth looked much rosier than they did elsewhere in Europe. Even by the end of the year, Germany's growth rate averaged between the 1 and 2 per cent mark, a positively bullish figure when compared with its big western European neighbours.

At the end of the year, however, the global financial crisis began to impinge, and by the end of December German growth had been throttled completely and unemployment figures were heading very much in the wrong direction. Full blown recession was believed, by more or less everyone, to be on the way. Merkel's reaction to the crisis had been heavily criticised. Merkel—by nature a consensual politician, loathe to act rashly in case the long term cost was higher than the short term gain—had refused to be drawn into the bidding wars, in which UK Prime Minister Gordon Brown and French President Nicolas Sarkozy were engaged, in the race to bolster flagging European economies. Instead, she chose to bide her time by showing financial restraint, and it was not long before commentators, who had once lauded her consensual, "big tent" style, were labelling her "Mrs No".

The first, 15 point stimulus package that Merkel's government finally agreed towards the end of 2008 was criticised both for being insufficient in scope and also far too late in coming. It had little direct effect and it was only a matter of days before commentators and politicians (both at home and abroad) were calling for a second set of more wide-ranging measures. (This, in fact, occurred early in January 2009.)

In terms of party politics, Merkel did at least find out who would be her main opponent in the 2009 federal election: Foreign Minister Frank-Walter Steinmeier. Steinmeier replaced Rhineland Palatinate's prime minister, Kurt Beck, as chairman of the Social Democratic Party (SPD) in a hectic few days in early September. Beck, a largely ineffective leader, had been head of the Social Democrats for a mere 15 months. His tenure in office had been blighted by a series of mainly tactical blunders, which had seen the SPD's opinion poll ratings plummet. The most obvious of these mistakes concerned the SPD's branch in the state (Land) of Hesse. Hesse's citizens went to the polls in a state election in January and the result was an almost dead heat between the Christian Democratic Union (CDU), with 36.8 per cent, and the SPD with 36.7 per cent. Neither party was subsequently able to form a coalition with its preferred partner (the liberal Free Democrats in the case of the CDU, and the Greens in the case of the SPD). Given that the incumbent CDU leader, Roland Koch, was widely loathed within the Social Democrats, a "grand coalition" that included him was also out of the question. For a period, it appeared as if either of two potential three-party coalitions might be a possibility, but, once again, negotiations broke down. This stalemate prompted Andrea Ypsilanti, the SPD leader in Hesse, to bring the radical socialist Left Party (Linkspartei, LP) into the coalition equation. After some equivocation, national SPD leader Beck supported her in this, thereby breaking the taboo of not working with what was, in essence, a former communist party in western Germany (different conventions were applied in the eastern states). More important still, Beck was blatantly breaking a pre-election promise expressly not to work with the LP, no matter what the election outcome. Ultimately, and in a moment of high drama, Ypsilanti's attempts to form a government with the Greens that was supported by the Left Party failed, on the very day that she was supposed to be inaugurated, 4 November. Four of her own parliamentarians decided more or less at the very last minute that they could not support a government that relied on LP votes. Ypsilanti, deprived of her majority, immediately admitted defeat and resigned from the leadership of the party. A new state election was called for early 2009.

Germany's three other Land elections in 2009 also had their noteworthy moments. The LP not only managed to enter the state parliament in Hesse, it did so also in Hamburg and Lower Saxony (and narrowly failed to win representation in Bavaria in September). These results were huge successes for a party that only came into being 12 months previously. Neither of its predecessors—the Electoral Alternative for Employment and Social Justice (WASG), and the Party of Democratic Socialism (PDS)—had ever even come close to gaining seats in a western German state parliament. The Left Party, on the other hand, seemed destined to stabilise itself as a genuine socialist force across the whole of the country.

The Bavarian Land election also witnessed a political upheaval. The Christian Social Union lost its overall majority in the state parliament for the first time in 46 years. The CSU had governed Bavaria for the majority of the post-war period, so the jolt not just of losing votes but also of having to enter into coalition with the Free Democrats was great. The twin leadership of local CSU chairman, Erwin Huber, and CSU state premier, Günther Beckstein, was seen to have been ineffectual in creating a new, modern narrative for Bavaria, and in the immediate aftermath of the September poll both stepped down from their positions. Federal Agriculture Minister Horst Seehofer returned to Bavaria to take over the leadership reins of both party and Land.

Dan Hough

FRANCE

CAPITAL: Paris   AREA: 551,500 sq km   POPULATION: 61,707,000 ('07) (metropolitan area only)
OFFICIAL LANGUAGES: French   POLITICAL SYSTEM: multiparty republic
HEAD OF STATE: President Nicolas Sarkozy (UMP) (since May '07)
RULING PARTY: Union for a Popular Movement (UMP) (since Nov '02)
HEAD OF GOVERNMENT: Prime Minister François Fillon (since May '07)
MAIN IGO MEMBERSHIPS (NON-UN): NATO, EU, OSCE, CE, OECD, G-8, PC, Francophonie
CURRENCY: euro (end-'08 £1=€1.0344, US$1=€0.7194)
GNI PER CAPITA: US$38,500 (incl DOMs), $33,470 at PPP ('07)

THROUGHOUT his 2007 election campaign President Nicolas Sarkozy called tirelessly for a "break" with many established policies and practices. But change is rarely comfortable or popular for long, and while his hyper-energetic approach to reform was initially well received, his attempts to achieve it against a backdrop of rising prices, a weakening economy, and parlous public finances brought a steady fall in his popularity.

Fifth Republic presidents have always been powerful figures, but in 2008 a nominally parliamentary system became effectively presidential. The prime minister was barely visible; ministers were frequently over-ruled or short-circuited. Thus, in February, Sarkozy abruptly decreed the abolition of advertising on the public television networks without warning or consulting relevant ministers, or indicating how the resulting gap in the networks' finances was to be filled. Earlier, he had no less unexpectedly decreed that the international news channel, France 24, should henceforth broadcast only in French.

That said, the government was kept busy preparing plans to reform the labour market, pensions, and the constitution, and to tackle the poverty, unemployment, and racial discrimination—endemic in the high-rise estates—that underlay the riots of 2005 (see AR 2005, pp. 41-42). Many of the measures considered were recommended in a report, *300 Decisions for Changing France*, from a commission established by Sarkozy and headed by Jacques Attali, a former adviser to the socialist president, François Mitterrand (1981-95). The report, published in January, suggested deregulation of a range of economic activities to improve the country's sluggish growth rate. "Whatever you propose, we will do", Sarkozy had told Attali. Yet, within days of the report's publication its proposals to deregulate taxis and pharmacies were abandoned in the face of the hostility of drivers and pharmacists: in many respects state intervention remained popular in France and even moves to increase retail competition received only lukewarm public backing.

With the public finances in a woeful state, programmes like the ambitious one billion euro vision of urban regeneration, also unveiled in January, would receive only a fraction of the promised funding. Given Sarkozy's highly personalised approach to governing, any public resentments inevitably turned on him. Although unemployment was at its lowest for over 20 years the public mood was particularly glum, not least because Sarkozy had not met expectations over high fuel and food prices and the drive for reform had lost momentum.

Meanwhile, he was also exposed on another flank. Having separated (by mutual consent) from his wife Cécilia Sarkozy in October 2007, within weeks he was very publicly courting a glamorous Italian singer and former model, Carla Bruni. Their liaison was signalled by an appearance at the Mickey Mouse parade at Disneyland Paris, followed by Christmas in the Middle East using a jet loaned by a friendly billionaire, where the world's media filmed their dalliance among the temples at great length. For many, this infringed a longstanding national reticence over the private life of public figures: the French expected greater dignity in their president. (The couple's wedding in March was more restrained and their relationship was subsequently generally accepted.)

Unsurprisingly, therefore, in municipal elections in March the left won back most of the ground it had lost in 2001, with 47.94 per cent of the vote in metropolitan communes with over 3,500 inhabitants, to 45.49 per cent for the right. The far left (1.49 per cent) and far right (0.66 per cent) did very poorly, while the centrists (3.22 per cent), who had hoped for a pivotal role, were badly squeezed in the second ballot.

Yet this was more a setback and a warning rather than a disaster. (Sarkozy was also fortunate in his opponents. As if oblivious to the crumbling economy, the Socialist Party spent most of the year in self-destructive irrelevance, wrangling over who should be the party's new first secretary, eventually selecting a former minister of labour, Martine Aubry, in November.) Responding characteristically to the poor election results, Sarkozy admitted mistakes but insisted that his reforms would continue. Among these would be the streamlining of public services by cutting staff and not replacing many who retired: thus 11,200 teachers would go before the new school year began in September. Public service strikes in May and June revealed a new weakness in the unions, which were now required to ensure provision of a minimum service during strikes in public transport and in schools. In July, new legislation undermined the unions' cherished 35-hour week. Overtime work was exempted from taxes and social charges. The retirement age was raised by one year and benefit rules were toughened to penalise unemployed people who refused more than two job offers.

Defence and the courts were also targeted for reorganisation. A defence white paper in June heralded the slimming down of the armed forces; over 50,000 posts would disappear over seven years, with the savings invested in intelligence and more modern equipment. Unenthusiastically accepted by the military, the proposals caused anger and anguish in the autumn when the consequences for local economies became apparent for towns that would lose their garrisons. It was much the same with the "rationalisation" of the courts, the geographical distribution of which had changed little for decades. Loss of a barracks or *tribunal* struck hard at local pride and the minister of justice who pushed her reforms through during the autumn incurred immense unpopularity.

In his presidential election campaign Sarkozy had pledged a reform of France's institutions, to give greater weight to the weak Parliament established under Charles de Gaulle. The resulting proposals were many and varied, some commanding general support, others furiously controversial. Among the major changes proposed were limiting the president to two five-year terms, subjecting some presidential appointments to parliamentary approval, giving Parliament a greater say in setting its own agenda (hitherto dominated by the government), requiring parliamentary approval for military operations abroad lasting over four months, and the possibility of approving accession of new member-states to the EU by parliamentary approval rather than referendum. Opponents were particularly hostile, for reasons reaching back to the 19th century, to allowing the president to address Parliament directly, the lack of a statutory right of reply to presidential television appearances, and to the perpetuation of a voting system for the upper house (Senate) designed to ensure a permanent conservative majority. Approval of the reform proposals required a three-fifths majority of the two chambers of Parliament meeting in congress in July, and it was clear that the outcome would be very close. After much intense lobbying and horse-trading, the requisite majority was achieved by a single vote, 539-357. "A victory for French democracy", said Sarkozy; another step towards "monocracy" said opponents.

Among other measures approved during the year was a lifting of the long-standing bar on the teaching of minority languages, which provoked a furious riposte from the French Academy at "an attack on French identity", and a decision that the government would appoint the head of France Télévisions, curiously presented as a measure of democratisation. The idea of "SarkoTV" went down badly. An active solidarity revenue (RSA), to help the unemployed and poor workers, financed by a 1.1 per cent tax on income from investments and real estate, was carried in August despite opposition from many government supporters. Yet not every battle was won. In November, plans to establish a database including many personal details about individuals were withdrawn in the face of widespread criticism, and in December reforms of the high school curriculum and teaching hours were deferred in the face of widespread demonstrations and fears of contagion from violence then taking place in Greece (see pp. 82-83).

French political scandals invariably take a long while to work through. In November, the former prime minister, Dominique de Villepin, was ordered to stand trial, with four others, for his alleged role in the Clearstream affair in 2004 (see AR 2007, pp. 43-44). The affair allegedly amounted to a conspiracy to blacken Sarkozy's character at a time when the two men were rivals to succeed Jacques Chirac as president. De Villepin accused Sarkozy of meddling in the judicial process. The case was expected to come to trial in 2010.

For much of the year France was encouraged to see herself as less vulnerable in the gathering global financial and economic crisis, due to the virtues of "the French model" over the Anglo-Saxon one, the flaws of which had now been so vividly exposed. True, there were some problems. In January a "rogue" trader at Société Générale, one of the country's largest banks, was charged with the biggest individual fraud in French history: €4.9 billion. In October, the Caisse d'Epargne, a large savings bank, admitted that rogue traders had lost it €600 million; and BNP Paribas, initially seen as a safe haven, was found to have been affected by the collapse of US investment bank Lehman Brothers. Even so, French financial institutions suffered less damage than those in the USA or Britain. Nevertheless, by the autumn France was clearly moving into recession. The economy was contracting, the stock market was down over 40 per cent over the year, the trade balance was worryingly negative, and the budget deficit was bumping against the EU ceiling of 3 per cent of GDP. Industrial production had fallen and unemployment had risen to 8.2 per cent.

FOREIGN AFFAIRS. France was a particularly active player on the world stage. Much of this activity was in the context of the EU presidency, which, as usual, offered opportunities to promote specifically French concerns like the Mediterranean Union and immigration policy. Sarkozy's highly visible involvement in rescuing the EU constitutional treaty (the Lisbon Treaty) and his intervention in the conflict between Russia and Georgia were surely a factor in the improved standing in the polls with which he ended the year.

In January Sarkozy announced the intention to establish a military base in the United Arab Emirates. This would be France's first permanent base in the Gulf, where it had no colonial ties. In February he said that France would renegotiate her defence pacts with her former African colonies; it was "no longer conceivable" that the French should be dragged into their internal conflicts. France would engage with the African Union to build a system of collective security. How great a difference this would make in practice remained unclear. Avowedly pro-American, Sarkozy made great efforts to mend fences with the USA, committing an additional 700 troops to Afghanistan. This was not a popular move, and still less so when 10 soldiers were killed and 21 wounded, in a Taliban ambush in August, the worst loss in a single incident for 25 years. His intention to restore links to NATO's military command structure, severed by de Gaulle in 1966, also raised hostility to his "Atlanticist obsession". Firm in his parliamentary support, he brushed aside an essentially symbolic opposition censure motion. France, he said, was independent, not subordinate. Yet he was prepared to annoy the Americans by inviting President Bashar Assad of Syria, still considered a terrorist by the USA, to the Bastille Day celebrations; and in November he ruffled Western feathers more widely by joining Russia in condemning US plans to install missile bases in Central Europe and supporting President Dmitry Medvedev's call for a pan-European pact (see p. 126).

Over China, by contrast, he was uncharacteristically hesitant, as he struggled to reconcile his commitment to human rights with a substantial expansion of trade. The disruption of the Paris leg of the Olympic torch relay produced Chinese demonstrations and threats against French companies that forced profuse apologies. There was uncertainty about whether he would boycott the Olympic opening ceremony; eventually he made a lightning visit. There was even greater uncertainty over whether he would brave Chinese wrath by meeting the Dalai Lama. Initially he sent his wife in his stead before, after more havering, opting for a private meeting in the course of a visit to Poland in December.

The happiest and least contentious moment of the year was the rescue of Ingrid Betancourt, a Franco-Colombian politician, after six years as a hostage of the rebel Revolutionary Armed Forces of Colombia (FARC) guerrillas there (see pp. 197-98; AR 2002, p. 196). Both Nicolas and Cécilia Sarkozy had long championed her cause, though France had no operational role in freeing her.

Martin Harrison

ITALY

CAPITAL: Rome   AREA: 301,340 sq km   POPULATION: 59,375,000 ('07)
OFFICIAL LANGUAGE: Italian   POLITICAL SYSTEM: multiparty republic
HEAD OF STATE: President Giorgio Napolitano (since May '06)
RULING PARTIES: People of Freedom (PDL) grouping, Northern League, & Movement for Autonomy
HEAD OF GOVERNMENT: Prime Minister Silvio Berlusconi (PDL) (since May '08)
MAIN IGO MEMBERSHIPS (NON-UN): NATO, EU, OSCE, CE, CEI, OECD, G-8
CURRENCY: euro (end-'08 £1=€1.0344, US$1=€0.7194)
GNI PER CAPITA: US$33,540, $29,900 at PPP ('07)

EARLY elections held on 13-14 April were deemed particularly significant by many, but in what way exactly was disputed. Many saw them as marking a new phase in Italy's transition towards a stronger governmental system; others were concerned by the strengthening of the right. Their disquiet was reinforced by the suggestion of the new minister of defence (and president of the National Alliance), Ignazio La Russa, during the 8 September anniversary of the beginning of the anti-Fascist Resistance, that the combatants of the 1943-45 Fascist continuity regime, the Republic of Salò, should also be honoured as defenders of the fatherland.

The centre-left administration of Prime Minister Romano Prodi fell after less than two years in office, defeated by Silvio Berlusconi, who won his third election in 15 years, this time with both a convincing majority and, apparently, a more cohesive one. The great surprise of the election was the failure of the radical left to gain parliamentary representation. The dominance of Italy's left by the Italian Communist Party (PCI) had been a defining feature of the so-called First Republic (c. 1948-93), along with its permanent exclusion from government at the national level, and the left had continued to attract some 5 to 10 per cent of the vote subsequently.

The Prodi government had had only a minimal parliamentary majority in the Senate (the upper house) and had quickly lost public support. Beset by internal challenges from both its radical and conservative fringes and assailed by Berlusconi's mobilisation of centre-right voters against it throughout its 20-month life, the government fell on 24 January, notwithstanding its creditable economic performance. The early election forced the postponement of three referendums on the electoral system, which had been approved by the Constitutional Court on 16 January.

As a consequence of the very different alliance strategies of the main parties compared to previous years, the party system was transformed by the election. It remained fundamentally bipolar, but saw a drastic reduction in its fragmentation. In 2006 both left and right had sought to include every political force possible in their electoral lists, resulting in a fragmented Parliament and a government (Prodi's) comprising nine parties. In 2008, Walter Veltroni, the leader of the newly formed Democratic Party (PD), sought to make his party one with a majority vocation, proffering the possibility of single party government. Challenged by this radical innovation, Berlusconi responded similarly, leading to the amalgamation of the two largest forces on the right, Forza Italia and the National Alliance, along with a number of minor formations, in the People of Freedom (PDL) grouping. In the event, neither the PD nor the PDL actually ran alone. The PD, comprising the former Democrats of the Left and the Margherita, hosted candidates from the small, strongly lay, Radical Party. It also allied with Italy of Values (IDV), led by Antonio Di Pietro, the former public prosecutor who had come to symbolise the campaign against political corruption of the early 1990s. The PDL allied with the Northern League (LN) and the very small Movement for Autonomy (MPA), a southern and essentially Sicilian party.

The PDL won 276 of the Chamber's (lower house's) 630 deputies and the centre-right alliance as a whole took 344; the MPA gaining just eight deputies, and Umberto Bossi's Northern League 60. The Union of Centre and Christian Democrats (UDC), which had been an awkward coalition partner in Berlusconi's 2001-06 governments, refused to accept dissolution within the PDL and ran independently, securing 36 deputies. It was the only party not belonging to one of the two major alliances to gain representation (other than tiny minority language parties). The radical Rainbow Left alliance failed in this respect, as did The Right, the former gaining 3.1 per cent of the Chamber vote, the latter 2.4 per cent (the threshold for representation was 4 per cent).

The PD won 217 deputies, and IDV 29. The centre-right's lead, in vote terms, was convincing: 46.3 per cent in the Chamber compared to 37.5 per cent for the left, with a similar 9-point lead in the Senate. Third-party votes accounted for some 16 per cent of the total. Abstention also grew, most notably on the left, its more radical voters splitting roughly evenly between loyalty, abstention—in the event, in vain—and the much-championed "useful vote" for the PD. The size of the third-party vote plus abstention plus uncertainty about the solidity of the two new large parties (the PDL and PD) left room for doubt about the stability of the new party system configuration.

Berlusconi's fourth executive appeared to be strong and the prime minister secured his personal position via an early and controversial piece of legislation, which rendered immune from prosecution the incumbents of the four highest public offices. This did not, however, prevent the opening at the end of the year of the trial of David Mills, a British lawyer accused of receiving a US$600,000 bribe for testifying in favour of Berlusconi in two trials a decade previously.

The challenges facing the new government were formidable. Already formally in recession at the end of the third quarter, Italy found its economic problems exacerbated by the sharp worsening of the international financial crisis. In November the Organisation for Economic Co-operation and Development (OECD) forecast that Italy would see two successive years of negative growth, in 2008 and 2009, something not yet seen in the Republic's history, with unemployment rising from 6.2 per cent to 7.8 per cent. The scale of the crisis lent force to speculation that the new, less europhile government might default on its euro debt, withdrawing Italy from the eurozone, especially given the electoral success of the eurosceptic Northern League, which had doubled its vote share. The likelihood of this remained remote, however, given Italy's national debt—at approximately 104 per cent of GDP still the third largest in the world—and the harsh international credit climate. One indication of Italy's continuing commitment to the EU was Parliament's unanimous ratification of the Lisbon Treaty in July.

The new government built on its election success with a string of initiatives designed to symbolise its, and above all Berlusconi's, efficiency. First, the process of government formation itself was the fastest ever in the Republic's history, the president being presented with a list of candidates immediately upon mandating Berlusconi to form a government. Second, the new cabinet adhered fully, for the first time, to legislation passed a decade earlier, which had reduced the number of cabinet ministers to just 12. The number of junior ministers was also small, the government numbering just over 60 in total, whereas for many years it had been closer to 100 in order to satisfy the demands of the many coalition participants. Third, the first cabinet meeting was held, for reasons of high symbolic impact, in Naples rather than Rome. In fact, the city's (and Campania region's) rubbish disposal crisis had been a prominent feature of the election campaign, identified by the then opposition as symbolising the left's inability to manage Italy's problems, at both the local and national level. Now, Berlusconi made the head of Italy's department for civil protection an undersecretary attached to the prime minister's office with direct responsibility for resolving the crisis.

Other symbolically significant measures announced at this meeting included the complete abolition of local domestic rates (the "ICI", actually already abolished for the 40 per cent of the population on the lowest incomes by the Prodi government), and the announcement of a "security package". This latter included the declaration of a state of emergency with regard to Roma (nomad) encampments in Lazio (embracing Rome), Campania, and Lombardy, and responded to a powerful wave of popular anxiety about crime and disorder in 2007, which some saw as having been fuelled by media outlets that were not merely sensationalist but also sympathetic to the right's agenda of fomenting discontent with the then government. The package was particularly controversial for its inclusion of provisions regarding fingerprinting, including of minors, as part of a census programme of the more than 160 encampments. Eight of the Roma encampments, a quarter of which were unauthorised, had been burnt down in the three months following the election and the atmosphere of intolerance and the harsh way in which the government and police forces acted over the summer became a matter of concern reported on by the European Parliament's committee on civil liberties, justice and home affairs. At the end of the year the government decided to fingerprint only those over 14 years of age. Italy was home to an estimated 200,000 Roma, 80,000 of whom were Italian citizens. Polls consistently showed the interior minister, Roberto Maroni, to be Italy's most popular government minister.

The government also began a campaign to render the country's 3.65 million public employees more efficient; embarked on education reform that aroused strong popular opposition; and followed up its aim, championed during the election, of maintaining the bankrupted national airline, Alitalia, as, in part at least, a national company. A major issue at stake here was the fate of Milan's airports, with the Northern League in particular championing the importance of maintaining Milan as an international hub.

By the end of the year, the left had still not recovered from its defeat, indeed double defeat. The radical left remained fragmented. The attempt at quasi-unification in a single list had failed to maintain parliamentary representation independent of the moderate left, whilst Communist Refoundation, the major component of the radical left, split almost exactly in two over its strategic stance: principled opposition or reformist party of government. The PD was disappointed by its failure to make an electoral breakthrough either outside the PCI's historical territorial strongholds in the so-called "red belt" regions (Tuscany, Emilia-Romagna, the Marches, and Umbria), or at the centre of the left-right spectrum. There was much speculation that Veltroni's campaign strategy— which had made no attempt to defend the incumbent Prodi government, focusing instead on the novelty of the PD and his leadership of it—was misconceived. As a party seeking to consolidate a moderate reformist identity it was, too, consistently outperformed in the opinion polls by its more vocally anti-Berlusconi ally, the IDV. Indeed, the two parties' continuing alliance was challenged by a minority within the party, while the whole question of alliance strategy remained unresolved. The possibility loomed large that the next election, though still four years away, could, for the first time since the 1990s crisis, see an incumbent government re-elected.

Mark Donovan

BELGIUM, THE NETHERLANDS, AND LUXEMBOURG

Belgium

CAPITAL: Brussels   AREA: 30,530 sq km   POPULATION: 10,626,000 ('07)
OFFICIAL LANGUAGES: French, Flemish & German   POLITICAL SYSTEM: multiparty monarchy
HEAD OF STATE: King Albert II (since Aug '93)
RULING PARTIES: Christian Democrats and Flemish (CDV), Flemish Liberals and Democrats
    (VLD), Reform Movement (MR), Socialist Party-Walloon (PS), Democratic and Humanist
    Centre (CDH)
HEAD OF GOVERNMENT: caretaker Prime Minister Herman Van Rompuy (CDV) (since Dec '08)
MAIN IGO MEMBERSHIPS (NON-UN): NATO, EU, Benelux, OSCE, CE, OECD, Francophonie
CURRENCY: euro (end-'08 £1=€1.0344, US$1=€0.7194)
GNI PER CAPITA: US$40,710, $35,110 at PPP ('07)

The Netherlands

CAPITAL: Amsterdam   AREA: 41,530 sq km   POPULATION: 16,381,000 ('07)
OFFICIAL LANGUAGE: Dutch   POLITICAL SYSTEM: multiparty monarchy
HEAD OF STATE: Queen Beatrix (since April '80)
RULING PARTIES: coalition of Christian Democratic Appeal (CDA), Labour Party (PvdA), and
    Christian Union (CU)
HEAD OF GOVERNMENT: Prime Minister Jan Peter Balkenende (CDA) (since July '02)
MAIN IGO MEMBERSHIPS (NON-UN): NATO, EU, Benelux, OSCE, CE, OECD
CURRENCY: euro (end-'08 £1=€1.0344, US$1=€0.7194)
GNI PER CAPITA: US$45,820 $39,500 at PPP ('07)

Luxembourg

CAPITAL: Luxembourg   AREA: 2,590 sq km   POPULATION: 480,000 ('07)
OFFICIAL LANGUAGE: Letzeburgish   POLITICAL SYSTEM: multiparty monarchy
HEAD OF STATE: Grand Duke Henri (since Oct '00)
RULING PARTIES: coalition of the Christian Social People's Party (CSV/PCS) and the Luxembourg
    Socialist Workers' Party (LSAP/POSL) (since July '04)
HEAD OF GOVERNMENT: Prime Minister Jean-Claude Juncker (CSV/PCS) (since Jan '95)
MAIN IGO MEMBERSHIPS (NON-UN): NATO, EU, Benelux, OSCE, CE, OECD, Francophonie
CURRENCY: euro (end-'08 £1=€1.0344, US$1=€0.7194)
GNI PER CAPITA: US$75,880, $64,400 at PPP ('07)

BELGIUM.   It took 192 days of manoeuvring, bargaining, and bickering following parliamentary elections in June 2007 (see AR 2008, p. 50) for a five-party coalition government of limited duration to be formed under Guy Verhofstadt, a Flemish Liberal. Its task was to agree the 2008 federal budget and prepare the way for constitutional reform by 15 March. A nominally balanced budget was approved, together with a package of minor measures of devolution, proposed by a committee of "wise men", as a contribution to building confidence in the more ambitious constitutional negotiations to follow. However, more substantial proposals on fiscal, healthcare, and labour policies were not agreed. Verhofstadt resigned when his mandate expired and was replaced by a Flemish Christian Democrat, Yves Leterme, who was seen as the real winner of the 2007 elections.

Leterme's government included conservatives and liberals from both the main language groups as well as francophone socialists. It was committed to a tough line on immigration, cuts in taxation, and higher pensions, but what really counted politically was its handling of the constitutional question. The issue, as always, was the clash of cultures and a battle for resources between wealthier Dutch-speaking Flanders and the poorer French-speaking Walloons in the south. Leterme set himself a deadline of 15 July for presenting proposals. The sharpest differences were over the bilingual electoral constituency of Brussels-Halle-Vilvoorde, where Fleming nationalists wanted to merge Halle and Vilvoorde into monoglot neighbouring Flemish areas, while francophones pressed for protection of their language rights. Leterme, whose room for negotiation was increasingly circumscribed by his nationalist-conservative allies, offered his resignation. King Albert II maintained him as a caretaker and appointed a three-person panel representing Belgium's linguistic communities to examine how to restart the reform process. However, the issues remained unresolved and positions became increasingly entrenched.

There were, of course, other issues requiring attention. In July, Parliament ratified the EU's Treaty of Lisbon by 116 votes to 18. In December, a long-standing issue was tackled when the banks and the government agreed to pay US$170 million in Holocaust restitution. The economy became an increasing preoccupation; high energy prices drove inflation up to 5.9 per cent in July, its highest level for 24 years. As the international economic storm gathered, the government remained optimistic that the public finances would be in structural balance for 2008 after the small deficit inherited from 2007. However, the situation deteriorated during the autumn. In December many companies were reported to be cutting production, investment, or staff; unemployment exceeded 10 per cent and the economy was expected to shrink in 2009. The government announced a €2 billion package of tax cuts, lower energy prices, and accelerated infrastructure projects to prop up the economy.

In October Belgium joined France and Luxembourg in supporting Dexla, the world's largest municipal lender, and it joined Luxembourg and the Netherlands in the partial nationalisation of the Fortis bank, Belgium's largest private sector employer. The bank had been much weakened by the high price it had paid in 2007 in the takeover of the Dutch ABN-Amro bank. Later, it was alleged that Leterme and the justice minister, Jo Vandeurzen, had tried to influence the judges in a case relating to shareholders' rights in the Fortis sale. Both men resigned in December, protesting their innocence, and at the very end of the year, the king appointed a Flemish Christian Democrat, Herman Van Rompuy, prime minister to head another five-party coalition government.

THE NETHERLANDS. The government of Jan Peter Balkenende met the global economic and financial crisis in a stronger position than many of its neighbours. Although elevated energy costs drove inflation higher than forecast, the economy was still growing relatively fast well into the year. At 4.5 per cent unemployment was low, the public finances were healthy, and the debt level of 45.4 per cent of GDP was comfortably below the EU average. Well into the third quarter the budget memorandum recognised that the country had not escaped unscathed by the global financial turbulence, but confidently asserted that the economy was in good shape, the coalition's agreed programme was being implemented, and purchasing power was being maintained.

Nevertheless, the government took a number of measures to strengthen the economy. Taxes on diesel were frozen in the summer after protests by hauliers. Providing pay rises were kept within "reasonable" bounds, employees' unemployment insurance contributions would be scrapped, generating an annual gain of some €500 for people on average incomes and €800 for working parents. There would also be a bonus of up to €3,000 for people continuing to work after the age of 62. Plans to increase VAT were shelved. The government expected the budget surplus for 2009 would reach 1.2 per cent and that state debt would fall to 39.6 per cent. It would press ahead with plans to invest in education, community regeneration, public safety, and national security. More would be spent on urban renewal, assistance to asylum seekers, tackling school dropouts, recruiting more police, and doubling parental leave to 26 weeks.

Nevertheless, the economic crisis was leaving its mark. By mid-year house prices had declined for the first time in 18 years. In October the trade surplus had fallen, though the balance still remained enviably healthy, and unemployment was rising. Local and provincial governments had at least €250 million in deposits in foreign banks that had run into difficulty. In September, the government joined Belgium and Luxembourg in the partial nationalisation of the Fortis bank. Several large pension funds found themselves unable to maintain payments in line with inflation; the Central Bank gave pension funds until April 2009 to rectify the situation. The government also guaranteed loans to banks and between banks. The prime minister warned that 2009 would be a difficult year; the economy might not begin recovering until 2011.

In a trial at the International Court of Justice (ICJ) at The Hague, the Court dismissed a case brought by a Bosnian family alleging that the Dutch state had failed to protect them during the Srebrenica massacre in 1995. The Court ruled that responsibility lay with the United Nations.

Other developments included ratification of the Treaty of Lisbon in July, warnings that The Netherlands remained a target for terrorism, not least because of the continued presence of Dutch troops in Afghanistan, and the release of a strongly anti-Islamic film by Geert Wilders, the leader of the anti-immigration Dutch Freedom Party (PVV). (In January a gathering of far-right politicians had called for a charter against the "Islamisation of European cities".) Finally, work began on a project to clean up and redevelop Amsterdam's notorious red-light district.

LUXEMBOURG. For many years Luxembourg enjoyed above average growth and steadily increasing prosperity thanks to the seemingly endless expansion of the financial sector. Yet although the global financial crisis was well underway when Prime Minister Jean-Claude Juncker delivered his annual state of the nation address on 1 June, the prevailing mood was sunny optimism. He was mindful of crises in the wider world but, for Luxembourg, "on average we live in a wholly favourable situation", with "few reasons to complain and no grounds for collective lamentations". He warned against the dangers of inflation and emphasised the need for moderation in wage increases. Yet he still felt able to announce modest reductions in taxes, introduction of a long-discussed unification of white- and blue-collar welfare regimes, a clutch of reforms of the education system, the phased introduction of free childcare, and ambitious plans for infrastructure development and for a friendlier and more open style of administration. Justice reforms were promised, particularly dealing with divorce and stalking. Poverty and weaknesses in social cohesion must be tackled, but pessimism would be out of place—"there will be no recession in Europe"—he expected growth of between 3 and 4 per cent for 2008 and 2009. The 2009 budget, which was adopted in December, looked for a 7.3 per cent increase in receipts, with expenditure rising 6.9 per cent to give a surplus of €13.2 million. The economy remained buoyant, with only a 0.1 per cent increase in unemployment over the year. One change that he set his face against was Sunday working.

Parliament ratified the Treaty of Lisbon by a large majority in May. The prime minister "profoundly" deplored Ireland's rejection of the Treaty and pressed for the process of ratification to continue. Legislation was introduced to reduce the delay before EU citizens would be eligible to vote in European and local elections. However, despite Luxembourg's stoutly pro-European commitment, it was anxious when the EU proposed a directive on the taxation of savings, insisting on preserving its traditional banking secrecy.

The country's relatively low-key politics was shaken by an unprecedented minor constitutional earthquake in December. Hitherto, bills had become law only after they had been signed by the archduke; effectively he had a veto, though that power had not been used for decades. However, when a bill to legalise euthanasia and assisted suicide came before the Chamber of Deputies, Grand Duke Henri let it be known that, as a matter of conscience, he would refuse to sign it. Though his stand earned warm words from Pope Benedict XVI, with quite remarkable speed, and amid considerable controversy, the constitution was amended in a matter of days; his signature would no longer be needed.

Martin Harrison

DENMARK—ICELAND—NORWAY—SWEDEN—FINLAND—AUSTRIA—
SWITZERLAND—EUROPEAN MINI-STATES

NORDIC COUNTRIES

Denmark

CAPITAL: Copenhagen   AREA: 43,090 sq km   POPULATION: 5,460,000 ('07)
OFFICIAL LANGUAGE: Danish   POLITICAL SYSTEM: multiparty monarchy
HEAD OF STATE: Queen Margrethe II (since Jan '72)
RULING PARTIES: Liberal Party (V) in coalition with the Conservative People's Party (KF) (since Nov '01)
HEAD OF GOVERNMENT: Prime Minister Anders Fogh Rasmussen (V) (since Dec '01)
MAIN IGO MEMBERSHIPS (NON-UN): NATO, EU, NC, CBSS, AC, OSCE, CE, OECD
CURRENCY: Danish krone (end-'08 £1=DKr7.6987, US$1=DKr5.3547)
GNI PER CAPITA: US$54,910, $36,740 at PPP ('07)

Iceland

CAPITAL: Reykjavík   AREA: 103,000 sq km   POPULATION: 311,000 ('07)
OFFICIAL LANGUAGE: Icelandic   POLITICAL SYSTEM: multiparty republic
HEAD OF STATE: President Ólafur Ragnar Grímsson (since Aug '96)
RULING PARTIES: Independence Party (IP) & Social Democratic Alliance (SF)
HEAD OF GOVERNMENT: Prime Minister Geir H. Haarde (IP) (since June '06)
MAIN IGO MEMBERSHIPS (NON-UN): NATO, EFTA/EEA, NC, AC, OSCE, CE, OECD
CURRENCY: Icelandic króna (end-'08 £1=IKr175.154, US$1=IKr121.825)
GNI PER CAPITA: US$54,100, $34,060 at PPP ('07)

Norway

CAPITAL: Oslo   AREA: 323,800 sq km   POPULATION: 4,709,000 ('07)
OFFICIAL LANGUAGE: Norwegian   POLITICAL SYSTEM: multiparty monarchy
HEAD OF STATE: King Harald V (since Jan '91)
RULING PARTIES: coalition of Labour Party (AP), Socialist Left Party (SV), and Centre Party (Sp)
HEAD OF GOVERNMENT: Prime Minister Jens Stoltenberg (AP) (since Oct '05)
MAIN IGO MEMBERSHIPS (NON-UN): NATO, EFTA/EEA, NC, CBSS, AC, OSCE, CE, OECD
CURRENCY: Norwegian krone (end-'08 £1=K10.0673, US$1=K7.0021)
GNI PER CAPITA: US$76,450, $53,690 at PPP ('07)

Sweden

CAPITAL: Stockholm   AREA: 450,290 sq km   POPULATION: 9,148,000 ('07)
OFFICIAL LANGUAGE: Swedish   POLITICAL SYSTEM: multiparty monarchy
HEAD OF STATE: King Carl XVI Gustav (since Sept '73)
RULING PARTIES: Alliance for Sweden coalition (MP, FpL, CP and KdS)
HEAD OF GOVERNMENT: Prime Minister Fredrik Reinfeldt (MUP) (since Oct '06)
MAIN IGO MEMBERSHIPS (NON-UN): EU, NC, CBSS, AC, PFP, OSCE, CE, OECD
CURRENCY: Swedish krona (end-'08 £1=K11.3697, US$1=K7.9080)
GNI PER CAPITA: US$46,060, $35,840 at PPP ('07)

Finland

CAPITAL: Helsinki   AREA: 338,150 sq km   POPULATION: 5,289,000 ('07)
OFFICIAL LANGUAGES: Finnish & Swedish   POLITICAL SYSTEM: multiparty republic
HEAD OF STATE: President Tarja Halonen (SSDP) (since February '00)
RULING PARTIES: Centre Party (KESK) in coalition with the National Coalition Party (KOK), the Greens (VIHR), and the Swedish People's Party (SFP)
HEAD OF GOVERNMENT: Prime Minister Matti Vanhanen (since June '03)
MAIN IGO MEMBERSHIPS (NON-UN): EU, NC, CBSS, AC, PFP, OSCE, CE, OECD
CURRENCY: euro (end-'08 £1=€1.0344, US$1=€0.7194)
GNI PER CAPITA: US$44,400, $35,270 at PPP ('07)

THE year 2008 was a tumultuous one in Iceland, with the country experiencing what the IMF described as "a banking crisis of extraordinary proportions". Already in the spring some economists were describing Iceland as the "canary in the coalmine". Concerns were raised about the level of bank indebtedness—estimated to be over 10 times national income—and the ability of the state to support its banks, were they to default on loans as a result of the international credit squeeze. Others were more optimistic, insisting that the banks still had "ample liquidity". By the summer, however, the IMF was making gloomy predictions about the prospects for the Icelandic economy and, more significantly, the Icelandic króna began to depreciate drastically. This had particularly severe repercussions for Icelandic homeowners, many of whom had taken out loans in foreign currency, and inflation reached levels not seen since 1990. By September, confidence in the Icelandic economy was evaporating fast and the króna continued to slide.

An acute crisis began on 29 September when the state announced that it was taking a 75 per cent stake in Glitnir, one of the country's largest banks. The collapse of the US investment bank, Lehman Brothers, earlier that month was blamed as one of the main causes for this drastic action. Glitnir's share price dropped by 85 per cent and the króna once again fell rapidly against other currencies. According to the international agency, Standard & Poor's, this measure, which cost the government at least €600 million, severely damaged Iceland's "long-term foreign currency sovereign credit rating". The following weekend, amid a mounting sense of crisis, the government entered emergency talks with the bank leaders and rumours about the health of the entire Icelandic financial system began to circulate both at home and abroad, as foreign journalists descended upon Reykjavík to cover what they called "the end of the party".

On Monday 6 October the Althing (legislature) passed an emergency bill to give the government sweeping and historically unprecedented powers of control over the banking system. Trading in six of the banks was suspended on the Icelandic stock exchange, but this could not prevent the króna losing a further 30 per cent of its value in a single day. Prime Minister Geir H. Haarde appeared on national television and acknowledged that there was now a real risk of national bankruptcy. The following day, it was announced that the government would take control of Landsbanki, the country's second largest bank.

The situation had repercussions in other European countries, especially in the UK and The Netherlands, where savers had deposited in Icelandic banks and now feared the loss of their money. The British government's own scheme guaranteed the deposits of domestic savers, but it was feared that local authorities and other corporate savers in the UK stood to lose substantial sums of money deposited in accounts held with Icelandic banks or their subsidiaries. The British and Dutch governments threatened to pursue legal action against Iceland to recover these funds and, in a move which angered many Icelanders, the British government used its anti-terrorist legislation to freeze Icelandic assets held in the UK. For their part, the leaders of the Icelandic bank, Kaupthing, blamed the British actions for helping to precipitate its collapse. Haarde attempted to defuse this diplomatic row, suggesting that the assets of the Icelandic banks were in fact sufficient to cover

British deposits, but inevitable comparisons were made with the "cod wars" between the UK and Iceland in the 1970s. Eventually the authorities of all three countries agreed that the UK and The Netherlands would make a loan to Iceland to enable it to compensate foreign holders of Icelandic accounts.

The settlement of this dispute was one of the main conditions imposed by the IMF before it could approve a US$2.1 billion loan to Iceland. This loan was also conditional upon Iceland's acceptance of an economic stabilisation programme, which included tight monetary restrictions and very high interest rates, stabilisation of the exchange rate, and a "comprehensive strategy for bank restructuring". The governments of the other four Nordic countries also declared their willingness to help, both in providing extra loans worth US$2.5 billion in total and in helping to implement the stabilisation package. Loans were also made by Poland, the UK, The Netherlands, and Germany, the whole package amounting to US$10.2 billion in total. As part of the stabilisation measures, interest rates were raised to 18 per cent and in November the prime minister asked the wage council responsible for determining the salaries of public officials to impose wage cuts of between 5 and 15 per cent for all public sector employees. Many large scale capital projects were also halted, including the construction of a new concert hall in Reykjavík. Despite this, the IMF forecasts for the economic future at the end of the year were extremely bleak: it predicted a fall in GDP of 9.6 per cent in 2009, and a rise in unemployment to 5.7 per cent. The inflation rate for 2008 was expected to be over 20 per cent. The total cost of the banking crisis was expected to amount to over 80 per cent of Iceland's GDP.

Inevitably all of this had far-reaching political consequences. Although the government blamed the international credit crunch as the main source of the country's difficulties, others, including the chairman of the Baugur group, Jón Ásgeir Jóhannesson, perhaps the best-known representative internationally of Icelandic venture capitalism, blamed the government itself for its handling of the crisis. Jóhannesson had in June been found guilty on one of 59 charges brought against him for alleged financial irregularities, following trials lasting six years. The government appealed for national unity in the face of the crisis, but popular anger could not be contained for long and by November daily demonstrations were taking place in Reykjavík. These were partly directed against the small number of high-profile entrepreneurs—like Jóhannesson—whose apparent recklessness many Icelanders blamed for the difficulties, but also the government and above all the former prime minister and governor of the Bank of Iceland, David Oddsson, who had presided over the deregulation of the banking system in 2003. By the end of November the opposition parties were calling for a vote of no confidence in the governing coalition and a national newspaper opinion poll found that 68.4 per cent of those interviewed declared themselves to be against the government. Above all, it seemed likely that the experience would provoke a rethinking of traditional Icelandic hostility towards membership of the EU and the euro, and some sources suggested that an application could even come as early as 2009.

The other Nordic countries were also affected by the international financial crisis, though not to the same extent as Iceland. At the start of 2008 economic confidence was high, and labour shortages and rising inflation seemed to be the most pressing problems facing governments. The spring and early summer period in Sweden, Denmark, and Norway was dominated by strikes in education, healthcare, childcare, and air transport, as employees in these sectors sought wage rises to offset the effects of inflation. By the end of the year, however, the situation had changed drastically and all the Nordic countries entered 2009 facing gloomy predictions of slow growth and rising unemployment.

There were serious problems in the Danish banking sector. In July, Roskilde Bank was forced to take a DKr 750 million loan from the state. Like the British bank, Northern Rock, it had become over exposed to housing loans and was severely affected by the downturn in the Danish property market, including a 10 per cent fall in Copenhagen property prices. The bank was put up for sale but failed to attract any offers, necessitating a DKr 4.5 billion buy-out by the Danish National Bank (the central bank) at the end of August. This followed an earlier merger of Bank Trelleborg and Sydbank, and further amalgamations were expected in a sector dominated by an unusually large number of small banks. In September it was reported that a further six Danish banks could be in danger of bankruptcy, as customers withdrew their savings to bring them within the limit guaranteed by the government. The state was also forced to provide liquidity to EBH Bank, the country's sixth largest. On 6 October, the government announced a scheme to guarantee all bank deposits in Denmark, as part of a deal by which the banks themselves agreed to make DKr 30 billion available to a central fund to improve liquidity.

The financial institutions of the other three Nordic countries seemed to be more robust. In Sweden and Finland this was partly because of the tighter financial regulations introduced in the wake of the banking crises of the early 1990s; indeed, the then Swedish finance minister, Bo Lundgren, was consulted in the USA and elsewhere about the Swedish response to the 1992 crisis. Norway was, as ever, partly shielded by its massive state oil fund, although this suffered substantial losses following the collapse of Lehman Brothers. The minister of finance, Kristin Halvorsen, who had ultimate responsibility for the fund's investment strategy, was strongly criticised when it was revealed that the fund had earlier in the year substantially increased its investments in Lehman Brothers. Previously, the fund had been cited at home and abroad as an example of enlightened long-term policy, particularly for its investments in schemes to reduce Norway's carbon emissions. In October, the Parliament passed a crisis package costing NKr350 billion, which was intended to improve liquidity and confidence in the banking sector.

Towards the end of 2008, however, it was becoming clear that none of the Nordic countries was immune from the impact of the global economic recession. Indeed, as small, open economies highly dependent on exports they could hardly avoid it, and in July Denmark became the first European country to confirm that it was in recession. It was followed in November by Sweden, where 50,000 jobs were lost in the last quarter of 2008. Car manufacturers Volvo and Saab (owned by Ford and General Motors respectively) faced particular difficulties. In December the Swedish government agreed to make up to SwKr25 billion available in the form of emergency credit and loan guarantees, together with some funds to support research into more environmentally-friendly car manufacture, but ruled out state ownership in the sector. By the end of the year the Swedish employment agency was predicting that unemployment would rise to 9 per cent in 2010, with young people and those born outside Sweden likely to be the worst affected. Moreover, as a result of controversial policies introduced after the election of the centre right government in 2006, it was reported that now only one-third of all employees were members of unemployment insurance funds (the so-called "a-kassa"), so this situation would place a heavy burden on social benefits.

Finland's relative economic stability was partly attributed to its membership of the eurozone, though here too there were signs of recession by the end of the year. The national statistics bureau reported signs of extremely weak consumer confidence before Christmas, as a result of fears of rising unemployment. Like Sweden, Norway, and Denmark, the Finnish government introduced expansionary fiscal policies intended to stimulate demand. A large part of these packages was based on public investments in transport and healthcare and (in Sweden) some tax relief for the construction sector. In both Norway and Sweden it seemed likely that the recession would have substantial political consequences, with general elections due in 2009 and 2010 respectively. Like his British counterpart, Gordon Brown, the Labour prime minister of Norway, Jens Stoltenberg, seemed to respond to the crisis with considerable confidence. In Sweden, the centre left parties—the Social Democrats, the Greens, and the Left—announced the formation of a new electoral coalition in December, raising the possibility of the emergence of a more permanent left-right bloc arrangement in Swedish politics. It seemed likely that the economic crisis would also spark fresh debates in Sweden and Denmark over entry to the eurozone.

Finland experienced another fatal school shooting, less than 12 months after the tragedy in Jokela in November 2007 (see AR 2008, p. 56). On 23 September a 22-year old male student shot and killed 11 people, including himself, at a vocational college in Kauhajoki in western Finland. Just before the incident the student had posted videos with violent content on the Internet site, "YouTube". It was later revealed that he had been interviewed by the police in relation to these only a day before the shootings, but no action had been taken. The shootings provoked renewed debate about Finland's laws on firearms and relatively high rate of gun ownership, as a result of which the government promised to draft new legislation tightening the law.

The summer conflict between Russia and Georgia was followed closely in Finland, but politicians of all parties agreed that the crisis did not require any change in Finland's security policy regarding its giant neighbour and there were no signs of increased popular support for NATO membership.

Greenlanders went to the polls on 25 November to vote in a referendum on self rule. The result was a resounding majority for increased autonomy from Denmark, with 75.54 per cent voting in favour, and 23.57 against. The result was welcomed with great emotion by the head of local government in Greenland, Hans Enoksen, and also by the Danish prime minister, Anders Fogh Rasmussen. Under the new arrangements, due to come into effect in June 2009, Greenland would take a greater share of its oil revenues, against a corresponding reduction in its annual subsidy from Denmark, and would also resume responsibility for the police, courts, and coastguard. The Inuit language, Kalaallisut, was also likely to replace Danish as the official language.

Mary Hilson

AUSTRIA

CAPITAL: Vienna   AREA: 83,870 sq km   POPULATION: 8,315,000 ('07)
OFFICIAL LANGUAGE: German   POLITICAL SYSTEM: multiparty republic
HEAD OF STATE: Federal President Heinz Fischer (since July '04)
RULING PARTIES: "Grand Coalition" of Social Democratic Party (SPÖ) and People's Party (ÖVP)
HEAD OF GOVERNMENT: Federal Chancellor Werner Faymann (SPÖ) (since Oct '08)
MAIN IGO MEMBERSHIPS (NON-UN): EU, OSCE, CE, PFP, OECD
CURRENCY: euro (end-'08 £1=€1.0344, US$1=€0.7194)
GNI PER CAPITA: US$42,700, $38,090 at PPP ('07)

OVER the course of the 20 years since 1989, it was not unusual for the enigmatic politician Jörg Haider to grab the headlines in Austria. The former leader of the right-wing Freedom Party (FPÖ) made all the news bulletins for the final time on the evening of 11 October. Speeding drunk along a dangerous road (where he had narrowly avoided death in the past), Haider careered off the highway and into a concrete pole. His death, at the age of 58, sent a shock wave through Austrian politics (see Obituary). Compounding the drama was the admission, by Haider's deputy, Stefan Petzner, in an Austrian Radio interview on 12 October, that they had had a "special relationship that went far beyond friendship".

Quite what effect this would have was another matter. Haider died just 13 days after the most recent in a depressing series of all too frequent Austrian federal elections (the poll took place on 28 September). This latest election came less than two years after the previous one (see AR 2007, pp. 58-59), as the unhappy "Grand Coalition" of Social Democrats (SPÖ) and the Austrian People's Party (ÖVP), under Federal Chancellor Alfred Gusenbauer (ÖVP), finally—and not unexpectedly—collapsed. Both parties performed dismally, recording their lowest ever vote shares in a national election, which was unsurprising given their ineffectiveness in government over the previous 18 months.

Indeed, both Haider's original creation, the FPÖ, and its far right competitor, Austria's Future (BZÖ), which Haider was leading by the time of the September election, performed remarkably well. The election result should once again be understood as a protest at the ineffectual grand coalitions formed by the two large centre parties, rather than a fundamental shift to the right in Austrian politics. However, even though this protest was not in itself a surprise, the BZÖ's remarkably good showing (10.7 per cent) and the ÖVP's weak showing (25.9 per cent) did cause major shockwaves.

Haider could (and did) also quite legitimately claim credit for the BZÖ's revival. Although he was the party's founder, Haider only took over the leadership of the BZÖ in August 2008, after the previous leader, Peter Westenthaler, was convicted of giving false testimony in a legal case. The result was subsequently (another) great success for Haider. However, it did little to clarify where Austrian politics was heading and, indeed, by the end of 2008 little genuine progress had been made towards forming a government. The most probable result seemed likely to be yet another grand coalition, as Werner Faymann, the Social Democrats' leader, had ruled out a coalition with either of the far right parties and major policy discrepancies existed between the SPÖ and the only other party to win seats in the Nationalrat (the lower house of the bicameral legislature), the Greens. The future of the negotiations on forming a new coalition would therefore hinge to a large extent on the direction in which the new leadership of the ÖVP wished to take the party.

Despite reasonable economic statistics—higher than normal inflation figures in 2008 (of over 3 per cent) were matched by decent (when compared with other European economies) economic growth forecasts (of around 2 per cent)—the federal government remained nothing less than a shambles for the first half of the year. Voters grew increasingly tired of the bickering and arguing between the main parties, and there was a palpable feeling of relief when the ÖVP leader, Wilhelm Molterer, finally pulled the People's Party out of government on 7 July.

Molterer no doubt hoped that the opinion polls, which showed his party in the lead, would remain constant until polling day. He was to be mistaken. As the tempo of the campaign quickened, the Social Democrats overhauled the ÖVP and on 28 September polled over 4 per cent more of the vote than its largest competitor. The charismatic Faymann, who had replaced the rather dour and, by the end of his term in office, exceptionally unpopular Gusenbauer as chairman of the SPÖ, did much to transform the party's position with his 5-point plan for boosting incomes in the face of creeping inflation. Reductions in the rate of VAT, the abolition of student tuition fees, increases in family allowances, and a subsidy for healthcare all proved popular and these policy measures played a significant role in reviving social democratic fortunes.

Away from politics, Austrian society was appalled by the case of a father, Josef Fritzl, who was arrested in April when it was discovered that he had kept his daughter, Elisabeth Fritzl, imprisoned in a cellar beneath his house in Amstetten since 1984 and fathered seven children by her. Three of the children were raised by Fritzl's wife, Rosmarie Fritzl, who was apparently unaware of her daughter's whereabouts, convinced by her husband's explanation that the children had been abandoned on their doorstep by Elisabeth, who had joined a sect. The other three children (one child died shortly after birth) had remained in the cellar with their mother. It was when one of these children, 19-year old Kerstin Fritzl, became seriously ill and was admitted to hospital, that the police were alerted. By the end of the year, Fritzl's trial (on charges of murder, rape, slavery, incest, imprisonment and abuse) had not yet begun, apparently because not enough jurors could be found who were willing to hear the evidence.

Dan Hough

SWITZERLAND

CAPITAL: Berne   AREA: 41,280 sq km   POPULATION: 7,550,000 ('07)
OFFICIAL LANGUAGES: German, French, Italian & Rhaeto-Romanic   POLITICAL SYSTEM: multiparty
republic
HEAD OF STATE: seven-member Federal Council
RULING PARTIES: Coalition of Swiss People's Party (SVP/UDC), Social Democratic Party (SPS/PSS),
    Radical Democratic Party (FDP/PRD) and Christian Democratic People's Party (CVP/PDC)
HEAD OF GOVERNMENT: Pascal Couchepin (FDP) (president of the Federal Council for 2008)
MAIN IGO MEMBERSHIPS (NON-UN): OECD, OSCE, CE, EFTA, PFP, Francophonie
CURRENCY: Swiss franc (end-'08 £1=SFr1.5303, US$1=SFr1.0644)
GNI PER CAPITA: US$59,880, $43,080 at PPP ('07)

WITH even the Swiss starting to feel the economic pinch, it was clear that the
global economy was facing real problems. Not that 2008 was a year of large
downturns or recessions, but economic development in the Alpine state undoubtedly took a turn for the worse. Inflation declined (as, thanks to the credit crunch,
it did in most countries), but by the end of the year it was still hovering at around
the 2.5 per cent mark. Growth was minimal (nearer 1.5 than 2 per cent) and the
forecast for 2009 even worse (barely 0.5 per cent). The financial crises that developed through the latter half of 2008 also left Swiss financial institutions in unusually delicate positions.

Political life in Switzerland was also thrown into a state of turmoil in late 2008
when the defence minister, Samuel Schmid of the Swiss People's Party (SVP),
announced his resignation on 12 November. Schmid's downfall came about when
it was revealed that he had failed to announce—both in public and, more perti-
nently, to any of his cabinet colleagues in private—that he knew about sexual misconduct allegations against Roland Nef, who became head of the Swiss armed
forces (thanks to a recommendation from Schmid) early in 2008. As ever, the
actual details of the indiscretion soon became a secondary issue; it was the nature
of Schmid's cover up that ultimately forced him to step down.

A ministerial resignation was normally nothing more than an uncomfortable
hiccup for a government, but Switzerland's delicate power-sharing constitutional
settlement rendered Schmid's departure particularly difficult. More specifically,
it offered the country's largest opposition party, the boisterously right wing SVP,
an opportunity to return to national government.

The SVP, out of national government and in opposition for most of 2008 (a
position that, given its populist and oppositionist style, remained its natural
home), was nonetheless never far from the political headlines and its campaign
to force Schmid out was only the tip of the iceberg. The departure of the SVP's
talismanic leader, Christoph Blocher, from the cabinet in late 2007 did not prevent the party from setting the political agenda throughout 2008. Eveline
Widmer-Schlumpf, a much more moderate member of the SVP, replaced
Blocher as the SVP's representative in government alongside Schmid, but she
did so against the wishes of her party and was bundled out of the parliamentary
party altogether. She subsequently joined fellow SVP member Schmid in
falling very much out of love with a party that was still infatuated with long-
time leader Blocher; the two party dissidents (Schmid and Widmer-Schlumpf)

ultimately helped form a new, conservative (although much more moderate) political organisation independent of the SVP, the Conservative Democratic Party (BDP).

Switzerland's unique model of direct democracy threw up its usual bag of interesting initiatives, with the SVP once more at the centre of some of the more controversial ones. On 1 July the Swiss rejected a proposal to tighten citizenship rules. In the referendum, 64 per cent said "no" to what was one of the SVP's most dearly held causes. Blocher also managed to turn a proposed "no" to the expansion of freedom of movement laws within the EU in July into a "yes" by November, much to the amazement of the party rank and file, illustrating once more his ability to perform verbal gymnastics like no other politician in recent Swiss memory. By the end of 2008, however, the SVP was once again officially represented in the Federal Council, and therefore constrained, at least theoretically, by government responsibility. Whether the appointment of Ueli Maurer (SVP) in place of Schmid on 10 December would prompt Blocher to moderate his political behaviour remained to be seen.

By the end of the summer, party political machinations were being eclipsed by the rapidly developing global financial crisis. In mid-October, the financial services company UBS—already in crisis—was only saved from bankruptcy by massive state intervention to the tune of SFr68 million. One person not involved in the discussions surrounding the bailout was Finance Minister Hans-Rudolf Merz. He collapsed on 21 September and had to be rushed into hospital to have an emergency heart operation. Merz recovered, and by the beginning of November had resumed his duties. It was Merz who found himself defending the state's decision to save a private company on the basis that it helped to secure Switzerland's reputation as a financial centre. More prickly were the criticisms about bonuses paid to underperforming UBS managers and the lack of any apparent democratic oversight in the government's decision-making processes: the decision to save UBS had been made in late summer by emergency decree over the heads of the Swiss people, who only found out about it on 16 October.

Dan Hough

EUROPEAN MINI-STATES

Andorra

CAPITAL: Andorra la Vella   AREA: 470 sq km   POPULATION: 67,000 ('07)
OFFICIAL LANGUAGE: Catalan   POLITICAL SYSTEM: multiparty monarchy (co-principality)
HEADS OF STATE: President Nicolas Sarkozy of France & Bishop Joan Enric Vives of Urgel (co-princes)
RULING PARTIES: National Andorran Coalition, dominated by Liberal Party of Andorra (PLA)
HEAD OF GOVERNMENT: President of Executive Council Albert Pintat Santolària (PLA), (since May '05)
MAIN IGO MEMBERSHIPS (NON-UN): CE, OSCE
CURRENCY: euro (end-'08 £1=€1.0344, US$1=€0.7194)
GNI PER CAPITA: high income: US$11,456 or more ('07 est), -

Holy See (Vatican City State)

CAPITAL: Vatican City   AREA: 0.44 sq km   POPULATION: 890
OFFICIAL LANGUAGES: Italian & Latin   POLITICAL SYSTEM: non-party papacy
HEAD OF STATE: Pope Benedict XVI (since April '05)
HEAD OF GOVERNMENT: Secretary of State Cardinal Tarcisio Bertone (since Sept '06)
MAIN IGO MEMBERSHIPS: OSCE. The Holy See is not a member of the UN.
CURRENCY: euro (end-'08 £1=€1.0344, US$1=€0.7194)
GNI PER CAPITA: n/a

Liechtenstein

CAPITAL: Vaduz   AREA: 160 sq km   POPULATION: 35,000 ('07)
OFFICIAL LANGUAGE: German   POLITICAL SYSTEM: multiparty monarchy
HEAD OF STATE: Prince Hans Adam II (since Nov '89)
RULING PARTIES: coalition of the Progressive Citizens' Party (FBP) and the Patriot Union (VU) (since April '05)
HEAD OF GOVERNMENT: Prime Minister Otmar Hasler (since April '01)
MAIN IGO MEMBERSHIPS (NON-UN): EFTA/EEA, OSCE, CE
CURRENCY: Swiss franc (end-'08 £1=SFr1.5303, US$1=SFr1.0644)
GNI PER CAPITA: high income: US$11,456 or more ('07 est), -

Monaco

CAPITAL: Monaco-Ville   AREA: 2 sq km   POPULATION: 33,000
OFFICIAL LANGUAGE: French   POLITICAL SYSTEM: non-party monarchy
HEAD OF STATE: Prince Albert II (since April '05)
RULING PARTY: the Union for Monaco (UNAM) (since Feb '03)
HEAD OF GOVERNMENT: Minister of State Patrick Leclercq (since Jan '00)
MAIN IGO MEMBERSHIPS (NON-UN): OSCE, Francophonie
CURRENCY: euro (end-'08 £1=€1.0344, US$1=€0.7194)
GNI PER CAPITA: high income: US$11,456 or more ('07 est), -

San Marino

CAPITAL: San Marino   AREA: 60 sq km   POPULATION: 29,000 ('07)
OFFICIAL LANGUAGE: Italian   POLITICAL SYSTEM: multiparty republic
HEADS OF STATE AND GOVERNMENT: Captains-Regent Ernesto Benedettini and Assunta Meloni (Oct '08 to April '09)
RULING PARTIES: Pact for San Marino (PSM) four-party coalition
MAIN IGO MEMBERSHIPS (NON-UN): OSCE, CE
CURRENCY: euro (end-'08 £1=€1.0344, US$1=€0.7194)
GNI PER CAPITA: US$45,130, $37,080 at PPP ('07 est based on regression)

FOR several years the Andorran authorities had been attempting to move the economy from its narrow focus on tourism and finance. Legislation adopted in April was designed to help the conversion of the economy. Foreign investors would now be allowed to control 100 per cent of companies in many economic sectors; in others, maximum holdings were increased from 33 to 49 per cent. Corporation tax and value added tax would be introduced. These measures were also intended to improve relations with Spain, which had imposed a 25 per cent tax on services provided by Andorran companies, and with the Organisation for Economic Co-operation and Development (OECD), which considered Andorra an "unco-operative tax haven". However, the economy was showing signs of weakness even before the international financial crisis. Tax receipts for 2007 were already €68 million in deficit, due to a decline in construction, and house prices fell 15 per cent in 2008, with public finances deteriorating still further.

The Holy See was a very active participant on the international scene, with a profusion of statements on world problems including bioethics, the global financial crisis (which required a "new economic order"), the connection between poverty and world peace, ratification of the convention banning cluster bombs, and the elimination of nuclear weapons; and refusal to accept a UN proposal that would have given gender identity and sexual orientation human rights protection. In a policy paper at the end of the year Pope Benedict XVI laid much of the blame for the international financial crisis on "off-shore centres", including tax havens. However, a senior official of the Vatican bank assured that the Holy See's own finances were unshaken because it had avoided speculative investments. The pope spoke much about the environment, suggesting that it was a cause upon which different faiths might find common ground. He worked hard at raising dialogue with Muslims from its low point in 2006 (see AR 2007, pp. 61; 475). Aware of Jewish sensitivities, he defended Pope Pius XII's actions during World War II but imposed a period of reflection before making a decision on his sainthood.

It emerged in February that the German tax authorities had paid a former employee of LGT Bank, owned by "the princely House of Liechtenstein", €4.2 million for hundreds of confidential account details that he took from the bank. The German authorities were pursuing tax defaulters and pressing the EU for action against the tax havens. Questions were raised within Germany about the ethics and legality of the action, the regent of Liechtenstein described the investigations as an "attack" on Liechtenstein, and the chief prosecutor of Liechtenstein initiated legal action over "violations of company secrecy for a foreign country". The royal family cancelled an exhibition of paintings in Munich as long as "the implementation of the basic principle of the rule of law appears questionable". However, cooler heads soon advised negotiation "with our good neighbours". In December the USA and Liechtenstein moved towards an agreement on banking clients that would diminish the appeal of Liechtenstein to rich Americans.

Monaco's head of state, Prince Albert II, was greatly concerned at being lumped with Liechtenstein as an unco-operative tax haven. He argued that Monaco operated a completely different system. Monegasque banking institutions were controlled by the French Banking Commission and the Bank of France (France's central bank). However, Monaco remained on the OECD black list because it refused to sign an agreement on sharing information about individuals' tax affairs. The principality's finance minister dismissed this as a technicality.

In November, the Council of Europe's group of states against corruption published its report on Monaco. In essence, while it found very little corruption, in its low-key language it laid bare a system in which little or no thought had been given to issues relating to corruption; essentially there was almost nothing in place to prevent, detect, and combat corruption, or to provide officials with appropriate training, though there were the beginnings of policies to provide stricter penalties and protect the confidentiality of investigations. Monaco should adopt an anti-corruption work programme to identify what further reforms were needed to raise awareness of the importance of combating corruption, said the report.

Elections to San Marino's Grand & General Council (legislature) were held on 9 November. For the first time the election was fought between two broad coalitions, rather than a host of individual parties. It was hoped that the newly introduced threshold of 3.5 per cent for representation would promote greater political stability. On a turnout of 68.48 per cent the centre-right Pact for San Marino gained 35 of the 60 seats with 11,373 votes (54.22 per cent) and the centre-left Reforms and Freedom coalition took the remaining 25 seats with 9,602 votes (45.78 per cent).

Martin Harrison

SPAIN—GIBRALTAR—PORTUGAL—MALTA—GREECE—CYPRUS—TURKEY

SPAIN

CAPITAL: Madrid   AREA: 505,370 sq km   POPULATION: 44,879,000 ('07)
OFFICIAL LANGUAGE: Spanish   POLITICAL SYSTEM: multiparty monarchy
HEAD OF STATE: King Juan Carlos (since Nov '75)
RULING PARTY: Spanish Socialist Workers' Party (PSOE)
HEAD OF GOVERNMENT: Prime Minister José Luis Rodríguez Zapatero (since April '04)
MAIN IGO MEMBERSHIPS (NON-UN): NATO, EU, OSCE, CE, OECD
CURRENCY: euro (end-'08 £1=€1.0344, US$1=€0.7194)
GNI PER CAPITA: US$29,450, $30,110 at PPP ('07)

THE Spanish Socialist Workers' Party (PSOE) of José Luis Rodríguez Zapatero was returned to power at the 9 March general election and spent the year grappling with an economy entering recession after 14 years of sustained growth. The Socialists won 43.8 per cent of the vote and 169 of the 350 seats in the Congress of Deputies (the lower house of the bicameral legislature), five more than in 2004. The right wing Popular Party (PP) polled 39.9 per cent and took 154 seats, six more than in 2004. The conservative nationalist Catalan party, Convergence and Union (CiU), finished third with an unchanged 10 seats, while the Basque Nationalist Party (PNV) dropped one to six. The main losers were the Catalan Republican Left (ERC), which supported independence for Catalonia and only won three seats, five fewer than in 2004, and the United Left (IU), which won two seats, three fewer than in the previous contest. The other six seats went to the Galician Nationalist Bloc (two), the Canarian Coalition (two), and one each for Progress and Democracy Union, and Navarre Yes. The Socialists and the PP together won almost 84 per cent of the vote, up from 80 per cent in 2004.

The Socialists benefited from a still booming economy at the time of the election and from a lacklustre PP campaign, which consisted of little more than relentlessly attacking the government while offering few constructive alternatives. Although the result meant that Mariano Rajoy Brey, the PP's leader, lost a general election for the second time, he remained the party's president. The Socialists' victory also showed that Zapatero was not an "accidental" prime minister, as the PP claimed, catapulted into office by the deadly Islamists bombings, which had occurred two days before the March 2004 election (see AR 2004, pp. 64-65), in response to the PP government's backing of the US-led invasion of Iraq.

For the first time ever, there were more female than male ministers in the new administration. Nine of the 17 ministers were women, two of whom, Bibiano Aído Almagro and Cristina Garmendia Mendizibál, respectively occupied the newly created ministries of equality and science, and innovation. Another woman, Carme Chacón Piqueras, was named defence minister. María Teresa Fernández de la Vega remained as first deputy prime minister and minister of the presidency; Pedro Solbes Mira as second deputy prime minister and economy and finance minister; and Miguel Ángel Moratinos Cuyaubé as foreign minister.

The election was overshadowed by the killing by the terrorist group, Basque Homeland and Freedom (ETA), of a former Socialist town councillor, Isaías Carrasco Miguel, in Mondragón. It came after a court in Madrid sentenced 47 people to prison terms of up to 20 years for their links to ETA. The Communist Party of the Basque Lands (PCTV) and Basque Nationalist Action (ANV) were barred from taking part in the election for having similar links; the activities of the two parties were suspended for three years. ETA had killed six people since ending its 15-month ceasefire in June 2007, four of them during 2008.

The Socialists had put out feelers for some kind of political negotiation with ETA during the truce (the details of which were never made clear), a move virulently opposed by the PP. However, the PP eased its stance against the Socialists after Prime Minister Zapatero stepped up the pursuit of ETA activists. Among those arrested by Spanish and French police in France were Javier López Peña, known as Thierry, who had been on the run for 25 years, and Garikoitz Aspiazu Rubina, said to be responsible for ETA's military strategy since it ended its ceasefire. The Constitutional Court declared illegal the referendum that the Basque government wanted to hold on 25 October, under which voters in the region (not in Spain as a whole) would have been asked whether they supported a process aimed at negotiating an end to ETA's 40 years of political violence and the region's right of self-determination.

The fraught relations between the central government and some of the autonomous regions, particularly the Basque Country and Catalonia, were epitomised by the discord produced by new lyrics for the national anthem. The previous lyrics had been dropped after the death of the dictator General Francisco

Franco Bahamonde in 1975, leaving the anthem wordless. The proposed new lyrics were abandoned after objections to including the words "Viva España" (Long live Spain) in the opening line. The next line, "We all sing together with different voices and one heart", was not sufficient to calm passions.

In foreign policy, Spain and Morocco ended their standoff triggered by the visit in November 2007 of King Juan Carlos to Spain's North African enclaves of Ceuta and Melilla, territories claimed by Morocco (see AR 2008, p. 65). The number of Spanish peacekeeping troops in Afghanistan was increased to close to 800; the ceiling of 3,000 troops abroad at any one time, set in 2005, was raised to 7,700 as of 2009. Relations with Turkey, whose EU membership application the government actively backed, were upgraded with the holding of an annual summit from 2009. Barcelona won its bid to be the headquarters of the Union for the Mediterranean, the new body grouping European and southern Mediterranean countries. The initiative that grabbed the headlines, however, was Prime Minister Zapatero's successful campaign to get Spain invited to the November G-20 summit on financial reform in Washington, DC. Despite being the world's eighth largest economy, Spain had not been invited as it was neither a G-8 country nor one of the nations (mainly emerging countries) that formed the G-20 during the 1990s.

The economy, which slowed down at a much faster pace than anyone expected because of the impact of the global financial crisis, dominated the new government's agenda. The country's banking system escaped largely unscathed because of almost a decade of very tight supervision and regulation by the Bank of Spain (the central bank); the accumulation of high levels of provisions to cover non-performing loans; no direct exposure to the US "subprime" debt crisis; and few toxic assets. Indeed, Spain's banking system was applauded in the international financial community as an example to follow. However, there were home grown problems, particularly in the residential construction sector, which slumped massively after a decade long boom and was the main driver of the steep rise in the unemployment rate, from 8.3 per cent at the end of 2007 to close to 13 per cent. The estimated stock of unsold homes stood at more than one million at the end of 2008.

In a bid to create jobs government pumped €11 billion into infrastructure, the car industry, and other areas, as well as providing an income tax rebate of €400, mortgage relief, and credit lines for businesses. It also created a €50 billion fund to buy assets from banks that needed liquidity and agreed to underwrite up to €100 billion in new bank debt.

GDP growth decelerated from 3.7 per cent in 2007 to just over 1 per cent; in the second half of the year the economy entered recession for the first time since 1993. Inflation was 1.4 per cent, the lowest level in a decade, the current account deficit remained at around 10 per cent, and the general government budget registered a deficit of more than 3 per cent of GDP, its first deficit since 2005 and breaching the EU ceiling. The Ibex-35 index of the Madrid stock exchange dropped 39.4 per cent.

The country's large immigrant community was particularly hard hit by the crash in the construction sector. Foreigners in Spain officially accounted for more than 11 per cent of the total population, which stood at 46.1 million at the beginning of 2008 according to government estimates, with the largest numbers coming from

Romania (729,000) and Morocco (645,000). The government sought to encourage jobless immigrants to return to their country of origin. Those legally resident in Spain and paying social security were entitled to receive their unemployment benefit in the form of a lump sum if they agreed to surrender their residence and work permits and sign a commitment not to return to Spain for three years. It was believed that most immigrants eligible for the deal would find ways to tough it out in Spain rather than return to an equally uncertain future in their own countries.

The downturn in the domestic market did not dent the profits of Spain's main companies and banks as much as it might have done because of the significant investments abroad made by them in recent years to increase and diversify revenue sources and risk origin. The number of Spanish companies in the Fortune Global 500 (the annual ranking by *Fortune* magazine of the top 500 corporations worldwide) increased by two to 11. The stock of outward investment stood at US$636.8 billion at the end of 2007 and represented 44.3 per cent of GDP, larger in these terms not only than Italy's (24.7 per cent) but also Germany's (37.3 per cent). Santander, the largest bank in the eurozone by market capitalisation, snapped up two failed UK banks (Alliance & Leicester and Bradford & Bingley) which, coupled with the one it bought in 2004 (Abbey), catapulted it into a top spot in the UK in terms of deposits (10 per cent of market share) and branches (1,286). Santander also acquired the 75 per cent of Sovereign Bancorp, based in Philadelphia, that it did not already own for a tenth of the price agreed when it took a minority stake three years previously. BBVA, Spain's second largest bank, doubled its stake in China's state-owned Citis Group to 10.1 per cent and Telefónica, the world's third largest telecommunications group by market value, acquired a further 5.7 per cent of China Netcom, giving it a significant position in the new company resulting from the merger of the mobile operator and Netcom, China's second largest fixed line operator.

Spain continued to grapple with the legacy of the Franco dictatorship. Baltasar Garzón, a maverick judge, was forced to abandon his controversial probe into the disappearance of more than 100,000 people during the 1936-39 Spanish Civil War and the ensuing 36-year dictatorship of General Franco after a court overruled him and amidst protests from the PP and the Roman Catholic Church. He had ordered exhumations from 25 mass graves containing the bodies of those shot by firing squad or on the orders of summary tribunals. The matter was left in the hands of the 62 courts in the areas where the graves were located. Garzón said that the amnesty for Francoist officials did not apply to the crimes he was investigating as they were crimes against humanity; he argued that if the Allies had followed the same reasoning as the public prosecutor's office, the "horrors of Nazism would not have been prosecuted". The last public statue of Franco on the Spanish mainland was removed from a square in Santander, in accordance with a provision in the 2007 Law of Historical Memory that called for the removal of symbols of repression under the dictatorship (see AR 2008, p. 66). Franco's heirs lost their battle with the regional government of Galicia and were ordered to open up El Pazo de Meirás, his summer estate, to the public for four days per month.

William Chislett

GIBRALTAR

CAPITAL: Gibraltar   AREA: 6.5 sq km   POPULATION: 28,779 ('05)
OFFICIAL LANGUAGE: English   POLITICAL SYSTEM: semi-autonomous UK overseas territory
HEAD OF STATE: Queen Elizabeth II
GOVERNOR-GENERAL: Sir Francis Richards (since May '03)
RULING PARTY: Gibraltar Social Democrats (GSD)
HEAD OF GOVERNMENT: Chief Minister Peter Caruana (since May '96)
CURRENCY: Gibraltar pound (end-'08 UK£=Gib£1.0000, US$1=Gib£0.6955)
GNI PER CAPITA: n/a

THE European Court of First Instance authorised Gibraltar to levy an effective corporate tax rate of only 15 per cent of profits on offshore companies after it threw
out an earlier ruling by the European Commission that the territory's tax reforms
amounted to illegal state aid. The Court ruled in December that the Commission
had gone beyond the limits of its review by deciding, in effect, that Gibraltar was
a "region" of the UK and had no powers to set its own tax regime.

In July, the UK, Spain, and Gibraltar held their second ministerial meeting of
the Forum of Dialogue on Gibraltar, set up in 2004 to air longstanding grievances
between the three parties (see AR 2004, p. 67), and agreed to co-operate on six
areas: the environment; maritime communications; judicial, customs and police
matters; financial services and taxation; visa related issues; and education.

In other signs of co-operation, the UK government paid the second tranche of
the lump sum to Spanish pensioners who had worked in Gibraltar; and the government of Gibraltar made available premises for Spain's Cervantes Institute, over
which Spain's flag would be able to fly on the Rock for the first time.

William Chislett

PORTUGAL

CAPITAL: Lisbon   AREA: 92,120 sq km   POPULATION: 10,608,000 ('07)
OFFICIAL LANGUAGE: Portuguese   POLITICAL SYSTEM: multiparty republic
HEAD OF STATE: President Aníbal Cavaco Silva (PSD) (since March '06)
RULING PARTY: Socialist Party (PS) (since March '05)
HEAD OF GOVERNMENT: Prime Minister José Sócrates (PS) (since March '05)
MAIN IGO MEMBERSHIPS (NON-UN): NATO, OECD, EU, OSCE, CE, CPLP
CURRENCY: euro (end-'08 £1=€1.0344, US$1=€0.7194)
GNI PER CAPITA: US$18,950, $20,640 at PPP ('07)

PORTUGAL'S recession-hit economy was again brought into focus in 2008. The
Socialist Party (PS) government sought to introduce groundbreaking reforms on
labour legislation but struggled to contain mass demonstrations from teachers and
truckers alike. All of these difficulties were compounded by the ongoing investigation into the disappearance of British toddler Madeleine McCann in 2007 and
the culmination of the Casa Pia criminal trial into an alleged paedophile ring.
Alongside this were corruption scandals surrounding leading football clubs, as
well as growing levels of poverty, a falling birth rate, increased infant mortality,
and a poorly performing health service, with the result that widespread uncertainty
gripped Portuguese society.

In the spring, the government pushed ahead with proposals to introduce its "flexicurity" labour practice. In April, Minister of Labour and Social Welfare José Vieira da Silva outlined a policy that was designed to combine flexible conditions for employers to hire and fire workers more easily but also provide for better worker security through increased unemployment benefits. The proposals proved controversial and provoked widespread protest throughout central and northern parts of the country. In June, the truck drivers' union, ANTRAM, organised a week-long blockade of fuel stations in opposition to rising transport costs for haulers. The action brought many areas close to standstill and forced the government into concessions. These included a reduction of toll duties for haulage trucks at night and a freezing of heavy goods vehicle taxes for the next three budgets, as well as investment in professional driver training schemes and the introduction of particle filters on lorries as standard. In the autumn, teachers added their voices to the cacophony of public protest by striking for the suspension of government imposed job evaluation measures. Once again, unions organised a series of national and regional expressions of dissent, culminating in over 100,000 teachers staying away from schools in a nationwide walkout on 6 December.

For much of the year, international media attention focused on the mystery surrounding Madeleine McCann (see AR 2008, p. 68). After a 14-month investigation costing an estimated £2.5 million, Portuguese police admitted having made little progress nor found any evidence to support their suspicions against the girl's parents. On 21 July, Attorney General Fernando José Pinto Monteiro formally shelved the case and lifted Kate and Gerry McCann's arguido (official suspect) status. A third arguido, Robert Murat, was also cleared, with the case remaining open but unsolved. For much of the rest of the year, the McCann family's legal representatives pored over the release of 11,000 pages of police files, searching for clues to the child's disappearance. Controversy surrounding the case was further fuelled in August with the publication of Gonçalo Amaral's book, *A Verdade da Mentira* (*The Truth of the Lie*). In it, the former leading detective on the case alleged that the toddler died in the couple's holiday apartment as the result of an unspecified "tragic accident". In other speculative accounts, newspapers suggested that an international paedophile network had abducted the child. As a result, media reports drew parallels with the Casa Pia court case (see AR 2004, p. 69), which closed on 9 December. After four years of proceedings (the longest in Portuguese legal history), seven suspects accused of sexually abusing 32 minors saw their trial draw to an end. Those indicted included a driver at the Casa Pia children's home, as well as a former diplomat, a TV presenter, a doctor, a lawyer, a business supplier, and a woman in whose house the alleged abuse took place. The high profile of those arrested and subsequent revelations shook Portuguese society to its foundations, with the long awaited verdicts expected in February 2009.

Environmental issues assumed importance with the announcement that the number of forest fires (an annual scourge) had been halved in 2008. More significantly, on 2 December, Europe's largest onshore wind farm became operational. Based in Viana do Castelo, 120 windmills helped to generate 1 per cent of Portu-

gal's total energy needs and was enough to power 300,000 homes in the neighbouring Minho region. When combined with advances in provision of solar electricity generation (see AR 2008, p. 69) and inauguration of the world's first commercial wave power plant in the Atlantic Ocean off Aguçadoura, the country
forged forward in its bid to become a major player in the renewable energies field.

Public gloom was heightened by limited sporting success at the 2008 European
Football Championship (Portugal was eliminated at the quarter final stage, losing
2-3 to Germany), as well as by the corruption scandals that enveloped two of the
country's leading football clubs and several referees. In May, FC Porto was docked
six points and fined €150,000 for match fixing and bribery of referees in the 2003-
04 championship winning season. In addition, club president Jorge Nuno Pinto da
Costa was suspended from football for two years and informed that he was to face
criminal charges. As part of a protracted investigation ("operation golden whistle",
see AR 2004, p. 69), Boavista FC was also found guilty of bribing match officials
and, in addition to being fined €180,000, suffered demotion to the second division.
In a further blow, in September, authorities investigating alleged tax evasion seized
Boavista's Bessa stadium. The ground was subsequently put up for sale, leaving
many supporters to reflect on the malaise afflicting the national sport.

As the year ended, the global financial crisis cast an additional shadow over
Portugal's economy. In common with many other cities, Lisbon's stock market
suffered its worst ever performance on 6 October when 10 per cent was wiped off
the value of stocks and shares. In swift response, Prime Minister José Sócrates's
PS government announced a halving of company tax (from 25 to 12.5 per cent)
alongside increased credit facilities and grants of low interest loans to small and
medium enterprises. While these bold measures were widely welcomed, projections from the Organisation for Economic Co-operation and Development
(OECD) and INE (the Portuguese national statistics institute) suggested that, in
the short term, a lowered national economic growth rate could be expected. President Aníbal Cavaco Silva called for "unity" amongst the Portuguese population
(both politicians and public) in the face of "tough times ahead".

Martin Eaton

MALTA

CAPITAL: Valletta   AREA: 320 sq km   POPULATION: 409,000 ('07)
OFFICIAL LANGUAGES: Maltese & English   POLITICAL SYSTEM: multiparty republic
HEAD OF STATE: President Edward Fenech Adami (since March '04)
RULING PARTY: Nationalist Party (PN)
HEAD OF GOVERNMENT: Prime Minister Lawrence Gonzi (since March '04)
MAIN IGO MEMBERSHIPS (NON-UN): CWTH, OSCE, CE, EU, PFP
CURRENCY: euro (end-'08 £1=€1.0344, US$1=€0.7194)
GNI PER CAPITA: US$15,310, $20,990 at PPP ('07)

POLITICS dominated the news during this election year. The general election of
8 March gave the Nationalist Party (PN) its third consecutive victory. Following several years of slack economic performance and overspending, the PN

government had been extremely skilful in presenting a picture of an upbeat economy and settled public finances. It addressed rising prices of oil and cereals and other harbingers of recession with the same panacea prescribed in the 2008 budget, namely, by pledging to put more money into people's pockets if re-elected. Aware that challenging the government's optimism could alienate a pampered electorate, the Labour opposition (MLP) promised munificence to match, thus implicitly endorsing the government's claims. Banking on the electorate's natural desire for change, the MLP focused on government arrogance and slackness and its own promises of better governance. Even here, however, the PN campaign deftly set the relatively new leadership of its head, Lawrence Gonzi, against the bruised vintage reputation of Labour's Alfred Sant. Labour's overconfidence caused it to fail by a slim 0.5 per cent, a decisive enough margin in this virtual two-party system. The smaller parties, as usual, polled negligible amounts.

The loss bewildered the MLP, which had been pining in opposition since 1987, bar the turbulent 22 months in which it held office in 1996-98. When Sant finally stepped down, the party entered a period of soul-searching regarding its policies, style, and even raison d'être. An extended leadership contest between advocates of continuity and those calling for a fundamental overhaul ended in victory for the former, who perceived change enough in the youth and approachability of Joseph Muscat, a member of the European Parliament.

Uninhibited by the narrowness of its victory or by its election slogan of "together, everything is possible", the government immediately took two controversial decisions without any consultation. The first, contentious on account of the country's neutrality, was to re-join NATO's Partnership for Peace, having done so once already in 1995, only for the Labour government to pull out in 1996. The second was to set in motion the process of privatising the shipyards, the historical core of Maltese industrialisation and a mainstay of MLP support, but also one that had long survived on state subsidies, which EU rules no longer permitted.

Unsurprisingly, it was a sedate government that was confirmed in office, not least because its recent open-handedness had pushed the deficit back up, so that instead of delivering on electoral promises it was hard put to settle its pre-election bills. Austerity opened with a stiff hike in utility prices to cover the losses incurred by the state energy monopoly. Post-election sobriety was evident in the budget for 2009, which offered a token relaxation in income tax but announced a spate of mainly environment-related taxes, which few doubted were intended to boost revenue.

The international financial crisis did not have too serious an impact on the country's banks, mostly thanks to a culture of caution in lending, borrowing, and personal investment practices. Nevertheless, Malta was not immune to the effects of the global economic slowdown, which were already beginning to be felt in manufacturing and tourism by the year's end.

Dominic Fenech

GREECE

CAPITAL: Athens   AREA: 131,960 sq km   POPULATION: 11,193,000 ('07)
OFFICIAL LANGUAGE: Greek   POLITICAL SYSTEM: multiparty republic
HEAD OF STATE: President Karolos Papoulias (since March '05)
RULING PARTY: New Democracy (ND)
HEAD OF GOVERNMENT: Prime Minister Kostas Karamanlis (since March '04)
MAIN IGO MEMBERSHIPS (NON-UN): NATO, EU, OSCE, CE, BSEC, OECD
CURRENCY: euro (end-'08 £1=€1.0344, US$1=€0.7194)
GNI PER CAPITA: US$29,630, $32,520 at PPP ('07)

FOR more than two weeks in December, Greece was convulsed by daily demon-strations and considerable violence, attracting international media attention and triggering sympathy demonstrations in other countries. Widely regarded as the first response to the international financial crisis, the unrest was also the climax of a year that saw a dramatic decline in the legitimacy of the domestic political system. New political scandals were added to the long list of previous years, while the concept of political responsibility was conspicuously absent, with min-isterial resignations rare and belated. The separation of powers did not appear to be working. On only one occasion was the legislature given the opportunity to examine a government scandal, while the judiciary systematically found there was no case to answer, creating a climate of immunity and a perception that the rule of law did not apply to the political class.

Even before the financial crisis, most households were heavily indebted to the banks, on a scale unprecedented in the past. Interest rates, higher than the euro-zone average, aggravated individual financial insecurity. New labour market entrants, the so-called "€700 generation", could expect salaries below a living wage and insecure employment conditions without full insurance rights, even in the public sector. The environmental degradation, which could no longer be ignored after the 2007 forest fires, suggested that the older generations were jeop-ardising the country's future.

The credibility of both major parties was damaged when the German investi-gation into unethical practices by the technology conglomerate Siemens revealed that the company, a longterm beneficiary of Greek public works con-tracts, had allocated tens of millions of euros for bribery in Greece. It emerged that under the previous socialist government a close adviser to the prime minis-ter had received 1 million German marks, channelled to his party. From the cur-rent governing party, the culture minister (and cousin to the prime minister) had enjoyed a Siemens-sponsored international trip, while an MP (and son of a former prime minister) received telephone equipment. When the independent administrative authority against money laundering announced an investigation, the government dissolved it.

The second major scandal concerned the allocation of 200 million euros of state subsidies for shipping services to less frequented islands. The chairman of the parliamentary committee on institutions, aware for over a year of corruption alle-gations, did nothing about them. The Supreme Court prosecutor declined to send the case to Parliament, although it concerned possible criminal responsibilities of a government minister.

The discrediting of trusted institutions included the traditionally respected Orthodox Church. The year's biggest scandal centred on monks who had eschewed the ascetic life to build a business empire based on lucrative sales of public land, in collaboration with government ministers who signed away state property rights worth hundreds of millions of euros, later blaming committees of their own appointees for misleading them. Two deputy prosecutors resigned when their superiors overturned their recommendation to refer the case to Parliament, leading the official opposition to file a suit against the Supreme Court prosecutor on the grounds of undermining the constitutional order. Subsequently, a parliamentary committee was established to investigate political, but not criminal, responsibilities of the ministers concerned.

The passage of a bill amalgamating social insurance funds provoked repeated demonstrations and strikes in February and March. Following the failure of the attempted constitutional revision to permit private universities, a new law providing for non-state tertiary education institutions recognised the plethora of private institutes of varying quality, which had been functioning for the previous decade. The anger of the academic and student community was fuelled by a European Court of Justice ruling that excluded the Greek government from supervisory rights over franchise operations run by EU (usually British) universities.

The government's reform programme also included the sale of the state's shares and management rights in the national telecommunications company to Deutsche Telecom and the launching of yet another privatisation plan for Olympic Airways.

In the first six months of the year, state spending grew by 10 per cent and revenue by 4 per cent, with tax receipts amounting to less that half of the 2008 budget target. The growing deficit raised the prospect of a return to eurozone surveillance, from which Greece had emerged in June 2007; meanwhile, reduced financial credibility meant higher interest rates for public borrowing. Following the onset of the international financial crisis, the offer of a massive €28 billion support package to the banking sector was followed by tough negotiations, with the banks reluctant to accept state intervention or reduced interest rates. The 2009 budget, based on expectations of 2.7 per cent economic growth, appeared unduly optimistic.

On 6 December, the shooting of 15-year old schoolboy, Alexandros Grigoropoulos, catalysed popular discontent. The official announcement that two police officers fired in the air when attacked by a mob was unanimously refuted by all eyewitnesses and by a mobile phone video showing the police calmly leaving the scene. The response was a spontaneous and inchoate youth revolt. Secondary schoolchildren played a leading role in countrywide demonstrations, while in Athens city centre hooded demonstrators burned buildings in nightly battles with the police. The latter were widely criticised, both for failing to protect property and for the violence employed against young demonstrators, while the systematic use of teargas raised public health concerns. Mass arrests included 14 schoolchildren charged in one provincial city under the anti-terrorism law.

The year closed with another violent event, the attempted murder of a trade unionist, Katerina Kouneva, on 22 December. A Bulgarian immigrant and history graduate who worked as a contract cleaner, Kouneva suffered irreparable damage to her health when her attackers threw acid in her face and then forced her to drink it. The attack focused attention on the practice of contracting out public sector services to private companies with political connections and in which employment conditions systematically violated labour legislation.

In foreign policy, Greece was one of five EU member states not to recognise Kosovo's declaration of independence during 2008 (see map, p. 111). In the long-running nomenclature dispute with Macedonia (known at Greece's insistence as the Former Yugoslav Republic of Macedonia to distinguish it from the Greek province), Greece declared that it would accept a compound name, including the word "Macedonia", but demanded that this should be for universal international use, not only bilateral Greek-Macedonian relations. At April's biannual NATO summit, Greece vetoed Macedonia's entry into the alliance (see pp. 109-10; AR 2008, p. 101). In the same month, the Greek and Russian governments signed an agreement for Greek participation in the "South Stream" natural gas pipeline project (see map, p. 103). Both developments caused some tension in relations with the USA. In May, in a surprising move for a country embedded in the EU security community, a change was announced in the national defence doctrine, from defensive to deterrent. Massive new armaments purchases simultaneously announced were explained as a lever to gain foreign support for Greece's Macedonian policy, using the lure of lucrative weapons contracts. The year also saw Greece become the first country to be temporarily suspended from the Kyoto Protocol for non-compliance, underlining the country's poor record in environmental management.

Susannah Verney

CYPRUS

CAPITAL: Nicosia   AREA: 9,250 sq km   POPULATION: 787,000 ('07); TRNC 264,172 (May '06 census)
POLITICAL SYSTEM: separate multiparty republics: Republic of Cyprus (recognised by UN), Turkish Republic of Northern Cyprus (TRNC—recognised only by Turkey)
HEAD OF STATE AND GOVERNMENT: Republic of Cyprus: President Demetris Christofias (since Feb '08); in the TRNC, President Mehmet Ali Talat (since April '05), Ferdi Sabit Soyer (CTP), Prime Minister (since April '05)
RULING PARTIES: Republic of Cyprus: representatives of the Progressive Party of the Working People (AKEL), the Democratic Party (DIKO) and the Socialist Party of Cyprus (EDEK) form the cabinet; in TRNC Republican Turkish Party (CTP) and Freedom and Reform Party (ORP) form coalition
MAIN IGO MEMBERSHIPS (NON-UN): Republic of Cyprus: EU, OSCE, CE, CWTH
CURRENCY: Republic of Cyprus: euro (end-'08 £1=€1.0344, US$1=€0.7194); TRNC: Turkish new lira (end-'08 £1=TL2.2192, US$1=TL1.5435)
GNI PER CAPITA: Republic of Cyprus: US$24,940, $26,370 at PPP ('07); TRNC: n/a

THE election as president of the Republic of Cyprus in February of communist party leader Demetris Christofias spurred a renewed negotiating process that initially prompted hopes of a rapid resolution of the 34-year division of the island. But in a joint statement issued on 23 December with the Turkish Cypriot president, Mehmet Ali Talat, the two community leaders admitted that, "although some progress has been made, it has been insufficient".

Historically, the Progressive Party of the Working People (AKEL) had been the king-maker in Greek Cypriot politics. It was the largest and best organised party and its endorsement of the candidate of another centre-left party usually ensured the latter's victory, while giving the communists a considerable say in public appointments and the workings of government. This was the case in 2003 when AKEL, long a proponent of a settlement on the island, supported as presidential candidate Tassos Papadopoulos, former head of the centrist Democratic Party (DIKO). However, after Papadopoulos urged Greek Cypriots to vote against the federation scheme proposed by UN Secretary-General Kofi Annan ahead of Cyprus's entry into the EU in 2004 (see AR 2004, pp. 74-75), the communists began to disengage from the coalition. They withdrew entirely in July 2007 and in the February 2008 elections for the first time ran their own presidential candidate, AKEL secretary general Christofias. Papadopoulos was eliminated in the first round of balloting on 17 February, having polled 32 per cent compared with 34 per cent for the conservative Democratic Rally (DISY) candidate and 33 per cent for Christofias. After an intense debate over which way DIKO should cast its votes in the run-off contest, the party decided to endorse Christofias, who comfortably won the second ballot on 24 February with 53 per cent. This left Christofias with a strong mandate to lead the Greek Cypriots into fresh negotiations, but also beholden to the rejectionist DIKO camp.

Talat, the president since 2005 of the Turkish Republic of Northern Cyprus (TRNC), was former head of the Republican Turkish Party (CTP), once styled a Marxist party but now deemed to be of centre-left persuasion. AKEL and the CTP both had strong links with the island's trade union movement, which was historically the prime mover in maintaining inter-communal contacts. Thus, the stage seemed to be set for rapid progress to be made towards a settlement.

Within three weeks of Christofias's election, the two leaders met for three hours in the presence of Michael Moller, the UN secretary-general's special representative on the island, and committed themselves to a formal structure for a negotiating process. Each appointed a special delegate: George Iacovou, a former foreign minister, as the presidential commissioner for the Greek Cypriots, and Ozdil Nami as special advisor for the Turkish Cypriots. The pair agreed to establish six working groups and seven technical committees.

On 3 April the two communities agreed as a confidence-building measure to re-open Ledra Street, the former main shopping street of the ancient walled city of Nicosia. (The UN reported that the thoroughfare was used for nearly half a million of the 1.5 million crossings of the demilitarised zone during the latter half of the year.)

Formal negotiations between the two camps commenced on 22 April and there were 270 meetings between the respective groups before Christofias and Talat met on 25 July to review the results. The two agreed 15 confidence-building measures (related to the environment, crisis management, crime, and cultural heritage) and endorsed six others on more quotidian matters, such as road safety and healthcare, which had earlier been agreed by their representatives. The two leaders agreed to start formal negotiations on 3 September. Secretary-General Ban Ki Moon stepped up the UN's efforts to promote the talks by renewing his representation for the island and appointing Australia's former foreign minister, Alexander Downer, as the secretary-general's special advisor with direct responsibility for hosting the talks between the community presidents.

Formal talks duly commenced in September at UN headquarters in the demilitarised zone. There were 13 sessions before the end of the year with a commitment to a resumption of talks in 2009. On 23 December, the two leaders made their statement to the effect that they had not made as much progress as they had hoped, yet Downer added that he thought the talks had momentum and that 2009 would be "productive". An unofficial timetable hoped to see the talks sufficiently close to completion that the Turkish Cypriots would be able to participate in European Parliament elections in June 2009.

The talks were held under a strict news blackout, which both sides observed. According to sources claiming to be close to the talks, the failure to make more progress faster was over the issue of sovereignty. In a joint statement on 23 May Christofias and Talat reiterated long agreed positions that the re-united island would be a bizonal, bicommunal federation with political equality. The island would have a federal government with a single international identity and Greek and Turkish Cypriot constituent states of equal status. According to the sources, however, the Turkish Cypriot side resurrected demands that the Turkish Republic of Northern Cyprus should be recognised before entering into the federation. This, the Greek Cypriots had historically argued, would be tantamount to confederation and would fall outside the federal brief.

On 12 December, Tassos Papadopoulos died suddenly. His death removed from the Greek Cypriot political scene the last major player from the days of the Greek Cypriots' struggle against British colonial rule for enosis, union with Greece (see Obituary). Papadopoulos had been a leading figure in EOKA, the Greek Cypriot guerrilla movement, and while he had been intimately involved with settlement talks since 1974, his covert goal had always been restoration of Greek Cypriot hegemony on the island. His removal from the political scene was expected to add impetus to the settlement process.

Talat's negotiating posture had to receive endorsement from the Islamist, but pro-European, Justice and Development Party (AKP) government in Turkey. It had confronted the Turkish armed forces establishment to promote the 2004 Annan federal scheme, and lost considerable domestic face after Papadopoulos urged the Greek Cypriots to reject the scheme in order to pursue a settlement of a more unitary nature. The AKP was embroiled during 2008 in a confrontation with Turkey's secularists, who had sought through the courts to have the party dissolved (see pp. 87-89). This made it difficult, if not impossible, for the AKP government to support any Turkish Cypriot negotiating posture that would be contrary to the security oriented stance over Cyprus of the Turkish military. At the end of 2008, it was unclear whether this situation might moderate in future, as Turkey sought to improve its relations with the EU, for which it was a membership candidate.

Robert McDonald

TURKEY

CAPITAL: Ankara   AREA: 783,560 sq km   POPULATION: 73,888,000 ('07)
OFFICIAL LANGUAGE: Turkish   POLITICAL SYSTEM: multiparty republic
HEAD OF STATE: President Abdullah Gul (AKP) (since Aug '07)
RULING PARTY: Justice and Development Party (AKP) (since Nov '02)
HEAD OF GOVERNMENT: Prime Minister Recep Tayyip Erdogan (since March '03)
MAIN IGO MEMBERSHIPS (NON-UN): NATO, OSCE, OECD, CE, OIC, ECO, BSEC
CURRENCY: new lira (end-'08 £1=TL2.2192, US$1=TL1.5435)
GNI PER CAPITA: US$8,020, $12,090 at PPP ('07)

THE government of Recep Tayyip Erdogan, leader of the conservative Justice and Development Party (AKP), which had won a second term in the elections held in July 2007, survived the legal process launched against it by the secularist and nationalist opposition.

On 5 June the Constitutional Court accepted a petition by the opposition Republican People's Party (CHP) and invalidated a constitutional amendment passed by the Grand National Assembly (the unicameral parliament) on 9 February, which would have had the effect of allowing women university students to wear the Muslim headscarf. Then, on 30 July, the Constitutional Court accepted a claim by the chief prosecutor of the republic that the AKP had become "the focus of activity against the secular order of the republic". This decision would have led to the closure of the party and the banning of its leadership from political activity for five years, if it had been supported by seven out of the 11 members of the Constitutional Court. However, as only six judges voted for it, the Court imposed on the AKP the lesser penalty of forfeiting 50 per cent of state funding. The government was again in trouble with the judiciary at the end of the year, when the Council of State (the highest administrative tribunal) allowed elections to over 800 town councils, which the government wanted to abolish on the grounds of population loss.

Prominent nationalists had in the meantime found themselves in the dock, accused of plotting to overthrow the government by force. According to the indictment drawn up by a prosecutor in Istanbul, the plot, codenamed Ergenekon (a mythical mountain pass in Central Asia, through which Turkish tribes were said to have emerged to conquer neighbouring countries), aimed at destabilising the regime by terrorist attacks in order to prompt a military coup. Investigations started when a store of army issue grenades was discovered in Istanbul in June 2007 in the home of a retired officer. The indictment named 86 defendants, 46 of whom were remanded in custody. They included two retired four-star generals, one of whom had been the main organiser of anti-government rallies in the summer of 2007, and also the leader of the small nationalist Turkish Workers Party, executives of a nationalist television channel, and the leader of an association of nationalist lawyers who had promoted the prosecution of Turkish liberal intellectuals (including the Nobel laureate novelist Orhan Pamuk). Other prominent defendants, such as the editor of the staunchly nationalist newspaper *Cumhuriyet*, and a former rector of Istanbul University, were granted bail. Hearings started on 20 October with the reading of an indictment of nearly 2,500 pages. Interest in the trial, which was intense at first, gradually decreased as it became clear that proceedings were likely to stretch out into the distant future.

The legal challenges prompted Prime Minister Erdogan to put off his plans to liberalise the constitution. His government's consequent failure to push ahead with reforms was criticised by the European Commission in its latest annual report covering progress to October 2008 in the negotiations on Turkey's accession. Yet, while the prospect of EU membership receded, Erdogan gradually regained the initiative in the second half of the year. He established good working relations with the new chief of the general staff, General Ilker Basbug, who took over from General Yasar Buyukanit at the end of August. The failure to stop by military means alone the armed campaign waged by the Kurdish nationalists of the PKK (Kurdistan Workers Party) from their main base in the mountains of northern Iraq persuaded the armed forces that military efforts had to be supplemented by political and economic measures. The AKP, which had received more votes in Kurdish majority areas than had the Kurdish nationalist Democratic Society Party (DTP), favoured by PKK supporters, was in any case anxious to gain the confidence of Turkey's Kurds prior to the local government elections on 29 March 2009. Programmes for economic aid to Kurdish majority areas were extended. In addition, the government introduced round-the-clock television broadcasts in Kurdish (which started on 1 January 2009), and plans were announced to promote Kurdish studies in Turkish universities. Old taboos were swept aside, as Kurdish demands for cultural rights were widely discussed by think tanks and in the media.

The continuation of the PKK armed campaign gave urgency to the discussion. During the year, PKK militants infiltrating from northern Iraq, mounted some 150 attacks on Turkish security forces, which lost 110 men. The worst terrorist attack against civilians occurred in Istanbul on 27 July when 17 people were killed by a bomb explosion in a crowded suburban market. The Turkish air force repeatedly bombed PKK targets in northern Iraq, and the Turkish army launched a major raid across the border in February, when it claimed to have killed 250 militants. Military measures were supplemented by diplomatic moves. There were tripartite meetings with US and Iraqi government representatives in Baghdad, and in December the Iraqi prime minister, Nouri al-Maliki, paid a working visit to Ankara, during which agreement was reached on an institutional framework to link the economies of the two countries. Contacts with the Kurdish regional government (KRG) in northern Iraq were also extended discreetly and cross-border travel by road and air increased.

While accession negotiations with the EU marked time, Turkish diplomacy concentrated on regional peace initiatives. The Turkish government welcomed the talks held under UN auspices between the Greek Cypriot president Demetris Christofias and Mehmet Ali Talat, the president of the Turkish Republic of Northern Cyprus (which Turkey was alone in recognising). However the failure of the two leaders to make significant progress did not cause any surprise in Ankara (see pp. 85-86).

When fighting erupted between Russia and Georgia in August, Turkey proposed the conclusion of a peace and co-operation pact for the Caucasus. Prime Minister Erdogan promoted the initiative in a series of meetings with the ministers of the countries concerned. President Abdullah Gul took the unprecedented step of accepting an invitation to a football match between the national teams of Turkey and Armenia in Yerevan, the capital of Armenia, even although there were no diplomatic relations between the two countries pending the resolution of the Nagorno-Karabakh dispute between Armenia and Azerbaijan (see p. 138). However, the land frontier between Turkey and Armenia remained closed, while air traffic between the two countries continued unimpeded. The campaign commitment by US President-elect Barack Obama to support a congressional move to characterise the treatment of Armenians in the Ottoman empire in 1915 as an act of genocide caused apprehension in Turkey, where Obama's election was otherwise widely welcomed.

Turkey took an active part in Middle East peace efforts. In August the Syrian president, Bashar Assad, and his Iranian counterpart, Mahmoud Ahmadinejad, visited Turkey. Turkish mediation between Israel and Syria was further discussed when Israel's prime minister, Ehud Olmert, paid a one-day visit to Ankara in December. Israel's decision a few days later to launch an all-out assault on Hamas in Gaza caused particular disappointment to Prime Minister Erdogan, who described it as a demonstration of disrespect for Turkey's mediation. Erdogan subsequently visited in quick succession Syria, Jordan (where he met the Palestinian president, Mahmoud Abbas), Egypt, and Saudi Arabia to promote a common peace initiative.

Economic growth slowed down in response to the global financial crisis, but there were no casualties among Turkish banks, which had been restructured a decade earlier when there had been a collapse of confidence in Turkey. Gross domestic product grew by 3 per cent in the first nine months of the year, as compared with 4.6 per cent in 2007. In spite of a drop in the import bill as a result of lower economic activity, the external payments deficit rose from US$29 billion to US$38 billion year-on-year in the first 10 months of the year. The worst effect was felt on the Istanbul stock exchange, where the index fell by 52 per cent over the year (as compared with a gain of 42 per cent in 2007), as foreign investors withdrew funds. Consumer prices rose by 10 per cent during the year. The Turkish government hesitated at first to apply for IMF aid for fear that it would be conditional on fiscal tightening, but as fiscal expansion gained in popularity worldwide, negotiations for a new IMF credit began at the end of the year.

A.J.A. Mango

III CENTRAL AND EASTERN EUROPE

POLAND—BALTIC STATES—CZECH REPUBLIC—SLOVAKIA—HUNGARY—
ROMANIA—BULGARIA

POLAND

CAPITAL: Warsaw   AREA: 312,690 sq km   POPULATION: 38,061,000 ('07)
OFFICIAL LANGUAGE: Polish   POLTICAL SYSTEM: multiparty republic
HEAD OF STATE: President Lech Kaczynski (PiS) (since Dec '05)
RULING PARTIES: coalition of Citizens' Platform (PO) and Polish Peasants' Party (PSL)
HEAD OF GOVERNMENT: Prime Minister Donald Tusk (PO) (since Nov '07)
MAIN IGO MEMBERSHIPS (NON-UN): NATO, OSCE, CE, CEI, CBSS, OECD, Francophonie, EU
CURRENCY: zloty (end-'08 £1=ZI4.2601, US$1=ZI2.9630)
GNI PER CAPITA: US$9,840, $15,590 at PPP ('07)

POLAND enjoyed relative political and economic stability in 2008. This was in marked contrast to the tensions of the immediately preceding two years, dominated by the Kaczynski brothers, their Law and Justice (PiS) party, national Catholicism, and the antics of the populist Andrzej Lepper (see AR 2008, pp. 80-81). Much was expected from the popular new Citizens' Platform (PO) and Polish Peasants' Party (PSL) government led by Donald Tusk, which set about refurbishing Poland's international image. Economic growth tailed off only slightly, while the National Bank of Poland (NBP, the central bank) kept inflation down to 4 per cent and the zloty strong as labour emigration weakened. Poland was thus in a strong position to weather the global financial crisis. The main domestic problem was the strained political cohabitation between President Lech Kaczynski and Prime Minister Tusk. They represented rival, centre-right political camps. Kaczynski's efforts to influence foreign policy, as in his UN address in September, and to gain domestic support were widely regarded as the early stages of a struggle with Tusk for the presidency in 2010.

Foreign Minister Radoslaw Sikorski defined foreign policy priorities in the Sejm (the lower house of the bicameral legislature) in April as: improving Poland's international image, further integration in the EU and NATO, strategic partnership with the USA, military modernisation, and pragmatic dialogue with Russia. Tusk's Moscow visit in early February and Russian Foreign Minister Sergei Lavrov's Warsaw visit in October could not resolve their fundamental disagreements over the US missile shield and Ukraine, however. Poland was also united in opposing the Russo-German North Stream gas pipeline. This would bypass Poland by pumping gas directly to Germany under the Baltic (see map, p. 103). Historical interpretation also continued to affect Polish-Russian relations: Andrzej Wajda's film, *Katyn*, dealing with the Stalinist massacre of about 22,000 Polish prisoners of war in spring 1940, had its premiere in Moscow in March. The Polish side in the Joint Historical Commission on Katyn failed to make much headway in October. The Russian judiciary refused to declassify its early 1990s investigation, and the Russian government also refused to publish the truth about Katyn in school textbooks. The debate on Polish historical memory and World War II continued with the film *Defiance*, starring Daniel Craig as a Jewish partisan leader whose activities in Belarus were regarded by many Poles as anti-Polish and pro-Soviet, while Hollywood's glaring neglect and distortion of the role of the Home Army (AK) was resented.

Tusk and Sikorski found it easier, after the abrasiveness of the Kaczynski brothers, to collaborate with Germany, Poland's largest trading partner by far. This was confirmed by a very friendly visit by Chancellor Angela Merkel to Gdansk in June. She endorsed Poland's regional initiatives in Scandinavia and over the proposed EU "eastern partnership" (a forum for relations with the EU's eastern neighbours). Substantive differences of public opinion nevertheless remained over German expellees and other emotional World War II legacies.

Sikorski continued his tough negotiating stance of bargaining Polish support for the US missile shield in exchange for Patriot defence missiles during his July meeting in Washington, DC with US Secretary of State Condoleezza Rice (see AR 2008, p. 82). This, accelerated by the Russian intervention in Georgia in August, led to agreement for the siting, by 2011-13, of 10 interceptor missiles at a base in northern Poland, supported by a radar tracking system in the Czech Republic. The USA's popularity in Poland diminished, until Barack Obama's election in November, because the USA had maintained its visa requirement for Poles and because of the growing perception that it was slow to reward Polish support, both financially and militarily.

Agreement between Kaczynski and Tusk enabled the Sejm to ratify the EU's Lisbon Treaty by 348 to 56 votes (a two-thirds majority obviating the need for a referendum) in early April. The "no" in the Irish referendum, however, allowed Kaczynski to delay the Treaty's signing as "pointless", despite much pressure from France's President Nicolas Sarkozy. Kaczynski was disappointed by NATO's failure to offer a membership action plan (MAP) to Ukraine and Georgia at its April Bucharest summit. The president reflected the hostility of Polish public opinion to Russia's brutal intervention in Abkhazia and South Ossetia in August (see map, p. 137) and Poland provided €5.5 million in reconstruction aid to Georgia. Tusk and Sikorski, however, pressed ahead with Poland's integration within NATO and military modernisation, especially with regard to the missile shield. Poland's growing weight as a close US ally within NATO produced rumours at the end of the year that both Sikorski and the former president, Aleksander Kwasniewski (1995-2005), were being considered for the post of NATO secretary general.

The crucial decision was taken to abolish conscription in 2009 and to complete the transformation of the Polish army into a fully professional, slimmed down, and modernised force. The 900-strong Polish contingent (down from a peak of 3,200) withdrew from south-central Iraq in July. Their five-year presence had cost 22 Polish lives and caused much domestic opposition. The indictment of seven soldiers for illegally killing five civilians in a remote village in Afghanistan increased, if anything, the unpopularity of the Polish redeployment to Ghazin province.

Economic liberalisation was promoted although there were no major policy reforms. GDP grew by 5.2 per cent in 2008, a comparatively minor slowdown from the 2007 level of 6.6 per cent, mainly caused by the global economic downturn. Unemployment had halved over a three-year period to 9.7 per cent, while exports had trebled and imports doubled since 2000. This brought GDP per capita up to US$17,560. Finance Minister Jacek Rostowski flattened tax rates, but concessions to demands for pay rises by doctors, nurses, and border guards blew away his ambitious tax cutting and budget deficit reduction plans. Although the Organisation for Economic Co-operation and Development (OECD) praised Poland's economic buoyancy, the IMF criticised its slowness in tackling economic de-regulation and structural problems such as the low, 54 per cent, labour participation rate. A much publicised Sejm commission on the "friendly state" attacked bureaucracy but its effectiveness was undermined by the quarrels that its controversial chairman, Jan Palikot, was having with his own PO party.

By early 2008 more Poles were leaving the UK than entering it for work purposes, because of growing employment in Poland, the collapse of the UK construction industry, and the strong zloty and weak pound sterling (see p. 39). The global financial crisis affected the Polish economy from October onwards, with significant declines in the stock exchange, the property market, and vehicle production, as well as increasing unemployment and tighter bank credit. Good credit ratings were maintained although the growth forecast for 2009 was cut to as low as 2.8 per cent in some estimates. The government reacted to the economic slowdown and financial crisis by presenting a stabilisation and development plan in early December. This introduced a budgetary stimulus of Zl91 billion, higher spending on infrastructure, and loan guarantees.

As the Polish economy was heavily dependent upon coal for energy (94 per cent) the government had to negotiate hard to limit the damage that would be caused by proposed EU CO_2 emission quota cuts of 20 per cent by 2020. Poland gained concessions over phasing in the EU's climate and energy package, agreed in December, as well as considerable financial aid (€15 billion) for green technologies. Awareness of the issue was raised by the 12-day UN climate change conference held in Poznan in December, which was attended by 190 countries.

The post-communist SLD (Alliance of the Democratic Left), broke up the LiD (Left & Democracy) coalition in March by splitting from the more reformist centre-left Democratic Party. Soon afterwards, the left wing and anti-clerical 34-year old Grzegorz Napieralski defeated Wojciech Olejniczak for the SLD leadership.

A Warsaw court opened legal proceedings over the Institute of National Remembrance (INP) indictment of former President Wojciech Jaruzelski and seven other communist functionaries for the declaration of martial law in December 1981 (see AR 1981, pp. 112-18). Equally controversially, an INP publication reiterated the claim that Jaruzelski's anti-communist successor, Lech Walesa, had been "agent Bolek" for the security service in the early 1970s.

Universal tributes were paid to the Solidarity former foreign minister, Bronislaw Geremek, who was killed in a car crash in July, as well as to Irena Sendler, who had saved Jewish children from the Warsaw ghetto during Nazi occupation. The reaction was more mixed to the death of Mieczyslaw Rakowski, a reform-communist but strongly anti-Solidarity figure, later in the year (see Obituary).

George Sanford

ESTONIA—LATVIA—LITHUANIA

Estonia

CAPITAL: Tallinn   AREA: 45,230 sq km   POPULATION: 1,342,000 ('07)
OFFICIAL LANGUAGE: Estonian   POLTICAL SYSTEM: multiparty republic
HEAD OF STATE: President Toomas Hendrik Ilves (ESDP) (since Sept '06)
RULING PARTIES: Estonian Reform Party (ER) in coalition with Union of Pro Patria and Res Publica
    (IRPL) and Estonian Social Democratic Party (ESDP)
HEAD OF GOVERNMENT: Prime Minister Andrus Ansip (ER) (since April '05)
MAIN IGO MEMBERSHIPS (NON-UN): OSCE, CE, PFP, BC, CBSS, EU, NATO
CURRENCY: kroon (end-'08 £1=K16.1835, US$1=K11.2561)
GNI PER CAPITA: US$13,200 $19,680 at PPP ('07)

Latvia

CAPITAL: Riga   AREA: 64,590 sq km   POPULATION: 2,276,000 ('07)
OFFICIAL LANGUAGE: Latvian   POLTICAL SYSTEM: multiparty republic
HEAD OF STATE: President Valdis Zatlers (since July '07)
RULING PARTIES: People's Party (TP) leads four-party coalition
HEAD OF GOVERNMENT: Prime Minister Ivars Godmanis (LC) (since Dec '07)
MAIN IGO MEMBERSHIPS (NON-UN): OSCE, CE, PFP, BC, CBSS, EU, NATO
CURRENCY: lats (end-'08 £1=L0.7326, US$1=L0.5096)
GNI PER CAPITA: US$9,930, $16,890 at PPP ('07)

Lithuania

CAPITAL: Vilnius   AREA: 65,300 sq km   POPULATION: 3,376,000 ('07)
OFFICIAL LANGUAGE: Lithuanian   POLTICAL SYSTEM: multiparty republic
HEAD OF STATE: President Valdas Adamkus (since July '04)
RULING PARTY: Homeland Union-Lithuanian Christian Democrats (TS-LKD)
HEAD OF GOVERNMENT: Prime Minister Andrius Kubilius (TS-LKD) (since Oct '08)
MAIN IGO MEMBERSHIPS (NON-UN): OSCE, CE, PFP, BC, CBSS, Francophonie, EU, NATO
CURRENCY: litas (end-'08 £1=L3.5713, US$1=L2.4840)
GNI PER CAPITA: US$9,920, $17,180 at PPP ('07)

WHILE the Baltic States did not witness a repeat of the violence that had occurred in Tallinn in April 2007 (see AR 2008, p. 83), there was no lack of political and economic turmoil in 2008, with government infighting, disputes with Russia and the EU, corruption, political scandals, and the threat of financial collapse. The various crises triggered a change of government in Lithuania and prompted anti-government demonstrations and direct action in Estonia and Latvia.

POLITICS AND SOCIETY. Although Ivars Godmanis's ruling coalition stayed in power in Latvia throughout 2008 (no mean feat for a Latvian government), the already fragmented political scene became even more splintered in February when a wave of legislators and former ministers from the ruling People's Party (TP)-led coalition and the opposition New Era (JL) left their respective parties to establish new political forces and thereby capitalise on popular discontent with the incumbent government. Sandra Kalniete of New Era and Girts Valdis Kristovskis of the nationalist For Fatherland and Freedom (TB/LNNK) party joined forces to set up the right-of-centre Civic Union (PS), whilst at the other end of the political spectrum, Artis Pabriks and Aigars Stockenbergs, two former ministers from the ruling

People's Party, set up the new left-of-centre Society for a Different Politics with the aim of ending the dominance that centre-right coalitions had enjoyed in Latvia since independence in 1991. Both new parties declared their intention to sever the ties between politics and big business and fight corruption, issues that raised their ugly heads repeatedly throughout the year. In March two Riga city council officials were arrested for soliciting a bribe; in May Ina Gudele, minister for electronic government affairs, was forced to resign when it was revealed that she had used government money to pay for her birthday party; and in October a date was finally set for the trial of the businessman and mayor of Ventspils, Aivars Lembergs, who was arrested in 2007 on suspicion of money laundering and bribery. The effectiveness of the Latvian anti-corruption agency (the Corruption Prevention and Control Bureau, KNAB) was called into question in July after the sacking of its head, Aleksejs Loskutovs, following the theft by two KNAB officers of €190,000 of confiscated money. Loskutovs himself was not implicated in the crime and his removal from office was seen by the public and the media as a political move aimed at derailing his investigation into irregularities in party financing and electoral spending (an issue that had contributed to the removal of former Prime Minister Aigars Kalvitis in December 2007, see AR 2008, pp. 84-85). The corruption scandals and sacking of the popular anti-corruption chief undermined public confidence in the government and prompted a signature campaign to hold a plebiscite on dissolving parliament by referendum. The "yes" vote was high, but it failed due to a low turn-out.

Politically, 2008 was a relatively quiet year in Estonia compared with the previous 12 months. The visit by Foreign Minister Urmas Paet in March to meet Russia's deputy foreign minister, Vladimir Titov, was a sign that, one year after the clashes between Russian youths and Estonian police, diplomatic relations between the two states were slowly returning to normal.

While Estonia and Latvia's relations with Russia normalised slowly during the year, Lithuania's took a turn for the worse following the government's decision in May to veto the resumption of talks between the EU and Russia, which were aimed at drafting a new partnership and co-operation agreement (PCA) on trade and energy. Lithuania insisted that the negotiations also address a number of what it considered to be vital issues, with energy security top of the agenda. Lithuania insisted that Russia resume gas supplies along the Druzhba pipeline, which Moscow had shut down—ostensibly for repairs—in retaliation at Lithuania's having sold its Mazeikiai oil refinery to a Polish rather than a Russian firm in 2006. In addition, the Lithuanians wanted assurances that Russia would bring to justice the men responsible for the Medininkai massacre of June 1991, when Soviet special troops had attacked a Lithuanian border post, killing seven officers, and provide compensation to those deported from the Baltic republics during the period of Soviet rule. The already tense relations with Russia were not eased by speculation in the summer that Lithuania might host US missiles, nor by the law adopted in August to ban Soviet symbols.

The country's domestic politics were equally turbulent. In January the opposition called on President Adamkus to hold an early election but he refused.

Prime Minister Gediminas Kirkilas survived a vote of no confidence in April, only to be removed from power in the subsequent general election. After two rounds of voting for seats in the Seimas (unicameral legislature), on 12 and 26 October, the conservative Homeland Union-Lithuanian Christian Democrats (TS-LKD) emerged the winner with almost 20 per cent of the vote, pushing the incumbent Social Democrats (LSDP) into fourth place with 12 per cent. The surprise runner-up was the newly established National Resurrection Party (TPP), a group of television celebrities and pop stars, which garnered over 15 per cent. In third place, with about 13 per cent, was the populist Order and Justice Party (TiT), led by Rolandas Paksas, a former president with the dubious honour of being the first European head of state to be removed from office by impeachment. The remaining parties (the Labour Party (DP), the Liberals' Movement (LRLS) and the Liberal and Centre Union (LCS)) each polled under 10 per cent, while the outgoing coalition partners—the Social Liberals and Peasants' Union—failed to cross the 5 per cent threshold required to enter the Seimas. Andrius Kubilius, leader of TS-LKD, was called on to form the government, which he cobbled together out of four parties: TS-LKD, TPP, and the two small liberal parties (LRLS and LCS).

At the same time as voting for a new government, the Lithuanian electorate was asked to support a referendum calling for the Ignalina nuclear power station to stay in operation beyond the 2009 deadline set for its closure, which had been agreed when Lithuania joined the EU. The motion received over 90 per cent support but the EU refused to bend. The new government showed itself as adept as its predecessor at taking on the EU when in November it attacked the European Commission for reopening the strategic partnership talks with Russia that had been suspended following the invasion of Georgia. However, the Lithuanian position may have had less to do with solidarity with Tbilisi and more to do with the announcement by Russian President Dmitry Medvedev of Russia's intention to deploy short-range missiles in the enclave of Kaliningrad to counter the USA's proposed missile defence shield in central Europe (see p. 125).

THE ECONOMY. Economically, Estonia continued to suffer from the aftermath of the "bronze soldier riots" of 2007. The agricultural sector was hit hard by the boycott of Estonian produce by Russian supermarkets. Even worse affected was the transit trade, with the port of Tallinn reporting that the volume of goods passing through it from the Commonwealth of Independent States had fallen by one-third, year-on-year, in March, with oil freight down 16 per cent and coal transit all but coming to a standstill, plummeting 97 per cent. Not all of Estonia's economic woes could be attributed to Russian actions, however. As a result of the US "subprime" mortgage crisis and ensuing credit crunch in Europe, domestic demand fell 9.5 per cent, exports were down, and unemployment went up. The economy officially entered recession in the third quarter of 2008, following two quarters of negative growth. There were positive signs: inflation waned from a high of 11 per cent at the start of the year to 7 per cent and the current account deficit shrank. Differences of opinion arose between the government coalition partners on how best to tackle the economic difficulties, with Prime Minister Ansip's Reform Party (ER) pushing to make the labour market more flexible in a bid to increase Estonia's international competitiveness, while the Social Democrats (ESDP) argued that the proposed changes to the employment law would seriously undermine workers' rights and job security.

The economic situation in Latvia was equally if not more serious in 2008. Gross domestic product fell 4.6 per cent in the third quarter as did exports (down some €400 million), and industrial production, which dived by 9 per cent. On the banking front, heavy bank lending in tandem with weak financial regulation, the pegging of the currency to the euro, and loose fiscal policy initially produced a financial sector bubble, which spectacularly burst in November. Combined with the low level of foreign direct investment (covering only 34 per cent of the current account deficit), the weak fundamentals meant that, when the global banking system went into freefall, the government was forced to appeal to the IMF for financial support.

The Lithuanian economy was the only one of the three to post continued growth in 2008. Moreover, Lithuanian export expansion was the highest in the EU. On the downside, wage inflation rose 19 per cent, while unemployment—and particularly youth unemployment—climbed continuously over the year. While Lithuania's economic fundamentals were not as shaky as those of its northern neighbours, the biggest problem was the huge current account deficit, which could only rise as the country became more dependent on foreign energy after the closure of Ignalina.

Richard Mole

CZECH REPUBLIC

CAPITAL: Prague   AREA: 78,870 sq km   POPULATION: 10,334,000 ('07)
OFFICIAL LANGUAGE: Czech   POLTICAL SYSTEM: multiparty republic
HEAD OF STATE: President Vaclav Klaus (ODS) (since Feb '03)
RULING PARTIES: Civic Democratic Party (ODS), Christian Democratic Union-Czech People's Party (KDU-CSL), and Green Party (SZ)
HEAD OF GOVERNMENT: Prime Minister Mirek Topolanek (ODS) (since Sept '06)
MAIN IGO MEMBERSHIPS (NON-UN): NATO, OSCE, CE, CEI, OECD, Francophonie, EU
CURRENCY: koruna (end-'08 £1=Kor27.7662, US$1=Kor19.3123)
GNI PER CAPITA: US$14,450 $21,820 at PPP ('07)

THE Czech Republic experienced rising uncertainty in 2008, as the cabinet's position weakened and the economy faltered. After six inconclusive rounds of voting, the Czech parliament re-elected Vaclav Klaus as the country's president by the narrowest possible margin on 15 February. Klaus relied primarily on representatives of the senior ruling Civic Democratic Party (ODS), which at the time held a majority in the 81-member Czech Senate and a plurality in the 200-member lower house (the Chamber of Deputies). Lacking enough votes from the ODS alone, Klaus was also forced to scour other parties for support, and the election was accompanied by several complaints about attempted intimidation.

Klaus's challenger, the US-Czech economist and former government adviser Jan Svejnar, was backed by the junior ruling Green Party (SZ) and the opposition Social Democrats (CSSD). Although both the candidates broadly adhered to centre-right values, Svejnar supported a more liberal, open stance toward the EU and more attention to the environment. In contrast, Klaus had a sceptical view on both EU integration and global warming.

While Svejnar's election as president could have triggered the government's collapse, Klaus's electoral success failed to guarantee unity. Indeed, pushing forward with further reforms while maintaining political stability proved challenging for Prime Minister Mirek Topolanek. Formed in early 2007, the government lacked a formal legislative majority and depended instead on defectors from the CSSD (see AR 2008, pp. 86-87). By June 2008, four CSSD deputies had left their party; however, the government's stability was complicated throughout 2008 by disputes within and among the three ruling parties.

While the Greens' backing of Svejnar in the presidential election helped to quell criticism from within the party that chairman Martin Bursik was pandering to the ODS, the reprieve was only temporary. Arguing that Bursik and his allies had deviated from the party programme, the party's first deputy chairwoman, Dana Kuchtova, challenged Bursik as party leader at an extraordinary congress in September. Bursik prevailed, but several SZ deputies considered leaving the party.

Controversy also emerged within the ODS in September, as party deputy Jan Morava was caught on hidden camera gathering sensitive information about politicians, making them vulnerable to extortion. Morava, who forfeited his parliamentary mandate in early September, claimed he had been provoked by former Finance Minister Vlastimil Tlusty, a Topolanek rival within the ODS. Several Tlusty allies from the ODS quit the party's parliamentary caucus, bringing the government's official supporters down below the original 100 deputies. Klaus sided with Topolanek's critics in mid-September, and the prime minister confirmed that the government was in its worst position since taking office.

The third party within the ruling coalition, the Christian and Democratic Union-Czech People's Party (KDU-CSL), regained its footing after chairman Jiri Cunek was cleared of corruption charges and allowed to return to the government in April 2008, following a five-month suspension. Nonetheless, some Green representatives remained suspicious of Cunek.

Compounding this instability was the crushing blow dealt to the ruling parties in the second half of October, as the CSSD scored a landslide victory in elections to the Senate and regional assemblies. With 27 out of 81 seats being contested in the Senate elections, the CSSD won 23, compared with just three for the ODS. As a result the ODS lost its majority in the upper house. The CSSD also pulled off an impressive victory in the regional elections, dominating in all 13 regions. Bolstered by these results, the CSSD initiated another parliamentary no confidence vote in late October, marking the fourth such attempt since the administration had taken office. Although Topolanek publicly worried that his cabinet might not survive, it did narrowly prevail, and the 2009 state budget draft bill was approved in December.

A main factor promoting government unity in 2008 related to the fact that the Czech Republic was scheduled to hold the EU presidency during the first half of 2009. Had the government collapsed before that time, it would have sent a negative signal to other EU members. Still, the administration did not seem overly embarrassed by the delayed ratification of the EU Lisbon Treaty. Arguing that the Treaty violated Czech law, eurosceptics in the Senate had referred the document to the Constitutional Court in April, and although the Court ruled in late November that the Treaty was indeed compatible, the Czech parliament failed to ratify the document before the country's EU presidency began.

Another divisive issue in foreign relations was the bilateral treaty with the USA concerning the installation of a radar tracking station on Czech soil as part of the US missile defence shield. The Czech government backed the treaty in May, and US Secretary of State Condoleezza Rice visited Prague in early July to sign the agreement. In July-August, Russia reduced oil supplies to the Czech Republic. Although Russia argued that the cuts were made for technical reasons and were "not political", many Czechs saw them as punishment for the government's decision to move forward on the missile defence deal, and by the end of 2008 parliamentary approval for the radar base had yet to be secured.

On the legislative front, the year's greatest challenges related to healthcare and pension reform, particularly given the country's aging population. Although the three ruling parties agreed in early April on an outline for restructuring healthcare, the ODS failed to reach a joint position with its two junior partners on several key issues, such as the privatisation of health insurance companies, university hospitals, and healthcare fees, introduced at the start of 2008. In late June, parliament backed a bill that would gradually raise the retirement age to 65 by the year 2030, marking the first step in pension reform. The bill was approved despite criticism from the opposition and the trade unions, which organised a one-hour general strike the day before the parliamentary vote. Still, more changes were needed, and Topolanek vowed that the government would not set a target date for adopting the European single currency (the euro) until further pension and healthcare reforms were approved.

Czech economic growth slowed moderately in 2008, after the record high rates of 2005-07. The Czech economy suffered from the international financial crisis as well as from the strong koruna. Meanwhile, the fiscal reforms that took effect at the start of 2008 drove up inflation to the highest level in years (at 6.3 per cent on average), boosted further by high food and fuel costs during the first half of the year. On a positive note, the Czech Republic recorded a foreign trade surplus for the fourth consecutive year.

Sharon Fisher

SLOVAKIA

CAPITAL: Bratislava   AREA: 49,030 sq km   POPULATION: 5,396,000 ('07)
OFFICIAL LANGUAGE: Slovak   POLTICAL SYSTEM: multiparty republic
HEAD OF STATE: President Ivan Gasparovic (since June '04)
RULING PARTIES: Direction-Social Democracy Party (S-SD), Slovak National Party (SNS), and
   People's Party-Movement for a Democratic Slovakia (LS-HZDS)
HEAD OF GOVERNMENT: Prime Minister Robert Fico (S-SD) (since July '06)
MAIN IGO MEMBERSHIPS (NON-UN): OSCE, CE, PFP, CEI, OECD, EU, NATO
CURRENCY: Slovak koruna (end-'08 £1=K31.1598, US$1=K21.6726)
GNI PER CAPITA: US$11,730, $19,330 at PPP ('07)

THE year was a positive one for Slovakia, particularly on the economic front as the approval of eurozone membership brought added stability. The Slovak economy performed relatively well, continuing to benefit from reform measures implemented by the previous government. Several foreign investors ramped up production, while falling unemployment and rising wages drove household demand. It was not until November that the international financial crisis began to have a serious effect on industrial production and exports. As a result, Slovak GDP growth in 2008 was much faster than in most other EU countries.

Despite scepticism over Slovakia's medium-term inflation prospects, the European Commission approved the country's eurozone membership in May, with accession scheduled for January 2009. Slovakia was the second state in post-communist Europe—after Slovenia—to be admitted to the eurozone, while others were at least three or four years behind. While Slovakia's convergence with the richer EU states had been relatively rapid, with GDP per capita in purchasing power terms rising from 50 per cent of the EU average in 2000 to 67 per cent in 2007, the country still had the dubious distinction of becoming the poorest eurozone member.

Many Slovaks feared that euro adoption would have a negative impact upon inflation, but the approval of eurozone accession was nonetheless a source of pride. Moreover, it was also a source of stability and confidence as it offered protection against the exchange rate fluctuations which affected several other EU member states in 2008. The final koruna-euro conversion rate was set at €1.00=K30.126, a level that was much stronger than originally expected and an increase on the 2007 average of €1.00=K33.78.

Prime Minister Robert Fico received another boost to his popularity from Europe in February, as the Party of European Socialists (PES) readmitted his party, Smer (Direction). The PES, an umbrella group for left-wing parties within the EU, had suspended Smer's membership after the 2006 elections, when Fico formed a government with two parties that were viewed as outside the European leftist mainstream, particularly in the case of the far-right Slovak National Party (SNS) (see AR 2007, p. 87). According to the PES, the decision to restore Smer's membership was based on Fico's proven social-democratic orientation and commitment to minority rights. Fico's favourable attitude toward further European integration, including euro adoption, was also a likely factor.

From a political perspective, Slovakia was relatively stable in 2008 as the ruling parties continued to record strong public support while the opposition struggled to find its voice. The ruling coalition was not without controversy and scandal, as three ministers were replaced and calls were made for the resignation of several others. Nonetheless, the opposition had few tools to use against the ruling coalition, particularly given Slovakia's strong economic performance.

One issue of particular concern to the opposition was a controversial press bill that was seen as limiting editorial freedom. The opposition parties attempted to link the press bill with the ratification of the EU Lisbon Treaty, blocking the Treaty's approval as long as the government insisted on the press bill. The Treaty needed to be ratified by at least 90 deputies in the 150-member National Council (unicameral legislature), but the ruling coalition held just 85 seats. Following several months of wrangling, the National Council backed both the Treaty and the press bill in April, and the opposition parties' tactics failed as one of the three—the Party of the Hungarian Coalition (SMK)—ended up voting in favour of the Lisbon Treaty.

While relations between Slovaks and ethnic Hungarians had been strained ever since the Fico government took office in 2006, tensions heightened further in 2008. Politicians in Budapest occasionally came to the defence of Slovakia's Hungarian minority, leading to accusations that Hungary was interfering in Slovak politics and fuelling separatist tendencies.

Sharon Fisher

HUNGARY

CAPITAL: Budapest   AREA: 93,030 sq km   POPULATION: 10,056,000 ('07)
OFFICIAL LANGUAGE: Hungarian   POLITICAL SYSTEM: multiparty republic
HEAD OF STATE: President Laszlo Solyom (since Aug '05)
RULING PARTY: Hungarian Socialist Party (MSzP) forms minority government
HEAD OF GOVERNMENT: Prime Minister Ferenc Gyurcsany (MSzP) (since Sept '04)
MAIN IGO MEMBERSHIPS (NON-UN): NATO, OSCE, CE, CEI, PFP, OECD, EU
CURRENCY: forint (end-'08 £1=Ft274.999, US$1=Ft191.270)
GNI PER CAPITA: US$11,570, $17,430 at PPP ('07)

HUNGARY entered 2008 with weak economic fundamentals stemming from the rather imprudent spending policies of consecutive governments between 2001 and 2006 and the consequent austerity measures. Problems manifested themselves in autumn when the global financial crisis hit the country. Slow economic growth, around 0.8 per cent in the third quarter compared to the same period of 2007, and high public debt of over 70 per cent of GDP made the economy vulnerable, even though the large budget deficits of recent years had already been reined in.

On 9 October an alleged speculative attack against Hungary's biggest commercial bank, OTP, sent the Budapest stock exchange into turmoil while the Hungarian forint lost value rapidly. Hungary faced insolvency as foreign currency markets suddenly dried up and investors lost interest in buying Hungarian state bonds, previously a steady source of external financing. The government and the Hungarian National Bank (the central bank) turned to the IMF, the European Central Bank, and the World Bank for help. On 29 October, a US$25.1 billion 17-month standby loan was offered by the three institutions, the IMF providing the bulk of it (US$15.7 billion), on condition that the government further cut back state spending and relaunched structural reforms. Industrial production and exports, which were the main source of economic growth in Hungary, quickly contracted. Economists forecast recession for 2009 and negative GDP growth of at least 1.5 per cent. Unemployment, already at 7.8 per cent in 2008, was also set to grow. A positive side effect of the economic crisis was a brief truce between government and opposition.

Until summer, however, politics centred upon the referendum on government policies, initiated by opposition leader and former prime minister Viktor Orban of Fidesz-Hungarian Civic Alliance in October 2006 to force Prime Minister Ferenc Gyurcsany to resign, after Gyurcsany had admitted lying to the public about the state of the economy in order to win the 2006 general election (see AR 2007, pp. 88-90). On 9 March an overwhelming majority of Hungarians voted against abolishing tuition fees in higher education, the contributory payments to doctors, and fees for hospital stays (the three issues approved for referendum), thereby practically vetoing all major reform initiatives by the deeply unpopular coalition government of the Hungarian Socialist Party (MSzP) and the liberal Alliance of Free Democrats (SzDSz). The referendum had significant ramifications for the coalition. On 29 March, fearful of the increasing dissent among the rank and file of the MSzP, Gyurcsany announced the shelving of the much needed structural reforms and spoke of more gentle changes or "velvety reforms" in a dramatic political volte face. This prompted the SzDSz to quit the Socialist-led government on 30 April. On 1 May, Gyurcsany formed a minority cabinet, relying for the rest of the year on occasional support from SzDSz and opposition Hungarian Democratic Forum (MDF) deputies to pass legislation.

Energy security remained high on the agenda as Hungary continued to be heavily dependent on Russian gas. On 28 February, Prime Minister Gyurcsany and Russia's President Vladimir Putin agreed in Moscow that the northern branch of the proposed South Stream gas pipeline would reach Austria via Hungary. The US government, which strongly supported plans for the rival, EU-sponsored Nabucco pipeline to circumvent Russia, raised concerns (see map, p. 103). On 17 November, however, US-Hungarian relations were boosted as Hungarians were finally offered visa-free travel to the USA after decades of lobbying.

The Austrian oil and gas firm, OMV, on 23 April failed to take over its Hungarian rival, MOL, when shareholders rejected a hostile bid, launched in September 2007 (see AR 2007, pp. 90-92). The European Commission also objected to the merger, on the grounds that it would create major competition problems and lead to higher prices. On 6 August, OMV officially withdrew its proposal but retained control of 20.2 per cent of shares in MOL.

On 23 June, another Austro-Hungarian economic battlefield opened when Vienna stock exchange operator, Wiener Börse, and its partner, Österreichische Kontrollbank, became majority stakeholders in the Budapest stock exchange.

Wiener Börse made similar acquisitions in Prague and Ljubljana in 2008. Unhappy with the acquisition, MOL and OTP Bank were reported to be in secret talks to set up a rival stock exchange. The two companies together represented around 70-80 per cent of the daily trade in Budapest.

Economic hardship apparently added to growing racism. On 3 June, petrol bombs were thrown into three houses of Roma people in the village of Patka in central Hungary. This set off a wave of similar attacks: by the end of the year 15 such incidents had taken place elsewhere in the country. In another development, on 16 December, the Budapest Municipal Court disbanded the extreme-right Magyar Garda (Hungarian Guard) association, which continued to hold marches in paramilitary uniform to "protect" Hungarians, for inciting hatred against the Roma and other minorities (see AR 2007, pp. 90-92). The Garda's representatives said they would appeal against the ruling.

Diplomatic tit-for-tat continued with Slovakia. On 1 November, a group of Hungarian football fans was beaten up by the Slovak police in Dunajska Streda for allegedly insulting Slovak national sentiment. Some fans were flying flags with symbols of the Kingdom of Hungary, in an alleged reference to Hungarian domination of Slovakia before 1920 (see AR 1920, pp. 224-25). Hungary demanded an explanation for the ferocity of the police intervention, which only fuelled an already bitter polemic between the presidents and governments of the two countries. On 15 November, a meeting in Komarno, Slovakia, between Gyurcsany and Prime Minister Robert Fico of Slovakia did little to ease tensions. Meanwhile, a group created on the popular social networking website, "Facebook", by Slovak and Hungarian users to express their dismay at the current state of official relations quickly gained popularity and thousands joined. Members said that politicians had exaggerated problems and focused too much on extremists.

In a year with little to celebrate, many Hungarians were putting their hopes in the Beijing Olympic Games. Instead, it triggered national soul searching when the Hungarian team ended the games with only three gold medals, their worst result ever relative to others. On 24 August, the men's water polo team offered consolation by beating the USA and winning their third Olympic gold medal in a row.

Daniel Izsak

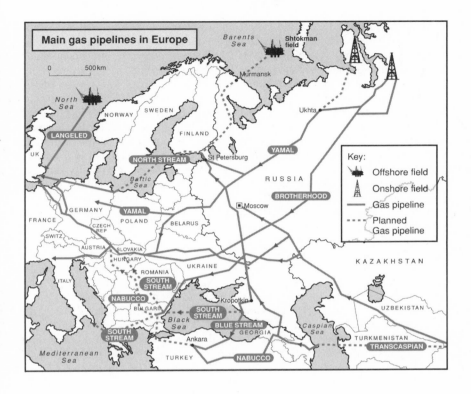

ROMANIA

CAPITAL: Bucharest   AREA: 238,390 sq km   POPULATION: 21,547,000 ('07)
OFFICIAL LANGUAGE: Romanian   POLTICAL SYSTEM: multiparty republic
HEAD OF STATE: President Traian Basescu (PD) (since Dec '04)
RULING PARTIES: Democratic Liberal Party (PD-L) and Social Democratic Party (PSD) coalition
HEAD OF GOVERNMENT: Emil Boc (PD-L) (since Dec '08)
MAIN IGO MEMBERSHIPS (NON-UN): OSCE, CE, CEI, PFP, BSEC, Francophonie, NATO, EU
CURRENCY: new leu (end-'08 £1=NL4.1714, US$1=NL2.9013)
GNI PER CAPITA: US$6,150, $10,980 at PPP ('07)

THE year began with a shaky minority government, which represented barely one-fifth of the electorate, struggling to complete its term in office, and ended with the formation of a grand coalition by Romania's two largest parties that united 70 per cent of the members of Parliament. The unexpected alliance between the Democratic Liberal Party (PD-L) and the Social Democratic Party (PSD), which emerged after the inconclusive election of 30 November, signalled that Romania's main political forces might be more willing to work together to tackle the challenges that lay ahead as nine successive years of robust economic growth ground to a halt in the final months of the year.

Preparations for the elections started early in the year. The opposition Democratic Party (PD), closely associated with the nominally non-partisan president, Traian Basescu, sought to consolidate its lead, demonstrated in the elections for the European Parliament in November 2007 (see AR 2008, p. 93), by merging with the much smaller Liberal Democratic Party in January to form the PD-L. On the other side of the political divide, Prime Minister Calin Popescu-Tariceanu's beleaguered National Liberal Party (PNL) formalised its collaboration with the opposition PSD by concluding a pact in March. By keeping Tariceanu's strongly pro-market minority administration in power, the centre-left PSD was hoping that the wave of support for the PD-L, which had followed its departure from the governing coalition with the PNL, would eventually subside.

An early test of the PSD's tactics came with nationwide local authority elections in June. The PSD and the PD-L finished neck-and-neck in the voting for county councils, with each party winning a 28 per cent share of the vote. The closeness of the race was replicated in the parliamentary elections six months later when the votes cast for the two parties were separated by only 0.6 per cent.

The PD-L gained 115 seats in the Chamber of Deputies (the lower house) against 114 won by the PSD in association with its junior partner, the Conservative Party. In the Senate the PD-L's tally was 51 and that of the PSD, 49. The PNL came third with 65 deputies and 28 senators, and the Hungarian Democratic Union of Romania (UDMR) made up the fourth parliamentary group with 22 deputies and nine senators.

The outcome of the elections was unusual in several ways. For the first time since the restoration of multi-party politics in 1990 (following the collapse of the communist regime), no overtly nationalist political force had succeeded in gaining a foothold in Parliament. The once influential Greater Romania Party failed to get any of its candidates elected, either in the newly-established single-member constituencies or by clearing the 5 per cent threshold required to benefit from proportional representation. The ethnic Hungarian UDMR, which had participated in every government since 1996, was not invited to join the new coalition. The turnout, at 39.2 per cent, was the lowest in the entire post-communist era, reflecting widespread apathy among the electorate. In addition, the elections were held on a Sunday before a public holiday, when many people were away from their local polling stations, contributing to the high level of absenteeism.

Given their history of co-operation over the previous 18 months, there was an expectation that the PNL and the PSD would form the new government. Instead, the coalition that emerged consisted of the PD-L and the PSD, perhaps because the PSD was concerned that an administration that excluded the PD-L would be undermined by an energetic and interventionist president. Basescu picked an experienced former head of government, Theodor Stolojan, as his first choice to lead the new administration, but the prime minister designate withdrew his candidacy, saying that he wanted to make way for the younger generation.

The post of prime minister went to Emil Boc, the 42-year old leader of the PD-L, mayor of the Transylvanian city of Cluj-Napoca, and a close associate of

Basescu. Boc declared that he would lead an "anti-crisis government", which would cut administration costs by 20 per cent, introduce judicial reforms, and tackle widespread corruption. However, the presence of the PSD in the coalition cast doubt on the determination of the new government to root out corruption, a policy strongly advocated by Basescu. Several PSD officials, including a former prime minister, Adrian Nastase, who were facing investigation over corruption charges, had escaped possible trials because of mass abstentions by their party's deputies in a parliamentary vote in June, thereby depriving prosecutors of the majority required to proceed against the suspects.

The Romanian Parliament's failure to act against corruption prompted particularly harsh criticism in the biennial report of the European Commission on progress in judicial reform in its two newest members. The report, published in July, noted that no progress had been made in 10 Romanian corruption cases involving former ministers. Unlike Bulgaria, however, Romania avoided the imposition of financial penalties (see p. 106).

Romania was among a minority of five EU states that refused to recognise Kosovo's declaration of independence from Serbia in February (see map, p. 111). Opposition to Kosovo's independence united Romania's political establishment and a joint session of Parliament's two chambers in February voted overwhelmingly against recognition. The Romanian stance was based on concern that the precedent set by Kosovo might induce the pro-Russian breakaway region of Transdniestr in neighbouring Moldova to follow suit, and could, in the longer term, encourage the large Hungarian minority in Romania to make similar demands. However, Romania was at one with its EU partners in supporting the territorial integrity of Georgia after its conflict with Russia in August, and in condemning Russia's subsequent move to recognise the independence of South Ossetia and Abkhazia (see map, p. 137).

Romania's economy enjoyed another outstanding year, with real GDP growth reaching 8 per cent, the highest growth rate in the EU. The continuing economic boom and resulting prosperity brought a surge in imports, resulting in a current account deficit amounting to 13 per cent of GDP. However, as the year drew to an end, there were signs of a rapid deceleration in growth, as the global economic downturn began to reduce access to credit and investment in Romania. Extended holidays over the Christmas period at major manufacturers, such as the Dacia car plant—whose domestic sales in December plummeted by over 50 per cent—indicated that the outlook for the economy had turned bleak almost overnight.

Gabriel Partos

BULGARIA

CAPITAL: Sofia   AREA: 111,000 sq km   POPULATION: 7,642,000 ('07)
OFFICIAL LANGUAGE: Bulgarian   POLITICAL SYSTEM: multiparty republic
HEAD OF STATE: President Georgi Purvanov (since Nov '01)
RULING PARTIES: coalition of the Bulgarian Socialist Party (BSP), the National Movement Simeon
    II, and the Turkish Movement for Rights and Freedoms (DPS)
HEAD OF GOVERNMENT: Prime Minister Sergei Stanishev (BSP) (since Aug '05)
MAIN IGO MEMBERSHIPS (NON-UN): OSCE, CE, PFP, CEI, BSEC, Francophonie, NATO, EU
CURRENCY: lev (end-'08 £1=L2.0226, US$1=L1.4068)
GNI PER CAPITA: US$4,590, $11,180 at PPP ('07)

BULGARIA registered strong economic performance throughout the year, with GDP growing by more than 6 per cent. The economy ran on a substantial budget surplus, and in the first half of the year the government moved to clear a large part of the country's foreign debt. To help stimulate the economy, and particularly to develop the potential of small and medium sized businesses, in April the National Assembly (unicameral legislature) approved the creation of a Bulgarian Development Bank.

In July, the National Assembly ratified Bulgaria's agreement with Russia for the construction of the South Stream gas pipeline, a joint venture between the two state gas monopolies, Gazprom and Bulgargaz, with a transit capacity of 31 billion cubic metres of natural gas per year. Western industry experts saw the pipeline as a threat to an EU-backed project, the Nabucco pipeline, which would bring Caspian Sea gas to central Europe without crossing Russian territory (see map, p. 103).

The coalition government, led by the socialist prime minister, Sergei Stanishev, was criticised for failing to make sufficient progress in the fight against corruption and organised crime. Earlier in the year, the parliamentary opposition initiated a no-confidence motion against the government, which saw off the challenge thanks to its comfortable majority. However, polls continued to show a slump in the government's popularity, with the main threat coming from the Citizens for European Development of Bulgaria (CEDB), under the leadership of the mayor of Sofia, Boiko Borisov, who enjoyed the highest approval ratings in the country. Nevertheless, with the opposition alliance of right-of-centre parties remaining fragmented, the governing coalition did not feel threatened.

The country's performance against EU benchmarks came under unprecedented external scrutiny from the European Commission. Whilst praising progress made in areas such as constitutional and judicial reform, the Commission, in its interim reports in February and July, expressed concern at the authorities' failure to deliver results in tackling corruption and stopping EU funds from being diverted. The outcome was suspension of some €950 million of EU funding, earmarked for improvements to Bulgaria's roads, institution building, agriculture, and rural development. Later, in November, the Commission announced that it was definitively stripping Bulgaria of €220 million from those funds. The Commission's action prompted a quick government response. It outlined a series of measures, including the creation of an agency responsible for monitoring the use of EU funds and improving communication with the EU. To lead the agency, the government appointed Miglena Plugchieva, a deputy prime minister.

The EU measures galvanised political debate. More controversy, however, was triggered by the arrest in March of Ivan Ivanov, the second most senior police officer in charge of combating organised crime. His arrest came after recordings of telephone conversations were brought to the attention of the chief prosecutor, allegedly showing that Ivanov had accepted bribes from a drugs gang in return for disclosing classified documents. The opposition parties called for the resignation of the interior minister, Rumen Petkov, claiming that he had failed to act against Ivanov. A controversial figure, Petkov lost his job in April after heavy pressure from the EU. Petkov admitted to having met two businessmen with alleged links to organised crime, but explained his contact with them as an attempt to stop mafia style killings, a serious problem since 2001.

There was also concern about the state of the country's health and education systems. Following persistent criticism, the prime minister changed his health minister in April, giving the post to a former mayor. The move signalled an attempt to revive health service reforms, which had stuttered in recent years.

Genc Lamani

ALBANIA—MACEDONIA—KOSOVO—SERBIA—MONTENEGRO— BOSNIA & HERZEGOVINA—CROATIA—SLOVENIA

ALBANIA

CAPITAL: Tirana   AREA: 28,750 sq km   POPULATION: 3,181,000 ('07)
OFFICIAL LANGUAGE: Albanian   POLTICAL SYSTEM: multiparty republic
HEAD OF STATE: President Bamir Topi (PDSh) (since July '07)
RULING PARTIES: Democratic Party of Albania (PDSh)-led coalition
HEAD OF GOVERNMENT: Prime Minister Sali Berisha (PDSh) (since Sept '05)
MAIN IGO MEMBERSHIPS (NON-UN): OSCE, PFP, CE, CEI, BSEC, OIC, Francophonie
CURRENCY: lek (end-'08 £1=AL127.996, US$1=AL89.0250)
GNI PER CAPITA: US$3,290, $6,580 at PPP ('07)

ALBANIA stepped up efforts in its quest for membership of NATO and the EU. It was rewarded at the NATO summit in Bucharest in April with an invitation to join the Alliance. This was the outcome of serious reforms by successive governments since the early 1990s, which enjoyed strong popular support. The signing of the NATO accession protocols in July launched the process of ratification by the Alliance members. Confirming that ratification was progressing, NATO foreign ministers said in December that they expected Albania, along with Croatia, to become NATO's newest members by April 2009.

Albania's EU integration efforts were less rewarding. Whilst some aspects of reform, including the government's zero tolerance policy on corruption, were praised by the European Commission, the Commission's progress report in November expressed concern about Albania's efforts. It noted that the declared commitment by the authorities to combat corruption lacked any rigorous imple-mentation. Corruption remained a problem, especially in the judiciary, police, health, and customs sectors. Reform of the judiciary was sluggish, despite a pledge of co-operation between the two main parliamentary parties, the governing Democratic Party (PDSh) and the opposition Socialist Party.

The country was shaken by a series of explosions at an ammunition depot at Gerdec, just outside Tirana, in March. The blasts, which killed 26 people and injured another 300, raised questions about the failure to enforce health and safety regulations. Hundreds of people, including women and children, were reported to be working at the military facility when the explosions occurred. The authorities were also accused of acting irresponsibly by allowing the ammunition depot to operate near a residential area close to Tirana's international airport, in order to facilitate controversial weapons and ammunition dealings, allegedly involving a state owned company (MEICO). The government rejected the allegations. The defence minister, Fatmir Mehdiu, resigned and was subsequently placed under investigation for the blasts and the weapons trade.

Another scandal—the so-called "Basha affair", relating to the foreign minister, Lulzim Basha—made headlines throughout the year, until he was indicted on corruption charges in December. The charges related to Basha's stint as minister of public works, transport and telecommunications. He was accused of abuse of power over alleged irregularities and misuse of public funds in the construction of the Albania-Kosovo highway, which was estimated to have cost the taxpayer an extra €230 million. Basha denied any wrongdoing, saying his indictment was politically motivated.

In a rare sign of co-operation between Albania's two largest political parties, in April Parliament adopted a package of constitutional amendments covering the electoral system, election of the president, and the mandate of the prosecutor general.

The amendments changed the electoral system from a mixed to a regional proportional system (140 seats filled by proportional representation from party lists, in regions corresponding to existing constituencies). The new system aimed to avoid the widespread tactical voting that the old system had promoted. Smaller parties fiercely contested the change, fearing that their influence would decline. A new election code, drafted with help from international experts, was adopted in November, together with a series of other measures, including the computerisation of citizen registers and voter lists.

Relations between Parliament and the president, who came from the ranks of the governing PDSh, became difficult at times. In what was seen as a politically motivated confrontation, the government mobilised its majority in Parliament to reject the presidential appointments of High Court judges in June, eventually approving a second set of nominees in July. The clash raised concerns about the independence of state institutions from the executive branch, as well as the role of personal interests and prejudices in shaping national political life.

The economy grew by about 6 percent. Inflation was kept under control, with the exception of some months of the year when it exceeded 4 per cent, mainly due to higher food and energy prices. The management of public finances improved, due to large scale tax administration measures. The introduction in January of a flat 10 per cent income tax rate led to an increase in tax revenues and an improvement of the investment climate.

Genc Lamani

MACEDONIA

CAPITAL: Skopje   AREA: 25,710 sq km   POPULATION: 2,037,000 ('07)
OFFICIAL LANGUAGE: Macedonian   POLTICAL SYSTEM: multiparty republic
HEAD OF STATE: President Branko Crvenkovski (since May '04)
RULING PARTY: VMRO-DPMNE heads For a Better Macedonia (ZpM) coalition
HEAD OF GOVERNMENT: Prime Minister Nikola Gruevski (VMRO-DPMNE) (since Aug '06)
MAIN IGO MEMBERSHIPS (NON-UN): OSCE, PFP, CE, CEFTA, CEI, Francophonie
CURRENCY: Macedonian denar (end-'08 £1=D62.7148, US$1=D43.6200)
GNI PER CAPITA: US$3,460, $8,510 at PPP ('07)

THE year was disappointing for Macedonia, marked by failure to win admission to NATO at the Alliance's summit in Bucharest in April, violent general elections in June, and another failure in the autumn to receive a firm date for a start to accession talks with the EU.

The year began with tragedy on 12 January, when all 11 soldiers and crew on board a Macedonian army helicopter returning from a peacekeeping mission in Bosnia & Herzegovina were killed after it crashed while preparing to land at Skopje airport.

NATO and EU membership issues cast longer shadows, however. As an EU candidate and contributor to the US-led war in Afghanistan, Macedonia expected to seal membership of both organisations in 2008. On 6 March, the EU enlargement commissioner, Olli Rehn, duly presented the centre-right government of Nikola Gruevski with a list of "benchmarks" that the country needed to meet in order to obtain a recommendation for the start to accession talks.

While the Gruevski government addressed EU demands, disaster struck on 3 April at NATO's Bucharest summit when Greece acted on earlier threats to veto Macedonia's admission to the Alliance (see AR 2008, pp. 101-02). Greece declared that it would not relent until Macedonia had resolved the long-running dispute over the country's nomenclature to Greece's satisfaction. Since Macedonia's independence in 1992, Greece had consistently claimed that use of the term "Macedonia" by the new country implied a territorial claim to the northern Greek province of the same name. Right up to the opening of the NATO summit, however, Macedonia had hoped that its US ally would force Greece to back down.

The debacle at Bucharest had immediate domestic political ramifications, prompting Gruevski on 13 April to go for early elections in search of a fresh mandate for his policy of resistance to Greek demands. For Gruevski's Internal Macedonian Revolutionary Organisation—Democratic Party for Macedonian National Unity (VMRO-DPMNE), the elections were a triumph. The opposition Social Democrats, under their uncharismatic leader, Radmila Sekerinska, struggled to find a narrative that did not make them appear weak in relation to Greece. For Gruevski's team, on the other hand, rejection of Greek demands proved comfortable political terrain and the party benefited accordingly, moving up from 45 to 63 seats in the 120-seat Sobranje (unicameral legislature), while the Socialists fell from 32 to 27. Whether the country's international image benefited from the elections was less clear. On 1 June, as voting got underway, one person was killed and at least six injured in mainly ethnic Albanian western districts. The violence and overall handling of the election drew unfavourable comment in European circles, damaging Macedonia's EU chances. The time wasted on the campaign, meanwhile, delayed action on the EU's shortlist of reforms.

On 28 July the Sobranje approved a new government led by Gruevski, who vowed to make economic prosperity and EU and NATO integration his priority. The Social Democrats, in disarray, elected a new leader, Zoran Zaev.

The new government made some proactive moves. Defying Serbia (and many of the ruling party's nationalist, anti-Albanian supporters), on 9 October Macedonia recognised the independence of neighbouring Kosovo. Work also began on completing demarcation of the border with Kosovo. But the year ended on the same note of disappointment as it had begun. Since the Bucharest NATO summit, the country had feared that Greece would apply the same veto to Macedonia's EU integration as it had to the NATO application. In the event, the blow fell from the European Commission itself, on 5 November, when an EU progress report on the Balkans signally failed to recommend a starting date for Macedonia's accession talks.

Meanwhile, the government in mid-November opened a law suit against Greece in the International Court of Justice (ICJ) in The Hague, charging it with breaking a 1995 UN interim accord when it vetoed Macedonia's application to join NATO. The accord bound Greece not to veto Macedonia's membership of any international organisation, so long as the country applied to join under its provisional UN name, the Former Yugoslav Republic of Macedonia, FYROM. Whether or not Macedonia won its suit, the move undoubtedly dimmed hopes of an early end to the "name" dispute with Greece. It was increasingly clear that Macedonia's hopes of joining the EU alongside Croatia within the next few years were receding.

Marcus Tanner

KOSOVO

CAPITAL: Pristina   AREA: 10,887 sq km   POPULATION: 2,100,000 (UN estimate '06)
OFFICIAL LANGUAGES: Albanian, Serbian   POLTICAL SYSTEM: multiparty republic
HEAD OF STATE: President Fatmir Sejdiu (since Feb '06)
RULING PARTIES: Democratic Party of Kosovo (PDK) in coalition with Albanian Democratic League of Kosovo (LDK)
HEAD OF GOVERNMENT: Prime Minister Hashim Thaci (PDK) (since Jan '08)
MAIN IGO MEMBERSHIPS (NON-UN): CEFTA
CURRENCY: euro (not formal member of eurozone) (end-'08 £1=€1.0344, US$1=€0.7194); and
   Serbian dinar (end-'08 £1=D92.7925, US$1=D64.5400)
GNI PER CAPITA: n/a

IN the former Serbian province, under UN control since 1999, the calamitous economic situation and an unemployment level of 45 per cent were all overshadowed by the question of Kosovo's "final status".

Responding to public pressure to resolve the issue, and emboldened by the report on Kosovo compiled in 2007 by the UN envoy, Martti Ahtisaari, which called for the province's "monitored" independence, the government of Hashim Thaci, head of the Democratic Party of Kosovo (PDK) and prime minister since 2007, declared Kosovo independent on 17 February (see Documents). In the 120-

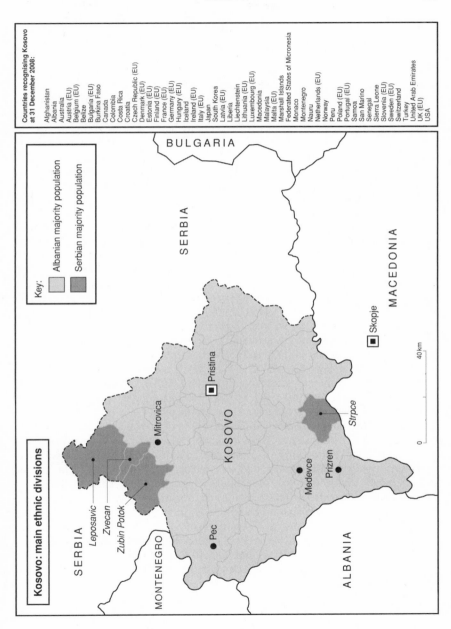

Kosovo: main ethnic divisions

Key:
Albanian majority population
Serbian majority population

Countries recognising Kosovo at 31 December 2008:

Afghanistan
Albania
Australia
Austria (EU)
Belgium (EU)
Belize
Bulgaria (EU)
Burkina Faso
Canada
Colombia
Costa Rica
Croatia
Czech Republic (EU)
Denmark (EU)
Estonia (EU)
Finland (EU)
France (EU)
Germany (EU)
Hungary (EU)
Iceland
Ireland (EU)
Italy (EU)
Japan
South Korea
Latvia (EU)
Liberia
Liechtenstein
Lithuania (EU)
Luxembourg (EU)
Macedonia
Malaysia
Malta (EU)
Marshall Islands
Federated States of Micronesia
Monaco
Montenegro
Nauru
Netherlands (EU)
Norway
Peru
Poland (EU)
Portugal (EU)
Samoa
San Marino
Senegal
Sierra Leone
Slovenia (EU)
Sweden (EU)
Switzerland
Turkey
United Arab Emirates
UK (EU)
USA

BULGARIA

SERBIA

MACEDONIA

Skopje

Pristina

Mitrovica

KOSOVO

Strpce

Medevce

Prizren

Pec

SERBIA

Leposavic
Zvecan
Zubin Potok

MONTENEGRO

ALBANIA

0   40 km

seat National Assembly in Pristina, 109 deputies voted in favour of the resolution and none against, though all 11 deputies representing Kosovo's Serbian minority boycotted the session. In spite of Serbia's strenuous opposition, in the form of threats to block Kosovo's membership of major international organisations and a move to undermine the independence declaration by seeking the opinion of the International Court of Justice (ICJ) in The Hague, 53 of the 192 members of the UN had recognised the new state by 31 December. These included the USA and all but five of the 27 EU states (the exceptions being Slovakia, Spain, Greece, Cyprus, and Romania). The UN Security Council was evenly split, with the USA, the UK, and France supporting recognition and China and Russia opposing. That same split was reflected in the former Yugoslavia, where Slovenia and Croatia offered recognition early on, Macedonia and Montenegro followed suit months later, while Bosnia & Herzegovina (and of course Serbia) made no moves at all to recognise the new state.

Widespread fears that independence would trigger pogroms against Kosovo's remaining 100,000 or so Serbs proved unfounded, however, as celebrations in the capital, Pristina, passed off peacefully, in contrast to violent riots in Serbia's capital, Belgrade. Indeed, independence appeared to defuse rather than fuel nationalist tension on the Albanian side. At the same time, independence cemented an existing "de facto" separation from Kosovo of the northern, Serb-run, municipalities of Leposavic, Zvecan, and Zubin Potok, and the northern half of the town and municipality of Mitrovica (see map, p. 111). Adjacent to Serbia and supported financially by the Serbian government, these areas rejected the authority of the Kosovo government and initially refused to consent to the deployment locally of a new EU rule of law mission, EULEX, which under the Ahtisaari plan was intended to replace the outgoing UN mission in Kosovo, UNMIK.

For its part, following the advice of its Western allies, Thaci's government resolved not to enter into avoidable physical confrontations with Serbian hardliners in the north, in spite of the National Assembly's adoption of a new constitution on 15 June that restated Kosovo's territorial integrity. The government's "good neighbour" policy also included keeping a distance from ethnic Albanian agitation in western Macedonia, southern Serbia and Montenegro. This pacific policy aroused relatively little discontent at home, where the focus of public opinion was drifting away from "national" to economic issues, such as unemployment, energy failures, corruption, and the malfunctioning judiciary.

Here, the picture was dismal. According to an EU report on the western Balkans issued in November, progress in combating money laundering was poor, while courts lacked both expertise and the will to challenge economic and financial crime. Drug trafficking was also described as a serious problem. "Kosovo is one of the main trafficking routes for drugs in the southern Balkans," the report said. "There is no action plan or strategy to combat drug trafficking... Statistics are unreliable and intelligence gathering capacity is insufficient." Ordinary people remained most preoccupied with unemployment, which at 45 per cent was by far the highest in the former Yugoslavia. With an estimated 28,000 youngsters entering the job market each year, and an average of only 6,500 finding employment, the chances of significantly cutting the jobless tally, even with healthy growth rates, looked bleak. One ray of light was that the 2009 budget, unveiled on 4 November, at €1.43 billion, was 15 per cent up on the budget for 2008. But in the absence of massive sustained investment—which looked highly unlikely— Kosovo's only realistic hope of economic survival rested on obtaining agreements to permit Kosovars to work legally in Europe and North America, thereby increasing the flow of remittances back home. This, too, looked far from hopeful.

Some local academics in 2008 were already loudly predicting violent social unrest, now that the Serbian threat had receded. However, it was also possible that a combination of the Albanians' traditionally strong and resourceful family networks, nationalist pride, and generally low material expectations would keep the new country on track and at peace.

Marcus Tanner

SERBIA

CAPITAL: Belgrade   AREA: 88,361 sq km   POPULATION: 7,386,000 ('07, excl. Kosovo and Metohija)
OFFICIAL LANGUAGE: Serbo-Croat   POLTICAL SYSTEM: multiparty republic
HEAD OF STATE: President Boris Tadic (DS) (since June '06)
RULING PARTIES: coalition of For a European Serbia, led by Democratic Party (DS) and Socialist Party of Serbia (SPS)
HEAD OF GOVERNMENT: Prime Minister Mirko Cvetkovic (DS) (since July '08)
MAIN IGO MEMBERSHIPS (NON-UN): OSCE, CE, CEI, EBRD, PFP, CEFTA
CURRENCY: dinar (end-'08 £1=D92.7925, US$1=D64.5400)
GNI PER CAPITA: US$4,730 (excl. Kosovo and Metohija), $10,220 at PPP ('07)

Two questions dominated Serbia in 2008: whether the nationalist Serbian Radical Party (SRS) would finally take power, and whether the breakaway province of Kosovo, under UN control since 1999, would declare independence. Many observers were convinced that if Kosovo declared independence, this would fatally undermine the country's fractious centrist government and give the Radicals the fillip they needed.

In the event, these dire predictions were disproved. Kosovo's formal secession on 17 February sparked a night of nationalist rioting in Belgrade, including vandalistic assaults on the US embassy, but in the ensuing elections the centre not only held its own but strengthened its position. Subsequent splits in the ranks of the Radicals left the pro-European moderates, led by Boris Tadic, in clearer control of the field at the end of 2008 than at any time since the fall of the regime of Slobodan Milosevic in 2000.

This was all the more surprising because Tadic's Democratic Party (DS) had failed to form a working relationship with its more nationalist partner in government since the January 2007 elections, the Democratic Party of Serbia (DSS), led by Vojislav Kostunica. Relations were so poor that Kostunica, then prime minister, refused to back his so-called partner, Tadic, in the presidential elections in January 2008. Partly as a result of this, Tomislav Nikolic, the acting head of the SRS, won the first round on 20 January. (SRS leader, Vojislav Seselj, was on trial before the war crimes tribunal, the International Criminal Tribunal for the former Yugoslavia (ICTY), in The Hague.) As had happened before, however, the threat of a Radical takeover galvanised moderates and ethnic minorities, rallying them to Tadic's support, and he won the second round with just over 51 per cent of the vote.

Relations between Tadic, now president, and Prime Minister Kostunica never recovered. Kosovo's independence on 17 February brought the farce of a Democrat-DSS coalition to a close, after Kostunica insisted on an early general election, called for 11 May. Unsurprisingly, the prime minister did not campaign alongside the Democrats but with a small nationalist coalition of his own. The Democrats assembled their own coalition, "For a European Serbia", while the Radicals campaigned independently. Widespread expectations of an SRS landslide on the back of a wave of popular rage over Kosovo were confounded.

Three developments aided Tadic's pro-European team in the days leading up to the vote: Serbia signed a stabilisation and association agreement (SAA) with the EU; the EU liberalised visa applications from Serbia; and the Italian car manufacturing giant, Fiat, announced a €700 million investment into the ailing Serbian car company, Zastava, delighting locals in the central city of Kragujevac, Zastava's headquarters.

The signing of the SAA was largely symbolic, as the deal could not take effect until Serbia's co-operation with the ICTY had been deemed complete, which meant Serbia handing over the last two fugitive indictees, the former Bosnian Serb general, Ratko Mladic, and the former Croatian Serb leader, Goran Hadzic. Nevertheless, the signing of the SAA boosted the pro-Europeans, divided nationalists, and contributed to the Democrat-led coalition's surprisingly good showing of 39 per cent, while the SRS won just under 30 per cent, and Kostunica's coalition won around 12 per cent.

The results left Milosevic's old Socialist Party of Serbia (SPS), led by Ivica Dacic, which won about 8 per cent, in the agreeable position of kingmaker. In spite of the SPS's nationalist heritage and previous fierce opposition to the ICTY, Dacic surprised observers—and many of his own voters—by forming a coalition with the Democrats instead of the Radicals, on the grounds that it was better to ally with the rising rather than the setting sun. Thus, Serbia received a new government firmly committed to a pro-European course. The secession in October from the SPS of several key figures, including Nikolic himself, to form a new nationalist, pro-EU, party, the Serbian Progressive Party, completed the disarray of the once monolithic Radical bloc.

For all its apparent pro-EU fervour, however, the new government showed it was prepared to risk irritating the USA and other Western countries by pursuing Serbia's claim to Kosovo, albeit using diplomatic, not military, methods. Ambassadors continued to be withdrawn (temporarily) from countries that had recognised Kosovo, while the foreign minister, Vuk Jeremic, spearheaded a busy campaign against Kosovo's recognition in the UN. This scored a success in early October, when the UN General Assembly backed a resolution endorsing Serbia's request for the International Court of Justice (ICJ) to deliver an opinion on the legality of Kosovo's independence. The vote was 77 to six. Kosovo's Western allies were among the 74 abstentions, justifying their inaction on the grounds that an ICJ opinion would be advisory and non-binding.

At the same time, Serbia's government softened its earlier rigid opposition to the deployment of the EU's rule of law mission, EULEX, in Serb-run areas of northern Kosovo, signalling that it would be satisfied by clarification that EULEX would be "status neutral" regarding the issue of Kosovo's independence. Therefore, hopes grew that this particular boil had been lanced. With the Kosovo issue "parked" in the ICJ, the Serbian public became more concerned with economic issues, and with whether the global recession was about to hit Serbia. Optimists maintained that Serbia's former economic isolation under UN sanctions might serve as a form of "windbreak" from the gale, and there was no sign of local banks experiencing credit shortages or of "runs" by customers panicking about savings. But by November, most economists were warning the country to brace for recession, suggesting that Serbia was not as disengaged from Western financial systems as the public appeared to believe.

Marcus Tanner

MONTENEGRO

CAPITAL: Podgorica   AREA: 14,026 sq km   POPULATION: 600,000 ('07)
OFFICIAL LANGUAGE: Montenegrin   POLTICAL SYSTEM: multiparty republic
HEAD OF STATE: President Filip Vujanovic (since May '03)
RULING PARTIES: coalition led by Democratic Party of Socialists (DPS)
HEAD OF GOVERNMENT: Prime Minister Milo Djukanovic (DPS) (since Feb '08)
MAIN IGO MEMBERSHIPS (NON-UN): OSCE, PFP, EBRD, IMF, CE, CEFTA
CURRENCY: euro (adopted unilaterally) (end-'08 £1=€1.0344, US$1=€0.7194)
GNI PER CAPITA: US$5,180, $10,290 at PPP ('07)

PRESIDENTIAL elections held in late spring proved the first major test of the popularity of the pro-independence establishment surrounding Milo Djukanovic and his Democratic Party of Socialists (DPS), which had navigated the country through an independence referendum, and out of a loose "state union" with Serbia, in 2006 (see AR 2007, pp. 104-05).

In the event, the election was a walkover, confirming the collapse of the once muscular pro-Serbian opposition. Filip Vujanovic, the incumbent president, standing as candidate for Prime Minister Djukanovic's bloc, won almost 52 per cent in the first round held on 6 April, making a second round unnecessary. He crushed his nearest rival, Andrija Mandic of the Serbian People's Party, who won 19 per cent as the candidate of the Serb List bloc. Djukanovic's continuing hegemony over the post-independence scene in Montenegro looked set to continue.

The principal factor behind the loss of confidence by the Serbian bloc, even though Serbs comprised at least 30 per cent of the population, was the strong economy. Dire warnings from Europe, Belgrade, and from within Montenegro itself, that independence would condemn the country to third world poverty levels and to isolation, proved very misplaced. Instead, tourism and property boomed, enabling the government to adopt a 2009 budget on 6 November that boosted spending by 15 per cent to €1.6 billion. Although economic growth was expected to fall from 8.2 per cent to just over 7 per cent in 2009, there was still an air of optimism that rebounded to the credit of the government.

Neither the government, nor most of the population, seemed much worried by descriptions of Djukanovic's Montenegro as a dumping ground for the ill-gotten gains of Russian tycoons, or by the nickname "Moscow-on-Sea". Aside from Russian billionaires, Montenegro was increasingly a playground for the super-rich of the Arab world. A high-profile visit in November by representatives of the royal family of Abu Dhabi, in connection with a planned €5 billion development on the sands near the port of Ulcinj, received enthusiastic publicity in the pro-government media.

As a result, the government simply shrugged off attempts by the opposition to create a showdown over the issue of Kosovo's independence. When pro-Serbian rioters took to the streets of the capital, Podgorica, after the government had recognised the former Serbian province on 9 October, Mandic's bloc, Serb List, was embarrassed by charges of having encouraged hooliganism. Mandic's personal attempt to force the government to rescind recognition by going on hunger strike was judged a total failure.

There were persistent suggestions that Russia's growing economic influence in Montenegro might lead to the government slowing, or even reversing, its moves to join NATO. However, early in November Djukanovic again showed that he was capable of riding two horses at once when he submitted Montenegro's request to join the alliance's membership action plan (MAP) to the NATO secretary general, Jaap de Hoop Scheffer.

Marcus Tanner

BOSNIA & HERZEGOVINA

CONSTITUENT REPUBLICS: Federation of Bosnia & Herzegovina, FBiH (Muslim-Croat Federation); and Republika Srpska, RS (Serb Rebublic)
CAPITAL: Sarajevo   AREA: 51,210 sq km   POPULATION: 3,773,000 ('07)
OFFICIAL LANGUAGES: Bosnian, Croatian, Serbian   POLTICAL SYSTEM: multiparty republic
HEADS OF STATE: Haris Silajdzic (SBiH), Bosniak (chairman); Nebojsa Radmanovic (SNSD), Serb; Zeljko Komsic (SDP), Croat (since Oct '06)
PRESIDENTS OF REPUBLICS: FBiH: Borjana Kristo (HDZ) (since Feb '07); RS: Igor Radojcic (acting) (SNSD) (since Oct '06)
HEADS OF GOVERNMENT: Prime Minister Nikola Spiric (SNSD) (since Jan '07); FBiH: Nedzad Brankovic (SDA) (since March '07); RS: Milorad Dodic (SNSD) (since Feb '06)
MAIN IGO MEMBERSHIPS (NON-UN): OSCE, EBRD, CE, CEI, PFP, CEFTA
CURRENCY: marka (end-'08 £1=M2.0230, US$1=M1.4071)
GNI PER CAPITA: US$3,790, $7,280 at PPP ('07)

THE single most important development of 2008 in Bosnia & Herzegovina did not occur inside the country but in Belgrade, Serbia's capital, where on 22 July the former Bosnian Serb leader Radovan Karadzic was arrested. The news brought thousands of Sarajevans onto the streets, rejoicing over the belated capture of the man who, as president of the Republika Srpska, had exercised overall command responsibility over the 1992-95 siege of Sarajevo, the deaths of tens of thousands of Bosniaks in detention camps, and the mass execution of 6,000 men and boys in Srebrenica, eastern Bosnia, after the enclave fell to Karadzic's military commander, General Ratko Mladic, in July 1995.

Disguised by a long white beard and living a new life as an alternative health guru, faith healer, and journalist, Karadzic was picked up in New Belgrade, where he had apparently been living for several years, and dispatched to The Hague for trial before the International Criminal Tribunal for the Former Yugoslavia (ICTY).

Yet Karadzic's capture did not bring "closure" to Bosnia. Indeed, the contrast between the joy felt in Sarajevo and the dismay in the Republika Srpska only underlined Bosnia's deepening divisions. Throughout 2008, talk of the eventual breakup of the country was increasingly heard, and not quelled by an otherwise major development: the passage of a long delayed law on police reform at the end of April, followed by the signing of a stabilisation and association agreement (SAA) with the European Union on 16 June. This was hailed as a step forward and, for a while, the abolition of the international community's administrator, the Office of the High Representative, OHR, again seemed back on the agenda. The hopes raised by the SAA soon gave way to familiar despondency as the two "entities"—the Republika Srpska and the Federation of Bosnia and Herzegovina (FBiH)—returned to their usual politics of mutual confrontation, with some Bosniak leaders demanding the abolition of the Bosnian Serb entity and the Bosnian Serb leader, Milorad Dodik, threatening to emulate Kosovo's example by seceding.

Local elections on 5 October proved a triumph for Dodik and his Party of Independent Social Democrats (SNSD) in the Republika Srpska, and for the old nationalist Bosniak and Croat parties in the FBiH: the (Bosniak) Party of Democratic Action (SDA), and the Croat Democratic Union (HDZ). These trounced their respective rivals: the Party for Bosnia and Herzegovina (SZBiH), led by Haris Silajdzic, and HDZ 1990.

The EU's November progress report on the western Balkans was predictably harsh on Bosnia & Herzegovina, condemning the elite's selfish politics of confrontation and the failure to build on the SAA. Adding to the drama, Lord (Paddy) Ashdown, high representative from 2002-06, and Richard Holbrooke, chief architect of the 1995 Dayton peace agreement for Bosnia & Herzegovina, jointly launched a public attack on Dodik, accusing him of intending to break up the country. Worried by the air of drift, Olli Rehn, the EU's enlargement commissioner, and Javier Solana, EU foreign affairs supremo, drafted an action plan for Bosnia that was approved by an EU foreign ministers' meeting on 11 November. The report underlined the deteriorating political situation, noting that while most Bosnians supported EU membership, their leaders remained "mired in the nationalist logic and talk of the past". It added: "A stronger engagement of the EU is today more essential than ever before." Among other things, the Rehn-Solana report recommended the closure of the OHR and the transfer of its remaining authorities to a new EU governor, the EU special representative (EUSR). Whether closer EU engagement would change anything in Bosnia was uncertain, for Dodik remained cheerfully indifferent to outside criticism, buoyed by his ascendancy among the Bosnian Serbs and by the relative economic success of the Republika Srpska compared to the ailing, indebted FBiH. One hopeful sign in late autumn was the unexpected agreement reached on 8 November between the leaders of the country's three biggest parties—the Bosniak SDA (Party for Democratic Action); the Serb SNSD (Party of Independent Social Democrats); and the Croat HDZ (Croatian Democratic Union)—to work together to overcome the current impasse in several key policy fields, such as the future of the district of Brcko and the sale of state enterprises. Thus, towards the end of 2008, there were faint signs that Bosnia's quarrelling leaders were aware of the need to draw back from the brink.

Marcus Tanner

CROATIA

CAPITAL: Zagreb   AREA: 56,540 sq km   POPULATION: 4,438,000 ('07)
OFFICIAL LANGUAGE: Croatian   POLITICAL SYSTEM: multiparty republic
HEAD OF STATE: President Stipe Mesic (HNS) (since Feb '00)
RULING PARTIES: Croatian Democratic Union (HDZ) in coalition with the Croatian Social Liberal Party (HSLS), Croatian Peasants' Party (HSS), and Independent Democratic Serbian Party (SDSS)
HEAD OF GOVERNMENT: Prime Minister Ivo Sanader (HDZ) (since Dec '03)
MAIN IGO MEMBERSHIPS (NON-UN): OSCE, CE, CEFTA, CEI, PFP
CURRENCY: kuna (end-'08 £1=K7.6242, US$1=K5.3029)
GNI PER CAPITA: US$10,460, $15,050 at PPP ('07)

THE issue of Croatia's membership of key Euro-Atlantic international organisations, the EU and NATO, dominated public discourse in the first half of the year, before the phenomenon of mobster violence assumed prominence in the autumn.

In March, polls showed support for EU membership tipping over the 50 per cent level for the first time in years, as fears of regional instability, linked to Kosovo's February independence declaration, outweighed both anger over EU pressure on Croatia to disband its planned "no-fishing" zone in the Adriatic, and worries that EU membership might result in Croatia being forced to concede to Slovenia in their maritime border dispute in the Piran Bay. Quarrels over the "protected ecological fishery zone", known by the acronym ZERP, mainly with Italy and Slovenia, had much excited the Croatian public in recent years and strengthened the large anti-EU lobby, which felt that EU membership was coming at too high a price.

NATO membership was far less controversial, however, in spite of the country's coolness towards the US-led war in Iraq. Prime Minister Ivo Sanader, head of the Croatian Democratic Union (HDZ), and President Stipe Mesic were both boosted when the NATO summit in Bucharest on 2-4 April announced that it wished to admit Croatia and Albania, even while the regional ally of both, Macedonia, was rejected. US President George W. Bush bestowed the seal of approval by making a brief one-day stopover in Croatia on 4 April, en route to Russia.

While the affair of the ZERP, the Piran Bay dispute with Slovenia, and the business of the EU "chapters" in the accession process filled the newspapers for months, a series of high-profile mobster murders later drew attention in another direction, partly because they embarrassed the country's much cultivated reputation as an oasis of peace in a turbulent region. The murders of a well-known publisher, Ivo Pukanic, and of Ivana Hodak, a lawyer's daughter, shocked the country, drawing attention to the increasingly violent criminal underworld and prompting Sanader to pledge that he would not allow Zagreb to become "another Beirut". Pukanic, owner and editor of the newspaper *Nacional*, among others, and a close friend to President Mesic, was killed on 23 October after a bomb was planted in his car outside his Zagreb office. He died alongside his marketing director shortly before he had been due to testify as a prosecution witness in a trial of tobacco smugglers. Two weeks earlier, Hodak, daughter of a prominent defence lawyer then engaged on behalf of a retired general on trial for theft, was also shot dead.

While the authorities moved to allay disquiet by launching a swoop on a number of suspected mafia bosses in December, fears remained that the killings might adversely affect Croatia's EU bid, especially as "justice" remained a key concern of the EU enlargement commissioner, Olli Rehn, when it came to Croatia. On 12 November, Rehn reiterated to Sanader that the fight against organised crime and reform of the judiciary needed to be Croatia's priorities. For his part, Sanader was still hoping to close the last chapters in the EU negotiations by the end of 2008 and secure an admission date in 2010 or 2011 at the latest.

While Slovenia's unresolved disputes with Croatia posed a direct threat to the country's EU accession hopes, a marked cooling of relations with Serbia was less significant, though unfortunate all the same, given the two countries' earlier remarkable progress towards reconciliation. The first upset came in mid-March, when Croatia, alongside Hungary, recognised the former Serbian province of Kosovo as an independent state. A worse spat unfolded on 18 November, when the International Court of Justice (ICJ) in The Hague ruled that it was willing to hear Croatia's case against Serbia accusing the latter, as the successor state to the former Yugoslavia, of genocide in the early 1990s. The case had been lodged against Yugoslavia in 1999, and largely forgotten by the public in both countries since then. But the ICJ's ruling reinvigorated the war crimes issue, prompting an aggrieved Serbia to announce that it would bring a similar case in the same court, accusing Croatia of the same offence in connection with the 1995 offensive against rebel Croatian Serbs, codenamed "operation storm".

With Macedonia simultaneously suing Greece in the ICJ (see p. 110), the danger was growing that the whole region could become encumbered in tit-for-tat lawsuits that could drag on for years, slowing the process of integration and reconciliation in south east Europe.

Marcus Tanner

SLOVENIA

CAPITAL: Ljubljana   AREA: 20,270 sq km   POPULATION: 2,018,000 ('07)
OFFICIAL LANGUAGE: Slovene   POLTICAL SYSTEM: multiparty republic
HEAD OF STATE: President Danilo Turk (since Dec '07)
RULING PARTIES: Social Democrats (SD) lead coalition
HEAD OF GOVERNMENT: Prime Minister Borut Pahor (SD) (since Nov '08)
MAIN IGO MEMBERSHIPS (NON-UN): OSCE, CE, NATO, CEI, Francophonie, EU, NATO
CURRENCY: euro (end-'08 £1=€1.0344, US$1=€0.7194)
GNI PER CAPITA: US$20,960, $26,640 at PPP ('07)

THE year began with a much-prized honour for Slovenia, as the country took over the rotating EU presidency for six months, starting 1 January, before handing over to France. It was the first time that a former eastern European communist state had held the EU presidency and the first occasion that a former Yugoslav republic had done so, too. Foreign Minister Dimitrij Rupel said that, alongside climate change and the unfinished Lisbon Treaty, he intended to make closer co-operation between the EU and the Balkans the presidency's priority. "We in Slovenia believe it is high time the Yugoslavian crisis came to an end," he said in Brussels, referring to the likely impact of Kosovo's imminent declaration of independence. While supporting moves to bring Serbia into the EU fold—to "help Serbia find its European footing"—as he put it, Rupel left no one in any doubt that Slovenia would lobby in support of Kosovo's independence, duly declared in February (see Documents).

While Rupel and Janez Jansa, prime minister and head of the right-of-centre Slovene Democratic Party (SDS), basked in Slovenia's high profile, culminating in a 10 June EU-US summit, held at Brdo and attended by US President George W. Bush, this political capital failed to translate into votes in the early autumn general election. In some ways this was a surprise. Jansa's conservative coalition had presided over steadily rising living standards and ever closer international integration since winning the 2004 elections, achievements symbolised by the country's adoption of the euro in 2007. But rising inflation—which at about 6 per cent was the highest in the eurozone—accusations of intolerance towards journalists, and more serious accusations of bribery in connection with a Finnish defence contract (aired on Finnish television on 1 September) dented Jansa's cultivated image as a "clean hands" politician.

In spite of this, on the eve of the elections on 21 September, several opinion polls put Jansa's party a couple of percentage points ahead of its nearest rival, the Social Democrats (SD), led by Borut Pahor. However, at the election itself, voters handed the crown—albeit by the closest of margins—to Pahor, after the SD won just over 30 per cent of the vote, less than 1 per cent more than Jansa's SDS. In third and fourth positions, the centrist Zares party and a pensioners' party won 9.4 and 7.5 per cent respectively.

Although the Social Democrats won only one more seat in Parliament than Jansa's Democrats, the fact that they almost tripled their seats, to 29 up from 10 in 2004, underscored the extent of their political comeback. After President Danilo Turk finally gave Pahor a mandate to form a government in November, a coalition of the Social Democrats, Liberal Democrats and Zares looked likely to take the reins in 2009.

The changing of the guard—while disappointing for Jansa and still more so for the veteran Rupel, who lost his seat in Parliament—appeared unlikely to lead to any very noticeable policy changes either at home or abroad, Pahor having made it clear he intended to make caution his watchword.   Certainly, there was no change in Slovenia's acrimonious relations with Croatia over the vexed issue of their land and maritime border in the Piran Bay. Indeed, Slovenia upped the ante in late December, dismaying its EU partners when it delayed Croatia's further EU accession in an apparent move to force Croatia's hand. This development was especially ironic given that it was Slovenia, under Rupel, that had once championed the idea of a pact between all the western Balkan states, by which each would promise not to use bilateral disputes as a motive for blocking the others' integration into the EU or NATO.

Marcus Tanner

RUSSIA, WESTERN CIS, AND THE CAUCASUS

RUSSIA

CAPITAL: Moscow   AREA: 17,098,240 sq km   POPULATION: 141,636,000 ('07)
OFFICIAL LANGUAGE: Russian   POLTICAL SYSTEM: multiparty republic
HEAD OF STATE: President Dmitry Medvedev (since May '08)
RULING PARTY: Unified Russia
HEAD OF GOVERNMENT: Prime Minister Vladimir Putin (since May '08)
MAIN IGO MEMBERSHIPS (NON-UN): CIS, APEC, OSCE, G-8, CE, PFP, CBSS, BSEC, AC
CURRENCY: rouble (end-'08 £1=R43.9017, US$1=R30.5350)
GNI PER CAPITA: US$7,560, $14,400 at PPP ('07)

RUSSIA began the year apparently well placed to weather the financial turmoil that was beginning to spread from the "subprime" mortgage crisis in the USA to affect developed economies. The political establishment could congratulate itself on a smooth, constitutional transition in March from President Vladimir Putin, at the end of his second consecutive term in office, to Dmitry Medvedev, his chosen successor. The two men's joint appearance at a rock concert in Moscow's Red Square on 2 March to celebrate this smooth transition symbolised what Medvedev called their "tandem" of power. Yet, by the end of the year the global financial crisis had hit Russia with unanticipated suddenness and the first signs of discontent were discernable in the hitherto quiescent populace.
    The choice of Dmitry Medvedev, a lawyer from St Petersburg and, at 42, the youngest Russian leader since the last Tsar, Nicholas II, seemed to indicate that Russia was pointing towards a modern, liberal future, rather than seeking the retrenchment of authoritarianism. Yet, in order to achieve this, the election itself was conducted among some of the tightest controls on freedom of speech since the Soviet era. The elite was taking no chances of an upset in the planned transfer of power. That the outgoing president was stepping down in constitutional fashion, rather than leaving "in a coffin, in ill health or under duress", as the

Financial Times put it, was a positive sign; but Putin remained very much at the pinnacle of power, becoming prime minister under his protégé, Medvedev. The election was held on 2 March and won by Medvedev with just over 70 per cent of the vote, on a turnout of 69.6 per cent. In second place was the perennial opposition candidate, Gennady Zyuganov of the Communist Party of the Russian Federation (KPRF), with nearly 18 per cent. This was higher than the KPRF usually polled, suggesting that Zyuganov had picked up protest votes. The other two candidates—another perennial oppositionist, Vladimir Zhirinovsky, and Andrei Bodganov of the Democratic Party of Russia—each polled less than 10 per cent. The liberal opposition candidate and former prime minister, Mikhail Kasyanov, was barred from standing on a technicality. As he had not been nominated by a political party represented in the Duma, he had to collect 2 million signatures in support of his candidacy; but 13 per cent of the signatures were ruled invalid by the Central Electoral Commission in January, although Kasyanov activists said that there had been a systematic campaign of intimidation to force them to admit forgery. The only Western group to monitor the elections—the Parliamentary Assembly of the Council of Europe (PACE)—said that voters' choices were "limited". Russian opposition groups reported numerous instances of pressure on people to vote, and it was evident that media coverage before the election had been heavily slanted towards Medvedev.

In an interview given to Western media before his inauguration, and again during his inauguration speech on 7 May, Medvedev said that he wanted to embed the rule of law in Russia, a place which he described as "a country of legal nihilism". These were grounds for hope. Another positive sign of his intentions was an assertion that placed him firmly in the "westerniser" intellectual tradition of Russia. Rejecting the line of argument, voiced in both Russia and in the West, that Russia was in some way inherently "unsuited" to democracy, Medvedev stated that "Russia is a European country and Russia is absolutely capable of developing together with other states that have chosen this democratic path of development." Nevertheless, the biggest constitutional change of 2008 was an amendment, rushed through the legislature at the end of the year, that would extend the presidential term from four to six years and the Duma's term from four to five years. (The changes would not apply to the current president and legislators.) Many pundits predicted that the amendment had been made to smooth the path for a return to the presidency by Putin for potentially a further 12 years, after the next presidential elections, due in 2012. But the rapidity with which the amendment was enacted—from Medvedev's announcement in his state of the nation speech on 5 November to his signing the bill into law on 30 December took less than 2 months—suggested that it might rather have been a panic measure by the elite to extend stability in the face of a developing economic and social crisis. How the relationship between the two men would develop remained to be seen. In a televised interview in December, Medvedev demonstrated a growing assertiveness. "The final responsibility for what happens in the country and for the important decisions taken would rest on my shoulders alone," he said, "I would not be able to share this responsibility with anyone."

The new government and presidential administration, formed by Putin and Medvedev in May, reshuffled leading figures from the cabinet and among the president's aides. A former senior presidential aide to Putin, Igor Shuvalov, became one of two first deputy prime ministers, the other being the former prime minister, Viktor Zubkov. The latter had been named prime minister in September 2007, a stop-gap appointment during the carefully choreographed Putin—Medvedev transition (see AR 2008, p. 107). Meanwhile, the former first deputy prime minister, Sergei Ivanov, who had been viewed as a possible presidential candidate from a security or "silovik" background, was demoted to the ranks of the deputy prime ministers. A former deputy prime minister, Sergei Naryshkin, was made presidential chief of staff, replacing the powerful Igor Sechin, who became a deputy prime minister. In addition, Nikolai Patrushev was replaced as head of the Federal Security Service (FSB), and the justice, telecommunications, and energy ministers were dismissed. According to some observers, the reshuffle was an attempt to curb the authority of the various "silovik" clans at the top of the presidential and government administration, whose infighting was hindering the progress of reform.

The liberal opposition, which under the umbrella "Other Russia" group had held "dissenters' marches" in 2007 that were roughly broken up by security forces (see AR 2008, p. 108), was largely quiescent in 2008, apparently ground down by the relentless harrassment of the authorities, although it did organise protests in March, to coincide with the presidential elections. However, towards the end of the year, there were signs that popular discontent with the increasingly difficult economic situation was giving new life to the opposition. In December, protests took place in Vladivostok and some 30 other cities against government plans to raise import tariffs on foreign made cars as a protectionist measure for the Russian automobile industry. Motorists who wanted to purchase foreign vehicles and those who made a living from vehicle imports objected, and whilst these protests were focused on a specific economic grievance, it seemed likely that they could broaden to embrace a broader economic and political agenda. Thus, "Other Russia" organised more "dissenters' marches" in mid-December in Moscow and St Petersburg. As in 2007, the protests were broken up by the police and tens of people were arrested, but the opposition was evidently attempting to capitalise on the growing social discontent, and attempted to highlight tightening political control by linking criticism of the government's handling of the economic crisis with protest against the measure to extend presidential terms of office.

ECONOMY. Russia's economy was one of the worst affected by the global financial crisis. Having grown at an average annual rate of around 7 per cent since 2000, the Russian economy faced recession in 2009. In large part, this was due to the collapse in the oil price. Russia had benefited from the surge in the price of oil, which reached a peak of US$147 per barrel in July, but in December, oil was selling at less than US$40 per barrel, well below the US$70 per barrel needed to balance the Russian budget. As had already become clear in 2007, insufficient state investment in the country's infrastructure meant that the fundamentals of the economy were weak; the recent boom had rested almost totally on high energy prices.

The Russian rouble declined 15 per cent against the US dollar and 12 per cent against the euro in 2008. The government responded to pressure on the currency by allowing, from November, a slow slide in the value of the rouble. Each gradual depreciation prompted further the withdrawal of rouble deposits and the Russian Central Bank's attempts to prop up the currency cost it some US$6 billion to US$10 billion per week, depleting its foreign currency reserves from a high point of US$597 billion in August to US$451 billion. Whilst the RCB's foreign currency reserves remained the third largest in the world at the end of the year, the declining oil price limited its ability to replenish them. A 20 per cent fall in the value of the rouble was thought necessary by many analysts to boost the economy, but Prime Minister Putin repeatedly rejected such a sharp correction. Memories of the financial crisis of August 1998, when a 70 per cent fall in the value of the rouble caused millions of Russians to lose their savings overnight, meant that the political consequences of a sharp devaluation were unthinkable.

The freeze in international credit markets affected businesses' abilities to refinance their foreign debt. Russian companies had taken out large loans with Western banks to finance expansion, pledging shares in their companies as collateral. However, as a result of the global financial crisis, much of the value was wiped off these shares, as Russia's two stock exchanges (the rouble denominated Moscow Interbank Currency Exchange—MICEX, and the dollar denominated Russian Trading System—RTS) fell dramatically in September, causing trading to be suspended on several occasions. The government earmarked US$50 billion to be extended to Russian companies for refinancing their loans, but a further US$170 billion of debt was due in 2009 and it was unclear whether companies could sustain their loans. An attempt to inject liquidity into the banking system comprising funds amounting to more than US$130 billion in September and a further US$36.5 billion in October failed to alleviate fears of a banking collapse, because the three main state banks in receipt of the funds were apparently failing to pass them on to second- and third-tier banks. President Medvedev told bankers and economic ministers on 16 October that they must repair "trust between creditor and debtor". The sliding rouble fed into the lending freeze, because of expectations that the rouble would devalue further. One Western banker quoted in the *Financial Times* said that Russia's "whole payments system is suffering from indigestion". Meanwhile, industrial production fell sharply at the end of the year. The figures for November showed an 8.7 per cent decline, year-on-year, which was the sharpest drop since August 1998. Wage arrears stood at R8.7 billion in December, having risen sharply from October by 33.4 per cent that month, and were estimated to be affecting 2 per cent of the workforce; there were dire predictions of mass unemployment. Inflation was running well above its annual target figure of 10.5 per cent, reaching 15 per cent in June.

A social backlash was widely anticipated, as figures suggested that up to 20 per cent of the population was affected by the crisis because of joblessness and wage arrears and the falling rouble. The fall in the RCB's currency reserves made it unlikely that discontent could be defused by social spending, unlike in 2003, when the government had spent liberally to halt a wave of unrest over attempts to cut social benefits.

FOREIGN AFFAIRS. Breaking with tradition, Medvedev's first foreign trip as president (on 23-24 May) was to China, via Kazakhstan, rather than to the USA and Europe, signalling the importance of Russian-Chinese co-operation in energy matters and the developing geopolitical alliance between the two neighbours. In a joint statement, Medvedev and China's President Hu Jintao condemned US plans for a missile defence system as inimical to "international efforts to control arms". Throughout the year, it was this US missile defence system or shield (MDS) that continued to be the main irritant in Russia's international relations, because of the plan to station elements of it in Poland and the Czech Republic (see AR 2008, p. 109). In November, Medvedev warned in his first state of the nation address that Russia would be prepared to station its short-range nuclear capable Iskander-M missiles (known by NATO as the SS-26) in Kaliningrad, Russia's exclave between Poland and Lithuania. From here they would be able to target the US sites in Poland and the Czech Republic. Russia was further infuriated by the insistence of the Bush administration that Georgia and Ukraine should be offered a membership action plan (MAP) as the first stage towards membership of NATO, something that Vladimir Putin had already indicated would be unacceptable to Russia, which viewed the eastward expansion of NATO (which now included nine former Soviet bloc states) as a provocation. France and Germany both opposed MAP status for the two former Soviet republics, and the meetings of NATO foreign ministers in both April and December limited themselves to vague suggestions about "eventual" membership.

The dangers of NATO expansion into areas Russia viewed as its own sphere were manifested in August, when the leadership of Georgia appeared to have taken at face value the expressions of US support. (Tellingly, Medvedev wrote later that President Saakashvili of Georgia had acted "with the complicity and encouragement of the US and some other NATO members".) Georgian artillery shelled the capital of the separatist enclave of South Ossetia on the night of 6-7 August, hours after announcing a ceasefire. The Georgian side claimed to be repelling a Russian attack: Russia said it entered South Ossetia to protect its civilians only after the Georgian barrage. Swift EU reaction brought an end to the fighting (see map p. 137), but Russia went on to recognise the independent status of South Ossetia and Abkhazia (another separatist region in Georgia). This, Russia argued, was no more inflammatory than the recognition by a number of states of Kosovo's independence (see map p. 111).

As a demonstration of its global reach, Russia sent warships, including the nuclear powered heavy missile cruiser *Peter the Great*, to South America in the autumn for military exercises off the coast of Venezuela. The naval expedition included a visit to Cuba in December, the first such since the end of the Cold War. A more assertive Russia did not necessarily mean a hostile Russia, however. NATO-Russia Council meetings would resume, it was announced in December, and the EU-Russia partnership agreement negotiations would also resume. (Both forums had been suspended after the Georgian hostilities.) With the election of Barack Obama in the USA and the anticipation of his administration's much heralded change in US foreign policy, there was hope for a new start. Medvedev, too, had indicated that he might take a different attitude from the belligerence so frequently displayed by Putin. In June and again in October he proposed a new European security structure for "the entire Euro-Atlantic space, from Vancouver to Vladivostok". Improved relations between NATO and Russia were essential for tackling issues such as Iran's nuclear weapons' programme and reviving disarmament treaties. Russia had suspended participation in the Conventional Forces in Europe (CFE) treaty in December 2007 (see AR 2008, p. 110) and the important US-Soviet nuclear disarmament treaty from 1991, START I, was due to expire in December 2009.

Two figures of great significance for both Soviet and post-Soviet Russia died in 2008. Alexander Solzhenitsyn, the novelist and chronicler of the Soviet prison camp (GULag) system, whose *One Day in the Life of Ivan Denisovich* had been a key text in the partial unveiling of Stalinist terror in the 1960s, died in August at the age of 89. In December, Patriarch Aleksii II of Moscow and All Russia, the head of the Russian Orthodox Church during its transformation from a tightly controlled body to an influential state-sponsored organisation, died at the age of 79 (see Obituary).

At the end of the year, a television poll, *Name of Russia*, decided that the warrior prince, Alexander Nevsky, who drove foreign invaders from medieval Russia, deserved the title of the "greatest Russian of all time". In second place came the pre-Revolutionary prime minister Peter Stolypin, an economic reformer but a supporter of tsarism; and third place went to Stalin. However, there was much grumbling that the voting figures had been massaged to produce a result that would send the right message: rather than the authoritarian Stalin, it was Alexander Nevsky who should be emulated, as should the economic liberal and political conservative Stolypin. Ironically enough, it was Nevsky who had also served as a rallying cry to the cause of national unity promoted by Stalin during the Great Patriotic War against Nazi Germany.

Wendy Slater

BELARUS—UKRAINE—MOLDOVA

Belarus

CAPITAL: Minsk   AREA: 207,600 sq km   POPULATION: 9,702,000 ('07)
OFFICIAL LANGUAGES: Belarusian & Russian   POLITICAL SYSTEM: multiparty republic
HEAD OF STATE: President Alyaksandr Lukashenka (since July '94)
RULING PARTY: Non-party supporters of President Lukashenka
HEAD OF GOVERNMENT: Prime Minister Syarhey Sidorski (since Dec '03)
MAIN IGO MEMBERSHIPS (NON-UN): CIS, OSCE, PFP, CEI, NAM
CURRENCY: Belarusian rouble (end-'08 £1=BR3,164.49, US$1=BR2,201.00)
GNI PER CAPITA: US$4,220, $10,740 at PPP ('07)

Ukraine

CAPITAL: Kyiv (Kiev)   AREA: 603,550 sq km   POPULATION: 46,383,000 ('07)
OFFICIAL LANGUAGE: Ukrainian   POLITICAL SYSTEM: multiparty republic
HEAD OF STATE: President Viktor Yushchenko (NUNS) (since Jan '05)
RULING PARTIES: Yuliya Tymoshenko Bloc (BYuT), Our Ukraine-People's Self-Defence Bloc
(NU-NS), Volodymyr Lytvyn Bloc form coalition
HEAD OF GOVERNMENT: Prime Minister Yuliya Tymoshenko (BYuT) (since Dec '07)
MAIN IGO MEMBERSHIPS (NON-UN): CIS, OSCE, CE, PFP, BSEC, CEI
CURRENCY: hryvna (end-'08 £1=H11.0348, US$1=H7.6750)
GNI PER CAPITA: US$2,550, $6,810 at PPP ('07)

Moldova

CAPITAL: Chisinau (Kishinev)   AREA: 33,840 sq km   POPULATION: 3,792,000 ('07)
(incl Transdniestr republic)
OFFICIAL LANGUAGE: Moldovan   POLITICAL SYSTEM: multiparty republic
HEAD OF STATE: President Vladimir Voronin (since April '01)
RULING PARTY: Communist Party of Moldova (PCM)
HEAD OF GOVERNMENT: Prime Minister Zinaida Grecianii (PCM) (since March '08)
MAIN IGO MEMBERSHIPS (NON-UN): CIS, OSCE, CE, PFP, BSEC, CEI, Francophonie, CEFTA
CURRENCY: leu (end-'08 £1=ML14.9526, US$1=ML10.4000)
GNI PER CAPITA: US$1,260 (excl Transdniestr republic), $2,930 at PPP ('07)

DEVELOPMENTS in the three western CIS states in 2008 were shaped by their relations with Russia. Belarus, for years subsidised by cheap Russian energy, began to move towards improved relations with the West, particularly the EU, as the Russian gas price rose. In Ukraine, relations with Russia—including the price Russia charged for gas—were a factor in the political squabbles that marred the year. Meanwhile, there were signs in Moldova that the "frozen conflict" with its separatist, pro-Russian Transdniestr region might be resolved with Russia's involvement.

BELARUS. Achieving better relations with the West would require the Belarusian authorities to relax their hardline attitude towards political opposition and, somewhat reluctantly, they demonstrated readiness to do so in 2008. (Belarus's President Alyaksandr Lukashenka also hired a UK public relations agency in 2008 to improve his and Belarus's image in the West.) Towards the end of the year, the EU responded with the easing of some sanctions against the "last dictatorship in Europe". This rapprochement was motivated, on both sides, by relations with Russia. Russia no longer guaranteed Belarus subsidised energy (gas prices had doubled in December 2006); the EU, meanwhile, saw Belarus as a potential buffer against Russia and an important transit route for its own supplies of Russian gas.

In January and February, six people considered political prisoners by the international community were unexpectedly released, in what Lukashenka described as "a goodwill gesture". Those released included two leaders of the Youth Front, two businessmen, the editor of the independent *Zgoda* newspaper, and opposition leader Andrei Klimaw of the United Civic Party. The most prominent prisoner release, however, came in August, when Alyaksandr Kazulin received a presidential pardon. Kazulin had been sentenced to five-and-a-half years in prison in July 2006 on public order charges stemming from mass protests against the conduct of the presidential elections in March 2006, in which he had been a candidate (see AR 2007, p. 110). In February, Kazulin had been granted a three-day reprieve from his prison sentence in order to attend the funeral of his wife, Irina Kazulina. This became a public event, attracting 1,000 people. Meanwhile, in December, another prominent opposition leader, Alyaksandr Milinkevich, successfully registered his Movement for Freedom at the fourth attempt (see AR 2008, p. 111).

This relaxation was not consistent, however, and numerous instances of pressure on the opposition occurred throughout the year. In January, riot police broke up a demonstration against tax increases on small businesses; in March, dozens of opposition protesters at a rally in Minsk were arrested. KGB (state security) agents subsequently searched independent journalists' homes and offices throughout Belarus and arrested 30 people.

In the general election on 28 September to the House of Representatives (lower chamber of the bicameral legislature), all 110 seats were won by supporters of Lukashenka. The poll was assessed by the Organisation for Security and Co-operation in Europe (OSCE) as falling short of OSCE standards, although observers noted "some minor improvements" in the conduct of the vote. This provided the opportunity for the EU to suspend for six months from October an entry visa ban against Lukashenka and a number of other officials, which had been instigated in 2006 after the presidential elections. (A visa entry ban remained in place, however, against officials suspected of involvement in the disappearances of opposition figures in 1999 and 2000.) The EU move was also a reward for the government's resistance to Russian pressure that Belarus follow it in recognising the separatist Georgian regions of South Ossetia and Abkhazia as independent states (see p. 136).

Relations with the USA remained strained. A diplomatic dispute in the early part of 2008 over US sanctions on the Belarusian state petrochemical company resulted in the recall of ambassadors and reciprocal expulsions of diplomats, which left the US embassy in Minsk with just four staff members in May, down from 32 in February.

Domestically, Lukashenka's position appeared secure. In July, he dismissed two longterm allies—Viktor Sheyman, secretary of the security council, and Henadz Nyavyhlas, head of the presidential administration—in the aftermath of a bombing incident at an outdoor concert in Minsk. It was suggested that their dismissal represented the climax of an internal power struggle, in which Lukashenka had prevailed. A factor in Lukashenka's longevity had been Belarus's relatively stable Soviet-style economy. Nevertheless, this was before the global financial crisis began to bite, and on 31 December the IMF announced a 15-month US$2.5 billion loan to Belarus to help it adjust to external shocks. In an indication that the Belarusian economy was set to change, there were moves in 2008 to privatise the country's major assets, including banks, mobile telephone operators, and factories. What effect this would have on the country's political structure remained to be seen.

UKRAINE. It was a bad year for Ukraine. Tensions with Russia over Ukraine's ambitions to join NATO and the price of Russian gas were played out in the country's domestic politics. The governing coalition in the Verkhovna Rada (unicameral legislature) fragmented and much effort was expended in the rivalry between President Viktor Yushchenko and Prime Minister Yuliya Tymoshenko. However, towards the end of the year Ukraine found itself heavily exposed to the growing global financial crisis, forcing Yushchenko to abandon his attempts to remove the prime minister, whilst a massive IMF loan was swiftly arranged in an attempt to restore macroeconomic stability.

The governing coalition, formed late in 2007 and consisting of the pro-presidential Our Ukraine-People's Self-Defence Bloc (NUNS) and the Yuliya Tymoshenko Bloc (BYuT) (see AR 2008, pp. 112-13), collapsed on 16 September when BYuT legislators voted with the opposition to curtail some of the president's powers of appointment. Indeed, the NUNS—BYuT alliance had never been strong, producing dramatic scenes in the Verkhovna Rada in May, when pro-Tymoshenko deputies blocked the speaker's rostrum to prevent President Yushchenko from delivering his annual state of the nation address. Yushchenko's efforts to dissolve the Verkhovna Rada and call early elections for December failed after BYuT deputies refused to pass enabling legislation. The political dispute coincided with the economic crisis and the negotiations to obtain an IMF loan (see below). Apparently this concentrated the minds of politicians. As Yushchenko's chief of staff Viktor Baloha said, on 30 November, early elections were "not the priority at the moment". On 16 December, a new coalition agreement was signed, uniting the NUNS, BYuT, and the 20-strong Lytvyn bloc, whose leader, Volodymyr Lytvyn, was elected speaker of the Verkhovna Rada for the second time in his career. He characterised his role in the new coalition as that of a "peacemaker", although whether he could smooth the differences between Yushchenko and Tymoshenko remained doubtful, since both were expected to contest the presidential elections due in late 2009 or early 2010, a rivalry that fuelled their political differences.

The political turmoil left Ukraine in a weakened state to cope with a dramatic economic downturn that resulted from the global financial crisis. Ukraine had been one of Europe's fastest growing economies, with average annual growth of 7 per cent since 2000, including projected 6 per cent growth in 2008. By the end of 2008, however, the IMF was forecasting an economic contraction of 3 per cent in 2009.

Ukraine's spectacular growth rates had been heavily dependent upon international borrowing, which raised the ratio of external debt to GDP from 45 per cent in 2005 to nearly 60 per cent in 2007, with 78 per cent forecast for 2009. The international "credit crunch", therefore, hit Ukraine's banks and private companies particularly hard as they struggled to refinance their debts whilst the value of their assets fell. At the same time, global demand for steel collapsed, striking a savage blow to a country where ferrous metals accounted for 40 per cent of export revenue and 25 per cent of industrial production. The result was a dramatic slide in the value of the currency, the hryvna, which fell from 4.6 hryvnas to the US dollar in July to 7.38 hryvnas to the dollar in late November. In the real economy, with inflation of around 25 per cent and industrial output falling, there were fears of mass unemployment and bankrupties. The deal reached with the IMF on 5 November envisaged a massive loan of US$16.4 billion over two years, which was designed to restore macroeconomic stability. Ukraine, in turn, promised to reduce the budget deficit to zero for 2009, adopt a flexible exchange rate, and tighten monetary policy.

A further serious problem for Ukraine in 2009 was likely to be a sharp rise in the price of natural gas supplied from Russia. The traditional new year's eve dispute over the price of gas for the coming year duly took place, with Russia's gas monopoly, Gazprom, seeking to more than double the 2008 contract price of US$179.5 per 1,000 cubic metres (tcm) to a level comparable with that paid for gas by EU countries of around US$400 per tcm. Gazprom was also seeking US$2.1 billion for gas supplied in November and December, and threatened to halt gas supplies to Ukraine on 1 January 2009 if these issues were not resolved.

A dispute between Gazprom and Ukraine over unpaid gas debts earlier in the year, which had resulted in the suspension of supplies in March, appeared to have been resolved. But the agreement did not succeed in removing from the equation the intermediary company, RosUkrEnergo, which supplied Ukraine's gas distribution company, Naftohaz Ukrainy, with gas from Central Asia. It was widely suspected that the Ukrainian and Russian oligarchs behind RosUkrEnergo were benefiting spectacularly from the gas trade, and presumably influencing officials to keep the company in place. One estimate suggested that the undeclared earnings of RosUkrEnergo (at 2007 gas prices) could be as high as US$4.35 billion. Prime Minister Tymoshenko had pledged to remove RosUkrEnergo from the gas supply chain. She failed, describing the contract reached in April between Naftohaz Ukrainy and RosUkrEnergo for gas deliveries for the remainder of 2008 "a compromise, but a victory in the circumstances".

A resolution to the perennial Ukraine-Russia gas dispute was a priority for the EU, which received 25 per cent of its natural gas from Russia, and 80 per cent of this through pipelines through Ukraine. Thus, the development of new pipelines that would avoid Ukraine (North Stream, South Stream, and Nabucco) was a priority, both for Russia and for EU countries (see map, p. 103).

Ukraine's internal chaos played to Russia's advantage on many levels. Domestically, whereas Russia in 2008 saw the election of a handpicked successor to President Vladimir Putin, Ukraine's messy politics could be characterised as the failure of its post-Orange revolution democracy. But the principal benefit to Russia was the increasingly distant prospect of Ukrainian membership of NATO. Ukraine's membership bid, which had strong US support as symbolised by a visit to Kiev by US President George W. Bush in April, was one of the main irritants in relations between Russia and the West in 2008. It was repeatedly made clear by Russian officials that Russia would view Ukraine's (and Georgia's) membership of the Western military alliance as a security threat. Popular support in Ukraine for NATO membership was not strong, and indeed Ukraine fell short of NATO standards in military readiness and political reform. Unsurprisingly, therefore, NATO's second foreign ministers' meeting of 2008, in December, reiterated the decisions of its first, in April, that neither Ukraine nor Georgia should be offered a NATO membership action plan (MAP—the first stage to membership).

The Russian intervention in Georgia in August nevertheless prompted President Yushchenko to demand Ukraine's swifter integration into "Euro-Atlantic structures". Ukraine, he said, had "become a hostage in the war waged by Russia". Some of this ringing of alarm bells was aimed at a domestic audience, the implication being that rival politicians, including Tymoshenko, were pro-Russian. Nevertheless, a serious point of contention between Russia and Ukraine, which would need to be resolved in the near future, was the question of whether Russia's Black Sea Fleet would be able to renew its lease on the Ukrainian port of Sevastopol, which was due to expire in 2017.

MOLDOVA. Whilst most international attention in 2008 was directed at the Russian-Georgian war, arising from the "frozen conflicts" of Georgia's separatist regions, the way in which Russia was dealing with another "frozen conflict", in Moldova, largely escaped notice.

Over the year, Russia exerted "soft power" on the separatist, Russian-speaking, self-proclaimed "Transdniestr Republic" in order to force its reintegration into Moldova proper. In September, Russia's President Dmitry Medvedev deployed both stick and carrot at a meeting with the recalcitrant Transdniestr leader, Igor Smirnov, persuading him to "abandon his crusade for sovereignty", according to Russia's Kommersant newspaper. Medvedev pointed out that the Transdniestr region owed Russia US$1.5 billion in gas debts and promised education and healthcare programmes, and pensions for Russian nationals in Transdniestr. Earlier, in August, Medvedev had also met Moldova's President Vladimir Voronin to urge resolution of the Transdniestr problem.

The first direct meeting between Voronin and Smirnov since 2001 had been held earlier in the year, in April, in the Transdniestr town of Bendery. The "five plus two" talks were mediated by Russia, Ukraine, and the OSCE, with the EU and USA as observers, and agreed to form a joint working group to draft confidence building measures.

Russia's condition for pressing the "Transdniestr Republic" to reintegrate into Moldova proper was that Moldova should abandon any plans to join NATO. In May, Moldova signed into law a national security strategy that reaffirmed its neutral status. Russian officials made pointed comparisons with the Georgia situation. Georgia, intent upon joining NATO, had provoked Russia into using force: Moldova, in affirming its neutrality, was making a commitment not to attempt NATO membership. *Kommersant* quoted a Russian foreign ministry official: "We are convinced that it is possible to find a political solution to the problem so that territorial integrity of Moldova will be preserved with some special status for the Transdniestr region...the atmosphere there is very different from the Caucasus."

Meanwhile, political developments in Moldova focused on the general election approaching in 2009, which the ruling Communist Party of Moldova (PCM) appeared less than certain of winning. On 19 March, the government of Vasile Tarlev, prime minister since 2001, resigned in what the opposition claimed was a tactical move to give the PCM greater credibility before the 2009 elections. Tarlev—a non-party figure—was replaced by Moldova's first woman prime minister, Zinaida Grecianii, of the PCM, a Russian-born economist and first deputy prime minister since 2005.

According to the European Bank for Reconstruction and Development (EBRD), Moldova's economy was expected to grow by 6 per cent in 2008, up from 3 per cent in 2007, thanks to improved access to EU markets for Moldovan products and the resumption in late 2007 of Moldovan wine exports to Russia (see AR 2008, p. 114). The EBRD predicted growth of 4.1 per cent in 2009, however, because of the global financial crisis. The main effect of the crisis was expected to be a decrease in remittances, estimated to total US$1.8 billion in 2008, from the 450,000 Moldovans working abroad.

Wendy Slater

ARMENIA—GEORGIA—AZERBAIJAN

Armenia

CAPITAL: Yerevan   AREA: 29,800 sq km   POPULATION: 3,001,000 ('07)
OFFICIAL LANGUAGE: Armenian   POLTICAL SYSTEM: multiparty republic
HEAD OF STATE: President Serzh Sarkisian (since April '08)
RULING PARTIES: coalition comprising Republican Party of Armenia (NHK), Law Based State
   (OY), Prosperous Armenia party (BH), and Armenian Revolutionary Federation—
   Dashnaktsutiun (HHD)
HEAD OF GOVERNMENT: Prime Minister Tigran Sargsyan (ind) (since April '08)
MAIN IGO MEMBERSHIPS (NON-UN): CIS, OSCE, PFP, BSEC, CE, CEI
CURRENCY: dram (end-'08 £1=D441.405, US$1=D307.000)
GNI PER CAPITA: US$2,640, $5,900 at PPP ('07)

Georgia

CAPITAL: Tbilisi   AREA: 69,700 sq km   POPULATION: 4,396,000 ('07)
OFFICIAL LANGUAGE: Georgian   POLTICAL SYSTEM: multiparty republic
HEAD OF STATE: President Mikheil Saakashvili (since Jan '04)
RULING PARTY: United National Movement for a Victorious Georgia
HEAD OF GOVERNMENT: Prime Minister Grigol Mgaloblishvili (since Oct '08)
MAIN IGO MEMBERSHIPS (NON-UN): CIS, CE, OSCE, PFP, BSEC
CURRENCY: lari (end-'08 £1=L2.4001, US$1=L1.6694)
GNI PER CAPITA: US$2,120, $4,770 at PPP ('07)

Azerbaijan

CAPITAL: Baku   AREA: 86,600 sq km   POPULATION: 8,571,000 ('07)
OFFICIAL LANGUAGE: Azeri   POLTICAL SYSTEM: multiparty republic
HEAD OF STATE: President Ilham Aliyev (since Oct '03)
RULING PARTY: New Azerbaijan Party (YAP)
HEAD OF GOVERNMENT: Artur Rasizade
MAIN IGO MEMBERSHIPS (NON-UN): CIS, OSCE, PFP, BSEC, OIC, ECO, CE
CURRENCY: new manat (end-'08 £1=NM1.1676, US$1=NM0.8121)
GNI PER CAPITA: US$2,550, $6,370 at PPP ('07)

THE five-day war in August between Russia and Georgia over South Ossetia resulted in the recognition by Russia on 26 August, and by Nicaragua on 4 September, of Georgia's separatist regions of Abkhazia and South Ossetia as independent states. The conflict had a major impact throughout the south Caucasus, highlighting both the vulnerability of transport routes, including strategic oil and gas pipelines, and the limitations of international diplomacy. Armenia responded by seeking closer co-operation with Georgia, while Azerbaijan tilted more closely towards Russia, and Turkey unveiled a new proposal for strengthening regional stability.

In all three south Caucasus states, the ruling elite succeeded in retaining its hold on power in 2008, in elections that were deemed by international monitors as having failed to meet accepted standards for a free and fair ballot.

ARMENIA.   Prime Minister Serzh Sarkisian was pronounced the official victor in the Armenian presidential election on 19 February, in which incumbent Robert Kocharian was barred by the constitution from seeking a third term. Supporters of Sarkisian's closest challenger, former President Levon Ter-Petrossian, rejected the official results, according to which Sarkisian polled over 52 per cent of the vote compared with 21.5 per cent for Ter-Petrossian, and staged daily protests in Yerevan, which were brutally suppressed by police and security forces on 1-2 March. Ten people, including two policemen, died in the violence. President Kocharian imposed a nationwide state of emergency and media restrictions on 1 March, which were lifted three weeks later.

Dozens of supporters of Ter-Petrossian were arrested; seven of the most prominent, including a former foreign minister, Alexander Arzoumanian, went on trial on 19 December on charges of seeking to seize power by force. Two defeated presidential candidates, former Parliament speaker Artur Baghdasarian (Law-Based State (OY)) and Vahan Hovannisian (Armenian Revolutionary Federation—Dashnaktsutiun (HHD)), accepted Sarkisian's invitation to join a coalition government. They signed a formal agreement to that effect on 21 March with Sarkisian's Republican Party of Armenia (HHK) and the Prosperous Armenia party (BH) headed by Gagik Tsarukian. Baghdasarian was also named National Security Council secretary in late February.

Under pressure from the international community, in particular the Parliamentary Assembly of the Council of Europe (PACE), the Armenian authorities set up an ad hoc Parliamentary commission to investigate the events that had culminated in the 1-2 March violence and to establish who gave the order to open fire on the protesters. Ter-Petrossian declined an invitation to nominate a representative to serve on the commission, and a separate international body was established in October to conduct a parallel probe.

In August, 16 parties and movements that supported Ter-Petrossian aligned in an umbrella group, the Armenian National Congress. Ter-Petrossian suspended indefinitely on 17 October sporadic public protests against the post-election crackdown which had resumed on 20 June.

Tigran Torosian resigned under pressure on 19 September as Parliamentary speaker, and former Deputy Prime Minister Hovik Abrahamian was elected to replace him.

AZERBAIJAN. Protracted talks between the Azerbaijani authorities and Council of Europe experts failed to yield an agreement on liberalising election legislation, and all major opposition parties opted to boycott the 15 October presidential election, on the grounds that the law did not create conditions for a fair ballot. As universally expected, incumbent President Ilham Aliyev was re-elected for a second term with 88.7 per cent of the vote, defeating six rival candidates representing small, mostly pro-government political parties. International observers ruled that the election failed to meet some OSCE (Organisation for Security and Co-operation in Europe) commitments. The ruling New Azerbaijan Party (YAP) subsequently proposed amending the constitution to permit Aliyev, who celebrated his 47th birthday in December, to serve a third, and possibly a fourth term.

Two people died on 17 August in an explosion at the Abu Bekr mosque in Baku, the congregation of which was reputed to include Islamic radicals. The mosque was subsequently closed. In late December, the Azerbaijani authorities banned the rebroadcasting of foreign radio stations, including the BBC.

GEORGIA. Incumbent President Mikheil Saakashvili was re-elected in a pre-term ballot on 5 January that his closest challenger, businessman Levan Gachechiladze, protested was rigged to preclude a second round run-off between himself and Saakashvili. The international community expressed concern at procedural irregularities during the voting and count, but stopped short of endorsing opposition demands for the annulment of the results and a repeat election.

The Georgian Parliament then amended the election law in such a way as virtually to guarantee a victory for Saakashvili's United National Movement in the general election that Saakashvili scheduled for 21 May. Saakashvili's party indeed garnered 119 of the 150 seats in the unicameral Parliament; several opposition deputies rejected their mandates to protest against the perceived falsification of the vote.

Saakashvili reshuffled the Georgian government in late January, naming banker Vladimir Gurgenidze to head a new cabinet; and again following the May parliamentary election. Then, in late October, he named a little-known diplomat, 35-year old Grigol Mgaloblishvili, to succeed Gurgenidze as prime minister. He also dismissed the foreign and defence ministers, Eka Tkeshalashvili and Davit Kezerashvili.

Meanwhile, several of Saakashvili's former close allies, including former Parliament speaker Nino Burdjanadze, former Prime Minister Zurab Noghaideli, and human rights ombudsman Sozar Subari, publicly criticised either the conduct of the August war with Russia (see below) or domestic political repression and the lack of media freedom, and established their own political parties or movements. In early December, Irakli Alasania resigned as ambassador to the UN amid reports that he would align with a new opposition grouping formed by the merger of the Republican Party and the New Rightists. A Georgian Parliament commission, established on 26 September to evaluate the events that immediately preceded the outbreak of hostilities, concluded, after three months' hearings, that responsibility for the fighting lay exclusively with Russia which, it said, had "planned and provoked the war". The commission's final 200-page report contained no criticism of Saakashvili's actions. At the same time, and despite a massive public relations campaign by the Georgian leadership, many Western commentators increasingly questioned the official Georgian version of the events that led to the August war, and began reassessing Saakashvili's reputation in the light of persistent reports of human rights violations and repression of the independent media.

NAGORNO KARABAKH. Renewed diplomatic activity failed to yield a formal settlement of the Nagorno-Karabakh conflict between Armenia and Azerbaijan. On 14 March, at Azerbaijan's initiative, the UN General Assembly adopted by 39 votes to seven with 100 abstentions a non-binding resolution calling for an immediate Armenian withdrawal from occupied Azerbaijani territory.

Following an initial meeting in St Petersburg in June under the aegis of the OSCE Minsk Group (formed in 1992 to encourage a negotiated solution to the Nagorno-Karabakh dispute), Presidents Sarkisian and Aliyev met in Moscow on 2 November at the invitation of Russia's President Dmitry Medvedev. They signed a declaration affirming their shared commitment, in the wake of the Russia-Georgia war, to a peaceful solution to the Karabakh conflict that would draw on the so-called "Madrid principles" drafted by the Minsk Group in November 2007.

WAR BETWEEN GEORGIA AND RUSSIA. Georgia's already tense relations with Russia (see AR 2008, p. 118) deteriorated further in mid-April, when outgoing Russian President Vladimir Putin issued a decree ordering the Russian government to establish closer ties with the separatist Georgian regions of Abkhazia and South Ossetia, which were aligned with Russia. Abkhazia rejected new peace proposals unveiled by Saakashvili on 28 March and by German Foreign Minister Frank-Walter Steinmeier on 17 July.

Following several weeks of sporadic exchanges of fire between Georgian troops and Ossetian militants, Saakashvili ordered Georgian troops into South Ossetia on 7 August—just hours after announcing a unilateral ceasefire—and launched an artillery attack on the South Ossetian capital, Tskhinvali. Russian tanks and troops advanced into South Ossetia on 8 August, allegedly to protect those residents of South Ossetia who held Russian citizenship. Tskhinvali changed hands several times during three days of intense fighting, which caused widespread destruction. Russian forces then advanced southwards towards the internal border between South Ossetia and the rest of Georgia. The Russian forces bombed Gori, the Black Sea port of Poti, and several military bases on 9 August, and occupied Gori on 11 August, meeting little resistance (see map).

In western Georgia, Russian forces opened a second front and expelled Georgian troops from the Kodori Gorge, which straddled Abkhazia and Georgia proper, advancing south to occupy the strategic military base at Senaki. Several hundred Georgian servicemen and civilians died during the fighting and tens of thousands of civilians were forced to flee their homes.

Talks on 12 August in Moscow between Russian President Dmitry Medvedev and French President Nicolas Sarkozy yielded a ceasefire, which was augmented on 8 September with an agreement on the deployment along the borders between the two breakaway regions and the rest of Georgia of some 200 EU observers. Russian troops withdrew from the conflict zones by the 10 October deadline, but sporadic low level violence continued, with irregular Ossetian and Abkhaz militias targeting Georgian civilians.

Saakashvili announced on 12 August that Georgia would quit the Commonwealth of Independent States (CIS) in protest at the Russian military operation. On 26 August, Russia formally recognized Abkhazia and South Ossetia as independent states, whereupon Georgia, on 29 August, severed diplomatic ties with Russia. Russia subsequently announced plans to establish military bases in both Abkhazia and South Ossetia, and signed friendship and co-operation agreements, which included military guarantees, with their leaders, Sergei Bagapsh of Abkhazia and Eduard Kokoity of South Ossetia.

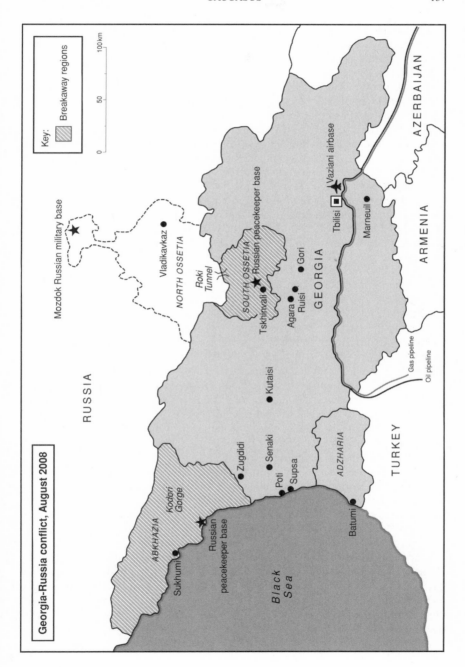

Georgia-Russia conflict, August 2008

Key:

Breakaway regions

100 km
50
0

RUSSIA

Mozdok Russian military base

Vladikavkaz

NORTH OSSETIA

Roki Tunnel

SOUTH OSSETIA

Russian peacekeeper base

Tskhinvali

Agara
Ruisi
Gori

GEORGIA

Kutaisi

Zugdidi

Senaki

Poti
Supsa

ABKHAZIA

Kodori Gorge

Russian peacekeeper base

Sukhumi

ADZHARIA

Batumi

Black Sea

Tbilisi

Vaziani airbase

Marneuli

AZERBAIJAN

ARMENIA

TURKEY

Gas pipeline
Oil pipeline

The EU, the OSCE, and the USA and most European governments unequivocally condemned what they termed Russia's disproportionate use of force, deployed to protect residents of South Ossetia who had Russian citizenship, and consistently affirmed their support for Georgia's sovereignty and territorial integrity.

The EU convened a conference in Brussels on 22 October, at which participants pledged US$4.5 billion for Georgia in post-conflict reconstruction aid. Three successive rounds of talks sponsored by the UN and the EU in Geneva on 15-16 October, 18-19 November, and 17-18 December failed to reach agreement on security provisions that would enable Georgian displaced persons to return to Abkhazia and South Ossetia. In late December, Russia vetoed an extension of the mandate of the OSCE mission in Georgia. (The mission had been established in December 1992 to assist in resolution of the South Ossetia and Abkhazia issue.)

The August war put paid to any hopes that Georgia might be offered a NATO membership action plan (MAP) at the NATO foreign ministers' meeting in December. No such offer to Georgia (or Ukraine) had been forthcoming at the Bucharest NATO summit in April, despite strong US support for the two states' being offered an MAP. Many analysts noted that the US administration's advocacy of NATO membership for Georgia, and backing of Saakashvili personally, had encouraged the Georgian leadership vigorously to prosecute the war in the expectation—swiftly disappointed—that it would receive active US support.

The August war between Georgia and Russia demonstrated the vulnerability of neighbouring states to any interruption in transport communications between them, and served as the catalyst for a broad reassessment of the geo-political landscape, prompting Turkey to propose a south Caucasus stability pact, in which Russia, too, would be invited to participate.

Even before the August crisis, Armenian President Sarkisian had sought a rapprochement with Turkey, and in June he invited his Turkish counterpart, Abdullah Gul, to Yerevan to watch a football match between the two countries' national teams. Despite hopes on both sides, this landmark visit on 6 September did not lead to the establishment of formal diplomatic relations or to the opening of the border between the two countries (see p. 89).

The August war also led to a new economic co-operation agreement between Armenia and Georgia. US diplomatic overtures to Azerbaijan, including a September visit by Vice President Dick Cheney, met a cool response.

The economies of all three countries, which had grappled with double-digit inflation from the start of the year, suffered from the effects of both the August war and the global financial crisis. Annual GDP growth in Armenia dipped below 10 per cent for the first time in six years, while the foreign trade deficit grew by 29 per cent to almost US$3 billion. Azerbaijan was hit by plummeting world oil prices that it was thought might necessitate a sequester of the 2009 annual budget, predicated on an average price of US$70 per barrel. In addition to causing millions of dollars of damage to infrastructure, the war led to a 14 per cent fall in the value of the Georgian currency, the lari.

Elizabeth Fuller

IV THE AMERICAS AND THE CARIBBEAN

UNITED STATES OF AMERICA

CAPITAL: Washington, DC   AREA: 9,632,030 sq km   POPULATION: 301,621,000 ('07)
OFFICIAL LANGUAGES: English (de facto); Spanish widely used   POLTICAL SYSTEM: multiparty republic
HEAD OF STATE AND GOVERNMENT: President George W. Bush, Republican, since Jan '01
PRESIDENT ELECT: Barack Obama, Democrat
RULING PARTY: Congress is controlled by the Democrats
MAIN IGO MEMBERSHIPS (NON-UN): NATO, OSCE, OECD, G-8, OAS, NAFTA, APEC, AC, CP, PC, ANZUS, DR-CAFTA
CURRENCY: US dollar (end-'08 £1=US$1.4378, €1=$1.3901)
GNI PER CAPITA: US$46,040, $45,850 at PPP ('07)

THE election campaign for president dominated much of the year. Every major public issue—the economy and society, the culture wars and the real wars, domestic policy and foreign policy—was subsumed by the unrelenting focus on this seemingly eternal contest. That is, until September, when a globe-engulfing economic crisis finally proved large enough to overshadow the campaign. As economic crisis became the context for the election campaign, rather than the campaign being the context for everything else, the candidates found that the fear regarding the nation's economic future would prove to be a far larger force to be reckoned with than even the foreign wars that it was thought, back in the mists of the campaign's beginnings, would be the dominant political issue of the contest. Yet, when it was finally over, even the worst economic crisis since the Great Depression of the 1930s could not obscure the historic election of Barack Obama to the highest office in the land.

ECONOMY. The impact of the "subprime" mortgage crisis expanded and intensified. The year was studded with evidence that there was scarcely an area of the national and global economies that the US mortgage debacle had not undermined. The house of profit built, with minimal regulation, on the intricate assembling of subprime mortgages, mortgage-backed securities, collateralised debt obligations, and all the other imaginative financial instruments designed to make money from nothing, came crashing down. From individual home owners to some of the world's largest financial companies, the "credit crunch" would take a heavy toll in what most observers viewed as the worst economic crisis since the Great Depression. This crisis, and the federal government's response to it, proved the only issues that could challenge the presidential election for media and public attention.

In his State of the Union address on 28 January, President George W. Bush noted with delicate understatement that "our economy is undergoing a period of uncertainty." While jobs and wages were still rising, so too were prices, he claimed, noting also that "the housing market has declined." While the housing market continued to decline, jobs did not continue to rise for long. In February, for the first time in over four years, jobs were lost from the economy. In December alone, over half a million jobs were lost, across most sectors of the economy. By the end of the year, 11.1 million people, or 7.2 per cent of the workforce, were unemployed, up 3.6 million and 2.3 per cent respectively from one year earlier. International stock markets fell throughout the year. The Dow Jones industrial average began the year at 13,044 and ended it down 4,268 points at 8,776. Oil prices continued to soar through the first part of the year, peaking in July at $147 per barrel. Prices fell over the remaining months to under $50 at year's end. For the consumer, this translated into petrol prices of over $4 per gallon in July. By December the average price was under $1.70, a welcome drop for the public but one that went relatively unnoticed in the midst of growing economic turmoil. The nation's dependence on foreign oil and the question of whether the government should encourage off-shore drilling in the USA developed as important election issues.

The higher cost of petrol and, consequently, of many everyday goods and services, contributed to the woes of a US public also hit hard by housing foreclosures and rising unemployment. The hardest hit were, of course, those losing their homes and their jobs. But the crisis, and the sense of crisis, spread far beyond those directly affected. Even those currently housed, employed, and solvent felt anxiety about the future. Many held company or private pension plans closely tied to the state of the stock market. Many people and businesses in sound financial condition found it increasingly difficult to get mortgages or loans as lending of all kinds dried up. Many large businesses and financial institutions also teetered on the brink, as losses mounted and capital dried up. The large investment bank of Bear Stearns, for example, had made fortunes in mortgage-backed securities, but now faced critical liquidity problems as those investments collapsed.

The year saw a series of attempts to deal with the worsening crisis. In January, Bush proposed an economic stimulus package, consisting of measures such as tax rebates for families and increased tax deductions for businesses. Congress (the bicameral legislature) passed a package close to $170 billion in February. It would prove to be the first of a series of extraordinary government expenditures over the course of the year. The Federal Reserve (the central bank) had a busy March as it sought both to ease, and to deal with, the consequences of the heightening liquidity crisis. It cut short-term borrowing interest rates by three-quarters of 1 per cent, the largest single cut in its history. It facilitated the takeover by giant financial services company JP Morgan Chase Bank of investment bank Bear Stearns, by guaranteeing $30 billion of the latter's debt. It also sought to ease the credit crunch by expanding its securities lending programme, making available up to $200 billion in Treasury bonds to banks and brokers, while accepting as collateral the troubled mortgage-backed securities that could find no buyers in the current market. These March measures would ultimately pale compared to the federal intervention in the economy that would occur later in the year (see below). Taken together, these financial interventions would contribute to an ever-increasing national debt and to a growing national deficit that by year's end was predicted to exceed $1 trillion.

NATIONAL SECURITY. In Iraq, the year began badly as a suicide attack on a group mourning the victim of a bombing killed dozens more, while six US soldiers died entering a booby-trapped home in Diyala province. Over 70 people died and more than twice that number were injured in an especially horrific attack in February when bombs attached to two women, thought to be mentally disabled, were detonated by remote control at a Baghdad pet market. Such brutality spoke not only to the depravity of the perpetrators but also, it was argued, to their desperation, as their ability to create carnage appeared to be reduced by the growing success of US and Iraqi forces. Terrible deadly attacks continued throughout the year, yet violence was much reduced across the country. According to army officials, the average daily number of attacks in Iraq had shrunk from 180 to 10, bringing with it far fewer civilian deaths and casualties. The total number of US military dead passed 4,000 in March, when four soldiers died in a roadside bomb attack in Baghdad. Overall, however, the death toll for the US forces for the year was down significantly. According to Pentagon (department of defence) figures, 309 US military personnel died, 222 of them in combat. This compared to 906 in 2007 and over 800 each year from 2004 to 2006.

Supporters of the continued vigorous prosecution of the war credited the decline in violence to the new military strategy implemented in 2007 under the leadership of General David H. Petraeus. Popularly known as "the surge", this new strategy included more US troops taking a more aggressive approach to clearing areas of insurgents and retaining control of those areas with the help of Iraqi forces. In April, Petraeus took over as head of Central Command (CENTCOM), the command unit responsible for the Middle East and Central Asia. Observers more sceptical about how well the war was now going emphasised other aspects of the larger change in policy, especially the co-opting to the coalition side of many Sunnis who had once fought against it. Disillusioned with al-Qaida and reconstituted as the Sons of Iraq, and paid well by the government, these forces proved important in keeping many areas free from terrorist groups. Some questioned the solidity of this support as they did the de facto truce being observed by Shia militias such as that of Muqtada al Sadr in Baghdad. Clearly, however, the violence was significantly reduced, something that even some of the Democratic candidates grudgingly acknowledged.

Petraeus himself emphasised that the ultimate success of the strategy depended on political progress being made in the more stable environment created by military activity. There were some signs of such progress early in the year. In February several laws were passed, dealing with such things as provincial elections, as well as a Justice and Accountability Law intended to provide amnesty for many current detainees and former members of the Baath Party. It was hoped, in turn, that this legislation would help pave the way for increased Sunni participation in the political process and the national government. Petraeus acknowledged these political gains, but insisted that there had not been "sufficient progress by any means in the area of national reconciliation" or in rebuilding the nation's infrastructure and services. In April, he testified before Congress that the "significant" military progress was still "fragile and reversible" and, therefore, that any troop withdrawal in the near term would be premature. President Bush offered a more fulsome interpretation of recent events, speaking on 19 March, the fifth anniversary of the war's beginning. Recognising that "the battle in Iraq has been longer and harder and more costly than we anticipated," the president remained certain that it "is noble, it is necessary, and it is just." Adopting a robust optimism with regard to recent military developments, he claimed that they had turned Iraq into a "place where Arabs joined with Americans to drive al-Qaida out," while the surge had "opened the door to a major strategic victory in the broader war on terror".

In November, the cabinet of Iraqi Prime Minister Nouri al-Maliki approved an agreement drawn up with the USA to deal with the status of US troops, whose UN mandate was set to expire on 31 December. The Status of Forces Agreement (SOFA) called for the withdrawal of US troops from the streets of Iraq's towns and cities and the handing over of US bases to Iraq in 2009, as well as the removal of those troops' authority to raid homes without Iraqi judicial approval (see Documents). The Agreement was ratified by the Iraqi parliament on 27 November. Many Iraqis, however, remained opposed to an agreement that they believed left the way open for the continued indefinite presence of US troops after the major withdrawals had taken place.

In Afghanistan, few observers were optimistic enough to identify any significant movement either towards military victory for the Afghan government and its coalition allies or towards political stability, particularly in the provinces at a distance from the capital, Kabul. Indeed, in the eyes of most observers the military and political challenges facing "Operation Enduring Freedom" only grew over the course of the year. Attacks on both civilian and military targets increased. February saw the deadliest single insurgent attack since the war began, when a suicide bomber killed 80 people, including a local police chief, and wounded many more attending a dog fight near Kandahar. Roadside bombs took an increasing toll on coalition troops: 155 US troops died, the largest single-year total of the war, up from 115 in 2007, and almost one-quarter of US deaths in the entire war to date. In August the Pentagon approved a request from the NATO commander in Afghanistan, US General David McKiernan, for three more brigades to be sent to the country. The addition of an estimated 12,000-15,000 troops would bring the US presence to about 50,000 troops. Given the deteriorating situation, the expectation was that it would not be the last increase. Both presidential candidates favoured greater attention being paid to the war in Afghanistan, with Barack Obama consistently maintaining that one advantage of withdrawing from Iraq would be the increased capacity to prosecute the war against the Taliban and al-Qaida.

Elsewhere, the USA showed itself willing to ignore national borders in prosecuting the "war on terror". As it had done in 2007, the USA launched missile attacks against targets inside Somalia. An attack in May killed at least 10 people, including Aden Hashi Ayro, a prominent militia commander with links to al-Qaida. The USA also increased its attacks on targets inside Pakistan, often using unmanned "drone" aircraft to deliver missiles. The resurgent Taliban's use of the country's north-western territories as both haven and staging ground and the administration's determination to inflict more damage on al-Qaida before the end of Bush's presidential term were both factors in this increased activity. In January, for example, a missile attack killed a senior member of al-Qaida, Abu Laith al-Libi, who was on the US military's "most wanted" list. While most attacks were conducted from the air, a mission in September by helicopter-borne US Special Forces troops was the first reported ground attack carried out on Pakistani territory.

FOREIGN AFFAIRS. These increased attacks on targets within a sovereign state, and an allied one at that, did not help the cause of US diplomacy in Pakistan. The attacks generated intense resentment in Pakistan, as well as complaints from US-leaning politicians that they made it more difficult to support US anti-terrorist efforts while also maintaining the support of the Pakistani people. In general it was a difficult year in South Asia for the USA's efforts to develop further its ties with Pakistan and India, and to encourage better relations between the two nuclear neighbours. The region lived with the aftermath of Benazir Bhutto's assassination at the end of 2007, the resignation of President Pervez Musharraf in 2008, as well as continuing terrorist attacks in both India and Pakistan, culminating in the series of co-ordinated terrorist attacks which hit various targets in Bombay (Mumbai)—India's financial capital—in December (see pp. 316-17).

Closer to the homeland, Fidel Castro Ruz stood down as president of Cuba in February, less than one year from the 50th anniversary of the revolution that overthrew the dictator General Fulgencio Batista and established Castro's own marathon run as ruler. He had been seriously ill for some time and presidential power had temporarily passed to his brother Raúl Castro Ruz in 2006. Now, the change was made permanent. Such was the saturation coverage of the early stages of the US elections and the growing attention paid to the nation's economic problems that the resignation of the USA's longest-surviving nemesis passed with very little public discussion. To many, other than the still energetically anti-Castro majority of Cuban émigrés, the continuing US embargo of Cuba spoke of an earlier Cold War era of US-Soviet superpower conflict, which already seemed part of distant history. The history seemed a little less distant in August, however, when Russian tanks and troops rolled into Georgia in support of separatist opponents of the Georgian government in the province of South Ossetia (see map, p. 137). Russian leaders claimed that the invasion was necessary to protect their fellow Russians—who made up a substantial part of the former Soviet republic's population—from Georgia's intensified military attack on the secessionists. The conflict exacerbated already strained relations between Russia and the USA, adding to the tensions engendered by NATO expansion to the borders of Russia and its plans to locate elements of a missile defence shield in countries such as Poland and the Czech Republic.

President Bush met several times over the course of the year with the leaders of Israel and Palestine, Ehud Olmert and Mahmoud Abbas, a reflection in part of the administration's belated hopes to make significant progress towards a peace agreement before the end of its term. Although Bush was the first US president to call explicitly for an independent Palestinian state as part of an enduring peace for the region, he had been criticised for not making the Israeli-Palestinian conflict a priority earlier in his presidency. Fears and criticisms that the late push was too little and too late proved prescient by the year's end, as Israel launched a large-scale military assault upon the Palestinian territory of Gaza in an effort to bring an end to the firing of crude rockets from the Hamas-controlled area.

POLITICS. The world of politics beyond the presidential campaign began with an event that, had it not been for the saturation coverage given to the early caucuses and primaries, might have received more national attention. On 14 January, Piyush Jindal was sworn in as governor of Louisiana. Known since childhood as Bobby, supposedly after a character in *The Brady Bunch* situation comedy, Jindal became the first Indian-American to become a governor of a state as well as, at the age of 36, the youngest sitting governor in the country. Jindal became the fourth Asian-American governor in the country's history, and the first of South Asian background.

March saw a swing to the other end of the "only in America" spectrum, when New York Governor Elliot Spitzer resigned after the *New York Times* revealed his efforts to engage the services, not for the first time, of a prostitute from a sex ring known as Emperor's Club VIP. Spitzer, or Client 9 as he was known by the service, admitted his involvement and resigned on 12 March. He was succeeded by David Paterson, a legally blind former lieutenant governor of the state and the third African-American governor in US history.

PRESIDENTIAL ELECTION. The presidential campaign had been seriously underway for almost a year before the primary and caucus voting commenced in early January in Iowa and New Hampshire. In keeping with precedents established in the decades since World War II, these states voted first. Proponents of their primacy have argued that starting in such relatively small states has allowed lesser-known candidates to make an impression on the voters through the relatively low budget "retail" politics of going door-to-door and holding "town hall meetings", rather than having to depend on expensive television advertising. Critics countered that these very homogeneous states (both having predominantly white populations) did not reflect the nation's diversity, and that their disproportionate influence often meant that the process was effectively over before the citizens of larger states could have their say.

In 2008, Florida and Michigan became the latest states to attempt to exert more influence by moving their primaries to an earlier stage in the process. In response, Iowa and New Hampshire moved their contests even earlier (state law in New Hampshire requiring that its primary be first). The Democratic party had already consented to earlier events for Nevada and South Carolina, to provide more regional balance, but agreed not to accept any other contests in January. Consequently, it ruled that the Florida and Michigan delegates would not be seated at the party convention. The party's candidates undertook not to campaign in either state. Whether the results in these states were to be taken into account, and if so how, would prove to be a controversial issue for the Democrats.

As the primary season progressed, great attention was, of course, paid to which candidates won and lost in each state. But also crucial to keep in mind was that these were not direct elections. Rather, the popular vote translated into "pledged" delegates: party members who would attend their party's national convention and vote for the candidate to whom they had been committed by the popular vote. In some contests on the Republican side all delegates went to the winner. In others, and in all of the Democratic party contests, delegates were distributed on a pro-portional formula based on the popular vote. Thus, the key target for all candi-dates was to win more than half of the available delegates. For the Republicans the magic number was 1,191; for the Democrats 2,118. Further complicating the most cumbersome electoral process on earth, the Democratic party also had a cat-egory of "superdelegates", made up of 796 party members, including state gover-nors and members of Congress, as well as party workers and luminaries. These delegates could support the candidate of their choice, declare their support at any time, and, indeed, change their mind at any time. Thus the support of these superdelegates was ardently pursued by all candidates.

On 3 January, Iowans caucused in homes and schools and other meeting places across the state, and selected Senator Barack Obama of Illinois and former gov-ernor of Arkansas Mike Huckabee as their favourite Democrat and Republican, respectively. Both victories were something of a surprise. Former senator John Edwards of North Carolina finished in second place in the Democratic contest, with frontrunner Senator Hillary Clinton coming in third. With the caucus system allowing participants to move their support to other candidates if their first choice could not win, Obama finished with 38 per cent, 8 per cent ahead of Edwards, who edged out Clinton by just 1 percentage point. Obama's victory offered many cit-izens a first glimpse of what would prove to be his campaign's consistent and prodigious ability to raise funds and organise and inspire supporters.

On the Republican side, former governor of Massachusetts Mitt Romney fin-ished second with another former senator, Fred Thompson of Tennessee, coming third. Two Republican candidates, expecting to have a prominent role before pro-ceedings concluded, campaigned little in Iowa: former mayor of New York City, Rudy Giuliani, and Senator John McCain of Arizona. For the latter—the only leading candidate from either party brave enough to oppose the government sub-sidies for ethanol so beloved of Iowans—extensive campaigning there was assumed to be a poor use of his limited funds. McCain nevertheless won 13 per cent of the vote, sharing third place with Thompson. Both men lagged a long way behind the 35 per cent garnered by Huckabee, whose blend of conservative poli-tics, evangelical beliefs, amiable personality, and impressive powers of communi-cation helped to make him one of the early hits of the campaign season.

Once held in March and, as recently as 1996, in the second half of February, the New Hampshire primary called voters to the polls on 8 January. This gave little time to Romney and Clinton to regain momentum and achieve the strong showing, if not victory, that many observers felt essential to their continued viability. On the Republican side, McCain was also pinning all his early hopes on a positive result in New Hampshire. The state had been very good to McCain in his previous run for the nomination, giving him a sound victory over George W. Bush in 2000. It repeated the treat in 2008, giving McCain the victory with 37 per cent of the vote to Romney's 31.5 per cent. Huckabee came in a distant third with just over 11 per cent, and no other candidate reached double figures. While Huckabee was not expected to do well in the north east, Romney's defeat in a neighbouring state (much of whose media came from his own Massachusetts) proved a serious blow to his candidacy. McCain outpolled Romney among independents (who were allowed to vote in New Hampshire primaries) and did best among those deserting the already sinking campaigns of Giuliani and Thompson. The win resurrected a campaign declared dead and broke in the summer of 2007. For Romney, who had already outspent his rivals by millions, much of it coming from his own personal fortune, two second place finishes were not what he had expected.

As expected—since he had grown up there and his father had been a popular governor of the state—Romney did win the Michigan primary on 15 January with 39 per cent of the vote, 9 per cent ahead of second placed McCain. Four days later he won the Nevada caucus. The same day, however, McCain took the South Carolina primary with one-third of the vote, only 3 per cent ahead of second placed Mike Huckabee, but winning more than twice as many votes as Romney, who trailed in fourth with 15 per cent. Tennessee's Thompson finished third, a poor result in terms of his own expectations for the first southern contest, and he withdrew from the race soon afterwards. In the last contest of the month, in Florida, McCain pulled off an impressive victory in a state where, not long before, success had seemed beyond him. Mitt Romney finished with 31 per cent, 5 points behind McCain and 15 ahead of Giuliani, for whom the poll provided final confirmation that his strategy of saving himself, and his money, for Florida had been a strategic blunder. Giuliani withdrew from the race and endorsed McCain.

In the Democratic race, Iowa appeared to have answered the question of whether or not Obama could translate his growing public profile and popularity into actual votes. Yes, he could. His victory in almost all-white Iowa was credited with helping to convince black voters that Obama had a viable shot at the nomination. This, in turn, contributed to the black surge to Obama and away from Clinton, at one time the most popular candidate among black Democrats. For her part, the impressive performance of Obama and his campaign in Iowa piled pressure on Clinton to show that she was capable of waging a strong campaign, now that hopes of a procession of victories leading to an early capture of the nomination had been dashed. As it turned out, she proved that she could. With most polls showing solid leads for Obama, the Clinton campaign worked frantically to lower expectations for the New Hampshire primary to a narrow defeat. Fuelled by some suspect polling, which appeared to have failed to capture the unusually large number of voters who decided very late, much of the media breathlessly predicted a contest-ending New Hampshire victory for Obama. Yet the senator from New York pulled off a narrow victory, beating her opponent by 3 per cent.

Pausing briefly for some light self-flagellation, the pundit army then got down to explaining an outcome that most of them had declared highly unlikely only hours before. Perhaps it was because Clinton had shed a tear in a New Hampshire diner, thus revealing a "human side". Perhaps it was because she had reminded people that, being a woman, she too embodied the possibility of radical change in the nation's politics. Perhaps the people of New Hampshire had grown tired of hearing that the contest was over before they had even voted. Whatever the impact of these events, it was clear that, of the very high number of late-deciding voters, the majority had opted for Clinton. Furthermore, almost 60 per cent of those who voted were women and a majority of them voted for Clinton. In a pattern that would persist, Clinton did better among registered Democrats, while Obama was more successful in attracting Independents in contests that allowed registered Independents to vote. Clinton was clearly grateful to the people who had saved her campaign. "I come tonight with a very, very full heart, and I want especially to thank New Hampshire," declared the senator in her victory speech in Manchester, New Hampshire. "Over the last week, I listened to you, and in the process I found my own voice." Third place in New Hampshire went to John Edwards, who finished almost 20 percentage points behind Obama with 17 per cent of the vote. Edwards stayed in the race, but New Mexico governor Bill Richardson dropped out after two fourth-place finishes, joining Senators Biden and Dodd, who had called it a day after the Iowa caucus. Responding to defeat, Obama presciently predicted that "the battle ahead will be long" but would eventually be won by the "millions of voices calling for change".

January brought further Democratic contests in Michigan, Nevada, South Carolina, and Florida, which left Clinton and Obama as the last remaining major candidates. Squeezed by the big two for attention and money, Edwards left the race after more poor results, including in his native state of South Carolina. Obama's overwhelming victory in that state, where black Americans made up about 30 per cent of the population, was interpreted as further evidence that black Democrats—consistently the staunchest of Clintonians going back to the presidency of Bill Clinton—now believed that Obama could really win. Obama received over 55 per cent of the vote, almost 30 points more than Clinton. The latter scored a rare caucus victory in Nevada, and also won Michigan and Florida handily, beating "uncommitted" by 15 per cent in the former (other significant candidates having removed their name from the ballot) and Obama by 17 per cent in Florida where, again, candidates had agreed not to campaign. Heading into the contests to be held on 5 February in 22 states—the appropriately if unimaginatively dubbed "super Tuesday"—Obama and Clinton remained the only two major candidates in the Democratic race. On the Republican side, McCain's comeback had made him the frontrunner, with Romney his major challenger and Huckabee still insisting that he could make a challenge, despite disappointing results in South Carolina and Florida.

As the fields narrowed, so too did the areas of debate between the candidates. On the Republican side, the question of which candidate was the best conservative preoccupied much of the early discussion. As the campaign proceeded, who would be the best steward of the nation's economy in difficult times came to the fore. Romney made much of his background as a successful capitalist. McCain responded that his forte was "leadership, not management," but he was challenged throughout the primaries by claims that for him the economy was not a major area either of interest or expertise. He did not help himself in this regard with various comments about his knowledge of economics from earlier in the campaign. In December he acknowledged that "the issue of economics is not something I've understood as well as I should." While a palpable sense of personal antagonism between the two leading candidates ran throughout the race, it could not obscure their broad agreement on such Republican staples as abortion, taxes, and national security.

The absence of substantive policy differences was even more evident among the Democrats. As much was suggested by a televised Clinton-Obama debate held in February in Cleveland, Ohio, which began with a 16-minute discussion on one aspect of their respective universal healthcare plans: whether or not all people would be required to purchase insurance. While this was an important issue, it hardly represented an ideological gulf between the two. Instead, claim and counterclaim regarding experience and judgement, of who was best equipped to bring "change" to the country, predominated. In foreign policy, Clinton emphasised her experience and sought to paint Obama as naïve, even reckless, for his views that enemies such as Iran should be engaged diplomatically at the highest level and that military strikes inside Pakistan would be legitimate as a means to kill Osama bin Laden or other senior al-Qaida targets. Obama contrasted his judgement to Clinton's experience, emphasising his opposition, before he himself was a member, to the 2002 Senate authorisation to use military forces in Iraq, which Senator Clinton had supported. Yet on the issue of how to get out of Iraq, differences were increasingly difficult to identify. As the situation in Iraq stabilised, both candidates spoke of the matter in increasingly cautious terms.

McCain emerged from "super Tuesday" with his frontrunner status significantly strengthened. He won only nine of the 21 contests on the Republican side, but those included the largest state, California, and two other large states, New Jersey and New York, which allotted their delegates on a winner-takes-all basis. Romney won seven contests, mostly in more lightly-populated states, and lost more ground. This was due, in significant part, to the unexpectedly strong performance of Huckabee across the states of the South, from his home state of Arkansas to West Virginia. That so many conservative Republicans in these states did not turn their scepticism regarding McCain's poor conservative credentials into a vote for the remaining candidate capable of beating him offered strong evidence that Romney, too, had failed to win over that same conservative base. On 7 February, he announced the suspension of his campaign, and a week later formally withdrew from the race and offered his support to his bitter rival, McCain. Huckabee showed no sign of following suit, continuing to campaign throughout February, even as growing numbers of Republicans called on him to accept the inevitability of McCain's eventual victory and to bow out. He did withdraw from the race, but not until McCain had clinched the requisite number of delegates with four more victories, including Ohio and Texas, in early March. There was an ironic quality to this outcome. In a debate focused on the questions of who was the most reliably conservative and, later, who was most qualified to lead the country in troubled economic times, the candidate deemed by few as best qualified on either count had won the day. What had helped McCain was the perception that he was the most electable of the Republicans, given his appeal to Independents (an attraction that itself owed something to his less than solid reputation with right-wing Republicans).

"Super Tuesday" resolved little with regard to which of the two leading Democrats would eventually triumph. Obama won 14 of the contests, showing his popularity in all regions of the country, from Alaska to Alabama, Colorado to Connecticut. While Clinton claimed only eight victories, these included the large prizes of California, New Jersey, and her own New York. Clinton also won in Massachusetts, where both sitting senators, John Kerry and Edward Kennedy, were active Obama supporters. In total votes and delegates assigned, the candidates emerged fairly even, with Clinton having a slight lead in pledged delegates. While not decisive, "super Tuesday" handed an advantage to Obama, the candidate whose strategy had always planned for the long haul, assiduously building organisations and support in many of the states still to vote. The confidence in the Clinton camp that the nomination would be theirs no later than early February left them poorly placed—in terms of money and strategy—to conduct a campaign that would now extend far beyond that point. Obama went on to win the nine remaining contests held in February, including Virginia, Maryland, Louisiana, Oregon, and his adopted state of Hawaii. These victories maintained his momentum while bringing a pledged delegate lead that he would never relinquish.

Nevertheless, Clinton was determined to press on. Despite money problems (she twice had to loan her own campaign millions of dollars) and growing analysis which suggested that she could not overtake Obama, she entered what was arguably her most successful period of campaigning. She sharpened her attacks on Obama, increasingly engaging in negative campaigning. Shortly before the "must-win" primaries in Ohio and Texas, she released a controversial television advertisement—"the three a.m. phone call"—which juxtaposed a child sleeping safely at home with the sound of a telephone ringing in the White House, because "something is happening in the world." The viewer was asked to consider whom they would want to answer the phone, suggesting obviously that Clinton, with all her experience, would be that person. The advertisement made no mention of Obama, and the Clinton campaign argued that it was merely pointing out the importance of having an experienced president in times of threat. The Obama campaign dismissed it as politics-as-usual, designed to play on the fears of the electorate rather than appeal to its hopes. Clinton did win both primaries in those big states on 5 March, as well as winning in Rhode Island. Obama won Vermont.

Yet Clinton's big day at the polls did not translate into significant gains in the pledged delegate race. Her wins in Texas and Ohio, by 3 per cent and 8 per cent respectively, netted her a total gain of only 12 pledged delegates. Furthermore, Texas held a caucus as well as a primary, at which a further 67 pledged delegates were at stake. Obama won this by 5,000 votes from less than 50,000, and received 38 delegates to Clinton's 29. This compared to Clinton's receiving 65 delegates to Obama's 61 for outpolling him by 100,000 votes from a total of over 2.8 million cast. Thus, in Texas Obama garnered more delegates than Clinton, 99 to 94, for receiving 95,000 fewer of the votes cast. While Texas was somewhat anomalous, given its holding of both a primary and a caucus, other results, too, brought Clinton limited delegate gains on her opponent despite solid victories.

Given the proportional distribution of delegates and the disproportionate impact of winning caucuses (which usually had far fewer participants than did primaries), victory was already beyond Clinton, barring some extraordinary event. By mid-March, she could have won all of the remaining contests and still been extremely unlikely to overtake Obama among the pledged delegates. Thus, by this point the campaign had entered a paradoxical stage. As Clinton's appetite for the fight appeared to increase in inverse proportion to her chances of winning it, so, too, did her negative attacks upon her opponent. In particular her campaign emphasised his lack of experience as well as his supposed inability to attract support from essential Democratic constituencies, such as women and working class white people. Clinton also continued to mock her opponent's immense oratorical skills, attempting to portray this strength as actually a lack of substance. On 7 March, addressing a crowd of supporters drawn from the military, Clinton sneered that, "Senator McCain will bring a lifetime of experience to the campaign, I will bring a lifetime of experience, and Senator Obama will bring a speech he gave in 2002."

Adding to the somewhat unreal quality of the contest was the fact that much of the media coverage recognised the inevitability of an Obama victory even as it continued to cover the contests as if Clinton could really win the nomination. While Clinton seemed energised, Obama appeared to be on the defensive. March was a tough month for the young Illinois senator. It brought film footage of his Chicago pastor, the Reverend Jeremiah Wright, making harsh criticisms of the USA in some of his sermons. The Obama family had been long-time members of Wright's church and Obama had claimed the pastor as a mentor (even borrowing one of Wright's phrases—"the audacity of hope"—for the title of one of his books). Obama had faced questions earlier about some of Wright's comments, but the newly available video footage took the story to an entirely different level of interest and concern. Obama heard calls to distance himself from Wright's remarks, which he did, and from Wright himself, which he did not. In Philadelphia Obama made a remarkable speech in which he addressed the issue of race, for so long an unspoken component of the campaign, head on. He condemned Wright's remarks, but insisted that simply to condemn without seeking to understand the anger and resentment felt by many black people, and indeed many white people, was simply to prolong the "racial stalemate we've been stuck in for years". Obama stated his "firm conviction—a conviction rooted in my faith in God and my faith in the American people—that working together we can move beyond some of our old racial wounds, and that in fact we have no choice if we are to continue on the path of a more perfect union." After further controversial remarks by Wright to the National Press Club in April, Obama did break with him and with the Trinity United Church of Christ in Chicago. Despite the approving reception given to his speech, the Wright controversy and Clinton's attacks seemed to take some toll on Obama's popularity, enough to slow perhaps, but not prevent, his march to the nomination.

Faced with Obama's inexorable progress and increasing questions as to why Clinton was continuing the contest (not least from anxious Democrats who were unnerved by the severity of Clinton's attacks and the damage that they were doing to the likely nominee), Clinton's supporters offered various rationales for staying in the race. Increasingly, they focused on the impressive numbers of voters that Clinton was attracting to the polls rather than on the delegate count. They emphasised how, by the campaign's end, it was quite possible that Clinton would have more popular votes than Obama (and to this end, they increasingly pushed for the votes in the disallowed Florida and Michigan primaries "to be counted", where once all had agreed they would not be recognised). Increasingly they stressed the strong support of women for a woman candidate, where once Clinton had been as assiduous in de-emphasising her sex as Obama continued to be in downplaying his race. They presented Clinton's growing popular success—especially among groups such as women and the white working class, where Democrats usually polled well—as a "movement" rather than a mere campaign. Clinton's supporters were not slow to contrast their candidate's success within these traditional Democratic blocs with Obama's failure to "close the sale" with these same groups. Without the enthusiastic support of these voters, the Democrats could not win the presidency. The argument that some Democrats would not vote for the Democratic nominee in the presidential election just because they had voted for another candidate in the primary had its flaws, of course, but was given strength by the growing bitterness and division between the two campaigns. With Clinton surrogates assiduously pushing the suggestion—itself heavily laden with covert racism—that Obama was unelectable, the continuing campaign fuelled a growing feeling among Clinton supporters that they were being ignored and even "disrespected" by Obama and his followers. Clinton's newfound populism served her well as her supporters resisted calls for her to withdraw, characterising these as disrespectful to the millions who had joined her movement, and in so doing fuelled a sense both of identity with Clinton and an increased antagonism towards Obama among many of those followers.

Clinton's growing emphasis on the popular vote rather than the delegate totals brought with it an increasing focus on the role of the superdelegates. The category of superdelegate had been created, in part, to lessen the chances that the party would nominate a candidate who, while popular with segments of the party, might not be acceptable to the general population. The not-so-subtle suggestion from Clinton circles was that the superdelegates should get in line with the popular vote and support the supposedly more electable candidate from New York. Many Democrats, and not just Obama supporters, were quick to point out that any such move would surely outrage and alienate Obama's supporters, particularly his black supporters, without whom no Democrat could win a presidential election. One way or another, many superdelegates made it clear that this was not going to happen, and indeed over this period more and more of them respected the official results of the primary process and declared for Obama.

As ever more Democrats worried that the only person being helped by Clinton's continuing campaign was McCain, Clinton did indeed go on to record more victories, winning six of the 11 remaining contests, including Pennsylvania and West Virginia, states which provided further strong evidence of the New York senator's popularity among white working class and rural voters. Yet, Obama had his own impressive victories, including in North Carolina and Oregon, and, as had been long predicted, it was Obama who passed the number of delegates necessary to clinch the nomination. Although Clinton still refused to concede as the last contests were completed, Obama claimed victory. "After 54 hard-fought contests, our primary season has finally come to an end," he declared on 3 June in Minneapolis. "Tonight, I can stand here before you and say that I will be the Democratic nominee for the president of the United States of America."

Obama's victory did little to reduce the media hysteria surrounding the question of what Clinton would do next. Would she continue to refuse to concede and instead take the contest all the way to the floor of the convention? Would she concede but refuse to throw her support behind Obama unless she got what she wanted (the vice-presidential nomination, for example)? Would she really encourage her disappointed and embittered supporters to get behind Obama? These clouds would hang over Obama's campaign for some time, but they were well on the way to being dispersed by the time that he accepted the nomination on a spectacular August night in Denver. At the Democratic convention, Clinton did everything expected of her in the name of party unity. Obama's selection, shortly before the convention, of Senator Joe Biden as his running mate was well received as a safe choice that added a popular Democrat with extensive foreign policy experience to the ticket.

In accepting the nomination Obama spoke in the open air on a sparkling night to an audience of over 80,000 in Invesco Field stadium in Denver and to almost 40 million on television across the country. Speaking on the themes of "change" and "the American promise", he offered a departure from the "broken politics" of the past and the "failed policies" of the Bush administration. "America, we are better than these last eight years," he declared, "We are a better country than this." Blending rhetoric intended to inspire with lists of issues and aims designed to persuade, Obama set out familiar pledges to work for universal healthcare, better education and a greener economy, to provide tax cuts for the middle class and small businesses, and to "end this war in Iraq responsibly, and finish the fight against al-Qaida and the Taliban in Afghanistan." Obama also set out the core of his case against McCain, insistently linking his opponent to the current administration. "John McCain has voted with George Bush ninety per cent of the time. Senator McCain likes to talk about judgement, but really, what does it say about your judgement when you think George Bush has been right more than ninety per cent of the time? I don't know about you, but I'm not ready to take a ten per cent chance on change." It was not that McCain "doesn't care what's going on in the lives of Americans. I just think he doesn't know." Contrasting the record of the past eight years with the promise of the future, Obama declared, "Tonight, I say to the American people, to Democrats and Republicans and Independents across this great land: Enough! This moment—this election—is our chance to keep, in the 21st century, the American promise alive."

If Obama's speech did not give his candidacy as big a "bounce" as many had predicted, the reason may have been McCain's announcement the following day that he had chosen the 44-year old governor of Alaska, Sarah Palin, to be his running mate. Palin's name had come up occasionally in the swirl of rumour that surrounds such decisions, but most attention was focused elsewhere by the time that McCain introduced his running mate to a crowd of 15,000 in Dayton, Ohio. Palin was only the second woman to be chosen as the vice-presidential nominee of a major party, and the first Alaskan to occupy any place at the top of a major party ticket. These would be far from the only characteristics that made Palin such a unique and transformative presence in the election. She proved an instant hit with the right wing of the party. Her convention speech on 3 September was understandably heavy on introducing herself, her family, and her political record to a public that knew little about her. She described herself as "just your average hockey mom," and to delighted applause characterised "the difference between a hockey mom and a pit bull: lipstick". She was also quick to take the fight to opponents whose "plan" was "to make government bigger, and take more of your money, and give you more orders from Washington, and to reduce the strength of America in a dangerous world". Referring throughout to McCain's military record and principled approach to politics, Palin closed by exhorting those assembled to "join our cause and help America elect a great man as the next president of the United States".

Accepting the nomination, McCain also made much of his military record and his years as a prisoner of war in Vietnam. Using the word, or one of its variants, 25 times, McCain made clear his willingness to "fight" for "your future", for "Americans", for the restoration of the "pride and principles of our party" and for "country". Like Obama, McCain listed his policy ambitions if elected and warned of the harmful results should his opponent win. He made a strong appeal for national unity, promoting his willingness and ability to work with opponents for the greater good. In conclusion, he returned to his central theme and exhorted his audience to "Stand up, stand up, stand up and fight. Nothing is inevitable here. We're Americans, and we never give up. We never quit. We never hide from history. We make history."

Neither candidate's acceptance speech broke new ground, either in terms of his own aims or his opponent's deficiencies. Indeed, Obama and McCain had been campaigning against one another long before their nominations became official. Thus, the conventions marked a point of continuity in the campaign itself. Obama continued to tie McCain to the "failed policies" of the Bush administration and to paint him as unversed in economic matters and out of touch with the lives of most citizens. McCain did not help himself in this regard when he was unable to tell a questioner how many homes he owned. More damaging was his claim that the fundamentals of the nation's economy were strong, long past the time when most people thought that the economy could be facing a catastrophe. McCain continued to paint Obama as unqualified and to belittle his record of public service. Following Clinton (and sometimes using her very words), the McCain campaign sought to turn positives into negatives: Obama's eloquence masked inexperience and ineffectiveness; his popularity was mere celebrity. "He's the biggest celebrity in the world. But is he ready to lead?" ran part of one advertisement, as it interspersed clips of Obama appearing before huge crowds in Berlin (see p. 49) with images of the less than universally respected celebrities, Britney Spears and Paris Hilton, both of whom had expressed support for him.

These attacks had some resonance for a public that could certainly see that Obama was a man with a good conceit of himself. Nevertheless, it was not so much Spears and Hilton with whom the public increasingly compared him, but rather that new celebrity in the political firmament, Sarah Palin. The conservative base of the party welcomed her with open arms, liking her folksiness, her looks, her confidence, her evangelical faith, and her uncompromisingly conservative beliefs. Palin brought a sorely needed energy to the Republican ticket and attracted the huge crowds that had mostly eluded McCain. A successful convention and the Palin selection helped McCain to an early September lead in some opinion polls. Yet Palin's wider popularity was less secure, and consistently declined as more voters became familiar with her, believing her to be too conservative or too inexperienced. Many commentators, including many Republicans, questioned McCain's judgement in choosing someone who undercut one of his major weapons against Obama: that he lacked experience. If a 44-year old former small town mayor and one term governor could be a breath away from being president, why could a 47-year old former state senator and one term US senator not be president? Most damaging, however, was the growing public perception that Palin was simply not up to the job. Despite intensive coaching and protection by her Republican media handlers, the more she revealed about herself in speeches and interviews, the more doubts were raised about her suitability. Her folksy style could not conceal a level of ignorance, particularly in relation to the world outside the USA (of which she had almost no direct experience), that was shocking. Her glamour was undermined by revelations concerning her extravagant shopping habits (particularly when others were picking up the bills); her freshness was offset by unsavoury revelations concerning her family; and even her much vaunted reformist credentials were undermined by her record in office and the pall of corruption allegations over "Troopergate", which drifted south from Alaska and entered the media mainstream. The more Palin imposed herself on the campaign, the more independent voters, essential to McCain's chances of victory, gravitated away from the Republican ticket. On balance, it was difficult to escape the conclusion that the choice of Palin was a grave mistake for, although it galvanised the party faithful, it undermined McCain's assets: his claim to have good judgement, his emphasis on experience in a dangerous and complex world, and, perhaps most important of all, his ability to attract middle-of-the-road independent voters.

Obama also looked increasingly mature and serious in contrast to McCain. This was especially true of the period during and after the major turning point of the election campaign. This turning point consisted of several events that took place during September and which elevated the ongoing economic crisis to a new level. On 7 September, the federal government took control of the Federal National Mortgage Association and the Federal Home Loan Mortgage Corporation (known colloquially as Fannie Mae and Freddie Mac respectively). These two massive mortgage finance companies dominated the secondary mortgage market, buying mortgages from the original lenders and either holding them or packaging them as securities and selling them on to investors. Between them they held or guaranteed almost half the mortgages in the USA. According to Treasury Secretary Henry Paulson, "Fannie Mae and Freddie Mac are so large and so interwoven in our financial system that a failure of either of them would cause great turmoil in our financial markets here at home and around the globe." On 15 September, the investment bank of Lehman Brothers filed for bankruptcy. In terms of the company's assets, it was the largest bankruptcy in US history. Founded in 1850, and with a long-held reputation for financial probity, it had become the largest casualty to date of the developing economic crisis. On the same day, which soon became known as "meltdown Monday", the Bank of America purchased Merrill Lynch, an established brokerage house desperately weakened by $50 billion in losses; and on 16 September the Federal Reserve announced an emergency government loan of $85 billion to the massive insurance company, AIG.

The various crises of September were all tied, in one way or another, to the mortgage crisis. Fannie Mae and Freddie Mac had bundled mortgages and other credit items into mortgage backed securities and sold them on. Companies like Lehman Brothers and Merrill Lynch had bought and sold them. Companies like AIG had insured them. When the housing bubble burst, all suffered. Once the public grasped the mammoth scale and interconnected character of the economic crisis facing the nation and, indeed, most of the world, this in turn pushed almost everything else to the periphery of the national consciousness. Even the election was now conducted in its shadow.

Warning that "without immediate action by Congress, America can slip into a major panic," President Bush asked Congress on 20 September to approve a plan aimed at breaking the liquidity logjam. The plan called for the government to spend $700 billion on buying mortgage backed securities from banks in order to restore confidence, inject money into the system, and encourage banks to start lending again. Government intervention on such a massive scale aroused great debate. For some, it was a denial of free market principles. For others, it was too focused on "bailing out" the Wall Street entities that had created the crisis in the first place, rather than helping the suffering citizens of "Main Street". Both Obama and McCain had a dual role to play in this debate, as candidates but also as sitting US senators. Judgements as to their suitability to lead were increasingly tested against their response to the crisis. McCain sought to portray himself as a man of action (unlike Obama, the intellectual dilettante), by flying to Washington, DC and proclaiming his determination to stay there until a deal had been worked out, even if that meant his missing the first presidential debate scheduled for 26 September in Oxford, Mississippi. This gambit did not work, in part because most people appeared to agree with Obama that anyone running for president should be able to do more than one thing at a time, and in part because McCain's role in proceedings was far from pivotal. With no agreement between Congress and the Treasury in place, McCain attended the debate after all, appearing ineffective and indecisive, even opportunistic, rather than the country-first statesman he had sought to portray. By contrast, Obama's thoughtful pronouncements on the financial crisis enhanced his reputation as a cool head in a time of crisis.

The three presidential debates were even more devoid of substance than usual. Pundits speculated who needed to deliver the "knock-out punch", who could deliver one, who, if anyone, had delivered one, and so on. The reality, however, was that none of the varied debate formats made such a blow possible. Instead, both candidates reiterated familiar arguments and critiques regarding taxes and healthcare, war and foreign policy, and the judgement or otherwise of each other's political decisions and beliefs. In the battle of ideas, Obama came out on top, according to post-debate polls, particularly in the area of greatest importance to voters: the economy. But perhaps the strongest overall impression derived from the debates was of demeanour rather than of policy proposals. Leading in the polls, Obama was all coolness and caution, too much caution for many of his supporters, who felt he should have hit back hard at some of McCain's claims and charges. McCain was feistier, more frenetic, desperate to score the victory that might translate into momentum with the voters and, therefore, more prepared to attack his opponent. These attacks appeared to backfire, with polls suggesting that they contributed to a sense of McCain as angry and lacking in poise. The first debate, which focused mostly on McCain's strong suit, national security, left the polls unchanged, with Obama leading by an average of 5 per cent. Polls taken after the remaining debates recorded convincing wins for Obama (by as much as 53 to 22 per cent in one CBS survey), as well as a growing public faith in his knowledge and competence, in his composure, and in his ability to lead. Perhaps this, rather than the platitudes spoken, was the real message of the debates, and indeed of the closing weeks of the campaign. McCain was the old man yelling at the kids to get off his lawn, too tetchy, too fidgety, too negative. His flailing campaign and ailing candidacy lacked focus and a consistent message. By contrast, Obama was cool; not just celebrity cool, but competent cool, confidence cool. A class act, he remained poised and relentlessly on message, whatever the provocations of opponents or the urgings of supporters.

The economic crisis seemed to have stopped the presidential campaign in its tracks. A growing public debate on the pros and cons of both candidates seemed to have been resolved by the debates and then frozen by circumstances in favour of Obama. He maintained a consistent lead in the many polls taken in October, with McCain seldom coming any closer than within 5 per cent. Almost all showed

Obama with more than 50 per cent support among likely voters. All the eve-of-election polls had Obama ahead by at least 5 percentage points and usually more, and all showed him with 50 per cent or more of the vote.

In the one poll that counted, this time the predictions were borne out. As the results of the election on 4 November came in, the turning point was the moment that the various networks called Ohio for Obama. No Republican had ever won the presidency without carrying that state. In the end, Obama won by 53 per cent to 46 per cent, and by 365 electoral votes to 173. It was a great day for the Democrats, who also increased their majorities in both the House of Representatives and the Senate (see maps). Speaking in Chicago on election night, Obama embodied the message of "change" that he had emphasised throughout the campaign. "If there is anyone out there who still doubts that America is a place where all things are possible, who still wonders if the dream of our founders is alive in our time, who still questions the power of our democracy, tonight is your answer."

Obama's victory was striking in several respects beyond the most obvious one that the USA had elected its first black president. After the losses of 2000 and 2004 some Democrats had called for the party to abandon apparently rock-ribbed Republican areas such as the South and the Mountain West, and to focus on areas of strength, and on crucial swing states. Howard Dean, the party chairman, however, had insisted on a 50-state strategy. While the Republicans carried most of the states that they were expected to win, and won by large margins in most of the Deep South, Obama proved himself capable of winning states in all areas of the country. He won Virginia, North Carolina, and Florida in the South; Colorado and Nevada in the West; as well as sweeping the West Coast, the Mid-West, and New England.

America basked in the glow of a genuinely historic moment: the election of its first African-American president. Despite the rancour of the election, the weeks after the poll saw Obama's popularity growing along with the public's good wishes for his success. In part, this was a consequence of the widespread awareness of the economic challenges facing the nation. In part, it stemmed from Obama's actions after the election when, by all appearances, he made genuine efforts to practise what he had preached during the campaign about bringing people together and bridging the divides that obscured more profound, shared hopes. He reached out to John McCain. He announced his intention to keep Republican Robert Gates as his secretary of defence. Most surprising of all, for many, he asked Hillary Clinton to be his secretary of state. She agreed. Obama received high praise for his conduct during the transition period, as did President Bush for his gracious co-operation. As the year ended the national mood seemed sombre yet hopeful, aware of present difficulties but ready to work for change in the future, and perhaps a little more patient than usual. In those respects, the country appeared to mirror the demeanour of its next president.

James D. Miller

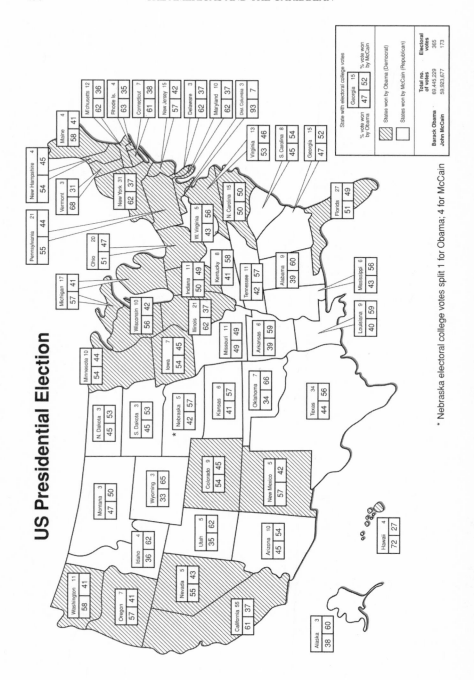

US Presidential Election

State	Electoral votes	% vote won by Obama	% vote won by McCain
Massachusetts	12	62	36
Rhode Is.	4	63	35
Connecticut	7	61	38
New Jersey	15	57	42
Delaware	3	62	37
Maryland	10	62	37
Dist. Columbia	3	93	7
Maine	4	58	41
New Hampshire	4	54	45
Vermont	3	68	31
New York	31	62	37
Pennsylvania	21	55	44
Ohio	20	51	47
Michigan	17	57	41
Wisconsin	10	56	42
Minnesota	10	54	44
N. Dakota	3	45	53
S. Dakota	3	45	53
Nebraska*	5	42	57
Montana	3	47	50
Wyoming	3	33	65
Idaho	4	36	62
Utah	5	35	62
Washington	11	58	41
Oregon	7	57	41
Nevada	5	55	43
California	55	61	37
Alaska	3	38	60
Arizona	10	45	54
New Mexico	5	57	42
Colorado	9	54	45
Kansas	6	41	57
Oklahoma	7	34	66
Texas	34	44	56
Hawaii	4	72	27
Iowa	7	54	45
Missouri	11	49	49
Arkansas	6	39	59
Louisiana	9	40	59
Mississippi	6	43	56
Alabama	9	39	60
Tennessee	11	42	57
Kentucky	8	41	58
Indiana	11	50	49
Illinois	21	62	37
W. Virginia	5	43	56
Virginia	13	53	46
S. Carolina	8	45	54
Georgia	15	47	52
N. Carolina	15	50	50
Florida	27	51	49

State with electoral college votes

Georgia	15
% vote won by Obama	% vote won by McCain
47	52

States won by Obama (Democrat)

States won by McCain (Republican)

	Total no. of votes	Electoral votes
Barack Obama	69,445,229	365
John McCain	59,923,677	173

* Nebraska electoral college votes split 1 for Obama; 4 for McCain

House of Representatives Election

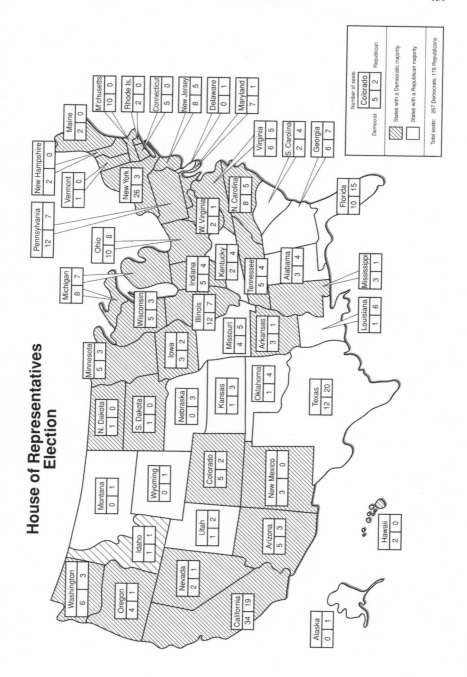

Number of seats

Colorado	5	2
Democrat		Republican

▨ States with a Democratic majority

☐ States with a Republican majority

Total seats: 257 Democrats, 178 Republicans

State	Dem	Rep
M'chusetts	10	0
Rhode Is.	2	0
Connecticut	5	0
New Jersey	8	5
Delaware	0	1
Maryland	7	1
Maine	2	0
New Hampshire	2	0
Vermont	1	0
New York	26	3
Pennsylvania	12	7
Ohio	10	8
Michigan	8	7
Wisconsin	5	3
Illinois	12	7
Indiana	5	4
Virginia	6	5
S. Carolina	2	4
Georgia	6	7
Florida	10	15
N. Carolina	8	5
W. Virginia	2	1
Kentucky	2	4
Tennessee	5	4
Alabama	3	4
Mississippi	3	1
Louisiana	1	6
Missouri	4	5
Arkansas	3	1
Minnesota	5	3
Iowa	3	2
Kansas	1	3
Oklahoma	1	4
Texas	12	20
Nebraska	0	3
N. Dakota	1	0
S. Dakota	1	0
Montana	0	1
Wyoming	0	1
Colorado	5	2
New Mexico	3	0
Utah	1	2
Arizona	5	3
Idaho	1	1
Nevada	2	1
Washington	6	3
Oregon	4	1
California	34	19
Hawaii	2	0
Alaska	0	1

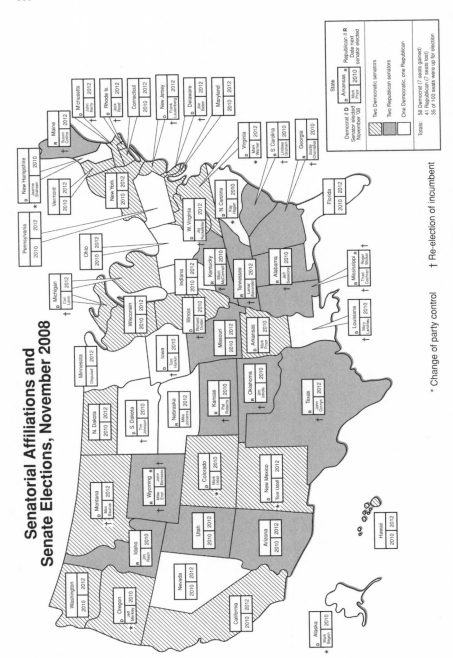

Senatorial Affiliations and
Senate Elections, November 2008

* Change of party control   † Re-election of incumbent

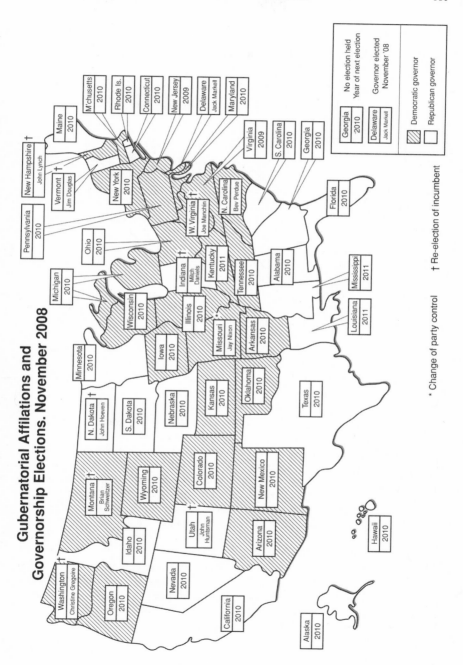

Gubernatorial Affilations and Governorship Elections. November 2008

Maine 2010

New Hampshire †
John Lynch

Vermont †
Jim Douglas

M'chusetts 2010

Rhode Is. 2010

Connecticut 2010

New Jersey 2009

Delaware
Jack Markell

Maryland 2010

New York 2010

Pennsylvania 2010

Ohio 2010

W. Virginia †
Joe Manchin

Virginia 2009

N. Carolina
Bev Perdue

S. Carolina 2010

Georgia 2010

Florida 2010

Michigan 2010

Indiana †
Mitch Daniels

Kentucky 2011

Tennessee 2010

Alabama 2010

Mississippi 2011

Wisconsin 2010

Illinois 2010

Missouri *
Jay Nixon

Arkansas 2010

Louisiana 2011

Minnesota 2010

Iowa 2010

Kansas 2010

Oklahoma 2010

Texas 2010

N. Dakota †
John Hoeven

S. Dakota 2010

Nebraska 2010

Colorado 2010

New Mexico 2010

Montana †
Brian Schweitzer

Wyoming 2010

Utah †
John Huntsman

Arizona 2010

Idaho 2010

Nevada 2010

Hawaii 2010

Washington †
Christine Gregoire

Oregon 2010

California 2010

Alaska 2010

Georgia
2010 — No election held / Year of next election

Delaware
Jack Markell — Governor elected November '08

Democratic governor

Republican governor

* Change of party control   † Re-election of incumbent

CANADA

CAPITAL: Ottawa   AREA: 9,984,670 sq km   POPULATION: 32,976,000 ('07)
OFFICIAL LANGUAGES: English & French   POLTICAL SYSTEM: multiparty system
HEAD OF STATE: Queen Elizabeth II (since Feb '52)
GOVERNOR-GENERAL: Michaëlle Jean (since Sept '05)
RULING PARTY: Conservative Party of Canada (CPC) (since Jan '06)
HEAD OF GOVERNMENT: Prime Minister Stephen Harper (since Feb '06)
MAIN IGO MEMBERSHIPS (NON-UN): NATO, OECD, OSCE, G-7, OAS, NAFTA, APEC, CP, AC,
   CWTH, Francophonie
CURRENCY: Canadian dollar (end-'08 £1=C$1.7749, US$1=C$1.2345)
GNI PER CAPITA: US$39,420, $35,310 at PPP ('07)

PRIME Minister Stephen Harper's centre-right Conservative Party of Canada
(CPC) prevailed at the polls on 14 October in the country's third general election since 2004. The Conservatives took 143 of 308 constituency seats, making
significant gains in Ontario and British Columbia. The centre-left Liberal Party,
led by Stéphane Dion, achieved its worst share of the popular vote in modern
Canadian history at just over 26 percent, although its 77 seats ensured that the
party retained its status as the country's official opposition. Gilles Duceppe's
separatist Bloc Québécois won 49 of the 75 ridings it contested in Québec, and
Jack Layton's left-wing New Democrats achieved victory in 37 seats across the
country. Canada's environmentalist Green Party became the only major political party to increase the total number of votes it received compared with the previous election, as voter turnout hit a historic low of only 59.1 per cent; however,
the party, under Elizabeth May's leadership, failed to win any seats in the House
of Commons (the lower chamber) and lost its sole representative when former
Liberal and Independent MP Blair Wilson, who had switched allegiance to the
Greens shortly before the election, was defeated in his British Columbia constituency. Two independent MPs were also re-elected.

Contravening a fixed-date election law passed by his own government, Harper
said he had called an early election because he believed Parliament was becoming
dysfunctional. The CPC used an effective advertising strategy to paint the main
opposition leader, Dion, as ineffective, unsteady, and risky. Polls in the first few
weeks of the campaign suggested that the Conservatives were achieving levels of
popular support sufficient to produce a majority government, despite several blunders from CPC candidates. However, the party's expected breakthrough in
Québec failed to materialise after the Conservatives introduced two policies that
were overwhelmingly unpopular in the predominantly French-speaking province.
The party's plans to make some cuts to arts and culture programmes and to
toughen youth justice sentencing were received poorly in a province that was generally liberal in social affairs and which used the arts to express its distinct identity. Harper's ill-considered initial reaction to a sudden fall in the stock market in
the midst of the campaign, when he said that the fundamentals of the Canadian
economy were strong and that the stock market decline presented good buying
opportunities, also hurt his party's popularity nationally.

Yet the Liberals were unable to turn Conservative gaffes and campaign problems to their advantage. A central plank in the Liberal platform—the introduc-

tion of a carbon tax called the "green shift" that would cut income taxes and raise taxes on carbon-based fuels—proved unpopular at a time of soaring energy prices and was difficult to explain concisely to voters. Moreover, Dion's difficulties in communicating in English—encapsulated in a widely publicised gaffe, in which he asked for a television interview to be restarted numerous times because he could not understand a question about his party's economic plans—caused the leader's personal standing to act as a drag on the party's fortune. In the aftermath of his election defeat and after only two years as leader of the Liberal Party, Dion announced on 20 October that he would resign his position as soon as a new leader was chosen.

Notwithstanding his re-election and a widely praised formal apology in June to Canada's aboriginal residential school survivors for the emotional, physical, and cultural abuse, which they had suffered in the discontinued government-run assimilation program (see Documents), 2008 proved to be a tough and tumultuous year for the prime minister and his party. In early March Harper's chief of staff, Ian Brodie, and Canada's ambassador to the USA, Michael Wilson, faced accusations that they played a role in a damaging political leak to the news media during the US Democratic presidential primaries. Brodie and Wilson were both named as possible sources for a leak, in which Democratic candidate Barack Obama's campaign team had privately suggested that, contrary to Obama's campaign rhetoric, a Democratic administration would not seek to renegotiate the North American Free Trade Agreement (NAFTA). Although an internal investigation cleared Brodie, he later resigned from his position.

Another to resign was Foreign Affairs Minister Maxime Bernier, who stood down on 26 May following a series of embarrassing gaffes and shortly before allegations surfaced that he had left secret NATO briefing documents at the home of Julie Couillard, a woman he had been dating and who had previously had relationships with men connected to Québec's infamous biker gangs.

Harper also faced intense criticism for tape-recorded statements that he made to an author, in which he allegedly acknowledged that his party had offered financial incentives to Independent MP Chuck Cadman to vote for a no-confidence motion against a previous Liberal minority government that was on the brink of falling. It was contrary to Canadian law to promise monetary inducements to a parliamentarian in exchange for a vote.

Harper's government suffered its greatest political challenge shortly after being re-elected, however. In the weeks following his party's moderate success at the polls, Harper offered a more conciliatory tone in speeches and promised a less divisive and less partisan atmosphere in the House of Commons. His government, which had previously refused to run a budgetary deficit and had promoted a neo-liberal political ideology stressing minimal government intervention, also appeared to change course following the global economic downturn and made announcements to the effect that increased government spending was needed to combat the looming recession.

Nevertheless, a government fiscal update presented by Finance Minister Jim Flaherty on 27 November predicted a series of small, yet unlikely, surpluses for the next few years and included a number of policies, which the opposition parties found to be overtly partisan, including the elimination of public financing for political parties, temporary suspension of the federal public service's right to strike, and the interruption of programmes aimed at helping women fight for pay equity. All opposition parties announced plans to defeat the fiscal update, which included pieces of legislation that were confidence matters and could result in the defeat of the recently re-elected Conservative minority government. Rather than return to the polls immediately, the Liberals and New Democrats agreed to form a coalition government, if they were called upon to do so by Governor General Michaëlle Jean. Although not formally part of the proposed coalition government, the Bloc Québécois agreed to support this coalition on matters of confidence for a period of 18 months.

Public reaction to the proposed coalition was mixed, but tended to be opposed to the proposal in spite of public anger about the CPC's overly-partisan fiscal update. In the face of imminent defeat in the House of Commons, on 4 December Harper took the extraordinary step of asking the governor general to prorogue Parliament mere weeks after a new session had begun. She agreed to his request to open a new session of Parliament on 26 January, 2009. Harper pledged to work with the opposition to create an early budget with a large economic stimulus package, upon which his government's fate would rest. Political pundits, who had previously praised the prime minister as being a master strategist with an iron grip upon his party, suggested that the episode had seriously damaged him politically. Commentators also noted that Harper's initial strategy—to attack the credibility of the proposed coalition because it required the support of the separatist Bloc Québécois to govern—would undermine his party's chances of winning over soft-nationalist voters in Québec, who tended to view the Bloc as primarily a tool to protect the province's interests.

Dion, who would have led the proposed coalition (as he was still temporarily leader of the Liberals), also emerged mortally wounded in political terms from the episode. Following several poor performances in defending the legitimacy of the coalition, and an amateurish episode in which his party had delivered a poorly-produced taped message late to national television networks, he resigned as Liberal leader earlier than he had planned. Liberal MP Michael Ignatieff, a frontrunner in the campaign to replace Dion, was named interim leader of the party when two other leadership contenders stepped aside. Ignatieff pledged to revive the coalition if he and the other opposition leaders were not satisfied with the 2009 budget.

All federal, provincial, and territorial governments tabled balanced budgets during the first half of 2008; however, the autumn's swift economic downturn prompted numerous governments to issue updates that warned of potential deficits. Canada's federal government had posted surpluses since 1998. Although during the federal election campaign both Harper and Dion pledged not to post budgetary deficits, the worsening global economic climate prompted a significant reversal in the appetite of politicians and the public for deficit spending. Canada's 2008-09 budget, tabled on 26 February, was the smallest in 11 years in terms of spending increases.

On 23 October the Bank of Canada (the central bank) announced that Canada was likely to enter a recession, which could be deep and protracted. The statements followed a 20 per cent stock market loss over the previous two months, a plunging Canadian dollar, and the lowest levels of consumer confidence in 26 years.

Will Stos

MEXICO AND CENTRAL AMERICA

MEXICO—GUATEMALA—EL SALVADOR—HONDURAS—NICARAGUA— COSTA RICA—PANAMA

MEXICO

CAPITAL: Mexico City   AREA: 1,964,380 sq km   POPULATION: 105,281,000 ('07)
OFFICIAL LANGUAGE: Spanish   POLITICAL SYSTEM: multiparty republic
HEAD OF STATE AND GOVERNMENT: President Felipe Calderón (PAN) (since Dec '06)
RULING PARTY: National Action Party (PAN)
MAIN IGO MEMBERSHIPS (NON-UN): OAS, SELA, ALADI, ACS, APEC, NAFTA, OECD
CURRENCY: Mexican peso (end-'08 £1=MP19.9107, US$1=MP13.8485)
GNI PER CAPITA: US$8,340, $12,580 at PPP ('07)

VIOLENT gang-related crime was the dominant issue for Mexico. The national daily newspaper, *El Universal*, reported that 5,630 people were killed by gangs in 2008. The number was twice as high as in 2007. The state with the highest number of gang killings was Chihuahua, followed by Sinaloa and Baja California. These were the areas where the Sinaloa cartel, led by Mexico's most-wanted man, Joaquin "Shorty" Guzman, fought with his rival Vicente Carrillo. Only one of Mexico's 32 states, Tlaxcala, did not see a single gang killing in 2008. The government argued that the upsurge in killings was due largely to increased feuding between the main drug gangs, and there was some evidence to support this view. The rivalry between the gangs was very hard fought because of the potentially vast financial gains. Mexican gangs dominated the wholesale distribution of cocaine in the USA, controlled methamphetamine distribution, and supervised the drug transit routes through Mexico from South America. In its annual national drug threat assessment, the US justice department's National Drugs Intelligence Centre asserted that "Mexican drug trafficking organisations represent the greatest organised crime threat to the United States." The report estimated that Mexican and Colombian drug traffickers made and laundered between US$18 billion and US$39 billion in wholesale drug profits annually.

Those affected by the violence, however, went far beyond the gangs, and included the police and the public. For example, in September a grenade attack in the main square of Morelia, the capital of the state of Michoacán, killed eight people and badly injured a further 50; while in December eight soldiers and one policeman were killed, and then decapitated, in the southern state of Guerrero. The government seemed unable to stem, let alone defeat, the drug gangs. There were a number of reasons for this: the corruption of police officers by the gangs, especially at the municipal and state level; the poor performance of "clean" police officers; the growing exhaustion of the army, deployed to help the police; and the growing sophistication of the gangs themselves. There was also evidence to indicate that the political structures of Mexico were being infiltrated. In July, the procurator general said that at least 80 local authorities were controlled by gangs, and the head of the intelligence service suggested that Congress (the bicameral legislature) was not exempt from the effects of the drug gangs. "We cannot discount the possibility that drug money has been used in [some congressmen's] election campaigns," he said, "Drug traffickers have become the principal threat because they are trying to take power from the state." To protest against the growing levels of crime and the government's failure to address the issue a series of marches was held on 30 August. The largest of the demonstrations was in Mexico City, but similar marches took place in 70 cities across the country.

In early October, President Felipe Calderón announced plans for a US$4.3 billion emergency spending programme to help Mexico deal with the impact of the global financial crisis. The proposals included increasing public spending on infrastructure, especially roads, schools, housing, and prisons; the construction of a new oil refinery; and a programme of assistance for small and medium-sized businesses. Calderón warned that Mexico faced a fall in exports, investment, and remittances as a result of the US economic slowdown. Later in the month, Congress passed a series of energy reforms, including controversial plans to allow private investment in the struggling state oil company, Pemex. The measures gave Pemex more autonomy and allowed it to keep more of its profits for investment in technology and exploration. The reforms also made it possible for private contractors to gain bonuses for early completion of projects and for transferring technology to Pemex. However, some of the initial reforms were watered down, including proposals that would have allowed private companies to invest in oil refining and to own storage and transport facilities. Mexico's constitution stated that the oil industry must remain under state control; thus, even the suggestion of allowing more private involvement was controversial.

Peter Clegg

CENTRAL AMERICA

Guatemala

CAPITAL: Guatemala City   AREA: 108,890 sq km   POPULATION: 13,348,000 ('07)
OFFICIAL LANGUAGE: Spanish   POLTICAL SYSTEM: multiparty republic
HEAD OF STATE AND GOVERNMENT: President Álvaro Colom Caballeros (UNE) (since Jan '08)
RULING PARTY: National Union for Hope (UNE)
MAIN IGO MEMBERSHIPS (NON-UN): OAS, SELA, CACM, ACM, ACS, NAM, DR-CAFTA
CURRENCY: quetzal (end-'08 £1=Q11.1376, US$1=Q7.7465)
GNI PER CAPITA: US$2,440, $4,520 at PPP ('07 est based on regression)

El Salvador

CAPITAL: San Salvador   AREA: 21,040 sq km   POPULATION: 6,853,000 ('07)
OFFICIAL LANGUAGE: Spanish   POLTICAL SYSTEM: multiparty republic
HEAD OF STATE AND GOVERNMENT: President Antonio Elías (Tony) Saca (ARENA) (since June '04)
RULING PARTIES: Nationalist Republican Alliance (ARENA) in coalition with the National
   Conciliation Party (PCN)
MAIN IGO MEMBERSHIPS (NON-UN): OAS, SELA, CACM, ACS, DR-CAFTA
CURRENCY: Salvadorian colón (end-'08 £1=C12.5832, US$1=C8.7520)
GNI PER CAPITA: US$2,850, $5,640 at PPP ('07 est based on regression)

Honduras

CAPITAL: Tegucigalpa   AREA: 112,090 sq km   POPULATION: 7,091,000 ('07)
OFFICIAL LANGUAGE: Spanish   POLTICAL SYSTEM: multiparty republic
HEAD OF STATE AND GOVERNMENT: President Jose Manuel "Mel" Zelaya (since Jan '06)
RULING PARTY: Liberal Party of Honduras (PLH)
MAIN IGO MEMBERSHIPS (NON-UN): OAS, SELA, CACM, ACS, NAM, DR-CAFTA
CURRENCY: lempira (end-'08 £1=L27.1663, US$1=L18.8950)
GNI PER CAPITA: US$1,600, $3,620 at PPP ('07 est based on regression)

Nicaragua

CAPITAL: Managua   AREA: 130,000 sq km   POPULATION: 5,605,000 ('07)
OFFICIAL LANGUAGE: Spanish   POLTICAL SYSTEM: multiparty republic
HEAD OF STATE AND GOVERNMENT: President Daniel Ortega Saavedra (FSLN) (since Jan '07)
RULING PARTY: Sandinista National Liberation Front (FSLN)
MAIN IGO MEMBERSHIPS (NON-UN): OAS, SELA, CACM, ACS, NAM, DR-CAFTA
CURRENCY: gold córdoba (end-'08 £1=C28.5367, US$1=C19.8481)
GNI PER CAPITA: US$980, $2,520 at PPP ('07 est based on regression)

Costa Rica

CAPITAL: San José   AREA: 51,100 sq km   POPULATION: 4,462,000 ('07)
OFFICIAL LANGUAGE: Spanish   POLTICAL SYSTEM: multiparty republic
HEAD OF STATE AND GOVERNMENT: President Oscar Arias Sánchez (since May '06)
RULING PARTY: National Liberation Party (PLN)
MAIN IGO MEMBERSHIPS (NON-UN): OAS, SELA, CACM, ACS
CURRENCY: colón (end-'08 £1=C798.622, US$1=C555.465)
GNI PER CAPITA: US$5,560, $10,700 at PPP ('07 est based on regression)

Panama

CAPITAL: Panama City   AREA: 75,520 sq km   POPULATION: 3,341,000 ('07)
OFFICIAL LANGUAGE: Spanish   POLTICAL SYSTEM: multiparty republic
HEAD OF STATE AND GOVERNMENT: President Martín Torrijos Espino (PRD) (since Sept '04)
RULING PARTIES: New Nation alliance (PN) composed of Democratic Revolutionary Party (PRD)
   and Popular Party (PP)
MAIN IGO MEMBERSHIPS (NON-UN): OAS, SELA, NAM
CURRENCY: balboa (end-'08 £1=B1.4378, US$1=B1.0000)
GNI PER CAPITA: US$5,510, $10,610 at PPP ('07 est based on regression)

GUATEMALA was affected by serious political and social divisions during the year. Álvaro Colom Caballeros was sworn in as president on 14 January, the country's first "social democratic" leader in over half a century. However, from the outset Colom was faced with government, party, and parliamentary instability. Even before taking office, Colom delayed the announcement of his cabinet because of internal divisions within his party. In March, the economy minister resigned, in July the health and agriculture ministers were sacked, while the attorney general also left his post. On 6 December, a legislator from Colom's National Unity of Hope (UNE) party, Manuel Baldizón, left Guatemala for the USA, saying that he had received death threats after declaring his intention, a week earlier, to stand as a candidate for the post of UNE secretary general. Then, four days later, 10 UNE legislators resigned from the party, upset over an announced change in the party's congressional leadership. The move undermined Colom's attempts to push his legislative agenda through Congress (the unicameral legislature), a task which was already proving difficult as the UNE did not have a majority. The work of Congress was further hampered by a split in the main opposition Grand National Alliance (GANA) party in February and corruption allegations against several legislators from both the government and opposition benches in June.

The scourge of drug trafficking and drug related crime was the key policy concern. Much of it was attributed to the growing role of Mexican drug cartels in the country. President Colom implemented a number of reforms, including the establishment of a national security council to co-ordinate the institutions dealing with security in Guatemala and the reform of the police force, and revealed plans to increase the size of the army. Despite such measures, violent crime continued to increase. In response, the director of the UN-supported International Commission against Impunity in Guatemala (CICIG) warned that if the authorities were unable to halt the worsening security situation, Mexican drug cartels could soon be running the country. Indeed, by December the authorities admitted that they were unable to cope with the level of organised crime.

One consequence was the dismissal of the head of the army, the defence minister, and other senior army and defence personnel. Another was an agreement worth US$3.9 million with the G-13 countries (composed of European countries plus Canada), aimed at addressing the violence in the country. The "pact", which was due to take effect in 2009 and last two years, helped to restructure and modernise the prison system, improve the transparency of the Supreme Court, combat corruption, and establish a new witness protection service. Colom also proposed the creation of a "multinational" force to combat drug trafficking, to be based in Guatemala and comprise representatives from South American countries.

EL SALVADOR. The year 2008 was dominated by campaigning for the presidential election, scheduled for March 2009. The governing right-wing Nationalist Republican Alliance (ARENA) was forced to develop a more social democratic image in response to the resurgence of support for the left-wing Martí National Liberation Front (FMLN), led by the moderate Mauricio Funes. This was seen in the national budget for 2009, which gave education, health, and social security additional funds, in contrast to the beginning of ARENA's current term in office (in 2004) when the emphasis had been on combating organised crime. In addition, ARENA's presidential candidate, Rodrigo Avila, and his running mate, Arturo Zablah, wooed the electorate by criticising mistakes made by previous ARENA administrations and promising to create 250,000 jobs and alleviate poverty. However, one issue that ARENA had often used against the FMLN—the status of the amnesty law shielding those accused of human rights abuses during the civil war (1980-92)—was used again. ARENA claimed that if the FMLN won power it would repeal the law. This assertion was made despite the fact that FMLN leader Funes ruled out revising the amnesty law on the grounds that to do so would "open wounds". Nevertheless, ARENA saw the charge as a useful line of attack in the election campaign, particularly as two human rights groups filed a suit in a Spanish court in November against El Salvador's former president, Alfredo Cristiani, and 14 military officers, relating to the murder of six Jesuit priests, their housekeeper, and her daughter in 1989 (see AR 1989, p. 80).

El Salvador's armed forces were recognised in a much more positive way on 12 June, when the country's Legislative Assembly agreed that they would participate in their first UN peacekeeping mission, in Lebanon. A visiting team from the UN had approved the army's involvement in peacekeeping missions in December 2007, stating that El Salvador's experience since the end of its civil war in 1992 would help it to bring peace to other conflict areas.

HONDURAS. Congress (the unicameral legislature) agreed to postpone the primary elections for the ruling Liberal Party (PL) and the opposition National Party (PN) by two weeks until 30 November, after heavy rains and flooding hit the country. At least 46 people were killed, close to 70,000 people were evacuated from their homes, and US$150 million of damage was caused. In the build up to the elections, four politicians were murdered, including Mario Fernando Hernández, a vice president of Congress and PL member. Despite government denials, the local media suggested that the crime was possibly drug related, as Hernández had been a member of the Congressional committee on security and drug trafficking. In the PL election, Mauricio Villeda secured the party's nomination for the presidential election scheduled for November 2009, after an acrimonious campaign. However, he made it clear that he was acting as a political surrogate for Vice President Elvin Santos, who had been prevented from standing by the supreme electoral tribunal (TSE). The TSE ruled that Santos could not stand because he had served as president during President Manuel Zelaya's absences from the country. However, Santos claimed that the TSE had been "influenced" to rule against him after he had fallen out with Zelaya. Santos then sought to overturn the TSE's ruling and replace Villeda on the PL ticket, but many in the party declared that they would not support his candidacy. The PN's primary election was more straightforward, with Porfirio Lobo winning a convincing victory.

In the policy arena, Zelaya signed up to the Bolivarian Alternative for Latin America (ALBA)—a proposed alternative to the moribund US-sponsored Free Trade Area of the Americas (FTAA)—on 25 August, and the decision was ratified subsequently by Congress. However, the PN abstained from the vote, while the umbrella business organisation, Cohep, described ALBA as a "political, military and ideological alliance, contrary to our history, values and ethical beliefs". Earlier in the year Congress had agreed to join Petrocaribe, the Venezuelan initiative to sell oil with soft financing.

NICARAGUA. The country ended the year once again in political crisis after disputed municipal elections were held in early November. The supreme electoral court published the official results on 20 November, almost two weeks after the voting. The ruling National Liberation Front (FSLN) was declared as the clear winner, taking 105 of the 146 municipalities in which voting took place and 13 of the 16 provincial capitals, including the capital, Managua. The opposition Constitutional Liberal Party (PLC) won 37 municipalities, 20 fewer than in the previous elections in 2004. The remaining four municipalities went to the Nicaraguan Liberal Alliance. However, there were allegations of widespread fraud. The extent of the fraud was hard to discern because, for the first time since 1990, foreign and local independent observers were refused accreditation to monitor the elections. Nevertheless, the opposition refused to accept the results.

Due to the fragmented nature of the distribution of seats within the National Assembly (unicameral legislature), the government was unable to authorise the results and the opposition was unable to cancel them. In response, on 24 November, the speaker of the National Assembly and FSLN member, René Núñez, announced that the Assembly would be suspended until "better conditions" prevailed. A new Assembly session was then scheduled for mid-December but did not take place, as the PLC and several other opposition parties refused to attend, meaning that the session was not quorate. The paralysis of the National Assembly meant that no decision on the election results was possible, several important economic initiatives were held up, and international aid was jeopardised. On the latter issue, the USA announced that US$64 million-worth of aid to fight poverty would be suspended in light of "democracy concerns", whilst the EU froze nearly US$37 million in budgetary assistance. A further US$40 million from the World Bank and Inter-American Development Bank (IDB) was also at risk.

COSTA RICA. In November, the unicameral Legislative Assembly finally approved the last law—on intellectual property—required for the implementation of the Central American-Dominican Republic-US (CAFTA-DR) free trade treaty. It had been hoped that the agreement would come into force at the end of February, but strong resistance from the opposition Citizens' Action Party (PAC) caused a delay. However, with approval of the final law, Costa Rica was scheduled to enter CAFTA-DR on 1 January, 2009.

Another foreign policy success for the government was the first visit of China's President Hu Jintao to Costa Rica and, indeed to Central America more generally. Several agreements were signed between the two countries, including a pledge that China's National Petroleum Corporation would invest in enlarging and modernising the facilities at Costa Rica's state oil refinery. The visit by Hu was also important for China, as Costa Rica was the only country in Central America with which it had diplomatic relations. The other countries in the region recognised Taiwan.

Finally, Costa Rica was awarded the title of most environmentally friendly country in Latin America, by researchers from the Universities of Yale and Columbia in the USA.

PANAMA. The government, led by President Martín Torrijos and his Revolutionary Democratic Party (PRD), became increasingly unpopular due to a number of controversies. In February nationwide protests took place after a construction worker was shot dead by a policeman during a demonstration over lax safety standards. Then, in June, the National Assembly (unicameral legislature) controversially voted to allow Torrijos to assume the authority to rule by decree for two months in order to restructure Panama's law enforcement and security services. Five decrees were issued in August, the most controversial being that which established the National Intelligence and Security Service (Senis), which was given wide-ranging powers but was answerable only to the president. The executive secretary of the government's national council of transparency against corruption (CNTCC), Alma Montenegro, warned that the creation of the new service would place "excessive power" in the hands of one agency and risked jeopardising Panama's democratic and political system. The media and the Roman Catholic Church, which were generally sympathetic to the government, also highlighted the agency's potential threat to civil liberties. Other critics feared that this measure and others were symptomatic of attempts by the government to re-militarise the country.

At the end of the year a Russian warship passed through the Panama Canal, the first to do so since the end of World War II. The *Admiral Chabanenko* arrived on 5 December at Panama's Pacific port of Balboa, which was once the hub of US naval activities in the region.

Finally, Irving Saladino won a gold medal in the Olympic long jump competition, with a jump of 8.34 metres, becoming Panama's first ever Olympic champion. This was also the first ever Olympic gold medal won in a men's event by a Central American athlete.

Peter Clegg

THE CARIBBEAN

CUBA—JAMAICA—DOMINICAN REPUBLIC AND HAITI—WINDWARD & LEEWARD ISLANDS—BARBADOS—TRINIDAD & TOBAGO—THE BAHAMAS—GUYANA, BELIZE AND SURINAME—UK DEPENDENCIES—NETHERLANDS ANTILLES AND ARUBA— US DEPENDENCIES

CUBA, JAMAICA, DOMINICAN REPUBLIC AND HAITI

Cuba

CAPITAL: Havana AREA: 110,860 sq km POPULATION: 11,257,000 ('07)
OFFICIAL LANGUAGE: Spanish POLTICAL SYSTEM: one-party republic
HEAD OF STATE AND GOVERNMENT: President Raúl Castro Ruz (since Feb '08)
RULING PARTY: Cuban Communist Party (PCC)
MAIN IGO MEMBERSHIPS (NON-UN): OAS (suspended), ALADI, ACS, SELA, NAM
CURRENCY: Cuban peso (end-'08 £1=Cub1.4378, US$1=Cub1.0000); conv peso (end-'08 £1=1.3228, US$1=0.8200)
GNI PER CAPITA: Upper middle income: US$3,706 to US$11,455 ('07 est), -

Jamaica

CAPITAL: Kingston AREA: 10,990 sq km POPULATION: 2,677,000 ('07)
OFFICIAL LANGUAGE: English POLTICAL SYSTEM: multiparty system
HEAD OF STATE: Queen Elizabeth II
GOVERNOR-GENERAL: Kenneth Octavius Hall (since Feb '06)
RULING PARTY: Jamaica Labour Party (JLP)
HEAD OF GOVERNMENT: Prime Minister Bruce Golding (JLP) (since Sept '07)
MAIN IGO MEMBERSHIPS (NON-UN): OAS, SELA, ACS, Caricom, ACP, CWTH, NAM
CURRENCY: Jamaican dollar (end-'08 £1=J$114.301, US$1=J$79.5000)
GNI PER CAPITA: US$3,710, $6,210 at PPP ('07)

Dominican Republic

CAPITAL: Santo Domingo AREA: 48,730 sq km POPULATION: 9,752,000 ('07)
OFFICIAL LANGUAGE: Spanish POLTICAL SYSTEM: multiparty republic
HEAD OF STATE AND GOVERNMENT: President Leonel Fernández Reyna (PLD) (since Aug '04)
RULING PARTIES: Dominican Liberation Party (PLD)-led alliance
MAIN IGO MEMBERSHIPS (NON-UN): OAS, SELA, ACS, ACP, NAM, DR-CAFTA
CURRENCY: Dominican Republic peso (end-'08 £1=DP50.8606, US$1=35.3750)
GNI PER CAPITA: US$3,550, $6,340 at PPP ('07 est based on regression)

Haiti

CAPITAL: Port-au-Prince AREA: 27,750 sq km POPULATION: 9,612,000 ('07)
OFFICIAL LANGUAGE: French POLTICAL SYSTEM: multiparty republic
HEAD OF STATE: President René Préval (Lespwa) (since May '06)
RULING PARTIES: Lespwa (Hope)-led coalition
HEAD OF GOVERNMENT: Michèle Duvivier Pierre-Louis (since July '08)
MAIN IGO MEMBERSHIPS (NON-UN): OAS, SELA, Caricom, ACS, ACP, Francophonie, NAM
CURRENCY: gourde (end-'08 £1=G56.4317, US$1=G39.2500)
GNI PER CAPITA: US$560, $1,150 at PPP ('07 est based on regression)

ALL four countries suffered hurricane damage, with Cuba and Haiti being particularly badly affected. Successive hurricanes in late August and early September cost the Cuban economy US$10 billion. More than 450,000 homes were damaged, and at least 200,000 Cubans were left homeless. In addition, most of the country's sugar crop was destroyed, and the tobacco, coffee, and rice crops were seriously damaged. Nickel production was also disrupted. In response the government took several emergency measures to ensure that the basic food needs of Cubans were met, imposing upper price limits on 16 basic products, including root vegetables and rice. In Haiti, meanwhile, the damage caused by Hurricanes Gustav, Hanna, and Ike and tropical storm Fay set the country back "several years", so said President René Préval. At least 800 people were killed, and more than 800,000 people were left requiring food, water, or shelter. Sixty per cent of the country's agriculture harvest was also lost. A World Bank report in December described the overall impact of the storms as "the largest disaster for Haiti in more than 100 years". In Jamaica, Hurricane Gustav caused nine deaths and damaged a majority of the country's banana and plantain farms; in the Dominican Republic tropical storm damage killed over a dozen people, and cost the economy US$28 million.

CUBA. Raúl Castro Ruz succeeded his brother, Fidel Castro Ruz, as president of Cuba on 24 February. Five days earlier Fidel had informed the National Assembly (unicameral legislature) that he would not accept another term as president. His resignation marked an end to 49 years in power, although Raúl had acted as president since July 2007 (see AR 2007, pp. 149-50).

The theme of Raúl's presidency during the year was stability but with gradual and considered change, particularly in regard to improving the functioning of the economy and making government institutions more efficient. Examples of reform included redistributing idle state land to farmers, ending the ban on buying computers and video equipment, and easing restrictions on the ownership and use of mobile telephones. Yet the economic situation became increasingly difficult, with the impact of the global financial crisis, the hurricanes, and the US trade embargo all having a deleterious effect. Economic growth was 4.3 per cent and not the 8 per cent which had been forecast at the start of the year. In December, spending cuts were announced, the retirement age was raised, and some relaxation of the country's egalitarian wage system was considered.

In foreign policy matters EU foreign ministers agreed in June to lift diplomatic sanctions against Cuba that had been in place since 2003. Meanwhile Cuba strengthened its ties with Russia, in the form of a visit by Russia's President Dmitry Medvedev in November and the arrival of three Russian warships in December, the first such deployment since the end of the Cold War.

JAMAICA. The two main political parties faced problems during the year. The governing Jamaica Labour Party (JLP) was shaken by a court challenge against four of its members of Parliament accused of holding dual nationality. The case had been brought by a member of the opposition People's National Party (PNP), who had been an unsuccessful candidate in the 2007 general election. He claimed that it was unconstitutional to hold a seat in Parliament when "owing allegiance" to a foreign power. The Supreme Court ruled that, indeed, those MPs with dual citizenship should give up their seats; the Court of Appeal was asked to consider the case, but a decision was not expected until early 2009. The PNP, meanwhile, was distracted by a leadership contest between its leader, the former prime minister Portia Simpson Miller, and Peter Phillips, vice president of the party and a longstanding rival. After a hard fought campaign, Simpson Miller won the vote, but was undermined by the resignation of a number of shadow cabinet members, including Phillips himself.

Violent crime continued to be an issue of serious concern. In May alone a record 197 people were murdered, which prompted the declaration by Prime Minister Bruce Golding that the country was facing "terrorism of a different kind".

DOMINICAN REPUBLIC. Incumbent Leonel Fernández Reyna won the presidential election on 16 May by a clear margin. Although in the months prior to the election his government had faced allegations of corruption as well as labour unrest, Fernández's strong standing amongst the electorate and his administration's good economic record helped him to victory. In addition, the close links of the main opposition candidate to the discredited regime of President Hipólito Mejía Domínguez (2000-04) undermined his electoral chances.

At the start of his new term, Fernández was faced by a wide range of problems, not least the continuing power cuts across the country. In mid-August, violent protests erupted over the interruptions to power supply, which left two people dead and dozens more injured. There were further demonstrations in early November, which saw another two people killed, including one policeman. The government admitted that the problems were due largely to its failure to maintain regular payments to power generators and distributors. However, the government also passed legislation to criminalise the theft of electricity. It was estimated that 47 per cent of the power for domestic consumption, and 33.5 per cent of that for commercial consumption, was being stolen.

HAITI. Sharp increases in the cost of fuel and food in the first half of the year undermined the government and the relative political stability that had existed since the election of René Préval as president in 2006. In April there were several days of violent protests, which left six people dead. In response the Senate (the upper chamber of the bicameral legislature) approved a motion of no confidence in Prime Minister Jacques-Edouard Alexis on the basis that he had failed to meet the basic needs and demands of the population. President Préval nominated Ericq Pierre, an Inter-American Development Bank (IDB) official, for the post of prime minister, but this was rejected by the Chamber of Deputies (the lower house); so, too, was the nomination of Robert Manuel, a close friend of the president. Préval's third choice proved to more acceptable, and thus economist Michèle Pierre-Louis became prime minister in August.

In other news, the UN Security Council extended the mandate of the UN peacekeeping mission in Haiti for a further year until 15 October, 2009. The Brazilian-led UN Stabilisation Mission (MINUSTAH) was made up of 7,000 troops and 2,000 police. In early November over 100 children and teachers died after a school collapsed in the Port-au-Prince suburb of Petionville.

Peter Clegg

WINDWARD AND LEEWARD ISLANDS

Antigua & Barbuda

CAPITAL: St John's   AREA: 440 sq km   POPULATION: 85,000 ('07)
OFFICIAL LANGUAGE: English   POLTICAL SYSTEM: multiparty system
HEAD OF STATE: Queen Elizabeth II (since Feb '52)
GOVERNOR-GENERAL: Louise Lake-Tack (since July '07)
RULING PARTY: United Progressive Party (UPP)
HEAD OF GOVERNMENT: Prime Minister Baldwin Spencer (since March '04)
MAIN IGO MEMBERSHIPS (NON-UN): OAS, OECS, Caricom, ACS, ACP, CWTH, NAM
CURRENCY: East Caribbean dollar (end-'08 £1=EC$3.8820, US$1=EC$2.7000)
GNI PER CAPITA: US$11,520, $17,620 at PPP ('07 est based on regression)

Dominica

CAPITAL: Roseau   AREA: 750 sq km   POPULATION: 73,000 ('07)
OFFICIAL LANGUAGE: English   POLTICAL SYSTEM: multiparty republic
HEAD OF STATE: President Nicholas Liverpool (since Oct '03)
RULING PARTY: Dominica Labour Party (DLP)
HEAD OF GOVERNMENT: Prime Minister Roosevelt Skerrit (since Jan '04)
MAIN IGO MEMBERSHIPS (NON-UN): OAS, ACS, OECS, Caricom, ACP, CWTH, NAM, Francophonie
CURRENCY: East Caribbean dollar (see above)
GNI PER CAPITA: US$4,250, $7,410 at PPP ('07 est based on regression)

St Christopher (Kitts) & Nevis

CAPITAL: Basseterre   AREA: 260 sq km   POPULATION: 49,000 ('07)
OFFICIAL LANGUAGE: English   POLITICAL SYSTEM: multiparty system
HEAD OF STATE: Queen Elizabeth II (since Feb '52)
GOVERNOR-GENERAL: Sir Cuthbert Sebastian (since Jan '96)
RULING PARTY: St Kitts-Nevis Labour Party (SKNLP)
HEAD OF GOVERNMENT: Prime Minister Denzil Douglas (since July '95)
MAIN IGO MEMBERSHIPS (NON-UN): OAS, ACS, Caricom, OECS, ACP, CWTH, NAM
CURRENCY: East Caribbean dollar (see above)
GNI PER CAPITA: US$9,630, $13,320 at PPP ('07 est based on regression)

St Lucia

CAPITAL: Castries   AREA: 620 sq km   POPULATION: 168,000 ('07)
OFFICIAL LANGUAGE: English   POLITICAL SYSTEM: multiparty system
HEAD OF STATE: Queen Elizabeth II (since Feb '52)
GOVERNOR-GENERAL: Perlette Louisy (since Sept '97)
RULING PARTY: United Workers' Party (UWP)
HEAD OF GOVERNMENT: Prime Minister Stephenson King (UWP) (since Sept '07; acting since May '07)
MAIN IGO MEMBERSHIPS (NON-UN): OAS, ACS, OECS, Caricom, ACP, CWTH, NAM, Francophonie
CURRENCY: East Caribbean dollar (see above)
GNI PER CAPITA: US$5,530, $9,430 at PPP ('07 est based on regression)

St Vincent & the Grenadines

CAPITAL: Kingstown   AREA: 390 sq km   POPULATION: 120,000 ('07)
OFFICIAL LANGUAGE: English   POLITICAL SYSTEM: multiparty system
HEAD OF STATE: Queen Elizabeth II (since Feb '52)
GOVERNOR-GENERAL: Freddy Ballantyne (since Sept '02)
RULING PARTY: Unity Labour Party (ULP)
HEAD OF GOVERNMENT: Prime Minister Ralph Gonsalves (since April '01)
MAIN IGO MEMBERSHIPS (NON-UN): OAS, ACS, OECS, Caricom, ACP, CWTH, NAM
CURRENCY: East Caribbean dollar (see above)
GNI PER CAPITA: US$4,210, $7,170 at PPP ('07 est based on regression)

Grenada

CAPITAL: St George's   AREA: 340 sq km   POPULATION: 108,000 ('07)
OFFICIAL LANGUAGE: English   POLTICAL SYSTEM: multiparty system
HEAD OF STATE: Queen Elizabeth II (since Feb '52)
GOVERNOR-GENERAL: Carlyle Glean (since Nov '08)
RULING PARTY: National Democratic Congress (NDC)
HEAD OF GOVERNMENT: Prime Minister Tillman Thomas (NDC) (since July '08)
MAIN IGO MEMBERSHIPS (NON-UN): OAS, SELA, ACS, Caricom, OECS, ACP, CWTH, NAM
CURRENCY: East Caribbean dollar (see above)
GNI PER CAPITA: US$4,670, $6,910 at PPP ('07 est based on regression)

THERE was only one general election held in the Islands in 2008. It occurred in Grenada, 8 July, and saw the opposition National Democratic Congress (NDC) achieve victory over the three-term government of the New National Party (NNP). The NDC, led by Tillman Thomas, won 51 per cent of the vote and 11 of the 15 seats in the House of Representatives (the lower chamber of the bicameral Parliament). The NNP took 48 per cent and the remaining four seats. Turnout was high, at over 80 per cent.

In St Lucia, meanwhile, the governing United Workers' Party (UWP) was weakened by deep internal divisions. These were caused after the ailing former prime minister, Sir John Compton (who died on 7 September, 2007, see AR 2008, pp. 152; 611), had dismissed the foreign affairs minister, Rufus Bousquet, in June 2007 after he had established diplomatic relations with Taiwan without the leader's knowledge. Once Stephenson King replaced Compton, several UWP members agitated for Bousquet's return. Furthermore, Bousquet and others demanded the removal of Finance Minister Ausbert d'Auvergne. D'Auvergne— a senator—was accused by Bousquet of being "an unelected MP who fields far too much influence on the governance of this country". It was also alleged that d'Auvergne had business links with two men convicted in the USA.

In April and May matters came to a head. In April there were reports that several members of the government were ready to support the opposition to vote down the 2008-09 budget if Bousquet was not brought back into the cabinet. Then, in May, d'Auvergne resigned his portfolio after some MPs, including Bousquet, threatened to withdraw their support from the government if d'Auvergne was not removed. Soon after the resignation, a cabinet reshuffle was undertaken that saw the appointment of Bousquet as minister for trade, industry, commerce, consumer affairs and investment. Some in the UWP were unhappy, seeing this as a sign of weakness on the part of Stephenson, and an act contrary to the legacy of Compton.

In other developments, the UK's department of culture, media and sport added Antigua & Barbuda to the list of gaming jurisdictions (the so-called "white list") in which licensed gambling operators were allowed to advertise in the UK.

Dominica ratified membership of the Bolivarian Alternative for Latin America (ALBA) (the proposed alternative to the moribund US-sponsored Free Trade Area of the Americas (FTAA)) in January, becoming the first Caribbean country to do so. Meanwhile, in June, Prime Minister Roosevelt Skerrit announced that Dominica would no longer vote with Japan in favour of commercial whaling.

St Vincent & the Grenadines established diplomatic ties with Iran in August and Iran in turn pledged to assist in the construction of St Vincent's planned US$200 million international airport.

In St Kitts & Nevis the first execution in the English-speaking Caribbean for eight years took place on 19 December. Charles Laplace was hanged for killing his wife. All independent English-speaking Caribbean counties retained the death penalty.

Peter Clegg

BARBADOS, TRINIDAD & TOBAGO, THE BAHAMAS

Barbados

CAPITAL: Bridgetown   AREA: 430 sq km   POPULATION: 294,000 ('07)
OFFICIAL LANGUAGE: English   POLTICAL SYSTEM: multiparty system
HEAD OF STATE: Queen Elizabeth II (since Feb '52)
GOVERNOR-GENERAL: Sir Clifford Husbands (since June '96)
RULING PARTY: Democratic Labour Party (DLP)
HEAD OF GOVERNMENT: Prime Minister David Thompson (since Jan '08)
MAIN IGO MEMBERSHIPS (NON-UN): OAS, SELA, ACS, Caricom, ACP, CWTH, NAM
CURRENCY: Barbados dollar (end-'08 £1=Bd$2.8755, US$1=Bd$2.0000)
GNI PER CAPITA: high income: US$11,456 or more ('07 est), $16,140 at PPP ('07 est based on regression)

Trinidad & Tobago

CAPITAL: Port of Spain   AREA: 5,130 sq km   POPULATION: 1,333,000 ('07)
OFFICIAL LANGUAGE: English   POLTICAL SYSTEM: multiparty republic
HEAD OF STATE: President Max Richards (since Feb '03)
RULING PARTY: People's National Movement (PNM) (since Oct '02)
HEAD OF GOVERNMENT: Prime Minister Patrick Manning (PNM) (since Dec '01)
MAIN IGO MEMBERSHIPS (NON-UN): OAS, SELA, ACS, Caricom, ACP, CWTH, NAM
CURRENCY: Trinidad & Tobago dollar (end-'08 £1=TT$9.0390, US$1=TT$6.2869)
GNI PER CAPITA: US$14,100, $22,490 at PPP ('07)

The Bahamas

CAPITAL: Nassau   AREA: 13,880 sq km   POPULATION: 331,000 ('07)
OFFICIAL LANGUAGE: English   POLTICAL SYSTEM: multiparty system
HEAD OF STATE: Queen Elizabeth II (since Feb '52)
GOVERNOR-GENERAL: Arthur Dion Hanna (since Feb '06)
RULING PARTY: Free National Movement (FNM)
HEAD OF GOVERNMENT: Prime Minister Hubert Ingraham (FNM) (since May '07)
MAIN IGO MEMBERSHIPS (NON-UN): OAS, SELA, ACS, Caricom, ACP, CWTH, NAM
CURRENCY: Bahamian dollar (end-'08 £1=B$1.4378, US$1=B$1.0000)
GNI PER CAPITA: high income: US$11,456 or more ('07 est), -

A GENERAL election was held in Barbados in early January with the opposition Democratic Labour Party (DLP), led by David Thompson, winning a clear victory. The DLP won 20 seats and 53 per cent of the vote, with the governing Barbados Labour Party (in office since 1994) securing the remaining 10 seats and 47 per cent. Thompson campaigned on the pledge of "change", and this struck a chord with voters. Several other issues influenced voting behaviour, including the rising cost of living, and concerns over healthcare and the transport network. Nine ministers lost their seats, although the former prime minister, Owen Arthur, was re-elected. Following the defeat he stepped down as party leader in favour of the former deputy prime minister, Mia Mottley.

Issues relating to crime and the criminal justice system were of concern to both Trindad & Tobago and The Bahamas. In June the government of Trinidad & Tobago cancelled the holiday leave of more than 500 police officers and placed them on duty in order to help combat a surge in violent crime. The country had seen an unprecedented number of murders—over 200 in the first five months of the year, almost double the number for the same period in 2007. Approximately 80 per cent of the murders were believed to be gang and drug related. The detection rate was low. In The Bahamas, doubts were raised about the credibility of the judicial system after the Judicial and Legal Services Commission in April appointed a Supreme Court judge, Rubie Nottage, who was wanted by the USA for alleged money laundering of drugs proceeds.

A further concern for both countries was the impact of the global economic crisis. In November, the Trinidad & Tobago government predicted a revenue shortfall of US$1 billion in the 2008-09 fiscal year, and announced plans to defer a number of capital projects. In The Bahamas, the economy slowed down rapidly as a consequence of its heavy dependence on the USA for investment, trade, and tourism. Prime Minister Hubert Ingraham said that the country's tourism sector was in a "terrible shape", as visitor arrivals dropped significantly, and property purchases by foreigners—an important contributor to construction sector growth—slumped. As a consequence, unemployment increased and government revenues fell.

Peter Clegg

GUYANA, BELIZE, AND SURINAME

Guyana

CAPITAL: Georgetown   AREA: 214,970 sq km   POPULATION: 739,000 ('07)
OFFICIAL LANGUAGE: English   POLTICAL SYSTEM: multiparty republic
HEAD OF STATE: President Bharrat Jagdeo (since Aug '99)
RULING PARTY: People's Progressive Party-Civic (PPP-C)
HEAD OF GOVERNMENT: Prime Minister Samuel Hinds (since Dec '97)
MAIN IGO MEMBERSHIPS (NON-UN): OAS, SELA, AP, ACS, Caricom, ACP, CWTH, NAM
CURRENCY: Guyanese dollar (end-'08 £1=G$292.197, US$1=G$203.225)
GNI PER CAPITA: US$1,300, $2,880 at PPP ('07 est based on regression)

Belize

CAPITAL: Belmopan   AREA: 22,970 sq km   POPULATION: 304,000 ('07)
OFFICIAL LANGUAGE: English   POLTICAL SYSTEM: multiparty system
HEAD OF STATE: Queen Elizabeth II (since Feb '52)
GOVERNOR-GENERAL: Sir Colville Young (since Nov '93)
RULING PARTY: United Democratic Party (UDP)
HEAD OF GOVERNMENT: Prime Minister Dean Barrow (since Feb '08)
MAIN IGO MEMBERSHIPS (NON-UN): OAS, SELA, ACS, Caricom, ACP, CWTH, NAM
CURRENCY: Belize dollar (end-'08 £1=Bz$2.8036, US$1=Bz$1.9500)
GNI PER CAPITA: US$3,800, $6,200 at PPP ('07 est based on regression)

Suriname

CAPITAL: Paramaribo   AREA: 163,270 sq km   POPULATION: 458,000 ('07)
OFFICIAL LANGUAGE: Dutch   POLITICAL SYSTEM: multiparty republic
HEAD OF STATE: President Ronald Venetiaan (since Aug '00)
RULING PARTIES: New Front for Democracy (NF) coalition supported by the A-Combination
   (A-Com) coalition
HEAD OF GOVERNMENT: Vice-President Ram Sardjoe (since Aug '05)
MAIN IGO MEMBERSHIPS (NON-UN): OAS, SELA, AP, ACS, Caricom, ACP, OIC, NAM
CURRENCY: Surinam dollar (end-'08 £1=S$3.9467, US$1=S$2.7450)
GNI PER CAPITA: US$4,730, $7,640 at PPP ('07 est based on regression)

VIOLENT crime was the foremost issue in Guyana. On 26 January gunmen shot and killed 11 Indo-Guyanese people in the coastal village of Lusignan. The government claimed that the attack had been carried out to increase tension between the Afro- and Indo-Guyanese communities. Then, in mid-February, 13 people were shot dead in the small mining town of Bartica. In response, on 6 June soldiers and police undertook a failed assault against the gang suspected of carrying out the massacres. On 21 June the bodies of eight miners were discovered in Lindo Creek, and the same gang was implicated in the deaths. In August security forces killed the alleged gang leader, Rondell Rawlins, a former member of the Guyana Defence Force, and two other suspected gang members. A further three gang members were shot dead by police in late November. Although the authorities gained some credit for their actions against this particular gang, the underlying problem of armed criminal gangs, which included some disaffected ex-soldiers, remained a serious concern.

Fortunately, the increasingly fractious relationship between the government and the opposition People's National Congress/Reform, which was in part caused by the worsening security situation, eased in the latter part of the year.

In Belize, the opposition United Democratic Party (UDP) won a landslide victory in the 7 February general election. UDP leader Dean Barrow became the country's first black prime minister. The UDP won 25 of the 31 seats in the House of Representatives and 57 per cent of the vote. The People's United Party, which had been in office for 10 years, lost 16 seats. In November, the defeated former prime minister, Said Musa, was charged with misappropriating US$10 million provided by the Venezuelan government.

In Suriname, the government confirmed its intention to establish a permanent jungle warfare school, in which foreign countries could train their troops. Suriname had hosted US and Dutch troops for special training for a number of years. In May, Suriname and Guyana signed an anti-crime co-operation agreement to help stem the movement of criminals and the flow of guns and drugs across their borders.

Peter Clegg

UK OVERSEAS TERRITORIES

Anguilla

CAPITAL: The Valley   AREA: 96 sq km   POPULATION: n/a
OFFICIAL LANGUAGE: English   POLTICAL SYSTEM: semi-autonomous UK overseas territory
GOVERNOR-GENERAL: Andrew George (since July '06)
RULING PARTIES: Anguilla National Alliance (ANA) & Anguilla Democratic Party (ADP) form
    United Front coalition
HEAD OF GOVERNMENT: Chief Minister Osbourne Fleming (ANA) (since March '00)
MAIN IGO MEMBERSHIPS (NON-UN): Caricom (associate), OECS (associate)
CURRENCY: East Caribbean dollar (end-'08 £1=EC$3.8820, US$1=EC$2.7000)
GNI PER CAPITA: n/a

Bermuda

CAPITAL: Hamilton   AREA: 50 sq km   POPULATION: 64,000 ('07)
OFFICIAL LANGUAGE: English   POLTICAL SYSTEM: semi-autonomous UK overseas territory
GOVERNOR-GENERAL: Sir Richard Gozney (since Dec '07)
RULING PARTY: Progressive Labour Party (PLP)
HEAD OF GOVERNMENT: Prime Minister Ewart Brown (PLP), (since Oct '06)
MAIN IGO MEMBERSHIPS (NON-UN): Caricom (obs.)
CURRENCY: Bermudian dollar (end-'08 £1=Bm$1.4378, US$1=Bm$1.0000)
GNI PER CAPITA: high income: US$11,456 or more ('07 est), -

British Virgin Islands

CAPITAL: Road Town   AREA: 153 sq km   POPULATION: 27,000 ('05 est)
OFFICIAL LANGUAGE: English   POLTICAL SYSTEM: semi-autonomous UK overseas territory
GOVERNOR-GENERAL: David Pearey (since April '06)
RULING PARTY: Virgin Islands Party (VIP)
HEAD OF GOVERNMENT: Premier Ralph O'Neal (since July '07)
MAIN IGO MEMBERSHIPS (NON-UN): OECS (assoc.), Caricom (assoc.)
CURRENCY: US dollar (end '08 £1=1.4378)
GNI PER CAPITA: n/a

Cayman Islands

CAPITAL: George Town, Grand Cayman   AREA: 260 sq km   POPULATION: 47,000 ('07)
OFFICIAL LANGUAGE: English   POLTICAL SYSTEM: semi-autonomous UK overseas territory
GOVERNOR-GENERAL: Stuart Jack (since Nov '05)
RULING PARTY: People's Progressive Movement (PPM)
HEAD OF GOVERNMENT: Kurt Tibbetts (since May '05)
MAIN IGO MEMBERSHIPS (NON-UN): Caricom (obs.)
CURRENCY: Cayman Island dollar (end-'08 £1=CI$1.1790, US$1=CI$0.8200)
GNI PER CAPITA: High income: US$11,456 or more ('07 est), -

Montserrat

CAPITAL: Plymouth   AREA: 102 sq km   POPULATION: 4,655
OFFICIAL LANGUAGE: English   POLTICAL SYSTEM: semi-autonomous UK overseas territory
GOVERNOR-GENERAL: Deborah Barnes-Jones (since May '04)
RULING PARTIES: coalition between Montserrat Democratic Party (MDP), New People's Liberation
     Movement, and Independents
HEAD OF GOVERNMENT: Chief Minister Lowell Lyttleton Lewis (MDP) (since June '06)
MAIN IGO MEMBERSHIPS (NON-UN): OECS, Caricom, ACS
CURRENCY: East Caribbean dollar (see above)
GNI PER CAPITA: n/a

Turks & Caicos Islands

CAPITAL: Cockburn Town   AREA: 430 sq km   POPULATION: 32,000 ('06 census est)
OFFICIAL LANGUAGE: English   POLTICAL SYSTEM: semi-autonomous UK overseas territory
GOVERNOR-GENERAL: Gordon Wetherell (since Aug '08)
RULING PARTY: Progressive National Party (PNP)
HEAD OF GOVERNMENT: Chief Minister Michael Misick (PNP) (since Aug '03)
MAIN IGO MEMBERSHIPS (NON-UN): Caricom (assoc.), ACS (assoc.)
CURRENCY: US dollar (end-'08 £1=1.4378)
GNI PER CAPITA: n/a

THE UK House of Commons foreign affairs committee scrutinised the systems of governance in Anguilla, Bermuda, the British Virgin Islands, the Cayman Islands, Montserrat, and the Turks & Caicos Islands (and in the UK's other Overseas Territories). The committee's conclusions were published in July. Several issues were considered, including the constitutional relationship between the UK and the Overseas Territories, the rule of law, human rights, and standards of governance. On the latter issue, the committee made a number of particularly strong recommendations. For example, the committee asked the UK government to put pressure on the government of Anguilla to establish an independent inquiry "into allegations that Anguillan ministers accepted bribes from developers in the Territory".

The committee also highlighted concerns regarding corruption in the Turks & Caicos Islands (TCI), including allegations that Crown land was being sold for the personal benefit of TCI government members and their relatives and sup-porters; the improper distribution of contracts and development agreements; the illegal granting of Belongerships (a status which indicated freedom from any immigration restrictions and also conferred rights normally associated with cit-izenship, including the right to vote); and the misuse of public funds. The report also criticised the "climate of fear" in the territory, suggesting that some citizens were too afraid to discuss their concerns about what was happening. In order to investigate fully these allegations and possible past corruption, the foreign affairs committee called for a commission of inquiry, and this was duly established by the UK government. It was still undertaking its work at year's end.

It was predicted that Chief Minister Michael Misick would resign in early 2009 after losing the support of most of his cabinet in December. Misick's position had been undermined by the corruption allegations, an ongoing investigation by the US Federal Bureau of Investigation (FBI) into an alleged rape committed by Misick, and his bitter public divorce.

Peter Clegg

NETHERLANDS ANTILLES AND ARUBA

Netherlands Antilles

CAPITAL: Willemstad (Curaçao)   AREA: 800 sq km   POPULATION: 191,000 ('07)
OFFICIAL LANGUAGES: Dutch, Papiamento & English   POLTICAL SYSTEM: autonomous dependency of The Netherlands
GOVERNOR-GENERAL: Fritz Goedgedrag (since July '02)
RULING PARTY: Antillean Restructuring Party (PAR) heads coalition
HEAD OF GOVERNMENT: Prime Minister Emily de Jongh-Elhage (PAR) (since March '06)
MAIN IGO MEMBERSHIPS (NON-UN): n/a
CURRENCY: Neth. Antilles guilder (end-'08 £1=AG2.5736, US$1=AG1.7900)
GNI PER CAPITA: High income: US$11,456 or more ('07 est), -

Aruba

CAPITAL: Oranjestad   AREA: 180 sq km   POPULATION: 101,000 ('07)
OFFICIAL LANGUAGE: Dutch   POLTICAL SYSTEM: autonomous dependency of the Netherlands
GOVERNOR-GENERAL: Fredis Refunjol (since May '04)
RULING PARTY: People's Electoral Movement (MEP)
HEAD OF GOVERNMENT: Prime Minister Nelson O. Oduber (MEP) (since Sept '01)
MAIN IGO MEMBERSHIPS (NON-UN): n/a
CURRENCY: Aruba guilder (end-'08 £1=AG2.5736, US$1=AG1.7900)
GNI PER CAPITA: high income: US$11,456 or more ('07 est), -

IN December an outline agreement was signed between the island authorities of the Netherlands Antilles and the Netherlands, which paved the way for the dismantling of the island group. One part of the December deal was a Dutch pledge to assume 70 per cent of the Netherlands Antilles' combined debt—some €1.7 billion—in return for legal and financial controls. The islands of Curaçao and St Maarten, which would be granted new, independent country status, agreed to strict Dutch supervision of their budgets and the creation of a Public Prosecutor's Office. However, the process of negotiation was not an easy one. For example, the decision to place Curaçao's finances under Dutch control was not welcomed by some within the island. After the local council agreed to the proposals in June, riots broke out with protestors targeting Dutch nationals. The prime minister of the Netherlands Antilles, Emily de Jongh-Elhage, condemned the outbreak of "racist violence". On the Dutch side, meanwhile, several legislators from across the political divide argued that St Maarten was not ready to attain country status, due to what they saw as its poor record in dealing with organised crime and drug trafficking. These sources of opposition, however, were unable to stop the December agreement being signed. Nevertheless, it had been announced earlier in the year that the target date for completing the constitutional changes would be the beginning of 2010, rather than the original date of 15 December 2008 (see AR 2007, p. 159). Under the changes Bonaire, St Eustatius, and Saba would become municipalities of The Netherlands.

In related developments, it was decided that financial assistance from The Netherlands to Curaçao and St Maarten would be reduced in the period 2008-12, and end completely in 2013. Also, the Dutch stated that assistance for Aruba, which had separated from the Netherlands Antilles in 1986 but remained part of the Kingdom of the Netherlands, would end in 2009.

Peter Clegg

US DEPENDENCIES

Puerto Rico

CAPITAL: San Juan   AREA: 8,950 sq km   POPULATION: 3,943,000 ('07)
OFFICIAL LANGUAGES: Spanish & English   POLITICAL SYSTEM: multiparty system in US
    Commonwealth
GOVERNOR-GENERAL: Luis Fortuño (PNP) (since Nov '08)
RULING PARTY: New Progressive Party (PNP)
CURRENCY: US dollar (end-'08 £1=1.4378)
GNI PER CAPITA: High income: US$11,456 or more ('07 est), -

US Virgin Islands

CAPITAL: Charlotte Amalie   AREA: 350 sq km   POPULATION: 108,000 ('07)
OFFICIAL LANGUAGE: English   POLTICAL SYSTEM: semi-autonomous overseas territory of the USA
GOVERNOR-GENERAL: John de Jongh Jr (Democratic Party) (since Jan '07)
RULING PARTY: Democrats
CURRENCY: US dollar (end-'08 £1=1.4378)
GNI PER CAPITA: High income: US$11,456 or more ('07 est), -

THE economic downturn in the USA had an impact on both Puerto Rico and the US Virgin Islands. The San Juan Popular Bank, the largest financial institution in Puerto Rico, lost US$669 million in the third quarter of the year, and was lent US$935 million by the US Treasury to secure its business. The US Virgin Islands (USVI) was given a two-year extension to its rum tax formula, which was worth an additional US$40 million to the government. The formula fixed the amount of tax to be returned to the USVI from rum sold in the USA.

Puerto Rico's governor and leader of the Popular Democratic Party (PPD), Aníbal Acevedo Vilá, was defeated by a large margin in the 4 November gubernatorial election by Luis Fortuño of the New Progressive Party (PNP). Fortuño won by over 220,000 votes, the widest margin of victory in 44 years, and gave the PNP its largest ever victory. The PNP also won the post of resident commissioner, a clear majority of seats in both the House of Representatives and the Senate, as well as most of the mayoralties. Prior to the elections the PPD's chances of securing victory were damaged severely after Acevedo Vilá was indicted by US federal prosecutors on charges of campaign finance fraud. After the election most of the charges were dropped, but Acevedo Vilá was scheduled to face trial on nine of the 24 original charges in February 2009.

The governor of the USVI, John de Jongh Jr, announced on 24 June a landmark 30-year public-private initiative with drinks manufacturer Diageo for the construction and operation of a new distillery on St Croix. From 2012 it was expected that the plant would supply all bulk rum used to make Captain Morgan branded products for the US market, and bring in an additional US$3 billion of revenue over the term of the agreement.

In other news, the former commissioners of the department of planning and natural resources, and the department of property procurement were sentenced to long prison terms for having accepted bribes in relation to the award of government contracts to a shell company, which then failed to carry out the promised works.

Peter Clegg

SOUTH AMERICA

BRAZIL—ARGENTINA—PARAGUAY—URUGUAY—CHILE—PERU—BOLIVIA—
ECUADOR—COLOMBIA—VENEZUELA

BRAZIL

CAPITAL: Brasília   AREA: 8,514,880 sq km   POPULATION: 191,601,000 ('07)
OFFICIAL LANGUAGE: Portuguese   POLTICAL SYSTEM: multiparty republic
HEAD OF STATE AND GOVERNMENT: President Luiz Inácio "Lula" da Silva (since Jan '03)
RULING PARTIES: Workers' Party (PT) heads coalition
MAIN IGO MEMBERSHIPS (NON-UN): OAS, ALADI, SELA, Mercosur, AP, CPLP
CURRENCY: real (end-'08 £1=R3.3529, US$1=R2.3320)
GNI PER CAPITA: US$5,910, $9,370 at PPP ('07)

BRAZIL'S status as an emerging global power received a boost on 23 December
when France's president, Nicolas Sarkozy, endorsed the South American country's
long-standing ambition to secure a permanent seat on the UN Security Council and
said that Brazil had a key role to play in global decision-making. The French president's support for Brazil's growing international influence was demonstrated
whilst he was attending a summit with President Luiz Inácio "Lula" da Silva in Rio
de Janeiro. At the summit, the two leaders signed a series of defence agreements
worth an estimated US$11.1 billion. The agreements included plans to use French
military technology to build 50 EC725 Super Cougar helicopters in Brazil and
develop one nuclear-powered submarine and four diesel-powered submarines. The
signing of the accords in December followed a meeting in February, during which
da Silva and Sarkozy had reached agreement on a "strategic alliance", featuring the
transfer to Brazil of French military technology and reciprocal diplomatic support
in international affairs. During an EU-Brazil summit hosted on 22 December, also
in Rio de Janeiro, da Silva and Sarkozy (who held the rotating post of EU president) agreed that the EU and Brazil would adopt a common position on ways to
deal with the ongoing global economic crisis. The two leaders gave no details
about their common position, but it was thought that their proposals would be
revealed at the next G-20 summit, to be hosted in London in April 2009.

In November, da Silva also signed a series of agreements with Russian President Dmitry Medvedev. The agreements were aimed at deepening bilateral
relations between Brazil and Russia and it was thought that the two leaders'
talks, held in Rio de Janeiro, focused on boosting bilateral trade and increasing
co-operation in the agriculture, energy, and railways sectors. In other developments affecting Brazil's foreign relations, da Silva hosted the Latin American
and Caribbean summit on integration and development in December, attended
by 31 of the region's 33 heads of state and held in the north-eastern city of Salvador de Bahia. Some observers regarded the hosting of the two-day gathering
as an attempt by da Silva's administration to show that Brazil—and not the
USA—was the leading political power in the region. The fact that the regional
summit marked the first occasion on which senior officials from every country

in South America and the Caribbean had met without the presence of the USA or Europe only served to confirm the widely held perception that Brazil was continuing to grow in confidence as a key player in regional and global affairs.

Despite the global economic crisis, Brazil experienced a cascade of positive economic news throughout the year, prompting several analysts to suggest that the country was better equipped to deal with the crisis than many other South American countries. On 9 December, da Silva assured Brazilians that there was "no country in the world better prepared" to face the economic crisis, adding that Brazil had reserves and markets and "a growing economy". Most Brazilians appeared to agree with the president's optimism; an opinion poll published by the research company, Instituto Sensus, in late December found that 80.3 per cent of respondents approved of da Silva's performance as president.

A boom in global commodity prices meant that Brazil, the largest economy in South America and the 10th largest in the world, continued to achieve powerful growth rates in 2008. Brazil's economic status was notably boosted in May, when Standard and Poor's, the international credit ratings agency, awarded the country an investment grade credit rating of BBB- (the lowest on the investment grade scale). Analysts expected the rating upgrade, which da Silva described as a "magical moment" in Brazil's history, to accelerate and increase inward investment in Brazil.

Brazil's growing status as a leading player in the global energy industry, which was boosted in 2007 by the discovery of vast new offshore oil and natural gas reserves (see AR 2008, p. 163), suffered some setbacks in 2008, however. In July, employees from Petrobras, the state-owned energy company, staged a five-day strike that cut Brazil's oil production by around 7 per cent, according to the company's estimates, or by up to 22 per cent, according to trade union claims. Employees from 42 oil platforms based off the coast of Rio de Janeiro participated in the strike, which was called in protest against the company's unwillingness to allow workers a day off in exchange for the time that they spent travelling to and from offshore platforms. A nationwide strike planned for 5 August was called off, however, after Petrobras agreed to increase the amount of profit that it shared with employees to 15.2 per cent (from 12.9 per cent). In September, da Silva announced that revenues from recently discovered offshore oil and gas reserves would be invested in education and poverty eradication programmes.

In February Petrobras officials had disclosed that four laptop computers (and two memory chips) holding data about earlier Brazilian offshore oil and gas discoveries had been stolen the previous month. It was thought that the computer equipment was stolen from a container on a ship, which had been chartered by Halliburton, a US-based multinational oilfield service company and Petrobras business partner. President da Silva said that the information held on the stolen equipment included "secrets of state", whilst the police revealed that they were treating the theft as a case of industrial espionage.

The emergence of fresh corruption scandals in 2008 served as a reminder that Brazil had not yet overcome the pervasive sleaze for which the country had been renowned before it began its transformation towards democratic normality. On 1 February, Minister of the Special Secretariat for the Promotion of Racial Equality

Matilde Ribeiro resigned from her post after it emerged that she had bought goods worth some R171,000 on her government credit card in 2007. It was revealed that Ribeiro's purchases included luxury goods from duty-free shops, meals in expensive restaurants, and rentals of high-performance cars. However, a subsequent congressional inquiry into the use of corporate credit cards by government officials concluded without charges being filed.

On 2 December Daniel Dantas, a notorious executive of a Brazilian asset management company, was fined R12 million and sentenced to 10 years in prison after being convicted of attempting to bribe police officers to remove his name from a list of people being investigated for a range of financial crimes. Dantas was arrested in July (along with his sister, Veronica Dantas, and at least 10 others) on charges of corruption, money laundering, and racketeering, following a four-year police investigation into a series of alleged financial crimes, some of which also implicated prominent political figures. The police believed that Dantas had used his asset management company to launder money, avoid tax liabilities, and illegally divert public funds to overseas bank accounts. Shortly after the arrest of Dantas, however, a Supreme Court ruling criticised Judge Fausto Martin de Sanctis's decision to detain the executive, and Dantas was released from custody on the grounds that there was "insufficient evidence" to warrant his detention. Dantas was subsequently re-arrested but the Supreme Court ruling had provoked widespread anger within the judicial community, prompting at least 130 judges to sign a statement supporting de Sanctis's original decision to order the arrest.

In April, more than 50 people, including 16 mayors and a federal judge, were accused of involvement in the embezzlement of more than US$100 million of public funds from Brazil's social security agency. Further corruption allegations emerged in September, when the leadership of the Brazilian Intelligence Agency (Abin), including agency chief Paulo Lacerda, was ordered to step down "temporarily" for allegedly tapping a telephone conversation between Gilmar Mendes, the Supreme Court president, and an opposition legislator. The suspension of Abin's leadership followed the publication of allegations, by an unnamed intelligence agent, that the illegal telephone tapping of senior judicial, legislative, and government officials was common practice for Abin agents.

Despite the announcement of a series of new initiatives, which the government said were aimed at protecting the environment, Brazil's status as the custodian of large swathes of the Amazon rainforest suffered several setbacks in 2008. As early as 24 January, the government unveiled a series of new measures designed to reduce deforestation of the Amazon. The measures included the deployment of soldiers to conduct inspections and a freeze on new deforestation requests in some of the worst affected areas of the rainforest. However, the government's environmental challenges were highlighted in February, when several hundred federal police officers were deployed to regain control of the remote town of Tailandia, in Para state. The town had been the scene of angry protests against the government's environmental policies, with a mob of around 2,000 people, many of whom worked in illegal logging mills, overpowering the local authorities. Similar scenes were witnessed in the town of Paragominas, in northern Para state, in

November, when a mob of around 3,000 people attacked offices used by the Ibama environmental protection agency in protest against the government's crackdown on illegal logging. Government officials said that the protests began after environment officials seized some 400 cubic metres of wood, which was thought to have been cut illegally from an Indian reservation. Environment Minister Carlos Minc responded to the unrest by deploying troops to restore order.

Minc, a founder of Brazil's Green Party (Partido Verde, PV), was appointed to the post of environment minister on 27 May, following the resignation of Marina Silva. Silva revealed that she had resigned because she had struggled "for some time" to implement the government's environmental agenda. Many environmentalists expressed "dismay" at Silva's departure from government, which came only days after a court overturned the conviction of Vitalmiro Bastos Moura, a landowner and rancher in the Amazon, for ordering the killing of US-born environmentalist and human rights activist Dorothy Stang in 2005 (see AR 2008, p. 162).

In late July President da Silva launched an international campaign to protect the Amazon rainforest and to help combat climate change. The campaign aimed to raise some US$21 billion of overseas investment to promote land conservation and sustainable development. Environment Minister Minc said that the government was "committed to reducing the destruction of the rainforest, to eliminating illegal burning and to guaranteeing a better quality of life for all". However, official statistics released on 30 August revealed that the rate of deforestation in the Amazon had increased by 69 per cent between August 2007 and August 2008, news which prompted the environment ministry to announce a series of new measures to protect the environment in September. The new measures included plans to plant a greater number of trees by 2015 than the number lost through logging, and the creation of a special force comprising 3,000 troops to monitor Brazil's ecosystems. The measures also included proposals to re-chart the country's Amazon region and extend satellite monitoring of the rainforest to other environmentally sensitive areas. In December, the government also pledged to reduce deforestation rates by 72 per cent before 2017.

On 9 July the justice and constitution committee in the Chamber of Deputies (the lower house of Congress, the bicameral federal legislature) rejected a controversial bill to legalise abortion. The public debate on abortion was a controversial issue in Brazil, the world's most populous Roman Catholic country, mainly because the church advocated sexual abstinence outside marriage and strongly opposed the termination of pregnancy. It was illegal to have an abortion in Brazil except in cases involving rape or a health risk to the expectant mother. Proponents of legalisation claimed that the debate should focus on public health issues, not religious beliefs. Some estimates suggested that one-third of Brazilian schoolgirls between the ages of 14 and 17 became pregnant each year, whilst the World Health Organisation estimate indicated that over 1 million illegal abortions were carried out in Brazil annually. It was revealed in November that at least 30 women had been sentenced to community work, whilst 150 others had been charged, in connection with a police investigation into allegations that some 1,200 women had had abortions in a clinic in the city of Campo Grande, in Mato Grosso Do Sul state. Some human rights organisations and women's groups protested against the investigation when it emerged that prosecutors were demanding that the women involved undergo intimate medical examinations.

In November the Supreme Court overruled Congress when it upheld a March 2007 ruling by the electoral court, which stated that electoral mandates belonged to political parties and not individual legislators. The case was brought before the Supreme Court after some opposition legislators claimed that the electoral court ruling was unconstitutional. It was common in Brazil for legislators to switch parties after being elected to office, often to gain favour with the government, and some observers predicted that the Supreme Court ruling could result in as many as 2,000 legislators (both federal and provincial) losing their electoral mandates.

The worst air crash in Brazil's history, at Sao Paulo's Congonhas airport in July 2007 (see AR 2008, pp. 164-15), was the fault of 10 government and airline officials, the Sao Paulo state police authorities concluded in November. A police investigation into the disaster found that government officials, including the former director of Brazil's National Civil Aviation Agency (ANAC), Denise Abreu, had failed to maintain the airport's drainage systems and implement adequate rules for aircraft landing during heavy rain. The investigation also found that TAM Linhas Aereas, the operators of the aeroplane, had failed properly to train its pilots. Public prosecutors, who were required to decide whether to prosecute the individuals concerned, had not filed any charges as the year ended.

Also in November, at least 109 people died in the southern state of Santa Catarina after prolonged and heavy rainfall triggered severe flooding and landslides in the region. Around 1.5 million people were affected by the flooding and landslides, including some 80,000 who were displaced by the disaster. The government declared some of the affected areas as disaster zones and pledged more than US$1 billion in emergency relief aid.

In other developments, Culture Minister Gilberto Gil announced on 30 July that he was resigning from his ministerial post. Gil, a globally renowned musician, revealed that his artistic work had been under "pressure" since assuming his post in the cabinet in January 2003. Juca Ferreira, an executive secretary in the culture ministry, was appointed to replace Gil. In an earlier government change, on 21 January, Edison Lobao, a senator from the Brazilian Democratic Movement (PMDB), was appointed as the new mines and energy minister. Lobao's appointment was controversial because he was embroiled in corruption allegations involving his son and had no previous experience of the mining and energy sector. Some observers claimed that Lobao's appointment was a political gesture to the PMDB, a coalition partner on which the government was heavily reliant for congressional support.

Kurt Perry

ARGENTINA

CAPITAL: Buenos Aires   AREA: 2,780,400 sq km   POPULATION: 39,503,000 ('07)
OFFICIAL LANGUAGE: Spanish   POLTICAL SYSTEM: multiparty republic
HEAD OF STATE AND GOVERNMENT: President Cristina Fernández de Kirchner (PJ) (since Oct '07)
RULING PARTY: Justicialist Party (PJ)
MAIN IGO MEMBERSHIPS (NON-UN): OAS, SELA, ALADI, Mercosur
CURRENCY: peso (end-'08 £1=AP4.9649, US$1=AP3.4533)
GNI PER CAPITA: US$6,050, $12,990 at PPP ('07)

As the year 2008 ended, slowing economic growth and speculation that Argentina might default on its sovereign debt prompted some analysts to describe the country as one of the most vulnerable in Latin America to the ongoing global financial crisis. The economic policies of President Cristina Fernández de Kirchner were widely blamed for Argentina's precarious economic position. Fernández was swept to power in October 2007 amid a wave of electoral support that had been at least partially generated by affection towards former President Nestor Kirchner (2003-07), her predecessor and husband, whose popularity was attributed to a widely held belief that he had steered Argentina towards its recovery from economic collapse in 2001 (see AR 2001, pp. 204-207). Faith in Nestor Kirchner's economic policies had had the knock-on effect of transforming his wife's election campaign in 2007 into what some observers described as a "coronation ceremony" (see AR 2008, pp. 165-66).

When she assumed office in December 2007, Fernández pledged to continue her husband's policies and appointed several members of his outgoing government to her own cabinet. As 2008 progressed, however, Fernández found herself unable to match the high popularity ratings that her husband had achieved. Argentina, Latin America's second largest economy, had enjoyed five continuous years of economic growth of more than 8 per cent per annum, but as 2008 ended many analysts were forecasting that the country's economy would enter a recession in 2009, whilst others claimed that it was already there. Faced with a deteriorating economic climate, Fernández resorted to interventionist measures, drawing fierce criticism from her opponents and from many political commentators.

The president faced her first serious test in January, when protesters took to the streets of Buenos Aires to vent their anger over power shortages that cut water supplies and left some parts of the city without electricity for 36 hours. She was dealt a more dramatic blow in July, when the 72-member Senate (the upper house of Congress, the bicameral legislature) narrowly rejected a presidential decree increasing taxes on some agricultural exports, such as soya beans, wheat, and corn. Fernández claimed that the decree, which she had signed in March, was required to help redistribute wealth, but the plans triggered some four months of protests, strikes, and roadblocks by members of Argentina's four largest farming unions. The defeat in the Senate was deeply embarrassing for Fernández, particularly because Vice President Julio Cobos, who was also the president of the upper house, cast the deciding negative vote. Some analysts said that the defeat, which forced the president to revoke the decree, effectively marked the end of a five-year period during which Fernández and Kirchner had enjoyed largely unchallenged political authority in Argentina. "Kirchnerism" suffered another setback on 23 December, when a court announced an investigation into Nestor Kirchner and other former government officials over alleged irregularities, dating back to the Kirchner presidency, in the award of government contracts and over Argentina's links to Venezuelan President Hugo Chávez Frías.

Government attempts to secure funds were more successful in November, when Congress approved a bill nationalising Argentina's private pension system. Announcing the plans on 21 October, Fernández claimed that the bill would help protect the pension funds from the negative effects of the global financial crisis. However, her critics claimed that the government would attempt to "grab" the pension funds, worth around US$26 billion, to help avert a default on Argentina's sovereign debt. In the following weeks the Buenos Aires stock exchange index fell by 27 per cent, prompting citizens to withdraw around 5 per cent of their deposits from Argentinian banks.

Despite government assurances that Argentina could meet its debt obligations, the international ratings agency, Standard & Poor's, on 31 October downgraded the country's debt rating to B-, six levels below investment grade. It was thought that Argentina's financing requirements for 2009 amounted to some US$16.5 billion, which, with the budget for 2009 estimating a primary surplus of US$8 billion, left a funding gap of around US$8.5 billion. In response to the economic problems, on 26 November Chief of Cabinet Sergio Massa announced a US$3.9 billion fiscal stimulus package to promote employment, production, and consumer confidence. The package included tax breaks to encourage companies to retain their employees and incentives for savers and companies to repatriate savings that had been deposited overseas. On 4 December the government also announced a US$21 billion public works programme, designed to more than double the number of jobs in the construction sector; some ten days later Massa revealed that a further US$11 billion of funds were being allocated to the public works programme.

The government also intervened in the private sector in December, when Congress approved the expropriation of Aerolineas Argentinas, an ailing international airline that operated more than 80 per cent of Argentina's domestic flights and which had debts of up to US$900 million. The Chamber of Deputies (the lower house) and the Senate approved a bill declaring the airline (and its sister airline, Austral) a "public good subject to expropriation". Spanish travel company Marsans, which had bought the airline in 2001, responded to the expropriation by vowing to initiate an arbitration claim with the World Bank's International Centre for Settlement of Investment Disputes.

The judiciary made progress in 2008 in its attempts to bring to justice the perpetrators of human rights violations committed during Argentina's "dirty war" era (1976-83), during which up to 30,000 opponents of the country's military dictatorship were thought to have been killed or kidnapped. The Spanish authorities on 15 February agreed to Argentina's extradition request for former police officer Rodolfo Eduardo Almiron Sena, who faced a series of charges of crimes against humanity allegedly committed in the run-up to the "dirty war". Almiron was wanted in connection with an ongoing investigation into the Argentinian Anti-Communist Alliance (AAA, or Triple A), a government-linked right-wing paramilitary organisation, which was accused of kidnapping and killing up to 2,000 dissidents in Argentina in 1974-76. He was extradited to Argentina on 19 March. On 31 March, the Spanish authorities also extradited Ricardo Miguel Cavallo (formerly known as "Serpico" or "Marcelo"), a former Argentinian naval officer, who faced a series of charges of crimes against humanity during the "dirty war". In another case involving the Spanish authorities, the National Court of Spain on 28 April ruled against the extradition to Argentina of former Argentinian President María Estela Martínez de Perón (also known as Isabel Martínez de Perón) (1974-76). Perón had been under house arrest in Spain since her arrest in January 2007 and was wanted in Argentina in connection with the disappearance and presumed murder of two government opponents in 1976.

On 28 August General (retd) Antonio Domingo Bussi and General (retd) Luciano Benjamin Menendez were sentenced to life in prison after being convicted of kidnapping, torturing, and murdering Guillermo Vargas Aignasse, an Argentinian legislator who had disappeared on 24 March, 1976, during the military coup that ushered in Argentina's "dirty war". Menendez, commander of the third army corps in the northern city of Córdoba in the mid-1970s, was also convicted in July (along with six other former military officials and one civilian) of the kidnap, torture, and murder of four dissidents in 1977. Former President General Jorge Rafael Videla, Argentina's military dictator in 1976-81, was transferred from house arrest to prison on 11 October. Videla was sentenced to life imprisonment in 1985 after being convicted of human rights violations. He was pardoned in 1990 by former President Carlos Saúl Menem (1989-99), but had been held under house arrest since April 2007, when a court overturned the pardon of 1990. On 19 December, a court suspended its decision taken the previous day to release from custody nearly 20 former navy officers accused of human rights violations during the "dirty war", including Alfredo Astiz (also known as the "Blond Angel of Death"). The court ruled to release the former officers on bail on the grounds that they had been held without trial for over two years. Amid widespread public anger, an appeal against the ruling was filed by prosecutors, meaning that the men would remain in prison pending a ruling by the Supreme Court.

Protracted tensions in Argentina's relations with the UK and with Iran continued to simmer in 2008. The approval in the UK of a new constitution for the disputed Falkland (Malvinas) Islands provoked sharp criticism from Foreign Minister Jorge Taiana on 6 November. Taiana described the new constitution, effective from 1 January, 2009, as a "flagrant violation" of the mandate granted to Argentina by the UN, adding that the UK was perpetuating "an anachronistic colonial situation".

On 16 December an Argentinian judge seized property in Buenos Aires owned by a former Iranian diplomat, who was wanted in Argentina on charges related to a bomb attack in July 1994 on a Jewish community centre in the Argentinian capital. Relations with Iran had soured in November 2006 (see AR 2007, p. 168) when Argentina issued international arrest warrants against former Iranian President Ali Akbar Hashemi Rafsanjani and seven of his officials for allegedly masterminding the bomb attack.

Kurt Perry

PARAGUAY—URUGUAY—CHILE—PERU—BOLIVIA—ECUADOR—COLOMBIA—VENEZUELA

Paraguay

CAPITAL: Asunción   AREA: 406,750 sq km   POPULATION: 6,120,000 ('07)
OFFICIAL LANGUAGE: Spanish   POLTICAL SYSTEM: multiparty republic
HEAD OF STATE AND GOVERNMENT: President Fernando Lugo Méndez (APC) (since Aug '08)
RULING PARTY: Patriotic Alliance for Change (APC)
MAIN IGO MEMBERSHIPS (NON-UN): OAS, ALADI, SELA, Mercosur
CURRENCY: guarani (end-'08 £1=G7,066.57, US$1=G4,915.00)
GNI PER CAPITA: US$1,670, $4,380 at PPP ('07)

Uruguay

CAPITAL: Montevideo   AREA: 176,220 sq km   POPULATION: 3,319,000 ('07)
OFFICIAL LANGUAGE: Spanish   POLTICAL SYSTEM: multiparty republic
HEAD OF STATE AND GOVERNMENT: President Tabaré Vázquez (EP-FA) (since March '05)
RULING PARTY: Progressive Encounter-Broad Front (EP-FA)
MAIN IGO MEMBERSHIPS (NON-UN): OAS, ALADI, SELA, Mercosur
CURRENCY: peso Uruguay (end-'08 £1=UP35.0812, US$1=UP24.4000)
GNI PER CAPITA: US$6,380, $11,040 at PPP ('07)

Chile

CAPITAL: Santiago   AREA: 756,630 sq km   POPULATION: 16,595,000 ('07)
OFFICIAL LANGUAGE: Spanish   POLTICAL SYSTEM: multiparty republic
HEAD OF STATE AND GOVERNMENT: President Michelle Bachelet (since March '06)
RULING PARTIES: Concertación coalition, comprising Party for Democracy (PPD), Socialist (PSC), Christian Democratic (PDC), & Social Democratic Radical (PRSD) parties
MAIN IGO MEMBERSHIPS (NON-UN): OAS, ALADI, SELA, APEC, NAM, Mercosur
CURRENCY: Chilean peso (end-'08 £1=Ch916.207, US$1=Ch637.250)
GNI PER CAPITA: US$8,350, $12,590 at PPP ('07)

Peru

CAPITAL: Lima   AREA: 1,285,220 sq km   POPULATION: 27,898,000 ('07)
OFFICIAL LANGUAGES: Spanish, Quechua, Aymará   POLTICAL SYSTEM: multiparty republic
HEAD OF STATE AND GOVERNMENT: President Alan García Pérez (APRA) (since July '06)
RULING PARTIES: Union for Perú (UPP) largest party in Congress; Peruvian Aprista Party (APRA) holds presidency
MAIN IGO MEMBERSHIPS (NON-UN): OAS, APEC, ALADI, SELA, CA, AP, NAM
CURRENCY: new sol (end-'08 £1=S4.5139, US$1=S3.1395)
GNI PER CAPITA: US$3,450, $7,240 at PPP ('07)

Bolivia

CAPITAL: La Paz and Sucre   AREA: 1,098,580 sq km   POPULATION: 9,518,000 ('07)
OFFICIAL LANGUAGES: Spanish, Quechua, Aymará   POLTICAL SYSTEM: multiparty republic
HEAD OF STATE AND GOVERNMENT: President Evo Morales (since Jan '06)
RULING PARTY: Movement Towards Socialism (MAS)
MAIN IGO MEMBERSHIPS (NON-UN): OAS, ALADI, SELA, AG, CA, NAM, Mercosur
CURRENCY: boliviano (end-'08 £1=B10.0931, US$1=B7.0200)
GNI PER CAPITA: US$1,260, $4,140 at PPP ('07)

Ecuador

CAPITAL: Quito　AREA: 283,560 sq km　POPULATION: 13,340,000 ('07)
OFFICIAL LANGUAGE: Spanish　POLTICAL SYSTEM: multiparty republic
HEAD OF STATE AND GOVERNMENT: President Rafael Correa Delgado (MPAIS/PS-FA) (since Jan '07)
RULING PARTY: Institutional Renewal Party of National Action (PRIAN)
MAIN IGO MEMBERSHIPS (NON-UN): OAS, ALADI, SELA, AG, CA, NAM
CURRENCY: sucre (end-'08 £1=S35,943.80, US$1=S25,000.0)
GNI PER CAPITA: US$3,080, $7,040 at PPP ('07)

Colombia

CAPITAL: Santa Fe de Bogotá　AREA: 1,141,750 sq km　POPULATION: 46,117,000 ('07)
OFFICIAL LANGUAGE: Spanish　POLTICAL SYSTEM: multiparty republic
HEAD OF STATE AND GOVERNMENT: President Alvaro Uribe Velez (Colombia First, PC) (since Aug. '02)
RULING PARTIES: parties allied with Uribe: Party of the "U" (UP), Colombian Conservative Party
　(PCC), and Radical Change (CR)
MAIN IGO MEMBERSHIPS (NON-UN): OAS, ALADI, SELA, AG, CA, ACS, NAM
CURRENCY: Colombian peso (end-'08 £1=Col3,232.90 US$1=Col2,248.58)
GNI PER CAPITA: US$3,250, $6,640 at PPP ('07)

Venezuela

CAPITAL: Caracas　AREA: 912,050 sq km　POPULATION: 27,467,000 ('07)
OFFICIAL LANGUAGE: Spanish　POLTICAL SYSTEM: multiparty republic
HEAD OF STATE AND GOVERNMENT: President Hugo Chávez Frías (since Feb '99)
RULING PARTY: Fifth Republic Movement (MVR)
MAIN IGO MEMBERSHIPS (NON-UN): OAS, ALADI, SELA, CA, ACS, OPEC, NAM
CURRENCY: bolívar (end-'08 £1=Bs3.0873, US$1=Bs2.1473)
GNI PER CAPITA: US$7,320, $11,920 at PPP ('07)

A SERIOUS regional diplomatic crisis erupted in March when Colombian military forces launched air and ground attacks against a target in the Ecuadorean
province of Sucumbíos, about 2 km from the Colombian border. The attacks
were launched against a remote camp used by rebels from the Colombian Revolutionary Armed Forces (FARC), Colombia's largest leftist guerrilla organisation. In the immediate aftermath, it was revealed that the Colombian airforce had strafed the FARC camp after rebels had "fled" across Colombia's
border into Ecuador. Raul Reyes, the second most senior member of the
FARC's secretariat, was amongst 21 people killed in the attacks, all of whom
were presumed to be rebels.

Colombia's President Alvaro Uribe Velez defended the military action,
describing the strikes as a "legitimate defence" of Colombia's national security.
However, Ecuador's President Rafael Correa condemned the military strikes as
"premeditated...aggression", before withdrawing his country's ambassador to
Colombia, and then expelling Colombia's ambassador to Ecuador. In a gesture
of solidarity with Ecuador, Venezuela's President Hugo Chávez Frías, a frequent
critic of Uribe's "pro-US" policies, followed suit by closing Venezuela's
embassy in Bogota and expelling Colombia's ambassador from Venezuela. The
crisis swiftly escalated into a tense military standoff, when Chávez announced
that he was deploying 10 battalions (around 9,000 troops), along with fighter
jets and tanks, to Venezuela's long border with Colombia. Hours later, Correa
announced that Ecuador was also deploying troops to its border with Colombia,

raising the spectre of the region's first armed clash since 1995, when a border dispute had escalated into a 22-day war between Peru and Ecuador. Correa and Chávez strongly denied Colombia's allegations that Ecuador and Venezuela were politically and financially supporting the FARC. The allegations were made when Colombian officials revealed that they were in possession of evidence, gathered from laptop computers seized from the site of the attacks, that proved the complicity of Ecuador and Venezuela.

Following several days of tense international efforts to avert an armed confrontation, the crisis was resolved peacefully on 7 March, when Uribe publicly apologised for Colombia's violation of Ecuador's territory, pledging "not to repeat" such attacks. Normal diplomatic relations between Colombia and Venezuela were restored on 9 March, but it was not until June that Ecuador announced an intention to restore diplomatic relations with Colombia at the level of chargés d'affaires. However, Colombia's foreign minister, Fernando Araujo, revealed on 24 June that Colombia was postponing a resumption of its diplomatic relations with Ecuador as a result of "aggressive remarks" that Correa had made about the initial attacks in an interview published in Argentina. In the interview, Correa was quoted as saying that the Colombian airforce had used "North American" bombs, and that survivors of the aerial raids had been shot and killed by Colombian soldiers.

Tensions between Venezuela and Colombia emerged once again on 17 May, when Venezuela's foreign minister, Nicolas Maduro, protested to Colombia about an alleged incursion by around 60 Colombian troops into Venezuelan territory the day before. Maduro said that the alleged incursion had been incited by the USA and was an attempt by Colombia to destabilise the region's "new democratic and progressive leaderships". Colombia responded to the allegations by repeating its claims that Venezuela was covertly supporting the FARC's long-running armed resistance.

REGIONAL AND FOREIGN RELATIONS. Colombia was widely regarded as the USA's strongest ally in the region, but close diplomatic ties were insufficient to ensure ratification of the United States—Colombia Trade Promotion Agreement (CTPA), a free trade agreement signed by the two countries in November 2006. On 10 April, the Democrat-controlled US House of Representatives (the lower house of the US Congress) voted to delay indefinitely ratification of the CTPA, amid concerns over Colombia's labour and human rights laws.

Established diplomatic tensions between Chávez and the US administration of President George W. Bush did not lessen in 2008. On 11 September, for example, Chávez ordered the USA's ambassador to Venezuela to leave the country within 72 hours and recalled Venezuela's ambassador from Washington, DC. Many observers regarded the move as a show of support for Bolivia's President Evo Morales, who had expelled the USA's ambassador to Bolivia a day earlier, after accusing the US government of fomenting the violence that erupted in Bolivia that month (see below). Chávez did, however, revive Venezuela's strained relations with Spain in 2008. On 25 July, on the Spanish island of Mallorca, the Venezuelan president and King Juan Carlos of Spain publicly shook hands, a gesture which symbolically normalised relations following the diplomatic spat which had erupted in November 2007 when the Spanish king told Chávez to "shut up" during an Ibero-American summit in Chile (see AR 2008, p. 178).

Chávez and Morales further strengthened their close links in May, when the self-declared "socialists" signed a "memorandum of understanding in the area of security and defence" in Venezuela's capital. The agreement provided for bilateral co-operation in training, capacity-building, and logistics, in what Chávez described as a move "to assure our defence and our democracy".

In contrast with the close rapport between Bolivia and Venezuela, Peru on 16 January instigated proceedings against neighbouring Chile at the International Court of Justice (ICJ) in connection with a long-standing maritime boundary dispute between the two countries. Peru's President García said that his country had instigated the action because its negotiations with Chile had failed to resolve the dispute. The boundary dispute had simmered between the two countries since Chile took swathes of Peruvian territory during the War of the Pacific (1879-1883). Chile's historically tense relations with Bolivia, however, warmed slightly in June, when the Chilean and Bolivian defence ministers, José Goñi and Walker San Miguel, respectively, signed an "historic" framework agreement on defence co-operation. The agreement, signed in La Paz (the administrative capital of Bolivia), included mutual pledges to strengthen military academic exchanges and plans for more transparency in peacekeeping operations and military budgets. Relations between Chile and Bolivia had remained tense since the former defeated the latter—and gained coastal territory as a result—in wars fought in the 19th century over the issue of Bolivian access to the Pacific Ocean.

Many of the countries in the region continued in 2008 to strengthen their trade and economic relations with states such as China, Russia, and Iran, all of which were regarded as traditional foes of the USA. Successive US government had since the 1970s exerted significant (and largely unchallenged) influence in the South America region, an area commonly referred to as the USA's "backyard". However, the rise of Chinese, Russian, and Iranian influence in South American territory was regarded by some observers as evidence that the USA's influence in the region was waning. In September, Venezuelan and Chinese officials signed a series of economic agreements in Beijing, including projects aimed at increasing the amount of Venezuelan oil sold to China and China's investments in Venezuela's telecommunications and agriculture sectors. The two countries also agreed to increase to US$12 billion the amount of capital that they held in a joint investment fund, which had been created to fund bilateral co-operation and the development of agriculture, infrastructure, communications, education, industry, and culture.

China's growing influence in South America was also evident in Peru and Chile. It was announced on 19 November that Peru's President Alan García Pérez and China's President Hu Jintao had signed a series of bilateral accords, including agreements on health and technology. The accords, which were expected to lead in 2009 to the signing of a free trade agreement (FTA) between Peru and China, were signed in Lima where Hu was attending a summit of the Asia Pacific Economic Co-operation (APEC) forum on 22-23 November. Earlier in the year, in April, Chile's President Michelle Bachelet paid an official state visit to China, and signed a series of bilateral trade agreements to boost economic ties between the two countries. The agreements reportedly included plans that granted Chilean companies access to 23 service industries in China and Chinese companies access to 37 industrial sectors in Chile.

In Bolivia on 17 March, executives from the Bolivian state energy company YPFB, signed an agreement with Gazprom, Russia's state-controlled gas monopoly, to "explore and exploit" natural gas reserves in southern Bolivia. The agreement, thought to be worth up to US$2 billion, involved a "strategic alliance" to identify potential natural gas exploration projects in the Sunchal gas field, Tarija province, and two other areas in the Subandino Sur basin of south east Bolivia.

Meanwhile, in September, during an official state visit to Russia by President Chávez, it was announced that the Russian government had agreed to lend Venezuela US$1 billion to purchase arms and military equipment from Russian manufacturers; in November, Russia's President Dmitry Medvedev met Chávez in Caracas, where the two leaders signed a series of bilateral agreements designed to enhance co-operation in the energy, military, economic, trade, technology, and financial sectors.

DRUGS, TERRORISM, AND CIVIL CONFLICT. Colombia witnessed the region's most dramatic event in 2008: the successful execution of a military rescue operation, which resulted in 15 high-profile hostages held by the FARC being freed from captivity. The rescue operation ("Operation Check") took place in the southern Colombian province of Guaviare in July, when Colombian security agents, posing as international aid workers, tricked the rebels into handing over the prisoners, telling the guerrillas that they had been instructed by senior FARC commanders to fly the hostages to a new rebel camp in southern Colombia. The hostages were handed over to the agents, who guided the captives, along with rebels Gerardo Antonio Aguilar Ramirez (alias Cesar) and Alexander Farfan Suarez (alias Enrique Gafas), to board a Colombian military helicopter, which had been painted white to conceal its military association. Once the helicopter was in the air, the agents disarmed and detained the two rebels and revealed their true identities to the hostages, explaining that they were being moved not to a new rebel camp but to freedom.

Those liberated were: Ingrid Betancourt, a French-Colombian citizen, who had been abducted by FARC rebels in February 2002; three US defence contractors (Thomas Howes, Keith Stansell, and Marc Gonsalves), who had been captured in 2003; and 11 members of the Colombian security forces. The daring rescue operation was executed in 22 minutes and involved no bloodshed, according to Colombian Defence Minister Juan Manuel Santos. President Uribe described the rescue as "an intelligence operation comparable with the greatest epics of human history". Santos also revealed that Colombian intelligence agents had prepared meticulously for the secret operation after infiltrating the rebel cell that was holding the hostages. Upon her release from captivity, Betancourt, a former Colombian presidential candidate, described the rescue as "a miracle" and soon afterwards urged the FARC to release immediately and unconditionally an estimated 700 remaining hostages. Several prominent international figures, including former Cuban President Fidel Castro Ruz, Correa, Chávez, and Morales, also called on the FARC to release the remaining hostages.

The rescue of the hostages, along with the death of senior FARC member Raul Reyes in Colombia's military attack against the FARC camp in Ecuador in March (see above), were crushing blows for the rebels. The FARC also suffered a series of other setbacks in 2008. In January, Ricardo Palmera (also known as Simón Trinidad), a senior FARC commander who was extradited to the USA in December 2004, was convicted in a US court and sentenced to 60 years in prison for conspiring to kidnap Howes, Stansell, and Gonsalves, the three US defence contractors freed in July. Also in January, the FARC released two high-profile hostages: Consuelo Gonzalez, a former legislator who had been kidnapped by the rebels in 2001, and Clara Rojas, who had been kidnapped, along with Betancourt, in 2002. The freeing of the two women followed months of sensitive negotiations between rebel leaders and Venezuela's President Chávez, who had been invited by Uribe to negotiate with the FARC in August 2007, after Colombian negotiations were stalled by rebel demands for a withdrawal of government security forces from some jungle provinces and a suspension of US-backed operations against the FARC (see AR 2008, p. 177). On 4 February, in a sign of growing public resentment towards the FARC, more than a million people in Colombia, supported by groups in some 130 cities across the world, participated in protest marches to demand the release of other hostages. The protests, along with further mediation efforts led by Chávez, were followed later in February by the release of former Colombian legislators Gloria Polanco de Lozada, Orlando Beltran, Luis Eladio Perez, and Jorge Gechem, who had been held captive by the FARC since 2001 and 2002.

In another setback for the rebels, Nelly Avila Moreno (also known as "Karina") surrendered to Colombian security forces on 18 May. Avila Moreno was commander of the FARC's 47th front in the north-western Antioquia region and had become notorious as the most senior female rebel leader. It was also confirmed in May that Manuel Marulanda Velez, the nom de guerre of Pedro Antonio Marín, also known as Tirofijo ("Sureshot"), who had led the FARC since its creation in 1964, had died of a heart attack on 26 March at the reported age of 78. It was thought that leadership of the FARC had since been assumed by Alfonso Cano, regarded as the rebels' chief ideologist. In another demoralising blow for the rebels, Oscar Lizcano, a former Colombian legislator who had been held hostage since 2000 by the FARC, escaped from captivity on 24 October, after one of the rebels who had been holding him and who was known as "Isaza" broke ranks with the guerrillas and fled his remote rebel camp with the former legislator in tow.

Mounting public disquiet over Colombia's civil conflict also prompted the remaining 45 members of the Guevarista Revolutionary Army (ERG), a small faction of the leftist National Liberation Army (ELN), to demobilise on 21 August. Olimpo Sanchez Caro (also known as Cristobal), the ERG leader, claimed that the group's demobilisation was driven by a realisation that most Colombians "rejected the armed struggle". Despite the widespread anger against the FARC's armed campaign, the FARC was widely believed to have been responsible for a series of bomb attacks in 2008, including one in the town of Ituango on 14 August which left seven people dead and at least 51 others injured. A car bomb attack on 1 September, which killed four people and wounded at least 28 others in the city of Cali, was blamed on the Manuel Cepeda Vargas faction of the FARC.

In developments affecting the former United Self Defence Forces of Colombia (AUC), a demobilised right-wing paramilitary organisation, Mario Uribe Escobar, a former legislator and a cousin of President Uribe, was detained by the authorities on 22 April after being accused of links to paramilitaries. Uribe Escobar was accused of having met with senior AUC commanders in 2002 to seek their political support and plan operations designed to take control of farmland. His arrest was part of the widening "para-political" scandal, in which several leading figures in Colombia (including legislators) were accused of having had links with illegal right-wing paramilitaries (see AR 2008, p. 176). On 29 April Miguel Angel Mejia Munera, a former paramilitary leader who was wanted in the USA on charges of drug trafficking, was shot dead by the Colombian police. Mejia, widely described in the media as one of Colombia's most notorious drug barons, was killed during a shootout in a rural area near the northern town of Taraza. In May, Uribe extradited 14 AUC warlords to the USA, where they faced drug trafficking charges. One of these, Diego Adolfo Murillo Bejarano (also known as Adolfo Paz or Don Berna), on 17 June pleaded guilty in a US court to conspiring to smuggle cocaine into the USA. Also in the USA, on 9 October, a court convicted AUC commanders Ramiro Vanoy Murillo and Francisco Javier Zuluaga Lindo of drug trafficking offences and sentenced each man to more than 20 years in prison. Finally, in December, Diego Montoya, alleged to be one of Colombia's most powerful drug lords, was also extradited to the USA, where he faced murder and drug trafficking charges.

In Peru, rebels from the Shining Path (Sendero Luminoso), a Maoist guerrilla movement, some members of which had in recent years become involved in the illegal drug trafficking trade, were blamed for a series of attacks in 2008 against police officers and citizens. On 10 October, at least 12 soldiers and seven civilians were killed in an ambush on a military convoy. The attack happened in a remote coca-growing area of the Huancavelica region of south eastern Peru. Just five days later, two soldiers were killed in an ambush in Vizcatan, in south eastern Peru. Three police officers were also killed in an ambush in Luricocha, in the region of Ayacucho, on 17 November. The authorities blamed all three attacks on rebels from the resurgent Shining Path.

ELECTORAL DEVELOPMENTS. In Paraguay, Fernando Lugo Méndez, the leader of the Patriotic Alliance for Change (APC), a broad coalition of political parties and social movements, was on 15 August inaugurated as the country's new president. Lugo, a moderate leftist and former Roman Catholic bishop, won Paraguay's presidential election on 20 April, thereby marking the end of more than 60 years of rule by the National Republican Association—Colorado Party (ANR-PC). Lugo won the election with some 40 per cent of the vote, whilst his closest rival, the ANR-PC's presidential candidate, former education minister Blanca Ovelar, secured around 30 per cent. Voter turnout was around 65 per cent. During his election victory speech, Lugo vowed to govern with honesty, not corruption, and pledged to forge a "consensus cabinet" that would lead to a broad and pluralist administration. During his election campaign, Lugo had pledged to carry out agrarian reforms to redistribute land to Paraguay's poor peasant farmers. In simultaneous elections to Congress (the bicameral legislature), no single party won a majority of seats in either chamber, meaning that Lugo would be forced to negotiate with his political rivals to secure the passage of his legislative agenda.

In regional elections held in Venezuela on 23 November, the opposition made some notable gains but the left-wing and pro-presidential Unified Socialist Party of Venezuela (PSUV), which was formally inaugurated in January, won the majority of states and municipalities. Candidates from the PSUV, a party which President Chávez described in January as the "spearhead and vanguard" of Venezuela's ongoing "[Bolivarian] revolution", won 17 of the 22 governorships and 267 of the 328 mayoral posts contested. Opposition candidates won five governorships, including two in the most populous states of Miranda and Zulia, and the powerful mayoralty of Caracas.

Meanwhile, in municipal elections held in Chile on 23 October, the ruling Concertación coalition suffered its first nationwide electoral defeat since it assumed power in 1990 after the end of the military dictatorship of General Augusto Pinochet Ugarte. Official results indicated that Alliance, a coalition of centre-right opposition parties, won eight of the 14 regional capitals after securing some 41 per cent of the vote for mayors. Some observers speculated that Alliance's strong performance in the municipal elections had paved the way for the coalition to win power in presidential elections scheduled to take place in December 2009.

CONSTITUTIONAL, JUDICIAL, AND LEGISLATIVE DEVELOPMENTS. Divisions in Bolivia over attempts by President Morales to introduce a new constitution escalated into a constitutional crisis, which erupted in widespread violence and civil unrest in September. The crisis was compounded by government plans to divert tax revenue derived from natural gas resources from regional governments to Bolivia's federal pension fund, and attempts by opposition-controlled departments to secure regional autonomy. During the unrest, which occurred mainly in the wealthy opposition-controlled departments of Beni, Pando, Santa Cruz, and Tarija, opponents of Morales stormed government buildings, sabotaged natural gas pipelines, and fought with government supporters. At least 15 government supporters were shot dead during violence in Pando on 11 September, whilst more than 35 others were injured. Morales responded by imposing martial law in that department a day later, whilst Leopoldo Fernández, Pando's prefect (governor), was arrested and charged with genocide, after being accused of having hired foreign gunmen to perpetrate the killings. The unrest followed the holding of unofficial referendums in Santa Cruz on 4 May and in Beni, Pando, and Tarija on 22 June. Morales described the referendums as "illegal" and "resounding failures", but a substantial majority of voters, in all four departments, approved greater regional autonomy.

In an attempt to regain the initiative, Morales on 12 May signed a bill passed by the Senate (the upper chamber of Congress), which allowed the holding of a "recall referendum", in which the electorate would have the opportunity to reverse the election both of Morales in December 2005 and of nine departmental prefects. In the "recall referendum", duly held on 10 August, the mandates of Morales and six of the nine departmental prefects were confirmed. Official results showed that 67.41 per cent of participating voters confirmed Morales's presidential mandate, whilst the departmental prefects of Beni, Pando, Santa Cruz, and Tarija were confirmed in office by securing 64.25 per cent, 56.21 per cent, 66.43 per cent, and 58.06 per cent of the vote respectively.

In what was regarded as a triumph for Morales, Congress on 21 October agreed that a revised version of the proposed new constitution would be put to a national referendum in January 2009. Morales secured congressional approval for the revised version of the proposed constitution after agreeing to make concessions on 105 of the draft charter's 411 articles. Most notably, the revised text allowed Bolivia's president to seek only one five-year term in office, whereas the draft constitution approved by Congress in December 2007 permitted two consecutive five-year presidential terms (see AR 2008, pp. 172-73).

In a national referendum held in Ecuador on 28 September, 63.93 per cent of voters ratified a new constitution that had been approved in July by the country's 130-member Constituent Assembly. Voter turnout was 75.72 per cent. President Correa said that the results of the referendum were a "clear, historic victory" and urged citizens to help his government "achieve a brave, sovereign and dignified homeland...equitable, just and without misery". The new constitution became effective in October, thereby fulfilling one of the key pledges that Correa had made during his election campaign in 2006. Under the new constitution, Ecuador's president was entitled to seek a second consecutive four-year term in office and the government would assume new powers, including the authority to set interest rates.

In Venezuela, Chávez announced on 10 June that a controversial presidential decree on intelligence and counter-intelligence legislation, which he had enacted in May, had been repealed. The decree had been the subject of widespread criticism amongst opposition legislators, senior officers in the armed forces, and human rights groups. The criticism focused on a series of controversial articles contained in the legislation, most notably Article 16, which made provisions for punishing citizens who failed to co-operate with the security services by up to six years in prison. Chávez claimed that the legislation was necessary to protect national security, but he later acknowledged that the decree contained "errors" and assumed responsibility for the mistakes.

In July, Chávez also signed 26 decrees designed to increase state control over the armed forces, public administration, social security, banks, agricultural production, and the tourism industry. The decrees were signed on 31 July, the expiry date of the "enabling law" that the National Assembly (the unicameral legislature) had approved in January 2007. The "enabling law" had given Chávez authority to rule by decree for a period of 18 months in 11 specific areas of governance. In December, following the PSUV's victory in municipal elections, Chávez initiated a campaign to secure public support for the holding of a new referendum on constitutional reform. Most observers regarded the campaign as a renewed effort by Chávez to remove Venezuela's two-term presidential limit, following the government's narrow defeat in December 2007 in a national referendum on constitutional reforms (see AR 2008, p. 172).

In Colombia on 26 June, the legality of President Uribe's landslide election victory in May 2006 was challenged by the country's Supreme Court, which ruled that the Constitutional Court should review the legislation that had permitted Uribe to seek his unprecedented second consecutive term in office (see AR 2007, p. 173). The ruling came after former legislator Yidis Medina was convicted for accepting bribes in 2004 in exchange for supporting a bill that approved the constitutional changes, which allowed Uribe to seek his second consecutive term. Uribe dismissed the court's ruling as "political bias".

In Paraguay, President Nicanor Duarte Frutos submitted his resignation on 23 June, almost two months before the end of his five-year term in office. Duarte's resignation was widely regarded as an attempt to assume a seat in the Senate (the upper house), which he had won in legislative elections held in April. The president had contested the legislative elections because, under the constitution, he was barred from running for a second consecutive five-year term in presidential elections also held in April. However, legislators in the Senate were due to be sworn in on 1 July, six weeks before the end of Duarte's presidential term. Many opposition legislators opposed Duarte's resignation, claiming that he was constitutionally prohibited from running for another public office while occupying the presidency. When the Senate convened on 24 June to debate the issue, its members failed to muster a quorum, thereby preventing Duarte's resignation.

In Uruguay, President Tabare Vazquez on 12 November vetoed a bill (approved by Congress in early November) that legalised abortion in the first 12 weeks of pregnancy. If approved, the bill would have allowed women to terminate their pregnancy without restriction in the first 12 weeks of gestation. Under Uruguay's 1938 abortion law, the termination of a pregnancy was only permitted in cases involving rape or when the life of the woman or the foetus was endangered. Women who had abortions in Uruguay faced up to nine months in prison.

In Chile, President Bachelet's administration announced in September that it would use discretionary funds, constitutionally set aside for national emergencies, to help finance the beleaguered Transantiago transport system in Santiago. The announcement was made after the Constitutional Court ruled as unconstitutional a presidential decree issued in June that requested a US$400 million loan for Transantiago from the Inter-American Development Bank (IDB). The ruling stated that the use of discretionary funds required congressional approval. Bachelet's administration also suffered a setback on 4 April when the Constitutional Court overturned a presidential decree of 2006 that allowed public health centres to distribute the "morning-after" contraceptive pill to women aged 14 years or over. The ruling was made after opposition legislators asked the Court to ban the pill, on the grounds that it was equivalent to abortion, which was illegal in Chile.

THE ECONOMY. Many economies in the region had flourished for a decade amid favourable economic conditions, but it became increasingly clear in 2008 that the global financial crisis, the effects of which were first felt in 2007 in the USA, had infected South America. Amid the global turmoil, most of the region's stock exchanges suffered volatility in 2008 whilst currencies plummeted in value and projections of future growth were downgraded. GDP growth in Colombia, for example, slowed to around 3.4 per cent in 2008, according to *The Economist*. The need to reduce debt in tightening credit conditions and stimulate economic activity was evident in Colombia's US$62.5 billion budget for 2009, which Finance Minister Oscar Iván Zuluaga presented to Congress on 20 October. The budget included plans to spend US$16.5 billion on servicing Colombia's national debt and US$13.2 billion on public investment projects.

Even in Chile, a country that most analysts regarded as relatively well placed to weather the negative effects of the economic crisis, due to the country's sound public finances and a comfortable cushion of reserves, business and consumer confidence was falling sharply as the year ended. Peru, widely regarded as one of the region's strongest economies, managed to maintain robust domestic growth of around 9 per cent in 2008. However, President García in early December announced that his government would spend up to US$13.2 billion in 2009 on a range of public infrastructure projects, as part of broader attempts to maintain Peru's status as one of the world's best-performing economies.

Some analysts predicted that an economic downturn in oil-rich Venezuela, which suffered the effects of 2008's sharp fall in crude oil prices, could heighten opposition to Chavez's administration in 2009. In Ecuador, which also experienced the impact of falling oil prices in 2008, the central bank revealed on 22 December that its reserves were falling rapidly, prompting Correa to threaten what credit-rating agencies described as a possible "selective default" on Ecuador's foreign debt.

CORRUPTION AND HUMAN RIGHTS DEVELOPMENTS. In Peru, a bribery scandal that surfaced in October forced García to reshuffle his cabinet. The scandal emerged when audio tapes, which were broadcast on local television, implicated Alberto Quimper, a senior official of Perupetro, the state-owned oil licensing company, and Rómulo León, a prominent lobbyist and former legislator, in an alleged arrangement to steer profitable state oil contracts to Discover Petroleum, a small petroleum company based in Norway, in exchange for cash. Energy and Mines Minister Juan Valdivia Romero and César Gutiérrez, the head of Petroperu, the state-owned oil operations company, resigned on 6 October, after being implicated in the scandal, which Peruvian media inevitably dubbed "Petrogate". Prime Minister Jorge del Castillo became embroiled in the scandal on 7 October, prompting him and all other members of the cabinet to resign from their posts. Two days later, García reinstated 10 of his ministers and appointed seven new ones, including Yehude Simon, a popular left-wing governor of the northern region of Lambayeque, who replaced del Castillo as prime minister. On 21 October prosecutors brought charges, including those of corruption, influence trafficking, and criminal conspiracy, against 14 people accused of involvement in the scandal.

In a corruption scandal involving Venezuela (dubbed the "suitcase scandal" by the media), a US court on 3 November convicted Venezuelan national Franklin Duran as guilty of having acted and conspired in the USA as an unregistered foreign agent of Venezuela. Duran was one of five men charged in December 2007 in connection with what US prosecutors described as a conspiracy by the Venezuelan government to take US$800,000 in cash to Argentina to help fund the presidential election campaign of Cristina Fernández de Kirchner. Carlos Kauffmann, a Venezuelan businessman, pleaded guilty to similar charges in March, as did Uruguayan citizen Rodolfo Edgardo Wanseele Paciello in April.

In human rights developments in Peru, the then prime minister del Castillo on 18 January accused Peru's former president, Alberto Keinya Fujimori, of having ordered a paramilitary group to kidnap Castillo during Fujimori's seizure of power (known as a "self coup" or "autogolpe") in 1992. Castillo claimed that after Fujimori suspended Peru's legislature and judiciary in April 1992, he had been held captive and tortured and that Fujimori's security forces had also tried to assassinate current President García. Castillo's accusations were part of his testimony to a court, which was trying Fujimori on human rights charges relating to his alleged authorisation of the deployment of death squads to carry out two massacres and two kidnappings in the 1990s. During the same trial, Pedro Supo, a former member of the notorious death squad "grupo colina", testified that an amnesty law approved by Fujimori in 1995 had been negotiated with the paramilitaries in exchange for a promise never to disclose the government's involvement in the massacres. Supo admitted to having participated in five operations to "eliminate" suspected guerrillas of the Shining Path and said that the attacks were authorised by Peru's "high command". The trial of Fujimori on human rights charges resumed on 14 July, after being temporarily suspended to allow the former president to undergo surgery to remove a pre-cancerous lesion on his tongue. The trial, which had opened in Lima on 10 December 2007, was entering its final phases as the year ended. If convicted in the human rights case, Fujimori faced up to 30 years in prison.

In a separate case involving Fujimori, Peru's Supreme Court on 15 April upheld a six-year prison sentence handed down to the former president in December 2007, following his conviction for abuse of authority. The sentence was delivered after Fujimori was found guilty of having ordered an aide in November 2000 to break into a house where evidence documenting corruption in the government had been hidden (see AR 2008, pp. 169-70).

Also in Peru, the authorities announced in May that the remains of at least 25 people had been discovered in a mass grave in the highland town of Putis, in the southern region of Ayacucho. The discovery of the grave, which was thought to contain the remains of people executed by the military on suspicion of having links with the Shining Path, was part of an ongoing investigation into atrocities committed by the security forces and Shining Path guerrillas in 1980-2000.

In Colombia, President Uribe dismissed 25 senior army officers in October over the extra-judicial killings of at least 11 civilians, who disappeared from Bogota in early 2008. The bodies of the 11 civilians (all men) were discovered in August and September in mass graves in north east Colombia. Colombian officials believed that the men were killed after rogue military officers (or criminals working for them) kidnapped or lured them from poor areas of Bogota with the false promise of work.

Maria del Pilar Hurtado, the head of the Administrative Department of Security (DAS), Colombia's intelligence service, resigned from her post on 23 October after the agency was accused of spying on politicians from opposition parties. Allegations that intelligence agents were "spying" on legislators also emerged in Ecuador in May when Correa was forced to admit that some military intelligence agents had spied on members of the country's Constituent Assembly. Correa denied having authorised the "spying", claiming that middle-ranking officers had, on their own initiative, intercepted communications between assembly members in December 2007 and January 2008.

The authorities in Chile continued their attempts to bring to justice the perpetrators of human rights violations committed during the country's "dirty war" era (1973-90). On 30 June, for example, General (retd) Manuel Contreras Sepúlveda, the former head of the National Intelligence Directorate (DINA—the notorious secret police), was handed two consecutive life sentences for the murders of General Carlos Prats, the former commander in chief of the armed forces, and his wife Sofia Cuthbert. Prats and Cuthbert were killed in a car bomb attack in Buenos Aires (the capital of Argentina) in 1974. Contreras was already serving prison sentences for other crimes committed during Chile's "dirty war". In May, 98 former employees of DINA were arrested in connection with an ongoing investigation into the kidnapping and murder of 42 people during "Operation Colombo", a campaign in 1974-75 against opponents of the military regime. DINA had operated notorious detention centres in the "dirty war".

In Bolivia, the authorities on 11 November formally requested the extradition from the USA of the former president, Gonzálo Sánchez de Lozada, in office 1993-97 and again 2002-03; the former defence minister, Carlos Sanchez Berzain; and the former hydrocarbons minister, Jorge Berindoague Alcocer. In October 2007, public prosecutors had brought nine criminal charges, including that of genocide, against Sánchez de Lozada.

Earlier in the year, in Uruguay, President Vázquez repealed a "secret of state" immunity provision, which had allowed police and military officers to withhold information about their role in human rights violations during the country's military dictatorship of 1973-85. Under the terms of the repeal, enacted on 25 February, police and army personnel were to be held accountable if they had carried out orders deemed "manifestly illegal".

Kurt Perry

V MIDDLE EAST AND NORTH AFRICA

ISRAEL

CAPITAL: Jerusalem   AREA: 22,070 sq km   POPULATION: 7,172,000 ('07)
OFFICIAL LANGUAGE: Hebrew   POLITICAL SYSTEM: multiparty republic
HEAD OF STATE: President Shimon Peres (since July '07)
RULING PARTIES: Kadima leads coalition, with Labour Party, Sephardic Torah Guardians (Shas), and
   Pensioners of Israel to the Knesset (Gil)
HEAD OF GOVERNMENT: Prime Minister Ehud Olmert (Kadima) (caretaker since Sept. '08)
CURRENCY: shekel (end-'08 £1=Sh5.4304, US$1=Sh3.7770)
GNI PER CAPITA: US $21,900, $25,930 at PPP ('07)

On 8 May celebrations took place across Israel to mark the 60th anniversary of the founding of the Jewish state. Israel had declared itself independent on 14 May, 1948, three years after the end of World War II, a conflict which had included the extermination of 6 million Jews in the Nazi Holocaust. (The commemoration of independence was calculated according to the Jewish lunar calendar.) Palestinians marked this same anniversary as al-Nakba ("the Catastrophe") and they held demonstrations on 8 May and 15 May to commemorate the suffering, which had befallen them since Israel's creation (see AR 1948, pp. 301-08).

Almost 60 years after its foundation, Israel began the year in a state of some anxiety—a hangover from its failed war in Lebanon in mid-2006—and ended it in serious conflict with the Iranian-backed Islamist Hamas, which controlled the Gaza Strip. In a busy year both domestically and externally, the possibility—the probability—of Iran constructing a viable nuclear arsenal was a constant, nagging, underlying concern. In early June, Lieutenant-General (retd) Shaul Mofaz, the Iranian-born transport minister and former chief of the general staff of the Israeli Defence Forces (IDF), told *Yedioth Ahronoth*, the country's most widely circulated newspaper, that an attack on Iran's nuclear sites was becoming "unavoidable". If Iran continued with its programme for developing nuclear weapons, Mofaz warned, "we will attack it". Internationally, the concern was that Israel might need to use its own nuclear weapons to destroy the Islamic Republic's nascent programme. In what appeared to some to be a well-timed intervention, former US President Jimmy Carter had in May—at the annual literary Hay-on-Wye festival in Wales, of all places—publicly acknowledged one of the world's worst-kept secrets: that Israel possessed at least 150 of its own nuclear weapons.

The Winograd commission established in September 2006 (see AR 2007, p. 185) to examine the government's and the military's handling of Israel's war in Lebanon issued its final report on 30 January. Prime Minister Ehud Olmert escaped any serious criticism over the handling of the war, although Eliyahu Winograd, a respected retired judge, found "serious failings and shortcomings" in Israel's political and military leadership. The former president of the Tel Aviv district court said that Israel had "embarked on a prolonged war that it initiated, which ended without a clear Israeli victory from a military standpoint". The Lebanese Shia Hezbullah movement, "a quasi-military organisation", had, Winograd said, managed to withstand "the strongest army in the Middle East for weeks". Winograd found "serious failings and shortcomings in the decision-making processes and staff-work in the political and the military echelons" and "serious failings and flaws in the quality of preparedness, decision-making and performance" in the high command of the IDF, especially in the army. Furthermore, he found "serious failings and flaws in the lack of strategic thinking and planning, in both the political and the military echelons" and "severe failings and flaws in the defence of the civilian population and in coping with its being attacked by rockets".

The year proved somewhat testing for Olmert, who ended it at the helm of a lame duck administration. Olmert, a former mayor of Jerusalem, had become prime minister in early 2006, when Ariel Sharon had suffered a severe stroke (see AR 2007, p. 183). He experienced a major setback in January when the far-right Yisrael Beiteinu withdrew from his Kadima-led ruling coalition in protest at the government's decision to hold talks with the Palestinians (which proved fruitless) on the "core issues" of the conflict, including borders, refugees, and the status of Jerusalem. Yisrael Beiteinu, which controlled 11 seats in the 120-member Knesset (the unicameral legislature), had joined the coalition in October 2006. The withdrawal of Yisrael Beiteinu—which advocated the reduction of Israel's Arab population through the redrawing of its borders with a future Palestinian state, in conjunction with efforts to increase Jewish immigration—left Olmert's coalition with only a slim majority in the Knesset. The leader of Yisrael Beiteinu, Avigdor Lieberman, a former Moldovan nightclub bouncer, resigned as deputy prime minister with responsibility for strategic threats against Israel, a post that he had held since October 2006.

Ultimately though, Olmert was brought down by the constant barrage of corruption charges levelled against him. In early May it emerged that the police had opened a new, and ultimately damning, investigation into Olmert, questioning him over his alleged receipt of campaign donations from Morris Talansky—a Long Island financier, who had a reputation as a big political donor in the USA—several years before he became prime minister in early 2006. Olmert was questioned at his official residence about donations raised by Talansky to fund elections for the mayoralty of Jerusalem and primary elections in Likud, the political party to which Olmert belonged at the time. Olmert was already under police investigation over his purchase of a house in Jerusalem, the city he had once served as mayor. Furthermore, in April 2007 the state comptroller had recommended a police investigation into allegations that Olmert had procured investment opportunities for an associate when he was in office as industry and trade minister (2003-05). Appearing before the Jerusalem District Court in late May, Talansky testified that he had given Olmert around US$150,000 over 15 years, including payments in envelopes stuffed with cash.

Olmert finally bowed to steadily mounting pressure in late July, announcing his intention to resign as prime minister. In a dramatic televised address, a tearful prime minister declared that he would not stand in the Kadima party leadership contest scheduled for 17 September and would leave office as soon as a new party leader was chosen. He told the nation: "I will step aside properly in an honourable and responsible way, and afterwards I will prove my innocence." Tzipi Livni, the vice prime minister and foreign minister, was subsequently elected as the new leader of Kadima, putting her on track to replace Olmert as prime minister. Livni, who had served as a lieutenant in the IDF and had worked for Mossad (the Israeli intelligence agency) during the early 1980s, defeated Shaul Mofaz in a tight contest. Following his narrow defeat, Mofaz announced that he would not accept a ministerial post in a future government headed by Livni, saying that he intended to find "additional ways to contribute to the state of Israel and my family". Following the poll, Olmert handed in his resignation as prime minister to President Shimon Peres, but was asked to remain in office in a caretaker capacity while Livni attempted to form a working coalition.

In late October Livni announced that she had been unable to form a new government and asked Peres to declare early elections. Although the Labour Party, headed by Defence Minister Ehud Barak, had agreed to join a Livni-led coalition, smaller parties—which held the balance of power in the Knesset—made far-reaching political and budgetary demands. Crucially, the ultra-Orthodox Sephardic Torah Guardians (Shas), announced that it would not join Livni's government after failing to reach agreement on a pledge to increase child allowance for large families and a promise to keep Jerusalem entirely under Israeli sovereignty and off the negotiating table with the Palestinians.

The Knesset was dissolved on 10 November ahead of elections scheduled for 10 February, 2009. Shortly afterwards it was revealed that renowned Israeli author Amos Oz had joined a number of intellectuals and public figures to form a new left-wing party in an attempt to defeat the resurgent right-wing Likud, which was leading in the opinion polls. Among those who attended a meeting in Tel Aviv to launch the new, as yet unnamed party, were former Labour cabinet minister Uzi Baram, Peace Now founder and former Labour member of the Knesset Tzali Reshef, and former Knesset Speaker Avraham Burg.

Elections for the new mayor of Jerusalem were held on 11 November and resulted in victory for Nir Barkat, a secular, hawkish entrepreneur who had made a fortune selling antivirus software. Barkat, a 49-year old former paratroops commander, had narrowly lost to the ultra-Orthodox incumbent Uri Lupoliansky when he ran for mayor in 2003. On this occasion, Barkat won some 52 per cent of the vote and defeated Meir Porush, an ultra-Orthodox rabbi, by 9 percentage points. After his victory, Barkat pledged that he would "protect Jerusalem" and "be the mayor of everyone". He promised to attract tourism and investment, "especially high-tech and biotech".

Several eminent Israelis died during the year. Major General Dan Shomron, who led the epic rescue of over 100 Israelis and French Jews from Entebbe airport in Uganda in 1976 (see AR 1976, pp. 179, 220), died in February, aged 70. Yosef "Tommy" Lapid, television presenter, journalist, and leader of the staunchly secularist and liberal Shinui Party, died in June, aged 76.

There were a number of high profile visitors to Israel during the year to celebrate the Jewish state's 60th anniversary. In mid-May, US President George W.

Bush addressed the Knesset, telling its members that the USA was proud to be the "closest ally and best friend in the world" of a nation that was a "homeland for the chosen people" and had "worked tirelessly for peace and...fought valiantly for freedom". President Nicolas Sarkozy of France visited Israel in June, but he proved to be a more critical guest than his US counterpart. In an address to the Knesset, Sarkozy called on Israel to share sovereignty of Jerusalem with the Palestinians and to stop building settlements in the occupied territories.

Darren Sagar

PALESTINE—EGYPT—JORDAN—SYRIA—LEBANON—IRAQ

PALESTINE

ADMINISTRATIVE CAPITAL: Ramallah   INTENDED CAPITAL: East Jerusalem   AREA: 6,020 sq km
  (West Bank & Gaza)   POPULATION: 3,869,000 ('07)
OFFICIAL LANGUAGE: Arabic   POLITICAL SYSTEM: multiparty republic under partial Israeli occupation
HEAD OF STATE: President Mahmoud Abbas (since Jan '05)
RULING PARTIES: Hamas (in Gaza); Fatah (in West Bank)
HEAD OF GOVERNMENT: Prime Minister Salam Khalid Abdallah Fayyad (since June '07)
CURRENCY: Jordanian dinar (end '08 £1=JD1.0190, US$1=JD0.7088), and Israeli shekel (end-'08 £1=Sh5.4304, US$1=Sh3.7770)
GNI PER CAPITA: US$1,230, -

ON 27 December Israel launched a military campaign in the Gaza Strip, code-named "Operation Cast Lead", with the stated intent of halting Hamas rocket attacks and targeting the Islamic Resistance Movement's members and infrastructure. A six-month truce between Hamas and Israel had expired on 19 December, after the two sides failed to agree on conditions to extend the ceasefire, which had been brokered by Egyptian intelligence officials (see p. 214). Hamas denounced Israel for not lifting its blockade of the Gaza Strip, which was the cause of huge civilian hardship, whilst Israel blamed Hamas for the continued rocket attacks against Israeli towns close to the border with Gaza.

In a statement posted on its website on 19 December, Hamas—the controlling Palestinian faction in the Gaza Strip since June 2007 (see AR 2008, pp. 184-88)— said that Israel had violated agreements by continuing its economic blockade of Gaza, launching military attacks into the territory, and continuing to target Hamas members in the West Bank. The statement said: "We hold the enemy fully responsible for ending the truce and we confirm that the Palestinian resistance factions headed by Hamas will act." There was no immediate Israeli response to the Hamas statement and over the weekend of 20-21 December Palestinian militants—generally believed to be members of Islamic Jihad, rather than of Hamas— fired in excess of 50 rockets and mortar shells into Israel. The rockets, largely rudimentary home-made Qassams (simple steel structures filled with explosives), failed to kill any Israelis, but they disrupted the lives of those living in settlements close to Gaza, including Beersheba and Ashdod, and caused widespread fear and anxiety. Militants continued to fire rockets into Israel, once again causing no injuries but generating widespread panic. Israel made no military response and, on 26 December, even re-opened its border with the Gaza Strip to allow the delivery of relief supplies. Close to 100 trucks were allowed into the Strip to deliver medicine, fuel, cooking gas, and other vital goods. Israel had severely restricted access to the Gaza Strip since Hamas had taken control of the territory in June 2007, a blockade that was bitterly resented by the Palestinians, who saw it as a collective punishment of the civilian population.

The Israeli military finally acted on 27 December, launching a major air assault on the Gaza Strip, using fighter jets, helicopter gunships, and unmanned drones to hit a huge array of targets. The air assault was the largest offensive targeted at the Gaza Strip since the June 1967 Six Day War, when the territory was seized from Egypt. The Israeli air force, supported by the navy, attacked Hamas bases, training camps, headquarters, and offices in Gaza. Civilian infrastructure, including mosques, houses, and schools, were also targeted. Israel claimed that many of these buildings had stocked weapons or militant personnel, a claim denied by Hamas. In one air raid, carried out on 28 December, dozens of tunnels running under the border between Gaza and Egypt, and which were used for smuggling arms and civilian supplies, were destroyed. As the year drew to a close, Israel threatened to escalate its offensive, placing tanks and armoured troop carriers close to the border with Gaza and calling up reservists for a possible ground incursion into the territory. Israeli Defence Minister Ehud Barak told US television on 28 December that "if boots on the ground will be needed, they will be there." By 29 December, Palestinian medical officials claimed that the death toll in Gaza had risen to 325. The UN, meanwhile, stated that 62 women and children were among the dead.

The UN Security Council, meeting late on 27 December, had expressed "serious concern" at the escalation of the situation in Gaza and called for an immediate halt to all violence. The USA, Israel's chief sponsor, refrained from criticising the military offensive. A statement issued on behalf of US President George W. Bush on 28 December simply said that it was "completely unacceptable" for Hamas to launch attacks on Israel. On the same day, US President-elect Barack Obama appeared to line up behind the Bush administration in support of Israel's military operation. Speaking on US television, Obama's senior adviser, David Axelrod, initially repeated the Obama team's formula that there could only be one US president at a time and that the president was currently George Bush. However, he then went on to recall comments that Obama had made in July at Sderot, the Israeli frontline town that was the main target of rocket attacks from Palestinian militants in Gaza. At the time, Obama said: "If somebody was sending rockets into my house where my two daughters sleep at night, I'm going to do everything in my power to stop that. I would expect Israelis to do the same thing." A similar sentiment had earlier been expressed by Condoleezza Rice, the outgoing US secretary of state, who said: "the United States strongly condemns the repeated rocket and mortar attacks against Israel and holds Hamas responsible for breaking the ceasefire and for the renewal of violence in Gaza."

The Israeli military assault sparked anti-Israeli protests across the wider Arab world. Speaking on 28 December, Sheikh Hassan Nasrallah, secretary general of the Shia Lebanese group Hezbullah, urged Egyptians to protest in their "millions" to force open their country's border with Gaza. He said that if the Egyptian government did not comply, it would be complicit with the Israeli military in killing Palestinians. On 30 December President Mohammed Hosni Mubarak of Egypt gave his strongest condemnation of the Israeli offensive, reflecting mounting pressure from protesters at home and across the Arab world. In a televised address to the nation, Mubarak accused Israeli leaders of "savage aggression against the Palestinians" and warned, "Your blood-stained hands are stirring up feelings of enormous anger."

As the year ended, Israeli ground forces were poised on the border with Gaza. Whilst the inevitable expansion of the operation into the urban battlefields represented Hamas's greatest tactical opportunity for inflicting losses on the Israeli Defence Forces (IDF), many analysts believed that Israel might succeed, at least temporarily, in depleting the military wing of Hamas, the Izz al-Din Qassem battalions. However, many agreed that if Hamas remained in a position to reassert its control over Gaza following the Israeli assault, then the conflict was likely to have the effect of strengthening the organisation and increasing its level of popular support. Somewhat ironically, the Israeli military operation also appeared to have removed the most obvious path to Hamas's demise: Palestinian presidential and parliamentary elections, scheduled for, but unlikely to be held in, either 2009 (according to Hamas) or 2010 (according to Fatah). The Israeli attack had also had a seriously negative impact on the secular and moderate West Bank-based Fatah. Charges of collusion between some senior Fatah leaders—including President Mahmoud Abbas himself—and Israel had put Fatah on the defensive. The effect was not only to undercut Fatah's level of popular support but also to divide the movement over its future direction.

Perhaps the most alarming possibility was that Salafi jihadists with ideological links to al-Qaida would be in a position to benefit from a weakened Hamas. By most estimates, the Salafi jihadist presence in Gaza did not exceed 200 fighters, so a serious political challenge to Hamas from the more extremist flank of Palestinian politics was unlikely. However, as Palestinians buried their dead—several hundred of them civilians—the general climate was one that favoured calls for revenge.

On the surface, the Hamas-Fatah split of 2007 had appeared to serve well both Abbas and Israel. In the West Bank, Abbas had formed an administration based on his own nationalist Fatah movement, which supported a two-state solution. Following the November 2007 Annapolis Middle East peace conference (see AR 2008, p. 188), Abbas's government had regained widespread international support and Israel had resumed final status negotiations with Fatah. However, whilst the year saw the usual rounds of high-level diplomatic manoeuvring, Fatah and the Israelis failed to make any progress in negotiations related to a future Palestinian state. The Annapolis conference had set a deadline of the end of 2008 for the two sides to reach agreement on the core issues (including borders, the future status of Jerusalem, and the fate of the families of Palestinian refugees who had fled or been forced from their homes in the war of 1948), but negotiations failed to make any progress. The Fatah-Hamas split meant that neither the Israeli nor the Palestinian public appeared to take the negotiating process seriously. Palestinians wanted a state that included the Gaza Strip, an aspiration that Abbas could not achieve. Israelis, on the other hand, saw little point in concessions when Abbas evidently could not sign on behalf of all Palestinians and had little chance of bringing a semblance of peace on the Gaza front. Furthermore, contrary to Israeli and US expectations, the siege of Gaza throughout 2008 did not provoke popular rebellion against Hamas. Instead, the organisation solidified its rule, its authority growing amid worsening humanitarian conditions as it provided essential support to many Palestinian families.

Throughout the year humanitarian conditions in Gaza continued to deteriorate due to the acute shortages in food and medical supplies needed by approximately 1.5 million Palestinian civilians living in the Strip. A press release issued by the Palestinian Centre for Human Rights (PCHR) in mid-November claimed that the amounts of food and medicines allowed into Gaza by Israel did not meet the minimum daily needs of the Palestinian civilian population and, in fact, constituted less than 10 per cent of the amounts that had been allowed into the territory before the Israeli blockade had been imposed in June 2007. The PCHR noted that Israel had further tightened the siege in early November and that, as a consequence, Gaza's sole power plant had been shut down and at least 30 per cent of the population lacked electricity. There was also a shortage of drinking water, especially in high buildings, due to repeated cuts in electricity supply. Many bakeries had ceased production because of a lack of cooking gas, electricity, and flour. Health facilities were facing a serious crisis due to the shortage in electrical and fuel supplies, which had in effect limited their ability to provide even basic medical services to patients.

Nobel Peace Prize laureate Archbishop Desmond Tutu of South Africa visited Gaza in late May at the head of a UN Human Rights Council (UNHRC) delegation, charged with investigating the shelling by the Israeli military of a house in Beit Hanoun in November 2006 that had resulted in the deaths of 19 Palestinians, including 13 members of the Athamneh family (see AR 2007, p. 190). At the end of his visit, Tutu said that he was in a "state of shock" and described Gaza as "a forlorn, deserted, desolate and eerie place". He called for an end to the "abominable" Israeli blockade of the territory and condemned a "culture of impunity" on both sides of the conflict.

In October the government of Japan convened the fourth conference for confidence-building between the Israelis and the Palestinians. The Israeli delegation was led by Interior Minister Meir Sheetrit and the Palestinian delegation by chief negotiator Saeb Erekat. Topics under discussion at the conference included the Japanese-promoted "Corridor for Peace and Prosperity" initiative, which consisted of establishing an agro-industrial park in the West Bank and exporting manufactured goods through Jordan to the Gulf countries.

The Palestinian national football team played its first ever game on home soil on 26 October, drawing 1-1 in a friendly match with Jordan. The match took place at a newly refurbished stadium in the West Bank town of al-Ram and had the blessing of both rival Palestinian factions, Fatah and Hamas.

George Habash, founder of the radical Marxist-Leninist Popular Front for the Liberation of Palestine (PFLP), died in Jordan on 26 January, aged 81 or 82. Habash had been one of the main leaders of the "rejectionist" wing of the Palestinian national movement and had been resolute in his insistence that under no circumstances should any negotiations be held with the Israeli state for a peaceful resolution of the Israeli-Palestinian conflict. During the 1970s, Habash had carried out a number of joint terrorist operations with other revolutionaries, such as the Japanese Red Army (at the Lod airport attack in 1972), the West German Red Army Faction, and the Venezuelan Ilich Ramírez Sánchez ("Carlos the Jackal"). Although his tactics softened in the 1980s, Habash was a stubborn opponent of the 1993 Oslo Accords and he refused to set foot in the areas under the nominal control of the Palestinian authority.

Darren Sagar

EGYPT

CAPITAL: Cairo   AREA: 1,001,450 sq km   POPULATION: 75,467,000 ('07)
OFFICIAL LANGUAGE: Arabic   POLITICAL SYSTEM: multiparty republic
HEAD OF STATE: President Mohammed Hosni Mubarak (since '81)
RULING PARTY: National Democratic Party (NDP)
HEAD OF GOVERNMENT: Prime Minister Ahmed Mahmud Mohammed Nazif (since July '04)
MAIN IGO MEMBERSHIPS (NON-UN): AL, OAPEC, AU, COMESA, OIC, NAM, Francophonie
CURRENCY: Egyptian pound (end-'08 £1=E£7.9238, US$1=E£5.5113)
GNI PER CAPITA: US$1,580, $5,400 at PPP ('07)

THE situation of the Palestinians in Gaza was a constant preoccupation of the Egyptian government during 2008. The year started with Palestinians forcing their way over the closed border with Egypt in search of relief from the Israeli blockade that had been in place since the takeover of Gaza by Hamas, the main Palestinian Islamist group, in mid-2007. This incident was followed by a series of military confrontations between Israeli and Palestinian forces in and around Gaza until a six-month ceasefire, achieved through the mediation of Egypt's chief of military intelligence Omar Suleiman, went into effect in June. Egypt made use of the relative calm to try to promote reconciliation between the rival Palestinian factions (Fatah and Hamas).

One of Egypt's goals was to enable officials of the Palestinian National Authority (PNA), which had been ousted from the Gaza Strip in 2007, to return to man the crossing points into Egypt under EU supervision, as had been stipulated in a 2005 international agreement covering access to the territory after Israel's withdrawal during that year (see AR 2005, pp. 176-77). However, the reconciliation talks foundered on the refusal of Hamas to attend, owing to its perception that Egypt was biased towards the PNA. The Gaza ceasefire broke down in early November after an Israeli cross-border raid, ostensibly carried out in order to destroy a tunnel that Israel considered to pose a threat to the security of its soldiers. Egypt strongly urged

Hamas to seek a renewal of the ceasefire, to take effect once the existing one formally expired on 19 December. However, Hamas persisted in firing rockets over the border, thus giving Israel grounds to launch a major offensive against Gaza on 27 December, which had clearly been carefully prepared over many months (see pp. 210-12). Egypt came under intense pressure from Hamas's allies, both around the Middle East—notably Syria, Iran, and the Lebanese Hezbullah movement—and from the domestic opposition, to open its borders with Gaza to allow unrestricted entry of food, fuel, and medicines, as well as fighters and weapons. However, the Egyptian president, Mohammed Hosni Mubarak, insisted that he would only do this as part of a negotiated settlement based on the 2005 agreement. With the support of France, Egypt embarked on a diplomatic effort to resolve the Gaza crisis, using its unique position as mediator between Hamas and Israel.

Besides the Gaza problem, the state of the domestic economy was a major concern for the Egyptian government during 2008. The rise in world prices of fuel and staple foods in 2007 and in the first half of 2008 resulted in a surge in Egypt's inflation rate, which rose to over 20 per cent. The government's problems were exacerbated when demand for subsidised flour and bread increased sharply, as relatively well-off consumers could no longer afford to pay the higher prices of better quality unsubsidised foodstuffs. Shortages of bread prompted sporadic outbreaks of unrest in early 2008. However, the government ultimately managed to keep the situation under control, through increasing its purchases of wheat and through restructuring its subsidised bread system by separating the operations of flour wholesalers from those of bakeries. It also imposed a ban on the export of rice, in order to safeguard supplies for the local market. At the start of May Mubarak announced a package of measures aimed at alleviating the hardship of poorer Egyptians. These included a 30 per cent increase in all public sector salaries; a 50 per cent rise in the pay levels of local government employees; a 20 per cent hike in pensions; and the extension of the ration card system to 15 million new beneficiaries, enabling them to gain access to subsidised sugar, rice, and cooking oil. In order to cover some of the costs of these salary and benefit increases, the government pushed through a number of revenue raising measures, including increasing prices for petrol, natural gas (for heavy industrial users), cigarettes, and vehicle duties.

The grievances of Egypt's poorer citizens against the government were amplified in October when more than 100 people were killed in a landslide in eastern Cairo, when several tonnes of rock fell from the Mokattam hills onto slum dwellings. The official rescue efforts were widely criticised for being tardy and ineffective, prompting accusations that the government discriminated against the poor.

Thus, the Mubarak regime survived an increasingly difficult year, but only managed to maintain basic civil order through resorting to costly fiscal measures and to heavy repression of dissent, cracking down particularly hard on the Muslim Brotherhood, which had a strong ideological connection with the Palestinian Hamas movement. Despite rising popular resentment at the pro-business government, which he appointed in 2004, Mubarak made no cabinet changes during the year, and kept faith with Ahmed Nazif as prime minister.

David Butter

JORDAN

CAPITAL: Amman   AREA: 88,780 sq km   POPULATION: 5,719,000 ('0 7)
OFFICIAL LANGUAGE: Arabic   POLITICAL SYSTEM: multiparty monarchy
HEAD OF STATE: King Abdullah ibn al-Husain (since Feb '99)
HEAD OF GOVERNMENT: Prime Minister Nader Dahabi (since Nov '07)
MAIN IGO MEMBERSHIPS (NON-UN): AL, OIC, NAM
CURRENCY: Jordanian dinar (end-'08 £1=JD1.0190, US$1=JD0.7088)
GNI PER CAPITA: US$2,850, $5,160 at PPP ('07)

THE role of the Palestinian majority in Jordan and its connections with the Islamic Action Front (IAF)—the local arm of the Muslim Brotherhood—was a persistent concern for King Abdullah II in 2008. At the start of the year, the IAF underwent a process of review and reorganisation following its poor showing in the November 2007 general election, when it won only six seats in the 110-seat Chamber of Deputies (the lower house of the bicameral National Assembly), compared with 17 in the previous election (see AR 2008, pp. 191-92). In March the Jordanian Muslim Brotherhood elected a new Shura Council, its main policy body, in which hardliners made significant advances. The movement also elected a new leader, Hammam Said, a Palestinian associated with the hardline camp. He was the first Palestinian to take charge of the Jordanian Muslim Brotherhood. The same month several thousand people in Jordan took part in demonstrations in solidarity with Hamas, the main Palestinian Islamist movement, after it came under military attack from Israel in Gaza.

Over the next few months the king sanctioned a shift in policy towards Hamas, as his chief of military intelligence, Mohammed Dahabi—a brother of the prime minister, Nader Dahabi, who was appointed in November 2007—sought to open a dialogue with the Palestinian group. However, when tensions between Israel and Hamas rose again at the end of 2008, the king signalled an end to this policy by replacing the intelligence chief.

In another important change of personnel at the highest levels of the Jordanian state, King Abdullah in September dismissed Bassem Awadallah from his position as head of the Royal Court. Awadallah had long been one of the king's closest confidants, but had often attracted controversy through appearing to overstep his powers. His departure from the Royal Court position appeared to be related to criticism from sections of the media of a number of lucrative sales of land to Arab real estate developers. The king responded to the criticism in a lengthy interview with Petra, the state news agency, in August, maintaining that there was no impropriety. However, it was clear that there was a strong public perception that members of the king's inner circle may have been exploiting their privileged position for gain, and Awadallah appeared to have paid the price. His replacement was Nasser Lozi, a former had of the national airline, who pledged to work closely with other institutions in the government. One of the criticisms of Awadallah, both in the Royal Court position (which he had held since November 2007) and in earlier posts, was that he tended to build up parallel centres of power, accountable to neither the government nor the National Assembly.

David Butter

SYRIA

CAPITAL: Damascus   AREA: 185,180 sq km   POPULATION: 19,891,000 ('07)
OFFICIAL LANGUAGE: Arabic   POLITICAL SYSTEM: multiparty republic
HEAD OF STATE: President Bashar Assad (since July '00)
RULING PARTIES: Baath Arab Socialist Party and six allies in the National Progressive Front
HEAD OF GOVERNMENT: Prime Minister Mohammed Naji al-Atri (since Sept '03)
MAIN IGO MEMBERSHIPS (NON-UN): AL, OAPEC, OIC, NAM
CURRENCY: Syrian pound (end-'08 £1=S£66.2107, US$1=S£46.0500)
GNI PER CAPITA: US$1,760, $4,370 at PPP ('07)

PRESIDENT Bashar Assad made significant progress in 2008 in improving Syria's international relations. Ties with France were put back on an even keel, mainly owing to Assad's decision to establish diplomatic relations with Lebanon; at the end of the year, Syria initialled an amended text of its association agreement with the EU, which had been frozen since 2004. However, Syria's ties with a number of powerful Arab states, notably Saudi Arabia and Egypt, remained fraught, and the USA continued to maintain a largely hostile stance towards the Syrian government.

At the start of the year Assad's primary focus was to ensure the success of the Arab League summit meeting, which was to be held in Damascus in March, marking the first time that Syria had hosted such an event since the Arab League was founded in 1945. These preparations were disturbed on 12 February, when Imad Mughniyeh, the head of military operations in Lebanon's Hezbullah movement, was assassinated in Damascus by a bomb placed in his car. Mughniyeh had been implicated in a series of bomb attacks on Western targets in Beirut and in the Gulf in the 1980s, since when he had dropped out of view. He was widely assumed to have taken refuge in the Iranian capital, Tehran. His continued active role in Hezbullah only came to light after the assassination, when the movement arranged an elaborate funeral for him in Beirut. The Syrian government did not furnish an explanation of what he was doing in Damascus, and it did not announce any conclusions from its investigation into the incident. Hezbullah made it clear that it was convinced that Israel was responsible.

The Damascus Arab summit went ahead at the end of March, but the event was overshadowed by the conflicts between Syria and pro-Western Arab states, led by Saudi Arabia and Egypt, which blamed Assad for the continuing deadlock in Lebanon, following the failure to elect a new president after the expiry of the term of the pro-Syrian Emile Lahoud in November 2007. Only half of the Arab League member states took part, and Saudi Arabia, Egypt, and Jordan were all represented at the lowest possible level, sending their Arab League ambassadors.

The Lebanese crisis came to a head in May when Syria's local allies, led by Hezbullah, the dominant Shia force in the country, overran central Beirut, the base of the anti-Syrian and Saudi-supported March 14 bloc, which held the majority of seats in the Lebanese Parliament. The crisis was resolved at a conference organised by the government of Qatar. This led to the election of Michel Suleiman as the new president of Lebanon and the formation of a national unity government, in which the opposition held sufficient seats to block decisions (see pp. 219-20). This resolution was broadly favourable to Syria, and led to an improvement in its relations with Lebanon, culminating in an agreement in October to establish formal diplomatic relations for the fist time since the two countries became independent from France in the 1940s. Syria had previously been reluctant to take this step, owing to its lingering resentment at the division of the two states under the French mandate.

In the first half of 2008 the Assad government also took decisive action in its domestic economic policy by pushing through a sharp increase in prices for diesel, the most heavily subsidised and widely used fuel in Syria. The general price for diesel was increased from S£7 (equivalent to about 12 US cents) per litre to S£25. At the same time, the government announced that each family would be entitled to buy 1,000 litres of diesel per year at S£9 per litre, and public sector salaries were increased by 20 per cent. The measures went into effect from 1 May. An attack on fuel subsidies had been under consideration for over a year, but the government had hesitated to go ahead for fear of a popular backlash. The new market price was still less than half the price of diesel on the world market in mid-2008, although the differential narrowed later in the year when the oil price fell. The introduction of the price increases passed off without incident, a testament both to the government's efforts to explain the dire need to cut subsidies and to the general fear of the security services on the part of the Syrian public.

The resolution of the Lebanon crisis paid immediate dividends to Syria in its relations with the EU. Assad was invited to Paris in July to attend the launch of the Union for the Mediterranean, an initiative of France's President Nicolas Sarkozy; in September Sarkozy visited Syria, the first Western head of state or government to do so in more than five years.

However, Syria continued to be dogged by security issues. On 27 September a large car bomb exploded in southern Damascus, resulting in the deaths of 17 people, the first such attack on Syrian civilians since the mid-1980s. The government blamed the attack on extreme Sunni Islamists. On 6 November Syrian television broadcast the purported confessions of 10 people said to have been implicated in the bomb attack. They indicated that they had been based in Sunni areas of Lebanon and that they had received financial backing from the Future Movement, led by Saad Hariri, the son of Rafiq Hariri, the former Lebanese prime minister who was assassinated in Beirut in 2005 (see AR 2005, pp. 182-83).

On 26 October four US helicopters flew across the Iraqi border and raided the Syrian village of Sukariya. Syria claimed that the raid had resulted in the deaths of several civilians; the USA said that it was targeting a leader of al-Qaida responsible for smuggling fighters and weapons into Iraq across the Syrian border. The incident demonstrated that Syrian relations with the USA remained fraught, despite the improvements in ties with the EU. However, the Syrian government welcomed the indications from US President-elect Barack Obama that he was interested in opening dialogue with states, such as Syria and Iran, that had been ostracised by the outgoing US administration.

David Butter

LEBANON

CAPITAL: Beirut   AREA: 10,400 sq km   POPULATION: 4,097,000 ('07)
OFFICIAL LANGUAGE: Arabic   POLITICAL SYSTEM: multiparty republic
HEAD OF STATE: Gen. Michel Suleiman (since July '08)
RULING PARTY: March 14 movement
HEAD OF GOVERNMENT: Prime Minister Fouad Siniora (since June '05)
MAIN IGO MEMBERSHIPS (NON-UN): AL, OIC, NAM, Francophonie
CURRENCY: Lebanese pound (end-'08 £1=L£2,160.22, US$1=L£1,502.50)
GNI PER CAPITA: US$5,770, $10,050 at PPP ('07)

LEBANON overcame a constitutional crisis in May, which briefly threatened to plunge the country back into civil war, and subsequently enjoyed more stable political conditions with the election of Michel Suleiman as president at the end of that month. The various political factions, which had been at loggerheads over the election of a successor to Emile Lahoud, who left office in November 2007, agreed to join a government of national unity after Suleiman's election and were gearing up at the end of 2008 for parliamentary elections, scheduled to take place in June 2009.

In January, the Arab League sought to break the deadlock over the Lebanese presidential election by drawing up a plan to bridge the differences between the parliamentary majority—known as March 14, and made up of a coalition of Western-backed groups united by their determination to rid Lebanon of Syrian influence—and the Syrian-backed opposition. Both sides had indicated that they were in favour of electing Suleiman, the commander of the Lebanese army, as president, but they disagreed over the distribution of cabinet posts in any post-election government. The opposition sought a guarantee that it would have at least one-third of the cabinet posts, which would enable it to veto any government decision to which it objected. This demand was first tabled in late 2006, when the opposition withdrew its ministers from the cabinet as part of an ultimately unsuccessful effort to block approval of the establishment of a mixed Lebanese-international tribunal for those charged with the February 2005 assassination of Rafiq Hariri, a former prime minister (see AR 2007, p. 202). The opposition was also concerned to prevent any move by the government to place restrictions on the autonomous military activities of Hezbullah, the dominant Shia Muslim movement in Lebanon.

Matters came to a head on 5 May when the cabinet held a lengthy meeting to discuss a number of critical economic and security issues. These included demands from trade unions for a big increase in wages to match the sharp rise in fuel and food prices; the question of security at Beirut airport, following claims that Hezbullah had set up a surveillance system near the runways; and the long-running issue of the unlicensed telecommunications network operated by Hezbullah in its main areas of control. The government decided to raise the monthly minimum wage by two-thirds to L£500,000 (US$330), which was considerably less than the rise demanded by the trade unions; it also ordered the dismissal of Brigadier-General Wafiq Shuqair as chief of airport security and declared the Hezbullah telecoms network to be illegal and unconstitutional.

Hezbullah described the government's measures at the airport and with respect to its telecoms network as tantamount to an attack on the movement's capability to defend Lebanon against Israel. After the government affirmed its determination to stand by its decisions, Hezbullah took matters into its own hands and launched a military thrust into the central areas of Beirut, housing the offices of the March 14 movement. Security guards employed by March 14 put up only token resistance, and Hezbullah and its militia allies were able to seize control of the city centre within a few hours. The army did not intervene. Hezbullah fighters also sought to capture territory in the hills to the south of Beirut, but were repulsed by fighters loyal to Walid Jumblatt, the leader of the minority Druze community and a key figure in March 14.

The crisis was eventually resolved after intervention by Qatar, one of the few Arab states trusted by both sides in Lebanon to act as a mediator. Leaders of the Lebanese factions involved gathered in the Qatari capital, Doha, on 16 May, and after five days of deliberations they thrashed out an agreement. The breakthrough came when March 14 accepted a formula that would allow the opposition effective veto powers in a national unity government to be formed after Suleiman's election. The new cabinet was to have 16 ministers from March 14, 11 from the opposition, and three nominees of the president, and all parties to the agreement pledged not to resign from the cabinet or otherwise hamper the operations of the government.

There were also tough negotiations in Doha over the proposed reforms to the system to be used for the 2009 general election. The opposition maintained that the existing law, drawn up under Syrian supervision in 2000, had worked to the advantage of March 14 and that it prevented the Free Patriotic Movement (FPM) of Michel Aoun, a key Hezbullah ally, from capitalising fully on its strong electoral appeal among sections of the Christian community. The Doha deal entailed tinkering with the electoral districts, through setting the local caza (county) as the standard constituency rather than the province, while leaving the system applied to Beirut unchanged, in a sop to Saad Hariri, the leader of March 14. The formula established at the 1989 Taef peace conference, whereby the 128 seats in Parliament were allocated on a 50:50 basis between Christians and Muslims (with parity for Sunnis and Shias), was also retained.

The Doha agreement contained only an oblique reference to the issue of Hezbullah's weapons and related military infrastructure, stipulating that no party could use weapons for political ends within Lebanon. It called for dialogue about ways to consolidate the authority of the Lebanese state over the entire territory of the country, and about defining the state's relations with various organisations in such a way as to safeguard the security of the state and its citizens.

Suleiman was duly elected president by the Lebanese Parliament on 25 May. In his acceptance speech he emphasised the need to foster national unity, and he advocated harnessing the military assets of Hezbullah to serve a national defence strategy. He also called for the establishment of normal diplomatic relations with Syria—with embassies in the respective capitals—and for a resolution of Lebanon's outstanding border issues with its powerful neighbour. Syria responded positively to these overtures, and the two sides agreed in October to establish diplomatic relations for the first time since they became independent from France (1943 in Lebanon's case; 1946 for Syria). The Syrian embassy in Beirut opened in December. However, there was little progress in discussions about border demarcation. Fouad Siniora, a pivotal figure in March 14, was reappointed as prime minister.

The Doha agreement and the election of Suleiman produced a more settled political environment in the second half of the year. However, the threat of renewed instability remained. On 10 September, Saleh Aridi, a prominent Druze politician, was killed when a bomb planted in his car exploded. Aridi was an aide to Talal Arslan, a political rival to Jumblatt. He had played a central role in forging a rapprochement between the two Druze leaders, and his assassination was widely interpreted as being aimed at disrupting that process. Towards the end of September, it emerged that Syria had deployed a significant number of troops along the border with north-eastern Lebanon. The Lebanese government said that Syria had indicated that the deployment was aimed at curbing the smuggling of weapons and terrorists into its territory from the Tripoli area of Lebanon, where a number of Sunni Islamist groups were based. On 27 September a car bomb exploded in Damascus, killing 17 people. Syria said that Islamist extremists were to blame, and implied that they had used Lebanon as a base for the attack on Syria. These Syrian moves and accusations were interpreted by March 14 as constituting an effort by Syria to sow divisions in the Sunni Muslim community in Lebanon with a view to affecting the result of the 2009 election. Syria gave a further strong hint as to its preferences in this contest by helping to arrange a five-day visit to Syria by Aoun in December.

The Doha agreement also provided a fillip for the Lebanese economy, as the tourism and retail sectors benefited from the improved perceptions of the country's security. Real GDP grew by about 4 per cent in 2008, the best performance in many years. However, Lebanon also started to feel the effects of the global financial crisis in the latter part of the year. Remittances from Lebanese working in the Gulf and in developed economies started to fall, and increasing numbers of expatriate workers began to return home, having lost their jobs.

David Butter

IRAQ

CAPITAL: Baghdad   AREA: 438,320 sq km   POPULATION: 28,100,000 (UN '04 est)
OFFICIAL LANGUAGES: Arabic and Kurdish   POLITICAL SYSTEM: multiparty republic under partial US
   occupation
HEAD OF STATE: President Jalal Talabani (since April '05)
RULING PARTY: United Iraq Alliance (UIA)
HEAD OF GOVERNMENT: Prime Minister Nouri al-Maliki (UIA, Da'wa Party) (since April '06)
MAIN IGO MEMBERSHIPS (NON-UN): AL, OPEC, OAPEC, OIC, NAM
CURRENCY: New Iraqi dinar(2) (end-'08 £1=NID1,665.12, US$1=NID1,158.10)
GNI PER CAPITA: Lower middle income: US$936-US$3,705 ('07 est)

AFTER months of tortuous negotiation, the government of Prime Minister Nouri al-Maliki in late November finally won the approval of the legislature, the Council of Representatives, for a Status of Forces Agreement (SOFA) that provided for a US military withdrawal from Iraq and set rules under which US forces would operate until final withdrawal in three years' time. The "Agreement Between the

United States of America and the Republic of Iraq On the Withdrawal of United States Forces from Iraq and the Organization of Their Activities during Their Temporary Presence in Iraq" provided for the withdrawal of all US combat forces from cities, towns, and villages "on a date no later than 30 June, 2009". Subsequently, all US forces would be withdrawn from "all Iraqi territory, water and airspace" no later than 31 December, 2011 (see Documents).

SECURITY. The US military had been operating in Iraq under a UN Security Council mandate that had last been renewed in December 2007 and which was scheduled to expire on 31 December 2008. The two countries could have gone back to the UN for another 12-month extension, or even signed a bland bilateral agreement that was not as intricate or involved as the SOFA, which was eventually approved by the Council of Representatives. However, the election in early November of Barack Obama as US president had undoubtedly altered Iran's perception, and so the Shia Islamic Republic—the key regional player in Shia-led Iraq—shifted its position on the Agreement. As a result, many Shia politicians in Iraq, who were either influenced by Iran or who were outright Iranian clients, suddenly lent their support to the Agreement. For months, the USA had blamed Iran for sabotaging the prospect for an agreement, and there is little doubt that had Republican John McCain won the US election, Iran would have concluded that the likelihood was very high that Iraq would be used as a base for attacking Iran over its controversial nuclear programme. Many analysts noted that the passage of the SOFA was an important sign from the Iranian leadership to President-elect Obama that Iran was willing to communicate and eventually deal with the USA.

Amongst other things, the SOFA made it unlawful for US forces to arrest an Iraqi "unless it is in accordance with an Iraqi decision" and, furthermore, US forces would not be able to search premises without "an Iraqi judicial order". Crucially, the agreement also removed the legal immunity of US "contractors" operating in Iraq. Chief amongst such "contractors" were employees of North Carolina-based Blackwater Security Consulting, who had a highly visible presence in Iraq and were regarded by many as little more than highly-paid mercenaries. In September 2007 Blackwater guards had shot and killed 17 Iraqi civilians in Nisour Square, Baghdad, whilst escorting US state department personnel to a meeting with officials from the US Agency for International Development (AID). The killings proved to be a public relations disaster, serving only to unite Iraq in its opposition to the ubiquitous "contractors".

Inevitably, there had been some opposition to the SOFA. It had sparked noisy debate when put before the Council of Representatives and at times it appeared that the vote would have to be delayed, after Sunni politicians said that they would refuse to participate unless additional demands were met. One session of the Council collapsed in chaos as a discussion about the SOFA boiled over into shouting and physical confrontation. Earlier, more than 10,000 supporters of firebrand Shia cleric Muqtada al-Sadr had congregated in Baghdad's Firdos Square to protest against the agreement. Excitable Sadrists had hanged a black-hooded effigy of US President George W. Bush from the column that once supported the statue of Saddam Hussein, toppled by US troops in April 2003. Removing the hood to beat the effigy with a shoe—a particularly deep Iraqi insult—they put a whip in its right hand and in its left a briefcase, on which was written, "The security agreement is shame and dishonour." The effigy was hooded, some of the Sadrists said, as a reminder of Saddam Hussein's execution at the hands of the US military and the new Maliki regime that owed its existence to the USA: except that Saddam was not hooded when he was hanged in late 2006 (see AR 2007, pp. 203-05), famously refusing his executioner's offer. (In another development concerning footwear—considered ritually unclean in the Muslim faith—an Iraqi journalist, Muntadar al-Zaidi, had in mid-December thrown his shoes at visiting US President Bush during a Baghdad press conference, shouting, "This is a farewell kiss, you dog!")

President Mahmoud Ahmadinejad of Iran paid a historic two-day official visit to Iraq in early March. The Shia-led Iraqi government rolled out the red carpet, literally, for Ahmadinejad as he became the first Iranian president to visit Iraq, a country that had been a bitter enemy when Saddam Hussein's Sunni government was in power. Ahmadinejad, at a joint news conference with Iraqi President Jalal Talabani, said that the trip "opens a new chapter in bilateral ties with Iraq". Later in the day, Ahmadinejad met Iraqi Prime Minister al-Maliki. Both Maliki and Talabani had made official trips to Iran since taking office.

Seven memorandums of understanding were signed during Ahmadinejad's visit, covering co-operation on customs and insurance affairs as well as co-operation in the fields of industry, transport, and development of mining industries. Furthermore, it was reported that Iran had offered a US$1 billion loan to Iraq for projects to be handled by Iranian companies. However, the pan-Arab daily newspaper *Al-Sharq al-Awsat* reported on 11 March that Iraqi Foreign Minister Hoshyar Zebari had said that Iraq had refused Iran's offer of a soft loan.

Some analysts portrayed Ahmadinejad's visit as a calculated snub to the USA, which had regularly accused Iran of backing Iraqi Shia militias, as well as seeking to develop nuclear weapons and supporting terrorism elsewhere in the Middle East. More specifically, the USA had accused Iran of supplying explosively formed penetrators or explosively formed projectiles (EFPs), the deadliest and most sophisticated type of roadside bomb, to Shia militias. At a joint news conference with Maliki in Baghdad's heavily protected "Green Zone", the Iranian leader did not hide his disdain for the USA and its leadership. President Bush, he said, "always accuses others without evidence and this increases problems... The Americans have to understand that Iraqi people do not like America."

Shortly after President Ahmadinejad's visit—on 25 March—the Iraqi armed forces launched a major military operation in the southern port city of Basra in an attempt to dismantle Muqtada al-Sadr's "Mahdi Army" militia, which controlled as many as five neighbourhoods in the city. Operation Sawlat al-Fursan (Charge of the Knights) was launched the day after Prime Minister Maliki had arrived in Basra and pledged to restore "security and stability" to "a city where civilians cannot even secure their lives and property". At least 700 people were killed as Shia militiamen, most of them Sadrists, battled the police and troops who raided their strongholds. By early April the fierce fighting that had marked the first week of the operation had given way to slower, more focused house-by-house searches by Iraqi troops, mainly in areas dominated by "Mahdi Army" militiamen. In late April the interior ministry announced that all areas of Basra were under the command of the security forces. A number of reports noted that music stores had reopened, with US movies, cassettes, and CDs on the shelves for the first time in years, as residents held parties now that alcohol was once more available, albeit surreptitiously. However, the security operation had not been without severe problems: in early April 1,300 police and soldiers were dismissed for desertion, refusing to fight, or for failing to perform their duties.

In early April the government launched a similar operation in Sadr City, the Sadrists' eastern Baghdad bastion. Eventually, on 12 May Muqtada al-Sadr authorised a ceasefire, a move regarded by many as a tactical retreat. Prime Minister Maliki emerged strengthened by his confrontation with the "Mahdi Army" and his government appeared increasingly confident that it had the upper hand over its enemies in both the Shia and Sunni communities. Shortly before al-Sadr had announced the ceasefire in Sadr City, the Iraqi army had launched a major offensive against al-Qaida in Iraq—the hardline Sunni group, buttressed by foreign jihadists—in the northern city of Mosul.

In an interview published by the *Washington Post* on 30 May, the director of the CIA, Michael Hayden, said that there had been a "near strategic defeat" of al-Qaida in Iraq, as well as "significant setbacks" for the network globally. Furthermore, Hayden contended that the leader of al-Qaida, Osama bin Laden, had lost the battle for hearts and minds in the Islamic world and had largely lost his ability to exploit the Iraq war to recruit new members. In Iraq, Hayden said that he was encouraged by US success against al-Qaida's affiliates and by what he described as the steadily rising competence of the Iraqi military and a growing popular antipathy toward jihadism.

The US military handed over security control of the province of Anbar to Iraqi government forces on 1 September in what appeared to be a significant milestone in US efforts to withdraw its troops from Iraq. Anbar had been the heartland of the al-Qaida-led Sunni Arab insurgency against the US occupation of Iraq (see map, AR 2005, p. 187). Over 1,300 of the 4,150 US soldiers killed in Iraq since 2003 had perished in Anbar, which had supplied many soldiers and security officials to the Saddam regime. The security situation had shifted markedly in 2006, when Sunni tribal leaders began forming Awakening Councils (Sahwa or Sons of Iraq), in opposition to al-Qaida and in support of the USA. The Iraqi authorities on 1 October officially took command of some 54,000 members of the Awakening Councils in Baghdad. The operation was delicate because the Shia-led government in Baghdad was wary of the Councils, which included many former Sunni insurgents.

In its quarterly assessment of the security situation in Iraq from September to November 2008, the US department of defence (the Pentagon) warned that Iran "continues to reflect a fundamental desire to oppose the development of a fully secure and stable Iraq", despite its "persistent promises to the contrary". The report accused Iran of trying to undermine the SOFA and claimed that it continued "to host, train, fund, arm, and direct militant groups intent on destabilising Iraq". Countering "malign influence and balancing soft Iranian influence" remained priorities in the effort to stabilise Iraq and ensure the sovereignty of its people, the report said.

The Pentagon report cited improvements in politics, security, economics, diplomacy, and rule of law, but emphasised their fragility. The overall security situation in Iraq "continues to improve", the report said, crediting, among other things, improved Iraqi security forces and the political will of the government to fight militants. It said that the insurgency had diminished as some militants embraced the Iraqi government. Although the number of civilians killed had dropped, assassinations of judicial and legislative officials had increased and violence against Christians in Nineveh province had stirred concern. The report raised fears that the mishandling of key political efforts in the country could reverse gains. Crucial areas included forthcoming provincial elections, resolving disputes over areas such as Kirkuk city, resettling displaced people, and providing permanent employment for members of the Awakening Councils.

US military deaths in Iraq dropped dramatically during 2008, a trend observers attributed to the lasting effects of the US-led "surge" offensive, more robust Iraqi security performance, and civilians' growing antipathy towards warfare. According to Pentagon figures, 309 US service members in Iraq died during the year: 222 in hostilities such as combat and attacks, and 87 in non-hostile circumstances such as traffic accidents, suicides, and natural deaths. The US death toll had been much higher in past years. In 2007, 906 personnel had died: 768 in combat and attacks, and 138 in non-hostile circumstances. There were more than 800 deaths in each of 2004, 2005, and 2006 as well. The decline in deaths coincided with a decrease in attacks, down from 180 attacks per day to an average of 10 per day in late 2008.

Despite the generally positive assessment of the security situation during the year, Iraq remained one of the most violent and dangerous countries in the world and some attacks still had the power to shock a nation hardened by years of bloodshed. One such incident occurred on 1 February, when two female suicide bombers carried out what appeared to be co-ordinated attacks on two pet markets in Baghdad, killing almost 100 people. A number of reports claimed that the bombers were mentally impaired and that their explosives had been set off by remote control. Iraqi and US officials blamed al-Qaida in Iraq for the attacks and accused the organisation of plumbing new depths of depravity. It was subsequently reported that the acting director of the al-Rashad psychiatric hospital in east Baghdad had been arrested on suspicion of supplying al-Qaida in Iraq with the mentally impaired women used in the attacks. The director of the hospital had apparently been shot dead by al-Qaida in December 2007 after he had refused to co-operate with them.

The attacks on the pet markets were part of a wider trend of suicide bombings carried out by women. In an attack on 10 November, a 13-year old girl exploded a suicide vest in Baquba, the capital of Diyala province, north east of Baghdad, killing four people. The target of the teenage bomber was a patrol of the Awakening Councils. Baquba had become notorious for suicide attacks by female bombers. It was reported that the teenage girl's death had taken to 27 the number of female bombers from Diyala province in the past 18 months. The trend led to an urgent country-wide security review, which was likely to involve more intrusive searches of women at checkpoints. Women were able to shroud their weapons underneath their abayas (their Islamic dress), and Islamic tradition generally prevented men from searching Iraqi women. As there were very few female officers working in the Iraqi police and army, Iraqi security forces announced plans to recruit more women to face the growing threat from female insurgents.

INTERNAL POLITICAL DEVELOPMENTS. On 12 January the Council of Representatives passed the Accountability and Justice Act, designed to reverse the catastrophic de-Ba'athification order issued in 2004 by the US Coalition Provisional Authority (CPA, the occupying power in Iraq in 2003-04). The new legislation removed many restrictions that had been imposed on lower- and middle-ranking members of the mainly Sunni Muslim former ruling Ba'ath Party. Passage of the new law, the first of the so-called "political benchmark" measures to be passed by the Council, opened the door for the re-instatement of thousands of former Ba'athists, who had been unable to work or stand for office since the US-led invasion of March 2003. Some Sunni leaders criticised the new law for not going far enough in reversing anti-Ba'athist measures, whilst many Shia leaders also opposed a law, which, they contended, would allow Ba'athists to infiltrate security organs and launch a coup.

On 18 March Prime Minister Maliki opened a two-day national conference in Baghdad aimed at reconciling the country's rival political, religious, and ethnic factions. In his opening statement to the conference, Maliki said that reconciliation was not intended to harm the interests of any group, but was "a boat that saves us and takes us to safety". However, the conference was boycotted by the Iraqi Consensus Front (ICF, or Tawafiq), the largest Sunni Arab block in the Council of Representatives, and by the Iraqi List, led by former interim Prime Minister Ayad Allawi, a secular Shia. Supporters of Muqtada al-Sadr initially attended the conference, but then walked out, describing it as a public relations ploy by the Maliki government.

In a more positive development, the Council of Representatives on 19 July approved the appointment of six Sunnis as members of the cabinet. The new ministers were all members of the ICF, which had boycotted the Maliki government since August 2007. Sunni leaders had decided to return to government following the passage in February of a general amnesty law, which would cover thousands of the detainees held in Iraqi prisons, and the Iraqi army's recent crackdown on Shia militias.

Rafi Hiyad al-Isawi, minister of state for foreign affairs until the ICF's withdrawal from the cabinet, was appointed as deputy prime minister. Abd Dhiyab al-Ajili was reappointed to his old post as minister of higher education and scientific research. Mahar Dilli al-Hadithi was appointed as minister of culture, Faruq Abd al-Qadir Abd al-Rahman as minister of communications, Nawal Majid al-Samarra as minister of state for women's affairs, and Muhammad Munajid al-Dulaymi as minister of state for foreign affairs.

The presidential council—the body comprising the president and two vice presidents—on 3 October approved legislation that cleared the path for provincial elections to be held before the end of January 2009 in most areas of the country. After months of acrimonious wrangling, the Council of Representatives had finally approved the legislation on 24 September. A previous effort to pass the law had been blocked largely because of a dispute between Arabs, Kurds, and Turkmen over power-sharing in the ethnically mixed, oil-rich city of Kirkuk. Kirkuk was claimed by some local Kurdish leaders as the "Kurdish Jerusalem", and viewed as the economic and political hub of any future Kurdish entity or state. The provincial election legislation was only approved after Kurdish, Arab, and Turkmen members of the Council of Representatives agreed to a UN-brokered compromise that called for a parliamentary committee to review the status of Kirkuk.

Darren Sagar

SAUDI ARABIA—YEMEN—ARAB STATES OF THE GULF

SAUDI ARABIA

CAPITAL: Riyadh   AREA: 2,000,000 sq km   POPULATION: 24,196,000 ('07)
OFFICIAL LANGUAGE: Arabic   POLITICAL SYSTEM: non-party monarchy
HEAD OF STATE AND GOVERNMENT: King Abdullah ibn Abdul Aziz (since Aug '05), also Prime Minister
HEIR APPARENT: Crown Prince Sultan ibn Abdul Aziz (since Aug '05), also Deputy Prime Minister
MAIN IGO MEMBERSHIPS (NON-UN): AL, OPEC, OAPEC, GCC, OIC, NAM
CURRENCY: Saudi riyal (end-'08 £1=SR5.3961, US$1=SR3.7531)
GNI PER CAPITA: US$15,440, $22,910 at PPP ('07)

SAUDI Arabia found itself courted abroad as the global financial crisis took hold towards the latter part of 2008 and Western governments looked to the kingdom to provide a semblance of stability in a tormented world market. At home, King Abdullah ibn Abdul Aziz al-Saud underlined the importance of reform, placing greater emphasis on education and tackling religious extremism. The year also saw the security situation in the kingdom remain stable, on the back of some successes achieved by security forces in dismantling jihadist militant networks.

In domestic affairs, the most important thrust was in social policy. Education received renewed attention, with the allocation of new funds and a sustained focus on attacking the ideological roots of jihadism, under the banner of the King Abdullah ibn Abdul Aziz project for developing public education. The ministry of education announced that school pupils would be denied access to supposedly extremist works by, or about, the founder of the Muslim Brotherhood, Sayyid Qutb (1906-66), who was regarded as the ideological precursor of al-Qaida. More controversially, the list of proscribed works of literature included a key text by Mohammed ibn Abdelwahhab, the 18th century cleric responsible for developing Saudi Arabia's official, conservative interpretation of Islam. Despite some murmurs of discontent at the prohibition of important Wahhabi texts, most Saudi clerics accepted the ministry of education's strictures. Meanwhile, the government stepped up its dismissal of clerics deemed to have breached official guidelines, with opposition circles claiming that up to 3,000 clerics had been removed from their positions.

King Abdullah persisted with his interfaith dialogue, which brought him into controversial contact with Israel's President Shimon Peres at a dinner held during a conference convened by the Saudi leader at the UN headquarters in New York in November. The issue of reaching out to other religions was one that proved to be close to the king's heart. In July, he sponsored the interfaith World Conference on Dialogue in Madrid, organised by the Muslim World League, which invited Jewish and Christian religious leaders, as well as representatives of other world religions, to discuss key issues. The conference adopted the Madrid Declaration, recognising "diversity and differences among peoples".

The Saudi leadership's domestic record on religious tolerance came under scrutiny, notably its attitude towards the Shia communities: both the Twelver Shia Muslims in the Eastern province and the Ismailis in south-western Najran province. Saudi domestic intelligence forces in early May arrested an Ismaili leader, Shaikh Ahmad bin Turki al-Sab, after he had led an Ismaili delegation presenting grievances to King Abdullah in late April. In June, the authorities briefly arrested a Shia cleric, Tawfiq al-Amir, after he criticised a statement by leading Wahhabi clerics that declared Shia Muslims to be "unbelievers". In August, Saudi intelligence forces arrested a Shia religious leader, Nimr al-Nimr, over comments he had made in a sermon criticising the government for allegedly failing to pursue real reforms. Furthermore, in October, a Saudi religious scholar declared in a fatwa that Sunni Muslims were forbidden from selling property to the Shia.

However, the government did make some moves to realise its tolerance agenda. On 4 November Najran's governor, Prince Mishal bin Saud, whom Ismailis considered a divisive figure, was forced to resign after 12 years in office in an overt display of King Abdullah's desire to improve communal relations in the south west. Nevertheless, it was unclear whether the king's raft of changes had the full support of the Saudi clerical establishment, or to what extent the kingdom was committed to a more tolerant domestic agenda.

Success in security measures continued throughout 2008 as indicated by the absence of serious incidents. An unsuccessful attempt on 14 October to stop a terrorist vehicle in eastern Riyadh made headlines, when four suspects attempted to attack the Jedawal compound in the city, which was a residential centre for US expatriates. This attack provided further confirmation that jihadist elements would continue to seek opportunities to mount assaults on foreign targets, although their chances of success were much reduced from the heyday of terrorism in 2004-05.

Saudi Arabia's foreign policy was more activist in 2008 than in previous years, partly through King Abdullah's attempts to galvanise interest in his interfaith dialogue programme. But many of the kingdom's foreign policy initiatives were driven by global interest in Saudi Arabia's perceived insulation from the worst economic trends and its capacity to rescue the international system by playing a more significant role. As the world's financial system faced severe crisis in November, UK Prime Minister Gordon Brown embarked on a visit to the Saudi capital, in order to request Saudi funds to bolster the IMF's aid package for failing nations. Foreign governments also sought Saudi Arabia's participation in the G-20 group of developed countries, in which the country was primed to play a significant role as a "voice" for the entire Middle East region. It was unclear, however, whether Saudi Arabia would be willing to assume this mantle. King Abdullah appeared reluctant to provide resources to plug the IMF's funding shortfall at the G-20 financial summit meeting in Washington, DC in November. With the oil price registering a stark decline in late 2008, the kingdom faced a dramatic slide in its own revenues, which would take priority over bailing out the international system.

In addition to Saudi Arabia's apparent reluctance to assume the economic role envisaged by some Western policymakers, there was also little evidence that Saudi diplomacy would be deployed across the region's trouble spots. Although NATO forces had sought Saudi mediation in order to encourage the Taliban to negotiate with President Hamid Karzai's pro-Western government in Afghanistan, there was little real enthusiasm from Saudi Arabia to do so. Similarly, although King Abdullah's "land-for-peace" proposal of 2002 to end the Arab-Israeli conflict remained up for discussion (see AR 2002, p. 206), there was evidence that Saudi Arabia had serious doubts about any genuine chances for peace between Israel and Palestine. Israel's launch of a military assault on the Gaza Strip in late December drew a stinging response from Saudi Arabia. The most telling contribution came from the former Saudi intelligence chief and ambassador to the USA and the UK, Prince Turki al-Faisal, who, in an unprecedented break with diplomatic niceties, launched a strong attack on the administration of US President George W. Bush for its support for Israel. Writing in the *Financial Times* in January 2009, just days after the end of Israel's three-week Gaza offensive, he claimed that the Bush administration had left a "sickening legacy in the region". Although Prince Turki had no official role in the government, his views reflected widespread anger within the Saudi royal family, and suggested that the government wanted to push US President-elect Barack Obama to take a stronger line towards Israel than his predecessor.

The other serious foreign challenge for Saudi Arabia was the worsening security situation on the high seas. There were more than 100 reported pirate attacks in the shipping lanes off eastern and northern Somalia in 2008, leading to the seizure in November of a Saudi super-tanker, the *MV Sirius Star*, fully laden with 2 million barrels of crude oil. It was returned in January 2009 to Saudi Aramco, in return for a ransom payment estimated at US$3 million. The kingdom was expected to co-operate with a US-led regional initiative to secure shipping lanes.

James Gavin

YEMEN

CAPITAL: Sana'a   AREA: 527,970 sq km   POPULATION: 22,383,000 ('07)
OFFICIAL LANGUAGE: Arabic   POLITICAL SYSTEM: multiparty republic
HEAD OF STATE AND GOVERNMENT: President (Lt-Gen.) Ali Abdullah Saleh (GPC) (since May '90)
RULING PARTY: General People's Congress (GPC)
PRIME MINISTER: Ali Mohammed Majur (since March '07)
MAIN IGO MEMBERSHIPS (NON-UN): AL, OIC, NAM
CURRENCY: Yemeni rial (end-'08 £1=YR287.658, US$1=YR200.075)
GNI PER CAPITA: US$870, $2,200 at PPP ('07)

PRESIDENT Ali Abdullah Saleh faced a plethora of domestic and foreign policy challenges in 2008, with civil conflict in the north of the country, a secessionist movement in the south, and an increasingly potent jihadist threat. This was in addition to domestic political opposition from the increasingly confident Joint Meeting Parties (JMP) alliance, which included the powerful Islamist Islah party. Yemen's vicinity to failed states like Somalia and its exposure to piracy in the Gulf of Aden complicated the challenges facing the Yemeni leadership.

Although Yemen boasted the paraphernalia of a modern democracy, with an elected legislature and president, Saleh exercised his rule via an extensive patronage system involving the northern tribal networks. One of his key props was the Islamist academic Sheikh Abdulmajeed al-Zindani, a prominent member of Islah and alleged, by the US treasury department, to be an affiliate of al-Qaida. However, the president's manipulation of the tribal system proved of relatively little value in containing the northern Shia Zaydi rebellion, which had intensified in 2007 (see AR 2008 p. 208), and the uprising was brought to an end only with a ceasefire engineered with the help of Qatar. The state of emergency in the northern province of Sa'ada was lifted at the end of August, after President Saleh announced on 17 July that the four-year civil war there had ended. This appeared to be confirmed by a letter issued by the rebel Zaydi leader, Abdel-Malek al-Houthi, in which he stated that the movement was no longer at war with the government and had met all peace conditions set by Saleh. According to the letter, the rebels would end hostilities, re-open roads and remove landmines, return from mountain bases and evacuate farms and houses, handing over weapons to the state and permitting the return of displaced citizens.

That peace agreement followed an intensification of fighting over the early summer months, which was quelled after state security forces routed rebels who had attempted to block the main road connecting Sa'ada with the capital. Meanwhile, although the government managed to contain the sporadic protests by southerners angry at their exclusion from power and access to state resources, Yemen remained at risk of further civil strife. Kidnappings increased towards the end of the year. In mid-December three Germans were taken hostage by tribesmen who were bargaining for the release of two tribal members.

With the northern rebellion losing momentum, the state faced more pressure to deal with Islamic militancy, including al-Qaida in Yemen, a local offshoot that sharpened its focus in 2008. In a shift in strategy, the al-Qaida organisation began to view the country not just as a convenient base for mounting attacks on

Western targets, but as a target of value in itself. Militants showed a heightened willingness to engage state security forces, leading to numerous clashes. On 17 September, a major car bomb attack on the US embassy compound in Sana'a left 16 people dead and exposed once more the weakness of the Yemeni security forces.

The rising influence of political Islam was another key trend. In mid-July, religious scholars issued a fatwa forbidding women from participating in public and political affairs. The country's self-styled moral police, the Committee for Protecting Virtue and Fighting Vice, mounted a campaign against the imposition of a quota of 15 per cent of seats for women in the parliamentary elections due in 2009. With political backing from the Islah party, this new group was poised to play an influential role in Yemeni society.

James Gavin

ARAB STATES OF THE GULF

United Arab Emirates (UAE)

CONSTITUENT REPUBLICS: Abu Dhabi, Dubai, Sharjah, Ras al-Khaimah, Fujairah, Umm al-Qaiwin, Ajman

CAPITAL: Abu Dhabi   AREA: 83,600 sq km   POPULATION: 4,365,000 ('07)

OFFICIAL LANGUAGE: Arabic   POLITICAL SYSTEM: non-party republic, comprising federation of monarchies

HEAD OF STATE AND GOVERNMENT: Shaikh Khalifa Bin Zayed al-Nahyan (Ruler of Abu Dhabi), UAE President (since Nov '04)

PRIME MINISTER: Gen. Shaikh Mohammed bin Rashid al-Maktoum (ruler of Dubai), UAE Vice-President and Prime Minister (since Jan '06)

MAIN IGO MEMBERSHIPS (NON-UN): AL, OPEC, OAPEC, GCC, OIC, NAM

CURRENCY: UAE dirham (end-'08 £1=Dh5.2810, US$1=Dh3.6731)

GNI PER CAPITA: High income: US$11,456 or more ('07 est), -

Kuwait

CAPITAL: Kuwait   AREA: 17,820 sq km   POPULATION: 2,663,000 ('07)

OFFICIAL LANGUAGE: Arabic   POLITICAL SYSTEM: non-party monarchy

HEAD OF STATE AND GOVERNMENT: Sheikh Sabah al-Ahmad al-Jabir al-Sabah (since Jan '06)

PRESIDENT ELECT: Crown Prince Sheikh Nawwaf al-Ahmad al-Jabir al-Sabah

PRIME MINISTER: Sheikh Nasser al-Mohammad al-Ahmad al-Sabah (since Feb '06)

MAIN IGO MEMBERSHIPS (NON-UN): AL, OPEC, OAPEC, GCC, OIC, NAM

CURRENCY: Kuwaiti dinar (end-'08 £1=KwD0.3977, US$1=KwD0.2766)

GNI PER CAPITA: US$31,640, $49,970 at PPP ('07)

Oman

CAPITAL: Muscat   AREA: 309,500 sq km   POPULATION: 2,600,000 ('07)

OFFICIAL LANGUAGE: Arabic   POLITICAL SYSTEM: non-party monarchy

HEAD OF STATE AND GOVERNMENT: Shaikh Qaboos bin Said (since July '70)

MAIN IGO MEMBERSHIPS (NON-UN): AL, GCC, OIC, NAM

CURRENCY: Omani riyal (end-'08 £1=RO0.5536, US$1=RO0.3851)

GNI PER CAPITA: US$11,120, $19,740 at PPP ('07)

Qatar

CAPITAL: Doha   AREA: 11,000 sq km   POPULATION: 836,000 ('07)
OFFICIAL LANGUAGE: Arabic   POLITICAL SYSTEM: non-party monarchy
HEAD OF STATE: Sheikh Hamad bin Khalifa al-Thani (since June '95)
HEIR APPARENT: Crown Prince Shaikh Tamin Bin Hamad al-Thani (since Aug '03)
PRIME MINISTER: Sheikh Hamad Bin Jassem Bin Jabr al-Thani (since April '07)
MAIN IGO MEMBERSHIPS (NON-UN): AL, OPEC, OAPEC, GCC, OIC, NAM
CURRENCY: Qatar riyal (end-'08 £1=QR5.2364, US$1=QR3.6421)
GNI PER CAPITA: High income: US$11,456 or more ('07 est), -

Bahrain

CAPITAL: Manama   AREA: 710 sq km   POPULATION: 753,000 ('07)
OFFICIAL LANGUAGE: Arabic   POLITICAL SYSTEM: constitutional monarchy
HEAD OF STATE: Sheikh Hamad bin Isa al-Khalifa (since March '99)
PRIME MINISTER: Sheikh Khalifa bin Sulman al-Khalifa (since Jan '70)
MAIN IGO MEMBERSHIPS (NON-UN): AL, OAPEC, GCC, OIC, NAM
CURRENCY: dinar (end-'08 £1=BD0.5421, US$1=BD0.3770)
GNI PER CAPITA: US$19,350, $34,310 at PPP ('07)

BAHRAIN'S tentative political consensus took a battering in 2008, with a sharp deterioration in relations between the leadership of Sheikh Hamad bin Isa al-Khalifa and the largely Shia opposition, which represented the majority of Bahrainis. Throughout the year there were a number of reports of angry Shia mobs attacking police with Molotov cocktails. Further inciting sectarian tensions, opposition groups claimed that the government was deliberately naturalising Sunni citizens from overseas in order to alter the sectarian balance in favour of the overwhelmingly Sunni ruling elite. Anecdotal evidence suggested that large numbers of Egyptians and Yemenis had been made Bahraini citizens to help rebalance the numbers, although statistics were not available to prove this suspicion.

The government alleged that the opposition had been involved in a series of incidents, which it described as undermining the island's stability. In mid-December police announced the arrest of 15 men believed to have been plotting bomb attacks "to disrupt national security and threaten the lives of citizens" on 17 December, Bahrain's national day. According to police, canisters filled with flammable liquid had been found at the homes of the men. The interior minister, Sheikh Rashid bin Abdullah bin Ahmed al-Khalifa, said that the suspects had been trained to make explosive devices by Bahraini expatriates based in the UK.

In response to these incidents, Sheikh Rashid announced new legislation to bolster public security, including tighter laws governing public meetings and demonstrations. Under the proposed changes, the organisers of demonstrations would be held accountable for any damage incurred or laws broken during events staged by them. The minister also warned that Bahrainis who criticised the country overseas without official permission could face prosecution back home. This followed a briefing given by opposition activists to the US Congress in October, alleging that Shia Muslims were under-represented in decision making positions in Bahrain.

QATAR, in contrast, presented a picture of domestic stability. The government's efforts were focused overwhelmingly on foreign diplomacy, in which the most notable successes were Qatar's efforts to bridge the divide between Lebanon's warring pro-Western and pro-Syrian factions, and to halt conflict between Yemen's government and northern Zaydi rebels (see pp. 220; 230). Such initiatives helped the Qatar government to punch above its weight in international diplomatic circles, suggesting that its diplomacy might be deployed in other regional conflicts in future.

Prime Minister Sheikh Hamad Bin Jassim Bin Jabr al-Thani played an active role in negotiating the pact between Lebanon's government and opposition which was signed in Doha on 21 May. The emir, Sheikh Hamad Bin Khalifa al-Thani, also played a key role in ending the political paralysis in Lebanon wrought by Hezbullah's deployment of its supporters on the streets during May. His active courting of senior leaders, including Syria's President Bashar Assad, helped to set the stage for the formation of a unity government in Lebanon.

OMAN, too, remained another of the Gulf's bastions of stability. Sheikh Qaboos bin Said focused his attention on foreign policy and economic reform. However, the long-serving Omani ruler also showed some signs of sensitivity to international criticism over the lack of political reform in the sultanate. Announcing the establishing of a national human rights commission in November, he won immediate political reward with Oman's removal from an official US state department list of countries that were allegedly doing too little to stop human trafficking.

KUWAIT was subject to further instability, leaving the emirate with the unhappy track record of having seen two parliaments dissolved and four governments formed (and collapse) in the space of just three years. National Assembly elections on 17 May returned a legislature that included a greater representation for conservative Islamists. The country's legislators predictably proved combative in the following months, with a number of them launching campaigns against an oil refinery project promoted by the emir, Sheikh Sabah al-Ahmad al-Jabir al-Sabah. Ministers were subjected to parliamentary grilling over key policy issues, with repeated accusations of corruption and illegal profiteering, to the extent that the government was prompted to resign in late 2008. The trigger for this was a motion from Salafist Islamist legislators to question the prime minister, Sheikh Nasser al-Mohammad al-Sabah. The biggest casualty inflicted by the opposition, however, was the cancellation in late 2008 of a US$17 billion petrochemical joint venture with Dow Chemical of the USA, known as K-Dow, which legislators claimed was not in the national interest and had cost the country too much money.

Sheikh Nasser al-Mohammed submitted his own resignation on 25 November, though he retained the support of the emir, who held talks with Assembly members before inviting the prime minister to form a new administration. Although he retained some sympathy within the National Assembly and was reappointed prime minister on 17 December, there was growing dissatisfaction with Sheikh Nasser's leadership and no sign that Kuwait was any closer to resolving the perennial fractiousness between executive and legislature, with obvious ramifications for a range of proposed economic projects and policy initiatives in 2009.

The UAE's focus was absorbed by the impact of the "credit crunch" on Dubai's economy, heavily reliant as it was on real estate and an abundance of cheap credit. The city-state's economy suffered more than that of any other Gulf state as the global financial crisis developed, with rising numbers of expatriates leaving the emirate as projects were cancelled or shelved. The negative economic outlook for Dubai was expected to shift the balance of power in the UAE—traditionally split between Dubai and Abu Dhabi—in favour of the latter.

The Abu Dhabi government received a blow on 2 June when a helicopter crash killed a senior member of the royal family, Sheikh Nasser Bin Zayed al-Nahyan, the brother of UAE President Sheikh Khalifa Bin Zayed al-Nahyan.

Though considered a highly stable Gulf state, the UAE was nevertheless the recipient of an unprecedented UK foreign office travel warning on 14 June that claimed a "high" threat from terrorism. No terrorist incident occurred in the emirates in 2008, but the warning indicated that the UAE could, perhaps, not count on being immune from radical Islamist attacks.

James Gavin

SUDAN—LIBYA—TUNISIA—ALGERIA—MOROCCO—WESTERN SAHARA

SUDAN

CAPITAL: Khartoum   AREA: 2,505,810 sq km   POPULATION: 38,556,000 ('07)
OFFICIAL LANGUAGE: Arabic   POLITICAL SYSTEM: multiparty republic
HEAD OF STATE AND GOVERNMENT: President (Gen.) Omar Hasan Ahmed al-Bashir (since Oct '93),
    previously Chairman of Revolutionary Command Council (since June '89)
RULING PARTIES: government of national unity mainly comprising the National Congress Party (NCP)
MAIN IGO MEMBERSHIPS (NON-UN): AL, AU, COMESA, OIC, ACP, NAM
CURRENCY: Sudan pound (end '08 £1=S£3.1401, US$1=S£2.1840)
GNI PER CAPITA: US$960, $1,880 at PPP ('07)

THE volatile relations between Sudan and Chad worsened in February when the latter's president, Idriss Déby, accused Sudan of arming some 3,000 rebels who launched an attack on the capital, Ndjaména, in an attempt to topple the Déby regime (see p. 271). The attack was repulsed and in March Déby and his Sudanese counterpart, General Omar Hasan Ahmed al-Bashir, signed a non-aggression accord during a meeting of the Organisation of the Islamic Conference (OIC) in Dakar, Senegal. However, in May a group of armed men from the rebel Darfurian Justice and Equality Movement (JEM) drove a convoy of vehicles from western Sudan and attacked the city of Omdurman, west of Khartoum. President al-Bashir accused Chad of being behind the attack and Sudan severed diplomatic relations. These were later restored following a meeting of the foreign ministers of the two countries in Asmara, Eritrea, in September.

Both of these armed incursions were rooted in the ongoing Darfur conflict (see map, AR 2005, p. 202). Despite the arrival of UN peacekeepers from various countries, the hybrid UN and African Union (AU) force in the region, UNAMID, mandated in 2007 under UNSC Resolution 1796 (see AR 2008, pp. 214; 573-78), lacked sufficient equipment and personnel to patrol and protect civilians. In June, a new joint UN-AU chief mediator for Darfur was appointed. Foreign Minister Djibril Bassolé of Burkina Faso took over from the special envoys of the UN and AU (respectively, Jan Elisson and Salim Ahmed Salim). In July the UN Security Council agreed to extend the mandate of UNAMID in Darfur until July 2009. However, the Sudanese government's continuing disregard for international opinion had been demonstrated by the appointment, in January, of Sheikh Musa Hilal as a senior adviser to a government minister. Hilal was subject to a UN Security Council travel ban for involvement in recruiting pro-government Janjawid militia who were responsible for committing many atrocities within Darfur.

A major offensive in February by Sudanese government forces against rebels in western Darfur caused the displacement of 12,000 civilians, who fled to eastern Chad. In a rare diplomatic intervention, China's special envoy to Darfur, Liu Guijin, urged Sudan's government to accelerate the peace process. However, Western governments continued to criticise China for not using its considerable influence on Sudan's government—which stemmed from trade links and oil imports—to press for an end to the conflict. Nafi Ali Nafi, presidential adviser and deputy leader of the ruling Sudanese National Congress Party (NCP), declared that the military campaign in Darfur would continue irrespective of international criticism and pressure.

In protest against China's failure to exert pressure on Sudan to reach a solution to the conflict, the film director Steven Spielberg in February resigned as artistic adviser to the Olympic Games in Beijing and donated US$1 million to aid groups helping non-Arabs in Darfur. His stand was followed by an open letter on 14 February, signed by a number of prominent public figures, including Olympic athletes, calling on China to step up its efforts to resolve the Darfur conflict.

The security threats to vehicles transporting aid to Darfur led to a halving of food rations for nearly 3 million people, and Sir John Holmes, the UN under-secretary-general for humanitarian affairs, reported in April that the situation in Darfur had worsened, with up to 300,000 deaths as a result of the conflict.

In July the chief prosecutor of the International Criminal Court (ICC) in The Hague, Luis Moreno-Ocampo, sought an arrest warrant against President al-Bashir on the grounds that there was "reasonable evidence" that he had committed crimes against humanity, war crimes, and genocide in relation to the Darfur conflict. (The conflict had been referred to the ICC by the UN Security Council in 2005—see AR 2005, p. 203.) Supporters of al-Bashir protested and, despite its non-recognition of the jurisdiction of the ICC, the Sudanese government began a diplomatic campaign to gain support from countries within the Arab League (AL), the African Union (AU), and the Organisation of the Islamic Conference (OIC). In a speech in Darfur later in July, al-Bashir admitted problems and injustices in the region and, in a move designed to appease the ICC and the international community, the Sudanese government appointed a special prosecutor to investigate abuses committed in Darfur since the beginning of the rebellion in 2003. In November the Sudanese president declared a ceasefire in

Darfur and promised to disarm the Janjawid, although rebel groups dismissed the declaration as empty rhetoric. Meanwhile, the three judges appointed by the ICC (from Brazil, Ghana, and Latvia) were still deliberating at the end of 2008 over whether to indict al-Bashir.

In April the UN Security Council recognised in Resolution 1812 the success of the Comprehensive Peace Agreement (CPA), signed in January 2005 between the Sudanese government and the rebels operating in the south of the country, the Sudan People's Liberation Movement (SPLM) (see AR 2005, pp. 201-03). The Resolution extended until April 2009 the mandate of the UN Mission in Sudan (UNMIS), which had 10,000 peacekeepers in southern Sudan. To help humanitarian recovery and reconstruction in the whole of the country, the Sudan Consortium (a forum to review progress) held its third meeting in May, in Oslo, and donors pledged US$4.8 billion in aid for the period 2008-11.

Friction in March between the southern Sudanese forces and Arab cattle-herding Miseriyya tribesmen in the disputed oil-rich region of Abyei, which lay across the north-south divide in the country, resulted in a number of deaths. The ruling National Congress Party (NCP) denounced the SPLM's establishment of an administration in Abyei without consultation. Further clashes took place between the military wing of the SPLM (the Sudan People's Liberation Army, SPLA) and the national Sudanese army, resulting in the deaths of 50 people and the displacement of 50,000. The dispute between the government of Southern Sudan and the NCP over the demarcation of Abyei boundaries was referred to the Permanent Court of Arbitration in The Hague. In August, however, President al-Bashir appointed Arop Moyak Mong Toj of the SPLM as chief of Abyei administration and mandated Rahama Abdel Rahman al-Nour of the NCP, as his deputy, to formulate proposals for the administration of Abyei.

In preparation for the national elections envisaged under the CPA, the Sudanese government carried out a national census in April. Darfurian rebel groups—as well as Minni Minnawi, the leader of the main rebel faction which had signed the 2006 Darfur Peace Agreement and who was now a senior advisor to al-Bashir, and Imam Al-Sadig al-Mahdi of the Ansar movement and president of the Umma Party (UP)—criticised the government for excluding Darfur from the census and from future elections. After minor amendments in July, the National Assembly (the lower chamber of the bicameral Sudanese legislature) passed the National Elections Act, which provided for holding elections between January and April 2009.

The Sudanese economy remained heavily dependant on oil. China paid US$1 billion for two-thirds of Sudan's oil exports, and there were agreements in place for China to carry out further oil exploration. The French oil company, Total, which had abandoned its earlier oil exploration due to the civil war in the south, decided that it would resume operations, and Kuwait's Al-Kharfi Group bought a 3 per cent stake in the Sudanese oil company, Petrodar, for US$500 million. Concern over future food supplies prompted Abu Dhabi's Fund For Development to launch a large-scale agricultural project to develop more than 70,000 acres of land in Sudan. For similar reasons, Saudi Arabia and Egypt held talks with Sudan's government on developing agricultural projects. Lieutenant-General Salva Kiir Mayardit, the first vice president and president of the government of Southern Sudan, visited Egypt (in February) and the United Arab Emirates (in March) to promote trade and encourage investment in southern Sudan

In November Sayyid Ahmed al-Mirghani, the former president of the republic (1986-89) and brother of the religious head of the Khatmiyya Sufi order, and chairman of the Democratic Unionist Party (DUP), died in Cairo. Since 1989, when the army took power, he had lived in exile in Saudi Arabia and Egypt, but a rapprochement with President al-Bashir led to his return to Sudan in 2001 (see Obituary).

Ahmed Al-Shahi

LIBYA

CAPITAL: Tripoli   AREA: 1,759,540 sq km   POPULATION: 6,156,000 ('07)
OFFICIAL LANGUAGE: Arabic   POLITICAL SYSTEM: one-party republic
HEAD OF STATE: Col Moamar Kadhafi, "Leader of the Revolution" (since '69)
HEAD OF GOVERNMENT: Al-Baghdadi Ali al-Mahmudi, Secretary General of General People's Committee (since March '06)
MAIN IGO MEMBERSHIPS (NON-UN): AL, OPEC, OAPEC, AMU, AU, OIC, NAM
CURRENCY: Libyan dinar (end-'08 £1=LD1.7778, US$1=LD1.2365)
GNI PER CAPITA: US$9,010, $14,710 at PPP ('07 est based on regression)

THE diplomatic rehabilitation of Libya was confirmed during 2008 and was achieved without the regime of Colonel Moamar Kadhafi initiating any fundamental political changes domestically. The year began with the country taking a seat on the UN Security Council, and went on to encompass not merely Libya's engagement with the EU and the USA, but also a renewal of ties with Russia, which echoed the closeness of the relationship that had once existed between Libya and the Soviet Union.

In January, Foreign Minister Abdel Rahman Shalgam met US Secretary of State Condoleezza Rice in Washington, DC, the first official visit to the USA by a Libyan foreign minister since 1972. The two countries signed a science and technology accord and announced plans for future military, trade, and educational agreements. Outstanding issues remained, however, particularly over the final compensation payments for those killed in the destruction of Pan Am Flight 103 over Lockerbie in December 1988 (see AR 1988, p. 38) and the victims of the attack on a disco in West Berlin in 1986. Negotiations on these issues were underway, as well as in relation to Libyan civilians killed by the US bombing of Tripoli and Benghazi in April 1986 (see AR 1986, p. 57). Legislation approved in the USA in August prevented the full normalisation of bilateral relations until the issue of terrorism-related compensation had been definitively settled. This was finally achieved on 14 August with the signing of a Comprehensive Claims Settlement Agreement in Tripoli. The full terms of the agreement were not disclosed but it resolved the compensation issue and thereby opened the way for the normalisation of relations. It was followed by a visit to Tripoli in September by Condoleezza Rice, the first by a US secretary of state for over 50 years. In October Libya made its final compensation payments and in December a new US ambassador joined the US embassy in Tripoli.

Relations with Europe also witnessed remarkable developments in 2008. In April, outgoing Russian President Vladimir Putin visited Libya and agreed to cancel US$4.5 billion of Libyan debt in order to facilitate large military and civilian export orders. In November Kadhafi made a reciprocal visit to Moscow, during which he agreed deals on civilian energy and military purchases. In August Libya signed a treaty of friendship and co-operation with Italy. Under the terms of the agreement, Italy apologised for the crimes it had committed during the colonial period and agreed to provide compensation to Libya in the form of investment in infrastructure projects worth US$5 billion over a period of 25 years. Such projects included the construction of a 1,700km highway across the country, stretching from the Tunisian to the Egyptian border. In November Libya began negotiations with the EU over an association agreement.

Relations with Switzerland were less smooth, however, as Libya reacted angrily to the arrest by Swiss police in July of Kadhafi's disreputable youngest son, Hannibal al-Kadhafi, on charges of boisterous behaviour and abuse of employees. His arrest, and that of his wife Aline al-Kadhafi, took place at a luxury hotel in Geneva. The couple were later released on bail and left the country. The Libyan government denounced the charges as "fabricated" and retaliated by discontinuing oil shipments, arresting two Swiss citizens, recalling Libya's diplomatic envoy to Switzerland, reducing air links between the two countries, closing the offices of two Swiss corporations, and refusing to issue visas to Swiss citizens.

Domestically, little changed despite some grand rhetoric about forthcoming profound political and economic reforms to move the economy away from its reliance on state regulation. The regime appeared secure and dissent, whether secular or Islamist, remained actively discouraged. In a rare outbreak of unrest, fighting occurred in November in the remote south-east Kufra area between Libyan government forces and members of the Tabu tribe, which left at least 11 dead.

The economy, bolstered by high oil and gas prices in the early part of the year, performed strongly, achieving GDP growth of 7.3 per cent. Although there were slow advances towards the privatisation of Libya's five state-owned banks, the economy remained hamstrung by heavy bureaucracy and rampant corruption. The Libyan government signed energy agreements with Egypt in July, including the construction of a refinery in Egypt to treat Libyan crude oil. Libya also concluded a US$2.5 billion agreement with the UAE-based Star Consortium for the advancement of the largest Libyan refinery in Ras Lanuf. However, more interesting developments in the oil and gas sector concerned the discussions between the Russian giant, Gazprom, and the Libyan authorities regarding the former's offer to purchase oil and gas, and other possible projects including the construction of a trans-Mediterranean gas pipeline connecting Libya to Europe.

Yahia Zoubir

TUNISIA

CAPITAL: Tunis   AREA: 163,610 sq km   POPULATION: 10,248,000 ('07)
OFFICIAL LANGUAGE: Arabic   POLITICAL SYSTEM: multiparty republic
HEAD OF STATE AND GOVERNMENT: President (Gen.) Zine el-Abidine Ben Ali (since Nov '87)
RULING PARTY: Constitutional Democratic Rally (RCD)
PRIME MINISTER: Mohammed Ghannouchi (since Nov '99)
MAIN IGO MEMBERSHIPS (NON-UN): AL, AMU, ICO, AU, OIC, NAM, Francophonie
CURRENCY: Tunisian dinar (end-'08 £1=TD1.8933, US$1=TD1.3169)
GNI PER CAPITA: US$3,200, $7,130 at PPP ('07)

IN early January, Tunisia witnessed a significant popular rebellion in Redeyef in the phosphate-rich Gafsa area, close to the border with Algeria. The rebellion stemmed from the blatantly nepotistic employment policies of the phosphates company, abetted by the state-controlled trade union, the Union Générale des Travailleurs Tunisiens (UGTT), which meant that the children of company managers were recruited whilst overall youth unemployment in the region reached 40 per cent. The demonstrations spread to the Gafsa mining basin in places such as Oum Larayes, Metlaoui, and Feriana. To escape the ensuing brutal repression, entire families fled to the mountains or to neighbouring Algeria. Fearful that the disturbances could spread to the rest of the country, the authorities deployed troops and decided in April to seal the whole region. Another uprising occurred in June and resulted in the fatal shooting by police of a young demonstrator. In December, 38 people involved in the unrest faced trial in a court in Gafsa; six leaders of the revolt, including the movement's spokesman, Adnane Hajji, were sentenced to prison terms of more than 10 years.

In July, the ruling Constitutional Democratic Rally (RCD) exhorted President General Zine el-Abidine Ben Ali to run for a fifth term in the October 2009 elections, in order to "continue leading Tunisia in the path of progress and prosperity". No one doubted Ben Ali's re-election with more than 90 per cent of the votes. Despite assurances of a transparent and free election, harassment of potential candidates began as soon as opponents announced their candidacy. When Najib Chebbi of the best organised opposition party, the Democratic Progressive Party (PDP), announced in February that he would stand in the election, constitutional amendments were announced that effectively disqualified him, because he had not held his party leadership for "at least two consecutive years". In December, the PDP decided to maintain Chebbi as its presidential candidate, rather than boycott the election or nominate Maya Jéribi, PDP secretary general since December 2006 and the first woman to lead a political party in Tunisia.

Freedom of the press remained tightly controlled in Tunisia, although, during his visit to the country in April, France's President Nicolas Sarkozy commended the progress of human rights. In fact, at the time of Sarkozy's visit, two prominent figures, Rachid Khechana and Mongi Ellouze, respectively editor-in-chief and director of the PDP's weekly magazine, *Al-Mawqif*, were on hunger strike to protest against the "blockade" of their publication (they maintained their fast until 10 May). In October, former political prisoner Abdellatif Bouhajila went on hunger strike to protest against the authorities' refusal to allow him medical treatment and to issue him a passport. The Tunisian League for Human Rights (LTDH) was prevented from working, while the Tunisian Association of Democratic Women (ATFD) suffered continuous harassment. Although the use of the Internet increased considerably, the authorities regularly blocked various sites and resorted to interruptions to service, especially for journalists and human rights activists. In November, on the eve of the 21st anniversary of the "medical coup" that brought him to power, President Ben Ali freed 44 political prisoners, 21 of whom were former members of the Islamist En-Nahda movement who had been jailed for 18 years. However, one of those freed, Sadok Chourou, who headed En-Nahda in 1990, was re-arrested, charged, and then sentenced in December to one year in prison for allegedly renewing contacts with members of a banned organisation.

Despite the sophistication of the security apparatus, Tunisian authorities failed to foil the kidnapping in February of two Austrian tourists by the al-Qaida Organisation in the Islamic Maghreb (AQIM). Initially, AQIM, which transferred the two into Mali, demanded the liberation of its imprisoned members in Tunisia and Algeria but then settled for a ransom, which was duly paid in late October.

Tunisia enjoyed 5.1 per cent growth in GDP in 2008 (against 6.3 per cent in 2007), a respectable performance given the economic slowdown in the eurozone, Tunisia's main trading partner (a free trade agreement with the EU on industrial products became effective on 1 January). Inflation stabilised at 5 per cent. The banking sector, including the first private bank (Banque de Tunisie), produced remarkable results in spite of the global financial crisis. Tourism also witnessed important growth, with a 9 per cent increase in tourist revenue, according to figures published in October, and a projected US$2.4 billion income from tourism by the end of 2008. The government also approved a variety of gigantic investment projects, many funded by UAE-based companies. Other infrastructure projects nearing completion included the new US$700 million airport and the deepwater port near Enfidha, costing US$2 billion.

Yahia Zoubir

ALGERIA

CAPITAL: Algiers   AREA: 2,381,740 sq km   POPULATION: 33,853,000 ('07)
OFFICIAL LANGUAGE: Arabic   POLITICAL SYSTEM: multiparty republic
HEAD OF STATE AND GOVERNMENT: President Abdelaziz Bouteflika (FLN) (since April '99)
RULING PARTIES: Presidential Alliance coalition, consisting of National Liberation Front (FLN), National Democratic Rally (RND), and Movement for a Peaceful Society (MSP)
PRIME MINISTER: Ahmed Ouyahia (RND) (since June '08)
MAIN IGO MEMBERSHIPS (NON-UN): AL, OPEC, OAPEC, AMU, AU, OIC, NAM
CURRENCY: dinar (end-'08 £1=AD101.538, US$1=AD70.6227)
GNI PER CAPITA: US$3,620, $7,640 at PPP ('07 est based on regression)

THE terror campaign orchestrated in 2007 by al-Qaida's Maghreb affiliates (al-Qaida in the Islamic Maghreb—AQIM), targeting for the most part symbolic edifices in the Algerian capital (see AR 2008, pp. 220-21), subsided into significantly more limited terrorist activity in the central and eastern provinces of the country in 2008. Concentrated in the summer months of June, July, and August, the attacks perpetrated by AQIM suicide bombers claimed mainly civilian lives, reflecting in their irregularity the damage inflicted upon the Islamist organisation by the government's reinvigorated counter-terrorist strategy. Indeed, in addition to insulating the capital from further terrorist attacks, the security forces announced the elimination during 2008 of more than 162 AQIM personnel, including seven commanders ("emirs").

With an improved domestic security situation, the government of President Abdelaziz Bouteflika could concentrate its resources on the execution of the president's plan for constitutional reform. Aimed principally at removing the limit of two presidential terms imposed by the 1996 constitution, the planned amendments had to be enacted in time for the presidential election scheduled for the spring of 2009. Beginning with the return on 23 June of Ahmed Ouyahia as government head, replacing presidential ally Abdelaziz Belkhadem and thereby reversing the pecking order, which had been in place since a similar swap two years earlier (see AR 2007, p. 225), the presidential démarche culminated in the submission on 12 November of the proposed constitutional amendments to a parliamentary vote, rather than a referendum as had been initially envisaged.

Dubbed "partial and limited", the constitutional revision was approved by an overwhelming majority of legislators, thus obviating what many saw as the remaining obstacle to the re-election of Bouteflika for a third term. Notwithstanding the inclusion among the amendments of provisions for the promotion of women in civil and political society and for the protection of "national symbols", Bouteflika's constitutional reform was widely criticised as a reversal of Algeria's democratic progress. Breaking with tradition, former president Chadli Bendjedid (1979-92) added his voice, albeit obliquely, to those opposing the amendments. Many opponents went as far as soliciting another former president, Liamine Zeroual (1995-99), to run against Bouteflika in the forthcoming election, pointing to the lack of credible opposition to the current president. Accordingly, the focus of the national political debate shifted from the state of Bouteflika's health to ways of preventing or eventually discrediting his re-election through a boycott.

When presenting to Parliament his "action plan" for the implementation of the remainder of the president's programme, Prime Minister Ouyahia (following the constitutional change) praised the economic record of Bouteflika's presidency and promised policy continuity over the next five years. He indicated that a further US$150 billion government investment plan was being prepared, fuelling more controversy over Bouteflika's egregious style of governance. Indeed the president, in a public address at the end of July, delivered a self-critical verdict on his economic policy, claiming that it had been a total failure, particularly as regarded investment, privatisation, and diversification of the economy. Far from imputing failure to anyone or anything, however, the president's elliptical critique seemed like a one-off discursive reflection.

Despite the announced policy failures, the economy was expected to see a significant increase in GDP, owing to record oil prices on the international market. Sonatrach, the state's oil and gas company and the country's main source of income, expected to make an unprecedented US$80 billion from its hydrocarbon exports. However, the dramatic slump in oil prices in the latter part of the year in the face of the global economic downturn cost Algeria about US$5 billion in lost revenue. Still, record levels of export income allowed the country's commercial account surplus to grow by more than 40 per cent, reaching over US$40 billion. As a result, Algeria's foreign currency reserves exceeded US$140 billion by the end of the year. But against this rosy macroeconomic picture, the living standards of many Algerians remained below the level of their aspirations. The country's wealth trickled down to the grass roots of society only very slowly because of the enduring lethargy of other sectors of the economy. Policy-makers were yet again reminded of the urgent need to diversify the economy when oil prices fell to below US$40 per barrel towards the end of the year, jeopardising the government's ability to finance many of its ambitious infrastructure programmes. However, if anything, the inconsistency that characterised the declarations of cabinet members as to the impact of the global recession on the Algerian economy threw into sharper relief the government's general impotence in the economic sphere.

Diplomatically, 2008 began on a negative note for Algeria when the air force's dissatisfaction with the technical properties of the first batch of MiG-29 fighter jets delivered by Russia in 2007—as stipulated by a 2006 US$8 billion bilateral military contract—meant that President Bouteflika had to travel to Moscow to seek their replacement. Eager not to embarrass the Russian authorities, Algeria placed a surrogate order for more expensive military jets, thereby illustrating the value it attached to its longstanding strategic relationship with Russia.

On the European front, the launch of French President Nicolas Sarkozy's Union for the Mediterranean project in July reaffirmed Algeria's sceptical attitude towards EU policy initiatives. By offering a noticeably tepid reception to this regional venture, Algeria appeared intent on ensuring that its new-found confidence earned it more recognition from the EU for its strategic importance. Also, the fact that the proposed venture was a progeny of French diplomacy was a significant factor in the deliberations of Algerian policy-makers, who little appreciated Sarkozy's stated opposition to the concept of French repentance over its colonial record in Algeria. The arrest in France of an Algerian diplomat on suspicion of involvement in the murder in 1987 of prominent Algerian opposition figure Ali Mecili—a claim denied strongly by the Algerian government—increased further the tension within Franco-Algerian relations.

Relations with neighbouring Morocco remained acrimonious despite the kingdom's repeated calls for normalisation and opening of the border, which had been closed since 1994. The protracted question of Western Sahara remained the main issue of contention between the two countries.

Hakim Darbouche

MOROCCO

CAPITAL: Rabat   AREA: 446,550 sq km   POPULATION: 30,861,000 ('07)
OFFICIAL LANGUAGE: Arabic   POLITICAL SYSTEM: multiparty monarchy
HEAD OF STATE AND GOVERNMENT: King Mohammed VI (since July '99)
RULING PARTY: Istiqlal
PRIME MINISTER: Abbas el-Fassi (Istiqlal) (since Sept '07)
MAIN IGO MEMBERSHIPS (NON-UN): AL, AMU, OIC, NAM, Francophonie
CURRENCY: dirham (end-'08 £1=D11.6281, US$1=D8.0877)
GNI PER CAPITA: US$2,250, $3,990 at PPP ('07)

THE year began in Morocco with the spectacular dismantling in February of a terrorist group operationally linked to Belgium and led by Abdelkader Belliraj, a Belgian-Moroccan with an alleged history of mingling with Islamist groups and the secret services in both countries. The break-up of the "Belliraj" cell resulted in the arrest of over 30 people, the discovery of an important arms arsenal, and the shutting down of Al Badil Al Hadari, an official Islamist party in the kingdom. The trial of Belliraj began in October and was expected to uncover further international connections with the group. What became clear as the year progressed was that the security operation against Belliraj was merely the prelude to a much larger anti-terror campaign conducted by Moroccan government forces in the aftermath of the suicide attacks in Casablanca in 2007 (see AR 2008, p. 223). Numerous important arrests were announced in subsequent months, involving groups alleged to be affiliated with al-Qaida and with links to Iraq and Algeria. Despite its relative success in preventing further attacks from taking place, the government security clampdown received an embarrassing blow when, in April, nine prisoners convicted in connection with the 2003 Casablanca bombings (see AR 2003, p. 264) escaped from a Kenitra gaol, north of Rabat.

Politically, the year was marked by the creation of a new party backed by Fouad Ali al-Himma, a close friend of King Mohammed VI and who—to the surprise of most observers—had left government in 2007 to participate in the legislative elections. Growing out of an initial parliamentary "association of democrats" formed by al-Himma soon after his election to Parliament, the new Authenticity and Modernity Party (PAM) immediately attracted a number of legislators and succeeded in joining forces with the National Rally of Independents (RNI) to form the largest coalition bloc in Parliament. Many observers of Moroccan politics saw in this development a royal manoeuvre aimed at rationalising the party landscape and countering the growing influence of the moderate Islamists of the Party of Justice and Development (PJD). By adopting a discourse of modernity and democracy, PAM sought to appeal to young Moroccans who were increasingly disillusioned with the existing political parties. Local elections due in June 2009 promised to be the first electoral test of what was widely perceived as the "King's party".

For the most part, 2008 saw numerous signs of socio-economic distress throughout Morocco. A confluence of international economic and financial forces undermined the government's efforts to lift large portions of the population out of poverty. High energy and primary commodity prices on international markets caused additional inflationary pressure on the Moroccan economy, with immediate effects on popular purchasing power and living standards. Moreover, the dependence of the Moroccan economy on exports to European countries was adversely affected by the contraction of their economies as a result of the global financial crisis: a situation likely to worsen in 2009. Even the hundreds of thousands of dollars granted Morocco by its friends in the Gulf (Saudi Arabia and the UAE), in the form of subsidies for its energy and food imports bills, failed to help the government prevent economic deprivation from turning into social discontent. The food riots that took place in June in the port city of Sidi Ifni, in southern Morocco, were a stark reminder to the authorities of the urgency of an appropriate response to the desperate living conditions in many sections of society. Unfortunately, the brutal methods chosen by the authorities to disperse the rioters only exacerbated tensions and led to the reported death of eight protesters. Beyond local unrest, the events of Sidi Ifni had wider repercussions on Morocco's international standing as the government decided to impose a ban on the Qatar-based al-Jazeera television news channel, preventing it from operating within the kingdom on grounds of the "partiality" of its coverage of the riots. The conduct of the Moroccan authorities attracted criticism from local and international human rights organisations, especially following the prosecution of the al-Jazeera bureau chief and a Moroccan human rights activist.

Despite Morocco's microeconomic woes, other economic indicators bore more positive signs of progress. GDP growth reached more than 5 per cent and foreign direct investment in the service economy continued to constitute the linchpin of the government's long-term strategy for growth. Interest expressed in the vast Tangier-Med platform project—starting with Renault-Nissan, which announced the building of a €600 million car factory—was evidence of the country's strategic reorientation towards an export-driven economy, less dependant on the vagaries of rainfall. In this vein, the firmer anchoring of the Moroccan economy to that of the EU through an agreement reached in October, which granted the kingdom an "advanced status" in the framework of the European neighbourhood policy, not only set a new benchmark in EU-Mediterranean relations but assisted Morocco's quest for closer ties with Europe. The conclusion of this agreement under the auspices of the French presidency of the Council of the EU suggested that Franco-Moroccan relations were likely to remain privileged under French President Nicolas Sarkozy. The support within the French establishment for Morocco's autonomy proposal for Western Sahara, which often translated into lobbying on behalf of the kingdom within the UN and francophone Africa, was clearly visible throughout the year.

By contrast, relations with Algeria remained strained. The issue of Western Sahara still prevented both countries from overcoming their differences to allow the realisation of regional integration under the de facto suspended Arab Maghreb Union (AMU). Unusual rhetorical posturing over the issue of border closure, fuelled by Morocco's media campaign pillorying Algeria's refusal to normalise relations and open its side of the land border, which had been closed since 1994, added a new dimension to their traditional animosity. The fact that

King Mohammed VI added his explicit voice to that of his ministers when, in two of his speeches (July and November), he called upon Algeria to open its border, reflected the damaging impact that the status quo was having on the Moroccan economy. Strategic divergence between the two neighbours was reaffirmed by their different responses to the military coup in Mauritania in August (see pp. 264-65): Algeria refused to recognise the legitimacy of the junta, whereas Morocco showed a more accommodating attitude.

Hakim Darbouche

WESTERN SAHARA

CAPITAL: Al Aaiún AREA: 284,000 sq km POPULATION: 267,405 ('04 est)
STATUS: regarded by Morocco as under its sovereignty, whereas independent Sahrawi Arab
    Democratic Republic (SADR) was declared by Polisario Front in 1976
MAIN IGO MEMBERSHIPS (NON-UN): AU
CURRENCY: Moroccan dirham (de facto)
GNP PER CAPITA: n/a

PEACE talks on the resolution of the Western Sahara conflict, initiated in 2007 under the guidance of the UN secretary-general's personal envoy, Peter van Walsum (see AR 2008, pp. 224-25), continued between the two main protagonists for a third round (7-9 January) and a fourth (16-18 March) in Manhasset, New York. With both the government of Morocco and the Polisario Front reportedly unwilling to make concessions, the "Manhasset process" appeared incapable of achieving any meaningful rapprochement between Morocco's autonomy proposal and Polisario's attachment to the principle of self-determination. Acknowledging this failure when briefing the UN Security Council at the end of April, van Walsum openly questioned the plausibility of independence for Western Sahara in view of the Security Council's reluctance to support the legally legitimate right of the Sahrawi people to define their destiny through referendum. The Dutch diplomat elaborated on his reasoning when, in two separate newspaper interviews published in May and August, he explained that unless France and the USA supported it, independence for Western Sahara was "unrealistic". He added that the sooner the Security Council took account of this reality and encouraged the Sahrawi nationalist movement to accept it, the better it would be for all.

Although the Security Council chose not to take such a daring leap forward when adopting Resolution 1813, which renewed for a further year (until 30 April 2009) the mandate of the UN Mission for the Referendum in Western Sahara (MINURSO) and called for continued dialogue between the parties, the Polisario leadership announced its refusal to take part in further rounds of negotiation under the auspices of van Walsum, in whose impartiality it had lost confidence. Concerned about the future of the peace process, the UN Secretariat unceremoniously dismissed the secretary-general's personal envoy at the end of August by simply not renewing his contract. As a result, the diplomatic pro-activism of the last two years on the issue of Western Sahara looked set to subside. However, a regional tour in early September by US Secretary of State Condoleezza Rice, during which she met the leaders of Algeria and Morocco, brought—despite her reiterating the Bush administration's support for Morocco's autonomy plan—fresh hopes for the nomination of a new UN moderator, when the name of veteran US Middle East diplomat Christopher Ross was floated. Ross had attended the first four rounds of talks at Manhasset as a US observer, and was said to be highly respected by the regional players.

Meanwhile, Morocco's well-chronicled human rights abuses within the Western Saharan territories and Polisario's treatment of refugees in the Tindouf camps (in south-west Algeria) continued to be the subject of vigorous investigations, the latest of which was reported by Human Rights Watch (HRW) at the end of December. In their extensive document, deemed the most comprehensive and objective on these issues for many years, HRW reporters confirmed Morocco's systematic violation of Sahrawis' rights to expression, association, and assembly. In the Polisario refugee camps based in Algeria, HRW reported the marginalisation by the nationalist movement of people who directly opposed Polisario's leadership, but found no evidence of restrictions on the freedom of movement of refugees. The HRW report largely corroborated the findings of investigations published earlier in the year by Amnesty International and the Moroccan weekly magazine, *Telquel*.

Hakim Darbouche

VI EQUATORIAL AFRICA

HORN OF AFRICA—KENYA—TANZANIA—UGANDA

ETHIOPIA—ERITREA—SOMALIA—DJIBOUTI

Ethiopia

CAPITAL: Addis Ababa   AREA: 1,104,300 sq km   POPULATION: 79,087,000 ('07)
OFFICIAL LANGUAGE: Amharic   POLITICAL SYSTEM: multiparty republic
HEAD OF STATE: President Girma Woldegiorgis (since Oct '01)
RULING PARTY: Ethiopian People's Revolutionary Democratic Front (ERPDF)
HEAD OF GOVERNMENT: Prime Minister Meles Zenawi (since Aug '95)
MAIN IGO MEMBERSHIPS (NON-UN): AU, COMESA, ACP, NAM
CURRENCY: birr (end-'08 £1=Br14.3846, US$1=Br10.0049)
GNI PER CAPITA: US$220, $780 at PPP ('07)

Eritrea

CAPITAL: Asmara   AREA: 117,600 sq km   POPULATION: 4,842,000 ('07)
OFFICIAL LANGUAGES: Arabic & Tigrinyam   POLITICAL SYSTEM: transitional government
HEAD OF STATE AND GOVERNMENT: President Isayas Afewerki (since May '93)
RULING PARTY: People's Front for Democracy and Justice (PFDJ)
MAIN IGO MEMBERSHIPS (NON-UN): AU, COMESA, ACP, NAM
CURRENCY: nakfa (end-'08 £1=N21.8546, US$1=15.2000)
GNI PER CAPITA: US$230, $520 at PPP ('07 est based on regression)

Somalia

CAPITAL: Mogadishu   AREA: 637,660 sq km   POPULATION: 8,696,000 ('07)
OFFICIAL LANGUAGES: Somali & Arabic   POLITICAL SYSTEM: transitional government
HEAD OF STATE AND GOVERNMENT: acting President Sheikh Aden Madobe (since Dec '08)
PRIME MINISTER: Nur Hassan Hussein (since Nov '07)
MAIN IGO MEMBERSHIPS (NON-UN): AL, AU, ACP, OIC, NAM
CURRENCY: Somalia shilling (end-'08 £1=Ssh2,037.36, US$1=Ssh1,417.00)
GNI PER CAPITA: Low income: US$935 or less ('07 est)

Djibouti

CAPITAL: Djibouti   AREA: 23,200 sq km   POPULATION: 833,000 ('07)
OFFICIAL LANGUAGES: Arabic & French   POLITICAL SYSTEM: multiparty republic
HEAD OF STATE AND GOVERNMENT: President Ismail Omar Guelleh (since April '99)
RULING PARTIES: Union for a Presidential Majority (UMP) (coalition of the Popular Rally for
    Progress (RPP), the Front for the Restoration of Unity and Democracy (FRUD), the People's
    Social Democratic Party (PPSD), and the National Democratic Party (PND)
PRIME MINISTER: Dilleita Mohamed Dilleita (since March '01)
MAIN IGO MEMBERSHIPS (NON-UN): AL, AU, COMESA, ACP, OIC, Francophonie, NAM
CURRENCY: Djibouti franc (end-'08 £1=DFr250.997, US$1=DFr174.570)
GNI PER CAPITA: US$1,090, $2,260 at PPP ('07)

ETHIOPIA.   Local and regional elections were held in two stages across Ethiopia in April for wereda (district) and kebele (neighbourhood) councils, at the same time as parliamentary by-elections. An opposition coalition, the United Ethiopian Democratic Forces (UEDF), withdrew three days before polling began, complaining of harassment and procedural misconduct. The UEDF had been able to register only a handful of candidates against the ruling Ethiopian People's Revolutionary Democratic Front (EPRDF), led by Prime Minister Meles Zenawi.

The Oromo Federalist Democratic Movement (OFDM) withdrew from the second round on 20 April, complaining of vote rigging and intimidation. The US-based monitoring organisation Human Rights Watch described the elections as "a rubber stamp on the EPRDF's near-monopoly on power". In the final results, the EPRDF was declared to have won 559 seats in 623 districts, as well as 38 of the parliamentary seats, which had originally been won by opposition candidates in 2005 (see AR 2005, pp. 213-14). Unrest followed the announcement of the results, with arrests and some deaths reported. Later in the year, several OFDM leaders were arrested, and in late December opposition leader Birtukan Mideksa, who had been jailed in 2005 and later released, was re-arrested after comments she made on a European tour.

The Ogaden crisis worsened, with drought and a 13-year-long rebellion helping to create food vulnerability throughout the vast eastern Somali region. Despite claims of a good harvest in the June-October season, several areas of the country suffered serious food insecurity, with as many as 8 million people needing food assistance, especially in the Gode, Wardheer, Korahe, Dhagahbur, and Fiiq districts of the Somali region, which also suffered severe water shortages and livestock deaths from February onwards. The drought extended to Oromiya and other southern and eastern parts of the country. According to World Health Organisation figures, the national prevalence of malnutrition was above 40 per cent.

In January the Ogaden National Liberation Front (founded in 1984) issued a statement accusing Western aid agencies of allowing the government to use food aid as a weapon "to suppress the people's resistance". Human Rights Watch published a report in June, sub-titled "war crimes and crimes against humanity in the Ogaden area", which detailed mass rape, the torturing of children, and the displacement of tens of thousands of people in what was described as a "scorched earth" campaign.

Relations with Eritrea were tense as the frontier dispute remained unresolved, with the border still not demarcated and the town of Badme in Ethiopian hands. After a UN Security Council decision not to renew the mandate of the UN Mission in Ethiopia and Eritrea (UNMEE), the UN last units left the country in October.

Coffee exports earned US$525 million in 2007-08, out of total export earnings of US$1.7 billion from oil seeds, khat, cereals, leather products, gold, and cut flowers. Despite this, Ethiopia remained one of the world's poorest countries, ranking 170th on the UN Human Development Index.

ERITREA. As was the case with other nations in the Horn of Africa, Eritrea suffered from poor rainfall and a consequent fall in food production during the year. The United Nations Office for the Co-ordination of Humanitarian Affairs reported in September that many Eritreans crossing into Ethiopia's Afar region were in "very poor nutritional condition". By October it was clear that cereal production would reach only half the 2007 figure, and the UN's Central Emergency Response Fund set aside US$2 million for seeds, fertiliser, and agricultural instruments. Children, pregnant women, and pastoralists were considered especially vulnerable. Eritrea had previously met approximately 60 per cent of its food needs from domestic production.

Relations with both Ethiopia and Djibouti were strained as unresolved border disputes continued, and clashes in June left six Djibouti soldiers dead and over 50 wounded.

Eritrea's human rights record was criticised in a report by the US bureau of democracy, human rights and labour in March, although the government dismissed this as "politically motivated" and full of "exaggerations and fabrications". The report claimed that violations included illegal killings, torture, and the limitation of basic rights such as freedom of speech, assembly, and religion. Security police arrested several evangelical Christians in May, targeting the Berhane Hiwet group in Keren. It was believed that as many as 2,000 evangelicals were in jail for their beliefs, as the government only recognised the Ethiopian Orthodox, Catholic, and Lutheran churches apart from the majority faith, Islam. In August, 40 Muslim clerics of Saho origin were also arrested. Other violations included the press-ganging of young people for military service and the persecution of military service evaders. The armed forces remained the largest in sub-Saharan Africa and numbered at least 320,000 troops from a total population of 4.7 million, according to the World Bank. Military service was obligatory for a minimum period of between 12 and 18 months for everybody aged between 18 and 40.

The IMF estimated growth in the Eritrean economy at only 1.2 per cent in 2008.

On 8 December, the leading Eritrean intellectual and historian Jordan Gebre-Medhin died in the USA at the age of 64.

SOMALIA. Attacks on shipping and seizures of vessels on the high seas by pirates from Somalia increased sharply in 2008, and attracted considerable international media attention. The pirates were reportedly based mainly in the port of Eyl, in the self-declared autonomous region of Puntland. From the beginning of the year up to mid-November there were over 90 attacks, with 39 ships captured. According to International Maritime Bureau figures, this was a threefold increase over the 31 reported attacks in 2007. In one well-publicised hijacking in April, the pirates captured a French luxury yacht, *Le Ponant*, and, in another assault, in November, a Saudi Arabian oil super-tanker was seized over 800km from the coast. Estimates of the amount extorted in 2008 in (often undisclosed) ransoms ranged from US$50 million to US$150 million. Late in the year, raiders expanded operations into Kenyan sea lanes. Eighteen countries deployed warships in the Indian Ocean to counter the threat, and the EU launched its first naval operation in the area in early December. Shortly afterwards, the UN Security Council also approved measures to permit international anti-piracy operations inside territorial waters.

From January onwards, control of the southern part of Somalia began to slip away from the tottering transitional federal government (TFG), which was backed by a US-trained Ethiopian force, as orchestrated violence by the al-Shabaab militias of the deposed Union of Islamic Courts (UIC) and other groups escalated, beginning in Jubbada and Shabeellaha regions. By March, the African Union Mission to Somalia (AMISOM) had reached just one-third of its pledged strength of 8,000, with only Ugandan and a few Burundian soldiers in place. AMISOM was consequently able to play only a restricted peacekeeping role.

In March, a US navy submarine fired *Tomahawk* missiles into Somalia at a target described as a "known al-Qaida terrorist" and in early May another strike apparently killed Aden Hashi Ayro, an al-Shabaab commander who was also alleged to have links with al-Qaida. A bomb attack in Baidoa a few days later killed eight government soldiers, apparently in retaliation.

On 12 May, as violence continued to spread, peace talks started in Djibouti between the TFG and moderate members of the Alliance for the Re-liberation of Somalia, based in Eritrea, which had rejected earlier attempts at negotiations until the Ethiopian troops withdrew. At the beginning of June the TFG and one Alliance faction signed a ceasefire agreement, which was rejected by another Alliance splinter group in Asmara. Al-Shabaab militias were not represented, and by the end of 2008 military events on the ground had rendered the Djibouti talks—still continuing into November—largely irrelevant, especially as the TFG's President Ahmed Abdullahi Yusuf did not support the power-sharing arrangements that had been negotiated.

In mid-April, street fighting broke out in Mogadishu between Islamic militias and Ethiopian forces deploying artillery and tanks, with a reported death toll, mainly civilian, of 81. In May, clashes took place in Beledweyne, capital of Hiran region, when insurgents ambushed a convoy. Fighting in the capital continued intermittently and on 8 June clashes in the northern suburbs of Wardhigley and Yaqsin left dozens dead and thousands more homeless. Bakara market was also shelled. In September fighting between militia factions broke out in Jowhaar, capital of Shabeellaha Dhexe region and a former TFG stronghold, and further violence rocked Mogadishu, again especially around Bakara market, leading Ali Sheikh Yassin of Somalia's Elman Human Rights group to describe the situation as worse than 2007. In December, Yassin estimated casualty figures for the period 2007-08 at 16,210 dead and more than 29,000 injured.

In August, 10 ministers resigned from the TFG over the infighting between President Ahmed and Prime Minister Nur Hassan Hussein. By November, various rebel groups including al-Shabaab and clan militias had seized control of towns and localities across the country, including the port city of Marka. On 16 December the president tried unilaterally to sack the prime minister without parliamentary support, resulting in his own forced resignation two weeks later on 29 December. He was replaced by the speaker, Sheikh Aden Madobe, as acting president. By the end of December the TFG controlled only a few streets in Mogadishu; the Ethiopian army was preparing to leave; and fighting had broken out between the al-Shabaab militias and the Ahlu-Sunna wal-Jama movement, after al-Shabaab fighters allegedly desecrated the graves of clerics in Kismaayo. UN Secretary-General Ban Ki Moon reported in December that there was no support for a proposed UN intervention in Somalia.

DJIBOUTI. Candidates from the ruling Union for a Presidential Majority (UMP) of President Ismail Omar Guelleh were unopposed in legislative elections in February. Opposition parties, which had won 38 per cent of votes in elections in 2003 without gaining a single seat, boycotted the ballot in protest against the "undemocratic" polling system.

The food crisis continued through the year as poor rainfall resulted in livestock deaths. In May the World Bank ranked Djibouti second in the world (after Haiti) on a watch list for food insecure countries with a high probability of social unrest.

Relations between Djibouti and France remained close, despite a sour note as the "affaire Bernard Borrel" (a dispute over the death of a French judge, whose charred body had been found in a ravine in 1995) dragged on. The International Court of Justice held hearings in January on Djibouti's complaints, filed in early 2006, and delivered judgment in June, effectively dismissing them all. French courts subsequently convicted two senior Djiboutian officials in absentia of bribing witnesses in the case, a finding condemned as "overtly racist" by the Djibouti government. From January to June, intermittent border clashes with Eritrea over the area near Doumeira Island resulted in Djiboutian casualties. France, which had 2,600 soldiers permanently garrisoned in Djibouti, provided logistical and intelligence support for its former colony during the crisis.

At the end of July, the government granted 500 sq km of land to a consortium headed by a member of the Saudi Arabian bin Laden family, to build a new city and a bridge across the Mandab Strait to Yemen at a cost of US$200 billion. However, the plan was dismissed by the *Economist*, among others, as "a fantasy".

Colin Darch

KENYA

CAPITAL: Nairobi   AREA: 580,370 sq km   POPULATION: 37,531,000 ('07)
OFFICIAL LANGUAGES: Kiswahili & English   POLITICAL SYSTEM: multiparty republic
HEAD OF STATE AND GOVERNMENT: President Mwai Kibaki (PNU) (since Dec '02)
RULING PARTIES: Party for National Unity (PNU) and Orange Democratic Movement (ODM)
PRIME MINISTER: Raila Odinga (ODM)
MAIN IGO MEMBERSHIPS (NON-UN): AU, EAC, SADC, COMESA, ACP, CWTH, NAM
CURRENCY: Kenya shilling (end '08 £1=Ks112.432, US$1=Ks78.2000)
GNI PER CAPITA: US$680, $1,540 at PPP ('07)

THE June budget sought to promote economic recovery, following the widespread violence stemming from the disputed presidential elections of December 2007 (see AR 2008, pp. 231-32), which had caused some 1,500 deaths and displaced 600,000 people. The socioeconomic challenges included inflation, high fuel prices, unemployment, rising food costs, and uneven food distribution. Clearing congestion at the port of Mombasa and opening up blocked supply routes were tackled urgently, but little was done to redistribute income and wealth by a coalition government faced with the heavy cost of a 42-member cabinet and the huge salaries and allowances that the members of the National Assembly (unicameral legislature), also elected in December, awarded themselves.

The two main party leaders, who both claimed victory in the December 2007 presidential elections—Mwai Kibaki of the Party for National Unity (PNU) and Raila Odinga of the Orange Democratic Movement (ODM)—signed a power-sharing agreement on 28 February, subsequently cemented by the National Accord and Reconciliation Act. Under the terms of the agreement, Kibaki retained the presidency for a second term and Odinga became prime minister, supported by two deputy prime ministers, one nominated by each member of the ruling coalition. On 6 March the National Assembly elected a speaker from the ODM, which commanded a narrow majority of seats; 21 Assembly members (out of 210) were women. There were early disputes over the standing and powers of the prime minister, the size of the cabinet, and the distribution of portfolios; ODM secured local government, but most of the key ministries, including finance and internal security, went to the PNU. Old stagers were favoured over new and younger politicians.

Under pressure from Kofi Annan, the former UN secretary-general, and his group of eminent persons, two commissions were established. The Commission of Inquiry into the Post-Election Violence was chaired by Justice Philip Waki and produced a lengthy, hard-hitting report in October, which found that though there was spontaneous rioting and arson after the election results were declared, most of the killings and evictions were planned (see Documents). The police record was found to be poor. Ten key organisers and financiers of the violence were identified, but their names would only be revealed if the recommended special tribunal was not established. The second body was the Independent Review Commission, which looked closely at the election in all its stages, and reported in September. Chaired by Johann Kriegler, a South African judge, it recommended the immediate dissolution of the Electoral Commission of Kenya, radical electoral reform, and the introduction of a new voter regulation system. It was unable, however, on available evidence, to decide who had won the presidential poll.

Neither commission could change the ethnic base of Kenyan politics, which was at the root of long-standing grievances over the distribution of power, wealth, and land. While there was a strong case for taking legal action against the guilty, there was also the danger of exciting communal violence by doing so, for example, by charging Kalenjin politicians with the murder of Kikuyu in the North Rift Valley.

A new political alliance was said to be taking shape within the PNU, ready to take over the party and contest the presidential elections when Kibaki retired, as he was constitutionally required to do, in 2012. Early in July the National Assembly passed a no-confidence vote in Amos Kimunya, the finance minister, on the grounds that he had mishandled public funds and property; he was replaced by John Michuki, minister for the environment. Three cabinet ministers were among nine Assembly members across the political divide who were charged with corruption and other serious offences. Tension remained high in some parts of the country, including the slum areas of Nairobi and the Mount Elgin region, where the military proposed to build a training camp.

In other developments, the government approved a controversial biofuel project to establish a sugar cane plantation in the Tana river delta. Many thousands of Somali refugees crossed the border into the north-eastern province, in flight from Somalia's civil war, their numbers significantly increased on 2007, according to the UN high commissioner for refugees.

Meanwhile, there was widespread rejoicing in Kenya at the success of Barack Obama, with his Kenyan roots, in the US presidential election.

William Tordoff

TANZANIA

CAPITAL: Dodoma   AREA: 947,300 sq km   POPULATION: 40,432,000 ('07) (incl Zanzibar)
OFFICIAL LANGUAGES: Kiswahili & English   POLITICAL SYSTEM: multiparty republic
HEAD OF STATE AND GOVERNMENT: President Jakaya Kikwete (CCM) (since Dec '05)
RULING PARTY: Chama Cha Mapinduzi (CCM)
PRESIDENT OF ZANZIBAR: Amani Abeid Karume (since Oct '00)
PRIME MINISTER: Mizengo Kayanza Pinda (since Feb '08)
MAIN IGO MEMBERSHIPS (NON-UN): AU, EAC, COMESA, SADC, ACP, CWTH, NAM
CURRENCY: Tanzanian shilling (end-'08 £1=Tsh1,894.24, US$1=Tsh1,317.50)
GNI PER CAPITA: US$400 (mainland Tanzania only), $1,200 at PPP ('07)

IN what one analyst described as the "people's budget", spending was scheduled to rise by 19 per cent, with some 64 per cent going to education, roads, health, agriculture, water, and energy. To meet this extra cost, the government proposed to take advantage of record prices for gold and review its policy of providing tax exemptions for the mining sector. The country's reliance on external finance was to be reduced further. Because of the popularity of smoking nationwide, the government faced the dilemma of whether to cut back the highly profitable production of tobacco in favour of less harmful crops.

In February, following the resignation of Edward Lowassa, the prime minister, over a suspect power contract awarded in 2006, President Jakaya Kikwete reduced the size of his cabinet by merging some ministries and abolishing others. He dropped nine ministers, most of them veterans inherited from his predecessor's government. The new prime minister was Mizengo Kayanza Pinda, a virtual political newcomer. The proportion of women in the cabinet fell from 30 to 25 per cent.

In April a woman became the first albino member of the National Assembly (legislature) out of a total albino population of roughly 8,000. At the same time, a crackdown was launched on those responsible for the ritual murder of 26 albinos, mostly women and children. The murders were linked to witchcraft and a growing trade in albino body parts.

Investigations revealed mounting evidence of fraud in the country's central bank and of corrupt practices in public institutions generally. Greater emphasis was placed on asset recovery rather than the prosecution of offenders.

In a bid to end the acute political divisions that followed the 2005 and earlier elections in Zanzibar, the islands' ruling party, Chama cha Mapinduzi (CCM), and the opposition Civic United Front struck a deal in February whereby, because of the near equal support that each received, the president of Zanzibar would be drawn from the winning party and the prime minister from the runner-up party. Despite further party meetings, this arrangement was neither ratified nor written into the constitution.

William Tordoff

UGANDA

CAPITAL: Kampala   AREA: 241,040 sq km   POPULATION: 30,930,000 ('07)
OFFICIAL LANGUAGE: English   POLITICAL SYSTEM: multi-party republic
HEAD OF STATE AND GOVERNMENT: President Yoweri Museveni (since Jan '86)
RULING PARTY: National Resistance Movement (NRM) heads broad-based coalition
PRIME MINISTER: Apollo Nsibambi (since April '99)
MAIN IGO MEMBERSHIPS (NON-UN): AU, SADC, COMESA, ACP, CWTH, OIC, NAM
CURRENCY: new Uganda shilling (end-'08 £1=Ush2,792.83, US$1=Ush1,942.50)
GNI PER CAPITA: US$340, $920 at PPP ('07)

ECONOMIC growth of 8.9 per cent was offset by higher oil and fuel prices and an increase in inflation. The budget nearly doubled spending on roads, and steps were taken to ease slightly the national power shortage. Worrying trends included increases in corruption on the part of officials, the growing cost of public administration, and the rising cost of living. President Yoweri Museveni seemed certain to seek a fourth term; as his popularity waned, he became less tolerant of press criticism.

In February and March, and again in late December, there were real hopes that Ugandan and rebel Lord's Resistance Army (LRA) delegates would reach a lasting peace settlement. Each time, however, these hopes were dashed by LRA leader Joseph Kony's insistence, from his remote camp in the forests of the north-eastern Democratic Republic of Congo (DRC), that there could be no final settlement unless the International Criminal Court (ICC) withdrew the arrest warrants issued in 2005 against him and his senior commanders for war crimes and crimes against humanity. The ICC refused to comply and also rejected the Uganda government's proposal that the accused should be tried under a combination of Uganda's domestic court system and traditional Acholi justice, rather than at The Hague. In the interim, the LRA—in the form either of the main body of some 600 troops or smaller rebel groups—carried out brutal raids over a wide area, stretching from Uganda to the DRC and the Central African Republic. In December a regional offensive against the LRA, to include troops from the UN Mission in the Democratic Republic of Congo (MONUC), was suspended when James Obita, the LRA's new chief negotiator, asked that another attempt should be made to reach a settlement. When this came to nothing, LRA raids continued, resulting in the deaths of hundreds of people in the DRC.

Among the considerations that militated against an end to the conflict were the lack of will—as in Darfur—of the international community to impose a settlement; the understandable refusal of the ICC to deny the fundamental principles of human rights on which it was based; the fact that the LRA itself was divided into factions, whose leaders were concerned to safeguard their own future in Acholi politics; the equivocal stand sometimes taken by the government of Southern Sudan towards the peace negotiations; and the involvement of both the LRA and Uganda in the affairs of the DRC, each allegedly seeking to benefit from that country's rich mineral resources. The 21-year old conflict underlined the need for a rapid response force to avert warfare in the region, and in November African military chiefs met in Nairobi to finalise plans to set up the 13-nation Eastern Africa Standby Brigade, first mooted in 2007.

In other developments, the introduction of a controversial land amendment bill sharpened the divisions between President Museveni and King Ronald Mutebi of the traditional kingdom of Buganda in south-central Uganda; each took up seemingly irreconcilable positions over land and governance. King Mswati of Swaziland, a distant relative of Mutebi, tried to negotiate a settlement. Heritage Oil, a Canadian oil prospecting firm, announced that it had discovered a large oil deposit in the Lake Albert basin, bordering the DRC. Discontent was rife in Uganda's prisons, especially in the overcrowded Luzira maximum security prison in Kampala. Uganda joined Rwanda and the DRC in a 10-year conservation plan to prevent the extinction of the species of mountain gorillas, who lived along the borders between the three countries.

William Tordoff

NIGERIA—GHANA—SIERRA LEONE—THE GAMBIA—LIBERIA

NIGERIA

CAPITAL: Abuja   AREA: 923,770 sq km   POPULATION: 147,983,000 ('07)
OFFICIAL LANGUAGE: English   POLITICAL SYSTEM: multiparty republic
HEAD OF STATE AND GOVERNMENT: President Umaru Musa Yar Adua (PDP) (since May '07)
RULING PARTY: People's Democratic Party (PDP)
MAIN IGO MEMBERSHIPS (NON-UN): AU, ECOWAS, OPEC, ACP, OIC, NAM, CWTH
CURRENCY: naira (end-'08 £1=N200.854, US$1=N139.700)
GNI PER CAPITA: US$930, $1,770 at PPP ('07)

THE year 2008 was an uneasy one for Nigeria. Poverty and social indicators starkly revealed the problems facing its leaders: 71 per cent of the population lived below the international poverty line, one child in 10 died before the age of five, 7 million children were not in school; and more than 3 million people were living with HIV/AIDS, the second largest number in any country in the world (and, proportionately, some 3.1 per cent of the population).

Politically, although his own position appeared secure, President Umaru Musa Yar Adua faced growing opposition that successfully forced re-runs in some of the contested seats in the legislature, the bicameral National Assembly, to which elections had been held in April 2007 (see AR 2008, p. 235). The opposition focused additionally on targeting the slow level of promised reforms and the government's failure to quell the violence in the Niger Delta. Yar Adua himself, on 12 December, nearly two years after the April 2007 presidential elections that were deemed flawed by international observers, finally obtained a favourable ruling from the Supreme Court confirming his election victory. The presidential candidates of the opposition All Nigeria People's Party (ANPP) and Action Congress (AC) (respectively, Major-General Muhammadu Buhari and Alhaji Atiku Abubakar) had contested Yar Adua's victory, although their petitions were rejected in February by a special legal tribunal. They accepted the Supreme Court judgment, though neither was prepared to work for Yar Adua.

The courts also had to rule on the election of some state governors. In November, the court of appeal upheld the petition of Adams Oshiomhole of the Action Congress that he had won the April 2007 Edo state election against Osarheimen Osunbor, incumbent governor from the ruling People's Democratic Party (PDP). However, in the case of Cross River, Bayelsa, Kogi, Adamawa, and Sokoto states, the PDP governors, whose election victories had been nullified by the appellate courts in favour of opposition candidates, were returned after re-run elections. On 9 March Chief Vincent Ogbulafor emerged as the national chairman of the PDP.

On 18 December, Yar Adua carried out a major cabinet reshuffle: 16 new ministers were sworn in while many of the remaining ministers changed positions. Rikwana Lukman returned to office as petroleum minister. The key ministries of Niger Delta, commerce and industry, and finance went, as expected, to Achike Udenwa, Lukman Babalola, and Ufot Ekaette, respectively. Democracy agitators, however, expressed doubts as to whether the new cabinet would make much difference to the government's economic policy. The secretary general of the Alliance for Credible Election (Ace-Nigeria), Emma Eyeazu, said the cabinet "is colourless, so we are not expecting much. It looks like settling political friends and not anything serious." The convenor for United Action for Democracy, Abiodun Aremu, said he was under no illusion that the team would perform better than the previous one, since ministers simply acted out the script handed down by Yar Adua.

With a population close to 150 million, none of Nigeria's problems was easy to resolve and the economy was expected to be adversely affected by the world recession, especially as the collapse in the oil price curbed Nigeria's main source of income (oil revenues accounted for 40 per cent of GDP and 83 per cent of government revenue). Other, non-oil sectors of the economy were expanding slowly, and the new commerce and industry minister, Achike Udenwa, pointed to infrastructure as a major issue, including irregular power supply and inadequate transportation. The 2009 budget of N2.87 trillion, presented, after considerable delay, at the beginning of December, represented an 8.4 per cent increase on the previous budget, but had been pared down to take account of the drop in oil prices.

An anti-corruption drive was one of Yar Adua's election promises, but during the course of 2008, corruption in the health ministry became a major scandal. The minister, Professor Adenike Grange, and her deputy, Gabriel Yakubu Aduku, voluntarily submitted their resignations in March after corruption charges had been levelled against them by the economic and financial crimes commission (EFCC). Senator Iyabo Obasanjo-Bello, the chairman of the Senate committee on health, was also indicted, and several other senior officials suspended. The details of the charges centred on contracts worth a total of N300 million, which were awarded by the health ministry without following due process in the last days of 2007. The tasks to be contracted were broken down into small units of slightly over N40 million each and backdated. However, disagreements over sharing the illegal proceeds from the contracts brought the corruption into the public domain.

Violence in the Niger Delta region had become a running sore for Nigeria and government efforts to resolve it had met with little success. In June armed rebels opened a new front in their campaign against foreign oil companies when they attacked a Royal Dutch Shell platform 120 miles off the coast. Up to that point, deepwater platforms had been seen as safe from attack. The result was the closure of the Bonga field. Chevron, too, was forced to reduce production after a pipeline attack, resulting in a cut of 300,000 barrels per day on the world market. The president appointed a senior UN official to help find a solution to the Delta unrest. Ibrahim Gambari, a former Nigerian foreign minister and special adviser to UN Secretary-General Ban Ki Moon, said in June that he would seek a 90-day truce in the Delta as a first step towards formal peace talks. He said: "We will hold thorough consultations with the militants and stakeholders in the Niger Delta so that we can have a truce to create an atmosphere for the summit." A brief ceasefire was announced by the main militant group, the Movement for the Emancipation of the Niger Delta (MEND), in June and July; in September, however, MEND intensified its attacks in response to the actions of a Nigerian military task force, which had engaged MEND fighters in ground battles.

Later in September, MEND announced another truce, but at the end of December Nigerian soldiers arrested the Delta oil rebel, Sabomabo Jackrich, at peace talks organised by Delta community leaders, raising fears of new violence as a result. Tony Urantu, a member of the government panel looking at solutions for Delta violence, argued that the arrest of Jackrich would derail the peace process, because it would lead to "loss of trust in government on the part of the Niger Delta". The government panel said that all militants should be granted amnesty if peace were to be achieved in the Delta, and advocated the release of Harry Okah, the leader of MEND, who had been extradited to Nigeria from Angola in February and was on trial for gun-running and treason.

Poverty was the root cause of the violence. Since the 1970s, Nigeria had produced more than US$300 billion worth of crude oil from the Delta region, which held an estimated 30 billion barrels of top grade oil, but only an estimated 13 per cent of this revenue had returned to the local economy of the Delta, one of the most impoverished areas in the country. Militants and local gangs stole an estimated 100,000 barrels of oil per day from pipelines, in an operation known as "bunkering", and operated hundreds of illegal refineries in the Delta, producing oil either to sell locally or to transfer to ships waiting offshore to transport the oil to the global market. The revenue accrued enabled the rebels to withstand the Nigerian military, members of which were also widely suspected of being deeply involved in siphoning off oil for personal profit. According to Nigeria's Environment Minister Halima Alao, Nigeria recorded 1,260 oil spills between 2006 and June 2008, 419 of them in the first half of 2008.

Nigeria witnessed a substantial amount of communal violence in areas other than the Delta region during the year. At the end of November, in the worst example of civil unrest for some years, bitter clashes between Muslims and Christians resulted in some 400 deaths. The violence occurred in Jos, in Nigeria's middle belt of states at the crossroads between the Muslim north and Christian south. In December violence erupted between the Jukun and Kuteb ethnic groups over rival festivals, and police reinforcements were drafted into the area to assist the local police to maintain order. Twenty people were reported killed in the disturbances. Meanwhile, the town of Nsukka, in Enugu state, suffered from a spate of kidnappings of wealthy people, for whom high ransoms were demanded.

Guy Arnold

GHANA—SIERRA LEONE—THE GAMBIA—LIBERIA

Ghana

CAPITAL: Accra   AREA: 238,540 sq km   POPULATION: 23,462,000 ('07)
OFFICIAL LANGUAGE: English   POLITICAL SYSTEM: multiparty republic
HEAD OF STATE AND GOVERNMENT: President John Agyekum Kufuor (since Jan '01)
PRESIDENT ELECT: John Atta Mills
RULING PARTY: New Patriotic Party (NPP)
MAIN IGO MEMBERSHIPS (NON-UN): AU, ECOWAS, ACP, CWTH, NAM
CURRENCY: cedi (end-'08 £1=C1.8299, US$1=C1.2728)
GNI PER CAPITA: US$590, $1,330 at PPP ('07)

Sierra Leone

CAPITAL: Freetown   AREA: 71,740 sq km   POPULATION: 5,848,000 ('07)
OFFICIAL LANGUAGE: English   POLITICAL SYSTEM: multiparty republic
HEAD OF STATE AND GOVERNMENT: President Ernest Bai Koroma (APC) (since Sept '07)
RULING PARTY: All People's Congress (APC)
MAIN IGO MEMBERSHIPS (NON-UN): AU, ECOWAS, OIC, ACP, CWTH, NAM
CURRENCY: leone (end-'08 £1=Le4,364.08, US$1=Le3,035.35)
GNI PER CAPITA: US$260, $660 at PPP ('07)

The Gambia

CAPITAL: Banjul   AREA: 11,300 sq km   POPULATION: 1,707,000 ('07)
OFFICIAL LANGUAGE: English   POLITICAL SYSTEM: multiparty republic
HEAD OF STATE AND GOVERNMENT: President (Col) Yahya Jammeh (APRC) (since Sept '96)
RULING PARTY: Alliance for Patriotic Reorientation and Construction (APRC)
MAIN IGO MEMBERSHIPS (NON-UN): AU, ECOWAS, ACP, CWTH, OIC, NAM
CURRENCY: dalasi (end-'08 £1=D38.6756, US$1=D26.9000)
GNI PER CAPITA: US$320, $1,140 at PPP ('07)

Liberia

CAPITAL: Monrovia   AREA: 111,370 sq km   POPULATION: 3,753,000 ('07)
OFFICIAL LANGUAGE: English   POLITICAL SYSTEM: multiparty republic
HEAD OF STATE AND GOVERNMENT: President Ellen Johnson-Sirleaf (since Jan '06)
RULING PARTY: Unity Party
MAIN IGO MEMBERSHIPS (NON-UN): AU, ECOWAS, ACP, NAM
CURRENCY: Liberian dollar (end-'08 £1=L$91.0127, US$1=L$63.3000)
GNI PER CAPITA: US$150, $290 at PPP ('07)

GHANA. In one of the most exciting and close run elections to have occurred in Africa in 2008, John Atta Mills—a former vice-president, who had served as deputy to President Jerry Rawlings—was chosen as Ghana's new president. The initial presidential ballot, on 7 December, proved indecisive but Atta Mills, of the opposition National Democratic Congress (NDC), won the run-off contest (on 28 December), polling 50.23 per cent of the votes cast to defeat his rival, Nana Akufo-Addo, of the ruling New Patriotic Party (NPP), by less than half a percentage point. After his victory in the fiercely fought contest, confirmed on 3 January 2009, Atta Mills said: "I assure Ghanaians that I will be president for all." They were brave words from a man who, as he prepared to take office (on 7 January 2009), faced the prospect of dealing with the effects of a severe global recession. Nevertheless, the conduct of the election—both rounds of which were approved by foreign monitors—sent a welcome message to the outside world about the viability of African democracy at the end of a year in which violence had marred elections in Kenya, agreements had been ruthlessly bypassed in Zimbabwe, and coups had occurred in Mauritania and Guinea. The outgoing president and head of the NPP, John Kufuor, who had completed the maximum permitted two terms in office, said: "What excites me is that I have ended my tenure, I believe, on a good note with the entire nation showing readiness to select my successor."

The results of the legislative elections held simultaneously with the first round of presidential voting saw the NDC win 114 seats compared with 107 for the NPP. The remaining seats in the 228-member National Assembly were taken by minor parties or independent candidates.

The country's economic position deteriorated during 2008 with inflation peaking at 18.4 per cent in June and the country's international reserves falling below the critical three month threshold. Rising food and fuel prices caused popular discontent and were a factor in the election victory of Atta Mills, whose campaign included promises to address the problem. Nevertheless, the underlying position of Ghana's economy was relatively strong. Corruption was endemic but there were few formal obstacles to impede the free market. The country also had significant natural resources, in particular gold—where Ghana was second only to South Africa in the continent's gold production—and cocoa, where it was second only to Côte d'Ivoire. The discovery of oil also offered the prospect of transforming the economy. It was announced in May that the Anglo-Irish oil exploration company, Tullow Oil, had discovered a significant offshore oilfield. The National Petroleum Corporation predicted output of 120,000 barrels per day (b/d) in 2010, when commercial production was scheduled to begin, rising to 250,000 b/d within two years.

SIERRA LEONE. The month of August witnessed violent confrontations in Freetown between supporters of the ruling All People's Congress (APC) and the opposition Sierra Leone People's Party (SLPP). ACP supporters vandalised the SLPP headquarters and, according to the SLPP secretary general, Jacob Jusu Saffa, launched attacks upon party offices and assaulted party members all over the country. Mohamed Turay, a lecturer at the Fourah Bay College, commented gloomily that "We are moving in a circle. This was the same government in power when war broke out in 1990, and they are doing the same things that caused the war—suppressing opposition with thuggery, as they are doing now."

The violence was symptomatic of the ongoing divide between the supporters of the two rival parties, who constituted the country's two largest ethnic groups. The APC drew its support mainly from the Temne, who came from the north and west of the country, whilst the SLPP relied upon the allegiance of the Mende, who came from the southern and eastern provinces. When President Ernest Bai Koroma had assumed office in 2007 he promised to form a government of national unity, but in reality his 20-member cabinet contained 17 ministers who were either Temnes or from the north. The previous SLPP government had appointed ministers drawn from all parts of the country. Nevertheless, the president continued to enjoy a significant degree of popular support. On 15 November, the anniversary of his inauguration, Koroma dispensed with any attendants and walked "as an ordinary man" through the streets of Freetown. As his presence became known, huge crowds gathered to cheer him.

Although a major producer of gem-quality diamonds, most of Sierra Leone's output was smuggled out of the country, with little passing through official export channels. The country remained heavily dependent on foreign aid and two-thirds of the population practiced subsistence agriculture. At the beginning of 2008 the country was ranked at the bottom of the UNDP Human Development Index in 177th place; by the end of the year it was ranked at 179, still in last place.

THE GAMBIA. The regime of President Yahya Jammeh, in power since 1994, continued to exercise its iron control over all aspects of Gambian public life. Despite a history of coup attempts against him, Jammeh negotiated 2008 without any obvious challenges and appeared secure in office. Although his tight control gave The Gambia a degree of security, it did not encourage prosperity. With per capita income at the beginning of 2008 of only US$320, The Gambia remained one of the world's poorest countries.

The government was criticised by international exponents of civil rights, especially for its attitude towards freedom of the press. According to Reporters Without Borders (RSF) there is "absolute intolerance of any form of criticism", with journalists who did not support the government frequently finding themselves subject to death threats, surveillance, and night-time arrests. The country's private media faced severe restrictions and radio stations and newspapers had to pay large licence fees.

A British couple, David Fulton and his wife Fiona, who had worked as missionaries in The Gambia for 12 years, were arrested at the end of November and charged with treason. They were offered bail but this required four Gambian property owners willing to vouch for them and these were not forthcoming. In court at the end of December they were accused of spreading "hatred against the government" by means of a series of round robin emails, one of which had been taken to the police. Amongst the emails quoted from during their hearing was one entitled "Hell in The Gambia", in which the country, whose population was

97 per cent Muslim, was described as "sinking fast into a morass of Islam". The Fultons pleaded guilty, hoping that their punishment would amount to a fine and deportation. Instead they were fined and sentenced to a year's hard labour, with the presiding magistrate declaring himself shocked by their lack of "respect for the country, the government and the president" and intending that the punishment act as a deterrent to others.

LIBERIA. In November the IMF delivered a favourable report upon economic activity in Liberia, which it said remained buoyant despite the rise in international food and fuel prices. According to the head of the IMF delegation, the country had achieved GDP growth of some 7 per cent and this was expected to rise as a result of higher production of Liberia's two main commodities, rice and timber. Inflation had increased but was expected to fall back to single figures by the end of 2009. The IMF delegation commended the Liberian government for its commitment to strengthening public financial management and its efforts to improve governance and combat corruption. The IMF agreed to support the Liberian recovery programme in 2009; the aim of the programme was to limit expenditure to available cash resources and the foreign reserves of the Central Bank of Liberia (CBL). The IMF delegation leader said: "Liberia's medium term outlook remains bright, but several risks are emerging as a consequence of the current global financial crisis and economic slowdown." During 2008 the major sources of Liberia's revenue remained rubber exports and its maritime registry programme. Liberia was the second-largest maritime registry in the world, with 2,721 vessels from all over the world sailing under its "flag of convenience", and earning the country some US$16 million a year.

Years of conflict and mismanagement had bequeathed Liberia a huge debt burden. On 12 June, the USA became the first bilateral creditor to sign an agreement implementing the Paris Club of sovereign creditors' April 2008 debt treatment for Liberia. Other creditors also pledged debt relief.

In her end of year message to the people of Liberia, President Ellen Johnson-Sirleaf said that the country's poverty reduction strategy (PRS)—"Lift Liberia"—could succeed through the participation and involvement of every citizen. The president assured Liberians and foreign partners that her administration would leave no stone unturned to achieve its development goals and dedicated 2009 as the year of "Lifting Liberia".

Guy Arnold

WEST AFRICAN FRANCOPHONE STATES—CENTRAL AFRICAN FRANC ZONE

SENEGAL—MAURITANIA—MALI—GUINEA—CÔTE D'IVOIRE— BURKINA FASO—TOGO—BENIN—NIGER

Senegal

CAPITAL: Dakar   AREA: 196,720 sq km   POPULATION: 12,411,000 ('07)
OFFICIAL LANGUAGE: French   POLITICAL SYSTEM: multiparty republic
HEAD OF STATE AND GOVERNMENT: President Abdoulaye Wade (since April '00)
RULING PARTIES: Sopi (Change) 2007 coalition, led by Senegalese Democratic Party (PDS)
PRIME MINISTER: Cheikh Hadjibou Soumare (since June '07)
MAIN IGO MEMBERSHIPS (NON-UN): AU, ECOWAS, UEMOA, ACP, OIC, NAM, Francophonie
CURRENCY: CFA franc (end-'08 £1=CFAFr678.466, US$1=CFAFr471.895)
GNI PER CAPITA: US$820, $1,640 at PPP ('07)

Mauritania

CAPITAL: Nouakchott   AREA: 1,030,700 sq km   POPULATION: 3,121,000 ('07)
OFFICIAL LANGUAGES: French & Arabic   POLITICAL SYSTEM: multiparty republic under military rule
HEAD OF STATE AND GOVERNMENT: President (head of higher state council) Gen. Mohammed Ould
    Abdelaziz (since Aug '08)
RULING PARTY: Coalition of Forces for Democratic Change (CFCD)
PRIME MINISTER: Prime Minister Moulaye Ould Mohamed Laghdhaf (since Aug '08)
MAIN IGO MEMBERSHIPS (NON-UN): AU (suspended), UEMOA, AMU, AL, ACP, OIC, NAM,
    Francophonie
CURRENCY: ouguiya (end-'08 £1=O376.914, US$1=O262.155)
GNI PER CAPITA: US$840, $2,010 at PPP ('07)

Mali

CAPITAL: Bamako   AREA: 1,240,190 sq km   POPULATION: 12,334,000 ('07)
OFFICIAL LANGUAGE: French   POLITICAL SYSTEM: multiparty republic
HEAD OF STATE AND GOVERNMENT: President Gen. (retd) Amadou Toumani Touré (ADP) (since
    June '02)
RULING PARTY: Alliance for Democracy and Progress (ADP)
PRIME MINISTER: Modibo Sidibe (since Sept '07)
MAIN IGO MEMBERSHIPS (NON-UN): AU, ECOWAS, UEMOA, AL, ACP, OIC, NAM, Francophonie
CURRENCY: CFA franc (see above)
GNI PER CAPITA: US$500, $1,040 at PPP ('07)

Guinea

CAPITAL: Conakry   AREA: 245,860 sq km   POPULATION: 9,380,000 ('07)
OFFICIAL LANGUAGE: French   POLITICAL SYSTEM: multiparty republic
HEAD OF STATE AND GOVERNMENT: Captain Moussa Dadis Camara, head of National Council for
    Democracy and Development (CNDD) (since Dec '08)
RULING PARTY: Party of Unity and Progress (PUP)
PRIME MINISTER: Kabine Komara (since Dec '08)
MAIN IGO MEMBERSHIPS (NON-UN): AU (suspended), ECOWAS, ACP, OIC, NAM, Francophonie
CURRENCY: Guinean franc (end-'08 £1=GFr7,165.78, US$1=GFr4,984.00)
GNI PER CAPITA: US$400, $1,120 at PPP ('07)

Côte d'Ivoire

CAPITAL: Yamoussoukro (official); Abidjan (de facto)   AREA: 322,460 sq km   POPULATION: 19,268,000 ('07)
OFFICIAL LANGUAGE: French   POLITICAL SYSTEM: transitional government under international supervision
HEAD OF STATE AND GOVERNMENT: President Laurent Gbagbo (since Oct '00)
RULING PARTY: Ivoirian Popular Front government controls south; rebel New Forces control north
PRIME MINISTER: Guillaume Kigbafori Soro (since March '07)
MAIN IGO MEMBERSHIPS (NON-UN): AU, ECOWAS, UEMOA, ACP, OIC, NAM, Francophonie
CURRENCY: CFA franc (see above)
GNI PER CAPITA: US$910, $1,590 at PPP ('07)

Burkina Faso

CAPITAL: Ouagadougou   AREA: 274,000 sq km   POPULATION: 14,777,000 ('07)
OFFICIAL LANGUAGE: French   POLITICAL SYSTEM: multiparty republic
HEAD OF STATE AND GOVERNMENT: President (Capt.) Blaise Compaoré (CDP) (since Dec '91); previously Chairman of Popular Front (from Oct '87)
RULING PARTY: Congress for Democracy and Progress (CDP)
PRIME MINISTER: Tertius Zongo (since June '07)
MAIN IGO MEMBERSHIPS (NON-UN): AU, ECOWAS, UEMOA, ACP, OIC, NAM, Francophonie
CURRENCY: CFA franc (see above)
GNI PER CAPITA: US$430, $1,120 at PPP ('07)

Togo

CAPITAL: Lomé   AREA: 56,790 sq km   POPULATION: 6,581,000 ('07)
OFFICIAL LANGUAGES: French, Kabiye & Ewem   POLITICAL SYSTEM: multiparty republic
HEAD OF STATE AND GOVERNMENT: President Faure Gnassingbé (RPT) (since May '05)
RULING PARTY: Rally of the Togolese People (RPT)
PRIME MINISTER: Gilbert Fossoun Houngbo (since Sept '08)
MAIN IGO MEMBERSHIPS (NON-UN): AU, ECOWAS, ACP, OIC, NAM, Francophonie
CURRENCY: CFA franc (see above)
GNI PER CAPITA: US$360, $800 at PPP ('07)

Benin

CAPITAL: Porto Novo   AREA: 112,620 sq km   POPULATION: 9,025,000 ('07)
OFFICIAL LANGUAGE: French   POLITICAL SYSTEM: multiparty republic
HEAD OF STATE AND GOVERNMENT: President Yayi Boni (since April '06)
RULING PARTY: Cauri Forces for an Emerging Benin (FCBE)
MAIN IGO MEMBERSHIPS (NON-UN): AU, ECOWAS, UEMOA, ACP, OIC, NAM, Francophonie
CURRENCY: CFA franc (see above)
GNI PER CAPITA: US$570, $1,310 at PPP ('07)

Niger

CAPITAL: Niamey   AREA: 1,267,000 sq km   POPULATION: 14,195,000 ('07)
OFFICIAL LANGUAGE: French   POLITICAL SYSTEM: multiparty republic
HEAD OF STATE AND GOVERNMENT: President Mamadou Tandja (since Dec '99)
RULING PARTY: National Movement for a Society of Development (MNSD)
PRIME MINISTER: Sieni Oumarou (since June '07)
MAIN IGO MEMBERSHIPS (NON-UN): AU, ECOWAS, UEMOA, ACP, OIC, NAM, Francophonie
CURRENCY: CFA franc (see above)
GNI PER CAPITA: US$280, $630 at PPP ('07)

SENEGAL.   The repercussions of the previous year's unsatisfactory presidential and parliamentary elections (see AR 2008, pp. 243-44) were still being felt in 2008. While the increasingly autocratic behaviour of the octogenarian President

Abdoulaye Wade was causing further resentment, the lack of a clear successor and continuing divisions between the opposition parties made effective action to counter this unwelcome trend hard to pursue. In March Senegal staged the 11th summit of the Organisation of the Islamic Conference (OIC), postponed from before the previous year's election. This was the second time in 17 years that Senegal had hosted the OIC and, with 60 delegations, it was one of Wade's "grands projets", designed to project him as a continental leader; it duly produced a Dakar Declaration on world peace (see p. 423). Although much of the funding for the summit came from oil-producing Middle East states, it left the Senegalese public fairly unimpressed.

The entrusting of running the summit to the president's increasingly influential son, Karim Wade, also brought further criticism, partly because of suspicions that the elderly leader had dynastic ambitions. Criticism of Wade's rule was reinforced by the proposal, which was pushed through the National Assembly, to increase the presidential term from five to seven years, which would effectively keep him in office until the age of nearly 90 (although some would have him older). Ironically, the pro-democracy constitutional amendments introduced by Wade in 2001 shortly after he had come to power had included a reduction from seven to five years (see AR 2001, p. 274). There were also concerns at an increasingly repressive attitude towards media criticism.

In August, a group of opposition parties called a "national assizes" to consider the state of the nation, especially faced with the impact of deteriorating global economic conditions, but the ruling Senegalese Democratic Party (PDS) declined to take part. There were signs of increasing urban unrest, and in December there was anti-government violence in the eastern town of Kédougou. Meanwhile, the "no war, no peace" situation in the separatist-inclined southern province of Casamance continued, despite earlier settlements.

MAURITANIA. In a serious setback for multi-party democracy, a military coup on 6 August overthrew the regime of President Mohammed Ould Cheikh Abdellahi, which had been elected in June 2007 (see AR 2008, pp. 244-45). The coup was staged by Major-General Mohammed Ould Abdelaziz, commander of the powerful presidential guard, following the attempt by Abdellahi to dismiss four senior army officers, including Abdelaziz himself. A statement was broadcast by a new 11-man State Council, stating baldly that Abdellahi was now a "former president" and that General Abdelaziz was taking over the functions of president.

The coup was the culmination of a deepening political crisis since the president had dismissed the government earlier in the year, following protests over food price increases. In July there was a vote of no-confidence in the cabinet and a walkout by nearly 50 members of the National Assembly (the lower house of the bicameral legislature) belonging to the ruling party, a move which removed the president's legislative majority. The attempted dismissal of the four senior army officers was said to have been triggered by suspicions that they had orchestrated the walkout.

Although the coup was apparently bloodless, troops fired on a group of several hundred demonstrators who staged a protest in reaction to a pro-coup march. The new military regime promised to hold fresh elections as soon as possible, but it detained ex-President Abdellahi and former Prime Minister Yahia Ould Ahmed El-Waqef and appeared in no hurry to move forward to a new transition. The two had not been released by the end of the year despite periodic demonstrations calling for the detained president's release. An emergency session of the National Assembly, comprising a rump of supporters of the coup, met in August and again for a budget session in November, but without the Assembly's president, Messoude Ould Boulkhaire.

There was strong international condemnation. The African Union (AU) suspended Mauritania until a constitutional government was restored, and the EU suspended non-humanitarian assistance, as did the USA, whose aid included US$15 million-worth of military-to-military co-operation. Some members of the Organisation of the Islamic Conference (OIC) also called for the restoration of democracy and for Abdellahi's release. Prognostications were not encouraging, however, as it was widely reported that General Abdelaziz had for some time believed that it was his turn for power after that of his cousin, General Ely Ould Mohammed Vall, who had staged the coup that overthrew President Ould Taya in 2005 and then returned power to civilians in 2007 (see AR 2005, pp. 229-30). The north African wing of al-Qaida (al-Qaida in the Islamic Maghreb, AQIM) called for a holy war in Mauritania to establish Islamic rule, saying that the coup had "probably" had the approval of "infidel states America, France and Israel". Israel maintained its embassy in Nouakchott.

MALI. Faced with continued attacks by a rebel Touareg faction headed by Ibrahim Ag Bahanga, the government of President Amadou Toumani Touré entered into peace discussions with the rebels in Libya in March. These successfully secured the release of over 30 Malian soldiers kidnapped in a surprise ambush near the town of Tin-Zaouatene, but there were doubts as to how long the ceasefire would hold. A senior UN drugs official suggested that the Touareg revolts in Mali and Niger were as much due to the fact that the West African region had become a "black hole" for criminals and undesirables as to genuine movements, but the strength of the activity in both countries continued. There was a new period of heightened tension, following two fresh rebel attacks in northern Mali, but in general the government pursued a conciliatory line, not wishing to be on the front line of conflict with a movement that some saw as linked to the uncertain quantity known as AQIM (al-Qaida in the Islamic Maghreb).

Reports that President Touré was manoeuvring to change the constitution in order to drop the presidential limit of two terms proved unfounded, so far. The constitutional changes drafted by a commission headed by Daba Diawara and to be published early in 2009 envisaged greater democratisation and did not address the issue of term duration or limits.

GUINEA. The long decline of the increasingly ailing President Lansana Conté finally came to an end with his death during the night of 22-23 December (see Obituary). It was at 2am on 23 December that his passing was formally announced by a group of senior government ministers and military officers. However, only five hours later there was a broadcast by Captain Moussa Dadis Camara, announcing that the army had taken power and was setting up a National Council for Democracy and Development (CNDD). The takeover was cautiously welcomed by wide sections of the country, as the defunct military ruler had become increasingly unpopular.

Although the decision to accord Conté a state funeral with full military honours on 26 December was seen as a sign of a conciliatory attitude on the part of the new rulers, their true intentions were probably more closely revealed by their detention, two days later, of most of the senior army officers over the rank of captain, including, notably, the army chief of staff, General Diarra Camara (who was no relation to Captain Camara). This was perhaps inevitable, in view of the risk that any one of them might have been able to organise a counter-coup, but it was still seen as a delicate exercise, as were the new regime's anti-corruption statements, which seemed to go beyond the declared objective of organising free and fair elections.

Much attention was focused on the personality of the hitherto unknown new head of state, Captain Camara, who had been the head of the fuel distribution unit of the army but had come under suspicion from some of the senior officers, who had already had to deal earlier in the year with a widespread mutiny over pay. A 44-year old graduate in economics, Camara showed a propensity for loquacity that worried some commentators, and there was a perceived risk that he might develop a taste for power, even though his declared role model was President Toumani Touré ("ATT") of Mali, who, after staging a coup in 1991, handed over power within 12 months. The new Guinean leader promised elections in 2010, and appointed Kabine Komara as prime minister on 30 December.

The international reaction was lukewarm, especially as the coup led to Guinea's automatic suspension by the African Union (AU), even if the president of the AU commission, Jean Ping, had attended Conté's funeral. Many of the countries of ECOWAS (Economic Community of West African States) also deplored the coup, although the attitude of the two most important neighbours, Côte d'Ivoire and Senegal, was more circumspect. President Wade of Senegal had said, along with the Libyan leader, Colonel Kadhafi, that the new Guinean leaders deserved support rather than criticism.

The change was also cautiously welcomed by the leaders of Guinea's much-harassed political parties, which took the commitment to democracy at face value, while the well organised civil society bodies, including trade unions, also seemed willing to co-operate with the transition, recalling their struggle against the deviousness and repression of the Conté regime. In May there had been little reaction to Conté's sacking of Prime Minister Lansana Kouyaté, a former international bureaucrat, who had come to power in February 2007 on the back of popular demonstrations (see AR 2008, p. 246). Although Kouyaté had improved relations with international donors, he had been systematically undermined by Conté, and had delivered little to improve conditions for ordinary Guineans. Thus the CNDD's commitment to national reconstruction, perceived in the inclusion of the word "development" in the title of the new ruling Council, inevitably brought only guarded approval.

CÔTE D'IVOIRE. This was the year in which, once again, the long promised elections never happened. Elections had been overdue since the mandate of President Laurent Gbagbo expired in November 2005, but each year they had been postponed. There had been annual resolutions of the UN Security Council giving a deadline for elections, but each year these had been defied. The reason for the regular postponement was lack of preparedness, most notably the delayed implementation of the so-called "identification" process by which the Ivoirian nationality (or Ivoirité) of voters was to be established.

After assertions of varying confidence during the year that voter registration was advancing, it was announced at a meeting in Ouagadougou in November, at which President Gbagbo and his young northern colleague Prime Minister Guillaume Soro met with mediator Blaise Compaoré (president of Burkina Faso), that it was not possible to hold the planned elections on 30 November. Political manoeuvring still continued, especially between Soro and the leader of the strongest northern party, Alassane Ouattara. In December Gbagbo and Soro signed a new agreement to integrate the armed forces and police of the government and the former northern rebel New Forces (Forces nouvelles, FN) over a two-year period, paying demobilisation compensation to former rebels and members of pro-government militias.

In July, the UN Security Council resolved that the UN Operation in Côte d'Ivoire (UNOCI), now reduced to under 2,000 troops (mainly French soldiers of Opération Licorne), should remain in the country until January 2009, although this resolution was taken in the expectation that elections would be held. It was still anticipated at the end of 2008 that UNOCI would stay until the elections, which the UN optimistically predicted would be held in the first half of 2009, even though it expressed continued concern over the delays in the registration process.

BURKINA FASO. The long reign of President Blaise Compaoré, who came to power after a military coup in 1987, showed no sign of coming to an end, in spite of periodic evidence of discontent. In February the divided opposition groups that had been firmly beaten in elections the previous year came together in a coalition for change, but demonstrations organised that month to protest against rising food prices were severely contained.

Compaoré's two-year period as chair of the regional organisation ECOWAS, in which he had played a notable role in brokering a peace deal in the civil conflict in Côte d'Ivoire, came to an end in December. It seemed to have bought him considerable favour with donors, who had previously held him in suspicion because of his earlier wrecking role in Liberia and Sierra Leone.

TOGO. The regime of President Faure Gnassingbé appeared at long last to have returned to a certain international respectability. The key move was the decision of the EU to resume fully its economic aid programme, which in 1993 had been suspended, apart from emergency operations. Although some EU members, notably France, had maintained close relations, the window was now open since Togo had been given a 90 per cent clean bill of health after the parliamentary elections of October 2007 (see AR 2008, pp. 247-48). The remaining issue that caused some lingering doubts was the inability of the Gnassingbé regime to achieve full political reconciliation with the opposition. The main opposition group, the Union of Forces for Change (UFC), led by Gilchrist Olympio, which held well over one-third of the seats in the new National Assembly, continued to decline participation in a national government, although other smaller opposition parties had accepted. But the green light from the EU paved the way for other donors, following the lead from the IMF and the World Bank, to initiate new aid programmes in a country visibly starved of development for more than 15 years.

Recognition of these changes was seen in the appointment in September of a technocrat, Gilbert Fossoun Houngbo, formerly director of the United Nations Development Programme (UNDP) in Africa, as Togo's prime minister. It was felt that he would be better able to negotiate with the international donor community than his predecessor, Komlan Mally, who had been close to the UFC. Maximum efforts were made to try and give a semblance of normality, but in reality all eyes were now on the coming presidential elections in 2010 and the crucial issue of whether Olympio would be allowed to contest them. Legal ruses had been found to prevent him standing in both 2003—when Gnassingbé's father, President Eyadéma, was still alive—and in 2005, just after Gnassingbé's imposed succession, which inevitably inhibited the UFC's chances of success (see AR 2005, p. 233). It was expected that Gnassingbé's conciliatory personality and donor blandishments, especially from the EU, would ensure a more level playing field, as the opposition was still very strong especially in southern areas of Togo. However, the powerful ethno-military group around the president was known to be notoriously resistant to pressure.

BENIN. The regime of President Yayi Boni, elected in 2006, met its first political difficulties. These were occasioned by the desire of the non-political banker president to secure a working majority in the National Assembly (the 83-member unicameral legislature), home of the country's notoriously truculent politicians. In October he reshuffled his cabinet in an attempt to accommodate dissatisfaction within the G13 Alliance, a coalition of small political parties that held the majority of seats in the Assembly. The three new G13 cabinet members cited a "lack of structural confidence" between the president and "the political class", and resigned en bloc, so the ministerial posts had to filled from other small parties. The president thus faced the prospect of continued tensions with the legislature.

The president's highly praised record of over 6 per cent growth rates in his first two years in office seemed uncertain to last in view of the impact of global recession on the oil price, because much of Benin's success had been based on the Nigerian oil-fuelled economic boom of the previous five years. Much of the boom had been in the informal sector, but Cotonou port had helped relieve some of the congestion in Nigeria's ports.

NIGER. It was another difficult year because of the continuing rebellion of Touareg nomads, which meant that much of the vast desert area in the north of the country outside certain towns and forts was reportedly out of government control. The rebel Niger Justice Movement (MNJ) began the year with an attack in January on Tanout, a town in the east, and kept up pressure until, in August, there was a provisional peace deal brokered by Libya (parallel to one in Mali, see above), which was signed by the MNJ leader, Aghaly al Alambo. However, another Touareg faction, the Front des Forces de Redressement (FFR), led by Mohamed Ag Aoutchiki, denounced the agreement and vowed to continue the struggle.

The government of President Mamadou Tandja for the most part maintained an uncompromisingly hardline attitude to the rebels, declining to enter into any peace negotiations and denying access to most of the affected areas, including to humanitarian organisations disturbed by reports of displacement of populations. Insecurity remained high through the year: there were unconfirmed reports in June of the kidnapping of four executives of the all-important French uranium mining company, Areva, but this matter was said to have been quietly settled; in December two Canadians, including Robert Fowler, the UN special envoy to Niger, were reported missing. No foreign journalist had been allowed in the north of the country for two years and Tandja's draconian attitude extended to the local media, notably the Niamey correspondent of Radio France International, Moussa Kaka, who had remained in detention since 2007 for alleged contact with the rebels. The radio station, Sahara FM, was also closed down by the government after interviewing victims of abuse by government soldiers.

The high insecurity in the north did not prevent continued excitement about Niger's untapped uranium deposits, thanks to renewed international interest in nuclear power. The year began with record high prices for uranium and new deals were signed with China to develop a mine in a concession granted two years previously; two deals were also done with Indian companies for prospecting. The Niger government announced that it intended to treble uranium production to 10,500 tonnes in the next few years, in order to become the world's second largest producer after Australia. At the end of 2008, despite a fall in world prices, Areva signed a new deal to develop the mine at Imouraren and begin commercial production in 2012.

Kaye Whiteman

CAMEROON—CHAD—GABON—CONGO—CENTRAL AFRICAN REPUBLIC—EQUATORIAL GUINEA

Cameroon

CAPITAL: Yaoundé   AREA: 475,440 sq km   POPULATION: 18,533,000 ('07)
OFFICIAL LANGUAGES: French & English   POLITICAL SYSTEM: multiparty republic
HEAD OF STATE AND GOVERNMENT: President Paul Biya (since Nov '82)
RULING PARTY: Cameroon People's Democratic Movement (RDPC)
PRIME MINISTER: Ephraim Inoni (since Dec '04)
MAIN IGO MEMBERSHIPS (NON-UN): AU, CEEAC, ACP, OIC, CWTH, NAM, Francophonie
CURRENCY: CFA franc (end-'08 £1=CFAFr678.466, US$1=CFAFr471.895)
GNI PER CAPITA: US$1,050, $2,120 at PPP ('07)

Chad

CAPITAL: Ndjaména   AREA: 1,284,000 sq km   POPULATION: 10,764,000 ('07)
OFFICIAL LANGUAGES: French & Arabic   POLITICAL SYSTEM: multiparty republic
HEAD OF STATE AND GOVERNMENT: President (Col) Idriss Déby (MPS) (since Dec '90)
RULING PARTIES: Patriotic Salvation Movement (MPS), Union for Renewal and Democracy (URD), and National Union for Development and Renewal (UNDR)
PRIME MINISTER: Youssouf Saleh Abbas (since April '08)
MAIN IGO MEMBERSHIPS (NON-UN): AU, CEEAC, ACP, OIC, NAM, Francophonie
GNI PER CAPITA: US$540, $1,280 at PPP ('07)

Gabon

CAPITAL: Libreville   AREA: 267,670 sq km   POPULATION: 1,330,000 ('07)
OFFICIAL LANGUAGE: French   POLITICAL SYSTEM: multiparty republic
HEAD OF STATE AND GOVERNMENT: President Omar Bongo Ondimba (PDG) (since March '67)
RULING PARTY: Gabonese Democratic Party (PDG)
PRIME MINISTER: Jean Eyeghe Ndong (since Jan '06)
MAIN IGO MEMBERSHIPS (NON-UN): AU, CEEAC, ACP, OIC, NAM, Francophonie
CURRENCY: CFA franc (see above)
GNI PER CAPITA: US$6,670, $13,080 at PPP ('07)

Congo

CAPITAL: Brazzaville   AREA: 342,000 sq km   POPULATION: 3,767,000 ('07)
OFFICIAL LANGUAGE: French   POLITICAL SYSTEM: multiparty republic
HEAD OF STATE AND GOVERNMENT: President Dénis Sassou Nguesso (since Oct '97)
RULING PARTY: Congolese Labour Party (PCT) heads ruling alliance
MAIN IGO MEMBERSHIPS (NON-UN): CEEAC, ACP, NAM, Francophonie
CURRENCY: CFA franc (see above)
GNI PER CAPITA: US$1,540, $2,750 at PPP ('07)

Central African Republic (CAR)

CAPITAL: Bangui   AREA: 623,000 sq km   POPULATION: 4,343,000 ('07)
OFFICIAL LANGUAGE: French   POLITICAL SYSTEM: transitional government
HEAD OF STATE AND GOVERNMENT: President Gen. François Bozizé (since March '03)
RULING PARTY: National Convergence "Kwa Na Kwa" (KNK) coalition
PRIME MINISTER: Faustin-Archange Touadera (since Jan '08)
MAIN IGO MEMBERSHIPS (NON-UN): AU, CEEAC, ACP, OIC, NAM, Francophonie
CURRENCY: CFA franc (see above)
GNI PER CAPITA: US$380, $740 at PPP ('07)

Equatorial Guinea

CAPITAL: Malabo   AREA: 28,050 sq km   POPULATION: 508,000 ('07)
OFFICIAL LANGUAGES: Spanish & French   POLITICAL SYSTEM: multiparty republic
HEAD OF STATE AND GOVERNMENT: President (Brig.-Gen.) Teodoro Obiang Nguema Mbasogo (since Aug '79)
RULING PARTY: Equatorial Guinea Democratic Party (PDGE)
PRIME MINISTER: Ignacio Milam Tang (since July '08)
MAIN IGO MEMBERSHIPS (NON-UN): AU, CEEAC, ACP, NAM, Francophonie
CURRENCY: CFA franc (see above)
GNI PER CAPITA: US$12,860, $21,230 at PPP ('07)

CAMEROON. The year began badly in when in February the commercial capital, Douala, was hit by unprecedented riots which spread rapidly to the national capital, Yaoundé, and other cities. Although triggered by a limited-objective taxi drivers' strike, the protests grew into broader anti-government demonstrations. The causes were not hard to find. There had long been a feeling of disappointment in a tired and corrupt government, and the now definite proposal by President Paul Biya (who had been in power since 1982) to amend the constitution so that he could serve for a further seven years from the next presidential election in 2011, created a storm of criticism. However, it was the sharp rises in food and fuel prices that caused public exasperation to spill over into outright protest. Almost immediately this deteriorated into anarchy and looting, and was put down severely by the forces of law and order.

In the lull which followed this explosion of violence, the ruling party, the Cameroon People's Democratic Movement (RDPC), used its dominant position in the National Assembly—where it commanded well over the two-thirds majority required to enact constitutional amendments—effectively to extend the presidential term indefinitely. On 10 April legislation was approved (by 157 votes to five, with 15 abstentions) to remove term limits from the presidency and to provide immunity from prosecution for the president after leaving office. The removal of term limits meant that there was no prospect of Biya's leaving office voluntarily in the near future. This suited the party's ruling barons, who were still fighting each other over who should succeed the 75-year old ailing president.

In August there was a smooth handover to Cameroon by Nigeria of the final parts of the Bakassi peninsula in accordance with a ruling, which the International Court of Justice had made in 2002, thereby completing a process which had begun in 2006 (see AR 2002, pp. 471-72; AR 2007, p. 254). There had been much nervousness about the handover after some minor acts of violence on the Nigerian side, but the goodwill of both governments helped the difficult process proceed without incident.

CHAD. The central event of the year was an attack in early February by rebel forces upon the country's capital, Ndjaména. A group of some 3,000 heavily armed troops, reportedly involving three different dissident movements, travelling in a convoy of 300 vehicles (mainly Toyotas used in the war in Chad), crossed the border from Sudan on 28 January and captured the town of Adré. They moved two days later to take the strategic town of Oum Hadjer, in the centre of the country, on the main road to the capital, and on 31 January were at Massaguet, some 50km from Ndjaména. It was here that elements of President Idriss Déby's army made a stand but were beaten back, and the rebels were soon in the outskirts of the capital.

The attack followed a similar pattern to an incident in April 2006, although this time the rebels appeared briefly to have toppled the government and there were rumours that Déby had fled. As in the previous attack, the president adopted the high risk strategy of allowing the insurgents into the capital and then taking advantage of their extended supply lines and the urban environment to defeat them. Battles took place around the presidential palace and the airport, before Déby, who had kept his crack presidential guard in reserve, forced the rebels to retreat in disarray. In 2006 the rebels had possessed only 100 vehicles and the battle had lasted a day. This time the fighting was more prolonged and intense, with greater casualties and more damage inflicted, and some 20,000 people were forced to flee across the Chari river to Cameroon. On this occasion there was also a more direct role played by French troops, who prevented an attack on the airport, from which they were evacuating French nationals.

There were also reports that French intelligence intercepted phone calls to the rebels from opposition politicians in Ndjaména, who were then arrested by Déby. These included Lol Mahamat Choua (who had briefly served as president in 1979); prominent southern politician Ngarléjy Yorongar; a former foreign minister, Abdelkader Kamougué; and the head of one of the opposition parties, Ibn Oumar Mahamat Saleh. Although the first three subsequently emerged from detention, Saleh did not reappear and was presumed to have died in prison, although this was never admitted by the government. His disappearance provoked an international outcry, especially in French public opinion, and was one of the factors that caused the government of President Nicolas Sarkozy to seek ways of embarking upon the difficult task of disengaging militarily from Chad. This had not happened by the end of the year, although Sarkozy had indicated on a visit to South Africa in February that he was renegotiating France's defence agreements in Africa (see pp. 54-55).

Indeed, one of the reasons the rebels had acted when they did was the impending arrival in Chad of the French-inspired EUFOR Chad/CAR, a force of some 4,000 troops from the EU, endorsed by a resolution from the UN Security Council. This had been agreed in 2007 but it had taken some time to mobilise the force because of the reluctance of some EU members, such as Germany, to endorse the initiative (see AR 2008, pp. 387-88). Its objective was to monitor and protect the camps, in both Chad and the Central African Republic, of some 200,000 refugees from the conflict in Darfur. However, the rebels feared that the presence of these foreign troops might inhibit their own military activities, and the attack on the capital delayed the deployment of EUFOR by a month. Sudan had also been concerned at the EUFOR presence because of the impact that it might have on the situation in Darfur. In fact, the rebel fears were probably exaggerated, as by the end of the year the role of EUFOR seemed marginal, and occasional rebel incursions still occurred, in between a number of short-lived peace deals with Sudan. By the end of 2008, however, there had been no major new rebel attack, and the different movements were regrouping, amoeba-like, among themselves. There was also serious speculation as to whether the EUFOR operation would continue beyond the expiry of its mandate early in 2009.

An increasing disenchantment with Déby within the international community was illustrated by the decision of the World Bank to abandon the complex accountability agreement that had been entered into some years before, at the time of the Bank's approval of funding for the Chad-Cameroon oil pipeline. The president showed little concern with his reputation in the West, however, and continued to woo China, as if to demonstrate his independence. He appointed a new government in April, with Youssouf Saleh Abbas replacing Nouradine Delwa Kassire Koumakoye as prime minister. Although the new cabinet included a few opposition figures, there was no indication that it betokened any significant shift in policy.

GABON. There were various hiccups in relations with France during the course of the year, over matters such as the expulsion of Gabonese students and continued legal moves against the French assets of President Omar Bongo Ondimba. This latter trend was driven by the commonly held belief that Bongo, one of the richest leaders in the world, had garnered his huge wealth through embezzlement and corruption. It represented something of a departure from traditional practice in that France, in the past, had tended to be almost obsequious in its attitude to Bongo (who, in power since 1967, was Africa's longest-serving ruler), in part because Gabon's mineral wealth remained principally in French hands. Suspicions that French attitudes towards Bongo were changing were fuelled by speculation that one of the French African bases that President Nicolas Sarkozy was most likely to close was the one located in Gabon.

REPUBLIC OF CONGO. Much of the year was focused on preparations for the July 2009 presidential and parliamentary elections, which would mark 30 years of political dominance by President Dénis Sassou Nguesso. The president prepared for the elections by consolidating his position further and seeking to neutralise significant opponents. From having been a Marxist revolutionary military leader, Sassou Nguesso had slowly evolved, through surviving a succession of crises and even a period out of power, into a hardened and wily old civilian politician. Although seemingly secure in office, he was regarded almost as a "dinosaur", in the same manner as were neighbouring Presidents Bongo Ondimba of Gabon and Biya of Cameroon. Like Bongo, who was married to his daughter, Sassou Nguesso faced growing pressure from the French legal authorities over corruption allegations and an investigation into the legitimacy of his extensive assets held in France.

CENTRAL AFRICAN REPUBLIC. The year saw a series of peace agreements with different rebel groups, which in the past had made the northern and eastern parts of the country virtually ungovernable. The process began in January, but more substantial mediation was carried out by Gabon in June. It had been clear for some time that there were parts of the country that President François Bozizé did not control. This, together with mounting evidence of growing popular discontent, raised increasing fears within the international community that CAR could be on the way to becoming a failed state. This concern was one of the reasons that caused France to press for the EUFOR operation (see above), but there were also concerns that instability within the country could feed into the complexities of the Darfur crisis.

EQUATORIAL GUINEA. In domestic politics the central event was the municipal and legislative elections held in May, which, unsurprisingly, produced sweeping majorities in favour of the ruling party, the Equatorial Guinea Democratic Party (PDGE). Following the elections, Ignacio Milam Tang replaced Mangue Obama Nfube as prime minister, but there was no discernible change in government policy.

International attention focused more on the trial of Simon Mann, the British mercenary accused of plotting in 2005 to overthrow the government of President Teodoro Obiang Nguema Mbasogo. Mann and other co-plotters had been arrested in Zimbabwe and, after serving a prison sentence there, he had been extradited in early 2008 to Equatorial Guinea. Mann claimed to be only an accomplice of a "management team" that included Mark Thatcher (son of the former British prime minister) and the Lebanese millionaire, Ely Calil. He also claimed that the governments of Spain and South Africa had endorsed the plot, although the South Africans denied strongly any implication in mercenary activity. Despite his attempts at co-operation with the court, Mann was sentenced on 7 July to 34 years in prison. A Lebanese businessman, Mohamed Salaam, was sentenced to 18 years for his role in the affair, and five other men received lesser terms.

Prior to the trial, Severo Moto, opposition leader in exile, who was allegedly part of the coup plot (and its intended beneficiary), was arrested in Spain on charges of gun-running, but the Spanish authorities indicated they would not extradite him to Equatorial Guinea.

Kaye Whiteman

CAPE VERDE—GUINEA-BISSAU—SÃO TOMÉ & PRÍNCIPE

Cape Verde

CAPITAL: Praia   AREA: 4,030 sq km   POPULATION: 530,000 ('07)
OFFICIAL LANGUAGE: Portuguese   POLITICAL SYSTEM: multiparty republic
HEAD OF STATE: President Pedro Pires (since March '01)
RULING PARTY: African Party for the Independence of Cape Verde (PAICV)
HEAD OF GOVERNMENT: Prime Minister José Maria Pereira Neves (since Feb '01)
MAIN IGO MEMBERSHIPS (NON-UN): AU, ECOWAS, ACP, NAM, CPLP, Francophonie
CURRENCY: CV escudo (end-'08 £1=CVEsc113.464, US$1=CvEsc78.9150)
GNI PER CAPITA: US$2,430, $2,940 at PPP ('07)

Guinea-Bissau

CAPITAL: Bissau   AREA: 36,120 sq km   POPULATION: 1,695,000 ('07)
OFFICIAL LANGUAGE: Portuguese   POLITICAL SYSTEM: multiparty republic
HEAD OF STATE AND GOVERNMENT: President João Bernardo "Nino" Vieira (since Oct '05)
RULING PARTY: African Party for the Independence of Guinea-Bissau and Cape Verde (PAIGC)
PRIME MINISTER: Carlos Gomes jr (PAIGC) (since Dec '08)
MAIN IGO MEMBERSHIPS (NON-UN): AU, ECOWAS, UEMOA, ACP, OIC, NAM, CPLP, Francophonie
CURRENCY: CFA franc (end-'08 £1=CFAFr678.466, US$1=CFAFr471.895)
GNI PER CAPITA: US$200, $470 at PPP ('07)

São Tomé & Príncipe

CAPITAL: São Tomé   AREA: 960 sq km   POPULATION: 158,000 ('07)
OFFICIAL LANGUAGE: Portuguese   POLITICAL SYSTEM: multiparty republic
HEAD OF STATE AND GOVERNMENT: President Fradique de Menezes (since Sept '01)
RULING PARTIES: Democratic Movement Force for Change-Party of Democratic Governance (MDFM-PCD) coalition
PRIME MINISTER: Prime Minister Joaquim Rafael Branco (MLSTP-PSD) (since June '08)
MAIN IGO MEMBERSHIPS (NON-UN): AU, CEEAC, ACP, NAM, CPLP, Francophonie
CURRENCY: dobra (end-'08 £1=Db20,682.75, US$1=Db14,385.00)
GNI PER CAPITA: US$870, $1,630 ('07)

CAPE VERDE. The island state began 2008 on a high note. Since its independence from Portugal in the 1970s it had been categorised by the UN as a "least developed country", but it now became only the second African country (after Botswana) to be upgraded to a "middle income" country. After years of negotiations, it was invited the join the World Trade Organisation in December 2007, and it formally joined that body in July 2008. The second annual *Index of African Governance*, produced by Harvard University's Kennedy school of government and released in November, placed Cape Verde near the top of its list; the US-based Freedom House monitoring organisation rated it as the freest country in Africa. In December the country's National Statistics Institute (INE) announced that the poverty rate had fallen by almost 20 per cent in six years—from 36 per cent of the population in 2001 to 29 per cent in 2007—a remarkable achievement, given the island republic's lack of natural resources.

In the last months of the year, the global economic crisis began to threaten some of the archipelago's new-found prosperity, which was heavily based on tourism from Europe. In 2008, for the first time, tourism brought in more revenue than remittances sent by Cape Verdeans living and working abroad. The country remained heavily dependant on grants and aid—much of which was from the EU—and, as one of the few West African countries not considered for relief under the IMF's highly indebted poor countries (HIPC) scheme, had to grapple with the costs of servicing a large foreign debt. In December President Pedro Pires travelled to oil-rich Angola to try to strengthen relations with that country. Whether the economic downturn would undermine Cape Verde's impressive political stability remained to be seen.

GUINEA-BISSAU. As one of the world's poorest countries, fifth from the bottom in the UN world development index, Guinea-Bissau had few effectively functioning institutions and its civil servants went for long periods without pay.

The stability pact between the three most important political parties fell apart in early 2008, ahead of the legislative elections scheduled to take place later in the year, and in July the African Party for the Independence of Guinea-Bissau and Cape Verde (PAIGC), the leading party since independence from Portugal in 1975, pulled out of the coalition government. The National Assembly (unicameral legislature) was dissolved and in August—after another failed coup attempt, this time by the former head of the navy—President João Bernardo Vieira swore in a caretaker government, mainly made up of former allies, under Carlos Correia as prime minister.

International attention was largely focused on the fact that the country had become a prime transit point for trafficking in drugs, especially cocaine, from Latin America to Europe. By 2008, the value of the drugs trade was said to be larger than the national income, and in the election campaign politicians traded mutual accusations of being involved in drug trafficking and of accepting money from drug traffickers to fund their campaigns. The international community put a lot of effort into trying to ensure a smooth election on 16 November. There was a relatively high turnout and voting was orderly, but after it was announced that the PAIGC had again won most seats in the National Assembly, elements of the armed forces attacked the president's residence, as Viera and his family hid inside, and he was fortunate to escape injury. In December the PAIGC leader, Carlos Gomes jr, formed a new government, which pledged to tackle drug trafficking. The year ended with the country politically still very fragile and with little hope of economic recovery.

SÃO TOMÉ AND PRÍNCIPE. The steep rise in the oil price in 2008 brought no benefits to the twin-island state, because oil had yet to be produced from its waters, despite the sale of the rights to exploit blocks offshore to various multinationals and consortia. Onshore there were hopes for greater political stability when, in February, the opposition Independent Democratic Action (ADI) party joined the governing coalition and its secretary general, Patrice Trovoada, became the new prime minister. Three months later, however, the coalition government lost a parliamentary vote of confidence after Trovoada was accused of corruption and lack of transparency in government affairs. The government of Portugal—the country's main donor—postponed its debt pardon and the Portuguese finance minister cancelled a visit to the islands.

President Fradique de Menezes, who was engaged in a struggle for power with the National Assembly (unicameral legislature), called for the legislative elections scheduled for 2010 to be brought forward, but this was rejected by the armed forces, the business community, trade unions, and others. In the face of this setback, the president in June appointed Joaquim Rafael Branco, the leader of the former ruling party, the Movement for the Liberation of São Tomé and Príncipe-Social Democratic Party (MLSTP-PSD), to head a new coalition government. Trovoada's ADI denounced Branco's appointment as unconstitutional, but he remained in office as the year ended, with the promised bonanza from oil still not in sight.

Christopher Saunders

VII CENTRAL AND SOUTHERN AFRICA

DEMOCRATIC REPUBLIC OF CONGO—BURUNDI AND RWANDA—
MOZAMBIQUE—ANGOLA

DEMOCRATIC REPUBLIC OF CONGO

CAPITAL: Kinshasa   AREA: 2,344,860 sq km   POPULATION: 62,399,000 ('07)
OFFICIAL LANGUAGE: French   POLITICAL SYSTEM: multiparty republic
HEAD OF STATE AND GOVERNMENT: President Maj.-Gen. Joseph Kabila (since Jan '01)
RULING PARTY: Alliance for the Presidential Majority (APM) coalition
PRIME MINISTER: Adolphe Muzito (since Oct '08)
MAIN IGO MEMBERSHIPS (NON-UN): AU, SADC, COMESA, CEEAC, ACP, Francophonie, NAM
CURRENCY: Congo franc (end-'08 £1=CFr920.576, US$1=CFr640.289)
GNI PER CAPITA: US$140, $290 at PPP ('07)

A PEACE agreement was signed in January between the government of the Democratic Republic of Congo and rebel forces in the east. It started to unravel almost immediately, and violence increased steadily throughout 2008, with the ceasefire effectively abandoned by mid-year. It was estimated that 4 million people had died in the Congolese conflict, the worst casualty rate in a single war since World War II. By October, a million people had been displaced from their homes by the fighting and were sheltering in overcrowded, unsanitary camps, with reported cases of cholera running well into the thousands.

The eight-day meeting (postponed from December 2007, see AR 2008, p. 258) to negotiate peace in North and South Kivu provinces opened on 6 January in Goma (the capital of North Kivu), but was not attended personally by either Congolese President Joseph Kabila or the ethnic Tutsi General Laurent Nkunda, leader of the rebel National Congress for the Defence of the People (CNDP). After two weeks of difficult bargaining, an agreement was reached that both sides would allow the creation of a buffer zone, which would be patrolled by soldiers from MONUC, the United Nations Mission in the Democratic Republic of the Congo. A joint commission, with representatives from the Congolese government as well as from the USA, the EU, and the African Union (AU), was established to supervise a ceasefire and the absorption of rebel soldiers into the national army, the Armed Forces of the Democratic Republic of Congo (FARDC). The pact, which covered other militias as well as the CNDP, promised amnesty for insurrection, but not for war crimes or human rights violations. It built upon and complemented an accord to disarm Hutu bands, which had been reached between the DRC and Rwandan governments in Nairobi in 2007.

Nkunda had refused to participate in earlier agreements because he maintained that the 6,000 ethnic Hutu extremists of the Democratic Forces for the Liberation of Rwanda (FDLR) constituted a special danger for Congolese Tutsi. The FDLR, a loose alliance of Hutu groups, was probably two-thirds Rwandan in origin. In March it was reported that FARDC lacked the capacity to disarm the FDLR and that the deadline for voluntary demobilisation had passed. By February Nkunda was boycotting the joint commission in protest against a MONUC report that accused his CNDP of killing civilians while the January peace talks were in progress.

By the end of April, MONUC reported optimistically that, although there had been several hundred ceasefire violations, most had been minor and there had been an overall reduction in fighting. Nevertheless, by October heavy fighting had broken out again, with the CNDP threatening to capture Goma town, aid workers being evacuated, and massive population displacement. In a BBC interview on 10 November, Nkunda stated that "if the Kinshasa government does not engage in serious dialogue on power-sharing" he would march on Kinshasa. On 4-5 November, about 150 people were killed by CNDP forces in Kiwanja town, North Kivu, with MONUC forces nearby. In a report published in December entitled *Killings in Kiwanja*, Human Rights Watch sharply criticised the UN for its "inability to protect civilians". At the same time, an independently researched report to the UN Security Council accused Rwanda directly of providing support to rebels in Congo.

Meanwhile, sporadic fighting in Ituri province against the Patriotic Resistance Front in Ituri (FRPI), and in the north east against the Ugandan rebel group, the Lord's Resistance Army (LRA), continued throughout 2008. In late February, attacks on rural populations by the FRPI started up again, and by October FARDC reinforcements had been sent to Ituri amidst reports of ongoing human rights violations. In September, FARDC mounted operations against the LRA, which was also accused of widespread abuses in the areas around Dungu and the Garamba National Park.

In July former rebel leader and former vice president Jean-Pierre Bemba, of the Congolese Liberation Movement (MLC), was arraigned before a preliminary hearing of the International Criminal Court in The Hague in connection with war crimes allegedly committed by his forces in the Central African Republic in 2002-2003.

On 22 December the UN Security Council renewed the mandate of the UN Mission in the DRC (MONUC) for a further year, authorising the deployment of nearly 20,000 troops, as well as observers and police. Under the terms of the renewed mandate, MONUC's role was to focus even more on the protection of civilians in the east and the prevention of cross-border support to rebel militias.

Sanitary and public health conditions remained difficult in 2008, especially in the Kivus, where displaced people were continuously on the move. In January there was a serious cholera outbreak in the southern Katanga province, centred on its capital Lubumbashi; in May there were cases reported in the districts of Masisi and Walikale in North Kivu. By the end of the year, Médecins sans Frontières reported that it had treated 7,000 cholera cases in North Kivu. Malaria remained a major problem, with an estimated 5 million cases a year across the country. Other outbreaks of disease included both haemorrhagic fever and wild polio, reported in northern Equateur province in June; 22 deaths from monkey pox in Equateur in July; over 600 new cases of Hansen's disease (leprosy); and an epidemic of Ebola in Kasai Occidental in late December. Sexual violence against women and minors was widespread in North Kivu, with over 5,000 rapes recorded in the first half of the year. President Kabila carried out a wide-ranging cabinet reshuffle in October, which included the promotion of Aldolphe Muzito, the budget minister, to the post of prime minister. Muzito replaced Antoine Gizenga who had announced his resignation in September, blaming the physical toll of the premiership, which he had held since December 2006. In April the government finalised a previously announced US$6 billion agreement with a private Chinese consortium to finance mining and other projects, including the building of roads, railways, and social infrastructure. In return China would gain access to copper and cobalt resources. Despite the continuing political crisis, economic growth rose to a projected 12 per cent in 2008, driven mainly by mining, trade, and construction. Generalised electrical power problems and an accelerating inflation rate had a negative impact on growth, however. In September, an IMF mission visited Kinshasa to discuss economic policy and the next budget. It was hoped that the visit would lead to a new IMF poverty reduction and growth facility (PRGF) for the country.

Colin Darch

BURUNDI AND RWANDA

Burundi

CAPITAL: Bujumbura   AREA: 27,830 sq km   POPULATION: 8,496,000 ('07)
OFFICIAL LANGUAGES: French & Kirundi   POLITICAL SYSTEM: multiparty republic
HEAD OF STATE AND GOVERNMENT: President Pierre Nkurunziza (CNDD-FDD) (since Aug '05)
RULING PARTY: National Council for the Defence of Democracy-Forces for the Defence of Democracy (CNDD-FDD)
MAIN IGO MEMBERSHIPS (NON-UN): AU, COMESA, EAC, CEEAC, ACP, NAM, Francophonie
CURRENCY: Burundi franc (end-'08 £1=BrF1,775.60, US$1=BrF1,234.98)
GNI PER CAPITA: US$110, $330 at PPP ('07)

Rwanda

CAPITAL: Kigali   AREA: 26,340 sq km   POPULATION: 9,736,000 ('07)
OFFICIAL LANGUAGES: French, Kinyarwanda & English   POLITICAL SYSTEM: multiparty republic
HEAD OF STATE AND GOVERNMENT: President Paul Kagame (RPF) (since April '00)
RULING PARTIES: Rwandan Patriotic Front (RPF) and six coalition allies
PRIME MINISTER: Bernard Mazuka (since April '00)
MAIN IGO MEMBERSHIPS (NON-UN): AU, COMESA, EAC, CEEAC, ACP, NAM, Francophonie
CURRENCY: Rwanda franc (end-'08 £1=RFr802.438, US$1=RFr558.120)
GNI PER CAPITA: US$320, $860 at PPP ('07)

BURUNDI. The post-conflict situation continued to present major challenges to the government through 2008. In the early part of the year the parliamentary paralysis of 2007 continued, as the fate of 22 deputies who had defected from President Pierre Nkurunziza's ruling coalition remained in the balance. Finally in June, the Constitutional Court ruled that the deputies, who included Hussein

Radjabu, the former head of the National Council for the Defence of Democracy—Forces for the Defence of Democracy (CNDD-FDD), had lost their seats by their defection and could legally be replaced. In April, Radjabu was sentenced to 13 years in prison on charges of rebellion and insulting the president. In late November, with the legislative programme unblocked, Parliament adopted a new legal code that integrated internationally-recognised elements on genocide and other crimes against humanity, as well as abolishing the death penalty for the first time. The code was criticised by human rights groups, however, for clauses that criminalised homosexuality.

In early 2008 hostilities between the government and the remaining rebel group, the National Forces for Freedom (FNL or FNL-Palipehutu), led by Agathon Rwasa, continued. Fighting resumed in Bujumbura in April, causing panic among civilians and leaving 100 dead. In May, UN Secretary General Ban Ki Moon described the security situation as "highly uneasy". However, on 26 May the FNL signed a ceasefire agreement mediated by the Regional Peace Initiative for Burundi (comprising Burundi, Rwanda, DRC, and Uganda), which included provisions for the demobilisation and reintegration of FNL fighters, according to the terms of the 2006 agreement between the FNL and the government (see AR 2007, p. 262). At the end of the month Agathon Rwasa returned from exile in Tanzania, a development warmly welcomed by Ban Ki Moon.

The process of cantonment of FNL fighters began in mid-June, as soldiers assembled in Rugazi and Gihanga communes. However, a month later the government accused the FNL of actively recruiting new members and of insisting on political recognition before the cantonment process was complete. In addition, although 2,450 fighters had reported to Rugazi, only 40 firearms had been surrendered. In December, after several months of sporadic progress, the FNL agreed to drop the word "palipehutu" from its title, as required by the constitution which banned ethnic references (the word was the acronym for the French "parti pour la liberation du peuple Hutu"). At the same time, President Nkurunziza agreed to appoint several senior FNL officials to government posts and to release FNL prisoners, who would then move to assembly points.

In May the government announced that the latest data available on HIV prevalence, for 2007, indicated an increase to 4.2 per cent compared with 3.5 per cent in 2002. There were about 250,000 people with HIV in the country, within a total population of over 7 million in 2007, but only 11,000 were receiving treatment. The history of conflict, combined with poverty and rural conservatism, complicated the issue, said the deputy minister in charge of fighting HIV/AIDS, Speciose Baransata. The repatriation of large numbers of refugees and the demobilisation of former fighters also remained major social tasks demanding considerable resources. According to the UN High Commissioner for Refugees, there were 338,000 Burundians still in exile in early 2008, most of them in Tanzania but some in the DRC and Rwanda. There were also about 150,000 internally displaced persons in 160 camps inside Burundi. The National Commission on Demobilisation, Reinsertion and Reintegration (NCDRR) estimated that 23,000 ex-combatants had been demobilised from a total of about 70,000.

The IMF predicted at the end of the year that overall economic growth in 2008 would reach 4.5 per cent, negatively affected by high import and fuel bills. In July the IMF approved a three-year poverty reduction and growth facility (PRGF) worth US$75.6 million for Burundi. The Burundi economy, one of Africa's smallest, remained largely agricultural with a high level of dependence on tea and coffee exports and a weak private sector.

RWANDA. In February, US President George W. Bush visited Rwanda on the third stage of a five-country tour of Africa. During the trip, seen by commentators as an endorsement of President Paul Kagame's administration and also an attempt to promote US-backed projects to fight AIDS and malaria, Bush laid a wreath in memory of genocide victims and visited the Kigali Memorial Centre, where 250,000 of the estimated 800,000 victims of the 1994 genocide were buried.

In December, the International Criminal Tribunal for Rwanda (ICTR), based in Arusha in Tanzania, convicted Théoneste Bagosora, a former Rwandan army colonel, and two accomplices, of genocide and crimes against humanity (one of the accused, Gratien Kabiligi, was acquitted, see AR 2008, p. 261). Bagosora had planned the genocide several years in advance and had trained armed militias to carry it out. He was sentenced to life imprisonment. The "Military 1" trial, which involved hundreds of witnesses and thousands of pages of testimony, began in 2002 and was seen as possessing great symbolic importance. The ICTR, set up in 1997, had already cost more than US$1 billion and had convicted only 36 accused in a decade of activity. Meanwhile, the traditional gacaca courts in Rwanda itself continued to try accused, and were apparently on course to complete over 10,000 cases by the end of 2009, when their mandate was due to expire.

In elections held in September, women candidates won 45 of the 80 seats in the Chamber of Deputies (the lower house of Parliament), making Rwanda the first country in the world to see women in the majority in a legislature. The ruling Rwandan Patriotic Front, at the head of a six-party coalition, won 42 seats; the remainder were won by parties also supporting President Kagame.

In December Théoneste Mutsindashyaka, the minister of education, announced that French would be phased out of Rwandan schools as a language of instruction by 2011, thus "joining the international system". Rwanda broke off diplomatic relations with France in 2006 over comments by a French judge about President Kagame's alleged involvement in the death of then President Juvénal Habyarimana in a plane crash in 1994 (see AR 1994, pp. 292-93; AR 2007, p. 264). In May, Kagame again criticised the "arrogance" of European courts when arrest warrants were issued in France and Spain against government officials.

In December, a UN report accused both Rwanda and Uganda of directly supporting the Tutsi rebellion of General Laurent Nkunda in the eastern Democratic Republic of Congo, and shortly afterwards both The Netherlands and Sweden announced a suspension of aid to Rwanda. President Kagame reacted angrily, and an editorial in the New Times described the report as "outrageous" and called on the population to prepare for life "after foreign aid". The government's plan for this phase appeared to rely at least partly on religious mobilisation around ideologies promulgated by US fundamentalist churches, and Rwanda continued to attract Christian missions of various denominations throughout 2008. In March Southern Baptist pastor Rick Warren, founder of the Saddleback mega-church in Lakeside, California, led a religious rally at Kigali's Amahoro stadium alongside Kagame. Rwanda officially adopted Warren's "purpose driven nation" programme in 2005.

In November the IMF predicted annual economic growth of 8.5 per cent for 2008, despite fluctuating inflation rates throughout the year. Weak agricultural performance continued to be a constraint on growth. The country's financial year—presently running concurrently with the calendar year—was to change in 2009 to run from July to June, in line with other countries in the East African Community.

In February an earthquake along the western Rift Valley fault killed 34 people in the districts of Rusizi and Nyamesheke, injuring another 250. In October, torrential rainfall in the north and west of the country destroyed over 500 houses, washed away over 2,000 hectares of crops, and damaged roads and bridges.

Colin Darch

MOZAMBIQUE

CAPITAL: Maputo   AREA: 799,380 sq km   POPULATION: 21,372,000 ('07)
OFFICIAL LANGUAGE: Portuguese   POLITICAL SYSTEM: multiparty republic
HEAD OF STATE: President Armando Emilio Guebuza (Frelimo) (since Feb '05)
RULING PARTY: Front for the Liberation of Mozambique (Frelimo)
PRIME MINISTER: Luisa Diogo (since Feb '04)
MAIN IGO MEMBERSHIPS (NON-UN): AU, SADC, ACP, CWTH, OIC, NAM, CPLP
CURRENCY: metical (end-'08 £1=M36.2685, US$1=M25.2250)
GNI PER CAPITA: US$320, $690 at PPP ('07)

MUNICIPAL elections were held to choose the mayors and local councils of 43 cities and towns in Mozambique on 19 November, after a lengthy and difficult three-stage voter registration process, dogged by technical failures, and a short official campaign. In the end, voter registration topped 88 per cent, or about 9 million people, which was regarded as a major success, and the campaign ran for 13 days, from 4 to 16 November.

The results were announced in early December, with Frelimo party mayoral candidates duly elected in 41 municipalities and Frelimo party majorities in 42 of the local assemblies. Mozambique's main opposition party, Renamo, performed badly, losing four of the five municipalities that it had previously controlled. In Beira, the country's second city and a Renamo stronghold, the independent Daviz Simango won with over 60 per cent of the vote, while Renamo lost its majority in the city council. An independent observer group, the Mission of International Observers, endorsed the elections as transparent and complying with the regulations. Renamo subsequently appealed unsuccessfully against the results, alleging irregularities.

Mozambique remained extremely vulnerable to natural disasters, with extensive flooding in January and February in the Zambezi and Save basins in the north and south of the country, as well as along the Punguè and Buzi rivers in Sofala province. By mid-January more than 60,000 people had been evacuated in the Zambezi valley, where flooding was described as more severe than in February 2007 (see AR 2008, p. 262). In Inhambane, the Save river burst its banks as water rose to a level of more than 7 metres, 2 metres above the alert level. In Sofala, around 54,000 people were displaced by flooding and four people drowned along the Punguè and Buzi valleys.

Cyclone Jokwe hit Nampula province in the north of the country on 8 March, killing six people and causing damage to homes, schools, and mosques, as well as destroying electricity pylons and cables in Angoche and Ilha de Moçambique. In March, a leader of Renamo, Maria Moreno, criticised government flood relief measures, which included resettlement of affected populations, as little more than a "return to the Communist dream of communal villages". At the end of the year the World Food Programme announced that 350,000 Mozambicans were living with "acute food insecurity" and needed immediate relief as the annual flood season started again.

In August Graça Machel, the widow of the late President Samora Machel, accused the former security minister, Sérgio Vieira, of "repugnant behaviour" after remarks that he made in a television interview about the 1986 Mbuzini air crash, in which Machel had been killed. Vieira had described the late Machel as "reckless". The South African government had promised to open a new inquiry into the crash, but never did so. Mbuzini was widely believed, but was never proven, to have been the result of sabotage by the South African apartheid regime.

On 5 February rioting broke out in Maputo and Matola when it was announced that minibus fares were to rise by 50 per cent in response to fuel price increases. Four people died and over 100 were injured during the violence, some of them from rubber bullets fired by police or from inhaling tear gas. On 23 February Finance Minister Manuel Chang announced a state subsidy on the diesel used in urban passenger transport.

In April President Armando Guebuza embarked on a major reshuffle of his cabinet, replacing the ministers of defence, foreign affairs, the environment, transport, and justice. Earlier he had also appointed a new chief of staff and a new deputy chief of staff for the Mozambican armed forces.

According to the Bank of Mozambique (the central bank), GDP growth faltered in 2008, with a first quarter figure of only 3.5 per cent, compared to 7 per cent in 2007, mainly because of a sharp drop in manufacturing productivity. The balance of trade also worsened, with imports up by nearly 20 per cent. There was some recovery in the second quarter, but the economy remained largely reliant on mega-projects such as gas, aluminium smelting, and the planned Moatize coal project.

HIV prevalence among people aged between 15 and 49 reportedly stabilised at 16 per cent, while the government distributed 4.3 million condoms in the first half of the year and about 100,000 people, of the estimated 300,000 who would benefit from the therapy, were receiving anti-retroviral (ARV) drugs.

After outbreaks of xenophobic violence in South African cities in May, in which at least 23 Mozambicans were killed by enraged township mobs, the government evacuated over 600 Mozambican citizens by bus; it was initially estimated that at least 10,000 others had made their way home from South Africa unaided. Altogether over 36,000 Mozambicans fled the fighting.

In December, Aníbal "Anibalzinho" dos Santos Junior, who was serving a sentence for his involvement in the assassination in November 2000 of the investigative journalist Carlos Cardoso, escaped from prison for the third time (see AR 2003, p. 307).

Colin Darch

ANGOLA

CAPITAL: Luanda   AREA: 1,246,700 sq km   POPULATION: 17,019,000 ('07)
OFFICIAL LANGUAGE: Portuguese   POLITICAL SYSTEM: multiparty republic
HEAD OF STATE AND GOVERNMENT: President José Eduardo dos Santos (since Sept '79)
RULING PARTY: Popular Movement for the Liberation of Angola-Workers' Party (MPLA)
PRIME MINISTER: Col António Paulo Kassoma (since Sept '08)
MAIN IGO MEMBERSHIPS (NON-UN): AU, COMESA, SADC, CEEAC, ACP, NAM, CPLP
CURRENCY: readj. kwanza (end-'08 £1=Kw108.077, US$1=Kw75.1685)
GNI PER CAPITA: US$2,560, $4,400 at PPP ('07)

AFTER years of delay, parliamentary elections were finally held in September 2008, the first elections that the country had seen since 1992. It had been widely expected that the Popular Movement for the Liberation of Angola (MPLA), which had ruled since independence in 1975, would defeat the largest opposition party, the National Union for the Total Independence for Angola (UNITA), led by Isaias Samakuva, but the scale of the MPLA's victory still surprised many observers. Voter turnout was high, estimated at 87.4 per cent of registered voters. The large EU monitoring mission, the most critical of the international observer missions, said that the election fell "short of basic international standards", and UNITA had complained of many irregularities and of intimidation during the campaign, but the MPLA's victory was so overwhelming that UNITA could not challenge it.

Under the terms of the peace agreement signed in 1994 in Lusaka, UNITA had been given several ministerial and vice-ministerial posts in a government of unity and national reconstruction (GURN). With the election, this arrangement came to an end. The UNITA appointees were replaced by MPLA ones, and the GURN was formally abolished in October. As a result of the election, in which it gained 81.6 per cent of the 6.4 million valid ballots, the MPLA held 191 of the 220 seats in the National Assembly (unicameral legislature); UNITA, which won only 10.4 per cent of the vote took 16 seats; and the third largest party, the Social Reconstruction Party (PRS), which had strong ethnic support among the Lunda people, eight. After the election all parties that failed to poll more than 0.5 per cent of the vote were dissolved, leaving the country with six officially registered parties. With so large a majority, the MPLA was well placed to change the constitution to allow for longer presidential terms.

It was widely expected that, despite rumours of ill-health, President José Eduardo dos Santos would stand in the presidential election due to take place in 2009 and win comfortably. After the legislative elections, he expanded his cabinet to 35 ministers, headed by a new prime minister, Colonel António Paulo Kassoma, proposed by the MPLA. The appointment of Manuel Nunes Júnior, the MPLA's chief of economic and social policy, to the new post of economics minister would ensure that the party kept control of economic policy. One new appointee to the cabinet was António Bento Bembe, a member of the Cabinda separatist movement, the Front for the Liberation of the Enclave of Cabinda (FLEC). His appointment as minister without portfolio represented an attempt to ensure that Cabinda separatism did not revive; however, another faction of FLEC continued to mount low level hit and run attacks on government installations in the enclave.

Angola now rivalled Nigeria as the largest oil producer in sub-Saharan Africa, producing close to 2 million barrels per day (b/d) in early 2008 as the price of oil rose to a record high of US$150 per barrel. In the second half of the year, however, the price of oil fell steeply because of the global recession, until it was below the government's 2009 budget assumption of US$55 per barrel. In line with the decision of the Organisation of Petroleum Exporting Countries (OPEC) taken at its September meeting to reduce total production to 2007 levels, Angola cut production by 99,000 b/d. In 2008 Angola overtook Saudi Arabia as the main supplier of crude to China, and more Angolan oil went to China than to the USA, although the USA remained Angola's main trading partner overall.

Much of what happened to the vast wealth from oil remained under wraps, though there were rumours that leading officials had secreted large amounts abroad, especially in Brazil, with which Angola had good relations. Not surprisingly, the Angolan elite who benefited from the lack of transparency were not pleased when the French began to investigate the payment of bribes by French officials to Angolans in the 1990s. France's President Nicolas Sarkozy visited Angola in May to try to improve relations that had been soured by the investigation. In October, 42 people, including Jean-Christophe Mitterrand, the son of former French President François Mitterrand, went on trial in France over the "arms to Angola" scandal, in which it was alleged that US$790 million-worth of arms, much from stockpiles left after the Soviet Union collapsed, had been sent to Angola at the height of the civil war in the mid-1990s. Although no Angolans were charged, it emerged in the trial that many had received tens of millions of dollars in clandestine payments.

Angola's oil-fuelled economic growth was said to be the highest in the world, averaging over 20 per cent per annum from 2005, although the estimate for 2008 was closer to 15 per cent because of the global economic downturn. The government continued with its multi-billion dollar programme of investment in infrastructure: some of it to repair what had been destroyed in the civil war; some of it new building. Large areas of Luanda were cleared for new suburbs and commercial developments, and vast new housing schemes were beginning to change the face of other urban centres. While plans for the state-owned oil company, Sonangol, and China Petroleum Corporation to build a US$3.5 billion oil refinery at the country's second largest port, Lobito, remained on hold, the reconstruction of the Benguela railway from Lobito into the interior, towards the eastern border with Zambia and the Democratic Republic of Congo (DRC), continued and the restored line reached Huambo, 220 km from Benguela. Much of the interior remained devastated by the war, and efforts to revive agricultural production were still hampered by the millions of landmines left from the war. But the emergence of Angola as a regional economic powerhouse was reflected in the rapid growth of trade with Namibia and South Africa in particular, and in the way in which Angola was beginning to play a larger role on the international stage. The fact that it was to host the African Cup of Nations football championship in 2010 was already bringing Angola much attention on the continent.

Christopher Saunders

ZAMBIA—MALAWI—ZIMBABWE—BLNS STATES

ZAMBIA

CAPITAL: Lusaka   AREA: 752,610 sq km   POPULATION: 11,920,000 ('07)
OFFICIAL LANGUAGE: English   POLITICAL SYSTEM: multiparty republic
HEAD OF STATE AND GOVERNMENT: President Rupiah Banda (since Nov '08; acting president since June '08)
RULING PARTY: Movement for Multi-Party Democracy (MMD)
MAIN IGO MEMBERSHIPS (NON-UN): AU, COMESA, SADC, ACP, CWTH, NAM
CURRENCY: Zambian kwacha (end-'08 £1=Kw6,894.01, US$1=Kw4,795.00)
GNI PER CAPITA: US$800, $1,220 at PPP ('07)

THE key political event of 2008 in Zambia was the death in August of 59-year old President Levy Mwanawasa, seven weeks after he had suffered a stroke when attending the 11th African Union heads of state meeting in Egypt (see Obituary). His vice president, former diplomat Rupiah Banda, took over as acting president. Under the terms of the constitution, an election had to be held within 90 days. After defeating a challenge as the nominee of the ruling Movement for Multiparty Democracy (MMD) for president, Banda promised continuity in his election campaign. The leading opposition figure, the populist and charismatic Michael Sata of the Patriotic Front, who had narrowly lost to Mwanawasa in the 2006 elections and had had a heart attack in May, called for change and criticised the government's pro-business policies.

After a fiercely fought but peaceful contest, Banda won the election on 30 October by a mere 32,000 vote margin on a low turnout, and he was immediately sworn in as the new president. Sata and his party claimed that the Electoral Commission had rigged the poll, but did not produce credible evidence in support of the charge and there was little post-election violence. The new president promised to be more active than his predecessor in tackling corruption: the court cases against the former president, Frederick Chiluba (1991-2001), and others for corruption had dragged on for years and remained unresolved.

Although the country had enjoyed sustained economic growth for some time thanks to the high price of copper and Mwanawasa's fiscal discipline, most Zambians remained very poor. By the time of the election, the price of copper, the mainstay of the Zambian economy, had begun to plummet and inflation to spiral, while the kwacha sank against the US dollar. Though some thought that increased copper production might help to offset a lower price, it was clear that the new president faced tough economic conditions. His main challenge in the region was how to deal with Zambia's southern neighbour. Mwanawasa had called Zimbabwe "a sinking Titanic" but had failed to effect change there, and Banda was unlikely to take any lead on Zimbabwe in the Southern African Development Community (SADC). Instead, he seemed destined to be absorbed by internal problems: the need to take charge of the ruling MMD— within which he was seen as an outsider—and to try to tackle the deep seated poverty in which so many of his countrymen were mired. Yet Zambia could not but be affected as Zimbabwe's prolonged economic, social, and political collapse continued.

Christopher Saunders

MALAWI

CAPITAL: Lilongwe   AREA: 118,480 sq km   POPULATION: 13,920,000 ('07)
OFFICIAL LANGUAGE: English   POLITICAL SYSTEM: multiparty republic
HEAD OF STATE AND GOVERNMENT: President Bingu wa Mutharika (DPP), since May '04
RULING PARTY: United Democratic Front (UDF)
MAIN IGO MEMBERSHIPS (NON-UN): AU, COMESA, SADC, ACP, CWTH, NAM
CURRENCY: Malawi kwacha (end-'08 £1=Kw202.148, US$1=Kw140.600)
GNI PER CAPITA: US$250, $750 at PPP ('07)

IN 2008 Malawi again had a bumper harvest of maize, its staple crop, which was grown by most of its adults and consumed by almost all of its people. Whereas in 2005 almost 5 million Malawians had needed food aid, in 2008 over 3 million tonnes of maize were produced, allowing more than 1 million tonnes to be exported. This was as a result of good rains and of hefty government subsidies for imported chemical fertiliser. There was also significant growth in the production of other crops, including rice and groundnuts, while the main export crop, tobacco, received record prices at auction, helping to push the country's economic growth to 8.6 per cent. By the end of the year an Australian mining company was beginning to exploit uranium oxide in the far north of the country, and uranium was expected soon to become the country's second-largest export after tobacco.

This economic recovery remained fragile, however, and had little impact on poverty levels. Malawi remained one of the poorest and least developed countries in Africa, with a maternal mortality rate among the highest in the world. Donors funded three-quarters of the country's development budget and half its recurrent budget, and donor funding paid for half of the fertiliser subsidy. There was much agonising in 2008 over whether Malawi should finalise an economic partnership agreement (EPA) with the EU, which took 40 per cent of its exports. In April the European Commission felt it necessary to reconfirm that the issue of signing an EPA was unrelated to Malawi's continued access to grants under the European Development Fund. Many in Malawi feared that the EPA would jeopardise Malawi's trading preferences with South Africa and mean that the country would not be able to protect its domestic industries via tariffs.

Meanwhile, political infighting also threatened the nascent economic recovery. President Bingu wa Mutharika continued to govern without a parliamentary majority, and the legislature continued to try to frustrate the executive. Legal wrangling continued over the use of section 65 of the constitution, which provided that the speaker could declare vacant the seat of those opposition members of the National Assembly who had crossed the floor to side with the government (see AR 2007, p. 269; AR 2008, p. 267). Former President Bakili Muluzi, the extra-parliamentary leader of the opposition United Democratic Front (UDF), had announced that he would be his party's candidate for president in the 2009 election. With the opposition accusing Mutharika of acting dictatorially, it was widely speculated that Muluzi might beat the incumbent in the forthcoming election and win a third term as president, especially if the global economic downturn led to a significant decline in donor funding.

Christopher Saunders

ZIMBABWE

CAPITAL: Harare   AREA: 390,760 sq km   POPULATION: 13,403,000 ('07)
OFFICIAL LANGUAGE: English   POLITICAL SYSTEM: multiparty republic
HEAD OF STATE AND GOVERNMENT: President Robert Mugabe (since Dec '87); previously Prime Minister (from April '80)
RULING PARTY: Zimbabwe African National Union-Patriotic Front (ZANU-PF)
MAIN IGO MEMBERSHIPS (NON-UN): AU, COMESA, SADC, ACP, NAM
CURRENCY: Zimbabwe dollar (end-'08 £1=Z$84,977.90, US$1=Z$80,808.10)
GNI PER CAPITA: US$340, -

THE crucial event in Zimbabwe's most dramatic year since independence in 1980 was the general election of 29 March. The announcement of the election date by President Robert Mugabe on 17 January forestalled negotiations between his ruling Zimbabwe African National Union-Patriotic Front (ZANU-PF) government and the opposition Movement for Democratic Change (MDC), led by Morgan Tsvangirai. The negotiations, brokered by South African president Thabo Mbeki on behalf of the Southern African Development Community (SADC), had sought to prepare the ground for a fair and open contest. For the first time in Zimbabwe the ballot would simultaneously elect the president, the House of Assembly and the Senate (the lower and upper chambers of the legislature), and local councils.

The campaign, like those of the elections of 2000 and 2005, was clearly unequal. The voters' roll was unrevised and out of date, while constituency boundaries had been manipulated to favour the ruling party. The MDC's election rallies were frequently disrupted, while those of ZANU-PF saw community leaders bribed with gifts of food, farm equipment, and vehicles. The MDC was denied access to the broadcasting media, while foreign press reporting was hampered. Each new obstacle made the MDC slogan—"chinja", or "change" in the majority Shona language—more pertinent.

Despite a restriction on independent observers and the illegal stationing of police officers within polling stations, election day proceeded peacefully. The MDC, alert to probable vote rigging—the government had printed 2 million more ballot forms than there were registered voters in the country—engineered a preliminary count at individual polling stations, photographed the results as they were posted, and emailed them to a co-ordinating office. Anticipating the formal count of the government-controlled Zimbabwe Electoral Commission (ZEC), the MDC's preliminary count pointed to an opposition victory in the parliamentary contest and the defeat of at least nine members of the ZANU-PF politburo. After two days the formal results began to trickle in, giving Tsvangirai's MDC 99 seats in the 210-seat House of Assembly to ZANU-PF's 97, with a breakaway MDC faction, led by Professor Arthur Mutambara, securing 10. (An independent candidate won one seat, and elections were postponed in three constituencies.) In at least eight constituencies, in which the MDC had fielded two candidates, the ZANU-PF candidate had won through. But for the first time in 28 years, Mugabe's party had lost control of the legislature.

For a few intense days, the world's press showed Mugabe's administration reeling in shock, while ordinary Zimbabweans took to the streets in celebration. The governing party narrowly won the Senate, but the MDC won the vast majority of council seats across the country, taking decisive control of all major conurbations. The results of the presidential poll, however, were delayed first for a week—the maximum allowed by the constitution—then indefinitely. The opposition responded by announcing its own tally, signalling an outright win for Tsvangirai by 51 per cent to Mugabe's 42 per cent, with the third candidate, Simba Makoni, a former government finance minister and senior ZANU-PF politburo member, on 7 per cent. For this bold presumption the secretary general of the MDC, Tendai Biti, was arrested and later charged with treason. On 3 May, after a secret count from which the opposition was barred, the ZEC announced the official result, which gave Tsvangirai 47.9 per cent of the vote to Mugabe's 43.2 per cent. A run-off election was secured and the president saved from elimination.

The ZANU-PF backlash began even before the final results were declared. MDC offices in Harare were attacked on 3 April. The following day 400 of Mugabe's war veterans staged an intimidating march through the streets of the capital. British and US journalists were detained and ZEC officials arrested for having committed "counting errors". Several newly elected MDC legislators were reported kidnapped, and retribution began against voters identified as having voted "the wrong way". Mugabe declared that the British would never "steal" his country, and established a joint operations command, led by his cabinet enforcer, Emmerson Mnangagwa, to ensure victory in the second round ballot.

The run-off seemed more a terror campaign than an electoral contest, with attacks on MDC activists, over 100 killings, some 5,000 abductions, and vindictive personalised attacks on the wives and children of elected officials. Tsvangirai was arrested, his driver murdered, and his vehicles impounded. Mugabe's reckless rhetoric both prejudiced the campaign and exposed his fears: he was prepared to "go to war" to prevent the MDC taking the presidency. In a speech on 21 June, he declared that a simple ballot would not persuade him to cede control, and that "only God" could remove him from office.

In hiding and at risk of assassination, Tsvangirai withdrew from the contest a week before the run-off, declaring he could not ask Zimbabweans to vote for him "when that vote could cost them their lives". Mugabe proceeded with the redundant poll on 27 June, this time announcing his victory—by 2,150,000 votes to 233,000—very promptly. Three sets of observers declared the poll undemocratic, and the opposition claimed that it would "block the arteries of dialogue". Though swiftly inaugurated for a new five-year term, Mugabe hesitated to form a government and continued to rule the country without parliament, without a cabinet, and by decree.

The vacuous nature of his re-election brought Mugabe international derision. Within the SADC, the governments of Botswana, Kenya, Rwanda, and Liberia refused to recognise Mugabe's victory. Jacob Zuma, leader of South Africa's ruling African National Congress (ANC) and the country's probable next president, declared that Zimbabwe's failure to recognise a democratic choice, and its brutality against its voters, had rendered it a police state. Western governments uniformly criticised the result: after the first round, Condoleezza Rice, the US secretary of state, had characterised the Mugabe regime as "a disgrace" to Africa.

In terms of the ongoing mediation of Thabo Mbeki, Mugabe's "victory" was an irrelevance. While an African Union (AU) summit at Sharm el-Sheikh in Egypt in early July failed to condemn the election, it backed negotiation between the parties and the formation of a government of national unity. Further meetings between ZANU-PF and the two MDC factions followed, and a tentative "memorandum of understanding" was signed in Harare on 22 July. An edgy public handshake between Mugabe and Tsvangirai presaged an intensive fortnight of talks in the South African capital, Pretoria. The core issues were the allocation of cabinet portfolios; the control of the army, police, and security services; the timing of fresh elections; and the relationship between Mugabe, as president, and Tsvangirai, as presumptive prime minister.

With these issues pending, the Zimbabwean Parliament reconvened for the first time in six months in August. The House of Assembly elected as its new speaker Lovemore Moyo, of the now majority MDC party. At the ceremonial opening of Parliament the following day, Mugabe was jeered and heckled as he attempted to deliver his opening address in the House of Assembly, an unprecedented humiliation after 28 years of unfettered power.

Finally, on 15 September, after weeks of mutual recrimination, the two parties signed a power-sharing deal at the Rainbow Towers Hotel in Harare. But almost immediately problems emerged, and the agreement was soon in deadlock over the control of the home affairs portfolio and of the security and intelligence services. The resignation of Mbeki as South Africa's president on 21 September appreciably weakened the status of the agreement's principal facilitator.

The political grandstanding of the party leaders sat awkwardly against the implosion of the country's economy and the desperate plight of its people. By the end of the year more than 90 per cent of Zimbabweans were jobless, with 3 million wholly sustained by the UN World Food Programme. The inflation rate, which started the year at over 10,000 per cent, rocketed to over 2 million per cent in July and an unimaginable 13 billion per cent in November, as the Zimbabwe Reserve Bank (the central bank) printed banknotes in ever escalating denominations. By the close of the year, the US dollar and South African rand had effectively supplanted Zimbabwe's own currency.

As the economy collapsed, the infrastructure of the country deconstructed. Schools and universities closed as teachers abandoned their worthless salaries in the struggle to survive. Strikes by doctors and public service workers closed down essential services. In early December a riot by soldiers over pay signalled growing alienation within the armed forces. Utilities barely functioned: in mid-June the entire country was without electricity for a full weekend. As Mugabe railed against the failures of the "colonial" powers, it was only Western aid and remittances from the millions of Zimbabweans working abroad that kept the country afloat.

With urban water supplies contaminated by sewage, instances of cholera increased in early September and swiftly turned into an epidemic. Despite an emergency aid package of £10 million from the UK, the outbreak resulted in over 2,000 avoidable deaths and many thousands stricken by the end of the year.

The government's response to the stalled power-sharing talks was to ramp up violence against its critics. It targeted human rights workers, and in December the widely admired Jestina Mukoko, executive director of the Zimbabwe Peace Project, was abducted. But Mugabe had run out of options: without a political settlement and external financial support there was no hope for the economy. The economic catastrophe and the profound suffering of the Zimbabwean people seemed likely to overtake the intractable power struggle between ruling party and opposition.

R.W. Baldock

BOTSWANA—LESOTHO—NAMIBIA—SWAZILAND

Botswana

CAPITAL: Gaborone   AREA: 581,730 sq km   POPULATION: 1,881,000 ('07)
OFFICIAL LANGUAGES: English and Setswana   POLITICAL SYSTEM: multiparty republic
HEAD OF STATE AND GOVERNMENT: President Lt-Gen. Seretse Khama Ian Khama (since April '08)
RULING PARTY: Botswana Democratic Party (BDP)
MAIN IGO MEMBERSHIPS (NON-UN): AU, SADC, SACU, ACP, CWTH, NAM
CURRENCY: pula (end-'08 £1=P10.8635, US$1=P7.5529)
GNI PER CAPITA: US$5,840, $12,420 at PPP ('07)

Lesotho

CAPITAL: Maseru   AREA: 30,350 sq km   POPULATION: 2,006,000 ('07)
OFFICIAL LANGUAGES: English & Sesotho   POLITICAL SYSTEM: multiparty monarchy
HEAD OF STATE: King Letsie III (since Jan '96)
RULING PARTY: Lesotho Congress for Democracy (LCD)
HEAD OF GOVERNMENT: Prime Minister Bethuel Pakalitha Mosisili (since June '98)
MAIN IGO MEMBERSHIPS (NON-UN): AU, SADC, SACU, ACP, CWTH, NAM
CURRENCY: maloti (end-'08 £1=M13.2920, US$1=M9.2450)
GNI PER CAPITA: US$1,000, $1,890 at PPP ('07)

Namibia

CAPITAL: Windhoek   AREA: 824,290 sq km   POPULATION: 2,074,000 ('07)
OFFICIAL LANGUAGES: Afrikaans & English   POLITICAL SYSTEM: multiparty republic
HEAD OF STATE: President Hifikepunye Pohamba (SWAPO) (since March '05)
RULING PARTY: South West Africa People's Organisation (SWAPO)
HEAD OF GOVERNMENT: Prime Minister Nahas Angula (since March '05)
MAIN IGO MEMBERSHIPS (NON-UN): AU, SADC, COMESA, SACU, ACP, CWTH, NAM
CURRENCY: Namibian dollar (end-'08 £1=N$13.2920, US$1=N$9.2450)
GNI PER CAPITA: US$3,360, $5,120 at PPP ('07)

Swaziland

CAPITAL: Mbabane   AREA: 17,360 sq km   POPULATION: 1,145,000 ('07)
OFFICIAL LANGUAGE: English & Siswati   POLITICAL SYSTEM: non-party monarchy
HEAD OF STATE: King Mswati III (since '86)
HEAD OF GOVERNMENT: Prime Minister Sibusiso Barnabas Dlamini (since Oct '08)
MAIN IGO MEMBERSHIPS (NON-UN): AU, COMESA, SADC, SACU, ACP, CWTH, NAM
CURRENCY: lilangeni/pl. emalangeni (end-'08 £1=E13.2920, US$1=E9.2450)
GNI PER CAPITA: US$2,580, $4,930 at PPP ('07)

BOTSWANA, Lesotho, Namibia, and Swaziland were intimately linked with South Africa through the Southern African Customs Union (SACU), which had been established in 1910 and was a major source of revenue for the BLNS states, especially Lesotho and Swaziland. During 2008, tensions continued between South Africa and its SACU partners over the economic partnership agreement (EPA) with the European Union. In 2007, South Africa had been alone in refusing to sign an interim EPA with the EU, citing unreasonable demands by the latter. It was feared that this split and the resultant differing trade regimes could imperil the future of SACU.

BOTSWANA.   President Festus Mogae stepped down on 1 April in favour of his vice president, Lieutenant General Seretse Khama Ian Khama, who immediately appointed a new cabinet. Mogae, who had been in power since 1998, was due to have concluded his second (and last term) in 2009. He subsequently continued activism around AIDS (a concern of his presidency), was appointed by UN Secretary General Ban Ki Moon as a special envoy on climate change, and was awarded the Mo Ibrahim prize for achievement in African leadership. Yet the manner in which power was passed on was criticised as "dynastic" and a blot on Botswana's democracy.

However, under President Khama, Botswana adopted a harder line against Zimbabwe, backing tougher measures against President Robert Mugabe. Khama refused to attend a Southern African Development Community (SADC) summit in August in protest at the presence of Mugabe after his fraudulent re-election (see p. 291). In November he called for a rerun of the election.

Botswana's push for greater benefit from its diamond resources was given impetus with the launch of a new diamond sorting facility in Gaborone in March and provision of training in the skills of sorting, valuing, and trading diamonds, which had previously been conducted elsewhere. In November the first "made in Botswana" diamonds began selling in the USA. The objective was to establish a Botswana brand and to add value, for example, by manufacturing jewellery in Botswana. However, the global financial crisis and fall in mineral prices began to affect mining operations, in particular by making funds for new operations difficult to obtain and by reducing international demand for diamonds and jewellery.

Botswana's treatment of its San minority continued to attract criticism from activists, as well as the US state department and the UN Human Rights Council. There were further allegations that the government was attempting to restrict access to water, in order to force the San from their lands. President Khama referred to the supposed desire of the San to subsist as hunter gatherers as "an archaic fantasy".

LESOTHO. Political uncertainty continued, harking back to the disputed election of 2007. The dispute centred on the allocation of seats in Parliament, which the opposition parties alleged favoured allies of the ruling Lesotho Congress for Democracy (see AR 2008, p. 272). Attempts in February, mandated by the SADC and led by the former president of Botswana, Ketumile Masire, to broker an end to the dispute proved fruitless. Masire said that he had difficulty in finding common ground between the parties and that it was "for Basotho [people] themselves to apply themselves seriously in this matter".

Media freedom came under the spotlight in relation to Harvest FM, the country's only private radio station. A radio journalist, Thabo Thakalekoala, appeared in court on charges of damaging the prime minister's reputation and subversion. He had broadcast a letter, which referred to the prime minister as an "unwanted ruler". He was sentenced to a fine of M200 (US$18) or two years in prison. Meanwhile, the station's manager, Reverend Adam Lekhoaba, was deported for holding dual citizenship, which was not permitted in Lesotho, and the station was closed for three months after complaints were laid against it by the police commissioner and an official in the communications ministry. The non-governmental

Media Institute of Southern Africa (MISA) condemned this action.

Socio-economic problems continued to afflict Lesotho. An ongoing drought and dependence by a large part of the population on food aid was aggravated by higher food and fuel prices. Rainfall predictions for 2008-09 were poor, and UNICEF and the Lesotho Vulnerability Assessment Committee (a joint UN agency, NGO, and government taskforce) estimated that some 353,000 people would need food assistance.

NAMIBIA. As the country prepared for elections in 2009, there were numerous indications that political intolerance would be a factor. This was linked in particular to the emergence of the Rally for Democracy and Progress (RDP), led by a former cabinet minister of the ruling South West African People's Organisation (SWAPO). Politicians and commentators expressed concern about the vitriolic language used in campaigns, and also the failure of senior politicians—including the president, Hifikepunye Pohamba—to rise above party politics. A number of political meetings saw violence and intimidation. During November, for example, a rally held by the RDP was disrupted by a crowd of SWAPO supporters, which left several people injured.

There was widespread speculation about Pohamba's future role in SWAPO. It was alleged that a faction, which included the SWAPO party youth league, wanted to remove him from the leadership and field a different candidate in the presidential elections, although SWAPO denied this.

In November, Pohamba launched Namibia's third development plan. This called for investments of some N$60 billion until March 2012, to further Namibia's ambition of becoming an industrialised country by 2030.

As in Botswana, the global financial crisis and fall in mineral prices were expected to hit Namibia's mining industry—a key element of its economy—hard. On the back of tumbling copper prices, Weatherly Mining Namibia decided to close its last two copper mines, shedding 600 jobs. The country's chamber of mines noted that further exploration and expansion in the industry would need to be limited under current circumstances.

SWAZILAND. The only absolute monarchy in Africa remained beset by political and economic problems. During September, the country held a joint celebration ("40-40"), commemorating 40 years of independence and the 40th birthday of the king, Mswati III, who was listed by Forbes magazine as one of the 15 richest royals in the world.

The costs and extravagance of the event—including sending some of the king's numerous wives abroad on an extensive shopping trip—provoked anger, and demonstrations were organised by HIV positive people and trade unions. In Swaziland some 26 per cent of people aged 15-49 were estimated to be HIV positive and some 48 per cent to live on less than US$1 per day.

Opposition groups, particularly the exiled political parties, received some support in their demands and in publicising their grievances from groups in South Africa, particularly the Congress of South African Trade Unions. In August, protests directed at King Mswati and Zimbabwe's President Robert Mugabe were held in Johannesburg at a SADC summit.

Swaziland also held elections under its Tinkhundla system. As political parties had been banned since 1973, candidates were required to stand as independents. Opposition groups denounced this as a sham and demanded multi-party elections. The SADC observer mission noted that "the vibrancy that is seen in most parts of the world during elections is not there in Swaziland", and the AU's Pan African Parliament called for change.

Elizabeth Sidiropoulos & Terence Corrigan

SOUTH AFRICA

CAPITAL: Pretoria   AREA: 1,219,090 sq km   POPULATION: 47,588,000 ('07)
OFFICIAL LANGUAGES: Afrikaans, English & nine African languages   POLITICAL SYSTEM: multiparty republic
HEAD OF STATE AND GOVERNMENT: President Kgalema Motlanthe (since Sept '08)
RULING PARTY: African National Congress (ANC)
MAIN IGO MEMBERSHIPS (NON-UN): AU, SADC, SACU, CWTH, NAM
CURRENCY: rand (end-'08 £1=R13.2920, US$1=R9.2450)
GNI PER CAPITA: US$5,760, $9,560 at PPP ('07)

DURING 2008, South Africa faced mounting economic difficulties. Whereas in 2007 the economy had grown by 5.1 per cent in real terms, in 2008 it experienced a large deficit on its current account and struggled with the effects of high fuel prices, inflation, and interest rates. Although some of these factors eased towards the end of the year, the overall difficulties were exacerbated by the global economic downturn and the expectation that South Africa could face a recession and large-scale retrenchments. On a positive note, however, the country seemed better placed to weather the crisis than some other economies, partly because of its more robust regulatory environment.

South Africa remained focused throughout 2008 on the strains within the ruling African National Congress (ANC) and their effect on the country's governance. Tensions had been exacerbated by the ousting of the country's president, Thabo Mbeki, from the ANC leadership at the party's conference in late 2007 (see AR 2008, p. 274). The assumption of the party leadership by Jacob Zuma, with backing from the ANC's leftist alliance partners (the South African Communist Party and the Congress of South African Trade Unions), opened the way for Zuma to become South Africa's president after the 2009 elections, and raised intense speculation over the direction that his administration would follow.

The prospects for Zuma's ascent to the presidency remained constrained, however, by corruption allegations embodied within a court case concerning a large arms purchase by the South African government (see below). Zuma conducted a protracted legal challenge to his prosecution, culminating in a judgment by Justice Chris Nicholson in September that the prosecution was invalid on technical grounds. Nicholson also remarked that the decision by the National Prosecuting Authority (NPA) to prosecute Zuma appeared to have been influenced by the executive. Both the NPA and Mbeki indicated an intention to appeal against the judgment.

The judgment provided the catalyst for the ANC's national executive committee to "recall" Mbeki from the presidency of the country in September "as a political way to deal with the implications of Judge Nicholson's ruling". Following Mbeki's recall, a number of cabinet ministers resigned, including the minister of finance, Trevor Manuel, who was respected internationally for his stewardship of the economy although disliked by the ANC's left wing. The resignations were motivated by loyalty to Mbeki, as well as a belief by some that it should be the president's prerogative to appoint his own cabinet.

The deputy president of the ANC, Kgalema Motlanthe, was on 25 September elected by the National Assembly (lower chamber of the Parliament) to the vacant presidency. Motlanthe had been a relatively recent addition to the National Assembly and the cabinet, having been appointed in July as minister without portfolio. The speaker of the National Assembly, Baleka Mbete, was appointed deputy president. Following his election Motlanthe reappointed most of Mbeki's ministers, including Manuel, although some were assigned new portfolios. A notable change was the appointment of the minister of health, Manto Tshabalala-Msimang, as minister in the presidency, while the health portfolio was passed to Barbara Hogan. Tshabalala-Msimang had been widely condemned for her handling of the country's HIV epidemic and groups active in the field, such as the Treatment Action Campaign, welcomed Hogan's appointment. Hogan's attitude towards the pandemic—including admitting that South Africa's response had been unsatisfactory—was seen as indicating a renewed determination to deal with the matter.

Throughout the year, the legislature appeared more assertive towards the executive than it had been for at least a decade, during which its quiescence had been viewed as a significant democratic liability by many analysts. This, however, may have been attributable to the victory of Zuma's supporters in the ANC leadership contest, and it was unclear if this assertiveness would endure.

South Africa's future policy orientation, especially regarding economic policy, was equally uncertain. Zuma, in particular, had repeatedly said that there would be no policy changes after the 2009 elections, but he was contradicted in November by the ANC secretary general, Gwede Mantashe, who told a business audience that economic policies would change, based on an "ideological shift". Changes would focus on "retaining and building on what is working and changing what is not working"; industrial policy would be implemented with "renewed vigour"; and state intervention would direct resources "to where they indeed must be". Policy proposals contained in a draft election manifesto suggested a significant increase in state involvement in the economy and an expansion of the welfare system. These included the extension of grants, an emphasis on "decent work", and prescribed investments. Some economists as well as the finance ministry cautioned that such moves would raise the cost of doing business and compound the problem of financing South Africa's current account deficit, standing at some US$20 billion per year.

The political fallout from Mbeki's recall further manifested itself in the resignation of several senior members of the ANC from the party. These included the premier of Gauteng province, Mbhazima Shilowa, and the erstwhile minister of defence, Mosiuoa Lekota. This group was seen as being broadly loyal to Mbeki (although the latter never publicly endorsed their actions), and began to mobilise support around the broad theme of defending the constitution. A formal party, named the Congress of the People (COPE), headed by Lekota, was formed at a congress in Bloemfontein in December. A number of ANC members resigned from the party to back COPE and this was evidently a source of confusion and concern for the ANC.

Allegations of corruption among senior government officials continued to present a formidable challenge to South Africa, while related government actions generated controversy. Jackie Selebi, the country's police commissioner and president of Interpol, who had been dogged by allegations of corruption and links to organised crime, took an "extended leave of absence" in January and resigned from the presidency of Interpol shortly thereafter. At the end of the month he appeared in court on charges of corruption and defeating the ends of justice.

Allegations around South Africa's multi-billion rand arms purchase of 1999 remained a prominent issue, with suspicions frequently raised that senior ANC officials, as well as the ANC itself, had either facilitated corruption, benefited from it, or were aware of what was transpiring. As president, Motlanthe had initially seemed open to a judicial commission of enquiry into the deal, but later rejected the notion.

Following a resolution at its 2007 conference, the ANC moved to abolish the directorate of special operations (the "Scorpions"), an elite crime-fighting unit in the NPA. Suspicions abounded that this was done in order to protect persons, including Zuma, who were under investigation. ANC officials argued that a consolidated unit within the police service would strengthen the fight against crime and corruption, and elsewhere suggested that the Scorpions had a "persistent hatred of the ANC". Parliament passed the legislation abolishing the unit in October.

The former director of the NPA, Vusi Pikoli, suspended in 2007 by Mbeki, was the subject of an enquiry by a former speaker of Parliament, Frene Ginwala, into his fitness to hold the office. She concluded that Pikoli was fit to do so, although he showed a "lack of appreciation for the sensitivities that are attendant on matters of national security". On the latter grounds, Motlanthe controversially refused to reinstate him.

Parliament's "travelgate" scandal, involving the abuse by MPs of their travel vouchers (see AR 2007, p. 278), concluded with the gazetting of a notice that the liquidators of a travel agency implicated in the scandal should "cease all litigation as against Members of Parliament". This implied that MPs who had defrauded Parliament would be let off lightly and, as no comprehensive list of such MPs had been made public, many would not be exposed for their actions.

The year exposed severe weaknesses in South Africa's infrastructure. A failure on government's part to allow the electricity utility, Eskom, to invest in expanding its generation capacity, a loss of skills, and low stocks of coal (among other factors), coupled with increasing demand, saw a serious shortfall in electricity supply and consequent repeated power cuts. One estimate, by the National Energy Regulator of South Africa, put the cost of the crisis between 1 November 2007 and 31 January 2008 at some R50 billion. To fund an expansion programme, tariffs would need to rise sharply. Road maintenance needs were extensive and the funds allocated to addressing them insufficient; concerns were also raised about the state of the country's water supply system.

The first set of pupils to take the school leaving examinations under South Africa's new outcomes based education (OBE) system graduated in 2008. Concerns abounded, including from the minister of education, Naledi Pandor, that the education system was not producing the skills needed to maintain a modern economy, especially in the hard sciences. The World Economic Forum's *Global Competitiveness Report* rated the quality of maths and science education in South Africa as among the poorest in the world.

Violence and crime remained key concerns. Some 18,487 people were murdered in the period between April 2007 and March 2008, compared with 19,202 in the comparable period of 2006-07. Political responses tended to be populist, including a call in April by the deputy minister of safety and security, Susan Shabangu, for police officers to "kill the bastards". In May, xenophobic riots erupted in numerous parts of the country, leading to some 62 deaths and the displacement of thousands. To deal with the crime problem, the government announced that it would be implementing the recommendations of a criminal justice review. This would entail co-ordinating the activities of the various aspects of the criminal justice system in order to produce a better and more focused response to crime. The effectiveness of these measures had yet to be seen.

In foreign affairs, South Africa, and specifically Mbeki, remained involved in mediating an end to the impasse in Zimbabwe, despite concerns that Mbeki was sympathetic to the ruling ZANU-PF and its leader, President Robert Mugabe. South Africa's efforts appeared to yield results when a power-sharing agreement was concluded in September, leaving Mugabe as head of state and the opposition leader, Morgan Tsvangirai, in the—yet to be created—position of prime minister. By the new year, such a government had still not been formed (see p. 292). South Africa had pledged that an aid package would not be delivered to Zimbabwe until this occurred, but in December announced that it would be sent as a part of a package by the Southern African Development Community (SADC), in the wake of a cholera outbreak.

South Africa also concluded its term on the UN Security Council. The government was pleased with its achievements: it had sought to advance the "African agenda" and had influenced a "large number and diversity of council outcomes". It had also encouraged debate on the relationship between the UN and regional organisations and the relationship between the UN and the African Union (AU). Other observers were disappointed with South Africa's performance, noting that it had used its position to shield despotic governments such as those of Burma and Zimbabwe.

Elizabeth Sidiropoulos & Terence Corrigan

VIII SOUTH ASIA AND INDIAN OCEAN

IRAN—AFGHANISTAN—CENTRAL ASIAN STATES

IRAN

CAPITAL: Tehran   AREA: 1,745,150 sq km POPULATION: 71,021,000 ('07)
OFFICIAL LANGUAGE: Farsi (Persian)   POLITICAL SYSTEM: multiparty republic, under religious
    leadership
SPIRITUAL GUIDE: Ayatollah Seyed Ali Khamenei (since June '89)
HEAD OF STATE: President Mahmoud Ahmadinejad (since Aug '05)
MAIN IGO MEMBERSHIPS (NON-UN): OPEC, ECO, CP, OIC, NAM
CURRENCY: Iranian rial (end-'08 £1=IR14,169.00, US$1=IR9,855.00)
GNP PER CAPITA: US$3,470, $10,800 at PPP ('07)

POLITICS in 2008 were dominated by interest in two elections—one in Iran and the
other in the United States—and a growing preoccupation with the state of the
economy. By the end of the year, the economic downturn and its projected consequences focused attention on another, forthcoming, election: that of the Iranian
president in 2009 and the likelihood of a second Ahmadinejad term.

As 2008 opened, Iranians looked forward to the elections to the Majlis (unicameral legislature) scheduled for 14 March. Considerable interest had been generated by the fact that President Mahmoud Ahmadinejad was losing popularity not
only among the elites but also among many ordinary people, who discovered, to
their continued frustration, that the economic promise of the Ahmadinejad presidency was not being fulfilled. Ahmadinejad was the quintessential populist, who
ignored the advice of technocrats to pursue an agenda, which sought to return the
country to the revolutionary purity of the early years of the Islamic Republic and,
more importantly, to consolidate the power of the hardline conservatives. Continued support from the supreme leader, Ayatollah Ali Khamenei, and high oil
prices enabled him to pursue this agenda with enthusiasm, galvanising the masses
with a heady mix of religious and nationalist rhetoric, while at the same time dismissing critics and suppressing opposition. Like populists before him, Ahmadinejad sought to present himself as the anti-establishment candidate, a position that
wore thin as his term in office proceeded and the real support from the hardline
establishment became increasingly obvious. Indeed, Ahmadinejad and his supporters had never yet won an election in Iran on terms that anyone could consider
fair, and as a result few Iranians had any illusions about the management of the
legislative elections.

As always, much depended on the level of vetting and whether sufficient candidates of varying political views would be allowed to stand to make the election
meaningful. In this respect, the authorities of the Islamic Republic were faced
with a persistent quandary. Ahmadinejad had singularly failed to earn popular
support for his brand of politics, despite the lavish expenditure of money. Cynicism had been reinforced and the authorities faced a choice: either relax control

and have a genuine competition, which would encourage a high turnout but risk losing control of the Majlis; or maintain tight control, risking a low turnout but ensuring the desired result.

As the election approached, it was increasingly clear that the authorities had opted for the safe option. The constitutional oversight body, the Council of Guardians, disqualified more than 2,000 reformist candidates, leaving voters basically with a choice between candidates from two wings of the "Principle-ist movement"—as the hardline conservatives had described themselves—who represented the pro- and anti-Ahmadinejad factions, with some disagreement over economic management but little else. Substantive policy alternatives were left to other factions, in particular the Reformists, who were limited to contesting a fraction of the seats in the 290-seat Majlis but who won most of those they contested. This was little compensation for the fact that the elections were the least transparent of any organised by the Islamic Republic since its inception. People stayed away in droves, and while the interior minister sought to stress that turnout was higher than 60 per cent, this was not supported by eyewitnesses, especially in the larger cities, where turnout was reportedly around 25 per cent. The real damage was to the credibility of the process itself. Iranians had grown to accept a degree of electoral manipulation, while at the same time recognising that, on balance, their vote could count. Since the legislative election of 2004 this faith had been gradually eroded, to the extent that by 2008 few believed it.

The final result, achieved after a second round on 25 April, gave the pro-Ahmadinejad Unified Principle-ist Front 117 seats and the more critical Broad Principle-ist Coalition 53 seats. The Reformists won 46 seats, and independents (many of whom were expected later to join one of the conservative factions) 69 seats, with five seats reserved for the recognised minorities.

For all the interest in the final composition of the Majlis and the focus on former nuclear negotiator Ali Larijani—an ostensible opponent of the president and leader of the Broad Principle-ist Coalition—as the new speaker, even conservatives began to voice concerns about the utility of an election that had been so ruthlessly managed. The real winner, everyone accepted, was Supreme Leader Ali Khamenei, upon whom candidates from all sides heaped praise.

The absence of political repercussions from the election reflected a number of realities. It was clear that society at large was turning its attention to economic difficulties and was losing interest in the machinations of the political leaders. These economic problems, while real, could be contained by the unprecedented liquidity in the economy (even if the money was not being spread very well), combined with the unerring optimism of the president, who assured the populace that Iran was now a great power. Ahmadinejad's growing unpopularity was, therefore, softened by the general belief that some things were going right. For persistent troublemakers, of course, the option of imprisonment always remained, though the government tended to target individuals who could be tarred with the opprobrium of colluding with foreign powers.

Furthermore, much of the foreign pressure on Iran had receded. Ahmadinejad had entered 2008 basking in what was generally regarded as the foreign policy triumph of the USA's National Intelligence Estimate (NIE) of December 2007, which asserted "with high confidence" that Iran had suspended its nuclear weapons programme as long ago as 2003 (see AR 2008, pp. 280-81; 584-86). At a stroke, this document not only undercut the EU negotiating strategy towards Iran (which was predicated on the fact that nobody knew the status of Iran's nuclear programme), but also effectively removed the military option from US President George W. Bush. In Iran, this was interpreted as a vindication for Ahmadinejad's robust foreign policy. Consequently, and despite mounting domestic difficulties, critics were dismissed by an increasingly hubristic and self-confident government. In his last report of 2008 on Iran's nuclear programme, International Atomic Energy Agency (IAEA) Director General Mohamed El-Baradei told the IAEA in November that Iran had increased its stocks of enriched uranium and concluded that "Contrary to the decisions of the [UN] Security Council, Iran has not suspended its enrichment-related activities." (UN Security Council Resolution 1835 (2008), adopted on 27 September, had reiterated demands that Iran should suspend all enrichment-related and reprocessing activities.)

By the autumn of 2008, however, the Iranian leadership was feeling less assured. In the first place, it was now apparent that in the USA Barack Obama was to be the presidential nominee of the Democratic party, and while his victory was by no means sure, his message and his rallies were beginning to attract serious attention. Iran's hardline politicians, including President Ahmadinejad, comforted themselves with the knowledge that the US "establishment" would never "allow" a black man to win the presidency, and, therefore, indulged themselves in a degree of magnanimous support without preparing for the eventuality of an Obama victory. This complacency was reinforced by the accelerating financial crisis, prompting a number of senior hardliners—most notably, Ayatollah Ahmad Jannati, the chairman of the Council of Guardians—to gloat that the demise of the West was nigh. It soon became apparent that Iran would not be immune from the consequences of this increasingly global financial meltdown, particularly as the oil price plummeted precipitously and the prospect of serious shortfalls in government revenue loomed. Voices which had been hitherto silent were suddenly heard again, and the government found itself under increasingly robust criticism. Criticism intensified after it became public knowledge that the oil stabilisation fund (OSF), established by former President Mohammad Khatami for just such an eventuality, had been accessed and to a large extent spent. As late as April, international assessments had placed the OSF at about US$80 billion, a figure that led some to believe that Iran could ride out the storm. By the autumn, it was revealed that the fund actually stood somewhere between US$9billion and US$25 billion, with most economists veering towards the lower figure.

It was precisely this sort of financial recklessness that caused consternation among even Ahmadinejad's supporters. In late spring, his interior minister, the noted hardliner Mostafa Pourmohammadi, resigned, citing differences thought to relate to the OSF. This resignation proved significant, not only because it marked a genuine rift among hardliners, but also because Ahmadinejad's response was to nominate in his place Ali Kordan, deputy oil minister, formerly of the state broadcasting service, and proud holder of an honorary doctorate in law from the University of Oxford. When members of the Majlis questioned this award, it rapidly became apparent that Kordan's claim was wholly false. In November, after only 90 days in office, Kordan was impeached by the Majlis for deception and replaced by Sadeq Mahsouli. Further damage had been done to the credibility of the system, especially when Ahmadinejad defended his nominee by arguing that loyalty was more important that the existence or otherwise of the degree.

This manifest economic and political incompetence encouraged Ahmadinejad's critics to become more vocal by the end of the year and to call for a more open election process in future. This demand was given greater urgency by the election of Barack Obama in November. The notion that change was coming to the USA encouraged critics in Iran to argue that Ahmadinejad was no longer the right person to engage with the United States. Of perhaps greater importance than the personality of the new US president, however, was the success of the process itself. Not only had US citizens elected a black president, they had done so in unprecedented numbers. Ordinary Iranians were impressed: perhaps the decline of the United States was not so inevitable. For the managers of Iran's political system, the pressure was on to ensure a high turnout in June 2009.

Ali M. Ansari

AFGHANISTAN

CAPITAL: Kabul   AREA: 652,090 sq km   POPULATION: n/a
OFFICIAL LANGUAGE/S: Pushtu, Dari (Persian)   POLITICAL SYSTEM: multiparty republic
HEAD OF STATE AND GOVERNMENT: President Hamid Karzai (since Dec '04)
MAIN IGO MEMBERSHIPS (NON-UN): ECO, CP, OIC, NAM
CURRENCY: afgani (end-'08 £1=Af67.5766, US$1=Af47.0000)
GNI PER CAPITA: low income: US$935 or less ('07 est), -

THERE was further compelling evidence during 2008 that the US-led war against the Taliban insurgents was being lost both militarily and politically. In much of southern and eastern Afghanistan the Taliban was already the de facto government: exercising authority, dispensing law, and raising revenue (see map, AR 2008, p. 285). In Kandahar, the county's third-largest population centre, the rebels openly controlled all but the very heart of the city. The Afghan government of President Hamid Karzai was hopelessly inefficient, deeply corrupt, and almost totally impotent. It was incapable of projecting its rule much beyond the boundaries of Kabul. Within 15 km of the capital there were permanent Taliban checkpoints. In this hostile environment the Western coalition forces, for all of their sophisticated weaponry, were largely confined to making limited forays from their heavily fortified bases. As they did so, they were subjected to frequent suicide attacks and increasingly deadly roadside bombs.

Almost 300 foreign troops were killed in Afghanistan during 2008, making it the costliest year for the coalition since the war began in 2001. Although some Western politicians and senior military figures continued to speak publicly of ultimate victory, increasingly, many of the war's most staunch supporters were privately admitting that the best that could be achieved was the perpetuation of a bloody stalemate. This private discourse concerning the progress of the war only occasionally broke into the public domain. In October, the UK ambassador to Afghanistan, Sir Sherard Cowper-Coles, reportedly admitted that the conflict could not be won and that the best of the possible outcomes was the installation of "an acceptable dictator" in Afghanistan. His remarks, apparently made during a briefing to a French diplomat and subsequently leaked to the press, also underlined the growing disenchantment of Western leaders with the ineffectual Karzai administration. It was, he said, a deeply corrupt government which would have collapsed were it not being propped up by the coalition's war effort. This pessimistic assessment was endorsed by the departing UK commander in war torn Helmand province, Brigadier Mark Carleton-Smith, who admitted that "we are not going to win this war" and warned that it was necessary to "lower our expectations" and not expect "a decisive military victory".

Even in the USA, where the concept of failure was considered antithetical to the self-defined national character, there was expert evidence to support the view that the war was slipping towards defeat. A draft National Intelligence Estimate (NIE)—a joint report by the country's intelligence agencies—was leaked to *The New York Times* in October and suggested that Afghanistan was in "a downward spiral". The report was said to highlight the breakdown in central authority and the growing success of the Taliban. It attributed this to the rampant corruption which riddled the Karzai government, the booming trade in heroin, and the increasingly sophisticated attacks by insurgents based across the border in Pakistan. At the end of the year General David McKiernan, the US commander of NATO's International Security Assistance Force (ISAF) and commander of US forces in Afghanistan, acknowledged that the struggle in much of southern Afghanistan had become a tactical "stalemate" and that the country had reached a "tipping point", with 2009 promising to be a "critical year for this campaign".

McKiernan's assessment of the importance of the coming year was characteristic of those supporters of the war who called for the deployment of greater numbers of troops to reverse the deteriorating military position. This strategy raised the delicate diplomatic question of which countries would supply the additional forces required for such an effort. By far the greatest contributor to the war was the USA, with some 35,000 troops split between "Operation Enduring Freedom", which had been in progress since 2001, and the NATO-led ISAF, a multinational force with a UN Security Council mandate, in existence since 2001 but which had been turned over to NATO command in 2003 (see AR 2001, p. 322; AR 2003, p. 329). During 2008 the USA increased its troop numbers still further (see p. 142) and ended the year with a commitment to provide a "surge" of fresh troops in 2009 in much the same way as it had done in 2007— with some success—in Iraq. There were also small increases by some of the minor contributing countries but the precise distribution of the burden amongst the allies remained an area of sharp dispute.

This dispute was complicated by the manner in which some contributing countries had attached conditions to their troop deployments, which prevented their soldiers from serving in the most dangerous areas of Afghanistan. There was a sharp diplomatic exchange over the issue between Germany and the USA in February with the leak of a letter from US Defence Secretary Robert Gates demanding that Germany's 3,200-strong contingent in Afghanistan be deployed in the south of the country, where the Taliban was most active. This had followed a threat from the government of Canada (a country which had suffered relatively heavy casualties in the south) that it would withdraw its 2,500 troops unless other countries showed greater commitment to the fight. In the same month, the issue of troop contributions was raised by US Secretary of State Condoleezza Rice, when she reminded US allies that NATO was "facing a real test" in Afghanistan and that the conflict was "not a peacekeeping mission". It was also central to the meeting of NATO defence ministers in Vilnius on 7-8 February and, a day later, Gates chided the Europeans for failing to "comprehend the magnitude of the direct threat to European security" posed by the war, warning that NATO risked destruction if it were to became a "two-tiered alliance of those who are willing to fight and those who are not".

The obvious reluctance of most European countries to avoid being sucked further into the Afghan quagmire was not evident in France where, with a customary flourish, President Nicolas Sarkozy promised additional French forces, numbering around 1,000 (including 700 combat troops), to join the 1,400 or so already serving in the country. There was also a commitment from the UK, the second-largest contributor, to raise its forces from around 7,800 to over 8,000 (see p. 35). Germany, too, indicated that it would increase its forces by one-third, although the restrictions on their deployment would remain (see p. 49).

In military terms, the year saw the continuation of the Taliban's attritional guerrilla campaign, enlivened with some headline-grabbing, high profile operations. Among these was the carefully planned and executed storming of the main prison in Kandahar in June, which involved the liberation of 1,200 prisoners, many of whom were Taliban fighters. In July the rebels overran an isolated US military position in the remote north-eastern province of Kunar, killing nine US soldiers and wounding a number of others. This success, achieved despite the defenders having called in artillery and air strikes, raised doubts about the US strategy of creating numerous small "combat outposts" in Afghanistan. Although these bases provided increased levels of intelligence and influence over local communities, they were also vulnerable to massed rebel attack. Another Taliban success came on 19 August when French troops suffered their worst loss of the war, when 10 were killed and 21 wounded in an ambush in the mountainous Sarobi district, east of Kabul (see p. 55).

Although a major Taliban offensive against Lashkar Gah, the capital of Helmand province, was repulsed in October with heavy losses, the year ended with further Taliban successes as the rebels stepped up their attacks on the main coalition supply line which ran, via the Khyber Pass, from Pakistan. This precarious route was already largely under Taliban control with private companies, which were subcontracted to supply Western military bases, routinely paying a hefty "tax" to Taliban commanders for safe passage.

Throughout the year the insurgents also continued their campaign of bombing, suicide attack and assassination. In January they illustrated that no area of the country was beyond reach when they launched an assault on the heavily guarded Serena Hotel in central Kabul, the country's only five-star hotel. The attack killed eight people, including several foreign nationals. The following month saw the worst suicide bombing in Afghanistan to date, with more than 80 people killed and many others wounded on 17 February as they watched a dog fight on the outskirts of Kandahar. The next day a further 37 were killed in a similar attack in the south of the province. Kabul suffered its worst suicide bombing on 7 July when at least 41 people were killed—including an Indian defence attaché and a senior Indian diplomat—and 139 injured, when a car packed with explosives was driven into a convoy of vehicles entering the compound of the Indian embassy.

Assassination was a common tactic used against foreign nationals, Afghan government officials, and politicians. President Karzai was an obvious target. On 27 April Taliban insurgents opened fire on a military parade, killing several people, including an Afghan legislator and a tribal leader. Karzai was present but escaped unscathed. Others were less fortunate. Amongst the Westerners who died during 2008 was UK aid worker Gayle Williams, who worked for a Christian charity involved in helping disabled Afghan children. She was shot dead near her home in Kabul on 20 October, executed by the Taliban for spreading Christianity. Women who pursued a role other than that prescribed by Taliban theology were particularly at risk. Amalalai Kakar, the country's most senior female police officer, was shot dead on 28 September in her car in Kandahar city. But perhaps the most repellent demonstration of the Taliban's views on gender came in Kandahar, on 12 November, when a group of girls had acid thrown into their faces as they walked to school. Their offence, it seemed, was to be female and to aspire to education.

This ugly incident was one small reminder of the misery endured by the civilian population of Afghanistan. Philip Alston, the special rapporteur of the UN Human Rights Council, released a report on 15 May in which he accused the international community, the Afghan government, and the Taliban of each being responsible for "gratuitous civilian killing". He also criticised the coalition forces for not keeping adequate records of civilian casualties and for adopting complicated and deliberately "opaque" procedures to obscure the details of civilian deaths.

Amongst the most controversial cause of civilian casualties were Western air strikes. Human Rights Watch reported in September on the inexorable rise in civilian deaths from US and NATO air strikes in recent years, and noted the "massive and unprecedented surge in the use of air power in Afghanistan in 2008", with the USA dropping approximately the same quantity of bombs in June and July alone as it had used during the whole of 2006.

It was unsurprising, therefore, that the year saw numerous appalling examples of the indiscriminate impact of aerial ordnance. On 6 July a US air strike hit a convoy that was escorting a bride to her new husband's village in the eastern province of Nangarhar. Of the 47 civilians killed, 39 were women and children, including the bride. A US air attack on the village of Azizabad, in western Herat, killed around 90 civilians, including 60 children, on 22 August. Although the US military initially insisted that the attack had been upon a legitimate Taliban target and denied that civilian casualties had been incurred, a UN investigation and the emergence of video footage of the mangled bodies established the awful nature of the incident. The US military authorities launched an inquiry. President Karzai condemned the attack as "irresponsible" and his government announced that it might renegotiate the terms under which foreign troops were operating. Nevertheless, the carnage continued. On 3 November at least 37 civilians, including 23 children and 10 women, were killed when a US aircraft bombed a wedding party at Shah Wali Kot, in Kandahar province. The US military promised an investigation and offered its condolences "if innocent people were killed in this operation". Karzai once again criticised the deaths, reasoning that "we cannot win the fight against terrorism with air strikes".

These incidents were only the most bloody in a year which saw the routine killing of civilians by coalition air strikes. The practice undermined the legitimacy of West's cause, undercut its humanitarian efforts in Afghanistan, and strengthened the appeal of the Taliban. It also provoked outrage amongst ordinary Afghans and exacerbated the growing divisions between President Karzai and his Western sponsors. All of this made the achievement of a political settlement in Afghanistan more difficult, at the very moment when such a solution increasingly appeared to be the only viable alternative to an unwinnable war. Although Western leaders continued publicly to rule out direct negotiations with the Taliban leadership, talks at local level were taking place in an effort to win over rebel commanders. The tactic had limited results, however, which were of dubious lasting value. Similarly ineffective was Karzai's direct appeal at the end of the year to the Taliban leadership to enter into negotiations with his government; his willingness to make such an unequivocal public overture was illustrative of the depth of his desperation. By contrast, buoyed by record profits from Afghanistan's flourishing opium trade, the Taliban's leaders appeared in no mood to negotiate as the year ended. It seemed as though they, like their US counterparts, viewed 2009 as redolent with military rather than political possibilities.

D.S. Lewis

KAZAKHSTAN—TURKMENISTAN—UZBEKISTAN— KYRGYZSTAN—TAJIKISTAN

Kazakhstan

CAPITAL: Astana   AREA: 2,724,900 sq km   POPULATION: 15,481,000 ('07)
OFFICIAL LANGUAGES: Kazakh & Russian   POLITICAL SYSTEM: multiparty republic
HEAD OF STATE AND GOVERNMENT: President Nursultan Nazarbayev (since Feb '90)
RULING PARTY: Nur-Otan People's Democratic Party
PRIME MINISTER: Karim Masimov (since Jan '07)
MAIN IGO MEMBERSHIPS (NON-UN): CIS, PFP, OSCE, OIC, ECO
CURRENCY: tenge (end-'08 £1=T173.788, US$1=T120.875)
GNI PER CAPITA: US$5,060, $9,700 at PPP ('07)

Turkmenistan

CAPITAL: Ashgabat   AREA: 488,100 sq km   POPULATION: 4,963,000 ('07)
OFFICIAL LANGUAGE: Turkmen   POLITICAL SYSTEM: multiparty republic
HEAD OF STATE AND GOVERNMENT: President and Prime Minister Gurbanguly Berdymukhamedov
   (since Feb '07)
RULING PARTY: Democratic Party of Turkmenistan (DPT)
MAIN IGO MEMBERSHIPS (NON-UN): CIS, PFP, OSCE, OIC, ECO, NAM
CURRENCY: Turkmen manat (end-'08 £1=2.6599, US$1=1.8500)
GNI PER CAPITA: Lower-middle income: US$936-US$3,705 ('07), US$4,350 at PPP (est based on
   regression)

Uzbekistan

CAPITAL: Tashkent   AREA: 447,400 sq km   POPULATION: 26,868,000 ('07)
OFFICIAL LANGUAGE: Uzbek   POLITICAL SYSTEM: multiparty republic
HEAD OF STATE AND GOVERNMENT: President Islam Karimov (since March '90)
RULING PARTY: People's Democratic Party (PDP)
PRIME MINISTER: Shavkat Mirzoyev (since Dec '03)
MAIN IGO MEMBERSHIPS (NON-UN): CIS, PFP, OSCE, OIC, ECO, NAM
CURRENCY: sum (end-'08 £1=S2,002.79, US$1=S1,393.00)
GNI PER CAPITA: US$730, $2,430 at PPP ('07 est based on regression)

Kyrgyzstan

CAPITAL: Bishkek   AREA: 199,900 sq km   POPULATION: 5,243,000 ('07)
OFFICIAL LANGUAGE: Kyrgyz & Russian   POLITICAL SYSTEM: multiparty republic
HEAD OF STATE AND GOVERNMENT: President Kurmanbek Bakiev (since March '05)
PRIME MINISTER: Igor Chudinov (since Dec '07)
MAIN IGO MEMBERSHIPS (NON-UN): CIS, PFP, OSCE, OIC, ECO
CURRENCY: som (end-'08 £1=S56.8631, US$1=S39.5500)
GNI PER CAPITA: US$590, $1,950 at PPP ('07)

Tajikistan

CAPITAL: Dushanbe   AREA: 142,550 sq km   POPULATION: 6,740,000 ('07)
OFFICIAL LANGUAGE: Tajik   POLITICAL SYSTEM: multiparty republic
HEAD OF STATE: President Imamoli Rahmon (formerly Rahmonov) (since Nov '92)
RULING PARTY: People's Democratic Party of Tajikistan
PRIME MINISTER: Akil Akilov (since Dec '99)
MAIN IGO MEMBERSHIPS (NON-UN): CIS, OSCE, OIC, ECO, PFP
CURRENCY: somoni (end-'08 £1=5.0205, US$1=3.4393)
GNI PER CAPITA: US$460, $1,710 at PPP ('07)

In Turkmenistan the dismantling of former President Saparmyrat Niyazov's legacy continued apace. On 26 September, after lengthy consultations, the Khalk Maslakhaty (People's Assembly), one of Niyazov's constitutional innovations, was abolished in favour of a unicameral parliament. Elections to this 125-member body were held on 14 December. Of the 288 candidates, some 90 per cent were members of the presidential Democratic Party; the remainder represented state-controlled organisations. Thus, the contest was not one of ideas, but of personalities. The electoral proceedings were monitored by observers from the Commonwealth of Independent States (CIS) and a few UN officials. In April, the calendar that President Niyazov had introduced (with months named after himself and his family) was abandoned and the international calendar re-instated. Niyazov's face was also removed from all but one denomination of the new banknotes that were to be issued on 1 January 2009. Yet these changes did not signal a new style of leadership: President Gurbanguly Berdymukhamedov proceeded to lay the foundations of his own personality cult, issuing coins bearing his portrait and publishing large editions of his speeches.

In Kazakhstan, the case of Rakhat Aliyev, ex-husband of the president's eldest daughter, rumbled on. Wanted on charges that included embezzlement and kidnapping, he had sought political asylum in Austria in 2007. When the Austrian authorities refused to extradite him, criminal proceedings were launched against him in absentia in Kazakhstan (see AR 2008, p. 289). In January 2008, after a trial that had lasted some eight months, a 20-year prison sentence was handed down. Aliyev's alleged accomplices, most of whom had also sought refuge abroad, received similar sentences. In March, at a second trial in absentia, a military court sentenced Aliyev to a further 20 years in prison for allegedly plotting a coup d'état.

In November the travel bans imposed on senior officials in Uzbekistan by the EU were not renewed. An arms embargo did remain in place, though this was largely symbolic as Uzbekistan did not in fact purchase arms from EU states. The sanctions had been introduced in 2005, when Uzbekistan was accused of using excessive force to quell civil disorder in the city of Andijan. The Uzbek government denied these accusations, insisting that they were based on inaccurate information. It rejected EU demands for an international investigation, claiming that its own judicial system was competent to deal with the matter. There was no public reaction from the Uzbek authorities to the relaxation of sanctions, which they had always regarded as unjustified.

The global financial crisis had a severe impact on the Central Asian states. Kazakhstan, which was most closely integrated into the international banking system, was the first to be affected. Inflation rose sharply and construction projects, previously a sign of its booming economy, were halted. International credit rating agencies such as Fitch, and Standard & Poor's, downgraded their earlier upbeat assessments of the country to reflect this negative trend. Kazakh banks were hit simultaneously by the drying up of international credit, shrinking assets, a falling oil price and a mountain of toxic debt. The Kazakh government took vigorous action to stabilise the situation, setting aside US$15 bil-

lion (15 per cent of GDP) for a bail-out programme. Measures to boost liquidity included the acquisition of stakes of some 25 per cent in the country's
four largest banks. There was also significant state support for the ailing property sector. By the end of the year, growth had slowed to around 4 per cent
(less than half that of recent years), but inflation had been held at just under 10
per cent.

Tajikistan, Kyrgyzstan, and Uzbekistan were also affected by the global
financial turmoil, but in a less direct way. They were hurt by the fall in the
price of export commodities and also by returning labour migrants who could
no longer find employment abroad. The migrant labour force, mostly
employed in the building sector, was unofficially estimated at around 800,000
Kyrgyz, 2 million Tajiks, and 3 million Uzbeks. Most went to Russia and
Kazakhstan, but some also to the Gulf States. They sent home remittances
worth billions of dollars annually, contributing an estimated 50 per cent to
Tajikistan's GDP and approximately 40 per cent to that of Kyrgyzstan. The
global recession caused a massive slowdown in the construction industry. As
a result, the Central Asian migrants not only lost their main source of income,
but were forced to return home to countries that were ill prepared to absorb an
influx of jobless labourers.

The spectre of large-scale unemployment in the region heightened concerns
about security and stability. The rise of militant Islamism, possibly financed in
part at least by drug trafficking and other forms of organised crime, was seen by
many as the chief threat. There were several arrests of suspected Muslim
extremists in all the Central Asian states. Even in Turkmenistan, hitherto free
of overt Islamist activity, there was a violent clash between the police and so-
called "radical Islamists" in the capital, Ashgabat, in September. Some 20
members of the Turkmen security forces were killed in the incident. Throughout the region, control over religious bodies was strengthened. New, more
restrictive draft laws were under consideration in Tajikistan and Kazakhstan,
while the legislation passed in Kyrgyzstan in November was said by critics to
breach international human rights standards. The Kyrgyz law included a ban on
private religious teaching and on the dissemination of religious literature in
public places. Instead, religious education was to be provided in public schools.

The rising cost of food, especially of grain products, compounded the problems of unemployment. In April, Kazakhstan introduced a temporary ban on
wheat exports (excluding flour) to safeguard domestic supplies. Uzbekistan, the
most populous country in the region, was self-sufficient in grain. However, in
order to safeguard food security in the future, various measures were put in
place to increase the production of staple crops. Particular emphasis was laid
on the need for better water management, including the introduction of modern
technology and water-saving agricultural practices.

There were signs of growing resource nationalism in Kazakhstan. This was
highlighted by the problems surrounding Kashagan, Kazakhstan's mega offshore oil field. In January, after months of negotiation, the Kazakh government
and the consortium of international oil companies that were developing the field

reached agreement on several key issues. These included increasing the stake of KazMunaiGaz, the state oil and gas company, to 16.81 per cent, placing it on a par with other major shareholders; the appointment of a new project operator to replace Eni-Agip; and the postponement of oil extraction to the end of 2011. Compensation due to Kazakhstan for the delay in production was set at US$5 billion. KazMunaiGaz would pay the six foreign shareholders US$1.78 billion for its new shares after the beginning of production. This, however, was not the end of the saga. In June the consortium announced that production would not begin until 2013. The Kazakh side responded by insisting on a major restructuring of the project. Included in the new terms of agreement were provisions such as a floating royalties structure linked to global oil prices.

Estimates of the hydrocarbon reserves of Central Asia were significantly upgraded. Publication of the audit conducted by the respected UK firm, Gaffney, Cline and Associates (GCA), confirmed that Turkmenistan's gas reserves were far greater than anticipated. The Yolotan field alone was conservatively estimated to hold a minimum of 4 trillion cubic metres (cm), with a possible maximum of 14 trillion cm, making it the fifth largest natural gas field in the world. Estimates for several other Turkmen gas fields were similarly promising. Elsewhere in the region, scientists reported findings of large oil and gas fields below the bed of the Aral Sea.

There was progress in the diversification of export pipelines. In June, China and Turkmenistan jointly launched the construction of a 10,000 km-long gas pipeline. Starting from the Turkmen side of the Amu-darya river, it would run across Uzbekistan and Kazakhstan and thence into China. Completion of the first phase was scheduled for late 2009, the second phase for late 2011. It would have the capacity to transport 40 billion cm annually. Meanwhile, work was also proceeding on the second phase of the Atasu-Alashankou oil pipeline between Kazakhstan and China.

There was also progress in implementing pipeline projects to Russia. In October, the intergovernmental agreement between Russia, Kazakhstan, and Turkmenistan on construction of the Pre-Caspian gas pipeline (originally signed by the participating countries in December 2007) was ratified by the Russian legislature. Construction, due to start in mid-2009, was scheduled for completion in 2010. It would carry up to 20 billion cm of natural gas per year, approximately half coming from Turkmenistan, the remainder from Kazakhstan.

In September, Russia's Prime Minister Vladimir Putin secured Uzbekistan's agreement to start building the Uzbek section of a new Central Asia-Centre (CAC) gas pipeline to Russia. The plan, which included a Kazakh leg, was first agreed in May 2007. However, owing to disagreements over pricing, the project was delayed for more than a year. The new pipeline would carry up to 30 billion cm of gas from Turkmenistan and Uzbekistan. It would be built alongside the existing Soviet-era CAC pipeline, which would be upgraded to double its capacity to around 90 billion cm. When completed, these pipelines would vastly increase the volume of Russian gas imports from Central Asia.

There were hopes that Turkmenistan might agree to contribute gas to the European Nabucco pipeline project (see map, p. 103), but the year ended with no firm commitment. However, another gas pipeline project, long moribund, was revived in April when India formally joined the steering committee of the trans-Afghan pipeline project, now renamed the Turkmenistan-Afghanistan-Pakistan-India pipeline (TAPI). A framework agreement was signed by the oil and gas ministers of the four countries. With a length of 1,680 km, the proposed pipeline was intended to deliver 90 million cubic metres of gas a day (mmcmd), to Afghanistan, India, and Pakistan. Afghanistan's share would initially be around 5 mmcmd, rising to 14 mmcmd in the third year; the remainder would be divided equally between India and Pakistan. The gas would be supplied from Turkmenistan (principally the Douletabad field).

Relations between the Central Asian states were generally cordial, but there were a number of contentious issues. A major area of disagreement was the pricing of gas supplies. Uzbekistan set a price of US$300 per 1,000 cubic metres for its gas sales for 2009. Russia, one of the largest importers of Uzbek gas (9 billion cm in 2008) assented to this as part of the package of energy deals agreed in September (see above). For the impoverished mountain states of Tajikistan and Kyrgyzstan, however, the price hike, almost double the amount paid in 2008, was a massive blow. The bitter winter of 2007-08, one of the coldest on record, was still fresh in the minds of the population; forecasts for the coming winter predicted equally severe conditions. Kyrgyzstan eventually succeeded in negotiating a reduced price of US$240 per 1,000 cubic metres for 2009. Tajikistan, already in dispute with Uzbekistan over unpaid debts for electricity supplies, was in a weaker bargaining position. The situation was complicated still further when, on 1 January 2009, Turkmenistan suspended electricity exports to Tajikistan. In 2007, Turkmenistan had agreed to supply 1.2 billion kWh of electricity per annum to Tajikistan via Uzbek power systems. However, Tajikistan failed to reach agreement with Uzbekistan over the transit fee, hence Turkmenistan's action. Negotiations continued into January 2009.

Russia remained a key partner for all the Central Asian states. In May, newly elected Russian President Dmitry Medvedev made his first state trip abroad to Kazakhstan (and thence to China), thereby emphasising the importance of this relationship (see p. 125). Kazakh-Russian ties were rooted in close economic co-operation. The other Central Asian states also maintained strong links with Russia. Trade was an important component of these relationships. The biggest percentage growth in trade turnover in 2008 was with Turkmenistan, owing mainly to large-scale joint ventures in the fuel and energy sector; growing imports of Russian tools, cars, and construction equipment also contributed to the favourable trend.

Iran's role as an economic partner increased steadily. There had long been close co-operation with Tajikistan, cemented by high level bilateral visits. In November, during the Tajik president's visit to Tehran, agreements were signed on co-operation in energy, petrochemicals, and transportation; also on the opening of an Iranian automobile manufacturing plant in Dushanbe. Relations with Turkmenistan were also strengthened. Turkmenistan supplied gas to northern Iran (some 25 million cm per day); previously there had been protracted disputes over terms and conditions, but negotiations over the price for 2009 were resolved amicably. Strategically, however, a key issue was the development of the Iranian-Uzbek transport corridor, linking the Central Asian hinterland in the north to warm water ports in the south. In May several Middle Eastern countries participated in an international conference on this emerging north-south artery.

South-East Asian countries were also active in Central Asia, especially in Uzbekistan. In November the Malaysian prime minister visited Tashkent and warmly supported the strengthening of ties between the two countries. Reciprocal trade grew rapidly; by October, the turnover stood at US$36.4 million, well above the figure for the whole of 2007. Malaysian investors were involved in a wide range of sectors in Uzbekistan. The Malaysian energy firm Petronas, already part of the consortium exploring hydrocarbon deposits in the Uzbek sector of the Aral Sea, expanded its activities in Uzbekistan, signing production sharing agreements for several new fields. Vietnam, a relative newcomer to Central Asia, aimed to secure reliable imports of Uzbek cotton for its garment sector, but was also diversifying its trade into new product areas. In August, PetroVietnam signed its first co-operation deal with the Uzbek state oil and gas company to acquire hydrocarbon assets in the country.

Shirin Akiner

INDIA—PAKISTAN—BANGLADESH—SRI LANKA—NEPAL—BHUTAN

India

CAPITAL: New Delhi   AREA: 3,287,260 sq km   POPULATION: 1,123,319,000 ('07)
OFFICIAL LANGUAGES: Hindi & English   POLITICAL SYSTEM: multiparty republic
HEAD OF STATE: President Pratibha Patil (since July '07)
RULING PARTIES: Congress (I)-led United Progressive Alliance (UPA) coalition
HEAD OF GOVERNMENT: Manmohan Singh (INC), Prime Minister (since May '04)
MAIN IGO MEMBERSHIPS (NON-UN): SAARC, CP, CWTH, NAM
CURRENCY: Indian rupee (end-'08 £1=Rs70.0472, US$1=Rs48.7200)
GNI PER CAPITA: US$950, $2,740 at PPP ('07)

Pakistan

CAPITAL: Islamabad   AREA: 796,100 sq km   POPULATION: 162,389,000 ('07)
OFFICIAL LANGUAGE: Urdu   POLITICAL SYSTEM: multiparty republic
HEAD OF STATE AND GOVERNMENT: President Asif Ali Zardari (PPP) (since Sept '08)
RULING PARTY: Pakistan People's Party (PPP)
PRIME MINISTER: Yusuf Raza Gillani (PPP) (since March '08)
MAIN IGO MEMBERSHIPS (NON-UN): OIC, SAARC, ECO, CP, NAM, CWTH
CURRENCY: Pakistani rupee (end-'08 £1=PRs113.762, US$1=PRs79.1250)
GNI PER CAPITA: US$870, $2,570 at PPP ('07)

Bangladesh

CAPITAL: Dhaka   AREA: 144,000 sq km   POPULATION: 158,572,000 ('07)
OFFICIAL LANGUAGE: Bengali   POLITICAL SYSTEM: multiparty republic
HEAD OF STATE: President Iajuddin Ahmed (since Sept '02)
RULING PARTIES: Bangladesh Nationalist Party (BNP) and Awami League (AL)-led coalition
HEAD OF GOVERNMENT: Fakhruddin Ahmed, chief adviser of caretaker government (since Jan '07)
MAIN IGO MEMBERSHIPS (NON-UN): SAARC, CP, OIC, CWTH, NAM
CURRENCY: taka (end-'08 £1=Tk99.0754 US$1=Tk68.9100)
GNI PER CAPITA: US$470, $1,340 at PPP ('07)

Sri Lanka

CAPITAL: Sri Jayawardenapura (Kotte)   AREA: 65,610 sq km   POPULATION: 19,945,000 ('07)
OFFICIAL LANGUAGES: Sinhala, Tamil & English   POLITICAL SYSTEM: multiparty republic
HEAD OF STATE AND GOVERNMENT: President Mahinda Rajapakse (SLFP) (since Nov '05)
RULING PARTIES: Sri Lanka Freedom Party (SLFP) heads United People's Freedom Alliance
    (UPFA) coalition
PRIME MINISTER: Ratnasiri Wickremanayake (since Nov '05)
MAIN IGO MEMBERSHIPS (NON-UN): SAARC, CP, CWTH, NAM
CURRENCY: Sri Lankan rupee (end-'08 £1=SRs162.466, US$1=SRs113.000)
GNI PER CAPITA: US$1,540, $4,210 at PPP ('07)

Nepal

CAPITAL: Kathmandu   AREA: 147,180 sq km   POPULATION: 28,108,000 ('07)
OFFICIAL LANGUAGE: Nepali   POLITICAL SYSTEM: multiparty federal republic
HEAD OF STATE: President Ram Baran Yadav (since July '08)
RULING PARTIES: coalition headed by Communist Party of Nepal-Maoist (CPN-M)
HEAD OF GOVERNMENT: Pushpa Kamal Dahal (Prachanda) (CPN-M) (since Aug '08)
MAIN IGO MEMBERSHIPS (NON-UN): SAARC, CP, NAM
CURRENCY: Nepalese rupee (end-'08 £1=NRs112.076, US$1=NRs77.9520)
GNI PER CAPITA: US$340, $1,040 at PPP ('07)

Bhutan

CAPITAL: Thimphu   AREA: 47,000 sq km   POPULATION: 657,000 ('07)
OFFICIAL LANGUAGES: Dzongkha, Lhotsan & English   POLITICAL SYSTEM: multi-party monarchy
HEAD OF STATE: Dragon King Jigme Khesar Namgyel Wangchuk (since Dec '06)
RULING PARTY: Bhutan Harmony Party (DPT)
HEAD OF GOVERNMENT: Prime Minister Jigme Yoser Thinley (since April '08)
MAIN IGO MEMBERSHIPS (NON-UN): SAARC, CP, NAM
CURRENCY: ngultrum (end '08 £1=Nu70.0472, US$1=Nu48.7200)
GNI PER CAPITA: US$1,770, $4,980 at PPP ('07)

THE year 2008 in South Asia was marked by extensive terrorist violence, especially in India and Pakistan, and by an intensification of Sri Lanka's civil war. It
also saw successful national elections in Bangladesh, Pakistan, Nepal, and
Bhutan. All the countries of the region were seriously affected by the world economic and financial crisis.

INDIA.   The earlier part of the year saw the political parties begin to gear up for the
elections scheduled to be held in 2009. In the middle of the year there was a political crisis provoked by the withdrawal of support from the Congress (I)-led ruling
coalition, the United Progressive Alliance (UPA), by the two Communist parties.
The immediate cause of this rupture was the government's insistence on going
ahead with the nuclear deal with the USA (see below), but more generally the

Communists felt that Manmohan Singh's administration was not sufficiently committed to its proclaimed programmes of social welfare and reform. In July the government was forced to seek a vote of confidence in order to continue in office. There were intensive manoeuvrings on all sides, including vocal assertions of inducements of various kinds being offered. In the end the UPA scraped through by 275 votes to 256. The key to the result was the way in which the various regional parties voted. The Bahujan Samaj Party (BSP), which controlled the government in the state of Uttar Pradesh under its powerful woman leader Mayawati, decided to support the opposition. Its bitter rival in Uttar Pradesh, the Samajwadi Party (SP), with its support among a major section of the lower castes, chose to back the UPA. While Congress and its allies survived the vote of confidence, the narrowness of the result indicated how much ground the coalition had lost since the 2004 elections. Mayawati in particular, whose power base lay among the lowest strata of Hindu society, strengthened her position during the year and appeared to be positioning herself as a potential prime minister.

One vital issue in Indian politics, as illustrated by the rise of Mayawati, was the allocation of benefits and resources on the basis of caste (which often overlapped to a very considerable extent with class). In April the Supreme Court approved a further extension of quotas in elite educational institutions for the so-called "other backward castes", the backbone of the SP's support. In May, the Gujjars, an important social group in northern India, continued their long-running campaign in Rajasthan to be given the status there of a "scheduled tribe" rather than "backward caste", again in order to gain economic advantages. Violence flared, and there were a number of deaths. Eventually, a face-saving compromise was reached between Gujjar leaders and the Bharatiya Janata Party (BJP) government of the state.

Regional demands for greater autonomy, usually at the expense of existing states of the Indian Union, were another area that could generate violent confrontation. The Nepali-speakers (also known as Gorkhas) of the hilly region around Darjeeling, in West Bengal, had long campaigned for a separate state. A compromise agreement had been reached some years previously between the most prominent leader of the Gorkha National Liberation Front (GNLF), Subash Ghising, and the West Bengal government. This was rejected, however, by a breakaway section of the party, which in February and again in June and July organised a series of strikes and blockades that led to a number of casualties and caused significant economic disruption. Ghising himself was forced to leave his Darjeeling base. In October there were bombs in Assam, which killed more than 80 people, and the following month the bans on the separatist United Front for the Liberation of Asom (ULFA) and the National Democratic Front of Bodoland were extended. A breakaway faction of ULFA announced a ceasefire in June and declared its willingness to talk with the government within the framework of the Indian constitution.

The Indian government faced renewed difficulties during the year in the Kashmir region. While the security situation had appeared to improve substantially in recent years, a dispute in June over the transfer of land to a Hindu religious trust sparked a series of increasingly agitated and widespread demonstrations, in which a number of people were killed by police bullets. Most sections of the Kashmiri Muslim population joined the protest. At the beginning of July the land transfer was revoked by the state government, but only at the cost of protests in the Hindu-majority areas of the state. The crisis then escalated with the collapse of the Congress-led coalition following the withdrawal of a major moderate Muslim group, the People's Democratic Party (PDP). The Union government imposed direct rule in advance of the state elections that were, in any case, scheduled for later in the year. This did nothing to stem the agitation, which went on for much of the rest of the year. On a number of occasions the security forces resorted to firing on demonstrators and the death toll mounted steadily, even if it did not reach the levels of earlier years. The elections were held, under tight security, in November and December. Many local political groups opposed them on the grounds that they would be used to legitimise the status quo, and called for a boycott. Nevertheless, there was a substantial turnout of voters. The results gave the National Conference—the party of the Abdullah family, Kashmir's "first family"—28 seats compared with 21 for the PDP. Congress won 17, enough to make it an essential part of any coalition. Negotiations to form a new government were under way at the end of the year.

Throughout the year there was a steady stream of bomb explosions, mainly without warning in crowded urban areas, resulting in high casualty levels. In May Jaipur was attacked, with 63 deaths; in July Ahmadabad and Surat, with over 50; and in September there were two separate attacks in Delhi. The latter three were claimed by a group called the Indian Mujahideen, and in September police in Mumbai (Bombay) arrested a number of individuals said to be the group's leaders. However, not all attacks were acknowledged, and several took place at the end of September in largely Muslim areas of towns such as Malegaon (in Maharashtra) and Modasa (in Gujarat), with the suspicion that local Hindu supremacist groups were responsible. In November a serving Indian army officer was arrested and charged with complicity in the attacks. He was also considered a suspect in the bombing of the Samjhauta Express in 2007 (see AR 2008, p. 296).

On 26 November Islamic militants launched a sustained and highly co-ordinated attack on Mumbai, India's principal commercial city. Over a period of three days, 10 armed fighters took over two of the city's leading hotels, including the iconic Taj Mahal hotel at the Gateway of India, as well as shooting indiscriminately at one of the main railway stations in the city and other locations. A local Jewish welfare centre was also occupied. Indian security forces eventually succeeded in regaining control, but were criticised in some quarters over the speed and efficacy of their response. The final death toll approached 200, principally Indian nationals but with some foreign casualties as well. While Mumbai had suffered worse terrorist attacks in terms of casualties—for example in 1993 (see AR 1993, p. 312)—the co-ordination of the 2008 attacks, and the attackers' ability to hold out for so long against police and army units, seemed especially shocking and led some local commentators to dub it India's 9/11 (referring to the attacks on the USA on 11 September 2001). There were no immediate revenge attacks on Muslim communities in Mumbai or elsewhere in India.

Responsibility for the attacks was claimed by a previously unknown group called the Deccan Mujahideen, but it was generally assumed that this was a nom de guerre. Recriminations began immediately between India and Pakistan over the identity of the terrorists and from whence the attacks had originated. Interrogation of the one militant captured alive, who the Indian authorities stated was from Pakistan, pointed towards the Pakistan-based group, the Lashkar-e-Toiba, well known for its activities in Kashmir, but this evidence was not accepted by the Pakistan government. By the end of the year, no resolution had been achieved over the issue (see below).

Politically, the attacks led to the resignation of the Union home minister, Shivraj Patil, who was succeeded by the former minister of finance and veteran Congress politician, P. Chidambaram. The national security advisor, M.K. Narayanan, also resigned but was asked to stay on. The government's firm but restrained handling of the crisis seemed to evoke a generally positive public response. The state elections that took place shortly afterwards did not seem to have been greatly influenced by the attacks. The UPA retained control of Delhi, and won Rajasthan from the BJP, as well as gaining control of Mizoram. The BJP in turn held Madhya Pradesh and Chhattisgarh. The more important issue in the elections appeared to have been the state of the economy, especially the high rate of inflation earlier in the year. Although it won control of none of the states, the BSP did well.

As in previous years, there was a steady trickle of clashes between police and Maoist rebels in several different parts of the country. Other concerns included violence between Hindu and Christian communities in Orissa. The genesis of these clashes was complex, including issues of land rights and other entitlements, as well as identity questions.

PAKISTAN. The general election, originally scheduled for 8 January but postponed because of the assassination of former Prime Minister Benazir Bhutto (see AR 2008, p. 299), was in the end held on 18 February. There were suggestions that it might be postponed for a much longer period, but the two main opposition parties—the Pakistan People's Party (PPP) and the Pakistan Muslim League (N) (PML(N))—together with the USA and other international actors, made it clear that this would be wholly unacceptable. Large numbers of troops were deployed to ensure security at polling stations and, despite widespread apprehensions that there might be violence either from militants opposed to the election or between rival political parties, the vote took place with only a couple of major incidents. These included a bomb at an Awami National Party (ANP) rally in Peshawar, which killed 29, and a bomb at a PPP rally in the tribal areas, which killed 37. The general view of observers was that the election was free and fair. Turnout, which was officially recorded at 44.5 per cent, was slightly higher than in recent elections.

The results gave the largest share of seats in the National Assembly (the lower house of the bicameral legislature) to the PPP, which won a total of 126 (including seats reserved for women and religious minorities and allocated in accordance with proportion of votes won), and a significant proportion to the PML(N), which won 91 in total. Other significant players were the Muttahida Qaumi Movement (MQM), which, as expected, dominated Karachi, winning a total of 25 seats; and the ANP, which won 13 seats in North-West Frontier Province (NWFP). The ANP, a party representing the secular interests of the Pathan population there, defeated the Jamiat-ul-Islam, one of the two major Islamist parties. Along with the Jamaat-e-Islami, this was one of the losers in the polls. The major loser, however, was the Pakistan Muslim League (Q) (PML(Q)), the so-called "King's Party" that had formed the government during the Musharraf era. It won only 53 seats in total. Independents were elected to 17 seats, although many of them subsequently joined one or other of the main parties.

In provincial elections that took place at the same time, the PPP emerged as the largest party in Sindh (with the MQM also performing strongly); the PML(N) in Punjab, the country's largest province; the ANP in NWFP; and, for local reasons, the PML(Q) in Balochistan. Each was able to put together a governing coalition.

As no party had secured an absolute majority in the national election, talks immediately began on possible coalitions. What rapidly emerged was an agreement between the PML(N) and the PPP, although there were reports that President Pervez Musharraf had hoped that the PPP would ally itself with the PML(Q), in order to exclude his arch-enemy, PML(N) leader Nawaz Sharif. The new National Assembly met in March and as its first task confirmed the election of PPP candidate Yusuf Raza Gillani as prime minister. PPP leader Asif Ali Zardari, Benazir Bhutto's widower, had not contested a seat in the National Assembly so was not eligible. Several candidates' names had been canvassed, and it was generally agreed that Gillani, a landowner from Southern Punjab, would act as a loyal lieutenant to the party leader. Key portfolios in the new cabinet were shared between the two main parties.

From the beginning, however, two related issues placed the system under great strain. The first was the demand for the reinstatement of all the judges who had been dismissed by President Musharraf in November 2007 (see AR 2008, p. 298), and the second was the future of Musharraf himself. Although both parties were publicly committed to the restoration of the judges, it was evident that Zardari had reservations, in part because of his own legal position and his apprehension, specifically, of the return of former Chief Justice Iftikhar Mohammed Chaudhry. There were thus convoluted and fruitless negotiations between Zardari and Nawaz Sharif over the mechanism for the judges' reinstatement. The failure of these talks led in May to the withdrawal of the PML(N) ministers from the cabinet, although Nawaz Sharif promised continuing support in the National Assembly.

In August, the PPP and PML(N) found common ground once again in threatening to impeach President Musharraf. Reportedly under pressure from countries such as the USA to step aside, and unsure whether he would receive support from the army if he chose to exercise his theoretical right to dismiss the government, Musharraf resigned on 18 August. An immediate consequence of his resignation was a final split between the PPP and the PML(N), with the latter demanding the immediate reinstatement of the judges and the choice of a non-partisan figure to succeed Musharraf. The PPP refused to accept this, and in September a contest for the presidency ensued between Zardari and a retired chief justice nominated by the PML(N), Saeed-uz-Zaman Siddiqi. With the help of the ANP and MQM, and other smaller groups, Zardari had no difficulty in defeating his opponent in the 8 September elections conducted in the federal legislature and provincial assemblies. In the short term at least, the PPP had been able to outmanoeuvre the PML(N).

The Pakistani state found itself under ever increasing pressure during the year from various militant groups which had established bases in the tribal areas. From here the militants attacked Western forces across the border in Afghanistan as well as launching attacks against the Pakistan government, which they perceived as in hock to the USA and the West in general. Although denied by the government, there were claims from US officials that Mullah Omar, leader of the Afghanistan Taliban insurgents, was in Pakistan, along with al-Qaida leader Osama bin Laden. Despite the firepower commanded by the Pakistan army, the militants were able on occasion to overwhelm isolated detachments and capture strongholds in areas such as South Waziristan. Casualties on both sides were substantial. Suicide bombings were a regular occurrence, especially in the tribal areas, although attacks also took place in Lahore, Islamabad, and Peshawar. The new government's initial approach included talks with militant leaders, and for a few weeks after it came to office there was an unofficial truce which included the release of a significant militant leader from Swat, Maulana Sufi Mohammad. The truce soon broke down. Later in the year the army launched a major operation in the Bajaur tribal agency, in which it was claimed that more than 1,000 militants were killed, while the frequency of suicide bombings and other attacks increased, including high profile attacks at a military munitions factory in August and on the Marriott Hotel in Islamabad in September. In the opinion of many observers, the government's approach to the whole question lacked coherence.

Pakistan found itself the focus of much negative attention after the Mumbai attacks in November (see above and below). Its immediate reaction was to deny that the attackers had any links with Pakistan. However, in December many arrests took place of individuals associated with the Jamaat ud Dawa, which was seen as a front for the Lashkar-e-Toiba, the organisation that India claimed was responsible. The founder of both organisations, Hafiz Mohammad Saeed, was placed under house arrest in Lahore, and another prominent member, Zaki ur Rahman Lakhvi, alleged by India to have organised the attacks, was arrested.

BANGLADESH. The year began with a military-backed government in power, and ended with a landslide election victory for the Awami League (AL) under Sheikh Hasina. The elections themselves, which had been postponed in January 2007 (see AR 2008, pp. 299-300), were announced in May. At that time, both leaders of the two major parties, Sheikh Hasina and the Bangladesh Nationalist Party (BNP)'s Begum Khaleda Zia, were in detention on charges of corruption during their respective terms in office. However, in June Hasina was released on bail in order to go abroad for medical treatment. Khaleda remained in jail until September. The government had, nevertheless, kept up the pressure on the corruption charges, with fresh allegations filed against Begum Khaleda in February, and continued to hope that the rank and file of the two parties would reject their leaders. No plausible alternatives emerged, although an attempt was made by a former minister, Hafizuddin Ahmed, supported by the government, to take control of the BNP.

Local elections were held in June in selected cities and municipalities as a sort of trial run for the national elections. Although conducted on a non-party basis, the results gave considerable comfort to the AL. The schedule for the forthcoming national elections was finally announced in November. A last-minute attempt was made by the BNP to postpone them, but in the end the party accepted a token delay in return for its participation, and it was clear that it was anxious not to be sidelined. The state of emergency, which had been in force since 2007, was lifted just 12 days before the date of the elections, although public campaigning had started a little earlier.

The elections took place on 29 December, and the large number of domestic and international observers concluded that they had been conducted fairly and freely on the basis of a recently revised electoral register that had weeded out many false entries. Turnout was reported to be a record 80 per cent. The results were a landslide for the AL and its smaller allies, principally the Jatiya Party of former president Hussein Muhammad Ershad, which won 263 of the total 300 seats available in the Jatiya Sangsad (unicameral legislature). The AL itself secured 230 and the Jatiya Party 27. The BNP won only 30 seats, while its ally, the Jamaat-e-Islami, which had had a significant influence on the BNP when it was in government, managed only two. While the operation of Bangladesh's first-past-the-post system no doubt exaggerated the results in terms of seats won (the AL won 49 per cent of the popular vote compared to the BNP's 33 per cent), the outcome was nevertheless a remarkable achievement for the AL. It had been able to shrug off the baggage of the past and present itself as a party oriented towards the future and capable of making a fresh start. By contrast, charges of corruption seemed to hit the BNP, which had formed the immediately previous government, harder.

The elections also appeared to be a rejection of the Islamist themes promoted by the Jamaat-e-Islami. At the same time, the activities of the Harkat-ul-Jihad-al-Islami (HUJI)—the banned Bangladesh wing of a militant Islamist group with links to al-Qaida—gave cause for concern both domestically and to India, which claimed that it was linked to the bombing campaigns there (see above). In October HUJI leaders established the Islamic Democratic Party as a separate organisation and applied to register it as a political party. The party held a number of public meetings thereafter but had no impact on the elections themselves.

In May the Dhaka High Court ruled that 150,000 individuals from the Bihari community—Urdu-speakers who had been marooned at the time of independence in 1971—were eligible for Bangladeshi citizenship. The ruling applied only to those born after 1971 or who had still been minors at that point, but was nevertheless a major development.

SRI LANKA.   In January the government officially announced that it considered the ceasefire with the Liberation Tigers of Tamil Eelam (LTTE), which had been brokered by the Norwegians in 2002 (see AR 2002, p. 326), to be at an end. This gave a signal for the army to intensify its attacks on LTTE strongholds in the Northern Province, especially the town of Kilinochchi, where the guerrillas had their administrative headquarters. Towards the end of the year, the army clearly began to gain the upper hand, and captured key positions on the main roads in the region, effectively tightening the siege of the town, which appeared to be in its concluding stages. However, at the end of December Kilinochchi remained under LTTE control. There were a number of bomb explosions in the commercial capital, Colombo, and other parts of the country, some carried out by suicide bombers, which were generally held to have been the work of the LTTE. Two government ministers and a senior retired general were killed, along with many civilians. The total death toll in the long-running civil war was estimated to have reached 70,000.

One major consequence of the intensified fighting was an increase in the number of internally displaced persons in the north, estimated at up to 300,000, some of whom were being forced to move for the second or third time and who were not allowed to leave the area, either by the army or the LTTE. Conditions were reported to be extremely poor, with only limited supplies of food and medicine. The situation appeared to have worsened at the end of the year, following the withdrawal from the region in September of the UN and other humanitarian agencies, on the instructions of the Sri Lankan government, which claimed that the situation was too unsafe for them to operate. Both the government and the LTTE were criticised by human rights groups for their disregard of civilian rights, and in the case of the LTTE the use of child soldiers. In May Sri Lanka failed in its bid to be re-elected to the UN Human Rights Council.

While the major focus remained on the military conflict, the Sri Lankan government continued to seek political means to contain the LTTE, principally through its support of the Tamil Makkal Viduthalai Puligal (TMVP), a breakaway group. In March the group won elections to local bodies in the Eastern Province, where the army had been able to re-establish control during the course of 2007; in May it won the provincial council elections. The deputy leader of the TMVP was then appointed as the province's first chief minister. The founder and leader of the group, Colonel Karuna Amman (real name Vinayagamoorti Muralitharan), had in the meantime been arrested and jailed in the UK on charges of illegal entry, amid suspicions that Sri Lankan officials had been complicit in providing him with forged documents. He was eventually deported to Sri Lanka in July, and was later appointed to a vacant seat in the Sri Lankan parliament on the government side.

NEPAL. The year was dominated by the elections to the country's first constituent assembly, held in the aftermath of the decision in 2007 to abolish the monarchy (see AR 2008, p. 301) and under the auspices of a coalition government that had been formed in 2006 at the end of the civil war (see AR 2007, pp. 298-99). The elections took place in April, following a campaign in which the main protagonists were the Communist Party of Nepal (Maoist) (CPN(M)), the political voice of the insurrectionists; the Nepali Congress (NC), which had dominated the previous government; and the Communist Party of Nepal—United Marxist-Leninist (CPN-UML). There were a number of reports of voter intimidation, although relatively little violence compared with recent elections. The turnout was estimated at 60 per cent, a high figure for the country.

The CPN(M) in the end did much better than had been predicted, and won 220 out of a total 575 elected seats, allocated according to a combined system of direct election and proportional representation. (A further 26 assembly members would also be appointed by the government.) This result put the CPN(M) in a strong position, although lacking an overall majority. The NC trailed in second place with 110 seats, closely followed by the CPN-UML with 103. Maoist support came primarily from the CPN(M)'s power bases in the rural areas, although the party had relatively less support in the cities and in the Terai, Nepal's plains region along the border with India. The Maoists' success in the elections marked the end of an armed struggle that had started in 1996 and had cost at least 12,000 lives.

Following the elections, the Constituent Assembly met at the end of May, and its first act, endorsed by an overwhelming majority of members, was to confirm the earlier decision to abolish the monarchy and transform Nepal into a parliamentary democracy. This also implied the end of Nepal's status as the world's only Hindu state. The king accepted the decision, and vacated the royal palace shortly thereafter, but remained in the country. Other issues proved more contentious, principally the question of choosing the country's new leadership. After two rounds of voting, Ram Baran Yadav, the candidate of the NC and CPN-UML, was elected president by the Constituent Assembly in July. Although the presidency was largely ceremonial, the election then made it possible for a new government to be formed. The Maoist leader, Prachanda (real name Pushpa Kamal Dahal), eventually emerged as prime minister over a rival from the NC, Sher Bahadur Deuba, and took office in August at the head of a coalition government.

Prachanda's first moves were cautious and designed to reassure the army and business interests that his government was not about to make fundamental changes. The budget, introduced in September, appeared to be welfarist rather than revolutionary in the measures it proposed, although some commentators felt that the apparent moderation might be intended to lull opponents into a false sense of security. By the end of the year, the new government had not in fact been able to implement any major new initiatives beyond the ending of the monarchy, and there was evidence of some discontent among the party rank and file. An area of great concern was the future of the more than 19,000 former guerrillas on the Maoist side, who, under the terms of the 2006 agreement, had been confined to demarcated camps. While the CPN(M) wanted them to be integrated into the regular army, the army itself—their former adversary—strongly resisted the idea. At the end of the year the issue remained unresolved.

A problem that the new government inherited was disaffection among the Madheshi population in the Terai. A regional movement, which had become active in earlier years, mounted a major campaign of civil disobedience in February and succeeded in blocking the main roads from India, along which almost all of Nepal's fuel supplies had to travel. Negotiation with the then government led to the blockade being lifted in return for political concessions. The demands of the Terai areas for greater autonomy had not previously been at the top of the political agenda. The new vice-president, Parmanand Jha, who was chosen as a gesture to the Terai areas, provoked widespread protest in the rest of the country by insisting on taking his oath of office in Hindi, on the basis that it was the language of the Terai.

BHUTAN. The year saw the country's first ever general election, as well as the coronation of the new king. The election, held in March, had been carefully planned to begin the process of allowing a moderate leadership to emerge to govern in partnership with the monarchy; both the contesting parties, which had been formed the previous year, were pro-monarchist. The successful party was the

Bhutan Harmony Party (DPT, also known as the Bhutan Peace and Prosperity Party), which won two-thirds of the popular vote and an overwhelming 45 out of the 47 seats in the National Assembly (the lower chamber of the bicameral legislature). Turnout was high at nearly 80 per cent. Jigme Thinley, leader of the party and a minister during the non-party period, took over as prime minister.

While the elections themselves were peaceful, a series of bomb explosions had taken place in January in the capital, Thimpu, and other urban centres. Although no-one claimed responsibility, it was widely believed that the attacks were the work of extremist groups among the ethnic Nepali population of Bhutan, many of whom had been in refugee camps in Nepal for many years. Even so, nine of the elected legislators came from the Nepali community. In pursuance of an offer made in 2006 to resettle 60,000 Nepali refugees in the USA, the first batch moved there at the beginning of the year.

The coronation of King Jigme Khesar Namgyel Wangchuck took place in Thimpu in November. Most foreign representation was at ambassadorial level, but India, whose close ties with Bhutan went back to the colonial period, was represented by its president, Pratibha Patil, while Sonia Gandhi and other leading personalities were also present. By contrast, no invitation was sent to the Nepali head of state, who in turn sent no message of congratulation.

INDIA AND THE GLOBAL ORDER.   France's President Nicolas Sarkozy was the guest of honour at India's prestigious Republic Day celebrations in January, and during his visit there were important talks on trade and development issues, including the possible supply of nuclear materials. The same month saw a visit by British Prime Minister Gordon Brown, who also held talks on economic co-operation, as well as publicly supporting India's ambition for a permanent seat on the UN Security Council.

Prime Minister Manmohan Singh made a major visit to China in January, where the focus was on trade issues. Both sides were keen to increase the volume of trade, while increasing the proportion of India's exports to China. Later in the year, the worldwide protests in run-up to Beijing Olympic Games over the status of Tibet tested Indian diplomacy. The government permitted limited protests during the passage of the Olympic flame through India but adopted a conciliatory stance towards China on the overall issue, including a public statement by the Indian foreign minister in April, warning the Dalai Lama against any activity which might damage Sino-Indian relations.

In April India hosted the first ever India-Africa summit. This focused on trade and investment relations, and was clearly an effort by India to recover some of the ground that it had lost in Africa to China. A number of senior African leaders attended the summit. In June, India received an official visit from Syria's President Bashar Assad, the first from a Syrian president in 30 years. Again, the focus was on economic relations.

INDIA AND THE NUCLEAR ISSUE.   In September, following years of discussion and an abortive attempt earlier in the year, the Nuclear Suppliers Group (NSG, the 45-country body that controlled the trade in material applicable to nuclear weapons development) lifted its ban on the provision to India of sensitive nuclear technology. This was largely at the instance of the USA, which had been in negotiation with India since 2005 to supply it with nuclear technology and materials, without the latter signing the Non-Proliferation Treaty and giving up its nuclear weapons. India was able to take advantage of the NSG's decision to conclude an agreement with France in September, which would allow the purchase of French civilian nuclear reactors. At the same time, the final voting took place in the US Congress to ratify the US-India nuclear agreements, and these were signed into law by President George W. Bush in October, just ahead of the US presidential and congressional elections.

The net result of these decisions was that India in effect became a recognised nuclear power, ending restrictions that in some cases dated back to 1974, when the country's first nuclear test had taken place. India would open its civilian nuclear facilities for outside inspection, but not its military installations, and it retained the right to carry out further nuclear tests if it considered these to be in its security interests. The USA made clear, however, that were this to happen it would reconsider its position on assured nuclear fuel supply for civilian reactors.

INDIA AND PAKISTAN.   At the beginning of 2008 the peace process between the two countries was making slow, but still perceptible, progress. India welcomed the installation of an elected government in Pakistan and official-level talks were held in May and again in July. There were some minor clashes along the line of control as the situation in Indian Kashmir worsened (see above), but not to the extent of threatening the broader dialogue. In September President Zardari and Prime Minister Singh met on the sidelines of the UN General Assembly, the first occasion that they had met. As a consequence, there were further official-level talks the following month.

The Mumbai attacks (see above) inevitably, in the words of the Indian foreign minister, Pranab Mukherjee, led to a pause in the peace process. India claimed from the beginning that all the evidence pointed to the attacks having been planned and executed from Pakistani territory, and singled out the Lashkar-e-Toiba, a militant organisation, which had in earlier years been patronised by Pakistani intelligence services. Some military moves were made on both sides, including Pakistan's shifting some of its troops from the battle against the militants in the tribal areas to the Indian border. However, these appeared to be mainly for domestic consumption. Condoleezza Rice, the US secretary of state, visited both countries at the beginning of December to advise restraint, but also firm action by Pakistan against terrorist groups. India asked Pakistan to hand over a list of 20 individuals, who it claimed were being harboured by Pakistan, but this request was refused. Pakistan insisted that it would take action against anyone involved in the Mumbai attacks but only on the basis of hard evidence, and rejected the information supplied by India as unreliable. It did, however, take some steps against the Lashkar-e-Toiba and those associated with it (see above).

PAKISTAN'S INTERNATIONAL RELATIONS.   Pakistan was under pressure during the year from the USA, which was anxious to see the government do more to eliminate foreign and domestic militants from the tribal areas and to minimise cross-border infiltration into Afghanistan. US officials, including the chairman of the Joint Chiefs of Staff, Admiral Mike Mullen, on several occasions during the year made statements that indicated dissatisfaction with the policy that Pakistan was pursuing. Yet domestic pressure, as well as the apprehension of further increasing militant activity, meant that Pakistan could not give free rein to its security forces, some of whom might themselves object to what they were asked to do. The US deputy secretary of state visited Pakistan shortly after the February general election to ensure that the new government understood the US position, and the Pakistan army engaged throughout the year in operations in several parts of the border areas, suffering substantial numbers of casualties (see above). The government accepted the reality of regular cross-border attacks on militant targets by US drones and missiles, although it protested where these inflicted civilian casualties, as was frequently the case. In September there were border incidents as US troops entered Pakistan territory in pursuit of militant targets, and this was discussed when Zardari met Bush at the UN General Assembly later in the month.

In July a car bomb exploded at the Indian embassy in the Afghanistan capital, Kabul, with many casualties, and was blamed by the Afghan side (as well as by India) on groups linked to Pakistan's intelligence services (see p. 306). Relations between the two governments remained tense throughout the year, with the Afghan foreign minister criticising Pakistan for its policy of talking with the militants (see above). However, Afghanistan's President Hamid Karzai attended the inauguration of President Zardari and in October both governments sponsored a peace jirga (assembly) in Islamabad, at which tribal leaders from both countries, together with politicians and other prominent individuals, agreed to hold talks with militant groups, but only on condition that the latter accepted the legitimacy of the two governments.

Pakistan's suspension from the Commonwealth (see AR 2008, p. 304) was lifted in May, following the legislative elections and the installation of an elected government.

REGIONAL RELATIONS WITHIN SOUTH ASIA. Nepal's new prime minister, Prachanda, visited India in September. Although India continued to be wary of the new Maoist government, fearful that it might encourage left-wing rebel groups in areas of the country bordering India as well as Nepal's links with China, the visit appeared to go well, with a focus on potential economic co-operation. Although the Maoists had in the past taken a tough anti-Indian line, Prachanda's visit was marked by a pragmatic understanding of the limits of Nepal's leverage.

In the case of Sri Lanka, India, which in the 1980s had intervened in earlier stages of that country's civil war, chose to remain at arm's length from the renewed fighting.

REGIONAL ECONOMIES. All the regional economies suffered badly from the global economic crisis in the last quarter of 2008. In the earlier part of the year, international energy prices rose to levels where governments could no longer afford to maintain subsidies and had to raise domestic prices significantly. Inflation began to rise to alarming levels. While the fall in energy prices towards the end of the year provided some relief, this was more than outweighed by the decline in global demand for South Asian exports. South Asia's greater integration in the world economy during the previous two decades meant that it could not easily avoid the impact of the global crisis. A separate issue that hit the whole region was shortages of the staple crops of wheat and rice, compounded by rises in global prices. In Nepal, for example, rice prices rose by 50 per cent compared to 2007. Most countries in the region, including India, imposed bans on exports to protect domestic consumers.

Compared with 2007, the year was disappointing for India. Growth rates began to decline in the first two quarters of the year, and then tumbled as the global crisis struck. The official growth estimate for the year was 7 per cent, although the actual figure was expected to be somewhat lower. Inflation was a serious problem, peaking at nearly 13 per cent in the middle of the year. The rupee declined significantly against the US dollar. The government was forced to raise fuel prices by 10 per cent in the middle of the year, leading predictably to vocal opposition protests.

As the impact of the world economic crisis was felt, India's stock markets fell rapidly and exports dropped sharply as demand in areas such as textiles declined. In the last quarter of the year, it was estimated that there had, for the first time, been negative growth in the manufacturing sector, with obvious consequences for employment. Foreign investment plans, for example by car manufacturers Nissan and Renault, were also delayed.

Initially, the Reserve Bank of India (the central bank) raised interest rates to attempt to restrain inflation, but this was replaced by measures towards the end of the year to stimulate growth, including a 1 per cent cut in interest rates and a US$4 billion package to boost economic activity. The February budget, seen by many observers as a pre-election budget, had also included measures to address poverty—principally a plan to extend a loan waiver scheme for subsistence farmers, in many ways the most vulnerable section of the population. The national rural employment guarantee scheme (see AR 2008, p. 295) was extended to the whole country, even though some analysts regarded it as an inefficient use of scarce resources, which had failed to achieve its goals of substantially reducing poverty. Plans were announced to expand the railway network, a key infrastructural constraint to increasing exports.

As in previous years, there was regular resistance from public sector unions to government moves towards greater liberalisation. In September, for example, there was a strike by public sector bank employees. A major mining initiative by the Vedanta Corporation in Orissa, which had aroused environmental concerns, was cleared to proceed.

Pakistan's economy was hit both by the global crisis and by its own internal political problems. Its reserves shrank rapidly during the year, while the value of the rupee also declined to its lowest ever level against the US dollar. Inflation in the latter part of the year reached 25 per cent, with food prices rising even more sharply. Towards the end of the year, talks began with the IMF on an assistance package and a US$7.6 billion loan was approved in November.

David Taylor

INDIAN OCEAN STATES

Maldives

CAPITAL: Malé   AREA: 300 sq km   POPULATION: 305,000 ('07)
OFFICIAL LANGUAGE: Divehi   POLITICAL SYSTEM: non-party republic
HEAD OF STATE AND GOVERNMENT: President Mohammed Nasheed (MDP) (since Nov '08)
RULING PARTIES: Maldivian Democratic Party (MDP)
MAIN IGO MEMBERSHIPS (NON-UN): SAARC, CP, OIC, CWTH, NAM
CURRENCY: rufiya (end-'08 £1=R18.4033, US$1=R12.8000)
GNI PER CAPITA: US$3,200, $5,040 at PPP ('07)

Seychelles

CAPITAL: Victoria   AREA: 460 sq km   POPULATION: 85,000 ('07)
OFFICIAL LANGUAGES: Séchellois, English & French   POLITICAL SYSTEM: multiparty republic
HEAD OF STATE AND GOVERNMENT: President James Michel (since April '04)
RULING PARTY: Seychelles People's Progressive Front (SPPF)
MAIN IGO MEMBERSHIPS (NON-UN): AU, COMESA, SADC, OIC, ACP, CWTH, Francophonie, NAM
CURRENCY: Seychelles rupee (end-'08 £1=SRs23.7232, US$1=SRs16.5000)
GNI PER CAPITA: US$8,960, $15,450 at PPP ('07 est based on regression)

Mauritius

CAPITAL: Port Louis   AREA: 2,040 sq km   POPULATION: 1,263,000 ('07)
OFFICIAL LANGUAGE: English   POLITICAL SYSTEM: multiparty republic
HEAD OF STATE: President Sir Anerood Jugnauth (since Oct '03)
RULING PARTY: Social Alliance (AS)
HEAD OF GOVERNMENT: Prime Minister Navin Ramgoolam (Mauritius Labour Party (MLP),
    member of AS) (since July '05)
MAIN IGO MEMBERSHIPS (NON-UN): AU, COMESA, SADC, ACP, CWTH, Francophonie, NAM
CURRENCY: Mauritian rupee (end-'08 £1=MRs45.6486, US$1=MRs31.7500)
GNI PER CAPITA: US$5,450, $11,390 at PPP ('07)

The Comoros

CONSTITUENT REPUBLICS: Anjouan, Grande Comore, Mohéli
CAPITAL: Moroni   AREA: 1,861 sq km   POPULATION: 626,000 ('07)
OFFICIAL LANGUAGES: Arabic & French   POLITICAL SYSTEM: multiparty federal republic
HEAD OF STATE AND GOVERNMENT: Union President Ahmed Abdallah Mohamed Sambi, (since May '06)
PRESIDENTS OF REPUBLICS: Anjouan President Moussa Toybou (since June '08); Grande Comore
    President Mohamed Abdoulwahab (since June '07); Moheli President Mohamed Ali Said
    (since June '07)
MAIN IGO MEMBERSHIPS (NON-UN): AU, COMESA, ACP, AL, OIC, Francophonie, NAM
CURRENCY: Comorian franc (end-'08 £1=Fr508.850, US$1=Fr353.921)
GNI PER CAPITA: US$680, $1,150 at PPP ('07)

Madagascar

CAPITAL: Antananarivo   AREA: 587,040 sq km   POPULATION: 19,670,000 ('07)
OFFICIAL LANGUAGES: Malagasy & French   POLITICAL SYSTEM: multiparty republic
HEAD OF STATE: President Marc Ravalomanana (since May '02)
RULING PARTY: I Love Madagascar Party (TIM)
HEAD OF GOVERNMENT: Prime Minister Gen. Charles Rabemananjara (since Jan '07)
MAIN IGO MEMBERSHIPS (NON-UN): AU, COMESA, OIC, ACP, Francophonie, NAM
CURRENCY: ariary (end-'08 £1=MGA2,674.22, US$1=MGA1,860.00)
GNI PER CAPITA: US$320, $920 at PPP ('07)

MALDIVES.   The long process of constitutional reform, which began with the legalisation of political parties in 2005, culminated in August 2008 when the president
ratified a new democratic constitution. This included a bill of rights and the sep-

aration of powers, and made provision for the direct election of the president. The sixth term of office of President Maumoon Abdul Gayoom, who had ruled the Maldives since 1978 and was Asia's longest-serving political leader, was due to end in November (he had last been re-elected, unopposed, in 2003).

Although there were problems establishing the multiparty commissions to implement the new constitution, free elections were held. In the first round, on 8 October, Gayoom polled 40 per cent and his main rival, Mohammed Nasheed, 25 per cent. In the second round runoff, on 28 October, Nasheed was backed by the Islamist party, Aadhalath, and the four candidates eliminated in the first round. He defeated Gayoom with 54 per cent of the vote compared to the president's 45 per cent. Nasheed was the founder and leader of the Maldives Democratic Party (MDP) and had been repeatedly imprisoned by his predecessor as he campaigned for political reform. He was on record as having said "in politics in this country you are either in government or in jail." Although Nasheed won a clear victory in the presidential elections, Gayoom's Dhivehi Rayyithunge Party still held a majority in the 50-seat Majlis (legislature).

Nasheed's election was seen as a triumph for peaceful democratic change, but the new constitution was widely criticised as it allowed only Muslims to become citizens of the Maldives; the Aadhalath party members soon gained an influential position in the new government, appointed by Nasheed in November.

The Maldives, heavily dependent on tourism, faced a variety of serious threats. Nasheed's election campaign focused on economic issues, as the global economic crisis limited tourist expansion. Refuse generated by the capital, Malé, and by the tourist industry was causing widespread pollution to the sea near the main island. Meanwhile, rising sea levels caused by climate change threatened to submerge the Maldives. The new president was reported as having said that the Maldivians might have to purchase a new homeland as their 1,200 islands gradually disappeared.

THE SEYCHELLES.   Seychelles was hit particularly hard by the global economic downturn. The IMF described the situation as "an acute balance of payments and public debt crisis, which jeopardizes [the population's] living standards and [the country's] economic development". The crisis brought the two major political parties, the ruling SPPF (Seychelles People's Progressive Front) of President James Michel, and the opposition SNP (Seychelles National Party) led by Wavel Ramakalawan, to adopt a common set of economic reform measures. Departing from some of its long held socialist policies, the ruling party agreed a reform pro-gramme, which included the removal of foreign exchange controls and subsidies, floating the rupee, a reduction in public employment, and privatisation measures. As a result the IMF granted a US$26 million standby credit in November. The policy of developing the upper end of the tourist market meant that revenue from tourism was less affected by the world economic crisis than might otherwise have been the case; close links had been developed with the Gulf States, which pro-vided the fourth largest number of foreign visitors. The rise of Somali-based piracy was, however, seen as an increasing security threat.

A report by an independent Irish judge, Michael Reilly, upheld complaints against the conduct of the Special Support Unit during the riots in 2006 (see AR

2007, p. 306) and recommended that it be incorporated into the armed forces. The government accepted the recommendations of the report.

MAURITIUS. There was no serious challenge to the dominance of the ruling Social Alliance (AS) coalition and the budget published in June was rated a success. In September there was a cabinet reshuffle and Prime Minister Navin Ramgoolam insisted that, faced with the global economic crisis, government measures should prioritise protection for the least well off. Tourism was particularly affected, with growth at only 0.1 per cent. Opinion polls showed that there would be strong electoral support for an alliance of the Mauritian Militant Movement (MMM), led by Paul Bérenger, and the Socialist Mauritian Movement (MSM), led by Pravind Jugnauth (the son of the president), but the two leaders continued to find co-operation difficult. Their alliance had fractured following defeat in the 2005 legislative elections. All parties in the National Assembly (unicameral legislature) united to re-elect unanimously Sir Anerood Jugnauth for a second term as president on 19 September, in spite of rumours that he might be seeking to re-enter party politics.

In November, the UK Privy Council dismissed an appeal against the 2007 verdict of the Mauritian Supreme Court, which had found Ashok Jugnauth (uncle of Pravind) guilty of electoral fraud, and he had to vacate his parliamentary seat. In the long running Chagos Island dispute, the UK's House of Lords declared that it was legal for the British government to refuse to allow the Chagos islanders the right of return. Paul Bérenger consequently suggested that the issue might be taken to the International Court of Justice at The Hague (see AR 2008, p. 308).

THE COMOROS. The failure of both African Union (AU) diplomacy led by South Africa, and of sanctions, to resolve the disputed election for the presidency of the island of Anjouan (see AR 2008, p. 308) led to demands for military intervention. In late March Comoros Union forces, supported by AU troops provided by Sudan, Libya, Tanzania, and Senegal, invaded Anjouan and the self-styled president, Mohamed Bacar, fled to the French overseas collectivity of Mayotte. The French refused either to extradite him or to grant him asylum and, after being sentenced for importing arms to Mayotte, he was allowed to go into exile in Benin. In June fresh elections were held in Anjouan and Moussa Toybou, the candidate supported by the Union president, won with 52.4 per cent of the vote in the second round runoff.

Having re-established Union authority, President Ahmed Sambi, who was widely known as the "Ayatollah", proposed an inter-island conference to discuss revisions to the constitution. Debate centred on ways to cut the expense of maintaining the four separate governments mandated by the federal constitution. Proposals for change were opposed by the president of Mohéli who, under the terms of the present constitution, was due to take over as president of the Union in 2010. French proposals to hold a referendum on the future of Mayotte, which could lead to Mayotte being granted the status of a French département, were strongly opposed, as the Comoros had claimed sovereignty over the island since independence in 1975.

The president of Grande Comore, Mohamed Abdoulwahab, who was an albino, publicly campaigned on behalf of albinos in Africa while on an official visit to Mali.

The economy of the Comoros showed no signs of reviving with the return of political stability. Fuel shortages led to a rise in prices while economic growth slowed to 0.5 per cent, falling far behind population increase. Demonstrations calling for the president to resign resulted from schools closures and civil servants remaining unpaid.

MADAGASCAR. In December 2007 the dominance of TIM (I Love Madagascar), the ruling party of President Marc Ravalomanana, was rudely shaken when an independent candidate, Andry Rajoelina, won a sweeping victory to become mayor of Antananarivo with 62.6 per cent of the vote. Rajoelina's supporters also gained control of the city council. The capital had been considered the heartland of support for the president, who in the past had also been the city's mayor, and the loss of electoral support was interpreted as criticism of Ravalomanana's increasingly dictatorial approach to politics. However, TIM won convincing victories outside the capital, taking control of all 22 regions and even winning in Taomasina, previously the stronghold of the former president, Didier Ratsiraka. After these victories the prime minister, Charles Rabemananjara, declared electoral reform—which would have established an independent electoral commission—to be off the agenda.

The opposition was increasingly leaderless. Herizo Razafimahaleo, a previous presidential candidate, died in July, and Roland Ratsiraka, son of the former president, was arrested in September on corruption charges. Following demonstrations in the capital, attempts were made to limit the powers of the new mayor of Antananarivo but he responded by publishing highly compromising audited accounts for the years when President Ravalomanana had been mayor.

The success of the Madagascar's EPZ (export processing zone), which had led to the rapid growth of the textile and mining sectors, was criticised by the IMF, which claimed it was responsible for the weak position of government revenue collection. As a result, the Madagascar action plan (MAP) was stalled because of a shortage of government investment funds. The mining boom attracted large scale foreign investment, which to some extent offset the damage caused by the cyclones earlier in the year that left 300,000 people homeless.

Malyn Newitt

IX SOUTH-EAST AND EAST ASIA

SOUTH-EAST ASIAN STATES

BURMA—THAILAND—MALAYSIA—BRUNEI—SINGAPORE—VIETNAM—CAMBODIA—LAOS

Burma (Myanmar)

CAPITAL: Naypyidaw (Pyinmana)   AREA: 676,580 sq km   POPULATION: 48,783,000 ('07)
OFFICIAL LANGUAGE: Burmese   POLITICAL SYSTEM: military regime
HEAD OF STATE AND GOVERNMENT: Gen. Than Shwe, Chairman of State Peace and Development
  Council (since April '92)
PRIME MINISTER: Lt-Gen. Thein Sein (since Oct '07; acting since June '07)
MAIN IGO MEMBERSHIPS (NON-UN): ASEAN, CP, NAM
CURRENCY: kyat (end-'08 £1=K9.2522, US$1=K6.4350)
GNI PER CAPITA: Low income: US$935 or less ('07 est)

Thailand

CAPITAL: Bangkok   AREA: 513,120 sq km   POPULATION: 63,832,000 ('07)
OFFICIAL LANGUAGE: Thai   POLITICAL SYSTEM: multiparty monarchy under martial law
HEAD OF STATE: King Bhumibol Adulyadej (Rama IX), since June '46
RULING PARTY: Democrat Party (DP) heads coalition
HEAD OF GOVERNMENT: Prime Minister Abhisit Vejjajiva (DP) (since Dec '08)
MAIN IGO MEMBERSHIPS (NON-UN): ASEAN, CP, APEC, NAM
CURRENCY: baht (end-'08 £1=Bt50.0050, US$1=Bt34.7800)
GNI PER CAPITA: US$3,400, $7,880 at PPP ('07)

Malaysia

CAPITAL: Kuala Lumpur   AREA: 329,740 sq km   POPULATION: 26,550,000 ('07)
OFFICIAL LANGUAGE: Bahasa Malaysia   POLITICAL SYSTEM: multiparty monarchy
HEAD OF STATE: King Mizan Zainal Abidin ibni Al-Marhum Sultan Mahmud Al-Muktafi Billah
  Shah, Sultan of Terengganu (since Nov '06)
RULING PARTY: National Front (BN) coalition
HEAD OF GOVERNMENT: Prime Minister Abdullah Ahmad Badawi (since Oct '03)
MAIN IGO MEMBERSHIPS (NON-UN): ASEAN, APEC, CP, OIC, CWTH, NAM
CURRENCY: ringgit Malaysia (end-'08 £1=RM4.9746, US$1=RM3.4600)
GNI PER CAPITA: US$6,540, $13,570 at PPP ('07)

Brunei

CAPITAL: Bandar Seri Bagawan   AREA: 5,770 sq km   POPULATION: 389,000 ('07)
OFFICIAL LANGUAGES: Malay & English   POLITICAL SYSTEM: non-party sultanate
HEAD OF STATE AND GOVERNMENT: Sultan Sir Hassanal Bolkiah (since '67)
MAIN IGO MEMBERSHIPS (NON-UN): ASEAN, APEC, OIC, CWTH, NAM
CURRENCY: Brunei dollar (end-'08 £1=Br$2.0715, US$1=Br$1.4408)
GNI PER CAPITA: US$26,930, $49,900 at PPP ('07)

Singapore

CAPITAL: Singapore   AREA: 699 sq km   POPULATION: 4,589,000 ('07)
OFFICIAL LANGUAGES: Malay, Chinese, Tamil & English   POLITICAL SYSTEM: multiparty republic
HEAD OF STATE: President S.R. Nathan (since Sept '99)
RULING PARTY: People's Action Party (PAP)
HEAD OF GOVERNMENT: Prime Minister Lee Hsien Loong (since August '04)
MAIN IGO MEMBERSHIPS (NON-UN): ASEAN, APEC, CP, CWTH, NAM
CURRENCY: Singapore dollar (end-'08 £1=S$2.0715, US$1=S$1.4408)
GNI PER CAPITA: US$32,470, $48,520 at PPP ('07)

Vietnam

CAPITAL: Hanoi   AREA: 329,310 sq km   POPULATION: 85,140,000 ('07)
OFFICIAL LANGUAGE: Vietnamese   POLITICAL SYSTEM: one-party republic
HEAD OF STATE: President Nguyen Minh Triet (since June '06)
RULING PARTY: Communist Party of Vietnam (CPV)
PARTY LEADER: Nong Duc Manh, CPV secretary general (since April '01)
PRIME MINISTER: Nguyen Tan Dung (since June '06)
MAIN IGO MEMBERSHIPS (NON-UN): ASEAN, APEC, NAM, WTO, Francophonie
CURRENCY: dong (end-'08 £1=Vnd25,136.20, US$1=Vnd17,483.00)
GNP PER CAPITA: US$790, $2,550 at PPP ('07)

Cambodia

CAPITAL: Phnom Penh   AREA: 181,040 sq km   POPULATION: 14,446,000 ('07)
OFFICIAL LANGUAGE: Khmer   POLITICAL SYSTEM: multiparty monarchy
HEAD OF STATE: King Norodom Sihamoni (elected Oct '04)
RULING PARTY: Cambodian People's Party (CPP)
HEAD OF GOVERNMENT: Prime Minister Hun Sen (since July '97)
MAIN IGO MEMBERSHIPS (NON-UN): ASEAN, CP, Francophonie, NAM
CURRENCY: riel (end-'08 £1=R5,823.09, US$1=R4,050.00)
GNI PER CAPITA: US$540, $1,690 at PPP ('07)

Laos

CAPITAL: Vientiane   AREA: 236,800 sq km   POPULATION: 5,860,000 ('07)
OFFICIAL LANGUAGE: Laotian   POLITICAL SYSTEM: one-party republic
HEAD OF STATE: President (Lt.-Gen.) Choummaly Sayasone (since June '06)
RULING PARTY: Lao People's Revolutionary Party (LPRP)
HEAD OF GOVERNMENT: Prime Minister Bouasone Bouphavanh (since June '06)
MAIN IGO MEMBERSHIPS (NON-UN): ASEAN, CP, Francophonie, NAM
CURRENCY: new kip (end-'08 £1=K12,182.48, US$1=K8,473.00)
GNI PER CAPITA: US$580, $1,940 at PPP ('07)

A POLITICAL stalemate continued in Thailand, disrupting efforts to restore democratically elected civilian rule in the aftermath of the September 2006 military coup. A stalemate of a different kind persisted in Burma, with efforts both within and outside the country to bring about democratic change continuing to have little discernible impact on the military regime.

THAILAND.   For Thailand, regarded until fairly recently as evolving towards a stable democratic system, legislative elections proved unable to overcome increasingly entrenched political divisions. The victory of the People's Power Party (PPP) in December 2007, in parliamentary elections following the return to barracks of the Thai military, brought to power Samak Sundaravej, seen as close to the man ousted by the military (and barred from Thai politics for at least five years), Thaksin Shinawatra (see AR 2008, p. 316).

The former prime minister returned from 17 months' exile in late February and declined an invitation from the finance minister to be one of his economic advisors. Thaksin's return led to suggestions of a possible amnesty for banned PPP politicians and the foreign minister called for Thaksin's diplomatic passport to be restored to him. In March, Thaksin urged his opponents to "let bygones be bygones" and pleaded innocent in a corruption case. In August, his wife—Pojaman Shinawatra—was found guilty of tax evasion and given a three-year prison sentence, against which she was scheduled to appeal. Although barred in July by the Supreme Court from leaving the country, both Thaksin and his wife flew to London, with Thaksin stating that he was unable to obtain a fair trial in Thailand. Thailand's Supreme Court issued arrest warrants for the couple—who divorced in November, apparently for financial reasons—as the two reportedly sought asylum in the UK (which revoked his visa in November). Speaking from exile in November, Thaksin addressed more than 60,000 people, who had gathered at a Bangkok stadium to hear him speak by videophone, stating that he wished to return, but that only "royal kindness or the power of the people" could bring him "home".

Allegations of electoral fraud jeopardised the PPP-led coalition government from the outset. In February, the Election Commission disqualified the speaker of the lower house (the House of Representatives), jeopardising the party's existence. In March, the Commission found that election fraud had been committed by two of the PPP's coalition partners. In July, a court decision barred the PPP's deputy leader from politics for five years.

Government proposals for a special committee to review Thailand's constitution (which came into force in August 2007 following a referendum, see AR 2008, p. 316) were seen as linked to efforts to lift the ban on political participation imposed on Thaksin and other leaders of his Thai Rak Thai (TRT) party. Proposed constitutional amendments, seen as intended to protect the PPP and its allies from court action, were accompanied by comments from Samak that the constitution should be rewritten. The prime minister's announcement in May of plans to hold another referendum, this time asking voters whether or not they wanted the constitution to be amended, led the anti-Thaksin People's Alliance for Democracy (PAD) to launch a campaign to bring about Samak's resignation, with the PAD also calling for the impeachment of legislators who sought to amend or replace the constitution. In June, several thousand people pushed past police protecting Government House (the seat of government) in Bangkok and surrounded the compound with the intent of maintaining a siege until the government's resignation.

The anti-government PAD protesters adopted the royal colour, yellow, as their symbol and became known as "yellow shirts". They were opposed by pro-Thaksin protesters, grouped in the United Front for Democracy against Dictatorship (UDD), who adopted the colour red and were labelled "red shirts". At the end of August, pro-government UDD demonstrators attacked PAD protesters occupying Government House; one person was killed and 40 were injured, as PAD protesters continued to refuse to leave the building or end their blockade until a new government was sworn in.

On 26 August, anti-government protesters broke into the compound housing the prime minister's office, took over a state-controlled television station, and besieged several ministries. The PAD blocked roads leading to Government House and police issued arrest warrants for five protest leaders. On 29 August, Thai police cleared barricades and regained control of access to Government House. Protesters continued their rally there, however, demanding the resignation of the prime minister.

On 1 September, Samak called an emergency session of Parliament in an attempt to end the protest and declared a state of emergency in Bangkok. Samak's tenure as prime minister ended six days later when he was forced from office by the Constitutional Court, which ruled that his hosting of a television cookery show whilst in office represented a conflict of interest. The ruling presented a further opportunity for the country to return to stable civilian-led government.

It was an opportunity not taken, however, as Thaksin's brother-in-law, Somchai Wongsawat, who had served as Samak's deputy prime minister, was chosen by the PPP as its new leader and elected by Parliament on 17 September as the country's new prime minister. In response, the anti-Thaksin forces who had demonstrated so strongly against Thaksin, and then against Samak, intensified their protests. Once again, demonstrators sought to make the country ungovernable. PAD protesters refused to end their siege of the prime minister's office and Somchai was forced to set up a temporary office elsewhere. On 7 October, two people died and more than 400 were injured in Bangkok street violence. The Thai military deployed unarmed troops to help police restore order. With the prime minister's authority eroded, once again a Thai court provided the final blow, removing Somchai in a ruling that also had the effect of depriving the governing party of its right to continue to participate in Thai politics. The court's decision that the PPP was little more than Thaksin's old TRT party—itself banned—meant that the PPP was ruled an illegal organisation; its members, including the prime minister and all of the cabinet, were barred from participating in Thai politics.

The possibility of yet another head of government from the pro-Thaksin camp being selected was avoided when the Thai Parliament on 15 December elected an opposition member, Abhisit Vejjajiva, as the country's new prime minister, Thailand's third in only four months. Abhisit had led his Democrat Party (DP) at the 2007 elections, only to fail to gain the premiership when Samak's PPP won more votes and parliamentary seats than the Democrats. Nevertheless, the inability of either Samak or Somchai to be regarded as legitimate leaders meant that finally, in December, he had his chance to govern, becoming, at 44, the country's youngest-ever prime minister.

The beginnings of Abhisit's premiership were far from auspicious. Demonstrators surrounded the Parliament building in an attempt to deny him access to the legislative chamber. As the Thai constitution stipulated that a new leader must give an address to Parliament within 15 days of taking office, the UDD protests introduced a further complicating constitutional element into the ongoing, and increasingly divisive, political stalemate. With thousands of protesters blocking entry to the Parliament building, Abhisit gave his speech on 30 December at the foreign ministry, rather than in Parliament.

While the prime minister had been able to deliver his constitutionally mandated inaugural policy address, there was little immediate sign that his legislative programme or political outlook would prove sufficient to reduce tensions in an increasingly brittle political system. The political acrimony within Thailand had broader consequences for the country and region. Thailand had been scheduled to host the Association of South-East Asian Nations (ASEAN) leaders' summit in December, but proved unable to provide a secure setting. Protesters occupying Bangkok's two international airports made the capital an unsuitable venue, while at the same time harming the country's image and damaging its tourist industry as thousands of visitors were stranded, unable to leave, and others were unable to arrive.

Although Thailand's highly respected King Bhumibol had on several occasions been able to resolve previous political crises, his capacity or willingness to intervene in this ongoing dispute appeared to have been more limited. Planned birthday celebrations for the king were muted due to illness; after swearing in Abhisit and his cabinet, the king called for "peace" and stability, but it was far from clear that those opposed to Abhisit's appointment were prepared to comply.

Meanwhile, a violent Islamic insurgency continued in the south of the country, with ongoing attacks, some fatal, on soldiers and civilians. In February, an exiled Muslim leader called for a referendum on independence for the Muslim-majority southern provinces of Pattani, Narathiwat, and Yala. The proposal, and suggestions for granting autonomy to the region, were criticised by the government. By late March, Thai police reported that the insurgency's death toll since January 2004 now exceeded 3,000. A government minister admitted to having "no idea" how to curb the unrest.

The year ended tragically for Thailand when a fire swept through a nightclub in Bangkok on 31 December, New Year's Eve, killing at least 59 people and injuring more than 200, with both Thai citizens and foreign nationals among the victims.

BURMA.   In contrast to Thailand's leadership instability, the military regime in Burma remained entrenched. In February, it was announced that a referendum on the regime's new constitution would be held in May and that new elections (the first since 1990, the results of which had not been honoured, see AR 1990, pp. 333-35) would be held in 2009. The opposition National League for Democracy, not having been consulted on these developments, reacted at first cautiously, and then increasingly negatively, to the announcement. In March, Buddhist monks issued a statement urging a "no" vote in the referendum. Monks and nuns were among those (including convicted felons and the mentally ill) who were prohibited from voting.

Scepticism about the regime's intentions was not confined to Burma, as regional and international reaction to the regime's political "road map" was far from uniformly supportive. Within the country, criticism of the referendum—

and of the constitutional document itself—soon became a punishable offence. The possibility of informed debate on the merits of the regime's constitution diminished further with the inability or unwillingness of the government to circulate copies of the constitution to the country's voters. The referendum itself lost whatever remaining credibility it might have had when the regime went ahead with the vote, despite the country having sustained heavy damage from Cyclone Nargis, which swept up the Irrawaddy river in May, devastating many communities, leaving thousands homeless and in need of emergency assistance. Dozens of villages were said to have been wiped out in the storm. As a result of the cyclone, which began on 2 May, more than 140,000 people were believed to have died. Foreign aid workers already in Burma were initially banned from the worst affected areas, and UN Secretary-General Ban Ki-Moon travelled to Burma to meet with its leaders in an attempt to remove the restrictions. Cyclone relief centres were briefly established, but homeless families were subsequently evicted and urged to return to their places of origin.

The regime lost further support, both regionally and internationally, through its tardy response to what had become a major humanitarian crisis. Unable to provide food, shelter, and medical supplies to the population, the government nevertheless initially declined offers of external assistance, and then accepted shipments of aid conditional on donors not delivering supplies directly to the countryside. Ships laden with aid remained off shore, not permitted to dock; only a few flights to the capital were allowed, their supplies taken off (often with painful inefficiency) by contingents of the Burmese military. US, French, and British navy ships with relief supplies were denied the opportunity to deliver their cargoes.

Despite submissions that the 10 May referendum be postponed, the vote went ahead on schedule, without the presence of external monitors or international media coverage. With much of the population struggling to survive the effects of Cyclone Nargis, the regime nevertheless reported a voter turnout of 92 per cent: a remarkable achievement for such a beleaguered electorate. The pro-constitution vote, in turn, was reported as 99 per cent, a result so unbalanced as to make it impossible to regard the referendum as either "free" or "fair", thereby further weakening the credibility of the regime's "seven step" process towards a new political system.

A regime indifferent to the plight of its own citizens, unwilling to accept offers of aid at a time of national crisis, could scarcely have been open to external influence on other matters considered pivotal to its own survival. Despite repeated calls for her release from years of house arrest, the regime extended for a further year the imprisonment and isolation of Nobel Peace Prize laureate Aung San Suu Kyi. Further visits to the country by the UN envoy, Ibrahim Gambari, proved even more futile than before. After initial regime resistance to another visit—his fifth since his appointment in 2006, and the first since November 2007—Gambari was able to obtain a visa and visited the country for a few days in March, but failed to hold a meeting with the country's leader, General Than Shwe. Gambari met with Suu Kyi, after being told by Burma's information minister that the country had no political prisoners and that the government had already done enough to hold a dialogue with Suu Kyi. The information minister rejected Gambari's suggested revisions of the government-drafted constitution and an offer of observers for the referendum.

The regime stated in March that Suu Kyi, who had been under house arrest since May 2003, would not be permitted to take part in elections in 2010, on the grounds that she had been married to a foreigner (the late Michael Aris). Nevertheless, in May, *Time Magazine* named her among the 100 most influential people in the world for 2008. In August, she began a hunger strike and, no doubt frustrated by the inability of the UN to assist, refused to meet Gambari during his August visit. Subsequently, in December, several members of Suu Kyi's National League for Democracy died in prison, following years of imprisonment.

In February, the USA introduced additional sanctions, freezing the assets of individuals or corporations linked to the regime and prohibiting US citizens from engaging in any financial or commercial transactions with them. Further measures were announced on 1 May against Burma's state-owned companies dealing in gems, timber, and pearls. President George W. Bush met Burmese activists in exile in Bangkok in August, during a brief halt en route to the Beijing Olympic Games, and his wife, Laura Bush, outspoken on the Burma issue and the continued detention of Suu Kyi, visited a refugee camp on the Thai-Burma border.

A move by the USA for a UN Security Council presidential statement on the constitutional referendum was initially opposed by China and Russia, but on 2 May—eight days before the referendum—a statement was unanimously adopted, urging that the constitutional referendum process be "inclusive and credible, including the full participation of all political actors and respect for fundamental freedoms". Support was also expressed for Gambari's mission. In December, the UN General Assembly adopted a resolution calling on Burma to free all political prisoners, including Suu Kyi, and criticising the human rights record of the regime. No ASEAN member state voted in favour of the resolution. In December, Suu Kyi's lawyer stated that the authorities had denied him permission to meet with her to discuss an appeal against her continued detention.

Elsewhere in South-East Asia, elections were held under conditions generally regarded as "free and fair", with varying results for the incumbent governments.

CAMBODIA. The governing Cambodian People's Party (CPP) was able to win yet another election, leaving Prime Minister Hun Sen firmly in control of the country. The campaign began in June, with 11 parties taking part in elections on 27 July for the 123-seat National Assembly, the lower house of the Cambodian legislature. The CPP won 90 seats, up from 73 in 2003; the opposition Sam Rainsy Party won 26 seats, a slight increase from its 24 seats. In September, King Norodom Sihamoni issued a pardon to his half-brother, Prince Norodom Ranariddh, making it possible for him to return from exile in Malaysia. In July, a Supreme Court judge had upheld a lower court's 2007 ruling in relation to a lawsuit against the prince filed by his former colleagues in the royalist Funcinpec party, which had removed Prince Ranariddh as its leader in 2006. The prince's Norodom Ranariddh Party won two seats in the 2008 elections, as did Funcinpec.

In July, Cambodians celebrated after an 11th century Hindu temple was declared a World Heritage site (as were two historic Malaysian trading towns) by UNESCO. The Preah Vihear temple along the disputed Thai-Cambodian border remained in contention between the two countries, despite a 1962 International Court of Justice decision awarding the temple and the land it occupied to Cambodia. Thailand had opposed the World Heritage site designation, but in May its then Prime Minister Samak Sundaravej, who visited Cambodia in March, endorsed Cambodia's application. Samak was threatened with impeachment by a group of senators for his endorsement and the government withdrew its support in late June. In July, Thailand's Constitutional Court ruled that the government should have received prior parliamentary approval before signing the communiqué. The Thai foreign minister subsequently resigned, shortly after the Democrat Party submitted an impeachment motion against him over the issue.

In August, the Thai and Cambodian foreign ministers met in an effort to settle the dispute. In October, the two countries agreed to hold joint patrols, after a skirmish near the temple killed two Cambodians and wounded three others; seven Thai troops were also wounded. Cambodia released 13 Thai paramilitary troops that it had taken prisoner.

The process of bringing at least several high-ranking former Khmer Rouge officials before a special UN-sponsored international genocide tribunal—the Extraordinary Chambers in the Court of Cambodia (ECCC)—continued at a desultory pace (see AR 2008, p. 320). The tribunal continued its efforts to persuade lower-ranking officials and police to co-operate in the face of concerns from some that they might also be prosecuted. In February, it sought a significant increase to its budget in order to continue operating until March 2011. In February, a Cambodian survivor of the genocide of 1975-79 confronted Nuon Chea, one of the five former Khmer Rouge leaders being held for trial, at an appeal for his release from pre-trial detention. It was the first time that a victim had been able to confront one of the accused in court. Another Khmer Rouge defendant awaiting trial, who was charged with responsibility for the torture and killing of 17,000 people, stated in an interview in February that "all the prisoners had to be eliminated". The former Khmer Rouge leaders, elderly and in poor health, lost their appeals against pre-trial detention.

In March, the Cambodian Supreme Court upheld life sentences for a Cambodian man and two Thais convicted of plotting attacks on the US and British embassies.

MALAYSIA. Elections in March proved a serious setback for the incumbent prime minister, Abdullah Ahmad Badawi. Already under attack from within his own party, and especially from his predecessor, Mahathir Mohammed, the prime minister was held responsible for electoral setbacks that saw the opposition emerge victorious in five states, winning 82 seats in the 222-seat legislature.

The prime minister emphasised that the governing party, the National Front (BN) coalition, had won the election, taking 140 seats, and had retained a substantial legislative majority. Nevertheless, the loss of support, and the gains made by the opposition—which quadrupled its representation from the 21 seats in 2004—led to repeated calls for his resignation, both as leader of the governing party and as prime minister.

Parliament had been dissolved on 13 February and the elections were held at a time when Badawi's popularity was already falling as a result of inflation, crime, and ethnic tensions involving Malays, Indians, and Chinese. An election co-operation agreement among three opposition parties—People's Justice Party, Islamic Party of Malaysia (PAS), and Democratic Action Party—meant that together they fielded only one candidate per constituency against the National Front, which had governed Malaysia since 1957. In 2004, Badawi had led the National Front to its best result ever, winning more than 90 per cent of parliamentary seats and 12 of the 13 state governments. The 2008 outcome, however, gave the ruling coalition only 62.6 percent of the seats in the legislature, its lowest proportion ever and the first time since 1969 that it had not been able to achieve a two-thirds majority. Four cabinet ministers lost their seats as the government forfeited support from ethnic Chinese and Indians, and also from some Malays choosing to vote for the Islamist PAS. The vote represented a protest against racial discrimination, crime, corruption, and rising prices. Afterwards, opposition-ruled states declared that they would no longer follow an affirmative action programme introduced to benefit ethnic Malays.

The prime minister's leadership of the United Malays National Organisation (UMNO)—the leading party in the National Front—was reconfirmed after the election at a special meeting of the UMNO, which ignored Mahathir's calls for Badawi to resign and urged him to continue as party president and prime minister. On 10 March, Badawi took the oath of office for a new five-year term and in May he again refused to resign, saying "I have work to do." Mahathir resigned from the ruling party, declaring that he would not remain a member of the UMNO so long as Badawi continued as its president. In September, Badawi announced that UMNO leadership elections scheduled for December would be postponed until March 2009. Then, in October, he announced that he would not contest the party presidency, opening the way for Deputy Prime Minister Najib Razak to assume the post and take over as prime minister. Razak, however, faced claims of sexual misconduct in connection with the murder of a Mongolian model in 2006.

The Malaysian opposition was led by former deputy prime minister, Anwar Ibrahim, whose parliamentary career had been disrupted in 1998 when he was imprisoned for sodomy and corruption offences. Released from prison in 2004 (when the sodomy conviction was overturned), he remained disqualified from the legislature until April 2008 (see AR 2004, p. 311). His wife, Wan Azizah Ismail, won Anwar's parliamentary seat in 2004—the only member of her party to be elected—and in 2008 she extended her majority in the constituency. Anwar's daughter was also elected, unseating a minister in winning her first

campaign. On 31 July, Anwar's wife resigned her seat, giving Anwar an opportunity to return to Parliament by contesting the resulting by-election. However,
on 7 August, Anwar was again charged with sodomy and was released on bail
after pleading innocent to the charge, which he characterised as "political".
Continuing his campaign, Anwar was elected on 26 August, re-entering Parliament on 28 August when he took the oath and was formally appointed leader of
the opposition. Anwar vowed to become prime minister (through defections by
government MPs) by 16 September, but failed to do so.

An Islamic court allowed a Muslim convert to return to Buddhism after her
marriage collapsed, despite a prohibition against the renunciation of Islam by
Muslim Malaysians. In August, the government warned a Christian newspaper
about running articles deemed political and insulting to Islam. In December,
Malaysia released seven people (held since 2002) accused of involvement in terrorism, including one who had been accused of helping the hijackers in the 11
September 2001 attacks, the home minister stating that they were no longer considered a threat. In August, Malaysia ordered more than 25,000 refugees who
had fled Indonesia after the 2004 tsunami to leave by early January 2009 (see
map, AR 2005, p. 296).

Economic growth, rather than electoral developments, remained the predomi-
nant issue elsewhere in the region.

BRUNEI benefited from the sharp rise in oil prices that occurred prior to the financial crisis. The sultan's feud over finances continued with his exiled brother,
Prince Jefri Bolkiah, as a court attempted yet again to gain control over the disputed funds (see AR 2007, pp. 317-18). A British judge issued an arrest warrant for the prince for violating a court order to hand over £3 billion to the
Brunei government, money that had allegedly gone missing while he was serving as the country's minister of finance.

VIETNAM continued to experience significant economic growth, while the country's rate of inflation also continued to rise. In April, Vietnam successfully
launched its first satellite, a telecommunications satellite. In December, the
government announced an economic stimulus package to maintain growth amid
the global downturn, the funds to be spent on schools, hospitals, housing, jobs
training, and infrastructure projects.

Relations with the USA continued to improve. In June, President Bush welcomed Prime Minister Nguyen Tan Dung to the White House. The two leaders
hailed strengthening economic ties, reflected in a growth in bilateral trade, with
the USA becoming Vietnam's leading export market. Relations with China also
appeared to improve, with reports of the two countries completing the demarcation of their long-disputed land border.

In December, Vietnam approved new regulations banning Internet diarists
(bloggers) from discussing subjects deemed by the government too sensitive or
inappropriate, with bloggers required to confine their writings to personal

issues. In April, a Vietnamese-born British citizen condemned to death for heroin trafficking had his sentence commuted to life imprisonment by Vietnam's president. The floods and landslides resulting from a tropical storm in August cost more than 100 lives in Vietnam.

SINGAPORE continued to play a major role in ASEAN, playing host to various regional meetings. Under its leadership, the organisation, meeting in Singapore in July, called for Burma's government to engage in "meaningful dialogue" with the opposition and expressed "deep disappointment" at the continued detention of Aung San Suu Kyi. The International Court of Justice ruled in May in favour of Singapore in its 28-year sovereignty dispute with Malaysia over a small, uninhabited island, strategically positioned in the Straits of Malacca (see pp. 482-83).

In February, a commander of the Jemaah Islamiah (JI) group in Singapore, imprisoned for plotting various terrorist attacks—allegedly including one to crash an aeroplane into the country's international airport—escaped from a detention centre, setting off a nationwide search. The prime minister described the escape as a "setback" to the country's reputation as a well-policed state.

LAOS. A feature film, *Sabaidee Luang Prabang*, considered the first "real" Lao movie in 33 years (that is, since the communist regime came to power in 1975), was released. The film, shot in Laos and with Lao actors in the starring roles, was made with private Lao and Thai funding and co-directed by Lao and Thai film-makers. Only three other Lao films had been made during this period, each narrating nationalistic tales of communist victories over foreign powers; they had been funded by the Lao and Vietnamese governments.

In June, Thailand deported 837 Hmong refugees to Laos, as several thousand Hmong walked out of a refugee camp in northern Thailand to demonstrate against their deportation. More than 500 of these were detained in provincial jails. Half the dwellings in the camp were burned down during several weeks preceding the deportation. About 8,000 Hmong had lived in the Huay Nam Khao refugee camp for several years, claiming that they would face persecution if returned to Laos.

The Chinese government provided funding for construction of a new sports stadium in the capital, Vientiane, for the 2009 South-East Asia Games to be hosted by Laos.

In August, severe flooding of towns, villages, and farmland along the Mekong river affected more than 150,000 people in Laos. Concern about public health problems brought assistance from various UN humanitarian agencies.

Stephen Levine

INDONESIA—EAST TIMOR—PHILIPPINES

Indonesia

CAPITAL: Jakarta   AREA: 1,904,570 sq km   POPULATION: 225,630,000 ('07)
OFFICIAL LANGUAGE: Bahasa Indonesia   POLITICAL SYSTEM: multiparty republic
HEAD OF STATE AND GOVERNMENT: President General (retd) Susilo Bambang Yudhoyono
   (since Oct '04)
RULING PARTY: Nationhood Coalition dominated by Golkar
MAIN IGO MEMBERSHIPS (NON-UN): ASEAN, APEC, CP, OIC, OPEC, NAM
CURRENCY: rupiah (end-'08 £1=Rp15,671.50, US$1=Rp10,900.00)
GNI PER CAPITA: US$1,650, $3,580 at PPP ('07)

East Timor

CAPITAL: Dili   AREA: 14,870 sq km   POPULATION: 1,066,000 ('07)
OFFICIAL LANGUAGES: Portuguese, Tetum and Bahasa Indonesian   POLITICAL SYSTEM: transitional
   government overseen by UNTAET
HEAD OF STATE: President José Ramos Horta (since May '07)
HEAD OF GOVERNMENT: Prime Minister Xanana Gusmão (since Aug '07)
MAIN IGO MEMBERSHIPS (NON-UN): NAM, G-77, CPLP
CURRENCY: US dollar (end-'08 £1=1.4378)
GNI PER CAPITA: US$1,510, $3,080 at PPP ('07 est based on regression)

Philippines

CAPITAL: Manila   AREA: 300,000 sq km   POPULATION: 87,892,000 ('07)
OFFICIAL LANGUAGE: Filipino   POLITICAL SYSTEM: multiparty republic
HEAD OF STATE AND GOVERNMENT: President Gloria Macapagal-Arroyo (since Jan '01)
RULING PARTY: TEAM (Together Everyone Achieves More) Unity coalition
MAIN IGO MEMBERSHIPS (NON-UN): ASEAN, APEC, CP, NAM
CURRENCY: Philippine peso (end-'08 £1=PP68.3651, US$1=PP47.5500)
GNI PER CAPITA: US$1,620 $3,730 at PPP ('07)

INDONESIA.   Compared to some recent years of high drama, 2008 was a relatively calm one for Indonesia (to the extent that any country could be said to
enjoy calm amidst the global economic crisis).   The government of President
Susilo Bambang Yudhoyono continued to move Indonesia along its—admittedly
occasionally chaotic—democratic road.   This was no mean achievement at a
time when the democratic process among some of Indonesia's neighbours,
notably Thailand and the Philippines, was under threat.   It was all the more
impressive in the world's most populous Muslim country, where real challenges
faced secular democracy.

The year began with the death of former President Suharto, who had ruled
Indonesia from the upheavals of the mid-1960s until his overthrow amidst the
South-East Asian economic collapse of the late 1990s (see Obituary).   In a characteristically Indonesian way, the passing of the old dictator was regarded with
ambivalence.   On the one hand, Suharto had been directly or indirectly responsible for perhaps a million deaths, from the anti-communist bloodletting of the
1960s through to the later conflicts in East Timor, West Papua, and Aceh.   Suharto
and his wider family and cronies had been guilty of financial corruption on a truly
stellar scale.   By the time of his death, he had amassed a personal fortune estimated by some to be in excess of US$35 billion.   Yet even after his downfall (see

AR 1998, pp. 355-57) and the emergence of a new, democratic culture, he had never been brought to trial for his crimes. At the same time, however, many Indonesians, even as they shared in the anger over this impunity, still regarded him as "Pak Harto" (father Suharto) who, whatever his faults, had navigated the nation more or less successfully through four turbulent decades.

The end of the year saw the passing of another key political figure from the pre-democratic era. In December the death was announced of Ali Alatas, who had been Suharto's foreign minister during the last 10 years of his rule. A diligent public servant rather than a committed member of the regime, Alatas was a career diplomat before being appointed to political office. He was held in high respect in diplomatic circles and had been mentioned as a candidate for the post of UN secretary-general in the 1990s.

In November three Islamists convicted of the Bali bombings of 2002 were finally executed, having exhausted all appeals (see AR 2002, p. 340). Indonesia (and the wider world) was on high alert in anticipation of an Islamist backlash. Despite various blood-curdling threats from different sources, however, there was no violent reaction to the executions, which were carried out by firing squad in a west Java prison. Although thousands of mourners turned out for the bombers' funerals, there seemed to be no appetite (or perhaps capacity) for revenge. This in itself was probably a testament to the success of the government's anti-terrorist policies. In recent years the main South-East Asian-wide terrorist movement, Jemaah Islamiah (JI), which had been blamed for most of Indonesia's Islamist violence (including the Bali bombings), had been severely weakened by the loss of key leaders. The government had in place an extremely effective intelligence network and a robust special police unit, known as "Detachment 88", which scored a number of successes during the year.

Even non-violent political Islamism had difficulty asserting itself in a culture which, though strongly religious in many respects, was also resolutely secular in day-to-day life. The inter-faith violence between Muslims and Christians that had marred communal politics in Indonesia in previous years, though far from eradicated, appeared to have declined in 2008.

This did not mean that the long-present spectre of regionalist and inter-ethnic tension in Indonesia was finally being laid to rest, for such an outcome was hardly likely in such a vast, culturally varied, and geographically fractured state. Separatist agitation and its violent suppression continued in 2008 in Indonesian West Papua, for example, and the potential for further violence remained throughout the national archipelago. There was, though, a considerable advance against the legacy of regionalist conflict in respect of East Timor. Relations between the two countries improved considerably during 2008, when Indonesia finally acknowledged its blame for the violence of 1999 from which East Timor had emerged into nationhood. The gesture came with the publication of the report of the joint Indonesia-East Timor Commission for Truth and Friendship, a body established by both countries and whose findings each had undertaken to accept. The Commission's report laid responsibility for the most serious crimes of 1999 at the door of Indonesia and its local clients (see below, East Timor).

Domestic political attention in Indonesia began to focus during the year on the presidential and parliamentary elections scheduled for 2009, as candidates and parties began their campaigns. One of the more interesting developments here was the return of Megawati Sukarnoputri, daughter of Indonesia's founding president, and Suharto's predecessor, Sukarno. Megawati herself had been a (rather lacklustre) head of state between 2001 and 2004. She and her grouping, the Indonesian Democratic Party of Struggle (PDI-P), posed a challenge to President Bambang and his own Democratic Party (a minority group within the governing coalition). One area where the current administration had a likely electoral advantage over Megawati and her party, however, was in the fight against Indonesia's institutionalised corruption. The record of Megawati's term in office was unimpressive in this area, and key members of her PDI-P were themselves accused of accepting bribes. Bambang's government, in contrast, continued to move ahead slowly but steadily in the investigation and prosecution of corrupt officials and politicians, even at the upper levels of the political and financial elite.

EAST TIMOR (TIMOR-LESTE). East Timor's year began with a dramatic expression of the country's fractured political and social structures, when both President José Ramos Horta and Prime Minister Xanana Gusmão were the targets of co-ordinated assassination attempts. On 11 February they were attacked by supporters of Alfredo Reinado, a former military police chief, in what appeared to be a coup attempt. Reinado had been the leading light in the regionalist anti-government violence of the previous year and had remained at large, despite the arrest of many of his key lieutenants (see AR 2007, p. 323). Although Gusmão escaped unhurt when his car was ambushed, Ramos Horta was badly wounded in an attack on his home. Reinado himself was killed by the presidential bodyguard at the scene. Treated initially by Australian military doctors in the capital, Dili, Ramos Horta was later transferred to Australia, where he underwent a series of life-saving operations.

Despite anxieties in both East Timor and more broadly in the Asia-Pacific region, the incident did not trigger a return to the widespread violence and disorder of 2007. In fact, the rapid supportive response of East Timor's key neighbours, Australia and Indonesia, actually improved what had often been fractious diplomatic relationships.

The Australian government quickly reinforced its police and military presence in the country, making clear that its forces were deployed in support of the democratically mandated government of Ramos Horta and Gusmão (who were described by Prime Minister Kevin Rudd in the Australian Parliament as "our friends in Dili"). A few days after the attacks, Rudd visited East Timor, where he had talks with Prime Minister Gusmão. Australian solidarity with East Timor's government was further reinforced at the end of the year when Australia's head of state, Governor General Quentin Bryce, made an official visit to the country.

Indonesia, too, was quick to express its support for the government after the events of February. In September, relations were further improved when the

Indonesian government and armed forces publicly acknowledged their role in the violence of 1999, which had prefigured the independence of East Timor (see AR 1999, pp. 347-48). This followed the publication of the report of the joint Indonesia-East Timor Commission for Truth and Friendship, which blamed Indonesia for serious crimes against the people of East Timor (see above).

Despite this generally benign diplomatic milieu, however, East Timor's intractable social and economic difficulties persisted during 2008. Although a number of the February conspirators gave themselves up, the conditions for further political violence remained. The hopes of the government and its foreign friends were focused on projected income from the vast underwater gas and oil reserves of the Timor Sea. Some, however, feared that sudden unearned wealth of this type could further complicate East Timor's problems, rather than solving them.

PHILIPPINES. In 2008 pressure was maintained against President Gloria Macapagal-Arroyo by a broad coalition of political and civil society representatives. The year also brought the prospect of a settlement of the long-running Muslim insurgency in the south of the country, only to see it squandered. All of this took place against a backdrop of increasingly harsh economic conditions.

In February, thousands of protesters representing opposition political groups, labour organisations, and the Roman Catholic Church, were joined by two former presidents, Corazon Aquino (1986-92) and Joseph Estrada (1998-2001), in calling for Arroyo's resignation. The demonstrations were the latest round in a campaign against a head of state who had become one of the great survivors of Philippine politics, having faced down three impeachment attempts and four coups in her seven years in office to date. Specifically, the 2008 protests grew out of a major bribery scandal from the previous year, in which her close family had been implicated (see AR 2007, p. 325). As long as she was able to rely on the acquiescence—if not the enthusiastic support—of the military high command, however, Arroyo remained immune from the sort of "people's power" that had removed previous Philippine presidents, including Estrada, her immediate predecessor.

In what was, perhaps, a warning to any dissident elements in the military who might be considering a move against her government, nine junior officers involved in a half-hearted putsch in 2003 were sentenced in April to prison terms ranging from six to 40 years (see AR 2003, p. 365). The harshness of the punishments surprised even the state prosecutors involved in the case.

In August the government prepared for the signing of an historic and definitive peace agreement with the Moro Islamic Liberation Front (MILF), which had been a key player in the Muslim insurgency that had affected the southern Philippine islands since the 1970s. The settlement, emerging from seven years of talks brokered by Malaysia, would have created a new political entity in the south, which was to enjoy a large degree of autonomy. As preparations for the ceremony (to be held in Malaysia's capital, Kuala Lumpur) were nearing completion, however, groups representing Christians in the south raised a legal action to halt the deal. Fearing for their own religious and cultural freedoms in a Muslim-controlled autonomous region, they challenged the constitutionality of the plan. The courts initially delayed the peace agreement and the Supreme Court subsequently blocked it as unconstitutional. After a period of growing tension, elements of the MILF launched attacks against government installations, provoking a return to widespread conflict.

The Arroyo administration found itself in a complicated political bind. On the one hand, there was limited national support for the agreement, which many non-Muslims saw as a concession to Islamism. Powerful elements in the military also had their doubts about such an accommodation with the "enemy". Against this, however, there was strong diplomatic pressure for a settlement (not least from Malaysia, a powerful Muslim country, which had been midwife to the deal). The USA, too, was keen to see a settlement concluded with the MILF to remove a distraction from the campaign against more radical groups linked with al-Qaida, such as Abu Sayyaf (AS). Now, the danger was that elements of the MILF might make common cause with AS, which they had previously kept at arm's length. Even if Arroyo had decided to push ahead with the deal, however, she would have faced considerable political and legal difficulties. So wary were her political opponents of her constitutional intentions, particularly in regard to the requirement for her to leave office at the end of her term in 2010, that she would have found it difficult to secure the amendments needed to restore the settlement terms to legality. At the end of 2008, therefore, fighting continued between the MILF and government forces in the south.

The government also remained locked in a parallel, long-running struggle with the leftist guerrillas of the New People's Army (NPA), the military wing of the Communist Party of the Philippines. This was primarily a "dirty war", in that it involved few direct clashes between armed groups, taking instead the form of the abduction and murder of left-wingers and community activists, perceived to be communists by shadowy paramilitary groups close to the Philippines armed forces (see AR 2007, p. 325). By 2008, between 900 and 1,000 people had "disappeared" in this way over the previous seven years. An old fear now returned to haunt the government: a possible alliance between the Muslim insurgents of the south and the NPA.

Aside from political violence, the country suffered a depressing number of civil disasters during the year. The most grave was the loss of about 800 lives in June when an inter-island ferry sank in a typhoon.

Rising food prices (by the beginning of 2008, the cost of rice had doubled in a year) led to government action to support the poorest in the country. By the end of 2008, however, the impact of the global economic crisis threatened much more dramatic social problems.

Norman MacQueen

EAST ASIAN STATES

PEOPLE'S REPUBLIC OF CHINA—HONG KONG—TAIWAN

People's Republic of China

CAPITAL: Beijing   AREA: 9,598,088 sq km   POPULATION: 1,319,983,000 ('07)
OFFICIAL LANGUAGE: Chinese   POLITICAL SYSTEM: one-party republic
HEAD OF STATE: President Hu Jintao (since March '03)
RULING PARTY: Chinese Communist Party (CCP)
PARTY LEADER: CCP General Secretary Hu Jintao (since Nov '02)
CCP POLITBURO STANDING COMMITTEE: Hu Jintao, Wu Bangguo, Wen Jiabao, Jia Qinglin, Li
   Changchun, Xi Jinping, Li Keqiang, He Guoqiang, Zhou Yongkang
CCP CENTRAL COMMITTEE SECRETARIAT: Xi Jinping, Liu Yunshan, Li Yuanchao, He Yong, Ling Jihua,
   Wang Huning
CENTRAL MILITARY COMMISSION: Hu Jintao, chairman (since March '04)
PRIME MINISTER: Wen Jiabao (since March '03)
MAIN IGO MEMBERSHIPS (NON-UN): APEC, SCO, ASEAN-plus 3
CURRENCY: renminbi (RMB) denominated in yuan (end-'08 £1=Y9.8098, US$1=Y6.8230)
GNP PER CAPITA: US$2,360, $5,370 at PPP ('07)

Hong Kong Special Administrative Region

CAPITAL: Victoria   AREA: 1,092 sq km   POPULATION: 6,926,000 ('07)
STATUS: Special Administrative Region of People's Republic of China (since 1 July 1997)
CHIEF EXECUTIVE: Donald Tsang Yam-Kuen (since June '05)
ADMINISTRATIVE SECRETARY: Henry Tang Ying-nian (since July '07)
MAIN IGO MEMBERSHIPS (NON-UN): APEC
CURRENCY: Hong Kong dollar (end-'08 £1=HK$11.1429, US$1=HK$7.7502)
GNP PER CAPITA: US$31,610, $44,050 at PPP ('07)

Taiwan

CAPITAL: Taipei   AREA: 35,980 sq km   POPULATION: 22,828,558 ('07)
OFFICIAL LANGUAGE: Chinese   POLITICAL SYSTEM: multiparty republic
HEAD OF STATE AND GOVERNMENT: President Ma Ying-jeou (KMT) (since May '08)
RULING PARTY: Kuomintang (KMT)
PRIME MINISTER: Liu Chao-shiuan (KMT) (since May '08)
MAIN IGO MEMBERSHIPS (NON-UN): APEC
CURRENCY: Taiwan dollar (end-'08 £1=NT$47.1841, US$1=NT$32.8180)
GNI PER CAPITA: US$15,122 ('07)

THE year 2008 was an eventful one for China. The much anticipated 29th Olympic Games were held in Beijing in August. On 25 September, China successfully launched its first space walk mission. December saw the 30th anniversary of the beginning of the economic reforms that have transformed China. The severe winter weather of February and the massive earthquake in central China in May challenged the government's ability to respond to large-scale natural disasters, while the outbreak of riots in Tibet in May and the scandal of the Sanlu contaminated milk powder reflected the continual political and social tensions within the country. The slowing during the course of the year of China's dramatic economic growth demonstrated how vulnerable the "workshop of the world" was to the global economic crisis. At the end of the year, the govern-

ment for the first time dispatched a naval squadron to the Bay of Aden to provide protection for China's commercial ships from pirate attacks. This was seen
as marking a symbolic turning point in the evolution of China's international
interests and China's capacity to pursue those interests.

The year began with the challenge of a large-scale, devastating natural disaster. Starting on 12 January, a strong cold front brought snow and frost to a dozen
provinces in southern China. This unusual winter storm paralysed airports and
major roads, cut electricity supplies to hundreds of thousands of households for
weeks, and left many hundreds of cities and towns in total isolation. Millions
of people on their way home for the Chinese New Year were stranded at airports,
train stations, and on motorways. The weather necessitated the emergency
evacuation of 1.5 million people. The month-long disaster resulted in a direct
economic loss of Y111 billion (about US$16 billion) and a death toll of 107.
The event put to the test the new nationwide emergency response system, which
the government had tried to put in place after the SARS (severe acute respira-
tory syndrome) outbreak in 2003 (see AR 2003, p. 371). In November 2007, the
government had passed the Emergency Response Law, which provided for the
establishment of a nationally co-ordinated, centrally controlled system, with
various responsibilities at different administrative levels. But the response to
the severe weather crisis showed that the government clearly was not able to
respond adequately to emergencies which developed with such speed and on
such a scale. It took the government two weeks to formulate a state-wide co-
ordinated response. The law stipulated a well-designed, very detailed system of
emergency measures, but the new bureaucracy-centred system proved ineffective. Facing criticism for its slow response, the government in the end resorted
to its traditional Communist Party and military systems to mobilise forces and
organise the huge relief effort.

Lessons were learnt. When a major earthquake struck in central China on 12
May, the government and the country at large were clearly much better prepared. The earthquake was measured at 8.0 on the Richter scale, making it the
strongest since 1950, and was followed by severe aftershocks, heavy rain and
landslides. The disaster killed 69,197 people, left 374,176 injured, 18,222
missing, and forced the relocation of many others. The government sent Prime
Minister Wen Jiabao to the affected areas immediately after the disaster, followed by 146,000 troops, rescue teams from all over the country, and, for the
first time, rescuers from Taiwan, Hong Kong, and many other counties. A special national command centre for co-ordinating the rescue and relief efforts was
established. As usual, the government turned the event into a rallying point for
the country, whereby the people were seen to support and help each other, the
party provided leadership, and the soldiers were heroes. A less publicised
aspect of the disaster was the disproportionate number of children who were
killed by the collapse of their schools in the earthquake, leading grieving parents to accuse the authorities of substandard levels of construction. There were
instances where the authorities harassed parents attempting to draw attention to
the issue.

With a smaller impact on the country at large, but no less politically significant for the government, were two events leading up to the Beijing Olympic
Games in August: the riots in Tibet and the government's swift response, and
the scandal of the Sanlu poisonous milk powder. The riots in Tibet began with
demonstrations in Lhasa, the capital, on 10 March, the anniversary of the failed
Tibetan uprising of 1959. The central government responded with a security
crackdown which included the dispersal of demonstrators and the arrest of
monks. The protests intensified and became more violent, involving the burning and looting of property and co-ordinated attacks upon ethnic Han Chinese.
The unrest also spread to neighbouring territories which had large concentrations of Tibetans. The authorities used soldiers and armed police to seal off
Lhasa and other areas, thereby making it impossible to gauge accurately the
numbers killed in the violence. Despite the news quarantine, the protests drew
enormous international attention, much of it sympathetic to the plight of the
Tibetans, at a time when the Chinese authorities were doing all that they could
to make sure that there were no political problems in the run-up to the Olympic
Games. The authorities accused the Dalai Lama—Tibet's spiritual and tempo-
ral leader and a renowned advocate of non-violent resistance—of masterminding the riots. Nevertheless, anxious to appease international opinion in order not
to jeopardise the Olympics, they agreed to hold a dialogue with personal representatives of the Dalai Lama, although no progress resulted from it.

The unrest in Tibet reflected a tension within the exiled Tibetan community
over strategy and tactics in their relations with China. There was discord between
the moderate group headed by the Dalai Lama himself, and the more radical
group, the Tibetan Youth Association. It also illustrated the degree to which the
Chinese authorities did not want the Tibetan issue to damage their relations with
Western countries, and, more specifically, threaten their years of effort in preparing for the Olympic Games.

Another issue presented the government with a serious challenge at both central and local levels. The story arose from the system of dairy production in
China. Milk companies obtained their raw milk from farmers through interme-
diate agents. To raise the quantity and grade (measured by protein levels) of raw
milk, and therefore profit, agents would add water as well as a chemical additive,
melamine, which helped to show a higher level of protein in milk when tested.
Consumption of a large mount of melamine, particularly by young babies, however, could cause kidney ailments and eventually kidney failure and death. In
March 2008, the news first broke of 10 cases of baby kidney failure at a hospital
in Nanjin. Over the next few months, there was an increasing number of cases
of baby kidney ailments and growing evidence of the link between the illness and
the infant formula (milk powder) which these babies had consumed. The milk
powder was produced by Sanlu, one of the country's largest brands, and contained melamine. The scandal led to the deaths of six babies, and a total of
290,000 infants had been adversely affected by the end of November. On 11
September, Sanlu recalled all the contaminated products. The state council (cabinet) formed a special committee to investigate the scandal, which led in Sep-

tember to the removal of four senior government officials and of the mayor of the city where Sanlu Corporation was located; plus the arrest of 19 people, including the senior executives of the company, and two milk powder suppliers. On 31 December, the company executives and the milk powder suppliers were put on trial, which ended in January 2009 with sentences of life imprisonment for the chairwoman of the board of directors of Sanlu, along with other Sanlu executives, and death sentences for the two milk powder suppliers.

The Sanlu scandal reflected multiple problems in China, concerning relations between government and business, central-local government relations, industrial safety and standards, and the public health system. It took seven months for the company to take action from the time that the problem first surfaced in March to the nationwide product recall in September. It was reported that the local government had received reports of the milk powder problem from the company in early August, but it did not pass these on to the central government for fear of distracting from the Olympic Games which were about to begin. Sanlu, which had discovered a possible link between its infant formula and the kidney ailments in children in April, tried to keep the information confined to its top executives and publicly denied such knowledge until 12 September. In the meantime, thousands of babies continued to be affected by the contaminated milk powder and the death toll was rising. When the families of the affected children demanded testing of the suspect infant formula, the certificates issued by the local government still showed that the products met quality standards. In fact, over the years, Sanlu was one of those companies whose products were exempted by the state from standard quality tests. In the nationwide tests conducted by the government in September, the products of 22 dairy companies were found to be contaminated with unnaturally high levels of melamine.

On 8 August, after seven years of preparations, the 29th Olympic Games opened in Beijing with an elaborate televised ceremony which was viewed by billions of people inside and outside China. The Games were seen in China as a major political event, symbolising the rise of China as a modern, strong, and powerful country after a hundred years of economic backwardness, political chaos, and international humiliation. Comparisons were drawn with the Olympic Games in Tokyo in 1966, and the Seoul Games of 1988, which represented significant points in the modern histories of Japan and South Korea.

By many standards, the Beijing Olympics were a huge success. They attracted the largest number of participants and the largest number of participating countries in Olympic history. The years of preparation meant that China presented a new, dynamic, modern and cosmopolitan Beijing to the world. In terms of sporting success, China for the first time surpassed the USA in the number of gold medals won. More importantly, the success of the Beijing Olympics was seen in China as a recognition by the international community of China's ability to play an important international role and as an opportunity for the world to understand China. The success of the Olympics gave the Chinese people the confidence and respect they needed amid the profound change that had taken place in China and in China's global position over the previous 30 years. There was however an alternative Olympic narrative, which lay behind the official spectacle. It was visible in the popular protests that occurred in almost every country through which the Chinese paraded the Olympic torch in its round-the-world journey in April, prior to the opening of the Games. What had been planned as a triumph descended into a public relations disaster as the repeated protests focused global media attention on China's poor human rights record in general and its policy towards Tibet in particular. This provoked reciprocal expressions of anger in China towards countries where such protests occurred. Similarly the counterpoint to the technical brilliance of the staging of the Olympics was the clampdown on dissent and the heavy-handed beautification measures which preceded the Games, and the intrusive security, the control of journalists, and the alarming air pollution levels which accompanied them. These elements, too, were emblematic of the development of modern China.

Another major event of the year was the 30th anniversary of China's economic reforms. At the Third Plenary Session of the Chinese Communist Party (CCP) on 18 December, 1978, the then Chinese leader, Deng Xiaoping, made a speech, in which he called on party members to "Open your mind, be truthful, and let us unite and move forward." China in 1978 had just emerged from Mao's radical economic, social, and political programme of the first 20 years of the People's Republic of China, followed by the 10 chaotic years of the Cultural Revolution. Deng's new line moved China away from ideological obsession and focused it on what worked, in order to bring China out of economic poverty and social backwardness. It may not have been Deng's original intention, but the 30 years since his speech had seen a socialist country on the brink of economic collapse transformed into a state capitalist entity with much improved living conditions, a dynamic economy with record rates of growth, and a much stronger position in the international system. Throughout 2008 a series of events celebrated the 30 years of reform and transformation. On 18 December, the CCP staged a major ceremony to mark the anniversary of Deng's speech. At the gathering, CCP Secretary General Hu Jintao reiterated Deng's line: let us not distract ourselves, but continue to focus on reform.

There was much for the Communist Party to celebrate. The 30 years of change had worked out a model of post-socialist reform and transformation which was radically different from that which had occurred in Eastern Europe and the Soviet Union. China's gradual, piecemeal change and its dual-track reform, which allowed the old system to continue while promoting a new one alongside it, effectively reduced the severity of resistance from the old system; gave greater space for new things to survive, adjust, and consolidate; and moderated the impact of the profound economic and social change on society and individuals. Nevertheless, the reform had its own problems. The dominance of the ideal and principles of a free market economy over the 30 years had changed the country's social and economic system, tilting it toward a principally market driven model. Public interest and the government's role in providing social welfare and security to its citizens seemed buried in the relentless pursuit of efficiency, profit, and rapid growth. Moreover, the gradual and dual track nature of the reform left a great level of uncertainty in the institutional environment for further economic development.

Health service reform was a case in point. Under the old socialist system, all healthcare was provided free of charge to citizens. The call for reform to the health sector came in the 1990s, driven primarily by the US model of health services. There was a government-led campaign for the transformation of the public health service from state provision to market provision, funded through insurance on the part of patients and financial self-sufficiency on the part of hospitals. This model led to rocketing medical costs and low quality of medical services. The failure of health service reform led the government to rethink its overall direction and recognise the state's role in providing and managing healthcare as a public service. In September, the state council introduced its "Document on Further Reform of Medical and Health Systems" for public comment, which was formally approved in January, 2009. Under the new plan, the government would invest Y850 billion over three years to establish a primary care system, develop state hospitals as public service rather than commercial operations, and reform the system of medicine manufacture and supply.

Another example was the reform of land rights. Under the old socialist system, all land in China was owned by the state. Because of the gradual and dual track nature of reform, the past 30 years had seen an ambiguous property rights environment develop. Farmers, for example, did not own their land, but had the contract rights to "use" it. The Property Rights Law of 2007, while it formally restored the legal status of private property, still left the land rights issue unresolved. The uncertainty surrounding farmers' legal rights over the land they managed clearly compromised the development of modern economic relations in rural areas. Consequently the gap between urban and rural areas continued to widen. To energise rural development under the existing institutional environment, the Communist Party in October issued a major policy directive to allow the formal transfer of contract land rights, hoping that this would promote the modernisation of the rural economy. Indeed, transfers of farmers' contract land rights had been going on informally for years. The government hoped to give state backing for this new development without the trouble of formulating a constitutional change over land rights. But the government was likely to face a great challenge in this area in the years ahead.

Towards the end of the year, another development attracted considerable attention. On 26 December, China dispatched two of its most advanced navy destroyers and a supply ship to the Gulf of Aden off the coast of Somalia to provide protection from pirate attacks for Chinese cargo ships. This was the first time that China had sent a naval squadron outside its territorial waters on a potential combat mission, and was seen by many as a landmark in the development of Chinese military capacity. The destroyers were two of the four most advanced ships in China's navy, sent on a patrol that was unlikely to require such advanced resources. It was, perhaps, a demonstration by China of how it defined and defended its national interests.

That 2008 was an eventful year was seen nowhere more clearly than in the development of the Chinese economy. At the end of 2007, there was a general consensus that the economy was overheating, with a danger of inflation and fears that the economic bubble would burst. China's GDP growth in 2007 was 11.4 per cent, posting growth above 10 per cent for the fifth consecutive year, with total GDP of Y24,662 billion, inflation of 4.8 per cent, retail sales up 7.6 per cent (the highest in 11 years), social consumption up 16.8 per cent, fixed capital investment up 24.8 per cent, and imports and exports up 23.5 per cent. The renminbi was under great pressure to appreciate. All the signs of a bubble economy were there, as had been seen in Japan in the 1990s. The government had been applying macro control policies for two years: in 2007 alone, the government raised the deposit-reserve ratio 10 times and the interest rate 6 times, but these measures clearly had little effect. At the end of 2007, the government announced the twin aims of its economic policy for 2008: to prevent economic growth from overheating, and to prevent price rises leading to inflation. However, the first half of 2008 saw various new forces come into play, which significantly changed the direction of the economy, and consequently of government economic policy in the middle of the year.

Several factors had a suppressing impact on the Chinese economy in 2008. The first was the global financial crisis, originating in the USA in 2007. In 2008, this financial crisis appeared increasingly to be a real economic crisis. The global crisis substantially reduced demand for Chinese exports, on which the Chinese economy was heavily dependent. This in turn slowed the growth of Chinese manufacturing. Industrial growth was up 12.9 per cent in 2008, 5.6 per cent less than in 2007. Retail sales were down 19.7 per cent. GDP growth in 2008 was 9 per cent, down from 11.4 per cent in 2007. By the end of the year, 20,000,000 migrant workers from rural areas had lost their jobs and returned to their farms. The second factor was the appreciation of the renminbi. The Chinese currency rose from Y8.1 to the US dollar at the start of the year to 6.84 at its end. The rising value of the Chinese currency led to higher prices for Chinese products in international markets. This further suppressed exports and manufacturing in China. Another important, though controversial, factor was the coming into effect of the new Employment Contract Law on 1 January 2008. This law stipulated higher standards for working conditions, which many believed ultimately added to the costs of production, although others argued that it was an essential step in China's economic and social development.

By the summer, it was clear that the major challenge for the Chinese economy was no longer the risk of inflation and overheating, but rather a possible recession. The government adjusted its economic policy to "maintain steady growth and prevent a fast rise of prices", and adopted a series of financial and monetary policies to halt the slowdown in the economy. On 5 November, the government announced that it would put together a two-year stimulus package amounting to Y4,000 billion to increase domestic demand. By December, when the central government held its annual economic decision-making conference, the government set one single goal for its economic policy in 2009: to "maintain steady economic growth", that is, in plain language, to keep GDP growth rate above 8 per cent.

Within the span of a single year, China's economic development went through some unexpected turns: from tight financial and monetary policy to battle overheating and inflation at the beginning of the year to a series of stimulus measures to re-energise the economy in the latter part of the year. To some, this was not completely unexpected. Firstly, it reflected the dependence of the Chinese economy on its export markets, and thus its vulnerability to the functioning of the international economic system. It also showed the challenges facing China as a newly industrialising economy.

Many inside and outside China expected 2008 to be a year of great challenges. At the end of the year, there was a general feeling that things were better than expected. The Olympic Games had taken place without major troubles. The Chinese economy had weathered the global financial crisis relatively well so far. The Chinese had gained confidence and a sense of achievement after 30 years of remarkable economic reform and development. Many believed that if China survived 2008, nothing could prevent it becoming once again a strong and wealthy country. Amid this over-confident feeling, however, were some unvoiced concerns about 2009, when China would face major hurdles in tackling essential economic, political, and social reforms.

TAIWAN. One source of the feeling that 2008 had been better than expected for China arose from Taiwan. Many predicted that the Olympic Games would present Taiwan with an opportunity to push its independence agenda, since China's government, wary of possible negative responses from the West during the Olympics, would find it difficult to respond. However, developments in Taiwan in 2008 pointed history in a different direction. The year started with a landslide victory for the opposition Kuomintang (KMT, the Nationalist Party), in the election on 12 January to the Legislative Yuan (unicameral legislature). The KMT and its Pan-Blue coalition won 85 of the total 113 seats. The ruling Democratic Progressive Party (DPP) won only 27 seats. These were the first elections to be held under a new electoral system, according to which 73 legislators were elected from single-member districts and 34 were chosen from party lists according to proportional representation by a separate vote. There were also six seats reserved for aboriginal people in two three-member aboriginal districts. This new electoral system may have been one of the factors in the results, which saw no small parties win any seats. The DPP-led democratic transfer of power in 2000 had ended the KMT's 50 year reign in Taiwan. The KMT's return to power in 2008 perhaps represented a healthy development in the maturing democratic system in Taiwan, but had come about sooner than many expected.

Faced with this major setback, the DPP continued to push its agenda, relying on the same political strategy and tactics that had proved effective in the past. In the presidential elections of 22 March, outgoing President Chen Shui-bian and his DPP positioned themselves as campaigning for Taiwan's sovereignty and international status, and forced a referendum on seeking UN membership under the name of "Taiwan". The KMT, meanwhile, proposed a referendum asking whether an application to rejoin the UN should be made under the name "Republic of China" (Taiwan's formal title). In the presidential election, the KMT's candidate, Ma Ying-jeou, won 58.45 per cent of the vote; Frank Hsieh, the DPP candidate, won 41.55 per cent. Ma Ying-jeou had long been a favourite political star, and the DPP's candidate was much less energetic and appealing. But the public was clearly unhappy with the DDP's performance of the past eight years, and rejected its increasingly radical political line. Neither referendum achieved the required 50-per cent turnout of eligible voters and so both were declared void.

The first challenge facing the new Ma administration was the global financial crisis, which severely affected Taiwan's economy. The economy, disrupted by internal politics in the eight years since 2000, was already weak and clearly lacked strategic direction, long-term investment, and government vision and support. Those years were a lost decade, in which Taiwan could have readjusted and upgraded its economy, after decades of rapid, successful industrialisation and economic growth. It was also a decade when Taiwan was increasingly marginalised in the region because of China's growing influence. The global financial crisis only made the situation worse. The Ma administration's wobbles in the first few months of 2008 delayed an effective government response to the impending financial crisis. In September, the government put forward a series of rescue and stimulus packages, including a long-term economic strategy that promoted Taiwan as an operational centre of the world and the Asia-Pacific region; measures to support important industries and assist in their modernisation; a NT$58.3 billion programme to expand domestic demand, and a NT$82.9 billion-scheme of purchase coupons (worth NT$3,600 for each resident); a NT$585 billion programme for economic revitalisation; and short-term financial and monetary policies to assist firms to weather the economic crisis.

President Ma put his hopes for a revitalised economy sustainable over the long term on Taiwan's improving relations with China. After Ma assumed the presidency on 20 May, the relations between China and Taiwan significantly improved. Senior officials exchanged visits. In July, holiday charter fights were extended to weekend charter flights. In December, direct flights (without a stopover in Hong Kong) were in operation as part of the package of "three directs": direct flights, direct shipping, and direct postal services across the straits. This was a landmark development in the cross-straits relationship, a policy long pursued by the KMT. The warming of relations led China's President Hu Jintao to declare on 31 December that China was ready to discuss Taiwan's international status, military confidence-building measures, and Taiwan's role in regional economic co-operation, all issues that had long been thorny points in the relationship.

Along with these developments in the cross-straits relations was the rapid downfall of the former president, Chen Shui-bian. While Chen was still president, he and his wife were indicted on corruption charges. Chen had been a member of the legal defence group for the democratic activists charged by the KMT government in the 1980s. The rise of the DPP since then had brought these former lawyers to political prominence. Soon after he stepped down as president on 20 May, Chen went immediately from lawyer to defendant. On 15 August, Chen appeared on television and admitted that he had failed to declare huge amounts of campaign funds and had sent the money overseas. He announced his resignation from the DPP. In the next few months, the special investigation team discovered that the Chen family had sent billions of Taiwanese dollars to their numerous secret accounts overseas. The scandal involved almost every member of Chen's family and a long list of senior government officials working for Chen and helping the Chen family to launder the money. On 11 November, Chen was taken into custody. On 12 December, the Procurator's Office formally indicted Chen and 14 other co-defendants, including his wife.

HONG KONG.   Along with China and Taiwan, Hong Kong was hit hard by the global financial crisis. The first half of 2008 appeared to be rosy for Hong Kong. With huge tax revenues from 2007, the government had a record HK$124 billion fiscal surplus for the year. The stock market's Hang Seng Index was at a record high. The government spent HK$40 billion on tax cuts early in the year, further adding to the continual expansion of the economy. In the mid-year, those affected by rocketing prices went onto the streets with demands for pay rises. By September, the impact of the global financial crisis started to be felt. Because of the nature of Kong Hong's economy, dominated by the service sector, and its role as a bridge between manufacturing in China and Taiwan and exports to international markets, the financial crisis hit Hong Kong directly and its impact was severe.

In September, Lehman Brothers investment bank in New York filed the largest bankruptcy in US history. In Hong Kong, 40,000 investors holding Lehman's mini-bonds immediately lost their one billion dollars of investment. For some of these small and medium investors, the Lehman bankruptcy cost their life savings. Social unrest soon spread. The investors went onto the streets, charging that the government had failed to protect them and demanding compensation. Subsequently, there were drastic movements on the HK stock market, driven primarily by the fluctuations of the international market. On 27 October, the Hang Seng Index dropped 12.7 per cent in a single day but rebounded by 14.35 per cent the following day. The Hang Seng started the year at 27,812 points but ended at 14,387, with a total loss of 13,425 points or 48.27 per cent. This was a 54.53 per cent fall from its historic high of 31,638 points on 30 October, 2007.

Like the governments of China and Taiwan, the Hong Kong government took steps to respond to the economic crisis with a mixture of long-term measures, to promote closer integration with the mainland's economy, and emergent programmes for crisis relief. In July, the Hong Kong government made more service areas eligible for benefits under the Mainland-Hong Kong closer economic partnership arrangement (CEPA) and further pushed the integration of Hong Kong with the Pearl River Delta region of southern China. In December, the chief executive (the head of the Hong Kong government) announced a plan to provide HK$100 billion in loan credits for businesses and 60,000 job opportunities in

oomy portents (22 January): Grim financial headlines play across a ticker in Times quare, New York, at the start of what will prove to be a calamitous year for the world onomy. (REUTERS/Jeff Zelevansky).

Capture of Karadzic (22 July): Fatima Mujic, who lost her husband and other relatives in the 1995 Srebrenica massacre, watches from a memorial room in Tuzla, Bosnia & Herzegovina, as the television news broadcasts details of Bosnian Serb wartime president Radovan Karadzic's arrest near Belgrade. (REUTERS/Nikola Solic).

Changing of the guard (14 April): A pregnant Carme Chacón, Spain's first female defence minister, reviews an honour guard with outgoing defence minister José Antonio Alonso at the defence ministry in Madrid. (REUTERS/Susana Vera).

residential celebration (2 March): Addressing the crowd at a concert in Moscow on election day, Russia's outgoing President Vladimir Putin (left) congratulates First Deputy Prime Minister Dmitry Medvedev, whose victory was a foregone conclusion. (REUTERS/RIA Novosti/Kremlin).

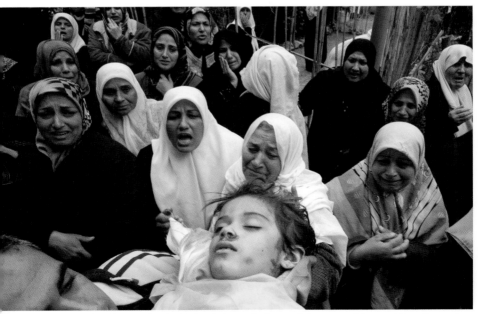

rieving in Gaza (30 December): Palestinian relatives of 4-year-old Lama Hamdan, who as killed together with her sister in an Israeli air raid, mourn during her funeral in the wn of Beit Hanoun in the northern Gaza Strip. (REUTERS/Mohammed Salem).

Olympic protests (7 April): Pro-Tibet demonstrators stage an anti-China protest at the Trocadero ahead of the Paris leg of the Olympic torch relay. (REUTERS/Thomas Samson)

Olympic pageantry (8 August): The Olympic Flame is lit during the opening ceremony of the Beijing 2008 Olympic Games at the National Stadium (also known as the Bird's Nest). (REUTERS/Gary Hershorn).

Surviving catastrophe (7 May): Survivors are seen near the ruins of their home, which was destroyed by Cyclone Nargis, near the town of Kyaiklat, south-west of Rangoon, Burma. (REUTERS/Stringer).

Mourning the dead (27 May): A mother mourns her dead son during a memorial service at the ruins of Juyuan Middle School in Dujiangyan, in China's Sichuan province, which was hit by a severe earthquake on 12 May. (REUTERS/Stringer).

epping down (26 July): Cuba's President Raul Castro addresses a rally at the former
ncada military barracks in Santiago de Cuba, from beneath a giant poster of his broth-
, retired Cuban leader Fidel Castro. (REUTERS/Claudia Daut).

Stepping up (4 November): US President-elect Barack Obama leads his family onstage during his election night victory celebration in Chicago; he holds his daughter Sasha's hand, as Malia (in red) and Michelle Obama follow. (REUTERS/Jason Reed).

2009. Mainland China also stepped in with a 14-point package to assist Hong Kong to respond to the financial crisis.

On the political front, in December 2007, the National People's Congress in Beijing issued an interpretation of the Basic Law (the de facto constitution of Hong Kong), and stipulated that the direct election by universal suffrage of the chief executive (the head of the Hong Kong government) would not take place until 2017, and that of the Legislative Council (LegCo) not until 2020. This subdued the heated debate among various political forces within Hong Kong. The overall political balance did not change much after the LegCo elections in September 2008. Of the total 60 seats—of which 30 were elected from five geographical districts and 30 elected from functional groups—the pro-Beijing coalition (the Democratic Alliance for the Betterment and Progress of Hong Kong, the Liberal Party, and others) won 35, two seats more than at the last election, in 2005, while the opposition camp (the Democratic Party, the Civic Party, the League of Social Democrats, and others) won 23, two seats fewer.

The year 2008 was also particularly notable for the development of the "principal official accountability system". This system was introduced in 2002 to restructure the relationships among senior government officials (ministerial level), and between them and the chief executive. Under the British colonial government, all government officials were civil servants and politically neutral. Under the new system, they were appointed by and accountable to the chief executive, providing a greater level of transparency and accountability. However, ministers under the new system were less independent and more responsive to public opinions and political pressure. A series of events in 2008 put this system in the spotlight: from the charge that the government had failed to protect investors in the Lehman Brothers case to the controversy over the government's decision not to send charter flights to Thailand to rescue stranded Hong Kong travellers (see p. 335); from the government's proposal to impose assets criteria for pension rises to the government's announcement of increased taxi fees. The process of appointing senior government officials in May also caused great controversy. Most of these cases ended with apologies by the government, withdrawal of policy proposals, or modifications of these policies. Clearly these senior government officials were still learning how to function as political appointees rather than civil servants.

Xiaoming Huang

JAPAN

CAPITAL: Tokyo   AREA: 377,910 sq km   POPULATION: 127,771,000 ('07)
OFFICIAL LANGUAGE: Japanese   POLITICAL SYSTEM: multiparty monarchy
HEAD OF STATE: Emperor Tsugu no Miya Akihito (since Jan '89)
RULING PARTIES: Liberal Democratic Party (LDP) in coalition with the New Komeito party;
    Democratic Party of Japan (DPJ) controls upper house
HEAD OF GOVERNMENT: Prime Minister Taro Aso (since Sept '08)
MAIN IGO MEMBERSHIPS (NON-UN): APEC, CP, OECD, G-8
CURRENCY: yen (end-'08 £1=Y130.332, US$1=Y90.6500)
GNI PER CAPITA: US$37,670, $34,600 at PPP ('07)

It was a bad year for the Liberal Democratic Party (LDP), which had ruled Japan almost continuously since the party's creation in 1955, most recently in coalition with the small New Komeito party. The LDP had been returned to office in elections to the House of Representatives (the lower chamber of the Diet, the legislature) in 2005 but in the elections to the House of Councillors (the upper chamber) in 2007 it was defeated. With the opposition, led by the Democratic Party of Japan (DPJ), in control of the upper house, the LDP government struggled to secure approval for its legislative programme. In the face of this impediment, the government had only a limited range of options. It could call an early election (constitutionally the lower house's term was due to end in September 2009), but with the LDP trailing consistently in the opinion polls such an option never seemed likely. Alternatively, the government could attempt to negotiate with the DPJ and its maverick leader, Ichiro Ozawa, in order to obtain co-operation over specific issues, a tactic which was deployed throughout the course of the year with varying degrees of success. The final option was to resolve the impasse by resorting to the provisions of the Japanese constitution, which allowed the more powerful lower house to force through legislation despite the objections of the upper chamber. Within the consensual political landscape of Japanese politics this option had rarely been used, but it was resorted to by the LDP during 2008 as a means of saving its political programme from stalemate.

The year began with Yasuo Fukuda—a pragmatist and a moderate, who had been elected president of the LDP (thereby also becoming prime minister) in September 2007 following the resignation of Shinzo Abe—facing a major political crisis. This centred upon the role of the Maritime Self Defence Force (SDF)—the Japanese navy—in refuelling and supplying vessels in the Indian Ocean, which were engaged in the war in Afghanistan. Abe's resignation had been due largely to his inability to secure opposition approval for an extension of the temporary mandate for this operation, a mandate which took the form of a piece of anti-terrorism legislation due to expire in November 2007. Upon taking office, Fukuda had gained approval in the lower chamber for an extension but was unsuccessful in his attempts to persuade the upper chamber to pass the measure (see AR 2008, pp. 340-41). With the legislation having expired, and facing strong US pressure to resume the refuelling mission, Fukuda acted decisively to break the deadlock. On 11 January, the LDP used its two-thirds majority in the lower house to pass the anti-terrorism special measures legislation, which amounted to renewal of the mandate for one year, despite the upper chamber's objections. The move provoked some consternation as it was the first occasion that such powers had been exercised since 1951.

A related matter arose over the US-led coalition's operations in Iraq. The Nagoya High Court ruled that the actions of Japan's Air SDF in airlifting multinational troops from Kuwait to Baghdad were illegal, being in violation of Japan's pacifist constitution. The government did not accept this ruling, arguing that Baghdad International Airport was not in a combat zone and no question of violating the constitution arose. These forces were eventually withdrawn in October after completing a successful mission.

Notwithstanding the resolution of the Indian Ocean refuelling dispute, the political impasse in the legislature continued. In March there was a bitter and protracted clash between the government and the opposition over the choice of a replacement for the governor of the Bank of Japan (BoJ, the central bank), whose term of office expired on 19 March. The candidate proposed by the LDP was turned down by the upper house and the position was left vacant. It was not until early April that the government managed to achieve consensus with the opposition and appointed the deputy governor, Masaaki Shirakawa, who had been holding the position ad interim. It was seen as an embarrassing climb down by Fukuda and contributed to a growing public perception of weakness.

Another source of conflict was the DPJ's unwillingness to countenance any extension of a long-term (although technically temporary) tax on petrol. The DPJ opposed the tax, which was earmarked to pay for road improvement schemes, on the grounds that it benefited the powerful construction lobby and was an example of the sort of "pork barrel" politics endemic within the Japanese political system. The DPJ's opposition forced the tax to lapse at the beginning of April, despite government claims that it was essential to the national finances. The popularity of the DPJ's stance was demonstrated at a by-election in Yamaguchi prefecture, which was dominated by the issue and which resulted on 27 April in a crushing defeat for the LDP. The petrol tax was eventually restored as Fukuda resorted to further use of the LDP's majority in the lower chamber to force through legislation in the face of upper house objections, but his action suggested a sense of desperation rather than one of strength. The opinion polls showed that the prime minister's support among the electorate was plummeting, as he seemed unable to select the correct issues upon which to fight and appeared unwilling to choose between the alternative courses of facing down the opposition or seeking consensus with it.

Much of the middle of the year was taken up with preparations for the G-8 meeting of industrialised countries, which Japan was to host in July. Fukuda hoped that the occasion would enable him to adopt the mantle of an international statesman and that this might staunch the haemorrhaging of his domestic support. He tried to meet a number of world leaders before the summit and toured the UK, Germany, and Italy for preliminary talks. He was energetic in preparing the ground for the topics that would dominate the summit, notably food, oil, and climate change. Similar meetings for specialised ministers from the G-8 were also held in various Japanese cities. At the summit itself, which met at the Lake Toya resort, Hokkaido, the representatives—including observers from China and India—discussed rising world energy and food prices and assistance for developing countries. But the question of climate change dominated discussions. It was agreed to aim at achieving at least a 50 per cent reduction in greenhouse gas emissions on a global basis by 2050. No short-term targets were set, however, and many disagreements with developing countries over emissions were left unresolved.

Although Fukuda had ably conducted the summit, he soon came under renewed domestic attack. The opposition-dominated upper house passed a motion of no-confidence in him in June, while the lower house, with its LDP majority, countered with a vote of confidence. Fukuda desperately sought to shore up his unpopular government by reshuffling his cabinet on 1 August, bringing in old-stagers who he hoped would enhance its reputation. The changes were extensive and meant that for the first time Fukuda had a cabinet chosen by him rather than merely inherited from his predecessor. But it was not enough to save him, for by now the global financial crisis was beginning to bite hard. Rising food and commodity prices were exacerbated by falling exports, as demand for Japanese products slackened. The Japanese economy, which had seen six years of unbroken growth, was now contracting. Notwithstanding his promise to enact an economic stimulus package, the prime minister was unable to shake off the aura of failure, which surrounded his administration. Bowing to the inevitable, on 1 September Fukuda announced his resignation. He cited his frustration over the political deadlock in the Diet, but also recognised that it was in the LDP's interests to choose a new leader if the party was to have any chance of retaining power at the forthcoming general election.

Even as the country waited to see who would be chosen as the new LDP leader and prime minister, the outgoing Fukuda administration—maintaining its accident prone reputation until the end—suffered a further ministerial casualty. Seiichi Ota, the minister for agriculture, forestry and fisheries, resigned on 19 September in connection with a scandal involving the sale of contaminated rice for human consumption. The rice, imported from China and elsewhere, had been found to be contaminated by pesticides and mould and had been consigned for use in industrial production. Nevertheless, some 400 tonnes of it had entered the food chain after being sold to food manufacturing companies by the Osaka-based Mikasa Foods company. Allegations that numerous civil servants within the department of agriculture had received corporate hospitality from Mikasa Foods led to a huge corruption investigation. Ota, who had only been appointed to the cabinet in the August reshuffle, found himself in an untenable position after he fuelled public outrage over the scandal by suggesting that the levels of contamination were not sufficient to cause fatalities and, therefore, there was no need to make "too much of a fuss over it".

Fukuda's resignation sparked perhaps the most open LDP leadership contest ever staged. The closely fought battle between five candidates ended on 22 September with the victory of Taro Aso, who was elected party president with 351 out of 525 votes. Two days later he was formally elected as prime minister, the country's fourth in only three years. In forming his new cabinet, he turned his back on ministers who had been associated with structural reform and favoured those who were his close allies and veteran politicians. It was widely predicted that Aso, who came from a prominent, conservative, Catholic family and who had served as a hawkish foreign minister under Fukuda's two predecessors, would take the LDP further to the right. However, hopes that the new government would prove less accident prone than the last were quickly diminished when, only four days after the appointment of the cabinet, the minister for land, transport, infrastructure and tourism, Nariaki Nakayama, resigned after making a number of verbal gaffes.

A further source of controversial views emerged with an essay written by General Toshio Tamogami, chief of staff of the Air SDF. He had written it for a public essay contest and won first prize. His theme was that Japan had not been an "aggressive nation" in the 1930s and 1940s and that history teaching was biased against Japan's "glorious history". For expressing these views, he was dismissed on 31 October. Journalists pursued the case and discovered that in a previous post as principal of the Joint Staff Defence College in 2002-04 he had included in the curriculum lectures by revisionist historians. Asked to defend his position before a committee of the upper house and at press conferences, Tamogami reiterated his views and said that they were widely held by politicians and SDF personnel. Moreover, he believed that the SDF should not be restricted in its role in international anti-terrorism campaigns.

Notwithstanding such distractions, Aso's new administration attempted to address the intensifying global financial crisis. Japan's export-driven economy was teetering on the brink of recession as markets in North America, China, and Europe contracted as a consequence of the crisis. Japanese exports were also hit by the strong rise in the value of the yen. With interest rates already at 0.5 per cent there was little scope for the use of monetary policy to restore business and consumer confidence. Instead the new government pursued a series of packages designed to stimulate domestic demand. A Y1,810 billion supplementary budget, associated with the stimulus package announced in August by Fukuda, was approved by the Diet in October, despite opposition grumbles that it contained too many "pet projects". The severity of the unfolding crisis, however, made it apparent that the measures were wholly inadequate in scale as the conflagration, which had begun in the USA, spread to Japan's financial markets. During October share prices plummeted (the Osaka and Tokyo stock markets were briefly forced to suspend trading at one point), and Yamato—a life insurance company, which had traded for almost a century—collapsed with debts of Y269 billion. Aso described the turmoil as "frankly beyond our imagination". At the end of the month he announced a new economic stimulus package, estimated to be worth some Y26,900 billion, and including Y5,000 billion in fresh state expenditure and some Y21,000 billion in loan guarantees for small- and medium-sized businesses. (The Bank of Japan also cut interest rates to 0.3 per cent.) Aso announced further stimulus measures in December, which overlapped with those already proposed, and which also sought to address the liquidity crisis facing the country's banks and financial institutions. The problem for the prime minister was that the second supplementary budget necessary for the financing of these stimulus measures remained, like the regular 2009 budget, unapproved by the legislature, both victims of the political deadlock within the Diet.

At the end of the year the political and economic scene looked bleak for the government. It had been confirmed in November that Japan was officially in a recession, its first in seven years, as the economy contracted for the second consecutive quarter in the period June-September. Although the Japanese financial sector, cleansed of many of its bad debts by the crisis of the 1990s, suffered less spectacularly than those of many countries (most notably, the USA), the underlying indicators were not good. Capital spending and industrial production were falling, domestic demand was sluggish, and in November it had been revealed that Japan had posted a trade deficit in the previous month of Y63.9 billion. These statistics raised fears that the country could be returning to the sort of deflation which had characterised the "lost decade" of the 1990s and the early part of the 21st century. Politically, the ratings of the Aso administration in the opinion polls had sunk to an all-time low and it was blamed for having responded slowly to the financial crisis. Despite the prime minister's proposed economic stimulus packages, in reality Aso's legislative programme remained becalmed in the Diet. The opposition indicated that it would unblock the legislative process if the government would agree to an early election. Aso, aware of the LDP's desperate position in the polls, appeared intent upon clinging to office. The result was that 2009 promised to be a highly significant year, containing the real possibility that the LDP would be swept from office and that the Japanese political landscape would be fundamentally reshaped.

In the sphere of foreign relations, Japan's relationship with its giant neighbour, China, was, as always, a subject of intense scrutiny. The year began badly as a number of Japanese fell ill from eating gyoza dumplings imported from China, which had allegedly been laced with a pesticide. The incident fuelled anti-Chinese feeling and fanned fears among the Japanese public over the adequacy of China's food safety standards. There were also some voluble anti-Chinese protests, particularly over the issue of Tibet, when, in the course of its worldwide journey, the Olympic torch came to Japan in April.

In contrast, the five-day visit to Japan in May of President Hu Jintao, the first by a Chinese head of state for 10 years, generated great cordiality. Widespread publicity was given to his playing table tennis, his speech to students at Waseda University, and goodwill gestures like the loan of a panda for Ueno Zoo to replace the one that had recently died. With China constituting Japan's major trading partner, both sides wanted to move on from years of political distrust. The talks attempted to make practical progress over current disagreements, notably the need to solve the issue of oil exploration rights in the East China Sea, associated with the Senkaku islands where both countries claimed to have exclusive economic zones. Japan and China later agreed that they would jointly develop the gas fields in this disputed area.

This mutual confidence was tested a few days after Hu's return by the Sichuan earthquake (see p. 348). At the Chinese president's wish, Japan was the first country to be asked for emergency aid. Japan despatched a search and rescue team and a medical team, and later helped with relief supplies, including tents and blankets. Japanese soldiers delivered aid on Chinese soil, the first time they had appeared there since 1945. When, however, it was proposed that further deliveries be carried by military aircraft, serious protests were made by Chinese nationalists, mainly through the Internet, and the idea was dropped on the grounds of sensitivity. The deliveries were, therefore, left to chartered civilian flights. Nonetheless, considering the continuing legacy of animosity associated with the Sino-Japanese war, it was remarkable how far Chinese attitudes had changed. As flooding from broken dams followed the earthquake, the Japanese destroyer *Sazanami* entered Zhanjiang (a naval base in southern China) on 26 June, carrying further blankets and emergency food supplies. Apart from its humanitarian aspect, this was a reciprocal visit for that paid by a Chinese missile destroyer, which had visited Japan in November 2007.

There were two serious earthquakes in Japan during the year: that on 16 June in Iwate prefecture and that on 24 July in western Japan, which recorded 7.2 and 6.8 on the Richter scale respectively.

Shuichi Kato, one of Japan's leading critics, died at the age of 89. A lecturer in many universities around the world, he was renowned in Japan and abroad for his extensive work in the fields of art, literature, philosophy, and culture, but also for forming a pacifist group to oppose the amendment of Article 9 of the constitution.

Ian Nish

SOUTH AND NORTH KOREA

South Korea

CAPITAL: Seoul   AREA: 99,260 sq km   POPULATION: 48,530,000 ('07)
OFFICIAL LANGUAGE: Korean   POLITICAL SYSTEM: multiparty republic
HEAD OF STATE AND GOVERNMENT: President Lee Myung Bak (GNP) (since Feb '08)
RULING PARTY: Grand National Party (GNP)
PRESIDENTS OF REPUBLICS: n/a
PRIME MINISTER: Han Seung Soo (GNP) (since Feb '08)
MAIN IGO MEMBERSHIPS (NON-UN): APEC, CP, OECD
CURRENCY: won (end-'08 £1=W1,810.92, US$1=W1,259.55)
GNI PER CAPITA: US$19,690, $24,750 at PPP ('07)

North Korea

CAPITAL: Pyongyang   AREA: 120,540 sq km   POPULATION: 23,783,000 ('07)
OFFICIAL LANGUAGE: Korean   POLITICAL SYSTEM: one-party republic
HEAD OF STATE: Kim Il Sung, Eternal President, died 1994
RULING PARTY: Korean Workers' Party (KWP)
PARTY LEADER: Kim Jong Il, KWP general secretary (since Oct '97)
PRIME MINISTER: Kim Yong Il (since April '07)
MAIN IGO MEMBERSHIPS (NON-UN): NAM
CURRENCY: won (end-'08 £1=W248.100, US$1=W142.450)
GNP PER CAPITA: Low income: US$935 or less ('07 est), -

SOUTH KOREA. Lee Myung Bak's election in December 2007 as the first conservative president of the Republic of Korea (ROK—South Korea) for 10 years promised major changes (see AR 2008, pp. 343-44). Lee, a former Hyundai chief executive officer and later mayor of Seoul, was nicknamed "the Bulldozer" for his approach to solving problems. He promised slimmer government, improved relations with the USA and Japan, and a more realistic policy towards the Democratic People's Republic of Korea (DPRK—North Korea). The country's economy would be improved through his "747" plan: it would grow 7 per cent per annum, with per capita income of US$40,000, and become the world's seventh-largest economy. These were ambitious targets: growth in 2007 was 4 per cent, income had just passed US$20,000 per capita, and South Korea was the world's 13th economy.

Although Lee assumed office enjoying popularity levels of around 75 per cent in opinion polls, there were signs that his plans might run into difficulties. Attempts to streamline the government fell in the face of opposition in the National Assembly (the 299-member unicameral legislature), where Lee's Grand National Party (GNP) did not command a majority. It also became obvious that the "747" model might not fly so easily in government as it had in opposition. Lee's style aroused adverse comment. He did not appear to consult, and was seen as too sympathetic to the conglomerates. By March, his opinion poll ranking was 51.8 per cent, a sharp fall for a new president.

National Assembly elections on 9 April added to Lee's difficulties. He had won the GNP nomination for president by defeating Park Geun Hye, daughter of President Park Chung Hee, the architect of South Korea's economic development. She remained popular, however, and her supporters stood as a separate group. The election result gave the GNP 153 seats against the Democratic Party's 81, while Park's supporters won 14 seats. A third conservative group, the Liberty Forward Party, took 18 seats. Even after a number of independent legislators had joined the GNP caucus, the party lacked the two-thirds majority required for amending the constitution. Although in practice the members of the other conservative parties tended to side with the government, such support could not be relied on.

Lee soon faced another problem. Visiting the USA in April shortly after the elections, and anxious to move forward the 2007 ROK-US free trade agreement (FTA, see AR 2008, p. 345), he agreed that US beef imports, banned because of bovine spongiform encephalopathy (BSE or "mad cow disease"), could resume. This may have seemed uncontroversial, since there were no known US deaths from BSE, but soon massive candlelight protests began in Seoul against the proposed reopening of the market. By early June, Lee's popularity had plunged to 17.2 per cent. Eventually, the president acknowledged that, over beef and other issues, he had behaved arrogantly and not taken public opinion into account, for which he apologised. He changed his secretariat and reshuffled his cabinet. The government also agreed that no US beef from cattle over 30 months old would be imported. US President George W. Bush's visit to South Korea in August passed quietly and US beef went on sale in the autumn. The president's popularity crept back to 25 per cent in September.

Lee's difficulties were not over. Lee—a Presbyterian and by no means the first senior South Korean politician with a Christian background—appeared to some to be more aggressively Christian than his predecessors. Buddhist groups staged protests, claiming that there had been a programme of discrimination against Buddhists since Lee had come to office, for 13 of Lee's 16-member cabinet were Christian, two had no religion, and only one was Buddhist. The demonstrations eventually petered out, but showed the need for caution.

The global economic downturn started to affect South Korea. In July the finance minister said that the ROK might be facing a crisis similar to that of 1997, and US$10.6 billion in foreign exchange reserves were used, unsuccessfully, to support the won. The government still took exception to adverse comments on the economy, pursuing one online commentator for damaging confidence and protesting at negative *Financial Times* reports. The "747" project faded and growth estimates were revised downwards. The government provided aid for the banking sector, including a US$100 billion guarantee to cover foreign debt. The economy still had strengths, including a strong information technology industry, major shipbuilding and automobile industries, and healthy foreign reserves; however, youth unemployment was growing, there was heavy dependence on overseas trade, and real estate was expensive. Industrial output declined by 14 per cent in November, and 18.6 per cent in December.

Despite the concessions on beef, the ROK-US FTA did not come into force. Negotiations over a free trade agreement with the EU also failed to make progress. There was a hope that negotiations might begin with Japan, but the ongoing sovereignty dispute over the Dokdo or Takeshima islands (see below) prevented progress. Preliminary FTA negotiations began with Australia and six Gulf states. With important trading partners such as Japan, the USA, and China experiencing economic downturns, 2009 would not be an easy year.

The Bush administration was more at home with Lee's conservatism. Lee's insistence that the ROK would no longer treat the DPRK as a special case was welcomed by the USA, although the US administration's wish for an agreement on denuclearisation meant that it did not want confrontation with North Korea. The USA removed an irritant in bilateral relations by concluding a visa waiver agreement, and it provided swap facilities for ROK banks. There were tough negotiations on trade matters and payment for the stationing of US forces in the ROK. Relations with Japan started well. Japan's Prime Minister Yasuo Fukuda attended Lee's presidential inauguration in February and the two leaders held talks. Lee said that he wanted no further apologies from Japan for past conduct and proposed the renewal of discussions on FTA and other issues. High level diplomatic exchanges resumed. The ROK and Japan found themselves in agreement on handling the DPRK, with the Lee government supporting Japan over the abductees issue (the Japanese citizens abducted from Japan by North Korea). The improved relations continued when Fukuda gave way to Taro Aso as prime minister in September. However, they broke down over reiterated Japanese claims that Dokdo (known in Japan as Takeshima)—a group of rocks under ROK occupation—were Japanese. The ROK ambassador was recalled, visits were cancelled, and Lee called on the Japanese emperor to apologise. Some contacts continued, especially in the margins of international gatherings and in the context of the growing global financial crisis, but the territorial dispute was an ill omen.

Relations with the People's Republic of China had their ups and downs. Bilateral trade totalled US$145 billion in 2007. Visitors each way reached 6 million, and there were 1,000 weekly flights. Yet Lee's more robust attitude towards the DPRK and wish for improved relations with the USA caused concern. Perhaps as a consequence, China courted the ROK, with a succession of high-level visits. Lee went to China in May, and in talks with President Hu Jintao the two sides agreed to raise their relationship from a "comprehensive and co-operative partnership" to a "strategic and co-operative partnership". Lee visited the Sichuan earthquake area (see p. 348), and the ROK donated US$5 million relief aid. Lee returned to China for the Beijing Olympic Games. Hu paid a state visit to the ROK later in August. The two presidents then met in December, together with the Japanese prime minister, to discuss economic matters and DPRK denuclearisation and agreed to hold regular trilateral meetings.

Tensions with China rose in April, however, when violent clashes occurred between pro- and anti-Chinese demonstrators as the Olympic torch passed through Seoul. The Chinese authorities largely ignored ROK government protests. The global economic downturn also had a negative effect on Sino-ROK relations, with reports that up to 30 per cent of smaller ROK companies in China were losing money. Some closed and left. Other irritants included contaminated Chinese foodstuffs, industrial espionage, and illegal fishing in ROK waters.

President Lee visited Russia in September. The two sides agreed to build a gas pipeline and to link the ROK railway system to the Trans-Siberian Railway. These proposals ignored the fact that both might depend on DPRK agreement, something that looked unlikely as the year progressed.

NORTH KOREA (DPRK).   Relations between the two Koreas plummeted in 2008. The DPRK remained silent about Lee Myung Bak during the presidential election campaign of 2007, and the silence continued after his inauguration in February 2008. Lee argued that engagement should be on a reciprocal basis. He offered to raise DPRK income levels to US$3,000 per capita ("Vision 3000"), if the DPRK co-operated on denuclearisation. He also indicated that projects agreed in 2000 and 2007 would be examined, and that his government would not ignore DPRK human rights issues. The DPRK made no comment, but at the end of March it expelled most ROK officials from the inter-Korean office at the Kaesong industrial zone just north of the Demilitarised Zone (DMZ) between the two countries, following a statement that development of the zone would be linked to denuclearisation. Then, on 1 April, the DPRK media launched a sweeping attack on Lee, which set the tone for relations for the remainder of the year.

Co-operation did not stop completely. South Korean non-governmental organisations (NGOs) continued operating in the DPRK, and energy-related items as required under the six party talks (see AR 2008, p. 347) were supplied. ROK tourists could still visit Kaesong and the Kumgang Mountains on the east coast. Trade in 2007 expanded to US$1.8 billion. Of this, commercial trade totalled US$1.4 billion. The Kaesong zone expanded, with over 38,000 North Koreans working there in some 90 factories by December. Since the DPRK was clearly making money, it seemed unlikely that such projects would be halted.

On 11 July, President Lee made his first speech to the South Korean National Assembly, in which he offered an olive branch to the DPRK. He would follow a policy of "mutual benefit and common prosperity", and pledged that agreements reached at the 2000 and 2007 inter-Korean summits would be honoured (see AR 2000, pp. 345-46; 2008, p. 348). The DPRK rejected the overture. That same day, a South Korean woman tourist, allegedly in a prohibited area, was shot dead by a North Korean soldier at the Kumgang resort. The DPRK expressed regret but would not allow an ROK enquiry. The ROK government then suspended tours. The standoff continued to the end of the year. With no visits by South Korean tourists, and none in prospect, the DPRK reduced the number of ROK personnel at Kumgang. Visits to Kaesong, however, continued.

The DPRK had another grievance. Before 2000, both sides had engaged in propaganda exchanges, despatching balloons carrying leaflets over each other's territory. The 2000 summit agreed to stop such activities. During 2008, ROK NGOs decided to use balloons to send information into the DPRK, especially as rumours developed about the health of party leader Kim Jong Il in the autumn (see below). First raised in May, the issue came to a head at working level military meetings in October. The DPRK demanded that the sending of balloons be stopped, or it would take "practical action", including the closure of the Kaesong zone. ROK attempts to dissuade the NGOs were unsuccessful.

Kaesong then came under pressure. On 6 November, the DPRK chief delegate to the military talks carried out an inspection at Kaesong, asking how quickly companies could leave. An announcement followed on 12 November that cross-border movements would be restricted from 1 December, while the DPRK Red Cross closed its liaison office at Panmunjom in the DMZ and cut cross-border telephone links. The ROK reaction was low key, noting that naval and aviation hotlines were still working. On 24 November, it was announced that from 1 December cross-border trains would stop running, tourism would be suspended, ROK staff at both Kaesong and Kumgang would be "selectively expelled", and there would be more control over border crossings. Two days later, the Hyundai Asan corporation was told to cut its Kumgang staff from 192 to 86, and on 1 December, the Kaesong measures came into force. As well as halting trains and tourists, border gate openings were reduced from 19 to three per day, and the number of South Korean residents at Kaesong was reduced from 4,200 to 880.

Some saw this as a major shift in power within the DPRK to a more hardline group, drawn from the military and security forces. The signals were mixed. Possibly the DPRK military were concerned at what they saw as the negative influences from the South and welcomed the opportunity to impose restrictions; but the DPRK actions followed from the Lee government's actions. Signs of continued engagement included the opening of a major Pyongyang-based joint venture and the continued acceptance of ROK NGOs.

From early September, rumours circulated about Kim Jong Il's health after he failed to appear at the celebrations marking the country's 60th anniversary, adding to speculation about a possible power struggle. Kim had named no successor and was known to suffer poor health. Some claimed that he was dead, others that he had suffered a stroke and was incapacitated. Photographs released by the DPRK were unconvincing. The ROK and US governments were cautious, saying that it was likely Kim had suffered a stroke but had recovered.

The food situation remained precarious, especially after August's heavy rains, and the World Food Programme and ROK NGOs predicted famine in the DPRK following bad harvests in 2007. The rise in international food costs and competing demands for international aid affected food availability, but in the event there was no famine. Meanwhile, an Egyptian company set up a mobile telephone network.

Relations remained close with China, the DPRK's main source of food and energy. Trade in 2007 reached US$1.97 billion, with Chinese investments at US$445 million. The two countries apparently agreed to tighten their border against defectors. During a visit by China's new vice president, Xi Jinping, in June, they agreed to celebrate 60 years of diplomatic relations in 2009. Russia continued to improve its links with the DPRK, with increases in trade and aid, but relations with Japan remain stalled. The outlook appeared brighter when the DPRK agreed to re-examine the Japanese abductees issue in return for the lifting of Japanese sanctions imposed in 2006. When the more hawkish Aso became Japanese premier, the DPRK postponed action until it had seen what policies he would follow. When the Japanese government renewed sanctions in October, the agreement fell away. The DPRK opposed Japanese membership of the six party talks, and condemned Japanese statements on Dokdo.

The New York Philharmonic Orchestra visited in February and performed in Pyongyang. Otherwise, denuclearisation dominated relations with the USA. Attempts continued to get a satisfactory statement on the DPRK nuclear programme. The DPRK blamed its failure to begin decommissioning on US failure to remove it from the list of countries deemed to support terrorism. Negotiations did not stop, and in May the DPRK handed over 18,000 pages of documentation. June saw a DPRK declaration to China on its nuclear programme, and the start of decommissioning of the nuclear reactor at Yongbyon by blowing up a cooling tower.

This allowed the resumption of the six party talks, but the DPRK demanded additional economic assistance to continue decommissioning. A verification subcommittee made little progress. At the end of August, the DPRK said that it would suspend the Yongbyon decommissioning because the USA had not removed it from the terrorism list and a month later that it was no longer interested in being removed from the list. US Assistant Secretary of State Christopher Hill's shuttle diplomacy appeared to pay off, however, when in October the DPRK agreed to a verification process and resumed the disablement of Yongbyon. The USA then finally delisted the DPRK as a state sponsoring terrorism and lifted some sanctions. US officials made it clear that other sanctions remained in force under the Trading with the Enemy Act. Despite these moves and continued frenetic diplomatic activity, it proved impossible to reach an agreement on sampling and other verification issues by the end of the year.

J.E. Hoare

MONGOLIA

CAPITAL: Ulan Bator   AREA: 1,566,500 sq km   POPULATION: 2,612,000 ('07)
OFFICIAL LANGUAGE: Halh (Khalkha) Mongolia   POLITICAL SYSTEM: multiparty republic
HEAD OF STATE: President Nambariyn Enkhbayar (MAHN) (since June '05)
RULING PARTIES: Mongolian People's Revolutionary Party (MAHN) and Democratic Party (AN)
HEAD OF GOVERNMENT: Prime Minister Sanj Bayar (MAHN) (since Nov '07)
MAIN IGO MEMBERSHIPS (NON-UN): NAM, EBRD
CURRENCY: tugrik (end-'08 £1=T1,852.92, US$1=T1,288.76)
GNI PER CAPITA: US$1,290, $3,160 at PPP ('07)

MONGOLIA on 29 June held its fifth legislative election since the demise of the socialist system in 1990. Although the Democratic Party (AN) disputed the victory claimed by the Mongolian People's Revolutionary Party (MAHN) in the contest for seats in the Great Hural (unicameral legislature) and claimed electoral fraud, a new coalition government was formed in September by the MAHN and the AN, with Prime Minister Sanj Bayar of the MAHN retaining his post.

A total of 356 candidates ran for 76 seats in the Great Hural, but by 28 August, when legislators were sworn in, only 69 results had been confirmed. As of the end of the year, and with two seats still under dispute, the MAHN had 44 seats and the AN 27; the Civil Will Party, the Citizen's Coalition, and independents had one apiece. Only three women won seats, the smallest number since the democratic reform of 1990. Most foreign observers declared that the election was free and fair. However, the country's Voter Education Centre and other non-governmental organisations, as well as independent lawyers, criticised many legal and practical aspects of the election as being unfair to challengers, new political movements, and female candidates. Observers from both the Asia Pacific Democracy Partnership and the International Republican Institute saw problems with the correlation between lists of registered voters and actual voters, and with the drawn out process of counting and recording the ballots, all of which gave room for potential fraud.

Protests rejecting the election results turned violent on the evening of 1 July and demonstrators set fire to the MAHN headquarters in central Ulan Bator. The police used tear gas, rubber bullets and water cannon, but instead of dispersing the protesters threw rocks at the police. Five protesters were killed and hundreds of people were injured, including some police. Around midnight, the president, Nambariyn Enkhbayar, declared a four-day state of emergency. He acknowledged the protesters' frustration, but called for a peaceful resolution of the dispute over alleged election fraud. All television channels, except National Public Television, were temporarily banned from broadcasting. Much significance was attributed to the fire in the theatre museum, which was adjacent to the MAHN's headquarters. Reports portrayed the damage to the museum as a crime against the national heritage. Several hundred protesters were arrested for alleged crimes of misconduct and burglary during the riots, and more people were arrested during the subsequent state of emergency. The interpretation of the riots shifted from an act of political protest to vandalism. Twenty human rights NGOs voluntarily conducted monitoring of the situation of detainees, and demanded that egregious violations of human rights be stopped immediately.

As the team of Mongolian athletes eased the trauma of the political turmoil by winning three gold and two silver medals during the Beijing Olympic Games, some achievements were also seen in the economic sphere. The government implemented a campaign to improve the wheat and vegetable harvests by recovering farmlands abandoned after the collapse of socialism. Mongolia hoped thereby to supply around half of its domestic requirements in these crops.

In December 2008 the Great Hural approved a resolution to exploit Mongolia's vast mineral resources. The resolution entitled the government to establish investment agreements with domestic and foreign investors, with the condition that the Mongolian government receive at least a 51 per cent ownership share in the Tavan Tolgoi coalfield and a 34 per cent stake in the Oyu Tolgoi copper and gold deposits. Meanwhile, as the global financial crisis began to affect Mongolia, the Great Hural authorised the injection of some T455 billion to stabilise the banking system.

Manduhai Buyandelger

X AUSTRALASIA AND THE PACIFIC

AUSTRALIA—PAPUA NEW GUINEA

AUSTRALIA

CAPITAL: Canberra   AREA: 7,741,220 sq km   POPULATION: 21,017,000 ('07)
OFFICIAL LANGUAGE: English   POLITICAL SYSTEM: multiparty system
HEAD OF STATE: Queen Elizabeth II (since Feb '52)
GOVERNOR-GENERAL: Quentin Bryce (since Sept '08)
RULING PARTY: Australian Labor Party (ALP)
HEAD OF GOVERNMENT: Prime Minister Kevin Rudd (since Nov '07)
MAIN IGO MEMBERSHIPS (NON-UN): APEC, PC, PIF, CP, ANZUS, OECD, CWTH
CURRENCY: Australian dollar (end-'08 £1=A$2.0622, US$1=A$1.4343)
GNI PER CAPITA: US$35,960, $33,340 at PPP ('07)

THE first full year of the Australian Labor Party (ALP) government, led by Prime Minister Kevin Rudd, saw it enjoying a strong lead in the opinion polls over an opposition which was showing signs of the tension between its two constituent parties, the Liberals and the National Party. The Liberals changed their leader from Brendan Nelson to Malcolm Turnbull on 16 September, but this had little impact on their popularity. Turnbull was a highly successful barrister and merchant banker, but was best known as chairman of the Australian Republican Movement between 1993 and 2000. The expiry of Senate (upper house) terms on 1 July, which brought in the new senators elected in the November 2007 general election, saw the end of the Australian Democrats as a parliamentary party after almost 30 years. The impact of the global financial crisis was strongly reflected in falling share prices and the exchange value of the Australian dollar, but was yet to show up in increased unemployment. The government followed a strategy of injecting large sums into the economy, including paying a major bonus, totalling A$8.7 billion, to pensioners and others on low incomes ahead of Christmas.

Domestic politics were dominated by the two global issues of climate change and the financial crisis. There were, however, several other matters left over from the previous government, which needed clearing up. The asylum seeker detention system was substantially reformed by ending the temporary protection visa scheme and closing down the detention centre on Nauru (see p. 381). Later in the year, the numbers of asylum seekers arriving by boat increased slightly, giving rise to accusations from the opposition that liberalisation was attracting more people to attempt the hazardous sea journey. However the numbers were very small, and all the voyagers were detained for processing on the Australian territory of Christmas Island, although not in rigorous conditions. The first group to be granted permanent residence in Australia left for the mainland in December. The government continued with its programme of withdrawing combat troops from Iraq, but committed itself to military involvement in Afghanistan.

The televised opening ceremony of the new Parliament on 13 February included Aboriginal elements for the first time. Prime Minister Rudd made a significant speech, breaking with the attitudes of his predecessor, John Howard, in formally apologising to Australia's Aboriginal peoples for their "past mistreatment" (see Documents).

Another major break from the Howard years had been Rudd's signature, immediately upon taking office, of the Kyoto Protocol on climate change (see AR 2008, p. 457). The new government was now faced with the conundrum of Australia's being a major exporter and domestic user of coal. While the opposition and most major companies accepted that global warming was a reality, there was an undercurrent of scepticism and a much greater concern with the economic impact of Kyoto's target of an average 5.5 per cent reduction in carbon emissions by 2012. State governments with strong interests in mining, especially those of Western Australia and Queensland, were anxious about the impact on their development. Support for the ALP waned in Western Australia for this and other reasons, to the point where the government lost its majority in state elections on 6 September. The ALP won 28 seats; the Liberals 24 seats; the Nationals four seats; the Greens no seats; and independents three seats. With the ALP unable to form a coalition, the Liberal Party announced that it would govern with National support, and its leader, Colin Barnett, became state premier.

New South Wales was another state with a strong interest in coal and declining support for its ALP government. Some unions affiliated to the ALP were anxious about the impact of policies to combat climate change on their membership. A related issue was the government's attempt to privatise the state's power generators. At the party's conference, this policy was opposed by 702 votes to 107, despite the strong support of the state premier, Maurice Iemma. In the ensuing crisis within the parliamentary party, Iemma resigned on 5 September and was replaced by Nathan Rees.

Another aspect of the issue of global warming was the long drought, which had affected some parts of Australia for several years and was starting to have an impact on water supplies to major cities, until it broke in November. The condition of the country's main river system, the Murray-Darling basin, was of continuing concern to four of the six states and affected the bulk of Australian agriculture and irrigation. After some resistance, Victoria agreed to support the new Commonwealth Murray-Darling Basin Commission on 26 March, provided the state's extensive irrigation agriculture received Commonwealth support. This extension of national government influence into state responsibilities was supported by all political parties and resulted from initial legislation passed by the former Commonwealth coalition government.

The global financial crisis had only a limited visible impact on Australia before the end of the year. Unemployment remained below 5 per cent, inflation was low, and interest rates were progressively reduced. Mortgage holders were well served but pensioners and shareholders had less to be happy about. Share prices dropped by 40 per cent during the year and the Australian dollar's value against major currencies showed a similar decline. Two of the major car producers, General Motors Holden and Chrysler, sought and received substantial financial support from the federal government. A pump priming strategy was adopted, including a A$10.4 billion stimulus package announced on 14 October, a large part of which was to be absorbed by the payments to low-income families to stimulate spending prior to Christmas. The government advocated major tax cuts and consequent reductions in public services, despite opposition criticism. The government's response was to criticise its predecessor for failing to consolidate and to develop infrastructure during its 11 years in office. For all the problems it faced, the Rudd government remained remarkably popular. It was only in some of the states, notably Western Australia and New South Wales, that ALP support declined (see above). But this was due more to internal party disputes and incompetence than to the national issues of global warming and the financial collapse.

Several important but unconnected criminal matters were wound up. The drug gang wars, which had killed about 30 people in Melbourne (see AR 2003, p. 389; AR 2004, p. 343), concluded with the trials and imprisonment of several remaining participants and the extradition of another from Greece. The case of Mohamed Haneef, the Indian doctor arrested in connection with bombing incidents in the UK in 2007 (see AR 2008, p. 352), was finalised with an official inquiry, which cleared him of any suspicion of terrorism and was highly critical of several security organisations but not of any individual. A successful prosecution was launched against a group led by an Islamic cleric, Abdul Nacer Benbrika. He and his followers were convicted on 15 September and imprisoned for supporting a terrorist organisation. Another case, against alleged supporters of Sri Lanka's Tamil Tigers (the LTTE) in Melbourne, was still in progress at the end of the year.

James Jupp

PAPUA NEW GUINEA

CAPITAL: Port Moresby   AREA: 462,840 sq km   POPULATION: 6,324,000 ('07)
OFFICIAL LANGUAGES: Pidgin, Motu & English   POLITICAL SYSTEM: multiparty system
HEAD OF STATE: Queen Elizabeth II
GOVERNOR-GENERAL: Sir Paulias Matane (since May '04)
RULING PARTY: National Alliance Party (NAP)
HEAD OF GOVERNMENT: Prime Minister Sir Michael Somare (NAP) (since August '02)
MAIN IGO MEMBERSHIPS (NON-UN): APEC, CP, PC, PIF, ACP, CWTH, NAM
CURRENCY: kina (end-'08 £1=K3.7812, US$1=K2.6300)
GNI PER CAPITA: US$850, $1,870 at PPP ('07 est based on regression)

PAPUA New Guinea muddled through a familiar set of problems in 2008. Crime and disorder, environmental threat, and complicated international relationships provided the principal themes of the year. But once again the country emerged more or less still functioning, in defiance of the predictions of some outside observers.

Tribal fighting in the highlands region cost scores if not hundreds of lives in 2008, with the Western Highlands and Enga provinces being worst affected. Most of these conflicts grew from pressure over land in an area of high population and limited agricultural fertility. A related problem, which had been growing over recent years in the highlands, became a major cause of concern: the murderous pursuit of supposed sorcerers. This cost at least 50 lives during the year and probably many more, with most of the killings being carried out in quite horrific circumstances. Typically, the world over, such witch hunts were an indication of societies under extreme stress.

"Ordinary" crime, too, continued to preoccupy the country. Perhaps the greatest single social and economic problem confronting Papua New Guinea since its independence, criminal activity had taken ever more organised and dramatic forms over recent years. Bank robbery, often accompanied by the violent abduction of employees, seemed to be the crime of choice in 2008. A new and particularly alarming feature of this was the widespread complicity of police officers. In July, the police commissioner, Gari Baki, acknowledged the problem when he announced that almost 80 officers in the capital, Port Moresby, had mysteriously gone missing when investigations began into police involvement in the current crime wave. The following month all eight police barracks in Moresby were placed under a night time curfew "to minimise unlawful activities conducted inside the barracks [which had] become safe havens and points of contact for criminals and their associates", according to police chiefs.

In April a Pacific-wide report into illegal timber trading identified Papua New Guinea as a major problem. According to the report, up to 80 per cent of logging in the country was carried out illegally. On current trends timber resources would be depleted within 10 years. The report reiterated the already widely recognised fact that the problem was driven by the involvement of the political elite, reaching right up to veteran Prime Minister Michael Somare himself. In September Greenpeace environmental activists drew attention to the situation by occupying a Malaysian logging ship in a remote part of the southern coast.

Another environmental problem, one not of the making of Papua New Guineans themselves, passed a landmark in 2008. Rising sea levels as a result of climate change required the large-scale and permanent resettlement of populations from low lying coastal areas in the Bismarck Sea.

On the diplomatic stage, relations with Australia improved markedly during the year. This had been widely anticipated at the end of 2007, when the Australian Labor Party returned to power. The new warmth was underlined in March with a successful visit to Port Moresby by the Australian prime minister, Kevin Rudd. Relations with the country's other large neighbour, Indonesia, were briefly a little more fraught. In July, border incursions by troops from Indonesian West Papua caused a spat reminiscent of the sensitive years of the 1980s, when many Papua New Guineans feared Indonesian expansionism. On this occasion, however, the matter was quickly resolved with what amounted to an apology from the Indonesian government.

At the end of October, the Bank of Papua New Guinea (the central bank) produced a sombre report on the likely effects on the country of the global economic downturn. Sharp declines in GDP, direct foreign investment, and export revenue were predicted. Against this, however, there was a promise of future relief in the form of a huge new natural gas field discovered in Gulf province.

Norman MacQueen

NEW ZEALAND—PACIFIC ISLAND STATES

NEW ZEALAND

CAPITAL: Wellington   AREA: 267,710 sq km   POPULATION: 4,228,000 ('07)
OFFICIAL LANGUAGE: English   POLITICAL SYSTEM: multiparty system
HEAD OF STATE: Queen Elizabeth II (since Feb '52)
GOVERNOR-GENERAL: Anand Satyanand (since April '06)
RULING PARTY: National Party (NP)
HEAD OF GOVERNMENT: Prime Minister John Key (NP) (since Nov '08)
MAIN IGO MEMBERSHIPS (NON-UN): ANZUS (suspended), APEC, PC, PIF, CP, OECD, CWTH
CURRENCY: New Zealand dollar (end-'08 £1=NZ$2.4602, US$1=NZ$1.7112)
GNI PER CAPITA: US$28,780, $26,340 at PPP ('07)

PARLIAMENTARY elections on 8 November produced the first change of government in New Zealand since 1999. The Labour Party's tenure at the head of a succession of coalition governments had lasted nine years, the same length of time as the National Party had been in office when it finally lost power in 1999 (see AR 1999, pp. 385-87). Prior to the election, National had been ahead in opinion polls for much of 2008 and its leader, John Key, fighting his first general election as party leader, had moved past Prime Minister Helen Clark as the public's choice of "preferred prime minister". At the election itself, New Zealand's fifth under a proportional electoral system, once again no party emerged with an overall majority of seats in the 122-member House of Representatives (the unicameral legislature). But National—which won 58 to Labour's 43—came close and was able to form a viable minority government by gaining assurances of support from two smaller parties, ACT and the Maori Party, which each won five seats, and United Future (UFNZ), which won one seat.

The election campaign coincided with the global financial crisis, giving both Labour and National opportunities to claim greater experience: Labour with its nine-year period in office, and National with an affluent leader who had made his fortune in the financial sector before deciding to stand for parliament in 2002. The government's reluctant short-term response to the crisis was to give New Zealanders a virtually unlimited guarantee on their bank deposits.

A succession of embarrassments for Labour preceded the opening of the election campaign. New restrictions on financial donations to candidates, parties and groups seeking to influence the election, introduced by Labour, proved controversial and confusing, with the ruling party itself becoming the first to fall foul of the new law. Campaign contributions dating from the previous election tarnished both Clark and her foreign minister, Winston Peters, leader of the New

Zealand First Party. There were claims that the donor of the contributions had sought appointment as honorary consul in Monaco (where he lived). The foreign minister's denial that he had received any financial support, or that the position had been offered, led to a series of inquiries and, in due course, to his being removed as foreign minister and censured by parliament.

National's election victory meant that Key became prime minister, with 19 of his colleagues gaining cabinet appointments and another being elected as speaker of the House. Clark announced her resignation as Labour leader on election night, a move followed the next day by her deputy leader and shortly thereafter by the party's president. The new Labour parliamentary team promptly elected two experienced MPs, Phil Goff and Annette King (both ministers in the outgoing cabinet), to serve as leader and deputy leader. The new legislature was without Winston Peters as all members of New Zealand First lost their seats.

The new administration included five ministers drawn from the three small parties which had agreed to support the government, although all of these remained formally outside the cabinet and, therefore, free from the obligation of collective responsibility. The right-wing ACT Party—a libertarian group committed to major tax reductions and a smaller role for the state—and the left-of-centre Maori Party—formed in 2004 and committed to stronger representation for the indigenous Maori population—each contributed two ministers, and the UFNZ leader, Peter Dunne, retained the portfolios which he had held under the previous administration.

Notwithstanding the impending election, the year had opened with matters far from partisan politics. On 11 January the country's national hero, Sir Edmund Hillary, the first climber to reach the top of Mount Everest, in 1953, died aged 88 (see Obituary). A state funeral on 22 January was held in Auckland, and in April Queen Elizabeth II held a memorial service at Windsor Castle in his honour, attended by the New Zealand prime minister and members of the Hillary family. In February, another event transcending the country's politics—the theft in 2007 of 96 New Zealand war medals (including nine Victoria Crosses) from the country's national military museum—was resolved, when negotiations succeeded in bringing about the surrender of the medals to the authorities.

The government achieved a number of significant policy successes during the year. In April, it intervened to block foreign ownership of Auckland's international airport. In July, the rail industry was renationalised. A climate change bill mandating an emissions trading scheme was enacted in September. Ownership of nine forests, covering 435,000 acres (176,038 hectares), was transferred in July to seven Maori tribes.

In October, the High Court ruled that neither the editor nor the publisher of Wellington's *Dominion Post* was guilty of contempt of court for the November 2007 publication of extracts of intercepted communications associated with police "terrorist" raids (see AR 2008, p. 356).

In the sphere of foreign relations, Prime Minister Clark travelled to Beijing in April to sign a free trade agreement (FTA) with China. The accord, endorsed by parliament in July, followed more than three years of negotiations and was expected to provide New Zealand with greater access to China's markets.

New Zealand continued its military deployments overseas. In East Timor the presence of a 200-member force was extended for a further year to deal with increased unrest following the attempted assassination of the country's president and prime minister in February (see p. 344). There were regular rotations of troops in the Solomon Islands and in the Sinai, and small additions to New Zealand's contribution to multinational forces in Afghanistan.

There were ambiguous signals with respect to relations with the USA. US Secretary of State Condoleezza Rice met the prime minister and the foreign minister in late July in Auckland, referring to New Zealand as a friend "and ally". Subsequently Prime Minister Clark distanced herself from the remark, denying that there was an "alliance" while acknowledging that the two countries were working together more closely in the Pacific, in maritime security, and in Afghanistan.

In August, the New Zealand team at the Beijing Olympics won nine medals, equalling New Zealand's combined total from the previous two Olympics.

Stephen Levine

PACIFIC ISLAND STATES

Fiji

CAPITAL: Suva   AREA: 18,270 sq km   POPULATION: 838,000 ('07)
OFFICIAL LANGUAGES: Fijian, Hindi & English   POLITICAL SYSTEM: multiparty republic under military rule
HEAD OF STATE: President Ratu Josefa Iloilo (since Jan '07)
HEAD OF GOVERNMENT: interim Prime Minister Commodore Josaia Voreqe (Frank) Bainimarama (since Jan '07)
MAIN IGO MEMBERSHIPS (NON-UN): CWTH (suspended), PC, PIF, CP, ACP
CURRENCY: Fiji dollar (end-'08 £1=F$2.5362, US$1=F$1.7640)
GNI PER CAPITA: US$3,800, $4,370 at PPP ('07)

Kiribati

CAPITAL: Tarawa   AREA: 810 sq km   POPULATION: 102,000 ('07)
OFFICIAL LANGUAGES: English & Kiribati   POLITICAL SYSTEM: multiparty republic
HEAD OF STATE AND GOVERNMENT: President Anote Tong (since July '03)
MAIN IGO MEMBERSHIPS (NON-UN): CWTH, PC, PIF, ACP
CURRENCY: Australian dollar (end-'08 £1=A$2.0622, US$1=A$1.4343)
GNI PER CAPITA: US$1,170, $2,240 at PPP ('07 est based on regression)

Marshall Islands

CAPITAL: Dalap-Uliga-Darrit   AREA: 180 sq km   POPULATION: 67,000 ('07)
OFFICIAL LANGUAGES: English & Marshallese   POLITICAL SYSTEM: multiparty republic in free association with USA
HEAD OF STATE AND GOVERNMENT: President Litokwa Tomeing (UPP) (since Jan '08)
RULING PARTIES: United People's Party in alliance with Aelon Kein Ad (AKA—Our Islands)
MAIN IGO MEMBERSHIPS (NON-UN): PC, PIF
CURRENCY: US dollar (end '08 £1=1.4378)
GNI PER CAPITA: US$3,070 ('07), -

Federated States of Micronesia

CAPITAL: Palikir (Pohnpei)   AREA: 700 sq km   POPULATION: 111,000 ('07)
OFFICIAL LANGUAGE: English   POLITICAL SYSTEM: multiparty republic in free association
  with USA
HEAD OF STATE AND GOVERNMENT: President Emanuel "Manny" Mori (since May '07)
MAIN IGO MEMBERSHIPS (NON-UN): PC, PIF
CURRENCY: US dollar (end-'08 £1=1.4378)
GNI PER CAPITA: US$2,470, $3,270 at PPP ('07 est based on regression)

Nauru

CAPITAL: Domaneab   AREA: 21.4 sq km   POPULATION: 10,131 ('06 est)
OFFICIAL LANGUAGES: Nauruan & English   POLITICAL SYSTEM: one-party republic
HEAD OF STATE AND GOVERNMENT: President Marcus Stephen (since Dec '07)
MAIN IGO MEMBERSHIPS (NON-UN): CWTH (special member), PC, PIF
CURRENCY: Australian dollar (see above)
GNI PER CAPITA: n/a

Palau (Belau)

CAPITAL: Koror   AREA: 460 sq km   POPULATION: 20,000 ('07)
OFFICIAL LANGUAGE: English   POLITICAL SYSTEM: multiparty republic in free association with USA
HEAD OF STATE AND GOVERNMENT: President Johnson Toribiong (since Nov '08)
MAIN IGO MEMBERSHIPS (NON-UN): PC, PIF
CURRENCY: US dollar (end-'08 £1=1.4378)
GNI PER CAPITA: US$8,210 ('07), -

Samoa

CAPITAL: Apia   AREA: 2,840 sq km   POPULATION: 187,000 ('07)
OFFICIAL LANGUAGES: English & Samoan   POLITICAL SYSTEM: multiparty monarchy
HEAD OF STATE: Tuiatua Tupua Tamasese Taisi Tupuola Tufuga Efi (since June '07)
RULING PARTY: Human Rights Protection Party (HRPP)
HEAD OF GOVERNMENT: Prime Minister Tuilaepa Sailele Malielegaoi (since Nov '98)
MAIN IGO MEMBERSHIPS (NON-UN): CWTH, PC, PIF, ACP
CURRENCY: tala (end-'08 £1=T4.2115, US$1=T2.9274)
GNI PER CAPITA: US$2,430, $3,930 at PPP ('07 est based on regression)

Solomon Islands

CAPITAL: Honiara   AREA: 28,900 sq km   POPULATION: 495,000 ('07)
OFFICIAL LANGUAGE: English   POLITICAL SYSTEM: multiparty system
HEAD OF STATE: Queen Elizabeth II (since Feb '52)
GOVERNOR-GENERAL: Nathaniel Waena (since July '04)
RULING PARTY: People's Alliance Party (PAP)
HEAD OF GOVERNMENT: Prime Minister Derek Sikua (since Dec '07)
MAIN IGO MEMBERSHIPS (NON-UN): CWTH, PC, PIF, ACP
CURRENCY: Solomon Island dollar (end-'08 £1=SI$11.0990, US$1=SI$7.7042)
GNI PER CAPITA: US$730, $1,680 at PPP ('07 est based on regression)

Tonga

CAPITAL: Nuku'alofa   AREA: 750 sq km   POPULATION: 101,000 ('07)
OFFICIAL LANGUAGES: Tongan & English   POLITICAL SYSTEM: non-party monarchy
HEAD OF STATE: King George (Siaosi) Tupou V (since Sept '06)
CURRENCY: Prime Minister Feleti (Fred) Sevele (since March '06)
MAIN IGO MEMBERSHIPS (NON-UN): CWTH, PC, PIF, ACP
CURRENCY: pa'anga (end-'08 £1=P3.0648, US$1=P2.1313)
GNI PER CAPITA: US$2,320, $3,650 at PPP ('07 est based on regression)

Tuvalu

CAPITAL: Fongafale   AREA: 26 sq km   POPULATION: 10,200
OFFICIAL LANGUAGE: English   POLITICAL SYSTEM: non-party monarchy
HEAD OF STATE: Queen Elizabeth II (since Feb '52)
GOVERNOR-GENERAL: Faimalaga Luka (since Sept '03)
HEAD OF GOVERNMENT: Prime Minister Apisai Ielemia (since Aug '06)
MAIN IGO MEMBERSHIPS (NON-UN): PC, PIF, ACP, CWTH (special member)
CURRENCY: Australian dollar (end-'08 £1=A$2.0622, US$1=A$1.4343)
GNI PER CAPITA: n/a

Vanuatu

CAPITAL: Port Vila   AREA: 12,190 sq km   POPULATION: 226,000 ('07)
OFFICIAL LANGUAGES: English, French & Bislama   POLITICAL SYSTEM: multiparty republic
HEAD OF STATE: President Kalkot Mataskelekele (since Aug '04)
RULING PARTIES: Vanua'aku Pati (VP)-led coalition
HEAD OF GOVERNMENT: Prime Minister Edward Natapei (VP) (since Sept '08)
MAIN IGO MEMBERSHIPS (NON-UN): CWTH, PC, PIF, ACP, Francophonie
CURRENCY: vatu (end-'08 £1=V163.552, US$1=V113.755)
GNI PER CAPITA: US$1,840, $3,410 at PPP ('07 est based on regression)

FIJI'S Prime Minister Commodore Josaia Voreqe (Frank) Bainimarama retreated from a promise he had made in October 2007 to the Pacific Islands Forum (PIF) to hold new elections by March 2009. The prime minister declined to attend the annual PIF summit, in August, at which the PIF unanimously agreed to consider suspending Fiji if it did not recommit itself to the March elections.

Bainimarama asserted that fresh elections—which would return Fiji to democratic rule after the military coup of December 2006 (see AR 2007, pp. 356-57)—needed to be preceded by implementation of the government-sponsored "people's charter for change, peace and progress" (see AR 2008, p. 360). On 5 August the charter was endorsed by the government-appointed National Council for Building a Better Fiji, and a day later it was released to the public. The charter articulated values for "building a better Fiji", and recommended a common electoral roll (rather than rolls based on communal or ethnic categories) for future elections. The final copy of the charter was presented to Fiji's president on 15 December; shortly afterwards, he authorised the government to begin implementing its recommendations.

In October, the Suva High Court ruled that the appointment by President Ratu Josefa Iloilo of an interim government following the 2006 military takeover had been valid. In characterising Iloilo's actions as lawful, the Court in effect ruled that the transition of power to Fiji's military leader, Bainimarama, whom Iloilo had appointed prime minister, had been legal. The USA stated that its suspension of aid to Fiji would continue, in spite of the Court ruling. In October, Bainimarama, who also served as finance minister, was denied a US visa to attend a meeting of the World Bank in Washington, DC.

Australia and New Zealand indicated that their sanctions also would remain, including travel bans on individuals associated with the regime (and their families). Deteriorating relations with Australia led to death threats against the Australian high commissioner in Fiji, as well as problems for Australian journalists seeking to enter the country. In December, the interim government rejected a visa request for an Australian military attaché to be based at the high commission. Relations between Fiji and New Zealand worsened in December when a Fiji university student was denied a visa to return to New Zealand to complete his studies. Fiji expelled New Zealand's high commissioner (whose predecessor had been expelled in June 2007) and also deported a New Zealand journalist. New Zealand responded by expelling the Fiji high commissioner.

Controversy surrounded other actions of the prime minister and his government. In February, Bainimarama appointed himself head of Fiji's prestigious Great Council of Chiefs (GCC). In April, lawyers representing suspended GCC members filed suit in the High Court, challenging "unlawful" changes, including the prime minister's self-appointment. In December, the government announced its intention to dissolve municipal government councils, stating that their operations were being hampered by political parties.

Difficulties also continued with respect to Fiji's news media. In February the publisher and chief executive of the *Fiji Sun* (who was an Australian citizen) was arrested and deported. On 1 May the publisher of the *Fiji Times* was also expelled from the country. In November, the government confirmed that it was seeking jail sentences against a newspaper editor and publisher over publication of a letter criticising the High Court's ruling on the legality of the coup.

In several other Pacific Island states and territories, electoral competition influenced political developments.

VANUATU. Legislative elections in September led to the election by the National Assembly (the 52-seat legislature) of Edward Natapei of the Vanua'aki Pati (VP) as the country's new prime minister on 22 September. Natapei defeated former prime minister Maxime Carlot Korman by a 27-25 vote margin and formed a multi-party coalition. The survival of the seven-party government was almost immediately put in jeopardy by defections among its members, but opposition legislators proved equally fickle, allowing the government to defeat a number of no-confidence motions. None of these manoeuvres had any effect on the country's ranking in the 178-nation "Happy Planet Index" (accessible on the Internet), which listed Vanuatu as the happiest nation on earth.

NAURU. The main police station was set on fire in March and Australian police on the island deputised 100 civilians to help prevent any further violence. On 20 April the president of Nauru, Marcus Stephen, declared a state of emergency, dissolved the 18-member parliament, and called new elections in six days' time. The Pacific Islands Forum sent two observers to monitor the snap election. Prior to the vote, parliament had been deadlocked with nine members each supporting the government and the opposition. Three opposition MPs lost their seats in the election, thereby giving the government a majority.

The Australian-funded detention centre on Nauru, part of Australia's "Pacific solution" for dealing with asylum seekers, was closed in February, following the election of a new government in Australia and the departure of the last remaining refugees (21 Sri Lankans). Asylum claims of those attempting to reach Australia by boat were to be processed in a new immigration detention centre on the Australian territory of Christmas Island (see p. 371).

Nauru participated in the Beijing Olympic Games, providing the event's only one-person delegation, a weightlifter.

PALAU. A general election on 4 November was won by Johnson Toribiong, who became president in place of Tommy Remengesau, who was constitutionally barred from seeking a third term. Remengesau became the first Palauan president to win a seat in the Senate (the upper house of the bicameral legislature) after his term had expired, in the legislative election held simultaneously with the presidential poll.

NIUE. Elections in June to the 20-member Legislative Assembly led to the choice of a new premier, Toke Talagi.

MARSHALL ISLANDS. The Nitijela (legislature) convened in January, following the November 2007 elections (see AR 2008, p. 363), and elected the former speaker, Litokwa Tomeing, as president. Although President Tomeing had called for links with the People's Republic of China during his election campaign, his United People's Party's preference for maintaining ties with Taiwan forestalled any immediate moves to change the country's allegiances. Taiwan remained the Marshall Islands' second largest aid donor, behind the USA, providing assistance to Air Marshall Islands in the early part of 2008 that enabled the national carrier to resume flights after both of its aircraft had been grounded for several months.

In December, the first Marshall Islands soldier to die in Iraq was killed in a suicide bombing. There were further casualties among troops from other Pacific island territories. Five soldiers from Guam, one from American Samoa, and two Fiji soldiers serving in the British Army were killed in the conflicts in Iraq and Afghanistan. In August, New Caledonia sustained its first casualty in Afghanistan, when an ethnic Kanak soldier serving with French forces was killed in an ambush. In December, Tonga completed withdrawal of all of its forces from Iraq, ending an involvement which began in 2004.

The US Congress (bicameral legislature) enacted legislation giving the Commonwealth of the Northern Mariana Islands (CNMI) a congressional delegate with limited voting powers, putting the CNMI on the same basis as Guam and American Samoa. In November, the first CMNI delegate to the House of Representatives was elected, with Gregorio Sablan, an independent candidate, defeating eight other candidates. Faleomavaega Eni Hunkin won his 10th consecutive two-year term as American Samoa's congressional delegate.

TONGA. Legislative elections were held in April, the first since the riots in the capital, Nuku'alofa, in late 2006 (see AR 2007, p. 358). Six of the nine incumbent people's representatives (commoner legislators) in the Fale Alea (unicameral legislature) were re-elected, and of the nine people's representatives, pro-democracy candidates won six seats. Tonga's 29 nobles also elected their nine representatives. The speaker lost his seat. In July, the Fale Alea passed a bill establishing a constitution and electoral commission to make recommendations for changing Tonga's electoral system (which would require constitutional change). The commission's five members—one nominated by the cabinet, one by the nobles, one by the people's representatives, and two by the Judicial Services Commission—were announced in November.

The coronation of King George (Siaosi) Tupou V was held on 31 July-1 August. The event had been scheduled to take place in 2007, following the king's accession in September 2006, but had been postponed because of the riots. The coronation was attended by several thousand visitors, including members of various European and Asian royal families as well as heads of state and government from many Pacific island countries. The coronation included both traditional Tongan and Western-style ceremonies, and the celebrations continued over a 22-day period, with the King travelling to each of Tonga's island groups.

There were other coronations as well, two on the French overseas territory of Wallis and Futuna. The new King of Wallis, Kapiliele (Gabriel) Faupala, was crowned on 25 July; his predecessor had ruled for 48 years (see AR 2008, p. 362). On 6 November Petelo Vikena, a former public servant, was crowned in the village of Alo as one of Futuna's two kings, replacing the incumbent, ousted in February in a decision taken by the island's four chiefly clans.

In French Polynesia, elections in January and February under a new two-round proportional representation system resulted in a defeat for the pro-independence territorial government, led by Oscar Temaru. On 23 February Gaston Flosse was elected president by the Legislative Assembly, for the sixth time since 1984. He lost power after only 52 days, however, when Gaston Tong Sang on 15 April successfully moved a motion of no-confidence and assumed the presidency.

The French territory of New Caledonia continued progress towards greater autonomy. In January a public contest was initiated to define "symbols of identity", including a national anthem, a motto, and a design for future banknotes. In June a new public holiday (26 June) was announced, aimed at promoting ideas of "reconciliation" and "common destiny", phrases enshrined in the territory's key autonomy agreements, the 1988 Matignon-Oudinot Accord and the 1998 Noumea Accord. In July, New Caledonia's lagoons and reef ecosystems were added to the UNESCO list of world heritage sites. The ecosystems, covering some 15,700 sq km, were believed to be the world's second largest such system, behind only Australia's Great Barrier Reef.

In January, Kiribati declared its Phoenix Islands—a group of eight mostly uninhabited atolls and two submerged coral reefs—to be a protected area, comprising 185,000 sq km off-limits to commercial fishing.

In October, victims of child sexual abuse on the British Pacific island territory of Pitcairn (see AR 2004, p. 352) succeeded in winning agreement from the UK government that they were entitled to financial compensation for physical and psychological injuries.

Demonstrations were held in the Indonesian province of West Papua (half of the island of New Guinea) calling for a referendum on Indonesia's "special autonomy" law and Papuan self-determination. Arrests were made during protests, in which the banned Papuan "Morning Star" flag was raised.

SOLOMON ISLANDS. The government of Prime Minister Derek Sikua, elected in December 2007 (see AR 2008, pp. 361-62), took steps to resolve ongoing problems, both domestic and with some of its neighbours. The prime minister met the prime ministers of Australia and Papua New Guinea, in a move to restore relations. The government also improved its position in parliament, gaining support as a result of defections from the opposition. A no-confidence vote moved by the former prime minister, Manasseh Sogavare, failed miserably. Another former prime minister, Allan Kemakeza (2001-06), was imprisoned, following his conviction in December on corruption charges.

In February, the government apologised to the capital's Chinese residents, victimised in the 2006 riots that had seen the burning of Honiara's Chinatown (see AR 2007, p. 356). Reconciliation between indigenous groups within the Solomon Islands proved more problematic, with several planned ceremonies having to be cancelled before one could be performed. The prime minister issued a public apology to the people of Malaita island in January, acknowledging that they had been made to feel unwelcome in other parts of the country.

Sikua expressed support for the multi-national intervention force, RAMSI (Regional Assistance Mission to Solomon Islands), which marked its fifth anniversary in 2008. A RAMSI police vehicle killed a Solomon Islands woman in a road accident in June, however, leading to calls from the opposition for a review of the legal framework governing RAMSI operations. Subsequently the Samoan officer was charged with manslaughter and dangerous driving.

Despite international criticism, the Solomon Islands continued its export of live dolphins. The government announced, however, that it would no longer be taking part in meetings of the International Whaling Commission, with Prime Minister Sikua declining an offer from the Japanese government to assist with the delegation's expenses. The country's foreign policy and aid and development strategy became more complex in October when the foreign minister travelled to Iran for talks.

The People's Republic of China, and Taiwan, continued to play rival roles in Pacific island states' development programmes. In January, China signed an agreement with the Fiji minister of finance, offering aid to Fiji to assist with the building of infrastructure projects. In April, Tonga's king made his first official visit to China, meeting the country's president. Support from China enabled reconstruction in Nuku'alofa to begin in November. Construction began in September in Rarotonga (Cook Islands) of an indoor sports complex, suitable for the 2009 Pacific Mini Games, funded by a loan from China. In December, a multi-million dollar loan from China led to the transfer of two aircraft to Vanuatu, enabling inter-island air links for the multi-island country. Meanwhile, in July Taiwan confirmed that it would fund the second stage of the Solomon Islands' Parliament House, with the building expected to be completed by the next Taiwan-Pacific Allies summit, scheduled to be hosted by the Solomon Islands in March 2009.

Stephen Levine

XI INTERNATIONAL ORGANISATIONS

UNITED NATIONS AND ITS AGENCIES

DATE OF FOUNDATION: 1945   HEADQUARTERS: New York, USA
OBJECTIVES: To promote international peace, security and co-operation on the basis of the equality of member-states, the right of self-determination of peoples and respect for human rights
MEMBERSHIP (END-'08): 192 sovereign states; those not in membership of the UN itself at end-2008 were the Holy See (Vatican) and Taiwan (Republic of China), although all except Taiwan were members of one or more UN specialised agency
SECRETARY GENERAL: Ban Ki Moon (South Korea) (since Jan '07)

THE secretary-general described 2008 as a year of multiple crises, in which he felt that the UN's record was mixed. Ban Ki Moon was pleased that the issue of climate change had remained at the top of the international agenda, that the UN had responded promptly to natural disasters and the food crises, and that quiet diplomacy had nurtured peace treaties and contained explosive situations. But he believed that the UN's record on human rights was on trial, because the organisation had been unable to protect innocent people from violence. He was concerned about the situations in Zimbabwe, a country on the brink of collapse; in Somalia, facing the continuing danger of anarchy; and in Afghanistan, where the humanitarian situation was growing worse. In 2008, at least 34 UN personnel lost their lives as a result of malicious acts while on active service; 10 personnel were taken hostage; and, on 14 December, the secretary-general's special envoy for Niger, Canadian diplomat Robert Fowler, together with his assistant and their UN driver, went missing near the capital, Niamey (see p. 269).

THE GENERAL ASSEMBLY.   The General Debate of the 63rd Session (23-27 and 29 September), which was attended by 111 heads of state and government, had as its major focus the impact of the global food crisis on poverty and hunger in the world, and the need to democratise the United Nations. Over the year, the General Assembly also held high level meetings on African development needs, on the Millennium Development Goals (MDGs), on the mid-term review of the 2003 Almaty Programme of Action for landlocked developing countries, and on the Culture of Peace (the years 2001-10 having been declared the international decade for the culture of peace). Interactive round tables were held on the impact of the financial crisis upon the food and energy crises, and on human rights. The president of the 63rd Session (Father Miguel d'Escoto Brockmann of Nicaragua) established an 18-member commission to review the workings of the global financial system.

To mark the 60th Anniversary of the Universal Declaration of Human Rights, the General Assembly reaffirmed the indivisibility of all fundamental rights and freedoms, pledging commitment to all internationally agreed development goals, the fulfilment of which would be instrumental to the enjoyment of human rights.

The Assembly also unanimously adopted an optional protocol to the International Covenant on Economic, Social and Cultural rights and recommended that it be open for signature in 2009. The protocol would allow any individual or group who claimed that their rights under the Covenant had been violated to submit a written communication for examination by the committee on economic, social and cultural rights.

The 63rd General Assembly on 17 October elected Austria, Turkey, Uganda, Japan, and Mexico to serve as non-permanent members of the UN Security Council for two-year terms, from 1 January, 2009. They would replace Belgium, Indonesia, Italy, Panama, and South Africa.

The General Assembly and the Security Council on 6 November elected, independently but concurrently, five judges to serve nine-year terms on the International Court of Justice (ICJ), starting in February 2009. These were Ronny Abraham of France, Awn Shawkat Al-Khasawneh of Jordan, Christopher Greenwood of the UK, Antonio Augusto Cançado Trindade of Brazil, and Abdulqawi Ahmed Yusuf of Somalia.

FINANCE. In a report released on 24 October, the secretary-general stated that, after considering the main financial indicators—assessments issued to member states, unpaid assessments, available cash, and the institution's outstanding debt to member states—the UN's financial health remained fragile.

Assessments and payments were both lower on 24 October than on 31 October 2007, by US$174 million and US$25 million, respectively. Because the reduction in assessments was greater than the reduction in payments, unpaid assessments were also lower, by US$80 million, at US$756 million compared with US$836 million on 31 October 2007. The reduced assessments for 2008 were the result of budget adjustments primarily for special political missions, which had been included in assessments for 2007. Seven more members had paid their regular assessments in full than had been the case on 31 October 2007 (133 compared with 126).

Of the US$756 million that remained outstanding on 24 October, 94 per cent was owed by one member—the USA—and 6 per cent by the remaining member states.

Cash for the regular budget was in the general fund, into which regular assessments were paid; in the working capital fund, which had US$150 million approved by the General Assembly; and in the special account. On 24 October, the general fund had a deficit of US$66 million, primarily due to special political mission expenditure during the first year of the budget biennium and the general weakening of the value of the US dollar compared with the budgeted exchange rate. If the USA failed to pay its outstanding assessment, it might be necessary to borrow US$148 million from reserve accounts; if it paid in full, there could be a positive cash balance at the end of 2008.

The secretary-general pointed out in his report that it was difficult to make a financial projection for peacekeeping, as the demand for peacekeeping activities was unpredictable. Peacekeeping had a different financial year from that of the regular budget (running from 1 July to 30 June, rather than from 1 January to 31

December). Assessments were issued separately for each operation, during the mandate period approved by the Security Council for each mission. Thus assessments were issued for different periods throughout the year.

Unpaid assessments on 24 October were over US$2.9 billion. The amount of unpaid assessments was, in part, related to the peacekeeping cycle and, in particular, included assessments that had been issued on 26 September. Like the regular budget, peacekeeping debt was highly concentrated with 62 per cent owed by two member states—the USA and Japan—and another 21 per cent by four other member states. The peacekeeping cash balance on 24 October was about US$3.1 billion, which was divided between active mission accounts (approximately US$2.5 billion), the peacekeeping reserve fund (US$142 million), and the completed mission accounts (US$467 million). There were restrictions, however, on the use of this money: the General Assembly routinely specified that no peacekeeping mission could be financed by borrowing from active missions; the terms of reference of the peacekeeping reserve fund restricted its use to new operations and the expansion of existing ones; and only some of the cash in closed mission accounts was currently available for cross-borrowing.

It was anticipated that the total cash available in the peacekeeping accounts at the end of 2008 would be slightly less than US$2.2 billion: comprising US$1.5 billion in the active peacekeeping accounts, US$522 million in the closed accounts, and US$142 million in the peacekeeping reserve fund. Of the US$522 million in the closed mission accounts, US$295 million was earmarked for payments, including for troops and equipment and credits due to member states. This would leave only US$227 million available for possible cross-borrowing by active peacekeeping operations and other accounts, including the regular budget and the international tribunals. The secretary-general remarked that this was a very thin margin for cross-borrowing: US$50 million had been cross-borrowed in 2007 for five active missions; but in 2008 US$117 million had already been borrowed for seven active missions (in Kosovo, Georgia, Western Sahara, Cyprus, Côte d'Ivoire, Haiti, and Liberia).

The financial position of the International Tribunals for Rwanda and the Former Yugoslavia was relatively acceptable. Assessments in 2008 were higher than those in 2007, but the amount outstanding was US$11 million less. By 24 October 97 member states had paid their assessments in full, five more than in the previous year.

The final financial position would depend on whether outstanding assessments were paid. There was a high concentration of debt, with one state (the USA) responsible for 85 per cent. If recent trends continued, however, the Tribunals should end 2008 with positive cash balances, although the position of the former Yugoslavia Tribunal was expected to be stronger than that of Rwanda.

The budget for the capital master plan for the renovation of the headquarters building in New York, approved in 2006, was US$1.88 billion. Twelve states had decided to meet their assessment in a single payment, while 180 states had decided to spread their assessment over several years. By 24 October, 120 states had paid their 2008 assessments in full, which amounted to US$766 million, while US$50 million remained outstanding for 2008. Payments to the working capital reserve were US$44.9 million.

The UN's debt to member states for providing troops and equipment for peacekeeping operations at the end of 2008 would be about US$645 million, which was below the May projection of US$728 million and the US$779 million outstanding at the end of 2007. Institutional debt had increased in 2008, mainly because of the deployment of troops to the African Union—UN Hybrid operation in Darfur (UNAMID), but this had been partly offset by a reduction in the mission in Liberia, reduced deployment in Lebanon, and the termination of the mission in Ethiopia and Eritrea. The total number of uniformed personnel deployed increased from 74,578 at the end of 2007 to 79,047 at 30 September 2008.

The secretary-general was committed to meeting the UN's obligations to member states for providing troops and equipment to peacekeeping operations as expeditiously as possible. The extent to which he could do this would depend upon the degree to which member states met their financial obligations and on the completion of memorandums of understanding with troop contributors for provision of equipment.

The General Assembly finally approved the regular budget on 24 December, after the fifth committee had worked through the night to reach agreement. The approved budget for 2009 was US$4.8 billion. One important development was the creation of 92 posts in the secretariat for development, and of 49 posts for preventive diplomacy in the department of political affairs.

THE SECURITY COUNCIL. The Council held 217 public meetings, adopted 64 resolutions, and issued 48 presidential statements. Only four resolutions required votes. One issue prompted overt disagreement in the Security Council. On 11 July the Council failed to adopt a resolution concerning the violence surrounding the presidential election in Zimbabwe, because of the vetoes of China and the Russian Federation. The resolution would have imposed an arms embargo on Zimbabwe, and travel and financial sanctions against President Robert Mugabe and 13 senior officials. But the permanent members disagreed about the extent to which the internal violence was a threat to international peace and security, with China and Russia arguing that there was no mandate for sanctions, because the violence remained domestic, while France and others stated that it threatened to destabilise southern Africa. Libya, Vietnam, and South Africa joined them in voting against the resolution; the USA, the UK, France, Belgium, Burkina Faso, Costa Rica, Croatia, Italy, and Panama voted in favour; Indonesia abstained. The Security Council's failure to adopt sanctions against Mugabe raised doubts about the organisation's readiness to intervene in a humanitarian and political crisis, and contributed to a souring of Russia's relations with the West, since Russia had backed a recent G-8 resolution calling for sanctions against Zimbabwe. The US representative said in the debate that Russia's actions raised "questions about its reliability as a G-8 partner".

The Security Council considered three new disputes. The first was in Kenya when, following the violent aftermath of the disputed presidential election of 27 December 2007, the Council issued a presidential statement on 6 February. The Council was concerned at the scale, volume, and severity of human suffering and the political, security and economic impact of this internal dispute upon the region. It welcomed the decisions by the high commissioner for human rights and the secretary-general's special advisor on the prevention of genocide to send missions to Kenya, and supported the African Union (AU) and the panel of eminent African persons, led by former UN Secretary-General Kofi Annan, in their efforts to stem the violence.

The second was when armed clashes started between Djibouti and Eritrea on 10 June. The Council condemned Eritrea's military action. It called upon the parties to agree to a ceasefire, withdraw their forces, and co-operate with efforts to resolve the dispute. It also asked that the secretary-general urgently use his good offices to facilitate bilateral negotiations and to despatch a fact finding mission to the region. Such a mission visited Djibouti and Ethiopia from 28 July to 6 August, but was unable to obtain visas to enter Eritrea. Although the mission reported that the situation needed urgent attention, and although members of the Council commented in the open meeting of 23 October that Eritrea had refused to co-operate and to withdraw its troops, the prevailing sentiment was simply to urge dialogue between the disputants and mediation through the AU, the Arab League, and the use of the secretary-general's good offices, with the Council taking no formal action.

The third crisis began when armed hostilities between Georgia and the Russian Federation began in the separatist Georgian region of South Ossetia on 7 August (see map, p. 137). Although the Council was unable to reach an agreement on a resolution, despite drafts being circulated by France and Russia on a 6-point peace plan, the consultations and the debates allowed the two protagonists to present their different views of the origins of the fighting. The debates also allowed other Council members to express their views on the need for restraint, especially as some believed that disproportionate force was being used. There was discussion of ways to achieve an immediate cessation of hostilities and the mitigation of the deteriorating humanitarian situation. Members expressed concerns about the territorial integrity of Georgia when Russia, subsequently, recognised the independence of South Ossetia and Abkhazia.

MIDDLE EAST—PALESTINE. The Council received monthly briefings on the situation in Gaza and the West Bank. The briefings highlighted the fluctuating fortunes of the Israeli-Palestine peace process, which had been re-launched at Annapolis in November 2007 (see AR 2008, p. 188). They also demonstrated the lack of unity among the Palestinians, including internecine violence; the appalling humanitarian situation in Gaza, which was exacerbated by the Israeli policy of allowing civilians to suffer by denying unimpeded delivery of fuel and basic necessities; and the intermittent violence and violations of the ceasefire by both Hamas and Israel. The secretary-general condemned Hamas's rocket attacks on southern Israel as terrorism and censured the Israeli land and air assault, launched in response, as a disproportionate and excessive use of force.

The Security Council met on five occasions to discuss Palestine, prior to the Israeli military assault on the Gaza Strip at the end of 2008 (see below). On four occasions the Council took no action: an emergency session on 1 March to discuss the escalation of violence in Gaza and southern Israel, with its attendant civilian toll; a ministerial level meeting on 26 September to consider the impact on the Annapolis peace process of continued Israeli settlement activity in the Palestinian territories; a session on 3 December to discuss Libya's claim that Israel had refused to allow a boat carrying humanitarian supplies to reach the port of Gaza; and an open debate on Palestine on 18 December. On 16 December, however, the Council adopted a resolution on Palestine for the first time for over four years, by 14 votes, with Libya abstaining. The resolution affirmed the Annapolis agreements and called upon the parties, regional states, other states, and international organisations to intensify their efforts to achieve a two-state solution to the Israeli-Palestine conflict, as well as peaceful co-existence among all states in the region.

On 27 December, Israel commenced an air campaign against Gaza, code-named "Operation Cast Lead", in an attempt to prevent Hamas and other groups from launching further rocket attacks against southern Israel. The Security Council issued a press statement on 28 December, negotiated between the USA and the Arab states, expressing serious concern at the situation in Gaza and calling for an immediate halt to all violence and for all parties to address the serious economic and humanitarian needs, including the opening of the border crossings. The Council met in emergency session on 31 December, partly because the call to end violence had remained unheeded, and Council members again expressed concern at the escalation of violence and the need to address the humanitarian situation, including the protection of civilians and access for all forms of humanitarian supplies.

DARFUR. The Council received regular briefings upon the AU-UN Hybrid mission in Darfur (UNAMID), which stressed the difficulties that the mission faced in the field. Political progress was essential for the cessation of attacks against civilians and for the provision of conditions for effective peacekeeping. But progress was hindered by political rivalry among the rebels, the parties normally preferring fighting to negotiations, with rebel advances being met by large-scale ground and air campaigns by the Sudanese government. The ability of the peacekeeping force to deploy at authorised strength, and quickly, was hindered by a number of factors. These included the harsh physical climate, the unpredictable security situation (the force lost 21 personnel in 2008), the difficulties in obtaining the requisite personnel, the absence of specialist equipment (particularly helicopters), the logistical problems of moving equipment over the vast distances to Darfur, and the protracted diplomatic negotiations with the Sudanese government. The revised aim was to have 85 per cent of UNAMID's authorised strength deployed by March 2009.

The prosecutor of the International Criminal Court (ICC), to which the Security Council had referred the Darfur conflict in 2005, stated that the entire Darfur region was a crime scene. Evidence showed that crimes on such a scale, throughout Darfur, over a period of five years, had required the sustained mobilisation of the entire state apparatus. Subsequently, on 14 July, the prosecutor requested a warrant for the arrest of President Omar Hasan Ahmed al-Bashir for genocide, war crimes, and crimes against humanity. This was the first attempt by the ICC to prosecute a serving head of state and the first case involving allegations of genocide (see p. 484). The prosecutor appeared before the Council on 3 December, seeking its support to ensure the execution of the warrant if the ICC in January 2009 decided to issue it. Previous warrants for other Sudanese officials had not been executed by the Sudanese government, despite the intervention of the secretary-general.

The Council, however, was still divided over the extent to which the government of Sudan should be subject to public criticism, if co-operation was to be enhanced and sustained for the peacekeeping operation. This was reflected in the Council's actions: a presidential statement on 10 May condemned the rebel Justice and Equality Movement attack on the outskirts of the capital, Khartoum (see p. 234). Another statement on 16 June urged the government to co-operate fully with the ICC in order to end impunity in Darfur. The issue of the potential arrest warrant for al-Bashir became entangled with the extension of UNAMID's mandate, which resulted in the USA abstaining on the resolution to extend the mandate. A paragraph in the resolution noted the concerns of the AU and some members of the Security Council about the potential negative effects of the warrant being issued. The USA believed that this sent the wrong message to al-Bashir.

SOMALIA. The Security Council met 16 times to explore how Somalia might be stabilised. The first issue was how the AU Mission to Somalia (AMISOM, which was unable to reach its authorised strength, could be helped. The first suggestion was for an international stabilisation force as a precursor to a UN peacekeeping force (both of which would incorporate AMISOM) but, although this was requested by the Somali parties that had signed the June Djibouti Agreement (see p. 250), the secretary-general—who canvassed support from national leaders during the General Debate in the General Assembly in September—was unable to secure significant pledges of troops, essential resources, and leadership. Although contingency planning continued for a UN peacekeeping force of 22,500 soldiers, appropriate police and civilian components, and a maritime and aviation task force to support the land operations, the secretary-general did not believe that the conditions currently existed for peacekeeping. He therefore proposed that the most realistic prospect was the strengthening of AMISOM through the provision of finance, logistical support, necessary training, and equipment, facilitated by the UN and member states.

The second issue was piracy off the coast of Somalia. By the end of November, 120 such attacks had been reported, with 35 ships seized and more than 600 seamen captured. On 2 June, in Resolution 1816 (2008), the Security Council authorised states for a period of six months (extended for a further 12 months in Resolution 1851 (2008) of 16 December) to enter the territorial waters of Somalia to suppress piracy by the use of force if necessary. In Resolution 1838 of 7 October, the Council called upon states interested in the security of maritime activities to deploy naval vessels and military aircraft to fight actively piracy on the high seas off the coast of Somalia. Subsequently, in Resolution 1851, the Council also authorised states and regional organisations to use land based operations in Somalia in the fight against piracy.

KOSOVO. Kosovo declared independence from Serbia on 17 February (see Documents). The secretary-general informed the Security Council that UNMIK, the UN Interim Administration Mission in Kosovo, would continue to implement its mandate, which sought to maintain stability in Kosovo and the wider region. The permanent members of the Council remained divided about the status of the independence declaration, with the USA, the UK, and France supporting recognition of Kosovo; China and, predictably, Russia against. This division meant that the Council was also unable to agree whether the EU's new police and rule of law mission (EULEX) would be able to supervise the emergence of a multi-ethnic and democratic Kosovo. Initially, there was also disagreement over the legal status and usefulness of the secretary-general's subsequent proposal of 15 July to reconfigure UNMIK to operate alongside NATO's Kosovo Force (KFOR) and an enhanced role for EULEX under a UN mantle. However, after receiving a briefing on 26 November from the special representative in Kosovo, who emphasised that EULEX was acting as a channel of communication between Kosovo and Serbia, the Council was sufficiently united to issue a presidential statement, which welcomed Kosovo's and Serbia's stated intentions to co-operate with UNMIK and EULEX.

The Council on 4 June received briefings from the presidents and chief prosecutors of the International Criminal Tribunals for the Former Yugoslavia and Rwanda on their trial completion strategy, and on 28 October in a private meeting, from the president of the International Court of Justice.

On 19 August the Council adopted a presidential statement in which it condemned the military overthrow on 6 August of the democratically elected government of Mauritania. The Council demanded the immediate release of President Sidi Mohammed Ould Cheikh Abdellahi and the restoration of legitimate, democratic institutions.

With regard to Cyprus, the Security Council on 4 September welcomed the launch of fully fledged negotiations between the leaders of the both the Greek and Turkish communities, aimed at the reunification of the island, under the auspices of the good offices mission of the secretary general.

Thematic debates were held on terrorism; the importance of mediation for the peaceful settlement of disputes; UN co-operation with regional organisations, in particular the AU; strengthening collective security through general regulation and reduction of armaments; the protection of civilians in armed conflicts; women and peace and security; children and armed conflict; post conflict peacebuilding; security sector reform; and—for the first time in 14 years—the working methods of the Council.

MISSIONS, PEACEKEEPING, SANCTIONS, AND FORCE.   There were two Security Council missions. The first was to Africa (1-10 June), which assessed progress in Sudan, Somalia, Chad, the Democratic Republic of Congo, and Côte d'Ivoire. The second, to Afghanistan on 21-28 November, visited Kabul and Herat to examine the multifaceted challenges facing the government and the international community.

Secretary-General Ban Ki Moon appointed Alain Le Roy of France as the new head of peacekeeping. He replaced Jean Marie Guehenno, who had held the post since October 2000. Susana Malcorra of Argentina was appointed under-secretary-general for field support.

Important developments in peacekeeping included the decision on 31 July not to renew the UN Mission in Ethiopia and Eritrea (UNMEE), largely because of a lack of co-operation by Eritrea (see p. 248). As part of the process of running down the UN Mission in Liberia (UNMIL), 1,460 military personnel were withdrawn and 240 police officers added. The mandate of the UN Mission in the Democratic Republic of the Congo (MONUC) was expanded to provide assistance to the Congolese authorities in preparing for local elections in 2009, and the force was increased and reconfigured to enable it to protect civilians in the eastern provinces from the continued violence (see pp. 278-79). The Security Council expressed its intention to authorise a UN military component to replace the EU troops (EUFOR Chad/CAR), who arrived in Chad in 2008 under the auspices of the UN Mission in the Central African Republic and Chad (MINUR-CAT) (see p. 272). The Council reviewed the findings of an investigation into the incident in Mitrovica, Kosovo, on 17 March, in which Serbian demonstrators had seized a courthouse operated by UNMIK in the ethnically-divided city (see map, p. 111). The investigation confirmed that UNMIK had acted within its mandate to regain control of the courthouse, but that the actions taken by UNMIK towards Serb demonstrators, who had held daily protests in front of the building since Kosovo's independence declaration, lacked both balance and an appreciation of the political and legal implications of the use of force. Finally, the Council heard the recommendations of the panel established by the secretary-general, which explored how the UN and the AU could enhance predictability, sustainability, and flexibility of financing for UN-mandated peace operations undertaken by the AU. The panel advised that a multi-donor trust fund should be established and that UN-assessed funding should be used for a period of six months.

The Security Council terminated one sanctions regime and made alterations to four others. In Resolution 1823 (10 July), the Council terminated the prohibition on the supply and use of arms by non-governmental groups in Rwanda. In Resolution 1803 (3 March), it broadened the scope of the embargo against Iran relating to the proliferation of sensitive nuclear activities and delivery systems for nuclear weapons. The same Resolution, drawing upon earlier resolutions, added more named individuals and entities subject to asset freezes, travel notification, and travel bans to earlier such resolutions. It also called upon states to exercise vigilance over public financial support for trade with Iran and over the activities of financial institutions with branches domiciled in Iran. In Resolution 1822 (20 June), with regard to sanctions relating to al-Qaida and the Taliban, the Council revised the rules for listing individuals subject to sanctions. The new rules asked states to identify information on each listed individual that could be made public, directed the sanctions committee to make available on its website narrative summaries of the reasons for listing an individual on the consolidated list, decided that the secretariat should inform within one week a member state's permanent mission that one of its nationals had been listed and that the member state concerned, on receiving notification, should inform the listed individual in a timely manner (a similar procedure was to be adopted for delisting), and directed the sanctions committee to conduct a review of all the names on the list before June 2010. In Resolution 1844 of 20 November the Council extended the sanctions relating to Somalia to include travel restrictions and an asset freeze on individuals and entities that threatened peace and the political process and obstructed humanitarian assistance. Finally, in Resolution 1857 of 22 December, the Council extended targeted sanctions in the Democratic Republic of Congo to include, in the eastern part of the DRC, individuals obstructing access to or the distribution of humanitarian assistance, and individuals and entities supporting illegal groups through the illicit trade of natural resources.

The Security Council extended the authorization of the AU Mission in Somalia (AMISOM) for two periods of six months, by Resolutions 1801 of 20 February and 1831 of 19 August. It also extended the mandate of the International Security Assistance Force (ISAF) in Afghanistan for one year beyond 13 October (Resolution 1833 of 22 September). Regarding Bosnia & Herzegovina, the Security Council extended for a further 12 months the mandate of the EU Stabilisation Force (EUFOR) and the continued presence of a headquarters for NATO (Resolution 1845 of 20 November).

On 4 December, Iraq ratified the Status of Force Agreement (SOFA), covering the presence of US armed forces in the country, which would take effect after the UN's authorisation for the multinational force in Iraq ended on 31 December 2008 (see Documents). The secretary-general on 12 December informed the Security Council that he intended to conclude an agreement with the US forces in Iraq to provide security for UN activities in that country.

David Travers

UNITED NATIONS PEACEKEEPING MISSIONS 2008

Mission	Established	Present Strength	Renewal Date
UNTSO: United Nations Truce Supervision Organisation	May 1948	151 military observers; 95 international civilians; 133 local civilians. Total personnel: 379. Fatalities: 49. Budget: $66,217,000.	
UNMOGIP: United Nations Military Observer Group in India and Pakistan	January 1949	44 military observers; 23 international civilians; 46 local civilians. Total personnel: 113. Fatalities: 11. Budget: $16,957,100.	
UNFICYP: United Nations Peacekeeping Force in Cyprus	March 1964	859 military; 68 civilian police; 39 international civilians; 106 local civilians. Total personnel: 1,072 Fatalities: 179. Budget: $57,392,000, including voluntary contributions of one-third from Cyprus and $6,500,000 million from Greece.	June 2009
UNDOF: United Nations Disengagement Observer Force	June 1974	1,039 military; 37 international civilians; 100 local civilians. Total personnel: 1,176. Fatalities: 43. Budget: $47,859,100.	June 2009
UNIFIL: United Nations Interim Force in Lebanon	March 1978	12,435 military; 317 international civilians; 640 local civilians. Total personnel: 13,392. Fatalities: 279. Budget: $680,932,600.	August 2009
MINURSO: United Nations Mission for the Referendum in Western Sahara	April 1991	20 troops; 197 military observers; 6 civilian police; 97 international civilians; 153 local civilians; 18 UN volunteers. Total personnel: 491. Fatalities: 15. Budget: $47,702,500.	April 2009
UNOMIG: United Nations Observer Mission in Georgia	August 1993	136 military observers; 20 civilian police; 103 international civilians; 195 local civilians; 1 UN volunteer. Total personnel: 455. Fatalities: 11. Budget: $36,084,000.	February 2009

UNITED NATIONS PEACEKEEPING MISSIONS 2008 *continued*

Mission	Established	Present Strength	Renewal Date
UNMIK: United Nations Interim Administration Mission in Kosovo	June 1999	22 military observers; 841 civilian police; 373 international civilians; 1,666 local civilians. 88 UN Volunteers. Total personnel: 2,990. Fatalities: 54. Budget: $207,203,100.	Established for an initial period of 12 months; to continue unless the Security Council decides otherwise.
MONUC: United Nations Organisation Mission in the Democratic Republic of Congo	November 1999	16,603 troops; 740 military observers; 1,079 civilian police; 951 international civilians; 2,206 local civilians; 595 UN volunteers. Total personnel: 22,174. Fatalities: 139. Budget: $1,242,729,000.	December 2009
UNMIL: United Nations Mission in Liberia	September 2003	10,607 troops; 180 military observers; 1,066 civilian police; 478 international civilians; 993 local civilians; 238 UN volunteers. Total personnel: 13,562. Fatalities: 123 Budget $631,689,100.	September 2009
UNOCI: United Nations Mission in Côte d'Ivoire	April 2004	7,830 troops; 197 military observers; 1,163 civilian police; 430 international civilians; 656 local civilians; 296 UN volunteers. Total personnel: 10,572. Fatalities: 54. Budget: $497,455,100.	January 2009
MINUSTAH: United Nations Stabilisation Mission in Haiti	June 2004	7,036 military; 2,053 civilian police; 492 international civilians; 1,211 local civilians; 210 UN volunteers. Total personnel: 11,002. Fatalities: 39. Budget: $601,580,100.	October 2009
UNMIS: United Nations Mission in Sudan	March 2005	8,726 military; 620 military observers; 679 civilian police; 774 international civilian; 2,475 local civilians; 271 UN volunteers. Total personnel: 13,545. Fatalities: 42. Budget: $858,771,200.	April 2009

UNITED NATIONS PEACEKEEPING MISSIONS 2008 *continued*

Mission	Established	Present Strength	Renewal Date
UNMIT: United Nations Integrated Mission in Timor-Leste (East Timor)	August 2006	33 military observers; 1,517 civilian police; 351 international civilians; 881 local civilians; 133 UN volunteers. Total personnel: 2,915. Fatalities: 4. Budget: $180,841,100.	February 2009
UNAMID: African Union/ United Nations Hybrid Operation in Darfur (mandated tasks to begin no later than 31 December 2007)	July 2007	Current strength: 12,194 military; 175 military observers; 2,767 civilian police; 786 international civilians; 1,405 local civilians; 266 UN volunteers. Total personnel: 17,593. Fatalities: 25. Authorised strength: 19,315 military; 240 military observers; 6,432 civilian police; 1,579 international civilians; 3,455 local civilians; 548 UN volunteers. Total personnel: 31,569. Budget: $1,569,255,200.	July 2009
MINURCAT: United Nations Mission in the Central African Republic and Chad	September 2007	Current strength: 44 military observers; 235 civilian police; 316 international civilians; 183 local civilians; 98 UN volunteers. Total personnel: 876. Fatalities: 2. Budget $315,083,400.	March 2009

NOTES.

Different categories of personnel serving in peacekeeping missions as of 31 December 2008:

Military troops, observers, and civilian police: 91,382 (77,349 troops; 11,494 civilian police; and 2,539 military observers).

Number of countries contributing uniformed personnel: 120.

International civilians (as at 30 November 2008): 5,662.

Local civilians (as at 30 November 2008): 13,049.

United Nations volunteers: 2,214.

Total number of personnel serving in the 16 peacekeeping operations: 112,307.

Total number of personnel serving in the 18 department of peacekeeping-led operations: 114,212.

Total number of fatalities from all categories in all peacekeeping operations between 1948 and 31 December 2008: 2,555.

Finance:

Approved budgets for the period 1 July 2008 to 30 June 2009: c. US$7.1 billion.

Estimated total cost of operations from 1948 to 30 June 2008: c. US$54 billion.

Outstanding contributions to peacekeeping (as at 30 November 2008): c. US$3.38 billion.

UNTSO and UNMOGIP are funded from the UN regular biennial budget. The costs to the UN of the 14 other current peacekeeping operations are financed from the operations' own separate accounts, on the basis of legal binding assessments on all member states.

Completed mission during 2008:

The United Nations Mission in Ethiopia and Eritrea (UNMEE), established in July 2000, was terminated on 31 July by Security Council Resolution 1827 (2008).

Number of peacekeeping operations since 1948: 63.

(Sources: UN background note 31 December 2008; UN current peacekeeping operations website; and UN press releases.)

UNITED NATIONS POLITICAL AND PEACEBUILDING MISSIONS 2008

Mission	Established	Present Strength	Current Authorisation
UNPOS: United Nations Political Office for Somalia	April 1995	Special Representative of the Secretary-General: Ahmedou Ould-Abdallah (Mauritania); 32 international civilians; 16 local civilians.	
UNOGBIS: United Nations Peace-building Support Office in Guinea-Bissau	March 1999	Representative of the Secretary-General: Shola Omoregie (Nigeria); 9 international civilians; 2 military advisers; 1 civilian police adviser; 14 local civilians.	30 June 2009
UNSCO: Office of the United Nations Special Co-ordinator for the Middle East.	October 1999	Special Co-ordinator for the Middle East Peace Process and Personal Representative of the Secretary-General to the Palestine Liberation Organisation and the Palestine Authority: Robert H. Serry (The Netherlands); 29 international civilians; 24 local civilians.	
BONUCA: United Nations Peace-building Office in the Central African Republic	February 2000	Representative of the Secretary-General: Francois Lonsey Fall (Guinea); 24 international civilians; 5 military advisers; 6 civilian police; 54 local civilians; 3 UN volunteers.	31 December 2009
Office of the United Nations Special Co-ordinator for Lebanon (formerly known as Office of the Personal Representative of the Secretary-General for Southern Lebanon)	February 2007	Special Co-ordinator for Lebanon: Michael C. Williams (UK); 14 international civilians; 28 local civilians.	

UNITED NATIONS POLITICAL AND PEACEBUILDING MISSIONS 2008 *continued*

Mission	Established	Present Strength	Current Authorisation
Office of the Special Representative of the Secretary-General for West Africa	November 2001	Special Representative of the Secretary-General: Saïd Djinnit (Algeria); 10 international civilians; 11 local civilians.	31 December 2010
UNAMA: United Nations Assistance Mission in Afghanistan	March 2002	Special Representative of the Secretary-General: Kai Eide (Norway); 250 international civilians; 1,163 local civilians; 16 military observers; 5 civilian police; 41 UN volunteers.	23 March 2009
UNAMI: United Nations Assistance Mission for Iraq	August 2003	Special Representative of the Secretary-General for Iraq: Staffan de Mistura (Sweden); authorised strength: 1,014 (463 international civilians; 551 local civilians). Current strength (staff are based in Iraq, Jordan and Kuwait): 296 international civilians; 389 local civilians; 222 troops; 6 military observers.	7 August 2009
UNIPSIL: United Nations Integrated Peacebuilding Office in Sierra Leone	October 2008	Executive Representative of the Secretary-General: Michael von der Schulenburg (Germany); 13 international civilians; 1 local civilian; 5 military observers; 2 civilian police; 9 UN volunteers.	1 October 2009
BINUB: United Nations Integrated Office in Burundi	January 2007	Executive Representative of the Secretary General: Youssef Mahmoud (Tunisia); 117 international civilians; 213 local civilians; 8 military observers; 12 civilian police; 50 UN volunteers.	31 December 2009

UNITED NATIONS POLITICAL AND PEACEBUILDING MISSIONS 2008 *continued*

Mission	Established	Present Strength	Current Authorisation
UNMIN: United Nations Mission in Nepal	January 2007	Special Representative in Nepal and Head of Mission: Ian Martin (UK); 104 international civilians; 158 local civilians; 61 military observers; 33 UN volunteers.	23 January 2009
UNRCCA: United Nations Regional Centre for Preventive Diplomacy for Central Asia	December 2007	Special Representative of the Secretary-General: Miroslav Jenca (Slovakia); 2 international civilians.	

NOTES.

UNAMA and BINUB, although political missions, were directed and supported by the department of peacekeeping operations. All the other political and peace-building missions were directed by the department of political affairs.

The following mission was completed in 2008:
UNIOSIL: United Nations Integrated Office in Sierra Leone (1 January 2006 to 30 September 2008). It was succeeded by **UNIPSIL** (see above).

Current number of Missions: 12

Personnel:

    International Civilians (as at 30 November 2008): 900.
    Uniformed personnel: 351.
    Local civilian personnel (as at 30 November 2008): 2,071.
    UN volunteers: 136.

Total number of personnel serving in political and peacebuilding missions: 3,458.

(Sources: UN Political and Peace-Building Missions background note 31 December 2008; and UN website.)

DEFENCE AND ECONOMIC ORGANISATIONS

DEFENCE ORGANISATIONS

North Atlantic Treaty Organisation (NATO)
DATE OF FOUNDATION: 1949   HEADQUARTERS: Brussels, Belgium
OBJECTIVES: To ensure the collective security of member states
MEMBERSHIP (END-'08): Belgium, Bulgaria, Canada, Czech Republic, Denmark, Estonia, France,
    Germany, Greece, Hungary, Iceland, Italy, Latvia, Lithuania, Luxembourg, Netherlands,
    Norway, Poland, Portugal, Romania, Slovakia, Slovenia, Spain, Turkey, UK, USA (total 26)
SECRETARY GENERAL: Jaap de Hoop Scheffer (Netherlands)

Partnership for Peace (PFP)
DATE OF FOUNDATION: 1994   HEADQUARTERS: Brussels, Belgium
OBJECTIVES: To provide a framework for co-operation between NATO and the former communist
    and neutral states of Europe and ex-Soviet Central Asia
MEMBERSHIP (END-'08): Albania, Armenia, Austria, Azerbaijan, Belarus, Bosnia & Herzegovina,
    Croatia, Finland, Georgia, Irish Republic, Kazakhstan, Kyrgyzstan, Macedonia, Malta,
    Moldova, Montenegro, Russia, Serbia, Sweden, Switzerland, Tajikistan, Turkmenistan,
    Ukraine, Uzbekistan (total 24)

For data on other organisations mentioned in this article, see specific entries.

THE year 2008 saw further evidence of the cyber-security threat. It was increasingly clear that the global information and communications technology (ICT) infrastructure was open to exploitation by a range of miscreants including political extremists, organised criminal groups, individual hackers, and cyber-hooligans. Some aspects of the cyber-security problem had been understood for several years: online fraud was scarcely a novel security challenge, and the Internet had long been a means by which to transmit and receive illegal images, for example. More recently, cyber-security had taken on a new dimension, with some governments apparently having taken the view that the Internet was little more than a battlefield where strategic conflict could be won or lost. It was also clear that the various cyber-security challenges could be interconnected: extremist groups might make use of low-level cyber-criminality in order to raise funds, while mass hacking was regarded as a valid tool in one state's conflict with another. It would be an exaggeration to suggest that these various manifestations of the cyber-security challenge were all elements of a unified conspiracy led by some cyber-mastermind. Yet when taken together, these different cyber-threats—occasionally, and perhaps accidentally, overlapping—did constitute a general challenge to developed economies and societies. Cyber-security, in other words, touched upon all aspects of life in economically developed, open societies: governmental, commercial and private.

Cyber-security had moved to the top of the agenda for national governments and international security organisations. Devising policy responses had not, however, been straightforward. In the first place, governments, institutions, commercial companies, and private individuals all confronted the problem described by one analyst as the "dilemma of the global technological commons". In other words, the ICT infrastructure exploited by extremists, criminals, and hackers was essentially indistinguishable from that used by society for entirely innocent and legitimate purposes. What was more, these legitimate uses were often not optional extras, which society might set aside for reasons of safety and security. Thus, the dilemma was that a restrictive approach to global ICT might narrow the scope of action of illegitimate users, but it would also constrain the behaviour of legitimate users, for whom a permissive (and perhaps even unregulated) ICT environment would be preferable. The second problem was derived simply from the fact that so much of society was challenged by the misuse of ICT. Different sectors of society responded in their own way to those aspects of the cyber-security challenge which concerned them most. As a result it was difficult to know how—and by whom—the response should be co-ordinated overall, and difficult to ensure that policies were complementary rather than conflicting.

European and international security and defence organisations responded in a variety of ways to the complex challenge of cyber-security. With its concern for human security, the Council of Europe's contribution to international cyber-security policy was in the form of a Convention on Cybercrime, which was opened for signature in November 2001 and which entered into force in July 2004. Directed at "terrorist groups, pornographers and paedophile networks, illegal traffickers in weapons, drugs and human beings, money launderers and cybercriminals", the Cybercrime Convention provided "guidelines for all governments wishing to develop legislation against cybercrime" in pursuit of closer co-ordination of national efforts. An additional protocol to the Convention also forbade "acts of a racist and xenophobic nature committed through computer systems". The distinctive feature of the Convention, however, was that it constituted a binding international treaty against cybercrime, and was the only one which had so far been brought into effect. The Convention detailed the crimes and offences which signatory governments should bring into domestic law and act against, ranging from illegal interception of data, to computer-related fraud, and offences related to child pornography. The Convention also set out procedures by which computer data could be restored and retrieved for the purposes of criminal investigation, and by which the signatories to the Convention "shall afford one another mutual assistance to the widest extent possible for the purpose of investigations or proceedings concerning criminal offences related to computer systems and data, or for the collection of evidence in electronic form of a criminal offence".

The Organisation for Security and Co-operation in Europe (OSCE) had also taken an interest in cyber-security. In December 2004 the OSCE ministerial council (comprising the foreign ministers of OSCE participating states) resolved to address "the extent of use of the Internet by terrorist organisations", including a range of activities such as terrorist recruitment, fundraising, organisation, and propaganda. Two years later, foreign ministers called for enhanced international co-operation and for more effort to protect "vital critical information infrastructures and networks against the threat of cyber attacks". Participating states were urged to monitor more closely the websites of terrorist and extremist organisations, and to exchange information with other governments in the OSCE and other appropriate forums. The permanent council of the OSCE had been a venue for debate and discussion concerning cyber-security. In June 2008, for example, Estonian Defence Minister Jaak Aaviksoo spoke of an "immense amount of work to be done" in the field of cyber-security. The organisation's forum for security co-operation (FSC) also contributed to the OSCE's involvement in the field of cyber-security. In October 2008 the FSC (in joint session with the permanent council), decided to convene an OSCE "workshop on a comprehensive OSCE approach to enhancing cyber security" in March 2009. The OSCE also supported national efforts, such as Armenia's task force on cybercrime and cyber-security.

In April 2008 reports were circulated of an attack against eight Internet sites operated by Radio Free Europe/Radio Liberty. In an orchestrated attempt to overwhelm the target sites, some 50,000 fake hits were recorded every second. This was scarcely the most sophisticated form of cyber-operation. Yet, far from being a low-level hacking or nuisance attack, the source of the operation was alleged to be none other than the authoritarian government of Belarus's Alyaksandr Lukashenka, concerned to limit media coverage of opposition protests against his regime. Moreover, the RFE/RL case illustrated a recent trend in Internet misuse, which was arguably more systematic and which could have consequences far more serious than nuisance hacking and the temporary jamming of radio broadcasts, and other low-level activities of that sort. In September 2000, Israeli hackers attacked and defaced websites owned by Hezbullah and the Palestinian National Authority. In the Palestinian response—described as a "cyber holy war"—Israeli government and financial websites came under assault. In 2001, following a dispute over damage to US and Chinese aircraft in the South China Sea, both countries suffered a series of cyber-attacks, and at one stage California's electricity grid was almost shut down. Neither government accepted responsibility for launching these operations, although both had reportedly conducted research into the viability and effect of cyber-weapons.

More recently, the cyber-attacks launched against Estonia in April and May 2007 captured the attention of Europe's security organisations. In a dispute over a Russian war memorial, Estonian government and banking websites and Internet providers were the targets of concentrated "distributed denial of service" (DDOS) attacks. These attacks were especially disabling for a country which held itself up as a pioneer of electronic government. There was some uncertainty as to who or what had orchestrated the attacks, although the Estonian authorities eventually prosecuted a lone hacker. One important lesson of the Estonian affair was that even very large organisations and government departments were vulnerable to disabling attacks of this sort, and the episode hastened NATO's development of the co-operative cyber defence centre of excellence, which had been established in Estonia (see below).

Drawing lessons from the long military tradition of electronic warfare, cyber-operations had also become a feature of conventional military attacks. In September 2007, for example, an Israeli air strike against a target in Syria was reportedly assisted by a parallel cyber-attack against Syrian air defences, enabling non-stealthy Israeli aircraft to move into Syrian airspace without fear of detection and interdiction. For one analyst, this was an indication of things to come, with cyber-aggression possibly serving to indicate that a more traditional, physical attack was in preparation. This warning rang true within a year, with the Russia-Georgia conflict over South Ossetia in August 2008 (see pp. 136-38). Seen by some commentators as the advent of a wholly new style of warfare, the Russia-Georgia conflict saw private computing power organised and co-ordinated in such a way as to have strategic effect on a national enemy. It was not clear that the Russian government was directly behind the DDOS attacks on Georgia, but it seems likely that the attacks were officially not prevented, even if not formally sanctioned. Although no serious long-term Georgian cyber damage was reported, the co-ordinated attack was an uncomfortably clear demonstration that the Internet could be used against the government and population of an adversary, creating the confusion and uncertainty usually associated with more traditional forms of armed conflict.

It was likely, if not certain that cyber-warfare would be an increasingly important feature of conflict between states in years to come. Indeed, losses and gains made in cyber-space might prove so decisive that the character of warfare could change fundamentally, as the physical and the territorial parameters of conflict gave way to the virtual and the digital. Analysis clearly pointed in this direction. It was estimated that a large-scale DDOS attack against the USA, for example, could have a devastating effect: if power and other services could be shut down for a period of three months, the damage could be equivalent to many hurricane-force storms all striking the country simultaneously. China's intentions and capabilities often featured prominently in analysis of this sort. The November 2008 *US-China Economic and Security Review*, published by the US Congress, found that China was "aggressively developing its power to wage cyber warfare and is now in a position to delay or disrupt the deployment of America's military forces around the world, potentially giving it the upper hand in any conflict". An increasing number of electronic "intrusions" were reported to have originated in China, although as with the Russia-Georgia conflict it was not entirely clear how far this activity had been officially approved. China was, nevertheless, thought to be allocating very significant resources to computer network operations, including computer network defence (CND). By reducing vulnerability to counter-measures, CND would be a crucial feature of cyber-dependent operations, and was consistent with the view that the Chinese People's Liberation Army would seek to dominate the electromagnetic spectrum early in any conflict, and would try to maintain that advantage.

If cyber-security were to become increasingly militarised, and if the Internet did become yet another weapon to be used in inter-state conflict, a number of intriguing political, technological, and ethical questions would be raised. What was the best form of defence in cyber-warfare? Would cyber-aggression contravene Article 51 of the UN Charter (the right of self-defence), and perhaps trigger action under Article 5 of NATO's Washington Treaty (the principle of collective defence)? How could the origin of a cyber-attack, and the identity of the perpetrator, be ascertained? What exactly were "cyber-weapons" and did they constitute weapons of war in the same way as combat aircraft and artillery? Should the Internet be regarded as essentially harmless technology, or as something that could be used to damage, destroy, and kill and, therefore, regulated as such? If so, should efforts be made to agree a "cyber-Geneva Convention" or something similar? Was it reasonable or useful to regard cyber-weapons as equivalent in magnitude to "weapons of mass destruction", as some commentators insisted? Finally, what response should be expected from organisations such as NATO and the EU, both of which had traditionally been at the heart of Europe's security and prosperity?

NATO had long been familiar with the use of, and defence against, electronic and information warfare. For several years NATO had been closely involved in the US-led efforts to "transform" military organisation and the conduct of operations through "network-centric warfare" and "network-enabled capability". At the Prague summit in November 2002, NATO leaders resolved to "strengthen our capabilities to defend against cyber attacks", resulting in a range of initiatives. A new NATO Cyber-Defence Programme was established, involving various NATO bodies: the NATO communication and information systems services agency (NCSA), described as the Alliance's "first line of defence against cyber terrorism"; the NATO information security technical centre (NITC), responsible for communications and computer security; the NATO information security operations centre, responsible for the management of cryptographic equipment and the co-ordination of responses to cyber attacks against NATO; and the NATO computer incident response capability (NCIRC), tasked with the protection of NATO's encrypted communications and systems.

Following the cyber-attacks against Estonia in April and May 2007, NATO ministers agreed the outlines of an Alliance-wide cyber-defence concept in October 2007, and this in turn developed into the NATO policy on cyber-defence, agreed in early 2008. Following the Alliance's April 2008 Bucharest summit, the NATO cyber-defence management authority (CDMA) was created in order to bring together the principal actors and agencies in NATO's cyber-defence programmes, and to provide support to NATO nations under cyber-threat or attack. At about the same time, Alliance leaders also agreed to the establishment of the NATO co-operative cyber defence centre of excellence (CCD-CoE), which had been under development since 2004. Based in Tallinn, the significance of the CCD-CoE was emphasised by the attacks on Estonia in 2007, and in October 2008 NATO's North Atlantic council granted the CCD-CoE full NATO accreditation as an international military organisation. The "mission and vision" of the CCD-CoE were "to enhance the co-operative cyber defence capability of NATO and NATO nations, thus improving the Alliance's interoperability in the field of co-operative cyber defence" and to be "a primary source of subject matter expertise for NATO in co-operative cyber defence related matters".

The EU's response to the challenge of cyber-security was vigorous, diverse, and largely unco-ordinated. Various EU bodies and agencies addressed aspects of the cyber-security challenge. Thus, in 2006 the European Commission proposed a "strategy for a secure information society", which called for a "multi-stakeholder approach" to information security and for the further development of a "dynamic, global strategy in Europe, based on a culture of security and founded on dialogue, partnership and empowerment". The Commission was also engaged with lower-level cyber-security challenges: the directorate-general for information society and media hosted a "safer Internet plus" programme, intended to "protect online environments from illegal and harmful online content, which ranges from racism and bullying to child pornography and child grooming". Most recently, in November 2008, the Commission launched a public consultation exercise on network and information security policy in Europe. Describing the ICT infrastructure as "the nervous system of our modern society", the Commission argued that "network and information security challenges will require a strong, co-ordinated European response. Recent cyber-attacks targeting individual countries have shown that one country on its own can be very vulnerable."

Under the auspices of the EU's inter-governmental Third Pillar—police and judicial co-operation (PJC)—cyber-security was addressed in a more direct and operational manner in the contexts of terrorism, organised crime, and financial crime. At the operational level, for example, the European police office (EUROPOL), an agency of the PJC, produced an annual *EU Terrorism Situation and Trend Report*, the 2008 edition of which noted the extensive use of the Internet for a wide range of terrorist purposes.

The EU also took a number of agency-level initiatives. In February 2002 the Commission established the contact network of spam authorities, an initiative by which EU governments could assist each other in the fight against spam. The European network and information security agency (ENISA), established in 2004, was intended to promote best practice in the field of network and information security, involving governments and the private sector in the process. ENISA described itself as a "centre of excellence" (and "expertise") in information security. Like NATO's CCD centre of excellence in Tallinn, ENISA was also based at some distance from Brussels, in Crete. For some critics, the choice of location was but one of many problems confronting ENISA. Across the EU there were very different levels of experience and understanding of information security and cyber-security, suggesting that there might be insufficient common ground upon which ENISA could construct a credible work programme. At the national level, important differences remained in the implementation of information security law, and it was not clear that ENISA would be able to overcome these differences.

By the end of 2008 it was difficult to identify an EU body or agency which did not have some interest or involvement in cyber-security concepts and policy on the one hand, and/or in delivery and operations on the other. It should also be borne in mind that each of the EU's 27 national governments was engaged with the problem of security, at one level or another. Yet for all the vigour and diversity of the EU's response to the cyber-security challenge, what was notably absent was a comprehensive strategy for cyber-security, which united all EU efforts. In a relatively brief passage covering cyber-security, the 2008 report on the implementation of the EU's security strategy made this point succinctly: "More work is required in this area, to explore a comprehensive EU approach, raise awareness and enhance international co-operation." In seeking to redress this deficiency, some analysts had begun to argue that the common foreign and security policy (CFSP, the Second Pillar of the EU) should have a role in cyber-security, and that an EU "cyber-security co-ordinator" should then be established (along similar lines to the EU counter-terrorism co-ordinator) and given the task of facilitating a common culture of cyber-security across the many bodies, functions, and governments of the EU. Some saw this approach as too timid, however, and insisted that nothing short of a full-scale institutional response by the EU (accompanied by a new strategy) would be sufficient to meet the cyber-security challenge. Others were more sceptical, and argued that until NATO and the EU were able to undertake relatively straightforward tasks, such as exchanging secret intelligence, there was little hope for a comprehensive response to the cyber-security challenge on the part of Europe's security and defence organisations.

Paul Cornish

ECONOMIC ORGANISATIONS

International Monetary Fund (IMF)

DATE OF FOUNDATION: 1945   HEADQUARTERS: Washington, DC, USA
OBJECTIVES: To promote international monetary co-operation and to assist member states in
establishing sound budgetary and trading policies
MEMBERSHIP (END-'08): 185 members
MANAGING DIRECTOR: Dominique Strauss-Kahn (France)

*World Bank (International Bank for Reconstruction and Development (IBRD) and
International Development Association (IDA)*

DATE OF FOUNDATION: 1945   HEADQUARTERS: Washington, DC, USA
OBJECTIVES: To make loans on reasonable terms to developing countries with the aim of increasing
their productive capacity
MEMBERSHIP (END-'08): 185 members
PRESIDENT: Robert Zoellick (USA)

World Trade Organisation (WTO)

DATE OF FOUNDATION: 1995 (successor to General Agreement on Tariffs and Trade, GATT)
HEADQUARTERS: Geneva, Switzerland
OBJECTIVES: To eliminate tariffs and other barriers to international trade and to facilitate
international financial settlements
MEMBERSHIP (END-'08): 153 members
DIRECTOR GENERAL: Pascal Lamy (France)

Organisation for Economic Co-operation and Development (OECD)

DATE OF FOUNDATION: 1961   HEADQUARTERS: Paris, France
OBJECTIVES: To promote economic growth in member states and the sound development of the
world economy
MEMBERSHIP (END-'08): Australia, Austria, Belgium, Canada, Czech Republic, Denmark, Finland,
France, Germany, Greece, Hungary, Iceland, Ireland, Italy, Japan, South Korea, Luxembourg,
Mexico, The Netherlands, New Zealand, Norway, Poland, Portugal, Slovakia, Spain, Sweden,
Switzerland, Turkey, UK, USA (total 30)
SECRETARY GENERAL: Angel Gurria (Mexico)

THE most severe financial and economic crisis since World War II led to
increased discussion in 2008 about the need for more effective international
institutions to improve co-operation among the governments of inter-dependent
economies and for better rules to help forestall similar crises in future. There
were calls for a "New Bretton Woods" but, although the G-20 meeting in
November reiterated these (see Documents), there was little precision as to what
this new "international architecture" might look like. The advanced economy
governments disagreed among themselves on whether there should be a global
regulatory authority for finance and, if so, whether or not it should be entrusted
to the IMF. The emerging market economies, especially Brazil, Russia, India,
and China (BRIC), who met formally as a group for the first time in November,
made it clear that they must be treated as equals in any new institutional order.
That was accepted in principle by the USA and the Europeans, but more influence for BRIC meant less for the Europeans and reaching agreement would not
be easy, as was shown by the continuing deadlock in the WTO over the Doha

Round of trade negotiations. This reflected not so much a "lack of political will" as the difficulties of reconciling real differences of national interest between countries at different levels of development.

INTERNATIONAL MONETARY FUND (IMF).   The IMF in recent years was being sidelined and its own financial situation was deteriorating. Countries in need of current account financing obtained it easily from the international capital markets, even if some of them had to pay somewhat more to avoid IMF conditionality. But as banks and other institutions, as well as non-financial companies, in the advanced economies began to repair their balance sheets in the wake of the financial crisis, the flow of finance to emerging and developing countries fell dramatically. In the closing months of 2008 several countries were forced to turn to the Fund for help and by the end of the year agreements had been reached with Belarus, Hungary, Iceland, Latvia, Pakistan, Serbia, and Ukraine. Altogether some US$48 billion was committed. A precautionary loan was agreed for El Salvador and talks were under way with Turkey. In September the Fund's exogenous shock facility was modified to provide easier and faster access for low-income countries affected by external shocks, such as the rise in world food prices. In December, Kyrgyzstan was provided with an 18-month standby of US$100 million under the arrangement. In October, the executive board created a new short-term liquidity facility to help emerging market economies with liquidity problems. This was targeted at a small number of countries with sound economic policies but which were suffering contagion from external sources of instability. The Fund had some US$250 billion in loanable resources at the end of 2008 but, given the worsening recession and the likelihood of a significant rise in the demands for help in 2009, it was seeking ways to double that amount. Even then, the sum would be relatively small when compared with the amounts spent on bank bailouts in the USA and Europe. Japan offered to lend the Fund US$100 billion. Other countries in large current account surplus did not follow Japan's example: Middle East oil producers were focused on their own priorities, while China and other Asian countries were unwilling to make contributions without being given increased influence within the institution.

The issue of voting rights' reform had been under discussion since 2006 (see AR 2007, p. 387) and in April 2008 the board of governors adopted a "quota and voice reform", intended to increase the voice of low-income countries in the Fund's decision making. The reform included a new quota formula, a tripling of basic votes, and an additional alternate executive director for the two African chairs at the board. The quota and voting shares were expected to be reviewed every five years. The net result in terms of voting rights was to reduce the share of the developed countries from 60.57 per cent to 57.93 per cent and to raise that of developing countries from 31.70 per cent to 34.49 per cent. The share of the transition economies of the former Soviet Union was also reduced, from 7.09 per cent to 6.82 per cent. The changes were smaller than those which the developing countries had hoped for and independent commentators considered that they fell short of what was required to turn the Fund into a truly global institution, reflecting the new realities of the global economy.

Recognising that more reforms of governance were needed, the managing director set up a group of eight eminent people (including Michel Camdessus, a former managing director, and Amartya Sen, a Nobel Laureate in economics), who would examine these issues and make recommendations.

The Fund saw the global crisis as an opportunity to show that it had a key role to play in restoring international financial stability and in any new system of global governance. Describing the central role of the Fund as "a crisis responder and a developer of ideas", the managing director, in December, set out its strategic priorities for the immediate future: (i) to respond quickly and effectively as the crisis unfolded in individual countries; and (ii) to analyse the causes of the current crisis and to find ways to avoid a repetition, with better surveillance and early warning, and to explore options for reform of the international financial system. (The managing director, however, did not see the Fund as a global regulator.) It was clear in 2008 that achieving the first objective would depend on the Fund obtaining extra resources. But, more generally, the BRIC group and other emerging economies insisted that more reforms were needed if the IMF was to be regarded as a legitimate global body instead of a Western-dominated club.

The Republic of Kosovo applied for admission to the IMF on 15 July.

THE WORLD BANK. It should be noted that the term "World Bank" is shorthand for the World Bank Group which consists of: (i) the International Bank for Reconstruction and Development (IBRD), which made loans to middle-income and credit-worthy low-income countries, and raised resources on the international capital markets; (ii) the International Development Association (IDA), whose resources came from donor governments, and which made interest-free, long-term loans and grants to the poorest countries, which had little or no possibility to borrow on market terms; (iii) the International Finance Corporation (IFC), which provided long-term loans, equity, and securitised products to private enterprises, which had limited access to capital markets and/or operated in markets that would be too risky for private investors without the IFC presence; (iv) the Multilateral Investment Guarantee Agency (MIGA), which provided political risk insurance or guarantees to promote foreign direct investment (FDI) in developing countries; and (v) the International Centre for the Settlement of Investment Disputes (ICSID), a conciliation and arbitration facility for handling disputes between foreign investors and host states.

The total commitments of the World Bank in fiscal 2008 (in June) were US$38.2 billion, 11.4 per cent higher than in 2007, and were distributed among the institutions of the Group as follows: IBRD US$13.5 billion; IDA US$11.2 billion; IFC US$11.4 billion; and MIGA US$2.1 billion. The global financial crisis did not impair the IBRD's ability to raise funds; indeed, as a triple-A rated institution it was one of the few beneficiaries of the "flight to safety" from other assets and jurisdictions. In fiscal 2008 it raised US$19 billion in medium- to long-term bonds, a significant increase on the US$10.7 billion raised in the previous year; and in October 2008 (which fell within fiscal 2009) it was still able to issue a five-year bond of US$1.5 billion at 3.5 per cent. Commitments by the IBRD were some 5 per cent up in 2008 after a fall of over 9 per cent in 2007; the Bank's loan book rose for the first time since 2003; and its operating income increased sharply to US$2.3 billion, its highest level for several years.

IDA funding was secured in December, when the donor countries pledged a record US$41.7 billion for the fiscal years 2009-11. The IBRD and the IFC were also committed to transfer another US$3.5 billion of their own resources to the IDA. This replenishment of the IDA was timely, given that the financial crisis was expected to lead to more calls for help in 2009, and should make available some US$14 billion per year to nearly 80 of the poorest countries.

An element of the new president's strategy for the Bank was to expand the activities of the IFC, and this appeared to have had some success in 2008: IFC provision of finance for private sector development increased by roughly one-third, and when the funds mobilised through syndicated loans and structural finance (US$4.8 billion) were added to those on its own account (US$11.4 billion), IFC commitments were actually larger than those of the IBRD.

The largest share of IBRD-IDA lending continued to go to Africa (23 per cent, nearly all IDA funds), followed by Latin America (19 per cent) and East Asia (18 per cent). Almost 60 per cent of all loans went to three sectors: law, justice, and public administration (21 per cent); transportation (19 per cent); and energy and mining (17 per cent). The Bank's priorities were also reflected in the distribution of lending by "themes"; 25 per cent of all loans went to support financial and private sector development and 20 per cent to public sector governance and the rule of law. The proportions varied from region to region but the support for public sector governance and the rule of law was a particularly high proportion of loans to Africa (some 30 per cent). The emphasis on governance reflected in part the 2007 Volcker Report's recommendations for the Bank's fight against corruption (see AR 2008, p. 393), and in particular the launch of the governance and anti-corruption strategy as a key element of the Bank's development efforts.

In October the board of governors agreed a number of reforms to increase the influence of developing countries. These changes included an extra seat on the board for sub-Saharan Africa, which gave developing countries a majority of the seats, and an increase in their share of total voting in the Bank to 44 per cent. It was agreed to work towards parity of voting power between developed and developing countries. In February, Justin Lin, professor at Beijing University and founding director of the China Centre for Economic Research, was appointed chief economist and senior vice-president for development economics at the World Bank.

THE WORLD TRADE ORGANISATION (WTO). The work of the WTO was dominated by the protracted negotiations on the Doha Trade Round, as it had been for seven years, and the cycle of raised and then frustrated hopes for a conclusion also followed the pattern of previous years (see AR 2008, pp. 393-94). In January the US and EU negotiators argued that a successful deal would boost confidence in a deteriorating economic climate; the reverse would undermine the world trade system and lead to protectionism and economic isolationism. Throughout the year the Round was serially presented as the key to solving the food crisis, the answer to the financial crisis, and the way to avoid a return to the protectionism of the 1930s. Officials and politicians kept repeating that a deal was close and that it was "one minute to midnight for Doha". Most of this rhetoric came from the EU and the USA. Trade rounds are about "enlightened mercantilism", or striking balanced deals among interest groups, but at the year's end the negotiators had still failed to find a balanced outcome.

For the developing countries the negotiations were essentially about correcting fundamental distortions in the trade rules, and these mainly concerned the high levels of subsidy and market protection of agriculture in the USA and Europe. Few concessions were offered on agriculture: the largely fallacious distinction between various types of subsidy, the offer to cap US farm subsidies at US$14.5 billion when their current level was US$9 billion, and the passage of the US farm bill into law in May did little to persuade most of the developing countries that they would obtain a good deal. The developed countries maintained their demands for much greater access to developing country markets for industrial goods and services, and opposed the demand of countries such as India for an enhanced "special safeguard mechanism" to protect small-scale farmers against sudden import surges.

In July a ministerial meeting collapsed after a fruitless nine-day search for agreement. Plans for another ministerial meeting in December, following the G-20's call in November for key agreements to be reached by the end of the year, were abandoned when the director general judged there was no "political drive" for a final push on the "special safeguard mechanism" and non-agricultural market access. Moreover, for the developing countries it no longer seemed a good time for them to liberalise financial services. Given the failure of regulation in the developed economies and the lack of consensus for dealing with cross-border banking and other financial failures, they were reluctant to accept proposals that would constrain their national prudential measures and increase their direct exposure to financial instability in the USA and Europe.

In previous rounds of trade negotiations, Europe and the USA had reached agreements that were then imposed upon the rest of the world. This approach was shown in 2008 to be no longer possible with a global body of over 150 members, many of whom were increasingly unwilling to accept lectures from developed countries on how to manage their economies.

Ukraine became the WTO's 152nd member on 16 May 2008. It had applied in 1993 and membership negotiations were completed in January 2008. Cape Verde became the WTO's 153rd member on 23 July 2008.

ORGANISATION FOR ECONOMIC CO-OPERATION AND DEVELOPMENT (OECD). When OECD ministers of finance met for their annual council meeting in June they were optimistic about the global economy: given the shocks to which it had been subjected, overall performance was much better than expected. Although credit conditions were still holding back investment, financial markets had improved since the spring and the ministers, with a touch of self-congratulation, held that the resilience of OECD countries could be attributed to the structural reforms and sound macroeconomic policies which they had pursued over the years. They were more concerned about inflationary pressures emerging in the expected upturn than a deepening recession. These views reflected the OECD secretariat's assessment of the previous November, but this was sharply revised in its *Economic Outlook* of November 2008: the forecast then was for a fall in output in 2009 "with many OECD economies in or on the verge of a protracted recession of a magnitude not experienced since the early 1980s". Thus the OECD was no better than any other organisation in anticipating the scope of the financial crisis and its effects on the real economy. Its economists were aware of the risks but these could not be quantified and their relation to the real economy was anyway not fully understood. As was commonly the case, what could not be quantified was usually relegated to parentheses or footnotes.

Following the G-8 request of June 2007, the OECD deepened its relations with emerging market economies in 2008: candidates for OECD membership (Chile, Estonia, Israel, Russia, and Slovenia) all attended the ministerial council meeting for the first time and the countries with which OECD was in "enhanced engagement" (Brazil, India, Indonesia, China, and South Africa) were also invited to all sessions of the council. The OECD saw itself as becoming a "real hub of dialogue on global issues", providing "coherent solutions to global challenges". Increasing the relevance and legitimacy of international organisations was seen as necessary "to stem the growing opposition to globalisation". This strategy was reflected in some of the council's priorities for the organisation: the economics of global climate change; analysis and advice for dealing with non-tariff obstacles to trade, especially in services; co-ordination with the IMF on developing a code of best practices for sovereign wealth funds (SWFs); work with the Food and Agriculture Organisation (FAO) on the long-term factors behind global food supply and the pressures for higher prices; and research on the "political economy of reform". The strategy was to be more than a "hub for dialogue": the OECD's growing membership increased the organisation's power to set international rules and standards, as ministers were well aware in June when they adopted their Declaration on SWFs and Recipient Country Policies.

In November the secretary general set out a plan for responding to the financial crisis. This integrated two sets of policies: (i) to provide tighter regulation and supervision of financial markets; and (ii) to improve and co-ordinate national policies to restore the conditions for economic growth. The organisation also launched a global drive to improve corporate governance, failures in which were seen as contributing to the financial crisis. At the same time, other important issues were not to be marginalised. In October the OECD published a major report, *Growing Unequal?*, which showed that in over three-quarters of OECD countries the gap between rich and poor had grown over the past 20 years. Ignoring the socially divisive effects of increasing inequality was not an option, in the view of the secretary general.

Paul Rayment

OTHER WORLD ORGANISATIONS

THE COMMONWEALTH

DATE OF FOUNDATION: 1949 (London Declaration) HEADQUARTERS: London, UK
OBJECTIVES: To maintain political, cultural and social links between (mainly English-speaking)
  countries of the former British Empire and others subscribing to Commonwealth democratic
  principles and aims
MEMBERSHIP (END-'08): Antigua & Barbuda, Australia, The Bahamas, Bangladesh, Barbados, Belize,
  Botswana, Brunei, Cameroon, Canada, Cyprus, Dominica, Fiji (suspended), the Gambia,
  Ghana, Grenada, Guyana, India, Jamaica, Kenya, Kiribati, Lesotho, Malawi, Malaysia,
  Maldives, Malta, Mauritius, Mozambique, Namibia, Nauru, New Zealand, Nigeria, Pakistan,
  Papua New Guinea, St Kitts & Nevis, St Lucia, St Vincent & the Grenadines, Samoa,
  Seychelles, Sierra Leone, Singapore, Solomon Islands, South Africa, Sri Lanka, Swaziland,
  Tanzania, Tonga, Trinidad & Tobago, Tuvalu, Uganda, UK, Vanuatu, Zambia (total 53)
SECRETARY GENERAL: Kamalesh Sharma (India)

Two countries were a focus of Commonwealth political attention in 2008: Pakistan and Zimbabwe. It had been five years since President Robert Mugabe had pulled Zimbabwe out of the Commonwealth (see AR 2003, p. 431), and for a long time the organisation had done little more than keep a watching brief on the deteriorating situation. Now strong feeling grew, mainly in civil society organisations, that the Commonwealth should re-engage. All of Zimbabwe's neighbours were Commonwealth members and non-governmental organisations (NGOs) began to look ahead to a post-Mugabe period, in which substantial human resources would be required to restore the country and it could return to the fold. When Kamalesh Sharma of India succeeded Don McKinnon of New Zealand as Commonwealth secretary general on 1 April, he put the problem high on his agenda.

Pakistan, meanwhile, had been suspended once more from the Commonwealth in November 2007 (see AR 2008, p. 397). Days afterwards, however, President Pervez Musharraf stepped down as army chief and elections in February 2008 saw defeat for his Pakistan Muslim League (Q) (see pp. 317-18). The nine-member Commonwealth Ministerial Action Group (CMAG) of foreign ministers (which had the task of addressing serious violations of Commonwealth values and principles), met in London on 12 May and restored full membership to Pakistan, noting that the state of emergency had been lifted, political detainees released, and the election commission was being reformed.

This left only Fiji still under suspension. In July, a visit by special Commonwealth envoy Sir Paul Reeves of New Zealand produced little satisfactory result, and when the CMAG met again in New York on 27 September it expressed disappointment at the lack of progress towards elections, which the interim government of army chief Prime Minister Commodore Josaia Voreqe (Frank) Bainimarama had promised by March 2009. Under Commonwealth rules, Fiji reached the two-year deadline for the restoration of democratic government in December 2008, leaving the problem for the next CMAG meeting to tackle.

In several instances the Commonwealth's steady consolidation of better governance among its members was producing results. The closely fought election in Ghana, to which Baroness Valerie Amos of the UK led a Commonwealth observer group, took place smoothly (see pp. 258-59). Another success was the Maldives election, which saw the end of the 30-year rule of President Maumoon Abdul Gayoom (see pp. 327-28). Elections in October under a new constitution and the smooth transfer of power to former political prisoner Mohammed Nasheed of the Maldives Democratic Party followed several years of work by the secretary general and his special envoys, notably Musa Hitam, former deputy prime minister of Malaysia. An observer group led by Owen Arthur, former prime minister of Barbados, found the two rounds of polling "credible overall", but made numerous recommendations for systemic improvements next time the country voted. The group found that Nasheed, unsurprisingly, was not too well versed in government and would need support.

In 2008 this diplomatic work continued in several other countries where democracy and good governance were still seen to be lacking in varying degrees. In Guyana the situation had steadily improved and the country was much calmer. Lesotho was making steady progress; but Swaziland was slow, and it was felt that, while the king was prepared for some constitutional change, his followers were determined to maintain his autocracy. Two countries showed little progress. In Cameroon Paul Biya remained president after 26 years, longer than any other Commonwealth leader; press freedom showed no improvement; and the quality of democracy was poor. In The Gambia, President Yahya Jammeh continued on his autocratic path.

The return of democratic government to Bangladesh after two years under a caretaker regime was a major step forward (see pp. 319-20). In September a human rights commission was set up there, with help from the Commonwealth secretariat's human rights unit.

The despatch of election observer groups was another part of this democratic work. In 2008 Commonwealth observers or expert teams were also sent to Belize, Swaziland, Sierra Leone (for local elections), and, at the tail end of the year, to Ghana and Bangladesh. The group despatched to Bangladesh was led by former president Cassam Uteem of Mauritius. The team sent to Swaziland, in reporting its unhappiness about the election and weaknesses in the constitutional and legal framework, hinted at the king's dominant role (see pp. 295-96).

One result of this steady advance in democracy was a greater turnover of faces at Commonwealth summits. By the end of 2008, there were as many as 14 new heads of government compared with the November 2007 summit in Kampala, Uganda. For a short period, after Helen Clark was defeated in New Zealand in November, not one of the 53 leaders was a woman: a reflection on the electorates rather than on the Commonwealth, which had made vigorous efforts over many years to increase greatly the number of elected women. When Sheikh Hasina Wazed was elected in Bangladesh on the last day of 2008, the Commonwealth once more included a woman leader. The Commonwealth, in line with the Millennium Development Goals, had pledged to achieve 30 per cent representation by women in its member states' legislatures by 2015; by 2008, only five of the 53 member states had reached that target.

Among various ministerial meetings that took place over the year, of special importance was the meeting of a group of Commonwealth heads of government in New York on 14 September to discuss efforts to expedite reform of the UN, the World Bank, and the IMF. The meeting took place in the shadow of the accelerating global financial crisis.

Derek Ingram

INTERNATIONAL ORGANISATION OF FRANCOPHONIE

DATE OF FOUNDATION: 1997   HEADQUARTERS: Paris, France
OBJECTIVES: To promote co-operation and exchange between countries wholly or partly French-speaking and to defend usage of the French language
MEMBERSHIP (END-'08): Albania, Andorra, Armenia, Belgium, French-speaking community of Belgium, Benin, Bulgaria, Burkina Faso, Burundi, Cambodia, Cameroon, Canada, New Brunswick (Canada), Québec (Canada), Cape Verde, Central African Republic, Chad, Comoros, Republic of Congo, Côte d'Ivoire, Democratic Republic of Congo, Djibouti, Dominica, Egypt, Equatorial Guinea, France, Gabon, Greece, Guinea, Guinea-Bissau, Haiti, Laos, Lebanon, Luxembourg, Macedonia, Madagascar, Mali, Mauritania (suspended), Mauritius, Moldova, Monaco, Morocco, Niger, Romania, Rwanda, St Lucia, São Tomé & Príncipe, Senegal, Seychelles, Switzerland, Togo, Tunisia, Vanuatu, Vietnam (total 54)
OBSERVER MEMBERS: Austria, Croatia, Czech Republic, Georgia, Hungary, Latvia, Lithuania, Mozambique, Poland, Serbia, Slovakia, Slovenia, Thailand, Ukraine (total 14)
ASSOCIATE MEMBERS: Cyprus, Ghana
SECRETARY GENERAL: Abdou Diouf (Senegal)

THE central feature of 2008 for the International Organisation of Francophonie (OIF) was the 12th summit. Indeed, there were no other ministerial meetings in 2008, except that of the foreign ministers prior to the summit, although there were the usual gatherings of specialised institutions and the celebration of the international day of Francophonie in March. The summit was held in Québec City on 17-19 October and was an emblematic moment for Canada's main French-speaking province. The year also saw a series of celebrations to mark the 400th anniversary of the founding of the city by Samuel de Champlain in 1609. It was the second time that Québec had held the summit, having hosted the second summit in 1987. Canada thus became the only country to have hosted the event three times (in 1999, it had been held in Moncton, New Brunswick), a reflection of the importance Canada attached to its OIF membership.

The summit was attended by almost all of the OIF's 70 members, observers, and associates (observers could speak and vote, while associates were simply passive participants), including some 40 heads of state and government. The membership broke down into 54 full members (including the suspended Mauritania), 14 observers, and two associates. Armenia switched from associate to full member, and Thailand and Latvia were welcomed as observers in 2008. Under the broad membership definition of "countries using the French language", there were as many as 23 countries from the EU in the OIF membership—many of them with very small francophone populations—as well as the French community of Belgium (separately from the Kingdom of Belgium). The president of Algeria, Abdelaziz Bouteflika, attended once more by special invitation, although Algeria had always resisted even observer status.

The conference had four themes—democracy and the rule of law, economic governance, the environment, and the French language—and their broad sweep was intended to show that La Francophonie was a fully mature international organisation of the stature of the Commonwealth (this was certainly how the Canadians wanted to see it). The 12th summit was strongly focused on the international financial crisis, which broke in full magnitude just a month before. As France's Prime Minister François Fillon said: "Nobody wants extra rules. Nobody wants protectionism. What we want is regulation of the financial system that is coherent and harmonious." Canada's Prime Minister Stephen Harper said that francophone countries "must work collectively" and that a targeted and efficient response was needed to address the crisis, damage from which was spreading to developing nations.

In this context, African leaders in particular made a variety of statements expressing their concern at the spread of the crisis. President Bouteflika, for example, observed that the future of developing countries could be gravely affected: "their economic and structural problems will be complicated with new threats and difficulties." The final Québec Declaration noted: "No country is immune from the turmoil that undermines global credit markets and the turbulence that rocked our markets requires urgent intervention and co-ordination."

The fourth theme, that of the French language, had always been an undercurrent at francophone summits—indeed, the promotion and protection of the French language was the OIF's original raison d'être—but had not necessarily dominated proceedings. At the 12th summit, however, far from being a routine exercise in reaffirmation, the subject reasserted itself, perhaps because of the ultra-francophone nature of the setting. The summit adopted a major separate "resolution on the French language" outside the Québec Declaration. This was placed very much in the context of protecting "cultural diversity", which the OIF had made its own cause in forums such as UNESCO.

The resolution asked the secretary general to pursue actions for "multi-lingualism" and conclude "linguistic pacts" with all governments seeking them, which would "encourage the use of the French language on their territories". There were several clauses on the development of multilingual education in schools and universities. The resolution also specifically called for a consolidation of the multilateral character of the Paris-based global television channel, TV5 Monde, for which Harper had already announced increased support from Canada.

There was much comment on the departure from Québec of French President Nicolas Sarkozy before the debate on the resolution. This was thought odd, given France's strong vested interest in the subject, but it was interpreted as a diplomatic and tactical withdrawal designed to suggest that it was not France that was particularly pushing for the resolution. Sarkozy's speeches in Québec itself, though full of fraternal sentiments, were not politically loaded. This was certainly no General de Gaulle of some 40 years before, declaiming "Vive le

Québec libre". It was, rather, a posture of wise and discreet counsel to the Québécois not to go too far, counsels Sarkozy repeated subsequently as a new separatist fervour seemed to been gaining ground in the province.

The Québec Declaration began by spectacularly reinforcing the resolution on the French language, calling on the OIF to increase the human and financial resources devoted to its promotion. It then proceeded to a range of other subjects, notably "peace, democratic governance and the rule of law". This followed from the OIF's basic texts of Bamako (2002) and St Boniface (2006), and found practical application in action on Mauritania, which was suspended from membership after the coup there of 6 August (see pp. 264-65). There was an appeal to free the former president, Mohammed Ould Cheikh Abdellahi, detained after the coup. Political situations in Djibouti, Haiti, Côte d'Ivoire, Democratic Republic of Congo (DRC), Chad, Central African Republic, Moldova, and Georgia (all in the OIF) were all also featured in the Declaration, as was the crisis in Palestine and the issue of piracy on the Indian Ocean.

It was decided that the next summit would be held in Antananarivo, capital of Madagascar, which had already hosted OIF foreign ministers three years previously. Antananarivo was chosen in favour of Kinshasa, capital of the DRC, although both venues entailed a certain amount of risk.

Kaye Whiteman

NON-ALIGNED MOVEMENT AND DEVELOPING COUNTRIES

Non-Aligned Movement (NAM)

DATE OF FOUNDATION: 1961   HEADQUARTERS: rotating with chair
OBJECTIVES: Originally to promote decolonisation and to avoid domination by either the Western industrialised world or the Communist bloc; since the early 1970s to provide a authoritative forum to set the political and economic priorities of developing countries; in addition, since the end of the Cold War to resist domination of the UN system by the USA
MEMBERSHIP (END-'08): Afghanistan, Algeria, Angola, Antigua & Barbuda, Bahamas, Bahrain, Bangladesh, Barbados, Belarus, Belize, Benin, Bhutan, Bolivia, Botswana, Brunei, Burkina Faso, Burma (Myanmar), Burundi, Cambodia, Cameroon, Cape Verde, Central African Republic, Chad, Chile, Colombia, Comoros, Congo, Côte d'Ivoire, Cuba, Democratic Republic of Congo, Djibouti, Dominica, Dominican Republic, East Timor, Ecuador, Egypt, Equatorial Guinea, Eritrea, Ethiopia, Gabon, the Gambia, Ghana, Grenada, Guatemala, Guinea, Guinea-Bissau, Guyana, Haiti, Honduras, India, Indonesia, Iran, Iraq, Jamaica, Jordan, Kenya, Kuwait, Laos, Lebanon, Lesotho, Liberia, Libya, Madagascar, Malawi, Malaysia, Maldives, Mali, Mauritania, Mauritius, Mongolia, Morocco, Mozambique, Namibia, Nepal, Nicaragua, Niger, Nigeria, North Korea, Oman, Pakistan, Palestine, Panama, Papua New Guinea, Peru, Philippines, Qatar, Rwanda, St Kitts & Nevis, St Lucia, St Vincent & the Grenadines, São Tomé and Príncipe, Saudi Arabia, Senegal, Seychelles, Sierra Leone, Singapore, Somalia, South Africa, Sri Lanka, Sudan, Suriname, Swaziland, Syria, Tanzania, Thailand, Togo, Trinidad & Tobago, Tunisia, Turkmenistan, Uganda, United Arab Emirates, Uzbekistan, Vanuatu, Venezuela, Vietnam, Yemen, Zambia, Zimbabwe (total 118)
CHAIRMAN: Raúl Castro (Cuba) (since Sept '06)

Group of 77 (G-77)

DATE OF FOUNDATION: 1964   HEADQUARTERS: UN centres
OBJECTIVES: To act as an international lobbying group for the concerns of developing countries
MEMBERSHIP (END-'08): Afghanistan, Algeria, Angola, Antigua & Barbuda, Argentina, Bahamas, Bahrain, Bangladesh, Barbados, Belize, Benin, Bhutan, Bolivia, Bosnia & Herzegovina, Botswana, Brazil, Brunei, Burkina Faso, Burma (Myanmar), Burundi, Cambodia, Cameroon, Cape Verde, Central African Republic, Chad, Chile, Colombia, Comoros, Congo, Costa Rica, Côte d'Ivoire, Cuba, Democratic Republic of Congo, Djibouti, Dominica, Dominican Republic, Ecuador, East Timor, Egypt, El Salvador, Equatorial Guinea, Eritrea, Ethiopia, Federated States of Micronesia, Fiji, Gabon, the Gambia, Ghana, Grenada, Guatemala, Guinea, Guinea-Bissau, Guyana, Haiti, Honduras, India, Indonesia, Iran, Iraq, Jamaica, Jordan, Kenya, Kuwait, Laos, Lebanon, Lesotho, Liberia, Libya, Madagascar, Malawi, Malaysia, Maldives, Mali, Marshall Islands, Mauritania, Mauritius, Mongolia, Morocco, Mozambique, Namibia, Nepal, Nicaragua, Niger, Nigeria, North Korea, Oman, Pakistan, Palau, Palestine, Panama, Papua New Guinea, Paraguay, Peru, Philippines, Qatar, Rwanda, St Kitts & Nevis, St Lucia, St Vincent & the Grenadines, Samoa, São Tomé and Príncipe, Saudi Arabia, Senegal, Seychelles, Sierra Leone, Singapore, Solomon Islands, Somalia, South Africa, Sri Lanka, Sudan, Suriname, Swaziland, Syria, Tanzania, Thailand, Togo, Tonga, Trinidad & Tobago, Tunisia, Turkmenistan, Uganda, United Arab Emirates, Uruguay, Vanuatu, Venezuela, Vietnam, Yemen, Zambia, Zimbabwe (total 130)
CHAIRMAN '08: Baldwin Spencer (Antigua & Barbuda)

THE triennial conference of foreign ministers of the Non-Aligned Movement (NAM) met in Tehran, Iran, on 29-30 July, to review the international situation and to prepare for the 15th summit conference due in 2009. The 32nd annual meeting of the Group of 77 (G-77) in New York was held on 26 September, at the start of the UN General Assembly session. There was also a series of more specialist NAM ministerial meetings during the year. For the first time for 32 years the NAM did not hold its annual foreign ministers meeting at the UN.

However, various NAM working groups did continue to sponsor draft resolutions in the Assembly on a wide range of topics.

At the NAM conference in July there was, surprisingly, no sense of a global financial crisis, which would affect developing countries. The over-riding concern was with dramatic increases in food prices, particularly for wheat and maize, which had reached record highs. By the September G-77 meeting, when the US "subprime" crisis was at its most dramatic, consideration of development was dominated by the challenge of "multiple inter-related and mutually reinforcing crises, including a global food crisis, a financial crisis, an energy crisis, a climate crisis and environment crisis as well as a crisis of confidence in some international institutions". However, it was not until the end of the year, when wheat and maize prices had sharply declined, that the developing countries were significantly engaged with the financial crisis. At a UN-sponsored conference in Doha, Qatar, in December (on the implementation of the 2002 Monterrey Consensus on financing for development), the G-77 chairman spoke of "clear and present dangers".

The economic upheaval radicalised the developing countries and the G-77 ended the year by pushing through the UN General Assembly on 19 December a reaffirmation of the 1970s "New International Economic Order", a set of proposals to improve the terms of trade for developing countries. Only the USA voted against the resolution, but virtually all Northern countries abstained. The vote was 123 in favour to one against, with 52 abstentions. The G-77 also for the first time tabled a resolution on "middle-income developing countries", recognising that they still faced challenges in the area of poverty eradication. There was also a significant change in NAM and G-77 attitudes to climate change: fears were expressed of the risks this entailed for developing countries.

At the NAM conference in Tehran, at the G-77 meeting in New York, and again in Doha, strong emphasis was placed on the desire to reform the international financial institutions in order to give a greater voice to developing countries. Neither the changes in the membership and votes in the Executive Board of the IMF adopted in April (see p. 410) nor the increased role given to the G-20 rather than the G-8 were regarded as more than "modest efforts", or, as the G-77 chairman put it, a "a nod in the right direction".

NAM members were pleased by their ability to take much of the sting out of the assessment of each country's human rights record under the Universal Periodic Review mechanism of the UN Human Rights Council, by means of adopting a standard, bland, formal conclusion for each of the first batch of reports in 2008. At Tehran, their next target was to end the General Assembly's continued practice of adopting resolutions criticising the record of individual countries. There was also an implied threat to the work of human rights NGOs in the call to "review modalities, in order to streamline their activities". On 10 December, the Co-ordinating Bureau of the NAM, operating in New York, issued a declaration to commemorate the 60th anniversary of the adoption of the Universal Declaration on Human Rights. It expressed a strong commitment to human rights, emphasising the right to development, but negated this by asserting respect for sovereignty.

The question of Palestine continued to be a priority for the NAM, but members were frustrated when, in September, the UN Security Council refused to allow Cuba's representative to speak on behalf of the Non-Aligned during a debate on Israeli settlements in Palestine. They protested at the Council's "lack of transparency" and reiterated Non-Aligned calls for "an urgent, thorough reform of that body, including its methods of work". At the end of November, the Bureau expressed great concern at the situation in Gaza, well before the Israeli assault had started. They referred to "the deteriorating situation on the ground"; to "Israel's continued use of force against the Palestinian civilian population"; and to the humanitarian crisis caused by the "inhumane closure and siege of Gaza". They showed prescience in saying, "the current transitional period is a fragile period". In December, as soon as the Israeli bombing of Gaza began, the Bureau met again to condemn Israeli military aggression and to call upon the Security Council to act urgently.

The seventh conference of ministers of information of the Non-Aligned Countries (COMINAC-VII) was held in Venezuela on 2-4 July, but only 64 of the 118 governments were represented. There was much rhetoric challenging the "lopsided information", "media terrorism", and "orchestrated smear campaigns" in the Western media and asserting the need to redress imbalances in flows of information. However, endorsement of pluralistic and professional media was negated by agreement to "encourage private practitioners to complement the information and communication efforts of government agencies within the context of social responsibility". Responsibility for co-operation on these questions for the following three years was handed over from Malaysia, the host of the previous conference in 2005, to Venezuela. Despite this, it was agreed that the NAM News Network, an Internet news service, would continue to be based in Kuala Lumpur. Venezuela was given the task of preparing a list of all developing country institutions that might contribute to South-South flows of information. As a contribution to lessening the disparities between different countries, Malaysia offered to provide training in media studies.

During the year there were also NAM ministerial meetings in Geneva on health in May and on labour questions in June, and a co-ordination committee on economic co-operation in June in Côte d'Ivoire. There was preliminary discussion on holding a third South Summit in Africa in 2010. At the end of 2008, Antigua & Barbuda handed the chairmanship of the Group of 77 to Sudan for 2009. There was no change in the membership of either the G-77 or the NAM during 2008.

Peter Willetts

ORGANISATION OF THE ISLAMIC CONFERENCE (OIC)

DATE OF FOUNDATION: 1969   HEADQUARTERS: Jeddah, Saudi Arabia
OBJECTIVES: To further co-operation among Islamic countries in the political, economic, social, cultural and scientific spheres
MEMBERSHIP (END-'08): Afghanistan, Albania, Algeria, Azerbaijan, Bahrain, Bangladesh, Benin, Brunei, Burkina Faso, Cameroon, Chad, Comoros, Côte d'Ivoire, Djibouti, Egypt, Gabon, the Gambia, Guinea, Guinea-Bissau, Guyana, Indonesia, Iran, Iraq, Jordan, Kazakhstan, Kuwait, Kyrgyzstan, Lebanon, Libya, Malaysia, Maldives, Mali, Mauritania, Morocco, Mozambique, Niger, Nigeria, Oman, Pakistan, Palestine, Qatar, Saudi Arabia, Senegal, Sierra Leone, Somalia, Sudan, Suriname, Syria, Tajikistan, Togo, Tunisia, Turkey, Turkmenistan, Uganda, United Arab Emirates, Uzbekistan, Yemen (total 57)
OBSERVER MEMBERS: Bosnia & Herzegovina, Central African Republic, Turkish Republic of Northern Cyprus, Thailand, Russia (total 5)
SECRETARY GENERAL: Ekmeleddin Ihsanoglu (Turkey)

THE Organisation of the Islamic Conference (OIC) held its 11th regular summit meeting in Dakar, the capital of Senegal, on 13-14 March. The 10th regular summit had taken place in Malaysia in October 2003 (see AR 2003, pp. 439-40); the organisation's third extraordinary summit had been held in Saudi Arabia in December 2005 (see AR 2005, pp. 367-68). The 11th summit ended with the adoption of the "Dakar Declaration", which noted that the early years of the third millennium had been "marked by major world developments at the ideological, political, economic, scientific and technological levels". The leaders stated: "We are proud to proclaim, once again, to the entire world that the Ummah is fortunate, in the face of such challenges, to find in the Holy Quran's lofty teachings the right solutions to the problems currently besetting human societies. Islam, a religion of total devotion to Allah the Almighty, is also an irreplaceable vector of progress in this world in that its message of human salvation encompasses all walks of life."

The summit approved a resolution hailing "the steadfastness of the Palestinian people and their valiant struggle to regain their inalienable national rights" and affirming the OIC's "determination to support the Palestinian people in order to recover their inalienable national rights through all possible ways and means". The resolution furthermore condemned "the ongoing and escalating Israeli military campaign against the Palestinian people through which Israel, the occupying power, continues to commit grave human rights violations and war crimes, including the killing and injuring of Palestinian civilians, including children, women, and the elderly".

A resolution was passed recognising the "inalienable right" of the Islamic Republic of Iran to develop nuclear energy for peaceful purposes. It rejected "discrimination and double standards" in peaceful uses of nuclear energy and any attempt to resort to unilateral action in resolving verification concerns. It expressed concern over any unwanted consequences, on the peace and security of the region and beyond, of threats and pressures on Iran by "certain circles".

OIC foreign ministers assembled for their 35th session in Kampala, the capital of Uganda, on 18-20 June. The session on "prosperity and development" ended with the adoption of the "Kampala Declaration" which noted "with concern" the negative impact of rising food and energy prices in some parts of the world and welcomed "the praiseworthy initiative" of the emir of Kuwait, Sheikh Sabah al-Ahmad al-Jabir al-Sabah, in setting up the "fund for dignified life" to help OIC countries respond to this challenge.

The Kampala Declaration strongly condemn terrorism "in all its forms and manifestations committed by whomsoever and wherever" and also condemned "the growing trend of Islamophobia" and the "systematic discrimination against the adherents of Islam". The foreign ministers called upon the international community to prevent incitement to hatred and discrimination against Muslims and take "effective measures to combat defamation of religions and acts of negative stereotyping of people based on religion, belief or ethnicity".

Darren Sagar

EUROPEAN ORGANISATIONS

THE EUROPEAN UNION

DATE OF FOUNDATION: 1952   HEADQUARTERS: Brussels, Belgium
OBJECTIVES: To seek ever-closer union of member states
MEMBERSHIP (END-'08): Austria, Belgium, Bulgaria, Cyprus, Czech Republic, Denmark, Estonia,
    Finland, France, Germany, Greece, Hungary, Ireland, Italy, Latvia, Lithuania, Luxembourg,
    Malta, Netherlands, Poland, Portugal, Romania, Slovakia, Slovenia, Spain, Sweden, UK
    (total 27)
PRESIDENT OF THE EUROPEAN COMMISSION: José Manuel Barroso (Portugal)

THE year began on a subdued note. The repercussions of the credit crisis, which began in the second half of 2007, as yet seemed relatively muted; the status of Kosovo was the main external relations question; and it was widely thought that all the effort invested in constructing a new reform treaty for the European Union (the Lisbon Treaty) would yield results by the end of the year.

On 12 June the EU's constitutional ambitions were thrown into confusion by Ireland's rejection of the Lisbon Treaty. It was assumed that resolving this crisis would be the main preoccupation of the French presidency, which took office on 1 July. However, the smouldering dispute between Russia and Georgia over South Ossetia took flame early in August, while the autumn saw a new phase in the credit crisis as sections of Europe's banking system faced collapse. France's President Nicolas Sarkozy found himself ideally placed to exercise his unbounded energy on behalf of the European Union.

THE LISBON TREATY.   Ratification of the Lisbon Treaty, the text of which had been finalised in 2007 (see AR 2008, pp. 406-08), required unanimous approval by all 27 of the EU member states. Ireland was the only one of these to require a positive popular vote, and the referendum was set for 12 June. As the date approached, there was increasing concern that the Treaty would be rejected. In the event these fears were realised. The Irish voted 862,415 against and 752,451 in favour, on a turnout of 53.4 per cent.

All the major political parties, business organisations, and trade unions had argued for a "yes" vote but, in a demonstration of popular disdain for political elites, their leadership was rejected, much as it had been in the 2005 referendums in France and the Netherlands on an earlier version of the treaty (see AR 2005, pp. 40; 48; 368-70). The "no" campaign produced extraordinary allegations, such as that all children would be microchipped, abortion legalised, and Irish youngsters conscripted for a European army; but the commonest complaint was that people did not understand the Treaty and refused to vote in favour of something they did not comprehend (see p. 47).

The president of the European Commission, José Manuel Barroso, said that the Commission respected the outcome, which should not be seen as a vote against the Union. He urged the eight member states, which yet had to ratify, to continue the process. It was clear, however, that the only way ahead was to hold a second Irish referendum. (This mirrored the situation of 2002, when a second Irish vote was held on the Treaty of Nice—the framework for EU enlargement—following a "no" in the first round, see AR 2002, pp. 49; 415.)

The Irish government looked for measures which might address popular concerns. At the European Council (summit) of 11-12 December, the Irish taoiseach (prime minister), Brian Cowen, told EU colleagues that he would seek a re-run of the referendum in the autumn of 2009, as long as some reassuring protocols could be agreed at the European level. These would deal with taxation, where there was deemed to be a threat to low Irish corporate tax rates; with abortion, where the EU would have no business to meddle; and with defence, where it should be clear that Irish neutrality was not in question.

The only demand that would imply a change in the draft treaty concerned the provision whereby the European Commission would be reduced in size from 2014, meaning that there would no longer be a member of the college from every EU country. The Irish government wanted to see this provision removed, so that even a small country like Ireland could be assured of a seat in the college.

The December Council agreed to this request "provided the Treaty of Lisbon enters into force". In a curious paradox, the Treaty of Nice, currently in force, provided for a reduction in the number of commissioners as from 1 November 2009, so if the Lisbon Treaty continued to be blocked and the Nice Treaty remained applicable, Ireland could in any case be deprived of its own commissioner. The Council also agreed draft protocols to meet Ireland's concerns on abortion, taxation, and defence.

CREDIT CRISIS. There were signs of economic trouble ahead in the early part of 2008, especially in the USA, but analysts were fairly confident of the capacity of the EU to get through a difficult period. "The EU economy is still in a relatively good position to weather these headwinds on the back of improved fundamentals," said the Commission in its spring 2008 economic forecast. The main concern was over the strength of the euro and the impact that this might have on industrial competitiveness. Germany's export performance was healthy enough in the first half of the year, whereas the Italian economy was facing increasing problems. The surge in fuel and food prices was building inflationary worries.

By the autumn the credit crisis had dealt a body blow to all growth forecasts. The Commission was describing the economic situation as "exceptionally uncertain". Growth projections had been cut by 1.5 percentage points and by the end of the year the eurozone as a whole was in technical recession.

On 15 September US investment bank Lehman Brothers filed for bankruptcy, triggering turmoil in financial markets worldwide. On 22 September, the European Central Bank (ECB) injected €27 billion into the money markets, but rejected the need for any major bailout on the scale of the USA's US$700 billion rescue plan (see p. 155). Although welcomed by European policy-makers, the US initiative was seen as dealing with a US problem, and whereas the Anglo-Saxon world was dominated by news of collapsing banks and bailouts, the eurozone seemed relatively immune. The ECB president, Jean-Claude Trichet, stressed that it was not the role of central banks to rush to the rescue of commercial banks: "We have a responsibility as regards the provision of liquidity, we have no responsibility as regards the solvency issue that might emerge here and there." That, he said, was for national governments to deal with. The German finance minister, Peter Steinbrück, blamed the US administration for its regulatory failures and told journalists that 2008 would be seen as "a fundamental rupture" in American domination of financial markets. He stressed that the German government would not be required to mount any bank rescue programmes.

Within a week of these somewhat detached reactions, continental Europe was hit by the "subprime" storm. Liquidity dried up, governments were forced to rescue their financial institutions, Iceland's banking system was close to meltdown, the Irish, Greek, Danish, and German governments were promising guarantees for bank deposits, and Commissioner for Trade Peter Mandelson was brought back to London to join Gordon Brown's cabinet (see p. 26).

Ireland's open-ended guarantees to depositors caused dismay to other EU members, especially the UK, as funds flowed out of British banks into Irish deposit accounts. EU Competition Commissioner Neelie Kroes fiercely attacked the Irish for not consulting the Commission in advance. Her insistence on applying the EU rules regulating state aid caused great impatience among finance ministers, although the guidelines ultimately issued by the Commission followed events rather than regulating them.

Criticism mounted over the EU's failure to come up with a common approach to the crisis. The French president floated the idea of a European bank bailout fund, but this attracted little support. On 7 October EU finance ministers met in Luxembourg to approve a set of principles for bank rescues. They agreed that governments could take various national measures, including recapitalisation, purchase of bank assets, and state-backed guarantees. A minimum of €50,000 in personal deposits would be guaranteed for one year, with some countries able to choose a higher figure. Calls for a tougher regulatory regime for financial services became increasingly vocal, obliging the European Commission to come up with modest proposals for more demanding capital requirements for banks and insurance companies, and for closer supervision of the rating agencies responsible for assessing the credit-worthiness of companies and governments, and which many perceived as the main culprits in the "subprime" disaster.

One curious consequence of the crisis was a transformed relationship between the eurozone and the UK, which had never adopted the European currency. British Prime Minister Gordon Brown was invited to a summit of the 15 eurozone countries on 12 October to set out his three-point model for underwriting inter-bank lending, recapitalising the banks, and protecting savers (see p. 26). He was regarded as the hero of the hour for his grasp of the policies required and the coherence of his approach. Brown even took his place in the official photo of the 15 eurozone leaders.

President Sarkozy saw the crisis as an opportunity to project Europe's role at an international level and called for a global summit, which would launch major reforms to the financial regulatory system at a worldwide level. He had the satisfaction of receiving an invitation from US President George W. Bush, extended to him and Commission President Barroso, to dine in Washington, DC on 17 October. The outcome was a commitment to hold a series of global summits, with the first to be held in Washington, DC on 15 November. This meeting agreed a programme to achieve world economic recovery, improve financial markets, and resist protectionism (see Documents).

In advance of the December European Council, Brown invited Sarkozy and Barroso to London to discuss the response to the global financial crisis. The absence of German Chancellor Angela Merkel was ascribed to Germany's rejection of the high spending approach of her colleagues (see p. 50). A European economic recovery plan was approved at the summit, amounting to about €200 billion, with sums to be allocated for small and medium enterprises, renewable energy, and clean transport, including support for the motor industry.

THE BALKANS. Accession to the European Union was the key ambition of most countries in the Balkans, although EU politicians and officials continued to express caution at the prospect, with President Sarkozy and the European Parliament president, Hans-Gert Pöttering, stating that no new membership could be contemplated before the Lisbon Treaty had taken effect. However, it was Kosovo which was the major regional issue in the early months of the year.

On 17 February the National Assembly in Pristina pronounced Kosovo to be an independent state and no longer part of Serbia (see Documents). The Serbs were furious and Russia was vehemently opposed, arguing that Kosovo's independence could only be granted in the context of a UN decision, which Russia itself continued to veto. The EU noted the terms of the independence resolution and said that each member country would decide "in accordance with national practice and international law" on whether or not to recognise Kosovo as a sovereign state. The EU communiqué stressed that Kosovo was a sui generis special case, which did not call into question the principles of the UN Charter, "such as sovereignty and territorial integrity".

In reality, Kosovo was becoming a protectorate of the European Union. A decision by the EU Council of Ministers, taken on 4 February, established a rule of law mission, consisting of more than 1,800 police, judicial, and customs officials, which would move into Kosovo to join the 16,000 NATO troops already there as the Kosovo Force (KFOR). All 27 EU member states approved the mission, known as EULEX Kosovo, although five EU governments continued to regard the country's independence as illegal and refused to grant formal recognition (see p. 112).

The aim of EULEX, which was supposed to begin operations in early summer, was to help establish effective judicial and law enforcement practices in the country, and strengthen an independent judiciary and police force, whilst KFOR was meant to guarantee security. Relations with KFOR did not work well to begin with, because of the diplomatic standoff between Turkey (a member of NATO but not the EU) and Cyprus (a member of the EU but not NATO). By the end of the year, oversight of policing had been transferred from the UN (which still had a mission in Kosovo, UNMIK) to the EU (see p. 392). Allegations of torture by the Kosovo police were under investigation in the latter part of the year.

Serbia's ambitions to join the EU received a major boost. A stabilisation and association agreement was signed in April and, notwithstanding Serbian anger over Kosovar independence, the May general election brought success for Boris Tadic's pro-European Democratic Party, much to the satisfaction of the European Commission. Formation of a government took time, as the Socialist Party of Serbia considered an alliance with the nationalist radicals, but Tadic persuaded them to form a coalition with him. The arrest in Belgrade in July of wartime Bosnian Serb leader Radovan Karadzic could be seen as further evidence of the new coalition's commitment to a mainstream European destiny for Serbia. Nevertheless, the Dutch in particular stressed that Ratko Mladic and Goran Hadzic, the last two wartime leaders under indictment by the International Criminal Tribunal for the former Yugoslavia (ICTY) and still at large, must also be caught, no doubt mindful of the Srebrenica massacre of 1995 (see pp. 114; 117).

As for Bosnia & Herzegovina, a free trade agreement came into effect during the summer and a stabilisation and association agreement was signed in June, while Montenegro submitted a formal application for EU membership in the final days of 2008. Progress continued to be made in accession talks with Croatia, although the Piran Bay border dispute with Slovenia was threatening an early outcome (see p. 121).

EU-RUSSIA RELATIONS. There were hopes that when Dmitry Medvedev took over as Russian president from Vladimir Putin on 7 May, it might signal a new direction in Russian foreign policy. The mood at the EU-Russia summit of 26-27 June in the Siberian town of Khanty-Mansiysk appeared to confirm Russia's regard for the EU, which it recognised as a vital trading partner and, perhaps, an ally in Russia's campaign to reduce the presence of the USA and NATO in Russia's "near abroad". The joint communiqué of the June summit was entitled "The start of a new age". President of the European Council, Slovenia's Prime Minister Janez Jansa, saw partner relations between the EU and Russia as "one of the key factors determining the success of the European Union as well as the Russian Federation in the 21st century". Negotiations were launched for a new EU-Russia partnership and co-operation agreement, to replace the one that expired at the end of 2007. There was reference to "resolving frozen conflicts in the shared neighbourhood".

Georgia's separatist regions of South Ossetia and Abkhazia were the most sensitive of these frozen conflicts, and a major irritant between Russia and Georgia. The EU had been actively promoting a peaceful resolution of the dispute for some years. On 7 July the EU foreign affairs chief, Javier Solana, spoke of his concern at rising tension. "A peaceful, sustainable solution to the conflicts can only be found through dialogue," he said. An EU envoy was sent to the region. However, pressure continued to build, with military exercises carried out on both sides of the Russian-Georgian border—including 1,000 US troops on the Georgian side—just before hostilities broke out. On the night of 7-8 August, according to observers from the Organisation for Security and Co-operation in Europe (OSCE), Georgia launched an artillery attack on Tskhinvali, the capital of South Ossetia, hours after Georgia's President Mikheil Saakashvili had announced a unilateral ceasefire in the ongoing skirmishing between Georgian troops and South Ossetian rebels. Russian troops then entered South Ossetia in force on 8 August, and the following day pushed further into Georgia and into the other separatist area of Abkhazia, destroying Georgian military capabilities in the process and seizing the port of Poti (see map, p. 137).

The French EU presidency immediately called for a ceasefire and on 12 August Sarkozy flew to Moscow and Tbilisi with outline proposals. A six point plan was eventually accepted by both sides, which provided for an end to hostilities, renounced the further use of force, allowed free access to humanitarian aid, and stipulated the withdrawal of troops by both sides to their former positions. The future of South Ossetia and Abkhazia would be subject to international discussion. Russia's unilateral recognition of the independence of the two enclaves on 26 August brought a formal protest from the EU, but the precedent of Kosovo's independence somewhat reduced its credibility. The EU continued to put pressure on Russia to respect the terms of the ceasefire. A team of 200 EU monitors was deployed in the region and, after some delay, they were allowed to move into areas under Russian control at the beginning of October.

An EU-Russia summit was held in Nice on 14 November, attended by President Medvedev, at which Sarkozy spoke approvingly of the Russian implementation of the ceasefire agreement. He said that the Russians had met the conditions for the withdrawal of their forces, except for two specific areas. They had accepted the deployment of EU observers, and participated in the first international talks in Geneva on the disputed enclaves. The EU welcomed negotiations initiated by the Russians to settle the conflict in Nagorno-Karabakh (see p. 136), an initiative which, it was said, could be a model for South Ossetia and Abkhazia. However, Sarkozy criticised the Russian threat to station nuclear missiles in Kaliningrad in reprisal for the US plans for a missile defence shield (see p. 125). It would complicate things, he said.

One consequence of the Russia-Georgia conflict was a greatly extended role for the European Union in the region. The EU effectively became the guarantor of peace, having negotiated the ceasefire, put in place the monitoring team, and brokered a longer term peace settlement. It convened a donors' conference in Brussels in October to work out a funding programme in conjunction with the World Bank to rebuild the Georgian economy after the conflict. For its part, the European Commission committed up to €500 million between 2008 and 2010.

The EU view on the conflict, rarely stated in public, was that Georgia had at least an equal responsibility, although Russia was deemed to have overreacted.

Contravention of human rights in Russia continued to trouble the EU. On 4 December the Council of Ministers issued a statement condemning the search by masked men of the St Petersburg offices of the Memorial Organisation human rights group, a body which investigated the fate of Stalin's victims. The action was perceived to be part of a government-inspired nationalist programme for Stalin's rehabilitation (see p. 126).

ENERGY AND CLIMATE CHANGE.   EU leaders reached agreement on a far-reaching energy and climate change package at their December summit, with the European Parliament giving its approval in the following week. The targets—all to be reached by the year 2020—were a reduction in greenhouse gas emissions by 20 per cent of 1990 levels, an increase in the share of renewable energy to 20 per cent of overall energy sources, and a 20 per cent improvement in energy efficiency. The strategic objective was to limit the global average temperature increase to not more than 2 degrees Celsius above pre-industrial levels.

The measures provided that the target for CO_2 reduction would be increased to 30 per cent by 2020, if other industrialised nations, plus "advanced developing countries" such as China and India, committed themselves to comparable reductions. This decision would be contingent on the outcome of the UN climate change conference in December 2009 in Copenhagen.

The agreement provided for completion of the internal market for gas and electricity; a boost to energy efficiency, including proposals for an international agreement on energy-efficient standards for consumer appliances; support for clean coal technology; an external energy policy to pursue European interests; and a strategic energy technology plan to focus research and development at the European level. Individual member states would determine their own policy on the use of nuclear power. Earlier in the year, the Commission had put forward detailed proposals for an emissions trading scheme, a communication on carbon capture and storage, and a proposal on renewable energy.

Proposals to open up gas and electricity markets had been highly contentious in some member states, because this would require unbundling the transmission assets from the biggest energy-producing companies. Both Germany and France were strongly opposed. It was finally agreed that the companies could remain intact, but with supervision to ensure that the different functions (production and transmission) were fully separate.

Another highly problematic question was posed by nine member states in central and eastern Europe, which were highly dependent on coal and therefore threatening to block the deal. Poland was the most determined that a special formula should be agreed and President Sarkozy, as chair of the European Council, attended a meeting in Gdansk on 6 December where all nine countries were represented. Their concerns were ultimately met by delaying the deadline for obligatory purchase of carbon permits. Those industrial sectors threatened by competition from non-EU countries, which had not introduced measures to cut CO_2 emissions, were reassured that they would continue to receive free CO_2 allowances.

Energy Commissioner Andris Piebalgs was pleased with the outcome. "There has been some tough negotiation and some long nights of debate, but the result is a truly remarkable piece of legislation, which puts the EU on track towards a low-carbon energy economy, in which renewable energy sources play a key role," he said. For Commission President Barroso the deal was "part of the solution both to the climate crisis and to the current economic and financial crisis". It was a green "new deal", which would enhance the competitiveness of EU industry in an increasingly carbon-constrained world, he said.

Europe's security of supply for energy was a major preoccupation during the year, in particular when oil prices soared and also when gas supplies from Russia through Ukraine were once again threatened. In order to strengthen the EU's energy position, the Commission proposed in November that the EU should create a new consortium to bring gas from Central Asia to Europe across the Caspian Sea. This was the centrepiece of a strategic energy plan, which would include the Nabucco project to transport gas from eastern Turkey to Austria (see map, p. 103). The proposed consortium would be called the Caspian Development Corporation. Its shareholders would include private companies, it would be backed by the European Investment Bank, and it would aim to channel the equivalent of between 12 and 25 per cent of current European gas consumption. Russia would be invited to use the pipeline capacity, but the main aim would be to access gas from Turkmenistan and Kazakhstan and so provide more diversity of supply. The pricing dispute between Ukraine and Russia at the end of the year gave these ideas particular impetus.

TRADE. The collapse of the World Trade Organisation's (WTO's) Doha Round of negotiations in July was a bitter disappointment for the European Commission, which had been striving for seven years to make progress towards a new international trade agreement. Various attempts were made during the remainder of the year to revive the talks, but without success (see p. 413). Speaking in Geneva when it became clear that the talks had foundered, EU Trade Commissioner Peter Mandelson said, "The prosperity of all of us in the world depends on a strong, rules-based global trading system. A Doha deal would have given it a much-needed boost." He told the European Parliament that he remained convinced "that a definitive collapse of the Doha Round—should we face this—would seriously dent confidence in the WTO's system of trade rules and future market openness, and have a significant knock-on effect on the multilateral system as a whole." The failure of the talks was a particular disappointment for Mandelson, who accepted UK Prime Minister Gordon Brown's invitation to leave Brussels in September, before his mandate expired. The UK's place in the Commission was taken by Baroness Ashton (for full list of EU commissioners see Documents).

UNION FOR THE MEDITERRANEAN. Conceived during the French presidential elections as an alternative to Turkey's membership of the EU, a Mediterranean Union was the brainchild of Nicolas Sarkozy, who saw it as a grouping of Mediterranean countries which would be led by France and would include Turkey. The idea was unacceptable to other EU members, and especially to Germany, not least because it envisaged having recourse to EU funds without giving the EU any control. It was also unacceptable to Turkey.

After discussion with German Chancellor Merkel, President Sarkozy modified his views and assured Turkey that the organisation would be a stepping stone to EU membership rather than an alternative, so the Union for the Mediterranean was born at a meeting in Paris on 13 July. It would consist of all the 27 EU countries and 16 other countries, most of them Muslim, but also including Israel. Libya took observer status, with Colonel Moamar Kadhafi asking how one could possibly envisage a union between the countries of North Africa and those of Scandinavia, "where it is common to see people walk around naked".

The organisation did have potential to contribute to progress in the Middle East peace process, and it had other practical long-term aims, such as cleaning up the Mediterranean Sea, managing water resources, developing solar power capabilities, improving transport links, and tackling natural disasters.

Michael Berendt

THE COUNCIL OF EUROPE

DATE OF FOUNDATION: 1949   HEADQUARTERS: Strasbourg, France
OBJECTIVES: To strengthen pluralist democracy, the rule of law and the maintenance of human rights in Europe and to further political, social and cultural co-operation between member states
MEMBERSHIP (END-'08): Albania, Andorra, Armenia, Austria, Azerbaijan, Belgium, Bosnia & Herzegovina, Bulgaria, Croatia, Cyprus, Czech Republic, Denmark, Estonia, Finland, France, Georgia, Germany, Greece, Hungary, Iceland, Ireland, Italy, Latvia, Liechtenstein, Lithuania, Luxembourg, Macedonia, Malta, Moldova, Monaco, Montenegro, Netherlands, Norway, Poland, Portugal, Romania, Russia, San Marino, Serbia, Slovakia, Slovenia, Spain, Sweden, Switzerland, Turkey, Ukraine, UK (total 47)
SECRETARY GENERAL: Terry Davis (UK)

ARMED conflict between Russia and Georgia, two of the Council of Europe's own member states, presented the organisation with an impossible challenge in August 2008. An institution whose whole raison d'être was the peaceful settlement of disputes, promotion of democracy, and protection of human rights could bring no pressure to bear in a crisis where military force was everything.

Russian troops invaded South Ossetia on 8 August and Abkhazia the following day, claiming that they were defending Russian citizens in the two disputed enclaves. Georgia, late on 7 August, had engaged in heavy shelling of the South

Ossetian capital, Tskhinvali, after announcing a ceasefire in its skirmishing with South Ossetian separatists (see map, p. 137). The Swedish foreign secretary Carl Bildt, currently chairing the Council of Europe committee of ministers, issued a statement on 9 August urging "the Russian Federation, Georgia and the separatist South Ossetian and Abkhaz administrations" to enter into a ceasefire and engage in direct talks.

On 11 August Bildt visited the Georgian capital, Tbilisi, to assess the situation, but his plans to fly to Moscow collapsed when the Russian government informed him that he would not be officially received there. In fact, the offices of the EU were more successful. A ceasefire was negotiated on 12 August and EU observers were deployed in October to monitor it (see pp. 136-38; 429-30). On 26 August a further Council of Europe statement was issued, condemning Russia's recognition of the independence of the two disputed territories.

The Swedish presidency described the conflict as a serious challenge to the Council of Europe, its credibility, and the values it defended. "The undertaking to settle disputes by peaceful means...made at the accession of both the Russian Federation and Georgia have been ignored," it said. An informal meeting of the Council's committee of ministers was convened in New York and in October an action plan was drawn up, but had not been adopted by the year's end.

The Council's human rights activity had led to a highly critical statement earlier in 2008 of Russian behaviour in the North Caucasus. A memorandum was issued by Dick Marty, rapporteur of the legal affairs committee of the Parliamentary Assembly of the Council of Europe (PACE). His report highlighted human rights violations by Russian security forces in Russia's North Caucasus republic of Chechnya, including disappearances, torture, and executions, with impunity for those responsible for these violations.

The Council was active in the Balkans, sending observers to elections in Montenegro—the Council's newest member-state—in April. These it pronounced as being in accordance with international standards (see p. 115). There was genuine choice of candidates, a calm environment and a focus on substantive issues. The Council's commissioner for human rights, Thomas Hammarberg, visited Montenegro in June to discuss human rights issues.

In July, the president of the PACE, Lluís Maria de Puig, welcomed the arrest in Belgrade (Serbia's capital) of Radovan Karadzic, the wartime Bosnian Serb leader, which he saw as a "clear, unequivocal signal of the determination...to bind Serbia ever more closely to the European institutions" (see pp. 116-17).

Efforts to persuade Russia to speed ratification of protocol 14 to the European Convention on Human Rights made no progress. This protocol would help the European Court of Human Rights to deal with the long backlog of cases that it faced (the majority of which related to Russia). A letter sent to Russian President Dmitry Medvedev by the Council presidency received no reply. The Court was therefore asked whether it could put into effect some of the provisions of the protocol, despite the Russian block.

Michael Berendt

ORGANIZATION FOR SECURITY AND CO-OPERATION IN EUROPE (OSCE)

DATE OF FOUNDATION: 1975   HEADQUARTERS: Vienna, Austria
OBJECTIVES: To promote security and co-operation among member states, particularly in respect of the resolution of internal and external conflicts
MEMBERSHIP (END-'08): Albania, Andorra, Armenia, Austria, Azerbaijan, Belarus, Belgium, Bosnia & Herzegovina, Bulgaria, Canada, Croatia, Cyprus, Czech Republic, Denmark, Estonia, Finland, France, Georgia, Germany, Greece, Holy See (Vatican), Hungary, Iceland, Ireland, Italy, Kazakhstan, Kyrgyzstan, Latvia, Liechtenstein, Lithuania, Luxembourg, Macedonia, Malta, Moldova, Monaco, Montenegro, Netherlands, Norway, Poland, Portugal, Romania, Russian Federation, San Marino, Serbia & Montenegro, Slovakia, Slovenia, Spain, Sweden, Switzerland, Tajikistan, Turkey, Turkmenistan, Ukraine, UK, USA, Uzbekistan (total 56)
SECRETARY GENERAL: Marc Perrin de Brichambaut (France)
CHAIRMAN-IN-OFFICE (2008): Alexander Stubb (Finland)

AT the start of the year, the incoming chairman-in-office, Alexander Stubb, foreign minister of Finland, outlined a programme of "three Cs": continuity, coherence, and co-operation. The war between Georgia and Russia—both OSCE members—in August, however, changed the priorities of the Finnish chairmanship. What was supposed to have been an interim period, dedicated to pondering the future of the organisation, turned into a "Georgia chairmanship", as Stubb described it. Underlining this focus for the OSCE, the organisation's annual ministerial council, held in Helsinki on 4-5 December, was attended by a record 50 foreign ministers and was dominated by two themes: the Caucasus, in particularly Georgia, and European security.

The OSCE had been active since 1992 in promoting resolution of the "frozen conflicts" between Georgia and its separatist regions of South Ossetia and Abkhazia, and maintained a 200-strong monitoring mission in the country. OSCE Chairman Stubb was instrumental in helping to negotiate a ceasefire in the brief August war, in conjunction with the French presidency of the EU. The small number of unarmed military monitors from the OSCE mission, stationed in areas adjacent to South Ossetia, was expanded to monitor the ceasefire (see pp. 136-38; 429-30). Significantly, some members of the OSCE mission later blamed Georgia for directing an "indiscriminate" artillery attack on Tskhinvali (the capital of South Ossetia) on the night of 7 August, contradicting the Georgian version that they were engaged in a defensive operation. Whilst the OSCE refused to discuss its monitors' findings, neither did it dispute them.

At the end of the year, however, the OSCE's civilian mission to Georgia was under threat after Russia, at a meeting on 22 December, blocked the extension of its mandate beyond 31 December 2008, on the grounds that the OSCE was not treating South Ossetia and Abkhazia separately from Georgia, and so had failed to accept Russia's recognition of the regions as independent states. The Russian decision was a further indication of the fractious relationship between Russia and the OSCE. Earlier in the year, the OSCE had decided not to send monitors from its office for democratic institutions and human rights (ODIHR) to the Russian presidential elections of 2 March, on the grounds that Russia had placed "unacceptable" restrictions on the election observers.

The OSCE was also one of the mediators in negotiations for a settlement of another "frozen conflict" left over from the Soviet collapse: the separatist Transdniestr region in Moldova. Significant steps were taken towards achieving resolution in 2008, with the first meeting in seven years between the Moldovan president and the Transdniestr leader, held in April. President Vladimir Voronin of Moldova and self-styled Transdniestr President Igor Smirnov were applauded by the head of the OSCE's mission to Moldova, Philip Remler, for the political will which they demonstrated. In large part, however, the progress made in 2008 towards resolving the conflict was achieved thanks to "soft pressure" exerted by Russia (see pp. 131-32).

Michael Kaser

EUROPEAN BANK FOR RECONSTRUCTION AND DEVELOPMENT (EBRD)

DATE OF FOUNDATION: 1991   HEADQUARTERS: London, UK
OBJECTIVES: To promote the economic reconstruction of former Communist-ruled countries on the
   basis of the free-market system and pluralism
MEMBERSHIP (END-'08): Albania, Armenia, Australia, Austria, Azerbaijan, Belarus, Belgium, Bosnia
   & Herzegovina, Bulgaria, Canada, Croatia, Cyprus, Czech Republic, Denmark, Egypt,
   Estonia, Finland, France, Georgia, Germany, Greece, Hungary, Iceland, Ireland, Israel, Italy,
   Japan, Kazakhstan, South Korea, Kyrgyzstan, Latvia, Liechtenstein, Lithuania, Luxembourg,
   Macedonia, Malta, Mexico, Moldova, Mongolia, Montenegro, Morocco, Netherlands, New
   Zealand, Norway, Poland, Portugal, Romania, Russia, Serbia, Slovakia, Slovenia, Spain,
   Sweden, Switzerland, Tajikistan, Turkey, Turkmenistan, Ukraine, UK, USA, Uzbekistan,
   European Community, European Investment Bank (total 63)
PRESIDENT: Thomas Mirow (Germany)

THE Bank returned to the Ukrainian capital, Kiev, for its annual meeting on 18-19 May—having convened there in 1998—and, appropriately, reviewed progress in the EBRD region during those 10 years. The EBRD resolved to continue shifting its activities further south and east, in line with the varying development record and needs of the area, but in conditions of generally slowing economic growth, financial market turbulence, and the new threat of rising inflation.

EBRD President Jean Lemierre, retiring after eight years in office, noted that the conditions in the Bank's region had improved dramatically over the decade, for in the year 2000 member economies were still affected by the Russian financial collapse of 1998 and "it was a time of poverty, corruption and pessimism about life in the free market". Current prospects were positive, but turbulent financial markets and increased investor hesitancy dictated caution. Lemierre proposed that 80 per cent of the Bank's net income in 2007 of €1.1 billion be earmarked for reserves, the remainder to be divided between a new fund for financing technical co-operation to facilitate future investments (€115 million) and helping to finance work to make safe the site of the Chernobyl nuclear plant (€135 million).

The USA had previously envisaged the payment of dividends to members, but was opposed by EU member states and non-EU states of Eastern Europe. Of the Bank's total investment of €5.6 billion in 2007, 90 per cent had gone to countries that were not among the eight that joined the EU in 2004. Funding had been provided for more than 3 million small- and medium-sized enterprises. Energy efficiency projects, which the Bank saw as a key priority, absorbed one-fifth of overall investments. The Bank's reserves would be maintained at a level sufficient to sustain investment at the 2007 level until the next five-year review due in 2010-11.

The EBRD's board of governors appointed Thomas Mirow, state secretary at the German ministry of finance, as the Bank's fifth president. Aged 55, Mirow had experience in both the private and the public sectors, notably in Hamburg and in the federal chancellery. At a press conference during the annual meeting, he expressed the intention to undertake earlier the general review of the Bank's operations scheduled for 2010.

The Bank's *Transition Report 2008*, released in November, was subtitled *Growth in Transition*. It argued that many countries in the region had failed to take advantage of the strong skills base at the start of the transition period, and that economic growth prospects could be improved substantially by raising education levels and skills. The report was gloomy about the prospects for the EBRD countries in the context of the accelerating global financial crisis, predicting that overall growth in EBRD countries would fall to 6.3 per cent in 2008 (having been 7.5 per cent in 2007), and to 3.0 per cent in 2009. Capital outflows from emerging markets and the recession in key developed economies were likely to test the resilience of transition countries, it warned. The report also highlighted the possibility of a particularly sharp contraction in countries that were running large current account deficits combined with high foreign currency debt, and warned that tightening credit conditions could have "undoubtedly severe" consequences for overall economic growth in transition countries.

Michael Kaser

OTHER EUROPEAN ORGANISATIONS

European Free Trade Association (EFTA)

DATE OF FOUNDATION: 1960   HEADQUARTERS: Geneva, Switzerland
OBJECTIVES: To eliminate barriers to non-agricultural trade between members
MEMBERSHIP (END-'08): Iceland, Liechtenstein, Norway, Switzerland (total 4)
SECRETARY GENERAL: Kare Bryn (Norway)

Visegrad Group

DATE OF FOUNDATION: 1991   HEADQUARTERS: rotating
OBJECTIVES: Originally, to reduce trade barriers between members with a view to their eventual
    membership of the European Union; since 2004, to continue developing the co-operation of
    the Visegrad Group countries as member states of the EU and NATO
MEMBERSHIP (END-'08): Czech Republic, Hungary, Poland, Slovakia (total 4)
PRESIDENCY: rotating ('07-'08: Czech Republic)

Nordic Council

DATE OF FOUNDATION: 1952   HEADQUARTERS: Stockholm, Sweden
OBJECTIVES: To facilitate legislative and governmental cooperation between member states, with
    particular reference to proposals of the Nordic Council of Ministers
MEMBERSHIP (END-'08): Denmark, Finland, Iceland, Norway, Sweden (total 5)
SECRETARY GENERAL: Halldor Asgrimsson (Iceland)

Council of the Baltic Sea States (CBSS)

DATE OF FOUNDATION: 1992   HEADQUARTERS: Stockholm, Sweden
OBJECTIVES: To promote political, economic and other co-operation between Baltic littoral and
    adjecent states
MEMBERSHIP (END-'08): Denmark, Estonia, Finland, Germany, Iceland, Latvia, Lithuania, Norway,
    Poland, Russia, Sweden, European Commission (total 12)
OBSERVER MEMBERS: France, Italy, Netherlands, Slovakia, Ukraine, UK, USA (total 7)
PRESIDENCY ('08-'09): Denmark

Central European Free Trade Agreement (CEFTA)

DATE OF FOUNDATION: 1992; CEFTA 2006   HEADQUARTERS: rotating
OBJECTIVES: to promote regional stability and further membership of the EU
MEMBERSHIP (END-'08): Albania, Bosnia & Herzegovina, Croatia, Kosovo, Macedonia, Moldova,
    Montenegro, Serbia (total 8)
PRESIDENCY ('08): Moldova

Central European Initiative (CEI)

DATE OF FOUNDATION: 1989   HEADQUARTERS: Trieste, Italy
OBJECTIVES: To promote the harmonisation of economic and other policies of member states
MEMBERSHIP (END-'08): Albania, Armenia, Belarus, Bosnia & Herzegovina, Bulgaria, Croatia, Czech
    Republic, Hungary, Italy, Macedonia, Moldova, Montenegro, Poland, Romania, Slovakia,
    Slovenia, Ukraine, Serbia (total 18)
DIRECTOR GENERAL: Pietro Ago (Italy)

Organisation of the Black Sea Economic Co-operation (BSEC)

DATE OF FOUNDATION: 1992   HEADQUARTERS: Istanbul, Turkey
OBJECTIVES: To promote economic co-operation between member states
MEMBERSHIP (END-'08): Albania, Armenia, Azerbaijan, Bulgaria, Georgia, Greece, Moldova,
    Romania, Russia, Serbia, Turkey, Ukraine (total 12)
SECRETARY GENERAL: Leonidas Chrysanthopoulos (Greece)

EUROPEAN FREE TRADE AREA (EFTA). Under Swiss and then Icelandic chairmanship in 2008, EFTA was intensively engaged in extending its range of free trade agreements. An agreement with the Southern Africa Customs Union (SACU)—the first concluded with another trading bloc—entered into force in May. Negotiations were successfully concluded with the Gulf Co-operation Council (GCC), an agreement was signed with Colombia in November, and negotiations with Algeria made substantial progress. Talks began with India and a ministerial meeting in November signalled readiness to embark on negotiations with Albania, Serbia, and Ukraine. Meanwhile, work was at a more exploratory stage in relation to Georgia, Pakistan, Thailand, Serbia and Indonesia, though political uncertainties made progress uncertain with some of these.

Considerable time was also given to wider issues, including the liberalisation of trade in agricultural produce, the implications of the outcome of the WTO's Doha Round of trade negotiations for trade with third countries, and the quality of south European infrastructure. Concern was also expressed that as the EU became ever more heterogeneous, it was becoming less able to respond to the special concerns of the European Economic Area (EEA) states (the EU member states plus Iceland, Liechtenstein, and Norway). A growing number of legal instruments and policy statements emanating from the European Commission were relevant to the EEA but were not covered by the EEA agreement.

VISEGRAD GROUP. Meeting in April, the Visegrad Group urged the EU to support democratisation in Belarus and the aspirations of Ukraine and Georgia—soon to be put on hold—to join NATO. In September the presidents of the four member states advocated further expansion of the EU, notably to include Croatia, while their environment ministers were concerned with CO_2 emissions from vehicles, greener tax systems, and the illegal transporting of waste to their countries. By the November meeting of prime ministers, darker and more immediate problems were to the fore. Leaders called for structural reforms by the EU in the face of the growing global financial crisis and for diversification of energy supplies. Also in November, the foreign ministers joined their counterparts from Bulgaria, Romania, the three Baltic states,and Sweden, in Warsaw, to agree a long statement, which included a call for the EU to be firm with Russia over Georgia, the need to develop new forms of co-operation with the EU's eastern partnership (discussed at the June 2008 EU summit), and the easing of EU visa rules.

NORDIC COUNCIL. The organisation's major preoccupations during the year included how its members could work together more closely on defence and security and how they might co-operate to end tax evasion. Meeting at Riksgränsen, Sweden, in December, the prime ministers identified cutting-edge scientific research as a prime area for increased co-operation and agreed on the need for joint action on climate change initiatives.

COUNCIL OF THE BALTIC SEA STATES (CBSS). At its annual summit in Riga in June, the Council followed up the commitment made by the 2007 meeting to reform and revitalise the organisation to make it more capable of concentrating on a limited range of priorities and developing regionally important strategic projects. These would include ensuring stable and secure energy supplies, the environment, education, culture and civil security (including the fight against organised crime, human trafficking, and illegal migration), and the protection of children's rights.

CENTRAL EUROPE FREE TRADE AGREEMENT (CEFTA). Under Moldovan presidency, the main focus of CEFTA's activity during the year was organisational. Particular attention was paid to the establishment of a CEFTA secretariat in Brussels and the work of sub-committees on agriculture, customs evaluations and tariff and non-tariff measures.

CENTRAL EUROPEAN INITIATIVE (CEI). The CEI group of 18 countries, also under Moldovan presidency in 2008, was principally engaged with the "repositioning" process agreed by the heads of government at their November 2007 meeting (see AR 2008, p. 421). This included redrafting the CEI plan of action to concentrate on economic and human development and inter-regional and cross-border co-operation. Progress with the repositioning process was reviewed by the CEI heads of government at their annual summit in Chisinau (Moldova) in November. Particular emphasis was laid on increased co-operation with the European Commission and other regional organisations and on strengthening the role of the CEI as a bridge between EU and non-EU countries, helping non-EU member-states in their progress towards integration. The CEI climate fund, launched during the year, and the know-how exchange programme were seen as useful tools in increasing CEI participation in EU programmes. (The climate fund was created to support environmentally-related projects, proposed by institutions from CEI countries, for developments benefiting non-EU members.) The CEI economic summit, also in November, focused on reforms and investments needed to foster regional integration, with particular attention to energy efficiency, infrastructure development, and the role of e-government in economic growth and competitiveness. It was recognised that the relative weakness of financial institutions in the CEI area had, to some extent, cushioned member states from the effects of the global financial crisis; nevertheless, economic development would require the development of stronger financial institutions.

ORGANISATION OF THE BLACK SEA ECONOMIC CO-OPERATION (BSEC). Foreign ministers of BSEC and the EU, meeting for the first time in Kiev, Ukraine, in February, discussed the implementation of the EU's 2007 initiative on Black Sea synergy (see AR 2008, p. 421). They agreed a joint statement backing closer co-operation on developing transport, energy infrastructure, security, and environmental protection, which was a growing problem as pollution levels increased. In April, a meeting of BSEC foreign ministers emphasised the need for institutionalising relations between BSEC and the EU. Also in April, a meeting of transport ministers, though marred by a spat between Armenia and Azerbaijan, agreed a joint declaration supporting the co-ordinated development of the long-cherished project for a Black Sea ring highway and the grandiosely titled "motorways of the sea" programme. On these, there were few concrete signs of progress. However, work on closer co-operation in transport and the easing of visa procedures offered hope.

Measures to improve the efficiency of BSEC's decision-making were initiated as far back as 2006, but progress was slow. A meeting of foreign ministers in October approved guidelines on the improvement of BSEC efficiency. The need for further work in this area to raise the organisation's "credibility" and also to improve its decision-making mechanisms still featured prominently on the agenda of the incoming Armenian presidency in November.

Martin Harrison

AMERICAN, ARAB, AFRICAN, EURASIAN, AND ASIA-PACIFIC ORGANISATIONS

AMERICAN AND CARIBBEAN ORGANISATIONS

Organisation of American States (OAS)

DATE OF FOUNDATION: 1951   HEADQUARTERS: Washington DC, USA
OBJECTIVES: To facilitate political, economic and other co-operation between member states and to defend their territorial integrity and independence
MEMBERSHIP (END-'08): Antigua & Barbuda, Argentina, Bahamas, Barbados, Belize, Bolivia, Brazil, Canada, Chile, Colombia, Costa Rica, Cuba (suspended), Dominica, Dominican Republic, Ecuador, El Salvador, Grenada, Guatemala, Guyana, Haiti, Honduras, Jamaica, Mexico, Nicaragua, Panama, Paraguay, Peru, St Kitts & Nevis, St Lucia, St Vincent & the Grenadines, Suriname, Trinidad & Tobago, USA, Uruguay, Venezuela (total 35)
SECRETARY GENERAL: José Miguel Insulza (Chile)

Rio Group

DATE OF FOUNDATION: 1986   HEADQUARTERS: rotating
OBJECTIVES: To provide a regional mechanism for joint political action
MEMBERSHIP(END-'08): Argentina, Belize, Bolivia, Brazil, Chile, Colombia, Costa Rica, Cuba, Dominican Republic, Ecuador, El Salvador, Guatemala, Guyana, Haiti, Honduras, Jamaica, Mexico, Nicaragua, Panama, Paraguay, Peru, Uruguay, Venezuela (total 23)

Southern Common Market (Mercosur)

DATE OF FOUNDATION: 1991   HEADQUARTERS: Montevideo, Uruguay
OBJECTIVES: To build a genuine common market between member states
MEMBERSHIP (END-'08): Argentina, Brazil, Paraguay, Uruguay (total 4; Venezuela's membership is awaiting formal ratification)
ASSOCIATE MEMBERS: Bolivia, Chile, Colombia, Ecuador, Peru (total 5)
PRO TEMPORE SECRETARY: Carlos Alvarez (Argentina)

Andean Community of Nations (Ancom/CAN)

DATE OF FOUNDATION: 1969   HEADQUARTERS: Lima, Peru
OBJECTIVES: To promote the economic development and integration of member states
MEMBERSHIP (END-'08): Bolivia, Colombia, Ecuador, Peru (total 4)
ASSOCIATE MEMBERS: Argentina, Brazil, Chile, Paraguay, Uruguay (total 5)
OBSERVER MEMBERS: Mexico, Panama
SECRETARY GENERAL: Freddy Ehlers Zurita (Ecuador)

Caribbean Community and Common Market (Caricom)

DATE OF FOUNDATION: 1973   HEADQUARTERS: Georgetown, Guyana
OBJECTIVES: To facilitate economic, political and other co-operation between member states and to operate certain regional services
MEMBERSHIP (END-'08): Antigua & Barbuda, Bahamas, Barbados, Belize, Dominica, Grenada, Guyana, Haiti, Jamaica, Montserrat, St Kitts & Nevis, St Lucia, St Vincent & the Grenadines, Suriname, Trinidad & Tobago (total 15)
ASSOCIATE MEMBERS: Anguilla, Bermuda, British Virgin Islands, Cayman Islands, Turk & Caicos Islands (total 5)
SECRETARY GENERAL: Edwin Carrington (Trinidad & Tobago)

Organisation of Eastern Caribbean States (OECS)

DATE OF FOUNDATION: 1981   HEADQUARTERS: Castries, St Lucia
OBJECTIVES: To co-ordinate the external, defence, trade and monetary policies of member states
MEMBERSHIP (END-'08): Antigua & Barbuda, Dominica, Grenada, Montserrat, St Lucia, St Kitts & Nevis, St Vincent & the Grenadines (total 7)
ASSOCIATE MEMBERS: Anguilla, British Virgin Islands,
DIRECTOR GENERAL: Len Ishmael (St Lucia)

ORGANISATION OF AMERICAN STATES (OAS).   The OAS and the Rio Group were both involved in dealing with a dispute between Colombia, Ecuador, and Venezuela in early March (see pp. 194-95). The cause of the hostilities was an attack by Colombia's armed forces on a guerrilla camp of the Revolutionary Armed Forces of Colombia (FARC) located just over the border with Ecuador. Ecuador and Venezuela criticised Colombia's action, broke off diplomatic ties, and sent troops to the border. Then, on 5 March the OAS approved, albeit without US support, a resolution stating that the bombing of the FARC camp had constituted "a violation of the sovereignty and territorial integrity of Ecuador and the principles of international law". However, it omitted explicitly to condemn Colombia for its action. Ecuador's president, Rafael Correa Delgado, said that the OAS should be consigned "to the dustbin of history" if it failed to issue Colombia with a stern rebuke. Although no such rebuke was forthcoming, the dispute was resolved just two days later. On 7 March at the Rio Group summit held in the Dominican Republic, President Hugo Chávez Frías of Venezuela, having failed to win regional backing for his aggressive stance against Colombia, reversed his position and acted as mediator. He urged everyone to step back from the brink and set aside their differences for the sake of peace. This prompted a somewhat uneasy rapprochement between Correa, Chávez and Colombian President Alvaro Uribe Velez.

RIO GROUP.   In mid-December the Rio Group formally accepted Cuba as its 23rd member. The decision was made during a brief, extraordinary Rio Group summit, held on the sidelines of the first ever meeting between all 33 Latin American and Caribbean countries in Brazil. Cuban President Raúl Castro Ruz welcomed membership as a "transcendental moment" for his country.

SOUTHERN COMMON MARKET (MERCOSUR).   Mercosur held its first presidential summit of the year, its 35th overall, in Argentina at the beginning of July. Two issues dominated proceedings: the rise in global food prices, and a newly adopted EU immigration measure. On the latter issue, Mercosur states condemned the

EU's approval of the Return Directive, which involved tougher terms for detention and expulsion of illegal immigrants, and a five-year ban on their return. In a joint declaration, the presidents rejected "every effort to criminalise irregular migration and the adoption of restrictive immigration policies, in particular against the most vulnerable sectors of society, women and children". The EU measure angered Mercosur leaders because there was significant illegal migration from Latin America to Spain.

At the second presidential summit, held in Brazil in mid-December, an unsuccessful attempt was made to eliminate the group's trade distorting double tariff system. Under the system, one tariff was charged on goods imported from countries outside Mercosur, and another when those same goods were exported from one member to another. Landlocked Paraguay, which sourced the majority of its imports from Argentina and Brazil, was reluctant to see the tariff removed, as it threatened to reduced its tax revenue.

ANDEAN COMMUNITY OF NATIONS (ANCOM/CAN). The members of the Andean Community and those of Mercosur, together with Chile, Guyana, Suriname, and Venezuela, signed a treaty on 23 May to create the Union of South American Nations (UNASUR). The objectives of the embryonic organisation were to improve political and economic integration in the region, as well as defence co-operation, via a number of initiatives such as the creation of a single market and a South American Defence Council. According to the constitutive treaty, UNASUR's headquarters would be located in Quito, Ecuador. A South American Parliament would be located in Cochabamba, Bolivia, and UNASUR's associated bank, the Bank of the South, would be located in Caracas, Venezuela.

CARIBBEAN COMMUNITY AND COMMON MARKET (CARICOM). On 15 October member states and the Dominican Republic signed an economic partnership agreement (EPA) with the EU. The agreement had been initialled in December 2007 (see AR 2008, pp. 424-25) but final ratification was delayed. Guyana and some of the smaller Caribbean states were concerned that the EPA would open up their economies too quickly and undermine their already limited economic sovereignty. In the end all states except Haiti signed up to the agreement. Haiti did not participate because of reservations over some of the EPA's provisions relating to regional preference, development aid, and tariff levels.

The divisions over the EPA were indicative of a wider malaise within Caricom. In January the launch of the Caricom competition commission, established to improve the operation of the Caribbean Single Market and Economy (CSME), was undermined from the outset by a shortage of funds because some member states refused to pay their full contributions. Then, in July, Caricom heads of government failed to resolve several key issues relating to the CSME, including setting out a specific timetable for the free movement of Caricom nationals. In the 15-page summit communiqué only one paragraph was devoted to the CSME. In December Trinidad & Tobago announced that the government would likely cut, or even halt, its monthly contributions to the Caribbean development fund (CDF) due to the global financial crisis. The CDF was created in July to provide financial and technical assistance to disadvantaged member states and sectors participating in the CSME.

There were also divisions in the area of foreign affairs. There was no unified position towards the competing claims of China and Taiwan, the Venezuelan-backed Bolivarian Alternative for Latin America (ALBA), or Venezuela's oil supply initiative, PetroCaribe (see p. 170). A number of serving and former heads of government criticised the growing discord and structural weaknesses within Caricom, while Norman Girvan, former secretary-general of the Association of Caribbean States, talked of "a real danger of disintegration".

ORGANISATION OF EASTERN CARIBBEAN STATES (OECS). Developments within the OECS, whose members were part of Caricom, also highlighted the problems facing the larger organisation. On 14 August OECS leaders committed themselves to achieving economic union by 2011 (four years before the planned inauguration of the CSME's single economy) and political union by 2013 (which was not an objective of Caricom). While on 11 September it was agreed that Trinidad & Tobago could join the OECS, in response Jamaica's prime minister, Bruce Golding, warned that the move would have implications "for the structure, and indeed future of Caricom". Other leaders claimed that the potential political union would be a "distraction" from greater Caricom integration.

Peter Clegg

ARAB ORGANISATIONS

League of Arab States (Arab League)

DATE OF FOUNDATION: 1945   HEADQUARTERS: Cairo, Egypt
OBJECTIVES: To co-ordinate political, economic, social and cultural co-operation between member states and to mediate in disputes between them
MEMBERSHIP (END-'08): Algeria, Bahrain, Comoros, Djibouti, Egypt, Iraq, Jordan, Kuwait, Lebanon, Libya, Mauritania, Morocco, Oman, Palestine, Qatar, Saudi Arabia, Somalia, Sudan, Syria, Tunisia, United Arab Emirates, Yemen (total 22)
SECRETARY GENERAL: Amr Moussa (Egypt)

Gulf Co-operation Council (GCC)

DATE OF FOUNDATION: 1981   HEADQUARTERS: Riyadh, Saudi Arabia
OBJECTIVES: To promote co-operation between member states in all fields with a view to achieving unity
MEMBERSHIP (END-'08): Bahrain, Kuwait, Oman, Qatar, Saudi Arabia, United Arab Emirates (total 6)
SECRETARY GENERAL: Abdulrahman al-Attiya (Qatar)

LEAGUE OF ARAB STATES (ARAB LEAGUE). The Arab League held its 20th regular summit meeting in Damascus, Syria, on 29-30 March (see p. 217). There was a disappointingly low turnout, with only 11 out of 22 heads of state attending the gathering. Lebanon boycotted the summit entirely, accusing Syria of blocking the election of a new Lebanese president after the pro-Syrian President Emile Lahoud's term had ended in November 2007 (see AR 2008, pp. 197-98). Key pro-Western Arab leaders, including Egyptian President Mohammed Hosni Mubarak, Saudi Arabian King Abdullah ibn Abdul Aziz, and Jordanian King Abdullah II, shunned the summit in solidarity with Lebanon.

The summit made no breakthrough on the Lebanese political crisis (see pp. 219-20). However, Syrian Foreign Minister Walid al-Mu'allim rejected the allegation that the summit's success had hinged on making progress on Lebanon. He said, "The issue of Lebanon was raised during the closed session, but the leaders decided it was not appropriate to discuss Lebanon during its absence."

The summit concluded its deliberations by issuing the "Damascus Declaration" on Arab solidarity, national security, and revitalising the mechanisms of the joint Arab action. The declaration, read by Arab League Secretary General Amr Moussa at a press conference, highlighted the following topics: (i) a commitment to bolstering Arab solidarity to protect Arab national security, and guarantee for each Arab country safety, sovereignty, the right to defend itself and non-interference in its internal affairs; (ii) working to surpass inter-Arab disputes through deep, serious dialogue and overcoming weaknesses in some aspects of Arab joint action; (iii) giving priority to the higher interests of the Arab nation over any arguments or disputes, and dealing firmly with any foreign interference that attempts to increase inter-Arab disputes; (iv) standing together in the face of economic and political pressure campaigns imposed by some countries on any Arab country and taking necessary steps to confront them; (v) giving the Arabic language special care, so that it could keep up with scientific developments in the age of globalisation and information and become a means to combat attempts to defame and Westernise Arab culture.

The declaration also vowed to continue to provide all types of political, material, and moral support to the Palestinian people in their struggle against Israeli occupation. It warned against the excessive Israeli policies of "laying siege and intensifying attacks", particularly in the Gaza Strip, characterising them as "war crimes" that required immediate action. It pledged to work to achieve a just and comprehensive peace in the Middle East, guaranteeing the restoration of legitimate Arab rights, including the return of Palestinian refugees to their homeland and the establishment of an independent Palestinian state with Jerusalem as its capital.

The declaration expressed great concern at the "mounting ferocious attack on Islam and the phenomena of anti-Islam" and noted that anti-Islamic abuse was on the rise in countries generally marked by diversity. This growing polarisation necessitated greater work to narrow the gap, which was widening between cultures and civilisations.

Arab foreign ministers had renewed their commitment to the Arab "land for peace" initiative as a basis for a just and comprehensive solution to the Arab-Israeli conflict during their one-day preparatory meeting on 28 March. The Arab peace initiative, first adopted at the Arab League's March 2002 summit in Beirut (see AR 2002, pp. 206-07), called for an Israeli withdrawal from the territories that were occupied in the 1967 Six-Day War, in exchange for a complete normalisation of relations with the Arab states. At the Arab League's 19th regular summit, held in Saudi Arabia in March 2007, Arab leaders had agreed to relaunch the 2002 "land for peace" initiative (see AR 2008, p. 426).

GULF CO-OPERATION COUNCIL (GCC). The 29th summit meeting of the GCC was held in Muscat, Oman, on 29-30 December. Leaders reviewed the progress of the GCC common market, which had been launched on 1 January 2008. The common market granted national treatment to all GCC companies and citizens in any other GCC country, and in doing so removed all barriers to cross-country investment and trade.

A final communiqué issued at the end of the summit stated that the leaders had considered the current global financial crisis, its consequences and its economic impacts, and had directed the concerned ministerial committees to intensify co-ordination among the member states and take the necessary measures to limit its negative effects on the economies of the GCC's member states. The leaders had also directed the concerned ministerial committee to exert "every possible effort that would contribute in stabilising oil prices in a manner that would achieve the pursed balance and joint interests of oil producing and consuming countries".

On the question of the future membership of Yemen, the leaders "hailed the growing co-operation between the GCC and the brotherly Republic of Yemen". They approved Yemen's accession to the GCC standardisation authority, the Gulf organisation for industrial consultancy, the GCC auditing and accounting authority, and the Gulf radio and television authority. They issued directives that all the necessary legal and administrative measures be taken in this regard, and that Yemen would have the same rights and obligations of GCC member states in these institutions.

On the issue of Palestine, the leaders requested Israel to refrain from "the obstinacy of power" and lift the blockade, which had been imposed on the Palestinian territories and especially the Gaza Strip. They called upon the international community to bear its full responsibilities and move immediately to halt the massacres and attacks perpetrated by "the Israeli killing machine". They expressed the hope that US President-elect Barack Obama would accord top priority in US foreign policy to the Palestinian problem and the Middle East peace process, in order to fulfil the promises and commitment of the establishment of a viable Palestinian state coexisting in peace and security alongside the state of Israel.

Darren Sagar

AFRICAN ORGANISATIONS AND CONFERENCES

African Union (AU)

DATE OF FOUNDATION: 2001   HEADQUARTERS: Addis Ababa, Ethiopia
OBJECTIVES: To promote the unity, solidarity and co-operation of African states, to defend their
   sovereignty, to promote democratic principles, human rights and sustainable development and
   to accelerate the political and socio-economic integration of the continent
MEMBERSHIP (END-'08): Algeria, Angola, Benin, Botswana, Burkina Faso, Burundi, Cameroon, Cape
   Verde, Central African Republic, Chad, Comoros, Congo, Côte d'Ivoire, Democratic Republic
   of Congo, Djibouti, Egypt, Equatorial Guinea, Eritrea, Ethiopia, Gabon, the Gambia, Ghana,
   Guinea (suspended), Guinea-Bissau, Kenya, Lesotho, Liberia, Libya, Madagascar, Malawi,
   Mali, Mauritania, Mauritius, Mozambique, Namibia, Niger, Nigeria, Rwanda, São Tomé and
   Príncipe, Senegal, Seychelles, Sierra Leone, Somalia, South Africa, Sudan, Swaziland,
   Tanzania, Togo, Tunisia, Uganda, Western Sahara, Zambia, Zimbabwe (total 53)
CHAIRMAN (END-'08): President Jakaya Kikwete (Tanzania); CHAIRMAN OF AU COMMISSION:
   Jean Ping (Gabon)

Southern African Development Community (SADC)

DATE OF FOUNDATION: 1992   HEADQUARTERS: Gaboro, Botswana
OBJECTIVES: To work towards the creation of a regional common market
MEMBERSHIP (END-'08): Angola, Botswana, Democratic Republic of Congo, Lesotho, Madagascar,
   Malawi, Mauritius, Mozambique, Namibia, Seychelles, South Africa, Swaziland, Tanzania,
   Zambia, Zimbabwe (total 15)
EXECUTIVE SECRETARY: Tomaz Augusto Salomão (Mozambique)

AFRICAN UNION (AU).   On 31 January, the first day of the 10th meeting of heads of
state and government of the AU, in Addis Ababa, Ethiopia, Tanzania's President
Jakaya Kikwete succeeded President John Kufuor of Ghana as chairman of the
AU. On the following day, the Gabonese foreign affairs minister, Jean Ping, was
elected as the new chairperson of the AU Commission, and in March he formally
took over from Alpha Omar Konare of Mali.

The 11th AU summit, held in Sharm-el-Sheikh, Egypt, between 24 June and
1 July, which had as its theme "meeting the Millennium Goals", achieved little
of significance. The AU's lack of capacity had been shown by its failure to help
settle the chaos in Kenya, which had followed the disputed election there in late
2007. It was also significant that from the beginning of 2008 the undermanned
AU Mission in Sudan (AMIS) became a joint UN-AU one (UNAMID), whilst
the largest peacekeeping force on the continent remained the UN's in the Democratic Republic of Congo (DRC). By the end of the year over 12,000 military
personnel were deployed in UNAMID and when in July the AU's peace and
security council reaffirmed its commitment to the mission, it combined this with
asking the International Criminal Court (ICC) not to pursue its case against the
Sudanese president (see p. 235). In December the AU decided to maintain its
peacekeeping force in Somalia, where Ethiopian troops had intervened on the
AU's behalf and from which Burundi and Uganda had threatened to pull out
their troops if they were not more adequately supported (see p. 250).

SOUTHERN AFRICAN DEVELOPMENT COMMUNITY (SADC).   The SADC and the AU both
failed to deal effectively with Robert Mugabe, who clung to power in Zimbabwe

despite suffering a defeat in the March election, and who instituted a campaign of violence against the opposition (see pp. 289-92). Throughout the year Thabo Mbeki of South Africa remained the SADC mediator on Zimbabwe, even after he had been recalled as South Africa's president (see pp. 296-98). Though he managed to broker a power-sharing deal in September, the initiative proved hopeless in the face of Mugabe's obduracy and intransigence. Perhaps the most significant development in SADC during the year was that Botswana's new president, Ian Khama, boycotted the August summit because Mugabe had been invited. By then, the authoritarian king of Swaziland, who lacked any credibility as the leader of a modern state, was the new chair of SADC's organ on politics, defence, and security co-operation. Mbeki inaugurated a SADC free trade area at the August summit, but with Angola and the DRC not signing up to it, half of the SADC area was not involved. The EU's economic partnership agreements further divided SADC and threatened the continued existence of the Southern African Customs Union (SACU) (see p. 293).

Mbeki's departure from office gravely weakened the New Partnership for Africa's Development (NEPAD), of which he had been the leading champion. In May he and Senegal's Abdoulaye Wade had announced the integration of NEPAD into the AU, but they also agreed that NEPAD would retain its headquarters in South Africa. After Mbeki's departure, little more was heard of the African Peer Review Mechanism, which had been held up as one of NEPAD's main achievements (see AR 2005, p. 387). The permanent committees of the Pan-African Parliament met in August in Midrand, South Africa, and the Parliament itself convened there for its 10th session in late October, but nothing significant was achieved at either meeting.

South Africa's proud record as a champion of human rights was badly blemished by its actions as a non-permanent member of the UN Security Council, when it refused to condemn human rights abuses in Zimbabwe and elsewhere on the flimsy grounds that there was no threat to international peace and security involved, and therefore the Security Council should not be involved (see p. 388).

In late December, after the military seized power in Guinea following the death of President Lansana Conté, the AU condemned the coup and suspended Guinea's membership of the organisation, but once again with no effect (see p. 266).

While the process of signing AU and other international instruments continued apace during the year, absorbing much energy and cost, they often meant little or nothing in practice, and their implementation often remained unmonitored. If the global economic downturn meant the withdrawal of donor funding, a number of African organisations could disappear. Some would not be much missed.

Christopher Saunders

EURASIAN ORGANISATIONS

Shanghai Co-operation Organisation (SCO)

DATE OF FOUNDATION: 2001   HEADQUARTERS: Beijing, China
OBJECTIVES: To strengthen mutual trust and good-neighbourly relations among member states
MEMBERSHIP (END-'08): China, Kazakhstan, Kyrgyzstan, Russia, Tajikistan, Uzbekistan (total 6)
OBSERVER MEMBERS: Pakistan, India, Iran, Mongolia
SECRETARY GENERAL: Bolat Nurgaliyev (Kazakhstan)

Commonwealth of Independent States (CIS)

DATE OF FOUNDATION: 1991   HEADQUARTERS: Minsk, Belarus
OBJECTIVES: To facilitate economic and humanitarian integration between member states
MEMBERSHIP (END-'08): Russia, Belarus, Kazakhstan, Kyrgyzstan, Azerbaijan, Armenia, Moldova, Tajikistan, Uzbekistan (total 9)
ASSOCIATE MEMBERS: Turkmenistan
EXECUTIVE SECRETARY: Gen. Sergei Lebedev (Russia)

Collective Security Treaty Organisation (CSTO)

DATE OF FOUNDATION: 2002   HEADQUARTERS: Moscow, Russia
OBJECTIVES: To further co-operation and develop joint structures in security, defence and intelligence
MEMBERSHIP (END-'08): Armenia, Belarus, Kazakhstan, Kyrgyzstan, Russia, Tajikistan, Uzbekistan · (total 7)
SECRETARY GENERAL: Gen. Nikolai Bordyuzha (Russia)

Eurasian Economic Community (EAEC/EurAsEC)

DATE OF FOUNDATION: 2000   HEADQUARTERS: Moscow, Russia
OBJECTIVES: To form a customs union and common market in the former Soviet space
MEMBERSHIP (END-'08): Belarus, Kazakhstan, Kyrgyzstan, Russia, Tajikistan (total 5)
OBSERVER MEMBERS: Armenia, Moldova, Ukraine
SECRETARY GENERAL: Tair Mansurov (Kazakhstan)

SHANGHAI CO-OPERATION ORGANISATION (SCO). The eighth summit meeting of the SCO—comprising China, Russia, Kazakhstan, Kyrgyzstan, Tajikistan, and Uzbekistan, with Pakistan, India, Iran, and Mongolia as observers—was held in Dushanbe, Tajikistan, on 28 August. The agenda included discussions on energy, transportation, the fight against terrorism, and drug trafficking. Contrary to expectations that the organisation would be enlarged, no new members were accepted.

The annual meeting of SCO prime ministers took place at the end of October in Astana, Kazakhstan. Following on from the August summit, it addressed issues of social, economic, and humanitarian co-operation among member states. Particular attention was devoted to co-ordinating an approach to the global financial crisis. In late December, the Chinese legislature finally ratified a multilateral pact on joint SCO military exercises (originally signed by defence ministers of member states in June 2007). The document covered issues involved in staging military exercises, including authorising institutions, decision making, consulting mechanisms, compensation of losses, and judicial issues.

COMMONWEALTH OF INDEPENDENT STATES (CIS). The annual summit of CIS leaders was held on 10 October in Bishkek, the capital of Kyrgyzstan, holder of the year's presidency of the organisation. Membership of the CIS at this stage comprised Russia, Belarus, Kazakhstan, Kyrgyzstan, Azerbaijan, Armenia, Moldova, Tajikistan, and Uzbekistan; Ukraine was a participating state but not formally a member, while Turkmenistan held associate status. Georgia had withdrawn from the CIS in August 2008, following the war with Russia over the separatist republic of South Ossetia (see p. 136). High on the Bishkek agenda was the drafting of a common economic development strategy until 2020 (previously raised at the informal meeting of CIS leaders in St Petersburg in June). The impact of the global financial crisis and regional and national responses to it were also discussed. Other issues included measures to improve co-operation in the energy sector, the fight against drug-trafficking, and illegal migration.

COLLECTIVE SECURITY TREATY ORGANISATION (CSTO). The CSTO marked its fifth anniversary since official registration at the UN as a regional international organisation. In March, Uzbekistan's legislature ratified a document formally restoring its membership of the organisation (which had been officially "frozen" since 1999). The CSTO thus comprised Russia, Belarus, Kazakhstan, Kyrgyzstan, Tajikistan, Uzbekistan, and Armenia. Structurally, it had expanded to include a number of specialised units such as the business council, aimed at fostering military-economic co-operation, and the emergency council, created to deal with natural disasters and other emergency situations. Regular meetings of these bodies underpinned inter-state co-ordination.

In September the CSTO announced an ambitious plan to set up an 11,000-strong regional army in Central Asia, to be based on the existing CSTO rapid reaction force. The new force would comprise a total of 10 battalions from Russia, Kazakhstan, Uzbekistan, Tajikistan, and Kyrgyzstan (the majority from Russia). The initiative was primarily a response to the worsening security situation in Afghanistan, but it was not clear precisely how it would be implemented. It was also not clear what the implications would be for co-operation with the NATO-led International Security Assistance Force (ISAF) in Afghanistan. However, it indicated some degree of common purpose within CSTO. Yet the limits of this solidarity were demonstrated by the fact that, although CSTO members backed Russia in its conflict with Georgia, they did not go so far as to follow Russia in recognising the independence of South Ossetia and Abkhazia.

EURASIAN ECONOMIC COMMUNITY (EAEC/EurAsEC). EurAsEC had an eventful year. In January 2008, three years earlier than anticipated, the core states of Belarus, Russia, and Kazakhstan signed a package of agreements that completed the process of forming a customs union. The other members of the organisation—Tajikistan, Kyrgyzstan, and Uzbekistan—confirmed their commitment to joining the customs union in due course.

In November, however, Uzbekistan suddenly announced that it was withdrawing from EurAsEC. The timing was significant, coming shortly after the

EU suspended the sanctions that it had imposed on Uzbekistan in 2005, following the alleged use of "disproportionate force" by the Uzbek authorities in suppressing an insurgency in the city of Andijan in May that year (see p. 309). This had precipitated Uzbekistan's application for membership of EurAsEC in October 2005; it formally acceded to the organisation in January 2006. Thus, in autumn 2008, the lifting of EU sanctions and Uzbekistan's unexpected withdrawal from EurAsEC seemed to be linked, suggesting a shift in Uzbek foreign policy away from Russia and back into the Western orbit. Yet a more probable explanation was the Uzbek government's irritation over EurAsEC's slow progress in implementing agreed resolutions. There was no indication at this stage that Uzbekistan was contemplating withdrawal from the CIS or from the CSTO. There was also no perceptible cooling in bilateral relations with Russia or with other EurAsEC members.

In August, foreign ministers of the 20-member Conference on Interaction and Confidence Building Measures in Asia (CICA) held their third meeting in Almaty, Kazakhstan. The Chinese delegation endorsed the "vigorous development" of CICA and pledged support for its policy of promoting mutual understanding and trust, inter-civilisation dialogue, and harmonious development in the region. Representatives of member states were joined by observers from Indonesia, Japan, the USA, and Vietnam. The UN, the Organisation for Security and Co-operation in Europe (OSCE), and the Arab League also sent representatives to the meeting.

The seventh ministerial Conference on Central Asia Regional Economic Co-operation (CAREC) was held in November in Baku, Azerbaijan. An initiative supported by the Asian Development Bank (ADB), the CAREC programme (comprising Azerbaijan, Kazakhstan, Kyrgyzstan, Mongolia, Tajikistan, Uzbekistan, Afghanistan, and China) financed infrastructure projects and aimed to improve the region's policy environment in the priority areas of transport, energy, trade policy, and trade facilitation.

Shirin Akiner

ASIA-PACIFIC ORGANISATIONS

Association of South-East Asian Nations (ASEAN)

DATE OF FOUNDATION: 1967 HEADQUARTERS: Jakarta, Indonesia
OBJECTIVES: To accelerate economic growth, social progress and cultural development in the region
MEMBERSHIP (END-'08): Brunei, Burma (Myanmar), Cambodia, Indonesia, Laos, Malaysia, Philippines, Singapore, Thailand, Vietnam (total 10)
SECRETARY GENERAL: Surin Pitsuwan (Thailand)

Asia-Pacific Economic Co-operation (APEC)

DATE OF FOUNDATION: 1989 HEADQUARTERS: Singapore
OBJECTIVES: To promote market-oriented economic development and co-operation in the Pacific Rim countries
MEMBERSHIP (END-'08): Australia, Brunei, Canada, Chile, China, Hong Kong, Indonesia, Japan, South Korea, Malaysia, Mexico, New Zealand, Papua New Guinea, Peru, Philippines, Russia, Singapore, Taiwan, Thailand, USA, Vietnam (total 21)
OBSERVER MEMBERS: Association of South East Asian Nations (ASEAN), Pacific Economic Co-operation Council (PECC), South Pacific Forum (SPF)
EXECUTIVE DIRECTOR (END-'08): Juan Carlos Capuñay (Peru)

Pacific Islands Forum (PIF)

DATE OF FOUNDATION: 1971 (as South Pacific Forum) HEADQUARTERS: Suva, Fiji
OBJECTIVES: To enhance the economic and social well-being of the people of the Pacific, in support of the efforts of the members' governments
MEMBERSHIP (END-'08): Australia, Cook Islands, Fiji, Kiribati, Marshall Islands, Federated States of Micronesia, Nauru, New Zealand, Niue, Palau, Papua New Guinea, Samoa, Solomon Islands, Tonga, Tuvalu, Vanuatu (total 16); associate members: New Caledonia, French Polynesia
SECRETARY GENERAL: Tuiloma Neroni Slade (Samoa)

Asian Development Bank (ADB)

DATE OF FOUNDATION: 1966 HEADQUARTERS: Manila, Philippines
OBJECTIVES: To improve the welfare of the people in Asia and the Pacific, particularly the 1.9 billion who live on less than $2 a day
MEMBERSHIP (END-'08): REGIONAL MEMBERS: Afghanistan, Armenia, Australia, Azerbaijan, Bangladesh, Bhutan, Brunei, Burma (Myanmar), Cambodia, China, Cook Islands, East Timor, Fiji, Georgia, Hong Kong, India, Indonesia, Japan, Kazakhstan, Kiribati, Kyrgyzstan, Laos, Malaysia, Maldives, Marshall Islands, Federated States of Micronesia, Mongolia, Nauru, Nepal, New Zealand, Pakistan, Palau, Papua New Guinea, Philippines, Samoa, Singapore, Solomon Islands, South Korea, Sri Lanka, Taiwan, Tajikistan, Thailand, Tonga, Turkmenistan, Tuvalu, Uzbekistan, Vanuatu, Vietnam (total 48); NON REGIONAL MEMBERS: Austria, Belgium, Canada, Denmark, Finland, France, Germany, Italy, Ireland, Luxembourg, the Netherlands, Norway, Portugal, Spain, Sweden, Switzerland, Turkey, UK, USA (total 19)
PRESIDENT: Haruhiko Kuroda (Japan)

South Asian Association for Regional Co-operation (SAARC)

DATE OF FOUNDATION: 1985 HEADQUARTERS: Kathmandu, Nepal
OBJECTIVES: To promote collaboration and mutual assistance in the economic, social, cultural and technical fields
MEMBERSHIP (END-'08): Afghanistan, Bangladesh, Bhutan, India, Maldives, Nepal, Pakistan, Sri Lanka (total 8)
OBSERVER MEMBERS: Australia, Burma (Myanmar), China, EU, Iran, Japan, Mauritius, South Korea, USA (total 9)
SECRETARY GENERAL: Sheel Kant Sharma (India)

ASSOCIATION OF SOUTH-EAST ASIAN NATIONS (ASEAN). On 15 December, following ratification during 2008 by each member of ASEAN, foreign ministers meeting in

Jakarta signed the ASEAN Charter (see AR 2008, p. 434), which then officially came into force. A proposed human rights body, provided for by the charter, remained to be established, with discussion planned for the next ASEAN leaders' summit, scheduled for Thailand in February 2009, having been postponed from December due to political turmoil (which led to the closure of the capital's international airports, see p. 335). In February, it was announced that ASEAN would establish a committee of permanent representatives, with each member country expected to appoint an ambassador to the ASEAN secretariat in Jakarta.

ASEAN sought to assist with humanitarian relief efforts in Burma (Myanmar) for the victims of Cyclone Nargis, which struck the country in May (see p. 336). In Singapore, an emergency meeting of ASEAN foreign ministers agreed to set up an ASEAN-led task force for distributing foreign aid, as Burma agreed to allow medical teams from ASEAN countries into the country. ASEAN's secretary-general, Surin Pitsuwan, issued a statement appealing to all member governments and to the private sector in the ASEAN region to provide emergency aid. On 30 June, however, Pitsuwan complained about Burma's unwillingness to allow ASEAN media representatives into the country to report on the humanitarian effort. In August, the ASEAN inter-parliamentary Myanmar caucus issued a statement of concern over the health of opposition leader Aung San Suu Kyi after reports that she was refusing food.

In July, ASEAN welcomed North Korea's decision to sign the organisation's non-aggression pact, the Treaty of Amity and Co-operation in Southeast Asia. The signing took place after the meeting of the ASEAN Regional Forum (ARF), at which 27 countries met to discuss regional security issues. In August, economic representatives of ASEAN confirmed that they expected to ratify a comprehensive free trade agreement (FTA) with Japan. ASEAN countries also reached a tentative agreement with Australia and New Zealand on an FTA, and similar negotiations were also concluded with India. In October, Taiwan expressed concern about being excluded from an ASEAN free trade area and expressed its wish for greater involvement with the organisation.

ASIA-PACIFIC ECONOMIC CO-OPERATION (APEC). The 20th annual leaders' summit, meeting in Lima, Peru, in November, agreed that the global economic crisis should be addressed through co-operation, arguing against new barriers to trade and investment. The leaders declared their opposition to global protectionism and called for "a new commitment to Asia-Pacific development". The conference communiqué also stressed the need for anti-corruption efforts and greater corporate social responsibility.

PACIFIC ISLANDS FORUM (PIF). The annual summit of the PIF was held on 18-20 August in Niue, a self-governing island in free association with New Zealand. The post-forum dialogue partners' meeting took place on 21 August. Fiji's prime minister boycotted the summit, at which the prime ministers of Australia and New Zealand, together with other Pacific leaders, were intending to press him to hold promised elections and restore democracy (see p. 379).

PIF foreign ministers had met in Auckland, New Zealand, in March to discuss Fiji's "roadmap" to democracy and its preparations for a 2009 election. In August, PIF leaders considered a report from the foreign ministers, who had visited Fiji in July. In a unanimous statement, the PIF asked Fiji's prime minister to explain why he had not kept to "undertakings given" at the 2007 PIF meeting in Tonga for elections in March 2009. The communiqué called on Fiji to maintain "respect for human rights and the rule of law". The communiqué was the first time that the organisation had threatened to suspend a member since its establishment in 1971. A decision about Fiji's suspension from the PIF was to be taken at a special Forum meeting to be held in Papua New Guinea in January 2009.

The PIF also reviewed progress on the region's "Pacific plan", and the final communiqué expressed concerns about increases in food and fuel prices, while issuing a special declaration on climate change. The French Pacific territory of Wallis and Futuna's application to become an associate member—following the conferring of this status upon French Polynesia and New Caledonia in 2006—was to be kept under review for further consideration in 2010. The PIF selected a new secretary general, Tuiloma Neroni Slade, of Samoa, a judge of the International Criminal Court (ICC), following the resignation of the incumbent, Australia's Greg Urwin, for medical reasons.

The PIF took part in several ministerial meetings with external partners, including the first such session intended to enhance "political dialogue" with the EU. Pacific trade ministers also met with the EU in October to discuss negotiations for a new trading relationship. In January, the Italian government announced its intention to convene an Italy-PIF meeting, following Italy's attendance at the 2007 PIF summit in Tonga as a "dialogue partner". The French government likewise announced plans for a third France-Oceania summit, to be held in 2009 in Noumea, New Caledonia, with France's President Nicolas Sarkozy in attendance. In April, PIF foreign ministers met in Istanbul, the Forum's first such meeting with Turkey, an emerging donor country in the Pacific islands region. The first ministerial meeting was held with Cuba in Havana in September, with representatives from 10 Pacific countries focusing on issues affecting small island states, including climate change. Cuba's provision of medical services and scholarships for Pacific island medical students was also emphasised. In October, Taiwan cancelled its summit with six Pacific island nations, scheduled for November, reflecting the new Taiwanese president's desire to improve relations with China. A meeting was still scheduled to take place in the Solomon Islands in 2009.

In May, the Pacific Islands Forum fisheries agency (FFA) came to an agreement on a new Japanese investment programme designed to assist in fisheries conservation and management programmes. New rules for conserving tuna stocks were approved at the fourth Forum fisheries ministerial meeting in Palau.

ASIAN DEVELOPMENT BANK (ADB). In January, the ADB stated that it was redefining its Pacific strategy to consider more emphasis on environmental management. The mid-term review of the ADB's Pacific strategy 2005-09 highlighted key initiatives to support Pacific developing countries and the steps needed to help deal with climate change. The ADB said in April that weak governance was having a negative effect on economic development in the Pacific.

SOUTH ASIAN ASSOCIATION FOR REGIONAL CO-OPERATION (SAARC).   In August SAARC held its 15th summit, meeting in Colombo, Sri Lanka. The organisation reaffirmed its commitment to the SAARC charter, with its emphasis on regional efforts to promote economic growth and cultural development. The summit's declaration, "Partnership for Growth for Our People", identified energy, the environment, water resources, and the alleviation of poverty as key issues, and the summit also "strongly condemned all forms of terrorist violence". Australia and Burma were welcomed to SAARC as new observers.

Stephen Levine

XII THE INTERNATIONAL ECONOMY IN 2008

"Wealth heaped on wealth, nor truth nor safety buys,
The dangers gather as the treasures rise."

Samuel Johnson. *The Vanity of Human Wishes.*

At the end of 2007 many governments in the advanced economies, as well as some international financial institutions, were confident that despite the financial turmoil a deep and synchronised downturn in the world economy would be avoided. A relatively sharp fall in the growth rate of the US economy, to 2 per cent or less, and a more moderate fall in Europe would still leave world output growing at nearly 5 per cent. This was the view, widely shared, of the IMF in October 2007 but it rested on two key assumptions: first, that the financial crisis would be stabilised and that confidence would be restored to the banking system; and second, that the developing or emerging market economies would "decouple" from developments in the advanced economies and continue to grow at an average rate above 6.5 per cent. Both assumptions proved to be false.

The financial turmoil continued throughout 2008 and, far from stabilising, the financial crisis intensified in the last quarter following the collapse of a major investment bank. There were also increasingly severe second-round effects from the deterioration in the real economy (the "negative feed-back loop", in the jargon of the day). The cumulative interaction between an enfeebled financial sector and a steady decline of output and employment in the advanced economies threatened to create a vicious downward spiral resulting in a deep and long recession. By the end of the year, a comparison with the 1930s had become commonplace, if not entirely accurate. The comparison was depressing in that it suggested the seriousness of the problems ahead, but also reassuring in that economists and policy-makers were confident that they knew how to avoid a repetition of anything resembling the pre-War depression. But on several occasions during 2008 key policy-makers faced imminent disaster: the US secretary of the treasury admitted in December that there had been three moments when he feared that the global financial system was in danger of meltdown (in August, mid-September, and late September). In the UK, the financial services secretary to the treasury thought the UK banking system was "very close to a systemic collapse" on 10 October, two days after the government's £50 billion rescue of the banks. At the start of 2009 distinguished commentators, including the 2008 Nobel Laureate in economics, were speaking of the advanced economies teetering on "the edge of an abyss" and threatening to take the rest of the world with them. In more measured language, the director of the Congressional budget office of the USA judged that without a fiscal stimulus the US economy was facing its worst recession "in duration and depth since the Depression of the 1930s".

A notable feature of developments in 2008 was the speed at which activity slowed in the second half of the year and especially in the last quarter, catching governments and businessmen by surprise. This was visible in the various revisions to the macroeconomic forecasts for 2008 and 2009. Taking those made by the IMF—others showed a more or less similar profile—the forecast for world economic growth in 2008 was lowered from 4.8 per cent in October 2007 to 4.1 per cent in January 2008 and 3.9 per cent in October. The outturn for 2008 was provisionally estimated at 3.4 per cent. More striking was the changing outlook for 2009: between April and July 2008 the IMF actually raised its forecast for the world economy (from 3.8 to 3.9 per cent) but then in three months from October it was lowered from 3 per cent to 0.5 per cent. This failure to keep up with events suggested serious shortcomings in the basic forecasting models, but a more general explanation was the imperfect understanding of the links between the financial sector and the real economy. A notable feature of 2008 was the increased attention given by policy-makers and commentators to hitherto obscure corners of the financial system. This was true not just of the more recent innovations, such as collateralised debt obligations and credit default swaps, but also of essential and longstanding parts of the economic "plumbing system" such as monoline and other insurers or letters of credit. Normally macroeconomists had been able to ignore such details, implicitly treating them as background constants, but the global crisis disturbed all parts of the system.

The world economy in 2008 was weakened by three principal factors: the worsening of the problems of the housing market in the USA and also in several European economies; increasing turmoil in the financial system triggered by the collapse of mortgage backed assets and related markets; and a sharp rise in commodity prices, which created a problem for monetary policy.

The first two factors were closely related. The practice of banks and building societies packaging mortgages into bond-like securities with varying degrees of security (collateralised debt obligations) had started nearly 40 years previously, but the demand for them by investors had boomed as a result of deregulation in the 1980s and 1990s. This practice of "securitisation" also expanded to other areas such as student loans, credit card debt, and commercial mortgages. The expansion of these markets was driven by a massive rise in lending by the unregulated sectors of the economy, although much of this consisted of off-balance sheet entities operated by the banks to escape capital and other forms of regulation. Hedge funds and other investors also took advantage of low short-term interest rates by borrowing on a very large scale to invest the funds in higher interest mortgage obligations. Insurance companies moved into the lucrative market by offering protection against default by mortgagees (credit default swaps), and this in turn encouraged yet more demand for mortgage-backed securities (including "subprime" assets) by hedge funds, pension funds, and investment banks. De-regulation enabled institutions such as hedge funds, investment banks, and private equity funds to operate with capital-asset ratios as high as 20-30, and so there arose an enormous volume of debt from a very narrow base.

When mortgage defaults began to rise rapidly at the end of 2007 the value of mortgage-backed securities started to fall and the whole inverted pyramid of debt began to implode (see AR 2008, pp. 437-40). Its accelerating rate of collapse, together with the increasingly energetic efforts of governments and central banks to check it and limit the damage both to the financial system itself and to the real economy, constituted the central narrative of the international economy in 2008. It was also a narrative without a conclusion at the end of the year: the efforts of policy-makers to resolve the financial crisis had made some progress but were hardly decisive and, as a result, the prospects for all regions of the global economy darkened considerably.

The course of events in 2008 was regularly punctuated by the crises of individual financial institutions, followed by moments of calm after intervention by the authorities to rescue them as well as the enactment of various general measures to boost the liquidity of the banks. But such moments of calm tended to be brief as a steady drip of negative macroeconomic data relentlessly pointed towards recession. One problem throughout the year was that due to the major role of the unregulated shadow banking sector in the system, there was little (and then often confused) information as to the scale and location of bad assets and thus how risk was distributed. Investors lacked confidence in the banks and in their disclosures, and for the same reason banks lacked trust in one another. The authorities, therefore, were uncertain as to where the next collapse might occur. For months before their takeover (see below), there had been assurances from their regulators and government officials that there was no problem with the levels of regulatory capital at Fannie Mae and Freddie Mac, the two giant US mortgage finance companies, but US treasury officials later found this was not the case. This increased doubts about the creditworthiness of banks and the cost of insuring against a default of the larger ones continued to rise.

The early months of 2008 were marked by very volatile stock markets and after record falls on "black Monday" (21 January) the Federal Reserve (the US central bank) introduced a surprise cut in its policy interest rate by 75 basis points, the largest reduction in 20 years. At the same time, emerging market equity prices fell across the board, despite a generally positive view of their macroeconomic positions. Falling government bond yields in the USA, Europe, and Japan indicated a general movement of funds into safe havens. In mid-February the UK government nationalised Northern Rock, a major mortgage lender, and some four weeks later the US treasury arranged the takeover of a major investment bank, Bear Stearns (see p. 140). These actions were interpreted to mean that no large bank would be allowed to fail and create a systemic crisis. But other banks were alarmed by the speed at which Bear Stearns' access to liquidity had disappeared and investors were worried that auditors had approved the bank's accounts only a short while before its collapse. Central bank interventions, which included extending the range of collateral that they would accept from the banks, had little impact on inter-bank lending rates and a worrying sign of mistrust was that many money market funds preferred to place their money in safe US treasury bills rather than in the banks.

From late spring through the summer there was rather more focus on the weakening real economy and on rising inflation. The commodity price shock had led to large increases in food and fuel prices throughout the world's economies and this led to central bankers, especially in Europe, worrying about the possibility of a wage-price spiral. The European Central Bank held its policy rate at 4.25 per cent despite eurozone output falling in the second and third quarters and steadily rising unemployment. It was cut to 3.75 per cent as part of the co-ordinated reduction with other central banks in early October and then gradually reduced to 2.5 per cent by the end of the year. In the UK, the Bank of England reduced its policy rate to 5 per cent in early April and maintained it there until early October, when it was lowered to 4.5 per cent. But it then moved rapidly to lower the rate to 2 per cent in December. This slowness in cutting interest rates—both central banks in September were still contemplating higher rates—attracted criticism from some governments in the EU and from a variety of commentators. They argued that the downside risks of the financial crisis for the real economy were being underestimated by the central banks and that fears of a surge in wage demands to compensate for high inflation were exaggerated, given the steady deterioration in output and the labour markets. After oil prices peaked in July, inflation expectations fell rapidly. The credit crunch, however, had weakened the impact of looser monetary policy on the economy—interest rate cuts were not passed on, or not passed on in full—to bank customers: consumers and especially companies suddenly found it harder to obtain or renew credit, which made it more difficult to meet their obligations, thus making the banks even more cautious.

In September and October the whole financial system faced its worst crisis since the 1920s and at several points, as quoted earlier, appeared close to a complete breakdown. On 7 September the US administration took the country's two major housing finance agencies, Fanny Mae and Freddie Mac, into conservatorship, a move which amounted to nationalisation. Between them they held about one-half of the USA's $12,000 billion home loan market and foreign central banks held nearly US$1,000 billion of their debt in mid-July. A collapse would have had disastrous national and international consequences. But the effect of the rescue on confidence was short-lived as it raised fears of more writedowns and losses elsewhere in the financial sector. Equity prices fell, credit spreads widened, and the difficulties for those dependent on the wholesale markets for funds greatly increased. When a large Asian investor withdrew from talks about investing in the investment bank, Lehman Brothers, the general presumption was that the authorities would rescue it. They did not, and Lehman filed for bankruptcy on 15 September (see p. 155).

The decision not to rescue Lehman Brothers was a signal event and a controversial one. At the time, there were many who regarded the US treasury's action as a risky but necessary step to set a limit to the number of bailouts. Some saw that as essential to check the growth of moral hazard in the financial sector. The US treasury argued that it lacked the legal authority to bail out Lehman because of collateral problems, but for many commentators the reasons for the authorities' decision remained unclear.

The immediate consequences were considerable. The price of credit default swaps (CDS), in which Lehman was believed (without hard evidence) to be heavily involved, rose considerably as investors sought protection. The rise in CDSs then led to the giant insurance company, AIG, facing default as it had a large short position in CDSs and had to be rescued by the US treasury with a US$85 billion loan. Lehman was also heavily involved in the commercial paper market. When a major fund, holding large quantities of Lehman paper, was forced to stop redeeming its shares at their face value of $1 (i.e. it "broke the buck", in the local argot) depositors panicked and, again, the treasury had to support the market to avoid a run on money market funds. The turmoil quickly spread. There was panic in equity markets and a general flight from virtually all asset classes to the safety of government bonds. There was a massive loss of trust and confidence in the banks and, as they became even more reluctant to deal with one another, the credit markets were paralysed.

The Lehman bankruptcy was widely regarded as the turning point when the credit crunch was transformed into a major economic crisis. The French finance minister called the bankruptcy "a genuine error" and many others, especially in the financial centres of Wall Street and the City of London, described it as perhaps the biggest blunder in the whole course of the crisis. There was, however, a degree of opportunistic bias and exaggeration in that interpretation by those who had failed to see what was coming. Policy-makers, central banks, and market participants had been slow to react to the deterioration in the real economy. Throughout the summer and into early September concerns were more focused on the risks of inflation rather than recession. The real economy, however, had been steadily weakening throughout the year. In the USA the national bureau of economic research (NBER) dated the start of recession at December 2007 and, on the same definition rather than the conventional two successive quarters of decline, the UK economy entered recession in April. In the eurozone industrial confidence and consumer confidence were falling rapidly from the start of the year and GDP fell in both the second and third quarters. Similarly in the USA, activity and non-farm payrolls were falling sharply, well before the post-Lehman escalation in the financial crisis. The negative feed-back loop was already operating before 15 September.

Another consequence of the Lehman bankruptcy was to create uncertainty as to whether the authorities were now prepared to let financial institutions collapse, however large they might be. But this was quickly dispelled by the US rescue of AIG, the UK nationalisation of another mortgage lender and its intervention to arrange the takeover of HBOS by Lloyds TSB (see p. 37), and the German government's rescue of Hypo Real Estate. After the chaos of September, governments began to move towards a more comprehensive and coherent approach to what was clearly a systemic and, by then, a global crisis. On 18 September the US treasury and Federal Reserve sought Congressional approval for a US$700 billion bailout programme for the banking system and, after initial rejection, a much revised version, the troubled asset relief programme (TARP), was agreed on 3 October. A week later the G-7 countries agreed to take "all necessary steps" to deal with the crisis and this was quickly followed by the UK government's comprehensive £400 billion support programme for the banking sector. In mid-November the G-20 countries promised united action on the global crisis (see Documents).

Nevertheless, ad hoc measures continued to flow, ranging from the USA's $326 billion rescue of Citigroup in late November, to the surprise announcement in December in the UK of a two-year holiday from mortgage interest payments for specific groups in an attempt to check the rise in house repossessions. But the patchwork of measures to boost liquidity in the financial system and encourage a recovery of bank lending had met with little success by the end of the year. Interest rates on the inter-bank lending market had fallen from their earlier peaks, but the availability of credit to the non-financial sector remained very tight and investors were still seeking safety in government bonds rather than banks. In Europe, corporate failures were rising, activity levels falling fast, and forecasts of recession in 2009 were increasingly pessimistic.

Against this background, governments started to prepare plans for fiscal stimuli and to postpone worries about rising levels of government debt until the beginnings of recovery were in sight. The members of the EU agreed to co-ordinate national efforts to produce a stimulus equivalent to 1.5 per cent of GDP, with Germany, which had earlier attacked "crass Keynesianism", preparing one of some 2 per cent (see p. 50). Considerable attention was focused on the USA where President-elect Barack Obama was preparing a large fiscal programme, initially of the order of some US$300 billion but climbing rapidly towards the US$700-800 billion that seemed likely to be presented to Congress in early 2009. As interest rates fell towards zero in the USA and the UK, the monetary authorities were preparing to adopt another Keynesian idea of the 1930s, namely, for the central banks to buy long-dated government bonds in order to drive down long-term interest rates, a policy now blessed with the name of "quantitative easing". There was nevertheless considerable uncertainty as to whether and when these policies would have the desired effects on restoring financial stability and checking the descent into a severe recession. Many observers detected a psychological fatigue among policymakers, financial market operators, and the general public at the end of the year: a condition that led to more and more people looking to the new, charismatic, US president-elect for leadership and inspiration.

At the end of 2007 it was hoped that the global economy, although slowing somewhat, would still perform quite strongly with slower growth in the advanced economies having a relatively minor effect on the rest of the world. The provisional estimates available in early 2009 were that the world economy grew some 3.4 per cent in 2008, with growth of just 1 per cent in the advanced economies and 6.3 per cent in emerging market and developing economies. However, given the unexpectedly rapid deceleration of growth in the last quarter, these estimates were likely to be lowered.

These annual averages were somewhat misleading because of the rapid deterioration of the global economy in the second half of 2008. Western Europe's GDP growth averaged just over 1 per cent but by the end of the year most of the region was in recession with much larger than expected falls in activity in the last quarter. Japan had also moved into recession in the second and third quarters. For most of the emerging and developing economies, GDP slowed but was still relatively robust: regional growth rates ranged between 4.3 per cent (Latin America) and 7 per cent (the CIS and Asia), but, as elsewhere, the deterioration was very rapid in the last quarter and most of the impact on developing countries of slower growth in the advanced economies would be felt in 2009.

The crisis originating in the advanced economies spread to the developing world as a result of falling demand for the latter's exports and through a fall in the availability of current account financing. Western banks and other investors were already withdrawing funds from developing countries in early 2008, not necessarily because the latter's economic fundamentals were unsound but to offset losses incurred elsewhere, rebalance portfolios, and move funds into the safety of US treasury bills. Such behaviour was not new—it had occurred in all of the previous crises of the last 20 years or so—but it underlined the risk of heavy reliance on foreign capital. As a result, many countries in central Europe, the CIS, Africa, and Latin America were judged to be facing potential shortages of foreign finance in 2009, thus increasing the balance of payments constraint on growth.

The latest (January 2009) forecasts, at the time of writing, were for a severe recession, with global expansion down to 0.5 per cent, output falling by some 2 per cent in the advanced economies and growth of just over 3 per cent in emerging market and developing economies. The uncertainty surrounding this outlook was still unusually large. It was clear however that 2008 had ended with the advanced economies facing their worst recession since World War II and, as a consequence, the emerging and developing countries would be dragged into a serious and painful slowdown.

The GROWTH OF WORLD TRADE decelerated sharply in the wake of slowing global output growth: from an 8.8 per cent volume growth in 2006 to 6.25 per cent in 2007. UN and World Trade Organisation (WTO) estimates pointed to an increase of some 4.5 per cent in 2008. Given the unexpectedly rapid fall in output growth in the last quarter and the general credit squeeze apparently reducing access to letters of credit, the final estimate could well be less. The dollar value of world trade, however, rose by some 19 per cent, largely reflecting the commodity price boom in the early part of the year.

Among the principal factors behind the slowdown in world trade was a fall of nearly 5 per cent in the import demand of the USA, driven by falling personal incomes and the cumulative depreciation of the dollar in recent years. Exports of developed Asia and Oceania also fell, but as most of the slowdown occurred in the second half of the year the full impact would appear in 2009, when it was estimated that the volume of world trade could fall for the first time since 1982.

The global CURRENT ACCOUNT IMBALANCES, which had played a central role in global economic developments in the previous decade and had been seen as an important underlying factor in the emergence of the current financial crisis, narrowed slightly in 2008 and were expected to continue to do so in 2009. The US current account deficit fell a little in 2008, to some US$690 billion from somewhat over US$700 billion in 2007. Most developing country regions remained in surplus—the oil exporters at US$813 billion, China at US$399 billion (according to IMF estimates)—but Germany (US$279 billion) and Japan (US$194 billion) also had huge surpluses. Fears for a disorderly adjustment of the imbalances increased in 2008 because of the considerable volatility of the US dollar. In the first half of 2008 the dollar fell against the euro and other currencies when there was still a perception that the financial crisis might be contained in the USA and that growth in the rest of the world would not be greatly affected. When this perception proved mistaken, the dollar appreciated markedly against most currencies (but not the yen), especially after the financial turmoil in September and October. The fear was that at some point, perhaps when the financial crisis had stabilised, doubts would re-appear about the sustainability of US debt levels and precipitate a rapid fall in the dollar and a disorderly adjustment of the imbalances.

The rising trend in INTERNATIONAL COMMODITY PRICES over the previous five years accelerated in the first half of 2008. Non-fuel products rose nearly 50 per cent (in dollars) between the last quarter of 2007 and the second of 2008, while the average price of the OPEC basket of 13 grades of crude increased by just under 40 per cent. Non-fuel prices peaked in June and then fell rapidly. The price of crude oil peaked at just over US$147 per barrel in July and had fallen to around US$40 by the end of the year. Food prices were down by nearly 30 per cent. The rapidity of the slump in prices caught most commentators and traders by surprise: in the financial markets in early July, call options (the right to buy at a given price at a given future date) were betting on the price of oil reaching US$200 plus by the end of the year. While it took some four years to climb from US$35 to US$147, the oil price was back to its 2004 level in less than five months.

The reasons for the rise in commodity prices included a mixture of short- and long-term factors. Among the longer-run influences were rising consumption in the emerging market economies and what the World Bank described as "complacency" about agricultural investment over the previous two decades. Poor harvests in Europe and Australia affected the supply of grains; producers of many commodities tried to offset the falling dollar exchange rate by raising dollar prices; and the increase in the price of oil raised production and transport costs for agricultural producers. More controversial was the influence of speculators. Speculation in physical markets appeared to have raised prices as commodities were bought and stored, anticipating further price increases. But the effect of speculation in futures markets (i.e. where no physical trade occurred) on price trends was controversial: some ministers in advanced economies blamed speculators for adding to the rise in the oil price, but regulators in the USA found no evidence of a systematic effect. There was more agreement on the influence of biofuel production on food prices. The World Bank, the IMF, and the UN's Food and Agriculture Organisation (FAO) all concluded that the diversion of agricultural acreage to biofuels was partly to blame for higher prices.

In October 2007 the director general of the FAO had warned that a continued rise in food prices could trigger riots and, indeed, there were at least 35 such disturbances recorded in the first half of 2008. The FAO warned that riots and instability could be frequent in coming years, a probability underlined by the deterioration of labour markets (see below). Although food prices fell after July they still remained higher than in 2005.

The strong growth of the global economy in recent years led to significant improvements in LABOUR MARKETS between 2004 and 2007, but the gathering recession in 2008 ended this favourable trend. The global unemployment rate was estimated by the International Labour Organisation (ILO) to have edged up from 5.7 per cent in 2007 to 6.0 per cent in 2008, a rise of nearly 11 million people and the largest increase since 1998. That left a total of some 190 million people without work. A worrisome aspect was that the unemployment rate for young people was nearly three times that for adults, the global number of unemployed youth reaching 76 million. Average unemployment rates in 2008 rose in virtually all regions, with the largest increase in the advanced economies, and ranged from 3.8 per cent in East Asia to 10.3 per cent in North Africa (according to preliminary ILO estimates). Employment, however, was not necessarily an escape from poverty. Just over one-fifth of the employed were living on US$1.25 a day (the new threshold for extreme poverty, as set by the World Bank in August 2008) and two-fifths on US$2 a day. Another category of the working population was "vulnerable employment", those without social protection and safety nets, and often without adequate personal savings to provide a cushion against unemployment or falling demand. This large army of poor and vulnerable workers, nearly all in developing countries, was severely affected by the large rise in food and energy prices in the first half of 2008 and there were numerous outbreaks of social unrest. The outlook for 2009 was that their situation would worsen following job losses in the export sectors.

The global financial crisis was widely seen outside the advanced economies, but also increasingly within them, as a major failure of globalisation and, in particular, of the principle of unfettered freedom for capital movements. The promises of the brave "new" world of finance, that it would allocate resources and manage risk more efficiently than the old, more regulated, system had proved false. Far from spreading and reducing risk, and making the global financial system more robust and resistant to shocks, risk was hidden and thus the innovations increased systemic vulnerability. Moreover, the system of bonuses and other rewards within the financial sector, as the governor of the Bank of England argued, distorted the incentive structures within the industry and led to reckless and irresponsible risk-taking. That was a key point. As Nobel Laureate Douglas North stressed, efficient markets depended on appropriate incentives, and these in turn were embedded in the framework of institutions and rules in which the markets operated. If the structure of incentives led to perverse outcomes, there was a clear case of market failure.

In a year that saw the governments of the USA and the UK—the two countries most attached to neo-liberalism—take large equity stakes in banks or nationalise important parts of the financial system, there were many cries predicting "the end of capitalism". That seemed unlikely. The neo-liberal ascendancy of the last three decades had been found to be seriously wanting, but the reaction would not be the end of the market economy. Rather, fundamental changes in the regulation of the financial sector were to be expected. An indication of this was President-elect Obama's appointment of the former Federal Reserve chairman, Paul A. Volcker, to head an independent economic advisory board which, inter alia, was to recommend specific reforms in this direction. Volcker, unlike his successor at the Federal Reserve, Alan Greenspan, was known for his views that financial markets had to be regulated. Professor John Kay described the modern financial services industry as "a casino attached to a utility", so a key task of reform was to separate the two and ensure that the gambling element, to paraphrase John Maynard Keynes, was no more than a bubble on the real economy rather than the reverse. Correcting systemic failure in the advanced economies, however, was only one part of an emerging agenda. Another reflected the growing impatience of many developing economies at the instabilities of the international financial system and especially the disruptions caused by the unfettered movements of foreign finance capital. The developing countries were expected to push harder to reduce what they regarded as the excessive influence of the G-7 countries in controlling and shaping the agenda of international institutions such as the WTO and the IMF.

The financial crisis of 2007-08 was also seen by many as raising fundamental issues, which went beyond the technicalities of how better to regulate the financial sector. The crisis had brought out important political and moral questions about a particular variety of capitalism that had not only tolerated irresponsible and incompetent behaviour on a huge scale, but which had also generated enormous disparities of income and wealth, which failed to find a justification in any Rawlsian-type principle of being for the general good of society.

During 2008 a number of religious leaders, including bishops in the UK and Germany, criticised the behaviour of certain banks and criticised government policies for short-sightedness. They were roundly attacked in turn for their weak grasp of the immediate macro-economic problem, but their fundamental points—concerning the morality of personal conduct and the subordination of so many political and social preferences to the priorities of high finance—were concerns that were shared by large proportions of the population in the advanced economies. Not only did their arguments reflect the Judaeo-Christian tradition—that the accumulation of wealth was acceptable if honestly acquired and used for the benefit of all—but they were also echoed in Adam Smith's *Theory of Moral Sentiments* and in Keynes's notion of a civilised society. The latter's distinguished biographer, Robert Skidelsky, who also argued that the present crisis raised moral issues, wrote that Keynes thought, "the pace of change should be adapted not to the requirements of what he called the 'economic juggernaut' but to what human beings found reasonably comfortable, what they could cope with. He believed that the economic environment should be challenging, even stimulating, but not destructive of most of what made life worth living." The incoming US president, in his speeches on the economy, appeared to have taken more from Keynes than simply his justification for a fiscal stimulus.

Paul Rayment

XIII THE SCIENCES

SCIENTIFIC, INDUSTRIAL AND MEDICAL RESEARCH

MANY within the scientific community were as excited as people in the rest of the world about the election on 4 November of Barack Obama as president of the USA. He was a figure who seemed to give a high priority to scientific research. In a radio address on 22 December he promised to "put science at the top of our agenda", pointing out that "science holds the key to our survival as a planet and our security and prosperity as a nation." Key appointments to his administration included John Holdren of Harvard University as science advisor, and Steven Chu, a Nobel Laureate from the University of California, Berkeley, as energy secretary. Announcing his team, Obama said: "My administration will value science. We will make decisions based on the facts, and we understand that the facts demand bold action."

MEDICAL AND BIOLOGICAL SCIENCES. The world's first "test-tube baby" celebrated her 13th birthday on 25 July. In-vitro fertilisation (IVF) currently accounted for 1.5 per cent of all births but in the UK only 30 per cent of IVF cycles resulted in a successful pregnancy. As two-thirds of IVF embryos had the wrong number of chromosomes, more sophisticated tests of recognition were needed. Pre-implantation genetic screening (PGS) was available, but carried risks to the tested embryo. More advanced PGS tests used at a later stage of embryonic development, currently being trialled at Oxford University and at the Colorado Centre for Reproductive Medicine, were producing more promising results. Non-invasive metabolic profiling examined the quality of the embryos from the culture medium in which they grew. Researchers at the University of Manchester identified three or four amino acids, taken up from the womb by the embryo, which were good quality indicators. At Yale University the technique of infra-red spectroscopy, which examined the light scattered by the culture medium, had been shown to be able to predict which embryos were more likely to implant.

In the UK, the updated Human Fertilization and Embryology Act included the controversial substitution "of the need of the child [conceived by IVF] for a father" for the term "for supportive parenting" to make the Act more acceptable to the 0.5 per cent lesbian and the 1.4 per cent single women IVF users. The same Act legalised the use of cybrid embryos (see AR 2007, p. 448) and opened up the use of genetically modified embryos for research.

The first commercially cloned puppies, derived from the frozen remains of an ear of a much lamented pit-bull terrier, not only delighted their mourning Californian owner but also brought back into the limelight scientists from the Seoul National University, who collaborated with a Californian company to produce the puppies. The company was a rival to one, which currently employed the formerly disgraced Hwang Woo Suk (see AR 2005, pp. 315-16, 405; AR 2007, p. 448).

The creation of induced pluripotent stem cells (IPS cells) by teams led by Professor Shinya Yamanaka of the University of Kyoto and Jamie Thomson of Wisconsin University (see AR 2007, p. 448) was named as the breakthrough of the year by the journal *Science*. The technique, which involved inducing adult skin cells to revert to pluripotent embryonic stem cells capable of being converted into different cellular types, had the benefit of retaining the individual's DNA, thereby eliminating the risk of immune rejection if transplanted.   Further progress was made by investigators at the California Scripps Research Institute and the German Max Planck Institute for Molecular Biomedicine into reducing the risks of using viruses or potentially cancer-causing genes in the genetic reprogramming process.   The IPS technique had been applied by researchers at the University of Wisconsin-Madison to turn back the clock in observing the progress of the childhood disease, spinal muscular atrophy. By taking skin from an affected child the researchers created stem cells and nerve cells that showed characteristics of the disease. They hoped that by understanding the basis of the disease, potential new therapies could be developed.

Regenerative surgery showed its potential with the successful transplantation of a bioengineered human airway into a 30-year old Colombian woman with a collapsed left main bronchus, caused by tuberculosis. The new graft was developed by a European team of scientists from Bristol, Padua, and Milan and was transplanted in Barcelona. The technique used a 7cm segment of donor trachea, which was stripped of all its potentially antigenic cells. The bare cartilage scaffold was reseeded, over a period of four days in a newly developed bioreactor, with living cells, grown from the lining of the patient's own right bronchus, and chondrocytes (cartilage cells) taken from a piece of her nasal cartilage. Because the new airway was developed using the patient's own stem cells she did not require immunosuppressant drugs. Following the operation the graft was reported to be functioning normally and there were no signs of rejection.

The Nobel Prize in Physiology or Medicine was awarded with one half to Harald zur Hausen of Germany, for his discovery of the role of human papilloma viruses (HPV) in causing cervical cancer, and the other half jointly to Françoise Barré-Sinoussi and Luc Montagnier, both of France, for their discovery of human immunodeficiency virus (HIV) (see Documents). Zur Hausen's discovery of the tumour-causing HPV types HPV16 and HPV18 enabled development of effective vaccines against these two forms of HPV, which offered protection to women against developing cervical cancer. Whilst HIV had thus far eluded the production of a vaccine, treatment with combinations of antiviral drugs had increased the lifespan and quality of life in people with the infection.

In July a man who, prior to gender-reassignment treatment, had previously been a woman, gave birth to a healthy baby girl. This was made possible by his decision to retain his female reproductive organs at the time he underwent male hormone treatment and mastectomies. His wife had previously had a hysterectomy. They together inseminated him with donor sperm after he had stopped his bimonthly testosterone injections. Although legally male, this "mother/father" raised many ethical issues.

Noise induced hearing loss, resulting in the presently irreversible loss of hair cells from the inner ear, had been highlighted in both civilian and military situations. A report from the EU's scientific committee on emerging and newly identified health risks emphasised the danger of listening to music, generated by personal media players and played through "in-the-ear" phones, at sound levels of greater than 89 decibels (dB). Under current regulations personal media players were allowed to reach 100dB but with "in-the-ear" phones the sound level at the eardrum could reach 120dB. The scientific committee concluded that, in order to prevent premature deafness in young people, a maximum limit of 80dB should be programmed into the personal media players. An increasing number of front-line British troops were suffering from hearing disability after combat in Iraq and Afghanistan. The resulting prospects of reduced availability of soldiers for deployment and compensation payment due to them was expected to encourage the ministry of defence to invest in more sophisticated hearing protection, which not only maintained but also enhanced normal hearing and at the same time excluded noise above 90dB.

The quest for ways of treating the ever increasing number of older people suffering from Alzheimer's disease continued. Researchers at the University of Manchester identified the DNA of the cold sore virus, herpes simplex (HSVI), in the formation of beta amyloid plaques in the brain cells of Alzheimer's patients. These plaques, or "tangles", first destroyed nerve cells linked to memory. Whilst recognising that much more research was needed to determine whether HSVI contributed to plaque formation whilst in a latent or active phase, there existed the attraction of potential treatment with known, cheap antiviral agents such as acyclovir (Zovirax). A research team at the University of Aberdeen demonstrated that a drug, Rember, directly attacked the "tangles" and slowed progression of the disease in up to 81 per cent of their study group.

Researchers at the Children's Hospital, Boston, USA, bred a transparent zebra fish, which allowed them to observe the migration of cancer cells; as an example, melanoma cells moved from the fish's abdominal cavity to the skin. Zebra fish were chosen for their strong genetic similarities to human beings.

Cancer therapy was moving into a new era of sophistication, whereby a joint project between the British Sanger Institute, Cambridge, and the Massachusetts General Hospital, Boston, aimed to produce a range of genetically distinct tumours and treatments. On the basis of DNA tests, they hoped to be able to predict which drug would be most likely to work. This concept acknowledged that tumours had different genetic characteristics and, despite being in the same part of the body, needed to be treated as separate diseases. Over 200 different types of cancer were already known. Many types could be further divided, driven by particular patterns of abnormal DNA, which would determine whether certain drugs would or would not work. This research, funded by the Wellcome Trust, promised to open up a more tailored drug/tumour-specific approach to cancer care and to revisit a range of drugs, which had hitherto not been suitable for specifically identified tumour subgroups.

A meeting of leading economists attending the four yearly Copenhagen Consensus Initiative placed the provision of micronutrient supplements (vitamin A and zinc) for children in developing countries as the single most cost-effective way of making the world a better place in which to live. Of 30 measures proposed, the top 10 were aimed at improvements in nutrition and education, whereas research into "global warming" and lowering carbon dioxide levels ranked 29th and 30th, respectively.

ARCHAEOLOGY AND PALAEONTOLOGY.   The fossilised remains of a feathered dinosaur, found in China in October, was believed to be indicative of the first stage in the evolution between early reptiles and modern birds. The creature, named *Epidexipteryx hui*, was flightless, but had long tail feathers, similar to a peacock, which were thought to have been used for display. Palaeontologists believed that it lived between 146 and 176 million years ago. Two new species of dinosaur—a giant flying pterosaur, and a plant-eating sauropod—were discovered in Morocco in December. The pterosaur, thought to have lived 100 million years ago, was unusual because the bones of such dinosaurs were light and fragile and therefore rarely found undamaged. Another rare find was a fossilised spider's web, 140 million years old, which was discovered in a piece of amber in England, showing that orb web-spinning spiders had lived many years earlier than previously thought.

The fossilised skull of a huge rat was unearthed in Uruguay in January. The rodent, which was 3 metres long and weighed an estimated 1.2 tonnes, was so huge that it was thought that it must have lived most of the time in water, supporting its vast weight in much the same way as did a modern hippopotamus. Living 4 million years ago, the rat had incisors 30cms long but appeared to have been herbivorous. Palaeontologists believed that the creatures might have used these teeth to fell trees in a similar way to modern beavers.

The ruins of an ancient city discovered in Peru in December were thought to be the capital city of the Moche, a civilisation important from AD 100 to AD 800.

SPACE AND ASTRONOMY.   Human understanding of Mars increased immensely during the year. In June, NASA's *Phoenix* lander dug up chunks of ice from below the planet's surface. In November huge glaciers—13 miles long, 60 miles wide, and up to half a mile thick—were found by NASA's *Reconnaissance* orbiter. The spacecraft also sent back photographs of the Martian surface, which clearly showed rings of rock graded by size. The most likely explanation for this was repeated freezing and thawing of ice at some stage in the planet's history. In August analytical equipment on *Phoenix* detected the presence of perchlorate (chorine and oxygen atoms combined) in Martian soil. This caused great excitement because it represented a possible source of oxygen, but tests suggested that it was present in concentrations high enough to be toxic.

There had long been speculation about the composition of apparent "lakes" on Titan, one of the moons of Saturn. In July it was confirmed that these were liquid, and spectrographic analysis of a lake near the south pole by *Cassini*, the spacecraft visiting Saturn, found that they contained liquid ethane at a temperature of minus 180 degrees Celsius.

The year saw NASA's *Messenger* spacecraft complete 60 per cent of its voyage to survey Mercury. Having travelled 3 billion miles since its launch in 2004, the vessel had sent back pictures of 80 per cent of the planet's surface, showing it to be covered in volcanic craters. This was a major finding because it had been thought that Mercury's landscape, unlike that of Earth, had not been formed by volcanic action.

India joined the small group of countries—the USA, Russia, Japan, and China—which had successfully sent spacecraft to the Moon. An unmanned mission, launched on 22 October from Sriharikota island, near Madras, orbited the Moon and sent a small probe onto the lunar surface. In September, China completed its first space walk when an astronaut left his capsule, which was orbiting Earth, and made a 15-minute walk in space.

For the first time, methane was found on a planet outside Earth's solar system. In May researchers used the Hubble space telescope to analyse spectra from a large planet 63 light years away. The atmosphere of the planet was 900 degrees Celsius, believed to be far too hot to support life.

Images of a collision between two galaxy clusters 100 million years ago provided new evidence for the existence of dark matter, the material that was believed to account for most of the universe. Photographed in August by the Hubble space telescope, the collision appeared to separate light and dark matter in a way that had not been seen before.

An electronic failure put the Hubble telescope out of action in September and it was not expected to be operating again until May 2009.

CHEMISTRY. Work on biofuels continued during the year. Catalytic production of methanol had been widely researched as a route to cheap fuel, but currently available processes required costly high temperatures and pressures. In December, Oxford University announced that researchers had produced methanol efficiently from glycerol for the first time under mild conditions, using a precious metal catalyst. Glycerol was cheap and widespread as a by-product of biodiesel manufacture, and much of it was currently incinerated as a waste product. Also in December, researchers at Montana State University announced that they had cultivated a fungus that could be used to convert cellulose directly into diesel fuel.

The deliberate adulteration of food products continued in China during the year. At least six children were killed and an estimated 300,000 made ill with kidney stones and other problems as a result of melamine added to powdered milk (see pp. 349-50). The melamine was added because it tested positive for nitrogen, which was used as a measure of protein levels in milk, thereby allowing unscrupulous manufacturers to dilute the milk without detection. Chocolate products were also found to contain melamine, leading to the withdrawal of a number of products.

Chemists were excited by the development of drug delivery systems based on nanofibre mesh, which allowed delivery of the active ingredient only in the presence of specific enzymes. This opened up the possibility of very specific targeting, for example drugs released only at the site of inflamed tissue or only into tumours.

The idea of an invisibility cloak had always excited the public imagination, and science came a step closer on 11 August when researchers at the University of California in Berkeley announced that they had developed nanoparticles, which could potentially bend light in three dimensions so that it curved around an object and continued unaltered on the other side. Two possible materials were tiny silver wires embedded in aluminium oxide and a fishnet pattern of strips of silver and magnesium fluoride.

The Nobel Prize in Chemistry was awarded, in equal shares, to Osamu Shimomura of the Marine Biological Laboratory, Boston, USA; Martin Chalfie of Columbia University, New York; and Roger Y. Tsien of the University of California, for isolating green fluorescent protein (GFP) from the jellyfish Aequorea Victoria in 1962 (see Documents). Using GFP, which glowed bright green under ultraviolet light, these researchers had developed ways to watch processes that were previously invisible, such as the development of nerve cells in the brain or the spread of cancer cells. Tsien extended the colour palette beyond green, thereby allowing researchers to tag various proteins and cells with different colours.

PHYSICS. The most eagerly awaited science news of the year was in the field of particle physics and involved the Large Hadron Collider (LHC) at CERN (the European Organisation for Nuclear Research) in Geneva. Having been delayed in 2007 (see AR 2008, p. 451), the LHC was finally activated on 10 September to a fanfare of excitement amongst scientists and most of the public. It did cause panic for a few, however, with some scientists receiving death threats amid rumours that a particle accelerator of this size could create a black hole. Worries proved unfounded, but following delay after delay in starting up, the operation of the Collider was short-lived. Failure of one of the magnets caused a leakage of helium, and it was switched off on 19 September. Work was then begun on installing a leakage early-warning system and it was not expected that the LHC would become operational again until July 2009. Scientists had been waiting for 20 years for results from the Collider and there was intense frustration that crucial experiments searching for the postulated Higg's boson, amongst other particles, could not be done for yet another year.

US researchers announced in December the development of a nanocoating of silicon dioxide and titanium dioxide, which stopped sunlight from being reflected. Used as a coating on solar cells, this increased the amount of light absorbed from 67 to 92 per cent, a major advance in efficiency.

The Casimir force was observed for the first time in January 2008 by researchers at the University of Stuttgart. Identified in 1948, but never before seen, this force was composed of photons created in a vacuum when particles and antiparticles annihilated each other.

The Nobel Prize in Physics was awarded with one half to Yoichiro Nambu of the University of Chicago, USA, "for the discovery of the mechanism of spontaneous broken symmetry in sub-atomic physics"; and the other half, jointly, to

Makoto Kobayashi of KEK Laboratory, Tsukuba, Japan, and Toshihide Maskawa of the University of Kyoto, Japan, "for the discovery of the origin of the broken symmetry which predicts the existence of at least three families of quarks in nature" (see Documents). Quarks were the elementary sub-units of protons and neutrons, which together made up the nuclei of atoms. The work was highly relevant in relation to the forthcoming experiments on the LHC.

Neil Weir (Medicine, Biology) and Lorelly Wilson (Archaeology, Space, Chemistry, Physics).

INFORMATION TECHNOLOGY

THE successful campaign of Barack Obama in the US presidential election of 2008 was the first to exploit fully the powers of the Internet and associated "new media". Although use of the Internet as a campaign organising tool had been pioneered in the 2004 presidential election by politicians such as Howard Dean, the Obama campaign was the first to be based almost entirely on its skilful harnessing of Internet technologies. The evolution of the Internet towards more interactive platforms—Web 2.0 (see AR 2005, pp. 410-11)—changed the tools available for political campaigns, and Obama's team took full advantage of this. Even before the official start of the primary and caucus voting in January 2008, the Obama campaign used social networking and Internet video broadcasting services to create and organise a formidable grassroots network that was able to maintain its candidate's momentum over the long-drawn-out primary, and then presidential, campaigns (see pp. 144-57). The impressive fundraising was a vital aspect of this: eschewing public campaign funds, the Obama team had raised over US$650 million for its candidate by the time of the general election, mainly from small donations via the Internet. Commenting after election night, Arianna Huffington, editor of the Internet newspaper, *The Huffington Post*, said: "Were it not for the Internet, Barack Obama would not be president. Were it not for the Internet, Barack Obama would not have been the nominee."

The issue over whether Internet service providers (ISPs) could lawfully prioritise certain types of network traffic or content providers over others—dubbed "net neutrality" (see AR 2007, pp. 447-48)—was given further clarity in February when the US federal communications commission (FCC) held that the ISP Comcast was wrong in deliberately throttling traffic from the BitTorrent peer-to-peer networking service. Although Comcast claimed to be attempting to improve Internet access for the majority of its customers, the FCC judged that maintaining the Internet's unfettered nature was of more importance. Despite the ruling, the FCC stopped short of indicating whether or not it supported introducing specific legislation to guarantee the Internet's neutrality, claiming that it already possessed the necessary legal tools to prevent undesirable traffic tampering by ISPs.

Cloud computing, where computer resources were remotely hosted by third parties and provided as a service over the Internet, matured from a concept into a recognisable industry in 2008. Microsoft, VMware, and Citrix all joined cloud computer pioneer, Amazon, in launching commercial cloud computer services. Cited as a key element in the future of computer infrastructure, cloud computing resources could dynamically shrink, or grow, on demand, achieving much higher levels of computer efficiency than with traditional infrastructure, where computers would be left running, but unused, during off-peak periods. With the cloud being maintained by the service provider and customers only paying for the computing resources they used, cloud computing proved particularly popular with small, technology businesses who found the low initial costs and the freedom from having to maintain an in-house computer support resource appealing. Many fast growing technology companies, particularly those developing Web 2.0 applications, declared they were building their products and services on top of cloud computing components.

Despite the potential advantages of cloud computing, those users relying on computer services, which were fundamentally outside their control, were given pause for thought when the Amazon "S3" cloud computing resource suffered several shut-downs during 2008, leaving services dependant upon it unable to function. Privacy concerns were also expressed, as user data would frequently be stored within the cloud. Canada, for example, expressly banned its public information technology projects from using US cloud computing resources, due to data protection concerns.

While social networking continued to grow in popularity, it was the "microblogging" site, Twitter, which attracted the most attention in 2008. The Twitter service, where users posted and read short messages (known as "tweets") concerning their current thoughts and activities, proved a hit due to its ease of use, non-invasive presence, and the fact that it was supported by a wide range of devices and media, through which users could send and read messages. High profile incidents illustrating the popularity of Twitter in 2008 included its role in the presidential election campaign of Barack Obama (see above), and its rapid dissemination of eye witness accounts of the terrorist attacks in Bombay (Mumbai).

Music distributors appeared to have realised, grudgingly, that their insistence on incorporating digital rights management (DRM) technology into digital music formats had done them more harm than good. This was evident in their capitulation to online music retailers, who were seeking to offer DRM-free downloads. Although DRM was designed to prevent piracy by tethering a particular piece of purchased music to certain digital music players, the outcome of the scheme had, in effect, been to hand a monopoly to Apple's iPod digital music player (Apple had some 70 per cent market share in digital music devices). Apple subsequently used this position to the music distributors' disadvantage, by insisting on selling music at lower prices. Apple began selling DRM-free music in May; meanwhile, eMusic established itself as the second largest online music retailer with its DRM-free service. By the end of the year, the four largest music distributors (Sony BMG, Universal Music Group, Warner

Music Group, and EMI) had all announced that they would sell their music free of DRM technology.

As an alternative to DRM, music distributors began experimenting with digital tracing techniques known as "watermarking". This placed hidden signatures within a digital file, enabling it to be identified (and potentially removed) were it to appear on servers and networks known to be used by music pirates.

The move from analogue to digital technologies resulted in parts of the wireless spectrum being recycled and reused, as analogue services were decommissioned. The largest instance of this in 2008 was the auction of sections within the 700MHz band of the US wireless spectrum (the auction raising US$19.6 billion). At the time of the auction, the range was in use to support analogue television broadcasts, a service due to be stopped in February 2009. The US federal communications commission (FCC) was also persuaded, principally by Internet search company, Google, to require open access to a particular section of the 700MHz spectrum, known as the "C block". The open access requirement would allow users to connect to the network with any handset or application, even those not approved by service providers. The FCC agreed to add the open access requirement to the C block licence, provided the licence reached its reserve price of US$4.6 billion. The reserve price was subsequently met, with wireless telecommunications company, Verizon, emerging with the winning bid. Although Verizon objected to the open access requirement attached to the licence, when its legal challenges failed, it agreed to honour the requirement and ensure that access to C block would be free to any handset or application. Google had argued that open network access would stimulate the provision of innovative new wireless services and handsets, while Verizon would have preferred to retain control over which devices could access its network, claiming that allowing anyone to connect could create interference or network problems.

In addition to those sections of the wireless spectrum abandoned by analogue services, a consortium of companies (including Microsoft, Google, HP, and Intel) lobbied the FCC for the small spaces between the currently allocated bandwidth slots of the wireless spectrum to be utilised in order to provide an open access wireless network. These small wireless channels, dubbed "whitespace", could be used to provide high speed wireless Internet access services, the consortium argued, although a group of wireless broadcasters opposed the proposition, citing fears of interference with existing services.

The deadlock in the race to become the de-facto standard in high definition video formats was broken early in the year when two of the major supporters of the HD-DVD format, Toshiba and Microsoft, announced that they would halt production of their HD-DVD players. Following this, Warner Brothers announced that it would stop distributing films on the HD-DVD format and focus exclusively on its only rival: Sony's Blu-ray. Other film distributors soon followed, abandoning HD-DVD and leaving Blu-ray looking like the victor; but with increasing interest in services whereby films were delivered straight to viewers' homes via the Internet, many suspected that Sony's victory would turn out to be a hollow one, as physical media of all kinds became obsolete.

In what was deemed an attempt to counter the increasing dominance of Google in many areas of the Internet, particularly Internet search in which Google was the clear leader, Microsoft on 1 February tabled a US$44 billion offer for Internet service provider, Yahoo!, the world's second most popular Internet search engine. The initial offer was quickly rejected by the Yahoo! board of directors, with incompatible corporate cultures being cited as much as financial reasons. This precipitated a struggle which lasted throughout the year. In an attempt to protect itself from Microsoft's increasingly predatory advances, Yahoo! announced a search advertising deal with its rival, Google. Events turned against Yahoo!, however, when the Google partnership was abandoned after the US department of justice indicated that it would attempt to block the deal. After Microsoft formally withdrew its final offer and the price of Yahoo! shares fell from a high of US$30.25 to below US$12, founder Jerry Yang was forced to resign as CEO.

Building on the success of the Wii games console, with its innovative, motion sensing controller (see AR 2007, p. 451), Nintendo continued to release new games and peripherals designed to attract new people to computer gaming (a pastime traditionally dominated by young men). Their Wii Fit accessories, which turned the games console into an interactive fitness machine, proved popular with woman and children, while their Nintendo DS handheld console, with its puzzle and general knowledge games, proved popular with older computer users. By October, Nintendo had sold 5 million Wii consoles, more than twice that of its closest competitor, Microsoft's Xbox 360, and also led the handheld console market, having sold over 8 million Nintendo DSs worldwide.

Kristian Saxton

THE ENVIRONMENT

THE POLITICS OF CLIMATE CHANGE. The year saw a widening of the chasm between the ever more urgent and detailed warnings from scientists on the likely fate of the planet if present levels of carbon-based greenhouse gas emissions (GGEs) were maintained, and the lumbering pace of global negotiations over a strategy to reduce them. This gulf was in part the product of the time lag between the collection of data, its publication, and the political attention that it then received. It also reflected the sheer complexity of the task of finding solutions that combined continually revised scientific assessments with political and economic contingencies.

The landmark political event of 2008 as regarded the question of climate change was a conference held on 1-13 December in Poznan, Poland, under the auspices of the 1992 UN Framework Convention on Climate Change (UNFCCC), at which agreement was reached on a framework for negotiating a successor to the 1997 Kyoto Protocol on reducing GGEs, which expired in 2012. The Poznan conference was, in turn, the product of the 13th conference of the parties to the UNFCCC, held in Bali, Indonesia, in December 2007, at which the parties had agreed in principle to the negotiation of a successor to Kyoto (see AR 2008, pp. 457-58). Poznan was the culmination of meetings in Bangkok (Thailand) in March, Bonn (Germany) in June, and Accra (Ghana) in August, and represented the fulcrum after which discussion was to tip over into serious negotiation. It was agreed that a first draft of a treaty would be produced for a conference in Bonn in June 2009, in preparation for a final text to be agreed at a conference in Copenhagen (Denmark) in December 2009.

Some aspects of the treaty were agreed, in outline if not in detail, at Poznan, notably the establishment of an adaptation fund, to enable poor developing countries, such as small island states, to adapt to the effects of global warming. A number of low-lying states, such as Bangladesh, the Maldives, and several Pacific islands, were already suffering the encroachment on their habitable land of rising sea levels. However, the initial announced budget for this fund was a less than lavish US$80 million. It was also agreed that the new treaty would include a mechanism for the protection of forests against logging and clearances for cultivation, through inclusion in the already existing carbon credits scheme, although there was as yet no consensus on what form this should take. Deforestation was estimated to account for at least 18 per cent of the carbon dioxide (CO_2) released annually into the atmosphere.

It was forecast that the most difficult part of the treaty to negotiate would be a formula to set reductions in carbon-based GGEs for major emerging economies, such as China, India, and Brazil, which were now rivalling the industrialised states in the quantity of their emissions as the development of their economies accelerated. The leading developing economies held to the position that continuing industrial development was essential to lift their populations out of poverty, and that the burden on reducing emissions should fall principally, for the near future, on the developed Western states whose industrialisation since the mid-18th century was largely responsible for the prevailing increased levels of greenhouse gases in the atmosphere. The Kyoto Protocol had set a range of targets—for those industrialised states that ratified it—for reducing GGEs from 1990 levels by an average of 5.5 per cent by 2012. Although China had initiated domestic policies to encourage energy efficiency, renewable energy, and pollution reduction, analysts said that the country was unlikely to accept binding emissions reduction targets in the near future. Its starting point for negotiations was that developed countries should devote at least 0.7 per cent of GDP to aid the transfer of clean technology to developing countries and to mitigate the effects on poor countries of global warming. However, some developing countries did give positive undertakings at Poznan. Brazil said that it could reduce deforestation in the Amazon by 70 per cent over the next decade, whilst Peru said that, with assistance, it could eliminate deforestation. Mexico pledged to halve its GGEs by 2050.

The negotiators at Poznan were hampered by the fact that the conference took place in a US presidential interregnum. In recent years, delegations sent by the administration of President George W. Bush had played a largely negative and obstructive role in climate change negotiations. In its last year, however, the Bush administration took a new approach, announcing in February that it was prepared to enter into a binding international agreement on climate change, individually adjusted to different countries' capabilities, if China and India would also accept legal commitments. This was initially seen as a positive step, but at a so-called major economies' meeting in Paris on 16-17 April that involved 16 countries, which between them accounted for about 80 per cent of global GGEs, Bush made the disappointing proposal that the USA's emissions would peak in 2025, and that thereafter there would be unspecified cuts. This was widely seen as inadequate in the context of the central proposal at the talks to cut global emissions by 50 per cent by 2020 and the EU's commitment to reduce its GGEs by 20 per cent by 2020. Barack Obama, who was elected president of the USA on 4 November, had in his campaign committed himself to negotiating a successor to Kyoto and backed the domestic adoption of renewable energy technology, but would not take office until January 2009, and so was a tantalising absence at Poznan. However, in a speech as president-elect in November, Obama made a commitment to setting the USA "strong annual targets" for emissions reductions.

Lord Stern of Brentford (formerly Sir Nicholas Stern), a former chief economist at the World Bank and author of a highly influential 2006 report, *The Economics of Climate Change* (see AR 2007, pp. 453; 561-64), said in June that he had revised his assessment of the proportion of global GDP that needed to be spent to combat climate change from 1 per cent to 2 per cent, in order to keep the atmospheric concentration of carbon-dioxide equivalent (CDE) gases below 500 parts per million (ppm). Above that level, there would be a 50 per cent probability of global temperatures rising 5 degrees Celsius above pre-industrial levels, with the potential for catastrophic environmental consequences. Stern had based his original assessment on the then best available scientific data from the 2001 Third Assessment Report (TAR) of the UN Intergovernmental Panel on Climate Change (IPCC), which he said had now been overtaken by subsequent research (see AR 2001, pp. 485; 487). In an interview in April, Stern rejected criticisms of his report by environmental sceptics, saying that if he were writing it today, taking into account the IPCC's 2007 Fourth Assessment Report (FAR) (see AR 2008, pp. 460-63; 591-602), his warnings of the consequences of not taking rapid action to counter climate change would have been even more bleak.

In October the UN Environment Programme (UNEP) sounded an optimistic note by launching the green economy initiative, claiming that the way to sustain economic growth and employment was to invest in clean technologies and the planet's ecosystem infrastructure. The initiative was intended to produce a comprehensive blueprint for a transition to an environmentally friendly economy within two years.

ENVIRONMENTAL SCIENCE. Preliminary data released in December by the UN World Meteorological Organisation (WMO) indicated that 2008 was likely to be the 10th warmest year since climate records began in 1850. The global average sea and land temperature was slightly lower than for the previous years of the 21st century, but this was thought to be due to the effects of a strong manifestation of the periodic La Niña weather phenomenon in the Pacific Ocean. The 2008 average was still estimated to be 0.31 degrees Celsius above the annual average for 1961-90 of 14 degrees Celsius. The warmest year on record was 1998, but eight of the top 10 years were in the 21st century. A variety of statistics was published on the level of atmospheric greenhouse gases that trapped heat in the atmosphere. The WMO's *Greenhouse Gas Bulletin 2007*, released in November, found that concentration of CO_2, the most prevalent greenhouse gas, had reached a record 383.1 ppm, a 0.5 per cent increase from 2006, whilst nitrous oxide (N_2O) and methane (CH_4) also reached record levels, increasing by 0.25 per cent and 0.34 per cent respectively. The level of CO_2 was said to be the highest for 650,000 years.

Using an index produced by the US National Oceanic and Atmospheric Administration (NOAA), it was calculated that the total warming effect of all long-lived greenhouse gases had increased by 1.06 per cent in 2007 from the previous year, and that the increase since 1990 had been 24.2 per cent. Since the mid-18th century concentrations of CO_2 in the atmosphere had risen by 37 per cent, largely through industrialisation and the accompanying use of fossil fuels. The consequent expanding human population had exacerbated the problem through increased consumption of fossil fuels and the clearance of forests for agriculture, thereby releasing more CO_2 into the atmosphere. In November the secretariat of the UNFCCC released its latest data on emissions reported to it by 41 industrialised countries, which indicated that GGEs in 2006 showed a decrease of 0.1 per cent from the 2005 level, which it was thought might have been the result of a milder than normal winter. This data did not include any of the major developing countries, such as China, India, Brazil, and South Korea. However, in December the US department of energy's environment information administration (EIA) published its statistics for CO_2 emissions in 2006 for every country and territory in the world, showing that total global emissions rose by 2.5 per cent from 2005, to 29.195 billion tonnes of CO_2. The growth in emissions from 1996 to 2006 was 28 per cent. China, with 6.018 billion tonnes, an increase of 11 per cent from 2005, had become the largest source of emissions, overtaking the USA, which emitted 5.903 billion tonnes, a decrease of 2 per cent compared with 2005. However, the per capita emissions for the USA were 19.8 tonnes against 4.6 tonnes for China.

It was reported in September that Russian, Swedish, and British scientists had detected hundreds of submarine plumes of methane in the Arctic Ocean, in the east Siberian Sea, and to the west of the Norwegian island of Svalbard. Methane (CH_4) was at least 20 times more powerful than CO_2 as a greenhouse gas, but was present in much smaller quantities in the atmosphere and degraded within about 12 years of its emission, whereas CO_2 persisted in the atmosphere for 100 years. Atmospheric levels of CH_4 had risen since the industrial revolution, largely due to oil and gas exploration and agriculture, but in the decade to 2007 concentrations had remained stable. In the Arctic region huge quantities of methane were locked as clathrates beneath permafrost on land and under the seabed, and scientists had warned that higher temperatures—which were rising faster in the Arctic than anywhere else on Earth—could cause a "feedback effect" by releasing million of tonnes of CH_4 from thawing permafrost. It was suggested that relatively warmer river water discharged into the ocean, combined with the warming caused by the shrinkage of sea ice, was beginning to thaw the subsea permafrost. Data released by the NOAA in May suggested that the rise in 2007 in the level of CH_4 to about 1,790 parts per billion (ppb) was largely accounted for by Arctic emissions and that the preponderance of the C-12 isotope in the methane indicated that it was of bacteriological origin. A study published in the journal, *Nature*, in May found that the Earth's most severe ice age had ended suddenly, 635 million years ago, when methane clathrates were released as a result of ice sheets becoming unstable.

About half of GGEs were thought to be neutralised by elements of the Earth's ecosystem, but the capacity of natural resources to perform this service was seen as increasingly fragile, partly because of deforestation and the stresses on plant life imposed by higher temperatures. New research also found that the subtraction of CO_2 from the atmosphere could have other undesirable consequences. Two studies of the Pacific Ocean found increasing ocean acidity caused by the absorption of CO_2.

A study by a team of more than 80 climate and environmental experts published in February in the *Proceedings of the National Academy of Sciences* identified nine climatic "tipping points", at which climate change would become uncontrollable and which could occur before the end of the century, given rises in temperature of between 2 degrees and 3 degrees Celsius. These included the complete disappearance of summer Arctic sea ice, the beginning of the irreversible melting and collapse of the Greenland and west Antarctic ice sheets (the latter causing a significant rise in sea levels), a 30 per cent reduction in rainfall in the Amazon basin, the dying off of the boreal forests of the northern hemisphere, and the failure of the Indian monsoon.

A report by the US Geological Survey presented in December said that the 2007 Fourth Assessment Report predictions of a rise in sea levels of between 28 cm and 42 cm by 2100 did not incorporate recent data on the acceleration of the rate of glacier flows into the oceans, especially in Greenland and west Antarctica. The report cited new estimates of between 40 cm and 150 cm. The latter would completely overwhelm many islands and low-lying coastal areas, affecting hundreds of millions of people.

ENVIRONMENTAL IMPACTS AND BIODIVERSITY. As in previous years the Arctic region, one of the most sensitive environments on Earth and the one undergoing the most rapid temperature rise, was a bellwether of the impact of climate change. According to figures released by the US National Snow and Ice Data Centre (NSIDC), the extent of Arctic sea ice at the end of the melting season in September was 4.67 million sq km, second only to the record low in 2007 of 4.28 million sq km. The 2008 area of ice was 34 per cent lower than the long-term September average of 1979-2000. Although in March (at the end of winter) ice covered 73 per cent of the Arctic basin, because of the extent of the 2007 melting much of it was thin, first-year ice prone to melting in summer. An NSIDC study presented at a scientific conference in December found that Arctic surface air temperatures where sea ice had been lost were between 3 and 5 degrees Celsius above average, an effect called "Arctic amplification" occurring some five to 10 years earlier than expected. The phenomenon was caused by the increased area of dark open water absorbing more heat after the sea ice melted in summer, then releasing some of the heat into the cooler autumn air. Computer models predicted that the first ice-free Arctic summer was probable in about 2070, but some scientists believed that this could occur as early as 2030.

It was reported that during the summer Canada's five ice shelves on the northern coast of Ellesmere island, which had already lost over the past 100 years about 90 per cent of their 10,000 sq km of ice, were continuing to break up, losing a further 150 sq km of ice, some of which was 4,500 years old. New NASA satellite data announced in December also showed that more than 2,000 billion tonnes of land ice had melted in Alaska, Greenland, and Antarctica since 2003, raising sea levels by about 5 mm. In Antarctica it was found in March that the Wilkins ice shelf, attached to the Antarctica Peninsula and covering some 13,680 sq km, was close to disintegration. The peninsula, which was the fastest-warming region of the Antarctic, experiencing a temperature rise of 0.5 degrees Celsius per decade, had lost several ice shelves over the past 30 years, including in 2002 the rapid collapse of the Larsen B shelf, which was thought to have been stable for 400 years. However, the Wilkins shelf was about four times larger in area than any of the previous losses. The retreat and disintegration of the ice shelves was directly attributed to climate change.

An international study published in *Nature* in May, based on analysis of environmental reports from 1970 to 2004, concluded that observed climate change, which could not be explained by natural variations alone, was already having a "significant impact on physical and biological systems globally". The survey, the most comprehensive yet conducted, compared reports from the period in question—when the average global temperature rose by 0.6 degrees Celsius—with historical records of the environmental impact of natural climate variations. The report concluded that 90 per cent of changes in physical and biological environmental systems, and 95 per cent of changes in reproductive and migratory behaviour amongst some 28,800 animal and plant species, were consistent with the effects of global warming.

According to the Zoological Society of London, climate change did not yet play a major direct role in threatening biodiversity, although it was expected to become a significant factor in the future. The society's *Living Planet Index*, published in May and produced with the charity WWF (formerly the World Wildlife Fund), tracked over 1,400 species of mammals, birds, reptiles, amphibians, and fish and found that overall populations had declined by an average of 27 per cent between 1970 and 2005. The society attributed this decline to human over-exploitation of natural resources leading to habitat destruction and degradation, pollution, over-fishing, and the wildlife trade. The report highlighted the importance of preserving biodiversity in sustaining the health of the planet.

The International Union for the Conservation of Nature (IUCN)'s *Red List of Threatened Species*, published in October, confirmed the ominous trend identified by the *Living Planet Index*. In its review of 5,487 known species of land mammal the IUCN found that 1,141 species were at risk of extinction, of which 188 were critically endangered. Amongst these were 303 of the 634 species of primate rated endangered, a rise to 48 per cent from 39 per cent in the 2007 list. Of the total of 44,838 species of animals and plants surveyed, 16,928 species (some 38 per cent) were classed as endangered, representing an increase of more than 600 endangered species from the 2007 list. Some 31 per cent of species of amphibian were endangered and 24 per cent of reptiles. Although most of these threats to species came from human agency, such as hunting or habitat loss, or else from viruses, rather than directly through climate change, a different IUCN study found that 35 per cent of bird species, 52 per cent of amphibians, and 71 per cent of warm-water corals were particularly susceptible to global warming, because of environmental changes that they were unable to escape.

There continued to be concern over the mass death of honeybees worldwide, a phenomenon known as colony collapse disorder (CCD), without any scientific consensus being reached on an explanation of bee losses, which beekeepers had reported at between 30 per cent and 90 per cent since CCD first emerged in 2006. In September Italy joined France, Germany, and Slovenia in suspending the use of the neonicotinoids group of pesticides after they were implicated in CCD, but a range of different parasites and viruses, changes in land use, and weather patterns had also been blamed for the phenomenon. Two-thirds of the world's crops relied on pollination, chiefly by honeybees.

An exception to the 1989 ban on the trade in ivory was made in July at a conference of the parties to the Convention on the International Trade in Endangered Species (CITES), which voted to allow a one-off auction to China and Japan of a stockpile of 108 tonnes of ivory kept by four southern African countries. A previous auction of 50 tonnes had been held in 1999, but at that time only Japan was allowed to bid because China's controls over illegal ivory were thought to be insufficiently rigorous. The 2008 sale, which took place in October, was strongly opposed by some conservation groups (and some other African countries) on the grounds that any sale of ivory would stimulate demand and encourage poaching.

Tim Curtis

XIV THE LAW

INTERNATIONAL LAW—EUROPEAN COMMUNITY LAW

INTERNATIONAL LAW

CONTROVERSIAL legal issues about secession and self-determination arose with regard to Kosovo, and subsequently South Ossetia and Abkhazia. On 17 February the National Assembly of Kosovo declared independence from Serbia (see pp. 110-112; Documents). The UN General Assembly requested the International Court of Justice to give an Advisory Opinion on the legality of the unilateral declaration. Although some states supporting independence for Kosovo argued that this was a special case, which should not serve as a precedent, Russia warned that it would have implications for other cases, and when Georgia took forcible action to reassert central government authority over the separatist region of South Ossetia in August, Russia responded by the use of force (see pp. 136-38). Russia sought to justify the legality of its military operation by reference to self-defence of its nationals abroad and of its peacekeeping forces in South Ossetia and Abkhazia. This conflict also led to legal action before the International Court of Justice.

INTERNATIONAL COURT OF JUSTICE (ICJ). The ICJ had what its president described as its most productive year ever. Six new cases were brought to the Court on a wide range of subject matter. Peru brought an action against Chile, concerning a dispute on the delimitation of their maritime boundary (see p. 196); Ecuador sued Colombia for aerial spraying of toxic herbicides over Ecuadorian territory; the Former Yugoslav Republic of Macedonia (FYROM) sued Greece for vetoing FYROM's application to join NATO because of differences over its name, in violation of Greece's obligations under the 1995 *Interim Accord* (see pp. 84; 109-10); Germany instituted proceedings against Italy for failing to respect its jurisdictional immunity as a sovereign state.

Mexico made a *Request for the Interpretation of the Avena Judgment of 31 March 2004*, and sought provisional measures in that case. This was the latest stage in litigation, which had begun in 2003 when Mexico brought the *Avena* case against the USA for violation of the Vienna Convention on Consular Relations in its treatment of foreign nationals. In the *Avena* case, the ICJ had held that the USA had violated the Convention, and that it was therefore obliged "to provide by means of its own choosing review and reconsideration" of the convictions and sentences of 51 Mexican nationals, whose rights under the Consular Convention had been violated (see AR 2004, p. 442). In 2005 US President George W. Bush had accordingly ordered state courts to obey the ICJ ruling, but constitutional problems arose. On 25 March the US Supreme Court ruled that the president did not have the power to order individual states to relax their criminal procedures in order to obey a ruling of the ICJ. Mexico then filed a request for interpretation by the ICJ of its *Avena* judgment. The ICJ held that it had prima facie jurisdiction to give such an interpretation under Article 60 of its Statute, even though the USA had terminated its acceptance of the ICJ's jurisdiction under the Consular Convention after losing the 2004 case. Provisional measures were urgently needed, as the execution of five of the Mexican nationals was likely before the ICJ's decision on the merits. The ICJ accordingly ordered by seven votes to five that the USA should take all measures necessary to ensure that the Mexican nationals were not executed pending its judgment on the merits, unless these nationals received review and reconsideration under the 2004 judgment. Nevertheless the State of Texas executed one of the Mexican nationals, José Medellin, in defiance of the ICJ order.

During the conflict in South Ossetia and Abkhazia, Georgia instituted proceedings against Russia before the ICJ. It claimed that Russia, through its state organs and also through separatist forces acting under its direction and control, had violated its obligations under the 1965 International Convention on the Elimination of All Forms of Racial Discrimination (CERD) during three periods of intervention from 1990 to 2008. Georgia sought provisional measures to preserve its rights to protect its citizens against violent discriminatory acts. Russia contested the ICJ's jurisdiction, arguing that the real dispute concerned the use of force rather than discrimination, that CERD did not apply extra-territorially, that Russia did not control the separatist forces, and that there had been no preliminary negotiations. The ICJ by eight votes to seven ordered provisional measures, but not in the terms sought by Georgia. It found that it had prima facie jurisdiction because there was a dispute between the parties on the territorial scope of the application of CERD, and there was an imminent risk of irreparable harm to the rights at stake. It indicated provisional measures against both parties, demanding that both refrain from racial discrimination and do all in their power to ensure security of persons, freedom of movement, and protection of property of displaced persons.

The ICJ gave judgment on the merits in two cases. *Certain Questions of Mutual Assistance in Criminal Matters* (Djibouti v France) was the first case decided under Article 38(5) of the Court's Rules; this allowed a state to bring a case even where the respondent state had not given its consent, inviting that other state to consent to the ICJ's jurisdiction in that particular case. On the merits the Court found that France had violated its obligations under the 1986 Convention on Mutual Assistance in Criminal Matters, through its failure to give reasons for its refusal of assistance (see p. 251).

In *Sovereignty over Pedra Branca, Middle Rocks and South Ledge* (Malaysia v Singapore) the ICJ decided on sovereignty over Pedra Branca, an uninhabited island situated in the entrance of the Straits of Singapore. Although Malaysia's predecessor (Johor) had possessed original title through its continuous and peaceful display of territorial sovereignty, the ICJ held that the subsequent conduct of the parties meant that sovereignty passed to Singapore by tacit agreement. As of 1953 Johor had come to understand that it did not have sovereignty; and after that date Singapore had carried out sovereign acts such as investigation of accidents, control over visits, and installation of military communications equipment. However, Malaysia retained its original sovereignty over the Middle Rocks (see p. 341).

Finally the ICJ decided by 10 votes to five that it had jurisdiction in *Application of the Convention on the Prevention and Punishment of the Crime of Genocide*, a case brought by Croatia against Serbia arising out of the conflict in the former Yugoslavia. Serbia claimed that, because it had not been a member of the UN or a party to the ICJ's Statute or a party to the Genocide Convention at the date Croatia brought the action, the Court had no jurisdiction. The ICJ was faced with apparently inconsistent earlier decisions on the status of Serbia and its capacity to appear before the Court. However, the Court ignored its own previous decisions, saying it was not bound by them. It adopted a flexible approach, holding that, although Serbia was not a member of the UN when Croatia's application was filed in 1999, its subsequent admission as a new member in 2000 meant that the case could proceed. Also Serbia had, by its own declaration in 1992 and its subsequent practice, made clear that it had become a party to the Genocide Convention after the breakup of the former Yugoslavia (see p. 119).

Five judges were elected to the Court: Awn Shawkat Al-Khasawneh (Jordan) and Ronny Abraham (France) were re-elected; Antonio Augusto Cançado Trindade (Brazil), Christopher Greenwood (UK) and Abdulqawi Ahmed Yusuf (Somalia) were elected as new members.

INTERNATIONAL CRIMINAL TRIBUNAL FOR RWANDA (ICTR). The ICTR worked to fulfil its completion strategy, imposed by the UN Security Council in Resolution 1503 (2003), in order to finish all work by 2010. However, the plans for completion were challenged: the ICTR was now confronted by up to 10 new cases, and it was also faced with the resignation of judges and other staff. Thirteen fugitives remained at large, and were not to be awarded impunity because of the end of the ICTR's mandate. Several decisions denying the prosecutor's requests for referral of cases to Rwandan courts also cast some doubt on the ability of the ICTR to implement its completion strategy.

The most important ICTR case was that of *Théoneste Bagosora*, chief-of-staff in the defence ministry, accused of masterminding the 1994 genocide. He played the central role in organising the army and extremist Hutu militias to start the massacre of Tutsis. He also ordered the murder of the prime minister and the president of the Constitutional Court and the killing of UN peacekeepers. Bagosora was sentenced to life imprisonment for genocide, crimes against humanity, and war crimes (see p. 282). Convictions were handed down in three further cases, and two final judgments were given by the Appeals Chamber in *Tharcisse Muvunyi* and *Athanase Seromba*. In the latter Seromba, a Roman Catholic priest, was found guilty of committing genocide for his participation in the bulldozing of Nyange church, resulting in the death of at least 1,500 Tutsis seeking refuge inside the building. The Appeals Chamber overturned the original conviction for aiding and abetting genocide, and substituted a conviction for committing genocide. The Chamber increased Seromba's sentence to life imprisonment. This was an important judgment on the different modes of participation in genocide.

INTERNATIONAL CRIMINAL TRIBUNAL FOR THE FORMER YUGOSLAVIA (ICTY).   The ICTY
also had a productive year. The most high-profile development was the arrest and
surrender to the Court of *Radovan Karadzic*, former president of the Republika
Srpska in Bosnia & Herzegovina, indicted for genocide, war crimes, and crimes
against humanity (see p. 117). Two fugitives remained at large, *Ratko Mladic* and
Goran Hadzic (see p. 114).

The Trial Chamber made a controversial judgment in the trial of three KLA
(Kosovo Liberation Army) commanders, acquitting *Ramush Haradinaj*, a former
Kosovan prime minister, of torturing and murdering Serbs in 1998-99 (for indictment see AR 2005, p. 423). The prosecutors had failed to prove a deliberate campaign to kill and expel Serb civilians from Kosovo. There were allegations that
witnesses in this case had been intimidated. In the only case related to the 2001
Macedonian conflict heard by the ICTY, *Ljube Boskoski*, the former Macedonian
interior minister was acquitted of crimes against ethnic Albanians. He was
charged with command responsibility for failure to investigate the crimes and to
ensure that those responsible were punished, but this was not established. His co-
accused, *Johan Tarculovski*, had a direct role in the murder and mistreatment of
ethnic Albanians, and was sentenced to 12 years' imprisonment. *Rasim Delic*, a
Bosnian Muslim commander, was convicted of crimes against captured Bosnian
Serb soldiers. He was one of the most senior military commanders to be tried on
charges of superior criminal responsibility for murder and cruel treatment, and the
sentence of three years' imprisonment was criticised by some as too lenient.

The ICTY Appeals Chamber upheld the conviction and sentence of *Milan Martic*,
former Serb leader in Croatia, for his participation in a joint criminal enterprise
whose common purpose was to displace the non-Serb population of Krajina. The
Chamber acquitted *Naser Oric*, commander of Bosnian Muslim forces, because the
Trial Chamber had made mistakes on the doctrine of command responsibility. It
considered this doctrine further in *Pavle Strugar*, where it extended the scope of the
accused's responsibility for the shelling of Dubrovnik, and in the case of *Enver Haz-
ihasanovic* and *Amir Kubura*, senior officers in the army of Bosnia & Herzegovina.

INTERNATIONAL CRIMINAL COURT (ICC).   Over one hundred states had ratified the
Rome Statute of the ICC by the end of the year. But progress in the conduct of
cases was slow, and the ICC faced problems in securing co-operation from states.
However, *Jean-Pierre Bemba* was surrendered to the Court by Belgium and faced
trial for war crimes and crimes against humanity committed in the Central African
Republic (see p. 279). The most controversial development was the application
by the prosecutor for an arrest warrant against *Omar Hasan Ahmed al-Bashir*,
president of Sudan, for genocide, war crimes, and crimes against humanity; this
was the first application for the arrest of an incumbent head of state (see p. 235).
The prosecution alleged that he had masterminded and implemented a plan to
destroy the Fur, Masalit, and Zaghawa groups in Darfur on account of their ethnicity. Some argued that the prosecutor's application threatened the peace process
in Sudan. On 31 July the African Union (AU) peace and security council appealed
to the UN Security Council to use its powers under Article 16 of the Rome Statute
to suspend the process for a year (see p. 446). ˙

As regards the cases arising from the conflict in the Democratic Republic of the Congo (DRC), *Mathieu Ngudjolo* was surrendered to the Court by the Congolese authorities and his case was joined to that of *Germain Katanga*; the charges against the two men for war crimes and crimes against humanity were confirmed by the Pre-Trial Chamber. Progress in the trial of *Thomas Lubanga Dyilo* for war crimes involving the conscription of children was delayed when the Trial Chamber decided on 13 June to impose a stay of proceedings because the prosecution had misused its powers to obtain information on condition of confidentiality, with the result that the opportunity for the accused to prepare his defence had been seriously impaired. On 2 July the Trial Chamber then ordered the release of Lubanga. However, on 21 October the Appeals Chamber reversed the decision to release Lubanga and referred the case back to the Trial Chamber, which later lifted the stay of proceedings after reconsideration of the issue.

The Appeals Chamber of the Special Court for Sierra Leone issued its first judgments; it upheld long sentences for three senior commanders of the Armed Forces Revolutionary Council, which seized power in May 1997. *Alex Tamba Brima*, *Brima Bazzy Kamara*, and *Santigie Borbor Kanu* were each convicted on 14 charges of war crimes and crimes against humanity, including the recruitment of child soldiers. The Appeals Chamber ruled that forced marriages were distinct crimes against humanity. In the case of *Moinina Fofana* and *Allieu Kondewa*, the Appeals Chamber quashed the original convictions for collective punishment and enlistment of children, but substituted others for murder and inhumane acts, and increased the original sentences. The trial of *Charles Taylor*, former president of Liberia, resumed on 7 January. This posed serious challenges to the prosecutors: it was necessary for them to show that the former president of one state was linked to crimes committed on the ground by rebel groups in another (see AR 2008, p. 472).

In marking the 60th anniversary of the Universal Declaration of Human Rights the UN General Assembly adopted a new Declaration, reaffirming the indivisibility of human rights and pledging commitment to development. It also unanimously adopted an Optional Protocol to the International Covenant on Economic, Social and Cultural Rights. This was the result of five years' preparation and was designed to strengthen the enforcement mechanism to bring it into line with that for civil and political rights (see p. 386). A new UN high commissioner for human rights, Navanethem Pillay, was appointed to replace Louise Arbour.

The African Union (AU) summit in June-July adopted the Protocol on the Statute of the African Court of Justice and Human Rights, merging two courts— the African Court on Human and Peoples' Rights, and the AU Court of Justice— into one with the aim of consolidating resources. The Protocol did not allow individuals to bring a case unless a state party had made an optional declaration.

EUROPEAN COURT OF HUMAN RIGHTS (ECHR). The ECHR continued to deal with a massive case load; it decided its 10,000th case during the year. The Grand Chamber issued its first Advisory Opinion under Article 47 of the European Convention for the Protection of Human Rights. Malta had submitted an all-male list of candidates to be judges on the Court. The Court was asked whether a list, which otherwise satisfied the criteria for office required in Article 21 of the Convention, could be rejected because it did not include any female candidates. In a conservative ruling, the Court held that the Parliamentary Assembly of the Council of Europe (PACE) could not reject lists where the parties had complied with the requirements of Article 21.

The Court decided several important cases reaffirming the absolute nature of the prohibition on torture. In *Saadi v Italy* the Grand Chamber held unanimously that it would breach Article 3 (prohibition of torture) to deport the applicant to Tunisia on suspicion of terrorism, given the risk that he would be subjected to torture in that state; it rejected the UK's argument as intervener that the prospect of serious danger to national security should outweigh the risk that the person might suffer harm once deported. Other similar cases ruled that deportation to Sri Lanka and Turkmenistan would violate Article 3 because of the risk of torture in those states. However, in *N v UK*, the Court held that it was permissible to return a failed asylum seeker with AIDS to Uganda, even though she was likely to receive a lower level of medical care there. In *Gäfgen v Germany*, the Court held that threat of torture by police in Germany to induce a child murderer to confess was in itself inhumane treatment, but that it did not amount to torture. This case was then referred to the Grand Chamber.

The Court also made significant decisions on the conditions governing national prosecutions for war crimes and crimes against humanity arising out of World War II and the 1956 Hungarian uprising. Under Article 7 no-one should be held guilty of a crime on account of an act that was not unlawful at the time it was committed. In *Kononov v Latvia* and *Korbely v Hungary*, the Court considered whether the offences had been defined with sufficient accessibility and foreseeability.

A broad-based coalition of states, international organisations, and civil society groups brought about the adoption of the Convention on Cluster Munitions in response to the devastating humanitarian impact of cluster munitions during, and long after, conflict. At least 15 states had used cluster munitions in at least 32 territories. Their most recent large-scale use was by Israel in 2006 in southern Lebanon. The Convention was opened for signature on 3 December, signed by 94 states, and ratified by four. This convention banned the use, production, acquisition, stockpiling, and transfer of cluster bombs. It obliged parties to destroy their stockpiles as soon as possible. It required states to clear cluster munitions remnants in areas under their jurisdiction or control within 10 years; other parties were to provide technical and financial assistance where possible. It also made provision for assistance to cluster bomb victims. However, many of the major users, producers, and stockpilers of cluster bombs did not agree to sign. These included the USA, China, Russia, Israel, India, and Pakistan.

The Convention on the Protection and Promotion of the Rights and Dignity of Persons with Disabilities came into force on 3 May, only 18 months from its adoption in 13 December 2006 (see AR 2006, pp. 464-65) after its 20th ratification. The Optional Protocol allowing individuals and groups to petition for relief also came into force. On 3 November the states parties elected 12 independent experts to the committee that would monitor the implementation of the Convention.

Christine Gray

EUROPEAN COMMUNITY LAW

By the end of 2008, the new Lisbon Treaty, reforming the institutions of the European Union (for summary see AR 2008, pp. 556-57) had been approved by all the member states bar two. One, the Czech Republic, was still going through the ratification process after its Constitutional Court had given its sanction (see p. 98). The other, Ireland, was the only member state to hold a referendum (which was a constitutional necessity), unlike the previous occasion, in 2005, when France and the Netherlands had held referendums, which both voted against the constitutional treaty, thus killing it and relieving Ireland and the UK of the need to hold their own promised votes (see AR 2005, pp. 368-69). This time, Ireland voted "no" (see p. 47). So the rest of the year was devoted to persuading Ireland to hold a second referendum, which would hopefully reverse the verdict of the first. By late December it was accepted that almost certainly a second referendum would be held, in the latter part of the following year, 2009. It was also agreed that when the Lisbon Treaty came into force, the provision in the Treaty of Nice limiting the number of commissioners would be reversed, so that each member state would continue to contribute a commissioner to the whole college (see pp. 424-25).

The change in the balance of power from Commission to member states foreshadowed by the new Treaty was, in fact, already clearly evident in practice throughout the year. Partly this was a result of the virtual completion of the Commission-dominated common market aspect of the Union and the transfer of energy to areas covered by the intergovernmental second and third pillars. A significant increase could be seen in legislation that was formally initiated by the Council or by the summit meetings of the European Council or by individual member states. There was a related increase in instruments that were adopted by the Council alone, particular in the fields of foreign affairs and the justice system. This had the incidental, but not unimportant, side effect of increasing the activity, experience and, hence, power of the secretariat of the Council, which was becoming a serious rival to the Commission.

A consequence of this shift was a massive increase in non-economic foreign relations activity. The long-standing complaint of the world community that they wished to deal with Europe, but could only get responses from the member states, was now being met. And this development was calling forth new forms both in EU and in international law practice. Of particular note was the shooting of the old canard that the European Union (as opposed to the European Community) did not have international personality. Although most bilateral international agreements were still being concluded with the European Community (the EC Treaty included an Article on legal personality—which did not, however, mention international personality—whereas the EU Treaty did not have such an Article) a by now significant number of such agreements were being signed by the European Union. From an international law perspective, it was clear that "Community" and "Union" were interchangeable terms.

Parallel to that was the gradual introduction into multilateral treaties and the constitutions of international organisations of special clauses, allowing "regional economic integration organisations" to be party, alongside the previously exclusive participation of sovereign states. Undoubtedly directly due to the EU, this was beginning to acquire the aura of a permanent change in international law practice.

These and other changes marked a new self-confidence of the EU in managing its role in international affairs. Increasingly it was legislating in furtherance of international legal instruments and specifically saying so in its preambles or even in its texts, which could even go so far as to incorporate the international instrument as part of EU law. It did this in its regulation on the recovery of maintenance payments which, for choice of law rules, merely referred to the Hague Protocol on Maintenance adopted by the Hague Conference on Private International Law in 2007. It also issued a formal notice expressing approval of the work of the Council of Europe in the field of criminal justice. Its steady stream of joint actions, common positions, and decisions on various forms of weaponry of mass destruction (biological and toxin weapons, ballistic missiles, military exports all featured) were all in furtherance of international conventions.

The strongest expression, however, of the EU's new strength of purpose internationally could well be its first venture in the exercise of naval power, traditionally a key indicator of rank among sovereign states. Faced with the depredations of pirates in the seas off the coast of Somalia, which had affected the ships and goods of European states among others, and supported by the UN Security Council, the EU in September set up a taskforce, codenamed Atalanta, using naval units of its member states to police the threatened sea areas. Although the EU was no stranger to military actions on land, the international law of sea warfare and piracy was new to it and it had to start putting together the legal instruments, including treaties with coastal states, needed to manage the venture. Its experience on land had already led in December to a major 20-page decision on the financial implications of its military capability and the allocation of costs between the Union and the member states.

In fact, it was not only the naval aspects of the sea that interested the EU. It had, of course, long been involved in fishery matters as part of the common fisheries policy, but now it was embarking on a wide-ranging series of instruments aimed at regulating and policing the conduct of fishery on the high seas. Much of this was in a context of international maritime region treaty systems, or the United Nations, or the UN Food and Agriculture Organisation. Some measures were for the protection of cod and bluefin tuna or of bottom-dwelling marine eco-systems through catch regulation or, in the latter case, the restriction of bottom trawling. Two far-reaching and major regulations codified the policing regime of fishery activities not only in Community waters but also in foreign waters and on the high seas. A decision was also issued governing the allocation of costs incurred by national fishery control operations (there being no EU fishery protection vessels).

The other main sector to which the EU devoted a major legislative effort was the justice system, and particularly the perceived need to unify, but without unification, the justice systems of the member states. This it was doing by developing a powerful structure of mutual recognition of national judgments and quasi-judicial decisions, similar but not identical to the USA's constitutional principle of "full faith and credit", which included rules of jurisdiction and choice of law rules applicable to national courts in civil, but not criminal, matters. This was a long-standing programme going back to the enormously influential Brussels Judgments Convention of 1968, but it now received a huge boost with the adoption just before the end of the year of a number of major legislative instruments. In civil law these included a regulation on recognition and enforcement of maintenance judgments and, earlier in the year, the Rome I Regulation on the choice of law in contract cases as well as a decision on parental responsibility. There was also a Council resolution on the training of judges.

In criminal law the output was even more impressive. In the pre-Christmas rush, the European Evidence Warrant framework decision was a clone of the earlier European Arrest Warrant and almost as intrusive on the freedom of individuals. It was accompanied by two more framework decisions: on the recognition and enforcement of penal judgments, and on probation orders, both aimed at ensuring the carrying out of criminal sentences on those outside the physical jurisdiction of the sentencing court. There was also a very important framework directive applying the principles of the Data Privacy Directive to the police and to data held by them.

Other important criminal law initiatives included a decision on a European Judicial Network, a strategy document on cybercrime, and a well-thought-out directive on the protection of "critical infrastructures" against terrorist attack. Two further framework decisions were concerned with organised crime and xenophobic and racist utterances, the latter containing disturbing overtones of censorship. A major pair of decisions dealt with cross-border crime at some length, and a substantial Environmental Crimes Directive was promulgated, which required the member states to criminalise breaches of environmental law.

In the field of criminal intelligence and surveillance, the two massive EU databases, SIS and VIS, were developed extensively. The Schengen Information System completed its transformation from SIS I to SIS II and also finalised its application to Switzerland. The Visa Information System (VIS) was supplemented by very substantial regulations on access to it by crime prevention agencies and on its application to short-stay visas.

Enforcement of judgments was not limited to civil and criminal matters. Administrative mutual assistance was also covered by two instruments, both in the field of tax: a regulation on mutual fiscal assistance and a directive on the recovery of tax.

Finally, the Aviation Security Regulation was re-enacted, with its secret annex—which included the unpublished rules on prohibited cabin baggage—now published.

Neville March Hunnings

LAW IN THE UNITED KINGDOM

PERHAPS the most memorable change of 2008 was the introduction of a new judicial uniform for non-criminal proceedings in England and Wales. From 1 October, judges no longer wore their traditional horse-hair wigs in civil cases. A modernised set of robes was also designed on a pro bono basis by British fashion designer Betty Jackson, CBE. The new gown incorporated coloured tabs at the collar to indicate the seniority of the judge (e.g. lilac for circuit judges, gold for the Court of Appeal). The new outfit was modelled for the cameras by the lord chief justice, Lord Phillips of Worth Matravers. Public reaction was mixed. One contributor to *The Times* thought that it looked "like a dressing gown that Noel Coward might have worn" and Professor Sir John Baker of Cambridge University deplored "judges wanting to look like warlords from outer space". Moreover, the Bar Council decided that no change would be made in its members' court dress, so barristers continued to appear bewigged and begowned before bare-headed civil judges. Bench and Bar alike would still wear wigs and old-fashioned robes in all criminal proceedings.

Building work on the new Supreme Court continued at Middlesex Guildhall (see AR 2008, p. 476). The official emblem for the new court was approved by the Queen in October. In the same month, Lord Phillips replaced the retiring Lord Bingham of Cornhill as senior law lord, and Lord Judge succeeded Lord Phillips as lord chief justice.

The British government was ultimately victorious in a number of important constitutional disputes. In the *Bancoult* case, former inhabitants of the British Indian Ocean Territory challenged the legality of a 2004 royal prerogative order renewing their exile from the Chagos Islands (including Diego Garcia). In 2007 the Court of Appeal had held that the order was unlawful (see AR 2008, pp. 308; 476). However, on appeal the House of Lords upheld the order's legality (see p. 329). Lord Hoffmann commented that the right of abode was not a "constitutional right" but "a creature of the law": "the law gives it and the law may take it away". In legislating for a Crown colony, the Queen (no doubt) had to take the interests of its inhabitants into account, but "in the event of a conflict of interest, she is entitled, on the advice of Her United Kingdom ministers, to prefer the interests of the United Kingdom." In dissenting speeches, Lord Bingham argued that the absence of any precedent "in which the royal prerogative had been exercised to exile an indigenous population from its homeland" showed that such a power did not exist, and Lord Mance suggested that the majority's decision allowed the government to behave like King Richard II exiling the Duke of Norfolk, in Shakespeare's play.

The applicants in *Regina (Corner House Research) v Director General of the Serious Fraud Office* questioned the decision to halt a criminal investigation into alleged bribery in a major defence procurement contract between British Aerospace and Saudi Arabia (see AR 2007, p. 212). The director general had intervened after Saudi warnings that intelligence co-operation with the UK would cease, if the corruption inquiry went ahead. In the High Court, Lord Justice Moses held that the director general's "abject surrender" to these threats seriously undermined the rule of law. His duty was to resist attempts to interfere with the course of justice. Accordingly, the decision to halt the fraud investigation had been illegal. But the Serious Fraud Office appealed successfully to the House of Lords. Lord Bingham stated that the director general had given careful thought to the damage that his decision might do to the rule of law, but he had been entitled to take into account the implications of the Saudi threats for public safety in the UK. He had balanced these competing public interests in good faith, and his discretion could not be impugned.

In *Regina (Gentle) v Prime Minister* the House of Lords held that the duty to protect life under Article 2 of the European Convention on Human Rights did not require an independent inquiry to be held into the legality of an armed conflict. The claims had been brought by the mothers of two British servicemen killed in Iraq. In *Regina (Wheeler) v Prime Minister* the applicant alleged that the government's decision to ratify the EU's Lisbon Treaty was an unlawful breach of its earlier promise to hold a referendum on the EU Constitutional Treaty. But the High Court held that it was "unthinkable" that such a promise could generate binding legal obligations: the subject matter lay "so deep in the macro-political field that the court should not enter the relevant area at all". It would violate the separation of powers for a court to order ministers to place a Bill before Parliament, as would have been necessary for such a referendum. By the time the case was decided, Parliament had anyway enacted the legislation necessary for the ratification of the Lisbon Treaty (European Union (Amendment) Act), rejecting calls for a referendum (see p. 33).

However, in the immigration case of *SK*, Mr Justice Munby reminded ministers that the rule of law extended to all persons, however unsympathetic (in casu, the successful applicant was a convicted sex offender who had claimed asylum fraudulently). The judge lambasted the home office for "serial shortcomings" in matters "going to the liberty of the subject": "I have to say that the melancholy facts that have been exposed as a result of these proceedings are both shocking and scandalous. They are shocking even to those who still live in the shadow of the damning admission by a former Secretary of State that a great Department of State is 'unfit for purpose'. They are scandalous for what they expose as the seeming inability of that Department to comply not merely with the law but with the very rule of law itself." (The reference was to then Home Secretary John Reid's condemnation of the immigration system in 2006.)

Elsewhere, Parliament set national carbon emissions reduction targets in the Climate Change Act; required every child to participate in education or training until the age of 18 (Education and Skills Act); and set up a scheme to confiscate the contents of bank accounts unused for more than 15 years, for the public use (Dormant Bank and Building Society Accounts Act). The Human Fertilisation and Embryology Act stated that where a woman bore a child after artificial insemination, her female civil partner would be the other legal parent. In *Re G* the House of Lords held that a Northern Ireland law prohibiting unmarried couples from adopting children was illegally discriminatory. Lord Hoffmann said that such an irrebutable presumption of parental unsuitability could not be justified when the law required the welfare of the child to be considered in each case, given that potential adopters' relationships might "vary from quasi-marital to ephemeral". But Lord Walker of Gestingthorpe, dissenting, argued that such a change would better have been made by the democratically-elected Northern Ireland Assembly.

In *Regina (G) v Nottinghamshire NHS Trust* the High Court held that legislation banning smoking in mental hospitals did not breach the right to private life of detained mental health patients. The importance of preventing passive smoking justified any limitation of the patients' rights. In *Regina (B) v Greenwich Magistrates' Court* the High Court held that magistrates had been entitled to issue an anti-social behaviour order (ASBO) prohibiting the applicant from wearing a hooded top in a certain London borough, since he had intended to cause fear and intimidation by wearing the garment. The Criminal Justice and Immigration Act abolished the ancient crime of blasphemy, while extending the offences of inciting hatred to cover hatred on grounds of sexual orientation. The Act also created a new offence of possessing "extreme pornography" (including bestiality or necrophilia).

Privacy litigation continued to perplex, outrage, and amuse. In *Murray v Express Newspapers*, publication of photographs of the claimant (the baby son of author J.K. Rowling) being pushed in his perambulator in a public place had violated his "reasonable expectation of privacy". The Court of Appeal stressed the claimant's extreme youth. In the notorious case of *Mosley v News Group Newspapers*, the claimant (son of the noted British fascist leader of the 1930s, Sir Oswald Mosley) had been filmed by hidden cameras taking part in sado-masochistic games with several "prostitutes and dominatrices" in a London flat. Mr Justice Eady held that the defendant newspaper's detailed description of the orgy, and publication of the film on its website, had unjustifiably breached the claimant's privacy. Sexual activity on private property between consenting adults, whether paid or unpaid, entitled the participants to a degree of privacy, however distasteful or undignified it might seem to some. Disapproval could not justify public exposure, "whether the motive for such intrusion is merely prurience or a moral crusade". Everyone may conduct himself as he pleases in private, within the limits of the criminal law, and "that a particular relationship happens to be adulterous, or that someone's tastes are unconventional or 'perverted', does not give the media carte blanche". The judge awarded Mosley £60,000 damages for breach of privacy. Journalists reacted with alarm. *Daily Mail* editor Paul Dacre attacked Eady personally for his "arrogant and amoral judgements" in a November speech. But at least the Mosley trial at the High Court in July had provided several days of highly entertaining copy for the press (and even the judgment contained some very evocative passages). As one door shuts, another opens.

Jonathan Morgan

LAW IN THE USA

In 2008 laws and other measures taken to detect and prevent terrorism continued to present challenging issues for the federal courts. On 12 June, in a five to four decision, the US Supreme Court in *Boumediene v Bush* held unconstitutional Section 7 of the Detainee Treatment Act of 2005, which prohibited the courts from granting writs of habeas corpus, on the narrow ground that Congress had failed to state unequivocally its intent to suspend that writ. The Fourth Circuit Court of Appeals ruled in *Ali Saleh Kahala al-Marri v Wright* that al-Marri, a Qatari student legally resident in the USA, could be held indefinitely as an enemy combatant in the country under the Authorization for the Use of Military Force—the joint resolution adopted by the US Congress on 14 September, 2001—if the allegations against him could be proved. The Court accepted the case for review and was expected to decide in 2009 if such detention was lawful. The Washington, DC District Court of Appeals overturned the Guantánamo Bay military tribunal's decision ordering the continued detention of Hazaifa Parhat, a Uighur taken prisoner in Afghanistan in 2001. The Second Circuit Court of Appeals held as a violation of the First Amendment a provision in the Patriot Act that allowed the Federal Bureau of Investigation to demand that recipients of national security letters, which had the legal effect of subpoenas, not reveal the information they were demanded thereunder to provide. The Northern California United States District Court held wiretapping by the National Security Agency was permissible, if at all, under the Foreign Intelligence Surveillance Act, and not independently under the president's powers as commander in chief.

The scorecard in the culture wars in the United States showed mixed results in the court decisions in 2008. In *District Court of Columbia v Heller* the Court, in a 5-4 decision on 26 June, held a suit could proceed against the District challenging the constitutionality of a law that required that owners procure licences for all handguns and that all firearms kept in the District be unloaded or safety locked, on the grounds that the Second Amendment to the constitution protected an individual's right to possess firearms. The Court had not addressed the meaning of the Second Amendment in nearly 70 years. The California Supreme Court, in a 4-3 decision, held the law that limited marriages to unions between men and women violated the equal rights of gays and lesbians as protected by the California constitution. The decision was reversed by a referendum in California in November. In *Schroer v Billington*, the Washington, DC United States District Court ruled that the Library of Congress had violated an applicant's right to equality when it rescinded a job offer upon learning she was a transgender person. The Fourth Circuit Court of Appeals, in a 2-1 decision, ruled unconstitutional a Virginia law that prohibited the intact dilation and extraction medical procedure, which involved removing an intact foetus and piercing or crushing its skull. The Supreme Court had previously upheld a federal law that banned such procedures, but the appeals court held the Virginia law, by failing to distinguish between intentional and accidental delivery of foetuses, violated a woman's right to an abortion.

The Eighth Circuit Court of Appeals upheld a South Dakota law that obligated a doctor prepared to perform an abortion to advise his or her patients: "An abortion will terminate the life of a whole, separate, unique, living human being." The California Supreme Court refused to hear an appeal from the California Appeal Court holding that San Diego County could not refuse to implement California's medical cannabis law, which required the counties to issue medical marijuana identity cards notwithstanding federal law to the contrary.

The trend in favour of business continued in the leading court decisions in 2008. In *Riegel v Medtronic, Inc.*, the Court, in an 8-1 decision, held a claim under state tort or breach of warranty law could not be maintained against medical devices approved by the Food and Drug Administration under the Medical Devices Act, as the latter federal law pre-empted state law regarding such devices. The Second Circuit Court of Appeals dismissed an $800 billion class action for fraud on behalf of smokers against cigarette manufacturers, who advertised that light cigarettes were safer than regular ones, on the ground that smokers might have had different reasons for preferring light, over regular, cigarettes. The US District Court in Miami, Florida, held that a decision of the Florida Supreme Court, which quashed a verdict in a class action against cigarette manufacturers but ruled that the verdict could be introduced as evidence in individual cases, denied due process to the manufacturers. The US Supreme Court reversed the punitive damages award of $5 billion in *Exxon Shipping Company v Baker*, which arose from the infamous oil spill in 1989 by the *Exxon Valdez* in Price William Sound, Alaska, and resulted in a compensatory damages award of $287 million. The Court held that since Exxon had not profited from the oil spill, punitive damages could not exceed the total compensatory damage award.

Two trends in the criminal law continued in 2008. The Court, in *Kennedy v Louisiana*, held that execution of a person convicted for rape of a child less than 12 years of age was not proportional to the crime, as the crime left the victim still alive. Executions in the USA dropped to 37 in 2008, compared with the high of 98 in 1999. In *Gall v United States*, the Court held that judges who imposed sentences did not have to apply the mandatory minimum sentences prescribed in the federal sentencing guidelines, which, since the decision of the Court in 2005, should have been interpreted as advisory. A judge would be allowed to consider mitigating factors that would have otherwise been disregarded if the sentencing guidelines had applied.

Robert J. Spjut

XV RELIGION

THE global economic crisis provoked a certain amount of commentary within the religious sphere. As Paul Rayment writes (see p. 464) "During 2008 a number of religious leaders, including bishops in the UK and Germany, criticised the behaviour of certain banks and criticised government policies for short-sightedness. They were roundly attacked in turn for their weak grasp of the immediate macroeconomic problem, but their fundamental points—concerning the morality of personal conduct and the subordination of so many political and social preferences to the priorities of high finance—were concerns that were shared by large proportions of the population in the advanced economies." In addition to Christian sermonising on greed, the crisis also saw anti-Semitic publications blame the financial collapse on machinations by the Jews. Meanwhile, Islamic scholars pointed out that almost all of the practices which lay at the root of the financial crisis were prohibited by Sharia law.

CHRISTIANITY. In the Roman Catholic Church—the largest Christian denomination—the year 2008 confirmed the style of Benedict XVI's papacy. After much comment about his sartorial elegance in the media, he claimed that he was dressed "not by Prada but by Christ". While less frenetic and quieter than his predecessor, he nevertheless made a number of important visits, including to the USA in April, where he celebrated Mass at the Yankee stadium. He flew to Australia in July for the 23rd World Youth Day, where he spoke to 400,000 people. During both visits he met victims of sexual abuse by Catholic clergy. In September he went to Lourdes, in south-west France, for the 150th anniversary celebrations of the Marian apparitions. His journeys passed without significant controversy. This changed in his end-of-year address, when he claimed that the blurring of gender was as great a problem for humanity as the destruction of rainforests, a statement that was interpreted by many as an attack on same-sex unions.

In October the 12th Synod of Bishops met in Rome amidst increasing conflict over the Latin Mass and the continued relevance or otherwise of the reforming Second Vatican Council (1962-65). Shortly afterwards, Benedict reaffirmed his debt to what he called that "extraordinary ecclesial event". The Synod encouraged Bible reading and engagement with those of other faiths, an issue that had become increasingly important: Vatican statistics revealed that the number of Muslims (19.5 per cent of the world's population) had overtaken Roman Catholics (17.4 per cent). In November the first seminar organised by the Catholic-Muslim Forum—established in response to "A common word", the 2007 call for dialogue by 138 Muslim scholars (see AR 2008, pp. 484-85)—was greeted as a success. Held in Rome, the Forum set out a cautious path for further discussion and scheduled another seminar in a Muslim-majority country in 2010. It was also disclosed that the Vatican had been in discussions with the authorities in Saudi Arabia about building churches there.

The Roman Catholic Church was not immune from inter-religious conflict: Cardinal Paulos Faraj Rahho, leader of the Chaldean church in Iraq (which had lost 300,000 members through emigration since 1980) was kidnapped on 29 February and found dead a few weeks later. Anti-Christian violence also erupted in Orissa, in north-east India, in November, which led to the displacement of about 50,000 people (see below; p. 317).

The Orthodox churches lost two prominent leaders in 2008: Christodoulos, Archbishop of Athens, who died in January, and Aleksii II, Patriarch of Moscow and all Russia since 1990, who died in December (see Obituary). Aleksii had steered the Russian Orthodox Church through the major social and cultural revolution following the end of the Cold War. In 2007 he had presided over the unification of the ROC with the émigré Russian Orthodox Church Outside Russia. In July, with Ecumenical Patriarch Bartholomew I, he had attended the celebration in Kiev to mark the 1,020th anniversary of Christianity in Ukraine. Yet, responding to nationalist elements within the ROC that claimed the Roman Catholic Church was proselytising in Russia, he had resisted any meeting with the Pope, despite the efforts of Cardinal Walter Kasper, president of the Pontifical council for promoting Christian unity.

Other notable losses in the Christian world were the death in March of Chiara Lubich, founder of the Focolari Movement, the leading lay Catholic organisation, and in December of Cardinal Avery Dulles, one of the church's most prominent theologians (see Obituary). John Templeton, leading benefactor of study into Christianity and science, died in July.

In the Anglican Communion (the third largest denomination), rifts over the issue of sexuality appeared to widen further. The Lambeth Conference, held in July in Canterbury, UK, to which nearly all the bishops of the Communion were invited, was boycotted by some 200 bishops (about a quarter), many of them from the developing world. A large number of these had earlier met at the Global Anglican Future Conference in Jerusalem, which issued a call for a separate Anglican church composed only of those with conservative attitudes to the Bible and sexuality. Despite this challenge the Lambeth Conference, which included a march against poverty in London, was declared a success. It introduced two novelties: bishops were encouraged to listen to one another, and no votes were taken. Later in the year, however, a number of conservative dioceses in the USA chose to realign with the tiny Anglican Church of the Southern Cone (Latin America), which provoked legal challenges from the mainstream US Episcopal Church.

The Evangelical world played an important part in the US presidential campaign. Rick Warren, pastor of the Saddleback mega-church in California, appeared to have supplanted Billy Graham as the leading Evangelical voice in politics: he hosted both Barack Obama and John McCain, and was invited to offer the closing prayer at Obama's inauguration in January 2009. Other Evangelicals proved more controversial: after the release of footage in which the Reverend Jeremiah Wright made harsh criticisms of the USA, Obama was forced to sever his long-standing links with the Trinity United Church of Christ in Chicago (see pp. 150-51). Political divisions within conservative Evangelicalism were highlighted in March, when a number of prominent Southern Baptists issued a statement that their denomination had been "too timid" over the issue of global warming.

HINDUISM.   In January, the financial information firm, Dow Jones and Company, launched a new "dharma index" to track the stocks of over 3,000 companies that observed the values of dharma-based religions, such as Hinduism and Buddhism. This represented the first attempt to measure dharma-compliant stocks. Dow Jones pioneered faith-based indexes with the Islamic market index in 1999, which monitored companies' compliance with Sharia law. The dharma index was arrived at in consultation with an international team of scholars of Hinduism assembled by the Oxford Centre for Hindu Studies.

The last Hindu monarchy had its day, following a landmark election to a Constituent Assembly in Nepal in May, in which the Communist Party of Nepal (Maoist) took a commanding lead. The Assembly confirmed the decision taken in 2007 to abolish the monarchy and began drawing up a republican constitution (see pp. 321-22).

Tensions between castes still ran high from time to time in India. In October 2008 at least three incidents of violence took place against Dalits (formerly known as "untouchables") during the festival of Navaratri, including the shooting of a young Dalit who had entered a temple to make offerings to the goddess Durga. Conversely, a Hindu temple was opened to Dalits in Tamil Nadu on the order of the Chennai High Court. The temple had been closed for nine months over a dispute between Dalits and the higher caste Vanniyar community. The Dalits celebrated the ruling, but the Vanniyars moved to a different temple.

In January the Sri Lankan tourism board identified 50 sites associated with the Hindu epic, *Ramayana*, to attract more pilgrim travellers from India to the island nation. Plans included the restoration and redevelopment of sacred sites. A difficulty that the tourism board would need to consider was the fact that Indians told a story recounting the victory of the good Rama over the bad Ravana, while many Sri Lankans preferred the version which portrayed Rama as the villain and Ravana as the hero.

In the UK, the anger felt by the Hindu community at the forcible euthanasia of a cow at Bhaktivedanata Manor by the Royal Society for the Prevention of Cruelty to Animals (RSPCA) in late 2007, and of a TB-infected bullock at a Hindu centre in Wales earlier that year by officials from the government department of the environment, farming and rural affairs (DEFRA) (see AR 2008, pp. 482-83), was somewhat mollified after high level talks with the RSPCA, encouraged by the Archbishop of Canterbury. In December the RSPCA offered Bhaktivedanata Manor a replacement cow, which the community gladly accepted. Other temples had clashed with the RSPCA and DEFRA over the care of sick animals, some Hindus believing that killing a cow even for merciful reasons was wrong. DEFRA released guidelines that tried to avoid offending the Hindu community on the care of sacred temple animals.

Culturally, Hindu topics featured prominently in other countries. In April Philip Glass's opera, *Satyagraha*, was restaged in New York to much acclaim. Indian culture and language were to be studied in China at Beijing university. In January scientists and Vedic experts came together at the Indian science congress in Visakhapatnam to explore the interface between science and the Vedanta spiritual tradition.

The Sanskrit dictionary project of the Deccan College of Pune, which had begun in 1948 and had seen three generations of lexicographers at work, announced in August that the project should be completed in another 50 years. Hindu culture at least had no problem with long-term planning.

ISLAM. The year 2008 was marked by controversial fatwas and ongoing efforts to evolve a form of consistency in the fatwa-making process and its institutions. A fatwa (formal religious edict) could in principle be issued by any qualified jurist, despite efforts to introduce national fatwa-making councils and international attempts at co-ordination across the diverse Islamic world.

An example of the confusion inherent in the process came in September, when a senior Moroccan scholar, Mohamed bin Abderrahmane Al-Maghraoui, provoked a storm of controversy by ruling that girls could be married as early as the age of nine. The country's High Council of Ulema (religious experts) reacted with its own fatwa, opposing the marriage of underage girls, and reaffirming the Moroccan legal age of marriage as 18. A passionate but unresolved debate ensued in Morocco over the right of individual scholars to issue rulings that differed from the view of religious officialdom.

At the other end of the Islamic world, the Malaysian national fatwa council issued its own controversial ruling prohibiting the use of yoga by Muslims. The council chairman, Abdul Shukor Husin, made the claim that yoga involved spiritual practices and states of mind proper to Hinduism that were incompatible with Muslim faith. A prolonged controversy ensued, with some scholars independent of the council objecting; by the end of the year the debate had spread to neighbouring Indonesia, where a similar national ruling was expected.

No less controversial was a fatwa issued by the Saudi Arabian council of jurists, which ruled that the use of Qur'anic verses in the ringtones of mobile telephones was forbidden. The scholars argued that answering a telephone might involve cutting off a Qur'anic passage in such as way as to affect its meaning.

In the United Arab Emirates the religious authorities moved to curb confusion over religious edicts by creating, on 28 August, an official fatwa office controlled by the state run Islamic Affairs Authority. Muhammad Mattar al-Kaabi, the Authority's general secretary, expressed his hope that believers, who had previously been confused by rival fatwas delivered by different scholars in the country's mosques or available on Internet sites, would now rely exclusively on what were, in effect, the government's official fatwas. This move, however, was opposed as retrograde by voices calling for a greater separation of religion from the state.

The move to centralise the authority to issue fatwas, which was already well advanced in many Muslim jurisdictions, came against the background of the ongoing struggle against extremism. In India, where the threat of Islamic radicalism was a theme in some Hindu nationalist rhetoric against the country's large Muslim minority, several major events were held to launch fatwas against terrorism. The largest of these took place in May, when over 200,000 Muslims gathered in Delhi to hear a fatwa from India's best-known Islamic university, the Darul Uloom (Deoband). Denouncing terrorism as "un-Islamic", the Deoband fatwa was widely seen as an attempt to distance mainstream Islam from forces destabilising neighbouring Pakistan, where Taliban militias, believed by some to have their roots in Deobandi interpretations of Islam, posed a growing threat to Pakistan's stability during the year.

In November, an international gathering of 6,000 Muslim scholars met in the Indian city of Hyderabad to agree a similar message. The meeting's final declaration, which echoed the Deoband fatwa, was hailed across the Muslim world as the most substantial international fatwa against al-Qaida and allied extremist groups, and the hope was expressed that it would be widely reported in the world media.

A similarly significant event took place in the Libyan capital, Tripoli, in October, when 460 major Islamic organisations from across the Muslim world agreed to endorse "A common word", the 2007 declaration on Muslim-Christian friendship (see AR 2008, pp. 484-85). The declaration was also the subject of a series of high-level encounters between Muslim and Christian leaders. One of these took place at Yale University in the USA, where Muslim scholars and Evangelical Christian leaders endorsed "A common word". Still more significant was the first Catholic-Muslim Forum, held in November at the Vatican (see above), where Pope Benedict XVI, whose remarks on Islam had two years earlier attracted controversy, effectively endorsed the "common word" initiative, stating that "we must show, by our mutual respect and solidarity, that we consider ourselves members of one family." The Pope's address was generally received with approval in the Muslim world.

JUDAISM. Despite a concerted campaign to convince US Jews that Barack Obama was insufficiently supportive of Israel, or even that he was a covert Muslim, over 78 per cent of US Jews voted for the Democratic candidate in the 2008 US presidential election, proportionately far outstripping Catholic, Protestant and other Christian denominational support. It was surpassed only by the 96 per cent vote of the black community.

The Bernard Madoff affair, a massive fraud involving the disappearance of an estimated US$50 billion in investments placed with a US financier who, it turned out, was running a Ponzi scheme, had a severe impact upon a wide range of US Jewish organisations. The well-known Fifth Avenue synagogue was estimated to have lost a collective US$2 billion. Its members included the writer and Holocaust survivor, Elie Wiesel, whose foundation lost US$37 million. At the same time, the fact that Madoff was himself a Jew meant that the affair provoked anti-Semitic comments in some quarters.

More generally, a poll conducted by the US Anti-Defamation League in seven European countries at the end of 2008 found that 31 per cent of respondents blamed Jews in the finance industry for the international economic crisis. Some 40 per cent believed that Jews had "an over-abundance of power in the business world". In numerous Asian countries, which typically did not possess Jewish communities, books appeared which traded on European stereotypes. A Chinese bestseller entitled *The Currency War* declared that the Jews were plotting to rule the world by orchestrating the international banking system. Other books purported to explain to Asian audiences the "factual" basis of an infamous anti-Semitic text, the 1903 Tsarist forgery, *The Protocols of the Elders of Zion*.

There were co-ordinated attacks by Islamist militants in Mumbai (Bombay) in November (see pp. 316-17), which killed nearly 200 people, including a number of Jews. Amongst the targets was Nariman House, a Jewish welfare centre, where Rabbi Gavriel Holtzberg, his wife, and four other Jews were tortured and killed. The institution was one of the many Chabad houses on the tourist trail run by the Lubavitch Hasidim, which offered kosher food and hospitality to the Jewish traveller.

In Israel the Reform movement revived its attempt to secure recognition from the state through the collection of signatures on a petition to President Shimon Peres. In the Israeli election campaign, Yisrael Beitenu, originally a party of Russian immigrants, argued for the introduction of civil marriage in Israel and an easing of the conversion process. Religious authority in Israel, firmly in the hands of the orthodox, remained unable to solve the problem of the religious status of an estimated 300,000 non-Jews, who had arrived with their families during the large-scale immigration from the former Soviet Union in the 1990s. The Israeli Masorti movement (a branch of Conservative Judaism which also advocated reform) called for a privatisation of religious authority and requested the Israeli cabinet dissolve the Chief Rabbinate as a government organisation.

The Israeli military assault on Gaza at the end of 2008 occasioned deep debate within diaspora Jewish communities. There was broad agreement that Israel was justified in taking action against Islamic militants who were continuing to fire crude rockets into Israel. Their range had increased in recent years and there was a marked increase in such attacks following the expiry of the Egyptian-brokered truce between Israel and the Islamist Hamas movement on 19 December. Nevertheless, there was growing anguish over the suffering of Palestinian civilians as it became clear that a large number of women and children were being killed in the operation. Some British Jews counselled against an extension of the operation in the form of an Israeli ground assault (which was anticipated, but had not yet begun, at the end of the year), and others called for an immediate ceasefire. Despite the absence of the international media (excluded from the war zone by the Israeli and Egyptian authorities), reports from Gaza suggested that close to 400 Palestinians had been killed in Israeli air attacks by the end of the year: four Israelis (including one soldier) had been killed by rocket and mortar fire from Gaza during the same period.

The World Congress of Imams and Rabbis met in Paris in December 2008. Despite a decision to issue joint responses to acts of terror, there were, amidst all the proclamations of friendship, profound differences of opinion and no final resolution was agreed. The Gaza crisis a few days later caused an inevitable deterioration in Jewish-Muslim relations. The Muslim Council of Britain had for several years refused to attend the Holocaust Memorial Day commemoration, held each year on 27 January. In 2008, it reversed its decision and participated. By the end of the year, however, it reverted to its earlier stance because of the developing conflict in Gaza. Shahid Malik, undersecretary of state in the UK justice ministry, criticised the Muslim Council of Britain for its decision not to attend the 2009 commemoration.

Peter Oppenheimer (convener); Mark D. Chapman (Christianity); Shaunaka Rishi Das (Hinduism); Timothy Winter (Islam); Colin Shindler (Judaism)

XVI THE ARTS

OPERA—MUSIC—BALLET & DANCE—THEATRE—CINEMA—TELEVISION & RADIO

OPERA

THE long-running conundrum of the Bayreuth succession was finally solved at the end of the 2008 festival, when an announcement was made that half-sisters Katharina Wagner and Eva Wagner-Pasquier would jointly take over the administration from their father, Wolfgang. It was the expected result and the one backed by Wolfgang himself, who had restarted Bayreuth in 1951 in tandem with his brother, Wieland, after a hiatus following World War II. Wolfgang had guided the Wagnerian jamboree ever since, assuming sole leadership upon Wieland's early death in 1966. With his various children from two marriages regularly at loggerheads not only with each other but also with him, the question of whether the succession would remain within the family had been a moot one. The ascendancy of Eva and Katharina seemed likely to hold the fort for many years to come.

Another festival that enjoyed a makeover was Wexford, which opened in October with the launch of Ireland's first-ever purpose-built opera house. A handsome, state-of-the-art auditorium with good acoustics replaced the old and increasingly dilapidated Theatre Royal, where the festival, launched in the small coastal town in 1951, had long struggled to maintain high artistic standards within a ramshackle venue. The new theatre proved a remarkable achievement, with no technical hiccoughs apparent in an opening weekend that featured stagings of Rimsky-Korsakov's *The Snow Maiden*, Richard Rodney Bennett's *The Mines of Sulphur*, and Carlo Pedrotti's *Tutti in maschera*.

In the USA, Charles McKay, the long-term general manager of the St Louis Festival, moved on, after 23 successful years, to Santa Fe. His final season included an outstanding production of Walton's *Troilus and Cressida* that put this fine but neglected work back on the international map. His chief executive's position was assumed by Timothy O'Leary, formerly of New York City Opera, while the company's search for a new artistic head following the death of Colin Graham resulted in the appointment of James Robinson.

At New York City Opera itself, however, a new appointee failed to materialise. Gerard Mortier, the former head of La Monnaie in Brussels, then the Salzburg Festival, and latterly the Paris Opera, had been selected to assume a similar post at New York's second opera house, to start in 2009. His plans, already announced in broad terms, would see the company have a virtually silent season (two concert performances of Samuel Barber's *Anthony and Cleopatra* excepted) during 2008-09, in preparation for a grand new strategy offering what was assumed to be a relatively conservative audience the great masterpieces of 20th-century opera, plus new commissions from Charles Wuorinen (on the subject of the film *Brokeback Mountain*) and Philip Glass.

After increasing hints in the press and on the Internet that Mortier would revoke his commitment to the company, he actually did so, citing as his reason the inadequacy of the promised budget, and leaving the company in dire straits with no season, no artistic leadership, and no shortage of people to tell them that Mortier's appointment had been a disastrous notion in the first place. Three weeks later Mortier announced that he would go to the Teatro Réal, Madrid, instead.

Meanwhile, the increasingly difficult global economic situation was beginning to have an impact on opera worldwide and on American opera, which relied heavily on individual and corporate donors, as opposed to the public funding of the European model, in particular. Many companies announced shorter or cheaper seasons: other smaller ventures—Opera Pacifica in Costa Mesa was the first—simply closed down. Tighter purse-strings were not confined, however, to the USA. In Italy, Prime Minister Silvio Berlusconi's expressed view that "museums, theatres and archaeological sites are now a luxury" sent further shockwaves through the country's 14 major houses, several of which were already in serious financial difficulty. The fact that the creation of opera consistently redounded to Italy's cultural credit internationally may have escaped him.

Of notable appointments, conductor Donald Runnicles was named as music director of the Deutsche Oper, Berlin; Kazushi Ono as principal conductor of the Opéra National de Lyon. The undeniably talented Mark Wigglesworth came and went quickly at Brussels, his departure (which in fact preceded the official start of his contract) apparently occasioned by dissatisfaction among the orchestral players. Peter Mussbach, intendant of the Berlin Staatsoper, also resigned following, it was suggested, increasing disagreements with music director Daniel Barenboim.

The closure in 2006 for renovation of the Teatro Colón in Buenos Aires, one of the world's great opera houses, was announced as likely to continue until 2010; that of the Bolshoi in Moscow—shut down for "emergency repairs" in 2005—was supposedly due to end during 2009.

The sudden death of conductor Richard Hickox at the age of 60 shocked the entire musical world (see Obituary). His tenure of Opera Australia had received criticism, though mostly from local singers no longer asked to appear with the company. His commitment to the task in hand was always total. Just four days following his fatal heart attack, English National Opera was able to mount a new production of Vaughan Williams's *Riders to the Sea*, which had been due to open under his baton, as a result of the ability of their music director, Edward Gardner, to pick up the reins. Others who departed the universal stage in 2008 included sopranos Inga Nielsen, Leyla Gencer, and Christel Goltz; tenors Guiseppe Di Stefano (see Obituary), Sergey Larin, and Gianni Raimondi; baritone Peter Glossop; bass Richard Van Allan; conductors Noel Davies, Nicola Rescigno, and Horst Stein; and composers Alun Hoddinott (see Obituary) and Mauricio Kagel.

Despite the negatives, major new operas continued to arrive. At London's Covent Garden Sir Harrison Birtwistle's *The Minotaur* received a fine production conducted by the house's versatile music director, Antonio Pappano, and starring Sir John Tomlinson in the title role, specially written for him. This tenaciously dark and troubling piece was well received. At Glyndebourne, the Hungarian Peter Eötvös's *Love and Other Demons*, based on the work of Colombian magical-realist novelist Gabriel García Márquez and conducted by Vladimir Jurowski, proved altogether less memorable. The delayed première of Michael Berkeley's *For You*, to a libretto by Ian McEwan, made little positive impact. Scottish Opera's *Five: 15*, a programme of short new works, provided a varied and worthwhile evening; the clear winner was composer Lyell Cresswell with *The Perfect Woman*.

George Hall

MUSIC

THE power of Western classical music to evolve within the rich variety of national traditions was clearly demonstrated in 2008. If traditions are to flourish, continuity and aesthetic purpose within a broad, national culture will enable them to grow, spread, and become international.

The range of American culture was celebrated in two very different festive events in 2008. The first was the release of the live recordings—after 10 years— of the tumultuous arrival of 22 Cuban musicians on the mainland American scene at the concert by the Buena Vista Social Club at New York's Carnegie Hall on 3 July 1998. The discs, released to great acclaim, showed the living folk tradition of Cuba and its power to change the life of its people through music.

The second event was the celebration of composer Elliott Carter's 100th birthday, on 11 December 2008. Concerts and performances in honour of the grand old man of American music took place during the year throughout Europe and America. Over a long period, his style had seen many changes and reverses, and its aesthetic complications of rhythm, tonality, and texture, particularly in the middle period of his life after 1951 (*String Quartet No.1*), called for sustained concentration by musicians and audiences alike. In later years a relaxed lyricism, a sense of fun, helped the listener gain access to the core of the music, which was perceived as embodying the mainstream Western tradition of instrumental and vocal works, chamber music, symphonic and concerted composition. The focus of the year's events was a retrospective at Tanglewood, when 47 of Carter's major works were played over five days. Prominent was the much-performed *Symphonia: Sum Fluxae Pretium Spei* (see AR 1998, p. 513). New compositions included *Sound Fields* for string orchestra and *Mad Regales* for six voices. Carter's strongest advocate, Daniel Barenboim, contributed both as conductor of the *Flute Concerto* at a concert in Jerusalem, and as solo pianist in *Interventions* with the Boston Symphony under James Levine, in Boston and New York. In London, *Wind Rose* was heard with the BBC Symphony Orchestra under Oliver Knussen.

The *Silk Road Project*, inspiring fusion between ancient Eastern and modern Western musical traditions (see AR 2001, p. 507), continued to exert a creative influence in 2008, particularly on Chinese-American musicians. Tan Dun had a busy year. His *Piano Concerto* was heard with the New York Philharmonic under Leonard Slatkin, while his opera, *The First Emperor*, a pageant of ancient China, was produced at the Metropolitan Opera. Tan Dun's music was also to be heard during the Beijing Olympic Games at all the award ceremonies and competition venues, featuring a symbolic meld of the old (ancient bronze bells of the 5th century BC) and the new (jade stone chimes). Other *Silk Road* composers also coloured the American scene. Bright Sheng had three important performances during the year: the ballet *The Nightingale and the Rose* with the New York City Ballet, the *String Quartet No.5 (The Miraculous)*, and the *Harp Concerto, Never Far Away*, with the San Diego Symphony Orchestra under Jahja Ling. Unsuk Chin's new orchestral work *Rocana*, commissioned by the Beijing Festival, the Seoul Philharmonic, and the Bavarian State Opera, following her opera *Alice in Wonderland* in 2007, continued to pursue a multi-layered, kaleidoscopic sound world of background harmonies and unrelated tonalities. After a première in Montreal, it was played in New York by the Chicago Symphony under Kent Nagano; later in Beijing and Munich. John Harbison's *Symphony No.5*—three settings of poems on the myth of Orpheus and Eurydice—was premièred in April by the Boston Symphony under James Levine with soloists Kate Lindsey (soprano) and Nathan Gunn (baritone). A new opera, *The Bonesetter's Daughter*, by a younger American composer, Stewart Wallace, which had been commissioned by the San Francisco Opera and was first heard in September 2008, was an American opera with roots in China, using Chinese instruments to forge a new rhythmic idiom.

While Elliott Carter was being feted in Tanglewood, other important anniversaries took place in 2008. It was the centenary of the birth of Olivier Messiaen, and the 50th anniversary of the death of Vaughan Williams; both occasions were widely celebrated. Another composer whose music was perceived as belonging to the living tradition was Krzysztof Penderecki. His 75th birthday was marked with a three day festival, when performances and recordings took place of his major symphonic and chamber music works, as well as two premières of new pieces: *String Quartet No.3* with the Shanghai Quartet, and the *Horn Concerto "Winterreise"*, first heard in Bremen in May, conducted by the composer and later performed in Taipei, Tokyo, Warsaw, and San Sebastian. Penderecki also conducted a recording of his *Symphony No.7, Seven Gates of Jerusalem* with the orchestra of the Kracow Academy of Music.

Two of Penderecki's four operas were revived in 2008: *Die Teufel von Loudun* in Freiburg and *Paradise Lost* in Wroclaw. It was a strong year for new opera generally, with premières in Nuremberg of Hans Werner Henze's *Boulevard Solitude*; at Glyndebourne of Peter Eötvös's multilingual opera *Love and other demons*; in Hamburg of Aribert Reimann's chamber opera *Die Gespenster-Sonate*, following a revival in Frankfurt of his *Lear*, as well as a host of other revivals and first nights of the established repertory.

The British musical year was dominated by two premières, both in April: James MacMillan's *St John Passion* at the Barbican on 27 April and Harrison Birtwistle's *The Minotaur* at the Royal Opera House on 15 April. MacMillan's oratorio achieved what few premières ever did: a level of expressive power to which all those present—musicians, orchestra, conductor, audience alike—could respond and in which they could share. Coming so soon after MacMillan's opera, *The Sacrifice*, premièred in 2007 (see AR 2008, p. 491), the brilliant performance by the London Symphony Orchestra and Chorus under Colin Davis announced nothing less than the revitalisation of the British choral tradition, of which Davis was an understanding interpreter. (He had long been the champion of Michael Tippett's music and had directed the *Visions of Paradise* festival, also with the LSO at the Barbican, in celebration of Tippett's 90th birthday in 1995, see AR 1995, p. 476).

Birtwistle's *The Minotaur* was a summary of his operatic style, developed over 40 years. It explored, and made violently explicit, the dark, labyrinthine side of human life, in this case the fantasy world of the legend of Theseus and Ariadne. Coming so close to the première of MacMillan's *St John Passion* allowed comparison of the aesthetic differences of structure and idiom between the two. The opera was dark, obfuscated, convoluted in structure, its idiom one of tonal anarchy, its impact arcane. The oratorio was direct, unambiguous in its traditional roots, dramatic and cumulative in structure, its idiom one of a many-layered tonal order, its impact spontaneous and total. Rarely was a new work greeted, as was this one, with a standing ovation led by the Archbishop of Canterbury Rowan Williams.

Recordings of the year consisted mainly of re-issues of existing material. EMI Classics re-issued the complete output of Herbert von Karajan (1946-1984) on 160 discs; works of the Viennese classics, Haydn, Mozart, and Beethoven, accounted for 50 discs each. Several labels competed to release sets of the complete Bach cantatas, performed on period instruments, and there were versions by Nikolaus Harnoncourt and Concentus musicus Wien (Teldec Das Alte Werk); Masaaki Suzuki and Bach Collegium, Japan (Bis); John Eliot Gardiner and English Baroque Soloists (Soli Deo Gloria). They all showed that the quest for authenticity in the performance of early music was not without its risks, since the playing of stringed instruments—violins in particular—without vibrato and using gut strings could lead to an undernourished, lifeless tone quality, devoid of cantabile, which in turn led to a lack of balance between the strings and wind instruments within the orchestra.

New releases in 2008 were mainly of opera, in the form of DVDs. These included Wolfgang Fortner's *Die Bluthochzeit* (Profil), Karl Amadeus Hartmann's *Simplicius Simplicissimus* (Arthaus Musik), Ferruccio Busoni's *Doktor Faust* (Arthaus Musik), Leos Janacek's *The Excursions of Mr Broucek* (DG), Vaughan Williams's *Riders to the sea* (Warner Music Entertainment), Benjamin Britten's *Peter Grimes* (EMI Classics), and Unsuk Chin's *Alice in Wonderland* (Media Arts).

It was a lean year for British composers on disc. Songs and chamber music by Frank Bridge were released by Dutton Epoch; Alan Rawsthorne's *Practical*

Cats (Dutton Epoch) and Edmund Rubbra's *Viola Concerto* (Hyperion) were well served by excellent performances; three orchestral works by George Benjamin (Nimbus) traced his stylistic evolution over 10 years. Discs of British piano music included the traditional John Ireland (Somm New Horizons); and two collections of new works by younger players, Richard Uttley (UH Recordings) and Nicholas Ashton (Delphian). This reflected not only the well-known reluctance on the part of UK officialdom to back native talent—that much-vaunted "British reserve", which, in the case of music, allowed just under 4 per cent of the total activity to British composers—but also the effect of the economic downturn on the record market. The pattern of public support for music had been formalised in 1946 when, with the setting up of the Arts Council of Great Britain, funding was allowed to orchestras, performing bodies, and opera houses, but withheld from composers. This fundamental division marked the breaking of the composer-performer-listener cycle; thus arose the fault-line in the management of British musical culture that had persisted ever since.

Those who died in 2008 included the composers Tristram Cary, Norman Dello Joio, Maurizio Kagel, Peter Henrik Nordgren; the oboist Evelyn Rothwell; the jazz trumpeter Humphrey Lyttleton (see Obituary); and the violinist Siegmund Nissel.

Francis Routh

BOOKS OF THE YEAR

Studies of composers: *Elliott Carter: a centennial portrait in letters and documents*, ed by Felix Meyer and Anne C.Shreffler; *George Gershwin: his life and works*, by Howard Pollack; *Landscapes of the mind: the music of John McCabe*, ed by George Odam; *The life of Messiaen*, by Christopher Dingle; *Olivier Messiaen: music ,art and literature*, ed by Christopher Dingle and Nigel Simeone; *Olivier Messiaen's system of signs: notes towards understanding his music*, by Andrew Shenton; *Olivier Messiaen: Oiseaux exotiques*, by Peter Hill and Nigel Simeone; *Edmund Rubbra, Symphonist*, by Leo Black; *Peter Sculthorpe: the making of an Australian composer*, by Graham Skinner; *Letters of Ralph Vaughan Williams, 1875-1958*, ed by Hugh Cobbe; *The music of Hugh Wood*, by Edward Venn.

Aesthetics of Music: *Everything is connected: the power of music*, by Daniel Barenboim; *Thresholds: rethinking spirituality through music*, by Marcel Corbusson; *Thomas Beecham: an obsession with music*, by John Lucas; *The rest is noise: listening to the twentieth century*, by Alex Ross; *Music at the limits*, by Edward W. Said; *Chasing a myth and a legend (Das land ohne Musik, by Oscar Schmitz 1914)*, by Jürgen Schaarwächter.

BALLET AND DANCE

IF there was one image that conjured up dance for the British public in 2008 it had to be the broadcaster, John Sergeant, blundering his way through the television series, *Strictly Come Dancing*. The critics questioned his skills on the dance floor, but the public revelled in the entertainment he provided. Ballroom dancing has been observed to acquire popularity at times of national crisis: little wonder that *Strictly Come Dancing*—and its offshoots on stage—were watched by so many. Another development that took hold was the transmission of "live" performances of dance, not just to big screens in parks and piazzas, but also to selected cinemas. This reflected a growing interest in using new technology and innovative ways of looking at dance, in part with the aim of reaching audiences beyond the catchment area of specific theatres. At the same time, one of the most exciting dance discoveries in 2008 was the screening, as the centrepiece at Pordenone "Silent" Film Festival, of pioneering dance films made 100 years ago by the character dancer, pedagogue, and newly recognised film pioneer, Alexander Shiryaev (1867-1941). The dances that Shiryaev had preserved on film focused on character work of considerable virtuosity and revealed the style of performance presented by the Imperial Ballet in St Petersburg in the earliest years of the 20th century.

Other ballets from the past that could be enjoyed in 2008 included *Puppenfee* (dating from 1888) presented by the Vienna Ballet, and Marius Petipa's 1896 character ballet, *The Cavalry Halt*, staged in London for the first time by St Petersburg's Mikhailovsky Theatre. This charming 19th century ballet contrasted with the Mikhailovsky's spectacular new *Spartacus*, which had a cast of 200 and an alleged price tag of £1.8 million. The dramatic epic *Spartacus* also contrasted with a *Giselle* apparently inspired by surviving evidence of 1840s productions. *Giselle* on those terms was not successful. The dyes and fabrics of the costumes were too modern and elements of the set in Act II jumped up and down like elevators. In another celebration of the past, Rome Opera Ballet presented a quadruple bill of ballets designed by Giorgio de Chirico. The contribution from reconstructors Millicent Hodson and Kenneth Archer gave convincing impressions of the Ballets Suédois creation, *La Jarra*, and the Ballets Russes' *Le Bal*. Both revealed how de Chirico could enhance a ballet. However, in the curious productions of *Apollon Musagète* and *Bacchus et Ariadne* the elaborate designs fought with mediocre and fussy choreography.

The centenary of master choreographer Antony Tudor passed remarkably quietly, although American Ballet Theatre dedicated their October 2008 season to him and showed a range of his ballets. The choreographer who really was saluted in 2008 was Jerome Robbins, whose ballets were presented world-wide. Robbins was also the subject of an excellent exhibition at New York Public Library, while Roland Petit was honoured with a magnificent display at the Paris Opéra.

Two traditionally great companies seemed to be less impressive than audiences expected on visits to the UK in 2008. The Kirov—or Mariinsky Ballet as it preferred to be called—was large enough to send out a number of parallel tours. The group that appeared in Manchester and Birmingham was competent in *Don Quixote* but audiences expected more, given the high ticket prices. New York saw a Mariinsky company led by stars at City Center in April, although the divertissements from ballets including *Raymonda* and *Paquita* looked a little squashed on that stage. In London, too, the company appeared at a smaller theatre than usual (Sadler's Wells) where they presented two mixed bills. Their performance of George Balanchine's *Apollo* was sabotaged by the music. Under Valery Gergiev the quality of the music was superb but played far too slowly for dance; significantly the conductor never looked at the stage. The cast, led by Igor Zelensky as the young god, had potential but, without the elements working together, the overall performance was dead.

It was fascinating to see New York City Ballet dance in London and Paris during visits less than six months apart. The lacklustre company that danced at the London Coliseum in March was energised and transformed when they performed at the Bastille in September. In both cities the Robbins programmes, including *The Four Seasons*, *Moves*, and *The Concert*, fared far better than the all-Balanchine evenings. In London programmes of more recently created work enabled Damian Woetzel, a major dancer whose career was virtually unseen in London, to be featured. He retired from performance two months later.

In dance, as elsewhere, China was celebrated. In appalling taste, but enormous fun, was the gymnastic *Swan Lake*, which combined just enough elements of Tchaikovsky's ballet with a round-the-world spectacular. No one who saw it would forget prize-winning gymnast Wu Zhengdan dancing en pointe on the head of her husband, Wei Baohua. Other companies visiting London included Mark Morris with his unemotional, happy ending, *Romeo and Juliet*. This, the choreographer alleged, was what Serge Prokofiev had really intended. By contrast, Stuttgart Ballet returned to London, after a long absence, with John Cranko's tragic *Romeo and Juliet*. Marcia Haydée appeared as Juliet's somewhat mature mother, reviving memories of her golden performances as the heroine in the 1970s. Memorable this time was the charismatic Romeo of Friedemann Vogel, who happily returned to the UK later in the year to dance with English National Ballet. As Des Grieux in *Manon*, Vogel brought the pure line, the virtuosity, and the drama which the role required. He danced with a fearless Daria Klimentová, in one of six satisfying casts that the company presented. Vogel was one of three significant male guest artists with English National Ballet, Guillaume Côté and Zdenek Konvalina also giving memorable performances.

Manon and Kenneth MacMillan's *The Sleeping Beauty* were well danced by English National Ballet, which had a busy year with new productions. *Strictly Gershwin*, Derek Deane's new Royal Albert Hall extravaganza including stagings of *Rhapsody in Blue* and *An American in Paris*, was acclaimed by a widely-based audience. The production was a mixture of ballet, ballroom (with Darren Bennett and Lilia Kopylova) and tap. However Deane's choreography was not memorable and it was easy to be distracted by the inappropriate and mediocre projections above the arena. In a more traditional mixed bill Wayne Eagling presented *Resolution*, which he developed from a earlier trio, to music by

Gustav Mahler, that he had created in response to the courage of boys suffering from Duchenne Muscular Dystrophy.

A trio of contrasting new works were presented by The Royal Ballet in 2008. In Wayne McGregor's *Infra*, grey dancers revealed the loneliness of the figure in the crowd, as they danced beneath Julian Opie's faceless, white virtual figures walking along a travelator. Christopher Wheeldon's *Electric Counterpoint* featured four of The Royal Ballet's most interesting dancers, moving against multiple images of themselves. The third creation was far less dependant on technology and more on emotion. *Rushes—Fragments of a Lost Story?* was Kim Brandstrup's first creation for Royal Opera House main stage. Inspired by Dostoevsky's *The Idiot*, it presented a montage of images to an arrangement of studies for a film score by Prokofiev.

Elsewhere one could hardly complain about the variety of the productions, although a number of companies presented works below their usual standards. Rambert had a less than exciting year but notably presented Siobhan Davies's reworking of her 26-year old witty *Carnival of Animals*. It was remarkable how the choreographer had altered virtually all of the choreography (except her brilliant rendition of *The Swan*) and yet retained the heart of the charming work. DV8 presented *To Be Straight with You*, with its multi-ethnic cast drawing on 85 verbatim interviews to explore sexuality, religion, and intolerance. Inevitably episodic, it left its audience with startling images, not least that of Ankur Bahl as a teenaged Muslim from Hull speed skipping with a rope while describing how his father had knifed him when he came out as homosexual.

Matthew Bourne's *Dorian Gray* became the biggest ticket-selling dance production in the history of the Edinburgh Festival. Oscar Wilde's story had been updated to become a cautionary tale for the 21st century. Among other productions, Peter Schaufuss's trio of *Divas* in three acts was redeemed by Irina Kolesnikova's embodiment of Judy Garland. *In-i*, a reflection on love by Akram Khan and Juliette Binoche, was derivative of other productions and self-indulgent. Christopher Wheeldon's company, Metamorphose, gelled better on its second outing and its repertoire was more varied than in 2007. *Commedia*, set to Igor Stravinsky's suite from *Pulcinella*, was an interesting response to the score, and only the established works, Frederick Ashton's *Monotones* and Jerome Robbins's *Other Dances*, were disappointing in performance. However *Other Dances* had received a wonderful performance earlier in the year from Alina Cojocaru and Johan Kobborg, making it more regrettable that by the time this critic saw The Royal Ballet's *Dances at a Gathering*, Cojocaru had been sidelined by injury. Jonathan Lunn's carefully constructed *Reading Room* acquired an elegiac quality, as part of its text had been written by his close friend, Anthony Minghella, who died shortly before the première of the extended work (see Obituary). Finally, Richard Alston celebrated his 60th birthday and 40 years of choreography with a celebration of male dancing, *The Men in My Life*, which consisted of extracts from nine of his major creations performed by glorious dancers.

Jane Pritchard

THEATRE

It may seem odd to think of an entire theatre year across two bustling cultural centres as defined by a pair of very distinct addresses, but so it was in New York and London during 2008. By year's end, the London playhouse of choice had without a doubt announced itself as the Old Vic, the venerable jewel-box that had fallen on critical hard times since Kevin Spacey, the two-time US Academy Award winner, took the reins in 2004. During the first season or two it seemed as if Spacey could not do anything right, but four years later his luck had turned. The New York theatre-trained actor had himself to thank for that, with an Old Vic revival in the winter of 2008 of the 1988 David Mamet play, *Speed-the-Plow*, in which Spacey joined forces with another Hollywood A-lister, Jeff Goldblum, to play two movie world hustlers at the end of their moral tether.

At first, the rapport between the two men looked like a great comic double-act ramped up a notch or two (or 10), as the pair played off one another for much of the play's first scene with extraordinary abandon. But once Mamet introduced the play's third character, a secretary temp called Karen (played in the Broadway premiere by Madonna), the equation shifted significantly, as all three characters found themselves fighting for survival to varying degrees. "Then how bad can life be!", said Spacey's increasingly desperate character, Charlie Fox, in the play's closing line. The implicit answer: pretty bad, in a world in which male bonding may be all that was left to us and where even those loyalties hang by an increasingly frayed thread. The two US guys centre-stage had a British woman—Olivier Award-winner Laura Michelle Kelly, late of the West End premiere of the stage musical version of *Mary Poppins*—to complete a trio in which Kelly was in every sense an outsider, which in this play amounted to no bad thing. As directed by Matthew Warchus, an Englishman whose wife, performer Lauren Ward, was from the USA, the rhythms of Mamet's play emerged at breathless speed and to often breathtaking effect. The paradoxical effect of this play, that delivered a knockout punch in the direction of film, was to want this cast preserved forever on celluloid; not a chance. An (inferior) Broadway revival of the same play later in the year delivered only a fraction of the verbal and emotional fireworks on view for too brief a time in London. (The New York version, to its credit, did feature an unusually credible Karen from TV actress Elisabeth Moss, one of the rising stars of the *Mad Men* series.)

Back at the Vic, it was once again over to Warchus for an end-of-year treat via the first major London revival of Alan Ayckbourn's glorious 1974 triptych, *The Norman Conquests*, three separate but interrelated plays about the sexual and moral needs, wants, and peccadilloes of six characters. The six come together in the family home of the unmarried Annie (a superlative performance from TV comedienne Jessica Stevenson Hynes), who lusts after local veterinarian, Tom (Ben Miles), even as she, and seemingly everyone else, also carries a torch for the very married Norman, played by Stephen Mangan with the puppyish, shaggy-haired appeal to suit a character who at several moments is compared to a sheepdog. For this production, the proscenium-arched Vic was transformed into an in-the-round playing space that allowed audiences seeing all three plays to get a trio of perspectives on characters whose own lives kept being transformed in our perspective on them. Faultlessly acted by its cast of six—all of them well-known in the theatre and from television but none of them huge stars—the production was quickly scooped up for a New York run, its London ensemble intact, to open in April, 2009. This was good news for a play at once blissfully funny and woundingly painful that famously flopped in Manhattan the first time around, as too many of the prolific Ayckbourn's works have tended to do when they cross the pond.

Many in New York were wondering how the Lincoln Center Theatre's glorious revival of the classic musical *South Pacific* might ever travel in the other direction, to London, so perfect was the director Bartlett Sher's vision of the 1949 Richard Rodgers-Oscar Hammerstein classic. It was realised in a long—a full three-hours—and utterly riveting performance that won seven Tony Awards and made an instant Broadway star out of the Brazilian baritone Paulo Szot in his New York theatre debut. His leading lady, fast-rising Broadway star Kelli O'Hara, would have won her own Tony to go with Szot's had O'Hara not had the misfortune to find herself nominated against a bona fide Broadway diva in Patti LuPone, who won the best actress in a musical Tony for her cyclonic performance as Mama Rose in the enduring musical favourite, *Gypsy*. These two revivals together reminded 21st century observers of a Broadway golden age whose inability to be matched by new work was painfully evident in most of the New York theatre season's original musicals, notwithstanding the raw power and sense of occasion of a "trippy", unclassifiable piece called *Passing Strange*. A transfer uptown from the Public Theatre down in Manhattan's East Village, the narrative picaresque represented a genuine commercial risk and did not make a dime. But it was filmed by the director Spike Lee, an act of artistic empathy that should introduce movie-goers to the work's singularly named leading man, Stew, a physically squat, cease-lessly droll beat poet for a new generation of hipsters. *Passing Strange* was easily the coolest show of the year. The most user-friendly, of the new Broadway musicals at least, was the sweet if innocuous *In the Heights*, a paean by creator and leading actor Lin-Manuel Miranda to that swathe of uptown Manhattan—Washington Heights—that he called home. If there was one success story that sang out across the Broadway season, it was the 28-year old Miranda's sudden and genuine claim to fame.

But Lincoln Center remained the address most worth noting, even if one of the subscription-theatre offerings—a rather over-praised Broadway premiere of *Dividing the Estate* by the nonagenarian author Horton Foote—played away from home base at the Booth Theatre in midtown. (That play gathered an added cachet when its esteemed, Oscar-winning playwright died the following March 2009.) Way too little, by contrast, was made of young writer Noah Haidle's compassionate and searching *Saturn Returns*, a layered, infinitely touching examination of a Michigan widower as seen at three points in his life, aged 28, 58, and 88. That eldest version of the same self allowed Broadway veteran John McMartin to move an audience genuinely and without sentimentality, playing someone who in a sense could be said to have outlived his own life. In a theatre city in which audiences could often offer up their own critiques by dint of sheer restlessness, the matinee crowd among whom this critic watched *Saturn Returns* paid it the greatest compliment: a deep, abiding stillness.

At least New York still seemed to be searching for the great new play, which explained the excitement with which Tracy Letts's three-and-a-half hour *August: Osage County* was greeted when it transferred to Broadway from Chicago's remarkable Steppenwolf Theatre. That same play, most of its original Chicago and New York cast along for the ride, detonated with comparable force when it reached the Lyttelton auditorium of London's National Theatre, where director Anna D. Shapiro's Tony-winning production showed Londoners that great acting was not the province of the British alone, tempting though it was sometimes to think this. As an Oklahoma mother and her eldest daughter—played by Deanna Dunagan and Steppenwolf regular Amy Morton—tore into one another with unfettered brio they turned the arc of the play's three acts into long-festering pain. That the play folded into its epic display of familial dysfunction an implicit critique of the USA gave *August: Osage County* a political clout to rival its fiery personal pyrotechnics. Suddenly, *The Norman Conquests* had serious competition for the London year's best ensemble.

Elsewhere, it was business as usual on the London stage, which is to say lots of play revivals, some pretty dumb and/or superfluous musicals, and a liberal smattering of stars. An eclectic cast headed by Michael Gambon, his *Harry Potter* co-star David Bradley, and a stage neophyte in the co-star of the *Little Britain* comedy series on the BBC, David Walliams, lent their not always fully attuned talents to a revival of the 1975 play *No Man's Land* by Harold Pinter. It was imported to the West End from Dublin and was still running when its eminent, Nobel laureate author died just before Christmas (see Obituary). That production's director, Rupert Goold, was ubiquitous, as was his wont, throughout the year, segueing from *No Man's Land* to yet another West End production of the perennial musical favourite *Oliver!*. However, the height of his year in many quarters was a dazzling reclamation of an Italian classic, *Six Characters In Search of An Author*, that made of Luigi Pirandello's existential roundelay an up-to-the-moment, alternately funny and searing enquiry into the hot topic of assisted suicide. The production's superb leading man, Scotsman Ian McDiarmid, suffered a mild heart attack on the London opening night (the show was first seen at the Chichester Festival Theatre south of London), only to be back on stage within a week or so: the show must go on writ large.

Wyndham's Theatre on Charing Cross Road hosted the long-overdue return to the West End of onetime wunderkind Kenneth Branagh, who plumbed newly soulful depths in a revival of the Anton Chekhov play *Ivanov* from a director, Michael Grandage who, even more than Goold, scarcely seemed to pause for breath during the year. True to the Grandage norm, though, this star vehicle was in fact an opportunity for a diverse array of talents to tackle an early Chekhov play that had been increasingly performed of late. This production benefited from a spiky, astringent new version of the Chekhov original from Britain's own Tom Stoppard and an ace supporting cast headed by Malcolm Sinclair, Kevin McNally, and the instantly charismatic Tom Hiddleston. The play was followed into Wyndham's by another Grandage venture, *Twelfth Night*, in which the redoubtable Derek Jacobi hammed it up amiably as Malvolio, while the beautiful Indira Varma's long-necked Olivia struck glamour puss poses, as if one of Shakespeare's most tantalising women had been reinvented as a *Vogue* model. The beachside set was courtesy of Christopher Oram, Grandage's real-life partner, the two cutting a path through the British theatre that many assumed would lead Grandage to running the National Theatre in due course.

While musical fare ranged from quick flops—like the Holocaust-themed *Imagine This* and an utterly ill-conceived stage musical take on *Gone With the Wind*—to the longer-lasting, but comparably ill-fated, Michel Legrand-scored *Marguerite*, the show *Zorro the Musical* garnered better reviews than it deserved, presumably for the mere fact of being fun (well, for some of the time). Trevor Nunn, Britain's most successful director of musicals ever, bounced back from *Gone With the Wind* with, somewhat surprisingly, his first-ever foray into the repertoire of the leading US composer-lyricist, Stephen Sondheim. Staging the elegant, thematically and visually capacious *A Little Night Music* within the intimate confines of south London's Menier Chocolate Factory might have looked like squaring one theatrical circle too many, but Sondheim always benefited from a close attention to detail and textual acumen, both of which Nunn's production offered in abundance. It also had a rare Desiree Armfeldt, the touring actress at the musical's aching heart, from Hannah Waddingham who actually sang a role written for a non-singer in Glynis Johns. Pondering "Isn't it rich?" in the opening of the most popular song Sondheim ever wrote, Waddingham made audiences feel the riches that come with a beloved show reconceived with care. Later on, the same song asked, "Isn't it bliss?". Those in attendance at Nunn's *Little Night Music* could only answer, "Yes".

Matt Wolf

CINEMA

THERE is never a good time, so producers say, to raise finance for films. But towards the end of 2008 it became doubly difficult. Even Oscar winners, usually given pride of place, found it tricky, causing some to feel that the world's premier film awards were not as powerful as they once were. Yet, earlier in the year and even at the year's end, huge fortunes were being made by those—admittedly few—movies that hit the box-office jackpot worldwide.

The Dark Knight, for instance, directed by Christopher Nolan, a film-maker who had previously orchestrated small budget projects, proved that Batman the Caped Crusader was still an attraction everywhere in the world. The film had made just over US$1 billion by early 2009, vying with *Titanic*, *The Lord of the Rings: The Return of the King*, and *Pirates of the Caribbean: Dead Man's Chest* as one of the most successful ever in financial terms.

Hollywood could clearly still throw the dice and win. But so could Britain, whose *Slumdog Millionaire* and Abba tribute, *Mama Mia*, carried all before them as "feelgood" movies appropriate for a "feelbad" time. Danny Boyle's *Slumdog* went on to win the Oscar for best picture, and both the Golden Globe and the British Academy's premier prizes for good measure. No one could possibly say that the film was much more than an entertaining fantasy made in India, which taught Bollywood a few lessons in expert direction. But it was right for the time and if you can do that—despite the fact that films are made two years before they actually hit the cinemas—anything can happen. As for *Mama Mia*, it made more money in the UK than any film ever, despite almost universal critical bashing.

Even so, the end of 2008 and the beginning of 2009 saw Hollywood, and Bollywood (India's highly profitable equivalent), being more than usually careful about the films they financed. It seemed ever more likely that the worldwide recession and credit crunch would affect the cinema as much as any other entertainment, even though it has long been established that in bad times people tend to keep on going to the cinema as the least expensive form of entertainment available. Even if they stopped, they would continue to rent or buy DVDs of the films they had missed in the theatres.

The problem for those who wanted to see something other than obviously commercial fare seemed to be that specialist cinemas, playing what were generally termed "art movies" (translation: foreign films with sub-titles or dubbed versions), were suffering more than the multiplexes. This meant that non-English-speaking films had a harder task than ever to break down barriers, except in their own countries, and distributors were wary of buying anything but those they hoped to be the most cast-iron of successes. With these films, the DVD rights were increasingly important because a number of good movies, which had very brief exposure in the cinemas, could still make a decent profit on home screens.

There were, during 2008, some excellent examples of so-called art house cinema, notably the Cannes winner, *The Class* (*Entre les murs*), in which Laurent Cantet filmed a teacher trying to get through to his racially diverse pupils in an ordinary French high school, and frequently failing. This was not a documentary, but it felt like one. So did the Israeli animated film, *Waltz with Bashir*, by Ari Folman, in which a former soldier (the director himself) recalled his true-to-life experiences during the Lebanese war, where he watched as Lebanese Christian militia, allied to Israel, slaughtered Palestinians in the 1982 massacre at the Sabra and Shatila refugee camps.

Both these films were well rewarded at the box-office as well as receiving critical plaudits. The same was true of Germany's *The Baader-Meinhof Gang*, which retold the story of the terrorists who made headlines in West Germany and around the world during the 1970s. There was also an extraordinary French-Algerian film, called *Cous Cous* in some territories and *The Mullet and the Grain* in others, in which a working class Algerian, a former docker, tried to keep himself and his family from poverty as the owner of a café. The UK produced *Hunger*, a remarkable film about Bobby Sands, the IRA member whose hunger strike protest ended in his death in a Northern Ireland jail in 1981. While Europe clearly could not boast the master film-makers of the post-War period—such as Bergman, Buñuel, Fellini, Fassbinder, and Tarkovsky—it could still produce highly individual films, and 2008 showed us a whole clutch of them. British director Mike Leigh, for instance, made *Happy-Go-Lucky*, a comedy starring Sally Hawkins as a learner driver and Eddie Marsan as her instructor, which won awards in the USA as well as in the UK.

It was a good sign that, almost everywhere, national films did better in their own countries compared with previous years. But it was still the films from Hollywood and Bollywood (profitable in Africa and the Arab world as well as in India and anywhere where the Indian diaspora was located) that received the vast majority of cinema audiences. Those who bemoaned this fact should be aware that, in the cinema, it was ever thus. But then, how many people chose to listen to Beethoven and Mozart rather than rock and rap, and how many read Shakespeare when they could read thrillers, romances, and *Harry Potter* books instead? The problem for any cinema critic was to persuade his or her readers that the cinema had produced some of the greatest artists of the 20th century, on a par with the greatest writers, painters, and playwrights. This notion was still surprising for some, and probably for a large proportion of those who went regularly to the cinema primarily for entertainment.

Critics themselves hardly had a good year. In the USA many were sacked in favour of syndicated columns, and everywhere bloggers or Internet diarists produced reviews—sometimes good but usually feeble—which competed with those of more orthodox film writers. Most bloggers, of course, were not paid for what they did.

During 2008, four great men of the cinema died. The best known of them was Paul Newman, one of Hollywood's most admired and popular stars, whose most famous film was *Butch Cassidy and the Sundance Kid* (see Obituary). He received 10 Academy nominations but only won once, for *The Color of Money* in 1987, though he was even better as a pool shark in *The Hustler*, made in 1961. A decent man, he raised US$250 million for charity with his own brand of salad dressing called Newman's Own. Another casualty of the year was director Xie Jin, one of the great survivors of Chinese cinema who was a Communist Party member and made the original non-musical version of *The Red Detachment of Women*, a famous propaganda piece, but also *Two Stage Sisters*, one of the first genuinely great Chinese films. His reputation in the West was as a women's director in the Cukor mould, but in China he was regarded as a Party member who frequently got on the wrong side of his political masters.

Youssef Chahine, one of the best-known and most original of Arab directors, also died. He was born in the Egyptian city of Alexandria and came of age during the golden age of the Egyptian cinema, when the "Hollywood of the Nile" lagged only behind Hollywood and Bollywood in the number of films produced. *Cairo Station*, in which he also acted as an impoverished cripple, was his most famous film, and he was an outspoken critic of government corruption and religious fundamentalism. The other well-known and highly respected director who died during 2008 was Japan's Kon Ichikawa. He made his 84th film in 2006 at the age of 91, but his most famous were *Alone in the Pacific*, the story of a young Japanese yachtsman trying to sail single-handed to San Francisco, and *The Burmese Harp*, about a World War II soldier holed up in Burma for years after the war had ended and, when finally discovered, refusing to leave the jungle.

Others who died during the year included British director Anthony Minghella, Oscar winner for *The English Patient* (see Obituary); Sydney Pollack, distinguished US actor-director (see Obituary); Eva Dahlbeck, Swedish star of Bergman's classic *Smiles of a Summer Night*; Hazel Court, British actress who worked for Hammer Films and director Roger Corman; Mel Ferrer, Hollywood leading man; Alain Robbe-Grillet, radical French writer and director (see Obituary); Gerard Damiano, director of *Deep Throat*, the most famous of pornographic films; Gopi, star of south Indian cinema; Van Johnson, reliable Hollywood leading man; Paul Scofield, actor who played Sir Thomas More in *A Man For All Seasons* (see Obituary); Harold Pinter, who wrote many screenplays as well as plays (see Obituary); Heath Ledger, Australian actor who played in *Brokeback Mountain* and *The Dark Knight*; Nina Foch, female star of *An American in Paris*; and Cyd Charisse, whom Fred Astaire accounted the best dancer among his many partners.

Derek Malcolm

TELEVISION AND RADIO

A NUMBER of media commentators came to the same surprising verdict about 2008: it was "the year of the BBC"—despite financial pressures, fines, scandals, embarrassments and profuse apologies.

The worst of the scandals occurred in October and involved the *Russell Brand Show* on Radio 2. The show's presenter, Russell Brand, and his guest, broadcaster Jonathan Ross, left lewd messages on the answer machine of veteran comic actor Andrew Sachs about his granddaughter, Georgina Baillie. The recorded calls were later broadcast on the late-night show. Only two people complained initially but the BBC was later inundated by thousands of complaints—eventually more than 42,000—after the story received widespread publicity in the *Mail on Sunday* and the *Daily Mail*. After a delay, for which the BBC was criticised, Mark Thompson, the BBC director-general, suspended Brand and Ross for "a gross lapse of taste". Brand quickly resigned and Ross, reputed to earn £6 million a year from the BBC, was banned from appearing on all BBC programmes for three months, a suspension that cost him around £1.5 million. Later Thompson accepted the resignation of Lesley Douglas, controller of Radio 2 and Radio 6, who had worked for the BBC for 23 years.

The affair divided the audience along age lines. Young listeners mounted a petition of support with thousands of signatures while older members of the public insisted that Ross should have been sacked. The issue led to questions about BBC management and, in particular, the wisdom of paying anyone, particularly Ross, £18 million of the public's money for his three-year contract. On the salary issue Ross had not helped matters by joking at a comedy awards ceremony that he was worth the pay of 1,000 journalists.

Prior to the Brand-Ross affair, there had been another embarrassment when, in July, Ofcom, the communications regulator, had fined the BBC a record £400,000 for misleading viewers in 2006 and 2007 over competitions in programmes such as *Children In Need*, *Comic Relief*, and *Sports Relief* (see AR 2008, p. 502). The BBC Trust, the body that replaced the board of governors, said that although no-one had profited from the deceptions, there would be "an unprecedented action plan" of staff training to make sure that such things did not happen again.

Further difficulties arose from one of BBC 1's most popular programmes, *Strictly Come Dancing*. First former political journalist John Sergeant continued to progress through the elimination rounds of the programme despite being one of the worst dancers that the series had even seen. Viewers voted for him in their hundreds of thousands, much to the annoyance of the judges, until Sergeant himself, apparently, decided that the joke had gone far enough and removed himself from the competition, thereby annoying viewers who had supported him. Another apology came from the BBC when three competitors had to be included in the final of *Strictly* instead of two because of a voting fiasco.

Nevertheless, 2008 could be called "the year of the BBC" because the £3.5 billion per year guaranteed income from the licence fee largely insulated the Corporation and its programme budgets from the effects of the deepening recession. The BBC also saw off the cruder attempts to "top-slice" its licence fee (taking part of its income and giving it to commercial broadcasters). As an alternative, the BBC offered unprecedented levels of co-operation and partnership with former rivals in order to save them money.

At the same time the BBC had a good year in news with its business editor Robert Peston following his Northern Rock exclusives of 2007 with a string of stories about the crisis in the British banking sector and the £49 billion government bailout of the merged HBOS-Lloyd's TSB (see p. 37).

The relative financial comfort of the BBC and satellite broadcaster BSkyB, whose main income came from subscription, contrasted starkly with broadcasters who were dependent on advertising such as ITV, Channel 4, and Five. They all suffered as advertising revenues plummeted. ITV's share price fell to new record lows and reached 38p by the end of the year. In August the broadcaster had reported a loss of £1.5 billion for the first half of 2008 partly because of a massive write-off on the value of its broadcasting licences. ITV also announced the loss of more than 1,000 jobs, 430 of them as a result of a "restructuring" of its local and regional news network with a concentration on a smaller number of regional centres.

In a dramatic move Michael Grade, the ITV executive chairman, warned an audience of MPs and opinion formers in October that ITV might have to give its broadcasting licence back unless the cost of its public service broadcasting (PSB) obligations was brought more in line with potential earnings. Unless something was done ITV could simply decide to broadcast a wholly commercial schedule via satellite. At the same time Grade suggested that another body could take over responsibility for producing regional television news, perhaps with public funding, and ITV would make the broadcast slots available without charge. Grade estimated that provision of regional news was now creating an annual deficit for ITV of more than £80 million, and was unsustainable in the long run. "The collapse of the old system and in particular its key ability to facilitate the cross-subsidy of PSB programmes has happened far faster than most of us expected," Grade argued.

The Grade speech was a symptom of a much broader debate between broadcasters, the government, and regulators about how to devise new structures to protect commercially funded public service broadcasting when the move to digital was complete by 2012. The main object of policy was to find a way of preserving "plurality" of public service provision through commercial competition for the BBC. This search was made much more pressing by the deepening economic recession.

The greatest concern was for the future of Channel 4, which estimated that it would face a shortfall of £150 million per year by 2012, thereby putting at risk some of the channel's most distinctive programmes such as *Channel 4 News* and the weekly one-hour documentary series *Despatches*. A number of new structures and funding methods were explored without any resolution by the end of the year. A merger between Channel 4 and the much more commercial Five had been suggested, although Channel 4 chief executive Andy Duncan opposed the idea, warning that "oil and water" did not mix. Another idea was for BBC Worldwide (the commercial arm of the BBC) and Channel 4 to explore co-operation and possible joint ventures, an initiative favoured—at least in terms of its exploration—by Secretary of State for Culture, Media and Sport Andy Burnham and Minister of Communications, Technology and Broadcasting, Baron Carter of Barnes.

Ofcom's second public service broadcasting review also addressed the issue of how to fund commercial local and regional television news in future. Ofcom believed that £30-50 million per year would be needed to fund a contract that would be put out to tender. The regulator suggested that the money could come from direct government subsidy, charging ITV for the spectrum it used for its commercial digital channels ITV2, ITV3, and ITV4 or, most likely, from the BBC's "digital dividend". This was the estimated £130 million per year that would become available from 2011. The money was part of the licence fee but had been set aside to pay for the transition from analogue to digital and had not been included in the BBC's programme budgets. Others also wanted to get their hands on the money, including Lord Carter, who wanted universal access to broadband for all within the UK.

During the year technology continued to change the way the audience viewed television. Use of the BBC iPlayer, which allowed the free downloading to computers of programmes which had been broadcast in the previous seven days, reached new heights. In the week from Christmas to New Year there were 8 million downloads of programmes such as *Wallace and Gromit: A Matter of Loaf and Death* and *Dr Who: The Next Doctor*. In 2008 as a whole there were no fewer than 271 million downloads.

A bid to create a commercial download service, known as Kangaroo, which would have linked the BBC, ITV and Channel 4, was blocked by competition authorities on the grounds that it would have too much power in the fledgling video-on-demand market. Each broadcaster was thus required to go its separate way in this field. In November the BBC began broadcasting all its channels live on the Internet, a good use of technology, but raising questions about how the licence fee would be collected and enforced in future.

But BBC management suffered a setback at the hands of the BBC Trust when plans for a new level of local television, distributed by broadband, were blocked under considerable pressure from local newspaper publishers and commercial radio. The Trust decided that improving the normal linear local and regional television service would be a better use of scarce resources.

Amidst all the gloom and uncertainty Peter Fincham, ITV's director of television and former controller of BBC 1, delivered an optimistic MacTaggart lecture on the future of television at the Edinburgh Television Festival. Television was a great medium with a great future, Fincham argued, as long as it remembered it was a popular mass medium. Even now, *Coronation Street* could still attract audiences of 8 to 9 million, he noted, and went on to insist that popular channels such as BBC 1 and ITV 1 had to be defended. "We can't resist fragmentation, or time-shifted viewing or multiple platforms. But unless we fight hard to assert the importance of mass audiences, we may find that broadcasting, as we know it, simply splits into a thousand pieces," said Fincham.

In the USA network television was facing a different form of crisis, one that went beyond recessionary pressures. Despite high viewing figures for the Beijing Olympics and the most dramatic presidential election campaign in a generation, the primetime audience share of the big four US broadcasting networks—ABC, CBS, NBC and Fox—fell during the year by 6 per cent to 32.7 per cent. By contrast, advertising-supported cable channels increased their share of viewing to 59.2 per cent. For the seventh year running Fox News was the leader in cable news ratings but CNN claimed a "transformational" performance on 4 November when it became the first cable channel to beat all the networks in terms of audience share on presidential election night.

A further period of uncertainty could be under way in the USA following the announcement that the country would switch off its analogue transmitters on 17 February 2009, despite evidence that millions of viewers were still unprepared for the change.

There were controversial changes in broadcasting in France as President Nicolas Sarkozy tried to transform public television by banning prime time advertising on state channels to create a public television service "to rival the quality of the BBC". There were strikes by French broadcasters who claimed that the aim of the changes was to channel money from state to private channels, even though €450 million a year compensation had been promised. Critics noted that Sarkozy also wanted the presidency to have the right to nominate the boss of France Télévisions (see pp. 52, 54).

Public broadcasters across the EU expressed concern when the European Commission in November issued a draft communication on a revision of public service broadcasting rules. The proposed new rules would, it was feared, require member states to control more strictly "commercial" activities by public broadcasters. The European Broadcasting Union, the grouping of public broadcasters, claimed that the Commission was giving too much power to the market "which makes little sense when you see the failures of the markets in the past few weeks".

In the Middle East, and much further afield, the satellite channel Al-Jazeera came into its own with its coverage of one of the biggest news stories of the year, the Israeli assault on Gaza in December. Unlike the Western media which was prevented by the Israeli government from entering Gaza, the Arabic channel and its English version had four reporters on the spot sending often gruesome coverage around the world. This explicit illustration of the effect of Israeli ordnance upon Palestinian civilians meant that media-savvy Israel was seen by many to have "lost the media war" which surrounded its military operation.

Radio had a difficult year and its advertising revenues were hit by the recession, along with the rest of the media, but in the UK at least new players brought with them the prospect of additional investment. The *Times of India* newspaper group paid £53 million for Virgin Radio and relaunched the station as Absolute Radio. In April Global Radio, a venture-capital backed group which in 2007 had bought Chryalis Radio, spent £375 million on GCap, owners of Capital Radio in London. Global was by far the biggest player in a UK commercial radio sector which was now largely in private hands. During the year commercial radio pulled back some of its listening share from the BBC and was currently listened to regularly by around 62 per cent of the population.

In December the government for the first time outlined a possible migration path to the switch-off of analogue radio broadcasts as early as 2017. A Digital Radio Working Group set three prior criteria: 50 per cent digital radio ownership, digital multiples coverage comparable to FM, and local digital multiplexes reaching 90 per cent of the population, including all major roads.

It was radio though that provided a telling sign of the times. Channel 4 had been pushing ahead with ambitious plans to launch digital radio stations to compete with the BBC, in particular a commercial rival for Radio 4. Bob Shennan, the former head of BBC Radio 5 Live, was hired to run the business. In October, before any of the stations had come on air, Channel 4 announced that the project had been shelved. In words that could have been uttered by many British broadcasters, Channel 4 chief executive Andy Duncan said: "Frustratingly our plans have been overtaken by a drastic recent downturn in our revenues and we will have to forgo this future profit stream."

Raymond Snoddy

VISUAL ARTS

THE year began with Chinese contemporary art and Russian early 20th-century paintings selling very well to national buyers. The fledgling Indian art market was booming, with local art investment funds driving prices up. But a downturn was already beginning to make itself felt in the vital New York market, with buyers hesitating over lesser known artists, and galleries talking of mergers.

In January, the Museum of Danish Cartoon Art, part of the Royal Library in Copenhagen, agreed to house cartoons of the Prophet Mohammed that had been published in a Danish newspaper in 2005 and had provoked a wave of global Islamic protest in which more than 50 people were killed (see AR 2007, pp. 54-55).

In February, directors of the major UK museums protested at the change in the tax regime for non-domiciled foreign residents, due to come into force on 5 April, as they feared that it would reduce donations and loans to museums. The 12 March budget softened the provisions, but did not drop them. However, the UK government demonstrated its faith in the importance of museums and contemporary art when it voted £50 million, the largest public sum since the building of the British Library, towards an extension to Tate Modern, the total cost of which was estimated to be four times as much.

The government appointed Neil MacGregor, director of the British Museum, as "chairman of world collections", a new diplomatic post to encourage links between London's main museums and the rest of the world, particularly Asia and Africa.

The British army in Iraq, supported by its commander, Major-General Barney White-Spunner, and John Curtis of the British Museum, agreed to back the Iraq antiquities board in its efforts to safeguard archaeological sites and museums. In November the army would offer help in turning a former palace of Saddam Hussein in Basra into a museum to exhibit works from Baghdad's National Museum. An international mission led by the British Museum in June found no signs of recent looting of archaeological sites in southern Iraq. On 25 September, the US Senate voted to ratify the 1954 Hague Convention, an international treaty aimed at reducing damage to cultural property by war. This was largely due to the widespread dismay at the looting of the National Museum in Baghdad and damage to the archaeology of Iraq which had occurred during the second Gulf War of 2003 (see AR 2003, p. 524).

In March, in protest at leaked details of secret bank accounts held in his state, Prince Hans Adam II of Liechtenstein cancelled all loans of works of art to German museums, including an entire exhibition of Biedermeier paintings due to go on display at the Neue Pinakothek in Munich (see p. 73).

The Berlin State Museum, the Hamburger Bahnhof, accepted the gift of 166 works of contemporary art by artists such as Bruce Nauman, Paul McCarthy and Martin Kippenberger from the Mercedes heir, Friedrich Christian Flick. Previously the cities of Zurich, Strasbourg and Dresden had declined to show the works because Flick's fortune was derived from his grandfather, who had supplied the Nazis with munitions during World War II and had used forced labour in his factories. Also in Berlin, a monumental, above-ground bomb shelter, dating from the war, reopened in March as a private museum to show the collection of the advertising millionaire, Christian Boros.

Early signs of a weakening art market were evident in the disappointing sales of Chinese contemporary art at Sotheby's on 17 March, but Korean galleries continued to open in New York on the back of a speculative bubble back home, and an assemblage of Chinese contemporary art called the Estella Collection—fresh from having been displayed in museums in Denmark and Israel—made record sums at Sotheby's auctions in Hong Kong.

In April, the director of the Uffizi Gallery in Florence protested at the Italian government forcing him to lend one of the stars of the museum, Titian's "Venus of Urbino", to Tokyo's Museum of Western Art. "The Uffizi is not a quarry to be mined," said Antonio Natali. In June, the new mayor of Verona cancelled an exhibition of masterpieces from the Louvre agreed by his predecessor, and for which the museum would have been paid €4 million. That same month, the Italian branch of the International Council of Museums (ICOM) published a paper criticising the practice of charging loan fees.

The authorities in Greece announced that the new Acropolis Museum in Athens would display casts of the Parthenon Marbles in the British Museum to which they laid claim. The Axum obelisk, taken from northern Ethiopia by Mussolini in 1937, was finally re-erected on its original site 60 years after the Italian government had promised to return it.

Sharjah, one of the United Arab Emirates, opened an Islamic art museum, overshadowed from November by the splendid new Museum of Islamic Art designed for the emir of Qatar in Doha by the Chinese-American architect, I.M. Pei.

A key to the Kaa'ba in Mecca, thought to date from the 12th century, was sold at Sotheby's for £9.2 million but it was subsequently revealed to have been a fake. In the summer, Francis Ronald Egerton, the 7th Duke of Sutherland, began negotiations to sell a pair of Titian paintings of Diana, goddess of hunting, to the National Galleries of Scotland (where they had been on loan since 1945) and the National Gallery in London, for the comparatively low price of £100 million. Efforts were made during the remainder of the year to raise the necessary funds, amid a widespread public debate over the sale. Defenders of the proposed acquisition emphasised the quality of the works—the painter Lucian Freud describing them as "the most beautiful pictures in the world"—whilst critics questioned the use of huge sums of public money for such a purpose.

As part of the market's recent enthusiasm for design, houses by famous architects began to be included in contemporary art auctions. Richard Neutra's Kaufmann House in Palm Springs sold for US$16.8 million in between a Richard Prince painting and a Damien Hirst butterfly canvas.

The State of Utah was lobbied by the New York-based Dia Art Foundation and others to stop exploratory drilling for oil five miles from Robert Smithson's huge "Spiral Jetty" of 1970, created in the Great Salt Lake. Enthusiasts said that this famous example of Land Art needed unspoilt landscape around it to be appreciated. The Dia Foundation raised US$1.1 million to keep developers away from another famous example of Land Art, Walter de Maria's "Lightning Field" in New Mexico.

The Californian billionaire Eli Broad opened his private museum of contemporary art in Los Angeles, a prominent example of the growing tendency in recent years for collectors to open their own museums, such as the Palazzo Grassi in Venice, the Ullens Centre in Beijing, and the Jumex Collection in Mexico City.

Leading US antiquities collector Shelby White, who was a trustee of the Metropolitan Museum, returned nine Greek and Etruscan items to Italy. Documents had traced their origin to Giacomo Medici, who had been convicted for trafficking in looted antiquities.

On 15 September, the much publicised sale at Sotheby's London of 223 "showy" works created specially for the occasion by the British artist Damien Hirst was wildly successful, the proceeds from the sale amounting to a total of £111 million. In May the *Sunday Times*'s annual "Rich List" had estimated Hirst to be worth £200 million, £70 million more than in 2007. Immediately after the sale, the credit crisis hit European and US banks and the US House of Representatives passed a US$700 billion rescue plan for the financial system (see p. 155). Within a month, the global art market began to slump. On 17 October, 45 per cent of the lots at Christie's contemporary art sale in London went unsold and the sale totalled £32 million compared with the pre-sale estimate of £57.8-£75.6 million. Other auction houses suffered similarly. Recently "hot" categories, such as Chinese and Indian contemporary, aboriginal and Islamic art slid particularly dramatically.

The British sculptor Anthony Caro, 84, finished the most important ecclesiastical commission since Rothko's 1971 chapel in Houston. The large sculptures, alluding to the Creation but without specific religious iconography, occupied the arches of the early Gothic church of Saint Jean-Baptiste in Bourbourg, northern France.

The post-Pop artist Jeff Koons was invited to show 15 large works from the collection of François Pinault in the palace of Versailles by its director, Jacques Aillagon, who had recently been director of Pinault's private museum in Venice. This provoked accusations that it was a gambit to increase the value of the pieces.

The German installation artist, Gregor Schneider, announced that he wanted to show a person dying as part of an exhibition in Haus Lange, Krefeld, and that a private clinic in Düsseldorf was prepared to help him find volunteers.

The São Paulo Bienal, since 1951 Latin America's most important international art exhibition, responded to a shortage of financing by leaving a whole floor of its building empty of art and simply calling it "The Void".

The Metropolitan Museum announced in September that an internal candidate, Thomas Campbell, 46, a British expert in tapestries, would succeed Philippe de Montebello, who had served as director of the museum for 31 years. At the Guggenheim Museum in New York, its new director, Richard Armstrong, said that it would cease trying to found satellite museums around the world and would concentrate on its role in Manhattan.

The best attended exhibition of the year was the display in the Nara Museum, Japan, of very rare and ancient objects from the Shoso-in treasure, normally housed in the Todaiji Temple complex: 263,765 people came to see the objects over a 14-day period.

Deaths in 2008 included Robert Rauschenberg, US neo-dada artist, on 12 May, aged 82; Cornell Capa, photographer and founder of the International Center for Photography in New York, on 23 May, aged 90; Beryl Cook, popular British artist, on 28 May, aged 81 (see Obituary); and Jan Krugier, Swiss dealer who handled the inheritance of Picasso's mistress Marie-Thérèse Walter and granddaughter Marina Picasso, on 15 November, aged 80.

Anna Somers Cocks

ARCHITECTURE

In considering 2008—a year in its way as profoundly cataclysmic as 2001—it is therapeutic to highlight significant architecture that was something more than the virtuosic demonstration of immateriality or irony that had constituted so much recent architecture. It was strangely encouraging to note, during the production of this edition of *The Annual Register*, that the steel frame of the tower of Beijing's 159-metre high Television Cultural Centre (TVCC), designed by Rem Koolhaas and Cecil Balmond, remained structurally intact after a fire on 9 February 2009 that destroyed the rest of the building's materials.

A number of European projects were outstanding during 2008, three of which were in Italy. With their Palazzo d'Oro, Gambardella Architetti transformed a redundant concrete skeleton structure at the sharp junction of two streets in Montesarchio, southern Italy, into a brilliantly contemporary version of an Italian palazzo, with an asymmetrical plan emphasised by a deeply cantilevered cornice. The urban qualities of this building—its use of materials, context, and fenestration in particular—were admirable. Despite its vivid architectural accents, the Palazzo d'Oro remained completely civil and an object lesson in how highly-contemporary design could fit into a relatively quiet milieu.

In Milan, and rather more forcefully, the extension of Luigi Bocconi University by the Irish practice Grafton Architects showed how a boldly critical contextual response could produce a building that was both monumental and responsive to the streetscape. Its inner courtyard had ambiguous qualities: the vista through it seem at once Brutalist and convivial. The treatment of the two main façades created a series of fragmented, asymmetrical projecting slabs faced with grey pietra di Grè. The articulations of these façades ensured that the sheer mass of this very large building remained in civil architectural dialogue with the two streets that it confronted.

The design of the D&G headquarters in Milan, by the Piuarch Studio, was entirely unradical, but no less satisfying. Here, the architects restructured two buildings, one from the 1920s, the other from the 1960s. The treatment of the latter was quite beautiful in the way it accepted the tough, rectilinear rhythm of the original structure and transformed it into something of great elegance and material restraint. There was not a single "look-at-me detail", and yet the eye lingered on the expressed grid of super-thin elements that punctuated the building's envelope. The tactile quality of the façades demonstrated the magical visual pull that can be exerted by ostensibly unremarkable architectural details.

The tactile quality of Herzog and de Meuron's CaixaForum in Madrid, which developed the city's oldest power station into an art and culture centre, was the obverse. The architects turned a building—referred to as "my factory of light" by the writer Edmundo Paz Soldan—into an extraordinarily gripping presence, dominated by three surreally different elevations. Three storeys of the worn 19th century brick facades rose into a roughly patinated copper carapace with patterned cut-outs at high points and these were confronted—in the plaza leading to the cantilevered entrance—by a high screen of lush vegetation. Despite their essential flatness, the contrasts of these surfaces seemed almost hallucinatory, or like a computer-manipulated image.

Producing a similarly hallucinatory effect were the vertically staggered, mesh-screened segments of the New Museum of Contemporary Art in New York, designed by SANNA; the semi-opaque rotunda for plants in Madrid's Ecoboulevard, designed by Ecosistema Urbano; and the landscape scheme for the High Line in New York by Diller Scofido + Renfro, and Field Operation. In the global environmental gloom, the natural was assuming heightened reality.

There was nothing surreal about Snohetta's Opera House in Oslo, however. They embedded the concert hall segment in a vast, sloping plane of concrete on which promenaders could view the city from a deck the equivalent of four storeys high, then walk down to the water's edge. Particularly striking was that this building was demonstrably democratic and humane in the Scandinavian tradition. It was a building for anybody who cared to wander into it, or over it, and its public quality was evident even in photographs, such as those in the art publisher Skira's interesting *Y08 Yearbook of World Architecture*.

Something equally striking was achieved by Giancarlo Mazzanti Arquitectos Ltda in Medellin, Colombia. The España Library took the form of three gigantic angular boulders, which sat on a high bluff overlooking the hillside shanties of one of the most dangerous parts of this drug trade-dominated city. This was architecture designed to convey a message of changing aspirations, symbolic in form, obdurate, spectacularly confident in its sprayed concrete structure and oxidised ceramic envelope. Could a building like this, in Colombia, encourage something like the "architecture is policy" slogan of France's President Nicolas Sarkozy? Or did it risk wandering into the specious terrain of Rem Koolhaas's declaration that "where there is nothing, anything is possible; where there is architecture, nothing else is possible."

Nothing, however, could exceed the oleaginous double-talk that surrounded Zaha Hadid's creation of a touring "mobile art pavilion" for Karl Lagerfeld of

Chanel. With a steel frame "constructed at a factory in Yorkshire", read the publicity from Chanel, the pavilion's "immersive field" loop-form folds into a sequence of darkened spaces "embracing visitors in intimate proximity to the art, and one another, before depositing them into the daylight-suffused central court at the end of the exhibition...a pavilion that, like a handbag, is a completely portable and functional container with vast symbolic potential." How very regrettable that a statement of such bathetic pretension was tainted by the presence of actual architecture.

In the Far East, a number of buildings reminded us of more essential architectural virtues, most notably in terms of their materiality. Liu Jaikun's Luyeyuan Stone Sculpture Art Museum in China's Sichuan province was certainly of modernist formal provenance, but its board-marked concrete and the atmosphere of both its indoor and outdoor spaces added the suggestion of layers of time, and something of Carlo Scarpa's conflations of water and mass. The Songzhuang Art Centre in Beijing by DnA Architects conveyed marvellous formal qualities by its relatively simple brick-clad volumes held aloft on a minimally detailed podium. Courtyard 104 in Beijing, designed by Ai Weiwei of Fake Design, demonstrated with magisterial conviction Jacques Herzog's dictum to "do the maximum thing". Weiwei did so with small, detail-free block-form houses clad in coarse brick. These were buildings to be shown to any student who doubted the potential importance of unrefined materials in architecture. The nearest equivalent to Weiwei's scheme in the UK was the Guest Street terrace in the inner city of Manchester, by de Metz Forbes Knight.

British architects produced a number of interesting buildings, including the Bodegas Protos winery in Peñafiel, Spain, by Rogers Stirk Harbour + Partners. Essentially the work of Graham Stirk, it revealed his trademark beautifully expressed structure and connections, which invested the production process with a sense of ordered calm and, in the underground barrel storage vaults, a cathedral-like atmosphere. In Coventry, Pringle Richards Sharratt delivered a finely wrought extension to the Herbert Museum, the central promenade space of which provided an important connection in the city with Sir Basil Spence's post-war Coventry cathedral. The extension revealed PRS's design genetics: the wave-form roof was distinctly Hopkinsonian, but original in its key details.

The Curve Theatre in Leicester, designed by one of the profession's international panjandrums, the US architect Rafael Vinoly, was undoubtedly programmatically and operationally brilliant. Stripped of the louvres that covered its glazed southern facade, this would have been a Willis Faber building for the 21st century. Foster + Partners, who designed the Ipswich headquarters for insurance company Willis, Faber & Dumas in the 1970s, produced another kind of excellence in 2008: the elephant house at Copenhagen Zoo. Its elemental form and tough features were something quite new to the practice. Architecture like this recalled the gnomic remark of Samuel Beckett's Vladimir (*Waiting for Godot*): "The essential never changes."

Jay Merrick

LITERATURE

THE arrival of new names in the literary firmament is always something to greet with pleasure. In 2008, the year under review, a number of authors emerged whose immediate success would at least guarantee them the oxygen of publicity when they next produced a book, whatever its quality. The award of the Man Booker Prize for Fiction to a first-time novelist, Aravind Adiga, was one such example. His book, *The White Tiger*, was not unanimously selected and there were many critics who thought it a surprising choice over the well-established Irish writer Sebastian Barry's *The Secret Scripture*. This appeared alongside *The White Tiger* on the Booker shortlist, and went on at the beginning of 2009 to win the Costa Prize, as grand a literary award as the Man Booker Prize. Adiga did not endear himself to his fellow Indian authors by appearing to claim uniqueness in having brought the poor of the sub-continent to the attention of the world, ignorant, it seemed, of two generations of compatriot novelists preceding him who had done just that.

By contrast the Jesuit priest turned short story writer, Uwem Akpan, astonished all who read his brilliant first collection, *Say You're One of Them*. Here was a truly original voice from the developing world. Each of the seven stories was set in an African conflict zone, which was seen through the eyes of a child. The horror of the episodes, combined with the compassion of the author's insights, made this for many critics the début of the year. Samson Kambalu from Malawi, Preeta Samarasan from Malaysia, and Alexis Wright from aboriginal Australia were new Commonwealth novelists to watch. Another author making a mark at a very early stage of his career as a novelist was John Burnside, who moved with ease from the world of poetry in which he was already a considerable figure to that of fiction in *Glister*, his remarkable crime novel set in a masculinist Scottish community.

In an age when predictions of the death of literature were increasingly commonplace—killed off by the computer, television, celebrity culture, young people's reluctance to read, and a myriad other explanations—it was encouraging to find that the number of novels published in the USA, India, and the UK (the three largest book markets in the world) remained consistent. Even allowing for the dross and for the growing inclination of publishing houses to commission ghost writers to produce tired narratives to be cynically marketed under the brand name of a fashion model, footballer, or film star, there was plenty to celebrate by way of good fiction from well established writers. Salman Rushdie, for example, was at the peak of his powers in his eclectic novel *The Enchantress of Florence*. John Le Carré, in *A Most Wanted Man*, was also thought to be at his best. John Updike produced *The Widows of Eastwick*, a lively sequel to one of his biggest international successes, *The Witches of Eastwick*. The Japanese writer Haruki Murakami, whose work had taken off internationally more vigorously than that of any of his compatriots, was as inventive as ever in *What I Talk About When I Talk About Running*, sensitively translated by Philip Gabriel. Peter Carey, Amitav Ghosh, Christopher Hope, Siri Hustvedt,

James Kelman, Hanif Kureishi, Annie Proulx, Philip Roth, and Tim Winton all produced good novels, even if none had a masterpiece of the kind that had put them into the front rank. Doris Lessing, Nobel Laureate for Literature in 2007, intimated that *Alfred and Emily*, based on her memories of her parents, might be her last novel, though few were inclined to believe it.

Once again J.K. Rowling seized many of the headlines in publishing news. *The Tales of Beedle the Bard* amounted to no more than wood shavings from the carpenter's floor, but nevertheless outsold almost everything else in the year. Rowling's experienced marketing team regularly plied the media with stories about the author: how she had contemplated suicide before the *Harry Potter* books took off, why she might write a sequel to the *Potter* cycle, how much she had donated to charity. More ingenious marketing came from the world of James Bond, master spy. Sebastian Faulkes, one of the most admired serious novelists, denied that, in writing a new James Bond novel, he had exactly taken a holiday from literature, though he acknowledged that the commission had been fun. *Devil May Care* was a brilliant parody masquerading as an original adventure novel. It was one of the biggest sellers Penguin had ever published. Even the so-called "queen of crime", P.D. James, could not, at the age of 88, compete with that sort of commercial success, but *The Private Patient* found her at her most intriguing, as well as sociologically tart.

A giant of modern fiction, Alexander Solzhenitsyn, died in August (see Obituary). The award to him of the Nobel Prize for Literature in 1970 had been politically controversial at a time of great strain between his native Soviet Union, where he was regarded as a dissident, and Western countries, where he was seen as something of a guru. By 2008, however, the world was united in its admiration for his literary achievements. *The First Circle, One Day in the Life of Ivan Denisovich*, and *Cancer Ward* were especially respected as modern classics. The innovative French novelist Alain Robbe-Grillet, who also died (see Obituary), may have had a more profound influence on the formal evolution of modern fiction, but he was never as widely read outside his native country as Solzhenitsyn. However, *Le Voyeur*, in particular, was recognised as one of the key mid-century novels, just as the film he scripted for Alain Resnais, *L'Année Dernière à Marienbad*, was regarded as a defining work for the cinema in the 1950s.

Other novelists who died in the year included Arthur C. Clarke, the master of science fiction (see Obituary); Siobhan Dowd, who before her early death had been seen as a rising hope among writers for children; Elaine Dundy, author of *The Dud Avocado*, telling of a young American girl's rites of passage in the late 1950s; George MacDonald Fraser, creator of the Flashman series of popular novels; the Irish journalist turned fiction writer Nuala O'Faolain; and Jeff Torrington, whose *Swing Hammer Swing!*, 30 years in the making, had been a liberating contribution to modern Scottish writing.

The poetry world was enlivened by strong collections from hitherto little regarded writers. Adam Foulds, Jane Griffiths, Jen Hadfield, and Mary Oliver all made a distinctive mark. Of more established poets, a second collection from Mick Imlah was particularly welcomed, there having been a gap of 20 years since his first book. Presciently entitled *The Lost Leader*—for Imlah, long regarded as one of the best poets of the generation now in their fifties but too sparsely published to act as its focal point, was to die in the first fortnight of 2009—this book had its roots in Scottish history, to which it was a kind of homage. John Ashbery of the USA and Ciaran Carson from Ireland were two prominent poets whose new poems did not disappoint. It was good to have the *Selected Poems* of another Irish writer, Bernard O'Donoghue, available in a single volume. For some, however, the collection of the year was the posthumous work of the New Zealand writer, Janet Frame (1924-2004), whose *Storms Will Tell: Selected Poems* reminded them of her nervy and luminous greatness. The year also saw the posthumous publication of her novel, *Towards Another Summer*.

Two giant poets died in 2008. They were Aimé Césaire from Martinique and Mahmoud Darwish from Palestine. Césaire was one of the most quoted and admired post-colonial writers in the Francophone world. *Cahier d'un retour au pays natal* (known in English as *Return to My Native Land*), one of the foundation stones of the négritude literary movement, had been published in 1939. Césaire's version of *The Tempest*, called simply *Une Tempête*, came out 30 years later, one of several verse plays in which he subtly subverted white European classics. Darwish, like Césaire, was a highly political poet. Both argued that their national circumstances could make them no other. Darwish was immensely prolific and often sought to be populist, working with well-known Arab musicians, for example. Two other poets of note who died during the year were E.A. Markham, from the small island of Montserrat who nevertheless had a world vision, and Hone Tuwhare, regarded by many as the voice of the Maori people.

It was as difficult as ever to decide, on their first showing in the theatre, which plays would stay the course and be recognised as lasting literature. There was no doubt, however, that the death of Harold Pinter in the final week of the year marked the departure of a great dramatist whose work had fundamentally changed the form of modern drama (see Obituary). Winner of the Nobel Prize for Literature in 2005, Pinter's stance on political matters such as the Iraq war had alienated some, but no one doubted his importance as one of the shapers of late 20th century Western culture. By sad coincidence, the playwright, novelist, and essayist Simon Gray, with whom Pinter had frequently worked, also died in 2008 (see Obituary). His final work was a memoir called *The Last Cigarette*, which with hindsight took on aspects of a valediction.

In the field of biography Christopher Bigsby memorialised another great playwright, Arthur Miller. His biography of Miller only went up to 1962, more than 40 years before his death, but Bigsby made it clear that in his opinion the dramatist's best work was by then behind him. Another theatrical biography, Michael Holroyd's *A Strange Eventful History*—an account of the interlocking lives of Henry Irving and Ellen Terry and their families—broke new ground in examining the interplay of dynasties rather than focusing on a single life.

By common consent one of the outstanding biographies of the year was Patrick French's authorised life of the writer V.S. Naipaul. Many people could not understand why Naipaul had allowed devastating personal information to appear in his lifetime. This was a cause for admiration in some readers and scorn in others, making it the most talked-about literary biography for many years. By comparison the elegant memoirs of the publisher Diana Athill or the more acerbic observations of the novelist J.G. Ballard seemed small beer, illuminating though they undoubtedly were. Among non-fiction titles of 2008, Richard Holmes's *The Age of Wonder* stood out because its analysis of the Romantics' re-discovery of science resonated so strongly with our own time.

The quatercentenary of John Milton's birth was celebrated throughout 2008 by a number of special lectures, exhibitions, and monographs. His place in the history of political radicalism was already assured, but as a poet he had dropped out of fashion in this more secular age. The anniversary celebrations rescued him from neglect and brought many people back not only to his great religious epic, *Paradise Lost*, but also to his essays. By comparison the 50th anniversary of the publication of Chinua Achebe's novel *Things Fall Apart* was a minor matter, but there was nonetheless global acknowledgement of this Nigerian book as the parent of modern African fiction.

The award of the Nobel Prize for Literature for 2008 to a writer almost entirely unknown outside his native France puzzled insular Anglophones, but the novelist Jean-Marie Gustave Le Clézio, a sophisticated and prolific writer with an international background including time spent as a child in Nigeria, was a worthy winner. Le Clézio's win carried with it an implicit indictment of the publishing world outside France, for his work had been little translated. It remained the case that in both the UK and the USA the percentage of books translated from other languages into English could be numbered on the fingers of one mutilated hand. Le Clézio's Nobel nomination was unlikely to have changed this, though France was proud of its first literature laureate since Claude Simon in 1985. It seemed equally unlikely that Le Clézio would concur with the spirit of his predecessor Doris Lessing's comment that the winning of the Prize the year before had been for her "a bloody disaster".

Alastair Niven

Among the books which appeared in 2008, the following are either referred to above or are of special note:

FICTION. Aravind Adiga, *The White Tiger* (Atlantic); Uwem Akpan, *Say You're One of Them* (Abacus); Alaa Al Aswany, trans. Farouk Abdel Wahab, *Chicago* (Fourth Estate); Paul Auster, *Man in the Dark* (Faber); Murray Bail, *The Pages* (Harvill Secker); Peter Carey, *His Illegal Self* (Faber); Sebastian Barry, *The Secret Scripture* (Faber); Melissa Benn, *One of Us* (Chatto); Louis de Bernières, *A Partisan's Daughter* (Harvill Secker); John Berger, *From A to X* (Verso); John Burnside, *Glister* (Cape); Jenny Diski, *Apology for the Woman Writing* (Virago); Siobhan Dowd, *Bog Child* (David Fickling); Helen Dunmore, *Counting the Stars* (Fig Tree/Penguin); Robert Edric, *In Zodiac Light* (Doubleday); Anne Enright, *Taking Pictures* (Cape); Bernardine Evaristo, *Blonde Roots*

(Penguin); Sebastian Faulks, *Devil May Care* (Penguin); Laura Fish, *Strange Music* (Cape); Janet Frame, *Towards Another Summer* (Virago); Damon Galgut, *The Impostor* (Atlantic); Helen Garner, *The Spare Room* (Canongate); Keith Gessen, *All the Sad Young Literary Men* (Heinemann); Amitav Ghosh, *Sea of Poppies* (John Murray); Linda Grant, *The Clothes on Their Backs* (Virago); Aleksandar Hemon, *The Lazarus Project* (Picador); Philip Hensher, *The Northern Clemency* (Fourth Estate); Christopher Hope, *The Garden of Bad Dreams* (Atlantic Books); Siri Hustvedt, *The Sorrows of an American* (Sceptre); Howard Jacobson, *The Act of Love* (Cape); P.D. James, *The Private Patient* (Faber); Ma Jin, trans. Flora Drew, *Beijing Coma* (Chatto); Samson Kambalu, *The Jive Talker: Or, How to Get a British Passport* (Cape); James Kelman, *Kieron Smith, Boy* (Hamish Hamilton); Malcolm Knox, *Jamaica* (Old Street); Michelle de Kretser, *The Lost Dog* (Chatto); Hanif Kureishi, *Something to Tell You* (Faber); Jhumpa Lahiri, *Unaccustomed Earth* (Bloomsbury); John Le Carré, *A Most Wanted Man* (Hodder and Stoughton); Doris Lessing, *Alfred and Emily* (Fourth Estate); David Lodge, *Deaf Sentence* (Harvill Secker); Patrick McGrath, *Trauma* (Bloomsbury); Deirdre Madden, *Molly Fox's Birthday* (Faber); Adam Mars-Jones, *Pilcrow* (Faber); Rebecca Miller, *The Private Lives of Pippa Lee* (Canongate); Haruki Murakami, trans. Philip Gabriel, *What I Talk About When I Talk About Running* (Harvill Secker); Joseph O'Neill, *Netherland* (Fourth Estate); Tim Parks, *Dream of Rivers and Seas* (Harvill Secker); Emily Perkins, *Novel About My Wife* (Bloomsbury); Annie Proulx, *Fine Just the Way It Is* (Fourth Estate); Philip Roth, *Indignation* (Cape); Salman Rushdie, *The Enchantress of Florence* (Cape); Preeta Samarasan, *Evening is the Whole Day* (Fourth Estate); José Saramago, trans. Margaret Jull Costa, *Death at Intervals* (Harvill Secker); Will Self, *The Butt* (Bloomsbury); Paul Torday, *The Irresistible Inheritance of Wilberforce* (Weidenfeld and Nicolson); Curtis Sittenfeld, *American Wife* (Doubleday); Ali Smith, *The First Person and Other Stories* (Hamish Hamilton); Adam Thorpe, *The Standing Pool* (Bloomsbury); John Updike, *The Widows of Eastwick* (Hamish Hamilton); M.G. Vassanji, *The Assassin's Song* (Canongate); Irvine Welsh, *Crime* (Cape); Tim Winton, *Breath* (Picador); Alexis Wright, *Carpentaria* (Constable).

POETRY. Moniza Alvi, *Europa* (Bloodaxe); Moniza Alvi, *Split World: Poems 1990-2005* (Bloodaxe); John Ashbery, *Notes from the Air: Selected Later Poems* (Carcanet); Peter Bennet, *The Glass Swarm* (Flambard); Alison Brackenbury, *Singing in the Dark* (Carcanet); Sujata Bhatt, *Pure Lizard* (Carcanet); Ciaran Carson, *For All We Know* (Gallery Press); Robert Crawford, *Full Volume* (Cape); Keki Daruwalla, *The Glass-Blower* (Arc); Maura Dooley, *Life Under Water* (Bloodaxe); Mark Doty, *Theories and Apparitions* (Cape); Adam Foulds, *The Broken Word* (Cape); Janet Frame, *Storms Will Tell: Selected Poems* (Bloodaxe); Matthew Francis, *Mandeville* (Faber); Jane Griffiths, *Another Country: New and Selected Poems* (Bloodaxe); Jen Hadfield, *Nigh-No-Place* (Bloodaxe); Selima Hill, *Gloria: Selected Poems* (Bloodaxe); Selima Hill, *The Hat* (Bloodaxe); Michael Hofmann, *Selected Poems* (Faber); Mick Imlah, *The Lost Leader* (Faber); Jackie Kay, *Lamplighter* (Bloodaxe); John Kinsella, *Shades of the Sublime and Beautiful* (Picador); Frances Levitson, *Public Dream* (Picador); Ian McMillan, *Talking Myself Home* (John Murray); Sarah Maguire, *The Pomegranates of Kandahar* (Chatto and Windus); Glyn Maxwell, *Hide Now* (Picador); Bernard O'Donoghue, *Selected Poems* (Faber); Mary Oliver, *Thirst* (Bloodaxe); Christopher Middleton, *Collected Poems* (Carcanet); Stephen Romer, *Yellow Studio* (Carcanet); Jackie Wills, *Commandments* (Arc).

AUTOBIOGRAPHY AND BIOGRAPHY. Peter Ackroyd, *Poe: A Life Cut Short* (Chatto and Windus); Julie Andrews, *Home: a Memoir of My Early Years* (Weidenfeld and Nicolson); Diana Athill, *Somewhere Towards the End* (Granta); J.G. Ballard, *Miracles of Life: Shanghai to Shepperton* (Fourth Estate); Anna Beer, *Milton: Poet, Pamphleteer and Patriot* (Bloomsbury); Christopher Bigsby, *Arthur Miller, 1915-62* (Weidenfeld and Nicolson); Mark Bostridge, *Florence Nightingale: The Woman and Her Legend* (Viking); Elinor Burkett, *Golda Meier: The Iron Lady of the Middle East* (Gibson Square); Anthony Butler, *Cyril Ramaphosa* (James Currey); Paul Delany, *George Gissing: A Life* (Weidenfeld and Nicolson); edit. Terence Dooley, *So I Have Thought of You: The Letters of Penelope Fitzgerald* (Fourth Estate); David Ellis, *Death and the Author: How D.H. Lawrence Died, and Was Remembered* (OUP); Patrick French, *The World is What It Is: The Authorised Biography of V.S. Naipaul* (Picador); Simon Gray, *The Last Cigarette* (Granta); Ffion Hague, *The Pain and the Privilege: The Women in Lloyd George's Life* (Harper Press); Václav Havel, trans. Paul Wilson, *To the Castle and Back* (Portobello); Richard Holmes, *The Age of Wonder: How the Romantic Generation Discovered the Beauty and Terror of Science* (Harper Press); Michael Holroyd, *A Strange Eventful History: The Dramatic Lives of Ellen Terry, Henry Irving and Their Remarkable Families* (Chatto and Windus); John Lucas, *Thomas Beecham: An Obsession with Music* (Boydell Press); Judith Mackrell, *The Bloomsbury Ballerina: Lydia Lopokova, Imperial Dancer and Mrs John Maynard Keynes* (Weidenfeld and Nicolson); Gerald Martin, *Gabriel García Márquez: A Life* (Bloomsbury); Owen Matthews, *Stalin's Children* (Bloomsbury); Ian Mortimer, *The Fears of Henry IV: The Life of England's Self-Made King* (Vintage); Philip Norman, *John Lennon: The Life* (HarperCollins); Barack Obama, *Dreams from My Father: A Story of Race and Inheritance* (Canongate); Carole Seymour-Jones, *A Dangerous Liaison: Simone de Beauvoir and Jean-Paul Sartre* (Century); Narendra Singh Saril, *Once a Prince of Sarila* (IB Tauris); David Starkey, *Henry: Virtuous Prince* (Harper Press); Frances Wilson, *The Ballad of Dorothy Wordsworth* (Faber and Faber); Jean Moorcroft Wilson, *Isaac Rosenberg: The Making of a Great War Poet* (Weidenfeld and Nicolson); Simon Winchester, *Bomb, Book and Compass: Joseph Needham and the Great Secrets of China* (Viking).

MISCELLANEOUS. Lisa Appignanesi, *Mad, Bad and Sad: A History of Women and the Mind Doctors from 1800 to the Present* (Virago); Catharine Arnold, *Bedlam: London and Its Mad* (Simon and Schuster); Daniel Barenboim, *Everything is Connected* (Weidenfeld and Nicolson); Mary Beard, *Pompeii: The Life of a Roman Town* (Profile); Benazir Bhutto, *Reconciliation: Islam, Democracy and the West* (Simon and Schuster); James Boyce, *Van Diemen's Land: A History* (Black); Michael Braddick, *God's Fury, England's Fire: a new History of the English Civil Wars* (Allen Lane); Ruth Brandon, *Other People's Daughters: The Life and Times of the Governess* (Weidenfeld and Nicolson); Michael Burleigh, *Blood and Rage: A Cultural History of Terrorism* (Harper Press); Sean B. Carroll, *The Making of the Fittest: DNA and the Ultimate Forensic Record of Evolution* (Quercus); Amit Chaudhuri, *Clearing a Space: Reflections on India, Literature and Culture* (Peter Lang); Steve Coll, *The Bin Ladens: The Story of a Family and its Fortune* (Allen Lane/Penguin); David Crystal, *Txting: the gr8 db8* (OUP); James Cuno, *Who Owns Antiquity? Museums and the Battle over our Ancient Heritage* (Princeton); James Davidson, *The Greeks and Greek Love* (Weidenfeld and Nicolson); Richard Dowden, *Africa: Altered States, Ordinary Miracles* (Portobello); Susan Faludi, *The Terror Dream: Fear and Fantasy in Post*

9/11 America (Atlantic); Ophelia Field, *The Kit-Cat Club: Friends Who Imagined a Nation* (HarperPress); Francisco Goldman, *The Art of Political Murder: Who Killed Bishop Gerardi?* (Atlantic); Andrew Graham-Dixon, *Michelangelo and the Sistine Chapel* (Weidenfeld and Nicolson); Kelly Grovier, *The Gaol: The Story of Newgate, London's Most Notorious Prison* (John Murray); Janie Hampton, *The Austerity Olympics: When the Games Came to London in 1948* (Aurum); Rosemary Hill, *Stonehenge* (Profile); Richard Holmes, *The Age of Wonder* (Harper Press); Alberto Manguel, *The Library at Night* (Yale); Geoffrey Moorhouse, *The Last Office: 1539 and the Dissolution of a Monastery* (Weidenfeld and Nicolson); Desmond Morris, *The Naked Man* (Cape); Jonathan Powell, *Great Hatred, Little Room: Making Peace in Northern Ireland* (Bodley Head); Philippe Sands, *Torture Team: Deception, Cruelty and the Compromise of Law* (Allen Lane); Simon Schama, *The American Future: A History* (Bodley Head); Neil Shubin, *Your Inner Fish: A Journey into the 3.5 Billion-Year History of the Human Body* (Allen Lane); Kate Summerscale, *The Suspicions of Mr Whicher, or The Murder at Road Hill House* (Blooms-bury); Colin Tudge, *Consider the Birds: Who They Are and What They Do* (Allen Lane); Stephen Wall, *A Stranger in Europe: Britain and the EU from Thatcher to Blair* (OUP); Richard Webber, *Fifty Years of Carry On* (Century); Philip Ziegler, *Legacy: Cecil Rhodes, the Rhodes Trust and Rhodes Scholarships* (Yale).

XVII SPORT

OLYMPIC GAMES. The choice of Beijing as the host city for the 2008 Olympics remained controversial throughout the build-up to the Games. Critics pointed to China's poor human rights record and in particular to the country's crackdown in Tibet. There were protests as the Olympic torch relay passed through a number of countries, but boycotts did not materialise and a record 204 teams took part in the sporting spectacle. It was estimated that China had invested US$40 billion in the Games and from the moment they opened with a dazzling ceremony in the "Bird's Nest" stadium it was clear that no expense had been spared. There had been fears that smog might affect the athletes, but there were few complaints, while a huge security presence ensured the Games were conducted peacefully (see pp. 350-51). The hosts topped the medals table. China won 51 gold medals, 15 more than the USA, and was the first country for 20 years to win more than 50 golds. Nevertheless there was huge national disappointment when Liu Xiang, China's best hope for an athletics gold, pulled out before his heat with a foot injury.

Russia (with 23 golds) finished third and Britain (19 golds) was fourth. It was Britain's most successful Olympics for 100 years, with 47 medals won overall. Sailing (four golds) and rowing (two golds) were once again successful British sports, but the best results came in cycling. Nicole Cooke started the gold rush with victory in the women's road race before Britain's track cyclists swept all before them, winning seven golds, three silvers, and two bronzes. Chris Hoy became the first British Olympian for 100 years to win three golds at a single Olympics, in the keirin and team and individual sprints. Bradley Wiggins won gold in the team and individual sprint, Victoria Pendleton won the women's sprint, and Rebecca Romero claimed the 3,000m pursuit gold to add to the rowing silver she had won in Athens, becoming the first British woman ever to win Olympic medals in two different summer sports. In sailing, Ben Ainslie won the Finn class to claim his third successive Olympic gold, while Iain Percy and Andrew Simpson (Star class), Sarah Ayton, Sarah Webb, and Pippa Wilson (Yngling) and Paul Goodison (Laser) also finished at the head of their fleets. Rebecca Adlington became the first female British swimmer to win gold for 48 years, winning the 400m and 800m freestyle. The British men's four and lightweight doubles sculls crews won gold on the rowing lake, where Tim Brabants won the K1 1,000m flatwater canoeing class. James DeGale won a boxing gold in the middleweight division.

Britain's success came after their preparations had been dogged by controversy over the sprinter Dwain Chambers. The British Olympic Association (BOA) had banned Chambers for life for taking performance-enhancing drugs, but he claimed that the ban was unlawful. The High Court in London ruled in the BOA's favour. Another British athlete, Christine Ohuruogu, served a one-year ban for missing three out-of-competition tests in 2006, but competed in Beijing and won the 400m gold.

Michael Phelps became the most successful Olympian ever when he won eight swimming golds, one more than another US citizen, Mark Spitz, had achieved in 1972. It took his career tally of Olympic gold medals to 14. One final was desperately close—Phelps beat Milorad Cavic by one hundredth of a second in the 100m butterfly—but most of his wins were emphatic. The others were in the 200m freestyle, 200m butterfly, 200m and 400m individual medley, 4 x 100m freestyle relay, 4 x 100m medley relay, and 4 x 200m freestyle relay. In 17 races over nine days Phelps set seven world records.

The star of track and field was the Jamaican sprinter, Usain Bolt, who won gold medals in the 100m and 200m sprints, breaking both world records in the process. Bolt won the 100m in 9.69sec, beating the record of 9.72sec that he had set earlier in the year. He crossed the line with time to glance to both sides. Bolt won the 200m in 19.30sec, two hundredths of a second quicker than Michael Johnson had achieved in 1996. He won a third gold as Jamaica took the 4 x 100m relay. Kenenisa Bekele won the 5,000m and 10,000m titles, with Tirunesh Dibaba emulating his achievements in the women's events. Yelena Isinbayeva set a world women's pole vault record for the second Games in succession.

The Paralympics were a similar success. China once again topped the medals table, with Britain finishing second, winning 42 gold medals. More than 100 world records were set in the swimming stadium and athletes at the "Bird's Nest" competed in front of full houses every day.

FOOTBALL.　Spain, so often the great underachievers of international football, ended 44 years without a major trophy by winning the European Championship. Luis Aragones's team were worthy winners of an exciting tournament that featured some glorious attacking football. Fernando Torres, Cesc Fabregas, Xavi and Andres Iniesta illuminated the competition with their inventive play from the moment that Spain trounced Russia 4-1 in their first match. Spain beat the same opponents 3-0 in the semi-finals, while a Torres goal defeated Germany in the final. The Netherlands shone in the early stages, trouncing Italy, France, and Romania before losing to Russia in the quarter-finals. Italy qualified for the last eight by beating France (who took only one point from their three group matches) but then lost to Spain on penalties. Croatia won all three of their group matches, only to lose to Turkey in the quarter-finals. Croatia went ahead with two minutes of extra time left before Turkey equalised in the last minute and then won the penalty shootout 3-1. It was Turkey's third late comeback. In the group stages, Fatih Terim's team had recovered from 1-0 down to score the winner in injury time against Switzerland and had beaten the Czech Republic 3-2, despite trailing 2-0 with only 16 minutes of the match remaining. Turkey's run eventually ended with defeat by Germany in the semi-finals.

No teams from the British Isles qualified for the tournament, but England made an excellent start to their 2010 World Cup qualifying campaign. Under a new coach, Fabio Capello, England were five points clear of their rivals after winning their first four group games. Against Croatia, in Zagreb, Theo Walcott, 19, became the youngest player to score a hat-trick for England and the first since

Michael Owen in 2001. The Republic of Ireland also put an Italian in charge of the national squad, with Giovanni Trapattoni succeeding Steve Staunton. George Burley took over as manager of Scotland.

Diego Maradona, the most famous player in Argentina's history, took charge of the national team, while Mexico appointed Sven Goran Eriksson, the former England coach. Liga de Quito beat Brazil's Fluminense on penalties to become the first club from Ecuador to win the Copa Libertadores. Egypt successfully defended their title in the Africa Cup of Nations, beating Cameroon 1-0 in the final in Accra.

Manchester United beat Chelsea in the first all-English Champions League final. United won 6-5 on penalties after the match finished in a 1-1 draw. John Terry, the Chelsea captain, failed to convert what would have been a match-winning penalty. Within a week of the final Avram Grant was sacked as Chelsea manager. He was replaced by the Brazilian Luiz Felipe Scolari, who had been coaching the Portuguese national team. Zenit St Petersburg won the Uefa Cup, beating Rangers 2-0 in the final.

Manchester United won their 17th league title and their 10th under Sir Alex Ferguson. Cristiano Ronaldo had an outstanding season, scoring 42 goals, and was European footballer of the year. Portsmouth beat Cardiff City 1-0 in the FA Cup final to win their first major trophy for 58 years, while Tottenham Hotspur beat Chelsea 2-1 in the Carling Cup final. Arsenal won the women's FA Cup final for a record ninth time by beating Leeds United 4-1 in front of a crowd of 24,582, a record for the fixture. Sheikh Mansour bin Zayed Al Nahyran, the brother of the ruler of Abu Dhabi, bought control of Manchester City from Thaksin Shinawatra for £210 million through his Abu Dhabi United Group. Within days, City had signed the Brazilian, Robinho, from Real Madrid for £32.6 million. Derby County became the fourth Premier League club to be taken over by US owners when the Detroit-based General Sports and Entertainment company took control. Celtic won their third successive Scottish championship. Rangers won the CIS Insurance Cup, overcoming Dundee United on penalties, and the Scottish Cup, beating Queen of the South.

CRICKET. The march of the Twenty20 game continued apace and Australia showed the first signs of decline during a turbulent year. The Indian Cricket Board's Indian Premier League, a Twenty20 competition, was a huge success, with matches played in full grounds before big television audiences. The England and Wales Cricket Board refused to release players to play in the league but accepted an offer from the multi-millionaire, Sir Allen Stanford, to play a Twenty20 challenge match in Antigua against a West Indian team, who clinched the winner-takes-all prize of US$20 million.

At the beginning of the year Australia completed a 2-1 home series victory over India, during which they equalled their own world record of 16 consecutive Test wins. However, the series was marred by a race controversy, with allegations that India's Harbhajan Singh had abused Australia's Andrew Symonds. Harbhajan was eventually cleared after pleading guilty to a lesser offence of using abusive language. Australia's defeat against India at Perth was their first loss for almost a decade at what had become their most successful ground. India won the return series later in the year 2-0 as Australia struggled following the retirements of Glenn McGrath, Shane Warne, and Adam Gilchrist. The year ended with South Africa recording their first Test victory on Australian soil for 14 years. Sachin Tendulkar became the highest Test run-scorer, overtaking Brian Lara's total of 11,953 runs, while another Indian, Virender Sehwag, matched the achievement of Lara and Don Bradman by scoring a second Test triple hundred.

Unrest in India and Pakistan disrupted the cricket calendar. A Twenty20 Champions League tournament in India was postponed, as was the Champions Trophy, which was scheduled for Pakistan. England's autumn tour of India was interrupted by the terrorist attacks in Mumbai (Bombay) (see pp. 316-17). A limited-overs series that England were losing 5-0 was abandoned as the touring team went home. However, England returned for the three-match Test series, which they lost 1-0. India won the first Test and thereafter appeared happy to settle for draws.

England began the year by winning a three-Test series in New Zealand. Victory in the second Test was England captain Michael Vaughan's first win for seven Tests. England secured the series when Monty Panesar took six wickets in the final innings of the third Test. England also won two Twenty20 internationals, but the hosts won the one-day series 3-1. England won the return series 2-0. Jacob Oram's final-day century earned New Zealand a draw at Lord's, but England won the second Test at Old Trafford by six wickets, Andrew Strauss helping to secure their best comeback since Headingley 1981 with a final-day century. England won the third Test at Trent Bridge by an innings and nine runs. They also won the only Twenty20 international, but New Zealand took the one-day series, despite losing the first match at Durham, where Kevin Pietersen struck a brilliant century that included two sixes which were hit left-handed with a reverse sweep. South Africa won a four-Test series 2-1, their first series win in England since 1965. The visitors won the second Test by 10 wickets. In the third Graeme Smith, the captain, scored an unbeaten 154 as South Africa successfully chased a target of 282. Vaughan, England's most successful captain, stepped down after the third Test. He was replaced by Pietersen, who hit a century as England won the fourth Test at the Oval. He went on to lead his team to a 4-0 victory in the one-day series.

Durham won the county championship for the first time, beating Kent on the final day to deny Nottinghamshire. Warwickshire won the second division title. Essex won the Friends Provident Trophy, beating Kent in the final at Lord's. Middlesex won the Twenty20 Cup, beating Kent in the final at the Rose Bowl. Sussex took the Pro40 title, their sixth trophy in as many years.

RUGBY. Wales won rugby union's Grand Slam for the second time in four seasons as Warren Gatland enjoyed immediate success in his first season as coach. Shane Williams, who broke Gareth Thomas's Welsh try-scoring record, was an outstanding talent in the backs, Martyn Williams superb in the pack, and Ryan Jones an inspirational leader. Nevertheless the championship could have finished very differently if England had not imploded midway through their opening match against Wales at Twickenham, losing 26-19 after leading 16-6 at half-time. Wales went on to beat Scotland and Italy at the Millennium Stadium. A 16-12 victory over Ireland in Dublin secured the Triple Crown and a 29-12 success at home to France clinched the Grand Slam. England finished as runners-up. After the opening shambles at Twickenham, Brian Ashton's team won in Rome and Paris. A defeat at Murrayfield was followed by victory over Ireland at Twickenham. Eddie O'Sullivan resigned as Ireland coach after his team finished fourth. He was replaced by Declan Kidney, the coach who guided Munster to four Heineken Cup finals in eight years.

In April Martin Johnson, England's World Cup-winning captain in 2003, was appointed team manager. He named Steve Borthwick, the Bath forward, as captain in succession to Phil Vickery. In the summer England lost twice away to New Zealand, but Johnson did not take full charge until the new season. His first match in the autumn internationals brought a win over the Pacific Islanders, but England then lost 28-14 to Australia and suffered their heaviest defeat at Twickenham, losing 42-6 to South Africa. New Zealand won 32-6 in the final match. The autumn internationals emphasised how far ahead the southern hemisphere teams were in comparison with their northern rivals. New Zealand, who had won the Tri-Nations for a record fourth straight year, completed a clean sweep, with wins away to England, Wales, Scotland, and Ireland. South Africa beat England, Wales and Scotland. The only bright spot for the Six Nations countries was a 21-18 victory by Wales over Australia at the Millennium Stadium.

Munster won the Heineken Cup for the second time in three seasons, beating Toulouse 16-13 in Cardiff. Bath beat Worcester in the European Challenge Cup final. Gloucester finished the regular season top of the Guinness Premiership, but Wasps won the championship, beating Leicester in the final in Lawrence Dallaglio's last game before retirement. Ospreys won the EDF Energy Cup final, beating Leicester at Twickenham, and Leinster won the Celtic League.

St Helens dominated the rugby league season, despite losing the Super League Grand Final. Daniel Anderson's team were unbeaten from April until their defeat to Leeds at Old Trafford in the season's finale. On the way they won the Challenge Cup for the third year in succession, beating Hull in the final at Wembley. New Zealand sprang a surprise by winning the Rugby League World Cup, beating Australia in the final in Brisbane.

TENNIS. Roger Federer's 237-week reign as world No 1 was finally ended by Rafael Nadal. The Spaniard had previously reigned only on clay, but in 2008 he claimed Federer's Wimbledon title and also won the Olympic gold medal. Federer had glandular fever before the Australian Open, where Novak Djokovic won his first Grand Slam title, beating the unseeded Jo-Wilfried Tsonga in the final. As in 2006 and 2007, Federer faced Nadal in the finals of the French Open and Wimbledon. Nadal won at Roland Garros for the fourth year in succession and ended Federer's run of five successive titles at Wimbledon. The final was one of the greatest ever at the All England Club, Nadal winning in near-darkness at 9.15pm to become the first man since Bjorn Borg in 1980 to complete the Roland Garros-

Wimbledon double. At four hours and 48 minutes it was the longest Wimbledon final in history. Federer was knocked out of the Olympic singles tournament in the quarter-finals, though he won gold in the doubles with Stanislas Wawrinka. Federer also won the year's last Grand Slam tournament, beating Andy Murray, who was playing in his first major final, to claim his fifth successive US Open title. Murray ended 2008 as the world No 4. The Scot won five titles, including successive Masters Series tournaments in Cincinnati and Madrid. Spain beat Argentina to win the Davis Cup, while Britain were relegated from the World Group after defeats to Argentina and Austria.

The women's game was shaken by the retirement of Justine Henin, the world No 1, just 11 days before the French Open. In her absence four different players won the Grand Slam titles. Maria Sharapova won the Australian Open, beating Ana Ivanovic in the final, but then suffered a serious shoulder injury. Ivanovic won her first Grand Slam title, beating Dinara Safina in Paris, while Wimbledon staged an all-Williams final for the third time. Venus won her fifth All England Club title, but the match was closer than the 7-5, 6-4 margin over her sister, Serena, suggested. Two months later Serena became the sixth woman in the Open era to win nine or more Grand Slam titles when she triumphed at the US Open, beating Jelena Jankovic in the final to become world No 1 for the first time for five years. Russia beat Spain to win the Fed Cup.

GOLF. Two days after winning the US Open, Tiger Woods announced that he was having surgery to repair anterior cruciate ligament damage in his left knee. Earlier in the year the world's leading player had had arthroscopic surgery after finishing runner-up in the US Masters to South Africa's Trevor Immelman. In rehabilitating the joint, Woods had suffered a double stress fracture in his leg and had been unable to play 18 holes in the two months between the US Masters and the US Open. Woods defied the pain to win the US Open at Torrey Pines. After an 18-hole play-off failed to separate Woods and Rocco Mediate, the contest went to sudden-death, with the former winning at the first hole. It was his 14th major. In the absence of Woods the last two majors both went to Padraig Harrington, who became the first European to win two in succession in the same season. The Irishman successfully defended his Open title at Royal Birkdale. Greg Norman, 53, led by two shots after the third day, but Harrington played magnificently in the final round, coming home in 32. Britain's Ian Poulter finished second, four strokes adrift. In the US PGA Championship at Oakland Hills, Harrington shot 66 in his last two rounds and won by two strokes from Sergio Garcia and Ben Curtis.

The USA, even without Woods, were emphatic winners of the Ryder Cup at Valhalla. Captained by Paul Azinger and inspired by the youthful Anthony Kim and Hunter Mahan, the Americans won for the first time since 1999. The final score—16-and-a-half points to 11-and-a-half—was their biggest winning margin since 1981. Robert Karlsson became the first Swede to win the European Order of Merit, while Vijay Singh topped the US money list.

In a year when Sweden's Annika Sorenstam, arguably the best female player of all time, retired, three of the four women's majors were won by Asians.

Tseng Yani of Taiwan beat Maria Hjorth in a play-off for the LPGA Championship; South Korea's Park Inbee, aged 19, became the youngest player to win the US Women's Open; while her compatriot, Shin Jiyai, took the British Open at Sunningdale. Lorena Ochoa of Mexico won the Kraft Nabisco Championship. The USA won the Curtis Cup, beating Great Britain and Ireland 13-7 at St Andrews.

ATHLETICS. Usain Bolt was virtually unknown at the start of the year but he broke the world 100m record by winning in 9.72sec in New York before going on to record his historic sprint double at the Olympic Games. At the world indoor championships in Valencia the USA finished top of the medals table ahead of Russia. Britain was fourth, with Phillips Idowu (triple jump) the only Briton to win gold. Dwain Chambers (60m), Jeanette Kwayke (60m), Chris Tomlinson (long jump), and Kelly Sotherton (pentathlon) all won silver. Kenya's Martin Lel won the London Marathon for the third time in four years. The women's race was won by Germany's Irina Mikitenko. Paula Radcliffe won the New York Marathon for a third time, while Haile Gebrselassie broke his own world marathon record, winning in Berlin in under two hours and four minutes.

Drugs controversies continued, with seven Russian women punished before the Olympics for tampering with their urine samples. Marion Jones, who gave back her medals from the 2000 Olympics after admitting to having used performance-enhancing drugs, served six months in jail for lying about her drug use. Tim Montgomery, the former 100m world record holder, was sentenced to 46 months in prison in New York for his role in a cheque fraud scheme. He also admitted using banned drugs during the 2000 Olympic Games.

MOTOR SPORT. Lewis Hamilton became the youngest Formula One world champion in history when he won a thrilling title race on the last lap of the final grand prix. Felipe Massa crossed the line first in his home Brazilian Grand Prix, knowing that 23-year-old Hamilton would have to finish fifth to deny him the title. The Briton was sixth going into the final lap but overtook Timo Glock, who had gambled on finishing the race on dry tyres as rain started to fall in the closing stages. Hamilton took the title by just one point from Massa, whose Ferrari colleague, Kimi Raikkonen, finished third, with the BMW driver, Robert Kubica, in fourth place. Hamilton, the first British champion since Damon Hill 12 years earlier, won five races and Massa six. Sebastian Vettel, 21, won the Italian Grand Prix to become Formula One's youngest race winner. David Coulthard, winner of 13 races for McLaren and Williams, retired at the age of 37, while Honda announced their withdrawal from Formula One in 2009 on the grounds of cost. Ferrari won the constructors' championship. Max Mosley, the president of Formula One's ruling body, the FIA, kept his job despite controversy over lurid newspaper reports concerning his private life (see p. 492).

Denmark's Tom Kristensen, alongside Allan McNish and Rinaldo Capello, won the Le Mans 24-hour race for a record eighth time, while Citroen's Sebastien Loeb claimed the world rally championship for a record fifth year in a row. Yvan Muller won the world touring car championship. Valentino Rossi won his sixth MotoGP world title, while Troy Bayliss secured his third world superbikes crown.

BOXING. The Ukrainian brothers Vitali and Wladimir Klitschko ended the year with three of the world heavyweight crowns. Wladimir held the International Boxing Federation and World Boxing Organisation titles, while Vitali had the World Boxing Council crown. Russia's Nikolay Valuev was the World Boxing Association champion. Britain's Joe Calzaghe beat the USA's Bernard Hopkins, one of the sport's greatest middleweight champions, in Las Vegas in the Welshman's first fight in the USA. It extended his winning run to 45 wins from 45 fights. Calzaghe went on to beat another of the sport's biggest names when he overcame Roy Jones Jr on points in New York to preserve his unbeaten 10-year record. Ricky Hatton, whose confidence had been shaken by defeat at the hands of Floyd Mayweather Jr in 2007, put his career back on track when he beat the previously undefeated American, Paulie Malignaggi, in Las Vegas.

HORSE RACING. Two Irish trainers, Aidan O'Brien and Jim Bolger, dominated the Flat season. O'Brien made a clean sweep of the Irish Classics and won the 2,000 Guineas at Newmarket, while Bolger's Derby winner, New Approach, was arguably the most exciting performer of the year. Henrythenavigator, ridden by Johnny Murtagh, gave O'Brien his fifth 2,000 Guineas and went on to win the Irish 2,000 Guineas at The Curragh. The 1,000 Guineas was won by Natagore, trained by Pascal Bary. New Approach, ridden by Kevin Manning, recorded a last-gasp victory in the Derby and went on to win the Champion Stakes in devastating style. Look Here took the Oaks, giving a first domestic Classic victory to her trainer, Ralph Beckett, and jockey, Seb Sanders. Frankie Dettori rode Conduit to victory in the St Leger, providing the trainer, Sir Michael Stoute, with his first winner in the race. Zarkava, ridden by Christophe Soumillon and trained by Alain de Roye-Dupré, became only the second filly in 25 years to win the Prix de l'Arc de Triomphe. John Gosden enjoyed a Breeders' Cup double with Donativum and Raven's Pass. Ryan Moore won the jockeys' championship, while one of his predecessors, Kieren Fallon, was suspended for 18 months following a failed drugs test.

The National Hunt Festival at Cheltenham was disrupted when high winds forced the abandonment of the Wednesday programme. The races were rescheduled for the following two days. In their eagerly awaited Gold Cup meeting, Denman, ridden by Sam Thomas, beat Kauto Star by seven lengths. With Neptune Collonges finishing third, Paul Nicholls trained the first three past the post. Katchit, trained by Alan King and ridden by Robert Thornton, became the first five-year-old for 23 years to win the Champion Hurdle. Comply or Die, ridden by Timmy Murphy and trained by David Pipe, won the Grand National.

MISCELLANEOUS. Spain's Carlos Sastre won the Tour de France, holding off Cadel Evans in the time trial on the penultimate day. The sprinter Mark Cavendish became the first British rider to win four stages in a single Tour and went on to claim 17 wins in the year, more than anyone else. The Tour was again troubled by doping controversies. Among those who failed drugs tests was Bernard Kohl, who finished third overall and won the king of the mountains competition. Italy's Alessandro Ballan won the men's title in the world road race championships in Varese. In the women's event, Britain's Nicole Cooke added the world title to her Olympic crown. Britain's cyclists dominated the world championships in Manchester, winning a record-breaking nine gold medals and two silvers. Chris Hoy became the first track rider to win four world championship titles in separate disciplines. However, arguably the biggest cycling story of the year was Lance Armstrong's announcement that he would return to competition in 2009, when he would seek a record eighth Tour de France victory.

The New York Giants pulled off a major surprise in the Super Bowl, beating the New England Patriots 17-14. The Philadelphia Phillies ended a 28-year wait for a World Series baseball title when they beat the Tampa Bay Rays 4-3, while the Boston Celtics won the National Basketball Association championship for the first time since 1986, beating the LA Lakers 4-2.

John Part won the PDC World Darts Championship, beating the outsider Kirk Shepherd in the final, while Ronnie O'Sullivan won the world snooker championship for the third time, beating Ali Carter 17-8. Swimmers, helped by innovative racing suits, set a remarkable total of 108 world records during the year. Nicolas Touzaint became the first Frenchman to win the Badminton International Horse Trials, while William Fox-Pitt won a record-equalling fifth title at Burghley. Oxford won the Boat Race, beating Cambridge by six lengths.

Paul Newman

XVIII DOCUMENTS AND REFERENCE

SPEECH BY BARACK OBAMA ACCEPTING VICTORY IN US PRESIDENTIAL ELECTION

Published below is the text of the speech delivered by Barack Obama, before a crowd of 240,000 people at Grant Park, Chicago, Illinois, accepting victory in the US presidential election on the night of 4 November 2008.

OBAMA: Hello, Chicago. (APPLAUSE)

If there is anyone out there who still doubts that America is a place where all things are possible, who still wonders if the dream of our founders is alive in our time, who still questions the power of our democracy, tonight is your answer. (APPLAUSE)

It's the answer told by lines that stretched around schools and churches in numbers this nation has never seen, by people who waited three hours and four hours, many for the first time in their lives, because they believed that this time must be different, that their voices could be that difference.

It's the answer spoken by young and old, rich and poor, Democrat and Republican, black, white, Hispanic, Asian, Native American, gay, straight, disabled and not disabled. Americans who sent a message to the world that we have never been just a collection of individuals or a collection of red states and blue states.

We are, and always will be, the United States of America. (APPLAUSE)

It's the answer that led those who've been told for so long by so many to be cynical and fearful and doubtful about what we can achieve to put their hands on the arc of history and bend it once more toward the hope of a better day.

It's been a long time coming, but tonight, because of what we did on this date in this election at this defining moment change has come to America. (APPLAUSE)

A little bit earlier this evening, I received an extraordinarily gracious call from Senator McCain. (APPLAUSE)

Senator McCain fought long and hard in this campaign. And he's fought even longer and harder for the country that he loves. He has endured sacrifices for America that most of us cannot begin to imagine. We are better off for the service rendered by this brave and selfless leader.

I congratulate him; I congratulate Governor Palin for all that they've achieved. And I look forward to working with them to renew this nation's promise in the months ahead. (APPLAUSE)

I want to thank my partner in this journey, a man who campaigned from his heart, and spoke for the men and women he grew up with on the streets of Scranton... (APPLAUSE) ... and rode with on the train home to Delaware, the vice president-elect of the United States, Joe Biden. (APPLAUSE)

And I would not be standing here tonight without the unyielding support of my best friend for the last 16 years... (APPLAUSE) ... the rock of our family, the love of my life, the nation's next first lady... (APPLAUSE) ... Michelle Obama. (APPLAUSE)

Sasha and Malia... (APPLAUSE) ... I love you both more than you can imagine. And you have earned the new puppy that's coming with us... (LAUGHTER) ... to the new White House. (APPLAUSE)

And while she's no longer with us, I know my grandmother's watching, along with the family that made me who I am. I miss them tonight. I know that my debt to them is beyond measure.

To my sister Maya, my sister Alma, all my other brothers and sisters, thank you so much for all the support that you've given me. I am grateful to them. (APPLAUSE)

And to my campaign manager, David Plouffe... (APPLAUSE) ... the unsung hero of this campaign, who built the best — the best political campaign, I think, in the history of the United States of America. (APPLAUSE)

To my chief strategist David Axelrod... (APPLAUSE) ... who's been a partner with me every step of the way.

To the best campaign team ever assembled in the history of politics... (APPLAUSE) ... you made this happen, and I am forever grateful for what you've sacrificed to get it done.

But above all, I will never forget who this victory truly belongs to. It belongs to you. It belongs to you.

I was never the likeliest candidate for this office. We didn't start with much money or many endorsements. Our campaign was not hatched in the halls of Washington. It began in the backyards of Des Moines and the living rooms of Concord and the front porches of Charleston. It was built by working men and women who dug into what little savings they had to give $5 and $10 and $20 to the cause.

It grew strength from the young people who rejected the myth of their generation's apathy... (APPLAUSE) ... who left their homes and their families for jobs that offered little pay and less sleep.

It drew strength from the not-so-young people who braved the bitter cold and scorching heat to knock on doors of perfect strangers, and from the millions of Americans who volunteered and organized and proved that more than two centuries later a government of the people, by the people, and for the people has not perished from the Earth.

This is your victory. (APPLAUSE)

And I know you didn't do this just to win an election. And I know you didn't do it for me.

You did it because you understand the enormity of the task that lies ahead. For even as we celebrate tonight, we know the challenges that tomorrow will bring are the greatest of our lifetime — two wars, a planet in peril, the worst financial crisis in a century.

Even as we stand here tonight, we know there are brave Americans waking up in the deserts of Iraq and the mountains of Afghanistan to risk their lives for us.

There are mothers and fathers who will lie awake after the children fall asleep and wonder how they'll make the mortgage or pay their doctors' bills or save enough for their child's college education.

There's new energy to harness, new jobs to be created, new schools to build, and threats to meet, alliances to repair.

The road ahead will be long. Our climb will be steep. We may not get there in one year or even in one term. But, America, I have never been more hopeful than I am tonight that we will get there.

I promise you, we as a people will get there. (APPLAUSE)

AUDIENCE: Yes we can! Yes we can! Yes we can!

OBAMA: There will be setbacks and false starts. There are many who won't agree with every decision or policy I make as president. And we know the government can't solve every problem.

But I will always be honest with you about the challenges we face. I will listen to you, especially when we disagree. And, above all, I will ask you to join in the work of remaking this nation, the only way it's been done in America for 221 years — block by block, brick by brick, calloused hand by calloused hand.

What began 21 months ago in the depths of winter cannot end on this autumn night.

This victory alone is not the change we seek. It is only the chance for us to make that change. And that cannot happen if we go back to the way things were.

It can't happen without you, without a new spirit of service, a new spirit of sacrifice.

So let us summon a new spirit of patriotism, of responsibility, where each of us resolves to pitch in and work harder and look after not only ourselves but each other.

Let us remember that, if this financial crisis taught us anything, it's that we cannot have a thriving Wall Street while Main Street suffers.

In this country, we rise or fall as one nation, as one people. Let's resist the temptation to fall back on the same partisanship and pettiness and immaturity that has poisoned our politics for so long.

Let's remember that it was a man from this state who first carried the banner of the Republican Party to the White House, a party founded on the values of self-reliance and individual liberty and national unity.

Those are values that we all share. And while the Democratic Party has won a great victory tonight, we do so with a measure of humility and determination to heal the divides that have held back our progress. (APPLAUSE)

As Lincoln said to a nation far more divided than ours, we are not enemies but friends. Though passion may have strained, it must not break our bonds of affection.

And to those Americans whose support I have yet to earn, I may not have won your vote tonight, but I hear your voices. I need your help. And I will be your president, too. (APPLAUSE)

And to all those watching tonight from beyond our shores, from parliaments and palaces, to those who are huddled around radios in the forgotten corners of the world, our stories are singular, but our destiny is shared, and a new dawn of American leadership is at hand. (APPLAUSE)

To those — to those who would tear the world down: We will defeat you. To those who seek peace and security: We support you. And to all those who have wondered if America's beacon still burns as bright: Tonight we proved once more that the true strength of our nation comes not from the might of our arms or the scale of our wealth, but from the enduring power of our ideals: democracy, liberty, opportunity and unyielding hope. (APPLAUSE)

That's the true genius of America: that America can change. Our union can be perfected. What we've already achieved gives us hope for what we can and must achieve tomorrow.

This election had many firsts and many stories that will be told for generations. But one that's on my mind tonight's about a woman who cast her ballot in Atlanta. She's a lot like the millions of others who stood in line to make their voice heard in this election except for one thing: Ann Nixon Cooper is 106 years old. (APPLAUSE)

She was born just a generation past slavery; a time when there were no cars on the road or planes in the sky; when someone like her couldn't vote for two reasons — because she was a woman and because of the color of her skin. And tonight, I think about all that she's seen throughout her century in America — the heartache and the hope; the struggle and the progress; the times we were told that we can't, and the people who pressed on with that American creed: Yes we can. At a time when women's voices were silenced and their hopes dismissed, she lived to see them stand up and speak out and reach for the ballot. Yes we can. When there was despair in the dust bowl and depression across the land, she saw a nation conquer fear itself with a New Deal, new jobs, a new sense of common purpose. Yes we can.

AUDIENCE: Yes we can.

OBAMA: When the bombs fell on our harbor and tyranny threatened the world, she was there to witness a generation rise to greatness and a democracy was saved. Yes we can.

AUDIENCE: Yes we can.

OBAMA: She was there for the buses in Montgomery, the hoses in Birmingham, a bridge in Selma, and a preacher from Atlanta who told a people that "We Shall Overcome." Yes we can.

AUDIENCE: Yes we can.

OBAMA: A man touched down on the moon, a wall came down in Berlin, a world was connected by our own science and imagination.

And this year, in this election, she touched her finger to a screen, and cast her vote, because after 106 years in America, through the best of times and the darkest of hours, she knows how America can change.

Yes we can.

AUDIENCE: Yes we can.

OBAMA: America, we have come so far. We have seen so much. But there is so much more to do. So tonight, let us ask ourselves — if our children should live to see the next century; if my daughters should be so lucky to live as long as Ann Nixon Cooper, what change will they see? What progress will we have made?

This is our chance to answer that call. This is our moment.

This is our time, to put our people back to work and open doors of opportunity for our kids; to restore prosperity and promote the cause of peace; to reclaim the American dream and reaffirm that fundamental truth, that, out of many, we are one; that while we breathe, we hope. And where we are met with cynicism and doubts and those who tell us that we can't, we will respond with that time-less creed that sums up the spirit of a people: Yes, we can. (APPLAUSE)

Thank you. God bless you. And may God bless the United States of America. (APPLAUSE)

(Source: CQ Transcripts)

STATEMENT BY US TREASURY SECRETARY ON PROPOSED BAILOUT OF BANKING SYSTEM.

Published below is a statement delivered in Washington, DC on 19 September 2008 by Treasury Secretary Henry M. Paulson entitled "A Comprehensive Approach to Market Developments". *The statement was made amid an intensifying financial crisis, which had seen the federal government forced to intervene in the financial markets on a scale not seen in the post-war period. The global crisis had developed from the "credit crunch" (a shortage of liquidity in the credit markets) as a result of the securitisation of high-risk, "subprime" mortgage debt into "toxic assets", which had poisoned the financial sector. Paulson's statement introduced a plan for a huge bailout of the stricken banking system by using public funds to purchase, and thereby remove, these "troubled assets".*

Last night, Federal Reserve Chairman Ben Bernanke, SEC [Securities and Exchange Commission] Chairman Chris Cox and I had a lengthy and productive working session with Congressional leaders. We began a substantive discussion on the need for a comprehensive approach to relieving the stresses on our financial institutions and markets.

We have acted on a case-by-case basis in recent weeks, addressing problems at Fannie Mae and Freddie Mac, working with market participants to prepare for the failure of Lehman Brothers, and lending to AIG so it can sell some of its assets in an orderly manner. And this morning we've taken a number of powerful tactical steps to increase confidence in the system, including the establishment of a temporary guaranty program for the U.S. money market mutual fund industry.

Despite these steps, more is needed. We must now take further, decisive action to fundamentally and comprehensively address the root cause of our financial system's stresses.

The underlying weakness in our financial system today is the illiquid mortgage assets that have lost value as the housing correction has proceeded. These illiquid assets are choking off the flow of credit that is so vitally important to our economy. When the financial system works as it should, money and capital flow to and from households and businesses to pay for home loans, school loans and investments that create jobs. As illiquid mortgage assets block the system, the clogging of our financial markets has the potential to have significant effects on our financial system and our economy.

As we all know, lax lending practices earlier this decade led to irresponsible lending and irresponsible borrowing. This simply put too many families into mortgages they could not afford. We are seeing the impact on homeowners and neighborhoods, with 5 million homeowners now delinquent or in foreclosure. What began as a sub-prime lending problem has spread to other, less-risky mortgages, and contributed to excess home inventories that have pushed down home prices for responsible homeowners.

A similar scenario is playing out among the lenders who made those mortgages, the securitizers who bought, repackaged and resold them, and the investors who bought them. These troubled loans are now parked, or frozen, on the balance sheets of banks and other financial institutions, preventing them from financing productive loans. The inability to determine their worth has fostered uncertainty about mortgage assets, and even about the financial condition of the institutions that own them. The normal buying and selling of nearly all types of mortgage assets has become challenged.

These illiquid assets are clogging up our financial system, and undermining the strength of our otherwise sound financial institutions. As a result, Americans' personal savings are threatened, and the ability of consumers and businesses to borrow and finance spending, investment, and job creation has been disrupted. To restore confidence in our markets and our financial institutions, so they can fuel continued growth and prosperity, we must address the underlying problem.

The federal government must implement a program to remove these illiquid assets that are weighing down our financial institutions and threatening our economy. This troubled asset relief program must be properly designed and sufficiently large to have maximum impact, while including features that protect the taxpayer to the maximum extent possible. The ultimate taxpayer protection will be the stability this troubled asset relief program provides to our financial system, even as it will involve a significant investment of taxpayer dollars. I am convinced that this bold approach will cost American families far less than the alternative - a continuing series of financial institution failures and frozen credit markets unable to fund economic expansion.

I believe many members of Congress share my conviction. I will spend the weekend working with members of Congress of both parties to examine approaches to alleviate the pressure of these bad loans on our system, so credit can flow once again to American consumers and companies. Our economic health requires that we work together for prompt, bipartisan action.

As we work with the Congress to pass this legislation over the next week, other immediate actions will provide relief.

First, to provide critical additional funding to our mortgage markets, the GSEs [government sponsored enterprises] Fannie Mae and Freddie Mac will increase their purchases of mortgage-backed securities (MBS). These two enterprises must carry out their mission to support the mortgage market.

Second, to increase the availability of capital for new home loans, Treasury will expand the MBS purchase program we announced earlier this month. This will complement the capital provided by the GSEs and will help facilitate mortgage availability and affordability.

These two steps will provide some initial support to mortgage assets, but they are not enough. Many of the illiquid assets clogging our system today do not meet the regulatory requirements to be eligible for purchase by the GSEs or by the Treasury program.

I look forward to working with Congress to pass necessary legislation to remove these troubled assets from our financial system. When we get through this difficult period, which we will, our next task must be to improve the financial regulatory structure so that these past excesses do not recur. This crisis demonstrates in vivid terms that our financial regulatory structure is sub-optimal, duplicative and outdated. I have put forward my ideas for a modernized financial oversight structure that matches our modern economy, and more closely links the regulatory structure to the reasons why we regulate. That is a critical debate for another day.

Right now, our focus is restoring the strength of our financial system so it can again finance economic growth. The financial security of all Americans—their retirement savings, their home values, their ability to borrow for college, and the opportunities for more and higher-paying jobs—depends on our ability to restore our financial institutions to a sound footing.

(Source: US Department of the Treasury)

DECLARATION OF THE G-20 SUMMIT ON FINANCIAL MARKETS AND THE WORLD ECONOMY

Published below is the text of the closing declaration of the G-20 Summit on Financial Markets and the World Economy, held in Washington, DC, on 15-16 November 2008. The summit, which brought together leaders of the major industrialised countries and leading emerging economies, met to assess efforts to combat the global financial crisis and agree on measures to reform the world's financial institutions.

DECLARATION
SUMMIT ON FINANCIAL MARKETS AND THE WORLD ECONOMY
November 15, 2008

1. We, the Leaders of the Group of Twenty, held an initial meeting in Washington on November 15, 2008, amid serious challenges to the world economy and financial markets. We are determined to enhance our cooperation and work together to restore global growth and achieve needed reforms in the world's financial systems.

2. Over the past months our countries have taken urgent and exceptional measures to support the global economy and stabilize financial markets. These efforts must continue. At the same time, we must lay the foundation for reform to help to ensure that a global crisis, such as this one, does not happen again. Our work will be guided by a shared belief that market principles, open trade and investment regimes, and effectively regulated financial markets foster the dynamism, innovation, and entrepreneurship that are essential for economic growth, employment, and poverty reduction.

Root Causes of the Current Crisis

3. During a period of strong global growth, growing capital flows, and prolonged stability earlier this decade, market participants sought higher yields without an adequate appreciation of the risks and failed to exercise proper due diligence. At the same time, weak underwriting standards, unsound risk management practices, increasingly complex and opaque financial products, and consequent excessive leverage combined to create vulnerabilities in the system. Policy-makers, regulators and supervisors, in some advanced countries, did not adequately appreciate and address the risks building up in financial markets, keep pace with financial innovation, or take into account the systemic ramifications of domestic regulatory actions.

4. Major underlying factors to the current situation were, among others, inconsistent and insufficiently coordinated macroeconomic policies, inadequate structural reforms, which led to unsustainable global macroeconomic outcomes. These developments, together, contributed to excesses and ultimately resulted in severe market disruption.

Actions Taken and to Be Taken

5. We have taken strong and significant actions to date to stimulate our economies, provide liquidity, strengthen the capital of financial institutions, protect savings and deposits, address regulatory deficiencies, unfreeze credit markets, and are working to ensure that international financial institutions (IFIs) can provide critical support for the global economy.

6. But more needs to be done to stabilize financial markets and support economic growth. Economic momentum is slowing substantially in major economies and the global outlook has weakened. Many emerging market economies, which helped sustain the world economy this decade, are still experiencing good growth but increasingly are being adversely impacted by the worldwide slowdown.

7. Against this background of deteriorating economic conditions worldwide, we agreed that a broader policy response is needed, based on closer macroeconomic cooperation, to restore growth, avoid negative spillovers and support emerging market economies and developing countries. As immediate steps to achieve these objectives, as well as to address longer-term challenges, we will:

- Continue our vigorous efforts and take whatever further actions are necessary to stabilize the financial system.
- Recognize the importance of monetary policy support, as deemed appropriate to domestic conditions.
- Use fiscal measures to stimulate domestic demand to rapid effect, as appropriate, while maintaining a policy framework conducive to fiscal sustainability.
- Help emerging and developing economies gain access to finance in current difficult financial conditions, including through liquidity facilities and program support. We stress the International Monetary Fund's (IMF) important role in crisis response, welcome its new short-term liquidity facility, and urge the ongoing review of its instruments and facilities to ensure flexibility.
- Encourage the World Bank and other multilateral development banks (MDBs) to use their full capacity in support of their development agenda, and we welcome the recent introduction of new facilities by the World Bank in the areas of infrastructure and trade finance.
- Ensure that the IMF, World Bank and other MDBs have sufficient resources to continue playing their role in overcoming the crisis.

Common Principles for Reform of Financial Markets

8. In addition to the actions taken above, we will implement reforms that will strengthen financial markets and regulatory regimes so as to avoid future crises. Regulation is first and foremost the responsibility of national regulators who constitute the first line of defense against market instability. However, our financial markets are global in scope, therefore, intensified international cooperation among regulators and strengthening of international standards, where necessary, and their consistent implementation is necessary to protect against adverse cross-border, regional and global developments affecting international financial stability. Regulators must ensure that their actions support market discipline, avoid potentially adverse impacts on other countries, including regulatory arbitrage, and support competition, dynamism and innovation in the marketplace. Financial institutions must also bear their responsibility for the turmoil and should do their part to overcome it including by recognizing losses, improving disclosure and strengthening their governance and risk management practices.

9. We commit to implementing policies consistent with the following common principles for reform.

- **Strengthening Transparency and Accountability:** We will strengthen financial market transparency, including by enhancing required disclosure on complex financial products and ensuring complete and accurate disclosure by firms of their financial conditions. Incentives should be aligned to avoid excessive risk-taking.
- **Enhancing Sound Regulation:** We pledge to strengthen our regulatory regimes, prudential oversight, and risk management, and ensure that all financial markets, products and participants are regulated or subject to oversight, as appropriate to their circumstances. We will exercise strong oversight over credit rating agencies, consistent with the agreed and strengthened international code of conduct. We will also make regulatory regimes more effective over the economic cycle, while ensuring that regulation is efficient, does not stifle innovation, and encourages expanded trade in financial products and services. We commit to transparent assessments of our national regulatory systems.
- **Promoting Integrity in Financial Markets:** We commit to protect the integrity of the world's financial markets by bolstering investor and consumer protection, avoiding conflicts of interest,

preventing illegal market manipulation, fraudulent activities and abuse, and protecting against illicit finance risks arising from non-cooperative jurisdictions. We will also promote information sharing, including with respect to jurisdictions that have yet to commit to international standards with respect to bank secrecy and transparency.

- **Reinforcing International Cooperation:** We call upon our national and regional regulators to formulate their regulations and other measures in a consistent manner. Regulators should enhance their coordination and cooperation across all segments of financial markets, including with respect to cross-border capital flows. Regulators and other relevant authorities as a matter of priority should strengthen cooperation on crisis prevention, management, and resolution.
- **Reforming International Financial Institutions:** We are committed to advancing the reform of the Bretton Woods Institutions so that they can more adequately reflect changing economic weights in the world economy in order to increase their legitimacy and effectiveness. In this respect, emerging and developing economies, including the poorest countries, should have greater voice and representation. The Financial Stability Forum (FSF) must expand urgently to a broader membership of emerging economies, and other major standard setting bodies should promptly review their membership. The IMF, in collaboration with the expanded FSF and other bodies, should work to better identify vulnerabilities, anticipate potential stresses, and act swiftly to play a key role in crisis response.

Tasking of Ministers and Experts

10. We are committed to taking rapid action to implement these principles. We instruct our Finance Ministers, as coordinated by their 2009 G-20 leadership (Brazil, UK, Republic of Korea), to initiate processes and a timeline to do so. An initial list of specific measures is set forth in the attached Action Plan, including high priority actions to be completed prior to March 31, 2009.

In consultation with other economies and existing bodies, drawing upon the recommendations of such eminent independent experts as they may appoint, we request our Finance Ministers to formulate additional recommendations, including in the following specific areas:

- Mitigating against pro-cyclicality in regulatory policy;
- Reviewing and aligning global accounting standards, particularly for complex securities in times of stress;
- Strengthening the resilience and transparency of credit derivatives markets and reducing their systemic risks, including by improving the infrastructure of over-the-counter markets;
- Reviewing compensation practices as they relate to incentives for risk taking and innovation;
- Reviewing the mandates, governance, and resource requirements of the IFIs; and
- Defining the scope of systemically important institutions and determining their appropriate regulation or oversight.

11. In view of the role of the G-20 in financial systems reform, we will meet again by April 30, 2009, to review the implementation of the principles and decisions agreed today.

Commitment to an Open Global Economy

12. We recognize that these reforms will only be successful if grounded in a commitment to free market principles, including the rule of law, respect for private property, open trade and investment, competitive markets, and efficient, effectively regulated financial systems. These principles are essential to economic growth and prosperity and have lifted millions out of poverty, and have significantly raised the global standard of living. Recognizing the necessity to improve financial sector regulation, we must avoid over-regulation that would hamper economic growth and exacerbate the contraction of capital flows, including to developing countries.

13. We underscore the critical importance of rejecting protectionism and not turning inward in times of financial uncertainty. In this regard, within the next 12 months, we will refrain from raising new barriers to investment or to trade in goods and services, imposing new export restrictions, or implementing World Trade Organization (WTO) inconsistent measures to stimulate exports. Further, we shall strive to reach agreement this year on modalities that leads to a successful conclusion to the WTO's Doha Development Agenda with an ambitious and balanced outcome. We instruct our Trade Ministers to achieve this objective and stand ready to assist directly, as necessary. We also agree that our countries have the largest stake in the global trading system and therefore each must make the positive contributions necessary to achieve such an outcome.

14. We are mindful of the impact of the current crisis on developing countries, particularly the most vulnerable. We reaffirm the importance of the Millennium Development Goals, the development assistance commitments we have made, and urge both developed and emerging economies to undertake commitments consistent with their capacities and roles in the global economy. In this regard, we reaffirm the development principles agreed at the 2002 United Nations Conference on Financing for Development in Monterrey, Mexico, which emphasized country ownership and mobilizing all sources of financing for development.

15. We remain committed to addressing other critical challenges such as energy security and climate change, food security, the rule of law, and the fight against terrorism, poverty and disease.

16. As we move forward, we are confident that through continued partnership, cooperation, and multilateralism, we will overcome the challenges before us and restore stability and prosperity to the world economy.

Action Plan to Implement Principles for Reform

This Action Plan sets forth a comprehensive work plan to implement the five agreed principles for reform. Our finance ministers will work to ensure that the taskings set forth in this Action Plan are fully and vigorously implemented. They are responsible for the development and implementation of these recommendations drawing on the ongoing work of relevant bodies, including the International Monetary Fund (IMF), an expanded Financial Stability Forum (FSF), and standard setting bodies.

Strengthening Transparency and Accountability
Immediate Actions by March 31, 2009
- The key global accounting standards bodies should work to enhance guidance for valuation of securities, also taking into account the valuation of complex, illiquid products, especially during times of stress.
- Accounting standard setters should significantly advance their work to address weaknesses in accounting and disclosure standards for off-balance sheet vehicles.
- Regulators and accounting standard setters should enhance the required disclosure of complex financial instruments by firms to market participants.
- With a view toward promoting financial stability, the governance of the international accounting standard setting body should be further enhanced, including by undertaking a review of its membership, in particular in order to ensure transparency, accountability, and an appropriate relationship between this independent body and the relevant authorities.
- Private sector bodies that have already developed best practices for private pools of capital and/or hedge funds should bring forward proposals for a set of unified best practices. Finance Ministers should assess the adequacy of these proposals, drawing upon the analysis of regulators, the expanded FSF, and other relevant bodies.

Medium-term actions
- The key global accounting standards bodies should work intensively toward the objective of creating a single high-quality global standard.

- Regulators, supervisors, and accounting standard setters, as appropriate, should work with each other and the private sector on an ongoing basis to ensure consistent application and enforcement of high-quality accounting standards.
- Financial institutions should provide enhanced risk disclosures in their reporting and disclose all losses on an ongoing basis, consistent with international best practice, as appropriate. Regulators should work to ensure that a financial institution' financial statements include a complete, accurate, and timely picture of the firm's activities (including off-balance sheet activities) and are reported on a consistent and regular basis.

Enhancing Sound Regulation
Regulatory Regimes
Immediate Actions by March 31, 2009
- The IMF, expanded FSF, and other regulators and bodies should develop recommendations to mitigate pro-cyclicality, including the review of how valuation and leverage, bank capital, executive compensation, and provisioning practices may exacerbate cyclical trends.

Medium-term actions
- To the extent countries or regions have not already done so, each country or region pledges to review and report on the structure and principles of its regulatory system to ensure it is compatible with a modern and increasingly globalized financial system. To this end, all G-20 members commit to undertake a Financial Sector Assessment Program (FSAP) report and support the transparent assessments of countries' national regulatory systems.
- The appropriate bodies should review the differentiated nature of regulation in the banking, securities, and insurance sectors and provide a report outlining the issue and making recommendations on needed improvements. A review of the scope of financial regulation, with a special emphasis on institutions, instruments, and markets that are currently unregulated, along with ensuring that all systemically-important institutions are appropriately regulated, should also be undertaken.
- National and regional authorities should review resolution regimes and bankruptcy laws in light of recent experience to ensure that they permit an orderly wind-down of large complex cross-border financial institutions.
- Definitions of capital should be harmonized in order to achieve consistent measures of capital and capital adequacy.

Prudential Oversight
Immediate Actions by March 31, 2009
- Regulators should take steps to ensure that credit rating agencies meet the highest standards of the international organization of securities regulators and that they avoid conflicts of interest, provide greater disclosure to investors and to issuers, and differentiate ratings for complex products. This will help ensure that credit rating agencies have the right incentives and appropriate oversight to enable them to perform their important role in providing unbiased information and assessments to markets.
- The international organization of securities regulators should review credit rating agencies' adoption of the standards and mechanisms for monitoring compliance.
- Authorities should ensure that financial institutions maintain adequate capital in amounts necessary to sustain confidence. International standard setters should set out strengthened capital requirements for banks' structured credit and securitization activities.
- Supervisors and regulators, building on the imminent launch of central counterparty services for credit default swaps (CDS) in some countries, should: speed efforts to reduce the systemic risks

of CDS and over-the-counter (OTC) derivatives transactions; insist that market participants support exchange traded or electronic trading platforms for CDS contracts; expand OTC derivatives market transparency; and ensure that the infrastructure for OTC derivatives can support growing volumes.

Medium-term actions
• Credit Ratings Agencies that provide public ratings should be registered.
• Supervisors and central banks should develop robust and internationally consistent approaches for liquidity supervision of, and central bank liquidity operations for, cross-border banks.

Risk Management
Immediate Actions by March 31, 2009
• Regulators should develop enhanced guidance to strengthen banks' risk management practices, in line with international best practices, and should encourage financial firms to reexamine their internal controls and implement strengthened policies for sound risk management.
• Regulators should develop and implement procedures to ensure that financial firms implement policies to better manage liquidity risk, including by creating strong liquidity cushions.
• Supervisors should ensure that financial firms develop processes that provide for timely and comprehensive measurement of risk concentrations and large counterparty risk positions across products and geographies.
• Firms should reassess their risk management models to guard against stress and report to supervisors on their efforts.
• The Basel Committee should study the need for and help develop firms' new stress testing models, as appropriate.
• Financial institutions should have clear internal incentives to promote stability, and action needs to be taken, through voluntary effort or regulatory action, to avoid compensation schemes which reward excessive short-term returns or risk taking.
• Banks should exercise effective risk management and due diligence over structured products and securitization.

Medium-term actions
• International standard setting bodies, working with a broad range of economies and other appropriate bodies, should ensure that regulatory policy makers are aware and able to respond rapidly to evolution and innovation in financial markets and products.
• Authorities should monitor substantial changes in asset prices and their implications for the macroeconomy and the financial system.

Promoting Integrity in Financial Markets
Immediate Actions by March 31, 2009
• Our national and regional authorities should work together to enhance regulatory cooperation between jurisdictions on a regional and international level.
• National and regional authorities should work to promote information sharing about domestic and cross-border threats to market stability and ensure that national (or regional, where applicable) legal provisions are adequate to address these threats.
• National and regional authorities should also review business conduct rules to protect markets and investors, especially against market manipulation and fraud and strengthen their cross-border cooperation to protect the international financial system from illicit actors. In case of misconduct, there should be an appropriate sanctions regime.

Medium-term actions
- National and regional authorities should implement national and international measures that protect the global financial system from uncooperative and non-transparent jurisdictions that pose risks of illicit financial activity.
- The Financial Action Task Force should continue its important work against money laundering and terrorist financing, and we support the efforts of the World Bank - UN Stolen Asset Recovery (StAR) Initiative.
- Tax authorities, drawing upon the work of relevant bodies such as the Organization for Economic Cooperation and Development (OECD), should continue efforts to promote tax information exchange. Lack of transparency and a failure to exchange tax information should be vigorously addressed.

Reinforcing International Cooperation
Immediate Actions by March 31, 2009
- Supervisors should collaborate to establish supervisory colleges for all major cross-border financial institutions, as part of efforts to strengthen the surveillance of cross-border firms. Major global banks should meet regularly with their supervisory college for comprehensive discussions of the firm's activities and assessment of the risks it faces.
- Regulators should take all steps necessary to strengthen cross-border crisis management arrangements, including on cooperation and communication with each other and with appropriate authorities, and develop comprehensive contact lists and conduct simulation exercises, as appropriate.

Medium-term actions
- Authorities, drawing especially on the work of regulators, should collect information on areas where convergence in regulatory practices such as accounting standards, auditing, and deposit insurance is making progress, is in need of accelerated progress, or where there may be potential for progress.
- Authorities should ensure that temporary measures to restore stability and confidence have minimal distortions and are unwound in a timely, well-sequenced and coordinated manner.

Reforming International Financial Institutions
Immediate Actions by March 31, 2009
- The FSF should expand to a broader membership of emerging economies.
- The IMF, with its focus on surveillance, and the expanded FSF, with its focus on standard setting, should strengthen their collaboration, enhancing efforts to better integrate regulatory and supervisory responses into the macro-prudential policy framework and conduct early warning exercises.
- The IMF, given its universal membership and core macro-financial expertise, should, in close coordination with the FSF and others, take a leading role in drawing lessons from the current crisis, consistent with its mandate.
- We should review the adequacy of the resources of the IMF, the World Bank Group and other multilateral development banks and stand ready to increase them where necessary. The IFIs should also continue to review and adapt their lending instruments to adequately meet their members' needs and revise their lending role in the light of the ongoing financial crisis.
- We should explore ways to restore emerging and developing countries' access to credit and resume private capital flows which are critical for sustainable growth and development, including ongoing infrastructure investment.
- In cases where severe market disruptions have limited access to the necessary financing for

counter-cyclical fiscal policies, multilateral development banks must ensure arrangements are in place to support, as needed, those countries with a good track record and sound policies.

Medium-term actions

- We underscored that the Bretton Woods Institutions must be comprehensively reformed so that they can more adequately reflect changing economic weights in the world economy and be more responsive to future challenges. Emerging and developing economies should have greater voice and representation in these institutions.
- The IMF should conduct vigorous and even-handed surveillance reviews of all countries, as well as giving greater attention to their financial sectors and better integrating the reviews with the joint IMF/World Bank financial sector assessment programs. On this basis, the role of the IMF in providing macro-financial policy advice would be strengthened.
- Advanced economies, the IMF, and other international organizations should provide capacity-building programs for emerging market economies and developing countries on the formulation and the implementation of new major regulations, consistent with international standards.

(Source: G-20)

STATUS OF FORCES AGREEMENT BETWEEN USA AND IRAQ

Published below is the (unofficial) text of the Status of Forces Agreement (SOFA) between the USA and Iraq, a long-term security pact, providing for the withdrawal of US combat forces from Iraqi "cities, villages, and localities" by 30 June 2009 and of all US forces in Iraqi territory by 31 December 2011 (Article 24), and governing the rules under which US forces in Iraq would operate in the interim. The SOFA was signed on 17 November 2008 by Ryan Crocker, the US ambassador to Iraq, and Hoshyar Zebari, Iraq's foreign minister, and approved by the Iraqi Council of Representatives (legislature) on 27 November. Although not officially made public, the report—which was due to enter into force on 1 January 2009—was widely leaked to the news media.

Agreement
Between the United States of America and the Republic of Iraq
On the Withdrawal of United States Forces from Iraq and the
Organization of Their Activities during Their Temporary Presence in Iraq
Preamble

The United States of America and the Republic of Iraq, referred to hereafter as "the Parties":

Recognizing the importance of: strengthening their joint security, contributing to world peace and stability, combating terrorism in Iraq, and cooperating in the security and defense spheres, thereby deterring aggression and threats against the sovereignty, security, and territorial integrity of Iraq and against its democratic, federal, and constitutional system;

Affirming that such cooperation is based on full respect for the sovereignty of each of them in accordance with the purposes and principles of the United Nations Charter;

Out of a desire to reach a common understanding that strengthens cooperation between them;

Without prejudice to Iraqi sovereignty over its territory, waters, and airspace; and

Pursuant to joint undertakings as two sovereign, independent, and coequal countries;

Have agreed to the following:

Article 1
Scope and Purpose

This Agreement shall determine the principal provisions and requirements that regulate the temporary presence, activities, and withdrawal of the United States Forces from Iraq.

Article 2
Definition of Terms

1. "Agreed facilities and areas" are those Iraqi facilities and areas owned by the Government of Iraq that are in use by the United States Forces during the period in which this Agreement is in force.

2. "United States Forces" means the entity comprising the members of the United States Armed Forces, their associated civilian component, and all property, equipment, and materiel of the United States Armed Forces present in the territory of Iraq.

3. "Member of the United States Forces" means any individual who is a member of the United States Army, Navy, Air Force, Marine Corps, or Coast Guard.

4. "Member of the civilian component" means any civilian employed by the United States Department of Defense. This term does not include individuals normally resident in Iraq.

5. "United States contractors" and "United States contractor employees" mean non-Iraqi persons or legal entities, and their employees, who are citizens of the United States or a third country and who are in Iraq to supply goods, services, and security in Iraq to or on behalf of the United States Forces under a contract or subcontract with or for the United States Forces. However, the terms do not include persons or legal entities normally resident in the territory of Iraq.

6. "Official vehicles" means commercial vehicles that may be modified for security purposes and are basically designed for movement on various roads and designated for transportation of personnel.

7. "Military vehicles" means all types of vehicles used by the United States Forces, which were originally designated for use in combat operations and display special distinguishing numbers and symbols according to applicable United States Forces instructions and regulations.

8. "Defense equipment" means systems, weapons, supplies, equipment, munitions, and materials exclusively used in conventional warfare that are required by the United States Forces in connection with agreed activities under this Agreement and are not related, either directly or indirectly, to systems of weapons of mass destruction (chemical weapons, nuclear weapons, radiological weapons, biological weapons, and related waste of such weapons).

9. "Storage" means the keeping of defense equipment required by the United States Forces in connection with agreed activities under this Agreement.

10. "Taxes and duties" means all taxes, duties (including customs duties), fees, of whatever kind, imposed by the Government of Iraq, or its agencies, or governorates under Iraqi laws and regulations. However, the term does not include charges by the Government of Iraq, its agencies, or governorates for services requested and received by the United States Forces.

Article 3
Laws

1. While conducting military operations pursuant to this Agreement, it is the duty of members of the United States Forces and of the civilian component to respect Iraqi laws, customs, traditions, and conventions and to refrain from any activities that are inconsistent with the letter and spirit of this Agreement. It is the duty of the United States to take all necessary measures for this purpose.

2. With the exception of members of the United States Forces and of the civilian component, the United States Forces may not transfer any person into or out of Iraq on vehicles, vessels, or aircraft covered by this Agreement, unless in accordance with applicable Iraqi laws and regulations, including implementing arrangements as may be agreed to by the Government of Iraq.

Article 4
Missions

1. The Government of Iraq requests the temporary assistance of the United States Forces for the purposes of supporting Iraq in its efforts to maintain security and stability in Iraq, including cooperation in the conduct of operations against al-Qaeda and other terrorist groups, outlaw groups, and remnants of the former regime.

2. All such military operations that are carried out pursuant to this Agreement shall be conducted with the agreement of the Government of Iraq. Such operations shall be fully coordinated with Iraqi authorities. The coordination of all such military operations shall be overseen by a Joint Military Operations Coordination Committee (JMOCC) to be established pursuant to this Agreement. Issues regarding proposed military operations that cannot be resolved by the JMOCC shall be forwarded to the Joint Ministerial Committee.

3. All such operations shall be conducted with full respect for the Iraqi Constitution and the laws of Iraq. Execution of such operations shall not infringe upon the sovereignty of Iraq and its national interests, as defined by the Government of Iraq. It is the duty of the United States Forces to respect the laws, customs, and traditions of Iraq and applicable international law.

4. The Parties shall continue their efforts to cooperate to strengthen Iraq's security capabilities including, as may be mutually agreed, on training, equipping, supporting, supplying, and establishing and upgrading logistical systems, including transportation, housing, and supplies for Iraqi Security Forces.

5. The Parties retain the right to legitimate self defense within Iraq, as defined in applicable international law.

Article 5
Property Ownership

1. Iraq owns all buildings, non-relocatable structures, and assemblies connected to the soil that exist on agreed facilities and areas, including those that are used, constructed, altered, or improved by the United States Forces.

2. Upon their withdrawal, the United States Forces shall return to the Government of Iraq all the facilities and areas provided for the use of the combat forces of the United States, based on two lists. The first list of agreed facilities and areas shall take effect upon the entry into force of the Agreement. The second list shall take effect no later than June 30, 2009, the date for the withdrawal of combat forces from the cities, villages, and localities. The Government of Iraq may agree to allow the United States Forces the use of some necessary facilities for the purposes of this Agreement on withdrawal.

3. The United States shall bear all costs for construction, alterations, or improvements in the agreed facilities and areas provided for its exclusive use. The United States Forces shall consult with the Government of Iraq regarding such construction, alterations, and improvements, and must seek approval of the Government of Iraq for major construction and alteration projects. In the event that the use of agreed facilities and areas is shared, the two Parties shall bear the costs of construction, alterations, or improvements proportionately.

4. The United States shall be responsible for paying the costs for services requested and received in the agreed facilities and areas exclusively used by it, and both Parties shall be proportionally responsible for paying the costs for services requested and received in joint agreed facilities and areas.

5. Upon the discovery of any historical or cultural site or finding any strategic resource in agreed facilities and areas, all works of construction, upgrading, or modification shall cease immediately and the Iraqi representatives at the Joint Committee shall be notified to determine appropriate steps in that regard.

6. The United States shall return agreed facilities and areas and any non-relocatable structures and assemblies on them that it had built, installed, or established during the term of this Agreement, according to mechanisms and priorities set forth by the Joint Committee. Such facilities and areas shall be handed over to the Government of Iraq free of any debts and financial burdens.

7. The United States Forces shall return to the Government of Iraq the agreed facilities and areas that have heritage, moral, and political significance and any non-relocatable structures and assemblies on them that it had built, installed, or established, according to mechanisms, priorities, and a time period as mutually agreed by the Joint Committee, free of any debts or financial burdens.

8. The United States Forces shall return the agreed facilities and areas to the Government of Iraq upon the expiration or termination of this Agreement, or earlier as mutually agreed by the Parties, or when such facilities are no longer required as determined by the JMOCC, free of any debts or financial burdens.

9. The United States Forces and United States contractors shall retain title to all equipment, materials, supplies, relocatable structures, and other movable property that was legitimately imported into or legitimately acquired within the territory of Iraq in connection with this Agreement.

Article 6
Use of Agreed Facilities and Areas

1. With full respect for the sovereignty of Iraq, and as part of exchanging views between the Parties pursuant to this Agreement, Iraq grants access and use of agreed facilities and areas to the United States Forces, United States contractors, United States contractor employees, and other individuals or entities as agreed upon by the Parties.

2. In accordance with this Agreement, Iraq authorizes the United States Forces to exercise within the agreed facilities and areas all rights and powers that may be necessary to establish, use, maintain, and secure such agreed facilities and areas. The Parties shall coordinate and cooperate regarding exercising these rights and powers in the agreed facilities and areas of joint use.

3. The United States Forces shall assume control of entry to agreed facilities and areas that have been provided for its exclusive use. The Parties shall coordinate the control of entry into agreed facilities and areas for joint use and in accordance with mechanisms set forth by the JMOCC. The Parties shall coordinate guard duties in areas adjacent to agreed facilities and areas through the JMOCC.

Article 7
Positioning and Storage of Defense Equipment

The United States Forces may place within agreed facilities and areas and in other temporary locations agreed upon by the Parties defense equipment, supplies, and materials that are required by the United States Forces in connection with agreed activities under this Agreement. The use and storage of such equipment shall be proportionate to the temporary missions of the United States Forces in Iraq pursuant to Article 4 of this Agreement and shall not be related, either directly or indirectly, to systems of weapons of mass destruction (chemical weapons, nuclear weapons, radiological weapons, biological weapons, and related waste of such weapons). The United States Forces shall control the use and relocation of defense equipment that they own and are stored in Iraq. The United States Forces shall ensure that no storage depots for explosives or munitions are near residential areas, and they shall remove such materials stored therein. The United States shall provide the Government of Iraq with essential information on the numbers and types of such stocks.

Article 8
Protecting the Environment

Both Parties shall implement this Agreement in a manner consistent with protecting the natural environment and human health and safety. The United States reaffirms its commitment to respecting applicable Iraqi environmental laws, regulations, and standards in the course of executing its policies for the purposes of implementing this Agreement.

Article 9
Movement of Vehicles, Vessels, and Aircraft

1. With full respect for the relevant rules of land and maritime safety and movement, vessels and vehicles operated by or at the time exclusively for the United States Forces may enter, exit, and move within the territory of Iraq for the purposes of implementing this Agreement. The JMOCC shall develop appropriate procedures and rules to facilitate and regulate the movement of vehicles.

2. With full respect for relevant rules of safety in aviation and air navigation, United States Government aircraft and civil aircraft that are at the time operating exclusively under a contract with the United States Department of Defense are authorized to over-fly, conduct airborne refueling exclusively for the purposes of implementing this Agreement over, and land and take off within, the territory of Iraq for the purposes of implementing this Agreement. The Iraqi authorities shall grant the aforementioned aircraft permission every year to land in and take off from Iraqi territory exclusively for the purposes of implementing this Agreement. United States Government aircraft and civil aircraft that are at the time operating exclusively under a contract with the United States Department of Defense, vessels, and vehicles shall not have any party boarding them without the consent of the authorities of the United States Forces. The Joint Sub-Committee concerned with this matter shall take appropriate action to facilitate the regulation of such traffic.

3. Surveillance and control over Iraqi airspace shall transfer to Iraqi authority immediately upon entry into force of this Agreement.

4. Iraq may request from the United States Forces temporary support for the Iraqi authorities in the mission of surveillance and control of Iraqi air space.

5. United States Government aircraft and civil aircraft that are at the time operating exclusively

under contract to the United States Department of Defense shall not be subject to payment of any taxes, duties, fees, or similar charges, including overflight or navigation fees, landing, and parking fees at government airfields. Vehicles and vessels owned or operated by or at the time exclusively for the United States Forces shall not be subject to payment of any taxes, duties, fees, or similar charges, including for vessels at government ports. Such vehicles, vessels, and aircraft shall be free from registration requirements within Iraq.

6. The United States Forces shall pay fees for services requested and received.

7. Each Party shall provide the other with maps and other available information on the location of mine fields and other obstacles that can hamper or jeopardize movement within the territory and waters of Iraq.

Article 10
Contracting Procedures

The United States Forces may select contractors and enter into contracts in accordance with United States law for the purchase of materials and services in Iraq, including services of construction and building. The United States Forces shall contract with Iraqi suppliers of materials and services to the extent feasible when their bids are competitive and constitute best value. The United States Forces shall respect Iraqi law when contracting with Iraqi suppliers and contractors and shall provide Iraqi authorities with the names of Iraqi suppliers and contractors, and the amounts of relevant contracts.

Article 11
Services and Communications

1. The United States Forces may produce and provide water, electricity, and other services to agreed facilities and areas in coordination with the Iraqi authorities through the Joint Sub-Committee concerned with this matter.

2. The Government of Iraq owns all frequencies. Pertinent Iraqi authorities shall allocate to the United States Forces such frequencies as coordinated by both Parties through the JMOCC. The United States Forces shall return frequencies allocated to them at the end of their use not later than the termination of this Agreement.

3. The United States Forces shall operate their own telecommunications systems in a manner that fully respects the Constitution and laws of Iraq and in accordance with the definition of the term "telecommunications" contained in the Constitution of the International Union of Telecommunications of 1992, including the right to use necessary means and services of their own systems to ensure the full capability to operate systems of telecommunications.

4. For the purposes of this Agreement, the United States Forces are exempt from the payment of fees to use transmission airwaves and existing and future frequencies, including any administrative fees or any other related charges.

5. The United States Forces must obtain the consent of the Government of Iraq regarding any projects of infrastructure for communications that are made outside agreed facilities and areas exclusively for the purposes of this Agreement in accordance with Article 4, except in the case of actual combat operations conducted pursuant to Article 4.

6. The United States Forces shall use telecommunications systems exclusively for the purposes of this Agreement.

Article 12
Jurisdiction

Recognizing Iraq's sovereign right to determine and enforce the rules of criminal and civil law in its territory, in light of Iraq's request for temporary assistance from the United States Forces set forth in Article 4, and consistent with the duty of the members of the United States Forces and the civilian component to respect Iraqi laws, customs, traditions, and conventions, the Parties have agreed as follows:

1. Iraq shall have the primary right to exercise jurisdiction over members of the United States Forces and of the civilian component for the grave premeditated felonies enumerated pursuant to paragraph 8, when such crimes are committed outside agreed facilities and areas and outside duty status.

2. Iraq shall have the primary right to exercise jurisdiction over United States contractors and United States contractor employees.

3. The United States shall have the primary right to exercise jurisdiction over members of the United States Forces and of the civilian component for matters arising inside agreed facilities and areas; during duty status outside agreed facilities and areas; and in circumstances not covered by paragraph 1.

4. At the request of either Party, the Parties shall assist each other in the investigation of incidents and the collection and exchange of evidence to ensure the due course of justice.

5. Members of the United States Forces and of the civilian component arrested or detained by Iraqi authorities shall be notified immediately to United States Forces authorities and handed over to them within 24 hours from the time of detention or arrest. Where Iraq exercises jurisdiction pursuant to paragraph 1 of this Article, custody of an accused member of the United States Forces or of the civilian component shall reside with United States Forces authorities. United States Forces authorities shall make such accused persons available to the Iraqi authorities for purposes of investigation and trial.

6. The authorities of either Party may request the authorities of the other Party to waive its primary right to jurisdiction in a particular case. The Government of Iraq agrees to exercise jurisdiction under paragraph 1 above, only after it has determined and notifies the United States in writing within 21 days of the discovery of an alleged offense, that it is of particular importance that such jurisdiction be exercised.

7. Where the United States exercises jurisdiction pursuant to paragraph 3 of this Article, members of the United States Forces and of the civilian component shall be entitled to due process standards and protections pursuant to the Constitution and laws of the United States. Where the offense arising under paragraph 3 of this Article may involve a victim who is not a member of the United States Forces or of the civilian component, the Parties shall establish procedures through the Joint Committee to keep such persons informed as appropriate of: the status of the investigation of the crime; the bringing of charges against a suspected offender; the scheduling of court proceedings and the results of plea negotiations; opportunity to be heard at public sentencing proceedings, and to confer with the attorney for the prosecution in the case; and, assistance with filing a claim under Article 21 of this Agreement. As mutually agreed by the Parties, United States Forces authorities shall seek to hold the trials of such cases inside Iraq. If the trial of such cases is to be conducted in the United States, efforts will be undertaken to facilitate the personal attendance of the victim at the trial.

8. Where Iraq exercises jurisdiction pursuant to paragraph 1 of this Article, members of the United States Forces and of the civilian component shall be entitled to due process standards and protections consistent with those available under United States and Iraqi law. The Joint Committee shall establish procedures and mechanisms for implementing this Article, including an enumeration of the grave premeditated felonies that are subject to paragraph 1 and procedures that meet such due process standards and protections. Any exercise of jurisdiction pursuant to paragraph 1 of this Article may proceed only in accordance with these procedures and mechanisms.

9. Pursuant to paragraphs 1 and 3 of this Article, United States Forces authorities shall certify whether an alleged offense arose during duty status. In those cases where Iraqi authorities believe the circumstances require a review of this determination, the Parties shall consult immediately through the Joint Committee, and United States Forces authorities shall take full account of the facts and circumstances and any information Iraqi authorities may present bearing on the determination by United States Forces authorities.

10. The Parties shall review the provisions of this Article every 6 months including by considering any proposed amendments to this Article taking into account the security situation in Iraq, the extent to which the United States Forces in Iraq are engaged in military operations, the growth and development of the Iraqi judicial system, and changes in United States and Iraqi law.

Article 13
Carrying Weapons and Apparel

Members of the United States Forces and of the civilian component may possess and carry weapons that are owned by the United States while in Iraq according to the authority granted to them under orders and according to their requirements and duties. Members of the United States Forces may also wear uniforms during duty in Iraq.

Article 14
Entry and Exit

1. For purposes of this Agreement, members of the United States Forces and of the civilian component may enter and leave Iraq through official places of embarkation and debarkation requiring only identification cards and travel orders issued for them by the United States. The Joint Committee shall assume the task of setting up a mechanism and a process of verification to be carried out by pertinent Iraqi authorities.

2. Iraqi authorities shall have the right to inspect and verify the lists of names of members of the United States Forces and of the civilian component entering and leaving Iraq directly through the agreed facilities and areas. Said lists shall be submitted to Iraqi authorities by the United States Forces. For purposes of this Agreement, members of the United States Forces and of the civilian component may enter and leave Iraq through agreed facilities and areas requiring only identification cards issued for them by the United States. The Joint Committee shall assume the task of setting up a mechanism and a process for inspecting and verifying the validity of these documents.

Article 15
Import and Export

1. For the exclusive purposes of implementing this Agreement, the United States Forces and United States contractors may import, export (items bought in Iraq), re-export, transport, and use in Iraq any equipment, supplies, materials, and technology, provided that the materials imported or brought in by them are not banned in Iraq as of the date this Agreement enters into force. The importation, re-exportation, transportation, and use of such items shall not be subject to any inspections, licenses, or other restrictions, taxes, customs duties, or any other charges imposed in Iraq, as defined in Article 2, paragraph 10. United States Forces authorities shall provide to relevant Iraqi authorities an appropriate certification that such items are being imported by the United States Forces or United States contractors for use by the United States Forces exclusively for the purposes of this Agreement. Based on security information that becomes available, Iraqi authorities have the right to request the United States Forces to open in their presence any container in which such items are being imported in order to verify its contents. In making such a request, Iraqi authorities shall honor the security requirements of the United States Forces and, if requested to do so by the United States Forces, shall make such verifications in facilities used by the United States Forces. The exportation of Iraqi goods by the United States Forces and United States contractors shall not be subject to inspections or any restrictions other than licensing requirements. The Joint Committee shall work with the Iraqi Ministry of Trade to expedite license requirements consistent with Iraqi law for the export of goods purchased in Iraq by the United States Forces for the purposes of this Agreement. Iraq has the right to demand review of any issues arising out of this para-

graph. The Parties shall consult immediately in such cases through the Joint Committee or, if necessary, the Joint Ministerial Committee.

2. Members of the United States Forces and of the civilian component may import into Iraq, re-export, and use personal effect materials and equipment for consumption or personal use. The import into, re-export from, transfer from, and use of such imported items in Iraq shall not be subjected to licenses, other restrictions, taxes, custom duties, or any other charges imposed in Iraq, as defined in Article 2, paragraph 10. The imported quantities shall be reasonable and proportionate to personal use. United States Forces authorities will take measures to ensure that no items or material of cultural or historic significance to Iraq are being exported.

3. Any inspections of materials pursuant to paragraph 2 by Iraqi authorities must be done urgently in an agreed upon place and according to procedures established by the Joint Committee.

4. Any material imported free of customs and fees in accordance with this Agreement shall be subjected to taxes and customs and fees as defined in Article 2, paragraph 10, or any other fees valued at the time of sale in Iraq, upon sale to individuals and entities not covered by tax exemption or special import privileges. Such taxes and fees (including custom duties) shall be paid by the transferee for the items sold.

5. Materials referred to in the paragraphs of this Article must not be imported or used for commercial purposes.

Article 16
Taxes

1. Any taxes, duties, or fees as defined in Article 2, paragraph 10, with their value determined and imposed in the territory of Iraq, shall not be imposed on goods and services purchased by or on behalf of the United States Forces in Iraq for official use or on goods and services that have been purchased in Iraq on behalf of the United States Forces.

2. Members of the United States Forces and of the civilian component shall not be responsible for payment of any tax, duty, or fee that has its value determined and imposed in the territory of Iraq, unless in return for services requested and received.

Article 17
Licenses or Permits

1. Valid driver's licenses issued by United States authorities to members of the United States Forces and of the civilian component, and to United States contractor employees, shall be deemed acceptable to Iraqi authorities. Such license holders shall not be subject to a test or fee for operating the vehicles, vessels, and aircraft belonging to the United States Forces in Iraq.

2. Valid driver's licenses issued by United States authorities to members of the United States Forces and of the civilian component, and to United States contractor employees, to operate personal cars within the territory of Iraq shall be deemed acceptable to Iraqi authorities. License holders shall not be subject to a test or fee.

3. All professional licenses issued by United States authorities to members of the United States Forces and of the civilian component, and to United States contractor employees shall be deemed valid by Iraqi authorities, provided such licenses are related to the services they provide within the framework of performing their official duties for or contracts in support of the United States Forces, members of the civilian component, United States contractors, and United States contractor employees, according to terms agreed upon by the Parties.

Article 18
Official and Military Vehicles

1. Official vehicles shall display official Iraqi license plates to be agreed upon between the Parties. Iraqi authorities shall, at the request of the authorities of the United States Forces, issue regis-

tration plates for official vehicles of the United States Forces without fees, according to procedures used for the Iraqi Armed Forces. The authorities of the United States Forces shall pay to Iraqi authorities the cost of such plates.

2. Valid registration and licenses issued by United States authorities for official vehicles of the United States Forces shall be deemed acceptable by Iraqi authorities.

3. Military vehicles exclusively used by the United States Forces will be exempted from the requirements of registration and licenses, and they shall be clearly marked with numbers on such vehicles.

Article 19
Support Activities Services

1. The United States Forces, or others acting on behalf of the United States Forces, may assume the duties of establishing and administering activities and entities inside agreed facilities and areas, through which they can provide services for members of the United States Forces, the civilian component, United States contractors, and United States contractor employees. These entities and activities include military post offices; financial services; shops selling food items, medicine, and other commodities and services; and various areas to provide entertainment and telecommunications services, including radio broadcasts. The establishment of such services does not require permits.

2. Broadcasting, media, and entertainment services that reach beyond the scope of the agreed facilities and areas shall be subject to Iraqi laws.

3. Access to the Support Activities Services shall be limited to members of the United States Forces and of the civilian component, United States contractors, United States contractor employees, and other persons and entities that are agreed upon. The authorities of the United States Forces shall take appropriate actions to prevent misuse of the services provided by the mentioned activities, and prevent the sale or resale of aforementioned goods and services to persons not authorized access to these entities or to benefit from their services. The United States Forces will determine broadcasting and television programs to authorized recipients.

4. The service support entities and activities referred to in this Article shall be granted the same financial and customs exemptions granted to the United States Forces, including exemptions guaranteed in Articles 15 and 16 of this Agreement. These entities and activities that offer services shall be operated and managed in accordance with United States regulations; these entities and activities shall not be obligated to collect nor pay taxes or other fees related to the activities in connection with their operations.

5. The mail sent through the military post service shall be certified by United States Forces authorities and shall be exempt from inspection, search, and seizure by Iraqi authorities, except for non-official mail that may be subject to electronic observation. Questions arising in the course of implementation of this paragraph shall be addressed by the concerned Joint Sub-Committee and resolved by mutual agreement. The concerned Joint Sub-Committee shall periodically inspect the mechanisms by which the United States Forces authorities certify military mail.

Article 20
Currency and foreign exchange

1. The United States Forces shall have the right to use any amount of cash in United States currency or financial instruments with a designated value in United States currency exclusively for the purposes of this Agreement. Use of Iraqi currency and special banks by the United States Forces shall be in accordance with Iraqi laws.

2. The United States Forces may not export Iraqi currency from Iraq, and shall take measures to ensure that members of the United States Forces, of the civilian component, and United States contractors and United States contractor employees do not export Iraqi currency from Iraq.

Article 21
Claims

1. With the exception of claims arising from contracts, each Party shall waive the right to claim compensation against the other Party for any damage, loss, or destruction of property, or compensation for injuries or deaths that could happen to members of the force or civilian component of either Party arising out of the performance of their official duties in Iraq.

2. United States Forces authorities shall pay just and reasonable compensation in settlement of meritorious third party claims arising out of acts, omissions, or negligence of members of the United States Forces and of the civilian component done in the performance of their official duties and incident to the non-combat activities of the United States Forces. United States Forces authorities may also settle meritorious claims not arising from the performance of official duties. All claims in this paragraph shall be settled expeditiously in accordance with the laws and regulations of the United States. In settling claims, United States Forces authorities shall take into account any report of investigation or opinion regarding liability or amount of damages issued by Iraqi authorities.

3. Upon the request of either Party, the Parties shall consult immediately through the Joint Committee or, if necessary, the Joint Ministerial Committee, where issues referred to in paragraphs 1 and 2 above require review.

Article 22
Detention

1. No detention or arrest may be carried out by the United States Forces (except with respect to detention or arrest of members of the United States Forces and of the civilian component) except through an Iraqi decision issued in accordance with Iraqi law and pursuant to Article 4.

2. In the event the United States Forces detain or arrest persons as authorized by this Agreement or Iraqi law, such persons must be handed over to competent Iraqi authorities within 24 hours from the time of their detention or arrest.

3. The Iraqi authorities may request assistance from the United States Forces in detaining or arresting wanted individuals.

4. Upon entry into force of this Agreement, the United States Forces shall provide to the Government of Iraq available information on all detainees who are being held by them. Competent Iraqi authorities shall issue arrest warrants for persons who are wanted by them. The United States Forces shall act in full and effective coordination with the Government of Iraq to turn over custody of such wanted detainees to Iraqi authorities pursuant to a valid Iraqi arrest warrant and shall release all the remaining detainees in a safe and orderly manner, unless otherwise requested by the Government of Iraq and in accordance with Article 4 of this Agreement.

5. The United States Forces may not search houses or other real estate properties except by order of an Iraqi judicial warrant and in full coordination with the Government of Iraq, except in the case of actual combat operations conducted pursuant to Article 4.

Article 23
Implementation

Implementation of this Agreement and the settlement of disputes arising from the interpretation and application thereof shall be vested in the following bodies:

1. A Joint Ministerial Committee shall be established with participation at the Ministerial level determined by both Parties. The Joint Ministerial Committee shall deal with issues that are fundamental to the interpretation and implementation of this Agreement.

2. The Joint Ministerial Committee shall establish a JMOCC consisting of representatives from both Parties. The JMOCC shall be co-chaired by representatives of each Party.

3. The Joint Ministerial Committee shall also establish a Joint Committee consisting of representatives to be determined by both Parties. The Joint Committee shall be co-chaired by representatives of each Party, and shall deal with all issues related to this Agreement outside the exclusive competence of the JMOCC.

4. In accordance with paragraph 3 of this Article, the Joint Committee shall establish Joint Sub-Committees in different areas to consider the issues arising under this Agreement according to their competencies.

Article 24
Withdrawal of the United States Forces from Iraq

Recognizing the performance and increasing capacity of the Iraqi Security Forces, the assumption of full security responsibility by those Forces, and based upon the strong relationship between the Parties, an agreement on the following has been reached:

1. All the United States Forces shall withdraw from all Iraqi territory no later than December 31, 2011.

2. All United States combat forces shall withdraw from Iraqi cities, villages, and localities no later than the time at which Iraqi Security Forces assume full responsibility for security in an Iraqi province, provided that such withdrawal is completed no later than June 30, 2009.

3. United States combat forces withdrawn pursuant to paragraph 2 above shall be stationed in the agreed facilities and areas outside cities, villages, and localities to be designated by the JMOCC before the date established in paragraph 2 above.

4. The United States recognizes the sovereign right of the Government of Iraq to request the departure of the United States Forces from Iraq at any time. The Government of Iraq recognizes the sovereign right of the United States to withdraw the United States Forces from Iraq at any time.

5. The Parties agree to establish mechanisms and arrangements to reduce the number of the United States Forces during the periods of time that have been determined, and they shall agree on the locations where the United States Forces will be present.

Article 25
Measures to Terminate the Application of Chapter VII to Iraq

Acknowledging the right of the Government of Iraq not to request renewal of the Chapter VII authorization for and mandate of the multinational forces contained in United Nations Security Council Resolution 1790 (2007) that ends on December 31, 2008;

Taking note of the letters to the UN Security Council from the Prime Minister of Iraq and the Secretary of State of the United States dated December 7 and December 10, 2007, respectively, which are annexed to Resolution 1790;

Taking note of section 3 of the Declaration of Principles for a Long-Term Relationship of Cooperation and Friendship, signed by the President of the United States and the Prime Minister of Iraq on November 26, 2007, which memorialized Iraq's call for extension of the above-mentioned mandate for a final period, to end not later than December 31, 2008:

Recognizing also the dramatic and positive developments in Iraq, and noting that the situation in Iraq is fundamentally different than that which existed when the UN Security Council adopted Resolution 661 in 1990, and in particular that the threat to international peace and security posed by the Government of Iraq no longer exists, the Parties affirm in this regard that with the termination on December 31, 2008 of the Chapter VII mandate and authorization for the multinational force contained in Resolution 1790, Iraq should return to the legal and international standing that it enjoyed prior to the adoption of UN Security Council Resolution 661 (1990), and that the United States shall use its best efforts to help Iraq take the steps necessary to achieve this by December 31, 2008.

Article 26
Iraqi Assets

1. To enable Iraq to continue to develop its national economy through the rehabilitation of its economic infrastructure, as well as providing necessary essential services to the Iraqi people, and to continue to safeguard Iraq's revenues from oil and gas and other Iraqi resources and its financial and economic assets located abroad, including the Development Fund for Iraq, the United States shall ensure maximum efforts to:

a. Support Iraq to obtain forgiveness of international debt resulting from the policies of the former regime.

b. Support Iraq to achieve a comprehensive and final resolution of outstanding reparation claims inherited from the previous regime, including compensation requirements imposed by the UN Security Council on Iraq.

2. Recognizing and understanding Iraq's concern with claims based on actions perpetrated by the former regime, the President of the United States has exercised his authority to protect from United States judicial process the Development Fund for Iraq and certain other property in which Iraq has an interest. The United States shall remain fully and actively engaged with the Government of Iraq with respect to continuation of such protections and with respect to such claims.

3. Consistent with a letter from the President of the United States to be sent to the Prime Minister of Iraq, the United States remains committed to assist Iraq in connection with its request that the UN Security Council extend the protections and other arrangements established in Resolution 1483 (2003) and Resolution 1546 (2003) for petroleum, petroleum products, and natural gas originating in Iraq, proceeds and obligations from sale thereof, and the Development Fund for Iraq.

Article 27
Deterrence of Security Threats

In order to strengthen security and stability in Iraq and to contribute to the maintenance of international peace and stability, the Parties shall work actively to strengthen the political and military capabilities of the Republic of Iraq to deter threats against its sovereignty, political independence, territorial integrity, and its constitutional federal democratic system. To that end, the Parties agree as follows:

In the event of any external or internal threat or aggression against Iraq that would violate its sovereignty, political independence, or territorial integrity, waters, airspace, its democratic system or its elected institutions, and upon request by the Government of Iraq, the Parties shall immediately initiate strategic deliberations and, as may be mutually agreed, the United States shall take appropriate measures, including diplomatic, economic, or military measures, or any other measure, to deter such a threat.

The Parties agree to continue close cooperation in strengthening and maintaining military and security institutions and democratic political institutions in Iraq, including, as may be mutually agreed, cooperation in training, equipping, and arming the Iraqi Security Forces, in order to combat domestic and international terrorism and outlaw groups, upon request by the Government of Iraq.

Iraqi land, sea, and air shall not be used as a launching or transit point for attacks against other countries.

Article 28
The Green Zone

Upon entry into force of this Agreement the Government of Iraq shall have full responsibility for the Green Zone. The Government of Iraq may request from the United States Forces limited and temporary support for the Iraqi authorities in the mission of security for the Green Zone. Upon such request, relevant Iraqi authorities shall work jointly with the United States Forces authorities on security for the Green Zone during the period determined by the Government of Iraq.

Article 29
Implementing Mechanisms

Whenever the need arises, the Parties shall establish appropriate mechanisms for implementation of Articles of this Agreement, including those that do not contain specific implementation mechanisms.

Article 30
The Period for which the Agreement is Effective

1. This Agreement shall be effective for a period of three years, unless terminated sooner by either Party pursuant to paragraph 3 of this Article.

2. This Agreement shall be amended only with the official agreement of the Parties in writing and in accordance with the constitutional procedures in effect in both countries.

3. This Agreement shall terminate one year after a Party provides written notification to the other Party to that effect.

4. This Agreement shall enter into force on January 1, 2009, following an exchange of diplomatic notes confirming that the actions by the Parties necessary to bring the Agreement into force in accordance with each Party's respective constitutional procedures have been completed.

Signed in duplicate in Baghdad on this 17th day of November, 2008, in the English and Arabic languages, each text being equally authentic.

FOR THE UNITED   FOR THE
STATES OF AMERICA: REPUBLIC OF IRAQ:

(Source: Iraq Oil Report)

KOSOVO DECLARATION OF INDEPENDENCE

Published below is the text of the Declaration of Independence, adopted by the Assembly of Kosovo on 17 February 2008.

Kosovo Declaration of Independence
Sunday, 17.02.2008 17:20

Assembly of Kosovo,

Convened in an extraordinary meeting on February 17, 2008, in Pristine, the capital of Kosovo,

Answering the call of the people to build a society that honours human dignity and affirms the pride and purpose of its citizens,

Committed to confront the painful legacy of the recent past in a spirit of reconciliation and forgiveness,

Dedicated to protecting, promoting and honouring the diversity of our people,

Reaffirming our wish to become fully integrated into the Euro-Atlantic family of democracies,

Observing that Kosovo is a special case arising from Yugoslavia's non-consensual breakup and is not a precedent for any other situation,

Recalling the years of strife and violence in Kosovo, that disturbed the conscience of all civilised people,

Grateful that in 1999 the world intervened, thereby removing Belgrade's governance over Kosovo and placing Kosovo under United Nations interim administration,

Proud that Kosovo has since developed functional, multi-ethnic institutions of democracy that express freely the will of our citizens,

Recalling the years of internationally-sponsored negotiations between Belgrade and Pristina over the question of our future political status,

Regretting that no mutually-acceptable status outcome was possible, in spite of the good-faith engagement of our leaders,

Confirming that the recommendations of UN Special Envoy Martti Ahtisaari provide Kosovo with a comprehensive framework for its future development and are in line with the highest European standards of human rights and good governance,

Determined to see our status resolved in order to give our people clarity about their future, move beyond the conflicts of the past and realise the full democratic potential of our society,

Honouring all the men and women who made great sacrifices to build a better future for Kosovo,

Approves

KOSOVA DECLARATION OF INDEPENDENCE

1. We, the democratically-elected leaders of our people, hereby declare Kosovo to be an independent and sovereign state. This declaration reflects the will of our people and it is in full accordance with the recommendations of UN Special Envoy Martti Ahtisaari and his Comprehensive Proposal for the Kosovo Status Settlement.

2. We declare Kosovo to be a democratic, secular and multi-ethnic republic, guided by the principles of non-discrimination and equal protection under the law. We shall protect and promote the rights of all communities in Kosovo and create the conditions necessary for their effective participation in political and decision-making processes.

3. We accept fully the obligations for Kosovo contained in the Ahtisaari Plan, and welcome the framework it proposes to guide Kosovo in the years ahead. We shall implement in full those obliga-

tions including through priority adoption of the legislation included in its Annex XII, particularly those that protect and promote the rights of communities and their members.

4. We shall adopt as soon as possible a Constitution that enshrines our commitment to respect the human rights and fundamental freedoms of all our citizens, particularly as defined by the European Convention on Human Rights. The Constitution shall incorporate all relevant principles of the Ahtisaari Plan and be adopted through a democratic and deliberative process.

5. We welcome the international community's continued support of our democratic development through international presences established in Kosovo on the basis of UN Security Council resolution 1244 (1999). We invite and welcome an international civilian presence to supervise our implementation of the Ahtisaari Plan, and a European Union-led rule of law mission. We also invite and welcome the North Atlantic Treaty Organization to retain the leadership role of the international military presence in Kosovo and to implement responsibilities assigned to it under UN Security Council resolution 1244 (1999) and the Ahtisaari Plan, until such time as Kosovo institutions are capable of assuming these responsibilities. We shall cooperate fully with these presences to ensure Kosovo's future peace, prosperity and stability.

6. For reasons of culture, geography and history, we believe our future lies with the European family. We therefore declare our intention to take all steps necessary to facilitate full membership in the European Union as soon as feasible and implement the reforms required for European and Euro-Atlantic integration.

7. We express our deep gratitude to the United Nations for the work it has done to help us recover and rebuild from war and build institutions of democracy. We are committed to working constructively with the United Nations as it continues its work in the period ahead.

8. With independence comes the duty of responsible membership in the international community. We accept fully this duty and shall abide by the principles of the United Nations Charter, the Helsinki Final Act, other acts of the Organization on Security and Cooperation in Europe, and the international legal obligations and principles of international comity that mark the relations among states. Kosovo shall have its international borders as set forth in Annex VIII of the Ahtisaari Plan, and shall fully respect the sovereignty and territorial integrity of all our neighbours. Kosovo shall also refrain from the threat or use of force in any manner inconsistent with the purposes of the United Nations.

9. We hereby undertake the international obligations of Kosovo, including those concluded on our behalf by the United Nations Interim Administration Mission in Kosovo (UNMIK) and treaty and other obligations of the former Socialist Federal Republic of Yugoslavia to which we are bound as a former constituent part, including the Vienna Conventions on diplomatic and consular relations. We shall cooperate fully with the International Criminal Tribunal for the Former Yugoslavia. We intend to seek membership in international organisations, in which Kosovo shall seek to contribute to the pursuit of international peace and stability.

10. Kosovo declares its commitment to peace and stability in our region of southeast Europe. Our independence brings to an end the process of Yugoslavia's violent dissolution. While this process has been a painful one, we shall work tirelessly to contribute to a reconciliation that would allow southeast Europe to move beyond the conflicts of our past and forge new links of regional cooperation. We shall therefore work together with our neighbours to advance a common European future.

11. We express, in particular, our desire to establish good relations with all our neighbours, including the Republic of Serbia with whom we have deep historical, commercial and social ties that we seek to develop further in the near future. We shall continue our efforts to contribute to relations of friendship and cooperation with the Republic of Serbia, while promoting reconciliation among our people.

12. We hereby affirm, clearly, specifically, and irrevocably, that Kosovo shall be legally bound to comply with the provisions contained in this Declaration, including, especially, the obligations for it under the Ahtisaari Plan. In all of these matters, we shall act consistent with principles of international law and resolutions of the Security Council of the United Nations, including resolution 1244 (1999). We declare publicly that all states are entitled to rely upon this declaration, and appeal to them to extend to us their support and friendship.

D- 001
Pristina, 17 February 2008
President of the Assembly of Kosova
Jakup KRASNIQI

(Source: Republic of Kosovo Assembly website)

THE ILULISSAT DECLARATION

Published below is the Ilulissat Declaration, adopted at the Arctic Ocean Conference in Ilulissat, Greenland, on 27-29 May 2008, by the five coastal states bordering on the Arctic Ocean. The Conference discussed the Arctic Ocean, climate change, the marine environment, maritime safety, and the division of emergency responsibilities in the event of new shipping routes being opened. The Ilulissat Declaration agreed that such issues would be decided within the terms of existing legal regimes, rather than under a new "Arctic Treaty".

The Ilulissat Declaration
Arctic Ocean Conference
Ilulissat, Greenland, 27-29 May 2008

At the invitation of the Danish Minister for Foreign Affairs and the Premier of Greenland, representatives of the five coastal States bordering on the Arctic Ocean—Canada, Denmark, Norway, the Russian Federation and the United States of America—met at the political level on 28 May 2008 in Ilulissat, Greenland, to hold discussions. They adopted the following declaration:

The Arctic Ocean stands at the threshold of significant changes. Climate change and the melting of ice have a potential impact on vulnerable ecosystems, the livelihoods of local inhabitants and indigenous communities, and the potential exploitation of natural resources.

By virtue of their sovereignty, sovereign rights and jurisdiction in large areas of the Arctic Ocean the five coastal states are in a unique position to address these possibilities and challenges. In this regard, we recall that an extensive international legal framework applies to the Arctic Ocean as discussed between our representatives at the meeting in Oslo on 15 and 16 October 2007 at the level of senior officials. Notably, the law of the sea provides for important rights and obligations concerning the delineation of the outer limits of the continental shelf, the protection of the marine environment, including ice-covered areas, freedom of navigation, marine scientific research, and other uses of the sea. We remain committed to this legal framework and to the orderly settlement of any possible overlapping claims.

This framework provides a solid foundation for responsible management by the five coastal States and other users of this Ocean through national implementation and application of relevant provisions. We therefore see no need to develop a new comprehensive international legal regime to govern the Arctic Ocean. We will keep abreast of the developments in the Arctic Ocean and continue to implement appropriate measures.

The Arctic Ocean is a unique ecosystem, which the five coastal states have a stewardship role in protecting. Experience has shown how shipping disasters and subsequent pollution of the marine environment may cause irreversible disturbance of the ecological balance and major harm to the livelihoods of local inhabitants and indigenous communities. We will take steps in accordance with international law both nationally and in cooperation among the five states and other interested parties to ensure the protection and preservation of the fragile marine environment of the Arctic Ocean. In this regard we intend to work together including through the International Maritime Organization to strengthen existing measures and develop new measures to improve the safety of maritime navigation and prevent or reduce the risk of ship-based pollution in the Arctic Ocean.

The increased use of Arctic waters for tourism, shipping, research and resource development also increases the risk of accidents and therefore the need to further strengthen search and rescue capabilities and capacity around the Arctic Ocean to ensure an appropriate response from states to any accident. Cooperation, including on the sharing of information, is a prerequisite for addressing these challenges. We will work to promote safety of life at sea in the Arctic Ocean, including through bilateral and multilateral arrangements between or among relevant states.

The five coastal states currently cooperate closely in the Arctic Ocean with each other and with other interested parties. This cooperation includes the collection of scientific data concerning the continental shelf, the protection of the marine environment and other scientific research. We will work to strengthen this cooperation, which is based on mutual trust and transparency, inter alia, through timely exchange of data and analyses.

The Arctic Council and other international fora, including the Barents Euro-Arctic Council, have already taken important steps on specific issues, for example with regard to safety of navigation, search and rescue, environmental monitoring and disaster response and scientific cooperation, which are relevant also to the Arctic Ocean. The five coastal states of the Arctic Ocean will continue to contribute actively to the work of the Arctic Council and other relevant international fora.

Ilulissat, 28 May 2008

(Source: the Danish ministry of foreign affairs)

AUSTRALIAN PRIME MINISTER KEVIN RUDD'S APOLOGY TO AUSTRALIA'S INDIGENOUS PEOPLES

Apology to Australia's Indigenous Peoples
House of Representatives
Parliament House, Canberra

Published below is the text of the "National Apology to the Stolen Generations", *offered by Australia's Prime Minister Kevin Rudd to the Aboriginal peoples of Australia, at the televised opening of Parliament on 13 February 2008.*

—I move:

That today we honour the Indigenous peoples of this land, the oldest continuing cultures in human history.

We reflect on their past mistreatment.

We reflect in particular on the mistreatment of those who were Stolen Generations—this blemished chapter in our nation's history.

The time has now come for the nation to turn a new page in Australia's history by righting the wrongs of the past and so moving forward with confidence to the future.

We apologise for the laws and policies of successive Parliaments and governments that have inflicted profound grief, suffering and loss on these our fellow Australians.

We apologise especially for the removal of Aboriginal and Torres Strait Islander children from their families, their communities and their country.

For the pain, suffering and hurt of these Stolen Generations, their descendants and for their families left behind, we say sorry.

To the mothers and the fathers, the brothers and the sisters, for the breaking up of families and communities, we say sorry.

And for the indignity and degradation thus inflicted on a proud people and a proud culture, we say sorry.

We the Parliament of Australia respectfully request that this apology be received in the spirit in which it is offered as part of the healing of the nation.

For the future we take heart; resolving that this new page in the history of our great continent can now be written.

We today take this first step by acknowledging the past and laying claim to a future that embraces all Australians.

A future where this Parliament resolves that the injustices of the past must never, never happen again.

A future where we harness the determination of all Australians, Indigenous and non-Indigenous, to close the gap that lies between us in life expectancy, educational achievement and economic opportunity.

A future where we embrace the possibility of new solutions to enduring problems where old approaches have failed.

A future based on mutual respect, mutual resolve and mutual responsibility.

A future where all Australians, whatever their origins, are truly equal partners, with equal opportunities and with an equal stake in shaping the next chapter in the history of this great country, Australia.

There comes a time in the history of nations when their peoples must become fully reconciled to their past if they are to go forward with confidence to embrace their future. Our nation, Australia, has reached such a time. And that is why the parliament is today here assembled: to deal with this unfinished business of the nation, to remove a great stain from the nation's soul and, in a true spirit of reconciliation, to open a new chapter in the history of this great land, Australia.

Last year I made a commitment to the Australian people that if we formed the next government of the Commonwealth we would in parliament say sorry to the Stolen Generations. Today I honour that commitment. I said we would do so early in the life of the new parliament. Again, today I honour that commitment by doing so at the commencement of this the 42nd parliament of the Commonwealth. Because the time has come, well and truly come, for all peoples of our great country, for all citizens of our great Commonwealth, for all Australians—those who are Indigenous and those who are not—to come together to reconcile and together build a new future for our nation.

...There are thousands, tens of thousands of ...stories of forced separation of Aboriginal and Torres Strait Islander children from their mums and dads over the better part of a century. Some of these stories are graphically told in Bringing Them Home, the report commissioned in 1995 by Prime Minister Keating and received in 1997 by Prime Minister Howard. There is something terribly primal about these firsthand accounts. The pain is searing; it screams from the pages. The hurt, the humiliation, the degradation and the sheer brutality of the act of physically separating a mother from her children is a deep assault on our senses and on our most elemental humanity.

These stories cry out to be heard; they cry out for an apology. Instead, from the nation's parliament there has been a stony and stubborn and deafening silence for more than a decade. A view that somehow we, the parliament, should suspend our most basic instincts of what is right and what is wrong. A view that, instead, we should look for any pretext to push this great wrong to one side, to leave it languishing with the historians, the academics and the cultural warriors, as if the Stolen Generations are little more than an interesting sociological phenomenon. But the Stolen Generations are not intellectual curiosities. They are human beings, human beings who have been damaged deeply by the decisions of parliaments and governments. But, as of today, the time for denial, the time for delay, has at last come to an end.

The nation is demanding of its political leadership to take us forward. Decency, human decency, universal human decency, demands that the nation now steps forward to right a historical wrong. That is what we are doing in this place today. But should there still be doubts as to why we must now act. Let the parliament reflect for a moment on the following facts: that, between 1910 and 1970, between 10 and 30 per cent of Indigenous children were forcibly taken from their mothers and fathers. That, as a result, up to 50,000 children were forcibly taken from their families. That this was the product of the deliberate, calculated policies of the state as reflected in the explicit powers given to them under statute. That this policy was taken to such extremes by some in administrative authority that the forced extractions of children of so-called 'mixed lineage' were seen as part of a broader policy of dealing with 'the problem of the Aboriginal population'...

...These are uncomfortable things to be brought out into the light. They are not pleasant. They are profoundly disturbing. But we must acknowledge these facts if we are to deal once and for all with the argument that the policy of generic forced separation was somehow well motivated, justified by its historical context and, as a result, unworthy of any apology today.

Then we come to the argument of intergenerational responsibility, also used by some to argue against giving an apology today. But let us remember the fact that the forced removal of Aboriginal children was happening as late as the early 1970s. The 1970s is not exactly a point in remote antiquity. There are still serving members of this parliament who were first elected to this place in the early 1970s. It is well within the adult memory span of many of us. The uncomfortable truth for us all is that the parliaments of the nation, individually and collectively, enacted statutes and delegated authority under those statutes that made the forced removal of children on racial grounds fully lawful.

There is a further reason for an apology as well: it is that reconciliation is in fact an expression of a core value of our nation—and that value is a fair go for all. There is a deep and abiding belief in the Australian community that, for the Stolen Generations, there was no fair go at all. And there is a pretty basic Aussie belief that says it is time to put right this most outrageous of wrongs. It is for these reasons, quite apart from concerns of fundamental human decency, that the governments and parliaments of this nation must make this apology. Because, put simply, the laws that our parliaments enacted made the Stolen Generations possible. We, the parliaments of the nation, are ultimately responsible, not those who gave effect to our laws, the problem lay with the laws themselves. As has been said of settler societies elsewhere, we are the bearers of many blessings from our ancestors and therefore we must also be the bearer of their burdens as well. Therefore, for our nation, the course of action is clear. Therefore for our people, the course of action is clear. And that is, to deal now with what has become one of the darkest chapters in Australia's history. In doing so, we are doing more than contending with the facts, the evidence and the often rancorous public debate. In doing so, we are also wrestling with our own soul. This is not, as some would argue, a black-armband view of history; it is just the truth: the cold, confronting, uncomfortable truth. Facing with it, dealing with it, moving on from it. And until we fully confront that truth, there will always be a shadow hanging over us and our future as a fully united and fully reconciled people. It is time to reconcile. It is time to recognise the injustices of the past. It is time to say sorry. It is time to move forward together.

To the Stolen Generations, I say the following: as Prime Minister of Australia, I am sorry. On behalf of the Government of Australia, I am sorry. On behalf of the Parliament of Australia, I am sorry. And I offer you this apology without qualification. We apologise for the hurt, the pain and suffering we, the parliament, have caused you by the laws that previous parliaments have enacted. We apologise for the indignity, the degradation and the humiliation these laws embodied. We offer this apology to the mothers, the fathers, the brothers, the sisters, the families and the communities whose lives were ripped apart by the actions of successive governments under successive parliaments. In making this apology, I would also like to speak personally to the members of the Stolen Generation and their families: to those here today, so many of you; to those listening across the nation—from Yuendumu, in the central west of the Northern Territory, to Yabara, in North Queensland, and to Pitjantjatjara in South Australia.

I know that, in offering this apology on behalf of the government and the parliament, there is nothing I can say today that can take away the pain you have suffered personally. Whatever words I speak today, I cannot undo that. Words alone are not that powerful. Grief is a very personal thing. I say to non-Indigenous Australians listening today who may not fully understand why what we are doing is so important, I ask those non-Indigenous Australians to imagine for a moment if this had happened to you. I say to honourable members here present: imagine if this had happened to us. Imagine the crippling effect. Imagine how hard it would be to forgive. But my proposal is this: if the apology we extend today is accepted in the spirit of reconciliation, in which it is offered, we can today resolve together that there be a new beginning for Australia. And it is to such a new beginning that I believe the nation is now calling us.

Australians are a passionate lot. We are also a very practical lot. For us, symbolism is important but, unless the great symbolism of reconciliation is accompanied by an even greater substance, it is little more than a clanging gong. It is not sentiment that makes history; it is our actions that make history. Today's apology, however inadequate, is aimed at righting past wrongs. It is also aimed at building a bridge between Indigenous and non-Indigenous Australians—a bridge based on a real respect rather than a thinly veiled contempt. Our challenge for the future is now to cross that bridge and, in so doing, embrace a new partnership between Indigenous and non-Indigenous Australians. Embracing, as part of that partnership, expanded link-up and other critical services to help the Stolen Generations to trace their families, if at all possible, and to provide dignity to their lives. But the core of this partnership for the future is to closing the gap between Indigenous and non-Indigenous Australians on life expectancy, educational achievement and employment opportunities. This new partnership on closing the gap will set concrete targets for the future: within a decade to halve the widening gap in literacy, numeracy and employment outcomes and opportunities for Indigenous children, within a decade to halve the appalling gap in infant mortality rates between Indigenous and non-Indigenous children and, within a generation, to close the equally appalling 17-year life gap between Indigenous and non-Indigenous when it comes when it comes to overall life expectancy.

The truth is: a business as usual approach towards Indigenous Australians is not working. Most old approaches are not working. We need a new beginning. A new beginning which contains real measures of policy success or policy failure. A new beginning, a new partnership, on closing the gap with sufficient flexibility not to insist on a one-size-fits-all approach for each of the hundreds of remote and regional Indigenous communities across the country but instead allows flexible, tailored, local approaches to achieve commonly-agreed national objectives that lie at the core of our proposed new partnership. And a new beginning that draws intelligently on the experiences of new policy settings across the nation. However, unless we as a parliament set a destination for the nation, we have no clear point to guide our policy, our programs or our purpose; no centralised organising principle.

So let us resolve today to begin with the little children—a fitting place to start on this day of apology for the Stolen Generations. Let us resolve over the next five years to have every Indigenous four-year-old in a remote Aboriginal community enrolled and attending a proper early childhood education centre or opportunity and engaged in proper preliteracy and prenumeracy programs. Let us resolve to build new educational opportunities for these little ones, year by year, step by step, following the completion of their crucial preschool year. Let us resolve to use this systematic approach to building future educational opportunities for Indigenous children to provide proper primary and preventive health care for the same children, to begin the task of rolling back the obscenity that we find today in infant mortality rates in remote Indigenous communities—up to four times higher than in other communities.

None of this will be easy. Most of it will be hard—very hard. But none of it, none of it, is impossible, and all of it is achievable with clear goals, clear thinking, and by placing an absolute premium on respect, cooperation and mutual responsibility as the guiding principles of this new partnership on closing the gap. The mood of the nation is for reconciliation now, between Indigenous and non-Indigenous Australians. The mood of the nation on Indigenous policy and politics is now very simple. The nation is calling on us, the politicians, to move beyond our infantile bickering, our point-scoring and our mindlessly partisan politics and elevate at least this one core area of national responsibility to a rare position beyond the partisan divide. Surely this is the spirit, the unfulfilled spirit, of the 1967 referendum. Surely, at least from this day forward, we should give it a go.

So let me take this one step further to take what some may see as a piece of political posturing and make a practical proposal to the opposition on this day, the first full sitting day of the new parliament. I said before the election the nation needed a kind of war cabinet on parts of Indigenous policy, because the challenges are too great and the consequences too great to just allow it all to become a political football, as it has been so often in the past. I therefore propose a joint policy commission, to be led by the Leader of the Opposition and myself and, with a mandate to develop and implement—to begin with—an effective housing strategy for remote communities over the next five years. It will be consistent with the government's policy framework, a new partnership for closing the gap. If this commission operates well, I then propose that it work on the further task of constitutional recognition of the first Australians, consistent with the longstanding platform commitments of my party and the pre-election position of the opposition. This would probably be desirable in any event because, unless such a proposition were absolutely bipartisan, it would fail at a referendum. As I have said before, the time has come for new approaches to enduring problems. And working constructively together on such defined projects, I believe, would meet with the support of the nation. It is time for fresh ideas to fashion the nation's future.

Today the parliament has come together to right a great wrong. We have come together to deal with the past so that we might fully embrace the future. And we have had sufficient audacity of faith to advance a pathway to that future, with arms extended rather than with fists still clenched. So let us seize the day. Let it not become a moment of mere sentimental reflection. Let us take it with both hands and allow this day, this day of national reconciliation, to become one of those rare moments in which we might just be able to transform the way in which the nation thinks about itself, whereby the injustice administered to these Stolen Generations in the name of these, our parliaments, causes all of us to reappraise, at the deepest level of our beliefs, the real possibility of reconciliation writ large. Reconciliation across all Indigenous Australia. Reconciliation across the entire history of the often bloody encounter between those who emerged from the Dreamtime a thousand generations ago and those who, like me, came across the seas only yesterday. Reconciliation which opens up whole new possibilities for the future.

For the nation to bring the first two centuries of our settled history to a close, as we begin a new chapter and which we embrace with pride, admiration and awe these great and ancient cultures we are blessed, truly blessed, to have among us. Cultures that provide a unique, uninterrupted human thread linking our Australian continent to the most ancient prehistory of our planet. And growing from this new respect, to see our Indigenous brothers and sisters with fresh eyes, with new eyes, and with our minds wide open as to how we might tackle, together, the great practical challenges that Indigenous Australia faces in the future.

So let us turn this page together: Indigenous and non-Indigenous Australians, Government and Opposition, Commonwealth and State, and write this new chapter in our nation's story together. First Australians, First Fleeters, and those who first took the Oath of Allegiance just a few weeks ago. Let's grasp this opportunity to craft a new future for this great land: Australia. I commend the motion to the House.

(Source: website of the Prime Minister of Australia)

CANADIAN PRIME MINISTER STEPHEN HARPER'S APOLOGY TO INDIAN NATIONS

Published below is the prepared text of the apology to the former students of Canada's Indian residential schools, which was delivered by Canada's Prime Minister Stephen Harper in the House of Commons on 11 June 2008. Harper asked forgiveness for the damage that the schools had done to aboriginal culture and for the students' suffering.

Mr. Speaker, I stand before you today to offer an apology to former students of Indian residential schools.

The treatment of children in Indian residential schools is a sad chapter in our history.

[In French] For over a century the residential schools separated over 150,000 native children from their families and communities.

In the 1870s, the federal government, partly in order to meet its obligation to educate aboriginal children, began to play a role in the development and administration of these schools.

Two primary objectives of the residential schools system were to remove and isolate children from the influence of their homes, families, traditions and cultures, and to assimilate them into the dominant culture.

These objectives were based on the assumption aboriginal cultures and spiritual beliefs were inferior and unequal.

Indeed, some sought, as it was infamously said, "to kill the Indian in the child."

Today, we recognize that this policy of assimilation was wrong, has caused great harm, and has no place in our country.

132 schools financed by the federal government were located in all provinces and territories with the exception of Newfoundland, New Brunswick and PEI.

Most schools were operated as "joint ventures" with Anglican, Catholic, Presbyterian or United Churches.

The government of Canada built an educational system in which very young children were often forcibly removed from their homes, often taken far from their communities.

Many were inadequately fed, clothed and housed.

All were deprived of the care and nurturing of their parents, grandparents and communities.

First Nations, Inuit and Metis languages and cultural practices were prohibited in these schools.

Tragically, some of these children died while attending residential schools and others never returned home.

The government now recognizes that the consequences of the Indian residential schools policy were profoundly negative and that this policy has had a lasting and damaging impact on aboriginal culture, heritage and language.

While some former students have spoken positively about their experiences at residential schools, these stories are far overshadowed by tragic accounts of the emotional, physical and sexual abuse and neglect of helpless children, and their separation from powerless families and communities.

The legacy of Indian residential schools has contributed to social problems that continue to exist in many communities today.

It has taken extraordinary courage for the thousands of survivors that have come forward to speak publicly about the abuse they suffered.

It is a testament to their resilience as individuals and to the strength of their cultures.

Regrettably, many former students are not with us today and died never having received a full apology from the government of Canada.

The government recognizes that the absence of an apology has been an impediment to healing and reconciliation.

Therefore, on behalf of the government of Canada and all Canadians, I stand before you, in this chamber so central to our life as a country, to apologize to aboriginal peoples for Canada's role in the Indian residential schools system.

To the approximately 80,000 living former students, and all family members and communities, the government of Canada now recognizes that it was wrong to forcibly remove children from their homes and we apologize for having done this.

We now recognize that it was wrong to separate children from rich and vibrant cultures and traditions, that it created a void in many lives and communities, and we apologize for having done this.

We now recognize that, in separating children from their families, we undermined the ability of many to adequately parent their own children and sowed the seeds for generations to follow, and we apologize for having done this.

We now recognize that, far too often, these institutions gave rise to abuse or neglect and were inadequately controlled, and we apologize for failing to protect you.

Not only did you suffer these abuses as children, but as you became parents, you were powerless to protect your own children from suffering the same experience, and for this we are sorry.

The burden of this experience has been on your shoulders for far too long.

The burden is properly ours as a government, and as a country.

There is no place in Canada for the attitudes that inspired the Indian residential schools system to ever again prevail.

You have been working on recovering from this experience for a long time and in a very real sense, we are now joining you on this journey.

The government of Canada sincerely apologizes and asks the forgiveness of the aboriginal peoples of this country for failing them so profoundly.

Nous le regrettons.

We are sorry.

In moving towards healing, reconciliation and resolution of the sad legacy of Indian residential schools, implementation of the Indian residential schools settlement agreement began on September 19, 2007.

Years of work by survivors, communities, and aboriginal organizations culminated in an agreement that gives us a new beginning and an opportunity to move forward together in partnership.

A cornerstone of the settlement agreement is the Indian residential schools truth and reconciliation commission.

This commission presents a unique opportunity to educate all Canadians on the Indian residential schools system.

It will be a positive step in forging a new relationship between aboriginal peoples and other Canadians, a relationship based on the knowledge of our shared history, a respect for each other and a desire to move forward together with a renewed understanding that strong families, strong communities and vibrant cultures and traditions will contribute to a stronger Canada for all of us.

(Source: First Nations Summit website)

VERDICT OF THE JURY IN THE CORONER'S INQUEST INTO THE DEATHS OF DIANA, PRINCESS OF WALES AND MR DODI AL FAYED

Published below is the transcript of the verdict of the jury given in the coroner's inquest into the deaths, in August 1997, of Diana, Princess of Wales, and Dodi Al-Fayed, in a car crash in Paris. The inquest was chaired initially by Dame Elizabeth Butler-Sloss, and then by Lord Justice Scott Baker. On 7 April 2008, the jury delivered majority 9-2 verdicts of unlawful killing arising from the negligent driving, by Henri Paul, of the Mercedes in which Diana and Dodi were passengers, and of those vehicles (carrying paparazzi photographers) that were following the couple's car. In his summing up, the coroner had directed the jury that the possible verdicts were accidental death, unlawful killing by gross negligence, or an open verdict. He had ruled that there was no evidence to support the contention of Al-Fayed's father, Mohammed Al-Fayed, that the couple had been murdered in a plot by the British establishment.

Hearing transcripts
7 April 2008 - Verdict of the jury

LORD JUSTICE SCOTT BAKER: I would ask that nobody leaves the court until the reading of both inquisitions is complete, please.

SECRETARY TO THE INQUEST: Would the jury foreman please rise?

Madam Foreman, in the matter of the death of Mr Emad El-Din Mohamed Abdel Moneim Al Fayed, have you reached a verdict on which a majority of the nine of you have agreed?

THE JURY FOREMAN: We have.

SECRETARY TO THE INQUEST: Could you give us the verdict and indicate the number of jurors assenting to the verdict?

THE JURY FOREMAN: The verdict is unlawful killing, grossly negligent driving of the following vehicles and of the Mercedes.

SECRETARY TO THE INQUEST: Thank you. Could you now read the rest of the narrative on the inquisition, indicating as appropriate the -

LORD JUSTICE SCOTT BAKER: How many agreed and how many dissented?

THE JURY FOREMAN: Nine, sir. The deceased is Emad El-Din Mohamed Abdel Moneim Al Fayed. The injury causing death: multiple injuries, including severe impact injury to the chest and the transaction of the aorta. Dodi Al Fayed died in the Alma Underpass in Paris at around 12.22 am on 31st August 1997 as a result of a motor crash. The crash was caused or contributed to by the speed and manner of driving of the Mercedes, the speed and manner of driving of the following vehicles, the impairment of the judgment of the driver of the Mercedes through alcohol. There are nine of those who agree on those conclusions.

In addition, the death of the deceased was caused or contributed to by the fact that the deceased was not wearing a seat-belt, the fact that the Mercedes struck the pillar in the Alma Tunnel rather than colliding with something else, and we are unanimous on those, sir.

SECRETARY TO THE INQUEST: Is that the conclusion of your narrative verdict?

THE JURY FOREMAN: It is.

SECRETARY TO THE INQUEST: In the matter of Diana, Princess of Wales, have you reached a verdict on which at least nine of you have agreed?

THE JURY FOREMAN: We have.

SECRETARY TO THE INQUEST: Could you give us the verdict, indicating the number of jurors that have dissented to that?

THE JURY FOREMAN: The verdict is unlawful killing, grossly negligent driving of the following vehicles and of the Mercedes, and that is nine of us, sir.

SECRETARY TO THE INQUEST: Could you please read the rest of the narrative of your inquisition, indicating, where appropriate, the number of jurors who have assented to the verdict?

THE JURY FOREMAN: The deceased is Diana, Princess of Wales. The cause of death is chest injury, laceration within the left pulmonary vein and the immediate adjacent portion of the left atrium of the heart. Diana, Princess of Wales, died La Pitie-Salpetriere Hospital in Paris at around 4 am on 31st August 1997 as a result of a motor crash which occurred in the Alma Underpass in Paris on 31st August 1997 at around 12.22 am. The crash was caused or contributed to by the speed and manner of driving of the Mercedes, the speed and manner of driving of the following vehicles, the impairment of the judgment of the driver of the Mercedes through alcohol. Nine of us are agreed on those points, sir.

In addition, the death of the deceased was caused or contributed to by the fact that the deceased was not wearing a seat-belt, the fact that the Mercedes struck the pillar in the Alma Tunnel, rather than colliding with something else, and we are unanimously agreed on that.

SECRETARY TO THE INQUEST: Have the assenting jurors signed both inquisition forms?

THE JURY FOREMAN: They have.

SECRETARY TO THE INQUEST: Could you pass the forms to the usher? You may be seated.

LORD JUSTICE SCOTT BAKER: Thank you very much.

Thank you very much, members of the jury. It simply remains for me, on behalf of everyone, to give thanks to you for the obviously very, very great care that you have given to this case, not only through the six months that we have been hearing the evidence, but also in your deliberations over these last days.

I may say that I think that it is almost astonishing that you have managed to be here on every day of the six months with no absences for illness, no lateness and no other problems, meaning that you could not be here, which shows a really very considerable devotion to duty and I am sure that everybody is very grateful to you for that.

In a moment, there will be an opportunity for you to be debriefed by the court staff, which may be of some assistance, particularly in view of the unique nature of this case.

Finally, I would like to thank everybody else in court for the expedition with which it has been possible to proceed. Six months is a long time, but we have covered a lot of territory and I am grateful to counsel for all the assistance that I have had in making that possible. Thank you very much.

Oh, I should have added one very important thing. I excuse you all from jury service for life, if you so wish, and you will be getting a letter which will indicate this.

(4.33 pm)

(The inquests were concluded).

(Source: Scott Baker inquests website)

REPORT OF THE COMMISSION OF ENQUIRY INTO POST-ELECTION VIOLENCE IN KENYA

Published below is the Executive Summary of the Commission of Enquiry into post-election violence in Kenya in 2007-08, chaired by Justice Philip Waki, a judge of Kenya's Court of Appeal. The Commission comprised two additional members: Gavin McFayden (New Zealand) and Pascal Kambale (DRC). It released its report on 15 October 2008. The Commission had been established as part of a power-sharing agreement, following Kenya's disputed legislative and presidential elections of December 2007. The report concluded that political and business leaders were, in part, responsible for orchestrating the ethnic violence that followed the elections and criticised the police and security services for their ineffectual response.

Executive Summary

The mandate of the Commission of Inquiry into Post-Election Violence (CIPEV) was to investigate the facts and circumstances surrounding the violence, the conduct of state security agencies in their handling of it, and to make recommendations concerning these and other matters.

The Report comprises 5 Parts. Part I of the Report is an Introduction which discusses the historical context of the violence; Part II is a narration of the violence province by province. Part III deals with four cross cutting issues: sexual violence, internally displaced persons, the media and the nature and impact of the violence. Part IV deals with acts and omissions of state security agencies and impunity; and Part V contains recommendations made with a view to the prevention of future reoccurrence of large scale violence; the investigation of alleged perpetrators; and how to tackle the culture of impunity that has become the hallmark of violence and other crimes in the country.

Sadly, violence has been a part of Kenya's electoral processes since the restoration of multi party politics in 1991. However, the violence that shook Kenya after the 2007 general elections was unprecedented. It was by far the most deadly and the most destructive violence ever experienced in Kenya. Also, unlike previous cycles of election related violence, much of it followed, rather than preceded elections. The 2007-2008 post-election violence was also more widespread than in the past. It affected all but 2 provinces and was felt in both urban and rural parts of the country. Previously violence around election periods concentrated in a smaller number of districts mainly in Rift Valley, Western, and Coast Provinces.

As regards the conduct of state security agencies, they failed institutionally to anticipate, prepare for, and contain the violence. Often individual members of the state security agencies were also guilty of acts of violence and gross violations of the human rights of the citizens.

In some ways the post-election violence resembled the ethnic clashes of the 1990s and was but an episode in a trend of institutionalization of violence in Kenya over the years. The fact that armed militias, most of whom developed as a result of the 1990s ethnic clashes, were never de-mobilized led to the ease with which political and business leaders reactivated them for the 2007 post-election violence. Secondly, the increasing personalization of power around the presidency continues to be a factor in facilitating election related violence. The widespread belief that the presidency brings advantages for the President's ethnic group makes communities willing to exert violence to attain and keep power. Inequalities and economic marginalization, often viewed in ethnogeographic terms, were also very much at play in the post-election violence in places like the slum areas of Nairobi.

One of the main findings of the Commission's investigations is that the postelection violence was spontaneous in some geographic areas and a result of planning and organization in other areas, often with the involvement of politicians and business leaders. Some areas witnessed a combination of the two forms of violence, where what started as a spontaneous violent reaction to the perceived rigging of elections later evolved into well organized and coordinated attacks on members of ethnic groups associated with the incumbent president or the PNU party. This happened where there was an expectation that violence was inevitable whatever the results of the elections.

The report concludes that the post-election violence was more than a mere juxtaposition of citizens-to-citizens opportunistic assaults. These were systematic attacks on Kenyans based on their ethnicity and their political leanings. Attackers organized along ethnic lines, assembled considerable logistical means and traveled long distances to burn houses, maim, kill and sexually assault their occupants because these were of particular ethnic groups and political persuasion. Guilty by association was the guiding force behind deadly "revenge" attacks, with victims being identified not for what they did but for their ethnic association to other perpetrators. This free-for-all was made possible by the lawlessness stemming from an apparent collapse of state institutions and security forces.

In general, the police were overwhelmed by the massive numbers of the attackers and the relatively effective coordination of the attacks. However, in most parts of the country affected by the violence, failure on the part of the Kenya Police and the Provincial Administration to act on intelligence and other early warning signs contributed to the escalation of the violence.

The post-election violence is also the story of lack of preparedness of, and poor coordination among, different state security agencies. While the National Security Intelligence Service seemed to possess actionable intelligence on the likelihood of violence in many parts of the country, it was not clear whether and through which channel such intelligence was shared with operational security agencies. The effectiveness of the Kenya Police Service and the Administration Police was also negatively affected by the lack of clear policing operational procedures and by political expediency's adverse impact on their policing priorities.

The report recommends concrete measures to improve performance and accountability of state security agencies and coordination within the state security mechanism, including strengthening joint operational preparedness arrangements; developing comprehensive operational review processes; merging the two police agencies; and establishing an Independent Police Complaints Authority.

To break the cycle of impunity which is at the heart of the post-election violence, the report recommends the creation of a special tribunal with the mandate to prosecute crimes committed as a result of post-election violence. The tribunal will have an international component in the form of the presence of non-Kenyans on the senior investigations and prosecution staff.

(Source: the Human Security Gateway. Human Security Report Project)

UNITED KINGDOM LABOUR GOVERNMENT

(as at 31 December 2008)

Members of the Cabinet

Prime Minister, First Lord of the Treasury and Minister for the Civil Service	Rt Hon. Gordon Brown, MP
Chancellor of the Exchequer	Rt Hon. Alistair Darling, MP
Secretary of State for Foreign and Commonwealth Affairs	Rt Hon. David Miliband, MP
Secretary of State for Justice and Lord Chancellor	Rt Hon. Jack Straw, MP
Secretary of State for the Home Department	Rt Hon. Jacqui Smith, MP
Secretary of State for Health	Rt Hon. Alan Johnson, MP
Secretary of State for Business, Enterprise and Regulatory Reform	Rt Hon. Lord Mandelson
Secretary of State for Environment, Food and Rural Affairs	Rt Hon. Hilary Benn, MP
Secretary of State for International Development	Rt Hon. Douglas Alexander, MP
Secretary of State for Defence	Rt Hon. John Hutton, MP
Leader of the House of Commons, Lord Privy Seal, and Minister for Women and Equalities	Rt Hon. Harriet Harman, QC, MP
Secretary of State for Communities and Local Government	Rt Hon. Hazel Blears, MP
Secretary of State for Transport	Rt Hon. Geoff Hoon, MP
Secretary of State for Children, Schools and Families	Rt Hon. Ed Balls, MP
Secretary of State for Energy and Climate Change	Rt Hon. Edward Miliband, MP
Secretary of State for Work and Pensions	Rt Hon. James Purnell, MP
Secretary of State for Northern Ireland	Rt Hon Shaun Woodward, MP
Leader of the House of Lords and Lord President of the Council	Rt Hon. Baroness Royall of Blaisdon
Secretary of State for Culture, Media and Sport	Rt Hon Andy Burnham, MP
Secretary of State for Innovation, Universities and Skills	Rt Hon. John Denham, MP
Chief Secretary to the Treasury	Rt Hon. Yvette Cooper, MP
Secretary of State for Wales	Rt Hon. Paul Murphy, MP
Secretary of State for Scotland	Rt Hon. Jim Murphy, MP

Also attending Cabinet meetings:

Parliamentary Secretary to the Treasury and Chief Whip	Rt Hon. Nicholas Brown, MP
Minister for the Cabinet Office and Chancellor of the Duchy of Lancaster	Rt Hon. Liam Byrne, MP
Minister of State for Housing	Rt Hon. Margaret Beckett, MP
Minister for Employment and London	Rt Hon. Tony McNulty, MP
Minister for Africa, Asia and UN	Rt Hon. Lord Malloch-Brown, KCMG
Minister for Science	Rt Hon. Lord Drayson
Minister for the Olympics and Paymaster General	Rt Hon. Tessa Jowell, MP
Attorney General	Rt Hon. Baroness Scotland of Asthal, QC
Minister of State for Europe	Rt Hon. Caroline Flint, MP
Minister for Children, Young People and Families	Rt Hon. Beverley Hughes, MP

UNITED STATES REPUBLICAN ADMINISTRATION

(as at 31 December 2008)

Members of the Cabinet

President	George W. Bush
Secretary of Agriculture	Ed Schafer
Secretary of Commerce	Carlos Gutierrez
Secretary of Defence	Robert M. Gates
Secretary of Education	Margaret Spellings
Secretary of Energy	Samuel W. Bodman
Secretary of Health and Human Services	Michael O. Leavitt
Secretary of Homeland Security	Michael Chertoff
Secretary of Housing and Urban Development	Steve Preston
Secretary of the Interior	Dirk Kempthorne
Attorney General and Head of Department of Justice	Michael Mukasey
Secretary of Labour	Elaine Chao
Secretary of State	Condoleezza Rice
Secretary of Transportation	Mary E. Peters
Secretary of the Treasury	Henry M. Paulson, Jr
Secretary of Veterans' Affairs	Dr James Peake

Cabinet Rank Members

Vice President	Richard B. Cheney
Director of Office of Management and Budget	Jim Nussle
Administrator of Environmental Protection Agency	Stephen Johnson
White House Chief of Staff	Joshua B. Bolten
United States Trade Representative	Ambassador Susan Schwab
Director of Office of National Drug Control Policy	John Walters

MEMBERS OF THE EUROPEAN COMMISSION

(as at 31 December 2008)

Members of the European Commission, 2004-2009

José Manuel Barroso (Portugal)	*President*
Margot Wallström(Sweden)	*Vice-President; Institutional Relations and Communication Strategy*
Günter Verheugen (Germany)	*Vice-President; Enterprise and Industry*
Jacques Barrot (France)	*Vice-President; Justice, Freedom and Security (previously in charge of transport)*
Siim Kallas (Estonia)	*Vice-President; Administrative Affairs, Audit and Anti-Fraud*
Antonio Tajani (Italy)	*Vice-President; Transport (replaced Franco Frattini on 9 May 2008)*
Viviane Reding (Luxembourg)	*Information Society and Media*
Stavros Dimas (Greece)	*Environment*
Joaquín Almunia (Spain)	*Economic and Monetary Affairs*
Danuta Hübner (Poland)	*Regional Policy*
Joe Borg (Malta)	*Maritime Affairs and Fisheries*
Dalia Grybauskaite (Lithuania)	*Financial Programming and Budget*
Janez Potocnik (Slovenia)	*Science and Research*
Ján Figel (Slovakia)	*Education, Training, Culture and Youth*
Olli Rehn (Finland)	*Enlargement*
Louis Michel (Belgium)	*Development and Humanitarian Aid*
László Kovács (Hungary)	*Taxation and Customs Union*
Neelie Kroes (Netherlands)	*Competition*
Mariann Fischer Boel (Denmark)	*Agriculture and Rural Development*
Benita Ferrero-Waldner (Austria)	*External Relations and European Neighbourhood Policy*
Charlie McCreevy (Ireland)	*Internal Market and Services*
Vladimír Spidla (Czech Republic)	*Employment, Social Affairs and Equal Opportunities*
Andris Piebalgs (Latvia)	*Energy*
Meglena Kuneva (Bulgaria)	*Consumer Protection*
Leonard Orban (Romania)	*Multilingualism*
Androulia Vassiliou (Cyprus)	*Health (replaced Markos Kyprianou on 10 April 2008)*
Catherine Ashton (UK)	*Trade (replaced Peter Mandelson on 6 October 2008)*

NOBEL LAUREATES 2008

THE NOBEL PRIZE IN PHYSICS 2008
"for the discovery of the mechanism of spontaneous broken symmetry in subatomic physics" (1/2 of the prize):
Yoichiro Nambu, USA, (b. 1921, in Tokyo, Japan); Enrico Fermi Institute, University of Chicago, USA.

"for the discovery of the origin of the broken symmetry which predicts the existence of at least three families of quarks in nature" (1/2 of the prize):
Makoto Kobayashi, Japan (b. 1944); High Energy Accelerator Research Organisation (KEK), Tsukuba, Japan.
Toshihide Maskawa, Japan (b. 1940); Kyoto Sangyo University; Yukawa Institute for Theoretical Physics (YITP), Kyoto University, Japan.

THE NOBEL PRIZE IN CHEMISTRY 2008
"for the discovery and development of the green fluorescent protein, GFP":
Osamu Shimomura, USA, (b. 1928, in Kyoto, Japan); Marine Biological Laboratory (MBL), Woods Hole; Boston University Medical School, Massachusetts, USA.
Martin Chalfie, USA, (b. 1947); Columbia University, New York, USA.
Roger Y. Tsien, USA, (b. 1952); University of California, San Diego, USA; Howard Hughes Medical Institute

THE NOBEL PRIZE IN PHYSIOLOGY OR MEDICINE 2008
"for his discovery of human papilloma viruses causing cervical cancer" (1/2 of the prize):
Harald zur Hausen, Germany (b. 1936); German Cancer Research Centre, Heidelberg, Germany

"for their discovery of human immunodeficiency virus" (1/2 of the prize):
Françoise Barré-Sinoussi, France, (b. 1947); Regulation of Retroviral Infections Unit, Virology Department, Institut Pasteur, Paris, France.
Luc Montagnier, France, (b. 1932); World Foundation for AIDS Research and Prevention, Paris, France.

THE NOBEL PRIZE IN LITERATURE 2008
"author of new departures, poetic adventure and sensual ecstasy, explorer of a humanity beyond and below the reigning civilization":
Jean-Marie Gustave Le Clézio, France, (b. 1940).

THE NOBEL PEACE PRIZE 2008
"for his important efforts, on several continents and over more than three decades, to resolve international conflicts":
Martti Ahtisaari, Finland, (b. 1937).

THE SVERIGES RIKSBANK PRIZE IN ECONOMIC SCIENCES IN MEMORY OF ALFRED NOBEL 2008
"for his analysis of trade patterns and location of economic activity":
Paul Krugman, USA, (b. 1953); Princeton University, USA

(Source: the Nobel Foundation)

INTERNATIONAL COMPARISONS:
POPULATION, GDP AND GROWTH

The following table gives population, gross domestic product (GDP) and growth data for the main member states of the Organisation for Economic Co-operation and Development, plus selected other countries.

(Source: World Bank, Washington, DC)

	Population (million)			GDP ($000mn)		
			Avg. annual % growth			Avg. annual % growth
	2006	**2007**	**2000-07**	**2006**	**2007**	**2000-07**
Algeria	33.3	33.9	1.5	114.7	135.3	4.5
Argentina	39.1	39.5	1.0	214.1	262.3	4.7
Australia	20.5	21.0	1.3	768.2	821.7	3.3
Austria	8.2	8.3	0.5	322.4	377.0	1.9
Bangladesh	144.3	158.6	1.8	62.0	67.7	5.8
Belgium	10.5	10.6	0.5	392.0	448.6	1.9
Brazil	188.7	191.6	1.4	1,068.0	1,314.2	3.3
Canada	32.6	33.0	1.0	1,251.5	1,326.4	2.7
Chile	16.5	16.6	1.1	145.8	163.9	4.5
China	1,311.8	1,320.0	0.6	2,668.1	3,280.1	10.2
Colombia	45.6	46.1	1.4	135.8	172.0	4.5
Denmark	5.4	5.5	0.3	275.2	308.1	1.8
Egypt	75.4	75.5	1.8	107.5	128.1	4.5
Finland	5.3	5.3	0.3	209.4	246.0	3.1
France	61.0	61.7	0.7	2,230.7	2,562.3	1.7
Germany	82.4	82.3	0.0	2,906.7	3,297.2	1.1
Greece	11.1	11.2	0.4	245.0	360.0	4.3
Hungary	10.1	10.0	-0.2	112.9	138.2	4.0
India	1,109.8	1,123.3	1.4	906.3	1,171.0	7.8
Indonesia	223.0	225.6	1.3	364.5	432.8	5.1
Iran	69.2	71.0	1.5	222.9	270.9	5.9
Irish Republic	4.2	4.4	2.0	222.7	255.0	5.2
Italy	58.6	59.4	0.6	1,844.7	2,107.5	0.8
Japan	127.6	127.8	0.1	4,340.1	4,376.7	1.7
Kenya	35.1	37.5	2.6	21.2	29.5	4.4
South Korea	48.4	48.5	0.5	888.0	969.8	4.7
Malaysia	25.8	26.6	1.9	148.9	180.7	5.1
Mexico	104.2	105.3	1.0	839.2	893.4	2.6
Netherlands	16.4	16.4	0.4	657.6	754.2	1.6
New Zealand	4.1	4.2	1.3	103.9	129.4	3.2
Nigeria	144.4	148.0	2.4	114.7	165.7	6.7
Norway	4.6	4.7	0.7	311.0	382.0	2.5
Pakistan	159.0	162.4	2.3	128.8	143.6	5.8
Philippines	84.6	87.9	2.0	116.9	144.1	5.1
Poland	38.1	38.1	-0.1	338.7	420.3	4.1
Portugal	10.6	10.6	0.5	192.6	220.2	0.8
Russia	142.4	141.6	-0.5	986.9	1,291.0	6.6
South Africa	47.4	47.6	1.1	255.0	277.6	4.3
Spain	43.5	44.9	1.6	1,224.0	1,429.2	3.4
Sweden	9.0	9.1	0.4	384.9	444.4	2.8
Switzerland	7.4	7.6	0.7	379.8	415.5	1.6
Thailand	64.7	63.8	0.7	206.2	245.8	5.4
Turkey	72.9	73.9	1.3	402.7	657.1	5.9
United Kingdom	60.4	61.0	0.5	2,345.0	2,727.8	2.6
USA	299.0	301.6	0.9	13,201.8	13,811.2	2.7
Venezuela	27.0	27.5	1.7	181.9	228.1	4.7
Vietnam	84.1	85.1	1.3	60.9	71.2	7.8

XIX OBITUARY

Abse, Leo (b. 1917), British lawyer and Labour MP for the Welsh constituency of Pontypool (renamed Torfaen in 1983) for 29 years, who introduced a number of social reforms. Educated at Howard Gardens high school and the London School of Economics, he became a solicitor in Cardiff, where he continued to practise all his working life. After serving in the RAF during World War II, he became chairman of the Cardiff city Labour party, and in 1958 successfully contested a by-election at Pontypool. He introduced a number of private member's bills on homosexual and divorce reform, and in 1967 successfully secured the passing of the Sexual Offences Act and, in the same year, the Family Planning Act. Subsequently he was active in the campaign to abolish capital punishment; sponsored a children's bill, which eventually became the Children's Act of 1975; and a divorce bill, which was taken over by the government to become the Matrimonial and Proceedings Act of 1985. He also took to writing, publishing—among other books—*Private Member* in 1973 and, after retiring from Parliament in 1987, books about Margaret Thatcher and Tony Blair. Died 19 August.

al-Mirghani, Sayyid Ahmed (b. 1941), president of Sudan 1986-89, during the country's brief period of democracy. Born in Khartoum, he was educated locally and was still at school when Sudan became independent in 1956 and when the elected government was ousted in a military coup two years later. Al-Mirghani then went to the University of London, where he studied economics. On his return, following another military coup, which brought Colonel Jafaar al-Nimeiri to power, he was eventually appointed Sudan's ambassador in Cairo. In 1986, following another coup, elections were held and Sadeq al-Mahdi became prime minister. Al-Mirghani, now head of the Democratic Unionist Party (DUP), was appointed president, heading a five-member presidency council. In 1988 the DUP signed an agreement with the Sudan People's Liberation Movement, which appeared to bring about an agreed settlement of the long-running civil war. Instead al-Mahdi's coalition government rejected the agreement, and shortly afterwards al-Mirghani lost his position in a coup which brought Omar al-Bashir to power. Al-Mirghani went into exile, returning 12 years later, in 2001, as moves began finally to bring about a comprehensive peace agreement, but suffered a stroke in 2008. Died 2 November.

Aleksii II (b. 1929), Patriarch of Moscow and All Russia, who restored the Russian Orthodox Church's authority following the collapse of the Soviet Union. Born Aleksei Ridiger in Tallinn, Estonia, he entered the Theological Seminary in Leningrad in 1947 and the Leningrad Theological Academy two years later. He was ordained deacon and appointed rector in Tallinn in 1950, becoming archpriest in 1958, bishop of Tallinn in 1961, archbishop in 1964, and metropolitan in 1968. The fact that his rise to power took place when the KGB had control of the Orthodox Church led some to believe that he collaborated with, or was even an active agent of, the KGB, a charge he always denied. In 1990 he succeeded Patriarch Pimen. He took advantage of the liberalising policies of Mikhail Gorbachev to push for greater freedom of religion, but later sought to promote the primacy of the Russian Orthodox Church, an agenda that suited the more nationalistic policies of Presidents Boris Yeltsin and Vladimir Putin. With their co-operation he was able to revive faith and the influence of the church in Russia. Many of the churches that had been destroyed, notably the Cathedral of Christ the Saviour in Moscow, which Josef Stalin had demolished, were rebuilt, and by the time of Aleksii's death it was estimated that some two-thirds of the Russian people were at least nominally members of the Orthodox Church. Died 5 December.

Armstrong, Anne (b. 1927), US ambassador to the UK and a dedicated supporter of the Republican party. Born Anne Legendre in New

Orleans, she was educated at Foxcroft school in Middleburg, Virginia, and at Vassar College, and had her first political experience working as a volunteer in Harry S. Truman's presidential campaign of 1948, but subsequently decided that she was a Republican rather than a Democrat. After marrying Tobin Armstrong, who ran a cattle ranch in Texas, in 1950 she confined herself to local politics until 1971, when she was appointed co-chairman of the Republican national committee. Two years later she was appointed counsellor, with cabinet rank, to President Richard Nixon, to whom she remained loyal until he was directly implicated in the Watergate scandal. After his resignation she became counsellor to President Gerald Ford and subsequently, in 1976, was appointed ambassador to the UK. Her elegance and informal style, together with her courage in making an early visit to Northern Ireland during the bombing campaign, made her a popular figure in Britain, but she had to resign following the election of Democratic President Jimmy Carter in 1977. Back in the USA she worked for Ronald Reagan's presidential campaign and from 1981 to 1990 was chairman of the president's foreign intelligence advisory board. She was awarded the Presidential Medal of Freedom in 1987. Died 30 July.

Buckley Jr, William F. (b. 1925), US author and political columnist, who championed the conservative cause. Born in New York, he was educated at schools in Venezuela, England, France, the USA and, for a time, at Mexico University before being drafted into the US Army, after which he went to Yale. His experiences there prompted him to write his first book, *God and Man at Yale*, published in 1951. After working on *The American Mercury* he founded, and edited, the *National Review* as an antidote—as he put it—to the liberal influence in US public affairs. He also wrote for many other publications and began a column, "A Conservative Voice", which was subsequently syndicated in some 300 newspapers. In 1966 he started a weekly television programme, *Firing Line,* in which he interviewed most of the leading politicians of the day. He ran unsuccessfully in 1964 for the mayoralty of New York City but later for a time served as a US delegate to the UN General Assembly. These experiences provided material for two more books: *The Unmaking of a Mayor* (1966), and *United Nations Journal* (1974). Two years later, with *Saving the Queen,* he began a series of best-selling novels, while continuing to write articles and essays promoting US conservatism and achieving some of its ambitions with the election of Ronald Reagan in 1981. Buckley was awarded the Presidential Medal of Freedom in 1991. Died 27 February.

Clarke, Sir Arthur C. (b. 1917), British writer of science fiction, who produced more than 100 books and pointed to the age of satellite communications, Moon landings, and compact computers. Born in Minehead, Somerset, he was educated at Huish's grammar school in Taunton and King's College, London, and worked initially in the civil service. During World War II he served in the RAF, where he joined a US team working on a microwave beam unit, which led him to suggest, in 1945, that radio signals might be bounced back from a satellite if it could be put into geosynchronous orbit. He published his first book, *Interplanetary Flight*, in 1950 and his second, *The Exploration of Space*, in 1951 when his first novel, *Prelude to Space*, was also published. He had, in addition, written a short story, subsequently published as *The Sentinel*, which described the discovery of a monolithic alien object on the Moon. The idea was eventually taken up by the film director Stanley Kubrick, and the two collaborated on a screenplay for the film *2001: A Space Odyssey*. By this time Clarke was living permanently in Sri Lanka, where he continued to write both fiction and non-fiction works at an average of about one a year, including the popular series of novels, beginning with *Rendezvous with Rama* in 1972 (subsequent books in the series being co-written with Gentry Lee). He also appeared in a television series, *Arthur C. Clarke's Mysterious Worlds*. He was appointed CBE in 1989 and knighted in 1998. Died 19 March.

Conté, Lansana (b. 1934), president of Guinea, who seized power in a military coup in 1984 and retained it for the rest of his life. Born in Moussaya, some 40 miles from the capital Conakry, he was educated locally before going to military schools in Senegal and Côte d'Ivoire. He enlisted in the French Army in 1955 and was posted to Algeria until Guinea was given its independence in 1958, when he returned to serve under President Ahmed Sékou Touré, becoming chief of staff in 1975. Elected to the National Assembly (the legislature) in 1980, he seized power in a bloodless coup on Sékou Touré's death in 1984, declaring himself president and abolishing the constitution. Once securely in power he encouraged overseas investment and development of the country's mineral wealth and, in 1990, allowed a referendum that seemed to introduce a democratic system of government. A new constitution was drafted, political parties made legal and, in 1993, the country experienced its first presidential election. Conté won, amid suspicions of ballot rigging, and won a second term in 1998. In 2001 the constitution was amended to allow him an unlimited number of terms as president. He duly won a third term in 2003, and his firm control saved Guinea from the wars that raged in the neighbouring countries of Sierra Leone, Liberia, and Côte d'Ivoire. But his health was now declining and so was the state of the country. Conté responded to riots and a general strike in 2007 by declaring martial law, and clinging to power, though now desperately ill. Died 22 December.

Cook, Beryl (b. 1926), British artist whose exuberant paintings of fat ladies and other unlikely subjects appealed to the public, if not to art critics. Born Beryl Lansley at Egham, in Surrey, she was educated at Kendrick girls' school, Reading, until the age of 14, when she left to train as a typist. In 1948 she married the boy next door, John Cook, a merchant seaman, and spent most of her first 10 years of marriage on her own, until her husband took jobs first in Rhodesia and later in Zambia. When they returned to England in 1964 they took a cottage in Cornwall and later a house in Plymouth, both of which needed something to hang on the walls. Beryl, who was untaught, began to sketch the subjects she found around her—sailors and holidaymakers on the beaches and in the pubs—taking home the sketches to transfer them into oils on board. Persuaded to exhibit them at the Plymouth arts centre, she sold out her paint-

ings, which from then on were much in demand and were eventually selling for about £30,000 each. In addition there were books, greetings cards, advertisements, and postage stamps, enough to keep her painting happily for the rest of her life. Died 28 May.

Cornioley, Pearl (b. 1914), wartime agent in France for the British Special Operations Executive (SOE). Born Pearl Witherington in Paris, she was working as a secretary in the British embassy when the Germans invaded and, after escaping with her family via Spain and Gibraltar, she joined the Women's Auxiliary Air Force. She later volunteered for the SOE and, after several weeks training, was dropped by parachute into France, where she joined a Resistance group in the southern Loire valley. Her main job was to act as a courier of coded messages until, in 1944, the leader of her network, Maurice Southgate, was captured and she took control of the résistants in the Sologne, soon to number about 3,000. Their task was to disrupt German supply lines and stop the Germans moving north or back to Germany; more than 18,000 Germans surrendered in their area. A price of 1 million francs was put on her head, but she was never betrayed. She eventually made her way back to England, where in October 1944 she married Henri Cornioley, with whom she had been working in the Resistance. Recommended for a Military Cross, Pearl was offered a civil MBE, which she refused on the grounds that there was nothing civil about what she had been doing. She was then awarded a military MBE and finally, in 2004, a CBE. Died 23 February.

Cotton, Sir Bill (b. 1928), British television executive whose understanding of show business and popular taste provided the BBC with some of its most successful programmes. Born in London, the son of the bandleader whose *Billy Cotton Band Show* had been a popular feature on radio, TV, and on the halls, Bill Cotton Jr was educated at Ardingly before establishing himself in music publishing. In 1956 he joined the BBC, where he produced *Six-Five Special* and, with some reluctance, his father's band show. He was appointed assistant head of BBC light entertainment in 1962, head of variety in 1967, and head of light entertainment in 1970, years in which he became associated with a number of successful programmes, recruiting Bruce Forsyth to *The Generation Game*, Michael Parkinson for his talk show, Ronnie Barker and Ronnie Corbett for *The Two Ronnies*, and capturing Eric Morecambe and Ernie Wise from ITV for *The Morecambe and Wise Show*. In 1977 Cotton was appointed controller of BBC1 and in 1984 he was made managing director of BBC Television, retiring four years later when he reached the BBC's retiring age of 60. He was knighted in 2001. Died 11 August.

Cox, Sir Geoffrey (b. 1910), New Zealand journalist, who became editor and chief executive of Independent Television News (ITN) in Britain. Educated at Southland high school and Otago University, he went on to Oriel College, Oxford as a Rhodes scholar before joining the *News Chronicle* as a reporter. Later he was appointed a foreign correspondent on the *Daily Express*, first in Vienna and later based in Paris, where he organised the escape of *Daily Express* staff as the Germans approached. In World War II Cox volunteered for the New Zealand Army, serving in Greece, Crete, Libya, and Italy and in 1943 was sent to Washington, DC as his country's representative on the Pacific War council. After the war, he rejoined the *News Chronicle* before being appointed editor and chief executive of ITN in 1956. His main achievements in the post, which he retained until 1968, were the breaking down of the limitations on reporting, such as the 14-day rule (which banned TV from discussing issues that were due to come before Parliament within 14 days), the restrictions on reporting parliamentary elections, and the reverential approach to the conduct of television interviews. He appointed Robin Day to become the grand inquisitor of political leaders and, following the introduction of satellite reporting, campaigned successfully to extend ITN news to a half-hour programme. When he left ITN, Cox became deputy chairman of Yorkshire Television and later chairman of Tyne Tees Television. He was knighted in 1966 and appointed a Companion of the New Zealand Order of Merit in 2000. Died 2 April.

Crichton, Michael (b. 1942), US novelist, film director, and producer whose successes included *Jurassic Park* and *Rising Sun*, as well as the TV series *ER*. Born in Chicago, he was educated at Harvard University, where he read anthropology, after which he spent a year at Cambridge University as a visiting lecturer. In 1966 he returned to Harvard to read medicine, and though he emerged with a medical degree he had also written a number of novels, under the names of John Lange and Jeffrey Hudson, and decided to make this his career. He confirmed his talent by writing the best-seller, *The Andromeda Strain* (1969), which was made into a film in 1971. A series of less successful novels followed until *Jurassic Park* hit the jackpot, both as a novel (1990) and the film which followed (1993). In 1994 he branched out into television with the medical drama *ER*, which became one of the most popular weekly series in the USA, the UK, and many other countries. Crichton was married five times, the first four marriages ending in divorce. Died 4 November.

Crick, Sir Bernard (b. 1929), political academic and theorist who edited the *Political Quarterly* and was knighted for his services to citizenship. Born in London, he was educated at Whitgift school in Croydon, at University College, London, and at the London School of Economics where, after brief teaching spells in several US universities, he returned in 1957 to become a lecturer in politics. He wrote *A Defence of Politics* in 1962, arguing that politics was not an ideology, but was about negotiation and compromise. In 1964 he published *The Reform of Parliament*, suggesting that it was not Parliament but general elections that formed an effective check on the executive. In 1965 he moved to Sheffield University to a chair in political theory and became joint editor of *The Political Quarterly*, a post he held until 1980, after which he became chairman of its editorial board. He had returned to London in 1971 as professor of politics at Birkbeck College, and while there he wrote the authorised biography of George Orwell, published in 1980 to mixed reviews. Later Crick set up the George Orwell Memorial Trust and the Orwell Prize for political writing. In 1997 he was appointed by the new

Labour government to chair a commission on the teaching of citizenship in schools, which formed the basis of changes in the national curriculum. He was knighted in 2002. Died 19 December.

Dalton, Professor Sir Howard (b. 1944), chief scientific adviser to the UK government's department for environment, food and rural affairs (Defra) who was not afraid of controversy. Born in New Malden, Surrey, he was educated at Raynes Park grammar school and Queen Elizabeth College, London University, took a doctorate at the University of Sussex, and became a fellow of Purdue University, Indiana, where he continued his research into microbes. In 1973 he became a lecturer at Warwick University and was appointed professor of microbiology in 1983. He was appointed to Defra in 2002, shortly after the outbreak of foot and mouth disease in the previous year, when the department was finding it hard to provide comprehensive, and comprehensible, advice to the government. The same applied to the trials of GM crops, about which Dalton eventually took the view that Britain would soon be growing them in a well controlled environment. He also found himself embroiled in the divisive subjects of the disposal of nuclear waste and of climate change. On the latter issue, he argued that science and technology could help in curbing greenhouse gas emissions. He did not support the government on all its ideas on the environment, expressing himself strongly against wind turbines, which he argued were too expensive as well as being an eyesore. Dalton retired from Defra in 2007, was knighted that year, and was subsequently involved, with his wife, Kira Dalton, in setting up a medical centre in The Gambia. Died 12 January.

Dassin, Jules (b. 1911), US film director who worked in Europe following allegations of communist sympathies. Born in Middletown, Connecticut, he was educated at Morris high school in the Bronx and after briefly studying drama in Europe joined the Yiddish Theatre in New York before moving to Hollywood in 1940. After making a series of short films for MGM, he directed a series of crime films: *Brute Force* (1947), *The Naked City* (1948), and *Thieves'*

Highway (1949). In 1950 he filmed *Night and the City* in London, but in the following year was named as a communist in the House of Representatives' un-American activities committee. He had briefly been a member of the party in the 1930s, but when he refused to declare his politics to the committee he was black-listed in Hollywood and went to live in France. Here, in 1955, he made *Rififi*, a film about a robbery in Paris, which won for him the director's award at the Cannes Film Festival. This was followed by a series of films starring the Greek actress Merlina Mercouri, culminating in the popular success *Never on Sunday* (1960). In 1964 Dassin was able to return to Hollywood, where he made *Topkapi,* a comedy-thriller set in Istanbul. Dassin married Mercouri in 1966 and both became involved in the campaign to oust the military junta that had seized power in Greece in 1967. Died 31 March.

DeBakey, Michael (b. 1908), US cardiovascular surgeon, who conducted the first coronary artery bypass. Born in Lake Charles, Louisiana, the son of Lebanese immigrants, he was educated locally and at Tulane University in New Orleans. While there he designed a roller pump, which became an essential part of the heart-lung apparatus used in open-heart surgery. During World War II DeBakey served in the US Army, working at the office of the surgeon general in Europe, where he proposed that surgeons should work in mobile army surgical hospitals close to the front line, a development that led to the creation of MASH units. After the war he became professor of surgery at Baylor University College of Medicine at Houston, Texas, where in 1952 he performed the first successful repair of an aortic aneurysm and the first successful carotid endarterectomy, clearing fat from the main artery to the brain. In 1953 he carried out the first Dacron graft for replacing a blood vessel, the synthetic material being durable enough to allow new tissue to grow over it. In 1968, the year after Christian Barnard had performed the first human heart transplant, DeBakey led five teams of surgeons in transplanting into four male patients the heart, two kidneys, and a lung from a woman who had committed suicide. He abandoned heart transplants for the next decade, until the drug Cyclosporine was developed to reduce the risk of tissue rejection, concentrating instead on the development of an artificial heart and of heart-assist devices such as miniaturised pumps. He was accorded many honours, including the Presidential Medal of Freedom and the Congressional Gold Medal. Died (in his hundredth year) 11 July.

Di Stefano, Giuseppe (b. 1921), Sicilian tenor whose lyrical voice and dazzling stage presence dominated opera houses in the 1950s. Born near Catania, he was taken with his parents to Milan when he was six, and began training for the priesthood until it was discovered that he had a good voice and he started taking singing lessons. Conscripted into the army in 1939, he was quickly released when it was recognised that he would be better employed singing before the troops than fighting alongside them. He made his operatic debut at Reggio Emilia as Des Grieux in Massenet's *Manon*, repeating the role for his debut at La Scala in 1947, and in the following year sang at the Metropolitan Opera as the Duke of Mantua in *Rigoletto*. In 1951 he sang in *La traviata* with Maria Callas, the start of a memorable partnership, which they were to repeat at La Scala in 1955 with Carlo Maria Giulini conducting. Di Stefano subsequently moved to heavier roles that did not suit his voice so well, but in 1972 he persuaded Callas to come out of retirement and join him in an international concert tour, which proved to be a mistake for both of them. In retirement Di Stefano divided his time between homes in Italy and in Kenya, where in 2004 he was badly injured by unknown intruders. Died 3 March.

Drnovsek, Dr Janez (b. 1950), president and former prime minister of Slovenia, who led his country, relatively peacefully, to independence from former Yugoslavia and brought it into Western structures. Born in Celjie, he was educated locally and at Ljubljana University, where he studied economics. He became an active member of the Communist Party and in 1986 was appointed to the Assembly of the Slovenian Republic. Three years later, when the Slovenian government decided to arrange free elections for

its representative to the central Yugoslav presidency in Belgrade, he defeated the government's preferred candidate for the post. At once he found himself embroiled in the convulsions that broke up Yugoslavia and, after striving unsuccessfully to prevent its collapse, he returned home. When Slovenia declared its independence in 1991, he became leader of the newly-formed Liberal Democratic Party and in 1992 was elected prime minister. Apart from a few months in 2000 he retained the post until 2002, and during this time he arranged to take his country into the EU and NATO. On his retirement as prime minister he was elected president, and remained a popular figure even though, having been diagnosed with cancer, he became increasingly eccentric. Rejecting conventional treatment, he moved out of the presidential palace in favour of a remote mountain hut, which he shared with his dog. In 2007 he chose not to run for a second term as president. Died 23 February.

Dulles, Cardinal Avery (b. 1918), US Roman Catholic theologian who was created cardinal by Pope John Paul II in 2001. Born in Auburn, New York, to a political family, several of whose forbears, including his father, had been secretaries of state to US presidents, he was educated at schools in New York, Switzerland, and New England, and finally at Harvard University, where he arrived as an agnostic but became converted to Catholicism. When Pearl Harbour was bombed in 1941 he joined the US Navy, serving initially in the Caribbean and finally with a French ship in the Mediterranean, where he was awarded the Croix de Guerre but succumbed to polio, from which he appeared to make a complete recovery. After World War II he joined the Society of Jesus, becoming a teacher at Fordham University in 1951. He was ordained priest in 1956, moving to the Jesuits' Woodstock Seminary in 1960, to the Catholic University of America in 1974, and finally returning to Fordham in 1988. He wrote 23 books during his life, including *Models of the Church* (1974) and *The Splendour of Faith* (1999), and published a collection of his lectures in 2008. He suffered a recurrence of polio which, in his final year, left him unable to speak. Died 12 December.

Dunwoody, Gwyneth (b. 1930), Labour MP who could never be relied upon to toe the party line. Born in Fulham, London, the daughter of Morgan Phillips, who became general secretary of the Labour Party, Gwyneth Phillips was educated at Fulham County secondary school and Notre Dame Convent. On leaving, she became a reporter on a local paper. In 1954 she married a general practitioner, Dr John Dunwoody, and moved to Totnes, in Devon. After twice standing unsuccessfully in elections, she was finally successful in winning the Exeter constituency in 1966, while her husband won Falmouth and Camborne. Gwyneth was appointed a junior minister at the board of trade in 1967, but both she and her husband lost their seats three years later. Gwyneth was elected for the safe Labour seat of Crewe in 1974 and she remained in Parliament for the rest of her life, though she was never appointed to another ministerial post. She nonetheless made her presence felt by her forceful presence on the back benches and on several parliamentary committees, notably as chairman of the transport committee. Her daughter, Tamsin Dunwoody, stood unsuccessfully for Labour in the Crewe and Nantwich by-election precipitated by her death. Died 17 April.

Febres Cordero, León (b. 1931), president of Ecuador 1984-88 who was renowned for his political toughness. Born in Guayaquil, in western Ecuador, he was educated at a local primary school and in the USA at the Charlotte Hall Military Academy in Maryland and at Stevens Institute of Technology in Hoboken, New Jersey. He returned to Ecuador to become a successful businessman and politician with the centre-right Social Christian Party, earning his reputation for toughness after being shot three times while campaigning, as well as surviving cancer and several heart by-pass operations. He won the presidential election of 1984, campaigning for "bread, roof and employment", and he began by introducing liberal economic policies, settling foreign debts, and developing the country's roads. But he soon faced an armed revolutionary movement, which he tackled by creating units that came to be known as death squads. After retiring in 1988 he was charged with embezzling public funds

and a commission was set up to investigate cases of disappearances during his presidency. He subsequently became mayor of Guayaquil, eventually retiring from politics in 2007. Died 15 December.

Fischer, Bobby (b. 1943), chess prodigy who became the only US player to win the world championship, but failed thereafter to defend his title. Born in Chicago, he moved with his mother to New York after his father, who was born in Germany, returned there when Bobby was two. He started learning chess when he was six and eventually dropped out of school to pursue what had become an obsession. In 1958, when he was 14, he won the US championship and in the same year qualified, at a tournament in Yugoslavia, as one of six challengers for the world championship. In 1960 in Argentina he tied for first place with Boris Spassky, in 1961 came second to the then world champion, Mikhail Tal, and in 1962 won the international tournament in Stockholm. This qualified him for the candidates' tournament in Curaçao, where he finished fourth, complaining that the Russians had deliberately drawn games against each other to ensure that he could not win. He then withdrew from international competitions for five years. When he returned in 1967 he again fell into dispute with other players, and with tournament officials, and it was not until 1970 that he was persuaded to play again and won the right, in 1972, to challenge Soviet World Champion Spassky. In a memorable contest held in Reykjavik and which became a metaphor for the Cold War, Fischer won by 12-and-a-half points to 8-and-a-half through a combination of brilliant play and gamesmanship. Fischer appeared for a while to enjoy his celebrity status, but in 1975 forfeited his title by refusing to defend it against Anatoly Karpov. Instead he joined an evangelical sect in Pasadena, and virtually disappeared from public view. He played a rematch with Spassky, for money, in 1992, but this was held in Belgrade and contravened a UN embargo on Yugoslavia. The USA issued an arrest warrant and Fischer became a virtual fugitive (the US administration's view was not helped by Fischer's description of the 2001 attacks on the USA as "wonderful news"). Detained in Japan in 2004, he fought extradition to the USA and was eventually given refuge in Iceland. Died 17 January.

Franks, Sir Dick (b. 1920), chief of the UK's Secret Intelligence Service (SIS, or MI6). Given the names Arthur Temple, he was always known as Dick and was educated at Rugby School and Queen's College, Oxford. During World War II he served with the Bedfordshire and Hertfordshire Regiment in the Middle East, where he was appointed an intelligence officer to the Libyan Arab Force before joining the Special Operations Executive (SOE) in Cairo. Later he was sent to Serbia, where his task was to monitor and harass enemy movements on the river Danube, and when war ended he worked in the Control Commission for Germany. After spending a few years on the *Daily Mirror* he joined the SIS in 1949. He became involved with the overthrow of Iran's Prime Minister Mohammed Mossadeq in 1953 and was then posted to Tehran to reopen the SIS station before moving to Bonn in 1962. Subsequently Franks was appointed deputy head of SIS, succeeding Sir Maurice Oldfield as "C", the top post, in 1978. It was during his term that there were several significant defections of KGB and other Soviet spies, while within the KGB Oleg Gordievsky continued to provide valuable information to the SIS. Franks retired in 1981. Died 12 October.

Gray, Simon (b. 1936), prolific and popular English playwright and novelist whose published diaries were equally entertaining and provocative. Born on Hayling Island, he was evacuated in 1939 to Canada, returning to England in 1946 to be educated at Westminster School in London and at Trinity College, Cambridge, where he became a supervisor in English and wrote his first novel, *Colmain*, published in 1963. This was followed by two other novels and a number of not very successful plays until, in 1971, he wrote his first major hit, *Butley*, directed by Harold Pinter with Alan Bates in the title role, which won many awards. It was followed by *Otherwise Engaged* (1975), which was voted best play by New York critics, and, among others, *The Rear Column* (1978), *Quartermaine's Terms*

(1981), and *The Common Pursuit* (1984), which was accompanied in 1985 by *An Unholy Pursuit*—a diary account of the play's production in England—and, in 1988, by *How's That For Telling 'Em, Fat Lady?*, the diary of the play's production in the USA. In 1995 he wrote *Cell Mates*, a play about the relationship between the Soviet spy George Blake and Sean Bourke, who helped Blake escape from prison. The play became notorious when the actor playing Blake, Stephen Fry, disappeared two days after its first night. In his last years Gray wrote *The Smoking Diaries*, a surprisingly entertaining account of his attempts to give up the addiction which finally killed him. Died 6 August.

Haider, Jörg (b. 1950), leader of the right-wing Freedom Party in Austria whose electoral success caused the EU temporarily to impose sanctions on his country. Born in Bad Goisern, the son of parents who joined the Nazi party in 1929 and who were subsequently punished for it, Haider studied law at the University of Vienna but soon became politically involved. He became leader of the Freedom Party's youth wing in Upper Austria when he was 20 and in 1979 was elected to the Nationalrat (lower house of the national legislature). He became party leader in 1986, ousting its liberal leader, Norbert Steger, who at the time was vice-chancellor in the coalition with the Social Democrats. Haider, who declared himself a Pan-German nationalist and was certainly a rabble-rouser, was not an acceptable partner to the Social Democrats, who expelled the Freedom Party from the government. In 1989 Haider became head of the regional coalition government in Carinthia, but had to resign two years later after making remarks favourable to the SS and the Third Reich. He regained the position in 1999, and in the general election of that year his party won 27 per cent of the vote and formed a coalition with the People's Party. Though Haider himself was not included in the new administration, his remarks indicating personal sympathy with the Nazi past persuaded the EU member states to impose diplomatic sanctions on Austria. These were withdrawn later in 2000. Haider was subsequently forced out of the party, later founding a rival party, the far-right Austria's Future.

He remained a popular, though controversial, figure until he was killed when his car skidded off the road. Died 11 October.

Harvey-Jones, Sir John (b. 1924), British industrialist who was chairman of ICI and subsequently became a television celebrity. Born in Hackney, he spent his early years in India, where his father was serving as a soldier. He was educated at a prep school in Kent and at the Royal Naval College in Dartmouth, and during World War II served in destroyers and submarines, subsequently working for naval intelligence. In 1956 he resigned his commission and joined Imperial Chemical Industries (ICI). By 1973 he had worked his way up to the main board, and in 1982 was appointed chairman, transforming the country's largest company from a loss-maker to earning profits of more than £1 billion in 1984. He did not always get on well with his fellow directors, who found him overbearing, but he became extraordinarily popular with the general public when, following his retirement from ICI in 1987, he starred in a television programme, *Troubleshooter*, in which he visited companies all over the country, looked at their books and performance, talked to management and workers, and gave hard-hitting advice, ranging from ideas for development to liquidation. He also took on many directorships and charitable work, as well as writing his memoirs, *Making it Happen* (1988), and a number of other books including *Getting it Together* (1991) and *Managing to Survive* (1993). He was knighted in 1985. Died 9 January.

Helms, Jesse (b. 1921), US senator who was an outspoken defender of conservative values. Born in Monroe, North Carolina, he was educated at Wingate Junior College and Wake Forest College. After serving during World War II as a Navy recruiter, he joined the local radio station until moving to Washington, DC in 1951 to work as an assistant to a number of Democratic senators. Later he became known for his newspaper editorials, widely syndicated throughout the USA, and his radio and television broadcasts in North Carolina, all critical of the civil rights campaign and the Civil Rights Act of 1964. In 1970 Helms became a Republican. Elected to the Senate two years later, he soon established himself on the far right of US politics, fervently anti-communist and consistently attacking what he saw as the moral degeneracy and decadence of his country. In 1994 he became chairman of the Senate foreign relations committee. As he had spent much of his time campaigning against the use of US troops to fight "other people's wars" and criticising foreign aid as a waste of money, his appointment was not welcomed by President Bill Clinton. Helms was instrumental in delaying the ratification of a number of the administration's foreign policy agreements and treaties, but he was helpful in some other ways, such as in demanding UN reforms before agreeing to the payment of unpaid arrears. He remained the committee's chairman until 2001, but did not stand for re-election in 2002. Died 4 July.

Heston, Charlton (b. 1924), US epic film actor renowned for his performances in biblical extravaganzas. Born Charles Carter (known as Chuck) in Evanston, Illinois, he grew up in the rural community around Lake Michigan after his parents divorced and his mother married a local business man, Chet Heston. Chuck was educated at the local high school and at North-Western University. During World War II he served in the Army Air Corps, then settled in New York, where he began making his mark in some classic roles in the new medium of television, including *Macbeth* and *Jane Eyre*, in which his performance as Mr Rochester earned him a contract in Hollywood. His film career took off when Cecil B. DeMille cast him as Moses in *The Ten Commandments* (1956). This was quickly followed by Orson Welles's *Touch of Evil* (1957) and *The Big Country* (1958), directed by William Wyler, who then cast Heston as *Ben-Hur* (1959), which won him an Oscar for best actor. More epic parts followed, including John the Baptist in *The Greatest Story Ever Told* and Michelangelo in *The Agony and the Ecstasy* (both in 1965). In later life Heston became active in defending the right of Americans to bear arms, becoming president of the National Rifle Association and conceding that, politically, he was "about as right-wing as a man can be". He was awarded the Presidential Medal of Freedom in 2003. Died 5 April.

Hickox, Richard (b. 1948), English orchestral conductor who put new life into modern English music. Born in Stokenchurch, Buckinghamshire, he was educated at the Royal Grammar School in High Wycombe, at the Royal Academy of Music and at Queen's College, Cambridge. In 1971 he formed the Richard Hickox Orchestra (later to become the City of London Sinfonia) and the Richard Hickox Singers, and made his debut as a professional conductor at St John's, Smith Square, in London in the same year. From 1972 to 1982 he was organist and master of music at St Margaret's, Westminster, was artistic director of the Spitalfields Festival in 1974, and was appointed director of the London Symphony Chorus in 1976 and of the Bradford Festival Chorus in 1978, as well as making his opera debut with English National Opera in 1979. In the 1980s he was artistic director of the Northern Sinfonia and associate conductor of the London Symphony Orchestra, as well as making his debut at Covent Garden and conducting orchestras in other parts of the world, including the USA. In 1990 he formed the Collegium Musicum 90, an ensemble for period instruments, and became director of the Spoleto Festival. He also concentrated on 20th century British music, including the work of Vaughan Williams, recording a complete cycle of the symphonies as well as many rarities. In later years, he spent half his time in Australia as music director of Opera Australia in Sydney, while continuing to carry out many engagements in the UK and elsewhere. His enthusiasms were contagious, but led him to take on a workload which probably contributed to his early death. He was appointed CBE in 2002. Died 23 November.

Hillary, Sir Edmund (b. 1919), New Zealand adventurer who became, with Tenzing Norgay (Sherpa Tenzing), the first to reach the summit of Mount Everest. Born in Auckland, he was educated at the local grammar school and at Auckland University, but stayed only two years there before returning home to help on his father's bee farm. During World War II he served in the Pacific with the Royal New Zealand Air Force, and on demobilisation returned to bee-keeping while spending his holidays climbing mountains. In 1946 he scaled Mount Cook, the highest moun-

tain in New Zealand, and in 1951 was one of four New Zealanders who went climbing in Nepal. Here Hillary joined Eric Shipton's reconnaissance team preparing to climbing Everest from Nepal, and was subsequently invited to take part in the attempt to conquer the mountain in 1953. When Shipton was replaced as leader by Colonel (later Lord) John Hunt, Hillary remained on the team, and after Tom Bourdillon and Charles Evans had returned from the first attempt to reach the summit, 500ft short, he and Tenzing were sent up and successfully reached the top on 29 May, 1953. They spent 15 minutes on the summit, Hillary taking a photograph of Tenzing but not bothering to have one taken of himself. The consequent publicity, and the award of a knighthood, deprived him of the quiet life for which he had hoped. He returned to Everest in 1954, leading an expedition by the New Zealand Alpine Club, but broke three ribs and, after trying to carry on, had to be carried down. In 1955 he was appointed leader of the New Zealand Antarctic team in support of the Commonwealth Trans-Antarctic Expedition, led by Sir Vivian Fuchs. The two did not get on, and Hillary was critical of Fuchs in his subsequent book, *No Latitude for Error*, but was himself accused of putting the project in jeopardy by making a dash for the South Pole instead of waiting at the depot. In 1960 Hillary set off in search of the yeti, or abominable snowman, but concluded that it was a myth. In 1961 he suffered a slight stroke when attempting to climb Mount Makalu without oxygen. It was here that he set up the Himalayan Trust, the project which occupied much of his later years, providing schools, hospitals, and other buildings for the Sherpas, whose mountaineers had helped him on his climbs. In 1985 Hillary became New Zealand's high commissioner in New Delhi. He was appointed to the Order of New Zealand in 1987 and made a Knight of the Garter in 1995. He wrote many books about his adventures. Died 11 January.

Hillery, Dr Patrick (b. 1923), Irish politician who became president of his country from 1976 to 1990. Born in Milton Malbay, he was a medical student at University College, Dublin, but gave up medical practice in 1951 when he was elected as a Fianna Fáil member of the Dáil (legislature).

He was appointed minister for education in 1959, minister for labour in 1966, and minister for external affairs in 1969. His main achievement in this last post was the negotiation of Ireland's entry into the European Economic Community, which took place in 1973, when Hillery was appointed Irish commissioner. He settled well with his colleagues in the Community, but in 1976 was persuaded to stand for the Irish presidency, and was elected unopposed. He deliberately stayed out of the political limelight during his two terms of office (he was re-elected unopposed in 1983), maintaining that this was necessary after the controversial resignation of his predecessor (Cearbhall Ó Dálaigh) following a row with the then minister of defence. Hillery successfully kept the presidency above party politics, dissolving the Dáil in 1982 instead of forming a minority Fianna Fáil government, as he was being urged to do. This, together with his remoteness, was seen to have helped clear the way for his successor, Mary Robinson, who campaigned for a more active presidency. On his retirement Hillery maintained his low profile and preserved his privacy. Died 12 April.

Hoddinott, Alun (b. 1929), Welsh composer who wrote 10 symphonies, six operas, and many other works. Born in Bargoed, Glamorganshire, he was introduced to classical music at a young age, when he was inspired to learn the violin. In 1945 he won a composition scholarship and abandoned the instrument in favour of composition studies at University College, Cardiff, and private tuition with Arthur Benjamin. In 1951 he was appointed lecturer at the Welsh College of Music and Drama and came to public attention three years later with a clarinet concerto at the Cheltenham Festival, which led to new commissions. In 1959 he became a lecturer at University College, Cardiff and, in 1967, professor and head of the music department. In the same year he joined with John Ogden in establishing the Cardiff Festival of 20th century music, and remained its artistic director until 1989. He wrote his first symphony in 1955 and his first opera, *The Beach of Falesá*, in 1974. He was appointed CBE in 1983 and received many other awards and musical prizes. Died 12 March.

Hua Guofeng (b. 1921), Chinese communist politician who succeeded Mao Zedong as Chinese Communist Party (CCP) chairman, arrested the "Gang of Four", but was soon to lose his influence. Born Su Zhu in Jiaocheng, Shanxi province, he joined the Red Army when he was 15, adopting the nom de guerre Hua Guofeng, and became a full party member in 1938. Later he became party secretary in Hunan province and was an enthusiastic supporter of Mao and the Cultural Revolution. He was appointed to the CCP central committee in 1969, joined the politburo in 1973, was appointed minister of public security in 1975, prime minister in January 1976, and first vice-chairman of the CCP in April 1976. This inevitably brought him into conflict with Mao's wife, Jiang Qing, and the other members of the "Gang of Four"—Wang Hongwen, Yao Wenyuan and Zhang Chunqiao—but when Mao died in September 1976, Hua, persuaded by colleagues in the politburo, ordered the Gang's arrest and subsequent trial. In doing so he probably averted further chaos. Although he was appointed CCP chairman in October 1976, what control he had was undermined by the fact that the country was beginning to reject the influence of Mao, his followers, and his policies, and by the rise to power of Deng Xiaoping. At the CCP congress in 1977, Deng established himself as a potential leader, and in the months that followed contrived to isolate Hua, reviving the post of general secretary of the party at the expense of the chairman. Hua lost his seat on the politburo in 1982, and though he remained on the central committee until 2002 he was deprived of all authority. Died 20 August.

Huntington, Samuel (b. 1927), US political scientist. Born in New York City, Huntington graduated from Yale University before undertaking a period of military service. He then earned an MA from the University of Chicago and a PhD from Harvard where, in 1962, he became a tenured professor and remained for 45 years. A frequent consultant for the state department, the national security council, and the CIA, Huntington was often criticised as a right-wing, "cold war liberal" by those on the left of the political spectrum. He published a number of books, many of which expounded controversial views, and was renowned (and criticised) for using mathematical models and pseudo-mathematical political science techniques to support his personal theories. His most famous book, *The Clash of Civilizations and the Remaking of World Order* (1996), ignited fierce debate within academic and intellectual circles by predicting that future conflicts would not be between ideologies but between global cultures. His last book, *Who are We? The Challenges to America's National Identity* (2004), predicted calamitous consequences arising from the undermining of the USA's defining "Anglo-Protestant culture" by the growth of the country's Hispanic community. Died 24 December.

Hurwicz, Leonid (b. 1917), economist who shared the Nobel Prize in 2007 for his work on the mechanism design theory. Born in Moscow to Jewish parents who fled to Poland in 1919, Hurwicz was educated at Warsaw University and the London School of Economics. In 1939 he moved to Geneva, then to Portugal and finally, in 1940, to the USA, where he was ultimately joined by his family who had briefly been interned in Soviet labour camps. During World War II Hurwicz went to Chicago University, where he taught in the department of economics. In 1948 he worked for the UN economic commission and in 1953 joined the University of Minnesota, becoming Regents' Professor of economics in 1969. Working with the economists Eric Maskin and Roger B. Myerson, who shared the Nobel prize with him, he sought alternatives to both state planning and uncontrolled capitalism as a means of obtaining socially acceptable results. The mechanism design theory aimed to establish that economic transactions could be arranged so that general satisfaction could be obtained if everyone worked towards their own self interest. Died 24 June.

Kantrowitz, Adrian (b. 1918), cardiac surgeon who carried out the first heart transplant in the USA and invented the intra-aortic balloon pump, which since saved many lives. Born in New York, he studied mathematics at New York University before going to the Long Island College

of Medicine. During World War II he served in the US Army Medical Corps as a surgeon, subsequently specialising in cardiac surgery at the Montefiore hospital in the Bronx. In 1967, three days after Christian Barnard carried out the world's first heart transplant, Kantrowitz transplanted the heart of a baby at the Maimonidas Medical Centre in Brooklyn. Although the recipient baby died some hours later, organ transplants in children were subsequently carried out with great success. Moving to Detroit in 1970 Kantrowitz taught at the Wayne State University School of Medicine, practising as a surgeon at Sinai Hospital and working with Michael DeBakey (for obituary see above) and others on the development of artificial devices to help in the treatment of heart patients, including the intra-aortic balloon pump and the implantable pacemaker. Died 14 November.

Khalil, Mustafa (b. 1920), Egyptian politician who was prime minister for a brief period and worked on the Camp David attempt to establish peace in the Middle East. Born in Kalyoubieh, he took a degree in civil engineering at Cairo University in 1941, and on graduation worked for some years with the state railway. After World War II he took a PhD at the University of Illinois in the USA, subsequently returning to Cairo to work in the engineering faculty at Ain Shaims University. When Gamal Abdel Nasser took power in 1956, Khalil became an adviser to the government and in 1958 was appointed transport minister. Following Nasser's death in 1970, his successor, Anwar Sadat, appointed Khalil information minister, charged with explaining Sadat's ambition to recover the Sinai Peninsula (lost in the war of 1967) by a negotiated peace with Israel. In 1978 Khalil, now prime minister, was charged with leading the team of negotiators, which went to the USA and concluded the Camp David agreement of 1979. Khalil ceased to be prime minister shortly before Sadat was assassinated in 1981, but remained politically active as vice-chairman of the ruling National Democratic Party until his retirement in 2007. Died 7 May.

Kitt, Eartha (b. 1927), US singer and entertainer, who described herself as a "sex-kitten" and

purred or growled her way through many sug-
gestive songs. Born illegitimate on a cotton plantation in South Carolina, she was brought up by
a foster mother, then sent to live in Harlem, New
York, with a woman who was said to be her aunt.
There she was eventually taken on by the
Katharine Dunham dancing school, appearing
with the dancers on tour and in a film, *Casbah*, in
1948. Subsequently, in Paris, she met Orson
Welles, who cast her in a modern version of Marlowe's *Doctor Faustus*. After touring with this
production she returned to New York to appear in
the revue, *New Faces of 1952*, going on to make
a record album, which included such songs as "I
want to be evil" and "Santa baby". She also
made a number of unmemorable films and plays
until, at a White House lunch given by President
Lyndon Johnson in 1968, she stood up and
inveighed against the Vietnam War and found
herself unable to find work in the USA for the
next few years. She returned to Broadway in
1978 to star in *Timbuktu!* and make more records.
She also continued to tour successfully in Europe
and, in 1989, to publish a third volume of memoirs, which she entitled *I'm Still Here: Confessions of a Sex Kitten*. Died 25 December.

Lamb, Willis (b. 1913), US professor of physics
who shared the Nobel Prize for his research on
the hydrogen atom. Born in Los Angeles, he was
educated locally and at the University of California at Berkeley, where he received a degree in
chemistry and went on as a postgraduate student
to gain a PhD in theoretical physics in 1938. He
stayed on at the university, becoming professor in
1948 while at the same time working at the
Columbia Radiation Laboratory, where he did
the research which brought him the Nobel Prize
for Physics in 1955. His identification of the
small difference of energy in the hydrogen atom,
which became known as the "Lamb shift", revolutionised the formula of quantum mechanics,
which had previously assumed that the two states
of the atom had the same energy. From 1951,
when he moved to Stanford University as professor of physics, Lamb was almost constantly on
the move. He was at Harvard in 1953 as Morris
Loeb lecturer, worked in the UK as a fellow of
New College and professor of physics at Oxford

University, returned to the USA in 1962 to
become professor at Yale University, and finally
moved to the University of Arizona at Tucson as
professor of physics and optical sciences in 1974,
where he remained until his retirement in 2002.
Died 15 May.

Lederberg, Joshua (b. 1925), US geneticist and
microbiologist who shared the 1958 Nobel Prize
for Physiology or Medicine for his discoveries
on genetic recombination and the organisation of
the genetic material of bacteria. Born in Mont-
clair, New Jersey, he was educated at the
Stuyvesant high school in Manhattan and
Columbia University, reading zoology and subsequently studying medicine at Columbia University College of Physicians and Surgeons. In
1946 he took up a research fellowship at Yale
University, obtaining a PhD for research in
genetics. He spent the next few years carrying
out basic genetic research at the University of
Wisconsin, discovering "viral transduction": the
fact that viruses infecting bacteria could transfer
bits of DNA from one bacterium to another. He
was 33 when he shared the 1958 Nobel Prize,
and in that year he became one of the founding
members of the Space Science Board set up by
the US National Academy of Sciences, reflecting his concern that space vehicles from Earth
could contaminate the environment of the Moon
or Mars, and that on returning they might bring
pathogens back to Earth to which man had no
immunity. In 1959 he was appointed first chairman of the new department of genetics at Stanford University School of Medicine, and in 1978
he moved to Rockefeller University in New York
City, becoming professor emeritus in 1990 and
continuing research on genetics while also
advising the US government on health policies
and on the relationship between science and
public affairs. Died 2 February.

Lorenz, Edward (b. 1917), US professor of
meteorology, who was a pioneer of the chaos
theory. Born in West Hartford, Connecticut, he
studied mathematics at Dartmouth College in
New Hampshire and obtained a masters degree at
Harvard University in 1940. During World War
II he served as a weather forecaster in the US

Army Air Corps, later studying meteorology at the Massachusetts Institute of Technology (MIT), becoming a member of the staff of the department of meteorology after receiving his doctorate, and being appointed professor in 1962. In the following year he published a paper, based on his computer experiments, which showed why weather was unpredictable. From his findings emerged the chaos theory. In a later presentation to the American Association for the Advancement of Science, he used the term "butterfly effect" to describe how a small disturbance, such as the flap of a butterfly's wing, in one place might set off a tornado or other catastrophic effects in another. After studying the mathematics of such a circumstance, Lorenz published a paper, *Deterministic Nonperiodic Flow*, describing how relatively simple equations could have extremely complex results. In 1977 he was appointed head of the department of earth, atmospheric and planetary sciences at MIT, and emeritus professor in 1987. Died 16 April.

Lyons, Jack (b. 1916), British businessman and philanthropist, whose later life was marred by a conviction for fraud. Born in Leeds, the son of a Polish immigrant, he was educated at Leeds Grammar School and at Columbia University in the USA, where he was when war broke out in 1939. He enlisted in the Canadian Army and was put in charge of clothing for the troops. After World War II he returned to Leeds and his father's company, which in 1954 was merged with the United Drapery Stores group, of which he became a director. His support for the arts began in the 1950s, when the Leeds Music Festival seemed likely to fail. He became its chairman in 1955, recruiting the Earl of Harewood as its artistic director and, in 1958, setting up the successful centenary festival. Three years later he was a founder of the Leeds International Pianoforte Competition and subsequently founded a concert hall and music school in York and became a benefactor of the London Symphony Orchestra. He was appointed a CBE in 1967 and knighted in 1973, but was stripped of these honours following his involvement in the Guinness battle to take over Distillers, when he was tried and convicted of fraudulent share-trad-

ing. Three other men involved were given prison sentences, but Lyons was spared because of ill-health and his philanthropic record. Died 18 February.

Lyttelton, Humphrey (b. 1925), English jazz band leader and trumpeter, who became widely known as chairman of the radio comedy programme, *I'm Sorry, I Haven't a Clue*. He was born at Eton College, where his father was a housemaster and where Humphrey was educated. There he took up playing the trumpet and formed his first band. During World War II he fought with the Grenadier Guards, carrying his trumpet with him. After the war, he joined *The Dixielanders*, a jazz band led by George Webb, and enrolled in the Camberwell School of Art, where he developed his skills as a cartoonist and met Wally Fawkes, creator of *Flook*, the popular strip cartoon serialised in the *Daily Mail*, for which Lyttelton also drew under the by-line "Humph". In 1948 he and his band recorded for Parlophone and later for his own label, Calligraph. In 1956 his *Bad Penny Blues* became the first British jazz record to reach the pop chart Top 20, but he upset followers of traditional jazz by bringing in saxophones and incorporating African and Caribbean rhythms as well as swing. He became a regular broadcaster in the 1960s, introducing *The Best of Jazz*, a weekly record programme which ran for more than 40 years. *I'm Sorry, I Haven't a Clue*, the programme which brought him more fame as he developed doubles entendres and the incomprehensible panel game, "Mornington Crescent", into something of an art, began in 1972 and ran until his death. During his life he also wrote a number of autobiographical books, as well as a two-volume work, *The Best of Jazz* (1978-79, reproduced as one volume in 1997). Died 25 April.

Mahesh Yogi, Maharishi (b. 1918), spiritual leader and advocate of transcendental meditation. Born as Mahesh Prasad Varma in Jabalpur, central India, he graduated from Allahabad University with a degree in physics, and studied Sanskrit and yoga under Guru Deva, a key figure within the Hindu community. After the latter's death in 1953, Mahesh spent several years in isolated meditation and contemplation, before emerging in 1958 as the self-proclaimed Maharishi and announcing the formation of a worldwide movement for spiritual regeneration based upon "transcendental meditation". The notion that life's stresses could be diminished through personal meditation found adherents in the West and the Maharishi built up a multi-billion dollar empire based on personal donations and the sale of meditation and spiritual techniques. With outlets throughout the world, the Maharishi had a global following which numbered several million, including many celebrities, most notably, for a time, the members of the Beatles. In 1972 he claimed to have a plan for reorganising the world in order to solve the basic problems of humanity. He also engaged in the political process in a number of countries though his Natural Law Party, which regularly fielded large numbers of candidates in UK elections in the 1990s with a singular lack of success. In his later years, the Maharishi championed the technique of "yogic flying", a form of levitation based upon cross-legged leaping which attracted widespread ridicule. Died 5 February.

Makeba, Miriam (b. 1932), South African singer who was often referred to as "Mama Africa", though she was exiled from her country for much of her life. Born in Prospect, a township outside Johannesburg, she was educated at a missionary school and won a talent show at the age of 13. She soon combined her employment as a servant with singing at weddings and other occasions. Her career as a singer took off when, after being given a small part in the anti-apartheid film, *Come Back, Africa*, she travelled to the USA, where she had a great success with her remarkable voice, which ranged from coloratura to an extraordinary variety of vocal tricks, notably in the "Click Song", with which she became most closely associated and which she performed in the Xhosa language. She won a Grammy award and sang at President John. F. Kennedy's 45th birthday party, but was still unable to return to South Africa. She also fell out with the US authorities when she married Stokely Carmichael, one of the leaders of the Black Pan-

ther movement. The couple left for Guinea, but were divorced in 1978. Makeba continued to perform in many African countries, and was finally invited back to South Africa by Nelson Mandela when he became president in 1991. Died 9 November.

McKusick, Victor (b. 1921), US doctor widely recognised as the father of genetics in medicine. Born in Parkman, Maine, he was educated at the local grammar school, at Tufts University, and at the Johns Hopkins University School of Medicine. In 1948 he headed the cardiovascular unit at Baltimore Marine Hospital, but soon began researching into inherited diseases and in 1957 founded the Johns Hopkins Division of Medical Genetics, where he attracted students from many parts of the world and, in 1966, published a catalogue of all known genes and genetic disorders, *Mendelian Inheritance in Man*. In 1969 he proposed, in a lecture delivered at The Hague, that a map of all human genes be produced, and this was eventually published in 2001. Meanwhile in 1973 McKusick was appointed physician-in-chief at the Johns Hopkins Hospital and chairman of the department of medicine. For researching genes that caused recessive diseases, McKusick worked with inbred communities, notably the Old Order Amish communities in Pennsylvania, which led to the publication of his *Medical Genetic Studies of the Amish* in 1978. He was awarded the National Medal of Science in 2001, and the Japan Prize for Medical Genetics in 2008. Died 22 July.

Minghella, Anthony (b. 1954), British film director who won an Oscar for *The English Patient*. Born at Ryde in the Isle of Wight, he was educated at the Fairway grammar school in Sandown, St John's College in Portsmouth, and Hull University, where he studied and taught drama. He worked initially in television, while also writing plays, for which he won a number of awards. He wrote and directed his first film, *Truly, Madly, Deeply* in 1990, originally for BBC television, and its success led to Hollywood, where in 1993 he made *Mr Wonderful*, which was not very well received, but followed it in 1997 with his greatest success, *The English*

Patient, which won nine awards in the Oscar ceremonies, including his own for best director. In 2000 he followed this with *The Talented Mr Ripley*, with *Cold Mountain* in 2003 and *Breaking and Entering* in 2006. This was his last film, much of his time being taken up with his responsibilities as chairman of the British Film Institute, though he directed an English National Opera production of *Madam Butterfly* and adapted the novel, *The No 1 Ladies Detective Agency*, for BBC television. Died 18 March.

Mwanawasa, Levy (b. 1948), president of Zambia, who battled against corruption and was an outspoken critic of Robert Mugabe's regime in Zimbabwe. Born in Mufulira, he was educated locally and at the University of Zambia, where he studied law. He set up a private practice and, in 1981, was vice-chairman of his country's Law Association. In 1985 he was appointed solicitor-general, but served for only one year before returning to private practice. In 1990 he joined with the trade union leader, Frederick Chiluba, to form the Movement for Multi-Party Democracy (MMD). The party convincingly won the election of 1991, when Chiluba became president, appointing Mwanawasa as his deputy. Later in the same year Mwanawasa was badly injured in a car crash, which put him in hospital for several months and from which he never fully recovered, though he remained as vice-president until 1994. He was elected president in 2001 when the MMD refused to support Chiluba for a third term. As president, Mwanawasa made the fight against corruption his main concern, and he did not interfere when Chiluba was arrested and charged with corruption. During his term of office he won the support of foreign investors and of the World Bank, which wrote off much of the country's overseas debt; by his outspoken criticisms of Mugabe he also attracted many tourists, who would previously have visited Zimbabwe. He was re-elected president in 2006 but suffered a stroke in 2008. Died 19 August.

Nasir, Ibrahim (b. 1926), first president of the Maldives who secured its independence but eventually went into voluntary exile. Born in Malé, the capital of the chain of islands, he was educated locally and in Sri Lanka. He entered politics in the 1950s, becoming a junior minister in 1954 and minister for public affairs in 1956 before becoming prime minister in 1957, when the islands were still a British protectorate ruled by a sultanate. In 1965 he signed an agreement with the UK that granted the Maldives full independence. At the time the sultanate still existed, but in 1968 Nasir organised a referendum that voted in favour of its abolition. The sultan was deposed and Nasir was appointed president. He was re-elected for a second term in 1973 but was not tolerant of opposition and in 1975 he accused his prime minister, Ahmed Zaki, of plotting against him, and had him arrested and sent to one of the remoter islands. Meanwhile he developed the islands' fishing and tourist industries, but was faced with a slump in the 1970s, aggravated by the UK's decision to close its airfield in the island of Gan. He resigned in 1978 and went to live in Singapore. Died 22 November.

Nerina, Nadia (b. 1927), prima ballerina with The Royal Ballet whose technique and charm inspired Frederick Ashton's ballet, *La Fille mal gardée*. Born Nadine Judd in Bloemfontein, South Africa, she took ballet lessons there until, aged 17, she joined the Rambert and Sadler's Wells schools in England, and after a period with the Sadler's Wells Ballet joined, in 1947, the Covent Garden opera (subsequently The Royal Ballet) as a soloist, adopting the name Nerina (after the flower). She made her mark in 1948 in Ashton's ballet *Cinderella*, dancing an exciting solo reflecting the onset of spring. She went on to dance leading roles in classical ballets such as *The Sleeping Beauty*, *Les Sylphides*, and *Coppelia*. In 1960 she danced Lise in the première of *La Fille mal gardée*, which gave her the opportunity to display her spectacular floating leaps and darting steps. Later in the same year she danced in Russia, where she became the first Royal Ballet star to perform with the Bolshoi and the Kirov. She travelled widely to fulfil guest appearances in many venues, as well as continuing to perform occasionally for The Royal Ballet until her retirement in 1969. Died 6 October.

Newman, Paul (b. 1925), US actor and director, who was nominated for Oscars seven times, but won only once. Born in Shaker Heights, Ohio, he was educated in local schools until war broke out, when he enlisted in the US Navy, serving as a radio operator in bombers operating in the Pacific. Following World War II, he went to Kenyon College in Ohio and studied acting for a year at the Yale University School of Drama and at the Actors Studio. After some television work he made his Broadway debut in *Picnic* (1953), which earned him a contract from Warner Brothers in Hollywood, where he made his mark in *Somebody Up There Likes Me* (1956). But after a series of less popular films he bought out of his contract and proceeded to make a series of more successful films, including *The Hustler* (1961), *Hud* (1963), and *Cool Hand Luke* (1967), as well as a number of flops. He returned to form in 1969, with one of the films for which he is best remembered—*Butch Cassidy and the Sundance Kid*—followed by the equally popular *The Sting* in 1973. Other successes followed, including *The Towering Inferno* (1974) and *The Color of Money* (1986), for which he finally won an Oscar as best actor. Newman also directed a number of films, many of them starring his wife, Joanne Woodward, whom he had married in 1958. The most memorable of these was *Rachel, Rachel* (1968), for which she won an Oscar nomination. In addition to his stage and screen work, Newman became enthralled with motor racing, competing at Le Mans and coming second in 1979. Sixteen years later, at the age of 70, he won the 24-hour Daytona Beach race. Another successful diversion from acting was his introduction of a range of food products, called Newman's Own, which included salad dressing, pasta sauce, and popcorn, and all the profits from which were donated to charitable causes. Died 26 September.

Nixon, Sir Edwin (b. 1925), British businessman who became chairman and chief executive of IBM and helped establish computers in the UK. Born in Leicester, he was educated at Alderman Newton's school there and at Selwyn College, Cambridge. He joined IBM United Kingdom in 1955 and became managing director 10 years later. During this time he was involved with the introduction of US computer technology to the UK, establishing a sizeable share of the country's computer market and building a company with some 11,000 employees and an innovative structure that brought management and workers closer together. He was appointed chairman and chief executive in 1979, remaining with IBM until 1986, when he became deputy chairman of National Westminster Bank. In 1988, he became chairman of Amersham International, a medical research company that became the first company privatised as part of Prime Minister Margaret Thatcher's policy. He was knighted in 1984, and among the many other responsibilities he assumed were the chairmanship of the University of Leicester, the chairmanship of the board of trustees of the Royal Opera House, Covent Garden, and the presidency of the National Association for Gifted Children. Died 17 August.

Nouhak Phoumsavan (b. 1910), former president of Laos who was one of the three main leaders of the Pathet Lao revolution of 1975. Born in Ban Phalouka in Mukdahan province, he moved as a young man to Savannakhet, where he worked as a truck driver. In 1945 he was one of the founding members of the revolutionary movement, becoming minister of finance in the Pathet Lao resistance government in 1950 and representing the Pathet Lao at the Geneva conference in 1954. He became a member of the politburo of the Lao People's Party in 1955 and a member of the National Assembly in 1957, but was arrested and sent to prison in 1959. He escaped to rejoin the revolutionaries; subsequently, in 1975, being appointed minister of finance and deputy prime minister in the first government of the Lao People's Democratic Republic. In 1989 he became president of the Supreme People's Assembly and was appointed chairman of the commission that drafted a new constitution, which came into force in 1991. Kaysone Phomvihan became president, and when he died in 1992, Nouhak was elected to succeed him. He remained in the post until 1998, when he retired. Died 9 September.

O'Brien, Conor Cruise (b. 1917), Irish politician, diplomat, historian, and journalist who made his presence felt in all his activities. Born in Dublin, he was educated at Sandford Park school and Trinity College, Dublin. After graduating he worked first for the Irish department of finance and then, in 1944, for the department of external affairs, where he was employed in the government's campaign against partition. He also found time to write, publishing a book of essays on Catholic writers, *Maria Cross*, in 1952 and, while working at Ireland's embassy to Paris in 1956, a study of Charles Stuart Parnell, *Parnell and his Party*. In 1961 he became the UN secretary-general's representative in the Democratic Republic of Congo province of Katanga, which was seeking to secede from the newly independent country. O'Brien authorised the use of force to oust foreign mercenaries who were helping Katanga, but was recalled to New York. He resigned from the UN at the end of that year, writing a book, *To Katanga and Back*, in which he blamed Dag Hammarskjöld, the UN secretary-general, who had been killed in an air crash, for making him a scapegoat. In 1962 he was appointed vice chancellor of the University of Ghana, where he remained until 1965 when he went to New York University as Albert Schweizer professor of humanities. In 1969 he returned to Ireland, was elected to the Dáil and became minister for posts and telegraphs, controversially banning the IRA and its spokesmen from Irish radio and television. He lost his seat in 1977 but became a member of the Senate (the upper chamber) until 1979, when he moved to London to become editor-in-chief of the *Observer*. He lost that post in 1981, subsequently teaching in a number of US universities and continuing to write books, notably a biography of Edmund Burke, *The Great Melody*, in 1992 and *Memoir: My Life and Themes* in 1998. Died 18 December.

Odetta Holmes Felious (b. 1930), singer, actress, and civil rights campaigner. Known throughout her career only by her first name, Odetta was born in Birmingham, Alabama and, after leaving school aged 13, she worked as a maid and studied classical music at night school. She first sang professionally in Los Angeles in 1944. Her powerful voice, vocal range, and expressive personality quickly won her critical acclaim and in the ensuing years she appeared regularly in clubs, musical theatre, films, and on television. Her repertoire included a wide range of traditional material and she was active in the civil rights movement, singing at the March on Washington in 1963 and accompanying the Reverend Martin Luther King on his march from Selma to Montgomery in 1965. She influenced many young performers, most notably Bob Dylan, who later claimed that she had inspired him to put aside the electric guitar of his youth and instead play acoustic folk music. She acknowledged Dylan's enormous influence upon the genre when she recorded an album of his songs in 1965 entitled *Odetta Sings Dylan*. As popular music evolved in the 1960s her popularity waned as she was eclipsed by a wave of Dylan-inspired singer-song writers, and her classically trained mezzo-soprano voice was increasingly at odds with the gospel/blues-derived vocal style, which came to dominate black music. She continued to record and perform, however, and in January 2008, despite ill health, undertook a major US tour, performing in a wheelchair. Honoured by President Bill Clinton, who presented her with a National Medal of the Arts in 1999, Odetta had been due to sing at President Barack Obama's inauguration in January 2009, but death intervened to deny her this honour. Died 2 December.

Palade, George (b. 1912), scientist who was described as one of the fathers of cell biology and was awarded the Nobel Prize for his work on the structure and functions of living cell components. Born in Moldova, he was educated at the Al Hasdeu Lyceum in Buzau and the University of Bucharest. During World War II he served in the medical corps of the Romanian army, and subsequently went to New York University. In 1947 he joined the Rockefeller Institute for Medical Research, working there with Albert Claude on developing the technique of cell structure, isolating smaller structures within cells and identifying their functions. He also discovered ribosomes. He became a US citizen in 1952 and in 1958 was appointed professor of cytology. In 1973 he moved to Yale as chairman of the new department of cell biology. He won the Nobel Prize in Medicine or Physiology in 1974, jointly with Albert Claude and Christian de Duve. In 1990 he moved again to become professor of medicine in residence and dean of scientific affairs at the University of California in San Diego, retiring in 2001, though he remained a consultant. Died 7 October.

Papadopoulos, Tassos (b. 1934), Greek Cypriot president who rejected the proposed reunification of the Greek and Turkish communities on the island. Born in Nicosia, he was educated at the Pancyprian Gymnasium there and at King's College, London, subsequently training as a barrister in Gray's Inn. In 1955 he began to practise law in Cyprus, and when the EOKA movement began its campaign against British rule he became a member of its political wing and took part in the London conference of 1959, which negotiated the island's independence. He was one of those who voted against the treaty, which he believed was being forced on the islanders, but subsequently took part in drafting the island's new constitution and assumed various ministerial roles when the island became an independent republic. He became president in 2003, declaring that his ambition was to take a united Cyprus into Europe. The island had been divided since 1974, when Turkish troops occupied its northern third, and for nearly three decades the UN had tried to mediate a federal settlement. A proposed new constitution, sponsored by the UN and supported by the international community, was put to the Greek and Turkish communities in 2004. Turkish Cypriots voted in favour but the Greek community, led by Papadopoulos, overwhelmingly rejected it. A week later Cyprus became a member of the EU, which set about trying to end the economic isolation of the Turkish sector. Papadopoulos successfully delayed peace procedures for his remaining years in office, claiming that he had prevented Cyprus from becoming a Turkish protectorate. He was defeated in elections held in 2007. Died 12 December.

Pinter, Harold (b. 1930), British playwright, actor, and director who was awarded the Nobel Prize for Literature. Born in Hackney, he was educated at Hackney Downs grammar school, where he acted Macbeth and Romeo, broke the school sprint record, and developed a life-long enthusiasm for cricket. He began working as an actor, using the stage name David Baron, in 1950, and his first play, *The Room*, was staged by the Bristol Old Vic School in 1957. His first full-length play, *The Birthday Party*, ran at the Lyric Theatre, Hammersmith, for six nights in 1958 before being withdrawn. Its complexity and air of mystery baffled the audiences and many critics, but it was later accepted as one of his masterpieces, as was *The Caretaker*, which played in the West End in 1960. The pauses (written into the scripts, and subsequently inspiring the word "Pinteresque"), the air of mystery and danger, and the humour became accepted and established his reputation as a dramatist. This was confirmed with *The Homecoming*, staged by the Royal Shakespeare Company in 1965, and, 10 years later, *No Man's Land*, which played at the National Theatre. In the meantime Pinter had turned his talent to the writing of screenplays, notably for the films *The Go-Between, Accident*, and *The French Lieutenant's Woman*, but his private life also became a subject of general interest when he left his wife, Vivienne Merchant, who had performed in some of his early plays, for Lady Antonia Fraser, who divorced her husband in order to marry him. Pinter's next play, *Betrayal*, a depressing account of infidelity, was produced at the National and proved to be his last full-length work of note. His increasing concern with politics coloured his later plays and provoked many angry public outbursts, but inspiration was lacking. He was diagnosed with cancer in 2003, and had to fight other health problems, which he did with courage. He was appointed a Companion of Honour in 2002 and awarded the Nobel Prize in 2005. Died 24 December.

Pippard, Sir Brian (b. 1920), British physicist who was an expert on the study of metals and superconductivity. Born in Leeds, he was educated at Clifton College and Clare College, Cambridge, going on to gain a PhD, having worked at the Radar Research and Development Establishment at Great Malvern during World War II. On returning to Cambridge he concentrated on research into low temperature physics and semiconductors. He was able to prove the existence of the Fermi surface in metals, which had previously existed in theory but was not understood. He became lecturer in physics in 1950 and professor of physics in 1960. In 1964 he also became a supportive member of the governing body of Clare College, and when it was decided to found Clare Hall as a centre for advanced study he was appointed its first president for a seven-year term in 1966. He retired as Cavendish professor of physics in 1982, becoming an emeritus fellow, and was made an honorary fellow of Clare Hall in 1998. He wrote a number of books based on his research and was co-author of a three-volume encyclopaedia, *Twentieth Century Physics*. He was elected a Fellow of the Royal Society in 1956 and was knighted in 1975. Died 21 September.

Pollack, Sydney (b. 1934), US film director and producer who won two Oscars for *Out of Africa* and later became a character actor. Born in Lafayette, Indiana, he was determined to become an actor and went to New York to study at the Neighbourhood Playhouse School of the Theatre, where he began to teach. He also began to direct some television dramas, and after moving to Hollywood made his first film, *The Slender Thread* (1955), finally making his mark there directing *They Shoot Horses, Don't They?* (1969) and *The Way We Were* (1973). Among his more successful later films were *Tootsie* (1982), *Out of Africa* (1985), and *The Firm* (1993). He also produced *The Talented Mr Ripley* (1999) and *Cold Mountain* (2003), both directed by Anthony Minghella (for obituary see above). As an actor in films Pollack also stood out in *Husbands and Wives* (1992), directed by Woody Allen, and *Eyes Wide Shut* (1999), directed by Stanley Kubrick. Died 26 May.

Pym, Lord (b. 1922), British politician who served under four prime ministers but was dismissed following his criticisms of Margaret Thatcher. Born Francis Leslie Pym, the son of

another Conservative MP, he was educated at Eton and Magdalene College, Cambridge, and commissioned during World War II into the 9th Lancers, then serving at El Alamein. He was twice mentioned in dispatches and in 1945 was awarded the Military Cross. He completed his studies at Cambridge after the war and after working for a time in business took up politics, winning a by-election in Cambridgeshire in 1961. He joined the Whips' Office in 1962, becoming deputy chief whip in 1967 and chief whip in 1970. He was later moved to the Northern Ireland office, but had only a few months there before the Conservatives were defeated in the 1974 election. When the Conservatives returned to power in 1979, Pym was appointed secretary of state for defence, and in 1981 became leader of the House. A year later, when Lord Carrington resigned following Argentina's invasion of the Falkland Islands (Malvinas), he was appointed foreign secretary, where he was able to gain considerable international support for the British military effort to recapture the islands. He was abruptly dismissed by Thatcher in 1983, having suggested, during the election campaign of that year, that the Conservatives did not need a large majority. He responded by publishing *The Politics of Consent* (1984), in which he argued the case for centrist policies. What seemed to be a potential revolt in the party soon fizzled out, and Pym retired from the Commons in 1987, when he was given a life peerage as Baron Pym of Sandy. Died 7 March.

Rakowski, Mieczyslaw (b. 1926), Polish newspaper editor and politician who briefly became prime minister in 1988. Born in Kowalewko, he was educated in the Higher School of Social Sciences in Cracow and the Institute of Social Sciences in Warsaw, and worked at the central committee of the ruling Polish United Workers' Party (PUWP) before joining the newspaper, *Polityka*, of which he was editor-in-chief from 1958 to 1982. Under his leadership the paper achieved a high reputation, both for its writing and for its independence in foreign and social reporting. But it had to work within the communist system, as did Rakowski, and he sullied his reputation in 1981 by supporting martial law and the crushing of Poland's independent trade union, Solidarity. He became deputy prime minister in that year, but failed to find an accord with Solidarity or to connect with its leader, Lech Walesa, and was partly responsible for sending him to prison. Appointed prime minister in September 1988, Rakowski, at the head of the PUWP, saw his party lose the election of June 1989 to Solidarity, led by Tadeusz Mazowiecki who duly became prime minister. In 1990, as the last leader of the communist PUWP, Rakowski presided over its transformation into a small social democratic party. Died 7 November.

Robbe-Grillet, Alain (b. 1922), French novelist, film director, and script writer who was a leading figure in the literary avant-garde. Born in Saint-Pierre-Quilbion, near Brest, he was educated in Paris at the Lycée Buffon, the Lycée St Louis and at the Institut Agronomique, going on to work at the National Institute of Statistics. He also began to write, completing his first novel, *Un Régicide*, in 1949 (though it was not published until 1978), and his second, *Les Gommes*, which was published in 1953 by the Éditions de Minuit, by whom he was employed as a reader in 1955. That year he completed *Le Voyeur*, which won the Prix des critiques, appealed to the avant-garde, but disturbed many other readers, as did his *La Jalousie* (1957), which was subsequently acclaimed as his masterpiece. Set in a West Indian banana plantation, it recorded the distorted account of a jealous husband watching his wife through the slats of the Venetian-style window shutters (generally given the French name of "jalousies" in the Caribbean). His books established the nouveau roman—well constructed and written works, which nonetheless seemed to suggest more than was actually described or revealed—and were sometimes criticised for concentrating on form rather than content. In 1961 Robbe-Grillet wrote the script for Alain Resnais's film *L'Année Dernière à Marienbad*, and followed this by directing a number of films, including *Trans-Europe-Express* (1967), *La Belle Captive* (1983), and *Un Bruit qui rend fou* (1995). His involvement with the cinema also led him to create the ciné-roman, which could be read as a film script or as a book.

He remained a provocative writer and academic to the end of his life, even using a semi-biographical work, *Le Miroir qui revient*, to challenge some of the literary principles he had previously laboured to establish. Died 18 February.

Rooke, Sir Denis (b. 1924), chairman of British Gas, who masterminded the company's privatisation after bringing natural gas from the North Sea to British homes. Born in London, he was educated at Westminster City school, at Addey and Stanhope school in Deptford, and at University College, London, where he studied engineering. He served with the Royal Electrical and Mechanical Engineers in 1944-49, then joined the South-Eastern Gas Board before working with North Thames Gas to research the use of imported natural gas. He took part in the first, experimental, voyage of the ship, *Methane Power*, from the Gulf of Mexico to Canvey Island with a cargo of methane in liquefied form, which established that gas could be imported in bulk. When natural gas was discovered in the North Sea, Rooke became involved with the Gas Council's formation of a consortium to search for the gas, as well as negotiating to buy it from the oil companies. He was appointed deputy chairman of the British Gas Corporation in 1972 and chairman in 1976, a post which he held until his retirement in 1989. It brought him into conflict with governments, both Labour and Conservative, the former wanting special taxes as well as lower prices for consumers and the latter moving towards privatisation. When British Gas was eventually privatised in 1986, after some tough battles between Rooke and Margaret Thatcher's government, it was done as Rooke had insisted: in one piece, rather than being broken up. Rooke was knighted in 1977, elected a Fellow of the Royal Society in 1978 and, in 1997, appointed to the Order of Merit. Died 2 September.

Saad al-Abdullah al-Salem al-Sabah, Sheikh (b. 1929), briefly emir of Kuwait, who as crown prince led its government in exile during the Iraqi occupation. Born in Kuwait, he was educated at the Mubarakiya school there and at the Hendon police college in England. In 1954 he became deputy chief of the Kuwait city police and in

1962, following Kuwait's independence, was appointed minister of the interior and, from 1964, minister of defence as well. He held these posts until 1978, when he became crown prince and, in 1979, prime minister. In 1989 he visited Baghdad, subsequently reporting that positive steps had been made towards resolving the border disputes between the two countries. Bilateral relations deteriorated, however, and when Saddam Hussein's army invaded Kuwait in1990, Sheikh Saad fled the country with the emir, Sheikh Jaber al-Ahmed al-Jaber al-Sabah, and set about forming a government-in-exile and creating a coalition of nations to liberate his country. He succeeded in persuading Egypt, Saudi Arabia, and Syria to join the US-led task force, and on his return to Kuwait was appointed military governor. In 1997 he began to suffer from ill-health, and spent much time receiving treatment abroad, but nonetheless he succeeded as emir when Sheikh Jaber died in January 2006. His appearance in a wheel-chair increased speculation that he was too ill to exercise power effectively and, following a meeting within the ruling family, he agreed to abdicate, only to find that the Kuwait assembly had already voted him out of office. Died 13 May.

Saint Laurent, Yves (b. 1936), French couturier whose designs dominated the world of fashion in the 1960s and 1970s. Born in Oran, French Algeria, he was educated at the local lycée but spent much of his time designing clothes for his mother and sister, and he subsequently went to the Paris school of the Chambre syndicale de la couture (the regulating commission for haute couture). In 1955 he was taken on by Christian Dior and two years later, when Dior died, Saint Laurent was appointed as his successor. He was then 21. His first solo collection, in 1958, was a triumph, discarding shoulder pads and introducing the trapeze dress and trouser suits. Subsequent collections for Dior were less successful. Soon after being conscripted into the army, Saint Laurent had a breakdown and was rescued by Pierre Bergé, an art dealer who became his business manager. When the Dior company refused to take Saint Laurent back, Bergé successfully sued for breach of contract and set up the designer with his own fashion house (YSL), which soon set new trends for others to follow. By the 1980s he was being criticised both for his reckless lifestyle and for apparently losing his flair for design. He declared that he was no longer concerned with sensation but with the perfection of his style; perhaps more effectively, he responded by becoming the first living designer to have a retrospective of his work presented at the Metropolitan Museum in New York. In the 1990s he gradually wound down his involvement, as YSL and Rive Gauche (the ready-to-wear line) were sold, though he continued to design the haute couture collection until 2002, when he retired to Marrakech. He was appointed a grand officer of the Légion d'honneur in 2007. Died 1 June.

Scofield, Paul (b. 1922), British actor, described as the greatest of his generation, whose main work was on the stage, though he won an Oscar for his film portrayal of Sir Thomas More in *A Man for All Seasons*. Born in Hurstpierpoint, Sussex, he was educated at Varndean school for boys, subsequently training for the stage at the Croydon Repertory theatre school and the London Mask theatre school. He later joined the Birmingham Repertory Theatre, where he met Peter Brook, and the two went on together to the Shakespeare Memorial Theatre in Stratford upon Avon, where Scofield gave memorable performances in Shakespeare's *Love's Labours Lost*, *Henry V*, and *Hamlet*, and in Marlowe's *Doctor Faustus*. In 1949 he moved to London to play Alexander the Great in *Adventure Story*, a role written for him by Terence Rattigan, and the twins in *Ring Round the Moon*, Christopher Fry's adaptation of the play by Jean Anouilh. In 1953 Scofield joined John Gielgud's company at the Lyric, Hammersmith, where the two actors performed memorably together in Thomas Otway's *Venice Preserv'd*. He played Hamlet again in 1955, in a Peter Brook production; and at Stratford in 1962-63, once again directed by Peter Brook, he gave perhaps his most memorable stage performance in *King Lear*, which he repeated in Paris and other European cities, and in New York. Never enthusiastic about films, he turned down a Hollywood offer early in his career, but he repeated his stage performance in *A Man for All Seasons* in the film of 1966 and was persuaded to make a number of other films. He also made a memorable television appearance as the Chuzzlewit brothers in the BBC's *Martin Chuzzlewit*. But he preferred the theatre, and in 1996, by then in his seventies, he played the title role in Ibsen's *John Gabriel Borkman* at the National Theatre. He reportedly turned down offers of a knighthood, but accepted the appointment of Companion of Honour in 2001. Died 19 March.

Singh, V.P. (b. 1931), Indian politician who constantly found himself in and out of office but who, during his brief term as prime minister, initiated the breakdown of the caste system. Born in Allahabad, Vishwanath Pratap (V.P.) Singh was educated at Allahabad and Poona universities then entered politics in Uttar Pradesh, becoming a member of the Lok Sabha, the lower house of Parliament, in 1971, and chief minister of Uttar Pradesh in 1980. He launched a campaign against the dacoits—bandits who controlled the surrounding area—and twice offered to resign because of his failure to defeat them. In 1984 he was appointed finance minister, but was moved to the defence portfolio when his campaign against tax evasion began to affect some influential supporters of the Congress party. He resigned from Parliament when he was dismissed from the cabinet for investigating an earlier defence scandal. He established a new party and allied it with others opposed to the Rajiv Gandhi government, and this coalition—the Janata Dal—defeated the Congress party in the election of 1989. As prime minister, Singh decided in the following year to implement some of the recommendations of the Mandal Commission of 1980, which included reserving some posts in the civil service for lower castes, and opening up jobs for the "untouchables". It was, in effect, a social revolution, and one that succeeded, though Singh himself lost office for the last time in November 1990. Died 27 November.

Sinowatz, Fred (b. 1929), Austrian politician who became chancellor at a time of increasing difficulty for his country. Born in Neufeld an der Leitha, near the Hungarian border, he was educated at a local grammar school and the University of Vienna. He joined the Burgenland provincial government service in 1953 and, as a member of the local Socialist Party, entered the provincial legislature in 1961. He was appointed federal minister of education and the arts in 1971 and vice-chancellor in 1981. When the Socialists lost their overall majority in 1983 and Chancellor Bruno Kreisky resigned, Sinowatz was chosen to lead the party into a coalition with the Freedom Party. As chancellor he ran into trouble almost immediately. He had to reduce the workforce in loss-making state industries, was faced with the scandal of contaminated Austrian wine (which had been laced with potentially lethal substances designed to give it added sweetness), and was confronted with the problem of Kurt Waldheim, the former UN secretary-general, who had decided to run for the Austrian presidency in spite of allegations about his Nazi past. When Waldheim was elected in 1986, Sinowatz resigned as chancellor and, two years later, as Socialist Party chairman. He retired to Burgenland, though he continued to be dragged into the ongoing Waldheim affair. Died 11 August.

Solzhenitsyn, Aleksandr (b. 1918), Russian author who survived the Gulag and wrote about its horrors, for which he was sent into exile. Born in Kislovodsk, in the Caucasus, he was educated at Rostov State University, where he studied mathematics and physics. When Germany invaded the Soviet Union in 1941, he was conscripted into the Red Army, commanding an artillery division and fighting in the battle of Königsberg. He was subsequently arrested, apparently for criticising Stalin in a letter to a friend, and sentenced, without trial, to eight years' detention, initially at the Lubyanka in Moscow and then at the Mavrino special prison for scientists, and finally at a labour camp. His influential first novel, *One Day in the Life of Ivan Denisovich* (published in the Soviet Union in 1962 and a key text in the process of destalinisation under Nikita Khrushchev), was based on his experience in a labour camp, and *The First Circle* (published overseas, following a Soviet ban, in 1968) was set in Mavrino. When he was released Solzhenitsyn went to Kazakhstan, where he suffered cancer, an experience which became the basis of *Cancer Ward* (published overseas in 1968). His writings and other activities were clearly a challenge to the Soviet authorities, as was the award of the Nobel Prize for Literature in 1970. The publication in the West in 1973 of his *Gulag Archipelago* (written between 1958 and 1968) precipitated his expulsion from the Soviet Union. He went first to Zurich and then to Vermont in the USA, where he began to criticise the moral degeneracy of the West whilst continuing to inveigh against the Soviet system. He continued his huge semi-fictional account of the history of Russia, which he had begun in the Soviet Union, but the published volumes were poorly received. In 1994 he returned to Russia, but did not endear himself to the new wave of Russian society by criticising its materialism in his writings and media appearances. His Russian nationalism, however, seemed to strike a chord with President Vladimir Putin, who in 2007 presented Solzhenitsyn with the State Prize of the Russian Federation for humanitarian achievement. Died 3 August.

Stokes, Lord (b. 1914), British industrial salesman who tried, and failed, to make a success of British Leyland. Born in Plymouth, Donald Stokes was educated at Blundell's school and the Harris Institute of Technology in Preston before becoming an engineering apprentice to Leyland Motors in 1930. During World War II he was commissioned as assistant director of mechanical engineering with the Central Mediterranean Forces, returning to Leyland in 1946 as export development manager, becoming general sales and service manager in 1949 and joining the company's main board in 1953. Leyland at this time was a truck and bus manufacturer, but in 1961 it took over Standard Triumph and was transformed into the Leyland Motor Corporation in 1963, with Stokes as managing director and deputy chairman. He also advised the government on exporting defence equipment. In 1965 (the year he was knighted) he became chairman of Leyland, which in the same year acquired the Rover Car Company and, in 1968, merged with British Motor Holdings to become Britain's largest exporter. It was a complex business, beset with labour disputes and saddled with cars that could not compete with those of Ford and General Motors. Stokes, fundamentally a brilliant salesman, was ill-equipped to carry out the necessary reorganisation of a business of this size and complexity, and in 1975 he resigned as chairman. He was made a life peer as Lord Stokes of Leyland in 1969. Died 21 July.

Suharto, General (b. 1921), dictator of Indonesia. Born in Kemusu, central Java, Suharto (he used only that name) was educated at local schools, and briefly worked at a bank before joining the Dutch colonial army and going to the military academy at Gombong. He served with the Japanese army after it had occupied Indonesia (then known as the Dutch East Indies) during World War II, and afterwards fought against the Dutch when they attempted to re-establish their colonial rule. After Indonesia achieved independence, he came to prominence when the country's six leading generals were assassinated in a failed coup attempt—the origins of which remain a source of dispute—apparently directed against the regime of Achmad Sukarno. As one of the most senior military survivors, Suharto played a key role in defeating the coup and blaming it upon the country's large communist party. He was instrumental in unleashing a genocidal purge of the county's communists: between October 1965 and early 1966 more than 500,000 people were massacred and more than 1 million imprisoned. With Sukarno having been reduced to little more than a figurehead since the coup attempt, Suharto formally succeeded him as president in 1968 and established a military dictatorship. He created a party, Golkar, which regularly won carefully controlled elections, while Suharto himself was acclaimed president every five years, unopposed. His austerity measures reduced the country's high inflation rate, and he was able to secure economic growth at around 7 per cent per annum, and return Indonesia to membership of the IMF and the UN. He also developed primary education and a public health service and enjoyed consistent US support as a bulwark against South East Asian communism. The strong support which he received from the West was damaged when Indonesia occupied East Timor in 1975, killing some 100,000 who tried to resist the annexation. Nevertheless, his coercive regime appeared relatively stable until struck by the East Asian financial crisis in 1997. Amid growing economic chaos and widespread unrest, Suharto was forced to resign in 1998. He retired to his home in Jakarta and was able to avoid prosecution for corruption by pleading ill health, despite evidence that he had appropriated a personal fortune of US$15-35 billion whilst in office. Died 27 January.

Terkel, Studs (b. 1912), US writer and broadcaster whose interviews documented the lives of those he called "non-celebrated" Americans. Born in the Bronx, New York, his family moved to Chicago early in his life, and it was there as a young man that he abandoned his real name of Louis in favour of Studs, adopted from the Chicago crime novels of James Farrell. He was educated at Chicago University, where he read law, and after working briefly as a civil servant he began work in radio and television as an actor, interviewer, and disc jockey, having his own TV programme, *Stud's Place*, and in 1953 beginning a daily radio interview programme, *Sound of the City*, which was syndicated throughout the USA. He adopted this oral history technique, prodding people to recall their experiences of Prohibition, the Depression, and all aspects of their daily lives, and skilfully blending these ingredients into his popular books, beginning with *Division Street: America* (1966), which took as its subject the class structure of Chicago. This he followed with *Hard Times: an oral history of the Great Depression* (1970), *Working People* (1974), *American Dreams: Lost and Found* (1980), and *The Good War: an oral history of World War Two* (1985), for which he was awarded a Pulitzer Prize. In none of these, nor in his later books and broadcasts, did he disguise his own generally leftist views, which fulfilled the epithet that he was once accorded as the "national hell-raiser". Died 31 October.

Utzon, Jorn (b. 1918), Danish architect whose finest memorial was the Sydney Opera House. Born in Copenhagen, he was educated at Aalborg

Katadralskole and at the Royal Academy of Fine Arts. After working in Sweden and Finland he moved to the USA to work for Frank Lloyd Wright before returning to Copenhagen in 1950 to set up his own practice. His first project was a development of 64 single-storey houses in Elsinore using what he called the additive method, which he saw as growing naturally like a tree. In 1957 he won the competition to build the Sydney Opera House with an extraordinary design that housed five performance halls under reinforced concrete shells set in a unique configuration of apparently floating geometric forms. Its construction began in 1959 but was beset with problems, and the original design of the shells was declared by the structural engineers, Ove Arup & Partners, to be impossible. Eventually a solution was found by Utzon himself, and the work continued. In 1966, a year after the construction had been due to be completed, Utzon resigned amid a bitter dispute with his client, the government of New South Wales (which had changed in 1965, with the incoming administration being markedly less enthusiastic towards the project and its foreign architect), over design fees and disagreement over the acoustics. The building eventually opened in 1973—by which time it was massively over budget—and rapidly attained the status of an icon of global architecture, although its creator never returned to the city to see the finished project. Utzon undertook other commissions, including Copenhagen's National Museum and gardens and the building housing the National Assembly in Kuwait, but nothing he designed achieved the same level of popular acclaim as the Sydney Opera House. Died 29 November.

Vansittart, Peter (b. 1920), writer who gained critical respect, if not wide popular readership. Educated at Haileybury College, and Worcester College, Oxford, Vansittart published his first novel in 1942 but it was poorly received by the critics. Undeterred, he continued to write fiction throughout the rest of his career, supplementing his meagre writing income with teaching and renting out rooms in his Hampstead house. In 1960, assisted by a modest inheritance, he became a full time writer although he continued to make few concessions to popular literary tastes. Best known for his historical novels, Vansittart never achieved a wide public following, and was known as an author whose preference was for the exploration of language, symbols, and myths, rather than conventional narrative. He produced more than 40 books during his career, including children's literature, anecdotal social history, and anthologies such as *Voices from the Great War* (1981) and *Voices 1879-1914* (1984). Died 4 October.

Weller, Thomas (b. 1915), US virologist who was awarded the Nobel Prize for research that led to polio vaccines. Born in Ann Arbor, Michigan, he was educated in the local high school and at the University of Michigan. In 1936 he entered the Harvard Medical School and after receiving his medical degree moved to the children's hospital in Boston for clinical training. This was interrupted by World War II, during which he served in the US Army Medical Corps, working in Puerto Rico on controlling malaria in the Caribbean. He returned to Boston in 1947, subsequently moving to Harvard's department of comparative pathology and tropical medicine, where he worked with John Enders and Frederick Robbins on growing the polio virus in the laboratory. In 1949 they published a paper, *Cultivation of poliomyelitis virus in cultures of human foreskin and embryonic tissues*, which led to the development of a vaccine that virtually eradicated the disease of polio. The three were jointly awarded the Nobel Prize in Physiology or Medicine in 1954. In the same year Weller became professor of tropical public health and head of his department, and further research enabled him to isolate the rubella virus (German measles) and the varicella zoster virus (chicken pox). Died 23 August.

Wheeler, Sir Charles (b. 1923), British journalist and BBC foreign correspondent. Born in Hamburg, Germany, where his father worked as a shipping agent, he was educated at Cranbrook school in England and joined the Royal Marines on the outbreak of World War II, being mentioned in dispatches. On demobilisation he worked for the BBC external services. In 1956

he became a producer in current affairs and on the television documentary series, *Panorama*, but he wanted to report rather than produce and in 1958 he was sent to Delhi as the BBC's South Asia correspondent. In 1962 he was posted to Berlin, and in 1965 to Washington, DC, becoming the BBC's chief US correspondent in 1969. His reports on the presidencies of Lyndon Johnson and Richard Nixon, and particularly his coverage of the Watergate affair, made him a well-known figure on British television, but with some reluctance he was persuaded to leave Washington in 1973 and move to Brussels where, since the UK had just joined the European Economic Community, it was assumed that there would be many interesting developments to report. He returned to Britain and became, in 1977, the anchorman for *Panorama*. It was not a success: Wheeler never seemed confident in front of a camera in a studio, unlike his assured performances when reporting from where the action was. He resigned from the BBC in order to avoid the compulsory retirement at 60 and joined *Newsnight*, first as a disastrous presenter and then as a roving reporter. He later began to concentrate on making special television features, including *The Road to War* (1989), *D-Day: The Battle for Normandy* (1994), and *Charles Wheeler's America* (1996). He was appointed CMG in 2001 and was knighted in 2006. Died 4 July.

Wheeler, John (b. 1911), US nuclear physicist who was one of the key figures in the development of the atomic bomb. Born in Jacksonville, Florida, he was educated at Baltimore City College in Maryland and at Johns Hopkins University in Baltimore. While an associate professor at the University of North Carolina and at Princeton University in the 1930s, he worked with the Danish physicist Niels Bohr on the structure of nuclear fission and shortly before the outbreak of World War II the two wrote an analysis of the mechanism of the fission process. In 1942 Wheeler joined the Manhattan Project, working on the reactor at Chicago University. He returned to Princeton after the war, becoming professor of physics in 1947, and from 1951-53 he directed Project Matterhorn, exploring the use of nuclear fusion in building what was to become the H-bomb. Under the influence of Albert Einstein, with whom he worked at Princeton, he began to study relativity, quantum theory, and black holes, which was the name he gave to dense objects in space formed by the collapse of a star and from which nothing, not even light, could escape. Wheeler contributed substantially to the advance of modern physics, a subject which he was also able to explain in simple terms. Died 13 April.

Wijetunga, Dingiri Banda (b. 1922), quiet man of Sri Lanka who surprisingly became its prime minister and president. Born in a village near the city of Kandy, he was educated locally and became an inspector for the co-operative department before beginning to take an interest in politics. He was elected to Parliament in 1965 and became minister of information in 1978, of power and highways in 1979, of posts and telecommunications in 1982, of agricultural development and research in 1987, and of finance and planning in 1989, the year in which he was surprisingly appointed prime minister by President Ranasinghe Premadasa over many, more likely candidates. When Premadasa was assassinated in 1993, Parliament appointed Wijetunga as acting president for the remaining 18 months of his term. The appointment seemed to come as a relief to the population after the tough authoritarianism of his predecessor, but the quieter tone he managed to introduce into Sri Lankan politics did not last long. Chandrika Kumaratunga, the daughter of two former prime ministers, became prime minister after winning the general election of August 1994, and took control of the country as Wijetunga effectively went into retirement for the remaining three months of his office (whereupon Kumaratunga won the presidential elections). Died 21 September.

James Bishop

XX CHRONICLE OF PRINCIPAL EVENTS IN 2008

JANUARY

1-31	**Kenya:** serious tribal violence ripped through the country in the aftermath of disputed elections, killing some 900 people and causing a further 250,000 to flee their homes.
2	**Pakistan:** The elections scheduled for 8 January were postponed until 18 February because of the rioting which had followed the assassination in December 2007 of Benazir Bhutto.
	Sri Lanka: The government renounced the ceasefire which had been agreed in 2002 with the separatist Liberation Tigers of Tamil Eelam but which had been largely ignored since 2006.
3	**USA:** The first contest for the presidential nomination of the Democratic Party saw victory for Barack Obama in the Iowa caucuses, with the favourite, Hillary Clinton, finishing in third place.
4	**Mauritania:** the annual Dakar motor rally was cancelled amid security fears after the murder of four French tourists.
	Somalia: Nur Hassan Hussein, who had been appointed prime minister in November 2007, announced a new cabinet.
5	**Georgia:** incumbent President Mikheil Saakashvili was re-elected for a further term.
6	**Iran:** armed Iranian speedboats were involved in a confrontation with US warships in the Strait of Hormuz.
7	**Marshall Islands:** the legislature elected Litokwa Tomeing as the country's new president.
8	**USA:** Clinton won the state of New Hampshire, in the first primary election to be held in the Democratic nominating process. In the parallel Republican contest, the state was won by John McCain.
12	**Taiwan:** the opposition Kuomintang (KMT) won a landslide victory in legislative elections.
13	**Croatia:** the legislature endorsed a new centre-right coalition government, under Prime Minister Ivo Sanader, which had emerged after intensive negotiations following the elections of November 2007.
14	**Afghanistan:** A group of Taliban fighters attacked the heavily guarded Serena Hotel in central Kabul, the country's only 5 star hotel, killing eight people, including several foreign nationals.
	Guatemala: Alvaro Colom Caballeros was inaugurated as president following his election victory in November.
15	**Barbados:** the opposition Democratic Labour Party defeated the governing Barbados Labour Party in a general election.
19	**Faroe Islands:** the opposition, pro-independence Republican Party (TF) made gains in legislative elections.
22-27	**World Economic Forum:** the WEF held its 38th annual meeting in Davos, Switzerland, attended by some 2,500 politicians, academics, business leaders, and representatives of non-governmental organisations.
23	**Central African Republic:** President François Bozizé appointed Faustin-Archange Touadera as prime minister after the resignation of his predecessor in the face of popular protests.

Democratic Republic of Congo: a peace agreement was signed between government and rebel forces led by Laurent Nkunda, a renegade ethnic Tutsi leader who had engaged with the forces of the DRC in an effort to protect the large number of Tutsis living in the eastern provinces.

Palestine: tens of thousands of Palestinians crossed into Egypt after Hamas militants blew up the fence at various points along the border.

24 **Cuba:** legislative elections were held in which all candidates (who stood unopposed) secured more than the required 50 per cent of valid votes cast.

France: it was revealed that unauthorised stock market speculation by a rogue trader had led to losses of almost €5 million by the country's second-largest bank, Société Générale.

Italy: Romano Prodi resigned after his centre-left coalition government was defeated in a confidence vote in the Senate.

25 **Zimbabwe:** President Robert Mugabe announced that presidential and legislative elections would be held in March.

27 **Indonesia:** former President Suharto, who had been forced from office in 1996, died at the age of 86.

28 **EU:** the foreign ministers of the EU formally launched a military operation in Chad and the Central African Republic in support of the UN operation in the two countries (MINURCAT), which had been established in 2007.

Thailand: Samak Sundaravej, the leader of the People Power Party, was elected prime minister at the head of a multiparty coalition government.

USA: President George W. Bush delivered the last his last State of the Union address to the joint houses of Congress.

30 **Israel:** the Winograd commission, established in the aftermath of Israel's unsuccessful war in Lebanon in mid-2006, issued its final report, finding that there had been serious failings in the country's military and political leadership.

FEBRUARY

1 **Iraq:** two female suicide bombers, who according to some reports were mentally impaired, carried out apparently co-ordinated attacks in Baghdad markets, killing 99 people.

31 January–
2 February **African Union:** the 10th summit meeting of the AU, held in Addis Ababa, endorsed a plan for accelerated industrial development of the continent.

3 **Monaco:** legislative elections were held, producing no change in the distribution of seats in the 24-member National Council.

Serbia: incumbent President Boris Tadic won the second round of presidential elections, defeating his nationalist rival Tomislav Nikolic.

4 **Colombia:** more than one million people demonstrated against the FARC (the Colombian Revolutionary Armed Forces), calling upon it to release its hostages.

Israel: a suicide attack by a Hamas bomber in a shopping centre in the southern Israeli town of Dimona killed one woman and injured 11 other Israelis.

5 **USA:** on "Super Tuesday" a record 24 states (and the territory of American Samoa) held either caucuses or primary elections in the Democratic and Republican Parties' contests to determine their presidential candidates.

6 **Thailand:** a new cabinet was sworn in under Prime Minister Samak Sundaravej, leader of the People Power Party.

7   **Belize:** the ruling People's United Party was defeated in legislative elections by the United Democratic Party (UDP) under Dean Barrow, who became the new prime minister.

     Tanzania: Prime Minister Edward Lowassa resigned, over a scandal relating to an energy sector tender. He was replaced by Mizengo Pinda, who formed a new government on 12 February.

8   **Djibouti:** legislative elections were won by the pro-government Union for a Presidential Majority (UMP), as opposition parties boycotted the poll.

     Palestine: Israel started to cut the electricity supply to the Gaza Strip in retaliation for the suicide bombing of 4 February.

     Sudan: government forces staged a major offensive against rebels in western Darfur, capturing three towns and resulting in the flight to Chad of up to 12,000 Darfuri civilians.

11   **East Timor:** a 48-hour state of emergency was declared following attacks on the president and prime minister by a group of rebel soldiers that left Prime Minister José Ramos Horta seriously wounded.

     USA: military prosecutors filed charges against six men held at Guantánamo Bay, Cuba, including Khaled Sheikh Mohammed, allegedly the mastermind of the 11 September 2001 attacks.

12   **Lebanon:** a senior commander in the Shia Hezbullah movement, Imad Mughniyeh, was killed by a car bomb in Syria.

13   **Australia:** Prime Minister Kevin Rudd, at the opening ceremony of Parliament, made a formal apologies for white Australia's maltreatment of Aborigines.

     São Tomé and Príncipé: Patrice Emery Trovoada became prime minister at the head of a new coalition government.

15   **Czech Republic:** President Vaclav Klaus was narrowly re-elected for a second term by the legislature in the third round of a second election, the first (on 8 February) having been inconclusive.

     Germany: disclosures of tax evasion by wealthy Germans including state officials, through the use of "foundations" in Liechtenstein, caused public outrage and led to a dispute between Liechtenstein and Germany.

17   **Serbia:** the province of Kosovo declared independence; Serbia denounced the move.

18   **Cuba:** Fidel Castro Ruz announced that he would not accept re-election as president, paving the way for the succession of his brother, Raul Castro Ruz.

     Pakistan: the Pakistan Muslim League-Qaid-i-Azam, the party of President General (rtd) Pervez Musharraf, was heavily defeated in legislative elections.

19   **Armenia:** Prime Minister Serzh Sarkisian won presidential elections.

21   **Africa:** US President George W. Bush ended a five-nation tour of Africa, which began on 16 February.

     UK: the Northern Rock mortgage bank was brought into "temporary" public ownership.

     Turkey: the Turkish military began a ground offensive against bases of the Kurdistan Workers' Party (PKK) in northern Iraq. Troops were withdrawn on February 29.

22   **Turkey:** President Abdullah Gul signed into law two constitutional reforms, rescinding a ban on the wearing by women of the hijab (Islamic headscarf) in universities.

24   **Cyprus:** presidential elections were won in a second round by main opposition communist party leader, Demetris Christofias.

26   **environment:** an international seed vault in Norway's Svalbard archipelago was formally inaugurated.

     North Korea: the New York Philharmonic Orchestra played a classical music concert in Pyongyang, a possible sign of a thaw in relations between the USA and North Korea.

28	**Kenya:** President Mwai Kibaki agreed to share power with opposition leader Raila Odinga, who also claimed victory in the disputed presidential election of December 2007.
	Thailand: the former prime minister, Thaksin Shinawatra, returned from voluntary exile to face corruption charges.
29	**Montenegro:** Milo Djukanovic of the ruling Democratic Party of Socialists became prime minister, replacing Zeljko Sturanovic.

MARCH

2	**Russia:** First Deputy Prime Minister and chairman of Gazprom Dmitry Medvedev won over 70 per cent of the vote in presidential elections.
2-3	**Iraq:** Iran's President Mahmoud Ahmadinejad made an official visit to Iraq, the first by an Iranian leader since 1979.
3	**Iran:** the UN Security Council unanimously approved Resolution 1803 (2008), imposing new sanctions against Iran for refusing to halt uranium enrichment.
	Palestine: Israel withdrew its ground forces from the Gaza Strip; the military offensive, in response to rocket attacks upon Israeli towns, had begun on 27 February and had killed some 60 Palestinians on 1 March alone.
5	**Georgia:** the separatist republic of South Ossetia appealed for international recognition of its independence; a similar appeal by the republic of Abkhazia followed on 7 March.
	USA: John McCain was endorsed as Republican Party presidential candidate by outgoing President George W. Bush having won a majority of delegates in his party's nominating contests.
5-18	**China:** the first session of the 11th National People's Congress (legislature) confirmed a second term in office for President Hu Jintao and Prime Minister Wen Jiabao and important changes to the composition of the state council (cabinet).
6	**Israel:** a Palestinian gunman shot dead eight religious students at a seminary (yeshiva) in west Jerusalem.
7	**Afghanistan:** diplomat Kai Eide (Norway) was appointed UN special envoy to Afghanistan.
8	**Malaysia:** legislative elections to the lower chamber were won by the ruling 14-party Barisan Nasional coalition with a reduced majority.
	Malta: in legislative elections the ruling Nationalist Party (PN) won a further term in office.
	Serbia: the coalition government collapsed over the issue of Serbia's relations with the EU in the context of Kosovo's independence declaration.
	USA: President George W. Bush vetoed a funding bill for government intelligence agencies; the measure had included a provision to apply US Army standards to the forms of interrogation that the agencies could use, and hence rule out techniques such as "waterboarding".
9	**Spain:** the ruling Spanish Socialist Workers' Party (PSOE) won a second term in legislative elections.
9 and 16	**France:** local elections reflected the unpopularity of President Nicolas Sarkozy, with substantial losses for the ruling Union for a Popular Movement (UMP).
10	**China:** protests in Lhasa, the Tibetan capital, began peacefully but turned violent and were brutally suppressed by the Chinese authorities.

11 **USA:** the US Federal Reserve injected US$200 billion into the banking system, in an attempt to ease the "credit crunch".

14 **Iran:** elections to the Majlis (legislature) returned a majority of conservative supporters of President Mahmoud Ahmadinejad.

Kosovo: Serbs stormed a courthouse in Mitrovica operated by the UN Interim Administration in Kosovo (UNMIK); the building was retaken by NATO-led K-For troops on 17 March amidst violent clashes.

16 **USA:** the investment bank, Bear Sterns, was sold to JP Morgan Chase, having collapsed on 13 March; the Federal Reserve underwrote US$30 billion of Bear Sterns's assets.

18 **Kenya:** the National Assembly unanimously approved constitutional changes agreed after the post-election violence of December 2007, which would see power shared between president and prime minister.

USA: Barack Obama made a speech confronting the issues of race and religion in the USA, in response to views aired by his pastor, Jeremiah Wright, that were potentially damaging to his candidacy for Democratic presidential nomination.

19 **Japan:** Bank of Japan governor Toshihiko Fukui stepped down, leaving the post vacant as the Diet (legislature) had failed to endorse either of the candidates nominated by Prime Minister Yasuo Fukuda.

20 **Belgium:** a new five-party coalition government was appointed, under Prime Minister Yves Leterme, to replace the caretaker administration of Guy Verhofstadt.

21 **Moldova:** Zinaida Grecianii of the ruling Communist Party of Moldova (PCM) was nominated prime minister, following the unexpected resignation of Vasile Tarlev on 19 March.

22 **Taiwan:** Ma Ying-jeou of the opposition Kuomintang (KMT) won a landslide victory in presidential elections, giving the KMT control of both legislature and executive.

24 **Bhutan:** elections to the new legislature, the National Assembly, were won by the Bhutan Harmony Party (DPT).

25 **Comoros:** the army took control of the rebel island of Anjouan but failed to capture its president, Colonel Mohamed Bacar.

Iraq: heavy fighting broke out in Basra between the Iraqi army and Shia militias in a government bid to restore control of the city.

27 **North Korea:** the government expelled 11 South Korean government officials working at the Kaesong joint venture industrial park in response to criticism of North Korea by new South Korean President Lee Myung Bak the previous day.

29 **Zimbabwe:** presidential and legislative elections were held, amid concerns that President Robert Mugabe and the ruling ZANU-PF were trying to rig the result.

31 **Pakistan:** a new coalition cabinet was sworn in under Prime Minister Yusuf Raza Gillani of the Pakistan People's Party (PPP).

APRIL

1 **Botswana:** President Festus Mogae voluntarily stepped down before the end of his term and handed power to his vice president, Lieutenant-General Seretse Khama Ian Khama, the son of the country's first president.

1-30 **China:** the Olympic flame was carried by Chinese athletes through a number of major cities on its round-the-world journey to publicise the holding of the Games in Beijing scheduled for August. The relay became a major source of embarrassment for the Chinese government as the progress of the flame was repeatedly disrupted by demonstrators protesting over China's human rights record and its policy in Tibet.

2-4 **NATO:** a summit meeting was held in Bucharest, attended on the final day by Russian President Vladimir Putin, who made clear his opposition to the extension of NATO membership to countries which had formerly been part of the Soviet bloc.

3 **Afghanistan:** French President Nicolas Sarkozy announced the deployment of a further 1,000 French forces (including some 700 frontline troops) to Afghanistan to support the NATO-led operation against the Taliban insurgency.

Kenya: an agreement was reached between rival political leaders to create a power-sharing government.

Mali: as a result of Libyan mediation, government representatives meeting in Tripoli signed a ceasefire agreement with Touareg rebels under the command of Ibrahim Ag Bahanga.

6 **Montenegro:** incumbent President Filip Vujanovic, of the ruling Democratic Party of Socialists, won a further term in office in presidential elections.

7 **UK:** the jury in the inquests in London into the deaths in a 1997 Paris car crash of Diana, Princess of Wales and her companion Dodi al Fayed delivered majority verdicts of unlawful killing.

8-9 **Africa:** India hosted the first Africa-India summit, in what was seen as an initiative demonstrating India's growing involvement with the African continent and its desire to counter the growth of China's influence in Africa.

USA: General David Petraeus, the commander of US forces in Iraq, and Ryan Crocker, the US ambassador in Baghdad, testified again before Congress on the success of the "surge" strategy.

9 **Armenia:** following his disputed victory in the February presidential election, Serzh Sarkisian was formally inaugurated as president. He appointed Tigran Sargsyan, hitherto chairman of the Central Bank of Armenia (CBA), as the new prime minister.

Burma: the State Peace and Development Council (the military government) published the text of the country's new constitution and arranged for its approval by referendum on 10 May.

Kosovo: having declared itself unilaterally independent of Serbia, the legislature in Kosovo adopted a new constitution, effective 15 June, which characterised Kosovo as a parliamentary republic.

South Korea: the conservative Grand National Party won a narrow legislative majority in elections to the National Assembly.

10 **Bhutan:** King Jigme Khesar Namgyel Wangchuk formally appointed Jigme Yoser Thinley, of the Bhutan Harmony Party, as the new prime minister, following the party's overwhelming victory in legislative elections in March.

11 **Uganda:** talks between the government and the rebel Lord's Resistance Army designed to arrive at a complete peace agreement collapsed.

13 **Haiti:** amid widespread looting and rioting, triggered by sharp price increases, the government of Prime Minister Jacques Edouard Alexis fell after losing a vote of confidence in the Senate.

13-14 **Italy:** Silvio Berlusconi secured a third term as prime minister when his opposition centre-right People of Freedom (PdL) coalition won 46 per cent of the vote to defeat the centre-left Democratic Party (PD) alliance led by Walter Veltroni.

14 **Cameroon:** the constitution was amended to enable President Paul Biya, who was due to step down at the next election in 2011, to seek another term of office.

14 **Spain:** having won a second term as prime minister in the March elections, José Luís Rodríguez Zapatero appointed his cabinet, the first in Spanish history to contained a female majority.

15 **Vatican:** Pope Benedict XVI began a six-day visit to the USA, during which he met President George W. Bush and addressed the UN General Assembly.

16 **Chad:** Nouradine Delwa Kassiré Koumakoye was dismissed as prime minister by President Idriss Déby, and replaced by Youssouf Saleh Abbas, who had hitherto served as Déby's diplomatic adviser.

16 **French Polynesia:** the pro-French government of President Gaston Flosse fell in a no-confidence vote only 52 days after taking power. It was replaced on the following day by an administration led by former President Gaston Tong Sang.

North Korea: the UN World Food Programme (WFP) warned that food shortages, caused by flooding and a poor harvest in 2007, were likely to deepen into a humanitarian crisis within three months.

USA: the Supreme Court ruled in favour of the constitutionality of lethal injection as a method of judicial execution.

20 **Paraguay:** former Roman Catholic bishop Fernando Lugo, the leader of a coalition of opposition parties, was elected president, thereby breaking a monopoly on power held by the Colorado Party for more than 60 years.

25 **Tonga:** in the last election to be held under the highly restrictive franchise of the country's existing constitution, pro-democracy supporters were returned to the nine seats in the country's legislature which were open to commoners.

26 **Nauru:** President Marcus Stephen won a snap legislative election called in order to break the impasse attendant upon the 18-member Parliament being evenly split between government and opposition members.

29 **Egypt:** President Mohammed Hosni Mubarak proposed a 30 per cent rise in state employees' wages, in response to a series of strikes by workers protesting at rising food prices, redundancies, and privatisation.

MAY

1 **Somalia:** a US air strike on the town of Dhuusa Mareeb killed Aden Hashi Ayro, reputedly the leader of the country's Islamist insurrection.

UK: the ruling Labour party suffered heavy defeats in local council elections in England and Wales, including for the post of mayor of London.

2 **Palestine:** representatives of the Middle East Quartet met in London for a high-level conference to assess the Israeli-Palestinian peace process.

Zimbabwe: the Zimbabwe Electoral Commission announced that opposition leader Morgan Tsvangirai had defeated President Robert Mugabe in the 29 March presidential elections but, having not won an outright majority, would have to contest a second round.

2-3 **Burma:** Cyclone Nargis caused massive destruction and loss of life in the Irrawaddy river delta and Rangoon.

4 **Equatorial Guinea:** the ruling Democratic Party of Equatorial Guinea (PDGE) overwhelmingly won elections to the unicameral legislature.

Georgia: officials in Abkhazia claimed that two unmanned Georgian reconnaissance drones had been shot down over the separatist republic. Russia endorsed the allegations, which Georgia denied.

6 **Lebanon:** the government declared Hezbullah's telecommunications network in Beirut illegal and dismissed head of security at Beirut airport Brigadier General Wafic Chucair, prompting violent conflict with Hezbullah.

Mauritania: Yahia Ould Ahmed El-Waqef was appointed prime minister in place of Zeine Ould Zeidane and formed a new cabinet.

Japan: China's President Hu Jintao began a five-day visit, becoming the first Chinese head of state to visit Japan since 1998.

7   **Ireland:** Deputy Prime Minister and Finance Minister Brian Cowen was elected prime minister by the Dáil (lower chamber of the legislature) to replace Bertie Ahern, who resigned on 6 May.

Slovakia: the European Commission approved the country's application to adopt the euro from 1 January 2009.

8   **Bhutan:** King Jigme Khesar Namgyel Wangchuk formally handed over power at the inaugural joint session of the bicameral legislature.

North Korea: operational logs dating back to 1986 from the Yongbyon nuclear power plant were handed over to US negotiators.

Russia: following the inauguration of President Dmitry Medvedev on 7 May, former President Vladimir Putin was confirmed as the new prime minister.

9   **Central African Republic:** the government signed a ceasefire and peace accord with the main rebel group, the People's Army for the Restoration of the Republic and Democracy (APRD).

11   **Serbia:** legislative elections were won by the pro-EU forces of President Boris Tadic, with the nationalist Serbian Radical Party (SRS) coming second.

Sudan: President Omar Hassan Ahmed al-Bashir announced the severing of diplomatic relations with Chad over the attack on the city of Omdurman on 10 May by Darfuri rebels who he claimed were backed by Chad.

12   **Bangladesh:** Chief Adviser Fakhruddin Ahmed (head of the interim government) announced legislative elections for December and the suspension of aspects of the emergency power rules.

China: an huge earthquake struck the province of Sichuan, killing at least 69,000 people and affecting 45.55 million. A large number of schools collapsed, allegedly because of substandard construction methods.

Commonwealth: Pakistan's full membership was restored, having been suspended in November 2007.

Iraq: Shia cleric Muqtada al-Sadr authorised a ceasefire that would allow the Iraqi army, but not US troops, to enter Sadr City in Baghdad; in return Sadr promised to halt his "Mahdi Army"'s attacks on the Green Zone government compound in the city.

Pakistan: the Pakistan Muslim League-Nawaz (PML-N) withdrew its ministers from the coalition government.

13   **India:** eight bombs exploded in Jaipur, killing at least 63 people.

16   **Dominican Republic:** President Leonel Fernández Reyna was returned to power in elections.

Iceland: a €1.5 billion funding package to support the Icelandic currency and banking system against the effects of the global credit crisis was announced by the central banks of Sweden, Denmark, and Norway.

17   **Kuwait:** early legislative elections were held to a new National Assembly, the previous legislature having been dissolved on 19 March amid complaints that legislators were obstructing the government.

17-18   **South Africa:** violence erupted in the poor townships of Johannesburg as mobs attacked foreigners, mostly Zimbabwean refugees.

20   **Guinea:** President Lansana Conté dismissed Prime Minister Lansana Kouyaté, replacing him with technocrat Ahmed Tidiane Souare.

USA: the results of Democratic Party primary elections held in Kentucky and Oregon gave Barack Obama a majority of the total number of pledged delegates, although Hillary Clinton remained technically in the race.

21 **Georgia:** President Mikheil Saakashvili's United National Movement for a Victorious Georgia won elections to Parliament.

Japan: the Diet enacted a law abandoning the "non-military" principle governing Japan's use of space.

23 **Burma:** under international pressure, the chairman of the military government, Than Shwe, agreed to allow foreign aid workers into the country to assist the relief effort following Cylone Nargis.

23-24 **Russia:** Dmitry Medvedev made his first foreign visit as president to China, rather than the traditional visit to the USA and Europe.

25 **Lebanon:** the National Assembly (unicameral legislature) elected Gen. Michel Suleiman president, as provided for under the Doha agreement concluded on 21 May to resolve the country's political crisis.

26 **Ethiopia:** the federal Supreme Court sentenced former President Mengistu Haile Mariam, currently living in Zimbabwe, to death in absentia for genocide and crimes against humanity.

Space: NASA's *Phoenix* spacecraft landed successfully on Mars in the planet's north polar region.

27 **Argentina:** four farming unions resumed their protest strike at increased taxes on agricultural exports.

Burma: the military government extended by 12 months the house arrest of opposition leader Aung San Suu Kyi.

28 **Iran:** Ali Larijani was elected speaker of the new legislature, which had been elected in March and April.

Kuwait: a new cabinet was appointed, under reinstated prime minister Sheikh Nasser al-Mohammad al-Ahmad al-Sabah. The former cabinet had been dissolved, along with the legislature, on 19 March.

Nepal: the Constituent Assembly held its first session and endorsed a proposal to abolish the monarchy and declare Nepal a federal republic.

JUNE

1 **Macedonia:** early legislative elections were won by the For a Better Macedonia (ZpM) coalition, led by the ruling party, the VMRO-DPMNE.

2 **Denmark:** al-Qaida claimed responsibility for a suicide bombing outside the Danish embassy in Islamabad (capital of Pakistan) in retaliation for the republication by Danish newspapers in February of a caricature of the Prophet Mohammed.

3 **USA:** Barack Obama claimed victory in the Democratic presidential nomination contest in a speech in St Paul, Minnesota, after the last primaries were held that day and the party's "superdelegates" announced their support for him.

3-6 **Food and Agriculture Organisation:** a summit disagreed over reasons for the 71 per cent rise in food prices over the past two years that had triggered food riots in some 30 countries.

5 **Northern Ireland:** the National Assembly elected as first minister Peter Robinson, the new leader of the Democratic Unionist Party; he replaced Ian Paisley, who had announced his resignation from both positions in March.

Turkey: the Constitutional Court annulled the government's lifting of a ban on women wearing the hijab in universities.

7   **Niue:** elections were held to the Fono (unicameral legislature) which, on 18 June, elected Toke Talagi as the new premier, replacing Young Vivian.

USA: Hillary Clinton formally conceded defeat at a rally of her supporters in Washington, DC, and urged them to support Barack Obama in the presidential election.

9   **Somalia:** the transitional national government, backed by Ethiopia, and the Eritrean-backed opposition Alliance of the Liberation and Reconstitution of Somalia (ALRS) signed a peace agreement brokered by the UN, with little effect on the continued fighting.

10   **South Korea:** the cabinet offered to resign in the wake of popular protests against the scheduled resumption of imports of US beef amidst fears that the meat might be contaminated with BSE ("mad cow disease").

11   **Canada:** Prime Minister Stephen Harper made a formal apology, in Parliament, for the impact that Canada's Indian residential schools (active until the 1970s) had had upon aboriginal culture, and for the suffering of their inmates.

Japan: the opposition-controlled House of Councillors (the upper chamber) passed a symbolically important, though non-binding, censure motion against the government of Prime Minister Yasuo Fukuda; this was countered on 12 June by a vote of confidence in the lower house, where the government had a majority.

South Africa: President Thabo Mbeki condemned the perpetrators of violent attacks in May against foreigners, many of them Zimbabwean refugees.

12   **Afghanistan:** a donors' meeting in Paris pledged more than US$20 million in aid to Afghanistan, but also voiced criticism of the Afghan government for failing to tackle corruption.

Ireland: over 53 per cent of those voting in a referendum rejected the EU's Lisbon Treaty on institutional reform, putting the treaty in jeopardy.

USA: the Supreme Court ruled by five to four that inmates in the US prison camp at Guantánamo Bay, Cuba, could challenge their detention through the civilian judicial system and called for a halt to plans to try around 80 of the remaining 270 prisoners in military commissions.

13   **Afghanistan:** the Taliban attacked a prison in the southern city of Kandahar, releasing some 1,000 prisoners, including 400 Taliban militants.

16   **Bosnia & Herzegovina:** the country signed a stabilisation and association agreement (SAA) with the EU.

17   **France:** a review of defence policy envisaged the reintegration of France into NATO's military command structure, from which it had withdrawn in 1966.

19   **Palestine:** a ceasefire mediated by Egypt came into force between Israel and Hamas.

22   **OPEC:** at an emergency summit, members of the Organisation of Petroleum Exporting Countries and other countries discussed the continuing steep rise in oil prices.

São Tomé and Príncipe: a coalition government under Prime Minister Joaquim Rafael Branco of the former opposition Movement for the Liberation of São Tomé and Príncipe-Social Democratic Party replaced the previous government, which had lost a vote of confidence on 20 May.

22-24   **Syria:** IAEA officials visited the al-Kibar facility in the north of the country that was bombed by Israel in September 2007 and was alleged to have housed a secret nuclear programme.

23   **Algeria:** a new prime minister, Ahmed Ouyahia, was appointed to the post he had left in May 2006.

Cuba: the EU formally lifted diplomatic sanctions against Cuba, despite US objections, in an attempt to encourage President Raul Castro Ruz to improve the country's human rights record.

Haiti: President René Préval nominated a third candidate for prime minister, following the rejection on 12 June of his second choice, Robert Manuel, by the Chamber of Deputies.

26 **North Korea:** the government transmitted what it claimed were complete records of its nuclear programmes to US officials in Beijing.

USA: the Supreme Court ruled by five to four that the second amendment to the US Constitution guaranteed an individual's right to bear arms.

27 **Thailand:** Prime Minister Samak Sundaravej and seven cabinet ministers survived motions of no-confidence in the House of Representatives, whilst daily demonstrations continued against Samak's proposed constitutional changes that many believed were designed to rehabilitate disgraced former Prime Minister Thaksin Shinawatra.

Zimbabwe: in the second round of presidential elections, President Robert Mugabe won 85.5 per cent of the vote. The poll had been stripped of any legitimacy after Mugabe's opponent, Morgan Tsvangirai, had withdrawn on 22 June because of state-sponsored violence against opposition supporters.

29 **Comoros:** a second round of presidential elections on the island of Anjouan was won by Moussa Toybou.

Mongolia: legislative elections were held to the Great Hural under a new system of proportional representation, and were won by the Mongolian People's Revolutionary Party (MAHN).

30 **India:** Prime Minister Manmohan Singh announced a national action plan to encourage sustainable sources of energy, but made no commitment to reduce carbon emissions.

JULY

2 **Colombia:** a successful rescue operation was carried out by Colombian security agents to free 15 hostages held by the Colombian Revolutionary Armed Forces (FARC). They included French-Colombian citizen Ingrid Betancourt.

Mongolia: a four-day state of emergency was declared following rioting in Ulan Bator after allegations of fraud in the 29 June legislative elections.

3 **Democratic Republic of Congo:** the Belgian authorities transferred Jean-Pierre Bemba, leader of the opposition Congolese Liberation Movement, to the International Criminal Court in The Hague to face war crimes charges.

6 **Afghanistan:** the authorities denounced a US air strike in Nangarhar province which reportedly killed 47 civilians, including 39 women and children.

7 **Afghanistan:** a suicide car bombing in Kabul killed at least 58 people, in the worst such attack since the overthrow of the Taliban in 2001. The Afghan authorities implied that Pakistan's intelligence agency was responsible.

7-9 **G-8:** leaders of the G-8 held a summit meeting in Toyako, Japan, where they discussed the credit crisis, rising fuel and food prices, climate change policy, and aid to developing countries.

8 **Czech Republic:** a formal treaty was signed that, pending ratification by the legislature, would allow the USA to build an anti-missile radar tracking station in the Brdy military area, as part of the USA's planned anti-missile shield.

Grenada: the opposition National Democratic Congress (NDC) won legislative elections, thereby ending the 13-year dominance of the New National Party. NDC leader Tillman Thomas was inaugurated as prime minister on 9 July.

9　　**Baltic states:** Russia announced that from 2015 it would transfer its export of oil and other goods from ports in Estonia, Latvia, and Lithuania, to the Russian port of Ust-Luga.

10　　**USA:** amendments to the 1978 Foreign Intelligence Surveillance Act (FISA) became law, providing the US government with sweeping powers to monitor communications between suspected terrorists.

10-12　　**North Korea:** six-party talks on dismantling the country's nuclear weapons programme resumed in Beijing for the first time since July 2007.

11　　**Lebanon:** a new cabinet, headed by Prime Minister Fouad Siniora, was formed, with the Hezbullah-led opposition parties having enough posts to give them veto powers, as provided for by the Doha accord of 21 May.

Zimbabwe: Russia and China vetoed a UN Security Council resolution that would have imposed an arms embargo on Zimbabwe and travel and financial restrictions on President Robert Mugabe and nine of his associates.

13　　**EU-Mediterranean:** the inaugural summit was held in Paris of the Union for the Mediterranean, attended by 27 EU member states and 16 non-EU Mediterranean countries.

14　　**Belgium:** Prime Minister Yves Leterme tendered his resignation, for the third time in 11 months, over the failure of French and Flemish-speaking parties in his coalition government to resolve constitutional reform issues.

Equatorial Guinea: a new cabinet was appointed under Prime Minister Ignacio Milam Tang, himself appointed on 8 July after legislative elections held in May.

Sudan: the prosecutor of the International Criminal Court, Luis Moreno Ocampo, requested an arrest warrant for Sudan's President Omar Hassan Ahmed al-Bashir, on the grounds that al-Bashir had committed genocide, crimes against humanity, and war crimes in Darfur.

16　　**Lebanon:** the Shia Hezbullah movement handed over to Israel the bodies of two Israeli soldiers whose capture in 2006 had sparked the war of that summer; in return, Israel transferred five Lebanese prisoners (the last held by Israel), and the remains of 199 Lebanese and Palestinian militants.

18　　**Argentina:** President Cristina Fernández de Kirchner revoked a decree increasing agricultural export taxes in the face of sustained opposition by the four largest farming unions.

19-24　　**USA:** Democratic presidential candidate Barack Obama conducted a "fact-finding tour" of the Middle East and Europe, ending with a speech before 200,000 people at an outdoor rally in Berlin.

21　　**France:** a joint session of the legislature approved a series of amendments to the 1958 constitution of the Fifth Republic, among them measures to strengthen the powers of the legislature.

Nepal: the country's first elected president was chosen after two rounds of voting by members of the Constituent Assembly. He was Ram Baran Yadav of the Nepali Congress Party.

Serbia: security officers captured Radovan Karadzic, the Bosnian Serb wartime leader, accused in 1995 of genocide by the International Criminal Tribunal for the former Yugoslavia (ICTY) for his actions against Bosnian Muslims.

USA: the trial opened at the Guantanamo Bay prison camp in Cuba of Salim Ahmed Hamdan, former driver and alleged bodyguard of Osama bin Laden. The trial, in a military tribunal that allowed hearsay evidence and evidence obtained under torture, was seen as a rehearsal for the trials of more significant detainees.

22   **Bangladesh:** a new electoral roll was completed, after an 11-month campaign. The roll included details of over 80 million voters, 13 million fewer than on the previous roll.
India: the government of Prime Minister Manmohan Singh survived a vote of confidence in Parliament, triggered by the withdrawal of support by the Left Front parties over the proposed agreement with the USA on civil nuclear technology co-operation.

27   **Cambodia:** the ruling Cambodian People's Party won a landslide victory in legislative elections.

30   **Israel:** Prime Minister Ehud Olmert announced his impending resignation, under pressure from corruption allegations.
Turkey: the Constitutional Court failed to endorse a call for the closure of the ruling Islamist Justice and Development Party (AKP) on the grounds of trying to undermine Turkey's constitutional secular status.
USA: the Housing and Economic Recovery Act became law. It included measures allowing for the emergency rescue of two giant mortgage companies, Fannie Mae and Freddie Mac, which were at risk from the global credit crunch caused by high-risk lending in the form of "subprime" mortgages.

31   **Haiti:** the ratification by the Senate of the nomination as prime minister of Michèle Duvivier Pierre-Louis ended a three month stalemate between the legislature and President René Préval over appointing a candidate to the post.

AUGUST

1   **Brazil:** an international campaign, designed to raise US$21 billion of foreign investment, was launched to protect the Amazon rainforest and combat climate change.
Japan: Prime Minister Yasuo Fukuda replaced 13 of his 17 cabinet ministers in a desperate bid to bolster his beleaguered government.
Tonga: the coronation was held of King Siaosi (George) Tupou V.

3   **Russia:** the Soviet dissident writer Alexander Solzhenitsyn died, aged 89.

4   **China:** sixteen paramilitary police were killed in Kashgar, a predominantly Uighur Muslim city, in a separatist attack.
Italy: the deployment began of some 3,000 soldiers in major cities as part of the government's initiative to tackle street crime and illegal immigration.

5   **Guinea-Bissau:** Carlos Correia was appointed prime minister and the legislature was dissolved, following the collapse of the coalition government in July.
Rwanda: a government commission of enquiry reported that a number of senior French government officials had been complicit in the 1994 genocide. France described the allegations as "unacceptable".
USA: Aafia Siddiqui, a Pakistani US-trained neuroscientist, appeared in court in New York on charges of attempted murder and assault. Siddiqui claimed she had been raped and tortured at a secret US detention facility since her disappearance in Pakistan in March 2003 with her three children, whose whereabouts remained unknown. The court ordered that she receive medical attention for a gunshot wound, which had been denied her hitherto.

6   **Mauritania:** an 11-member junta, led by the head of the presidential guard, General Mohammed Ould Abdelaziz, seized power from President Sidi Mohammed Ould Cheikh Abdellahi in a military coup.

7-8   **Georgia:** Georgia shelled Tskhinvali, capital of the separatist republic of South Ossetia; Russian forces entered the republic, and then occupied strategic areas of Georgia.

8-24	**China:** the 29th Olympic Games were held in Beijing.
11	**Iraq:** King Abdullah II of Jordan made a surprise visit and held talks with Prime Minister Nouri al-Maliki.
13	**Cambodia:** the Extraordinary Chambers in the Courts of Cambodia (ECCC)—a UN-backed tribunal—served its first indictment of a leader of the 1975-79 Khmer Rouge regime, when it charged Kang Kek Ieu (Duch) with crimes against humanity and war crimes.
14	**Cameroon:** Nigeria formally handed to Cameroon control of the Bakassi peninsula, the disputed ownership of which had been settled by a 2002 ruling by the International Court of Justice.
	EU: official figures showed a 0.2 per cent contraction of GDP in the eurozone in the second quarter of 2008.
	Paraguay: a new cabinet was sworn in under President-elect Fernando Lugo Méndez, a former Roman Catholic bishop, whose inauguration ceremony took place on 15 August.
15	**Nepal:** the Constituent Assembly elected Pushpa Kamal Dahal (Prachanda), chairman of the Communist Party of Nepal-Maoist, as the country's first republican prime minister. He named a coalition cabinet on 22 August.
15-16	**Georgia-Russia:** the presidents of Georgia and Russia signed an EU-brokered ceasefire agreement, although Russia insisted on retaining troops in and around South Ossetia and Abkhazia.
16	**Belarus:** prominent opposition leader Alyaksandr Kazulin was unexpectedly released from prison, having received a presidential pardon.
18	**India and Nepal:** the collapse of a dam in Nepal caused severe flooding in south-eastern Nepal and India's Bihar state.
	Pakistan: President General (rtd) Pervez Musharraf, under imminent threat of impeachment by the legislature, announced his resignation.
19	**Afghanistan:** a recently deployed contingent of French troops suffered serious casualties, including 10 fatalities, in an ambush south-east of Kabul.
	NATO: NATO foreign ministers suspended meetings of the consultative NATO-Russia Council in reaction to the continued presence of Russian troops in Georgia.
	Zambia: President Levy Mwanawasa died in hospital in France; he had suffered a stroke on 29 June.
20	**Poland:** a formal treaty with the USA was signed, allowing for the deployment in Poland of 10 US anti-missile interceptors as part of the planned US missile defence shield; Poland also obtained a promise for the permanent stationing of US Patriot missiles in Poland.
22	**Afghanistan:** a US airstrike in Herat province was thought to have killed 90 civilians, 60 of them children.
23	**India:** the murder of a Hindu religious leader, Swami Laxmanananda Saraswati, triggered violence by Hindu extremists against Christians in Orissa state.
25	**Palestine:** Israel released 198 Palestinian prisoners in the West Bank, a move designed to bolster the position of Palestinian President Mahmoud Abbas.
	Zimbabwe: a candidate of the opposition Movement for Democratic Change (MDC), Lovemore Moyo, was elected to the important post of speaker of the House of Assembly (lower chamber of the legislature).
25-28	**USA:** the Democratic National Convention, held in Denver, Colorado, formally nominated Barack Obama as the party's presidential candidate.
26	**Malaysia:** Anwar Ibrahim (a former deputy prime minister) resumed a seat in the legislature and took up leadership of the opposition, having convincingly won a by-election.

Russia: President Dmitry Medvedev formally recognised the independence of South Ossetia and Abkhazia, endorsing the unanimous votes by the two houses of the Russian legislature the previous day for the independence of the Georgian enclaves.

26-31 **Americas:** Hurricane Gustav caused extensive damage in Haiti, the Dominican Republic, Jamaica, the Cayman Islands, and Cuba; at least 90 people were killed.

29 **USA:** Republican Party presidential candidate John McCain named as his running mate the relatively inexperienced Sarah Palin, governor of Alaska.

31 **Sudan:** the UN Security Council extended the mandate of the hybrid African Union and UN peacekeeping operation for Darfur, UNAMID, for a further 12 months, just two hours before the UNAMID mandate was due to expire.

SEPTEMBER

1-30 **Democratic Republic of Congo:** fighting broke out in the east of the country between government forces and rebels from the National Congress for the Defence of the People (CNDP).

India: monsoon flooding affected eastern and northern states.

Americas: Hurricane Ike hit a number of countries, with the worst damage occurring in Haiti, already battered by Hurricane Gustav and Tropical Storms Fay and Hanna.

1 **Iraq:** government forces assumed control over security in Anbar province from the US military. It was the 11th of 18 provinces to return to Iraqi control.

Japan: Yasuo Fukuda resigned as prime minister and president of the ruling Liberal Democratic Party.

3 **Pakistan:** US commandos, acting independently of the NATO-led International Security Assistance Force (ISAF), made their first cross-border raid from Afghanistan.

USA: the acceptance speech of Sarah Palin, Republican vice-presidential nominee, energised the party's national convention in Minneapolis-St Paul, although in television interviews later in the month her ignorance of foreign policy issues became clear.

5 **Arctic:** it was confirmed by the US National Ice Centre that both the Northwest Passage and the Northeast Passage sea routes were simultaneously clear of ice for the first time.

5-6 **Angola:** elections to the 220-seat National Assembly were won by the ruling Popular Movement for the Liberation of Angola (MPLA).

Libya: US Secretary of State Condoleezza Rice held talks with Libyan leaders, becoming the most senior US official to visit Libya in 50 years.

6 **Haiti:** Michèle Duvivier Pierre-Louis and her cabinet were sworn in, finally replacing the government of Jacques Edouard Alexis, which was dismissed in April.

7 **Afghanistan:** the emergence of a video showing graphic footage of at least 40 mutilated bodies, including many children, threw into doubt US military denials that a US air strike on 22 August in western Herat had killed up to 92 civilians.

Hong Kong: elections to contested seats in the legislature saw the pro-China Democratic Alliance for the Betterment of Hong Kong win most seats.

Togo: Gilbert Fossoun Houngbo was appointed prime minister, replacing Komlan Mally, whose unexpected resignation was announced on 5 September.

USA: the government took into "conservatorship" Fannie Mae and Freddie Mac, the two giant institutions that owned or guaranteed almost half of all US mortgages and which had suffered major losses due to "subprime" mortgage liabilities.

8   **Georgia:** following talks in Moscow with Russia's President Dmitry Medvedev, France's President Nicolas Sarkozy, in his role as chairman of the European Council, announced that Russia had agreed to withdraw its troops from Georgia (with the exception of the disputed regions of South Ossetia and Abkhazia) within 10 days of the deployment of EU monitors, which was to take place by 1 October.

        Pakistan: Asif Ali Zardari, co-chairman of the PPP (Pakistan People's Party) and widower of Benazir Bhutto, was indirectly elected president of Pakistan and sworn in the following day.

9   **Cambodia:** Prime Minister Samak Sundaravej resigned following a Constitutional Court ruling that he had violated the constitution by continuing to appear on a television cookery programme after becoming prime minister in January.

        USA: the Congressional Budget Office (CBO) projected a budget deficit of $407 billion in 2008, rising to $438 billion in 2009.

10   **Scientific research:** the European Centre for Nuclear Research (CERN) started up its Large Hadron Collider particle accelerator, but closed it for repairs on 19 September.

13   **India:** five bomb explosions in New Delhi killed at least 21 people. The little-known Indian Mujaheddin group claimed responsibility.

15   **China:** the first arrests were made in the contaminated baby milk scandal. By late September, an estimated 100,000 children had become ill as a result of consuming infant formula to which the industrial chemical melamine had been added.

        USA: investment bank Lehman Brothers collapsed with liabilities of $613 billion and filed for bankruptcy.

        Zimbabwe: President Robert Mugabe and the leaders of the two wings of the opposition Movement for Democratic Change, Morgan Tsvangirai and Arthur Mutambara, signed a power-sharing agreement.

15-18   **Rwanda:** elections to the Chamber of Deputies were won by the ruling Rwandan Patriotic Front (FPR) and its six coalition allies.

16   **Ukraine:** the ruling coalition collapsed, amidst rivalry between President Viktor Yushchenko and Prime Minister Yuliya Tymoshenko.

        USA: the Federal Reserve provided an emergency credit liquidity facility of $85 billion to the insurance company, AIG, which was facing bankruptcy.

17   **Cambodia:** Somchai Wongsawat became prime minister, but was targeted by renewed protests from the opposition People's Alliance for Democracy.

        Israel: Tzipi Livni, vice prime minister and foreign minister, was elected leader of the ruling Kadima party.

        Russia: the government, central bank, and financial regulator met to agree an emergency rescue package following turmoil in the country's financial markets.

19   **Mongolia:** a new coalition government was formed by the Mongolian People's Revolutionary Party and the Mongolian Democratic Party.

        Swaziland: the first legislative elections under the 2005 constitution were held for the House of Assembly.

20   **Pakistan:** the Marriott hotel in Islamabad was attacked by a suicide bomber with some 600 kg of military explosives in a truck.

        South Africa: President Thabo Mbeki resigned, under pressure from senior members of the ruling African National Congress.

21   **France:** in indirect elections for 114 of 343 Senate seats, the opposition Socialist Party (PS) made gains, although the ruling Union for a Popular Movement (UMP) remained the largest party.

        Slovenia: in legislative elections the centre-left Social Democrats emerged as the strongest party.

22   **Vanuatu:** Edward Natapei of the Vanua'aki Pati (VP) was elected prime minister by the National Assembly, following legislative elections on 2 September.

24   **Burma:** the government released 9,002 prisoners in an amnesty, including seven political prisoners, the most prominent of whom was Win Tin.

    Japan: Taro Aso became prime minister, having on 22 September won a leadership election for the ruling Liberal Democratic Party.

25   **Cambodia:** the National Assembly re-elected Hun Sen for a further five-year term as prime minister.

    Space: China successfully launched its third manned space mission.

    Democratic Republic of Congo: Antoine Gizenga announced his resignation as prime minister.

26   **USA:** in the largest bank failure in US history, the Washington Mutual (WaMu) bank holding company declared bankruptcy.

28   **Austria:** an early general election was won by the senior coalition partner, the Social Democratic Party (SPÖ), but nationalist parties showed appreciable gains.

    Belarus: in elections, supporters of the president won all 110 seats in the House of Representatives (lower chamber of the legislature).

29   **Palestine:** Israeli Prime Minister Ehud Olmert said in an interview with an Israeli newspaper that Israel must withdraw from nearly all the West Bank and East Jerusalem in order to achieve peace with the Palestinians.

    UK: the Bradford and Bingley (B&B) mortgage bank was taken into public ownership following its near failure as a result of the global credit crisis.

    USA: the $700 billion Emergency Economic Stabilisation Bill (bank bailout) was rejected in the House of Representatives, causing panic on US and European financial markets.

30   **Angola:** Col António Paulo Kassoma was appointed prime minister.

OCTOBER

3   **USA:** the $700 billion banking bailout plan—the Emergency Economic Stabilisation Act—was signed into law, having been approved in the House of Representatives that day by 263 votes to 271.

5   **Germany:** Chancellor Angela Merkel unexpectedly announced a government guarantee of all personal bank deposits, followed by the announcement on 13 October of a €500 billion bank support package.

6   **Iceland:** the Althing (legislature) approved emergency legislation that would allow the nationalisation of banks after banking transactions with Icelandic banks froze as a result of the global credit crisis.

    Sri Lanka: a suicide bombing in North Central Province killed at least 27 people, including Major-General (rtd) Janaka Perera, the provincial leader, who had fought against the rebel Tamil Tigers in Jaffna peninsula.

7   **Thailand:** ongoing protests by the People's Alliance for Democracy (PAD), who had occupied government buildings in Bangkok, escalated into serious violence and street battles with the police.

8   **international economy:** the US Federal Reserve, the European Central Bank, the Bank of England, and the central banks of Canada, Sweden, and Switzerland, announced simultaneous interest rate cuts of half a percentage point.

    UK: measures to support the banking system by increasing liquidity were announced, followed by further measures on 13 October.

9	**Afghanistan:** the *New York Times* published a leaked US National Intelligence Estimate draft which suggested that Afghanistan was "in a downward spiral".
9-12	**China:** the third plenary session of the 17th Chinese Communist Party (CCP) central committee adopted a number of land reform measures aimed at improving the rural economy.
10	**G-7:** finance ministers met in Washington, DC, to produce a co-ordinated plan to tackle the global financial crisis that threatened a global recession.
11	**Austria:** Jörg Haider, the leader of the far-right Alliance for the Future of Austria (BZÖ), was killed in a car accident.
	North Korea: the US government removed North Korea from its list of countries sponsoring terrorism; North Korea subsequently reopened the Yongbyon plant to inspectors from the UN's International Atomic Energy Agency (IAEA).
	Peru: a cabinet reshuffle followed allegations of bribery involving state oil contracts and public protests against the government's economic policies.
13	**France:** the government announced a €360 billion package to support French banks, following an emergency eurozone summit on 12 October to encourage concerted bank rescue measures by eurozone members.
	USA: Treasury Secretary Henry Paulson met bankers to finalise details of a plan for the government to purchase equity in banks, using funds allocated in the bailout legislation.
13-14	**IMF/World Bank:** the annual meetings of the IMF and World Bank were held, dominated by the spreading global financial crisis.
14	**Canada:** elections to the House of Commons returned Prime Minister Stephen Harper's Conservative Party of Canada to power, although it remained a minority government.
	Sudan: it was reported that the Sudanese government had arrested Ali Muhammad Ali Abd-al-Rahman, a leader of the pro-government Janjawid militia in Darfur. The ICC had issued a warrant for his arrest in May 2007 on charges of war crimes and crimes against humanity.
15	**Azerbaijan:** a presidential election was won by the incumbent, Ilham Aliyev, with over 87 per cent of the vote.
	Kenya: the commission of enquiry, headed by Philip Waki, into the post-election ethnic violence in Kenya released its report.
17	**Swaziland:** Sibusiso Barnabas Dlamini, a staunch royalist, was appointed prime minister by King Mswati III, following September's legislative elections.
17-18	**Czech Republic:** elections to regional councils and partial elections to the Senate (with a second round on October 24-25) produced a landslide victory for the opposition leftist Czech Social Democratic Party (CSSD).
22	**British Indian Ocean Territory:** a ruling by the UK's House of Lords rejected the Chagos islanders' right of return to the Chagos archipelago from which they have been removed.
	Georgia: an EU-sponsored donors' conference pledged US$4.55 billion in aid for Georgia, a sum greater than the agreed target of around US$3.2 billion.
	India: the line of control between the state of Jammu and Kashmir and Pakistan-controlled Kashmir was opened for trade for the first time since 1948.
24	**OPEC:** an extraordinary meeting of OPEC members decided on a cut in oil production, in an attempt to halt sliding oil prices.
26	**Democratic Republic of Congo:** heavy fighting in the east of the country erupted between government forces and rebels from the National Congress for the Defence of the People (CNDP), led by renegade ethnic Tutsi leader, Brigadier-General Laurent Nkunda. The same day, President Joseph Kabila appointed Aldophe Muzito as prime minister as part of an extensive cabinet reshuffle.

Syria: US military helicopters flew from Iraq to Syria and attacked a farm, killing eight civilians and, reportedly, a senior al-Qaida agent.

27   **Georgia:** Prime Minister Vladimir (Lado) Gurgenidze was dismissed, to be replaced by Grigol Mgaloblishvili

Niger: in its first hearing of a case of slavery, the Court of Justice of the Economic Community of West African States (ECOWAS) found Niger's government guilty of failing to protect a woman who had been sold into slavery some 12 years previously.

28   **Maldives:** presidential elections were won by Mohammed Nasheed (known as Anni), a former political prisoner, who defeated President Maumoon Abdul Gayoom in the second round.

29   **Hungary:** the IMF, World Bank, and EU granted a US$25.1 billion rescue package to help Hungary deal with the effects of the global credit crisis.

30   **India:** in the state of Assam, 13 near simultaneous bomb explosions killed at least 77 people.

Japan: a second economic stimulus package in the space of one month was announced.

South Korea: the National Assembly approved a US$130 billion bailout package for the country's banks.

Zambia: presidential elections, following the death of Levy Mwanawasa in August, were won by Rupiah Banda, who had been acting president since Mwanawasa's stroke in June.

31   **Lithuania:** the leader of the opposition conservative Homeland Union-Lithuanian Christian Democrats (TS-LKD), Andrius Kubilius, was asked to form a government, following the victory of the TS-LKD in legislative elections held on 12 and 26 October.

NOVEMBER

3   **USA:** a military commission at the prison camp at Guantánamo Bay, Cuba, convicted Ali Hamza al-Bahlul, formerly media secretary of Osama bin Laden, of a total of 35 counts relating to the 11 September 2001 attacks on the USA.

4   **Iran:** Interior Minister Ali Kordan was impeached by the Majlis (legislature) for deception over a forged law degree from Oxford University.

Palau: at a general election, Johnson Toribiong was chosen as president.

Palestine: there were clashes between Israeli troops and Hamas fighters in the Gaza Strip (the first since an Egypt-mediated ceasefire in June), prompting Israel to close crossings into Gaza, thereby contributing to the deterioration of already desperate conditions for the 1.5 million people living there.

Taiwan: an agreement was signed to expand contacts between mainland China and Taiwan.

USA: The Democratic Party candidate, Senator Barack Obama of Illinois, won the presidential election with 53 per cent of the popular vote, compared with 46 per cent for his Republican rival, Senator John McCain of Arizona. Obama was to be the USA's first non-white president. The Democrats also won majorities in the House of Representatives and the Senate.

5   **Germany:** the federal cabinet approved a two-year, €12 billion fiscal stimulus package to combat the recession, opposing the more substantial spending measures advocated by the European Commission and the UK.

Russia: in his first state of the nation address, President Dmitry Medvedev blamed the USA for the global financial crisis; he also announced that Russia would deploy nuclear-capable Iskander-M (SS-26) missiles in Kaliningrad.

6   **Bhutan:** the coronation was held of King Jigme Khesar Namgyel Wangchuk.

        Ukraine: the IMF agreed a huge two-year standby arrangement worth US$16.4 billion
        to stabilise the economy, as the currency—the hryvna—continued its slide in value.

7   **Democratic Republic of Congo:** an emergency summit of regional leaders was held in
        Nairobi (Kenya) to consider the situation in the DRC, where heavy fighting had
        broken out in North Kivu, in the east, between government forces and rebel Tutsis.

8   **New Zealand:** the Labour government of Prime Minister Helen Clark was defeated in
        the general election by the opposition National Party. National's leader, John Key,
        became prime minister.

9   **China:** a huge economic stimulus package was announced, amounting to some Y4,000
        billion in spending for 2010 on infrastructure, amid growing evidence of an eco-
        nomic slowdown.

        Indonesia: the three men responsible for the Bali bombings of 2002 were executed.

10   **Burma (Myanmar):** special courts began sentencing democracy activists; over 100 dis-
        sidents had been sentenced by the end of November, many to harsh prison terms.

12   **Maldives:** a new cabinet was sworn in under newly-inaugurated president, Mohammed
        Nasheed.

        Sudan: President Omar Hassan Ahmed al-Bashir announced a unilateral ceasefire in the
        Darfur region.

15   **Somalia:** pirates hijacked a fully-laden Saudi super-tanker, the *MV Sirius Star*, some 770
        km off the coast of Somalia. There had already been 77 pirate attacks on vessels in
        the Gulf of Aden in 2008.

        Zambia: the new president, Rupiah Banda, appointed his cabinet.

15-16   **G-20:** a meeting of leaders of the Group of 20 major industrialised countries was held in
        Washington, DC to discuss the reform of financial institutions and efforts to counter
        the global financial crisis.

16   **Guinea-Bissau:** legislative elections were won by the ruling African Party for the Inde-
        pendence of Guinea-Bissau and Cape Verde (PAIGC), prompting an unsuccessful
        military coup attempt on 23 November.

17   **Colombia:** a state of emergency was declared to deal with popular unrest, stemming
        from the collapse of hundreds of "pyramid" investment schemes.

        Japan: the country's economy officially entered recession, the first for seven years.

19   **Georgia-Russia:** the first talks between the parties to the August conflict were held in
        Geneva.

        Iran: in his latest regular report, International Atomic Energy Agency (IAEA) Director
        General Mohamed El-Baradei said that Iran was rapidly increasing its stocks of
        enriched uranium.

20   **Iceland:** the government borrowed a total of US$10 billion (roughly equivalent to the
        country's GDP) from the IMF and other lenders to rescue the country's financial
        system.

        Russia: the government announced a R550 billion package of stimulus measures to help
        the ailing economy.

21   **Slovenia:** a new centre-left coalition government was approved, led by Borut Pahor of
        the Social Democrats, which had won legislative elections in September.

24   **Pakistan:** the IMF approved a 23-month standby loan worth US$7.6 billion to stabilise
        the economy.

        UK: the pre-budget report presented by Chancellor Alistair Darling included fiscal stim-
        ulus measures amounting to 0.6 per cent of GDP, a sum greater than had been
        planned in 2008-09.

Zimbabwe: South African leaders and a group of international eminent persons warned that Zimbabwe was on the brink of collapse.

25 **Bulgaria:** the European Commission cancelled €220 million in EU aid because of Bulgaria's failure to deal with corruption.

OECD: the latest biannual *Economic Outlook* from the Organisation for Economic Co-operation and Development warned that many advanced economies were entering a period of deep recession.

Thailand: anti-government protesters from the royalist People's Alliance for Democracy (PAD) occupied Bangkok's airports, blocking international flights and seriously disrupting the country's tourist industry.

USA: further measures to counter the economic crisis were announced, involving releasing US$800 billion to the mortgage and consumer credit market.

26-29 **India:** a group of heavily armed gunmen launched a series of co-ordinated attacks in Mumbai (Bombay), killing a total of 183 people. Amongst their targets were landmark tourist sites as well as the railway station and hospitals.

27 **Iraq:** the Council of Representatives (legislature) approved the Status of Forces Agreement (SOFA), which provided the terms upon which the US military would withdraw from all Iraqi territory by the end of 2011.

27-29 **Nigeria:** violent clashes between gangs of Muslim Hausas and mostly Christian Beroms killed some 400 people in the central city of Jos following disputed local elections.

28 **Italy:** an economic stimulus package amounting to €80 billion was announced.

Somalia: Ethiopia announced that it was to withdraw all its forces in Somalia by the end of 2008. On 15 November, Somali President Ahmed Abdullahi Yusuf admitted that Islamist insurgents controlled most of the country.

30 **Romania:** legislative elections were narrowly won by the centre-right Democratic Liberal Party (PDL).

DECEMBER

1 **USA:** President-elect Barack Obama announced the appointment of Hillary Clinton, his defeated rival for the Democratic presidential nomination, as secretary of state in his new administration.

1-13 **environment:** a UN conference on climate change was held in Poznan (Poland) in preparation for negotiating the successor treaty to the Kyoto Protocol.

2 **Austria:** a new "grand coalition" cabinet took office under Social Democrat (SPÖ) leader Werner Faymann, with the conservative People's Party (ÖVP) as junior partner.

3-4 **India-Pakistan:** US Secretary of State Condoleezza Rice visited India and Pakistan in the wake of the Mumbai attacks of 26-29 November, which had heightened tension between the two countries.

4 **France:** a €26 billion package of fiscal stimulus measures, amounting to 1.3 per cent of GDP, was announced.

San Marino: a new centre-right cabinet was appointed, following the victory in elections on 9 November of the opposition Pact for San Marino.

UK: the base UK interest rate was cut to 2 per cent, its lowest level since 1951.

Zimbabwe: the government declared a health emergency and requested international assistance to combat a cholera epidemic.

7   **Greece:** riots erupted after the fatal shooting by police of a schoolboy in central Athens. They continued throughout the month, evolving into anti-government protests by disaffected youth.

    USA: Bernard Madoff was charged with securities fraud after confessing that his investment scheme was, in fact, a pyramid operation and had lost investors an estimated US$50 billion.

8   **Democratic Republic of Congo:** negotiations for a ceasefire in the conflict in the eastern provinces between government and rebel Tutsi forces opened in Nairobi (Kenya).

    Somalia: the EU launched a naval operation, "Operation Atalanta", to combat piracy off the Somali coast.

8-11   **North Korea:** the six-party talks on dismantling the country's nuclear weapons programme resumed in Beijing after a five-month hiatus, but made no progress on verification procedures.

9   **Kosovo:** the EU rule of law mission (EULEX) began deploying throughout the country.

    Lithuania: following October's elections, a four-party centre-right coalition government was appointed, led by Andrius Kubilius of the Homeland Union-Lithuanian Christian Democrats (TS-LKD).

10   **Afghanistan:** plans were announced for additional US troops to be sent to Afghanistan in a bid to bolster the war against the Taliban.

11-12   **European Union:** a summit agreed a €200 billion economic recovery plan to combat the recession; the summit also adopted targets for energy and climate change policy.

12   **Japan:** a new stimulus package of Y23,000 billion was announced, containing "emergency measures" against recession. The measures were separate from those contained in a Y26,900 billion stimulus package announced in October, although there was some overlap between the two packages.

14   **Iraq:** outgoing US President George W. Bush visited Baghdad for talks with Iraqi leaders. At a press conference by Bush and Iraqi Prime Minister Nouri al-Maliki, Iraqi journalist Muntader al-Zaidi threw his shoes at the US president in a gesture of contempt. He did not hit his target.

    Russia: opposition demonstrations in Moscow and St Petersburg were broken up by police; more demonstrations were held throughout the country on 20 and 21 December, with those in Vladivostok being suppressed by special purpose police (OMON) summoned from Moscow.

16   **South Africa:** the Congress of the People (COPE) was launched in Bloemfontein by a faction of the ruling African National Congress loyal to the deposed former president, Thabo Mbeki.

    Ukraine: as the economic crisis deepened, a new governing coalition was formed in the legislature, replacing the one which collapsed in September.

17   **OPEC:** the 151st (extraordinary) meeting of the Organisation of Petroleum Exporting Countries in Oran, Algeria, agreed the largest cut in production in OPEC's history, amounting to a collective reduction of 2.2 million barrels per day from 1 January 2009, in an attempt to boost falling oil prices.

    Thailand: Abhisit Vejjajiva, leader of the Democratic Party, was appointed prime minister following a Constitutional Court ruling on 2 December that dissolved the former ruling People Power Party (PPP).

18   **China:** celebrations marking the 30th anniversary of China's economic reform programme were held, amidst concern over the impact of the global financial crisis on China's hitherto spectacular growth rates.

Rwanda: concluding a trial that had opened in 2002, the International Criminal Tribunal for Rwanda (ICTR) convicted three senior officers of genocide, crimes against humanity, and war crimes, and acquitted one officer.

19 **Belgium:** the five-party coalition government led by Yves Leterme resigned over allegations of attempting to influence judges in a case relating to the sale of the Fortis banking and insurance group.

22 **OSCE:** at a meeting in Vienna of the Organisation for Security and Co-operation in Europe, Russia refused to agree to the extension of the OSCE's mission in Georgia, which was due to expire on 31 December.

Romania: a new government took office under Emil Bloc of the Democratic Liberal Party (PDL), which had narrowly won elections in November. The government also included members of the Social Democratic Party (PSD).

23 **Guinea:** President Lansana Conté died, aged 74. Within hours, Captain Moussa Camara, a junior army officer, announced that the government had been dissolved and power assumed by the National Council for Democracy and Development.

Latvia: a loan totalling €7.5 billion was arranged with the IMF and other lenders to support economic stabilisation.

27 **Palestine:** Israel launched a huge air assault on the Gaza Strip against Hamas targets, codenamed "Operation Cast Lead", in retaliation for Hamas rocket and mortar fire against Israeli towns.

28 **Belgium:** Flemish Christian Democrat Herman Van Rompuy was named prime minister designate.

Ghana: a second round of presidential elections resulted in victory for John Atta Mills of the main opposition party, the National Democratic Congress (NDC). The NDC also won the legislative elections held on 7 December

29 **Bangladesh:** legislative elections were convincingly won by the Awami League-led "Grand Alliance", under former prime minister, Sheikh Hasina Wajed.

Somalia: President Ahmed Abdullahi Yusuf resigned, following a power struggle over his attempted dismissal, on 14 December, of Prime Minister Nur Hassan Hussein. Yusuf handed power ad interim to the speaker of the legislature, Sheikh Aden Madobe.

30 **Guinea:** the military junta that took power on 23 December appointed Kabine Komara, a former banker, as prime minister.

Russia: bills to extend the presidential and legislative terms in office were signed into law. Following the end of the current presidential term in 2012, presidents would be elected for a six- (not four-) year term.

MAJOR WORLD EVENTS FROM THE ANNUAL REGISTER ARCHIVE

Compiled by Philip M.H. Bell, Senior Research Fellow, University of Liverpool, nominated to the Advisory Board of The Annual Register by the Royal Historical Society.

1758 Halley's Comet returns, as calculated by Edmond Halley in 1705
1759 British conquer Quebec from the French; death of Montcalm and Wolfe
1760 Britain: accession of George III, the first British Hanoverian monarch
1761 Transit of Venus on 6 June helps understanding of the movement of planets
1762 Russia: assassination of Tsar Peter III; accession of Catherine the Great
1763 Peace of Paris ends Seven Years' War; British control in Canada and India
1764 Stanislaus Poniatowski elected King of Poland
1765 British Parliament passes Stamp Act, to tax American colonies
1766 Repeal of Stamp Act in face of American opposition
1767 Expulsion of the Jesuits from all Spanish dominions
1768 France purchases Corsica from Genoa; conquest of island
1769 Britain imposes Tea Duties on American colonies
1770 The "Boston Massacre": casualty list 4 dead, 7 wounded
1771 Dispute between Britain and Spain over Falkland Islands
1772 First Partition of Poland by Russia, Prussia and Austria
1773 "Boston Tea Party" staged as protest against Tea Duty
1774 Continental Congress in Philadelphia draws together the American colonies
1775 American victories over British forces at battles of Lexington and Concord
1776 American Declaration of Independence, 4 July
1777 Publication of A Voyage towards the South Pole and round the World by James Cook
1778 Death of Voltaire, 30 May
1779 Spanish and French forces begin siege of Gibraltar
1780 Gordon Riots in London; "No Popery!"
1781 Cornwallis surrenders at Yorktown; decisive defeat for British in America
1782 Admiral Rodney's victory over the French at the Saints; British naval recovery
1783 Treaty of Versailles: Britain recognises American independence
1784 Pitt the Younger becomes British prime minister at age 24

MAJOR WORLD EVENTS 1758 - 2008

1785 Flight of Blanchard and Jeffries by balloon from Dover to Calais
1786 Death of Frederick the Great, the creator of the new Kingdom of Prussia
1787 France: Louis XVI convenes Assembly of Notables; dissolved without result
1788 Russo-Turkish war: Potemkin besieges Ochakov
1789 Revolution in France; storming of the Bastille, 14 July
1790 Death of Benjamin Franklin, statesman and polymath
1791 France: Feast of the National Confederation to acclaim the Revolution
1792 Battle of Valmy, 20 September; victory of French revolutionary army
1793 Execution of Louis XVI of France
1794 Erasmus Darwin publishes Zoonomia, foreshadowing the idea of evolution
1795 Third and final partition of Poland; Poland disappears from the map
1796 Napoleon's victory at Lodi marks his emergence as a dominant figure
1797 First bank-notes issued in Britain; paper currency replaces specie
1798 Napoleon's expedition to Egypt results in conquest and scientific exploration
1799 Pitt introduces income tax in Britain
1800 Act of Union between Britain and Ireland passed; takes effect, 1 January 1801
1801 Thomas Jefferson becomes president of the USA
1802 Peace of Amiens brings war between Britain and France to temporary end
1803 Louisiana Purchase: USA buys Louisiana territories from France
1804 Napoleon crowns himself Emperor of the French
1805 Battle of Trafalgar establishes British naval dominance for a century
1806 Humphry Davy presents paper on electro-chemistry to Royal Society

1807 Abolition of slave trade in British Empire
1808 Napoleon imposes Joseph Bonaparte as King of Spain; Spanish revolt
1809 Napoleon defeats Austrians at Wagram, and imposes severe peace terms
1810 Venezuela revolts against Spain; rebellion spreads to other colonies
1811 Birth of a son to Napoleon and Marie Louise, thereby starting a dynasty
1812 Napoleon captures Moscow, but is forced into disastrous winter retreat
1813 Napoleon decisively defeated at Leipzig in the Battle of the Nations
1814 Napoleon abdicates and is exiled to Elba
1815 Napoleon returns for the "Hundred Days", is defeated at Waterloo and exiled to St Helena
1816 Declaration of Argentinian Independence at Buenos Aires
1817 Discontent and disorder in Britain; Habeas Corpus suspended
1818 France: abolition of slave trade in all French territories
1819 Britain: parliamentary reform rally in Manchester ends in "Peterloo" massacre
1820 Spain ratifies treaty for purchase of Florida by USA

MAJOR WORLD EVENTS 1758 - 2008

1821 Mexican independence declared, under Iturbide as generalissimo
1822 Declaration of Greek independence; Turkish massacre of Greeks at Chios
1823 Monroe Doctrine: American continent declared closed to European colonisation
1824 Death of Byron at Missolonghi marks the creation of a Romantic legend
1825 Russia: Decembrist rising crushed in St Petersburg
1826 Opening of Telford's suspension bridge across Menai Straits, the first of its kind
1827 Battle of Navarino: Turkish defeat assists Greek struggle for independence
1828 Frontier treaty between Brazil and Argentina; establishment of Uruguay
1829 Catholic Emancipation in Britain; extension of franchise to Catholics
1830 French expedition captures Algiers; beginning of French Algeria
1831 Five-power treaty on Belgian independence declares it to be perpetually neutral
1832 Great Reform Act in Britain provides limited but significant extension of franchise
1833 General Santanna elected President of Mexico; Texas declares independence
1834 Introduction of new Poor Law in Britain creates Poor Law Boards and houses
1835 Prussia establishes Zollverein, bringing all German states into a customs union
1836 Civil war in Spain involves intervention by British warships and volunteers
1837 Accession of Queen Victoria to British throne
1838 Insurrection in Canada; Lord Durham's enquiry into its causes
1839 Chartist movement in Britain; National Petition and People's Charter
1840 British expedition to Canton to force Chinese government to accept opium trade
1841 Union of the two Canadas (Upper and Lower) comes into effect
1842 Destruction of British army in Afghanistan
1843 South Africa: Britain annexes Natal
1844 New Zealand: Maori War
1845 USA: annexation of Texas approved by Congress
1846 Ireland: failure of potato crop; resulting famine leads to large-scale emigration
1847 Vatican: first year of Pius IX's papacy shows him to be a liberal pope
1848 Year of Revolutions in Europe; Marx and Engels issue Communist Manifesto
1849 Mazzini proclaims Roman Republic; crushed by French army
1850 USA: California admitted as a state of the Union
1851 Britain: Jews allowed to sit in Parliament
1852 France: Louis Napoleon is proclaimed Emperor Napoleon III
1853 Japan: US expedition under Commodore Perry forcibly opens Japan to US trade
1854 Crimean War begins: British and French troops lay siege to Sevastopol
1855 Henry Bessemer takes out patents, which transform steel production

1856 Treaty of Paris ends Crimean War
1857 Indian Mutiny: widespread uprising against British rule in India

MAJOR WORLD EVENTS 1758 - 2008

1858 British Crown takes over government of India from East India Company
1859 War in Italy: Sardinia and France against Austria; Battle of Magenta
1860 Election of Lincoln, an opponent of the extension of slavery, as US president
1861 American Civil War begins after secession of Confederate States
1862 Lincoln signs Emancipation Proclamation, which frees slaves in Confederate territory
1863 Battles of Vicksburg and Gettysburg mark turning-points in Civil War
1864 Prussia and Austria defeat Denmark over Schleswig-Holstein
1865 Defeat of Confederacy marks end of American Civil War; assassination of Lincoln
1866 Prussian victory over Austria at Sadowa; Prussian predominance in Germany
1867 Dual Monarchy established in Austria-Hungary
1868 British expedition to Abyssinia; capture of Magdala, and withdrawal
1869 Opening of Suez Canal, a channel for world commerce
1870 Franco-Prussian War: crushing French defeat at Sedan leads to fall of Napoleon III
1871 Darwin's The Descent of Man published, amid sharp debate
1872 Britain: Ballot Act introduces voting in elections by secret ballot
1873 Russian advance into Central Asia; occupation of Khiva
1874 Britain: defeat of Gladstone; Disraeli forms Conservative government
1875 Disraeli purchases Khedive's shares in Suez Canal Company for Britain
1876 Bulgarian revolt suppressed by Turks; Gladstone denounces Bulgarian massacres
1877 Invention of "talking phonograph", a recording machine, by Thomas Edison
1878 Congress of Berlin: independence of Balkan states from Turkey
1879 Zulu War: defeat of British army at Isandlwana; defence of Rorke's Drift
1880 Ireland: ostracism of Captain Boycott by the Land League creates new word
1881 International Medical Congress: Pasteur's account of vaccination experiments
1882 Egypt: British bombard Alexandria and occupy Egypt
1883 French occupation of Madagascar and expedition to Tonkin (Indo-China)
1884 Congo Conference in Berlin on partition of Africa
1885 Death of General Gordon at Khartoum
1886 Gladstone's first Home Rule Bill for Ireland; Liberal split and defeat
1887 Indian National Congress meets at Calcutta; demands representative institutions
1888 Accession of William II as Emperor of Germany
1889 Austria-Hungary: death of Crown Prince Rudolph at Mayerling
1890 USA: McKinley Tariff to protect US industry
1891 First rail of Trans-Siberian Railway laid by the future Tsar Nicholas II
1892 Britain: Gladstone forms his fourth administration after Liberals win election
1893 Arctic exploration: Nansen sails in *Fram*; Peary sets out for North Pole
1894 France: Captain Dreyfus convicted of treason; start of Dreyfus Affair
1895 Treaty of Shimonosiki ends First Sino-Japanese War; Japan annexes Formosa
1896 Ethiopia: Battle of Adowa; defeat of Italian army by Ethiopians
1897 German Navy Bill initiates naval expansion and maritime rivalry with Britain
1898 Spanish-American War; US annexation of Hawaii, Puerto Rico and Philippines
1899 Boer War begins between Britain and Boer Republics
1900 Australian Commonwealth Act: Commonwealth of Australia established
1901 Marconi sends first trans-Atlantic wireless communication
1902 Treaty of Vereeniging ends Boer War

MAJOR WORLD EVENTS 1758 - 2008

1903 Independence of Panama from Colombia; USA begins Panama Canal
1904 Signing of Entente Cordiale between Britain and France

1905 Russo-Japanese War: Russian fleet destroyed at Tsushima
1906 Huge earthquake destroys San Francisco
1907 Finland becomes first European country to grant female suffrage
1908 Orville Wright makes flight of 1 hour and 10 minutes
1909 Britain: House of Lords rejects Finance Bill, leading to constitutional crisis
1910 China asserts suzerainty in Tibet: expedition to Lhasa, flight of Dalai Lama
1911 Moroccan crisis: French expedition to Fez, German gunboat to Agadir
1912 Titanic sunk by collision with iceberg, 15-16 April
1913 Niels Bohr introduces new quantum theory of atomic structure
1914 Assassination of Archduke Franz Ferdinand leads to outbreak of World War I
1915 Dardanelles campaign; ANZAC troops in action
1916 Battles of Verdun and the Somme epitomise attritional war on Western Front
1917 USA enters war; Bolshevik Revolution in Russia
1918 Treaty of Brest-Litovsk, March; armistice in France, 11 November
1919 Paris Peace Conference and Treaty of Versailles redraw world map. Einstein's
        new theory of the principle of relativity changes views of the universe
1920 Britain accepts mandate for Palestine, to establish a "National Home" for the Jews
1921 Washington Conference on naval disarmament and the Pacific
1922 Mussolini assumes dictatorial power in Italy; creation of fascist regime
1923 French occupation of the Ruhr; hyper-inflation in Germany
1924 Death of Lenin; struggle for succession begins
1925 Treaties of Locarno normalise relations between Germany and former Allied Powers
1926 Britain: General Strike brings country almost to a standstill
1927 Lindbergh's journey from New York to Le Bourget marks first trans-Atlantic flight
1928 China denounces all unequal treaties imposed by outside powers
1929 The Wall Street Crash: symbol of the Great Depression
1930 India: Gandhi's salt march, to protest against tax on salt manufacture
1931 Mukden Incident: Japanese occupation of Manchuria
1932 Election of Franklin D. Roosevelt as president of the USA
1933 Hitler becomes chancellor of Germany, 30 January, with conservative support
1934 Discovery of induced radio-activity by the Joliot-Curies, Paris
1935 Italian invasion of Ethiopia; enactment of Nuremberg Laws in Germany
1936 Civil War in Spain: Franco attacks Madrid; arrival of International Brigades
1937 USA: Neutrality Act forbids export of arms to belligerent states
1938 Munich Conference marks high point of appeasement of Nazi Germany

MAJOR WORLD EVENTS 1758 - 2008

1939 German attack on Poland initiates World War II
1940 Fall of France and creation of Vichy government; German defeat in Battle of Britain
1941 German invasion of Soviet Union; Japanese attack on Pearl Harbour
1942 Decisive defeat of German army at Stalingrad and of Japanese navy at Midway
1943 Teheran Conference cements British-US-Soviet alliance; overthrow of Mussolini
1944 Normandy Landings lead to liberation of France
1945 Surrender of Germany and discovery of Nazi death camps; surrender of Japan after atomic bombs dropped on Hiroshima and Nagasaki
1946 First Session of General Assembly of United Nations, involving 51 member states
1947 End of British rule in India; partition between India and Pakistan
1948 Palestine: establishment of Israel; conflict with Arab states
1949 Communist victory in Chinese civil war leads to establishment of Mao's regime
1950 Communist North Korea invades South; intervention by US-led UN forces
1951 Soviet Union detonates its first atomic bomb
1952 Britain: death of George VI and accession of Queen Elizabeth II
1953 Death of Stalin

1954 Defeat of French garrison at Dien Bien Phu marks end of French rule in Indo-China
1955 Asian-African Conference at Bandung (Indonesia); emergence of "Third World"
1956 Suez Crisis: Nasser nationalises Canal, prompting British-French-Israeli attack
1957 Treaties of Rome, founding the European Economic Community. Launch of Sputnik, the first man-made earth satellite, by Soviet Union
1958 France: end of 4th Republic; de Gaulle becomes president of new 5th Republic
1959 China: disastrous consequences of "Great Leap Forward", begun in 1958
1960 CERN cyclotron in Geneva produces crucial results in particle acceleration
1961 Soviet Union puts first man into space; Yury Gagarin orbits the earth
1962 Cuban Missile Crisis brings USA and Soviet Union to the brink of nuclear war
1963 USA: assassination of President Kennedy, 22 November
1964 South Africa: Nelson Mandela is sentenced to life imprisonment
1965 Britain: death and state funeral of Winston Churchill
1966 China: Cultural Revolution, led by Red Guards
1967 Six-Day War: Israel attacks and defeats Egypt, Syria and Jordan
1968 France: establishment shaken by student revolt. Soviet invasion of Czechoslovakia
1969 USA lands first men on the moon
1970 Introduction of Boeing 747 airliner marks start of mass air travel
1971 War between India and Pakistan; independence of Bangladesh
1972 Germany: success of Brandt's Ostpolitik; treaty between West and East Germany
1973 Ceasefire agreement in Vietnam War; Arab attack on Israel starts Yom Kippur war

MAJOR WORLD EVENTS 1758 - 2008

1974 "Oil Shock" ends many years of economic growth
1975 North Vietnam conquers South. Death of General Franco in Spain
1976 China: deaths of Chou En-lai and Mao Tse-tung lead to power struggle
1977 Czechoslovakia: publication of Charter 77, against violations of human rights
1978 Election of Karol Wojtyla as Pope John Paul II, a Polish pope
1979 Islamic revolution in Iran overthrows the Shah; Ayatollah Khomeini takes power
1980 Soviet army struggles to subdue guerrillas in Afghanistan
1981 Poland: conflict between government and Solidarity trade union; martial law imposed
1982 Falklands War: Falkland Islands invaded by Argentina and recovered by Britain
1983 Missile crisis in Europe; deployment of US Pershing and Soviet SS-20 missiles
1984 India: storming of Sikh Golden Temple; Indira Gandhi assassinated by Sikhs
1985 Mikhail Gorbachev becomes Soviet leader and embarks on reform programme
1986 Explosion at Chernobyl nuclear reactor: fallout affects much of Europe
1987 Reagan-Gorbachev summit: abolition of medium and short range missiles
1988 Geneva agreement on phased withdrawal of Soviet troops from Afghanistan
1989 Fall of Berlin Wall, symbolising collapse of communism in Eastern Europe
1990 Russia declares sovereignty, heralding the demise of the Soviet Union in 1991
1991 USA and allied powers defeat Iraq after its invasion of Kuwait in 1990
1992 Former Yugoslavia: civil war in Bosnia; Croatia declares independence
1993 South Africa: new, non-racial constitution adopted
1994 Rwanda: massacre of Tutsis by Hutu militants leaves up to 500,000 dead
1995 World Health Organisation estimates number of AIDS sufferers at over one million
1996 Comprehensive Nuclear Test Ban Treaty adopted by UN General Assembly
1997 Cloning of Dolly the sheep by researchers in Edinburgh
1998 Nuclear tests conducted by India and Pakistan
1999 Russia: resignation of Boris Yeltsin; Vladimir Putin becomes acting president
2000 Completion of mapping of the human genome, the human genetic blueprint
2001 Terrorist attacks on 11 September against World Trade Centre and Pentagon
2002 European Union: introduction of single currency (the euro) by 11 member states

2003 War by USA and allies against Iraq leads to overthrow of Saddam Hussein
2004 Indian Ocean earthquake unleashes tsunami, which kills several hundred thousand
2005 Kyoto Protocol on Climate Change comes into effect
2006 Afghanistan: new government takes office, but Taliban opposition grows
2007 USA implements troop "surge" in attempt to achieve success in Iraq conflict
2008 Election of Barack Obama as US president

INDEX

Page references in bold indicate location of main coverage.